D1429697

Crafting and Executing Strategy

The Quest for Competitive Advantage

Concepts and Cases

Crafting and Executing Strategy

The Quest for Competitive Advantage

Concepts and Cases

European Edition

Arthur A. Thompson
The University of Alabama

A. J. Strickland III
The University of Alabama

Margaret A. Peteraf
Dartmouth College

Alex Janes
The University of Exeter

John E. Gamble
University of South Alabama

Ciara Sutton
Stockholm School of Economics

McGraw-Hill Irwin

London   Boston   Burr Ridge,IL   Dubuque, IA   Madison, WI   New York   San Francisco
St. Louis   Bangkok   Bogotá   Caracas   Kuala Lumpur   Lisbon   Madrid   Mexico City   Milan   Montreal
New Delhi   Santiago   Seoul   Singapore   Sydney   Taipei   Toronto

Crafting and Executing Strategy

Arthur A. Thompson, Margaret A. Peteraf, John E. Gamble, A. J. Strickland III, Alex Janes and Ciara Sutton

ISBN-13 9780077137236

ISBN-10 007713723X

Published by McGraw-Hill Education

Shoppenhangers Road

Maidenhead

Berkshire

SL6 2QL

Telephone: 44 (0) 1628 502 500

Fax: 44 (0) 1628 770 224

Website: www.mcgraw-hill.co.uk

British Library Cataloguing in Publication Data

A catalogue record for this book is available from the British Library

Library of Congress Cataloging in Publication Data

The Library of Congress data for this book has been applied for from the Library of Congress

Executive Editor: Caroline Prodger

Commissioning Editor: Peter Hooper

Production Editor: Alison Davis

Marketing Manager: Alexis Gibbs

Cover design by Adam Renvoize

Printed and bound in Singapore by Markono Print Media Pte Ltd

Published by McGraw-Hill Education (UK) Limited an imprint of The McGraw-Hill Companies, Inc., 1221 Avenue of the Americas, New York, NY 10020. Copyright © 2012 by McGraw-Hill Education (UK) Limited. All rights reserved. No part of this publication may be reproduced or distributed in any form or by any means, or stored in a database or retrieval system, without the prior written consent of The McGraw-Hill Companies, Inc., including, but not limited to, in any network or other electronic storage or transmission, or broadcast for distance learning.

Fictitious names of companies, products, people, characters and/or data that may be used herein (in case studies or in examples) are not intended to represent any real individual, company, product or event.

ISBN-13 9780077137236

ISBN-10 007713723X

© 2013. Exclusive rights by The McGraw-Hill Companies, Inc. for manufacture and export. This book cannot be re-exported from the country to which it is sold by McGraw-Hill.v

Dedication

Alex Janes
To Yve, for her patience and support.

Ciara Sutton
To Peter, Kris & Jess

Brief contents

Preface   xix

Acknowledgements   xxxvii

About the authors   xxxviii

Guided tour   xl

For students: support materials   xlv

Part One Concepts and techniques for crafting and executing strategy

Section A: Introduction and overview
1   What is strategy and why is it important?   2

2   Charting an organization's direction: vision and mission,
    objectives and strategy   24

Section B: Core concepts and analytical tools
3   Analysing an organization's external environment   56

4   Evaluating an organization's resources, capabilities and competitiveness   98

Section C: Crafting a strategy
5   Strategies for competitive advantage: generic strategies and beyond   142

6   Strategies for changing the game   180

7   Strategies for international growth   222

8   Corporate strategy   266

9   Ethics, corporate social responsibility, environmental
    sustainability and strategy   312

Section D: Executing the strategy
10 Building an organization capable of good strategy execution   352

11 Managing internal operations   390

12 Organizational culture and leadership   422

Part Two Cases in crafting and executing strategy

C1 Reinventing Accor   456

C2 Apple and the retail industry for specialist consumer electronics
    in the United Kingdom   466

C3   Netflix: can it recover from its strategy mistakes?   474

C4   The O-Fold innovation for preventing wrinkles: a good business
         opportunity?   499

C5   Studio 100: a showcase in show business   512

C6   Ferretti Group: navigating through stormy seas   527

C7   Starbucks: evolving into a dynamic global organization   538

C8   Rhino capture in Kruger National Park   570

C9   Robin Hood   585

C10 NIS: geopolitical breakthrough or strategic failure?   587

C11 Kyaia   595

C12 Microsoft's strategic alliance with Nokia   607

Index   621

Table of contents

Preface   xix
Acknowledgements   xxxvii
About the authors   xxxviii
Guided tour   xl
For students: support materials   xlv

Part One   Concepts and techniques for crafting and executing strategy

    Section A: Introduction and overview   2

1 **What is strategy and why is it important?**   2

    OPENING CASE   *Apple: riding the strategy rollercoaster*   3

    What do we mean by *strategy*?   4

    Strategy and the quest for competitive advantage   7

    ILLUSTRATION CAPSULE 1.1
    McDonald's strategy in the quick-service restaurant industry   8

    KEY DEBATE 1.1   *Is competitive advantage sustainable in the twenty-first century?*   9

    Why an organization's strategy evolves over time   10

    An organization's strategy is partly proactive and partly reactive   10

    The relationship between an organization's strategy and its business model   11

    What makes a good strategy?   12

    ILLUSTRATION CAPSULE 1.2
    Web-based financial services – Zopa.com, a peer to peer lending website and First Direct, a UK-based telephone and Internet bank   13

    CURRENT PRACTICE 1.1   *Testing an organization's strategy*   15

    Why crafting and executing strategy are important tasks   16

    Good strategy + good strategy execution = good management   16

    The road ahead   16

    EMERGING THEME 1.1   *Economics: competing for capital and the credit crunch*   17

KEY POINTS   17

CLOSING CASE   *A tale of two confectioners: Nestlé and Ferrero*   18

ASSURANCE OF LEARNING EXERCISES   20

EXERCISES FOR SIMULATION PARTICIPANTS   21

ENDNOTES   22

2 **Charting an organization's direction: vision and mission, objectives and strategy**   24

    OPENING CASE   *Lamborghini and the Audi vision*   25

    What does the strategy-making, strategy-executing process entail?   27

    Stage 1: Developing a strategic vision, a mission and a set of core values   27

    Developing a strategic vision   27

    Communicating the strategic vision   29

    ILLUSTRATION CAPSULE 2.1
    Examples of strategic visions – how well do they measure up?   30

    Crafting a mission statement   31

    KEY DEBATE 2.1   *Are mission statements truthful and effective?*   33

    Linking the vision and mission with organization values   34

    ILLUSTRATION CAPSULE 2.2
    Zappos family mission and core values   35

    Stage 2: Setting objectives   36

    What kinds of objectives to set   36

    ILLUSTRATION CAPSULE 2.3
    Examples of company objectives   38

    Stage 3: Crafting a strategy   39

    Strategy-making involves managers at all organizational levels   39

    A strategic vision + objectives + strategy = a strategic plan   43

    Stage 4: Executing the strategy   44

    Stage 5: Evaluating performance and initiating corrective adjustments   45

    Corporate governance: the role of the board of directors in the strategy-crafting, strategy-executing process   45

ILLUSTRATION CAPSULE 2.4
*Corporate governance failures at
Fannie Mae and Freddie Mac*   47
A DIFFERENT VIEW   *Shareholder
versus stakeholder approaches*   49
KEY POINTS   49
CLOSING CASE   *Embedding a vision:
Scandic hotels*   51
ASSURANCE OF LEARNING
EXERCISES   53
EXERCISES FOR SIMULATION
PARTICIPANTS   54
ENDNOTES   54

**Section B: Core concepts and
analytical tools**

**3   Analysing an organization's external
environment**   56
OPENING CASE   *Who will profit from
'Tesco Law'?*   57
The strategically relevant components
of an organization's macro-environment   58
Scenario planning   59
Building scenarios   61
CURRENT PRACTICE 3.1   *Scenario
planning at VisitScotland*   62
Thinking strategically about an
organization's industry and competitive
environment   62
Question 1: Does the industry offer
attractive opportunities?   63
Question 2: What kinds of competitive
forces are industry members facing
and how strong are they?   64
Competitive pressures created by
the rivalry among competing sellers   64
Competitive pressures associated
with the threat of new entrants   68
Competitive pressures from the
sellers of substitute products   70
Competitive pressures stemming
from supplier bargaining power   71
ILLUSTRATION CAPSULE 3.1
*Microsoft and Intel: the power
of dominant suppliers*   71
Competitive pressures stemming
from buyer bargaining power
and price sensitivity   73
Is the collective strength of the
five competitive forces conducive
to good profitability?   75
KEY DEBATE 3.1   *How useful is Porter's
five-forces model in the current
environment?*   76

Question 3: What factors are driving
industry change and what impacts
will they have?   77
Analysing industry dynamics   78
Identifying an industry's drivers
of change   78
ILLUSTRATION CAPSULE 3.2   *The
impact of the Internet on Finnish
magazine publishing*   81
Assessing the impact of the factors
driving industry change   82
Developing a strategy that takes
the changes in industry conditions
into account   82
Question 4: How are industry rivals
positioned – who is strongly positioned
and who is not?   83
Using strategic group maps to
assess the market positions of
key competitors   83
ILLUSTRATION CAPSULE 3.3
*Comparative market positions of
selected mobile telecoms handset
manufacturers: a strategic group
map example*   84
What can be learned from strategic
group maps?   84
Question 5: What strategic moves are
rivals likely to make next?   85
A DIFFERENT VIEW   Blue ocean
strategy   86
Question 6: What are the key factors for
future competitive success?   87
Question 7: Does the industry offer good
prospects for attractive profits?   88
KEY POINTS   89
CLOSING CASE   *Spotify go West*   91
ASSURANCE OF LEARNING
EXERCISES   94
EXERCISES FOR SIMULATION
PARTICIPANTS   94
ENDNOTES   95

**4   Evaluating an organization's
resources, capabilities and
competitiveness**   98
OPENING CASE   *H&M*   99
Question 1: How well is the organization's
present strategy working?   100
Question 2: What are the organization's
competitively important resources and
capabilities?   104
Identifying the organization's
resources and capabilities   104

Determining whether an organization's resources and capabilities are strong enough to produce a sustainable competitive advantage 107

Question 3: Is the organization able to take advantage of market opportunities and overcome external threats? 110

Identifying an organization's internal strengths 110

Identifying organizational weaknesses and competitive deficiencies 111

Identifying an organization's market opportunities 113

Identifying the threats to an organization's future profitability 113

What do the SWOT listings reveal? 114

Question 4: Are the organization's prices and costs competitive with those of key rivals, and does it have an appealing customer value proposition? 115

A DIFFERENT VIEW *A critical look at SWOT* 116

The concept of a value chain 117

ILLUSTRATION CAPSULE 4.1 *The value chain for Just Coffee, a producer of fair-trade organic coffee* 119

The value chain system for an entire industry 120

Benchmarking: a tool for assessing whether the costs and effectiveness of an organization's value chain activities are in line 121

Strategic options for remedying a disadvantage in costs or effectiveness 122

ILLUSTRATION CAPSULE 4.2 *Benchmarking and ethical conduct* 123

Translating proficient performance of value chain activities into competitive advantage 125

Question 5: Is the organization competitively stronger or weaker than key rivals? 127

Strategic implications of competitive strength assessments 129

KEY DEBATE 4.1 *Extending the resource-based view* 130

Question 6: What strategic issues and problems merit priority managerial attention? 132

KEY POINTS 133

CLOSING CASE *Haribo* 135

ASSURANCE OF LEARNING EXERCISES 137

EXERCISES FOR SIMULATION PARTICIPANTS 139

ENDNOTES 139

Section C: Crafting a strategy

5 Strategies for competitive advantage: generic strategies and beyond 142

OPENING CASE *The end of higher education as we know it?* 143

The five generic competitive strategies 144

Low-cost provider strategies 145

The two major avenues for achieving a cost advantage 146

ILLUSTRATION CAPSULE 5.1 *How Aldi and Lidl developed low-cost strategies that even Wal-Mart could not match* 150

The keys to being a successful low-cost provider 151

When a low-cost provider strategy works best 151

Pitfalls to avoid in pursuing a low-cost provider strategy 152

KEY DEBATE 5.1 *Is cost leadership a discrete position or just another type of differentiation?* 153

Broad differentiation strategies 155

Managing the value chain to create the differentiating attributes 156

Delivering superior value via a broad differentiation strategy 158

When a differentiation strategy works best 160

Pitfalls to avoid in pursuing a differentiation strategy 160

CURRENT PRACTICE 5.1 *Competing successfully with low-cost rivals* 162

Focused (or market niche) strategies 162

A focused low-cost strategy 163

A focused differentiation strategy 163

When a focused low-cost or focused differentiation strategy is attractive 164

EMERGING THEME 5.1 *Technology: is focus the strategy of the future?* 164

The risks of a focused low-cost or focused differentiation strategy 165

ILLUSTRATION CAPSULE 5.2 *Bang & Olufsen – can focused differentiation survive disruptive innovation?* 165

Best-cost provider strategies   166
  When a best-cost provider
  strategy works best   167
  ILLUSTRATION CAPSULE 5.3
  *Toyota's best-cost provider strategy
  for its Lexus line*   167
  Best-cost provider strategy – big risk
  or the only option in future?   168
The contrasting features of the five
generic competitive strategies: a
summary   169
  Successful competitive strategies
  are resource-based   169
  A DIFFERENT VIEW *Combining
  generic strategies with the resource-
  based view: the market-control/value
  matrix*   171
  KEY POINTS   172
  CLOSING CASE *LA Fitness – muscling
  up or slimming down?*   174
  ASSURANCE OF LEARNING
  EXERCISES   177
  EXERCISES FOR SIMULATION
  PARTICIPANTS   177
  ENDNOTES   178

6 **Strategies for changing the game**   180
  OPENING CASE *Can Nintendo keep
  winning in the video games' war?*   181
Going on the offensive – strategic
options to improve a company's
market position   182
  Choosing the basis for competitive
  attack   183
  Choosing which rivals to attack   185
  Blue ocean strategy – a special
  kind of offensive   186
Defensive strategies – protecting
market position and competitive
advantage   188
  Blocking the avenues open to
  challengers   188
  Signalling challengers that
  retaliation is likely   188
Timing a company's offensive and
defensive strategic moves   189
  The potential for first-mover
  advantages   189
  The potential for first-mover
  disadvantages or late-mover
  advantages   190
  ILLUSTRATION CAPSULE 6.1
  *Amazon.com's first-mover
  advantage in online retailing*   191

To be a first mover or not   192
  CURRENT PRACTICE 6.1 *New bases
  for competitive advantage*   192
Strengthening an organization market
position via its scope of operations   194
Horizontal merger and acquisition
strategies   194
  Why mergers and acquisitions
  sometimes fail to produce
  anticipated results   196
Vertical integration strategies   197
  The advantages of a vertical
  integration strategy   197
  The disadvantages of a vertical
  integration strategy   199
  Weighing the pros and cons of
  vertical integration   200
  ILLUSTRATION CAPSULE 6.2 *EDF's
  vertical integration strategy*   201
Outsourcing strategies: narrowing the
scope of operations   202
  A major risk of outsourcing value
  chain activities   203
  KEY DEBATE 6.1 *Is innovation
  better sited within or outside an
  organization?*   204
Strategic alliances and partnerships   205
  Why and how strategic alliances are
  advantageous   207
  Capturing the benefits of strategic
  alliances   208
  The drawbacks of strategic alliances
  and partnerships   209
  How to make strategic alliances
  work   210
  KEY POINTS   212
  CLOSING CASE *Safaricom and
  M-Pesa – innovation through
  partnership*   214
  ASSURANCE OF LEARNING
  EXERCISES   217
  EXERCISES FOR SIMULATION
  PARTICIPANTS   218
  ENDNOTES   218

7 **Strategies for international growth**   222
  OPENING CASE *Oriflame*   223
Why organizations decide to enter
international markets   224
Why competing across national
borders makes strategy-making more
complex   225
  Cross-country variation in factors
  that affect industry competitiveness 225

Locating value chain activities for competitive advantage   227

The impact of government policies and economic conditions in host countries   228

The risks of adverse exchange rate shifts   229

Cross-country differences in demographic, cultural and market conditions   230

CURRENT PRACTICE 7.1 *Diamond model revisited*   231

The concepts of multidomestic competition and global competition   232

Strategic options for entering and competing in international markets   234

Export strategies   234

Licensing strategies   235

Franchising strategies   235

Acquisition strategies   236

Greenfield venture strategies   236

Alliance and joint venture strategies   237

ILLUSTRATION CAPSULE 7.1 *Four examples of cross-border strategic alliances*   238

Competing internationally: the three main strategic approaches   240

Multidomestic strategy – think local, act local   240

Global strategy – think global, act global   242

Transnational strategy – think global, act local   243

The quest for competitive advantage in the international arena   243

Using location to build competitive advantage   243

Sharing and transferring resources and capabilities across borders to build competitive advantage   246

Using cross-border co-ordination for competitive advantage   247

Profit sanctuaries and cross-border strategic moves   247

Using cross-market subsidization to make a strategic move   248

Using cross-border tactics to defend against international rivals   249

Strategies for competing in the markets of developing countries   250

ILLUSTRATION CAPSULE 7.2 *Yum! brands' strategy for becoming the leading food service brand in China*   251

Strategy options for competing in developing country markets   251

Defending against global giants: strategies for local organizations in developing countries   253

ILLUSTRATION CAPSULE 7.3 *How Ctrip successfully defended against international rivals to become China's largest online travel agency*   255

KEY DEBATE 7.1 *Globalization*   256

KEY POINTS   257

CLOSING CASE *Manganese Bronze and Geely – a case of 'Carry on Cabbie'?*   259

ASSURANCE OF LEARNING EXERCISES   261

EXERCISES FOR SIMULATION PARTICIPANTS   262

ENDNOTES   262

8   Corporate strategy   266

OPENING CASE *Sanofi*   267

When to diversify   270

CURRENT PRACTICE 8.1   271

Building shareholder value: a primary justification for diversifying   271

Strategies for entering new businesses   272

Acquisition of an existing business   272

Internal development   273

Joint ventures   273

Choosing a mode of entry   274

Choosing the diversification path: related versus unrelated businesses   275

Strategic fit and diversification into related businesses   276

Identifying cross-business strategic fit along the value chain   278

A DIFFERENT VIEW *Related diversification as a pursuit of market adjacencies*   279

Strategic fit, economies of scope and competitive advantage   281

Diversification into unrelated businesses   282

Building shareholder value via unrelated diversification   283

The path to greater shareholder value through unrelated diversification   285

The drawbacks of unrelated diversification   285

Inadequate reasons for pursuing unrelated diversification   286

KEY DEBATE 8.1 *Theory on determinants of the boundaries of the firm*   287

Combination related–unrelated diversification strategies   288

Evaluating the strategy of a diversified organization   289

    Step 1: Evaluating industry attractiveness   289

    Step 2: Evaluating business-unit competitive strength   292

    Step 3: Checking the competitive advantage potential of cross-business strategic fit   296

    Step 4: Checking for resource fit   296

    Step 5: Ranking the performance prospects of business units and assigning a priority for resource allocation   299

    Step 6: Crafting new strategic moves to improve overall corporate performance   300

    ILLUSTRATION CAPSULE 8.1 *Managing diversification at Johnson & Johnson: the benefits of cross-business strategic fit*   302

    ILLUSTRATION CAPSULE 8.2 *VF's corporate restructuring strategy that made it the star of the apparel industry*   305

    KEY POINTS   305

    CLOSING CASE *Philips exits TV*   307

    ASSURANCE OF LEARNING EXERCISES   308

    EXERCISES FOR SIMULATION PARTICIPANTS   309

    ENDNOTES   310

9   Ethics, corporate social responsibility, environmental sustainability and strategy   312

    OPENING CASE *BP and the Gulf of Mexico disaster*   313

What do we mean by *business ethics*?   314

Where do ethical standards come from – are they universal or dependent on local norms?   314

    ILLUSTRATION CAPSULE 9.1 *Many of Apple's suppliers flunk the ethics test*   315

    The school of ethical universalism   316

    The school of ethical relativism   316

    Ethics and integrative social contracts theory   319

How and why ethical standards impact on the tasks of crafting and executing strategy   320

What are the drivers of unethical strategies and business behaviour?   322

    ILLUSTRATION CAPSULE 9.2 *Investment fraud at Bernard L. Madoff Investment Securities and Stanford Financial Group*   323

    ILLUSTRATION CAPSULE 9.3 *Rebuilding Siemens' reputation*   326

Why should an organization's strategies be ethical?   327

    The moral case for an ethical strategy   327

    EMERGING THEME 9.1 *Technology and socio-cultural change*   328

    The business case for ethical strategies   328

Strategy, corporate social responsibility and evironmental sustainability   330

    What do we mean by *CSR*?   331

    KEY DEBATE 9.1 *Who is responsible for CSR?*   333

    CURRENT PRACTICE 9.1 *Novo Nordisk's triple bottom line*   335

    What do we mean by *sustainability* and *sustainable business practices*?   337

    Crafting CSR and sustainability strategies   338

    The moral case for CSR and environmentally sustainable business practices   339

The business case for CSR and environmentally sustainable business practices   339

    KEY POINTS   342

    CLOSING CASE *News Corporation at bay*   344

    ASSURANCE OF LEARNING EXERCISES   348

    EXERCISES FOR SIMULATION PARTICIPANTS   348

    ENDNOTES   349

Section D: Executing the strategy

10   Building an organization capable of good strategy execution   352

    OPENING CASE *The National Trust – going local*   353

A framework for executing strategy   356
  The principal components of the
  strategy execution process   356
Building an organization capable of
good strategy execution: where
to begin   358
Staffing the organization   359
  Putting together a strong
  management team   360
  ILLUSTRATION CAPSULE 10.1 *How
  GE develops a talented and deep
  management team*   361
  Recruiting, training and retaining
  capable employees   362
Building and strengthening core
competences and competitive
capabilities   363
  Three approaches to building and
  strengthening capabilities   364
  ILLUSTRATION CAPSULE 10.2
  *Toyota's legendary production
  system: a capability that translates
  into competitive advantage*   365
  Upgrading employee skills and
  knowledge resources   368
  Strategy execution capabilities and
  competitive advantage   369
Organizing the work effort with a
supportive organizational structure   369
  Deciding which value chain activities
  to perform internally and which to
  outsource   369
  Aligning the firm's organizational
  structure with its strategy   371
  KEY DEBATE 10.1 *What is the
  relationship between structure and
  strategy?*   375
  Determining how much authority
  to delegate   376
  A DIFFERENT VIEW *The empty
  bird's nest*   379
  Facilitating collaboration with
  external partners and strategic allies   380
  Further perspectives on structuring
  the work effort   380
  KEY POINTS   381
  CLOSING CASE *Lego – the
  comeback kids*   383
  ASSURANCE OF LEARNING
  EXERCISES   385
  EXERCISES FOR SIMULATION
  PARTICIPANTS   386
  ENDNOTES   386

11 Managing internal operations   390
  OPENING CASE *Rogue traders or
  systems failure – a problem for
  banking*   391
Allocating resources to the strategy
execution effort   392
Instituting policies and procedures
that facilitate strategy execution   393
Using process management tools to
strive for continuous improvement   395
  How the process of identifying and
  incorporating best practices works   395
  Business process reengineering,
  total quality management (TQM)
  and Six Sigma quality programmes:
  tools for promoting operating
  excellence   396
  CURRENT PRACTICE 11.1 *Six Sigma
  at a display manufacturer*   399
  ILLUSTRATION CAPSULE 11.1
  *Kuehne + Nagel's use of Six Sigma to
  drive continuous improvement*   400
  Capturing the benefits of
  initiatives to improve operations   402
Installing information and operating
systems   403
  Instituting adequate information
  systems, performance tracking and
  controls   405
  A DIFFERENT VIEW *Dynamic control
  systems*   406
Tying rewards and incentives to
strategy execution   407
  Incentives and motivational
  practices that facilitate good
  strategy execution   407
  ILLUSTRATION CAPSULE 11.2
  *What organizations do to motivate
  and reward employees*   409
  Striking the right balance
  between rewards and punishment   410
  Linking rewards to strategically
  relevant performance outcomes   410
  KEY DEBATE 11.1 *What really
  motivates employees?*   411
  KEY POINTS   413
  CLOSING CASE *Devon County
  Council – lean times*   414
  ASSURANCE OF LEARNING
  EXERCISES   418
  EXERCISES FOR SIMULATION
  PARTICIPANTS   418
  ENDNOTES   419

12   Organizational culture and leadership   422

OPENING CASE *Expressing small town values in a global organization: IKEA*   423

Instilling an organizational culture that promotes good strategy execution   424

Identifying the key features of an organization's culture   424

ILLUSTRATION CAPSULE 12.1 *The organizational cultures at Google and Alberto-Culver*   425

A DIFFERENT VIEW *Schein's levels of culture*   430

Organizational cultures can be strongly or weakly embedded   430

Why organizational cultures matter to the strategy execution process   433

Healthy cultures that aid good strategy execution   434

Unhealthy cultures that impede good strategy execution   435

A DIFFERENT VIEW *A taxonomy of organizational culture*   437

Changing a problem culture: the role of leadership   439

ILLUSTRATION CAPSULE 12.2 *Changing the 'Old Detroit' culture at Chrysler*   442

Leading the strategy execution process   443

Staying on top of how well things are going   444

Putting constructive pressure on organizational units to execute the strategy well and achieve operating excellence   444

KEY DEBATE 12.1 *What is organizational culture?*   445

Leading the process of making corrective adjustments   447

A final word on leading the process of crafting and executing strategy   447

KEY POINTS   448

CLOSING CASE *Telia – subcultures at a time of change*   450

ASSURANCE OF LEARNING EXERCISES   452

EXERCISES FOR SIMULATION PARTICIPANTS   452

ENDNOTES   453

Part Two   Cases in crafting and executing strategy

C1   Reinventing Accor   456

History of Accor   456

Demerger   459

The global hotel industry   460

History   460

Current trends   461

Accor's strategy   462

Key players in the global hotel industry   463

ENDNOTES   464

C2   Apple and the retail industry for specialist consumer electronics in the United Kingdom   466

Background   466

Major industry participants   467

DSGi   467

Comet   468

Independents   469

Euronics   469

Apple retail   469

Apple suppliers   471

Others   471

ENDNOTES   473

C3   Netflix: can it recover from its strategy mistakes?   474

Industry environment   478

Market trends in home viewing of movies   481

Competitive intensity   482

Netflix's business model and strategy   485

Netflix's subscription-based business model   485

Netflix's strategy   487

International expansion strategy   495

Netflix's performance prospects in 2012   496

Highlights of Netflix's performance in the first quarter of 2012   496

ENDNOTES   497

C4   The O-Fold innovation for preventing wrinkles: a good business opportunity?   499

The luggage industry   500

Angel investing   502

Substitutes   504

Price points   504

Patent   507

Business models   507

Sell the idea   507

License the idea   507

Outsource production   508

Use a crawl-walk-run strategy   510

Decision   511

C5 Studio 100: a showcase in show business 512
Studio 100's early years 512
New characters 512
Theme parks 514
A girl's band 515
Merchandising and licensing 516
More formats 516
Some challenges 517
International exploration and exploitation 517
Expansion to French-speaking Belgium 517
Expansion into Germany 518
Studio 100 animation 518
Further internationalization 518
Studio 100's special DNA 518
Creativity, entrepreneurship, and innovation 519
From ideas to business 519
Managing people through an appropriate organizational climate 520
Control 521
A structured approach 521
Portfolio management 521
Communication 521
Creativity embedded in the organization structure 523
Expanding the DNA abroad 523
ENDNOTES 525

C6 Ferretti Group: navigating through stormy seas 527
Introduction 527
The luxury yacht market and industry 527
Ferretti Group profile 529
Organization 529
Marketing, sales and distribution 529
Engineering and manufacturing 529
Strategic development 530
Early growth 530
A period of expansion 530
The private equity role 531
A period of public ownership … and then private again 531
A new investor appears 532
The situation in 2008/9 532
Business development activities 533
Management and financial developments 533
The view from the bridge 533
Getting and staying shipshape 534
Setting and steering a new course 534
Planning for recovery 534

Continued business development efforts 535
Structural developments 535
Improving prospects … and a setback 535
A new strategic development 536
Postscript 537
ENDNOTE 537

C7 Starbucks: evolving into a dynamic global organization 538
Company background 539
Starbucks' coffee, tea, and spice 539
Howard Schultz enters the picture 539
Starbucks and Howard Schultz: the 1982–85 period 541
Schultz becomes frustrated 542
Starbucks as a private company: 1987–92 544
Market expansion outside the Pacific Northwest 545
Starbucks' stores: design, ambience, and expansion of locations 546
Store design 546
Store ambience 548
Store expansion strategy 548
Starbucks' strategy to expand its product offerings and enter new market segments 549
Starbucks' consumer products group 555
Advertising 556
Vertical integration 556
Howard Schultz's efforts to make Starbucks a great place to work 556
Instituting health-care coverage for all employees 556
A stock option plan for employees 557
Starbucks stock purchase plan for employees 557
The workplace environment 558
Employee training and recognition 558
Starbucks' values, business principles, and mission 560
Starbucks' mission statement 560
Starbucks' coffee purchasing strategy 562
Pricing and purchasing arrangements 562
Starbucks ethical sourcing practices for coffee beans 562
Coffee roasting operations 563
Starbucks' corporate social responsibility strategy 564

Top management changes: changing
roles for Howard Schultz   566
Howard Schultz's campaign to
reinvigorate Starbucks, 2008–11   567
Starbucks' future prospects   567
   ENDNOTES   568

C8   **Rhino capture in Kruger National
Park**   570
Kruger National Park   571
Income generation from game
capture   571
Park services   573
SANParks' game capture unit   573
Capturing a rhino   573
Rhino hunting   577
Poaching   582
Animal supermarket   583
SANParks' justification   583
   ENDNOTES   584

C9   **Robin Hood**   585

C10   **NIS: geopolitical breakthrough
or strategic failure?**   587
NIS (Naftna Industrija Srbije)   588
JSC Gazprom Neft   589
Republic of Serbia   589
NIS: challenges and solutions   590
Politics   590
Culture   592
Economics   592

C11   **Kyaia**   595
Introduction   595
The Portuguese footwear industry   595
History of the Kyaia Group   597
Organizational structure   598
The Fly London brand and products   600
Internationalization and overall
control of the value chain   600
Distribution strategies   602
Introducing the RFID technology
along the supply chain   604
The single-sequence production
technology   604
Conclusion   605
   References   606
   Respondents   606
   ENDNOTES   606

C12   **Microsoft's strategic alliance
with Nokia**   607
Joining forces in the smartphone
wars   607
About Microsoft   608
Microsoft and the mobile OS space   609
The changing mobile OS market   610
Microsoft and Nokia forge strategic
alliance   612
Google buys Motorola Mobility   614
The road ahead   615
   ENDNOTES   618

Index   621

Preface

The defining trait of this European edition is an invigorated and much sharpened presentation of the material in each of the 12 chapters, with an as up-to-date and engaging discussion of the core concepts and analytical tools as you will find anywhere. All this has been tailored specifically for our European readers. Complementing the text chapters is a fresh, engrossing collection of cases to ignite interest in strategy, translate enthusiasm into learning achievements and enable you to shine in the classroom.

This edition represents one of our most important and thoroughgoing revisions ever. The new author team has revised the text thoroughly throughout to bring it up to date and make it better suited for courses run in Europe. The overriding objectives were to inject new perspectives and the best academic thinking, strengthen linkages to the latest research findings, modify the coverage and exposition as needed to ensure the most relevant content, and give every chapter a major facelift. While this European edition retains the 12-chapter structure of the prior edition, every chapter has been totally refreshed. Coverage was trimmed in some areas and expanded in others. New material has been added. The presentations of some topics were recast, others fine-tuned and still others left largely intact. As with past editions, scores of new examples have been added, along with fresh Illustration Capsules, to make the content come alive and to provide a ringside view of strategy in action. We have also added new cases to begin and end each chapter to help put the key issues in context and demonstrate how strategy works in real life. You will also find coverage of the latest research, emerging issues and current practice. But none of the changes have altered the fundamental character that has driven the text's success over three decades. The chapter content continues to be solidly mainstream and balanced, mirroring *both* the penetrating insight of academic thought and the pragmatism of real-world strategic management. And, as always, we have taken great care to keep the chapters very reader-friendly and exceptionally teachable.

A differentiating feature of this text has always been the tight linkage between the content of the chapters and the cases. The line-up of cases that accompany the European edition is outstanding in this respect – an appealing mix of strategically relevant and thoughtfully crafted cases, certain to engage students and sharpen their skills in applying the concepts and tools of strategic analysis. Many involve high-profile companies that the students will immediately recognize and relate to; all are framed around key strategic issues and serve to add depth and context to the topical content of the chapters.

For some years now, growing numbers of business schools world-wide have been moving from a purely text-case course structure to a more robust and energizing text-case-simulation course structure. Incorporating a competition-based strategy simulation has the strong appeal of providing class members with an immediate and engaging opportunity to apply the concepts and analytical tools covered in the chapters and to become personally involved in crafting and executing a strategy for a virtual company that they have been assigned to manage and that competes head-to-head with companies run by other class members. Two widely used and pedagogically effective online strategy simulations, the *Business Strategy Game (BSG)* and *GLO-BUS,* are optional companions for this text. Both simulations were created by this text's senior author and, like the cases, are closely linked to the content of each chapter in the text. The Exercises for Simulation Participants, found at the end of each chapter, provide clear guidance to students in applying the concepts and analytical tools covered in the chapters to the issues and decisions that they have to wrestle with in managing their simulation company.

Through our experiences as lecturers, we understand the assessment demands on instructors teaching strategic management and business policy courses. The European edition includes a set of Assurance of Learning Exercises at the end of each chapter that link to the specific learning objectives appearing at the beginning of each chapter and highlighted throughout the text. *An important new instructional feature of the European edition is the linkage of selected chapter-end Assurance of Learning Exercises to the publisher's web-based assignment and assessment platform called Connect.* Students can use the online Connect supplement to (1) complete two or three of the Assurance of Learning Exercises appearing at the end of each of the 12 chapters, (2) complete chapter-end quizzes, and (3) enter their answers to a select number of the suggested assignment questions.

In addition, both of the companion strategy simulations have a built-in Learning Assurance Report that quantifies how well students performed on nine skills/learning measures *versus tens of thousands of other students world-wide* who completed the simulation in the past 12 months. The chapter-end Assurance of Learning Exercises, the all-new online and Connect exercises, and the Learning Assurance Report generated at the conclusion of the *BSG* and *GLO-BUS* simulations provides lecturers with easy-to-use, empirical measures of student learning in their course. All can be used in conjunction with other instructor-developed or school-developed scoring rubrics and assessment tools to comprehensively evaluate course or programme learning outcomes and measure compliance with the Association to Advance Collegiate Schools of Business (AACSB) accreditation standards.

Taken together, the various components of the European edition package and the supporting set of instructor and student resources provide enormous course design flexibility and a powerful kit of teaching/learning tools.

Revitalized and Effective Content: The Signature of the European Edition

Our objective in undertaking a major revision of this text was to ensure that its content was current, with respect to both scholarship and managerial practice, and was presented in as clear and compelling a fashion as possible. We established five criteria for meeting this objective, namely, that the final product must:

- Explain core concepts in language that students can grasp and provide first-rate examples of their relevance and use by actual companies.

- Thoroughly explain the tools of strategic analysis, how they are used and where they fit into the managerial process of crafting and executing strategy.

- Incorporate the latest developments in the theory and practice of strategic management in every chapter to keep the content solidly in the mainstream of contemporary strategic thinking – but also provide some challenges to these views from academia and practice.

- Focus squarely on what every student needs to know about crafting and executing business strategies in today's market environments.

- Provide an attractive set of contemporary cases that involve headline strategic issues and give students ample opportunity to apply what they have learned from the chapters.

We believe the European edition meets all five criteria. Chapter discussions are to the point but, at the same time, our explanations of core concepts and analytical tools are covered in enough depth to make them understandable and usable. Chapter content is driven by including well-settled strategic management principles, fresh examples that illustrate the principles through the practices of real-world companies, recent research findings and contributions to the literature on strategic management and the latest thinking from prominent academics and practitioners. There is a logical flow from one chapter to the next, as well as an unparalleled set of cases with which to illustrate the key points and concepts in practice.

Six stand-out features strongly differentiate this text and the accompanying instructional package from others in the field:

1. *Our coverage of the resource-based theory of the firm in the European edition is unsurpassed by any other leading strategy text.* Resourced-base view (RBV) principles and

concepts are prominently and comprehensively integrated into our coverage of crafting both single business and multibusiness strategies. In Chapters 3–8 it is repeatedly emphasized that a company's strategy must be matched *not only* to its external market circumstances *but also* to its internal resources and competitive capabilities. Moreover, an RBV perspective is thoroughly integrated into the presentation on strategy execution (Chapters 10, 11 and 12) to make it unequivocally clear how and why the tasks of assembling intellectual capital and building core competences and competitive capabilities are absolutely critical to successful strategy execution and operating excellence.

2. *Our coverage of the relational view, which focuses on co-operative strategies and the role that interorganizational activity can play in the pursuit of competitive advantage, is similarly unsurpassed by other leading texts.* The topics of alliances, joint ventures, franchising and other types of co-operative and collaborative relationships are featured prominently in a number of chapters and are integrated into other material throughout the text as well. We show how strategies of this nature can contribute to the success of single business companies as well as multibusiness enterprises. And while we begin with coverage of such topics with respect to firms operating in domestic markets, we extend our discussion of this material to the international realm as well.

3. *Our coverage of business ethics, core values, social responsibility and environmental sustainability is unsurpassed by any other leading strategy text.* In this new edition, we have embellished the highly important chapter 'Ethics, Corporate Social Responsibility, Environmental Sustainability and Strategy' with fresh content so that it can better fulfil the important functions of (1) alerting students to the role and importance of ethical and socially responsible decision-making and (2) addressing the accreditation requirement of the AACSB International that business ethics be visibly and thoroughly embedded in the core curriculum. Moreover, discussions of the roles of values and ethics are integrated into portions of other chapters to further reinforce why and how considerations relating to ethics, values, social responsibility and sustainability should figure prominently in the managerial task of crafting and executing company strategies.

4. *The calibre of the case collection in the European edition is first rate* from the standpoints of student appeal, teachability and suitability for drilling students in the use of the concepts and analytical treatments in Chapters 1–12. The cases included in this edition are the very latest, the best and the most on target that we could find. They range from well-kown multinationals and global brands to small- to medium-sized enterprises (SMEs) and a range of sectors including not-for-profit and services and tourism. Many of them have been tested in undergraduate and postgraduate classes over the last two years and modified as a result.

5. *The text is paired with the publisher's innovative web-based assignment and assessment platform called Connect.* This will enable lecturers to gauge students ability in accurately completing a range of interactive exercises written for this edition.

6. *Two cutting-edge and widely used strategy simulations – the BSG and GLO-BUS – are optional companions to the European edition.* These give you unmatched capability to employ a text-case-simulation model of course delivery.

Organization, Content and Features of the European-Edition Text Chapters

The following rundown summarizes the noteworthy features and topical emphasis in this new edition:

- Although Chapter 1 continues to focus on the central questions of '*What is strategy?*' and '*Why is it important?*' the presentation of this material has been sharpened considerably, with more concise definitions of the key concepts and significant updating to improve the currency of the material. We introduce students to the primary approaches to building competitive advantage and the key elements of business-level strategy. Following Henry Mintzberg's process approach, we explain why a company's strategy is partly planned and partly reactive and why a strategy and its environment tend to co-evolve over time. We discuss the importance of a viable business model that outlines the company's customer value proposition and its profit formula, framing this discussion in terms of key elements of value, price and cost. We show how the mark of a winning strategy is its ability to pass three tests: (1) the *fit test* (for internal and external fit); (2) the *competitive advantage test*; and (3) the *performance test*; And we explain why good company performance depends on good strategy execution as well as a sound strategy. In short, this brief chapter is a perfect accompaniment for your opening-day lecture on what the course is all about and why it matters.

- Chapter 2 delves more deeply into the managerial process of actually crafting and executing a strategy. The focal point of the chapter is the five-step managerial process of crafting and executing strategy: (1) forming a strategic vision of where the company is headed and why; (2) developing strategic as well as financial objectives with which to measure the company's progress; (3) crafting a strategy to achieve these targets and move the company toward its market destination; (4) implementing and executing the strategy; and (5) monitoring progress and making corrective adjustments as needed. Students are introduced to such core concepts as strategic visions, mission statements and core values, the balanced scorecard, strategic intent and business-level versus corporate-level strategies. There is a robust discussion of why *all managers are on a company's strategy-making, strategy-executing team* and why a company's strategic plan is a collection of strategies devised by different managers at different levels in the organizational hierarchy. The chapter ends with a section on how to exercise good corporate governance and examines the conditions that led to recent high-profile corporate governance failures.

- Chapter 3 sets on the now familiar analytical tools and concepts of industry and competitive analysis and demonstrates the importance of tailoring strategy to fit the circumstances of a company's industry and competitive environment. The stand-out feature of this chapter is a presentation of Michael Porter's 'five-forces model of competition' *that has long been the clearest, most straightforward discussion of any text in the field*. The text here has been enhanced by introducing a more critical assessment of industry analysis in the light of more recent ideas and concepts such as hyper-competition and opportunities for collaboration. This edition also provides expanded coverage of a company's macro-environment, moving beyond the basic PESTEL/STEEPLE style analysis by introducing students to Scenario Planning and the need to be alert to 'weak signals' – especially important after the events of 2007/8.

- Chapter 4 presents the resource-based view of the firm and convincingly argues why a company's strategy must be built around its most competitively valuable resources and capabilities. We provide students with a simple taxonomy for identifying a company's resources and capabilities and frame our discussion of how a firm's resources and capabilities can provide a sustainable competitive advantage with the *VRIN model*. We introduce the notion of a company's *dynamic capabilities* and cast SWOT (strengths, weaknesses, opportunities, threats) analysis as a simple, easy-to-use way to assess a company's overall situation in terms of its ability to seize market opportunities and ward off external threats. There is solid coverage of value chain analysis, benchmarking and competitive strength assessments – standard tools for appraising a company's relative cost position and customer value proposition *vis-à-vis* rivals. *An important feature of this chapter is a table showing how key financial and operating ratios are calculated and how to interpret them*; students will find this table handy in doing the number crunching needed to evaluate whether a company's strategy is delivering good financial performance.

- Chapter 5 deals with the basic approaches used to compete successfully and gain a competitive advantage over market rivals. This discussion is framed around the five generic competitive strategies – low-cost leadership, differentiation, best-cost provider, focused differentiation and focused low cost. We emphasize that regardless of a company's choice, competitive success depends on a company's capacity to deliver more customer value – one way or another. We provide a fuller treatment of *cost drivers* and *uniqueness drivers* as the keys to bringing down a company's cost and enhancing its differentiation, respectively, in support of this overall goal. This section also introduces a range of other generic strategy approaches which build on the classic framework above.

- Chapter 6 continues the theme of competitive strategies for single-business firms with its spotlight on *strategic actions (offensive and defensive) and their timing*, including Blue ocean strategies and first-mover advantages and disadvantages. It also serves to segue into the material covered in the next two chapters (on international and diversification strategies) by introducing the topic of *strategies that alter a company's scope of operations*. The chapter features sections on the strategic benefits and risks of horizontal mergers and acquisitions, vertical integration and outsourcing of certain value chain activities. The concluding section of this chapter covers the advantages and drawbacks of using strategic alliances and co-operative arrangements to alter a company's scope of operations, with some pointers on how to make strategic alliances work.

- Chapter 7 explores the full range of strategy options for expanding a company's geographic scope and competing in foreign markets: export strategies, licensing, franchising, establishing a wholly owned subsidiary via acquisition or 'greenfield' venture and alliance strategies. In the European edition, we have added new coverage of topics such as Porter's *Diamond of National Advantage*; the choice between *multidomestic, global, and transnational strategies; profit sanctuaries* and cross-border strategic moves; and *the quest for competitive advantage via sharing, transferring, or accessing valuable resources and capabilities across national borders*. The chapter concludes with a discussion of the special issues of competing in the markets of developing countries and the strategies that local companies can use to defend against global giants.

- Chapter 8 introduces the topic of corporate-level strategy – a topic of concern for multi-business companies pursuing diversification. This chapter begins by explaining why successful diversification strategies must create shareholder value and lays out the three essential tests that a strategy must pass to achieve this goal *(the industry attractiveness, cost-of-entry and better-off tests)*. We discuss alternative means of entering new businesses (acquisition, internal start-up or joint venture) and offer a method for discerning which choice is a firm's best option. Then we turn our attention to a comparison of related versus unrelated diversification strategies, showing that they differ in terms of the nature of their critical resources *(specialized versus general parenting capabilities)* and whether they can exploit cross-business strategic fit for competitive gain. The chapter's analytical spotlight is trained on the techniques and procedures for assessing the strategic attractiveness of a diversified company's business portfolio – the relative attractiveness of the various industries the company has diversified into, the company's competitive strength in each of its lines of business and the extent to which there is *strategic fit* and *resource fit* among its different businesses. The chapter concludes with a brief survey of a company's four main post-diversification strategy alternatives: (1) sticking closely with the existing business line-up; (2) broadening the diversification base; (3) divesting some businesses and retrenching to a narrower diversification base; and (4) restructuring the make-up of the company's business line-up.

- Chapter 9 reflects the very latest in the literature on (1) a company's duty to operate according to ethical standards; (2) a company's obligation to demonstrate socially responsible behaviour and corporate citizenship; and (3) why more companies are limiting strategic initiatives to those that meet the needs of consumers in a manner that protects natural resources and ecological support systems needed by future generations. The discussion includes approaches to ensuring consistent ethical standards for companies with international operations. The contents of this chapter will definitely give students some things to ponder and will help to make them more *ethically aware* and conscious of *why all companies should conduct their business in a socially responsible and sustainable manner*. Chapter 9 has been written as a stand-alone chapter that can be assigned in the early, middle or late part of the course.

- Chapter 10 begins a three-chapter module on executing strategy (Chapters 10–12), anchored around a pragmatic, compelling conceptual framework. Chapter 10 presents an overview of this 10-step framework and then develops the first three pieces of it; (1) *staffing the organization* with capable managers and employees; (2) *marshalling the resources and building the organizational capabilities* required for successful strategy execution; and (3) *creating a strategy-supportive organizational structure* and structuring the work effort. We discuss three approaches to building and strengthening a company's capabilities, ranging from internal development to acquisitions to collaborative arrangements, and consider outsourcing as an option for structuring the work effort. We argue for matching a company's organizational structure to its strategy execution requirements, describe four basic types of organizational structures (simple, functional, multidivisional and matrix) and discuss centralized versus decentralized decision-making. We conclude with some further perspectives on facilitating collaboration with external partners and structuring the company's work effort.

- Chapter 11 covers five important topics concerning strategy execution: (1) *allocating ample resources* to strategy-critical activities; (2) ensuring that *policies and procedures* facilitate rather than impede strategy execution; (3) employing *process management tools* and adopting *best practices* to drive continuous improvement in the performance of value chain activities; (4) installing *information and operating systems* that enable company personnel to better carry out their strategic roles proficiently; and (5) tying *rewards and incentives* directly to good strategy execution and the achievement of performance targets.

- Chapter 12 concludes the text with a discussion of corporate culture and leadership in relation to good strategy execution. The recurring theme throughout the final three chapters is that implementing strategy entails figuring out the specific actions, behaviours and conditions that are needed for a smooth strategy-supportive operation and then following through to get things done and deliver results. The goal here is to ensure that students understand that the strategy-executing phase is a make-things-happen and make-them-happen-right kind of managerial exercise – one that is critical for achieving operating excellence and reaching the goal of strong company performance.

These 12 chapters convey the best thinking of academics and practitioners in the field of strategic management. The ultimate test of the text, of course, is the positive pedagogical impact it has in seminars and lectures.

The Case Collection

The case line-up in this edition is full of interesting companies and valuable lessons for students in the art and science of crafting and executing strategy. There are shorter cases, such as the chapter opening and closing cases, and much longer ones at the back of the book to meet every need.

Some of the cases feature global brands and well-recognized names, others are about small to medium-sized enterises (SMEs). We have tried to make the cases as diverse as possible to allow students to appreciate strategy in a range of organizations, from public sector and not-for-profit to family businesses, entrepreneurial start-ups and multinationals. The line-up includes cases that will provide students with insight into the special demands of competing in industry environments where technological developments are an everyday event, product life cycles are short, and competitive manoeuvring among rivals comes fast and furious. Some of the cases involve situations in which company resources and competitive capabilities play as large a role in the strategy-making, strategy-executing scheme of things as industry and competitive conditions do. Most cases are from Europe but there are also plenty of international cases too to reflect the globalization of the world economy. This wide array of cases and examples are designed to give a well-rounded picture of contemporary and classic strategy.

The Two Strategy Simulation Supplements: The *BSG* and *GLO-BUS*

The *BSG* and *GLO-BUS: Developing Winning Competitive Strategies* – two competition-based strategy simulations that are delivered online and that feature automated processing and grading of performance – are available for use with the European edition.

- The *Business Strategy Game* is the world's most popular strategy simulation, having been used in courses involving over 600 000 students at more than 700 university campuses in over 40 countries.
- *GLO-BUS*, a somewhat simpler strategy simulation introduced in 2004, has been used at more than 400 university campuses world-wide in courses involving over 120 000 students.

How the Strategy Simulations Work

In both the *BSG* and *GLO-BUS*, class members are divided into teams of one to five persons and assigned to run a company that competes head-to-head against companies run by other class members.

- In *BSG*, team members run an athletic footwear company, producing and marketing both branded and private-label footwear.
- In *GLO-BUS*, team members operate a digital camera company that designs, assembles and markets entry-level digital cameras and upscale, multifeatured cameras.

In both simulations, companies compete in a global market arena, selling their products in four geographic regions – Europe-Africa, North America, Asia-Pacific and Latin America. Each management team is called upon to craft a strategy for their company and make decisions relating to plant operations, workforce compensation, pricing and marketing, social responsibility/citizenship and finance.

Company co-managers are held accountable for their decision-making. Each company's performance is scored on the basis of earnings per share, return on equity investment, stock price, credit rating and image rating. Rankings of company performance, along with a wealth of industry and company statistics, are available to company co-managers after each decision round to use in making strategy adjustments and operating decisions for the next competitive round. You can be certain that the market environment, strategic issues and operating challenges that company co-managers must contend with are *very tightly linked* to what your class mates will be reading about in the text chapters. The circumstances that co-managers face in running their simulation company embrace the very concepts, analytical tools and strategy options they encounter in the text chapters (this is something you can quickly confirm by skimming through some of the Exercises for Simulation Participants that appear at the end of each chapter).

We suggest that you complete 1 or 2 practice rounds and anywhere from 4 to 10 regular (scored) decision rounds (more rounds are better than fewer rounds). Each decision round represents a year of company operations and will entail roughly two hours of time for company co-managers to complete. In traditional 12-week, semester-long courses, there is merit in scheduling one decision round per week. In courses that run 5–10 weeks, it is wise to schedule two decision rounds per week for the last several weeks of the term (sample course schedules are provided for courses of varying length and varying numbers of class meetings).

When the instructor-specified deadline for a decision round arrives, the simulation server automatically accesses the saved decision entries of each company, determines the competitiveness and buyer appeal of each company's product offering relative to the other companies being run by students in your class, and then awards sales and market shares to the competing companies, geographic region by geographic region. The unit sales volumes awarded to each company *are totally governed by*:

- how its prices compare against the prices of rival brands;
- how its product quality compares against the quality of rival brands;
- how its product line breadth and selection compare;
- how its advertising effort compares;
- and so on, for a total of 11 competitive factors that determine unit sales and market shares.

The competitiveness and overall buyer appeal of each company's product offering *in comparison to the product offerings of rival companies* is all-decisive – this algorithmic feature is what makes *BSG* and *GLO-BUS* 'competition-based' strategy simulations. Once each company's sales and market shares are awarded based on the competitiveness of its respective overall product offering, the various company and industry reports detailing the outcomes of the decision round are then generated. Company co-managers can access the results of the decision round 15–20 minutes after the decision deadline.

The Compelling Case for Incorporating Use of a Strategy Simulation

There are *three exceptionally important benefits* associated with using a competition-based simulation in strategy courses:

1. *A three-pronged text-case-simulation course model delivers significantly more teaching learning power than the traditional text-case model.* Using *both* cases and a strategy simulation to drill students in thinking strategically and applying what they read in the text chapters is a stronger, more effective means of helping them connect theory with practice and develop better business judgement. What cases do that a simulation cannot is to give class members broad exposure to a variety of companies and industry situations and insight into the kinds of strategy-related problems managers face. But what a competition-based strategy simulation does far better than case analysis is thrust class members squarely into *an active, hands-on managerial role* where they are totally responsible for assessing market conditions, determining how to respond to the actions of competitors, forging a long-term direction and strategy for their company and making all kinds of operating decisions. Because they are held fully accountable for their decisions and their company's performance, *co-managers are strongly motivated* to dig deeply into company operations, probe for ways to be more cost-efficient and competitive and ferret out strategic moves and decisions calculated to boost company performance. *Consequently, incorporating both case assignments and a strategy simulation to develop the skills of class members in thinking strategically and applying the concepts and tools of strategic analysis turns out to be more pedagogically powerful than relying solely on case assignments – there is stronger retention of the lessons learned and better achievement of course learning objectives.*

   To provide you with quantitative evidence of the learning that occurs with using the *BSG* or *GLO-BUS,* there is a built-in Learning Assurance Report showing how well each class member performs on nine skills/learning measures versus tens of thousands of students world-wide who have completed the simulation in the past 12 months.

2. *The competitive nature of a strategy simulation arouses positive energy and steps up the whole tempo of the course by a notch or two.* Nothing sparks excitement quicker or better than the concerted efforts on the part of class members at each decision round to achieve a high industry ranking and avoid the perilous consequences of being outcompeted by other students. Students really enjoy taking on the role of a manager, running their own company, crafting strategies, making all kinds of operating decisions, trying to outcompete rival companies and getting immediate feedback on the resulting company performance. Lots of back-and-forth chatter occurs when the results of the latest simulation round become available and co-managers renew their quest for strategic moves and actions that will strengthen company performance. Co-managers become *emotionally invested* in running their company and figuring out what strategic moves to make to boost

their company's performance. Interest levels climb. All this stimulates learning and causes students to see the practical relevance of the subject matter and the benefits of taking your course. This translates into *a livelier, richer learning experience from a student perspective and better instructor course evaluations.*

3. *Use of a fully automated online simulation reduces the time lecturers spend on course preparation, course administration and grading.* Since the simulation exercise involves a 20- to 30-hour workload for student teams (roughly two hours per decision round times 10–12 rounds, plus optional assignments), simulation adopters often compensate by trimming the number of assigned cases from, say, 10–12 to perhaps 4–6. This significantly reduces the time instructors spend reading cases, studying teaching notes and otherwise getting ready to lead class discussion of a case or grade oral team presentations. Course preparation time is further cut because you can use several class days to have students meet in the computer lab to work on upcoming decision rounds or a three-year strategic plan (in lieu of lecturing on a chapter or covering an additional assigned case). Not only does use of a simulation permit assigning fewer cases, but it also permits you to eliminate at least one assignment that entails considerable grading on your part. Grading one less written case or essay exam or other written assignment saves enormous time. With *BSG* and *GLO-BUS,* grading is effortless and takes only minutes; once you enter percentage weights for each assignment in your online grade book, a suggested overall grade is calculated for you. You will be pleasantly surprised – and quite pleased – at how little time it takes to gear up for and to administer the *BSG* or *GLO-BUS.*

In sum, incorporating use of a strategy simulation turns out to be *a win-win proposition for both students and instructors.* Moreover, a very convincing argument can be made that a competition-based strategy simulation is *the single most effective teaching/learning tool that instructors can employ to teach the discipline of business and competitive strategy, to make learning more enjoyable and to promote better achievement of course learning objectives.*

A Bird's-eye View of the *BSG*

The setting for the *BSG* is the global athletic footwear industry (there can be little doubt in today's world that a globally competitive strategy simulation is *vastly superior* to a simulation with a domestic-only setting). Global market demand for footwear grows at the rate of 7–9 per cent annually for the first five years and 5–7 per cent annually for the second five years. However, market growth rates vary by geographic region – Europe-Africa, North America, Latin America and Asia-Pacific.

Companies begin the simulation producing branded and private-label footwear in two plants, one in North America and one in Asia. They have the option to establish production facilities in Latin America and Europe-Africa, either by constructing new plants or by buying previously constructed plants that have been sold by competing companies. Company co-managers exercise control over production costs on the basis of the styling and quality they opt to manufacture, plant location (wages and incentive compensation vary from region to region), the use of best practices and Six Sigma programmes to reduce the production of defective footwear and to boost worker productivity, and compensation practices.

All newly produced footwear is shipped in bulk containers to one of four geographic distribution centres. All sales in a geographic region are made from footwear inventories in that region's distribution centre. Costs at the four regional distribution centres are a function of inventory storage costs, packing and shipping fees, import tariffs paid on incoming pairs shipped from foreign plants and exchange rate impacts. At the start of the simulation, import tariffs average $3 per pair in Europe-Africa, $4 per pair in Latin America and $5 in the Asia-Pacific region. However, the Free Trade Treaty of the Americas allows tariff-free movement of footwear between North America and Latin America. Instructors have the option to alter tariffs as the game progresses.

Companies market their brand of athletic footwear to footwear retailers world-wide and to individuals buying online at the company's website. Each company's sales and market share in the branded footwear segments hinges on its competitiveness on 11 factors: attractive pricing; footwear styling and quality; product line breadth; advertising; use of mail-in rebates; appeal of celebrities endorsing a company's brand; success in convincing footwear retailers to carry its brand; number of weeks it takes to fill retailer orders, effectiveness of a company's online sales effort at its website; and customer loyalty. Sales of private-label footwear hinge solely on being the low-price bidder.

All told, company co-managers make as many as 53 types of decisions each period that cut across production operations (up to 10 decisions per plant, with a maximum of four plants), plant capacity additions/sales/upgrades (up to 6 decisions per plant), worker compensation and training (3 decisions per plant), shipping (up to 8 decisions per plant), pricing and marketing (up to 10 decisions in four geographic regions), bids to sign celebrities (2 decision entries per bid), financing of company operations (up to 8 decisions) and corporate social responsibility and environmental sustainability (up to 6 decisions).

Each time company co-managers make a decision entry, an assortment of on-screen calculations instantly shows the projected effects on unit sales, revenues, market shares, unit costs, profit, earnings per share, return an equity (ROE) and other operating statistics. The on-screen calculations help team members evaluate the relative merits of one decision entry versus another and put together a promising strategy.

Companies can employ any of the five generic competitive strategy options in selling branded footwear – low-cost leadership, differentiation, best-cost provider, focused low cost and focused differentiation. They can pursue essentially the same strategy world-wide or craft slightly or very different strategies for the Europe-Africa, Asia-Pacific, Latin America and North America markets. They can strive for competitive advantage based on more advertising, a wider selection of models, more appealing styling/quality, bigger rebates and so on.

Any well-conceived, well-executed competitive approach is capable of succeeding, provided it is not overpowered by the strategies of competitors or defeated by the presence of too many copycat strategies that dilute its effectiveness. The challenge for each company's management team is to craft and execute a competitive strategy that produces good performance on five measures: earnings per share, return on equity investment, stock price appreciation, credit rating and brand image.

All activity for the *Business Strategy Game* takes place at www.bsg-online.com.

A Bird's-eye View of *GLO-BUS*

The industry setting for *GLO-BUS* is the digital camera industry. Global market demand grows at the rate of 8–10 per cent annually for the first five years and 4–6 per cent annually for the second five years. Retail sales of digital cameras are seasonal, with about 20 per cent of consumer demand coming in each of the first three quarters of each calendar year and 40 per cent coming during the big fourth-quarter retailing season.

Companies produce entry-level and upscale, multifeatured cameras of varying designs and quality in a Taiwan assembly facility and ship assembled cameras directly to retailers in Europe-Africa, North America, Asia-Pacific, and Latin America. All cameras are assembled as retail orders come in and are shipped immediately upon completion of the assembly process – companies maintain no finished-goods inventories, and all parts and components are delivered on a just-in-time basis (which eliminates the need to track inventories and simplifies the accounting for plant operations and costs). Company co-managers exercise control over production costs on the basis of the designs and components they specify for their cameras, workforce compensation and training, the length of warranties offered (which affects warranty costs), the amount spent for technical support provided to buyers of the company's cameras and their management of the assembly process.

Competition in each of the two product market segments (entry-level and multifeatured digital cameras) is based on 10 factors: price, camera performance and quality; number of quarterly sales promotions; length of promotions in weeks; size of the promotional discounts offered;

advertising; number of camera models; size of retail dealer network; warranty period; and amount/calibre of technical support provided to camera buyers. Low-cost leadership, differentiation strategies, best-cost provider strategies and focus strategies are all viable competitive options. Rival companies can strive to be the clear market leader in either entry-level cameras or upscale multifeatured cameras or both. They can focus on one or two geographic regions or strive for geographic balance. They can pursue essentially the same strategy world-wide or craft slightly or very different strategies for the Europe-Africa, Asia-Pacific, Latin America and North America markets. Just as with the *BSG*, almost any well-conceived, well-executed competitive approach is capable of succeeding, *provided it is not overpowered by the strategies of competitors or defeated by the presence of too many copycat strategies that dilute its effectiveness.*

Company co-managers make 49 types of decisions each period, ranging from research and development (R&D), camera components and camera performance (10 decisions) to production operations and worker compensation (15 decisions) to pricing and marketing (15 decisions) to the financing of company operations (4 decisions) to corporate social responsibility (5 decisions). *Each time participants make a decision entry, an assortment of on-screen calculations instantly shows the projected effects on unit sales, revenues, market shares, unit costs, profit, earnings per share, ROE and other operating statistics. These on-screen calculations help team members evaluate the relative merits of one decision entry versus another and stitch the separate decisions into a cohesive and promising strategy.* Company performance is judged on five criteria: earnings per share; return on equity investment; stock price; credit rating; and brand image.

All activity for *GLO-BUS* occurs at www.glo-bus.com.

Administration and Operating Features of the Two Simulations

The Internet delivery and user-friendly designs of both *BSG* and *GLO-BUS* make them incredibly easy to administer, even for first-time users. And the menus and controls are so similar that you can readily switch between the two simulations or use one in your undergraduate class and the other in a graduate class. If you have not yet used either of the two simulations, you may find the following of particular interest:

- Setting up the simulation for your course is done online and takes about 10–15 minutes. Once set-up is completed, no other administrative actions are required beyond those of moving participants to a different team (should the need arise) and monitoring the progress of the simulation (to whatever extent desired).

- Participant's Guides are delivered electronically to class members at the website – students can read the guide on their monitors or print out a copy, as they prefer.

- There are 2–4-minute Video Tutorials scattered throughout the software (including each decision screen and each page of each report) that provide on-demand guidance to class members who may be uncertain about how to proceed.

- Complementing the Video Tutorials are detailed and clearly written Help sections explaining 'all there is to know' about (a) each decision entry and the relevant cause–effect relationships, (b) the information on each page of the Industry Reports, and (c) the numbers presented in the Company Reports. *The Video Tutorials and the Help screens allow company co-managers to figure things out for themselves, thereby curbing the need for students to ask the instructor 'how things work'.*

- Built-in chat capability on each screen enables company co-managers to collaborate online in the event that a face-to-face meeting to review results and make decision entries is not convenient (or feasible, as is usually the case for class members taking an online course). Company co-managers can also use their mobile phones to talk things over while online looking at the screens.

- Both simulations are quite suitable for use in distance learning or online courses (and are currently being used in such courses on numerous campuses).

- Participants and instructors are notified via email when the results are ready (usually about 15–20 minutes after the decision round deadline specified by the instructor/game administrator).

- Following each decision round, participants are provided with a complete set of reports – a six-page Industry Report, a one-page Competitive Intelligence report for each geographic region that includes strategic group maps and bulleted lists of competitive strengths and weaknesses, and a set of Company Reports (income statement, balance sheet, cash flow statement, and assorted production, marketing and cost statistics).

- Two 'open-book' multiple-choice tests of 20 questions are built into each simulation. The quizzes, which you can require or not as you see fit, are taken online and automatically graded, with scores reported instantaneously to participants and automatically recorded in the instructor's electronic grade book. Students are automatically provided with three sample questions for each test.

- Both simulations contain a three-year strategic plan option that you can assign. Scores on the plan are automatically recorded in the instructor's online grade book.

- At the end of the simulation, you can have students complete online peer evaluations (again, the scores are automatically recorded in your online grade book).

- Both simulations have a Company Presentation feature that enables each team of company co-managers to easily prepare PowerPoint slides for use in describing their strategy and summarizing their company's performance in a presentation to either the class, the instructor, or an 'outside' board of directors.

- *A Learning Assurance Report provides you with hard data concerning how well your students performed vis-à-vis students playing the simulation world-wide over the past 12 months.* The report is based on nine measures of student proficiency, business know-how, and decision-making skill and can also be used in evaluating the extent to which your school's academic curriculum produces the desired degree of student learning in so far as accreditation standards are concerned.

For more details on either simulation, please consult Section 2 of the Instructor's Manual accompanying this text or register as an instructor at the simulation websites (www.bsg-online. com and www.glo-bus.com) to access even more comprehensive information. You should also consider signing up for one of the webinars that the simulation authors conduct several times each month (sometimes several times weekly) to demonstrate how the software works, walk you through the various features and menu options and answer any questions. We think you will be quite impressed with the cutting-edge capabilities that have been programmemed into the *BSG* and *GLO-BUS,* the simplicity with which both simulations can be administered, and their exceptionally tight connection to the text chapters, core concepts and standard analytical tools.

Resources and Support Materials for the European Edition

For Students

Key points summaries   At the end of each chapter is a synopsis of the core concepts, analytical tools and other key points discussed in the chapter. These chapter-end synopses, along with the core concept definitions and margin notes scattered throughout each chapter, help students focus on basic strategy principles, digest the messages of each chapter and prepare for tests.

Two sets of chapter-end exercises   Each chapter concludes with two sets of exercises. The *Assurance of Learning Exercises* can be used as the basis for class discussion, oral presentation assignments, short written reports and substitutes for case assignments. The *Exercises* *for Simulation Participants* are designed expressly for use by adopters who have incorporated use of a simulation and want to go a step further in tightly and explicitly connecting the chapter content to the simulation company their students are running.

A value-added website The student section of the Online Learning Centre (OLC) at website **www.mcgraw-hill.co.uk/textbooks/thompson** contains a number of helpful aids:

● Ten-question self-scoring chapter tests that students can take to measure their grasp of the material presented in each of the 12 chapters.

● The 'Guide to Case Analysis', containing sections on what a case is, why cases are a standard part of courses in strategy, preparing a case for class discussion, doing a written case analysis, doing an oral presentation and using financial ratio analysis to assess a company's financial condition. We suggest having students read this guide before the first class discussion of a case.

● PowerPoint slides for each chapter.

● Selected Case Video clips.

The *Connect*™ *Management* web-based assignment and assessment platform Beginning with this edition, we have taken advantage of the publisher's innovative *Connect*™ assignment and assessment platform and created several features that simplify the task of assigning and grading three types of exercises for students:

● There are self-scoring chapter tests consisting of 20–25 multiple-choice questions that students can take to measure their grasp of the material presented in each of the 12 chapters.

● There are Interactive Application exercises for each of the 12 chapters that test students in the use and application of the concepts and tools of strategic analysis.

● The *Connect*™ platform also includes Interactive Application exercises for the cases within the book to test their comprehensive and analytical skills.

Many of the *Connect*™ exercises are automatically graded (others entail student entry of essay answers), thereby simplifying the task of evaluating each class member's performance and monitoring the learning outcomes. The progress-tracking function built into the *Connect*™ *Management* system enables you to:

● view scored work immediately and track individual or group performance with assignment and grade reports;

● access an instant view of student or class performance relative to learning objectives;

● collect data and generate reports required by many accreditation organizations, such as AACSB.

For Instructors

Online Learning Centre (OLC) In addition to the student resources, the instructor section of site **www.mcgraw-hill.co.uk/textbooks/thompson** includes an Instructor's Manual and other support materials.

Instructor's Manual (IM) The accompanying IM contains:

● a section on suggestions for organizing and structuring your course;

● sample syllabi and course outlines;

● a set of lecture notes on each chapter;

● answers to the chapter-end Assurance of Learning Exercises;

● a copy of the test bank;

- a comprehensive case teaching note for each of the end-of-book cases. These teaching notes are filled with suggestions for using the case effectively, have very thorough, analysis-based answers to the suggested assignment questions for the case and contain an epilogue detailing any important developments since the case was written.

Test bank and EZ test online   There is a test bank containing over 900 multiple-choice questions and short-answer/essay questions. It has been tagged with AACSB and Bloom's Taxonomy criteria. All of the test bank questions are also accessible within a computerized test bank powered by McGraw-Hill's flexible electronic testing programme EZ Test Online (**www.eztestonline.com**). Using EZ Test Online allows you to create paper and online tests or quizzes. With EZ Test Online, instructors can select questions from multiple McGraw-Hill test banks or author their own and then either print the test for paper distribution or give it online.

PowerPoint slides   To facilitate delivery preparation of your lectures and to serve as chapter outlines, you will have access to approximately 500 colourful and professional-looking slides displaying core concepts, analytical procedures, key points and all the figures in the text chapters.

Instructor's Resource CD   All of our instructor supplements are available on disk; the disk set includes the complete IM, computerized test bank (EZ Test), accompanying PowerPoint slides and the Digital Image Library with all of the figures from the text. It is a useful aid for compiling a syllabus and daily course schedule, preparing customized lectures and developing tests on the text chapters.

The *BSG* and *GLO-BUS* online simulations   Using one of the two companion simulations is a powerful and constructive way of emotionally connecting students to the subject matter of the course. We know of no more effective way to arouse the competitive energy of students and prepare them for the challenges of real-world business decision-making than to have them match strategic wits with classmates in running a company in head-to-head competition for global market leadership.

|MANAGEMENT

 STUDENTS...

Want to get **better grades**? *(Who doesn't?)*

Prefer to do your **homework online**? *(After all, you are online anyway...)*

Need **a better way** to **study** before the big test?

(A little peace of mind is a good thing...)

A: With **McGraw-Hill's *Connect*™ *Plus Management*,**

STUDENTS GET:

- **Easy online access** to homework, tests and quizzes assigned by your instructor.

- **Immediate feedback** on how you're doing. (No more wishing you could call your instructor at 1 a.m.)

- **Quick access** to lectures, practice materials, eBook, and more. (All the material you need to be successful is right at your fingertips.)

- A Self-Quiz and Study tool that **assesses your knowledge** and **recommends** specific readings, supplemental study materials, and additional practice work.

- Access to the e-book of this text.

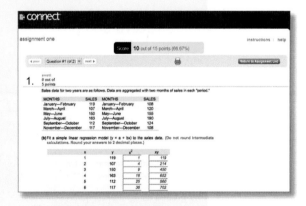

Less managing. More teaching. Greater learning.

INSTRUCTORS...

Would you like your **students** to show up for class **more prepared**?
(Let's face it, class is much more fun if everyone is engaged and prepared...)

Want an **easy way to assign** homework online and track student **progress**?
(Less time grading means more time teaching...)

Want an **instant view** of student or class performance? *(No more wondering if students understand...)*

Need to **collect data and generate reports** required for administration or accreditation? *(Say goodbye to manually tracking student learning outcomes...)*

Want to **record and post your lectures** for students to view online?

With **McGraw-Hill's** *Connect™ Plus Management,*

INSTRUCTORS GET:

- Simple **assignment management**, allowing you to spend more time teaching.

- **Auto-graded** assignments, quizzes and tests.

- **Detailed visual reporting** where student and section results can be viewed and analysed.

- Sophisticated **online testing** capability.

- A **filtering and reporting** function that allows you to easily assign and report on materials that are correlated to sections in the book and level of difficulty.

- An easy-to-use **lecture capture** tool.

- The option to **upload course documents** for student access.

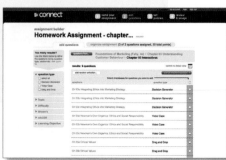

Want an online, **searchable version** of your textbook?

Wish your textbook could be **available online** while you're doing your assignments?

 ### Connect™ Plus Management eBook

If you choose to use *Connect™ Plus Marketing*, you have an affordable and searchable online version of your book integrated with your other online tools.

Connect™ Plus Management eBook offers a media-rich version of the book, including:

- Topic search
- Direct links from assignments
- Adjustable text size
- Jump to page number
- Print by section

 Want to get more **value** from your textbook purchase?

Think learning marketing should be a bit more **interesting**?

 ### Check out the STUDENT RESOURCES section under the *Connect™* Library tab.

Here you'll find a wealth of resources designed to help you achieve your goals in the course. Every student has different needs, so explore the STUDENT RESOURCES to find the materials best suited to you.

Let us help make our content your solution

At McGraw-Hill Education our aim is to help lecturers to find the most suitable content for their needs delivered to their students in the most appropriate way. Our **custom publishing solutions** offer the ideal combination of content delivered in the way which best suits lecturer and students.

Our custom publishing programme offers lecturers the opportunity to select just the chapters or sections of material they wish to deliver to their students from a database called CREATE™ at

www.mcgrawhillcreate.co.uk

CREATE™ contains over two million pages of content from:
- textbooks
- professional books
- case books – Harvard Articles, Insead, Ivey, Darden, Thunderbird and BusinessWeek
- Taking Sides – debate materials

Across the following imprints:
- McGraw-Hill Education
- Open University Press
- Harvard Business Publishing
- US and European material

There is also the option to include additional material authored by lecturers in the custom product – this does not necessarily have to be in English.

We take care of everything from start to finish in the process of developing and delivering a custom product to ensure that lecturers and students receive exactly the material needed in the most suitable way.

With a Custom Publishing Solution, students enjoy the best selection of material deemed to be the most suitable for learning everything they need for their courses – something of real value to support their learning. Teachers are able to use exactly the material they want, in the way they want, to support their teaching on the course.

Please contact **your local McGraw-Hill representative** with any questions or alternatively contact Warren Eels e: **warren_eels@mcgraw-hill.com**.

Acknowledgements

We heartily acknowledge the contributions of the case researchers whose case-writing efforts appear herein and the companies whose co-operation made the cases possible. To each one goes a very special thank you. We cannot overstate the importance of timely, carefully researched cases in contributing to a substantive study of strategic management issues and practices. From a research standpoint, strategy-related cases are invaluable in exposing the generic kinds of strategic issues that companies face, in forming hypotheses about strategic behaviour and in drawing experience-based generalizations about the practice of strategic management. From an instructional standpoint, strategy cases give students essential practice in diagnosing and evaluating the strategic situations of companies and organizations, in applying the concepts and tools of strategic analysis, in weighing strategic options and crafting strategies and in tackling the challenges of successful strategy execution. Without a continuing stream of fresh, well-researched and well-conceived cases, the discipline of strategic management would lose its close ties to the very institutions whose strategic actions and behaviour it is aimed at explaining. There is no question, therefore, that first-class case research constitutes a valuable scholarly contribution to the theory and practice of strategic management.

A great number of colleagues and students at various universities, business acquaintances and people at McGraw-Hill provided inspiration, encouragement and counsel during the course of this project. Like all text authors in the strategy field, we are intellectually indebted to the many academics whose research and writing have blazed new trails and advanced the discipline of strategic management.

Arthur A. Thompson

Margaret A. Peteraf

John E. Gamble

A. J. Strickland

Alex Janes

Ciara Sutton

About the authors

Arthur A. Thompson, Jr earned his BS and PhD degrees in economics from the University of Tennessee, spent three years on the economics faculty at Virginia Tech, and served on the faculty of the University of Alabama's College of Commerce and Business Administration for 24 years. In 1974 and again in 1982, Dr Thompson spent semester-long sabbaticals as a visiting scholar at the Harvard Business School.

His areas of specialization are business strategy, competition and market analysis, and the economics of business enterprises. In addition to publishing over 30 articles in some 25 different professional and trade publications, he has authored or co-authored five textbooks and six computer-based simulation exercises. His textbooks and strategy simulations have been used at well over 1000 college and university campuses world-wide.

Margaret A. Peteraf is the Leon E. Williams Professor of Management at the Tuck School of Business at Dartmouth College. She is an internationally recognized scholar of strategic management, with a long list of publications in top management journals. She has earned myriad honours and prizes for her contributions, including the 1999 Strategic Management Society Best Paper Award recognizing the deep influence of her work on the field of strategic management. Professor Peteraf is on the Board of Directors of the Strategic Management Society and has been elected as a Fellow of the Society. She served previously as a member of the Academy of Management's Board of Governors and as Chair of the Business Policy and Strategy Division of the Academy. She has also served in various editorial roles and is presently on nine editorial boards, including the *Strategic Management Journal,* the *Academy of Management Review* and *Organization Science.* She has taught in Executive Education programmes in various programmes around the world and has won teaching awards at the MBA and Executive level.

Professor Peteraf earned her PhD, MA and MPhil. at Yale University and held previous faculty appointments at Northwestern University's Kellogg Graduate School of Management and at the University of Minnesota's Carlson School of Management.

John E. Gamble is currently a Professor of Management in the Mitchell College of Business at the University of South Alabama. His teaching specialty at USA is strategic management and he also conducts a course in strategic management in Germany, which is sponsored by the University of Applied Sciences in Worms.

Dr Gamble's research interests centre on strategic issues in entrepreneurial, health care and manufacturing settings. His work has been published in various scholarly journals and he is the author or co-author of more than 50 case studies published in an assortment of strategic management and strategic marketing texts. He has done consulting on industry and market analysis for clients in a diverse mix of industries.

Dr A J (Lonnie) Strickland is the Thomas R. Miller Professor of Strategic Management at the Culverhouse School of Business at the University of Alabama. He is a native of North Georgia, and attended the University of Georgia, where he received a BSc degree in mathematics and physics; Georgia Institute of Technology, where he received an MS in industrial management; and Georgia State University, where he received his PhD in business administration.

Lonnie's experience in consulting and executive development is in the strategic management arena, with a concentration in industry and competitive analysis. He has developed strategic planning systems for numerous firms all over the world. He served as Director of Marketing and Strategy at Bell-South, has taken two companies to the New York Stock Exchange, is one of the founders and directors of American Equity Investment Life Holding (AEL) and serves on numerous boards of directors. He is a very popular speaker in the area of strategic management.

Alex Janes is Senior Lecturer in Strategy and Director of Education for Management at the University of Exeter Business School. Prior to joining Exeter in 2009, he gained over 20 years' management experience in both the public and private sectors. His commercial career included working in a range of diverse industries from antiques, tourism and electronics, to telecoms, trade exhibitions and education. He has worked in senior management roles and at board level in both an interim and permanent capacity for much of his career. Alex was also a part-time member of the Business School faculty at the Open and Plymouth Universities.

Alex has trained and coached hundreds of marketers and managers working for organizations, from small charities to FTSE 100 companies, including: American Express; Astra Zeneca; Burberry; BT plc, Corus, Cadbury, Dominos, KPMG, Microsoft, RNIB, Royal Bank of Canada, Siemens, Tate Gallery, Twentieth Century Fox, Wrigley, Wyeth Pharmaceuticals, and Xerox. He continues his consulting work in strategic management and marketing alongside his teaching and research.

Alex gained a postgraduate diploma in Marketing from the Chartered Institute of Marketing, where he is a subject examiner. More recently he completed an MBA and MEd with the Open University.

Ciara Sutton is a Research Fellow and lecturer in the Department of Marketing and Strategy at the Stockholm School of Economics. In addition she holds the position of Area Principal in Strategy and International Business at the Stockholm School of Economics in Russia.

Ciara teaches at Master's and Executive level in Strategy and International Business, with a particular interest in cross-cultural management, and is a coach and programme leader in change management, innovation, and business planning projects in various educational and corporate programmes, primarily in Sweden, Finland and Russia.

Ciara's research interests centre on strategic issues in international venture capital and private equity, as well as the concept of global leadership and the role and competencies of global leaders in multinational organizations.

She is Australian, with a BSc (Com.) from the University of New South Wales, Sydney and later earned her MSc and PhD from the Stockholm School of Economics in Sweden.

Guided tour

Chapter structure and organization

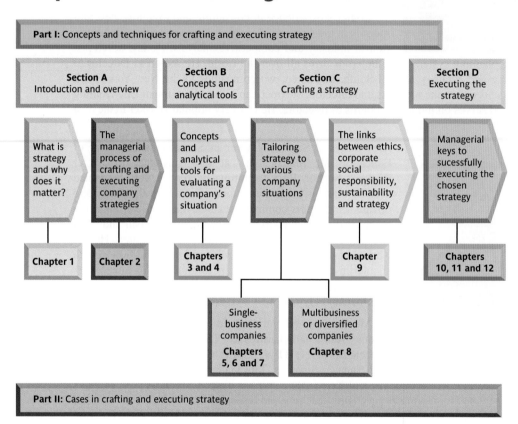

Part I: Concepts and techniques for crafting and executing strategy

Section A
Intoduction and overview

Section B
Concepts and analytical tools

Section C
Crafting a strategy

Section D
Executing the strategy

What is strategy and why does it matter?

The managerial process of crafting and executing company strategies

Concepts and analytical tools for evaluating a company's situation

Tailoring strategy to various company situations

The links between ethics, corporate social responsibility, sustainability and strategy

Managerial keys to sucessfully executing the chosen strategy

Chapter 1

Chapter 2

Chapters 3 and 4

Chapter 9

Chapters 10, 11 and 12

Single-business companies
Chapters 5, 6 and 7

Multibusiness or diversified companies
Chapter 8

Part II: Cases in crafting and executing strategy

Learning objectives

are listed at the beginning of each chapter; corresponding numbered indicators in the margins show where learning objectives are covered in the text.

Learning Objectives

When you have read this chapter you should be a

LO 3.1 Analyse an organization's external macro
identify which of these are the most stra

LO 3.2 Diagnose the factors that shape industry
attractiveness using both traditional app

LO 3.3 Identify the competitive forces at work i
relative strength.

LO 3.4 Describe different industry structures, in
within an industry or sector.

LO 3.5 Discuss the merits of other approaches t
force's concept.

LO 3.6 Explain why in-depth evaluation of a bu

Opening Case

APPLE: RIDING THE STRATEGY ROLLE

On 10 April 2012, Apple confirmed its postion as the wo
This remarkable performance, underpinned by better tha
the fact that Steve Jobs, the driving force behind the firm
picture was very different, as Jobs returned to run the org
went on to transform the organization, through a series o
(PC) manufacturer to one of the coolest organizations o
media player industries. His first move, however, was to s
a niche player in a highly competitive industry, PCs. From
the iMac computer and the iBook notebook. Distributio
sourced to Taiwan. Even in 2011 most manufacturing of A
Apple was back in profit and its share price was at an all-t

However, it was the launch of the iPod in 2001 followe
products moved the organization beyond their compute

Opening Cases

begin each chapter to help bring the subject to life
and feature companies such as Apple, H&M and BP.

Illustration Capsule 1.1

MCDONALD'S STRATEGY IN THE Q

In 2012, McDonald's was setting new sales records d
dence in the USA. Nearly 68 million customers visite
which allowed the organization to record 2011 reve
tively. McDonald's performance in the marketplace h
Industrial Average (the other was Walmart Stores, In
economic meltdown. The organization's sales were ho
with global sales as measured in constant currencies
bined operating margin had risen to nearly 32 per ce
well-conceived and executed Plan-to-Win strategy tha
to-Win strategy included:

● *Improved restaurant operations*. McDonald's global r
ing programmes ranging from on-the-job training f

Illustration Capsules

appear in boxes throughout each chapter to provide
in-depth examples, connect the text presentation to
real-world companies, and convincingly demonstrate
'strategy in action'. Some are appropriate for use as
mini-cases.

CURRENT PRACTICE 3.1

SCENARIO PLANNING AT VISITSCOT

VisitScotland, the national tourism organization for Sco
organization was the key adviser to the Scottish Governn
also supported organizations in the Scottish tourism ind
vision and improvement of tourist facilities in Scotland. I
respiratory syndrome (SARS) outbreak, which had caugh
to improve strategic management in the organization an

DEFINING THE SCOPE AND IDENTIFYING STAKEHO

The original scope of the scenarios was a time frame to 2(
as well as broader consumer needs and wants, plus sup
known and connected through its board.

Current Practice

goes beyond theory to examine how strategy is
being done *now by practitioners and leading
consultants in the field*.

Key Debate 1.1

IS COMPETITIVE ADVANTAGE SUS

In 1994 Professor Richard D'Aveni coined the term 'h
where the frequency of disruption and intensity of co
hope to achieve temporary competitive advantage wi
driven high-velocity industries such as computing or
sectors that illustrated these phenomena initially.
brought increasing numbers of competitors in to m
scope of innovation, and socio-cultural changes inclu
of successful entrepreneurs.

There is nothing new about markets being disru
1930s and 1940s. However, it is the scale and speed
hypercompetitive markets, D'Aveni contends, organiz

Key Debate

explore areas of conflicting views and stimulate discussion.

A Different View – Blue Ocean St

So far in this chapter we have focused on competing
sors, W. Chan Kim and Renee Mauborgne, suggested
this is no longer a recipe for sustained competitive ad
oceans (in reference to the blood spilled in cutthroa
exist but are then created by firms who move into ne

Blue oceans are more than just the unoccupied s
They are not found through benchmarking with con
industries. Chan Kim and Mauborgne cite Canadian
blue ocean strategy approach can be. Cirque du Sole
lectual and artistic content of great theatre shows. In
have previously gone to circus performances.

Cirque du Soleil did not recreate the features of tra
animal acts. All of these features were common to exi
product and in some cases, such as the use of anim

A Different View

encourages students to think critically and question some of the accepted views in strategy.

Core Concepts

A **competence** is an
activity that an
organization has learned
to perform with
proficiency—a
capability, in other
words.

Core Concept

A **core competence** is
an activity that an
organization performs
proficiently that is also
central to its strategy
and competitive success.

A **competence** is an inte
bility, in other words. A co
central to an organization's
iary of Unilever, has a core
keting them with catchy
Karamel Sutra and Phish Fo
zational strength than a co
strategy and the contributio
Often, core competences ca
the engine behind an orga
improvement and lean man

A **distinctive competer**
forms better than its rivals.
core competence. Because
rivals do not have, it qualifi
tage potential. This is partic
tion to deliver exceptional
performance or superior ser
uct innovation, as exemplifi

Margin Notes

define core concepts and call attention to important ideas and principles.

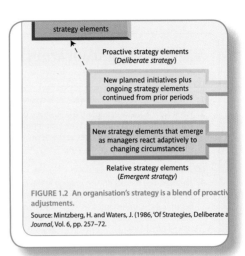

strategy elements

Proactive strategy elements
(*Deliberate strategy*)

New planned initiatives plus
ongoing strategy elements
continued from prior periods

New strategy elements that emerge
as managers react adaptively to
changing circumstances

Relative strategy elements
(*Emergent strategy*)

FIGURE 1.2 An organisation's strategy is a blend of proactiv
adjustments.

Source: Mintzberg, H. and Waters, J. (1986, 'Of Strategies, Deliberate a
Journal, Vol. 6, pp. 257–72.

Figures

scattered throughout the chapters provide
conceptual and analytical frameworks.

CLOSING CASE

A TALE OF TWO CONFECTIONERS: NESTLÉ AND FERRERO

In a small town just outside Turin, Italy, lies one of the
closely guarded secrets in the confectionery world. It
here in 1946 that Michele Ferrero's father and uncle d
oped a blend of hazelnut paste and chocolate, know
Giandujot, which helped them found the organizatio
has grown to be the fourth biggest confectionery man
turing organization in the world. In 2011, the Ferrero G
had a turnover in excess of $8.5 billion (€6.3 billion)
operated through 38 trading organizations, emplo
some 21 000 people world-wide. Ferrero's confectic
brands included Kinder, Nutella, Ferrero Rocher, Giotto

End of Chapter Cases

provide an opportunity for readers to explore the
chapter's key issues further and apply their learning.
Cases include News Corporation, Spotify and Lego.

KEY POINTS

The tasks of crafting and executing organization str
and winning in the marketplace. The key points to t

1. An organization's strategy consists of the overa
    and business approaches that they are employi
    business.

2. The central thrust of an organization's strategy
    long-term competitive position and financial p
    sustainable competitive advantage over them.

3. An organization achieves a sustainable compet
    effectively or efficiently than rivals and when th
    to match or surpass this advantage.

4. An organization's strategy typically evolves ove
    actions on the part of organization managers to
    responses to unanticipated developments and

5. An organization's business model is managem

Key Points

at the end of each chapter provide a handy summary
of essential ideas and things to remember.

EXERCISES FOR SIMULATION PA

LO 3.1, LO 3.2

1. Which of the five competitive forces is creating
2. What are the factors affecting the intensity of ri
   Use the relevant discussion in the chapter to he
   intensity. Would you characterize the rivalry am
   moderate or relatively weak? Why?

LO 3.3

3. Are there any factors driving change in the indu
   these drivers of change have? How will they ch
   become more or less intense? Will they act to b
   organization should consider taking in order to

LO 3.4

Exercises

at the end of each chapter, linked to learning objectives, provide a basis for class discussion, oral presentations and written assignments. Several chapters have exercises that qualify as mini-cases.

End of Book Cases

detail the strategic circumstances of actual companies and provide practice in applying the concepts and tools of strategic analysis.

Case 1

Reinventing Accor

Alex Janes
University of Exeter

Denis Hennequin became chief executive officer (CEO) of t
2010 with the vision to make the firm one of the world's top
2015. The group had decided to focus on its hotel brands in 20
to demerge this part of the business from its prepaid busi
Services (re-named Edenred in 2010). The stage was now se

For students: support materials

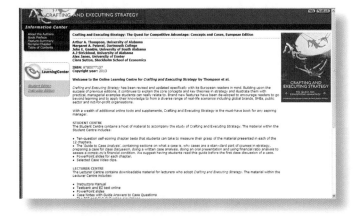

Website

www.mcgraw-hill.co.uk/textbooks/ thompson The student portion of the website features the 'Guide to Case Analysis,' with special sections on what a case is, why cases are a standard part of courses in strategy, preparing a case for class discussion, doing a written case analysis, doing an oral presentation and using financial ratio analysis to assess a company's financial condition. In addition, there are 10-question self-scoring chapter tests and a select number of PowerPoint slides for each chapter.

The *Business Strategy Game (BSG)* or *GLO-BUS* Simulation Exercises

Either one of these text supplements involves teams of students managing companies in a head-to-head contest for global market leadership. Company co-managers have to make decisions relating to product quality, production, workforce compensation and training, pricing and marketing and financing of company operations. The challenge is to craft and execute a strategy that is powerful enough to deliver good financial performance despite the competitive efforts of rival companies. Each company competes in Europe-Africa, America, Latin America and Asia-Pacific.

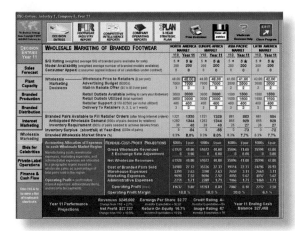

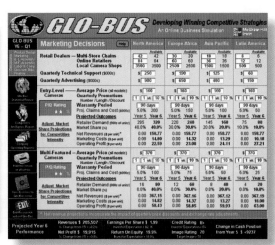

Improve your grades!

20% off any Study Skills book!

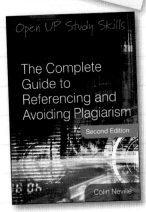

Our Study Skills books are packed with practical advice and tips that are easy to put into practice and will really improve the way you study. Our books will help you:

- ✓ Improve your grades
- ✓ Avoid plagiarism
- ✓ Save time
- ✓ Develop new skills

- ✓ Write confidently
- ✓ Undertake research projects
- ✓ Sail through exams
- ✓ Find the perfect job

Special offer!

As a valued customer, buy online and receive 20% off any of our Study Skills books by entering the promo code **BRILLIANT**

www.openup.co.uk/studyskills

PART ONE

Concepts and techniques for crafting and executing strategy

Part One	Concepts and techniques for crafting and executing strategy	1
Section A	Introduction and overview	
1	What is strategy and why is it important?	2
2	Charting an organization's direction: vision and mission, objectives and strategy	24
Section B	Core concepts and analytical tools	
3	Analysing an organization's external environment	56
4	Evaluating an organization's resources, capabilities and competitiveness	98
Section C	Crafting a strategy	
5	Strategies for competitive advantage: generic strategies and beyond	142
6	Strategies for changing the game	180
7	Strategies for international growth	222
8	Corporate strategy	266
9	Ethics, corporate social responsibility, environmental sustainability and strategy	312
Section D	Executing the strategy	
10	Building an organization capable of good strategy execution	352
11	Managing internal operations	390
12	Organizational culture and leadership	422

Chapter One

What is strategy and why is it important?

Strategy means making clear-cut choices about how to compete.

Jack Welch
Former CEO, General Electric

What's the use of running if you are not on the right road?

German proverb

One must have strategies to execute dreams.

Azim Premji
CEO Wipro Technologies and one of the world's richest people

Learning Objectives

When you have read this chapter you should be able to:

LO 1.1   Explain why every organization needs a sound strategy to compete successfully, manage the conduct of its business and strengthen its prospects for long-term success.

LO 1.2   Illustrate how an organization's strategy tends to evolve over time because of changing circumstances and ongoing management efforts to improve the organization's strategy.

LO 1.3   Justify why it is important for an organization to have a viable business model that outlines the organization's customer value proposition and its profit formula.

LO 1.4   Explain the tests that are used to identify a good strategy.

APPLE: RIDING THE STRATEGY ROLLERCOASTER

On 10 April 2012, Apple confirmed its postion as the world's most valuable firm with a market capitalization of over $600 billion. This remarkable performance, underpinned by better than expected sales of the firm's iPad and latest iPhone products, is despite the fact that Steve Jobs, the driving force behind the firm, died in October 2011. Just over 14 years earlier in September 1997, the picture was very different, as Jobs returned to run the organization he founded in the 1970s, Apple was close to bankruptcy. Jobs went on to transform the organization, through a series of well-crafted and executed strategies, from an ailing personal computer (PC) manufacturer to one of the coolest organizations on the planet with a stake in the music, mobile telephone and personal media player industries. His first move, however, was to scale Apple back to a size that matched its real industry position – that of a niche player in a highly competitive industry. From 1997 to 1999 the organization focused on a limited number of products – the iMac computer and the iBook notebook. Distribution and staffing levels were reduced and most manufacturing was outsourced to Taiwan. Even in 2011 most manufacturing of Apple gadgets was outsourced to a range of suppliers. By the end of 1999 Apple was back in profit and its share price was at an all-time high.

However, it was the launch of the iPod in 2001 followed by the iTunes service in 2003, that started Apple's transformation. These products moved the organization beyond their computer niche and into consumer electronics. Apple soon dominated the digital download market with a 70 per cent share despite not being the first or best digital music player on the market. Customers were attracted by the iPod's iconic design despite competitors such as Sony and Microsoft. In contrast, the iPhone, launched in 2007, was seen as a ground-breaking new product that took the integration of mobile telecoms, the Internet and other consumer electronic gadgets, started by organizations such as RIM and Nokia, to a higher level of sophistication. The iPhone had a wide range of unique product features and was hailed by *TIME* magazine as the Invention of the Year in 2007. The iPhone's launch coincided with a dramatic growth in the smartphone sector of the mobile telecoms handset industry and attracted other new entrants such as HTC (the organization behind Google's Nexus One), Samsung and Microsoft. Apple's most recent new venture was into the market for tablet computers with the iPad, launched in 2010. In each of the new sectors it has entered, Apple products appear to become the standard by which other devices are judged. For example, as each new smartphone was launched after 2007 the media would speculate whether this was an iPhone 'killer'. This may be because they have underestimated the strategy underpinning each launch. The electronic gadgets may be relatively easy to copy, which is why Apple has become involved in an increasingly bitter series of patent disputes with competitors. However, each gadget is part of a platform, rather than a standalone. The iPod has iTunes; the iPhone a huge range of apps from games to restaurant recommendations and the iPad combines an even wider range of functions including access to e-books, films and the Internet. Each gadget is also aimed at a high growth market, though how far each new product itself has added to the growth in that market is not clear.

Apple's performance has also demonstrated the success of their strategy to date. By April 2012 the firm had sold 67 million of its iPad devices, which were launched in 2010. It took 24 years to sell a similar number of Mac computers. This rapid growth also saw net income grow from $1.9 billion in 2006 to $11.6 billion in just the first quarter of 2012. Apple's profits are greater than Google's quarterly turnover and the firm's value is close to that of Microsoft's at the height of the dotcom boom in the late 1990s. Apple's shares have risen from $3.19 in 1997 to a staggering $644 in 2012 despite the global financial crisis.

QUESTION

1. What are the key factors underpinning Apple's success in the last 15 years?

Sources: BBC News (2012) 'Apple's market value hits $600bn', BBC News, 10 April. Available online at www.bbc.co.uk/news/business-17669078 (accessed 30 May 2012); BBC News (2012) 'Apple doubles quarterly profits to $11.6bn (£7.2bn)', BBC News, 25 April 2012. Available online at www.bbc.co.uk/news/business-17835234 (accessed 30 May 2012); Rumelt, R. (2011) *Good Strategy/Bad Strategy*, Profile Books, London; Marino, L. and Gamble, J. (2010) 'Apple Inc. in 2010', in Thompson, A., Peterhaf, M. Gamble, J. and Strickland, A. (2010) *Crafting and Executing Strategy*, New York, McGraw Hill Irwin, pp. 141–54; Weber, T. (2009) 'Why smartphones are not suffering in the recession', *BBC News*, 10 October.

In any given year, a group of organizations will stand out as the top performers, in terms of metrics such as profitability, sales growth, or growth in shareholder value or as a benchmark of best practice in their field. Some of these organizations will find that their star status fades quickly due to little more than a fortuitous constellation of circumstances, such as being in the right business at the right time. But other organizations somehow manage to rise to the top and stay there, year after year, pleasing their customers, shareholders and other stakeholders alike in the process. We can see evidence of this from the opening case on Apple and their performance over the last decade or more. Other organizations such as IKEA, Nintendo, Google, Coca-Cola, Unilever, Rolls Royce and BHP Billiton also come to mind but long-lived success is not just limited to developed world multinationals. Diverse kinds of organizations, both large and small, from many different countries, have been able to sustain strong performance records, including India's Tata Group (conglomerate), Bangladesh's Grameen Bank (in micro-credit), Korea's Hyundai Heavy Industries (in shipbuilding and construction), Mexico's Cemex (in construction), Taiwan's HTC (in telecommunications) and Britain's Autonomy (in software).

What can explain the ability of organizations like these to beat the odds and experience prolonged periods of profitability and growth? Why is it that some organizations, like Ryanair and John Lewis Partnership, continue to do well even when others in their industry are faltering? Why can some organizations survive and prosper even through economic downturns and industry turbulence?

Many factors enter into a full explanation of an organization's performance, of course. Some come from the external environment; others are internal to the organization. But only one thing can account for the kind of long-lived success records that we see in the world's greatest organizations and that is a cleverly crafted and well-executed *strategy,* one that facilitates the capture of emerging opportunities, produces enduringly good performance, is adaptable to changing business conditions and can withstand the competitive challenges from rival organizations.

In this opening chapter, we define the concept of strategy and describe its many facets. We explain what is meant by a competitive advantage, discuss the relationship between an organization's strategy and its business model and introduce you to some of the strategies that can give an organization an advantage over rivals in attracting customers and earning above-average profits. We will look at what sets a winning strategy apart from others and why the calibre of an organization's strategy can determine whether it will enjoy a competitive advantage over other organizations or be burdened by competitive disadvantage. By the end of this chapter, you will have a clear idea of why the tasks of crafting and executing strategy are core management functions and why for an organization to sustain success over the long term, the theory of how it conducts its business[1] should be synthesized with the practical management of each functional piece of that business.

What do we Mean by *Strategy*?

LO 1.1
Explain why every organization needs a sound strategy to compete successfully, manage the conduct of its business and strengthen its prospects for long-term success.

In moving an organization forward, managers of all types of organizations – family-owned businesses, rapidly growing entrepreneurial firms, not-for-profit organizations – such as community interest companies, state-owned enterprises, private equity partnerships, mutuals and co-operatives and the world's leading multinational corporations – face the same three central questions:

1. What is our present situation?
2. Where do we want to go from here?
3. How are we going to get there?

The first question, *'What is our present situation?'* usually prompts managers to evaluate industry conditions, the organization's current financial performance and market standing, its resources and capabilities, its competitive strengths and weaknesses and changes taking place in the business environment that might affect the organization. In essence this is the *context* within which the organization operates.[2] The answer to the question *'Where do we want to go from here?'* lies within management's vision of the organization's future direction – what new customer/client or stakeholder groups and customer/client or stakeholder needs to endeavour to satisfy and what new capabilities to build or acquire. We might see this as the *content* of the organization's strategy. The question *'How are we going to get there?'* challenges managers to craft and execute a strategy capable of moving the organization in the intended direction. This could be termed the *process* of putting the strategy into action and is probably the most difficult element of strategy for managers to control as the reality in most organizations is that planned, deliberate strategies are rarely, if ever, fully realized. However, this does not prevent many successful organizations from investing heavily in the execution element of the strategy process.

Developing clear answers to the question *'How are we going to get there?'* is the essence of managing strategically. However, there are many conflicting studies on and examples of how organizations approach this task. Some organizations, rather than relying on the status quo as a road-map and dealing with new opportunities or threats as they emerge, develop a full-blown game plan that spells out the competitive moves and business approaches that will be employed to compete successfully, attract and please customers and key stakeholders, conduct operations, achieve targeted levels of performance and grow the business.

Other organizations, especially those operating in dynamic and complex environments, have found little merit in the detailed, planned approaches that characterized strategic approaches in the 1960s and 1970s. In markets affected by technological change, convergence, the Internet and the rapid growth of information and communication technology (ICT), or in those that have experienced the rapid changes in regulation and privatization, such as in much of eastern Europe, other, less prescriptive approaches have been taken. Strategy has ceased to be the sole preserve of senior executives, with middle managers mere functionaries charged with the implementation of grand designs. The reality is often that while the chief executive officer (CEO) and directors may still set the overall direction of the organization and define its scope, increasingly staff closer to the front line are involved in strategic thinking and putting strategy into action. Many of these changes have intensified competition and the speed at which strategy is developed. So, in thinking about 'How are we going to get there?' managers need to consider the following:

- *How* to outcompete rivals.
- *How* to respond to changing economic and market conditions and capitalize on growth opportunities.
- *How* to manage each functional piece of the business (e.g. research and development (R&D), supply chain activities, production, sales and marketing, distribution, finance and human resources (HR).
- *How* to improve the organization's financial market and increasingly sustainability performance.

The specific elements that constitute management's answer to the question 'How are we going to get there?' define an organization's business strategy. So, part of an organization's strategy is management's *action plan* for competing successfully and operating profitably, based on an integrated array of considered choices.[3] The crafting of a strategy represents a managerial commitment to follow a particular course. In choosing a strategy, management is in effect saying, 'Among all the many different business approaches and ways of competing we could have chosen, we have decided to employ this particular combination of approaches in moving the organization in the intended direction, strengthening its *market position* and competitiveness and boosting performance.' The strategic choices an organization makes are seldom easy decisions and often involve difficult trade-offs, but that does not excuse failure to pursue a concrete course of action.[4]

In most industries, there are many different avenues for outcompeting rivals and boosting organizational performance, thus giving managers considerable freedom in choosing the specific elements of their organization's strategy.[5] Consequently, some organizations strive to improve their performance by employing strategies aimed at achieving lower costs than rivals, while others pursue strategies aimed at achieving product superiority or personalized customer service or quality dimensions that rivals cannot match. Some organizations opt for wide product lines, while others concentrate their energies on a narrow product line-up. Some position themselves in only one part of the industry's chain of production/distribution activities (preferring to be just in manufacturing or wholesale distribution or retailing), while others are partially or fully integrated, with operations ranging from components production to manufacturing and assembly to wholesale distribution and retailing. Some competitors deliberately confine their operations to local or regional markets; others opt to compete nationally, internationally (several countries) or globally (all or most of the major country markets world-wide). Some organizations decide to operate in only one industry, while others diversify broadly or narrowly into related or unrelated industries. Increasingly, organizations are also using alliances and networks to move their strategy forward. In a number of high-tech arenas groups of organizations share intellectual property through 'research commons', such as the Acer group in Taiwan and Blade.org, a collaborative group of over 100 organizations including IBM and Intel that are involved in the development of new blade platforms.[6] The Open Source movement, typified by Linux and Firefox, competes very successfully with industry giants such as Microsoft and relies on large networks of unpaid volunteers. As of May 2012, Firefox had just over 20 per cent of the browser market against Google Chrome's 19 per cent and Microsoft Explorer's 54 per cent. However, Mozilla only has 12 full-time paid programmers working on Firefox, virtually no marketing budget or influence with computer manufacturers and retailers – against several hundred programmers at Microsoft working on Explorer as well as the substantial market power the software giant has. Mozilla does have an army of several hundred thousand enthusiasts who volunteer advice, programming fixes and promote the product by word of mouth.[7]

There is no shortage of opportunity to fashion a strategy that both tightly fits an organization's own particular situation and is discernibly different from the strategies of rivals. In fact, competitive success requires an organization's managers to make strategic choices about the key building blocks of its strategy that differ from the choices made by competitors – not 100 per cent different but at least different in several important respects. A strategy stands a better chance of succeeding when it is predicated on actions, business approaches and competitive moves aimed at appealing to buyers *in ways that set an organization apart from rivals.* A successful organization's strategy tends to have some distinctive elements that draw in customers and produces a competitive edge. Strategy, at its essence, is about competing differently – doing what rival organizations *do not* do or what rival organizations *cannot* do. Thus, the *position* an organization chooses within its industry or market – however this may be defined – is also a key element of its strategy.[8]

An organization's strategy provides direction and guidance, in terms of not only what the organization *should* do but also what it *should not* do. Knowing what not to do can be as important as knowing what to do, strategically. At best, making the wrong strategic moves will prove a distraction and a waste of organization resources. At worst, it can bring about unintended long-term consequences that put the organization's very survival at risk. This overarching element of an organization's strategy can often be discerned from the *pattern* of decisions and actions over time.[9] It might also be apparent in an organization's vision or mission statement (we look at this in more detail in

> **Core Concept**
>
> An organization's strategy consists of the overarching direction set by managers, plus the competitive moves and business approaches that they are employing to compete successfully, improve performance and grow the business.

Chapter 2). Providing direction and guidance can be a particularly important element of an organization's strategy when it has a more emergent, bottom-up process and needs to ensure coherence and consistency between different parts of the business.

Figure 1.1 illustrates the broad types of actions and approaches that often characterize an organization's strategy in a particular business or industry. Using a simple framework such as this can be a useful starting point for analysing the pattern of strategic decisions made by an organization over time.

For a more concrete example of the specific actions constituting an organization's strategy, see Illustration Capsule 1.1 describing McDonald's strategy in the quick-service restaurant industry.

Strategy and the Quest for Competitive Advantage

Another key element of most organizations' strategy is the actions and moves in the marketplace that managers are taking to gain a competitive edge over rivals. A creative, distinctive strategy that sets an organization apart from rivals and provides a competitive advantage is an organization's most reliable ticket for earning above-average profits. Competing in the marketplace on the basis of a competitive advantage tends to be more profitable than competing with no advantage.

Competitive advantage generally comes from an ability to meet customer needs more *effectively*, with products or services that customers value more highly, or more *efficiently*, at a lower cost. Meeting customer needs more effectively can translate into the ability to command a higher price (e.g. Stella Artois lager) that can improve profits by boosting revenues. Meeting customer needs more cost-effectively can translate into being able to charge lower prices and achieve higher sales volumes (e.g. Carrefour), thereby improving profits on the revenue side as well as the cost side. Furthermore, if an organization's competitive edge holds promise for being sustainable (as opposed to just temporary), then so much the better for both the strategy and the organization's future profitability. What makes a competitive advantage **sustainable** (or durable), as

> **Core Concept**
> An organization achieves **sustainable competitive advantage** when it can meet customer needs more effectively or efficiently than rivals and when the basis for this is durable, despite the best efforts of competitors to match or surpass this advantage.

FIGURE 1.1 Identifying an organization's strategy – what to look for?

Illustration Capsule 1.1

MCDONALD'S STRATEGY IN THE QUICK-SERVICE RESTAURANT INDUSTRY

In 2012, McDonald's was setting new sales records despite a global economic slowdown and declining consumer confidence in the USA. Nearly 68 million customers visited one of McDonald's 33 000 restaurants in 119 countries each day, which allowed the organization to record 2011 revenues and earnings of more than $27 billion and $8.2 billion, respectively. McDonald's performance in the marketplace had made it one of only two organizations listed on the Dow Jones Industrial Average (the other was Walmart Stores, Inc.) that actually increased in share value in 2008–10 in spite of the economic meltdown. The organization's sales were holding up well amid the ongoing economic uncertainty in early 2012, with global sales as measured in constant currencies increasing by more than 3.3 per cent in the second quarter. Its combined operating margin had risen to nearly 32 per cent in December 2011. The organization's success was a result of its well-conceived and executed Plan-to-Win strategy that focused on 'being better, not just bigger'. Key initiatives of the Plan-to-Win strategy included:

- *Improved restaurant operations.* McDonald's global restaurant operations improvement process involved employee training programmes ranging from on-the-job training for new crew members to college-level management courses offered at the organization's Hamburger University. The organization also sent nearly 200 high-potential employees annually to its McDonald's Leadership Institute to build the leadership skills needed by its next generation of senior managers. McDonald's commitment to employee development earned the organization a place on *Fortune*'s list of Top 25 Global Organizations for Leaders in 2010. The organization also trained its store managers to closely monitor labour, food and utility costs.

- *Affordable pricing.* In addition to tackling operating costs in each of its restaurants, McDonald's kept its prices low by closely scrutinizing administrative costs and other corporate expenses. McDonald's saw the poor economy in the USA as an opportunity to renegotiate its advertising contracts with newspapers and TV networks in early 2009. The organization also began to replace its organization-owned vehicles with more fuel-efficient models when gasoline prices escalated dramatically in the USA during 2008. However, McDonald's did not choose to sacrifice product quality in order to offer lower prices. The organization implemented extensive supplier monitoring programmes to ensure that its suppliers did not change product specifications to lower costs. For example, the organization's chicken breasts were routinely checked for weight when arriving from suppliers' production facilities. The organization's broad approach to minimizing non-value-adding expenses allowed it to offer more items on its Dollar Menu in the USA, its Ein Mal Eins menu in Germany and its 100 yen menu in Japan.

- *Wide menu variety and beverage choices.* McDonald's has expanded its menu beyond the popular-selling Big Mac and Quarter Pounder to include such new, healthy quick-service items as grilled chicken salads, chicken snack wraps and premium chicken sandwiches in the USA, Lemon Shrimp Burgers in Germany, and Ebi shrimp wraps in Japan. The organization has also added an extensive line of premium coffees that include espressos, cappuccinos and lattes sold in its McCafe restaurant locations in the USA, Europe and the Asia/Pacific region. McDonald's latte was judged 'as good [as] or better' than lattes sold by Starbucks or Dunkin' Donuts in a review by the *Chicago Tribune*'s Good Eating and Dining staff in December 2008.

- *Convenience and expansion of dining opportunities.* The addition of McCafes helped McDonald's increase same store sales by extending traditional dining hours. Customers wanting a mid-morning coffee or an afternoon snack helped keep store traffic high after McDonald's had sold its last Egg McMuffin, McGriddle or chicken biscuit and before the lunch crowd arrived to order Big Macs, Quarter Pounders, chicken sandwiches or salads. The organization also extended its drive-through hours to 24 hours in more than 25 000 locations in cities around the world where consumers tended to eat at all hours of the day and night. At many high-traffic locations in the USA, double drive-through lanes were added to serve customers more quickly.

- *Ongoing restaurant reinvestment and international expansion.* With more than 14 000 restaurants in the USA, the focus of McDonald's expansion of units was in rapidly growing emerging markets such as Russia and China. The organization had opened over 500 restaurants in China and 314 restaurants in Russia by the end of 2011. The organization had also refurbished about 1500 of its locations in Europe by the end of 2011 as a part of its McCafe rollout and as a way to make its restaurants pleasant places for both customers to dine and employees to work.

Sources: Adamy Janet (2009) 'McDonald's seeks way to keep sizzling', *Wall Street Journal Online*, 10 March; various annual reports; various organization press releases.

opposed to temporary, are elements of the strategy that give buyers *lasting reasons to prefer* an organization's products or services over those of competitors – reasons that competitors are unable to nullify or overcome despite their best efforts.

The connection between competitive advantage and profitability means that many organizations continue to focus on creating a sustainable competitive advantage when crafting a strategy. The key to successful strategy-making is to come up with one or more strategy elements that act as a magnet to draw customers (and/or those providing funding) and that produce a lasting competitive edge over rivals. Indeed, what separates a powerful strategy from a run-of-the-mill or ineffective one is management's ability to forge a series of moves, both in the marketplace and internally, that sets the organization apart from its rivals, tilts the playing field in the organization's favour by giving buyers reason to prefer its products or services, and produces a sustainable competitive advantage over rivals. The bigger and more sustainable the competitive advantage, the better are an organization's prospects for winning in the marketplace and earning superior long-term profits relative to its rivals. Without a strategy that leads to competitive advantage, an organization risks being outcompeted by stronger rivals and locked into mediocre financial performance. The extent to which competitive advantage is truly sustainable in the current environment is explored in Key Debate 1.1 below.

Key Debate 1.1

IS COMPETITIVE ADVANTAGE SUSTAINABLE IN THE TWENTY-FIRST CENTURY?

In 1994 Professor Richard D'Aveni coined the term 'hypercompetiton', which he used to describe industry environments where the frequency of disruption and intensity of competition were such that organizations operating in them could only hope to achieve temporary competitive advantage without adopting a radically different approach to strategy. Technology-driven high-velocity industries such as computing or those affected by dramatic deregulation such as air travel were the sectors that illustrated these phenomena initially. The antecedents to hypercompetition were globalization – which brought increasing numbers of competitors into many markets, technology changes – which increased the pace and scope of innovation, and socio-cultural changes including increased short-termism in financial markets and the lionization of successful entrepreneurs.

There is nothing new about markets being disrupted by innovation, as the work of Schumpeter demonstrated in the 1930s and 1940s. However, it is the scale and speed of change that marks out hypercompetition as a greater threat. In hypercompetitive markets, D'Aveni contends, organizations are unable to build and defend positions in the long term and there is a constant cycle of aggressive manoeuvres as industry members seek to gain a temporary disruptive advantage over rivals. In this sort of environment it is difficult for one or two organizations to dominate an industry. In fact, industry-specific assets built up over time can prove to be a disadvantage as they lock organizations into a way of doing things and this can limit their strategic options. It is hard to predict rivals' moves and the environment facing the organization is unstable, making techniques such as forecasting difficult to rely on. In this sort of environment managers should seek to exploit short-term opportunities to create a series of temporary competitive advantages – perhaps by constantly introducing new products or services to gain frequent first-mover advantage.

Other strategy experts dispute the validity of D'Aveni's argument. Michael Porter (1996) has argued that by fearing and responding to potential hypercompetition, managers make it more likely to happen as they imitate competitors and chase each new technology without assessing its value. Porter's view is that organizations should focus on creating a unique position within an industry. Frequent changes to that position are costly as the organization will have developed a set of activities that support their strategic position and provide a suitable fit. So, it could be argued that managers create hypercompetition because they abandon effective approaches to strategy. This view was supported by Bogner and Barr whose research showed that managers in unstable environments often acted in ways that made their industry more unstable.

▶

◄

There is evidence that hypercompetitive environments are a reality in both developed and emerging economies. Research by Wiggins and Reufli in 2005 and Hermelo and Vassolo in 2010 both found evidence of hypercompetition. Hermelo and Vassolo's work showed that this state was not limited to developed markets and that there was evidence of a reduction in the time competitive advantage could be sustained in Latin America across a range of industries. Wiggins and Reufli's work came to similar conclusions after analysing manufacturing in the USA. Single industry studies, such as Cox and Bridwell's case study on the wine sector in 2007 also supported D'Aveni's theory. However, another study by McNamara, Vaaler and Devers suggested that while hypercompetition existed it was not new and had been in evidence prior to the 1990s.

QUESTIONS

1. Why might some industries be more prone to hypercompetition than others?
2. To what extent do the case studies on Apple and McDonald's in this chapter support the different points of view in this debate?

Sources: D'Aveni, R. (1994) *Hypercompetition: Managing the Dynamics of Strategic Maneuvering*, The Free Press, New York; Schumpeter, J. (1942) *Capitalism, Socialism and Democracy*, Harper, New York; Porter, M. (1996) 'What is strategy?' *Harvard Business Review*, 74(1): 61–78; Bogner, W. and Barr, P. (2000) 'Making sense in hypercompetitive environments: a cognitive explanation for the persistence of high velocity competition', *Organization Science*, 11: 212–26; Wiggins, R. and Reufli, T. (2005) 'Schumpeter's ghost: is hypercompetition making the best of times shorter?' *Strategic Management Journal*, 26: 887–91; Hermelo, F. and Vassolo, R. (2010) 'Institutional development and hypercompetition in emerging economies', *Strategic Management Journal*, 31: 1457–73; Cox, J. and Bridwell, L. (2007) 'Australian organizations using globalisation to disrupt the ancient wine industry', *Competitiveness Review*, 17(4): 209–21; McNamara, G., Vaaler, P. and Devers, C. (2003) 'Same as it ever was: the search for evidence of increasing hypercompetition', *Strategic Management Journal*, 24: 261–78.

Why an Organization's Strategy Evolves over Time

LO 1.2
Illustrate how an organization's strategy tends to evolve over time because of changing circumstances and ongoing management efforts to improve the organization's strategy.

The appeal of a strategy that yields a sustainable competitive advantage is that it offers the potential for an enduring edge over rivals. However, managers of every organization must be willing and ready to modify the strategy in response to changing market conditions, advancing technology, the fresh moves of competitors, shifting buyer needs, emerging market opportunities and new ideas for improving the strategy. In some industries, conditions change at a fairly slow pace, making it feasible for the major components of a good strategy to remain in place for long periods. But in industries where industry and competitive conditions change frequently and in sometimes dramatic ways, the life cycle of a given strategy is short. Industry environments characterized by high-velocity change require organizations to repeatedly adapt their strategies.[10] For example, organizations in industries with rapid-fire advances in technology like medical equipment, electronics and wireless devices often find it essential to adjust key elements of their strategies several times a year, sometimes even finding it necessary to 'reinvent' their approach to provide value to their customers.

Regardless of whether an organization's strategy changes gradually or swiftly, the important point is that the task of crafting strategy is not a one-time event but always a work in progress. Adapting to new conditions and constantly evaluating what is working well enough to continue and what needs to be improved are normal parts of the strategy-making process, resulting in an *evolving strategy*.[11]

An Organization's Strategy is Partly Proactive and Partly Reactive

The evolving nature of an organization's strategy means that typically it is a blend of (1) *proactive* actions to improve the organization's financial performance and secure a competitive edge and (2) *adaptive* reactions to unanticipated developments and fresh market conditions. In most cases, much of an organization's current strategy flows from previously initiated actions and business approaches that are working well enough to merit continuation and from newly launched initiatives aimed at boosting financial performance and edging out rivals. This part of management's action plan for running the organization is its deliberate strategy, consisting of strategy elements that are both planned and realized as planned (while other planned strategy elements may not work out).

But managers must always be willing to supplement or modify the proactive strategy elements with as-needed reactions to unanticipated conditions. Inevitably, there will be occasions when market and competitive conditions take an unexpected turn that calls for some kind of strategic reaction or adjustment. Hence, *a portion of an organization's strategy is always developed reactively,* coming as a response to fresh strategic manoeuvres on the part of rival organizations, unexpected shifts in customer requirements, fast-changing technological developments, newly appearing market opportunities, a changing political or economic climate, or other unanticipated happenings in the surrounding environment. Under conditions of high uncertainty, strategy elements are more likely to emerge from experimentation, trial and error and adaptive learning processes than from a proactive plan. These unplanned, reactive and adaptive strategy adjustments make up the organization's emergent strategy, consisting of the new strategy elements that emerge as changing conditions warrant. An organization's strategy in total (its *realized* strategy) thus tends to be a *combination* of proactive and reactive elements, with certain strategy elements being *abandoned* because they have become obsolete or ineffective – see Figure 1.2.[12] An organization's realized strategy can be observed in the pattern of its actions over time – a far better indicator than any of its strategic plans on paper or public pronouncements about its strategy.

The Relationship between an Organization's Strategy and its Business Model

Closely related to the concept of strategy is the organization's business model. An organization's business model is management's blueprint for delivering a valuable product or service to customers in a manner that will generate ample revenues to cover costs and yield an attractive profit.[13] It is management's story-line for how the strategy

> An organization's strategy is shaped partly by management analysis and choice and partly by the necessity of adapting and learning by doing.

> **Core Concepts**
>
> An organization's proactive (or deliberate) strategy consists of strategy elements that are both planned and realized as planned; its reactive (or emergent) strategy consists of new strategy elements that emerge as changing conditions warrant.

> **Core Concepts**
>
> An organization's business model sets forth the economic logic for making money in a business, given the organization's strategy. It describes two critical elements: (1) the customer value proposition and (2) the operating model.

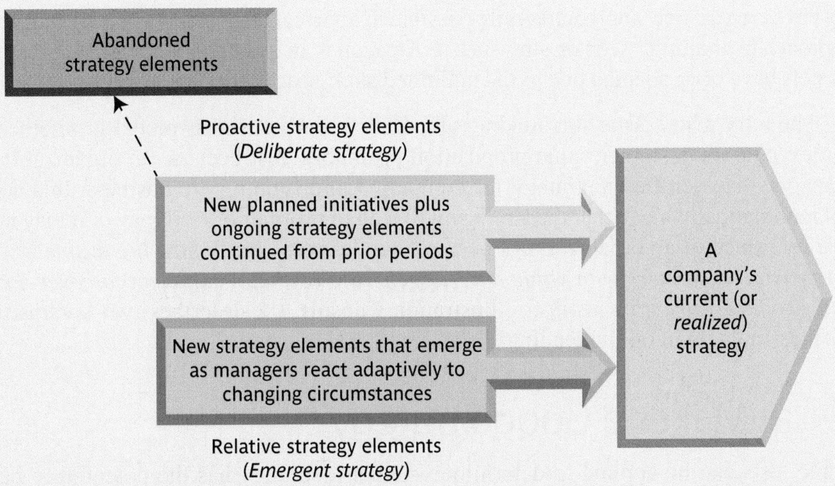

FIGURE 1.2 An organization's strategy is a blend of proactive initiatives and reactive adjustments.

Source: Mintzberg, H. and Waters, J. (1986), 'Of strategies, deliberate and emergent,' *Strategic Management Journal*, 6: 257–72.

will be a money-maker. Without the ability to deliver good profitability, the strategy is not viable and the survival of the business is in doubt.

LO 1.3
Justify why it is important for an organization to have a viable business model that outlines the organization's customer value proposition and its profit formula.

The two crucial elements of an organization's business model are (1) its *customer value proposition* and (2) its *operating model*. The customer value proposition describes the customers the organization is targeting, the products and services it will offer to satisfy their wants and needs at a price they will consider good value and how the organization will gain revenue. The greater the value provided (V) and the lower the price (P), the more attractive the value proposition is to customers. The operating model describes the organization's approach to determining a cost structure and set of activities that will allow for acceptable profits, given the pricing tied to its customer value proposition. More specifically, an organization's profit formula depends on three basic elements: V – the *value* provided to customers, in terms of how effectively the goods or services of the organization meet customers' wants and needs; P – the *price* charged to customers; and C – the organization's *costs*. The lower the costs (C), given the customer value proposition ($V - P$), the greater the ability of the business model to be a money-maker. Thus the operating model reveals how efficiently an organization can meet customer wants and needs and deliver on the value proposition.

Magazines and newspapers employ a business model keyed to delivering information and entertainment they believe readers will find valuable and a profit formula aimed at securing sufficient revenues from subscriptions and advertising to more than cover the costs of producing and delivering their products to readers. Mobile phone providers, satellite radio organizations and broadband providers also employ a subscription-based business model. The business model of network TV and radio broadcasters entails providing free programming to audiences but charging advertising fees based on audience size. Gillette's business model in razor blades involves selling a 'master product' – the razor – at an attractively low price and then making money on repeat purchases of razor blades that can be produced very cheaply and sold at high profit margins. Printer manufacturers like Hewlett-Packard, Lexmark and Epson pursue much the same business model as Gillette – selling printers at a low (virtually break-even) price and making large profit margins on the repeat purchases of printer supplies, especially ink cartridges. There are a range of other common business models including the brokerage model – here the organization charges a fee for bringing buyers and sellers together. This is common in areas such as property, travel and insurance and has been translated effectively into online businesses such as eBay. The growth of the Internet has spawned a large number of new business models. Some are variations on real-world operations and others have created new approaches only possible in a virtual environment. The 'Long Tail' approach to e-tailing[14] seen on sites such as Amazon is an example of how standard retail models have been adapted due to the unlimited shelf space virtual stores possess.

The nitty-gritty issue surrounding an organization's business model is whether it can execute its customer value proposition profitably. Just because an organization's managers have crafted a strategy for competing and running the business, this does not automatically mean that the strategy will lead to profitability – it may or it may not. The relevance of an organization's business model is to clarify *how the business will (1) provide customers with value and (2) generate revenues sufficient to cover costs and produce attractive profits.*[15] Illustration Capsule 1.2 describes two contrasting business models in online lending.

What Makes a Good Strategy?

LO 1.4
Explain the tests that are used to identify a good strategy.

Three tests can be applied to determine whether a strategy has the potential to be a winning strategy:

1. The Fit Test
2. The Competitive Advantage Test
3. The Performance Test

1. **The Fit Test:** *How well does the strategy fit the organization's situation?* A good strategy will be well matched to industry and competitive conditions, an organization's best market opportunities and other pertinent aspects of the business environment in which the organization operates. No strategy can work well unless it exhibits good *external fit* and is in sync with prevailing market conditions. At the same time, a winning strategy has to be tailored to the organization's resources and competitive capabilities and be supported by a complementary set of functional activities (i.e. activities in the realms of supply chain management, operations, sales and marketing, etc.). That is, it must also exhibit *internal fit* and be compatible with an organization's ability to execute the strategy in a competent manner. Unless a strategy exhibits good fit with both the external and internal aspects of an organization's overall situation, it is likely to underperform and fall short of producing the desired results. The best strategies also exhibit *dynamic fit* in the sense that they evolve over time in a manner that maintains close and effective alignment with the organization's situation even as external and internal conditions change.[16]

2. **The Competitive Advantage Test:** *Can the strategy help the organization achieve a sustainable competitive advantage?* Strategies that fail to achieve a durable competitive advantage over rivals are unlikely to produce superior performance for more than a brief period of time. Good strategies enable an organization to achieve a competitive advantage over key rivals that is long-lasting. The bigger and more durable the competitive advantage, the more powerful it is.

3. **The Performance Test:** *Is the strategy producing good organization performance?* The mark of a good strategy is strong organization performance. Performance indicators typically include (1) profitability and financial strength and (2) competitive strength and market standing. Above-average financial performance or gains in market share, competitive position or profitability are signs of a good strategy.

Illustration Capsule 1.2

WEB-BASED FINANCIAL SERVICES – ZOPA.COM, A PEER TO PEER LENDING WEBSITE AND FIRST DIRECT, A UK-BASED TELEPHONE AND INTERNET BANK

	Zopa.com	First Direct
Customer value proposition	**Target segments** The peer-to-peer lending site targets customers who want more transparency and equity in financial dealings than many banks offer. They are also likely to have a non-traditional career and lifestyle. For example, workers with portfolio careers, freelancers and entrepreneurs. Some of these consumers will find it difficult to get loans through high street banks. However, target segments will still need to have good credit histories	**Target segments** Segmented approach mainly aimed at converting existing account holders from high street banks. The telephone and Internet bank is aimed at time-poor, no-nonsense individuals who do not need the reassurance or the hassle of visiting their local high street branch. The bank's pricing structure seeks to attract those with a net income of £18 000 or higher

▶

	Product/service offering	**Product/service offering**
	The key element of Zopa's service is transparency – the website is offering to match people who want to borrow money with people who want to lend money. They agree the rate and terms of the loan and the whole process is transparent and simple	The bank offers most of the products associated with typical retail consumer banking, but through telephone and Internet platforms. Without a physical network the bank is able to offer competitively priced products/services ranging from mortgages and savings to insurance and current accounts
	Revenue model	**Revenue model**
	Zopa is not a bank and therefore its service is based on a brokerage approach; in other words, it brings buyers and sellers together, like eBay or an estate agency. Zopa charges lenders a fee based on the amount of the loan agreed and borrowers pay a one-off fixed fee to the organization. The interest rate for the loan is agreed between the lender and borrower.	The bank's current account is free if customers deposit £1500 a month or have bought a related product from the bank – so First Direct rely on attracting customers who they can then cross or upsell to a range of other products, such as overdrafts, loans, mortgages, insurance, investments and credit cards.
Operating model	**Value chain**	**Value chain**
	Zopa outsource most functions. They do not have to raise funds and they only offer two products in effect. In banking, risk management is one of the major activities in the value chain and Zopa outsource most of this activity, only keeping the underwriting and matching lenders to borrowers element in-house.	First Direct's operations follow a typical retail banking value chain model with primary activities starting with fundraising, then designing products for their target markets, marketing the products and providing after processing and other back office functions as after-sales service. Supporting activities differ from the traditional model with bank infrastructure lacking the physical branch networks but technological development accentuated.
	Cost model	**Cost model**
	Low fixed costs due to outsourcing of most functions. Mainly covering core staff at London office and costs associated with running a brokerage-style website. Variable costs cover elements such as risk assessment, credit checks, legal contracts, distribution of money between parties and matching lenders and borrowers.	Lower fixed costs than traditional retail banks due to the lack of branch network. Fixed costs cover call centres, staffing information technology and (IT) infrastructure, plus other costs associated with retail banking. Variable costs relate to volume of transactions.

Sources: Organization websites; Bogaerts, E. (2011) 'The 4 C's of core banking', *Journal of Internet Banking and Commerce*, 16(1): 1–4; Leichtfuss, R., Rhodes, D., Trascasa, C., Chai, S., Kumar, M. and Schmidt-Richter, R. (2007) *Retail Banking: Facing the Future*, Boston Consulting Group Report; Lamarque, E. (2005) 'Identifying key activities in banking firms: a competence-based analysis', *Competence Perspectives on Managing Internal Processes – Advances in Applied Business Strategy*, 7: 29–47; Carande, C. and Anzevino, A. (2009) *Beyond Turbulent Times: Transforming Banking Business Models*, KPMG Advisory paper; Financial Spread Betting Ltd (2012) 'Richard Duvall – founder of Zopa Borrowing Exchange' – interview on www.financial-spread-betting.com. Available online at www.financial-spread-betting.com/Richard-duvall-zopa.html (accessed 30 May, 2012).

Managers can use the same questions when evaluating either proposed or existing strategies. New initiatives that do not seem to match the organization's internal and external situations should be scrapped before they come to fruition, while existing strategies must be scrutinized on a regular basis to ensure they have good fit, offer a competitive advantage and are contributing to above-average performance or performance improvements. Organizations in not-for-profit or public arenas will be able to make effective use of the first test but will need to find equivalent measures for the other two tests.

CURRENT PRACTICE 1.1

TESTING AN ORGANIZATION'S STRATEGY

In a recent article three McKinsey consultants, set out a series of tests they have developed to assess the output of an organization's strategy processes. Chris Bradley, Martin Hirt and Sven Smit came up with a set of 10 questions that were refined through workshops with 700 strategy professionals and a questionnaire sent out to a global sample of over 2000 executives. The tests they developed are intended to work in the current environment, so had to work in situations with short planning cycles and bottom-up and emergent strategy processes as well as the more traditional planned rational approaches. The questions the consultants put forward are as follows:

1. 'Will your strategy beat the market?' – in other words does the strategy emphasize and build on the differences between your organization and the other key players in your industry. Sources of advantage need to be robust and capable of sustaining that advantage in dynamic conditions.

2. 'Does your strategy tap a true source of advantage?' – as seen in later chapters, this needs to be either a key positional advantage – such as being the lowest cost producer in an industry, or the result of the organization possessing distinctive capabilities – such as scarce resources or expertise.

3. 'Is your strategy granular about where to compete?' – organizations need to have a clear understanding of the segments they serve and the performance of those groups of customers in order to make the most effective allocation of resources.

4. 'Does your strategy put you ahead of trends?' – this test matters for both rapidly emerging trends and those that are slower to make an impact. As seen in Chapter 3, firms that are adept at scanning the environment and responding to current trends can gain an advantage or at least stay in the game. This test also challenges managers who may be locked into ways of operating as a result of previous successes or complacency.

5. 'Does your strategy rest on privileged insights?' – strategies that are based on newly commissioned field research, rather than widely available industry reports, or which have used a more challenging set of questions to test underlying assumptions can prove stronger because they give the organization insights into the direction of travel in the industry that its competitors may lack.

6. 'Does your strategy embrace uncertainty?' – to pass this test an organization needs first to understand the characteristics of its environment, whether it is fast moving and unpredictable, gives rise to a number of defined outcomes or is relatively predictable. Managers need to ensure that the organization's strategy is appropriate for the level of uncertainty in its environment.

7. 'Does your strategy balance commitment and flexibility?' – some decisions, especially those involving substantial long-term investments in, for example, organization-specific assets, require a commitment to a particular strategic position. However, in a time of uncertainty and rapid change, these must be balanced with a flexible approach to emerging opportunities and threats in the environment.

8. 'Is your strategy contaminated by bias?' – strategy is a future focused discipline, but this makes it hard to predict long-term outcomes with any real certainty. Relying on past performance can lead managers to make false assumptions. It is also possible that a strategy managers think gives their organization a competitive advantage, in reality, does not. This test cautions managers to be objective and to produce multiple options when crafting a strategy.

9. 'Is there conviction to act on your strategy?' – most strategies require change at all levels in the organization; the more radical, the more change is necessary. But whether it is the systems, structure or culture that needs to be changed, it is important that managers ensure there is broad support for the execution of their chosen strategy. It is easy for employees and other stakeholders to pay lip-service to the strategy without being convinced it is the right direction. Managers need to get face to face with key groups and see for themselves what stakeholder views really are.

10. 'Have you translated your strategy into an action plan?' – the process of putting the strategy into action is probably the hardest task. Managers need to be clear about the organization's starting point and also where it is going to. As mentioned above, having a good game plan, a clear business model and ensuring that everyone in the organization knows what to do is the final piece of the jigsaw.

Source: Bradley, C., Hirt, M. and Smit, S. (2011) 'Have you tested your strategy lately?' *McKinsey Quarterly*, January, pp. 1–14.

Why Crafting and Executing Strategy are Important Tasks

High performing organizations nearly always have well-crafted and effectively executed strategies. Even though we have seen in this chapter that strategies are in reality part prescription and part reaction, they provide direction for the organization. A good strategy will animate and orient[17] everyone connected with the organization – staff, suppliers, partners and customers, because it will provide a clear road-map for the future and a set of coherent actions aimed at engaging customers, gaining competitive advantage and improving performance. A good strategy will also help an organization convince those that supply the funds that what is planned is worth supporting. The best strategies allow an organization to attain and keep a unique position in their marketplace, to capitalize on opportunities, good fortune and lucky breaks. They provide an insightful analysis of the situation, support the critical choices made by management, co-ordinate the actions and objectives being pursued by different areas of the organization and provide clear benchmarks for measuring performance.

The CEO of one successful organization put it well when he said:

In the main, our competitors are acquainted with the same fundamental concepts and techniques and approaches that we follow, and they are as free to pursue them as we are. More often than not, the difference between their level of success and ours lies in the relative thoroughness and self-discipline with which we and they develop and execute our strategies for the future.

Good Strategy + Good Strategy Execution = Good Management

> How well an organization performs is directly attributable to the calibre of its strategy and the proficiency with which the strategy is executed.

Crafting and executing strategy are thus core management functions. Among all the things managers do, nothing affects an organization's ultimate success or failure more fundamentally than how well its management team charts the organization's direction, develops effective strategic moves and business approaches and pursues what needs to be done internally to produce good day-in, day-out strategy execution and operating excellence. Indeed, *good strategy and good strategy execution are the most telling signs of good management.* Managers do not deserve a gold star for designing a potentially brilliant strategy but failing to put the organizational means in place to carry it out in high-calibre fashion. Competent execution of a mediocre strategy scarcely merits enthusiastic applause for management's efforts either. The rationale for using the twin standards of good strategy-making and good strategy execution to determine whether an organization is well managed is therefore compelling: *The better conceived an organization's strategy and the more competently it is executed, the more likely that the organization will be a top performer in the marketplace.* In stark contrast, an organization that lacks clear-cut direction, has a flawed strategy, or cannot execute its strategy competently is an organization whose performance is probably suffering, whose survival is at long-term risk and whose management is sorely lacking.

The Road Ahead

The mission of this book is to provide a solid overview of what every business student and aspiring manager needs to know about crafting and executing strategy. We explore what good strategic thinking entails, describe the core concepts and tools of strategic analysis and examine the ins and outs of crafting and executing strategy. The accompanying cases will help build your skills both in diagnosing how well the strategy-making, strategy-executing task is being performed and in prescribing actions for how the strategy in question or its execution can be improved. In the process, we hope to

> ### Emerging Theme 1.1
>
> ## ECONOMICS: COMPETING FOR CAPITAL AND THE CREDIT CRUNCH
>
> In much of this chapter we have looked at competitive advantage from the point of view of customers and competitors. However, organizations are also often competing for capital – whether that is in the form of loans from banks, investments from shareholders/owners or venture capital, donations or taxes from the public or funds from central government or a corporate parent. Crafting and executing strategies often require a substantial injection of cash, for example, to acquire another organization or pursue a differentiation strategy underpinned by developing new products and promoting them to consumers.
>
> Since the events of 2007/8 organizations have found that although they can still raise debt, the interest rates being charged are higher than prior to the credit crunch and based more on the level of risk lenders perceive is involved. Lenders also expect organizations to put more of their own money into strategic moves such as acquisitions, which means organizations often need to raise more equity capital so their gearing is lower. So there is more need for organizations to attract investors and potential competition for a resource where demand may be outstripping supply. For an organization the ability to present a viable strategy to lenders or investors can therefore be a critical element in this process.

convince you that first-rate capabilities in crafting and executing strategy are basic to managing successfully and are skills every manager needs to possess.

In addition this book also asks you to think about and challenge some of the key concepts and ideas in the field of strategy. There are over 2000 books on the subject and this is growing year on year. To present a one-size-fits-all prescription for crafting and executing strategy is to dismiss the complexity and unpredictability that is often found in the environments faced by businesses and non-commercial organizations. Many of the ideas you will encounter in this book and the recommended readings simplify the environment, the choices available to managers and the task of putting strategy into action. That does not mean they cannot be used in real-world situations, in fact, their very simplicity is their major strength in that they provide an overview and some boundaries for managers. This is important because otherwise an overload of information can lead to a lack of action, 'paralysis by analysis'. However, it is important for managers and business students to understand the limitations of many of the standard models and frameworks they will commonly encounter in strategy. So, you will find a series of key debates, practitioner approaches and alternative views in the following chapters. These are all designed to help you think about the concepts you are using and apply them more effectively.

KEY POINTS

The tasks of crafting and executing organization strategies are the heart and soul of managing a business enterprise and winning in the marketplace. The key points to take away from this chapter include the following:

1. An organization's strategy consists of the overarching direction set by managers, plus the competitive moves and business approaches that they are employing to compete successfully, improve performance and grow the business.

2. The central thrust of an organization's strategy is undertaking moves to build and strengthen the organization's long-term competitive position and financial performance by *competing differently* from rivals and gaining a sustainable competitive advantage over them.

3. An organization achieves a sustainable competitive advantage when it can meet customer needs more effectively or efficiently than rivals and when the basis for this is durable, despite the best efforts of competitors to match or surpass this advantage.

4. An organization's strategy typically evolves over time, emerging from a blend of (1) proactive and deliberate actions on the part of organization managers to improve the strategy and (2) reactive, as-needed adaptive responses to unanticipated developments and fresh market conditions.

5. An organization's business model is management's story-line for how the strategy will be a money-maker. It contains two crucial elements: (1) the *customer value proposition* – a plan for satisfying customer wants and needs at a price customers will consider good value, and (2) the *operating model* – a plan for a cost structure that will enable the organization to deliver the customer value proposition profitably. In effect, an organization's business model sets forth the economic logic for making money in a particular business, given the organization's current strategy.

6. A good strategy will pass three tests: (1) *Fit* (external, internal and dynamic consistency); (2) *Competitive Advantage* (durable competitive advantage), and (3) *Performance* (outstanding financial and market performance).

7. Crafting and executing strategy are core management functions. How well an organization performs and the degree of market success it enjoys are directly attributable to the calibre of its strategy and the proficiency with which the strategy is executed.

CLOSING CASE

A TALE OF TWO CONFECTIONERS: NESTLÉ AND FERRERO

In a small town just outside Turin, Italy, lies one of the most closely guarded secrets in the confectionery world. It was here in 1946 that Michele Ferrero's father and uncle developed a blend of hazelnut paste and chocolate, known as Giandujot, which helped them found the organization that has grown to be the fourth biggest confectionery manufacturing organization in the world. In 2011, the Ferrero Group had a turnover in excess of $8.5 billion (€6.3 billion) and operated through 38 trading organizations, employing some 21 000 people world-wide. Ferrero's confectionery brands included Kinder, Nutella, Ferrero Rocher, Giotto and Tic-Tac. In addition to their facility at Alba, the organization had 17 factories in different regions of the world and exports to over 70 countries.

The majority of Ferrero's products sat in the sugar and chocolate confectionery segments of the industry and the organization had benefited from the continued global growth in this market in recent years. Growth rates in the industry have averaged 2.3 per cent globally over the five years to 2009. However, Ferrero had growth ambitions well above and beyond this. In the UK, for example, they were planning to double their sales over the five years to 2015. Even in the poor economic conditions following the credit crunch, sales in the UK rose by 10 per cent in 2010 and some products had seen spectacular growth even in mature markets. Nutella spread was introduced into the US market in 2009 and according to the organization had grown at nearly 80 per cent per year. The net profit recorded by the organization's Italian subsidiary in 2010 was 24.6 per cent up on the previous year and the turnover of their new Indian subsidiary, launched in 2008, reached $170 million by 2011.

So how did a small, family business become a giant of the confectionery world in three generations? Like many of the largest organizations in the industry, it had never been floated as a public organization, but unlike some of its competitors such as Mars, Wrigley and Hershey, it had taken secrecy to an altogether different level. Ferrero do not allow factory tours and the level of security at their HQ in Alba was described as 'like NASA' by a former employee. The organization had invested heavily in advanced manufacturing equipment in many of its factories world-wide. New automated, robotic packaging machinery and state-of-the-art warehouse management systems had been installed in its Canadian plant in Ontario and they had invested over $125 million dollars in a new production facility in Maharashtra, India. To prevent industrial espionage, more than 80 per cent of the production technology was developed by the organization's own in-house engineering division. Ferrero took a similar approach to R&D and had continued innovating new products and special packaging which improved the shelf life of their goods. The octogenarian owner of the organization, Michele, was rumoured to have a private research laboratory in Monte Carlo, where he spent time personally creating new products.

▶

◀

Ferrero was not as insular as its in-house approach inferred. They did run their own distribution network, but given the perishable nature of the product, this was not unusual in the food sector. Seeking greater control of the whole value chain could also be seen as a smart move in the industry. Most of the ingredients in the organization's products were commodities, such as sugar and cocoa, whose price had been very volatile in recent years. The hazelnuts in the key products containing Giandujot were mainly grown in the northern hemisphere. To ensure continuity of supply the organization had been growing a supply in South America and more recently, in 2008, shipped 450 000 trees to South Africa where it began working with local farmers on a shared basis.

This partnership with farmers was a new direction for the organization. Over the last 60 years they had never made an acquisition or merged with another organization. Ferrero were proud that their growth has been completely organic. However, since Michele's sons, Pietro and Giovanni, took over as joint CEOs, this stance had been under pressure. The first signs occurred in 2009 when it appeared that Ferrero were partnering Hershey in a bid for the UK confectionery organization Cadbury. Although they later pulled out of the deal and Cadbury was taken over by Kraft, the fact that Ferrero had expressed an interest in the acquisition marked a fundamental change in their approach to growth. In 2010, the organization also appointed a non-exclusive distributor in Sri Lanka, Delmege, to manage their grocery trade channel on the island. The managing director for the UK division of the organization, Christian Walter, recently stated that expansion would be driven by 'joint venture on distribution in some countries'. There is speculation over whether the organization's strategy will change following the death of Pietro Ferrero in an accident in 2011.

Ferrero were pursuing growth in a number of international markets. The BRIC countries provided significant opportunities and along with their Indian factories, they were also planning to open production facilities in Russia. Operations in former USSR states had been boosted by a judgment in the Ukraine against a local organization, Landrin, who were accused of counterfeiting Ferrero's Raffaello brand. However, the main markets they were targeting appeared to be in large English-speaking markets such as the UK, Canada and the USA. Given the size of these markets, perhaps it is no surprise that the makers of Kinder should focus here first.

Nestlé's route to the top flight in the confectionery industry had been rather different to Ferrero's. In a world of privately owned, closed chocolate manufacturers Nestlé was one of the first organizations to go public and to benefit from this injection of capital by being one of the early players in the consolidation of the industry. They acquired Rowntree back in 1988 but were also much more diversified than many of their competitors. A place at the top table seemed guaranteed until Mars' purchase of Wrigley in 2008 and Kraft's acquisition of Cadbury in 2010 pushed them into third place in the confectionery market. No single acquisition could now bridge the gap between Nestlé and the top two organizations in the industry. However, the organization remained the largest food and beverage organization in the world, with 283 000 employees and revenues of just under $100 billion. Their income from confectionery was over $11 billion in 2009.

Nestlé was an organization of contradictions and their CEO, Paul Bulcke, was faced with a range of critical decisions about the organization's future in 2011. Nestlé's number one objective according to Bulcke was to 'be recognised as the leader in Nutrition, Health and Wellness'. This was part of a long tradition at the organization, started in 1866 by Henri Nestlé to produce cereal-based baby food, but could be seen as at odds with the large-scale manufacture of confectionery. This issue had been brought into sharper relief as obesity and diabetes continued to rise dramatically in the developed world.

Emerging economies had also proved to be a controversial arena for the Swiss organization. Even as recently as 2007 Nestlé was being targeted by activists over their aggressive marketing of baby formula in countries such as Bangladesh. The organization had been described as the most boycotted organization in the world by some commentators. It was difficult to judge the extent to which this has impacted on their sales of confectionery products. The organization did have a truly global presence and had a long tradition of operating beyond its national base in Switzerland. In 2011 just over a third of its revenues came from emerging markets.

Nestlé also had to respond to allegations that they sourced cocoa from farms in the Ivory Coast that employed child labour. Against this they were one of the first major confectionery organizations to move to fair-trade supplies for their chocolate products. Since 2009, Kit Kat, one of the organization's major global brands, has been produced with fair-trade ingredients for the UK market. However, even this was not without its challenges; only 2 per cent of the world supply of cocoa was fair-trade certified and Nestlé's UK managing director, David Rennie, claimed that the organization could not source enough even to produce the full range of Kit Kat products for this market. Overall, the brand accounted for $2 billion of sales in

▶

70 countries including 23 per cent of Nestlé's confectionery sales in the UK.

The fact that Kit Kat had been adapted for the UK market, where consumers were more interested in the source of ingredients, illustrated Nestlé's flexible approach to international development. This local customization was not just limited to product attributes, branding and promotional aspects were also adapted. For example, the sweets branded as Rolo in the UK were known as Rossyia in Russia.

Nestlé did not just rely on their extensive portfolio of existing high-profile global brands and products. Over 5200 staff were employed in their product technology and R&D centres. Application groups located in their various factories world-wide worked with these staff to tailor products to local tastes and to ensure that they complied with local laws and regulations. However, their R&D capabilities were not just focused on confectionery, although they did launch the Chocolate Centre of Excellence at their facility in Broc, Switzerland, in 2008, to take account of the growth in the premium/luxury part of the market.

Some commentators have questioned Nestlé's commitment to the confectionery part of its business in the light of the recent consolidation in the industry. Despite this the organization was well positioned for the future. They had an increasing presence, through acquisition of local organizations, in some of the fastest growing emerging markets such as the Ukraine, Russia and parts of South America. Their range of confectionery products also covered all four of the main recognized sectors in confectionery; chocolate, gum, sugar and cereal bars. Only Mars and Kraft had similar coverage.

The fact that Nestlé was such a diversified organization with a greater focus on health and well-being and even cosmetics meant that the management of its portfolio could have a profound impact on the confectionery element of its business. It was arguably in a better position with regard to available capital than Kraft, who took on substantial debts to purchase Cadbury, but how it used this resource would be critical for future success.

QUESTIONS

1. Using Figure 1.1 identify the pattern of actions for each organization's strategy. Where are they similar and where are they different?

2. How similar are the two organizations' business models?

3. Is there evidence that either organization has modified their strategy in response to changes in the external environment? Which events are most likely to have been unpredictable?

4. Apply the three tests of a good strategy to the two organizations. Which meets the criteria best?

Sources: Ansa (2010) 'Food: Ferrero; Nutella + Kinder revenue and profit up; products in 70 countries, foreign turnover over 600 mln', *ANSA English Corporate Service*, 14 December; Ansa (2010) 'Ferrero success in battle over Raffaello in Ukraine', *ANSA English Corporate Service*, 2 March; Best, D. (2011) 'The just-food interview – Christian Walter, Ferrero', *just-food global news*, 2 February 2011; Beales, R. (2010) 'Ferrero to boost jobs', *Brantford Expositor* (Ontario), 22 October; Business Insights (2010) *The Top 10 Confectionery Organizations*, Business Insights, London; *Daily Mirror* (Sri Lanka) (2010) 'Ferrero partners Delmege Distributors', *Daily Mirror* (Sri Lanka), 6 September; Datamonitor (2010) *Industry Profile: Global Confectionery*, Datamonitor, London; Datamonitor (2010) *Nestlé SA Organization Profile*, Datamonitor, London; Finweek (2009) 'Ferrero: entrepreneurial and innovative', *Finweek*, 18 June; Hooper, J. (2010) 'Meltdown in Italy over EU Nutella ban that never was', *The Guardian* (London), 3 July; Keshri, G.K. (2010) 'Italy's Ferrero to set up $125 mn second chocolate unit in India', *Indo-Asian News Service*, 16 August; Marketing Week (2009) 'Politics of marketing: Kraft's Cadbury bid leaves Nestlé at crossroads', *Marketing Week*, 10 September; Moorhead, J. (2007) 'Milking it', *The Guardian*, Tuesday 15 May; Navach, G. (2009) 'Secretive family mulls first acquisition; Ferrero', *National Post* (Canada), 19 November; Nestlé (2011) *Nestlé Annual Report 2010*, Nestlé SA, Cham and Vevey (Switzerland); Russell, M. (2009) 'The just-food interview: David Rennie, Nestlé', *just-food global news*, Friday 25 December.

ASSURANCE OF LEARNING EXERCISES

LO 1.1, LO 1.2

1. Go to **www.rolls-royce.com**, click on the investors section, and explore Rolls-Royce's latest annual reports and financial statements to see if you can identify the key elements of the organization's strategy. Use the framework provided in Figure 1.1 to help identify these key elements. What approach towards winning a competitive advantage does Rolls-Royce seem to be pursuing?

LO 1.1, LO 1.2, LO 1.5

2. On the basis of what you know about the quick-service restaurant industry, does McDonald's strategy as described in Illustration Capsule 1.1 seem to be well matched to industry and competitive conditions? Does the strategy seem to be keyed to having a cost-based advantage, offering differentiating features, serving the unique needs of a narrow market niche, or being the best-cost provider? What is there about the action elements of McDonald's strategy that is consistent with its approach to competitive advantage? From the information provided, which tests of a good strategy does McDonald's strategy pass?

EXERCISES FOR SIMULATION PARTICIPANTS

This chapter discusses three questions that must be answered by managers of organizations of all sizes:

1. What is our present situation?
2. Where do we want to go from here?
3. How are we going to get there?

After you read the Participant's Guide or Player's Manual for the strategy simulation exercise that you will participate in this academic term, you and your co-managers should come up with brief one- or two-paragraph answers to these three questions *before* entering your first set of decisions. While the management team's answer to the first of the three questions can be developed from your reading of the manual, the second and third questions will require a collaborative discussion among the members of your organization's management team about how you intend to manage the organization you have been assigned to run.

LO 1.1, LO 1.2

1. *What is our organization's current situation?* A substantive answer to this question should cover the following issues:
- Is your organization in a good, average or weak competitive position *vis-à-vis* rival organizations?
- Does your organization appear to be in a sound financial condition?
- What problems does your organization have that need to be addressed?

LO 1.3, LO 1.5

2. *Where do we want to take the organization during the time we are in charge?* A complete answer to this question should say something about each of the following:
- What goals or aspirations do you have for your organization?
- What do you want the organization to be known for?
- What market share would you like your organization to have after the first five decision rounds?
- By what amount or percentage would you like to increase total profits of the organization by the end of the final decision round?
- What kinds of performance outcomes will signal that you and your co-managers are managing the organization in a successful manner?

LO 1.3, LO 1.4

3. *How are we going to get there?* Your answer should cover these issues:
- Which of the basic strategic and competitive approaches discussed in this chapter do you think makes the most sense to pursue?
- What kind of competitive advantage over rivals will you try to achieve?
- How would you describe the organization's business model?
- What kind of actions will support these objectives?

ENDNOTES

1. Drucker, P. (1996) *The Concept of the Corporation*, Transaction Publishers, New Jersey.

2. A good summary of the different elements of strategic change can be found in Pettigrew, A. (2003) 'Strategy as process, power and change', in Cummings, S. and Wilson, D. (eds) *Images of Strategy*, Blackwell, Oxford, pp. 301–30.

3. Rivkin, Jan (2001) 'An Alternative Approach to Making Strategic Choices', Harvard Business School, 9-702-433.

4. Markides, Costas (2004) 'What is strategy and how do you know if you have one?' *Business Strategy Review*, 15(2): 5–6. See also Collis, David J. and Rukstad, Michael F. (2008) 'Can you say what your strategy is?' *Harvard Business Review*, 86(4): 82–90.

5. For a discussion of the different ways that organizations can position themselves in the marketplace, see Porter, Michael E. (1996) 'What is strategy?' *Harvard Business Review*, 74(6): 65–7.

6. Miles, R., Miles, G., Snow, C., Blomqvist, K. and Rocha, H. (2009) 'The I-form organization', *California Management Review*, 51(4): 61–76.

7. Further details of Mozilla's approach can be found in Tapscott, D. and Williams, A. (2008) *Wikinomics*, Altantic Publishing, London. Details of the market shares of the main players in the browser market can be found at www.electronista.com/articles/12/05/01/ie.continues.comeback.safari.clear.mobile.leader/ (accessed 30 May 2012).

8. Porter, Michael E. (1996) 'What is strategy?' *Harvard Business Review*, 74(6): 65–7.

9. Although we give a relatively simplistic definition of strategy in the main text, it is also worth considering the true complexity of the subject. One of the best succinct articles to capture the multifaceted nature of strategy is Mintzberg, H. (1987) 'The Strategy Concept 1: five P's for strategy', *California Management Review*, 30(1): 11–24.

10. For more on the strategic challenges posed by high-velocity changes, see Brown, Shona L. and Eisenhardt, Kathleen M. (1998) *Competing on the Edge: Strategy as Structured Chaos*, Boston, MA, Harvard Business School Press, ch. 1.

11. For an excellent discussion of strategy as a dynamic process involving continuous, unending creation and recreation of strategy, see Montgomery, Cynthia A. (2008) 'Putting leadership back into strategy', *Harvard Business Review*, 86(1): 54–60.

12. See Mintzberg, Henry and Lampel, Joseph (1999) 'Reflecting on the strategy process', *Sloan Management Review*, 40(3): 21–30; Mintzberg, Henry and Waters, J. A. (1985) 'Of strategies, deliberate and emergent', *Strategic Management Journal*, 6: 257–72; Costas Markides (2001) 'Strategy as balance: from "either-or to and"', *Business Strategy Review*, 12(3): 1–10.

13. Johnson, Mark W. Christensen, Clayton M. and Kagermann, Henning (2008) 'Reinventing your business model', *Harvard Business Review*, 86(12): 52–53; Magretta, Joan (2002) 'Why business models matter', *Harvard Business Review*, 80(5): 87.

14. Anderson, C. (2009) *The Longer Long Tail*, Random House, London.

15. For further discussion of the meaning and role of an organization's customer value proposition and profit proposition, see Kim W. Chan and Mauborgne Renée (2009) 'How strategy shapes structure', *Harvard Business Review*, 87(9): 74–5.

16. For a discussion of the three types of fit, see Rivkin, Jan, 'An Alternative Approach to Making Strategic Choices'. For an example of managing internal fit dynamically, see Peteraf, M. and Reed, R. (2007) 'Managerial discretion and internal alignment under regulatory constraints and change', *Strategic Management Journal*, 28: 1089–112.

17. A more in-depth discussion of this measure of a good strategy is in Cummings, S. and Wilson, D. (2003) 'Images of strategy', in Cummings, S. and Wilson, D. (eds) *Images of Strategy*, Blackwell, Oxford, pp. 1–40.

Chapter Two

Charting an organization's direction: vision and mission, objectives and strategy

The vision we have … determines what we do and the opportunities we see or don't see.

Charles G. Koch
CEO of Koch Industries, the second largest privately held organization in the USA

If you don't know where you are going, any road will take you there.

Cheshire Cat to Alice
Lewis Carroll, Alice in Wonderland

A good goal is like a strenuous exercise – it makes you stretch.

Mary Kay Ash
Founder of Mary Kay Cosmetics

Learning Objectives

When you have read this chapter you should be able to:

LO 2.1 Know why it is essential for managers to have a clear strategic vision of where an organization needs to head and why.

LO 2.2 Understand the importance of setting both strategic and financial objectives.

LO 2.3 Understand why the strategic initiatives taken at various organizational levels should be tightly co-ordinated to achieve performance targets.

LO 2.4 Become aware of what an organization must do to achieve operating excellence and to execute its strategy proficiently.

LO 2.5 Become aware of the role and responsibility of the board of directors in overseeing the strategic management process.

LAMBORGHINI AND THE AUDI VISION

Founded in 1963, Automobili Lamborghini is headquartered in Sant'Agata Bolognese in north-eastern Italy. There it manufactures some of the world's most sought-after super sports cars. With the 2011 presentation of the best-in-class Aventador LP 700-4 at the Geneva Auto Show, Lamborghini marked another milestone in the history of luxury super sports cars. With more than 120 dealerships worldwide, Automobili Lamborghini is building on a succession of dynamic and elegant super sports cars.

Ferruccio Lamborghini, born in 1916, was the leading character in the foundation of Lamborghini and the early phases of its extraordinary history. By the time he decided to build a factory of luxury sports cars, Ferruccio had successfully built up a renowned tractor factory. In the early 1960s, Lamborghini was a powerful man who knew exactly what he wanted, and he wanted to build a super sports car to compete with Ferrari. He bought a large plot of land in Sant'Agata Bolognese, about 25 kilometres from Bologna, to build an ultramodern factory with a very functional structure that, at the time, was unrivalled in its field. The enormous and well-lit central building was located next to the office building, with only an internal car park in between, so that the management could constantly monitor the production situation. This was ideal for Lamborghini, who would often roll up his shirtsleeves and go to work on the cars personally.

Problems came in 1972–74 when Ferruccio lost a large tractor order. He had upgraded the tractor factory to build the numbers required and bought most of the raw materials needed to do so. He was forced to sell the controlling interest in Lamborghini to a Swiss businessman, Georges-Henri Rossetti. When the general world recession hit, the remaining shares were sold to Rene Leimer meaning that Lamborghini, the founder, was no longer a part of the company. The new shareholders did not undertake active involvement in the company and were reluctant to invest, and Automobili Lamborghini struggled to meet financial demands. Due to strategic mistakes, Lamborghini was bankrupt by 1977.

The company never closed down, a remarkable outcome, and one attributed to the determination of the employees, the passion and loyalty of its clients and the support of its distributors. In 1980 the Bologna Court sold the company to the Mimran brothers, food industry tycoons recognized for their passion for cars, and who started investment in plant, new products and the search for a skilled workforce.

By 1986 Lamborghini had taken off again. The growth was fast and demanding on capital expenditure, so much so that a corporate partner was needed to support the private company, and Chrysler came on board. So attracted was Chrysler to the motivated management, new products and skilled workforce, that it asked the Mimran family for total share capital. An agreement was signed in Sant'Agata on 23 April 1987. Both production and sales reached a new peak in 1991.

However, another recession was approaching. All automobile manufacturers were struggling and the luxury sports car market saw a significant fall in sales in 1992 before a slow recovery started during 1993 and 1994.

Despite signs of recovery, the Chrysler Corporation recognized incompatibilities with the management required of Lambourghini and their own mass-producer focus, and agreed to sell Automobili Lamborghini to MegaTech, part of the Indonesian group Sedtco. Then, its shareholding changed again and, in 1995, 60 per cent of its shareholding were controlled by an Indonesian company V-Power, and 40 per cent by Malaysian Company Mycom.

In 1988, following a period of Asian economic turmoil that probably forced the owners to look for an exit, an agreement between the shareholders of Lamborghini and Audi was signed in London for a complete takeover of the company. The 'House of the Bull' now had a strong owner, widely respected in the automotive world for its technical competence and commercial success.

AUDI GROUP

Audi's takeover of the company in 1998 instigated dramatic changes in how the cars were conceived, developed and constructed. To retain the brand's 'Italian-ness,' company headquarters stayed in Sant'Agata.

The new ownership resulted in shared platforms and a fundamental change in how emerging technologies were researched, developed and incorporated into the innovative world of super sports cars. Audi invested over 350 million euro in infrastructure, the development of new models, the renewal of lines and human resources (HR). Audi's ownership marked the beginning of a period of stability and increased productivity for Lamborghini, with sales increasing nearly tenfold over the following years.

But what was the added value of Lamborghini? According to Stephan Winkelmann, President and chief executive officer (CEO) of Automobili Lanborghini, the answer was obvious and simple and involved a mix of various factors: man, technology and the right spirit. At Sant'Agata Bolognese there was a solid and competent team, creating a good dialogue with the parent company, and which could count on highly advanced technological know-how. The spirit was always based on the brand identity of Lamborghini – a real Italian spirit. Emilia-Romagna also had a lot to offer. As well as the hundreds of Lamborghini employees, co-operation with the authorities of Bologna, Sant'Agata and other neighbouring communities had always been optimal, as was that with the trade unions.

AUDI GROUP VISION AND MISSION

With its **vision** of 'Audi: the number one premium brand', it has set itself the goal of taking on the lead role in the premium segment world-wide. The goals of Strategy 2020 focus on lasting corporate success, underpinned by sustainable actions. The Audi Group therefore regards it as a self-evident aspect of corporate responsibility that it takes account of the issues of ecology and social responsibility when defining the strategic direction of its core business.

The **mission** statement 'We delight customers worldwide' is at the very core of the Company's drive to become the number one in the premium segment. This means in practice that the Audi brand offers its customers emotional, technologically advanced products that are particularly noted for their sophistication and reliability. The brand with the four rings furthermore intends to delight its customers with the best brand experience available – hard evidence of the Audi brand values, 'sophisticated', 'progressive' and 'sporty' is provided at every point of contact with the customer.

QUESTIONS

1. What do you believe was the main motive for Audi group to acquire Lambourgini?
2. Does the Lambourghini organization and brand fit with the Audi group Vision and Mission?

Sources: Websites available online at www.lamborghini.com (accessed 7 December 2011); www.lambocars.com (accessed 7 December 2011); BBC News (1998) 'Audi in pole position for Lamborghini, 12 June 1998. www.bbc.co.uk (accessed 7 December 2011); www.wired.com (accessed 7 December 2011); www.audi.co.uk/audi-innovation/business/audi-and-lamborghini (accessed 7 December 2011); www.investinemiliaromagna.it (accessed 7 December 2011); www.audi.com (accessed 7 December 2011).

Crafting and executing strategy are the heart and soul of managing a business. But exactly what is involved in developing a strategy and executing it proficiently? What are the various components of the strategy-making, strategy-executing process and to what extent are employees – aside from senior management – involved in the process? In this chapter we present an overview of the ins and outs of crafting and executing organization strategies. Special attention is given to management's direction-setting responsibilities – charting a strategic course, setting performance targets and choosing a strategy capable of producing the desired outcomes. We also explain why strategy-making is a task for an organization's entire management team and discuss which kinds of strategic decision tend to be made at which levels of management. The chapter concludes with a look at the roles and responsibilities of an organization's board of directors in the strategy-making, strategy-executing process and how good corporate governance protects shareholder interests and promotes good management.

What does the Strategy-Making, Strategy-Executing Process Entail?

The process of crafting and executing an organization's strategy consists of five inter-related managerial stages:

1. *Developing a strategic vision* of the organization's long-term direction, a *mission* that describes the organization's purpose and a set of *values* to guide the pursuit of the vision and mission.
2. *Setting objectives* and using them to measure the organization's performance and progress.
3. *Crafting a strategy* to achieve the objectives and move the organization along the strategic course that management has defined.
4. *Executing the chosen strategy* efficiently and effectively.
5. *Monitoring developments, evaluating performance and initiating corrective adjustments* in the organization's vision and mission, objectives, strategy or execution in light of actual experience, changing conditions, new ideas and new opportunities.

Figure 2.1 displays this five-stage process, which we examine next in some detail.

Stage 1: Developing a Strategic Vision, a Mission and a Set of Core Values

Very early in the strategy-making process, an organization's senior managers must wrestle with the issue of what directional path the organization should take. Using information and ideas from throughout the organization they need to find a coherent path. Can the organization's prospects be improved by changing its product offerings and/or the markets in which it participates and/or the customers it caters to and/or the technologies it employs? Deciding to commit the organization to one path versus another pushes managers to draw some carefully reasoned conclusions about whether the organization's present strategic course offers attractive opportunities for growth and profitability or whether changes of one kind or another in the organization's strategy and long-term direction are needed.

Developing a Strategic Vision

Top management's views and conclusions about the organization's long-term direction and what product-customer-market-technology mix seems optimal for the road ahead constitute a **strategic vision** for the organization. A strategic vision delineates

> **LO 2.1** Know why it is essential for managers to have a clear strategic vision of where an organization needs to head and why.

> **Core Concept**
>
> A **strategic vision** describes management's aspirations for the future and delineates the organization's strategic course and long-term direction.

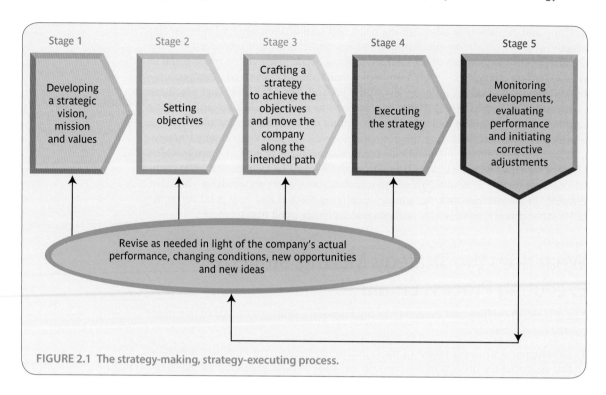

FIGURE 2.1 The strategy-making, strategy-executing process.

management's aspirations for the business, providing a panoramic view of 'where we are going' and a convincing rationale for why this makes good business sense for the organization. A strategic vision thus points an organization in a particular direction, charts a strategic path for it to follow in preparing for the future and builds commitment to the future course of action. A clearly articulated strategic vision communicates management's aspirations to stakeholders and helps steer the energies of employees in a common direction.

Well-conceived visions are *distinctive* and *specific* to a particular organization; they avoid generic, feel-good statements like 'We will become a global leader and the first choice of customers in every market we serve',which could apply to hundreds of organizations.[1] And they are not the product of a committee charged with coming up with an innocuous but well-meaning one-sentence vision that wins consensus approval from various stakeholders. Nicely worded vision statements with no specifics about the organization's product-market-customer-technology focus fall well short of what it takes for a vision to measure up.

A sampling of vision statements currently in use shows a range from strong and clear to overly general and generic. A surprising number of the vision statements found on company websites and in annual reports are vague and unrevealing, saying very little about the organization's future direction. Some could apply to almost any organization in any industry. Many read like a public relations statement – high-sounding words that someone came up with because it is fashionable for companies to have an official vision statement.[2] But the real purpose of a vision statement is to serve as a management tool to give the organization a sense of direction. Like any tool, it can be used properly or improperly, either clearly conveying an organization's future strategic path or not.

For a strategic vision to function as a valuable managerial tool, it must convey what management wants the business to look like and provide managers with a reference point in making strategic decisions and preparing the organization for the future. It must say something definitive about how the organization's leaders intend to position the organization beyond where it is today. Table 2.1 provides some dos and don'ts

TABLE 2.1 Wording a Vision Statement – the Dos and Don'ts

The Dos	The Don'ts
Be graphic. Paint a clear picture of where the organization is headed and the market position(s) the organization is striving for	**Don't be vague or incomplete.** Be specific about where the organization is headed and how the organization intends to prepare for the future
Be forward-looking and directional. Describe the strategic course that management has charted and the kinds of product-market-customer-technology changes that will help the organization prepare for the future	**Don't dwell on the present.** A vision is not about what an organization once did or does now; it is about 'where we are going'
Keep it focused. Be specific enough to provide managers with guidance in making decisions and allocating resources	**Don't use overly broad language.** All-inclusive language that allows the organization to head in almost any direction, pursue almost any opportunity or enter almost any business should be avoided
Have some wiggle room. Language that allows some flexibility is good. The directional course may have to be adjusted as market-customer-technology circumstances change, and coming up with a new vision statement every 1–3 years signals that management is drifting	**Don't state the vision in bland or uninspiring terms.** The best vision statements have the power to motivate employees and inspire shareholder confidence about the organization's direction and business outlook
Be sure the journey is feasible. The path and direction should be within the realm of what the organization can pursue and accomplish; over time, an organization should be able to demonstrate measurable progress in achieving the vision	**Don't be generic.** A vision statement that could apply to organizations in any of several industries (or to any of several organizations in the same industry) is incapable of giving an organization its own unique identity
Indicate why the directional path makes good business sense. The directional path should be in the long-term interests of stakeholders (for instance, shareholders, employees, and customers)	**Don't rely on superlatives only.** Visions that claim the organization's strategic course is one of being the 'best' or 'the most successful' or 'a recognized leader' or the 'global leader' usually deprive the essential and revealing specifics about the path the organization is taking to get there
Make it memorable. To give the organization a sense of direction and purpose, the vision needs to be easily communicated. Ideally, it should be reducible to a few lines or a memorable 'slogan' (like Henry Ford's famous vision of 'a car in every garage')	**Don't run on and on.** Vision statements that are overly long tend to be unfocused and meaningless. A vision statement that is not short and to the point will tend to lose its audience

Sources: Kotter, John P. (1996), *Leading Change* Boston, Harvard Business School Press, p. 72; Davidson, Hugh (2002) *The Committed Enterprise,* Oxford, Butterworth Heinemann, ch. 2; and Robert, Michel (1992) *Strategy Pure and Simple II,* New York, McGraw-Hill, chs 2, 3 and 6.

in composing an effectively worded vision statement. Illustration Capsule 2.1 provides a critique of the strategic visions of several prominent companies.

Communicating the Strategic Vision

Effectively communicating the strategic vision to lower-level managers and employees is as important as the strategic soundness of the long-term direction top management has chosen. Employees cannot be expected to unite behind managerial efforts to get the organization moving in the intended direction until they understand why the strategic course that management has charted is reasonable and beneficial. It is particularly important for executives to provide a compelling rationale for a dramatically *new* strategic vision and direction. When employees do not understand or accept the need for redirecting organizational efforts, they are prone to resist change. Hence, reiterating the basis for the new direction, addressing employee concerns head on,

> An effectively communicated vision is a tool for enlisting the commitment of employees to actions that move the organization forward in the intended direction.

Illustration Capsule 2.1

EXAMPLES OF STRATEGIC VISIONS – HOW WELL DO THEY MEASURE UP?

Vision Statement	Effective Elements	Shortcomings
Coca-Cola		
Our vision serves as the framework for our Roadmap and guides every aspect of our business by describing what we need to accomplish in order to continue achieving sustainable, quality growth. • People: Be a great place to work where people are inspired to be the best they can be. • Portfolio: Bring to the world a portfolio of quality beverage brands that anticipate and satisfy people's desires and needs. • Partners: Nurture a winning network of customers and suppliers; together we create mutual, enduring value. • Planet: Be a responsible citizen that makes a difference by helping build and support sustainable communities.	• Graphic • Focused • Flexible • Makes good business sense	• Long • Not forward-looking
• Profit: Maximize long-term return to shareowners while being mindful of our overall responsibilities. • Productivity: Be a highly effective, lean and fast-moving organization.		
UBS		
We are determined to be the best global financial services company. We focus on wealth and asset management, and on investment banking and securities businesses. We continually earn recognition and trust from clients, shareholders, and staff through our ability to anticipate, learn and shape our future. We share a common ambition to succeed by delivering quality in what we do. Our purpose is to help our clients make financial decisions with confidence. We use our resources to develop effective solutions and services for our clients. We foster a distinctive, meritocratic culture of ambition, performance and learning as this attracts, retains and develops the best talent for our company. By growing both our client and our talent franchises, we add sustainable value for our shareholders.	• Focused • Feasible • Desirable	• Not forward-looking • Bland or uninspiring • Hard to communicate
AstraZeneca		
At AstraZeneca, we are dedicated to the research, development and marketing of medicines that make a difference in healthcare. For us, this is at the core of our responsibility to our stakeholders and society. Successful pharmaceutical innovation, delivered responsibly, brings benefit for patients, creates value for shareholders and contributes to the economic development of the communities we serve.	• Feasible • Allows wiggle room • Desirable	• Vague • Overly broad

Sources: Company documents and websites (accessed 23 April 2010, 6 June 2010 and 5 December 2011).

calming fears, lifting spirits, facilitating involvement and providing updates and progress reports as events unfold all become part of the task in mobilizing support for the vision and winning commitment to needed actions.

Gaining the support of organizational members for the vision nearly always means putting 'where we are going and why' in writing, distributing the statement throughout the organization and having executives personally explain the vision and its rationale to as many people as feasible. *A strategic vision can usually be stated adequately in one to two paragraphs, and managers should be able to explain it to employees and outsiders in 5–10 minutes.* Ideally, executives should present their vision for the organization in a manner that reaches out and grabs people. An engaging and convincing strategic vision has enormous motivational value for the same reason that a stonemason is more inspired by building a great cathedral for the ages than simply laying stones to create floors and walls. When managers articulate a vivid and compelling case for where the organization is headed, organization members begin to say, 'This is interesting and has a lot of merit. I want to be involved and do my part to help make it happen'. The more that a vision evokes positive support and excitement, the greater its impact in terms of arousing a committed organizational effort and getting employees to move in a common direction.[3] Thus executive ability to paint a convincing and inspiring picture of an organization's journey and destination is an important element of effective strategic leadership.

> Strategic visions become real only when the vision statement is imprinted in the minds of organizational members and then translated into hard objectives and strategies.

Expressing the Essence of the Vision in a Slogan

The task of effectively conveying the vision to employees is assisted when management can capture the vision of where to head in a catchy or easily remembered slogan. A number of organizations have summed up their vision in a brief phrase:

- Levi Strauss & Company: 'We will clothe the world by marketing the most appealing and widely worn casual clothing in the world'.
- Nike: 'To bring innovation and inspiration to every athlete in the world'.
- Nova Nordisk: 'Committed to changing Diabetes'.
- The Metropolitan Police Service (Scotland Yard): 'To make London the safest major city in the world'.
- Greenpeace: 'To halt environmental abuse and promote environmental solutions'.

Creating a short slogan to illuminate an organization's direction and purpose helps rally organization members to deal with whatever obstacles lie in the organization's path and maintain their focus.

The Outcome of a Clear Vision Statement

While there is little evidence of a clear-cut relationship between the vision statement and the ultimate long-term performance of an organization, a well-conceived, skilfully communicated strategic vision lays the groundwork in several respects: (1) it crystallizes senior executives' own views about the firm's long-term direction; (2) it reduces the risk of aimless decision-making; (3) it is a tool for gaining the support of organization members for internal changes that will help make the vision a reality; (4) it provides a model for lower-level managers in setting departmental objectives and crafting departmental strategies that are in sync with the organization's overall strategy; and (5) it helps an organization prepare for the future. When management is able to demonstrate significant progress in achieving these five benefits, the first step in organizational direction-setting has been successfully completed.

> The distinction between a strategic vision and a mission statement is fairly clear-cut: a strategic vision portrays an organization's aspirations for its *future* ('where we are going'), whereas an organization's mission describes its *purpose* and its *present* business ('who we are, what we do and why we are here').

Crafting a Mission Statement

The defining characteristic of a strategic vision is what it says about the organization's *future strategic course* – 'the direction we are headed and our aspirations for the

> **Core Concept**
>
> A well-conceived **mission statement** conveys an organization's *purpose* in language specific enough to give the organization its own identity.

future'. In contrast, a **mission statement** describes the enterprise's *current business and purpose* – 'who we are, what we do and why we are here'. The mission statements that one finds in the organization's annual reports or posted on company websites are typically quite brief; some do a better job than others of conveying what the organization is all about. Consider, for example, the mission statement of **Sompo Japan Insurance Company of Europe Limited (SJE).**

- *SJE shall meet or exceed the expectations of clients while operating profitably in territories where we are authorized bearing in mind our risk strategy and our obligations and responsibilities under the regulatory system.*

  - *SJE's core competence lies in the strength of the Sompo Japan group's experience, network and relationship with clients. SJE shall focus on providing general insurance services to these clients.*

  - *SJE shall deliver such services through the provision of stable insurance cover over the long term at adequate and sustainable prices.*

  - *SJE shall enhance the reputation of the Sompo Japan Group by embedding a culture within its organization which embodies the Spirit of Fairness in decision-making and operations.*

Note that **the SJE's** mission statement does a good job of conveying 'who we are, what we do and why we are here', but it says nothing about the organization's long-term direction.

Another example of a well-stated mission statement with ample specifics about what the organization does is that of the Scandic hotel chain:

> *Our aim is to help Scandic's guests to recharge their batteries and to reinvigorate them by having an uncomplicated approach and by offering simple and accessible accommodation. We achieve this by simplifying our procedures, offering hotels in locations where many people travel to and taking account of our guests' various needs.*

Microsoft's grandiloquent mission statement – 'To help people and businesses throughout the world realise their full potential' – says so little about the customer needs it is satisfying that it could be applied to almost any firm. A well-conceived mission statement should employ language specific enough to give the organization its own identity.

Ideally, a mission statement is sufficiently descriptive to:

- identify the organization's product or services;
- specify the buyer needs it seeks to satisfy;
- identify the customer groups or markets it is endeavouring to serve;
- specify its approach to pleasing customers;
- give the organization its own identity.

Not many mission statements fully reveal *all* these facets of the business or employ language specific enough to give the organization an identity that is distinguishably different from those of other companies in much the same business or industry. A few companies have worded their mission statements so obscurely as to mask what they are all about. Occasionally, companies couch their mission in terms of making a profit. This is misguided. Profit is more correctly a *result* of what an organization does. Moreover, earning a profit is one of the obvious intentions of every commercial enterprise. Such companies as BMW, McDonald's, Shell Oil, Procter & Gamble, Nintendo and Nokia are each striving to earn a profit for shareholders; but plainly the fundamentals of their businesses are substantially different when it comes to 'who we are and what we do'. It is management's answer to 'make a profit doing what and for whom?' that reveals the substance of an organization's true mission and purpose.

Missions as Visions?

While we have presented clear definitions of vision and mission statements, and guidelines to their ideal content, it should be kept in mind that organizations may differ in their understanding of the hierarchy of definitions and their appropriate content. Some of the variety we see can be explained by the poor development of vision and mission statements, but the diversity of statements can also be attributed to country-specific differences and preferences. For instance, major differences are identified between the content of mission statements in the USA, Britain and France. While the US organizations generally follow a vision/mission hierarchy, British mission statements often encompass elements of company direction that we deem here as 'vision', while French mission statements, translated as 'the project of the enterprise' (project d'enterprise) frequently include elements of the vision, the strategy and the shared values of the organization.[4] Ultimately these differences do not appear to

---

Key Debate 2.1

ARE MISSION STATEMENTS TRUTHFUL AND EFFECTIVE?

Sometimes, researchers and practitioners make the claim that the link between mission statements and firm performance is not actually proven, and that a belief in their benefit as a strategic tool is only based on circumstantial evidence. Studies on the content, development processes and the performance outcomes of organizational direction statements provide a more nuanced understanding. Empirical studies on mission statements from Canada[5] and The Netherlands[6] stress that the existence of a mission statement is not automatically associated with an improved firm performance. To have a performance benefit there are additional criteria that must be fulfilled. First, the managers of the organization must be satisfied with the content of the mission statement, and must not just feel that they are nice-sounding words on a piece of paper. In connection with this, increasing both the manager's satisfaction with the mission statement and the performance effect, there must be a collective development process of the mission statement that includes all internal stakeholders. There is evidence that the involvement of the CEO and the top management is less important to the effectiveness of the mission statement than the collective input of all other hierarchical levels in the organization. It is also important that the evaluation system in the organization is aligned with the mission statement, both behaviourally and financially. Therefore, it is not a case of mission statements being always effective, nor never effective – the key to the mission statement being valuable for firm performance is the development process, management satisfaction and evaluation relevance.

ARE MISSION STATEMENTS TO BE BELIEVED?

When assessing an organization as an outsider, the accuracy of corporate mission statements should not be taken for granted. Studies[7] in this area also indicate some mixed results. Through studying the relationship between mission statement content and stakeholder management actions in the USA, it has been found that while social issues such as the environment and diversity are less frequently included, their mention in mission statements is significantly associated with behaviours regarding these issues. On the other hand the same study found no relationship between firms with mission statements that mention specific stakeholder groups (employees, customers and community) and behaviours regarding these stakeholders. This suggests that in some cases the inclusion of specific stakeholder groups in missions is likely to be the result of institutional pressures, while specifying social issues in missions is related to policy decisions.

QUESTIONS

1. Why would we find evidence that the performance benefits of mission statements are dependent on manager satisfaction? What would be the mechanisms behind this link?

2. Do organizations have a responsibility to be truthful in their mission statements? What are some acceptable reasons for differences between what is stated and the true actions of the organization?

matter as long as both the direction and purpose of the organization are clear and compelling.

Linking the Vision and Mission with Organization Values

> **Core Concept**
>
> An organization's **values** are the beliefs, traits and behavioural norms that employees are expected to display in conducting the organization's business and pursuing its strategic vision and mission.

The **values** of an organization (sometimes called *core values*) are the beliefs, traits and behavioural norms that management has determined should guide the pursuit of its vision and mission. They relate to such things as fair treatment, integrity, ethical behaviour, innovativeness, teamwork, top-notch quality, superior customer service, social responsibility and community citizenship. Many companies have developed a statement of values to emphasize the expectation that the values be reflected in the conduct of organizational operations and the behaviour of employees.

Many organizations have identified three to eight core values. At FedEx, the six core values concern people (valuing employees and promoting diversity), service (putting customers at the heart of all it does), innovation (inventing services and technologies to improve what it does), integrity (managing with honesty, efficiency and reliability) and loyalty (earning the respect of the FedEx people, customers and investors every day, in everything it does). Norwegian Air Shuttle ASA, commercially branded 'Norwegian' embraces three values – simplicity, directness and relevance in its quest to compete in the Scandinavian low-cost airline segment.

Do companies practise what they preach when it comes to their professed values? Sometimes no, sometimes yes – it runs the gamut. At one extreme are companies with window-dressing values; the values are given lip-service by top executives but have little discernible impact on either how employees behave or how the organization operates. Such companies have value statements because they are in vogue and make the organization look good. At the other extreme are companies whose executives are committed to infusing the organization with the desired character, traits and behavioural norms so that they are ingrained in the organization's culture – the core values thus become an integral part of the organization's DNA and what makes it tick. At such value-driven companies, executives 'walk the talk' and employees are held accountable for displaying the stated values.

At organizations where the stated values are real rather than cosmetic, managers connect values to the pursuit of the strategic vision and mission in one of two ways. In companies with long-standing values that are deeply entrenched in the culture, senior managers are careful to craft a vision, mission and strategy that match established values; they also reiterate how the value-based behavioural norms contribute to the organization's business success. If the organization changes to a different vision or strategy, executives take care to explain how and why the core values continue to be relevant. In new organizations or organizations having unspecified values, top management has to consider what values, behaviours and conduct should ideally characterize the organization and then draft a value statement that is circulated among managers and employees for discussion and possible modification. A final value statement that incorporates the desired behaviours and traits and that connects to the vision and mission is then officially adopted. This adoption can be an extremely long process requiring full commitment and persistence from managers as well as receptive employees who are convinced of the importance of the initiative. Some companies combine their vision, mission and values into a single statement or document, circulate it to all organization members, and in many instances post the vision, mission and value statement on the company's website. Illustration Capsule 2.2 describes how core values drive the mission at the Zappos Family of Companies, a quite successful online shoe and apparel retailer that was acquired recently by Amazon (but will continue to operate separately). The extreme nature of the statements, while effective for Zappos, may be unappealing to some due to an almost condescending simplicity. This illustrates that there is no universal way to develop, combine and transmit organizational values, visions and missions that would suit all organizations.

Illustration Capsule 2.2

ZAPPOS FAMILY MISSION AND CORE VALUES

We've been asked by a lot of people how we've grown so quickly, and the answer is actually really simple.... We've aligned the entire organization around one mission: *to provide the best customer service possible.* Internally, we call this our **WOW** philosophy.

These are the ten core values that we live by:

Deliver Wow through Service. *At the Zappos Family of Companies, anything worth doing is worth doing with WOW. WOW is such a short, simple word, but it really encompasses a lot of things. To WOW, you must differentiate yourself, which means doing something a little unconventional and innovative. You must do something that's above and beyond what's expected. And whatever you do must have an emotional impact on the receiver. We are not an average company, our service is not average, and we don't want our people to be average. We expect every employee to deliver WOW.*

Embrace and Drive Change. *Part of being in a growing company is that change is constant. For some people, especially those who come from bigger companies, the constant change can be somewhat unsettling at first. If you are not prepared to deal with constant change, then you probably are not a good fit for the company.*

Create Fun and a Little Weirdness. *At Zappos, We're Always Creating Fun and A Little Weirdness! One of the things that makes our company different from a lot of other companies is that we value being fun and being a little weird. We don't want to become one of those big companies that feels corporate and boring. We want to be able to laugh at ourselves. We look for both fun and humour in our daily work.*

Be Adventurous, Creative, and Open Minded. *We think it's important for people and the company as a whole to be bold and daring (but not reckless). We do not want people to be afraid to take risks and make mistakes. We believe if people aren't making mistakes, then that means they're not taking enough risks. Over time, we want everyone to develop his/her gut about business decisions. We want people to develop and improve their decision-making skills. We encourage people to make mistakes as long as they learn from them.*

Pursue Growth and Learning. *We think it's important for employees to grow both personally and professionally. It's important to constantly challenge and stretch yourself and not be stuck in a job where you don't feel like you are growing or learning.*

Build Open and Honest Relationships With Communication. *Fundamentally, we believe that openness and honesty make for the best relationships because that leads to trust and faith. We value strong relationships in all areas: with managers, direct reports, customers (internal and external), vendors, business partners, team members, and co-workers.*

Build a Positive Team and Family Spirit. *At our company, we place a lot of emphasis on our culture because we are both a team and a family. We want to create an environment that is friendly, warm, and exciting. We encourage diversity in ideas, opinions, and points of view.*

Do More with Less. *The Zappos Family of Companies has always been about being able to do more with less. While we may be casual in our interactions with each other, we are focused and serious about the operations of our business. We believe in working hard and putting in the extra effort to get things done.*

▶

Be Passionate and Determined. *Passion is the fuel that drives us and our company forward. We value passion, determination, perseverance, and the sense of urgency. We are inspired because we believe in what we are doing and where we are going. We don't take 'no' or 'that'll never work' for an answer because if we had, then our company would have never started in the first place.*

Be Humble. *While we have grown quickly in the past, we recognize that there are always challenges ahead to tackle. We believe that no matter what happens we should always be respectful of everyone.*

Source: Information posted at www.zappos.com (accessed 6 June 2010). © Zappos.com, Inc. 2011.

Stage 2: Setting Objectives

> **Core Concept**
>
> **Objectives** are an organization's performance targets – the specific results management wants to achieve.

The managerial purpose of setting **objectives** is to convert the vision and mission into specific performance targets. Well-stated objectives are *specific*, *quantifiable* or *measurable*, and contain a *deadline for achievement*. As Bill Hewlett, co-founder of Hewlett-Packard, shrewdly observed, 'You cannot manage what you cannot measure. . . . And what gets measured gets done'.[8] Concrete, measurable objectives are managerially valuable for three reasons: (1) they focus efforts and align actions throughout the organization, (2) they serve as standards for tracking an organization's performance and progress, and (3) they provide motivation and inspire employees to greater levels of effort. Ideally, managers should develop challenging yet achievable objectives that *stretch* an organization to perform at its full potential.

> **LO 2.2**
> Understand the importance of setting both strategic and financial objectives.

What Kinds of Objectives to Set

Two very distinct types of performance targets are required: those relating to financial performance and those relating to strategic performance. **Financial objectives** communicate management's targets for financial performance. **Strategic objectives** are related to an organization's marketing standing and competitive vitality. Examples of commonly used financial and strategic objectives include the following:

FINANCIAL VERSUS STRATEGIC OBJECTIVES

> **Core Concept**
>
> **Financial objectives** relate to the financial performance targets management has established for the organization to achieve. **Strategic objectives** relate to target outcomes that indicate an organization is strengthening its market standing, competitive vitality and future prospects.

Financial Objectives	Strategic Objectives
• An *x* percent increase in annual revenues	• Gaining an *x* percent market share
• Annual increases in after-tax profits *of x* percent	• Achieving lower overall costs than rivals
• Annual increases in earnings per share of *x* percent	• Overtaking key competitors on product performance or quality or customer service
• Annual dividend increases of *x* percent	• Deriving *x* percent of revenues from the sale of new products introduced within the past five years
• Profit margins of *x* percent	• Having broader or deeper technological capabilities than rivals
• An *x* percent return on capital employed (ROCE) or return on shareholders' equity investment (ROE)	• Having a wider product line than rivals
• Increased shareholder value – in the form of an upward-trending stock price	• Having a better-known or more powerful brand name than rivals
• Bond and credit ratings of *x*	• Having stronger national or global sales and distribution capabilities than rivals
• Internal cash flows of *x* to fund new capital investment	• Consistently getting new or improved products to market ahead of rivals

The importance of setting and achieving financial objectives is intuitive. Without adequate profitability and financial strength, an organization's long-term health and ultimate survival is vulnerable. Furthermore, insufficient earnings and a weak balance sheet alarm shareholders and creditors and put the jobs of senior executives at risk. However, good financial performance, by itself, is not enough.

The Balanced Scorecard: Improved Strategic Performance Fosters Better Financial Performance

An organization's financial performance measures are really *lagging indicators* that reflect the results of past decisions and organizational activities.[9] But an organization's past or current financial performance is not a reliable indicator of its future prospects – poor financial performers often turn things around and do better, while good financial performers can fall upon hard times. The best and most reliable *leading indicators* of an organization's future financial performance and business prospects are strategic outcomes that indicate whether the organization's competitiveness and market position are stronger or weaker. The accomplishment of strategic objectives signals that the organization is well positioned to sustain or improve its performance. For instance, if an organization is achieving ambitious strategic objectives such that its competitive strength and market position are on the rise, then there is reason to expect that its *future* financial performance will be better than its current or past performance. If an organization begins to lose competitive strength and fails to achieve important strategic objectives, then its ability to maintain its present profitability is highly suspect.

Consequently, utilizing a performance measurement system that strikes a *balance* between financial objectives and strategic objectives is optimal.[10] Just tracking an organization's financial performance overlooks the fact that what ultimately enables an organization to deliver better financial results from its operations is the achievement of strategic objectives that improve its competitiveness and market strength. Indeed, *the surest path to improving organizational profitability* period by period and year after year *is to continuously pursue strategic outcomes* that strengthen the organization's market position and produce a growing competitive advantage over rivals.

> **Core Concept**
>
> The **balanced scorecard** is a tool that is widely used to help an organization achieve its *financial objectives* by linking them to specific *strategic objectives* derived from the organization's business model.

The most widely used framework for balancing financial objectives with strategic objectives is known as the **balanced scorecard**.[11] This is a method for linking financial performance objectives to specific strategic objectives that derive from an organization's business model. It provides employees with clear guidelines about how their jobs are linked to the overall objectives of the organization, so they can contribute most productively and collaboratively to the achievement of these goals. In 2008, nearly 60 percent of global companies used a balanced-scorecard approach to measuring strategic and financial performance.[12] Examples of organizations that have adopted a balanced-scorecard approach to setting objectives and measuring performance include UPS, Ann Taylor Stores, UK Ministry of Defence, Caterpillar, Daimler AG, Hilton Hotels, Duke University Hospital and Siemens AG.[13] Illustration Capsule 2.3 provides selected strategic and financial objectives of four prominent companies.

The Merits of Setting Stretch Objectives

Ideally, managers ought to use the objective-setting exercise as a tool for *stretching an organization to perform at its full potential and deliver the best possible results*. Challenging employees to go all out and deliver 'stretch' gains in performance pushes an enterprise to be more inventive, to exhibit more urgency in improving both its financial performance and its business position and to be more intentional and focused in its actions. Stretch objectives spur exceptional performance and help prevent contentment with modest gains in organizational performance. As Mitchell Leibovitz, former CEO of the auto parts and service retailer Pep Boys, once said, 'If you want to have ho-hum results, have ho-hum objectives'. *There's no better way to avoid unimpressive results than by setting stretch objectives and using compensation incentives to motivate organization members to achieve the stretch performance targets.*

Illustration Capsule 2.3

EXAMPLES OF COMPANY OBJECTIVES

NORDSTROM

Increase same store sales by 2–4 per cent. Expand credit revenue by $25–$35 million while also reducing associated expenses by $10–$20 million as a result of lower bad debt expenses. Continue moderate store growth by opening three new Nordstrom stores, relocating one store and opening 17 Nordstrom Racks. Find more ways to connect with customers on a multi-channel basis, including plans for an enhanced online experience, improved mobile shopping capabilities and better engagement with customers through social networking. Improve customer focus: 'Most important, we continue to do everything in our power to elevate our focus on the customer. Our challenge is to keep building on this momentum. Our number one goal firmly remains improving customer service' (Blake Nordstrom, CEO).

MICROSOFT

On a broad level, deliver end-to-end experiences that connect users to information, communications, entertainment, and people in new and compelling ways across their lives at home, at work, and the broadest-possible range of mobile scenarios. Given the dramatic changes in the way people interact with technology, as touch, gestures, handwriting, and speech recognition become a normal part of how we control

devices, focus on making technology more accessible and simpler to use, which will create opportunities to reach new markets and deliver new kinds of computing experiences.

More specifically, grow revenue in the PC Division slightly faster than the overall PC market fuelled especially by emerging market trends. Launch Office 2010 for the business market and promote adoption followed by a 2011 launch of the Windows Phone 7 in the Entertainment and Devices Division. Grow annuity revenue between 4–6 per cent in the Server and Tools Business segment. Target overall gross margin increases of 1 per cent fuelled in part by improved operational efficiency. Operating expenses are targeted at $26.1–$26.3 billion for the year with projected capital spending at $2 billion.

MCDONALD'S

Reinvest $2.4 billion in the business; 50% of this will be spent on opening 1,000 new restaurants around the world, including roughly 500 in Asia Pacific, 250 in Europe, and 150 in the U.S. The other half will be allocated toward 're-imagining' the décor and menu of over 2,000 existing locations. Re-imagining has a direct positive impact on sales as market share increases after re-imagining restaurants in the U.S., France and Australia demonstrate. Continue to expand refranchising; 80% of restaurants have been refranchised and 200–300 restaurants will augment this in the next year. Focus on menu choice with a balance of familiar and popular core products as well as new items to keep products relevant.

Note: Developed with C. David Morgan.

Sources: 'Nordstrom 2009 Annual Report', www.phx.corporate-ir.net/phoenix.zhtml?c=93295&p=irol-irhome, www.materials. proxyvote.com/Approved/655664/20100312/AR_57243/images/Nordstrom-AR2009.pdf (accessed 4 April 2010); 'Nordstrom Fourth Quarter and Fiscal Year 2009 Earning, 22 February 2010', www.phxcorporate-ir.net/phoenix.zhtml?c=93295&p=irol-newsArticle&ID=1393755&highlight (accessed 30 April 2010); Nordstrom '4Q 2009 Financial Results', www.investor. nordstrom. com/phoenix.zhtml?c=93295&p=irol-audioArchives (accessed 30 April 2010); Thompson Reuters Street Events, 'JWN – Q4 2009 Nordstrom Earnings Conference Call', www.streetevents.com, February 2010 (transcribed version of webcast accessed 30 April 2010, through InvesText database); 'Microsoft Annual Report' www.microsoft.com/msft/reports/default.mspx (accessed 23 April 2010); 'Microsoft Third Quarter Earnings Call', www.microsoft.com/msft/earnings/fy10/earn_rel_q3_10.mspx (accessed 30 April 2010); Thompson Reuters Street Events, 'MCD – Q4 2009 McDonald's Corporate Earnings Conference Call', www. streetevents.com, January 2010 (transcribed version of webcast accessed 30 April 2010 through InvesText database).

Why Both Short-term and Long-term Objectives Are Needed

An organization's set of financial and strategic objectives should include both near-term and longer-term performance targets. Short-term (quarterly or annual) objectives focus attention on delivering performance improvements in the current period and satisfy shareholder expectations for near-term progress. Longer-term targets (three to five years off) force managers to consider what to do *now* to put the organization in a position to perform better later. Long-term objectives are critical for achieving optimal long-term performance and stand as a barrier to a near-sighted management philosophy and an undue focus on short-term results. When trade-offs have to be made between achieving long-run objectives and achieving short-run objectives, long-run objectives should take precedence (unless the achievement of one or more short-run performance targets has unique importance).

The Need for Objectives at All Organizational Levels

Objective-setting should not stop with top management's establishing organization-wide performance targets. Objectives need to be broken down into performance targets for each of the organization's separate businesses, product lines, functional departmens and individual work units. Organizational performance cannot reach full potential unless each organizational unit sets and pursues performance targets that contribute directly to the desired organization-wide outcomes and results. Objective-setting is thus generally a *top-down process* that must extend throughout the organization. And it means that each organizational unit must take care to set performance targets that support – rather than conflict with or negate – the achievement of organization-wide strategic and financial objectives.

The ideal situation is a team effort in which each organizational unit strives to produce results in its area of responsibility that contribute to the achievement of the organization's performance targets and strategic vision. Such consistency signals that organizational units know their strategic role and are on board in helping the organization move along the chosen strategic path and produce the desired results.

Stage 3: Crafting a Strategy

The task of stitching a strategy together entails addressing a series of 'hows': *how* to grow the business, *how* to please customers, *how* to outcompete rivals, *how* to respond to changing market conditions, *how* to manage each functional piece of the business, *how* to develop needed capabilities and *how* to achieve strategic and financial objectives. It also means choosing among the various strategic alternatives – proactively searching for opportunities to do new things or to do existing things in new or better ways.[14] The faster an organization's business environment is changing, the more critical it becomes for its managers to be good entrepreneurs in diagnosing the direction and force of the changes under way and in responding with timely adjustments in strategy. The organization needs to pay attention to early warnings of future change and be willing to experiment with dare-to-be-different ways to establish a market position in that future. When obstacles appear unexpectedly in an organization's path, it is up to management to adapt rapidly and innovatively. *Masterful strategies come from doing things differently from competitors where it counts – out-innovating them, being more efficient, being more imaginative, adapting faster – rather than running with the herd.* Good strategy-making is therefore inseparable from good business entrepreneurship. One cannot exist without the other.

Strategy-making Involves Managers at All Organizational Levels

An organization's senior executives obviously have important strategy-making roles. The CEO carries the mantles of chief direction-setter, chief objective-setter, chief

> **LO 2.3**
> Understand why the strategic initiatives taken at various organizational levels should be tightly co-ordinated to achieve performance targets.

strategy-maker and chief strategy implementer for the total organization. Ultimate responsibility for *leading* the strategy-making, strategy-executing process rests with the CEO. In some enterprises the CEO or owner functions as strategic visionary and chief architect of strategy, personally deciding what the key elements of the organization's strategy will be, although others may well assist with data-gathering and analysis and the CEO may seek the advice of senior executives or board members. A CEO-centred approach to strategy development is characteristic of small owner-managed companies and sometimes also large corporations that were founded by the present CEO or that have a CEO with strong strategic leadership skills. Steve Jobs at Apple, Andrea Jung at Avon and Howard Schultz at Starbucks are prominent examples of corporate CEOs who have wielded a heavy hand in shaping their organization's strategy.

Even here, however, it is a mistake to view strategy-making as a *top* management function, the exclusive province of owner-entrepreneurs CEOs, other senior executives and board members. The more an organization's operations cut across different products, industries and geographic areas, the more that headquarters executives have little option but to delegate considerable strategy-making authority to down-the-line managers in charge of particular subsidiaries, divisions, product lines, geographic sales offices, distribution centres and plants. On-the-scene managers who oversee specific operating units can be reliably counted on to have a more detailed command of the strategic issues and choices for the particular operating unit under their supervision – knowing the prevailing market and competitive conditions, customer requirements and expectations and all the other relevant aspects affecting the several strategic options available. Managers with day-to-day familiarity of, and authority over, a specific operating unit thus have a big edge over headquarters executives in making wise strategic choices for their operating unit.

> **Core Concept**
>
> In most companies, crafting and executing strategy is a *collaborative team effort* in which every manager has a role for the area he or she heads. It is flawed thinking to view crafting and executing strategy as something only high-level managers do.

Take, for example, an organization like General Electric (GE), a $183 billion global corporation with 325 000 employees, operations in some 100 countries and businesses that include jet engines, lighting, power generation, electric transmission and distribution equipment, housewares and appliances, medical equipment, media and entertainment, locomotives, security devices, water purification and financial services. While top-level headquarters executives may well be personally involved in shaping GE's *overall* strategy and fashioning *important* strategic moves, it does not follow that a few senior executives in GE's headquarters have either the expertise or a sufficiently detailed understanding of all the relevant factors to wisely craft all the strategic initiatives taken for hundreds of subsidiaries and thousands of products. They simply cannot know enough about the situation in every GE organizational unit to decide on every strategy detail and direct every strategic move made in GE's worldwide organization. Rather, it takes involvement on the part of GE's whole management team – top executives, business group heads, the heads of specific business units and product categories and key managers in plants, sales offices and distribution centres – to craft the thousands of strategic initiatives that end up constituting the whole of GE's strategy.

The *level* of strategy also has a bearing on who participates in crafting strategy. In diversified companies, where multiple businesses have to be managed, the strategy-making task involves four distinct levels of strategy. Each of these involves different facets of the organization's overall strategy and calls for the participation of different types of managers, as shown in Figure 2.2.

1. *Corporate strategy* is strategy at the multibusiness level – how to achieve a competitive edge through a multibusiness, multimarket strategy. It concerns how to improve the combined performance of *the set of businesses* the organization has diversified into and the means of capturing cross-business synergies and turning them into competitive advantage. It addresses the questions of what businesses to

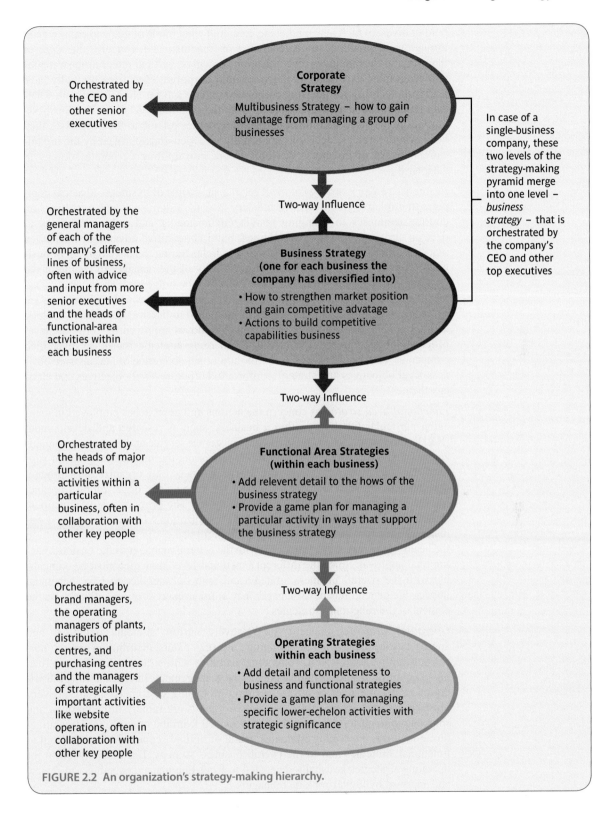

FIGURE 2.2 An organization's strategy-making hierarchy.

hold or divest, which new markets to enter and what mode of entry to employ (e.g. through an acquisition, strategic alliance or franchising). It concerns the *scope* of the firm and thus includes diversification strategies, vertical integration strategies and geographic expansion strategies. Senior corporate executives normally have lead responsibility for devising corporate strategy and for choosing among whatever recommended actions bubble up from the organization below. Key business-unit heads may also be influential regarding issues related to the businesses they head. Major strategic decisions are usually reviewed and approved by the organization's board of directors. We look deeper into crafting corporate strategy in Chapter 8.

2. *Business strategy* is strategy at the level of a single line of business – one that competes in a relatively well-defined industry or market domain. The key focus is on crafting responses to changing market circumstances and initiating actions to develop strong competitive capabilities, build competitive advantage, strengthen market position and enhance performance. Orchestrating the development of business-level strategy is typically the responsibility of the manager in charge of the business, although corporate-level managers may be influential. The business head has at least two other strategy-related roles: (1) seeing that lower-level strategies are well conceived, consistent and adequately matched to the overall business strategy and (2) getting major business-level strategic moves approved by corporate-level officers and keeping them informed of emerging strategic issues. In diversified companies, business-unit heads have the additional obligation of making sure business-level objectives and strategy conform to corporate-level objectives and strategy themes.

3. *Functional-area strategies* concern the actions and approaches employed in managing particular functions within a business, such as research and development (R&D), production, sales and marketing, customer service and finance. An organization's marketing strategy, for example, represents the managerial plan for running the sales and marketing part of the business. An organization's product development strategy represents the plan for keeping the organization's product line-up in tune with what buyers are looking for. The primary role of functional strategies is to flesh out the details of an organization's business strategy. Lead responsibility for functional strategies within a business is normally delegated to the heads of the respective functions, with the general manager of the business having final approval. Since the different functional-level strategies must be compatible with the overall business strategy and with one another to have beneficial impact, the general business manager may at times exert stronger influence on the content of the functional strategies.

4. *Operating strategies* concern the relatively narrow strategic initiatives and approaches for managing key operating units (e.g. plants, distribution centres, purchasing centres) and specific operating activities with strategic significance (e.g. quality control, materials purchasing, brand management, Internet sales). A distribution centre manager of an organization promising customers speedy delivery must have a strategy to ensure that finished goods are rapidly turned around and shipped out to customers once they are received from the organization's manufacturing facilities. Operating strategies, while of limited scope, add further detail to functional strategies and to the overall business strategy. Lead responsibility for operating strategies is usually delegated to front-line managers, subject to review and approval by higher-ranking managers.

Even though operating strategy is at the bottom of the strategy-making hierarchy, its importance should not be downplayed. A major plant that fails in its strategy to achieve production volume, unit cost and quality targets can damage the organization's reputation for quality products and undercut the achievement of the organization's sales and profit objectives. Front-line managers are thus an important part of an organization's strategy-making team. One cannot reliably judge the strategic importance of a given action simply by the strategy level or location within the managerial hierarchy where it is initiated.

In single-business enterprises, the corporate and business levels of strategy-making merge into one level – business strategy – because the strategy for the whole organization involves only one distinct line of business. Thus a single-business enterprise has three levels of strategy: (1) business strategy for the organization as a whole; (2) functional-area strategies for each main area within the business; (3) and operating strategies undertaken by lower-echelon managers to flesh out strategically significant aspects of the organization's business and functional-area strategies. Proprietorships, partnerships and owner-managed enterprises may have only one or two strategy-making levels since their strategy-making process can be handled by a few key people. The larger and more diverse the operations of an enterprise, the more points of strategic initiative it has and the more levels of management that have a significant strategy-making role.

The overall point is this: regardless of the type of organization and whether the strategy is primarily deliberate or primarily emergent, crafting strategy involves managers in various positions and at various organizational levels. And while managers farther down in the managerial hierarchy obviously have a narrower, more specific strategy-making role than managers closer to the top, the important understanding is that in most of today's organizations *every manager typically has a strategy-making role – ranging from minor to major – for the area he or she heads.* Hence, any notion that an organization's strategists are at the top of the management hierarchy and that mid-level and front-line employees merely carry out the strategic directives of senior managers needs to be cast aside. In organizations with wide-ranging operations, it is far more accurate to view strategy-making as a *collaborative team effort* involving managers (and sometimes other key employees) through the whole organizational hierarchy. A valuable strength of collaborative strategy-making is that the team of people charged with crafting the strategy include the very people who will also be charged with implementing and executing it. Giving people an influential stake in crafting the strategy they must later help execute not only builds motivation and commitment but also enhances accountability at multiple levels of management – removing the excuse of 'It wasn't my idea to do this'.

> In most organizations, crafting strategy is a *collaborative team effort* that includes managers in various positions and at various organizational levels. Crafting strategy is rarely something only high-level executives do.

A Strategic Vision + Objectives + Strategy = A Strategic Plan

Developing a strategic vision and mission, setting objectives and crafting a strategy are basic direction-setting tasks. They map out where an organization is headed, its purpose, the targeted strategic and financial outcomes, the basic business model and the competitive moves and internal action approaches to be used in achieving the desired business results. Together, they constitute a **strategic plan** for coping with industry conditions, outcompeting rivals, meeting objectives and making progress towards the strategic vision.[15] Typically, a strategic plan includes a commitment to allocate resources to the plan and specifies a time period for achieving goals (usually three to five years).

In some companies, the strategic plan is focused around achieving exceptionally bold strategic objectives – stretch goals requiring resources that are well beyond the current means of the organization. This type of strategic plan is more the expression of a **strategic intent** to rally the organization through an *unshakable – often obsessive – commitment* to do whatever it takes to acquire the resources and achieve the goals. Nike's strategic intent during the 1960s was to overtake Adidas – an objective far beyond Nike's means at the time. Starbucks strategic intent is to make the Starbucks brand the world's most recognized and respected brand.

In companies that do regular strategy reviews and develop explicit strategic plans, the strategic plan usually ends up as a written document that is circulated to most

> **Core Concept**
>
> An organization's **strategic plan** lays out its future direction and business purpose, performance targets and strategy.

> **Core Concept**
>
> An organization exhibits **strategic intent** when it relentlessly pursues an exceptionally ambitious strategic objective, committing to do whatever it takes to achieve the goals.

managers and selected employees. Near-term performance targets are the part of the strategic plan most often spelled out explicitly and communicated to managers and employees. A number of companies summarize key elements of their strategic plans in the organization's annual report to shareholders, in postings on their websites, or in statements provided to the business media, whereas others, perhaps for reasons of competitive sensitivity, make only vague, general statements about their strategic plans.[16] In small, privately owned companies, it is rare for strategic plans to exist in written form. Small-organization strategic plans tend to reside in the thinking and directives of owners/executives, with aspects of the plan being revealed in meetings and conversations with employees, and in the understandings and commitments among managers and key employees about where to head, what to accomplish and how to proceed.

Stage 4: Executing the Strategy

LO 2.4
Become aware of what an organization must do to achieve operating excellence and to execute its strategy proficiently.

Managing the implementation of a strategy is an operations-oriented, make-things-happen activity aimed at performing core business activities in a strategy-supportive manner. It is easily the most demanding and time-consuming part of the strategy management process. Converting strategic plans into actions and results tests a manager's ability to direct organizational action, motivate people, build and strengthen organizational competences and competitive capabilities, create and nurture a strategy-supportive climate and meet or beat performance targets. Initiatives to put the strategy in place and execute it proficiently have to be launched and managed on many organizational fronts.

Management's action agenda for executing the chosen strategy emerges from assessing what the organization will have to do to achieve the targeted financial and strategic performance. Each manager has to think through the answer to 'What has to be done in my area to execute my piece of the strategic plan, and what actions should I take to get the process under way?' How much internal change is needed depends on how much of the strategy is new, how far internal practices and competences deviate from what the strategy requires and how well the present climate/culture supports good strategy execution. Depending on the amount of internal change involved, full implementation and proficient execution of an organizational strategy (or important new pieces thereof) can take several months to several years.

In most situations, managing the strategy execution process includes the following principal aspects:

- Staffing the organization with the needed skills and expertise.
- Building and strengthening strategy-supporting resources and competitive capabilities.
- Organising the work effort along the lines of best practice.
- Allocating ample resources to the activities critical to strategic success.
- Ensuring that policies and procedures facilitate rather than impede effective strategy execution.
- Installing information and operating systems that enable employees to carry out their roles effectively and efficiently.
- Motivating people and tying rewards and incentives directly to the achievement of performance objectives.
- Creating an organizational culture and work climate conducive to successful strategy execution.
- Exerting the internal leadership needed to propel implementation forward and drive continuous improvement of the strategy execution processes.

Good strategy execution requires diligent pursuit of operating excellence. It is a job for an organization's whole management team. Success depends on the skills and co-operation of operating managers who can push for needed changes in their organizational units and consistently deliver good results. Management's handling of the strategy implementation process can be considered successful if things go smoothly enough that the organization meets or beats its strategic and financial performance targets and shows good progress in achieving management's strategic vision.

Stage 5: Evaluating Performance and Initiating Corrective Adjustments

The fifth component of the strategy management process – monitoring new external developments, evaluating the organization's progress and making corrective adjustments – is the trigger point for deciding whether to continue or change the organization's vision and mission, objectives, strategy and/or strategy execution methods.[17] As long as the organization's strategy continues to pass the three tests of a winning strategy (good fit, competitive advantage, strong performance), management may well decide to stay the course. Simply fine-tuning the strategic plan and continuing with efforts to improve strategy execution are sufficient.

However, whenever an organization encounters disruptive changes in its environment, questions need to be raised about the appropriateness of its direction and strategy. If an organization experiences a downturn in its market position or persistent shortfalls in performance, then managers are obligated to delve into the causes – do they relate to poor strategy, poor strategy execution or both? – and take timely corrective action. An organization's direction, objectives and strategy have to be revisited any time external or internal conditions warrant. It is to be expected that an organization will modify its strategic vision, direction, objectives and strategy over time.

> An organization's vision and mission, objectives, strategy and approach to strategy execution are never final; managing strategy is an ongoing process.

Likewise, it is not unusual for an organization to find that one or more aspects of its strategy execution are not going as well as intended. Proficient strategy execution is always the product of much organizational learning. It is achieved unevenly – coming quickly in some areas and proving difficult in others. It is both normal and desirable to periodically assess strategy execution to determine which aspects are working well and which need improving. Successful strategy execution entails vigilantly searching for ways to improve and then making corrective adjustments whenever and wherever it is useful to do so.

Corporate Governance: The Role of the Board of Directors in the Strategy-crafting, Strategy-executing Process

Although senior managers have *lead responsibility* for crafting and executing an organization's strategy, it is the duty of an organization's board of directors to exercise strong oversight and see that the five tasks of strategic management are conducted in a manner that is in the best interests of shareholders and other stakeholders.[18] An organization's board of directors has four important obligations to fulfil:

> **LO 2.5**
> Become aware of the role and responsibility of the board of directors in overseeing the strategic management process.

1. *Critically appraise the organization's direction, strategy and business approaches.* Board members must ask probing questions and draw on their business acumen to make independent judgements about whether strategy proposals have been

adequately analysed and whether proposed strategic actions appear to have greater promise than alternatives. Asking incisive questions is usually sufficient to test whether the case for management's proposals is compelling and to exercise vigilant oversight. However, when the organization's strategy is failing or is plagued with faulty execution, and certainly when there is a precipitous collapse in profitability, board members have a duty to be more proactive, expressing their concerns about the validity of the strategy and/or operating methods, initiating debate about the organization's strategic path, having one-on-one discussions with key executives and other board members and perhaps directly intervening as a group to alter the organization's executive leadership and, ultimately, its strategy and business approaches.

2. *Evaluate the calibre of senior executives' strategic leadership skills.* The board is always responsible for determining whether the current CEO is doing a good job of strategic leadership.[19] The board must also evaluate the leadership skills of other senior executives, since the board must elect a successor when the incumbent CEO steps down, either going with an insider or deciding that an outsider is needed. Evaluation of senior executives' skills is enhanced when outside directors visit the organization's facilities and talk with employees to personally evaluate whether the strategy is on track, how well the strategy is being executed and how well issues and problems are being addressed. Independent board members at GE visit operating executives at each major business unit once a year to assess the organization's talent pool and stay abreast of emerging strategic and operating issues affecting the organization's divisions.

3. *Institute a compensation plan for top executives that reward them for actions and results that serve stakeholder interests.* A basic principle of corporate governance is that the owners of a corporation (the shareholders) delegate managerial control to a team of executives who are compensated for their efforts on behalf of the owners. In their role as an *agent* of shareholders, corporate managers have a clear and unequivocal duty to make decisions and operate the organization in accord with shareholder interests. (This does not mean disregarding the interests of other stakeholders – employees, suppliers, the communities in which the organization operates and society at large.) Many boards of directors have a compensation committee, composed entirely of directors from *outside* the organization, to develop a salary and incentive compensation plan that rewards senior executives for boosting the organization's *long-term* performance and growing the economic value of the enterprise on behalf of shareholders; the compensation committee's recommendations are presented to the full board for approval. But during the past 10–15 years, many boards of directors have done a poor job of ensuring that executive salary increases, bonuses and stock option awards are tied tightly to performance measures that are truly in the long-term interests of shareholders. Rather, compensation packages at many organizations have increasingly rewarded executives for short-term performance improvements that led to undue risk-taking and compensation packages that, in the view of many people, were obscenely large. This has proved damaging to long-term organizational performance and has worked against shareholder interests – witness the huge loss of shareholder wealth that occurred at many financial institutions in 2008/9 because of executive risk-taking. As a consequence, the need to overhaul and reform executive compensation has become a hot topic in both public circles and corporate boardrooms. Illustration Capsule 2.4 discusses how weak governance at the mortgage companies Fannie Mae and Freddie Mac allowed opportunistic senior managers to boost their compensation while making decisions that risked the futures of the organizations they managed.

4. *Oversee the organization's financial accounting and financial reporting practices.* While top executives, particularly the organization's CEO and CFO (chief financial officer), are primarily responsible for seeing that the organization's finan-

Illustration Capsule 2.4

CORPORATE GOVERNANCE FAILURES AT FANNIE MAE AND FREDDIE MAC

Executive compensation in the financial services industry during the mid-2000s ranks high among examples of failed corporate governance. Corporate governance at the government-sponsored mortgage giants Fannie Mae and Freddie Mac was particularly weak. The politically appointed boards at both enterprises failed to understand the risks of the sub-prime loan strategies being employed, did not adequately monitor the decisions of the CEO, did not exercise effective oversight of the accounting principles being employed (which led to inflated earnings) and approved executive compensation systems that allowed management to manipulate earnings to receive lucrative performance bonuses. The audit and compensation committees at Fannie Mae were particularly ineffective in protecting

shareholder interests, with the audit committee allowing the company's financial officers to audit reports prepared under their direction and used to determine performance bonuses. Fannie Mae's audit committee also was aware of management's use of questionable accounting practices that reduced losses and recorded one-time gains to achieve financial targets linked to bonuses. In addition, the audit committee failed to investigate formal charges of accounting improprieties filed by a manager in the office of the controller.

Fannie Mae's compensation committee was equally ineffective. The committee allowed the company's CEO, Franklin Raines, to select the consultant employed to design the mortgage firm's executive compensation plan and agreed to a tiered bonus plan that would permit Raines and other senior managers to receive maximum bonuses without great difficulty. The compensation plan allowed Raines to earn performance-based bonuses of $52 million and total compensation of $90 million between 1999–2004. Raines was forced to resign in December 2004 when the Office of Federal Housing Enterprise Oversight found that Fannie Mae executives had fraudulently inflated earnings to receive bonuses linked to financial performance. Securities and Exchange Commission investigators also found evidence of improper accounting at Fannie Mae and required the company to restate its earnings between 2002–2004 by $6.3 billion.

Poor governance at Freddie Mac allowed its CEO and senior management to manipulate financial data to receive performance-based compensation as well. Freddie Mac CEO Richard Syron received 2007 compensation of $19.8 million while the mortgage company's share price declined from a high of $70 in 2005 to $25 at year-end 2007. During Syron's tenure as CEO, the company became embroiled in a multi-billion-dollar accounting scandal,

▶

◀

and Syron personally disregarded internal reports dating to 2004 that cautioned of an impending financial crisis at the company. Forewarnings within Freddie Mac and by federal regulators and outside industry observers proved to be correct, with loan underwriting policies at Freddie Mac and Fannie Mae leading to combined losses at the two firms in 2008 of more than $100 billion. The price of Freddie Mac's shares had fallen to below $1 by the time of Syron's resignation in September 2008.

Both organizations were placed into a conservatorship under the direction of the US government in September 2008 and were provided bailout funds of nearly $60 billion by April 2009. In May 2009, Fannie Mae requested another $19 billion of the $200 billion committed by the US government to cover the operating losses of the two government-sponsored mortgage firms. By June 2010, the bill for bailing out the two enterprises had risen to $145 billion, with the expectation that still more aid would be required to get them back on a sound financial footing.

Sources: 'Adding up the government's total bailout tab', *New York Times Online*, 4 February 2009; Dash, Eric 'Fannie Mae to restate results by $6.3 billion because of accounting', *New York Times Online*, 7 December 2006; Shin Annys, 'Fannie Mae sets executive salaries', *Washington Post*, 9 February 2006, p. D4; DeCarlo, Scott, Weiss, Eric, Jickling, Mark, Cristie, James R, (2006) *Fannie Mae and Freddie Mac: scandal in U.S housing*, New York, Nova, pp. 266–86; 'Chaffetz, Conyers, Smith, Issa and Bachus call for FOIA to apply to Fannie-Freddie', 17 June 2010 (June 2010 archives), www.chaffetz.house.gov/2010/06/ (accessed 24 June 2010).

cial statements fairly and accurately report the results of the organization's operations, board members have a fiduciary duty to protect shareholders by exercising oversight of the organization's financial practices. In addition, corporate boards must ensure that generally acceptable accounting principles are properly used in preparing the organization's financial statements and that proper financial controls are in place to prevent fraud and misuse of funds. Virtually all boards of directors have an audit committee, always composed entirely of *outside directors* (*inside directors* hold management positions in the organization and either directly or indirectly report to the CEO). The members of the audit committee have lead responsibility for overseeing the decisions of the organization's financial officers and consulting with both internal and external auditors to ensure that financial reports are accurate and that adequate financial controls are in place. Faulty oversight of corporate accounting and financial reporting practices by audit committees and corporate boards during the early 2000s resulted in the US federal investigation of more than 20 major corporations between 2000 and 2002. The investigations of such well-known companies as Global Crossing, Enron, Qwest Communications and WorldCom found that upper management had employed fraudulent or unsound accounting practices to artificially inflate revenues, overstate assets and reduce expenses. The scandals resulted in the conviction of a number of corporate executives and the passage of the Sarbanes–Oxley Act of 2002, which tightened financial reporting standards and created additional compliance requirements for public boards.

> Effective corporate governance requires the board of directors to oversee the organization's strategic direction, evaluate its senior executives, handle executive compensation and oversee financial reporting practices.

Every corporation should have a strong, independent board of directors that: (1) is well informed about the organization's performance; (2) guides and judges the CEO and other top executives; (3) has the courage to curb management actions the board believes are inappropriate or unduly risky; (4) certifies to shareholders that the CEO is doing what the board expects; (5) provides insight and advice to management; and (6) is intensely involved in debating the pros and cons of key decisions and actions.[20] Boards of directors that lack the backbone to challenge a strong-willed or 'imperial' CEO or that approve almost anything the CEO recommends without probing inquiry and debate (perhaps because the board is stacked with the CEO's cronies) abdicate their duty to represent and protect shareholder interests.

A Different View – Shareholder versus stakeholder approaches

In this chapter we have taken the perspective, somewhat tempered, that the primary purpose of an organization is to create value to shareholders. Certainly, it is made clear that employees, loan providers, customers and other stakeholders are considered important, and the company has *values* that guide their relationship and action to these stakeholders, but the main belief of the *shareholder capitalism* approach common to English-speaking countries, but primarily North America, is that the organization's main duty is to provide profits to shareholders. This can be contrasted to the *stakeholder* approach, found throughout western Europe, that problematizes the fundamental reason for the firms' existence. The logic in this approach is that the creating of value to *stakeholders* is the central objective of the organization, that the stakeholders should be considered and addressed in their own right, and shareholders are just one among many without assumed priority. The stakeholder approach[21] generally embraces a wider corporate responsibility, including corporate social responsibility and may include the local community and the wider community through environmental responsibility.

An organizational mission statement often reveals if a shareholder or stakeholder approach is followed. This also means that the approach will determine *how* to write a mission statement for the organization. With a stakeholder approach the mission statement will be broader, addressing a wider constituency of stakeholders whom the management regards as having a claim on the business and to whom it is accountable. For example, the Vision and Mission statements of Itella, one of the largest employers in Finland, who demonstrate a clear stakeholder approach:

Vision: Itella is the European benchmark in postal, logistics and information logistics services.

Mission: Itella's mission is to ensure the delivery of important items sent by our customers – in both physical and digital format. This mission is shared by all three business groups: Itella Information, Itella Logistics and Itella Mail Communications.

Everything we do must be based on sustainable development. Our goal is for Itella's success to support the well-being of our stakeholders by observing the environmental, financial and social aspects of corporate responsibility.

Source: www.itella.com.

KEY POINTS

The strategic management process consists of five interrelated and integrated stages:

1. *Developing a strategic vision* of the organization's future, a *mission* that defines the organization's current purpose, and a set of *core values* to guide the pursuit of the vision and mission. This managerial step provides direction for the organization, motivates and inspires employees, aligns and guides actions throughout the organization and communicates to stakeholders management's aspirations for the organization's future.

2. *Setting objectives* to convert the vision and mission into performance targets and using the targeted results as standards for measuring the organization's performance. Objectives need to spell out *how much* of *what kind* of performance *by when*. Two broad types of objectives are required: *financial objectives* and *strategic objectives*. A *balanced-scorecard* approach provides a popular method for linking financial objectives to specific, measurable strategic objectives.

3. *Crafting a strategy* to achieve the objectives and move the organization along the strategic course that management has charted. Crafting deliberate strategy calls for strategic analysis, based on the business model. Crafting emergent strategy is a learning-by-doing process involving experimentation. Who participates in the process of crafting strategy depends on (1) whether the process is emergent or deliberate and (2) the level of strategy concerned. Deliberate strategies are mostly top-down, while emergent strategies are bottom-up, although both cases require two-way interaction between different types of managers. In large, diversified companies, there are four levels

of strategy, each of which involves a corresponding level of management: corporate strategy (multibusiness strategy), business strategy (strategy for individual businesses that compete in a single industry), functional-area strategies within each business (e.g. marketing, R&D, logistics) and operating strategies (for key operating units, such as manufacturing plants). Thus, strategy-making is an inclusive, collaborative activity involving not only senior organization executives but also the heads of major business divisions, functional-area managers and operating managers on the front lines. The larger and more diverse the operations of an enterprise, the more points of strategic initiative it has and the more levels of management that play a significant strategy-making role.

4. *Executing the chosen strategy* and converting the strategic plan into action. Managing the execution of strategy is an operations-oriented, make-things-happen activity aimed at shaping the performance of core business activities in a strategy-supportive manner. Management's handling of the strategy implementation process can be considered successful if things go smoothly enough that the organization meets or beats its strategic and financial performance targets and shows good progress in achieving management's strategic vision.

5. *Monitoring developments, evaluating performance and initiating corrective adjustments* in light of actual experience, changing conditions, new ideas and new opportunities. This stage of the strategy management process is the trigger point for deciding whether to continue or change the organization's vision and mission, objectives, strategy and/or strategy execution methods.

The sum of an organization's strategic vision and mission, objectives and strategy constitutes a *strategic plan* for coping with industry conditions, outcompeting rivals, meeting objectives and making progress towards the strategic vision. An organization whose strategic plan is based around ambitious *stretch goals* that require an unwavering commitment to do whatever it takes to achieve them is said to have *strategic intent*.

Boards of directors have a duty to shareholders to play a vigilant role in overseeing management's handling of an organization's strategy-making, strategy-executing process. This entails four important obligations: (1) critically appraise the organization's direction, strategy and strategy execution; (2) evaluate the calibre of senior executives' strategic leadership skills; (3) institute a compensation plan for top executives that rewards them for actions and results that serve stakeholder interests – *especially those of shareholders*, and (4) ensure that the organization issues accurate financial reports and has adequate financial controls.

EMBEDDING A VISION: SCANDIC HOTELS

Scandic operates 160 hotels throughout Scandinavia and northern Europe, employing approximately 6600 people. Expansion plans are set for eastern Europe and Russia. Their slogan proclaims 'Easy and accessible travel for all'.

In 2011, Scandic formulated their goals, vision and mission as follows:

> Our aim is to help Scandic's guests to recharge their batteries and to reinvigorate them by having an uncomplicated approach and by offering simple and accessible accommodation. We achieve this by simplifying our procedures, offering hotels in locations where many people travel to and taking account of our guests' various needs.

> **'Creating value by being the place and inspiration for conscious people in a better world'.**

> We want to be more than just a hotel. We want to be a place where people can come together, meet others and be inspired, whether they are visiting Scandic on business or for pleasure. We want to be a source of inspiration for conscious people and we want to help make a better world. We believe that people are going to become increasingly conscious of the choices they make – and we want those conscious people to opt for Scandic because we are a good choice in every way – economically, socially and environmentally.

> As we proceed towards our vision, we measure Scandic's progress in three different dimensions – we call this our compass for sustainable development. The financial result shows how well we manage our stakeholders' money and create financial value. The environmental result shows to what degree we succeed in reducing Scandic's environmental impact. The ethical result shows how much we contribute as a committed member of society.

Founded in 1963 by Exxon as a motor hotel chain, Scandic went through various ownership changes and had little differentiation in the marketplace. Competitive advantage was sought through tangible amenities such as room decor, colour TVs and ironing boards, all of which were easily matched by competitors.

In the early 1990s, after a few years of consecutive losses, Scandic's market research showed that the basis for competition in the industry was increasingly shifting to intangible dimensions given this relative sameness of product offerings.

CEO Roland Nilsson and his senior management team became convinced that the leaders in the market of tomorrow would demonstrate business practices that were good for the organization and for society and would build consumer loyalty based on shared values. They saw an opportunity for Scandic to claim a leadership position in the hotel industry based on the concept of sustainability.

In consultation with a specialist partner 'The Natural Step', the executive committee set the company on a course of sustainability by issuing a clear policy in 1994 that stated:

> No company can avoid taking responsibility for the environment and focusing on environmental issues. Scandic shall, therefore, lead the way and work continuously to promote both a reduction in our environmental impact, and a better environment. Our goal is to be one of the most environmentally friendly companies in the hotel industry and to conduct our business on nature's terms.

Every Scandic hotel acts as a profit centre, with the manager evaluated by profit performance. The hotel industry is characterized by low margins and high competition therefore a programme for sustainability had to support managers in making good business decisions. It was important to Scandic's senior executives that the programme did not add an additional set of headquarter directives or create the perception of conflicting priorities. Sustainability had to be a strategic tool that served the business, or it would not work in the organization.

Scandic committed to building internal competence before rolling the programme out to line units. Training programmes started top-down. Internal trainers were developed from existing managers, and a programme developed with local adaptations in the content based on local regulatory conditions in the nine operating countries. The instigated pro-

▶

gramme, named 'The Environmental Dialogue', was a four-part programme that focused on an environmental guide, read by all current and new employees; environmental meetings, held once a week; an environmental programme of action plans for implementation of improvements, and an environmental barometer, a publication containing the status report of each hotel – later replaced by the Nordic Swan Criteria assessment. The word 'dialogue' was deliberately chosen to convey the message of two-way communication.

The programme was launched with a video featuring the CEO and the reasons behind it. The video was distributed organization-wide and also shared with suppliers.

Scandic's managers embarked on an integrated approach to implementation: initiating visible changes at the corporate level to demonstrate commitment and stimulating local ideas that were then collected, shared and quickly implemented.

At each hotel an employee was nominated as 'environmental' networker, to gather ideas from employees and suppliers. By 1995 this led to 64 per cent of all employees being involved in a local environmental activity.

At the corporate level, teams focused on identifying repetitive procedures carried out at all Scandic hotels, looking for changes that could produce a high impact throughout the system in terms of environmental quality and cost savings. The focus was on reducing and eliminating waste, as well as new product innovations.

Notable innovations included:

- **soap and shampoo dispenser system** – with natural products in recyclable dispenser bottles;
- **house-keeping chemicals** – using benign, multi-use chemicals;
- **dish washing** – highly concentrated detergents to reduce packaging and chemical discharge;
- **laundry** – supplier interaction to develop modified equipment to reduce wash cycles and water and oxygen bleach as a substitute for chlorine bleach;
- **waste management** – reducing solid waste and implementing guest room recycling containers;
- **energy efficiency** – central room temperature control to shut down heat in empty rooms as well as designing the 'recyclable' room for all new

renovations including natural materials of wood, wool, cotton and water-based paints.

Scandic gained significant press coverage and public awards for many of these innovations, gaining a 'first-mover' advantage over its competition.

In 1996 the group expanded by acquiring Reso Hotels, and became a publicly traded company on the Stockholm stock exchange. Further expansion followed into Finland via the Arctia Hotels group, and in 1999 the group expanded into Estonia. Scandia returned to profitability with healthy improvements in both sales and operating margin.

In 2001, Scandic was acquired by the London-based Hilton Group. The hotel chain changed ownership again in 2007, this time bought by EQT, a Swedish private equity firm.

In 2011 Scandic Hotels received the Nordic Council Environment Prize for the near 20-year commitment to sustainability. At the ceremony it was declared that since implementation over 11 000 employees had been trained in environmental issues, 19 000 rooms made of sustainable materials, water consumption reduced by 17 per cent, energy consumption by 22 per cent and CO_2 emissions by 38 per cent.

QUESTIONS

1. What elements contributed to the success of the sustainability concept at Scandic Hotels?

2. In your view, is the Scandic hotel Vision and Mission well grounded and worded to reflect the organizational intention?

3. By the late 1990s, Scandic hotels had created a competitive advantage through the sustainability concept. In your view, how well will this translate to a sustained source of future growth and profitability in this industry?

Sources: Lanahan Brian, 'Natural step case'. Available online at www.thenaturalstep.org (accessed 9 December 2011); Bohdanowicz, P., Simanic, B. and Martinac, I. (2004) 'Environmental training and measures at Scandic Hotel's, Sweden,' 'B.E.S.T. Sustainable Tourism Think Tank iv', Esbjerg, Denmark; Bohdanowicz, P., Simanic, B. and Martinac, I. (2004) 'Environmental education at Scandic Hotels – approach and results', *Regional Central and Eastern European Conference on Sustainable Building*, Warszawa, Poland; www.scandichotels.com (accessed 9 December 2011); 'Scandic hotels win the Nordic Council Environment Prize'. Available online at www.norden.org (accessed 9 December 2011).

ASSURANCE OF LEARNING EXERCISES

LO 2.1

1. Using the information in Table 2.1, critique the adequacy and merit of the following vision statements, listing effective elements and shortcomings. Rank the vision statements from best to worst once you complete your evaluation.

ASSURANCE OF LEARNING EXERCISE 1

Vision statement	Effective elements	Shortcomings
The Lego Group		
'Inventing the future of play': We want to pioneer new ways of playing, play materials and the business models of play – leveraging globalisation and digitalisation … it is not just about products, it is about realising the human possibility.		
Hilton Hotels Corporation		
Our vision is to be the first choice of the world's travellers. Hilton intends to build on the rich heritage and strength of our brands by: • Consistently delighting our customers • Investing in our team members • Delivering innovative products and services • Continuously improving performance • Increasing shareholder value • Creating a culture of pride • Strengthening the loyalty of our constituents		
The Dental Products Division of 3M Corporation		
Become THE supplier of choice to the global dental professional markets, providing world-class quality and innovative products.		
[Note: All employees of the division wear badges bearing these words, and whenever a new product or business procedure is being considered, management asks 'Is this representative of THE leading dental company?']		
H. J. Heinz Company		
Be the world's premier food company, offering nutritious, superior tasting foods to people everywhere. Being the premier food company does not mean being the biggest but it does mean being the best in terms of consumer value, customer service, employee talent, and consistent and predictable growth.		
Chevron		
To be *the* global energy company most admired for its people, partnership and performance. Our vision means we: • provide energy products vital to sustainable economic progress and human development throughout the world; • are people and an organization with superior capabilities and commitment; • are the partner of choice; • deliver world-class performance; • earn the admiration of all our stakeholders – investors, customers, host governments, local communities and our employees – not only for the goals we achieve but how we achieve them.		

Source: Company websites and annual reports.

▶

LO 2.2

2. Go to the websites for Tata Group (www.tata.com); Avon (www.avonorganization.com); and Inditex, one of the world's largest fashion retailers, brands including Zara, Pull & Bear, Massimo Dutti, Bershka, Stradivarius, Oysho, Zara Home and Uterqüe (www.inditex.com/en) to find some examples of strategic and financial objectives. Make a list of four objectives for each organization, and indicate which of these are strategic and which are financial.

LO 2.5

3. Go to www.dell.com/leadership, and read the sections dedicated to Dell's board of directors and corporate governance. Is there evidence of effective governance at Dell in regard to (1) accurate financial reports and controls, (2) a critical appraisal of strategic action plans, (3) evaluation of the strategic leadership skills of the CEO and (4) executive compensation?

EXERCISES FOR SIMULATION PARTICIPANTS

LO 2.1, LO 2.2, LO 2.3

1. Meet with your co-managers and prepare a strategic vision statement for your organization. It should be at least one sentence long and no longer than a brief paragraph. When you are finished, check to see if your vision statement is in compliance with the dos and don'ts set out in Table 2.1. If not, revise it accordingly. What would be a good slogan that captures the essence of your strategic vision and that could be used to help communicate the vision to organization employees, shareholders and other stakeholders?

2. What is your organization's strategic intent? Write a sentence that expresses your organization's strategic intent.

3. What are your organization's financial objectives?

4. What are your organization's strategic objectives?

5. What are the three or four key elements of your organization's strategy?

ENDNOTES

1. For a more in-depth discussion of the challenges of developing a well-conceived vision, as well as some good examples, see Davidson, Hugh (2002) *The Committed Enterprise: How to Make Vision and Values Work,* Oxford, Butterworth Heinemann, ch. 2; Chan Kim, W. and Mauborgne, Renée (2002) 'Charting Your Organization's Future', *Harvard Business Review,* 80(6): 77–83; Collins, James C. and Porras, Jerry I. (1996) 'Building your organization's vision', *Harvard Business Review,* 74(5): 65–77; Collins, Jim and Porras, Jerry (1994), *Built to Last: Successful Habits of Visionary Companies,* (New York, HarperCollins), ch. 11; Robert, Michel (1998), *Strategy Pure and Simple II: How Winning Companies Dominate Their Competitors*, New York, McGraw-Hill, chs. 2, 3 and 6.

2. Davidson, *The Committed Enterprise*, pp. 20 and 54.

3. Ibid., pp. 36 and 54.

4. Brabet, J. and Klemm, M. (1994) 'Sharing the vision: company mission statements in Britain and France', *Long Range Planning*, 27(1): 84–94.

5. Bart, C. and Baetz, M. (1998) 'The relationship between mission statements and firm performance: an exploratory study', *Journal of Management Studies*, 35(6): 823–53.

6. Sidhu, J. (2003) Mission statements: is it time to shelve them? *European Management Journal*, 21(4): 439–46.

7. Bartkus, B. and Glassman, M. (2008) 'Do firms practice what they preach? The relationship between mission statements and stakeholder management', *Journal of Business, Ethics*, 83(2): 207–16.

8. As quoted in House, Charles H. and Price, Raymond L. (1991) 'The return map: tracking product teams', *Harvard Business Review*, 60(1): 93.

9. Kaplan, Robert S. and Norton, David P. (2001) *The Strategy-Focused Organization*, Boston, Harvard Business School Press, p. 3. Also see Kaplan, Robert S. and Norton, David P. (1996) *The Balanced Scorecard: Translating Strategy into Action*, Boston, Harvard Business School Press, ch. 1.

10. Kaplan and Norton, p. 7. Also see Hendricks, Kevin B., Menor, Larry and Wiedman, Christine (2004) 'The balanced scorecard: to adopt or not to adopt', *Ivey Business Journal*, 69(2): 1–7; Richardson, Sandy (2004) 'The key elements of balanced scorecard success', *Ivey Business Journal*, 69(2): 7–9.

11. Kaplan and Norton, *The Balanced Scorecard*.

12. Information posted on the website of Bain and Organization, www.bain.com (accessed 27 May 2009).

13. Information posted on the website of Balanced Scorecard Institute, www.balancedscorecard.org/ (accessed 27 May 2009).

14. For a fuller discussion of strategy as an entrepreneurial process, see Mintzberg, Henry, Ahlstrand, Bruce and Lampel, Joseph (1998) *Strategy Safari: A Guided Tour through the Wilds of Strategic Management*, New York, Free Press, ch. 5. Also see Barringer, Bruce and Bluedorn, Allen C. (1999) 'The relationship between corporate entrepreneurship and strategic management', *Strategic Management Journal*, 20: 421–44; Covin, Jeffrey G. and Miles, Morgan P. (1999) 'Corporate entrepreneurship and the pursuit of competitive advantage', *Entrepreneurship: Theory and Practice*, 23(3): 47–63; Garvin, David A. and Levesque, Lynned C. (2006) 'Meeting the challenge of corporate entrepreneurship', *Harvard Business Review*, 84(10): 102–12.

15. For an excellent discussion of why a strategic plan needs to be more than a list of bullet points and should in fact tell an engaging, insightful, stage-setting story that lays out the industry and competitive situation as well as the vision, objectives and strategy, see Shaw, Gordon, Brown, Robert and Bromiley, Philip (1998) 'Strategic stories: how 3M Is rewriting business planning', *Harvard Business Review*, 76(3): 41–50.

16. In many companies, there is often confusion or ambiguity about exactly what an organization's strategy is; see Collis, David J. and Rukstad, Michael G. (2008) 'Can you say what your strategy is?' *Harvard Business Review*, 86(4): 82–90.

17. For an excellent discussion of why effective strategic leadership on the part of senior executives involves continuous recreation of an organization's strategy, see Montgomery, Cynthia A. (2008) 'Putting leadership back into strategy', *Harvard Business Review*, 86(1): 54–60.

18. For a timely and insightful discussion of the strategic and leadership functions of an organization's board of directors, see Lorsch, Jay W. and Clark, Robert C. (2008) 'Leading from the boardroom', *Harvard Business Review*, 86(4): 105–11.

19. For a deeper discussion of this function, see Kaufman, Stephen P. (2008) 'Evaluating the CEO', *Harvard Business Review*, 86(10): 53–57.

20. For a discussion of what it takes for the corporate governance system to function properly, see Nadler, David A. (2004) 'Building better boards', *Harvard Business Review*, 82(5): 102–5; Montgomery, Cynthia A. and Kaufman, Rhonda (2003) 'The board's missing link', *Harvard Business Review*, 8(3): 86–93; Carver, John (2003) 'What continues to be wrong with corporate governance and how to fix It', *Ivey Business Journal*, 68(1): 1–5. See also Donaldson, Gordon (1995) 'A new tool for boards: the strategic audit', *Harvard Business Review*, 73(4): 99–107.

21. Freeman, R.E. (1984) *Strategic Management: A Stakeholder Approach*, Boston, Pitman.

Chapter Three

Analysing an organization's external environment

Analysis is the critical starting point of strategic thinking.

Kenichi Ohmae
Consultant and Author

In essence, the job of a strategist is to understand and cope with competition.

Michael Porter
Harvard Business School professor and Co-founder of Monitor Consulting

The only way to beat the competition is to stop trying *to beat the competition.*

W. Chan Kim and Renée Mauborgne
Consultants and INSEAD Professors

Learning Objectives

When you have read this chapter you should be able to:

LO 3.1 Analyse an organization's external macro-environment using seven principal components and identify which of these are the most strategically relevant.

LO 3.2 Diagnose the factors that shape industry dynamics and forecast their effects on future industry attractiveness using both traditional approaches and alternatives such as scenario planning.

LO 3.3 Identify the competitive forces at work in an organization's industry or sector and assess their relative strength.

LO 3.4 Describe different industry structures, industry lifestyle stages and identify strategic groups within an industry or sector.

LO 3.5 Discuss the merits of other approaches to industry analysis that add to and challenge the five force's concept.

LO 3.6 Explain why in-depth evaluation of a business's strengths and weaknesses in relation to the specific industry conditions it confronts is an essential prerequisite to crafting a strategy that is well matched to its external situation.

WHO WILL PROFIT FROM 'TESCO LAW'?

In 2007 the UK government passed the Legal Services Act. Since then the legal profession has had just over four years to consider how the Act will affect their industry. This piece of legislation, which came into full force in October 2011, has been widely predicted to produce the biggest shake up in the sector for over a century. Even some of the top firms in the legal market, worth over £23 billon in 2011, have suggested it will present a risk to their profits in the future.

The Legal Services Act allows non-legal firms and individuals to own legal practices and offer a wider range of regulated legal services. It also allows lawyers to raise capital through shares and via the stock exchange. It is expected that the Act will encourage a wide range of new entrants to the market, from accountants to supermarkets – hence the term 'Tesco Law'. The legislation will make the UK one of the most deregulated markets in the world. This could also result in organizations from other countries setting up or acquiring firms capable of offering a range of legal services.

There has been oversupply in the UK legal profession for many years with over 10 500 firms of solicitors, of which 4500 are sole practitioners and 85 per cent would be described as small firms. At the other end of the scale are the so-called 'Magic Circle' law firms, the top five legal players headquartered in London, they include Linklaters and Clifford Chance. The top 10 firms account for almost 40 per cent of revenue in the UK market. The legal services sector saw annual growth of 3.8 per cent from 2005 to 2009 and this is predicted to increase further in the five years to 2014. Even without the impact of the Legal Services Act there is scope for significant consolidation in the industry.

The amount of work done by unregulated and unqualified individuals and organizations is a growing part of the UK legal market. Services such as will-writing, claims management for personal injuries and even divorce and employment-related work can all be carried out by non-lawyers. Some of the potential new entrants to the market, such as financial services organizations, have been providing Internet-based services, such as standard legal documents, for several years. A recent report by the UK's new Legal Ombudsman highlighted that customers of these unregulated firms had little redress under the current set-up. Once the Legal Services Act comes into force some of these organizations will have the option to become alternative business structures (ABSs) and join the regulated part of the sector. Even with this change it still does not cost much for customers to change their legal service provider.

In the past competition between legal firms, especially in more local markets, has been described as 'gentlemanly'. There is little evidence that solicitors compete on price but also in a recent survey conducted by YouGov, a market research firm, it was clear that few members of the public could name even the top firms of solicitors. The same survey found that 60 per cent of those questioned would consider buying legal services from retailers, such as the Co-operative and Tesco or from other organizations such as Barclays and the AA, a breakdown recovery service provider. Existing law firms have tended to compete on economies of scope rather than economies of scale and reputation has always been stressed as more important than brand. The low cost of changing service provider and the potential entry of powerful competitors is likely to make the legal sector in the UK a very challenging environment in the years to come.

Sources: Binham, C. (2011) 'Law firms fear "Tesco Law" will hit profits', *Financial Times*, 3 July. Available online at www.ft.com/cms/s/0/9e2bd112-a5c0-11e0-83b2-00144feabdc0.html#ixzz1TCVVyWCX (accessed 25 July 2011); Croft, J. (2011) 'Law firms expect lost work under "Tesco Law", *Financial Times*, 13 April. Available online at www.ft.com/cms/s/0/85babbdc-65e9-11e0-9d40-00144feab49a.html#ixzz1TCVmXzhd (accessed 25 July 2011); IRN Research (2010) *The UK Legal Services Market 2010*, IRN Research, Birmingham; Datamonitor (2010) *Industry Profile: Legal Services in the United Kingdom*, Datamonitor, London; BBC News (2010) 'New Legal Ombudsman warns rip-off lawyers', *BBC News*, 5 October. Available online at www.bbc.co.uk/news/uk-11473197 (accessed 25 July 2011); Rose, N. (2011) "Tesco law" – not the big bang, but it will change the face of legal services', *Guardian.co.uk*, 25 March, available online at http://www.guardian.co.uk/law/2011/mar/25/tesco-law-alternative-business-structures (accessed 25 July 2011).

QUESTIONS

1. What are the most important threats to the legal profession from the changes in regulation?
2. Which of these threats could an incumbent in the industry have predicted in 2007?

In Chapter 1, we learned that one of the three central questions managers must address in evaluating their business prospects is 'What's the organization's present situation?' Two facets of an organization's situation are especially pertinent: (1) general and competitive conditions for the industry in which the organization operates – its external environment; and (2) the organization's resources and organizational capabilities – its internal environment.

Insightful diagnosis of an organization's external and internal environments is often seen as the first step managers should take in crafting a strategy that is a good *fit* with the organization's situation. This is one of the key criteria for assessing a strategy. An appraisal of the organization's external environment and internal environment (as a basis for deciding on a long-term direction and developing a strategic vision) is often a vital part of the process of developing strategy, since it can underpin an evaluation of the most promising alternative strategies and business models, and inform managers in choosing a specific strategy. In organizations where strategy development processes are more emergent, a good *fit* with the firm's situation can also be an important consideration when assessing bottom-up strategies for consistency with the existing long-term direction of the organization.

This chapter presents the concepts and analytical tools for assessing those aspects of an organization's external environment that should be considered in making strategic choices about where and how to compete. Content includes the competitive arena in which an organization operates, the drivers of market change, the market positions of rival organizations and the factors that determine competitive success. The opening case is used to illustrate some of the key concepts and a final longer case can be used to practise applying some of the analytical tools. In Chapter 4 we explore the methods of evaluating an organization's internal circumstances and competitive capabilities.

The Strategically Relevant Components of an Organization's Macro-environment

Core Concept

The **macro-environment** encompasses the broad environmental context in which an organization's industry is situated.

Every organization operates in a larger environment that goes well beyond just the industry in which it operates. This 'macro-environment' includes seven principal components: population demographics; socio-cultural forces; political, legal and regulatory factors; the natural environment and ecological factors; technological factors; general economic conditions; and global forces. Each of these components has the potential to affect the firm's more immediate industry and competitive environment, although some are likely to have a more important effect than others (see Figure 3.1).

Since macro-economic factors affect different industries in different ways and to different degrees, it is important for managers to determine which of these represent the most *strategically relevant factors* outside the firm's industry boundaries. By *strategically relevant*, we mean important enough to have a bearing on the decisions the organization ultimately makes about its direction, objectives, strategy and business model. Strategically relevant influences coming from the outer ring of the external environment can sometimes have a high impact on an organization's business situation and have a very significant impact on the organization's direction and strategy. For example, in the opening case the changes in regulation of the legal profession are likely to have a profound effect on the incumbent firms in the sector. There are opportunities presented by the new access to capital they will enjoy but also threats in the form of potential new entrants to their industry. Motor vehicle companies must adapt their strategies to customer concerns about high petrol prices and to environmental concerns about carbon emissions. Organizations in the food processing, restaurant, sports and fitness industries have to pay special attention to changes in lifestyles, eating habits, leisure-time preferences and attitudes toward nutrition and fitness in fashioning their strategies. Table 3.1 provides a brief description of the components of the

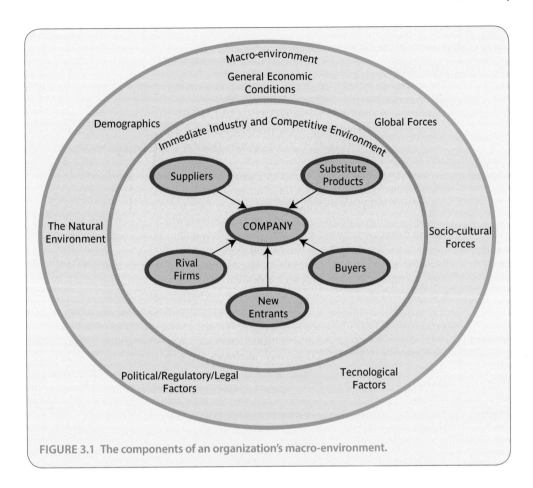

FIGURE 3.1 **The components of an organization's macro-environment.**

macro-environment and some examples of the industries or business situations that they might affect.

Happenings in the outer ring of the environment may occur rapidly or slowly, with or without advance warning. As managers scan the external environment, they must be alert for potentially important outer-ring developments, assess their impact and influence, and adapt the organization's direction and strategy as needed.

Scenario Planning

A traditional approach might be sufficient for industries or organizations with a relatively low level of uncertainty in their macro-environment. However, as events such as the banking crisis in 2008 and, more recently, the tsunami in Japan have shown there can be a high level of dynamism, complexity and unpredictability in the environment.[1] Both these events showed how complex systems have become in the global economy. For example, the tsunami disrupted many complex global supply chains and led to factories stopping production on other continents. In such circumstances managers have found scenario planning a useful enhancement to identifying strategically relevant factors. Scenario planning allows the organization to move beyond a single forecast and to create a series of coherent stories about the future. Royal Dutch Shell pioneered this approach to strategic analysis in the 1970s and was able to successfully predict the oil crisis in that decade and adapted its strategy accordingly.

Scenarios can help to make sense of the interaction between different factors in the macro-environment; for example, how technology trends may affect socio-cultural factors. The development of smartphones and the rise in people's use of social media

LO 3.1
Analyse an organization's external macro-environment using seven principal components and identify which of these are the most strategically relevant.

TABLE 3.1 The Seven Components of the Macro-environment

Component	Description
Demographics	Demographics includes the size, growth rate, and age distribution of different sectors of the population. It includes the geographic distribution of the population, the distribution of income across the population, and trends in these factors. Population demographics can have large implications for industries such as healthcare, where costs and service needs vary with demographic factors such as age and income distribution.
Socio-cultural forces	Socio-cultural forces include the societal values, attitudes, cultural factors and lifestyles that impact businesses. These forces vary by locale and change over time. An example includes the attitudes toward gender roles and diversity in the workforce. Another example is the trend toward healthier lifestyles, which can shift spending toward exercise equipment and health clubs and away from alcohol and snack foods.
Political, legal and regulatory factors	These factors include political policies and processes, as well as the regulations and laws with which organizations must comply. Examples include labour laws, antitrust laws, tax policy, regulatory policies, the political climate and the strength of institutions such as the court system. Some political factors, such as banking deregulation, are industry-specific. Others, such as minimum wage legislation, affect certain types of industries (low-wage, labour-intensive industries) more than others.
Natural environment	This includes ecological and environmental forces such as weather, climate, climate change and associated factors like water shortages. These factors can directly impact industries such as insurance, farming, energy production and tourism. They may have an indirect but substantial effect on other industries such as transportation and utilities.
Technological factors	Technological factors include the pace of technological change and technical developments that have the potential for wide-ranging effects on society, such as genetic engineering, the rise of the Internet, and changes in communication technologies. They include activities and institutions involved in creating new knowledge and controlling the use of technology, such as research and development (R&D) consortia, university-sponsored technology incubators, patent and copyright laws, and government control over the Internet. Technological change can encourage the birth of new industries, such as those based on nanotechnology, and disrupt others, such as the recording industry.
Global forces	Global forces include conditions and changes in global markets, including political events and policies toward international trade. They also include socio-cultural practices and the institutional environment in which global markets operate. Global forces influence the degree of international trade and investment through such mechanisms as trade barriers, tariffs, import restrictions and trade sanctions. Their effects are often industry-specific, such as import restrictions on steel.
General economic conditions	General economic conditions include economic factors at the local, state, national or international level that affect firms and industries. These include the rate of economic growth, unemployment rates, inflation rates, interest rates, trade deficits or surpluses, savings rates and per capita domestic product. Economic factors also include conditions in the markets for stocks and bonds, which can affect consumer confidence and discretionary income. Some industries, such as construction, are particularly vulnerable to economic downturns but are positively affected by factors such as low interest rates. Others, such as discount retailing, may benefit when general economic conditions weaken, as consumers become more price-conscious.

appear to be closely linked. Scenario planning allows organizations to explore a range of plausible future environments. This can then improve strategic decision-making and a firm's competitive advantage because it alerts managers to potential threats and opportunities that other firms may not have prepared for. For example, IBM came close to collapse because it failed to anticipate the rise of the desktop PC and remained in the mainframe business for too long. By considering a range of alternatives managers become more tuned to what Paul Schoemaker refers to as 'weak signals' in the environment.[2] For example, some players in the financial markets, such as Warren Buffet, were warning of the dangers of the housing bubble and the use of derivatives as early as 2003, yet the likes of Northern Rock, Bear Sterns and Lehman Brothers seemed oblivious to the risks they were taking until the crisis actually broke. The outcome of the crisis now look obvious and predictable, but back in 2003 these signs were peripheral and imprecise, not clear to most managers in the industry among the avalanche of other information crossing their desks and screens. Organizations' own systems and structures can also play a part in obscuring these signals. Scenarios allow organizations to get past some of these blocks in exploring possible futures, including those that may be at the extremes of the continuum (see Figure 3.2).

Building Scenarios

To ensure that the planning process is sufficiently focused, managers need to start by defining the scope of the scenarios. This usually involves setting a time frame and geographic or market/product boundaries. Shell build scenarios at three levels: global, country or business and individual project level.[3] The next step is to make use of the basic trends arising from analysis of the macro-environment such as the examples in Table 3.1. At the same time managers should be thinking about the key uncertainties in their environment. This is much harder than analysing the basic trends and can often involve consulting a range of experts who are external to the industry for opinions on possible future events and outcomes. Using the Delphi technique, which involves asking a panel of experts the same set of questions and then asking them to revise their answers in a second round, having seen an aggregate of the rest of the panels responses, can overcome organizational biases and improves the chances of predicting low probability events.

At this stage strategic planners need to make judgements about how the various trends and uncertainties interact with each other and build some initial scenarios. This will often involve setting the two extremes by looking at scenarios that would result from all negative or all positive outcomes for key uncertainties. From this a set of scenarios stories are developed and used not only to help the organization understand the potential futures but also as a tool to test different strategies/strategic options against. Current practice, below, shows how VisitScotland adapted this process to help the Scottish Government and tourism organizations become more forward-thinking about the industry.

LO 3.2
Diagnose the factors that shape industry dynamics and forecast their effects on future industry attractiveness using both traditional approaches and alternatives such as scenario planning.

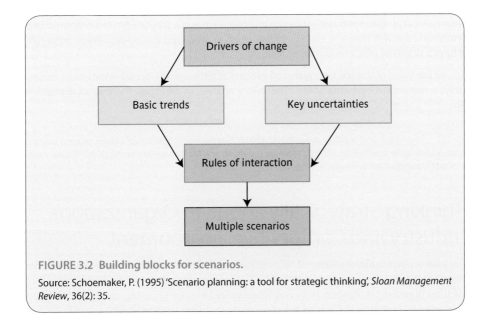

FIGURE 3.2 Building blocks for scenarios.

Source: Schoemaker, P. (1995) 'Scenario planning: a tool for strategic thinking', *Sloan Management Review*, 36(2): 35.

CURRENT PRACTICE 3.1

SCENARIO PLANNING AT VISITSCOTLAND

VisitScotland, the national tourism organization for Scotland, started developing scenarios in a systematic fashion in 2003. The organization was the key adviser to the Scottish Government for destination marketing and related policy and economic issues. It also supported organizations in the Scottish tourism industry by providing reports, advice and statistics and encouraging the provision and improvement of tourist facilities in Scotland. In the aftermath of the 9/11 and 7/7 terrorist bombs and the severe acute respiratory syndrome (SARS) outbreak, which had caught out many tourism organizations, scenario planning was seen as one way to improve strategic management in the organization and also the industry.

DEFINING THE SCOPE AND IDENTIFYING STAKEHOLDERS

The original scope of the scenarios was a time frame to 2025 and coverage of product offers and markets with the Scottish industry as well as broader consumer needs and wants, plus supply-side and structural issues. The organization's stakeholders were well known and connected through its board.

ENVIRONMENTAL SCANNING

VisitScotland worked closely with the Moffat Centre at Glasgow Caledonian University to identify key drivers for the Scottish tourism industry. These were used to make forecasts and quantify demographic, economic and technological trends that might impact on the tourism industry. For the key uncertainties, VisitScotland used a systems-based approach through a tool known as McTAFE developed by Strathclyde University and a loose group referred to as the Remarkable People network. This provided external experts to add rigour to the process and provide ideas from outside the industry and organization.

CONSTRUCTING SCENARIOS

Early on in the process it became clear to the scenario planning group that there was a high likelihood of a war in Iraq. This gave VisitScotland an opportunity to put their process into action. Having identified a range of key driving forces for Scottish tourism, including consumer confidence, GDP, oil prices, media stories and levels of disruption, these were combined to produce two underlying themes (see Figure 3.3 for details) – the nature of disruption and economic behaviour. The best and worst outcomes for each theme then formed the basis for developing scenarios. For example, economic behaviour ranged from a 'hiccup' in the world economy to 'merchants of doom', a full-blown global recession. The four scenarios developed were reduced to three as the *Into the valley of death* scenario was deemed too extreme. *New dawn* predicted a new world order following a major war in Iraq with tourism impacted by travel disruption and a brief economic downturn followed by recovery. *How the west was won* was seen as the most positive outcome for the industry with a limited and short period of disruption caused by war and terrorism and a similarly limited economic blip but consumer confidence remained relatively buoyant. *Global Northern Ireland* predicted limited disruption but a full-blown recession that would have a dramatic effect on domestic tourism.

The events of 2003/4 showed the value of the scenario planning process as although the actual events most closely resembled *How the west was won*, there were elements of the other two scenarios, in particular the level of disruption caused by ongoing terrorism.

Sources: Visit Scotland (2011) 'Management statement', available online at www.visitscotland.org/pdf/visitscotland_management_statement.pdf (accessed 31 July 2011); Yeoman, I. and McMahon-Beattie, U. (2005) 'Developing a scenario planning process using a blank piece of paper', *Tourism and Hospitality Research*, 5(3): 273–85; Yeoman, I., Galt, M. and McMahon-Beattie, U. (2005) 'A case study of how VisitScotland prepared for war', *Journal of Travel Research*, 44: 6–20.

Thinking Strategically about an Organization's Industry and Competitive Environment

To gain a deep understanding of an organization's industry and competitive environment, managers do not need to gather all the information they can find and spend lots of time digesting it. Rather, they can focus more directly on using some well-defined concepts and analytical tools to get clear answers to seven questions:

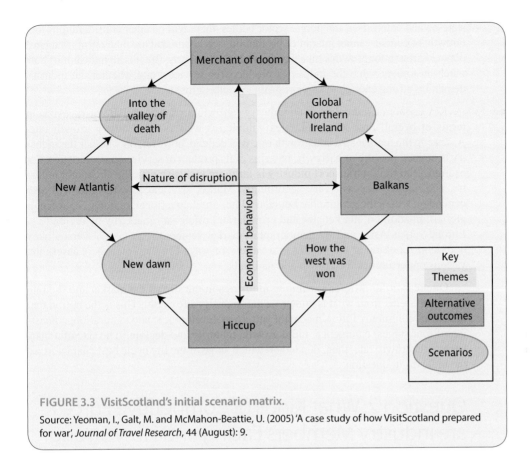

FIGURE 3.3 VisitScotland's initial scenario matrix.

Source: Yeoman, I., Galt, M. and McMahon-Beattie, U. (2005) 'A case study of how VisitScotland prepared for war', *Journal of Travel Research*, 44 (August): 9.

1. Does the industry offer attractive opportunities?
2. What kinds of competitive forces are industry members facing, and how strong is each force?
3. What factors are driving changes in the industry, and what impact will these changes have on competitive intensity and industry profitability?
4. What market positions do industry rivals occupy – who is strongly positioned and who is not?
5. What strategic moves are rivals likely to make next?
6. What are the key factors for competitive success in the industry?
7. Does the industry offer good prospects for attractive profits?

Analysis-based answers to these seven questions can, in many instances, provide managers with the understanding needed to craft a strategy that fits the organization's external situation and positions the organization to best meet its competitive challenges. The remainder of this chapter is devoted to describing the methods of obtaining solid answers to the seven questions and explaining how the nature of an organization's industry and competitive environment weighs upon the strategic choices of managers.

Question 1: Does the Industry Offer Attractive Opportunities?

Answering the question of whether or not an industry will offer the prospect of attractive opportunities begins with a consideration of what opportunities the organization is seeking. For most firms this will be growth and ultimately profit, but for a range of organizations such as social enterprises, B-corporations, co-operatives, mutuals, charities, state-owned enterprises and public sector bodies, there will be other considerations too. Growth, of course, cannot guarantee profitability – a lesson that too many firms that have pursued growth for growth's sake have learned the hard way. But it is an indicator of how much customers value the industry's products (or services) and whether the industry demand is strong enough to support profitable sales growth.

Key economic indicators of an industry's growth prospects include market size, in terms of overall unit sales and sales volume, as well as the industry growth rate. Assessing the market size and growth rate will depend, however, on whether the industry is defined broadly or narrowly, in terms of its product or service characteristics. For example, the freight transport industry is far more inclusive than the air freight industry, and market size will vary accordingly. Market size and growth rates will also depend on where the geographic boundary lines are drawn (local, regional, national or global). In addition, market size and growth rates often vary markedly by region (e.g. Europe versus Asia) and by demographic market segment (e.g. Gen Y versus baby boomers). Looking at the market in a variety of ways can help managers assess the various opportunities for growth and its limits.

One reason for differences among industries in the size of the market and the rate of growth stems from what is known as the 'industry life cycle'. This is the notion that industries commonly follow a general pattern of development and maturation, consisting of four stages: emergence, rapid growth, maturity and decline.[4] The size of a market and its growth rate, then, depend on which stage of the life cycle best characterizes the industry in question.

Question 2: What Kinds of Competitive Forces are Industry Members Facing and How Strong are They?

LO 3.3
Identify the competitive forces at work in an organization's industry or sector and assess their relative strength.

The character and strength of the competitive forces operating in an industry are never the same from one industry to another. Far and away the most powerful and widely used tool for systematically diagnosing the principal competitive pressures in a market is *Porter's five-forces model of competition*.[5] This model holds that the competitive forces affecting industry profitability go beyond rivalry among competing sellers and include pressures stemming from four coexisting sources. As depicted in Figure 3.4, the five competitive forces include: (1) competition from *rival sellers*; (2) competition from *potential new entrants* to the industry; (3) competition from producers of *substitute products*; (4) *supplier* bargaining power, and (5) *customer* bargaining power.

Using the five-forces model to determine the nature and strength of competitive pressures in a given industry involves building the picture of competition in three steps:

- *Step 1:* For each of the five forces, identify the different parties involved, along with the specific factors that bring about competitive pressures.
- *Step 2:* Evaluate how strong the pressures stemming from each of the five forces are (strong, moderate to normal or weak).
- *Step 3:* Determine whether the strength of the five competitive forces, overall, is conducive to earning attractive profits in the industry.

Competitive Pressures Created by the Rivalry among Competing Sellers

The strongest of the five competitive forces is often the market manoeuvring for buyer patronage that goes on among rival sellers of a product or service. In effect, *a market is a competitive battlefield* where the contest among competitors is ongoing and

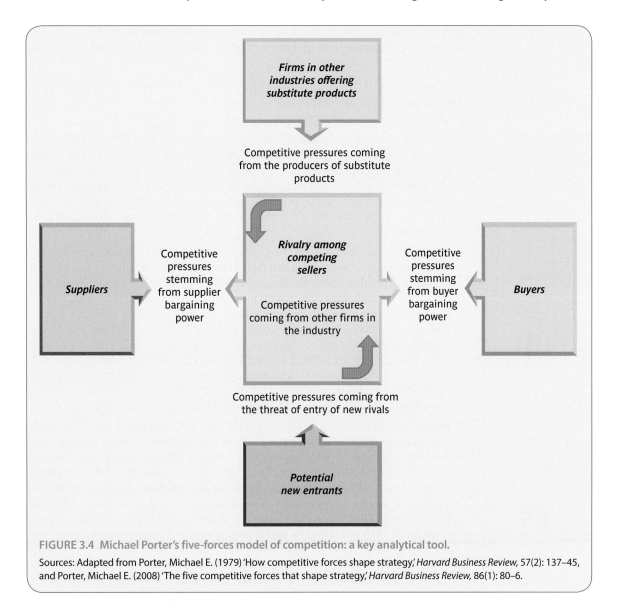

FIGURE 3.4 Michael Porter's five-forces model of competition: a key analytical tool.

Sources: Adapted from Porter, Michael E. (1979) 'How competitive forces shape strategy,' *Harvard Business Review,* 57(2): 137–45, and Porter, Michael E. (2008) 'The five competitive forces that shape strategy,' *Harvard Business Review,* 86(1): 80–6.

dynamic. Each competing organization endeavours to deploy whatever means in its business arsenal it believes will attract and retain buyers, strengthen its market position and yield good profits. The challenge is to craft a competitive strategy that, at the very least, allows an organization to hold its own against rivals and that, ideally, *produces a competitive edge over rivals.* But when one firm deploys a strategy or makes a new strategic move that produces good results, its rivals typically respond with offensive or defensive countermoves of their own. This pattern of action and reaction, move and countermove, produces a continually evolving competitive landscape where the market battle ebbs and flows, sometimes takes unpredictable twists and turns, and produces winners and losers.[6]

Competitive battles among rival sellers can assume many forms that extend well beyond lively price competition. For example, rival firms may resort to such marketing tactics as special sales promotions, heavy advertising, rebates or low-interest-rate financing to drum up additional sales. Active rivals may race one another to differentiate their products by offering better performance features or higher quality or improved customer service or a wider product selection. Rivals may also compete through the rapid introduction of next-generation products, frequent introduction of new or improved products, and efforts to build stronger dealer networks, establish positions in international markets, or otherwise expand distribution capabilities and market presence.

The intensity of rivalry varies from industry to industry and is often dependent on a number of identifiable factors.[7]

- *Rivalry is usually stronger in markets where buyer demand is growing slowly or declining, and it is often weaker in fast-growing markets.* Rapidly expanding buyer demand produces enough new business for all industry members to grow without using volume-boosting sales tactics to draw customers away from rival enterprises. But in markets where buyer demand is only growing slowly or is shrinking, organizations will typically employ price discounts, sales promotions and other tactics to boost their sales volumes, sometimes to the point of igniting a fierce battle for market share.

- *Rivalry increases as it becomes less costly for buyers to switch brands.* The less expensive it is for buyers to switch their purchases from the seller of one brand to the seller of another brand, the easier it is for sellers to steal customers away from rivals. But the higher the costs buyers incur to switch brands, the less prone they are to brand switching. Switching costs include not only monetary costs but also the time, inconvenience and psychological costs involved in switching brands. For example, distributors and retailers may not switch to the brands of rival manufacturers because they are hesitant to sever long-standing supplier relationships, incur any technical support costs or retraining expenses in making the switch-over, go to the trouble of testing the quality and reliability of the rival brand, or devote resources to marketing the new brand (especially if the brand is not well known).

- *Rivalry usually increases as the products of rival sellers become more alike, and it diminishes as the products of industry rivals become more strongly differentiated.* When the offerings of rivals are identical or weakly differentiated, buyers have less reason to be brand-loyal – a condition that makes it easier for rivals to convince buyers to switch to their offerings. And since the brands of different sellers have comparable attributes, buyers can shop the market for the best deal and switch brands at will. On the other hand, strongly differentiated product offerings among rivals breed high brand loyalty on the part of buyers – because many buyers view the attributes of certain brands as more appealing or better suited to their needs. Strong brand attachments make it tougher for sellers to draw customers away from rivals. Unless meaningful numbers of buyers are open to considering new or different product attributes being offered by rivals, the high degree of brand loyalty that accompanies strong product differentiation works against fierce rivalry among competing sellers. *The degree of product differentiation also affects switching costs.* When the offerings of rivals are identical or weakly differentiated, it is usually easy and inexpensive for buyers to switch their purchases from one seller to another. But in the case of strongly differentiated brands with quite different features and functionality (like rival brands of cell phones), buyers may be reluctant to go through the brand-switching hassle.

- *Rivalry is more intense when there is unused production capacity, especially if the industry's product has high fixed costs or high storage costs.* Where a market is oversupplied (such that sellers have unutilized production capacity and/or too much inventory), the result is a 'buyer's market' that intensifies rivalry perhaps even to the point of threatening the survival of competitively weak firms. A similar effect occurs when a product is perishable, seasonal or costly to hold in stock, since firms often engage in aggressive price cutting to ensure that they are not left with unwanted or costly inventories. Likewise, whenever fixed costs account for a large fraction of total cost so that unit costs are significantly lower at full capacity, firms come under significant pressure to cut prices to boost sales whenever they are operating below full capacity. Unused capacity imposes a significant cost-increasing penalty because there are fewer units over which to spread fixed costs. The pressure of high fixed or high storage costs can push rival firms into price concessions, special discounts, rebates and other volume-boosting competitive tactics.

- *Rivalry intensifies as the number of competitors increases and as competitors become more equal in size and competitive strength.* The greater the number of competitors, the higher the probability that one or more organizations will be engaged in a strategic offensive intended to enhance their market standing, thereby heating up competition and putting new pressures on rivals to respond with offensive or defensive moves of their own. In addition, when rivals are of comparable size and competitive strength, they can usually compete on a fairly equal footing – an evenly matched contest tends to be fiercer than a contest in which one or more industry members have commanding market shares and substantially greater resources and capabilities than their much smaller rivals.

- *Rivalry often becomes more intense – as well as more volatile and unpredictable – as the diversity of competitors increases in terms of long-term directions, objectives, strategies and countries of origin.* A diverse group of sellers often contains one or more mavericks willing to try novel or rule-breaking market approaches, thus generating a livelier and less predictable competitive environment. Globally competitive markets usually boost the intensity of rivalry, especially when aggressors having lower costs or products with more attractive features are intent on gaining a strong foothold in new country markets.

- *Rivalry is stronger when high exit barriers keep unprofitable firms from leaving the industry.* In industries where the assets cannot easily be sold or transferred to other uses, where workers are entitled to job protection, or where owners are committed to remaining in business for personal reasons, failing firms tend to hold on longer than they might otherwise. This increases rivalry in two ways. Firms that are losing ground or in financial trouble often resort to deep price discounting that can trigger a price war and destabilize an otherwise attractive industry. In addition, high exit barriers result in an industry being more overcrowded than it would otherwise be, and this boosts rivalry and forces the weakest organizations to scramble to win sufficient sales and revenues to stay in business.

Rivalry can be characterized as *cut-throat* or *brutal* when competitors engage in protracted price wars or habitually undertake other aggressive strategic moves that prove mutually destructive to profitability. Rivalry can be considered *fierce* to *strong* when the battle for market share is so vigorous that the profit margins of most industry members are squeezed to bare-bones levels. Rivalry can be characterized as *moderate* or *normal* when the manoeuvring among industry members, while lively and healthy,

TABLE 3.2 Types of industry structure

Industry type/features	Monopoly	Oligopoly	Monopolistic competition	Perfect competition
No. of firms				
Sustainability of competitive advantage	Total			None
Degree of competition	Low			High
Marketplace stability	High			Low
Typical strategic stance		Defensive		Aggressive

LO 3.4
Describe different industry structures, industry lifestyle stages and identify strategic groups within an industry or sector.

still allows most industry members to earn acceptable profits. Rivalry is *weak* when most organizations in the industry are relatively well satisfied with their sales growth and market shares, rarely undertake offensives to steal customers away from one another, and, because of weak competitive forces, earn consistently good profits and returns on investment.

Undertaking a five-forces analysis can help to categorize an industry into one of four distinct types. The general features of these types are covered in Table 3.2. These represent generic structures, so real industries may not conform to the descriptions exactly. However, they do offer managers a good insight of the likely features of each type of industry. For example, to enter the Chinese coupon website market, where there are over 2000 competing members, but significant growth potential,[8] a manager would have to accept that there would be little likelihood of gaining anything better than a temporary competitive advantage. As the industry appears to be close to a perfect competition type, it is likely an aggressive strategic approach would be required and that the market would be highly volatile with frequent entry and exit of players common. Unless the growth rate was very attractive this might be a market to avoid.

At the other end of the continuum, a monopoly player, such as a state-owned enterprise, serving a closed domestic market, will have a total advantage while it retains government support; there will be virtually no legitimate competition (although there may be in the informal economy of the country). The organization's market will be stable and predictable and the managers of the organization will typically adopt a defensive approach to strategy to maintain barriers to prevent entrants to the market. Oligopolistic structures are characterized by a few large organizations with substantial shares of the market, which try to maintain stability and their own long-term competitive advantage through crafting largely defensive strategies. Monopolistic competition has more rivals of a similar size that can result in less stability and shorter-term competitive advantage. This leads to aggressive strategic approaches and more intense competition.

Competitive Pressures Associated with the Threat of New Entrants

New entrants to a market often bring new production capacity, the desire to establish a secure place in the market and sometimes substantial resources. Just how serious the competitive threat of entry is in a particular market depends on two classes of factors: *barriers to entry* and the *expected reaction of incumbent firms to new entry*.[9]

Industry incumbents that are willing and able to launch strong defensive manoeuvres to maintain their positions can make it hard for a new entrant to gain a sufficient market foothold to survive and eventually become profitable. Entry candidates may have second thoughts if they conclude that existing firms are likely to give newcomers a hard time by offering price discounts (especially to the very customer groups a newcomer is seeking to attract), spending more on advertising, running frequent sales promotions, adding attractive new product features (to match or beat the newcomer's product offering) or providing additional services to customers. Such defensive manoeuvres on the part of incumbents raise an entrant's costs and risks and have to be considered likely if one or more incumbents have previously tried to strongly contest the entry of new firms into the marketplace.

A barrier to entry exists whenever it is hard for a newcomer to break into the market and/or the economics of the business put a potential entrant at a disadvantage. The most widely encountered such barriers that entry candidates must hurdle include the following:[10]

- *Significant economies of scale and/or learning curve effects in production, distribution, advertising or other areas of operation.* When incumbent organizations enjoy cost advantages associated with large-scale operations, outsiders must either enter on a large scale or accept a cost disadvantage and consequently lower profitability. Entering on a large scale in many industries also requires *high capital* outlay that will reduce the pool of potential entrants. Incumbent firms will often also have cost advantages that accrue from experience in performing certain activities (learning curve effects) such as manufacturing or new product development or inventory management. This gives incumbent firms a first-mover advantage over new entrants that may be difficult to overcome (we cover first-mover advantage in more depth in Chapter 6).

- *Other cost advantages enjoyed by industry incumbents.* Existing industry members may also have other types of cost advantages that are hard for a newcomer to replicate. These can stem from (1) preferential access to raw materials, components or other inputs, (2) cost savings accruing from patents or proprietary technology, (3) favourable locations and (4) low fixed costs (because they have older facilities that have been mostly depreciated). The bigger the cost advantages of industry incumbents, the more risky it becomes for outsiders to attempt entry (since they will have to accept thinner profit margins or even losses until the cost disadvantages can be overcome).

- *Strong brand preferences and high degrees of customer loyalty.* The stronger the attachment of buyers to established brands, the harder it is for a newcomer to break into the marketplace. Establishing brand recognition and building customer loyalty can be a slow and costly process. In addition, if it is difficult or costly for a customer to switch to a new brand, a new entrant may have to offer buyers a discounted price or an extra margin of quality or service. As we saw in the opening case this was not a significant barrier in the UK legal profession as incumbents had not invested in brand-building.

- *Strong 'network effects' in customer demand.* In industries where buyers are more attracted to a product when there are many other users of the product, there are said to be 'network effects', since demand is higher the larger the network of users. Video game systems are an example, since users prefer to have the same systems as their friends so that they can play together on systems they all know and share games. When incumbents have a larger base of users, new entrants with comparable products face a serious disadvantage in attracting buyers.

- *The difficulties of building a network of distributors or dealers and securing adequate space on retailers' shelves.* A potential entrant can face numerous distribution channel challenges. Wholesale distributors may be reluctant to take on a product that lacks buyer recognition. Retailers must be recruited and convinced to give a new brand ample display space and an adequate trial period. When existing sellers have strong, well-functioning distributor-dealer networks, a newcomer has an uphill struggle in squeezing its way into existing distribution channels.

- *Restrictive government policies.* Regulated industries like telecommunications, electric and gas utilities, radio and television broadcasting, alcohol retailing and railways entail government-controlled entry. Government agencies can also limit or even bar entry by requiring licences and permits, such as the plates and special driver's licence required for driving a taxi in London. Government-mandated safety regulations and environmental pollution standards also create entry barriers because they raise entry costs. In international markets, host governments commonly limit foreign entry and must approve all foreign investment applications. National governments commonly use tariffs and trade restrictions (anti-dumping rules, local content requirements, quotas etc.) to raise entry barriers for foreign firms and protect domestic producers from outside competition.

The threat of entry changes as the industry's prospects grow brighter or dimmer and as entry barriers rise or fall. For example, in the pharmaceutical industry the expiration of a key patent on a widely prescribed drug virtually guarantees that one or more drug-makers will enter with generic offerings of their own. Use of the Internet

High entry barriers and weak entry threats today do not always translate into high entry barriers and weak entry threats tomorrow.

for shopping is making it much easier for e-tailers to enter into competition against some of the best-known retail chains. Moreover, new strategic actions by incumbent firms to increase advertising, strengthen distributor-dealer relations, step up R&D or improve product quality can erect higher roadblocks to entry.

Additional Entry Threat Considerations

There are two additional factors that need to be considered in evaluating whether the threat of entry is strong or weak. The first concerns how attractive the growth and profit prospects are for new entrants. *Rapidly growing market demand and high potential profits frequently act as magnets, motivating potential entrants to commit the resources needed to hurdle entry barriers.*[11] When growth and profit opportunities are sufficiently attractive, certain types of entry barriers are unlikely to provide an effective entry deterrent. At most, they limit the pool of candidate entrants to enterprises with the requisite competences and resources and with the creativity to fashion a strategy for competing with incumbent firms. Hence, *one of the best tests of whether potential entry is a strong or weak competitive force in the marketplace is to ask if the industry's growth and profit prospects are strongly attractive to potential entry candidates with sufficient expertise and resources to hurdle prevailing entry barriers.*

The threat of entry is stronger when entry barriers are low, when incumbent firms are unable or unwilling to vigorously contest a newcomer's entry and when there is a sizeable pool of entry candidates with resources and capabilities well suited for competing in the industry.

A second factor concerns the pool of potential entrants and their capabilities in relation to the particular entry barriers in place. Organizations with sizeable financial resources, proven competitive capabilities and a respected brand name may be able to overcome certain types of entry barriers easily, while small start-up enterprises may find the same entry barriers insurmountable. Thus, how hard it will be for potential entrants to compete on a level playing field is relative to the financial resources and competitive capabilities of likely entrants. So, managers often find that when they question *whether an industry's entry barriers are high or low, the answer often depends on the resources and capabilities possessed by the pool of potential entrants.*[12] As a rule, the bigger the pool of entry candidates that have what it takes, the stronger is the threat of entry.

For example, as we saw in the opening case study, there was a large pool of potential entrants to the legal industry in the UK from a range of organizations with the brand reputation and financial resources to enter the market as the regulatory barriers changed. However, often competitive pressures associated with potential entry frequently come, not from outsiders, but from current industry participants with strong capabilities looking for growth opportunities. *Existing industry members are often strong candidates to enter market segments or geographic areas where they currently do not have a market presence.* Organizations already well established in certain product categories or geographic areas often possess the resources, competences and competitive capabilities to hurdle the barriers of entering a different market segment or new geographic area.

Competitive Pressures from the Sellers of Substitute Products

Organizations in one industry come under competitive pressure from the actions of organizations in a closely adjoining industry whenever buyers view the products of the two industries as good substitutes. For instance, newspapers are struggling to maintain their relevance to subscribers who can watch the news on any of the numerous TV channels and use Internet sources to get information about sports results, stock quotes and job opportunities.

To determine how strong the competitive pressures from substitute products are managers can focus on the following factors:

1. *Whether substitutes are readily available.* This creates competitive pressure by placing a ceiling on the prices industry members can charge without giving customers an incentive to switch to substitutes and risking sales erosion.[13] This price ceiling also puts a lid on the profits that industry members can earn unless they cut costs.

2. *Whether buyers view the substitutes as attractively priced in relation to their quality, performance and other relevant attributes.* In deciding whether to switch to a substitute product, customers compare its performance, features, ease of use and other attributes as well as price to see if the substitute offers more value for the money than the industry's product. The users of paper cartons constantly weigh the price/performance trade-offs with plastic containers and metal cans, for example. As seen in the closing case of this chapter, where the price of a product or service is considered 'free' by consumers, this can create major problems for industry incumbents.

3. *Whether the costs that buyers incur in switching to the substitutes are low or high.* Low switching costs make it easier for the sellers of attractive substitutes to lure buyers to their offerings; high switching costs deter buyers from purchasing substitute products.[14] Typical switching costs include the time and inconvenience involved in switching, the cost of any additional equipment needed, employee retraining costs and the psychological costs of severing old supplier relationships and establishing new ones.

Before assessing the competitive pressures coming from substitutes, managers must identify the substitutes, which is less easy than it sounds since it involves (1) determining where the industry boundaries lie and (2) figuring out which other products or services can address the same basic customer needs as those produced by industry members. Deciding on the industry boundaries is necessary for determining which firms are direct rivals and which produce substitutes.

As a rule, *the lower the price of substitutes, the higher their quality and performance; and the lower the user's switching costs, the more intense the competitive pressures posed by substitute products.* Other market indicators of the competitive strength of substitute products include: (1) whether the sales of substitutes are growing faster than the sales of the industry being analysed; (2) whether the producers of substitutes are moving to add new capacity, and (3) whether the profits of the producers of substitutes are on the rise.

Competitive Pressures Stemming from Supplier Bargaining Power

Whether the suppliers of industry members represent a weak or strong competitive force depends on the degree to which suppliers have sufficient *bargaining power* to influence the terms and conditions of supply in their favour. Suppliers with strong bargaining power can erode industry profitability by charging industry members higher prices, passing costs on to them and limiting their opportunities to find better deals.

Illustration Capsule 3.1

MICROSOFT AND INTEL: THE POWER OF DOMINANT SUPPLIERS

Microsoft and Intel, both of whom supply PC-makers with essential components, have been known to use their dominant market status not only to charge PC-makers' premium prices but also to leverage PC-makers in other ways. The bargaining power of these two organizations over their customers is so great that both organizations

▶

have faced antitrust charges on numerous occasions. Before a legal agreement ending the practice, Microsoft pressured PC-makers to load only Microsoft products onto the screens of new computers that come with factory-loaded software. Intel has also defended against antitrust charges but continues to give PC-makers who use the biggest percentages of Intel chips in their PC models top priority in filling orders for newly introduced Intel chips. Being on Intel's list of preferred customers helps a PC-maker get an allocation of the first production runs of Intel's latest chips and thus get new PC models to market ahead of rivals. Microsoft's and Intel's pressuring of PC-makers has helped them maintain their dominant positions in their industries.

A variety of factors determining the strength of suppliers' bargaining power are:[15]

- *Whether suppliers' products are in short supply.* Suppliers of items in short supply have pricing power and bargaining leverage, whereas a surge in the available supply of particular items shifts the bargaining power to the industry members.

- *Whether suppliers provide a differentiated input that enhances the performance or quality of the industry's product.* The more differentiated and valuable a particular input is in terms of enhancing the performance or quality of the products of industry members, the more bargaining leverage and pricing power suppliers have.

- *Whether the item being supplied is a standard item or a commodity that is readily available from a host of suppliers.* The suppliers of commodities (like copper or steel reinforcing rods or shipping cartons) are in a weak position to demand a premium price or insist on other favourable terms because industry members can readily obtain essentially the same item at the same price from many other suppliers eager to win their business.

- *Whether it is difficult or costly for industry members to switch their purchases from one supplier to another.* The higher the switching costs of industry members, the stronger the bargaining power of their suppliers. Low switching costs limit supplier bargaining power by enabling industry members to change suppliers if any one supplier attempts to raise prices by more than the costs of switching.

- *Whether there are good substitutes available for the suppliers' products.* The ready availability of substitute inputs lessens the bargaining power of suppliers by reducing the dependence of industry members on the suppliers. The better the price and performance characteristics of the substitute inputs, the weaker the bargaining power of suppliers.

- *Whether industry members account for a sizeable fraction of suppliers' total sales.* As a rule, suppliers have less bargaining leverage when their sales to members of the industry constitute a big percentage of their total sales. In such cases, the well-being of suppliers is closely tied to the well-being of their major customers. Suppliers have a big incentive to protect and enhance the competitiveness of their major customers via reasonable prices, exceptional quality and ongoing advances in the technology of the items supplied.

- *Whether the supplier industry is dominated by a few large organizations and whether it is more concentrated than the industry it sells to.* Suppliers with sizeable market shares and strong demand for the items they supply generally have sufficient bargaining power to charge high prices and deny requests from industry members for lower prices or other concessions.

- *Whether it makes good economic sense for industry members to integrate backward and self-manufacture items they have been buying from suppliers.* The make-or-buy issue generally boils down to whether suppliers who specialize in the production of particular parts or components and make them in volume for many different customers have the expertise and scale economies to supply as good or better components at a lower cost than industry members could achieve via self-manufacture. Frequently, it is difficult for industry members to self-manufacture parts and components more economically than they can obtain them from suppliers who specialize in making such items. For instance, most producers of outdoor power equipment (lawn mowers, rotary tillers, leaf blowers etc.) find it cheaper to source the small engines they need from outside manufacturers that specialize in small-engine manufacture than to make their own engines, because the quantity of engines they need is too small to justify the investment in manufacturing facilities, master the production process and capture scale economies. Specialists in small-engine manufacture, by supplying many kinds of engines to the whole power equipment industry, can obtain a big enough sales volume to fully realize scale economies, become proficient in all the manufacturing techniques and keep costs low. As a rule, suppliers are safe from the threat of self-manufacture by their customers *until* the volume of parts a customer needs becomes large enough for the customer to justify backward integration into self-manufacture of the component.

In identifying the degree of supplier power in an industry, it is important to recognize that different types of suppliers are likely to have different amounts of bargaining power. Thus, the first step is for managers to identify the different types of suppliers, paying particular attention to those that provide the industry with important inputs. The next step is to assess the bargaining power of each type of supplier separately.

Competitive Pressures Stemming from Buyer Bargaining Power and Price Sensitivity

Whether buyers are able to exert strong competitive pressures on industry members depends on (1) the degree to which buyers have bargaining power and (2) the extent to which buyers are price-sensitive. Buyers with strong bargaining power can limit industry profitability by demanding price concessions, better payment terms or additional features and services that increase industry members' costs. Buyer price sensitivity limits the profit potential of industry members by restricting the ability of sellers to raise prices without losing revenue.

The strength of buyers as a competitive force depends on a set of factors that predict the degree of bargaining power and price sensitivity, which may vary according to buyer group (e.g. wholesalers, large retail chains, small retailers, consumers). Retailers tend to have greater bargaining power over industry sellers if they have influence over the purchase decisions of the end-user or if they are critical in providing sellers with access to the end-user. For example, large retail chains like Carrefour, Staples, Tesco and the Metro Group typically have considerable negotiating leverage in purchasing products from manufacturers because of manufacturers' need for broad retail exposure and the most appealing shelf locations. Motor vehicle manufacturers have strong bargaining power in negotiating to buy original-equipment tyres from Goodyear, Michelin, Bridgestone/Firestone, Continental and Pirelli not only because they buy in large quantities but also because tyre-makers believe they gain an advantage in supplying replacement tyres to vehicle owners if their tyre brand is original equipment on the vehicle. In contrast, individual consumers rarely have any real bargaining power in negotiating price concessions or other favourable terms with sellers. Examples of factors affecting the bargaining power of buyers include:[16]

- *Buyers' bargaining power is greater when their costs of switching to competing brands or substitutes are relatively low.* Buyers who can readily switch brands have more leverage than buyers who have high switching costs. Switching costs limit industry profitability, in essence, by putting a cap on how much producers can raise price or reduce quality before they lose the buyer's business.

- *Buyer power increases when industry goods are standardized or differentiation is weak.* In such circumstances, buyers make their selections on the basis of price, which increases price competition among vendors. When products are differentiated, buyers' options are more limited and they are less focused on obtaining low prices, which may signal poor quality.

- *Buyers have more power when they are large and few in number relative to the number of sellers.* The smaller the number of buyers, the more sellers have to compete for their business and the less easy it is for sellers to find alternative buyers when a customer is lost to a competitor. The prospect of losing a customer not easily replaced often makes a seller more willing to grant concessions of one kind or another. The larger the buyer, the more important their business is to the seller and the more sellers will be willing to grant concessions.

- *Buyer power increases when buyer demand is weak and industry members are scrambling to sell more units.* Weak or declining demand creates a 'buyer's market', in which bargain-hunting buyers are able to press for better deals and special treatment; conversely, strong or rapidly growing demand creates a 'seller's market' and shifts bargaining power to sellers.

- *Buyers gain leverage if they are well informed about sellers' products, prices and costs.* The more information buyers have, the better bargaining position they are in. The mushrooming availability of product information on the Internet is giving added bargaining power to consumers. Buyers can easily use the Internet to compare prices and features of vacation packages, shop for the best interest rates on mortgages and loans and find the best prices on big-ticket items such as home entertainment centres.

- *Buyers' bargaining power is greater when they pose a credible threat of integrating backward into the business of sellers.* Organizations like Anheuser-Busch, Coors and Heinz have integrated backward into metal can manufacturing to gain bargaining power in obtaining the balance of their can requirements from otherwise powerful metal can manufacturers. Retailers gain bargaining power by stocking and promoting their own private-label brands alongside manufacturers' name brands.

- Also if buyers can *delay their purchase* or are *price-sensitive* (such as low-income consumers or where the product represents a large fraction of their total purchases), they are more likely to negotiate or simply walk away if they feel the price is too high.

The starting point for the analysis of buyers as a competitive force is to identify the different types of buyers along the value chain, then proceed to analysing the bargaining power and price sensitivity of each type separately. Overall, buyers exert strong competitive pressures and force industry profitability downwards if the majority of industry member sales are made to buyer groups that have either strong bargaining power or high price sensitivity. Buyers are able to exert only moderate competitive pressures on sellers when the majority of sellers' revenues come from buyers with intermediate levels of power or price sensitivity. Competitive pressures exerted by buyers are weak when a big portion of sellers' sales revenues comes from buyers with weak bargaining power and price sensitivity. It is also important to understand the underlying business models used in an industry to determine who the buyer is as opposed to the consumer. For example, the users of Google's search engine service consume the results, but it is the advertisers that might be labelled as the buyer since they pay for their promotional slots on the portal. Social businesses and public sector and not-for-profit organizations can have similar issues distinguishing between service users and funders. Sometimes it can be important to adapt parts of the five-forces framework to take account of the context of an industry or sector.

Is the Collective Strength of the Five Competitive Forces Conducive to Good Profitability?

Assessing whether each of the five competitive forces gives rise to strong, moderate or weak competitive pressures sets the stage for evaluating whether, overall, the strength of the five forces is conducive to good profitability. Is the state of competition in the industry stronger than 'normal'? Can organizations in this industry reasonably expect to earn decent profits in light of the prevailing competitive forces? Are some of the competitive forces sufficiently powerful to undermine industry profitability?

The most extreme case of a 'competitively unattractive' industry occurs when all five forces are producing strong competitive pressures: rivalry among sellers is vigorous, low entry barriers allow new rivals to gain a market foothold, competition from substitutes is intense and both suppliers and buyers are able to exercise considerable leverage. Fierce to strong competitive pressures coming from all five directions drive industry profitability to unacceptably low levels, frequently producing losses for many industry members and forcing some out of business. But an industry can be competitively unattractive without all five competitive forces being strong. In fact, intense competitive pressures *from just one or two* of the five forces may suffice to destroy the conditions for good profitability and prompt some organizations to exit the business.

As a rule, *the strongest competitive forces determine the extent of the competitive pressure on industry profitability.*[17] Thus, in evaluating the strength of the five forces overall and their effect on industry profitability, managers should look to the strongest forces. Having more than one strong force will not worsen the effect on industry profitability, but it does mean that the industry has multiple competitive challenges with which to cope. In that sense, an industry with three to five strong forces is even more 'unattractive' as a place to compete. Especially intense competitive conditions seem to be the norm in tyre manufacturing, apparel and commercial airlines, three industries where profit margins have historically been thin.

In contrast, when the overall impact of the five competitive forces is moderate to weak, an industry is 'attractive' in the sense that the *average* industry member can reasonably expect to earn good profits and a nice return on investment. The ideal competitive environment for earning superior profits is one in which both suppliers and customers are in weak bargaining positions, there are no good substitutes, high barriers block further entry and rivalry among present sellers generates only limited competitive pressures.

> **Core Concept**
>
> The strongest of the five forces determines how strong the forces of competition are overall and the extent of the downward pressure on an industry's level of profitability.

Matching Organizational Strategy to Competitive Conditions

Working through the five-forces model aids strategy-makers in assessing whether the intensity of competition allows good profitability. It can also help to better match an organization's strategy to the specific competitive character of the marketplace. Matching an organization's strategy to competitive conditions has three aspects:

1. Pursuing avenues that shield the firm from as many of the different competitive pressures as possible.

2. Initiating actions calculated to shift the competitive forces in the organization's favour by altering the underlying factors driving the five forces.

3. Spotting attractive arenas for expansion where competitive pressures in the industry are somewhat weaker.

> An organization's strategy is increasingly effective the more it provides some insulation from competitive pressures, shifts the competitive battle in the organization's favour and positions firms to take advantage of attractive growth opportunities.

But making headway on these three fronts first requires identifying competitive pressures, gauging the relative strength of each of the five competitive forces and gaining a deep enough understanding of the state of competition in the industry to know which strategy buttons to push.

Key Debate 3.1

HOW USEFUL IS PORTER'S FIVE-FORCES MODEL IN THE CURRENT ENVIRONMENT?

Although Michael Porter's seminal article introducing the five forces appeared in 1979, the economic theory underpinning it is much older. The key assumptions are based on the work of two US industrial economists, E.S. Mason, working in the late 1930s and J. Bain, writing in the 1950s and 1960s. As the business environment changes it is easy to see why the model has come in for criticism in recent times.

A SIXTH FORCE

One of the most frequent suggestions is that the model does not cover all the significant forces at work on an industry and that growing regulation means that the state should be added as a sixth force. The opening case in this chapter provides some evidence that regulation can have a significant impact on the structure of an industry and the conduct and performance of its members.

Another contender for the sixth force is that of complementors. As products and services have become more complex and involve a wider range of organizations in making and delivering them, firms develop relationships that are not just with suppliers or competitors but with other organizations whose products enhance their own. For example, apps on a smartphone could be seen as a complementary product because customers value their device more with apps on it. The value net model (see Figure 3.5) also highlights opportunities for firms to collaborate in creating value rather than just competing with each other in a zero-sum game as the five-forces model

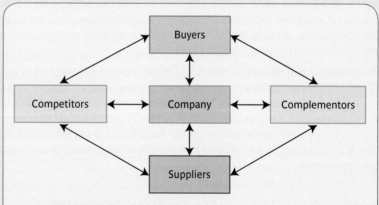

FIGURE 3.5 The value net model.

Source: Adapted from Brandenburger, A. and Nalebuff, B. (1995) 'The right game,' *Harvard Business Review*, July–August, pp.57–64.

assumes. Co-operation and even co-opetition exists in many industries. In trade exhibitions, the organisers are often competing with other forms of media for marketing spend, but it is usual to find the trade press producing exhibition catalogues and taking a booth at the exhibition while the organisers will purchase advertising and use direct marketing lists from magazines.

STATIC ANALYSIS

High velocity industries, especially those in technology-driven fields, are changing rapidly and it is often difficult for analysts to accurately define some industry's boundaries. The launch of the iPad and similar tablet devices has created an overlap between netbooks and smartphones. Many of the major players in China's burgeoning online business community, such as Alibaba, Baidu and Tencent, are increasingly offering similar services, despite starting out as Internet auction, search engine and chat service sites. Identifying potential new entrants, direct competitors

▶

◀

and substitutes in these circumstances can be a challenging task for managers. Defining an industry too narrowly can lead to incumbent players falling victim to disruptive innovators entering their market. Dyson's entry into the UK carpet cleaning market is an example of the dangers of this. They were able to achieve a market leading position in just two years before the existing firms in the industry responded effectively.

PORTER'S RESPONSE

In a recent (2008) article in *Harvard Business Review*, Porter acknowledged many of the criticisms but went on to defend his concept. In his view the model is useful even if managers are not able to draw industry boundaries correctly because it can still reveal a range of competitive threats. While the model is a snapshot of an industry, Porter contends that most industries evolve and their basic structures are persistent over time. Even with abrupt changes the model still provides a useful framework for analysing significant developments. Finally, Porter argues that there is no single element that constitutes a sixth force and that complementors, regulation and other factors should be analysed through their impact on the five forces.

QUESTIONS

1. What benefits are there in augmenting the five-forces model by adding additional forces?
2. Is the five-forces model effective for analysing all industries or only those that are more stable and predictable?

Sources: Brandenburger, A. and Nalebuff, B. (1995) 'The right game', *Harvard Business Review*, July–August, pp. 57–64; *The Economist* (2011) 'An internet with Chinese characteristics', *The Economist*, 30 July, pp. 55–6; Grundy, M. (2006) 'Rethinking and reinventing Michael Porter's five forces model', *Strategic Change*, 15: 213-29; Porter, M.E. (2008) 'The five competitive forces that shape strategy', *Harvard Business Review*, January, pp. 79–93.

Question 3: What Factors Are Driving Industry Change and What Impacts Will They Have?

LO 3.5 Discuss the merits of other approaches to industry analysis that add to and challenge the five-forces concept.

While it is critical to understand the nature and intensity of the competitive forces in an industry, it is just as important to understand that the intensity of these forces and the level of an industry's attractiveness are fluid and subject to change. All industries are affected by new developments and ongoing trends that alter industry conditions, some more speedily than others. Many of these changes are important enough to require a strategic response. Since the five competitive forces have such significance for an industry's profit potential, it is critical that managers remain alert to the changes most likely to affect the strength of the five forces. Environmental scanning for changes of this nature will enable managers to forecast changes in the expected profitability of the industry and to adjust their organization's strategy accordingly. As we saw at the beginning of the chapter some of these changes will come from the macro-environment. So it is important for managers to link their analysis of strategically relevant factors from outside the industry to their assessment of the competitive environment. In more complex and unpredictable environments this may also include the use of scenarios against which the organization's strategy can be tested.

LO 3.2 Diagnose the factors that shape industry dynamics and forecast their effects on future industry attractiveness using both traditional approaches and alternatives such as scenario planning.

Changes that affect the competitive forces in a positive manner may present opportunities for organizations to reposition themselves to take advantage of these forces. Changes that affect the five forces negatively may require a defensive strategic response. Regardless of the direction of change, managers will be able to react in a more timely fashion, with lower adjustment costs, if they have advance notice of the coming changes. Moreover, with early notice, managers may be able to influence the direction or scope of environmental change and improve the outlook.

Analysing Industry Dynamics

Managing under changing conditions begins with a strategic analysis of the industry dynamics. The earlier section on scenario planning showed how in less predictable environments it may be necessary for managers to look further into the future and develop several possible future states for an industry. However, this is often an expensive and time-consuming exercise and while it may be critical for organizations that have to make long-term strategic capital investments such as oil companies and utilities, it is not a process that all organizations can follow. In some industries, especially those where there is little or no basis on which to predict the future, it can actually be harmful as it gives managers false confidence that they have all the answers.[18] In other industries with a more stable structure and less dynamic environment a single forecast may be sufficient for making the necessary strategic decision.

> **Core Concept**
>
> Dynamic industry analysis involves determining how the drivers of change are affecting industry and competitive conditions.

As an alternative to an exhaustive scenario planning process firms can use the following three steps: (1) identifying the drivers of change; (2) assessing whether the drivers of change are, individually or collectively, acting to make the industry more or less attractive; and (3) determining what strategy changes are needed to prepare for the impacts of the anticipated change. All three steps merit further discussion.

Identifying an Industry's Drivers of Change

While many types of environmental change can affect industries in one way or another, it is important to focus on the most powerful agents of change – those with the biggest influence in reshaping the industry landscape and altering competitive conditions. Many drivers of change originate in the outer ring of the organization's external environment (see Figure 3.1), but others originate in the organization's more immediate industry and competitive environment. Some of the most common industry drivers are covered below:[19]

- *Changes in an industry's long-term growth rate.* Shifts in industry growth up or down are a key driver of industry change, affecting the balance between industry supply and buyer demand, entry and exit and the character and strength of competition. Whether demand is growing or declining is one of the key factors influencing the intensity of rivalry in an industry, as explained earlier. But the strength of this effect will depend on how changes in the industry growth rate affect entry and exit in the industry. If entry barriers are low, then growth in demand will attract new entrants, increasing the number of industry rivals. If exit barriers are low, then shrinking demand will induce exit, resulting in fewer remaining rivals. Since the numbers of firms in an industry also affect the strength of rivalry, these secondary effects via entry and exit would counteract the more direct effects of the change in demand on rivalry. Depending on how much entry or exit takes place, the net result might be that the overall force of rivals remains the same. A change in the long-term growth rate may affect industry conditions in other ways as well. For example, if growth prospects induce the entry of a large, established firm with ambitious growth goals, the intensity of rivalry may increase markedly due to the added diversity or changes in the size mix of incumbents. The exact effect of growth rate changes will vary depending on the specific industry situation. In analysing the effects of any change driver, managers need to keep in mind the various factors that influence the five forces.

- *Increasing globalization.* Globalization can be precipitated by the blossoming of consumer demand in more and more countries and by the actions of government officials in many countries to reduce trade barriers or open up once-closed markets to foreign competitors, as is occurring in many parts of Europe, Latin America and Asia. Significant differences in labour costs among countries give manufacturers a strong incentive to locate plants for labour-intensive products in low-wage countries and use these plants to supply market demand across the world. Wages in China, India, Singapore, Mexico and Brazil, for example, are about one-fourth those in the USA, Germany and Japan. Because globalization is a complex phenomenon that affects different industries in different ways, analysing its effects on industry dynamics is a challenging task that requires a consideration of how each of the five forces may be affected. For example, globalization increases the diversity and number of competitors, and this, in turn, increases the force of rivalry in an industry. At the same time, the lowering of trade barriers increases the threat of entry, putting further pressure on industry profitability. On the other hand, globalization is likely to weaken supplier power by increasing the number of suppliers and increasing the possibility of substituting cheap labour for other inputs. The specific effects vary by industry and will impact some industries more than others. Globalization is very much a driver of industry change in such industries as motor vehicles, steel, petroleum, personal computers, video games, public accounting and textbook publishing.

- *Changes in who buys the product and how they use it.* Shifts in buyer demographics and the ways products are used can greatly alter industry and competitive conditions. Longer life expectancies and growing percentages of relatively well-to-do retirees, for example, are driving demand growth in such industries as healthcare, prescription drugs, recreational living and vacation travel. This is the most common effect of changes in buyer demographics, and it affects industry rivalry, as observed above. But other effects are possible as well. Dell's 'buy direct' strategy lessened the buyer power of big-box retailers in the PC industry by cutting out the intermediate buyers and selling directly to end-users.

- *Technological change.* Advances in technology can cause disruptive change in an industry by introducing substitutes that offer buyers an irresistible price/performance combination. At the least, this increases the power of substitutes; it may change the business landscape in more fundamental ways if it has a devastating effect on demand. Technological change can also impact the manufacturing process in an industry. This might lead to greater economies of scale, for example, which would increase industry entry barriers. Or it could lead to greater product differentiation, as did the introduction of 'mass customization' techniques. Increasing product differentiation tends to lower buyer power, increase entry barriers and reduce rivalry, all of which have positive implications for industry profitability. On the other hand the spread of certain manufacturing technologies can lead to commoditization and potentially lower profits.

- *Emerging new Internet capabilities and applications.* The emergence of a high-speed Internet service and Voice over Internet Protocol (VoIP) technology, along with an ever-growing series of Internet applications, provides a special case of technological change that has been a major driver of change in industry after industry. It has reshaped many aspects of the business landscape and can affect the five forces in various ways. The ability of organizations to reach consumers via the Internet increases the number of rivals an organization faces and often escalates rivalry by pitting pure online sellers against combination brick-and-click sellers against pure brick-and-mortar sellers (increasing diversity and size mix). The Internet gives buyers increasing power through unprecedented ability to research the product offerings of competitors and shop the market for the best value (making buyers better informed). Widespread use of email has forever eroded the business of providing fax services and the first-class mail delivery revenues of government postal services world-wide (substitute power). Video-conferencing via the Internet erodes the demand for business travel (increasing rivalry in the travel market). The Internet of the future will feature faster speeds, dazzling applications and over a billion connected gadgets performing an array of functions, thus driving further industry and competitive changes. But Internet-related impacts vary from industry to industry. The challenges here are to assess precisely how emerging Internet developments are altering a particular industry's landscape and to factor these impacts into the strategy-making equation.

● *Product and marketing innovation.* An ongoing stream of product innovations tends to alter the pattern of competition in an industry by attracting more first-time buyers, rejuvenating industry growth and/or increasing product differentiation, with concomitant effects on rivalry, entry threat and buyer power. Product innovation has been a key driving force in such industries as digital cameras, golf clubs, video games, toys and prescription drugs. Similarly, when firms are successful in introducing *new ways* to market their products, they can spark a burst of buyer interest, widen industry demand, increase or lower entry barriers and increase product differentiation, any or all of which can alter the competitiveness of an industry.

● *Entry or exit of major firms.* The entry of one or more foreign organizations into a geographic market once dominated by domestic firms nearly always changes the balance between demand and supply and shakes up competitive conditions by adding diversity. Likewise, when an established domestic firm from another industry attempts entry, its fresh approach can drive the competition in new directions, with greater rivalry as the result. Similarly, exit of a major firm changes the competitive structure by reducing the number of market leaders and increasing the dominance of the leaders who remain.

● *Improvements in cost and efficiency in closely adjoining markets.* Big changes in the costs of substitute producers can dramatically alter the state of competition by changing the price/performance trade-off between an industry's products and that of substitute goods. For example, lower production costs and longer-life products have allowed the makers of super-efficient, fluorescent-based spiral light bulbs to cut deeply into the sales of incandescent light bulbs.

● *Regulatory influences and government policy changes.* Changes in regulations and government policies can affect competitive conditions in industries in a variety of ways. For example, regulatory actions can affect barriers to entry directly, as they have in industries such as airlines, banking and broadcasting. Regulations regarding product quality, safety and environmental protection can affect entry barriers more indirectly, by altering capital requirements or economies of scale. Government actions can also affect rivalry through antitrust policies, as they have in soft-drink bottling, where exclusive territorial rights were granted, and in automobile parts, where a loosening of restrictions led to increasing supplier power.[20]

● *Changing societal concerns, attitudes and lifestyles.* Emerging social issues and changing attitudes and lifestyles can be powerful instigators of industry change. Growing concerns about global warming have emerged as a major driver of change in the energy industry, changing the rate of industry growth in different sectors. The greater attention and care being given to household pets has driven growth across the whole pet industry. Changes in the industry growth rate, as we have seen, can affect the intensity of industry rivalry and entry conditions.

That there are so many different *potential* drivers of change explains why a full understanding of all types of change drivers is a fundamental part of analysing industry dynamics. However, for each industry no more than three or four of these drivers are likely to be powerful enough to qualify as the *major determinants* of why and how an industry's competitive conditions are changing. The true analytical task is to evaluate the forces of industry and competitive change carefully enough to separate major factors from minor ones.

Illustration Capsule 3.2

THE IMPACT OF THE INTERNET ON FINNISH MAGAZINE PUBLISHING

The Internet has been identified as a potentially disruptive factor for a whole range of media organizations and as we have seen above, is one of the most common drivers of change in an industry. Researchers at the Lappeenranta University of Technology in Finland carried out a study in 2007 into its impact on Finnish magazine publishers. They interviewed eight experts in the field and assessed the extent to which the Internet had changed the industry by tracing its positive and negative influence on each of the five forces (see Figure 3.6).

Despite the Internet's reputation as a significant disruptive factor, the study found that the effects on the Finnish magazine industry were limited. Although, in theory, the Internet should make it much easier for firms to enter the industry through a web-only magazine, there were still barriers to entry in terms of economies of scale enjoyed by the larger publishers, customer loyalty towards existing titles and access to distribution channels. All of these meant that new entrants would have to invest significant capital in marketing, sales and customer service. There was a balance between the opportunities and threats when it came to substitutes. While the Internet offers increasing amounts of specialist free content, it also gave incumbent industry members access to potential new customers through a range of other specialist online communities.

The Internet had not made significant changes to the relationship between magazines and suppliers but there was more potential for disruption when it came to buyers. Customers fall into two groups, readers and advertisers. Industry insiders felt that the differentiated nature of the magazines tended to insulate them from the worst effects of the Internet when it came to buyer bargaining power. The interviewees in the study described the magazine industry as mature and stable before the advent of the Internet. They did not believe that the Internet had resulted in major changes to the industry structure but it had resulted in a higher level of rivalry between firms as their web presence made benchmarking more feasible and could lead to a weakening

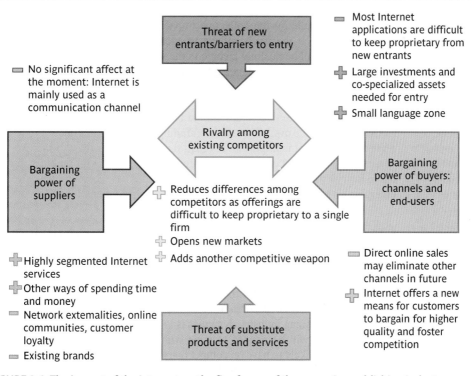

FIGURE 3.6 The impact of the Internet on the five forces of the magazine publishing industry.

◄

in the differentiation between industry members. It was acknowledged that the Finnish industry could have been insulated from the full effect of the Internet due to its size and specific language component.

> QUESTION
> 1. What impact do you think the Internet has had on the wider magazine industry?

Source: Ellonen, H-K., Kuivalanainen, O. and Jantunen, A. (2008) 'The strategic Impact of the Internet on magazine publishing', *International Journal of Innovation and Technology Management*, 5(3): 341–61.

Assessing the Impact of the Factors Driving Industry Change

Just identifying the factors driving industry change is not sufficient, however. The second, and more important step in dynamic industry analysis is to determine whether the prevailing change drivers, on the whole, are acting to make the industry environment more or less attractive. Answers to three questions are needed:

1. Overall, are the factors driving change causing demand for the industry's product to increase or decrease?
2. Is the collective impact of the drivers of change making competition more or less intense?
3. Will the combined impacts of the change drivers lead to higher or lower industry profitability?

The most important part of dynamic industry analysis is to determine whether the collective impact of the change drivers will be to increase or decrease market demand, make competition more or less intense and lead to higher or lower industry profitability.

Getting a handle on the collective impact of the factors driving industry change requires looking at the likely effects of each factor separately, since the drivers of change may not all be pushing change in the same direction. For example, one change driver may be acting to spur demand for the industry's product while another is working to curtail demand. Whether the net effect on industry demand is up or down hinges on which driver of change is the more powerful. Similarly, the effects of the drivers of change on each of the five forces should be looked at individually first, and then collectively, to view the overall effect. In summing up the overall effect of industry change on the five forces, it is important to recall that it is the *strongest* of the five forces that determines the degree of competitive pressure on industry profitability and therefore the industry's profit potential. The key question, then, is whether a new strong force is emerging or whether forces that are strong presently are beginning to weaken.

Developing a Strategy that Takes the Changes in Industry Conditions into Account

Dynamic industry analysis, when done properly, pushes managers to think about what is around the corner and what the organization needs to be doing to get ready for it.

The third step in the strategic analysis of industry dynamics – where the real payoff for strategy-making comes – is for managers to draw some conclusions about *what strategy adjustments will be needed to deal with the impacts of the changes in industry conditions*. The value of analysing industry dynamics is to gain a better understanding of what strategy adjustments will be needed to cope with the drivers of industry change and the impacts they are likely to have on competitive intensity and industry profitability. Indeed, without understanding the forces driving industry change and the impacts these forces will have on the character of the industry environment and on the organization's business over the next one to three years, managers are ill-prepared to craft a strategy tightly matched to emerging conditions. To the extent that managers are unclear about the drivers of industry change and their impacts, or if their views are off-base, the chances of making astute and timely strategy adjustments are slim. So dynamic industry analysis is not something to take lightly; it has practical value and is basic to the task of thinking strategically about where the industry is headed and how to prepare for the changes ahead.

Question 4: How are Industry Rivals Positioned – Who is Strongly Positioned and Who is Not?

> **LO 3.4**
> Describe different industry structures, industry lifestyle stages and identify strategic groups within an industry or sector.

Since competing organizations commonly sell in different price/quality ranges, emphasize different distribution channels, incorporate product features that appeal to different types of buyers, have different geographic coverage and so on, it stands to reason that some organizations enjoy stronger or more attractive market positions than other organizations. Understanding which organizations are strongly positioned and which are weakly positioned is an integral part of analysing an industry's competitive structure. The best technique for revealing the market positions of industry competitors is **strategic group mapping**.[21]

Using Strategic Group Maps to Assess the Market Positions of Key Competitors

> **Core Concept**
> A **strategic group** is a cluster of industry rivals that have similar competitive approaches and market positions.

A **strategic group** consists of those industry members with similar competitive approaches and positions in the market.[22] Organizations in the same strategic group can resemble one another in any of several ways: They may have comparable product-line breadth, sell in the same price/quality range, emphasize the same distribution channels, use essentially the same product attributes to appeal to similar types of buyers, depend on identical technological approaches, or offer buyers similar services and technical assistance.[23] An industry contains only one strategic group when all sellers pursue essentially identical strategies and have similar market positions. At the other extreme, an industry may contain as many strategic groups as there are competitors when each rival pursues a distinctively different competitive approach and occupies a substantially different market position.

> **Core Concept**
> **Strategic group mapping** is a technique for displaying the different market or competitive positions that rival firms occupy in the industry.

The procedure for constructing a *strategic group map* is straightforward:

- Identify the competitive characteristics that differentiate firms in the industry. Typical variables are price/quality range (high, medium, low), geographic coverage (local, regional, national, global), product-line breadth (wide, narrow), degree of service offered (no frills, limited, full) use of distribution channels (retail, wholesale, Internet, multiple), degree of vertical integration (none, partial, full) and degree of diversification into other industries (none, some, considerable).
- Plot the firms on a two-variable map using pairs of these differentiating characteristics.
- Assign firms occupying about the same map location to the same strategic group.
- Draw circles around each strategic group, making the circles proportional to the size of the group's share of total industry sales revenues.

This produces a two-dimensional diagram like the one for the mobile telecoms handset industry in Illustration Capsule 3.3.

Several guidelines need to be observed in creating strategic group maps.[24] First, the two variables selected as axes for the map should *not* be highly correlated; if they are, the circles on the map will fall along a diagonal and reveal nothing more about the relative positions of competitors than would be revealed by comparing the rivals on just one of the variables. For instance, if organizations with broad product lines use multiple distribution channels while organizations with narrow lines use a single

Illustration Capsule 3.3

COMPARATIVE MARKET POSITIONS OF SELECTED MOBILE TELECOMS HANDSET MANUFACTURERS: A STRATEGIC GROUP MAP EXAMPLE

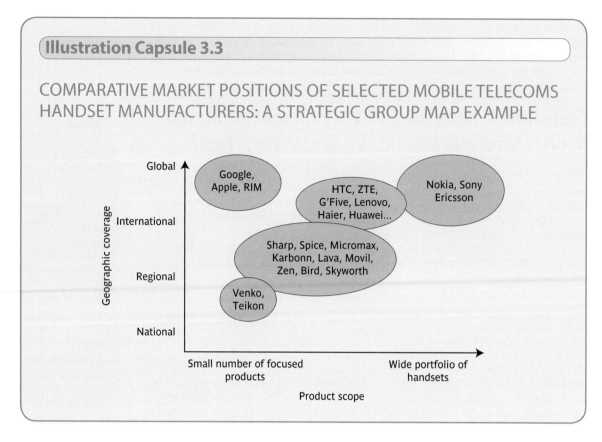

distribution channel, then looking at broad versus narrow product lines reveals just as much about industry positioning as looking at single versus multiple distribution channels; that is, one of the variables is redundant.

Second, the variables chosen as axes for the map should reflect key approaches to offering value to customers and expose big differences in how rivals position themselves to compete in the marketplace. This, of course, means analysts must identify the characteristics that differentiate rival firms and use these differences as variables for the axes and as the basis for deciding which firm belongs in which strategic group. Third, the variables used as axes do not have to be either quantitative or continuous; rather, they can be discrete variables, defined in terms of distinct classes and combinations. Fourth, drawing the sizes of the circles on the map proportional to the combined sales of the firms in each strategic group allows the map to reflect the relative sizes of each strategic group. Fifth, if more than two good variables can be used as axes for the map, then it is wise to draw several maps to give different views of the relationships among the competitive positions present in the industry's structure – there is not necessarily one best map for portraying how competing firms are positioned.

What Can Be Learned from Strategic Group Maps?

Strategic group maps are revealing in several respects. The most important has to do with identifying which industry members are close rivals and which are distant rivals. Firms in the same strategic group are the closest rivals; the next closest rivals are in the immediately adjacent groups. Often, firms in strategic groups that are far apart on the map hardly compete at all.

> Strategic group maps reveal which organizations are close competitors and which are distant competitors.

The second thing to be gleaned from strategic group mapping is that *not all positions on the map are equally attractive.*[25] There are two main reasons that account for why some positions can be more attractive than others:[26]

1. *Prevailing competitive pressures in the industry and drivers of change favour some strategic groups and hurt others.* Discerning which strategic groups are advantaged and disadvantaged requires scrutinizing the map in light of what has been learned from the prior analyses of competitive forces and industry dynamics. Quite often the strength of competition varies from group to group – there is little reason to believe that all firms in an industry feel the same degrees of competitive pressure, since their strategies and market positions may well differ in important respects. For instance, in the ready-to-eat cereal industry, there are significantly higher entry barriers (capital requirements, brand loyalty and so on.) for the strategic group comprising the large, branded cereal-makers than for the group of generic cereal-makers or the group of small natural cereal producers. Furthermore, industry dynamics may affect different groups in different ways. For example, the long-term growth in demand may be increasing for some strategic groups and shrinking for others – as is the case in the news industry, where Internet news services and cable news networks are gaining ground at the expense of newspapers and network television. The industry driving forces of emerging Internet capabilities and applications, changes in who buys the product and how they use it and changing societal concerns, attitudes and lifestyles are making it increasingly difficult for traditional media to increase audiences and attract new advertisers.

2. *Profit prospects vary from strategic group to strategic group.* The profit prospects of firms in different strategic groups can vary from good to poor because of differing growth rates for the principal buyer segments served by each group, differing degrees of competitive rivalry within strategic groups, differing pressures from potential entrants to each group, differing degrees of exposure to competition from substitute products outside the industry, differing degrees of supplier or customer bargaining power from group to group and differing impacts from the industry's drivers of change. As we can see from the map in Illustration Capsule 3.3, those handset manufacturers that have led the introduction of smartphones such as Apple are in a separate strategic group. They have overtaken many of the firms with much broader product portfolios such as Nokia in terms of their financial performance.

> Some strategic groups are more favourably positioned than others because they confront weaker competitive forces and/or because they are more favourably impacted by the drivers of industry change.

Thus, part of strategic group map analysis always entails drawing conclusions about where on the map is the 'best' place to be and why. Which organizations/strategic groups are destined to prosper because of their positions? Which organizations/strategic groups seem destined to struggle because of their positions? What accounts for why some parts of the map are better than others?

Question 5: What Strategic Moves are Rivals Likely to Make Next?

Unless an organization pays attention to the strategies and situations of competitors and has some inkling of what moves they will be making, it ends up flying blind into competitive battle. As in sports, scouting the opposition is an essential part of game plan development. **Competitive intelligence** about rivals' strategies, their latest actions and announcements, their financial performance, their strengths and weaknesses and the thinking and leadership styles of their executives is valuable for anticipating the strategic moves competitors are likely to make next. Having good information about the strategic direction and likely moves of key competitors allows an organization to prepare defensive countermoves, to craft its own strategic moves with some confidence about what market manoeuvres to expect from rivals in response and to exploit any openings that arise from competitors' mis-steps.

> Good **competitive intelligence** helps managers avoid the damage to sales and profits that comes from being caught napping by the surprise moves of rivals.

One indicator of the types of moves a rival is likely to make is its financial performance – how much pressure it is under to improve. Rivals with good financial performance are likely to continue their present strategy with only minor fine-tuning. Poorly performing rivals are more likely to make fresh strategic moves. Ambitious rivals looking to move up in the industry ranks are strong candidates for launching new strategic offensives to pursue emerging market opportunities and exploit the vulnerabilities of weaker rivals.

Other good clues about what actions a specific organization is likely to undertake can often be gleaned from an organization's press releases, their websites and public documents such as annual reports.[27] There are several useful questions that managers can pose to help predict the likely actions of important rivals:

1. Which competitors have strategies that are producing good results – and thus are likely to make only minor strategic adjustments?
2. Which competitors are losing ground in the marketplace or otherwise struggling to come up with a good strategy – and thus are strong candidates for adjusting important elements of their strategy?
3. Which competitors are poised to gain market share, and which ones seem destined to lose ground?
4. Which competitors are likely to rank among the industry leaders five years from now? Do the up-and-coming competitors have strong ambitions and the resources needed to overtake the current industry leader?
5. Which rivals badly need to increase their unit sales and market share? What strategic options are they most likely to pursue?
6. Which rivals are likely to enter new geographic markets or make major moves to substantially increase their sales and market share in a particular geographic region?
7. Which rivals are strong candidates to expand their product offerings and enter new product segments where they do not currently have a presence?
8. Which rivals are good candidates to be acquired? Which rivals may be looking to make an acquisition and are financially able to do so?

To succeed in predicting a competitor's next moves, an organization's strategists need to have a good understanding of each rival's situation, its pattern of behaviour in the past, how its managers think and what the rival's best strategic options are. Doing the necessary detective work can be time-consuming, and while it may be important in some industries such as oligopolies, with a relatively stable set of members, in other more dynamic, high-velocity environments speed of decision-making can be critical and there may not be time to cover every element in detail.

A Different View

BLUE OCEAN STRATEGY

So far in this chapter we have focused on competing directly with industry members. In their 2005 book, INSEAD professors, W. Chan Kim and Renee Mauborgne, suggested that as industries become overcrowded and increasingly competitive this is no longer a recipe for sustained competitive advantage or profitable growth. They refer to existing industries as red oceans (in reference to the blood spilled in cut-throat competition) and to blue oceans as industries that currently do not exist but are then created by firms who move into new and uncontested market space.

Blue oceans are more than just the unoccupied strategy space firms might identify through strategic groups analysis. They are not found through benchmarking with competitors in an industry but by breaking market boundaries between industries. Chan Kim and Mauborgne cite Canadian organization, Cirque du Soleil, as a clear example of how powerful a blue ocean strategy approach can be. Cirque du Soleil combined the best elements of circus performance with the intellectual and artistic content of great theatre shows. In doing so they attracted a new audience of customers who would not have previously gone to circus performances.

▶

◀

Cirque du Soleil did not recreate the features of traditional circuses. They did not use circus stars, run three rings or have animal acts. All of these features were common to existing industry members but were not the most valued element of the product and in some cases, such as the use of animals, were expensive and actually put off many potential customers. By focusing only on the most valued features of the circus, the acrobatic routines, the clowns and the big top atmosphere, Cirque du Soleil was able to operate at a lower cost than other circuses. But by adding in story-lines, music and dance they were also differentiated from the rest of the circus industry. In blue ocean strategy terms this is known as value innovation. We return to blue ocean strategy again in Chapter 6.

Activity:

1. Identify an organization in the video game, airline or the pharmaceutical sector that appears to have followed a blue ocean strategy.

Source: Chan Kim, W. and Mauborgne, R. (2005) *Blue Ocean Strategy*, Harvard Business Review Press, Boston, MA.

Question 6: What are the Key Factors for Future Competitive Success?

An industry's **key success factors (KSFs)** are those competitive factors that affect industry members' ability to survive and prosper in the marketplace – the particular strategy elements, product attributes, operational approaches, resources and competitive capabilities that spell the difference between being a strong competitor and a weak competitor – and between profit and loss. KSFs by their very nature are so important to competitive success that *all firms* in the industry must pay close attention to them or risk becoming an industry laggard or failure. To indicate the significance of KSFs another way, how well the elements of an organization's strategy measure up against an industry's KSFs determines just how financially and competitively successful that organization will be. Identifying KSFs, in light of the prevailing and anticipated industry and competitive conditions, is therefore always a top priority in analytical and strategy-making considerations. Strategists need to understand the industry landscape well enough to separate the factors most important to competitive success from those that are less important.

> **LO 3.5**
> Discuss the merits of other approaches to industry analysis that add to and challenge the five forces concept.

KSFs vary from industry to industry, and even from time to time within the same industry, as drivers of change and competitive conditions change. But regardless of the circumstances, an industry's KSFs can always be deduced by asking the same three questions:

1. On what basis do buyers of the industry's product choose between the competing brands of sellers? That is, what product attributes and service characteristics are crucial?
2. Given the nature of competitive rivalry and the competitive forces prevailing in the marketplace, what resources and competitive capabilities must an organization have to be competitively successful?
3. What shortcomings are almost certain to put an organization at a significant competitive disadvantage?

> **Core Concept**
> **Key success factors (KSFs)** are the strategy elements, product and service attributes, operational approaches, resources and competitive capabilities with the greatest impact on competitive success in the marketplace.

Only rarely are there more than five key factors for competitive success. When there appear to be more, usually some are of greater importance than others. Managers should therefore bear in mind the purpose of identifying KSFs – to determine which factors are most important to competitive success – and resist the temptation to label a factor that has only minor importance as a KSF. Compiling a list of every factor that matters even a little bit defeats the purpose of concentrating management attention on the factors truly critical to long-term competitive success.

LO 3.6
Explain why in-depth evaluation of a business's strengths and weaknesses in relation to the specific industry conditions it confronts is an essential prerequisite to crafting a strategy that is well matched to its external situation.

In the beer industry, for example, although there are many types of buyers (wholesale, retail, end-consumer), it is most important to understand the preferences and buying behaviour of the beer drinkers. Their purchase decisions are driven by price, taste, convenient access and marketing. Thus the KSFs include a *strong network of wholesale distributors* (to get the organization's brand stocked and favourably displayed in retail outlets, bars, restaurants and stadiums, where beer is sold) and *clever advertising* (to induce beer drinkers to buy the organization's brand and thereby pull beer sales through the established wholesale/retail channels). Because there is a potential for strong buyer power on the part of large distributors and retail chains, competitive success depends on some mechanism to offset that power, of which advertising (to create demand pull) is one. Thus, the KSFs also include *superior product differentiation* (as in microbrews) or *superior firm size and branding capabilities* (as in national brands). The KSFs also include *full utilization of brewing capacity* (to keep manufacturing costs low and offset the high advertising, branding and product differentiation costs).

Correctly diagnosing an industry's KSFs raises an organization's chances of crafting a sound strategy. The key success factors of an industry point to those things that every firm in the industry needs to attend to in order to retain customers and weather the competition. If the organization's strategy cannot deliver on the key success factors of its industry, it is unlikely to earn enough profits to remain a viable business. The goal of strategists, however, should be to do more than just meet the KSFs, since all firms in the industry need to clear this bar to survive. The goal of organization strategists should be to design a strategy that allows it to compare favourably *vis-à-vis* rivals on each and every one of the industry's KSFs and that aims at being *distinctively better* than rivals on one (or possibly two) of the KSFs.

Question 7: Does the Industry Offer Good Prospects for Attractive Profits?

The final step in evaluating the industry and competitive environment is to use the results of the analyses performed in answering questions 1–6 to determine whether the industry presents the organization with strong prospects for attractive profits. The important factors on which to base a conclusion include:

- the industry's growth potential;
- whether strong competitive forces are squeezing industry profitability to sub-par levels;
- whether industry profitability will be favourably or unfavourably affected by the prevailing drivers of change in the industry (i.e. whether the industry growth potential and competition appear destined to grow stronger or weaker).
- whether the organization occupies a stronger market position than rivals (one more capable of withstanding negative competitive forces) and whether this is likely to change in the course of competitive interactions.
- how well the organization's strategy delivers on the industry's key success factors.

As a general proposition, if an organization can conclude that its overall profit prospects are above average in the industry, then the industry environment is basically attractive (*for that organization*); if industry profit prospects are below average, conditions are unattractive (*for the organization*). However, it is a mistake to think of a particular industry as being equally attractive or unattractive to all industry participants and all potential entrants.[28] Attractiveness is relative, not absolute, and conclusions one way or the other have to be drawn from the perspective of a particular organization. For instance, a favourably positioned competitor may see ample opportunity to capitalize on the vulnerabilities of weaker rivals even though industry conditions are otherwise somewhat dismal. And even if an industry has appealing potential for growth and profitability, a weak competitor (one that may be part of an unfavourably positioned strategic group) may conclude that having to fight a steep uphill battle against much stronger rivals holds little promise of eventual market success or good return on shareholder investment. Similarly, industries attractive to insiders may be unattractive to outsiders because of the difficulty of challenging current market leaders with their particular resources and competences or because they have more attractive opportunities elsewhere.

When an organization decides an industry is fundamentally attractive and presents good opportunities, a strong case can be made that it should invest aggressively to capture the opportunities it sees and to improve its long-term competitive position in the business. When a strong competitor concludes an industry is becoming less attractive, it may elect to simply protect its present position, investing cautiously if at all and looking for opportunities in other industries. A competitively weak organization in an unattractive industry may see its best option as finding a buyer, perhaps a rival, to acquire its business.

> The degree to which an industry is attractive or unattractive is not the same for all industry participants and all potential entrants.

KEY POINTS

Thinking strategically about an organization's external situation involves probing for answers to the following seven questions:

1. *Does the industry offer attractive opportunities?* Industries differ significantly on such factors as market size and growth rate, geographic scope, life-cycle stage, the number and sizes of sellers, industry capacity and other conditions that describe the industry's demand–supply balance and opportunities for growth. Identifying the industry's basic economic features and growth potential sets the stage for the analysis to come, since they play an important role in determining an industry's potential for attractive profits.

2. *What kinds of competitive forces are industry members facing, and how strong is each force?* The strength of competition is a composite of five forces: (1) competitive pressures stemming from the competitive jockeying among industry rivals; (2) competitive pressures associated with the market inroads being made by the sellers of substitutes; (3) competitive pressures associated with the threat of new entrants into the market; (4) competitive pressures stemming from supplier bargaining power; and (5) competitive pressures stemming from buyer bargaining. The nature and strength of the competitive pressures have to be examined force by force and their collective strength must be evaluated. The strongest forces, however, are the ultimate determinant of the intensity of the competitive pressure on industry profitability. Working through the five-forces model aids strategy-makers in assessing how to insulate the organization from the strongest forces, identify attractive arenas for expansion or alter the competitive conditions so that they offer more favourable prospects for profitability.

3. *What factors are driving changes in the industry, and what impact will these changes have on competitive intensity and industry profitability?* Industry and competitive conditions change because of a variety of forces, some coming from the industry's macro-environment and others originating within the industry. The most common change drivers include changes in the long-term industry growth rate, increasing globalization, changing buyer demographics, technological change, Internet-related developments, product and marketing innovation, entry or exit of major firms, diffusion of know-how, efficiency improvements in adjacent markets, reductions in uncertainty and business risk, government policy changes and changing societal factors. Once an industry's change drivers have been identified, the analytical task becomes one of determining whether they are acting, individually and collectively, to make the industry environment more or less attractive. Are the change drivers causing demand for the industry's product to increase or decrease? Are they acting to make competition more or less intense? Will they lead to higher or lower industry profitability?

4. *What market positions do industry rivals occupy – who is strongly positioned and who is not?* Strategic group mapping is a valuable tool for understanding the similarities, differences, strengths and

weaknesses inherent in the market positions of rival organizations. Rivals in the same or nearby strategic groups are close competitors, whereas organizations in distant strategic groups usually pose little or no immediate threat. The lesson of strategic group mapping is that some positions on the map are more favourable than others. The profit potential of different strategic groups varies due to strengths and weaknesses in each group's market position. Often, industry competitive pressures and change drivers favour some strategic groups and hurt others.

5. *What strategic moves are rivals likely to make next?* Scouting competitors well enough to anticipate their actions can help an organization prepare effective countermoves (perhaps even beating a rival to the punch) and allows managers to take rivals' probable actions into account in designing their own organization's best course of action. Managers who fail to study competitors risk being caught unprepared by the strategic moves of rivals.

6. *What are the key factors for competitive success?* An industry's KSFs are the particular strategy elements, product attributes, operational approaches, resources and competitive capabilities that all industry members must have in order to survive and prosper in the industry. KSFs vary by industry and may vary over time as well. For any industry, however, they can be deduced by answering three basic questions: (1) on what basis do buyers of the industry's product choose between the competing brands of sellers; (2) what resources and competitive capabilities must a organization have to be competitively successful; and (3) what shortcomings are almost certain to put an organization at a significant competitive disadvantage? Correctly diagnosing an industry's KSFs raises an organization's chances of crafting a sound strategy.

7. *Does the outlook for the industry present the organization with sufficiently attractive prospects for profitability?* The last step in industry analysis is summing up the results from answering questions 1–6. If the answers reveal that an organization's overall profit prospects in that industry are above average, then the industry environment is basically attractive *for that organization;* if industry profit prospects are below average, conditions are unattractive for them. What may look like an attractive environment for one organization may appear to be unattractive from the perspective of a different organization.

Clear, insightful diagnosis of an organization's external situation is an essential first step in crafting strategies that are well matched to industry and competitive conditions. To do cutting-edge strategic thinking about the external environment, managers must know what questions to pose and what analytical tools to use in answering these questions. This is why this chapter has concentrated on suggesting the right questions to ask, explaining concepts and analytical approaches and indicating the kinds of things to look for. However, it is important to appreciate that there are a number of different approaches to this task that depend on the nature of the environment facing the organization. In more dynamic, less predictable environments using scenario planning may be an effective way of preparing an organization to exploit future opportunities and minimize threats more effectively. In industries where collaboration is the norm or products rely on a range of complementors to deliver value to the customer, an augmented approach to industry analysis may be needed. In highly competitive industries it may be effective to seek out blue oceans beyond established industry boundaries or find ways of responding to aggressive moves by rivals in these hypercompetitive conditions.

CLOSING CASE

SPOTIFY GO WEST

On 14 July 2011, Daniel Ek, Swedish founder of music streaming service, Spotify, announced that the firm was finally going to launch in the USA. Although this was not seen internally as an essential move, some commentators had already stated that they would judge the firm's overall strategy on how effective they were in breaking into the world's largest music market.

BACKGROUND

Spotify was founded in 2006 by Daniel Ek and Martin Lorentzon, both of whom had a history of launching and working in e-businesses. The two entrepreneurs started out in a small apartment/office with a broken coffee machine and a plan to tackle piracy in the music industry. By 2011 the firm had employed 250 people and had set up headquarters in London following an official launch in 2008. As an online music streaming service, Spotify offered users free access to 13 million tracks by the middle of 2011, provided they listened to advertising in between tracks. They also provided a premium service available for a monthly subscription without adverts.

The company had made a good start generating advertising revenue of £4.5 million and subscriptions of £6.8 million in its first year of operation. However, against this income they had costs of £27.9 million. Spotify needed to generate substantial growth to keep funders such as Hong Kong billionaire Li Ka-Shing, and Northzone Ventures (a venture capital company) satisfied. However, by March 2011 the Anglo-Swedish organization was being valued at £616 million, despite only have converted 10 per cent of its 10 million users to the premium service.

Spotify launched an iPhone app in 2009 to allow users to temporarily download and then listen to music off-line via their mobiles. Spotify felt they had a major advantage due to their agreement with Merlin, a digital music distributor/rights agency, which licensed over 6000 indie labels to the service to give it access to millions of tracks. However, it was agreements with the major labels that would secure their entry into the US market and this had proved harder to achieve. Although Universal stated that they believed Spotify's business model was commercially viable, in February 2010, Warner stated that they would be pulling out of streaming services as they were not providing sufficient income. This was followed in April 2010 by a strongly worded statement from the British Academy of Songwriters, Composers and Authors (BASCA) condemning the tiny payments their members were receiving from streaming websites. In April 2011, Spotify took the controversial step of limiting free access to their website, with users limited to 10 hours per month. It is widely believed that this finally secured the support of the major music labels for entry into the US market.

Not all of Spotify's users were satisfied with streaming and for those that wanted to own the music the firm also launched a premium download service at £9.99 per month. Potentially, this move took them into direct competition with Apple and their market leading service iTunes.

THE DIGITAL MUSIC INDUSTRY

It was at the end of the last century that a 19-year-old undergraduate in Boston turned the music business on its head. In June 1999 Shawn Fanning created the Napster programme and took music-sharing into the Internet age.

By 2011 Napster had become part of the Best Buy group, operating on a legitimate basis as a subscription service charging £5 per month for unlimited streaming plus five mp3 downloads.

Four major labels dominated the content creation element of the music business: Warner, EMI, Universal and Sony. Their reluctance to embrace new digital business models had created opportunities for experimentation in the industry – especially in terms of distribution.

In 2010 the digital music industry was growing globally at over 20 per cent per year and its estimated value was £4.5 billon. Some analysts forecast that the industry could be worth as much as £12.2 billon by 2015. However, these figures represented the legitimate element of the industry that was still plagued by illegal downloading. Most of the income in 2010 was generated by digital music retailers such as iTunes. The digital streaming services, such as Spotify, Last.fm and Pandora, generated much less revenue but were still a rapidly growing part of the sector.

DOWNLOADS

The legitimate digital music sector was dominated by Apple, which had just under 70 per cent of the market in 2011 through the iTunes download to own service. They had similar dominance in the digital music player market with the iPod accounting for 73 per cent of the market. Microsoft's Zune player had only managed to take a 2 per cent share since its launch in 2006 after encountering a number of technical problems.

▶

EXHIBIT 3.1: Digital music industry revenue for major players.

Digital Music Retailers	Revenues 2010 (£m)
iTunes music store	3013
Rhapsody (FY 2009)	98
Napster (FY 2008)	78
eMusic	41
Music Streaming Companies	
Pandora	55
Spotify	52
Last.fm	7

* All figures converted to pounds sterling to allow comparison between firms. Original figures in organization accounts quoted in a variety of currencies).
Source: Business Insights (2011) *The Digital Music Industry Outlook*, Business Insights Ltd, London.

7Digital and Amazon came into the market offering a similar download to own service and were seen as possible challengers to Apple's leadership in this sector. In September 2009 HMV, a traditional music retailer, bought a 50 per cent stake in 7Digital in order to boost its own development of a mobile music download service. The organization had links to Orange through its network of stores. Other mobile organizations such as Nokia were among those offering free music downloads as part of a service bundle with new handsets.

The record labels had also considered how they could tap into the digital music download sector, partly in response to Apple's dominance of the market. In September 2010, Sony announced that it would be launching a music download service to sit alongside its video-on-demand product in the USA by the end of 2010. Sony had previously launched a download service in 2004, but lack of sales led to its closure in 2007.

STREAMING

The free streaming model had proved popular with music fans. By July 2011, Spotify were claiming 10 million users in eight countries and We7 2.5 million in the UK alone. Other players such as MySpace, Mog and Rdio had also joined this market in the period 2008–10. The streaming model had also proved its viability in the USA, with one of the oldest sites, Pandora, finally turning a profit after 10 years' trading in 2010. Pandora's 65 million users provided a strong consumer base to sell to advertisers. Spotify would need to overcome their incumbent advantage to compete successfully in the US market.

Streaming started through computers, but by 2011 was migrating to mobile phones initially through apps on the iPhone and NexusOne. Pandora was also developing an in-car streaming service with Ford in the USA. The record labels were also exploring this part of the distribution element of the business with Sony trialling a streaming service known as bandit.fm in Australia and New Zealand. Even ISPs such as Virginmedia, BT and BSkyB had tried launching music subscription services, although Sky closed their offering at the end of 2010 due to lack of interest.

INTEGRATION

Spotify's move into download services was being matched by retailers moving into streaming, including Apple, whose purchase of Lala had given rise to speculation that they would include a streaming service in their new iCloud service.

DISINTERMEDIATION AND REINTERMEDIATION

In January 2006 the Arctic Monkeys made chart history with the fastest-selling debut album ever in the UK. The band successfully built a substantial fan base on the Internet and through live gigs without having a record deal (they signed to indie label Domino Records in 2005). Other bands such as Groove Armada and Radiohead had also exploited the Internet to market their music in innovative ways.

In contrast to the traditional music supply chain (see Figure 3.7), which meant artists reached the consumer via a record label and bricks and mortar retailer, the digital supply chain offered more routes. Apart from the direct route used by bands such as the Arctic Monkeys, artists could sell their music through aggregators such as CD Baby (who also acted as a retailer). The record labels could still be part of the equation and it appeared that the big losers in the disrupted supply chain were the traditional retailers.

PIRACY AND PROTECTION

Despite the problems high-profile illegal file-sharing sites such as the Pirate Bay had encountered (the owners were fined and jailed over breaches of copyright law and a takeover by a Swedish Games company was

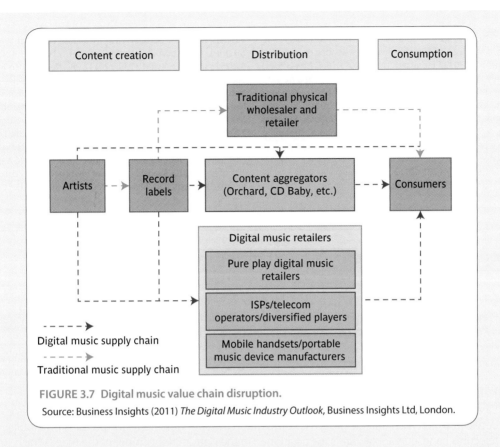

FIGURE 3.7 Digital music value chain disruption.

Source: Business Insights (2011) *The Digital Music Industry Outlook*, Business Insights Ltd, London.

in doubt after the firm's financial viability was brought into question), in 2010 it was estimated that there were 40 illegal downloads for every legal one. In 2008 online music piracy cost the music industry in the UK £180 millon according to estimates from the International Federation of the Phonographic Industry (IFPI). World-wide this amounted to billions of pounds of lost reve-nue for the industry. The main players have continued to lobby governments to tighten up on illegal file-shar-ing and were keen to force ISPs to cut off persistent offenders, although a landmark case in Ireland in October 2010 put this approach in doubt. In any event, neither the prospect of being cut off, nor the high-pro-file prosecutions and swingeing fines imposed in a handful of test cases had deterred the ongoing popu-larity of peer-to-peer (p2p) downloading services. A UK Music survey in 2009 found that over 60 per cent of 18–24-year-olds made use of these services, with the vast majority using them on a weekly basis. Many (over 77 per cent) stated that they still bought CDs and although this market had declined, it still rep-resented a substantial proportion of music sales. Whatever the future held for the music business, there was still a strong imperative to provide services that would compete with piracy and file-sharing. Jon Webster of the Music Managers' Forum offered a stark view of issues, 'The consumer is in a world where they

want things right here, right now, and if you don't give it to them they'll steal it'.

QUESTIONS

1. Using the case study and any other resources you can find on the digital music industry, draw a five-forces diagram for the industry from Spotify's per-spective. Briefly discuss the nature and strength of each of the five competitive forces.

2. What factors are driving change in the industry?

3. Does the five-forces model provide an adequate framework to assess the industry's attractiveness?

4. Using product/service line breadth and degree of diversification into other industries identify poten-tial strategic groups in the industry. Who are Spotify's closest rivals based on this analysis?

Sources: Cellan-Jones, R. (2011) 'Spotify heads West to the US … finally', *BBC News*, 14 July. Available online at: www.bbc.co.uk/news/technology-14157234 (accessed 31 July 2011); Spotify (2011) 'Background information', *Spotify* organization website available at: http://www.spotify.com/uk/about-us/press/background-info/ (accessed 31 July 2011); BBC News (2010) 'Spotify to expand music service despite losses of £16m', *BBC News*, 23 November 2010. Available online at www.bbc.co.uk/news/business-11821021 (accessed 31 July 2011); BBC News

(2011) 'Spotify hits milestone with 1 million subscribers', *BBC News*, 8 March 2011. Available online at www.bbc.co.uk/news/business-12676327 (accessed 31 July 2011); *BBC News* (2011) 'Spotify aims to take market share from iTunes', *BBC News*, 4 May 2011. Available online at www.bbc.co.uk/news/technology-13273135 (accessed 31 July 2011); Business Insights (2011) *The Digital Music Industry Outlook*, Business Insights Ltd, London; Malik, O. (2010) 'Pandora: streaming everywhere on everything,' *Business Week*, 12 January 2010. Available online at www.businessweek.com/technology/content/jan2010/tc201 00112_584610.htm (accessed 31 July 2011); Levy, A. (2010) 'Pandora's next frontier: your wheels', *Business Week*, 14 October 2010. Available online at www.businessweek.com/magazine/content/10_43/b42000 47925283.htm (accessed 31 July 2011); BBC News (2010) 'Irish court rules in favour of ISPs in piracy case', *BBC News*, 12 October 2010. Available online at www.bbc.co.uk/news/technology-11521949 (accessed 31 July 2011); Thompson, B. (2009) 'Downloading is not enough', *BBC News*, 13 August 2009. Available online at news.bbc.co.uk/1/hi/technology/8197574.stm (accessed 31 July 2011); Youngs, I. (2010) 'Warner retreats from free music streaming', *BBC News*, 10 February 2010. Available online at www.news.bbc.co.uk/1/hi/entertainment/ 8507885.stm (accessed 31 July 2011).

ASSURANCE OF LEARNING EXERCISES

LO 3.1, LO 3.2, LO3.3

1. Prepare a brief analysis of the snack-food industry using the information provided on industry trade association websites. On the basis of information provided on these websites, draw a five-forces diagram for the snack-food industry and briefly discuss the nature and strength of each of the five competitive forces. What factors are driving change in the industry?

LO 3.1, LO 3.3, LO 3.4

2. Based on the strategic group map in Illustration Capsule 3.3, who are Apple's closest competitors? Between which two strategic groups is competition the strongest? Why do you think no mobile telecoms handset manufacturers are positioned in the bottom right corner of the map? Which organization/strategic group faces the weakest competition from the members of other strategic groups?

LO 3.1, LO 3.2, LO 3.6

3. Using your knowledge as a snack-food consumer and your analysis of the five forces in that industry (from question 1), describe the key success factors for the snack-food industry. Your list should contain no more than six industry KSFs. In deciding on your list, it is important to distinguish between factors critical for the success of *any* firm in the industry and factors that pertain only to specific organizations.

LO 3.5

4. Choose an emerging industry and comment on how useful the concepts covered in this chapter are in analysing this market.

EXERCISES FOR SIMULATION PARTICIPANTS

LO 3.1, LO 3.2

1. Which of the five competitive forces is creating the strongest competitive pressures for your organization?

   What are the factors affecting the intensity of rivalry in the industry in which your organization is competing. Use the relevant discussion in the chapter to help you pinpoint the specific factors most affecting competitive intensity. Would you characterize the rivalry among the organizations in your industry as brutal, strong, moderate or relatively weak? Why?

LO 3.3

2. Are there any factors driving change in the industry in which your organization is competing? What impact will these drivers of change have? How will they change demand or supply? Will they cause competition to become more or less intense? Will they act to boost or squeeze profit margins? List at least two actions your organization should consider taking in order to combat any negative impacts of the factors driving change.

LO 3.4

3. Draw a strategic group map showing the market positions of the organizations in your industry. Which organizations do you believe are in the most attractive position on the map? Which organizations are the most weakly positioned? Which organizations do you believe are likely to try to move to a different position on the strategic group map?

LO3.6

4. What do you see as the key factors for being a successful competitor in an industry? List at least three.

ENDNOTES

1. Volberda, H.W. (1998) *Building the Flexible Firm*, Oxford, Oxford University Press.

2. For more details on scenario planning, see Schoemaker, P. (1995) 'Scenario planning: a tool for strategic thinking', *Sloan Management Review*, 36(2): 25–40; and Schoemaker, P. and Day, G. (2009) 'Why we miss the signs', *MIT Sloan Management Review*, 50(2): 43–4.

3. Cornelius, P., Van de Putte, A. and Romani, M. (2005) 'Three decades of scenario planning in Shell', *California Management Review*, 48(1): 92–109.

4. For a more extended discussion of the problems with the life-cycle hypothesis, see Porter, Michael E. (1980) *Competitive Strategy: Techniques for Analysing Industries and Competitors*, New York: Free Press, pp. 157–62.

5. The five-forces model of competition is the creation of Professor Michael Porter of the Harvard Business School. See Porter, Michael E. (1979) 'How competitive forces shape strategy', *Harvard Business Review*, 57(2): 137–45; Porter, *Competitive Strategy*, ch. 1; and Porter's most recent discussion of the model (2008) 'The five competitive forces that shape strategy', *Harvard Business Review*, 86(1): 78–93.

6. For a discussion of how an organization's actions to counter the moves of rival firms tend to escalate competitive pressures, see Derfus, Pamela J., Maggitti, Patrick G., Grimm, Curtis M. and Smith, Ken G. (2008) 'The red queen effect: competitive actions and firm performance', *Academy of Management Journal*, 51(1): 61–80.

7. Many of these indicators of whether rivalry produces intense competitive pressures are based on Porter, *Competitive Strategy*, pp. 17–21.

8. *The Economist* (2011) 'An internet with Chinese characteristics', *The Economist*, 30 July: 55–6.

9. Porter, *Competitive Strategy*, p. 7; Porter, 'The five competitive forces that shape strategy', p. 81.

10. The role of entry barriers in shaping the strength of competition in a particular market has long been a standard topic in the literature of micro-economics. For a discussion of how entry barriers affect competitive pressures associated with potential entry, see Bain, J.S. (1956) *Barriers to New Competition*, Cambridge, MA, Harvard University Press); Scherer, F.M. (1971) *Industrial Market Structure and Economic Performance*, Chicago, Rand McNally, pp. 216–20, 226–33; Porter *Competitive Strategy*, pp. 7–17; Porter, 'The five competitive forces that shape strategy', pp. 80–2.

11. For a good discussion of this point, see Yip, George S., (1982) 'Gateways to entry', *Harvard Business Review*, 60(5): 85–93.

12. Montgomery, C.A. and Hariharan, S. (1991) 'Diversified expansion by large established firms', *Journal of Economic Behavior & Organization*, 15(1): 71–89.

13. Porter, 'How competitive forces shape strategy', p. 142; Porter, *Competitive Strategy*, pp. 23–4.

14. Porter, *Competitive Strategy*, p. 10.

15. Ibid., pp. 27–8.

16. Ibid., pp. 24–7.

17. Porter, 'The five competitive forces that shape strategy', p. 80.

18. Roxburgh, C. (2010) 'Five scenario traps to avoid', *McKinsey Quarterly*, 1: 36–7.

19. Most of the candidate driving forces described here are based on the discussion in Porter, *Competitive Strategy*, pp. 164–83.

20. Yoffie, D. (2007) 'Cola Wars continue: Coke and Pepsi in 2006', Harvard Business School case 9-706-447, rev. 2 April; Lynn, B.C. (2009) 'How Detroit went bottom-up', *American Prospect*, October: 21–4.

21. Porter, *Competitive Strategy*, ch. 7.

22. Ibid., pp. 129–30.

23. For an excellent discussion of how to identify the factors that define strategic groups, see Gordon, Mary Ellen and Milne, George R. (1999) 'Selecting the dimensions that define strategic groups: a novel market-driven approach', *Journal of Managerial Issues*, 11(2): 213–33.

24. Porter, *Competitive Strategy*, pp. 152–4.

25. For other benefits of strategic group analysis, see Fiegenbaum, Avi and Thomas, Howard (1995) 'Strategic groups as reference groups: theory, modeling and empirical examination of industry and competitive strategy', *Strategic Management Journal*, 16: 461–76; Olusoga, S. Ade, Mokwa, Michael P. and Noble, Charles H. (1995) 'Strategic groups, mobility barriers, and competitive advantage', *Journal of Business Research*, 33: 153–64.

26. Porter, *Competitive Strategy*, pp. 130, 132–8 and 152–5.

27. For further discussion of legal and ethical ways of gathering competitive intelligence on rival organizations, see Kahaner, Larry (1996) *Competitive Intelligence*, New York, Simon & Schuster.

28. Wernerfelt, B. and Montgomery, C. (1986) 'What is an attractive industry?' *Management Science,* 32(10): 1223–30.

Chapter Four

Evaluating an organization's resources, capabilities and competitiveness

Before executives can chart a new strategy, they must reach common understanding of the company's current position.

W. Chan Kim and Renée Mauborgne
Consultants and INSEAD Professors

Organizations succeed in a competitive marketplace over the long run because they can do certain things their customers value better than can their competitors.

Robert Hayes, Gary Pisano and David Upton
Harvard Business School Professors

You have to learn to treat people as a resource . . . you have to ask not what do they cost, but what is the yield, what can they produce?

Peter F. Drucker
Business Thinker and Management Consultant

Only firms who are able to continually build new strategic assets faster and cheaper than their competitors will earn superior returns over the long term.

C.C. Markides and P.J. Williamson
London Business School Professors and Consultants

Learning Objectives

When you have read this chapter you should be able to:

LO 4.1   Evaluate how well an organization's strategy is working.

LO 4.2   Understand why an organization's resources and capabilities are central to its strategic approach and how to assess their potential for giving the organization a competitive edge over rivals.

LO 4.3   Evaluate the organization's strengths and weaknesses in light of market opportunities and external threats.

LO 4.4   Know how an organization's value chain activities can affect the organization's cost structure, degree of differentiation and competitive advantage.

LO 4.5   Understand how a comprehensive evaluation of an organization's competitive situation can assist managers in making critical decisions about their next strategic moves.

H&M

In terms of sales, Swedish H&M was the second largest actor on the fast fashion market in 2011. This did not mean, however, that they could be complacent about the future. Even with well-established financial, brand and organizational strength there were challenges ahead. Disappointing financial results in 2010 made these issues more tangible. One of these challenges stemmed from the stagnating growth in the established markets in Europe, others from the volatile raw material prices and logistics. These issues were critical for H&M as they held their position against a new range of strong competitors.

H&M engages in designing and retailing fashion apparel and accessories, with an aim to offering fast fashion that is priced considerably lower than designer clothing but is in line with current market trends. Collaborations with upmarket celebrities and guest designers such as Madonna, Karl Lagerfeld and Roberto Cavelli have added a touch of glamour and improved the appeal for the merchandise as a whole.

With retail distribution in 43 countries, the company core is the 140 in-house designers, who work together centrally with buyers and pattern makers at the organizations headquarters. Production is carried out through 16 production offices that work closely with over 700 independent suppliers located in Asia and Europe. The choice of low-cost suppliers places H&M's supply chain management under scrutiny; however, the company claims that they work hard on sustainability and own the responsibility for ensuring that all products are made under good working conditions and with the least possible impact on the environment.

The key to fast fashion is the short production and distribution lead times along with meeting current fashion trends. H&M refreshes the stores with new items daily. While exact times can vary, it takes approximately 15 weeks for H&M to get an item from design to retail. Traditional retail operates with lead times of at least six months. As for many retailers, online presence is increasingly relevant as a distribution channel for H&M with online shopping available in eight major markets.

H&M's attributes its speed to decisiveness. The people in charge of each collection can dream up and produce new fashions on their own authority. Only huge orders require approval from higher up. With a flat organization, decisions are made quickly. This decision-making forms part of the famous H&M team-oriented, entrepreneurial culture. Competitive pressures stem from a range of global and local players; however, Inditex, the parent company of Zara brand, is the strongest direct competitor to H&M. Zara has retail distribution in 77 countries and produces the majority of its designs in European and North African factories rather than outsourcing to cheaper Asian facilities. The Inditex business model is highly vertically integrated and supply chain management is a strong competence. The designers, factories and distribution centres are primarily on-site at its headquarters. The Inidex group directly controls the fabric supply, cutting and finishing while subcontracting the garment-making stage.

Merchandise is delivered from distribution hubs simultaneously to all stores twice a week. An advanced logistics system ensures that the order to delivery time from distribution centres is 24–48 hours. Compared to H&M's 15 weeks lead time, Inditex can get a garment from idea to store in just two weeks.

QUESTIONS

1. What are the main competitive strengths and weaknesses of H&M?

2. In your opinion, how well equipped is H&M to deal with current and future challenges?

Sources: Grant, R.M. (1996) 'Prospering in dynamically-competitive environments: organizational capability as knowledge integration', *Organization Science*, 7: 375–87; CBS H&M case competition. Available online at www.casecompetition.com (accessed 18 January 2012); Cachon, G. and Swimney, R. (2011) 'The value of fast fashion: quick response, enhanced design, and strategic consumer behaviour', *Management Science*, 57(4): 778–95; Bloomsberg Businessweek, 'H&M: It's the latest thing, really', 27 March 2006. Available online at www.businessweek.com/magazine/content/06_13/b3977004.htm; www.inditex.com/en.

In Chapter 3 we described how to use the tools of industry analysis to assess the profit potential and key success factors of an organization's external environment. This laid the groundwork for matching an organization's strategy to its external situation. In this chapter we discuss techniques for evaluating an organization's internal situation, including its collection of resources and capabilities and the activities it performs along its value chain.

Internal analysis enables managers to determine whether their strategy has appealing prospects for giving the organization a significant competitive edge over rival firms. Combined with external analysis, it facilitates an understanding of how to reposition a firm to take advantage of new opportunities and to cope with emerging competitive threats. The analytical spotlight focuses on six questions:

1. How well is the organization's present strategy working?
2. What are the organization's competitively important resources and capabilities?
3. Is the organization able to take advantage of market opportunities and overcome external threats to its well-being?
4. Are the organization's prices and costs competitive with those of key rivals, and does it have an appealing customer value proposition?
5. Is the organization competitively stronger or weaker than key rivals?
6. What strategic issues and problems merit urgent managerial attention?

In probing for answers to these questions, five analytical tools – resource and capability analysis, SWOT analysis, value chain analysis, benchmarking and competitive strength assessment – will be used. All five are valuable techniques for revealing an organization's competitiveness and for helping managers match their strategy to the organization's own particular circumstances.

Question 1: How Well is the Organization's Present Strategy Working?

In evaluating how well an organization's present strategy is working, the best way to start is with a clear view of what the strategy entails. Figure 4.1 shows the key components of a single-business organization's strategy. The first thing to examine is the organization's competitive approach. What moves has the organization made recently to attract customers and improve its market position; for instance, has it cut prices, improved the design of its product, added new features, increased advertising levels, entered a new geographic market (domestic or foreign) or merged with a competitor? Is it striving for a competitive advantage based on low costs or an appealingly different or better product offering? Is it concentrating on serving a broad spectrum of customers or a narrow market niche? The organization's functional strategies in research and development (R&D), production, marketing, finance, human resources (HR), information technology (IT) and so on further characterize organization strategy, as do any efforts to establish competitively valuable alliances or partnerships with other enterprises.

LO 4.1
Evaluate how well an organization's strategy is working.

The two best indicators of how well an organization's strategy is working are (1) whether the organization is achieving its stated financial and strategic objectives and (2) whether the organization is an above-average industry performer. Persistent shortfalls in meeting organization performance targets and weak performance relative to competitors are reliable warning signs that the organization has a weak strategy or suffers from poor strategy execution or both. Other indicators of how well an organization's strategy is working include:

● Whether the firm's sales are growing faster than, slower than, or about the same pace as the market as a whole, thus resulting in a rising, eroding or stable market share.

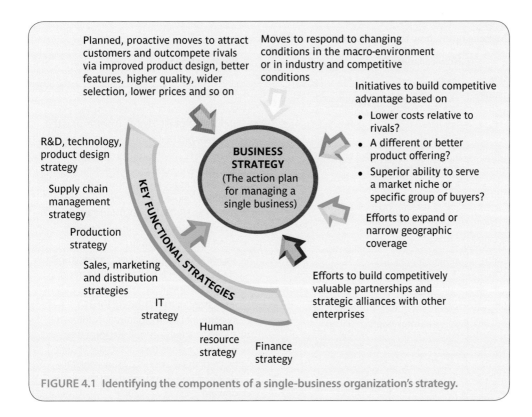

Planned, proactive moves to attract customers and outcompete rivals via improved product design, better features, higher quality, wider selection, lower prices and so on

Moves to respond to changing conditions in the macro-environment or in industry and competitive conditions

Initiatives to build competitive advantage based on

- Lower costs relative to rivals?
- A different or better product offering?
- Superior ability to serve a market niche or specific group of buyers?

Efforts to expand or narrow geographic coverage

R&D, technology, product design strategy

Supply chain management strategy

Production strategy

Sales, marketing and distribution strategies

IT strategy

Human resource strategy

Finance strategy

KEY FUNCTIONAL STRATEGIES

BUSINESS STRATEGY (The action plan for managing a single business)

Efforts to build competitively valuable partnerships and strategic alliances with other enterprises

FIGURE 4.1 Identifying the components of a single-business organization's strategy.

- Whether the organization is acquiring new customers at an attractive rate as well as retaining existing customers.
- Whether the firm's profit margins are increasing or decreasing and how well its margins compare to rival firms' margins.
- Trends in the firm's net profits and return on investment and how they compare to the same trends for other organizations in the industry.
- Whether the organization's overall financial strength and credit rating are improving or declining.
- How shareholders view the organization on the basis of trends in the organization's share prices and shareholder value (relative to the trends at other organizations in the industry).
- Whether the firm's image and reputation with its customers are growing stronger or weaker.
- How well the organization compares to rivals on technology, product innovation, customer service, product quality, delivery time, price, getting newly developed products to market quickly and other relevant factors on which buyers base their choices.
- Whether key measures of operating performance (such as days of inventory, employee productivity, unit cost, defect rate, scrap rate, order-filling accuracy, delivery times and warranty costs) are improving, remaining steady or deteriorating.

The stronger an organization's current overall performance, the less likely the need for radical changes in strategy. The weaker an organization's financial performance and market standing, the more its current strategy must be questioned. Weak performance is almost always a sign of weak strategy, weak execution or both.

Evaluating how well an organization's strategy is working should include quantitative as well as qualitative assessments. Table 4.1 provides a compilation of the financial ratios most commonly used to evaluate an organization's financial performance and balance sheet strength.

> The stronger an organization's financial performance and market position, the more likely it has a well-conceived, well-executed strategy.

TABLE 4.1 Key financial ratios: how to calculate them and what they mean

Ratio	How calculated	What it shows
Profitability ratios		
1. Gross profit margin	$$\frac{\text{Revenues} - \text{Cost of goods sold}}{\text{Revenues}}$$	Shows the percentage of revenues available to cover operating expenses and yield a profit. Higher is better and the trend should be upward
2. Operating profit margin (or return on sales)	$$\frac{\text{Revenues} - \text{Operating expenses}}{\text{Revenues}}$$ *or* $$\frac{\text{Operating income}}{\text{Revenues}}$$	Shows how much profit is earned on each currency unit of sales, before paying interest charges and income taxes. Earnings before interest and taxes are known as *EBIT* in financial and business accounting. Higher is better and the trend should be upward
3. Net profit margin (or net return on sales)	$$\frac{\text{Profits after taxes}}{\text{Revenues}}$$	Shows after-tax profits per currency unit of sales. Higher is better, and the trend should be upward
4. Return on total assets	$$\frac{\text{Profits after taxes} + \text{Interest}}{\text{Total assets}}$$	A measure of the return on total investment in the organization. Interest is added to after-tax profits to form the numerator, since total assets are financed by creditors as well as by shareholders. Higher is better and the trend should be upward
5. Return on shareholder's equity	$$\frac{\text{Profits after taxes}}{\text{Total shareholders equity}}$$	Shows the return shareholders are earning on their investment in the organization. A return in the 12 per cent to 15 per cent range is 'average', and the trend should be upward
6. Return on invested capital	$$\frac{\text{Profits after taxes}}{\text{Long-term debt} + \text{total equity}}$$	Shows how effectively an organization uses the monetary capital invested in its operations and the returns to those investments. Higher is better and the trend should be upward
7. Earnings per share	$$\frac{\text{Profits after taxes}}{\text{Number of shares of common stock outstanding}}$$	Shows the earnings for each share of common stock outstanding. The trend should be upward, and the bigger the annual percentage gains, the better
Liquidity ratios		
1. Current ratio	$$\frac{\text{Current assets}}{\text{Current liabilities}}$$	Shows a firm's ability to pay current liabilities using assets that can be converted to cash in the near term. The ratio should definitely be higher than 1.0; a ratio of 2.0 or higher is better still
2. Working capital	Current assets − Current liabilities	Shows the cash available for a firm's day-to-day operations. Bigger amounts are better because the organization has more internal funds available to (1) pay its current liabilities on a timely basis and (2) finance inventory expansion, additional accounts receivable and a larger base of operations without resorting to borrowing or raising more equity capital

TABLE 4.1 (*Continued*)

Ratio	How calculated	What it shows
Leverage ratios		
1. Debt-to-assets ratio	$$\frac{\text{Total debt}}{\text{Total assets}}$$	Measures the extent to which borrowed funds have been used to finance the firm's operations. A low fraction or ratio is better – a high fraction indicates overuse of debt and greater risk of bankruptcy
2. Long-term debt-to-capital ratio	$$\frac{\text{Long-term debt}}{\text{Long-term debt + Total shareholders' equity}}$$	An important measure of creditworthiness and balance sheet strength. It indicates the percentage of capital investment that has been financed by creditors and bondholders. A ratio below 0.25 is usually preferable since monies invested by shareholders account for 75 per cent or more of the organization's total capital. The lower the ratio, the greater the capacity to borrow additional funds. A debt-to-capital ratio above 0.50 and certainly above 0.75 indicates a heavy and perhaps excessive reliance on debt, lower creditworthiness and weak balance sheet strength
3. Debt-to-equity ratio	$$\frac{\text{Total debt}}{\text{Total shareholders' equity}}$$	Should usually be less than 1.0. A high ratio (especially above 1.0) signals excessive debt, lower creditworthiness and weaker balance sheet strength
4. Long-term debt-to-equity ratio	$$\frac{\text{Long-term debt}}{\text{Total stockholders' equity}}$$	Shows the balance between debt and equity in the firm's *long-term* capital structure. A low ratio indicates greater capacity to borrow additional funds if needed
5. Times-interest-earned (or coverage) ratio	$$\frac{\text{Operating income}}{\text{Interest expenses}}$$	Measures the ability to pay annual interest charges. Lenders usually insist on a minimum ratio of 2.0, but ratios above 3.0 signal better creditworthiness
Activity ratios		
1. Days of inventory	$$\frac{\text{Inventory}}{\text{Cost of goods sold} \div 365}$$	Measures inventory management efficiency. Fewer days of inventory are usually better
2. Inventory turnover	$$\frac{\text{Cost of goods sold}}{\text{Inventory}}$$	Measures the number of inventory turns per year. Higher is better
3. Average collection period	$$\frac{\text{Accounts receivable}}{\text{Total sales} \div 365}$$ *or* $$\frac{\text{Accounts receivable}}{\text{Average daily sales}}$$	Indicates the average length of time the firm must wait after making a sale to receive cash payment. A shorter collection time is better
Other important measures of financial performance		
1. Dividend yield on common stock	$$\frac{\text{Annual dividends per share}}{\text{Current market price per share}}$$	A measure of the return to owners received in the form of dividends

TABLE 4.1 Key financial ratios: how to calculate them and what they mean (*Continued*)

Ratio	How calculated	What it shows
2. Price-earnings ratio	$$\frac{\text{Current market price per share}}{\text{Earnings per share}}$$	A P/E ratio above 20 indicates strong investor confidence in a firm's outlook and earnings growth. Firms whose future earnings are at risk or likely to grow slowly typically have ratios below 12
3. Dividend payout ratio	$$\frac{\text{Annual dividends per share}}{\text{Earnings per share}}$$	Indicates the percentage of after-tax profits paid out as dividends
4. Internal cash flow	After tax profits + Depreciation	A quick and rough estimate of the cash an organization is generating after payment of operating expenses, interest and taxes. Such amounts can be used for dividend payments or funding capital expenditures
5. Free cash flow	After tax profits + Depreciation − Capital Expenditures − Dividends	A quick and rough estimate of the cash an organization is generating after payment of operating expenses, interest, taxes, dividends and desirable reinvestments in the business. The larger an organization's free cash flow, the greater is its ability to internally fund new strategic initiatives, repay debt, make new acquisitions, repurchase shares or increase dividend payments

Core Concept

An organization's resources and capabilities represent its **competitive assets** and are primary determinants of its competitiveness and ability to succeed in the marketplace.

LO 4.2
Understand why an organization's resources and capabilities are central to its strategic approach and how to evaluate their potential for giving the organization a competitive edge over rivals.

Question 2: What are the Organization's Competitively Important Resources and Capabilities?

Regardless of how well the strategy is working, it is important for managers to understand the underlying reasons. Clearly, this is critical if strategy changes are needed. But even when the strategy is working well, this can help managers to bolster a successful strategy and avoid harmful mis-steps. How well a strategy works depends a great deal on the relative strengths and weaknesses of an organization's resources and capabilities. An organization's resources and capabilities are its **competitive assets** and determine whether its competitive power in the marketplace will be impressively strong or disappointingly weak. Organizations with minimal or only ordinary competitive assets nearly always are relegated to a trailing position in the industry.

Resource and capability analysis provides managers with a powerful tool for assessing the organization's competitive assets and determining whether they can provide the foundation necessary for competitive success in the marketplace. This is a two-step process. The first step is for managers to identify the organization's resources and capabilities so that they have a better idea of what they have to work with in crafting the organization's competitive strategy. The second step is to examine the organization's resources and capabilities more closely to ascertain which of them are the most competitively valuable and to determine whether the best of them can help the firm attain a sustainable competitive advantage over rival firms.[1] This step involves applying the *four tests of a resource's competitive power*.

Identifying the Organization's Resources and Capabilities

A firm's resources and capabilities are the fundamental building blocks of its competitive strategy. In crafting strategy, it is essential for managers to be able to recognize a resource or an organizational capability for what it is and to know how to assess the organization's full complement of resources and capabilities. To do a good job with this, managers and strategists need to start with a basic understanding of what these terms mean.

In brief, a **resource** is a productive input or competitive asset that is owned or controlled by the organization. Organizations have many different types of resources at their disposal that vary not only in kind but in quality as well. Some are of a higher quality than others, and some are more competitively valuable, having greater potential to give a firm a competitive advantage over its rivals. For example, an organization's brand is a resource, as is an R&D team – yet some brands such as Coca-Cola and BMW are well known, with enduring value, while others have little more name recognition than generic products. In a similar fashion, some R&D teams are far more innovative and productive than others due to the outstanding talents of the individual team members, the team's composition and its chemistry.

A **capability** is the capacity of a firm to perform some activity proficiently. Capabilities also vary in form, quality and competitive importance, with some being more competitively valuable than others. Apple's product innovation capabilities are widely recognized as being far superior to those of its competitors; Spotify quickly became known for its customer service orientation; PepsiCo is admired for its marketing and brand management capabilities.

Types of Organizational Resources

A useful way to identify an organization's resources is to look for them within categories, as shown in Table 4.2. Broadly speaking, resources can be divided into two main categories: **tangible** and **intangible** resources. Although *human resources* (HR) make up one of the most important parts of an organization's resource base,

> **Core Concept**
>
> **Resource and capability analysis** is a powerful tool for assessing an organization's competitive assets and determining if they can support a sustainable competitive advantage over market rivals.

> A **resource** is a competitive asset that is owned or controlled by an organization; a **capability** is the capacity of a firm to perform some activity proficiently.

TABLE 4.2 Types of organizational resources

Tangible resources
• *Physical resources*: ownership of or access rights to natural resources (such as mineral deposits); state-of-the-art manufacturing plants, equipment and/or distribution facilities; land and real estate; the locations of stores, manufacturing plants or distribution centres, including the overall pattern of their physical locations
• *Financial resources*: cash and cash equivalents; marketable securities; other financial assets such as the borrowing capacity of the firm (as indicated from its balance sheet and credit rating)
• *Technological assets*: patents, copyrights and trade secrets; production technology, stock of other technologies, technological processes
• *Organizational resources*: IT and communication systems (servers, workstations etc.); other planning, co-ordination and control systems; the organizational design and reporting structure

Intangible resources
• *Human assets and intellectual capital*: the experience, cumulative learning and tacit knowledge of employees; the education, intellectual capital and know-how of specialized teams and workgroups; the knowledge of key employees concerning important business functions (e.g. skills in keeping operating costs low, improving product quality and providing customer service); managerial talent; the creativity and innovativeness of certain employees
• *Brands, image, and reputational assets*: brand names, trademarks, product image, buyer loyalty and goodwill; image, reputation for quality, service and reliability; reputation with suppliers and partners for fair dealing
• *Relationships*: alliances or joint ventures that provide access to technologies, specialized know-how or geographic markets; partnerships with suppliers that reduce costs and/or enhance product quality and performance; networks of dealers or distributors; the trust established with various partners
• *Organizational culture and incentive system*: the norms of behaviour, business principles and ingrained beliefs within the organization; the attachment of employees to the organization's ideals; the compensation system and the motivation level of employees

we include them in the intangible category to emphasize the role played by the skills, talents and knowledge of an organization's HR.

Tangible resources are the most easily identified, since tangible resources are those that can be touched or quantified readily. Obviously, they include various types of *physical resources* such as manufacturing facilities and mineral resources, but they also include an organization's *financial resources, technological resources* and *organizational resources* such as the organization's communication and control systems.

Intangible resources are harder to discern, but they are often among the most important of a firm's competitive assets. They include various sorts of *human assets and intellectual capital*, as well as an organization's *brands, image and reputational assets*. While intangible resources have no material existence on their own, they are often embodied in something material. Thus, the skills and knowledge resources of a firm are embodied in its managers and employees; an organization's brand name is embodied in the organization's logo or product labels. Other important kinds of intangible resources include an organization's *relationships* with suppliers, buyers or partners of various sorts and the *organization's culture and incentive system*. A more detailed listing of the various types of tangible and intangible resources is provided in Table 4.2.

Listing an organization's resources category by category can prevent managers from inadvertently overlooking some organizational resources that might be competitively important. At times, it can be difficult to decide exactly how to categorize certain types of resources. For example, resources such as a workgroup's specialized expertise in developing innovative products can be considered to be technological assets or human assets or intellectual capital and knowledge assets; the work ethic and drive of an organization's workforce could be included under the organization's human assets or its culture and incentive system. In this regard, it is important to remember that *it is not exactly how a resource is categorized that matters but, rather, that all of the organization's different types of resources are included in the inventory*. The real purpose of using categories in identifying an organization's resources is to ensure that none of an organization's resources go unnoticed when assessing the organization's competitive assets.

Identifying Capabilities

Organizational capabilities are more complex entities than resources; indeed, they are built up through the use of resources and draw on some combination of the firm's resources as they are exercised.[2] Virtually all organizational capabilities are *knowledge-based, residing in people and in an organization's intellectual capital or in organizational processes and systems, which embody tacit knowledge*. For example, L'Oréal's brand management capabilities draw on the knowledge of the organization's brand managers, the expertise of its marketing department and the organization's relationships with retailers and hair salons, since brand-building is a co-operative activity requiring retailer support. The capability in video game design for which Electronic Arts is known derives from the creative talents and technological expertise of its highly talented game developers, the organization's culture of creativity and a compensation system that generously rewards talented developers for creating best-selling video games.

Because of their complexity, capabilities are harder to categorize than resources and more challenging to search for as a result. There are, however, two approaches that can make the process of uncovering and identifying a firm's capabilities more systematic. The first method takes the completed listing of a firm's resources as its starting point. Since capabilities are built from resources and utilize resources as they are exercised, a firm's resources can provide a strong set of clues about the types of capabilities the firm is likely to have accumulated. This approach simply involves looking over the firm's resources and considering whether (and to what extent) the firm has built up any related capabilities. So, for example, a fleet of trucks, the latest tracking technology and a set of large automated distribution centres may be indicative of sophisticated capabilities in logistics and distribution. R&D teams composed of top scientists with expertise in genomics may suggest organizational capabilities in developing new gene therapies or in biotechnology more generally.

The second method of identifying a firm's capabilities takes a functional approach. Many capabilities relate to fairly specific functions; these draw on a limited set of resources and typically involve a single department or organizational unit. Capabilities in injection moulding or continuous casting or metal stamping are manufacturing-related; capabilities in direct selling, promotional pricing or database marketing all connect to the sales and marketing functions; capabilities in basic research, strategic innovation or new product development link to an organization's R&D function. This approach requires managers to survey the various functions a firm performs to find the different capabilities associated with each function.

A problem with this second method is that many of the most important capabilities of firms are inherently *cross-functional*. Cross-functional capabilities draw on a number of different kinds of resources and are generally multidisciplinary in nature – they arise from the effective collaboration among people with different expertise working in different organizational units. An example is the capability for fast-cycle, continuous product innovation that comes from teaming the efforts of groups with expertise in market research, new product R&D, design and engineering, advanced manufacturing and market testing. Cross-functional capabilities and other complex capabilities involving numerous linked and closely integrated competitive assets are sometimes referred to as **resource bundles**. Although resource bundles are not as easily pigeonholed as other types of resources and capabilities, they can still be identified by looking for organizational activities that link different types of resources, functions and departmental units. It is important not to miss identifying an organization's resource bundles, since they can be the most competitively important of a firm's competitive assets. Unless it includes an organization's cross-functional capabilities and resource bundles, no identification of an organization's resources and capabilities can be considered complete.

> **Core Concept**
>
> A **resource bundle** is a linked and closely integrated set of competitive assets centred around one or more cross-functional capabilities.

Determining Whether an Organization's Resources and Capabilities are Strong Enough to Produce a Sustainable Competitive Advantage

To determine the strategic relevance and competitive power of a firm's resources and capabilities, it is necessary to go beyond merely identifying an organization's resources and capabilities. The second step in resource and capability analysis is designed to ascertain which of an organization's resources and capabilities are competitively valuable and to what extent they can support an organization's quest for a sustainable competitive advantage over market rivals. This involves probing the *calibre* of a firm's competitive assets relative to those of its competitors.[3] When an organization has competitive assets that are central to its strategy and superior to those of rival firms, it has a competitive advantage over other firms. If this advantage proves durable despite the best efforts of competitors to overcome it, then the organization is said to have a *sustainable* **competitive advantage**. While it may be difficult for an organization to achieve a sustainable competitive advantage, it is an important strategic objective because it imparts a potential for attractive and long-lived profitability.

> **Core Concept**
>
> A *sustainable* **competitive advantage** is an advantage over market rivals that persists despite efforts of the rivals to overcome it.

The Four Tests of a Resource's Competitive Power

The competitive power of a resource or capability is measured by how many of the following four tests it can pass.[4] The first two tests determine whether a resource or capability can support a competitive advantage. The last two determine whether the competitive advantage can be sustained in the face of active competition.

1. *Is the resource (or capability) competitively valuable?* To be competitively valuable, a resource or capability must be directly relevant to the organization's strategy, making the organization a more effective competitor, able to exploit market opportunities and ward off external threats. Unless the resource contributes to the effectiveness of the organization's strategy, it cannot pass this first test. An indicator of its effectiveness is whether the resource enables the organization to strengthen its business model through a better customer value proposition and/or profit formula. Organizations have to guard against contending that something they do well is necessarily competitively valuable. Apple's operating system for its PCs is by most accounts superior (compared to Windows Vista and Windows 7), but Apple has so far failed miserably in converting its strength in operating system design into competitive success in the global PC market – it is lagging behind many competitors with a high of 5 per cent market share worldwide.[5]

2. *Is the resource rare – is it something rivals lack?* Resources and capabilities that are common among firms and widely available cannot be a source of competitive advantage. All makers of branded cereals have valuable marketing capabilities and brands, since the key success factors in the ready-to-eat cereal industry demand this. They are not rare. The brand strength of Cheerios, however, is uncommon and has provided Nestlé with a market share as well as the opportunity to benefit from brand extensions like Honey Cheerios. A resource or capability is considered rare if it is held by only a small number of firms in an industry or specific competitive domain. Thus, while general management capabilities are not rare in an absolute sense, they are relatively rare in some of the less-developed regions of the world and in some business domains.

3. *Is the resource hard to copy?* If a resource or capability is both valuable and rare, it will be competitively superior to comparable resources of rival firms. As such, it is a source of competitive advantage for the organization. The more difficult and more costly it is for competitors to imitate, the more likely that it can also provide a *sustainable* competitive advantage. Resources tend to be difficult to copy when they are unique (a fantastic real estate location, patent-protected technology, an unusually talented and motivated labour force), when they must be built over time in ways that are difficult to imitate (a well-known brand name, mastery of a complex process technology, a global network of dealers and distributors) and when they entail financial outlays or large-scale operations that few industry members can undertake. Imitation is also difficult for resources that reflect a high level of *social complexity* (organizational culture, interpersonal relationships among the managers or R&D teams, trust-based relations with customers or suppliers) and *causal ambiguity*, a term that signifies the hard-to-disentangle nature of the complex resources, such as a web of intricate processes enabling new drug discovery. Hard-to-copy resources and capabilities are important competitive assets, contributing to the longevity of an organization's market position and offering the potential for sustained profitability.

4. *Can the resource be trumped by different types of resources and capabilities – are there good substitutes available for the resource?* Even resources and capabilities that are valuable, rare and hard to copy can lose much of their competitive power if rivals have other types of resources and capabilities that are of equal or greater competitive power. An organization may have the most technologically advanced and sophisticated plants in its industry, but any efficiency advantage it enjoys may be nullified if rivals are able to produce equally good products at lower cost by locating their plants in countries where wage rates are relatively low and a labour force with adequate skills is available.

The vast majority of organizations are not well endowed with stand-out resources or capabilities, capable of passing all four tests with high marks. Most firms have a mixed bag of resources – one or two quite valuable, some good, many satisfactory to mediocre. Resources and capabilities that are valuable pass the first of the four tests.

Core Concepts

Social complexity and causal ambiguity are two factors that inhibit the ability of rivals to imitate a firm's most valuable resources and capabilities. Causal ambiguity makes it very hard to figure out how a complex resource contributes to competitive advantage and therefore exactly what to imitate.

As key contributors to the efficiency and effectiveness of the strategy, they are relevant to the firm's competitiveness but are no guarantee of competitive advantage. They may offer no more than competitive parity with competing firms.

Passing both of the first two tests requires more – it requires resources and capabilities that are not only valuable but also rare. This is a much higher hurdle that can be cleared only by resources and capabilities that are *competitively superior.* Resources and capabilities that are competitively superior are the organization's true strategic assets.[6] They provide the organization with a competitive advantage over its competitors, if only in the short run.

To pass the last two tests, a resource must be able to maintain its competitive superiority in the face of competition. It must be resistant to imitative attempts and efforts by competitors to find equally valuable substitute resources. Assessing the availability of substitutes is the most difficult of all the tests since substitutes are harder to recognize, but the key is to look for resources or capabilities held by other firms that *can serve the same function* as the organization's core resources and capabilities.[7]

Very few firms have resources and capabilities that can pass these tests, but those that do enjoy a sustainable competitive advantage with far greater profit potential. IKEA is a notable example, with capabilities in logistics and supply chain management that surpass those of its competitors. Toshiba specializes in flexible manufacturing and is able to switch from one product to another instantly at a low cost. This provides advantage by responding quickly to fast changing market demand, and making profit on low-volume runs.

An Organization's Resources and Capabilities must be Managed Dynamically

Even organizations like IKEA and Toshiba cannot afford to rest on their laurels. Rivals that are initially unable to replicate a key resource may develop better and better substitutes over time. Resources and capabilities can depreciate like other assets if they are managed with benign neglect. Disruptive environmental change can also destroy the value of key strategic assets, turning resources and capabilities 'from diamonds to rust'.[8] Some resources lose their clout quickly when there are rapid changes in technology, customer preferences, distribution channels or other competitive factors.

> An organization requires a dynamically evolving portfolio of resources and capabilities to sustain its competitiveness and help drive improvements in its performance.

For an organization's resources and capabilities to have *durable* value, they must be continually refined, updated and sometimes augmented with altogether new kinds of expertise. Not only are rival organizations endeavouring to sharpen and recalibrate their capabilities, customer needs and expectations are also undergoing constant change. Organizational capabilities grow stale unless they are kept freshly honed and on the cutting edge.[9] An organization's resources and capabilities are far more competitively potent when they are (1) in sync with changes in the organization's own strategy and its efforts to achieve a resource-based competitive advantage and (2) fully supportive of an organization's efforts to attract customers and contest competitors' newly launched offensives to win bigger sales and market shares. Management's challenge in managing the firm's resources and capabilities dynamically has two elements: attending to ongoing recalibration of existing competitive assets and casting a watchful eye for opportunities to develop totally new kinds of capabilities.

The Role of Dynamic Capabilities

Organizations that know the importance of recalibrating and upgrading their most valuable resources and capabilities ensure that these activities are done on a continual basis. By incorporating these activities into their routine managerial functions, they gain the experience necessary to be able to do them consistently well. At that point, their ability to freshen and renew their competitive assets becomes a capability in itself – a **dynamic capability**. A dynamic capability is the ability to modify or augment the organization's

> **Core Concept**
>
> A **dynamic capability** is the capacity of an organization to modify its existing resources and capabilities or create new ones.

existing resources and capabilities.[10] This includes the capacity to improve existing resources and capabilities incrementally, in the way that Roche continually upgrades the global systems connecting its innovation network of independent R&D centres, driving its product innovation strategy. It also includes the capacity to add new resources and capabilities to the organization's competitive asset portfolio. An example is Pfizer's acquisition capabilities, which have enabled it to replace degraded resources such as expiring patents with newly acquired capabilities in biotechnology.

Question 3: Is the organization able to take advantage of market opportunities and Overcome External Threats?

LO 4.3
Evaluate the organization's strengths and weaknesses in light of market opportunities and external threats.

An essential element in evaluating an organization's overall situation entails examining the organization's resources and competitive capabilities in terms of the degree to which they enable it to pursue its best market opportunities and defend against the external threats to its future well-being. The simplest and most easily applied tool for conducting this examination is widely known as *SWOT analysis*, so named because it focuses on an organization's internal **S**trengths and **W**eaknesses, as well as external **O**pportunities and **T**hreats. Just as important, a good SWOT analysis provides the basis for crafting a strategy that capitalizes on the organization's resource strengths, overcomes its resource weaknesses, aims squarely at capturing the organization's best opportunities and defends against the threats to its future well-being.

Identifying an Organization's Internal Strengths

SWOT analysis is a simple but powerful tool for focusing on organization's strengths and weaknesses, its market opportunities and the external threats to its future well-being.

A *strength* is something an organization is particularly good at doing or an attribute that enhances its competitiveness in the marketplace. An organization's strengths depend on the quality of its resources and capabilities. Resource and capability analysis provides a way for managers to assess the quality objectively. While resources and capabilities that pass the four tests of sustainable competitive advantage are among the organization's greatest strengths, other types can be counted among the organization's strengths as well. A capability that is not potent enough to produce a sustainable advantage over rivals may yet enable a series of temporary advantages if used as a basis for entry into a new market or market segment. A resource bundle that fails to match those of top-tier competitors may still allow an organization to compete successfully against the second tier.

Assessing an Organization's Competences – What Activities Does It Perform Well?

Basing an organization's strategy on its most competitively valuable resource and capability strengths gives the organization its best chance for market success.

One way to appraise the degree of an organization's strengths has to do with the organization's competence level in performing key pieces of its business, such as supply chain management, R&D, production, distribution, sales and marketing and customer service. Which activities does it perform especially well? And are there any activities it performs better than rivals? An organization's proficiency in conducting different facets of its operations can range from a mere competence in performing an activity to a core competence to a distinctive competence.

A **competence** is an internal activity an organization performs with proficiency – a capability, in other words. A **core competence** is a proficiently performed internal activity that is *central* to an organization's strategy and competitiveness. Ben & Jerry's Ice Cream, a subsidiary of Unilever, has a core competence in creating unusual flavours of ice cream and marketing them with catchy names like Chunky Monkey, Chubby Hubby, Cherry Garcia, Karamel Sutra and Phish Food. A core competence is a more competitively valuable organizational strength than a competence because of the activity's key role in the organization's strategy and the contribution it makes to the organization's market success and profitability. Often, core competences can be leveraged to create new markets or new product demand, as the engine behind an organization's growth. Toyota has a core competence in continuous improvement and lean manufacturing that is central to its strategy of growing its business.

A **distinctive competence** is a competitively valuable activity that an organization *performs better than its rivals*. A distinctive competence thus signifies greater proficiency than a core competence. Because a distinctive competence represents a level of proficiency that rivals do not have, it qualifies as a *competitively superior strength* with competitive advantage potential. This is particularly true when the distinctive competence enables an organization to deliver exceptional value to customers (in the form of lower prices, better product performance or superior service). For instance, Apple has a distinctive competence in product innovation, as exemplified by its iPod, iPhone and iPad products.

The conceptual differences between a competence, a core competence and a distinctive competence draw attention to the fact that an organization's strengths and competitive assets are not all equal.[11] Some competences merely enable market survival because most rivals have them – indeed, not having a competence or capability that rivals have can result in competitive disadvantage. If an apparel organization does not have the competence to produce its apparel items very cost-efficiently, it is unlikely to survive given the intensely price-competitive nature of the apparel industry. Every web retailer requires a basic competence in designing an appealing and user-friendly website. Core competences are *competitively* more important strengths than competences because they are central to the organization's strategy. Distinctive competences are even more competitively important. Because a distinctive competence is a competitively valuable capability that is unmatched by rivals, it can propel the organization to greater market success and profitability. A distinctive competence is thus potentially the impetus of an organization's success, unless it is trumped by other, even more powerful competences that rivals hold.

Organizational capabilities and competences that become deeply embedded can also have a down side if circumstances change – one time strengths and competitive assets can become *core rigidities*[12] that may hamper and inhibit the competitive position of the organization. Organizations therefore need to renew and replace competences over time to respond to a changing environment and competitive circumstances.

Identifying Organizational Weaknesses and Competitive Deficiencies

A weakness, or *competitive deficiency*, is something an organization lacks or does poorly (in comparison to others) or a condition that puts it at a competitive disadvantage in the marketplace. An organization's internal weaknesses can relate to: (1) inferior or unproven skills, expertise or intellectual capital in competitively important areas of the business; (2) deficiencies in competitively important physical, organizational or intangible assets; or (3) missing or competitively inferior capabilities in key areas. *Organizational weaknesses are thus internal shortcomings that constitute competitive liabilities.* Nearly all organizations have competitive liabilities of one kind or another. Whether an organization's internal weaknesses make it competitively vulnerable depends on how much they matter in the marketplace and whether they are offset by the organization's strengths.

Table 4.3 lists many of the things to consider in compiling an organization's **strengths** and **weaknesses**. Sizing up an organization's complement of strengths and deficiencies is akin to constructing a *strategic balance sheet*, where strengths represent *competitive assets* and weaknesses represent *competitive liabilities*. Obviously, the ideal condition is for the organization's competitive assets to outweigh its competitive liabilities by an ample margin – a 50–50 balance is definitely not the desired condition!

> **Core Concepts**
>
> A **competence** is an activity that an organization has learned to perform with proficiency – a capability, in other words.

> **Core Concept**
>
> A **core competence** is an activity that an organization performs proficiently that is also central to its strategy and competitive success.
>
> A **distinctive competence** is a competitively important activity that an organization performs better than its rivals – it thus represents *a competitively superior internal strength.*

> **Core Concept**
>
> An organization's **strengths** represent its competitive assets; its **weaknesses** are shortcomings that constitute competitive liabilities.

TABLE 4.3 What to look for in identifying an organization's strengths, weaknesses, opportunities and threats

Potential strengths and competitive assets	Potential weaknesses and competitive deficiencies
• Competences that are well matched to industry key success factors	• Competences that are not well-matched to industry key success factors
• Strong financial condition; ample financial resources to grow the business	• In the wrong strategic group _____
• Strong brand-name image/reputation	• Losing market share because
• Attractive customer base	• Lack of attention to customer needs
• Proprietary technology/superior technological skills/ important patents	• Weak balance sheet, short on financial resources to grow the firm, too much debt
• Superior intellectual capital	• Higher overall unit costs relative to those of key competitors
• Skills in advertising and promotion	• Weak or unproven product innovation capabilities
• Strong bargaining power over suppliers or buyers	• A product/service with ho-hum attributes or features inferior to the offerings of rivals
• Product innovation capabilities	• Too narrow a product line relative to rivals
• Proven capabilities in improving production processes	• Weak brand image or reputation
• Good supply chain management capabilities	• Weaker dealer network than key rivals and/or lack of adequate global distribution capability
• Good customer service capabilities	• Behind on product quality, R&D and/or technological know-how
• Superior product quality	• Lack of management depth
• Wide geographic coverage and/or strong global distribution capability	• Inferior intellectual capital relative to rivals
• Alliances/joint ventures that provide access to valuable technology, competences and/or attractive geographic markets	• Plagued with internal operating problems or obsolete facilities
• A product that is strongly differentiated from those of rivals	• Too much underutilized plant capacity
• Cost advantages over rivals	• No well-developed or proven core competences
• Core competences in _____	• No distinctive competences or competitively superior resources
• A distinctive competence in _____	• Resources that are readily copied or for which there are good substitutes
• Resources that are hard to copy and for which there are no good substitutes	• No clear strategic direction
Potential market opportunities	**Potential external threats to an organization's future profitability**
• Openings to win market share from rivals	• Increasing intensity of competition among industry rivals – may squeeze profit margins
• Sharply rising buyer demand for the industry's product	• Slowdowns in market growth
• Unserved customer groups or market segments	• Likely entry of potent new competitors
• Demand in new geographic markets	• Loss of sales to substitute products
• A broader range of customer needs than is currently served	• Growing bargaining power of customers or suppliers
• Online sales via the Internet	• Vulnerability to industry driving forces
• Integrating forward or backward	• Shift in buyer needs and tastes away from the industry's product
• Falling trade barriers in attractive foreign markets	• Adverse demographic changes that threaten to curtail demand for the industry's product

TABLE 4.3 What to look for in identifying an organization's strengths, weaknesses, opportunities and threats (*Continued*)

• Rival firms or organizations open for acquisition with attractive technological expertise or capabilities	• Adverse economic conditions that threaten critical suppliers or distributers
• Potential alliance or joint venture partners to expand the firm's market coverage or boost its competitive capability	• Changes in technology – particularly disruptive technology that can undermine the organization's distinctive competences
• Openings to exploit emerging new technologies	• Restrictive foreign trade policies
	• Costly new regulatory requirements
	• Tight credit conditions
	• Rising prices on energy or other key inputs

Identifying an Organization's Market Opportunities

Market opportunity is a big factor in shaping an organization's strategy. Indeed, managers cannot properly tailor strategy to the organization's situation without first identifying its market opportunities and appraising the growth and profit potential each one holds. Depending on the prevailing circumstances, an organization's opportunities can be plentiful or scarce, fleeting or lasting and can range from wildly attractive (an absolute 'must' to pursue) to marginally interesting (because of the high risks or questionable profit potentials) to unsuitable (because the organization's strengths are ill-suited to successfully capitalizing on the opportunities). A sampling of potential market opportunities is shown in Table 4.3.

Newly emerging and fast-changing markets sometimes present stunningly big or 'golden' opportunities, but it is typically hard for managers at one organization to peer into 'the fog of the future' and spot them much ahead of managers at other organizations.[13] But as the fog begins to clear, golden opportunities are nearly always seized rapidly – and the organizations that seize them are usually those that have been actively waiting, staying alert with diligent market reconnaissance and preparing themselves to capitalize on shifting market conditions by patiently assembling an arsenal of competitively valuable resources – talented personnel, technical know-how, strategic partnerships and cash to finance assertive action when the time comes.[14] In mature markets, unusually attractive market opportunities emerge sporadically, often after long periods of relative calm, but future market conditions may be more predictable, making emerging opportunities easier for industry members to detect.

> An organization is well advised to pass on a particular market opportunity unless it has or can acquire the competences needed to capture it.

In evaluating an organization's market opportunities and ranking their attractiveness, managers have to guard against viewing every *industry* opportunity as an *organizational* opportunity. Not every organization is equipped with the competences to successfully pursue each opportunity that exists in its industry. Some organizations are more capable of going after particular opportunities than others, and a few organizations may be hopelessly outclassed. *The market opportunities most relevant to an organization are those that match up well with the organization's competitive assets, offer the best growth and profitability and present the most potential for competitive advantage.*

Identifying the Threats to an Organization's Future Profitability

Often, certain factors in an organization's external environment pose *threats* to its profitability and competitive well-being. Threats can stem from the emergence of cheaper or better technologies, rivals' introduction of new or improved products, the entry of lower-cost foreign competitors into an organization's market stronghold, new regulations that are more burdensome to an organization than to its competitors, vulnerability to a rise in interest rates or tight credit conditions, unfavourable demographic shifts, adverse changes in foreign exchange rates, political upheaval in a foreign country where the organization has facilities and the like. A list of potential threats to an organization's future profitability and market position is shown in Table 4.3.

External threats may pose no more than a moderate degree of adversity (all organizations confront some threatening elements in the course of doing business), or they may be so imposing as to make an organization's situation and outlook quite tenuous. On rare occasions, market shocks can give birth to a *sudden-death* threat that throws an organization into an immediate crisis and a battle to survive. Many of the world's major airlines were plunged into an unprecedented financial crisis by the perfect storm of 9/11, rising prices for jet fuel, mounting competition from low-fare carriers, shifting traveller preferences for low fares as opposed to lots of in-flight amenities and higher labour costs. Similarly, the global economic crisis that began with the US's mortgage lenders, banks and insurance organizations has produced shock waves from which few industries have been insulated, causing even strong performers like General Electric (GE) to falter. While not all crises can be anticipated, it is management's job to identify the threats to the organization's future prospects and to evaluate what strategic actions can be taken to neutralize or lessen their impact.

What Do the SWOT Listings Reveal?

SWOT analysis involves more than making four lists. The two most important parts of SWOT analysis are *drawing conclusions* from the SWOT listings about the organization's overall situation and *translating these conclusions into strategic actions* to better match the organization's strategy to its internal strengths and market opportunities, to correct important weaknesses and to defend against external threats. Figure 4.2 shows the steps involved in gleaning insights from SWOT analysis.

Just what story the SWOT listings tell about the organization's overall situation is often revealed in the answers to the following set of questions:

- What aspects of the organization's situation are particularly attractive?
- What aspects are of the most concern?
- All things considered, where on a scale of 1 to 10 (where 1 is alarmingly weak and 10 is exceptionally strong) do the organization's overall situation and future prospects rank?
- Are the organization's internal strengths and competitive assets powerful enough to enable it to compete successfully?
- Are the organization's weaknesses and competitive deficiencies mostly inconsequential and readily correctable, or could one or more prove fatal if not remedied soon?
- Do the organization's strengths and competitive assets outweigh its weaknesses and competitive liabilities by an attractive margin?
- Does the organization have attractive market opportunities that are well suited to its internal strengths? Does the organization lack the competitive assets to pursue any of the most attractive opportunities?
- Are the threats alarming, or are they something the organization appears able to deal with and defend against?

The final piece of SWOT analysis is to translate the diagnosis of the organization's situation into actions for improving the organization's strategy and business prospects. *An organization's internal strengths should always serve as the basis of*

> Simply making lists of an organization's strengths, weaknesses, opportunities and threats is not enough; the payoff from SWOT analysis comes from the conclusions about an organization's situation and the implications for strategy improvement that flow from the four lists.

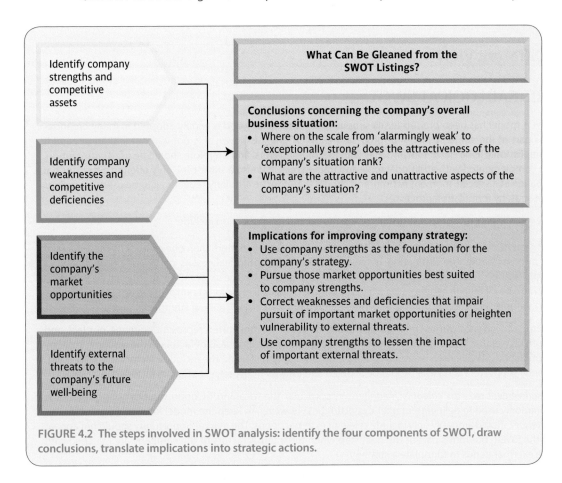

FIGURE 4.2 The steps involved in SWOT analysis: identify the four components of SWOT, draw conclusions, translate implications into strategic actions.

its strategy – placing heavy reliance on an organization's best competitive assets is the soundest route to attracting customers and competing successfully against rivals.[15] As a rule, strategies that place heavy demands on areas where the organization is weakest or has unproven competences are suspect and should be avoided. Plainly, managers have to look towards correcting competitive weaknesses that make the organization vulnerable, hold down profitability or disqualify it from pursuing an attractive opportunity. Furthermore, strategy has to be aimed at capturing those market opportunities that are most attractive and suited to the organization's collection of competences. How much attention to devote to defending against external threats to the organization's market position and future performance hinges on how vulnerable the organization is, whether there are attractive defensive moves that can be taken to lessen their impact and whether the costs of undertaking such moves represent the best use of competitive assets.

Question 4: Are the Organization's Prices and Costs Competitive with Those of Key Rivals, and Does It Have an Appealing Customer Value Proposition?

Managers are often stunned when a competitor cuts its price to 'unbelievably low' levels or when a new market entrant comes on strong with a very low price. The competitor may not, however, be 'dumping' (an economic term for selling at prices that are

LO 4.4 Know how an organization's value chain activities can affect the organization's cost structure, degree of differentiation and competitive advantage.

A Different View

A CRITICAL LOOK AT SWOT

The SWOT model has been praised for its simplicity and practicality and is widely adopted in many organizations as part of the strategic planning process. The SWOT analysis however is not without limitations, and if used simplistically it is a 'naïve' tool and may lead to strategic errors, and therefore should be used with caution, and be complemented with additional tools and frameworks. It is also a static tool, only offering a snapshot of the situation at a specific moment in time, and should therefore be regularly repeated if to be used as a serious input in strategy formulation processes.

The most widely recognized shortfalls of the model and its application include:

● *Inadequate definition of factors* – some factors may appear to fit in more than one category, others may not fit into any easily. The distinction between factors as strength/weakness is particularly problematic as many factors can be seen as possessing some elements of both. The external versus internal classification can also be difficult in certain cases when the degree of the organization's control of the factor is debatable, for example when image or reputation are deemed to be an organizational strength.

● *Factors are included without prioritizing and are subjective* – factors often represent opinions, not fact, and often no weightings are given. This can lead to over- or under-emphasis of factors in the resulting strategy formulation. SWOT analysis should therefore be a group activity, and the included factors should be sufficiently supported. Long lists should be avoided and only the most relevant factors included in a SWOT.

● *Disagreement over the category meanings*, in particular the meaning of 'opportunities': opportunities is commonly used to delineate 'market opportunities'; however, to keep the model internally consistent this category should arguably only include 'relevant external trends'. The market opportunity should not appear in the SWOT, but forms part of the next step when the internal factors of the company are matched with the external trends to formulate a strategy.

Sources: Pickton, D.W. and Wright, S. (1998) 'What's swot in strategic analysis?' *Strategic Change*, 7: 101–9; Hill, T. and Westbrook, R. (1997) 'SWOT analysis: it's time for a product recall', *Long Range Planning*, 30(1): 46–52.

---

below cost), buying its way into the market with a super-low price, or waging a desperate move to gain sales – it may simply have substantially lower costs. One of the most telling signs of whether an organization's business position is strong or precarious is if its prices and costs can remain competitive with industry rivals. For an organization to retain its market share, its costs must be *in line* with those of close rivals selling similar quality products.

While less common, new entrants can also enter the market with a product that pushes the quality level up so high that customers will abandon competing sellers even if they have to pay more for the new product. With its vastly greater storage capacity and lightweight, cool design, Apple's iPod left other makers of portable digital music players in the dust when it was first introduced. By introducing new models with even more attractive features, Apple has continued its world-wide dominance of this market. Apple's new iPad is doing the same in the market for e-readers and tablet PCs.

> The higher an organization's costs are above those of close rivals, the more competitively vulnerable it becomes.

Regardless of where on the quality spectrum an organization competes, it must also remain competitive in terms of its customer value proposition in order to stay in the game. Harrod's value proposition, for example, remains attractive to customers who want customer service, the assurance of quality and a high-status experience. Tesco's customer value proposition has done less well against the Aldi and Lidl low-price juggernaut despite attention to locally adapted product selection and pricing.

The value provided to the customer depends on how well a customer's needs are met for the price paid. How well customer needs are met depends on the perceived quality of a product or service as well as other, more tangible attributes. The greater the amount of customer value that the organization can offer profitably compared to its rivals, the less vulnerable it will be to competitive attack. For managers, the key is to keep close track of how *cost-effectively* the organization can deliver value to customers relative to its competitors. If they can deliver the same amount of value with lower expenditures (or more value at the same cost), they will maintain a competitive edge.

> The greater the amount of customer value that an organization can offer profitably relative to close rivals, the less competitively vulnerable it becomes.

Two analytical tools are particularly useful in determining whether an organization's prices, costs and customer value proposition are competitive: value chain analysis and benchmarking.

The Concept of a Value Chain

Every organization consists of a collection of activities undertaken in the course of designing, producing, marketing, delivering and supporting its product or service. All the various activities that an organization performs internally combine to form a **value chain** – so called because the underlying intent of an organization's activities is to do things that ultimately *create value for buyers*.

> **Core Concept**
>
> An organization's **value chain** identifies the primary activities that create customer value and the related support activities.

As shown in Figure 4.3, an organization's value chain consists of two broad categories of activities: the *primary activities* that are foremost in creating value for customers and the requisite *support activities* that facilitate and enhance the performance of the primary activities.[16] The exact nature of the primary and secondary activities that make up an organization's value chain vary according to the specifics of an organization's business; hence, the listing of the primary and support activities in Figure 4.3 is illustrative rather than definitive. For example, the primary value-creating activities for a manufacturer of bakery goods, such as Finnish Fazer, exporting to 15 countries, include supply chain management, baking and packaging operations, distribution and sales and marketing but are unlikely to include retail sales service. Its support activities include quality control as well as product R&D, HR management and administration. For a department store retailer, such as Debenham's, customer service is included among its primary activities, along with merchandise selection and buying, store layout and product display and advertising; its support activities include site selection, hiring and training and store maintenance, plus the usual assortment of administrative activities. For a hotel chain like Marriot, the primary activities and costs are in site selection and construction, reservations, operation of its hotel properties and marketing; principal support activities include accounting, hiring and training hotel staff, supply chain management and general administration.

With its focus on value-creating activities, the value chain is an ideal tool for examining how an organization delivers on its customer value proposition. It permits a deep look at the organization's cost structure and ability to offer low prices. It reveals the emphasis that an organization places on activities that enhance differentiation and support higher prices, such as service and marketing. Note that there is also a profit margin component to the value chain; this is because profits are necessary to compensate the organization's owners/shareholders and investors, who bear risks and provide capital. Tracking the profit margin along with the value-creating activities is critical because unless an enterprise succeeds in delivering customer value profitably (with a sufficient return on invested capital), it cannot survive for long. This is the essence of a sound business model.

Illustration Capsule 4.1 shows representative costs for various activities performed by Just Coffee, a co-operative producer and roaster of fair-trade organic coffee.

Comparing the Value Chains of Rival Organizations

The primary purpose of value chain analysis is to facilitate a comparison, activity-by-activity, of how effectively and efficiently an organization delivers value to its

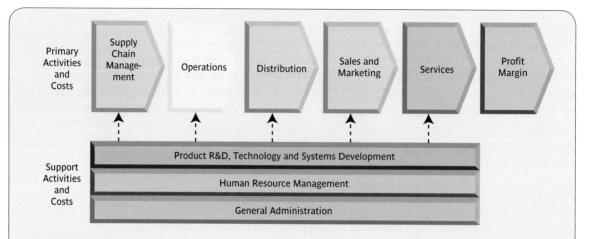

PRIMARY ACTIVITIES

- **Supply chain management** – Activities, costs and assets associated with purchasing fuel, energy, raw materials, parts and components, merchandise and consumable items from vendors; receiving, storing and disseminating inputs from suppliers; inspection; and inventory management.

- **Operations** – Activities, costs and assets associated with converting inputs into final product from (production, assembly, packaging, equipment maintenance, facilities, operations, quality assurance, environmental protection).

- **Distribution** – Activities, costs and assets dealing with physically distributing the product to buyers (finished goods warehousing, order processing, order picking and packing, shipping, delivery vehicle operations, establishing and maintaining a network of dealers and distributors).

- **Sales and Marketing** – Activities, costs and assets related to salesforce efforts, advertising and promotion, market research and planning and dealer/distributor support.

- **Service** – Activities, costs and assets associated with providing assistance to buyers, such as installation, spare parts delivery, maintenance and repair, technical assistance, buyer inquiries and compliants.

SUPPORT ACTIVITIES

- **Product R&D, Technology and Systems Development** – Activities, costs and assets relating to product R&D, process R&D, process design improvement, equipment design, computer software development, telecommunications systems, computer-assisted design and engineering, database capabilities and development of computerized support systems.

- **Human Resources Management** – Activities, costs and assets associated with the recruitment, hiring, training, development and compensation of all types of personnel; labour relations activities; and development of knowledge-based skills and core competences.

- **General Administration** – Activities costs and assets relating to general management, accounting and finance, legal and regulatory affairs, safety and security, management information systems, forming strategic alliances and collaborating with strategic partners and other 'overhead' functions.

FIGURE 4.3 A representative organizational value chain.

Source: Based on the discussion in Porter, Michael E. (1985) *Competitive Advantage,* New York, Free Press, pp. 37–43.

customers, relative to its competitors. Segregating the organization's operations into different types of primary and secondary activities is the first step in this comparison. The next is to do the same for the organization's most significant competitors.

Even rivals in the same industry may differ significantly in terms of the activities they perform. For instance, the 'operations' component of the value chain for a manufacturer that makes all of its own parts and components and assembles them into a finished product differs from the 'operations' of a rival producer that buys the needed

---

THE VALUE CHAIN FOR JUST COFFEE, A PRODUCER OF FAIR-TRADE ORGANIC COFFEE

Value chain activities and costs in producing, roasting and selling a 450 g bag of fair-trade organic coffee

1. Average cost of procuring the coffee from coffee-grower co-operatives	2.30
2. Import fees, storage costs and freight charges	.73
3. Labour cost of roasting and bagging	.89
4. Cost of labels and bag	.45
5. Average overhead costs	<u>3.03</u>
6. Total company costs	7.40
7. Average retail mark-up over company costs (company operating profit)	<u>2.59</u>
8. Average price to consumer at retail	9.99

Source: Developed by the authors with help from Jonathan D. Keith from information on Just Coffee's website, www.justcoffee.coop/the_coffee_dollar_breakdown (accessed 16 June 2010).

---

parts and components from outside suppliers and only performs assembly operations. How each activity is performed may affect an organization's relative cost position as well as its capacity for differentiation. Thus, even a simple comparison of how the activities of rivals' value chains differ can be revealing of competitive differences.

An Organization's Primary and Secondary Activities Identify the Major Components of Its Internal Cost Structure

Each activity in the value chain gives rise to costs and ties up assets. For an organization to remain competitive, it is critical for it to perform its activities cost-effectively, regardless of which it chooses to emphasize. Once the major value chain activities are identified, the next step is to evaluate the organization's cost competitiveness using what accountants call *activity-based costing* to determine the costs of performing each value chain activity (and assets required, including working capital).[17] The degree to which an organization's costs should be disaggregated into specific activities depends on how valuable it is to develop cost data for narrowly defined activities as opposed to broadly defined activities. Generally speaking, cost estimates are needed at least for each broad category of primary and secondary activities, but finer classifications may be needed if an organization discovers that it has a cost disadvantage *vis-à-vis* rivals and wants to pin down the exact source or activity causing the disadvantage. Quite often, there are links between activities such that the manner in which one activity is done can affect the costs of performing other activities. For instance, how a car is designed has a huge impact on the number of different parts and components, their respective manufacturing costs and the expense of assembling the various parts and components into a finished product.

The combined costs of all the various activities in an organization's value chain define the organization's internal cost structure. Further, the cost of each activity contributes to whether the organization's overall cost position relative to rivals is favourable or unfavourable. But an organization's own internal costs are insufficient to assess whether its costs are competitive with those of rivals. Cost and price differences among competing organizations can have their origins in activities performed by suppliers or by distribution allies involved in getting the product to the final customer or end-user of the product, in which case the organization's entire value chain system becomes relevant.

The Value Chain System for an Entire Industry

> An organization's cost competitiveness depends not only on the costs of internally performed activities (its own value chain) but also on costs in the value chains of its suppliers and distribution channel allies.

A company's value chain is embedded in a larger system of activities that includes the value chains of its suppliers and the value chains of whatever wholesale distributors and retailers it utilizes in getting its product or service to end-users. This *value chain system* has implications that extend far beyond the organization's costs. It can affect attributes like product quality that enhance differentiation and have importance for the organization's customer value proposition as well as its profitability.[18] Suppliers' value chains are relevant because suppliers perform activities and incur costs in creating and delivering the purchased inputs utilized in an organization's own value-creating activities. The costs, performance features and quality of these inputs influence an organization's own costs and product differentiation capabilities. Anything an organization can do to help its suppliers drive down the costs of their value chain activities or improve the quality and performance of the items being supplied can enhance its own competitiveness – a powerful reason for working collaboratively with suppliers in managing supply chain activities.[19]

Similarly, the value chains of an organization's distribution channel partners are relevant because (1) the costs and margins of an organization's distributors and retail dealers are part of the price the ultimate consumer pays and (2) the activities that distribution allies perform affect sales volumes and customer satisfaction. For these reasons, organizations normally work closely with their distribution allies (who are their direct customers) to perform value chain activities in mutually beneficial ways. For instance, motor vehicle manufacturers have a competitive interest in working closely with their car dealers to promote higher sales volumes and better customer satisfaction with dealers' repair and maintenance services. Producers of bathroom fixtures are heavily dependent on the sales and promotional activities of their distributors and building supply retailers and on whether distributors/retailers operate cost-effectively enough to be able to sell at prices that lead to attractive sales volumes.

As a consequence, *accurately assessing an organization's competitiveness entails scrutinizing the nature and costs of value chain activities throughout the entire value chain system for delivering its products or services to end-use customers.* A typical industry value chain system that incorporates the value chains of suppliers and forward channel allies (if any) is shown in Figure 4.4. As was the case with company value chains, the specific activities constituting industry value chains also vary significantly. The primary value chain system activities in the pulp and paper industry

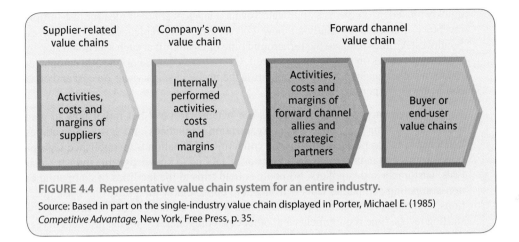

FIGURE 4.4 **Representative value chain system for an entire industry.**

Source: Based in part on the single-industry value chain displayed in Porter, Michael E. (1985) *Competitive Advantage,* New York, Free Press, p. 35.

(timber farming, logging, pulp mills and papermaking) differ from the primary value chain system activities in the home appliance industry (parts and components manufacture, assembly, wholesale distribution, retail sales). The value chain system in the soft-drink industry (syrup manufacture, bottling and can filling, wholesale distribution, advertising and retail merchandising) differs from that in the computer software industry (programming, disk loading, marketing, distribution).

Benchmarking: A Tool for Assessing Whether the Costs and Effectiveness of an Organization's Value Chain Activities are in Line

Once an organization has developed good estimates for the costs and effectiveness of each of the major activities in its own value chain and has sufficient data relating to the value chain activities of suppliers and distribution allies, then it is ready to explore how it compares on these dimensions with key rivals. This is where benchmarking comes in. **Benchmarking** entails comparing how different organizations perform various value chain activities – how inventories are managed, how products are assembled, how fast the organization can get new products to market, how customer orders are filled and shipped – and then making cross-organizational comparisons of the costs and effectiveness of these activities.[20] The objectives of benchmarking are to identify the best practices in performing an activity, to learn how other organizations have actually achieved lower costs or better results in performing benchmarked activities and to take action to improve an organization's competitiveness whenever benchmarking reveals that its costs and results of performing an activity are not on a par with what other organizations have achieved.

> **Core Concept**
>
> **Benchmarking** is a potent tool for improving an organization's own internal activities that is based on learning how other organizations perform them and borrowing their 'best practices'.

Xerox became one of the first organizations to use benchmarking in 1979 when Japanese manufacturers began selling mid-size copiers in the USA for $9600 each – less than Xerox's production costs.[21] Xerox management suspected its Japanese competitors were dumping, but it sent a team of line managers to Japan, including the head of manufacturing, to study competitors' business processes and costs. With the aid of Xerox's joint venture partner in Japan, Fuji-Xerox, which knew the competitors well, the team found that Xerox's costs were excessive due to gross inefficiencies in the company's manufacturing processes and business practices. The findings triggered a major internal effort at Xerox to become cost-competitive and prompted Xerox to begin benchmarking 67 of its key work processes against organizations identified as employing the best practices. Xerox quickly decided not to restrict its benchmarking efforts to its office equipment rivals but to extend them to any organization regarded as 'world class' in performing *any activity* relevant to Xerox's business. Other organizations quickly picked up on Xerox's approach. Toyota managers got their idea for just-in-time inventory deliveries by studying how US supermarkets replenished their shelves. Southwest Airlines reduced the turnaround time of its aircraft at each scheduled stop by studying pit crews on the racing car circuit. Over 80 per cent of Fortune 500 companies reportedly use benchmarking for comparing themselves against rivals on cost and other competitively important measures.

> Benchmarking the costs of organizational activities against rivals can provide hard evidence of whether an organization is cost-competitive.

The tough part of benchmarking is not whether to do it but rather how to gain access to information about other organization's practices and costs. Sometimes benchmarking can be accomplished by collecting information from published reports, trade groups and industry research firms or by talking to knowledgeable industry analysts, customers and suppliers. Sometimes field trips to the facilities of competing or non-competing companies can be arranged to observe how things are done, ask questions, compare practices and processes, and perhaps exchange data on productivity, staffing levels, time requirements and other cost components – but the problem here is that such organizations, even if they agree to host facilities tours and answer questions, are unlikely to share competitively sensitive cost information. Furthermore, comparing one organization's costs to another's costs may not involve comparing apples to apples if the two organizations employ different cost accounting principles to calculate the costs of particular activities.

However, a third and fairly reliable source of benchmarking information has emerged. The explosive interest of organizations in benchmarking costs and best practices has prompted numerous consulting firms and business organizations (e.g. Accenture, A.T. Kearney, Benchmark Consulting International, Comparison International) to gather benchmarking data, distribute information about best practices and provide comparative cost data without identifying the names of particular organizations. Having an independent group gather the information and report it in a manner that disguises the names of individual organizations protects competitively sensitive data and lessens the potential for unethical behaviour on the part of employees in gathering their own data about competitors. Illustration Capsule 4.2 presents a widely recommended European code of conduct for engaging in benchmarking.

Strategic Options for Remedying a Disadvantage in Costs or Effectiveness

Examining the costs of an organization's own value chain activities and comparing them to rivals' indicates who has how much cost advantage or disadvantage and which cost components are responsible. Similarly, much can be learned by comparisons at the activity level of how effectively an organization delivers on its value proposition relative to its competitors and which elements in its value chain system are responsible. Such information is vital in strategic actions to eliminate a cost disadvantage, deliver more customer value, enhance differentiation and improve profitability. Such information can also help an organization to recognize and reinforce activities in which it has a comparative advantage and to find new avenues for enhancing its competitiveness through lower costs, greater differentiation or a more attractive customer value proposition. There are three main areas in an organization's total value chain system where managers can try to improve its efficiency and effectiveness: (1) an organization's own activity segments; (2) suppliers' part of the overall value chain; and (3) the distribution channel portion of the chain.

Improving the Efficiency and Effectiveness of Internally Performed Value Chain Activities

Managers can pursue any of several strategic approaches to reduce the costs of internally performed value chain activities and improve an organization's cost competitiveness:[22]

Illustration Capsule 4.2

BENCHMARKING AND ETHICAL CONDUCT

Because discussions between benchmarking partners can involve competitively sensitive data, conceivably raising questions about possible restraint of trade or improper business conduct, many benchmarking organizations urge all individuals and organizations involved in benchmarking to abide by a code of conduct grounded in ethical business behaviour. The European benchmarking code of conduct is closely based on the widely used APQC/SPI Code of Conduct promoted by the International Benchmarking Clearinghouse. The wording has been modified to take into account the rules of European Union competition law. It is based on the following principles and guidelines:

- Avoid discussions or actions that could lead to or imply an interest in restraint of trade, market and/or customer allocation schemes, price fixing, dealing arrangements, bid rigging, or bribery. Don't discuss costs with competitors if costs are an element of pricing.

- Refrain from the acquisition of trade secrets from another by any means that could be interpreted as improper, including the breach of any duty to maintain secrecy. Do not disclose or use any trade secret that may have been obtained through improper means or that was disclosed by another in violation of duty to maintain its secrecy or limit its use.

- Be willing to provide to your benchmarking partner the same type and level of information that you request from that partner.

- Communicate fully and early in the relationship to clarify expectations, avoid misunderstanding, and establish mutual interest in the benchmarking exchange.

- Be honest and complete with the information submitted.

- The use or communication of a benchmarking partner's name with the data obtained or practices observed requires the prior permission of the benchmarking partner.

- Honour the wishes of benchmarking partners regarding how the information that is provided will be handled and used.

- In benchmarking with competitors, establish specific ground rules up front. For example, 'We don't want to talk about things that will give either of us a competitive advantage, but rather we want to see where we both can mutually improve or gain benefit'.

- Check with legal counsel if any information-gathering procedure is in doubt. If uncomfortable, do not proceed. Alternatively, negotiate and sign a specific nondisclosure agreement that will satisfy the attorneys representing each partner.

- Do not ask competitors for sensitive data or cause benchmarking partners to feel they must provide data to continue the process.

- Use an ethical third party to assemble and 'blind' competitive data, with inputs from legal counsel in direct competitor sharing. (Note: When cost is closely linked to price, sharing cost data can be considered to be the same as sharing price data.)

- Any information obtained from a benchmarking partner should be treated as internal, privileged communications. If 'confidential' or proprietary material is to be exchanged, then a specific agreement should be executed to specify the content of the material that needs to be protected, the duration of the period of protection, the conditions for permitting access to the material, and the specific handling requirements necessary for that material.

Sources: APQC, www.apqc.org; Qualserve Benchmarking Clearinghouse, www.awwa.org (accessed 8 October 2010); Best Practice Club, www.bpclub.com (accessed 29 January 2012).

1. Implement the use of best practices throughout the organization, particularly for high-cost activities.

2. Redesign the product and/or some of its components to eliminate high-cost components or facilitate speedier and more economical manufacture or assembly –

computer-chip makers regularly design around the patents held by others to avoid paying royalties; car-makers have substituted lower-cost plastic and rubber for metal at many exterior body locations.

3. Relocate high-cost activities (such as manufacturing) to lower cost geographic areas.

4. See if certain internally performed activities can be outsourced from vendors or performed by contractors more cheaply than they can be done in-house.

5. Shift to lower-cost technologies and/or invest in productivity-enhancing, cost-saving technological improvements (robotics, flexible manufacturing techniques, state-of-the-art information systems).

6. Stop performing activities that add little or no customer value. Examples include seldom-used customer services, training programmes that are of marginal value and maintaining large raw material or finished-goods inventories.

How successfully an organization competes depends on more than low costs. It also depends on how effectively it delivers value to the customer and on its ability to differentiate itself from rivals. To improve the effectiveness of its customer value proposition and enhance differentiation, there are several approaches a manager can take:[23]

1. Implement the use of best practices for quality throughout the organization, particularly for high-value activities (those that are important for creating value for the customer).

2. Adopt best practices and technologies that spur innovation, improve design and enhance creativity.

3. Implement the use of best practices in providing customer service.

4. Reallocate resources to devote more to activities that will have the biggest impact on the value delivered to the customer and that address buyers' most important purchase criteria.

5. For intermediate buyers (distributors or retailers, for example), gain an understanding of how the activities the organization performs impact the buyer's value chain. Improve the effectiveness of organizational activities that have the greatest impact on the efficiency or effectiveness of the buyer's value chain.

6. Adopt best practices for signalling the value of the product and for enhancing customer perceptions.

Improving the Efficiency and Effectiveness of Supplier-related Value Chain Activities

Improving the efficiency and effectiveness of the value chain activities of suppliers can also address an organization's competitive weaknesses with respect to costs and differentiation. On the cost side, an organization can gain savings in suppliers' part of the overall value chain by pressuring suppliers for lower prices, switching to lower-priced substitute inputs and collaborating closely with suppliers to identify mutual cost-saving opportunities.[24] For example, just-in-time deliveries from suppliers can lower an organization's inventory and internal logistics costs and may also allow suppliers to economize on their warehousing shipping and production scheduling costs – a win-win outcome for both. In a few instances, organizations may find that it is cheaper to integrate backward; into the business of high-cost suppliers and make the item in-house instead of buying it from outsiders.

Similarly, an organization can enhance its differentiation by working with or through its suppliers to do so. Some methods include selecting and retaining suppliers who meet higher-quality standards, co-ordinating with suppliers to enhance design or other features desired by customers, providing incentives to encourage suppliers to meet higher-quality standards and assisting suppliers in their efforts to improve. Fewer defects in parts from suppliers not only improve quality and enhance differentiation throughout the value chain system but can lower costs as well since there is less waste and disruption to the production processes.

Improving the Efficiency and Effectiveness of Distribution-related Value Chain Activities

Taking actions aimed at improvements with respect to the forward or downstream portion of the value chain system can also help to remedy an organization's competitive disadvantage with respect to either costs or differentiation. Any of three means can be used to achieve better cost competitiveness in the forward portion of the industry value chain: (1) pressure distributors, dealers and other forward channel allies to reduce their costs and mark-ups so as to make the final price to buyers more competitive with the prices of rivals; (2) collaborate with forward channel allies to identify win-win opportunities to reduce costs – a chocolate manufacturer, for example, learned that by shipping its bulk chocolate in liquid form in tank cars instead of as 4.5 kg moulded bars, it could not only save its chocolate-bar manufacturing customers the costs associated with unpacking and melting but also eliminate its own costs of moulding bars and packing them; and (3) change to a more economical distribution strategy, including switching to cheaper distribution channels (perhaps direct sales via the Internet) or perhaps integrating forward into company-owned retail outlets.

The means to enhance differentiation through activities at the forward end of the value chain system include: (1) engaging in co-operative advertising and promotions with forward allies (dealers, distributors, retailers, etc.); (2) creating exclusive arrangements with downstream sellers or other mechanisms that increase their incentives to enhance delivered customer value; and (3) creating and enforcing standards for downstream activities and assisting in training channel partners in business practices. Harley-Davidson, for example, enhances the shopping experience and perceptions of buyers by selling through retailers that sell Harley-Davidson motorcycles exclusively and meet Harley-Davidson standards.

Translating Proficient Performance of Value Chain Activities into Competitive Advantage

Value chain analysis and benchmarking are not only useful for identifying and remedying competitive disadvantages; they can also be used to uncover and strengthen competitive advantages. An organization's value-creating activities can offer a competitive advantage in one of two ways: (1) they can contribute to greater efficiency and lower costs relative to competitors; or (2) they can provide a basis for differentiation, so customers are willing to pay relatively more for the organization's goods and services. An organization that does a *first-rate job* of managing its value chain activities *relative to competitors* stands a good chance of profiting from its competitive advantage.

Achieving a cost-based competitive advantage requires determined organizational efforts to be cost-efficient in performing value chain activities. Such efforts have to be ongoing and persistent, and they have to involve each and every value chain activity. The goal must be a continuous cost reduction, not a one-time or on-again–off-again effort. Organizations whose managers are truly committed to low-cost performance of value chain activities and succeed in engaging employees to discover innovative ways to drive costs out of the business have a real chance of gaining a durable low-cost edge over rivals. It is not as easy as it seems to imitate an organization's low-cost practices. Organizations like Dollar General, Nucor Steel, Ryanair, Greyhound Lines and Carrefour have been highly successful in managing their values chains in a low-cost manner.

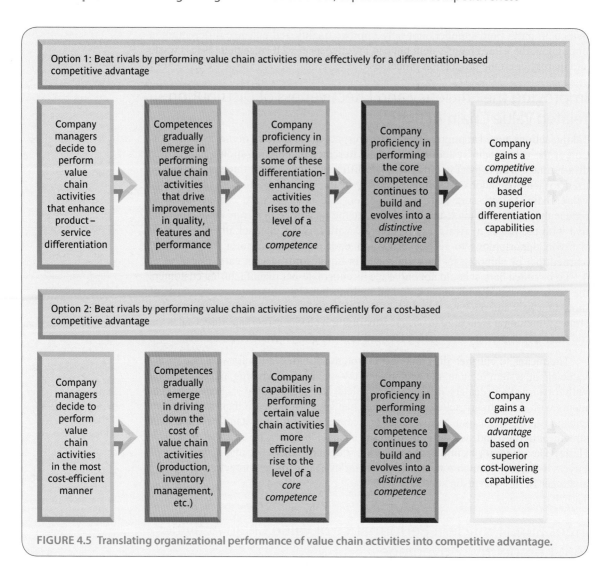

FIGURE 4.5 **Translating organizational performance of value chain activities into competitive advantage.**

Ongoing and persistent efforts are also required for a competitive advantage based on differentiation. Superior reputations and brands are built up slowly over time, through continuous investment and activities that deliver consistent, reinforcing messages. Differentiation based on quality requires vigilant management of activities for quality assurance throughout the value chain. While the basis for differentiation (e.g. status, design, innovation, customer service, reliability, image) may vary widely among organizations pursuing a differentiation advantage, those that succeed do so on the basis of a commitment to co-ordinated value chain activities aimed purposefully at this objective. Examples include Grey Goose Vodka (status), IKEA (design), FedEx (reliability), 3M (innovation), Body Shop (image) and Nordstrom (customer service).

How Activities Relate to Resources and Capabilities

There is a close relationship between the value-creating activities that an organization performs and its resources and capabilities. An organizational capability or competence implies a *capacity* for action; in contrast, a value-creating activity *is* the action. With respect to resources and capabilities, activities are 'the moment of truth'. When organizations engage in a value-creating activity, they do so by drawing on specific organizational resources and capabilities that underlie and enable the activity. For example, brand-building activities depend on HR, such as experienced brand managers (including their knowledge and expertise in this arena), as well as organizational capabilities in advertising and marketing. Cost-cutting activities may derive from organizational capabilities in inventory management, for example, and resources such as inventory tracking systems.

Because of this correspondence between activities and supporting resources and capabilities, value chain analysis can complement resource and capability analysis as tools for assessing an organization's competitive advantage. Resources and capabilities that are *both valuable and rare* provide an organization with *what it takes* for competitive advantage. For an organization with competitive assets of this sort, the potential is there. When these assets are deployed in the form of a value-creating activity, that potential is realized due to their competitive superiority. Resource analysis is one tool for identifying competitively superior resources and capabilities. Their value, however, and the competitive superiority of that value can only be assessed objectively *after* they are deployed. Value chain analysis and benchmarking provide the type of data needed to make that objective assessment.

There is also a dynamic relationship between an organization's activities and its resources and capabilities. Value-creating activities are more than just the embodiment of a resource's or capability's potential. They also contribute to the formation and development of capabilities. The road to competitive advantage begins with management efforts to build organizational expertise in performing certain competitively important value chain activities. With consistent practice and continuous investment of organizational resources, these activities rise to the level of a reliable organizational capability or a competence. To the extent that top management makes the growing capability a cornerstone of the organization's strategy, this capability becomes a core competence for the organization. Later, with further organizational learning and gains in proficiency, the core competence may evolve into a distinctive competence, giving the organization superiority over rivals in performing an important value chain activity. Such superiority, if it gives the organization significant competitive power in the marketplace, can produce an attractive competitive edge over rivals. Whether the resulting competitive advantage is on the cost side or on the differentiation side (or both) will depend on the organization's choice of which types of competence-building activities to engage in over this time period, as shown in Figure 4.5.

> Performing value chain activities in ways that give an organization the capabilities to either outmatch rivals on differentiation or beat them on costs will help the organization to secure a competitive advantage.

Question 5: Is the Organization Competitively Stronger or Weaker than Key Rivals?

Resource and capability analysis together with value chain analysis and benchmarking will reveal whether an organization has a competitive advantage over rivals on the basis of *individual* resources, capabilities and activities. These tools can also be used to assess the competitive advantage attributable to a *bundle* of resources and capabilities. Resource bundles can sometimes pass the four tests of a resource's competitive power even when the individual components of the resource bundle cannot. For example, although Callaway Golf's engineering capabilities and market research capabilities are matched relatively well by rivals Cobra Golf and Ping Golf, the organization's bundling of resources used in its product development process (including cross-functional development systems, technological capabilities, knowledge of consumer preferences and a collaborative organizational culture) gives it a competitive advantage that has allowed it to remain the largest seller of golf equipment for more than a decade.

> **LO 4.5**
> Understand how a comprehensive evaluation of an organization's competitive situation can assist managers in making critical decisions about their next strategic moves.

Resource analysis and value chain/benchmarking analysis of the organization's resources, capabilities and activities (both as individual entities and as bundles) are necessary for determining whether the organization is competitively stronger or weaker than key rivals. But they are not sufficient for gaining a complete picture of an organization's competitive situation. A more comprehensive assessment needs to be made of the organization's *overall* competitive strengths and weaknesses since a competitive advantage along one part of its value chain can be overwhelmed by competitive disadvantages along other parts of the chain. In making an overall assessment of an organization's competitiveness, the answers to two questions are of particular interest: First, how does the organization rank relative to competitors on each of the important factors that determine market success? Second, all things considered, does the organization have a *net* competitive advantage or disadvantage versus major competitors?

An easy-to-use method for answering these two questions involves developing quantitative strength ratings for the organization and its main competitors on each industry key success factor and each competitively pivotal resource and capability. Much of the information needed for doing a competitive strength assessment comes from previous analyses. Industry and five-forces analyses reveal the key success factors and competitive forces that separate industry winners from losers. Analysing benchmarking data and scouting key competitors provide a basis for judging the competitive strength of rivals on such factors as cost, key product attributes, customer service, image and reputation, financial strength, technological skills, distribution capability and other resources and capabilities. Resource and capability analysis reveals which factors are competitively important, given the external situation. Together with value chain analysis, it also shines a light on the competitive strengths of the organization. That is, it reveals whether the organization or its rivals have the advantage with respect to competitively important resources, capabilities and activities. The four tests of a resource's competitive power indicate, further, whether any of these advantages are sustainable. SWOT analysis provides a relatively comprehensive and forward-looking picture of the organization's overall situation by surveying the entire set of its strengths and weaknesses in relation to rivals and the external environment.

Step 1 in doing a competitive strength assessment is to make a list of the industry's key success factors and most telling measures of competitive strength or weakness (6 to 10 measures usually suffice). Step 2 is to assign weights to each of the measures of competitive strength based on their perceived importance – it is highly unlikely that the different measures are equally important. In an industry where the products/services of rivals are virtually identical, for instance, having low unit costs relative to rivals is nearly always the most important determinant of competitive strength. In an industry with strong product differentiation, the most significant measures of competitive strength may be brand awareness, brand image and reputation, product attractiveness and distribution capability. A weight could be as high as 0.75 (maybe even higher) in situations where one particular competitive variable is overwhelmingly decisive, or a weight could be as low as 0.20 when two or three strength measures are more important than the rest. Lesser competitive strength indicators can carry weights of 0.05 or 0.10. Whether the differences between the importance weights are big or little, *the sum of the weights must add up to 1.*

Step 3 is to rate the firm and its rivals on each competitive strength measure. Numerical rating scales (e.g. from 1 to 10) are best to use, although ratings of stronger (+), weaker (−), and about equal (=) may be appropriate when information is scanty and assigning numerical scores conveys false precision. Step 4 is to multiply each strength rating by its importance weight to obtain weighted strength scores (a strength rating of 4 times a weight of 0.20 gives a weighted strength score of 0.80). Step 5 is to sum the weighted scores on each measure to get overall weighted competitive strength ratings for each organization. Step 6 is to use the overall strength ratings to draw conclusions about the size and extent of the organization's net competitive advantage or disadvantage and to take specific note of areas of strength and weakness.

Table 4.4 provides an example of competitive strength assessment in which a hypothetical organization (ABC Company) competes against two rivals. In the example,

TABLE 4.4 A representative weighted competitive strength assessment

Key success factor/ strength measure	Importance weight	Competitive strength assessment (Rating scale: 1 = very weak; 10 = very strong)					
		ABC		Rival 1		Rival 2	
		Strength rating	Weighted score	Strength rating	Weighted score	Strength rating	Weighted score
Quality/product performance	0.10	8	0.80	5	0.50	1	0.10
Reputation/image	0.10	8	0.80	7	0.70	1	0.10
Manufacturing capability	0.10	2	0.20	10	1.00	5	0.50
Technological skills	0.05	10	0.50	1	0.05	3	0.15
Dealer network/ distribution capability	0.05	9	0.45	4	0.20	5	0.25
New product innovation capability	0.05	9	0.45	4	0.20	5	0.25
Financial resources	0.10	5	0.50	10	1.00	3	0.30
Relative cost position	0.30	5	1.50	10	3.00	1	0.30
Customer service capabilities	0.15	5	0.75	7	1.05	1	0.15
Sum of importance weights	**1.00**						
Overall weighted competitive strength rating			**5.95**		**7.70**		**2.10**

relative cost is the most telling measure of competitive strength, and the other strength measures are of lesser importance. The organization with the highest rating on a given measure has an implied competitive edge on that measure, with the size of its edge reflected in the difference between its weighted rating and rivals' weighted ratings. For instance, Rival 1's 3.00 weighted strength rating on relative cost signals a considerable cost advantage versus ABC Company (with a 1.50 weighted score on relative cost) and an even bigger cost advantage against Rival 2 (with a weighted score of 0.30). The measure-by-measure ratings reveal the competitive areas where an organization is strongest and weakest, and against whom.

The overall competitive strength scores indicate how all the different strength measures add up – whether the organization is at a net overall competitive advantage or disadvantage against each rival. The higher an organization's *overall weighted strength rating*, the stronger its *overall competitiveness* versus rivals. The bigger the difference between an organization's overall weighted rating and the scores of *lower-rated* rivals, the greater is its implied *net competitive advantage*. Thus, Rival 1's overall weighted score of 7.70 indicates a greater net competitive advantage over Rival 2 (with a score of 2.10) than over ABC Company (with a score of 5.95). Conversely, the bigger the difference between an organization's overall rating and the scores of *higher-rated* rivals, the greater its implied *net competitive disadvantage*. Rival 2's score of 2.10 gives it a smaller net competitive disadvantage against ABC Company (with an overall score of 5.95) than against Rival 1 (with an overall score of 7.70).

High weighted competitive strength ratings signal a strong competitive position and possession of competitive advantage; low ratings signal a weak position and competitive disadvantage.

Strategic Implications of Competitive Strength Assessments

Competitive strength assessments provide useful information about an organization's competitive situation. The ratings show how an organization compares against rivals,

Key Debate 4.1

EXTENDING THE RESOURCE-BASED VIEW

The resource-based view, first developed in the early 1990s, is one of the most influential theories in management, explaining the internal sources of a firm's sustained competitive advantage. Sometimes positioned to challenge the industrial organization (IO) view that places the determinants of company performance outside the firm, it has long been considered a complementary approach, with some of the key IO theorists as the main proponents.

In this chapter we explored some of the central propositions of the theory, being that if a firm is to attain sustained competitive advantage it must acquire and control valuable, rare, inimitable and non-substitutable resources, as well as be able to apply these resources. This central proposition has been developed over the years, and the original frameworks have been complemented with the analyses of core competences, dynamic capabilities and the knowledge-based view.

This theory is not without criticism, however, and theorizing on the internal sources of competitive advantage continues.

One of the simple critical observations is that the theory applies primarily to predictable environments. This is relatively easy to address, in that in unpredictable environments, when the value of resources can change drastically, then the resource-based view needs to be complemented with other approaches.

Some of the more complex key concerns stem from the limited managerial implications of the theory, as it is clear that understanding the resource requirements for competitive advantage does not help managers know how to acquire them, and even understanding the resource requirements is not a straightforward task. The concept of a 'resource' is quite complex, extended from tangible resources, to include intangible assets as well as knowledge and capabilities possessed by the firm.

With increasing comprehensiveness it becomes more crucial that it is known in what way different types of resources might contribute to a firm's sustained competitive advantage, and here the research is still incomplete. Even further it is likely that there is no objective definition of a resource but it must be defined by the situation or the context. Researchers have looked closer at capabilities as resources and can discern more fine-grained distinctions including the capability of integration of knowledge resources. The inclusion of knowledge as a resource creates some issues for the competitive power framework tests, as knowledge as a resource has the ability to increase with deployment, rather than be diminished, and it may create externalities that everyone can benefit from. This suggests co-operation and co-development behaviours for organizations, alongside competition, and makes null the requirements of rare and non-imitable as a test for a valuable resource. The distribution and creation of knowledge also has implications for the use of value chain analysis.

FROM VALUE CHAIN TO VALUE NETWORK

The concept of value chain has a dominant position in the strategic analysis of companies and industries. However, as products and services become more knowledge-based, fuelled by the rise of new communication technologies, the value chain becomes a less appropriate tool to uncover sources of value. This is particularly relevant in sectors such as entertainment, music, advertising and banking.

Many industries now exhibit strong co-operative behaviours with inter-firm relationships playing a significant role in competitive performance. While the value chain is designed around the activities required to produce a focal product, the reality for many firms today is that the value is co-created by a combination of players in the network, and hence the 'value network' concept has developed a strong following as an alternative approach.

In a network approach, organizations focus not on the company or the industry, but on the value-creating system itself within which the actors (which can include customers, partners and suppliers) work together to co-produce value. The network is also known as a 'value constellation', being inter-organizational networks linking firms with different assets and competences together.

Inter-organizational networks have many links with the idea of open versus closed innovation. Closed innovation posits that control over knowledge and other resources is needed for successful innovation. Open innovation is a paradigm that assumes that firms can and should use external ideas as well as internal ideas, and internal and external paths to market. This redefines the boundary between a firm and its surrounding environment. Implications for the resource-based view is the inclusion of these new processes of creation, whereby organizations have to combine their internal resources with those of their partners to generate value. A value network analysis would therefore be an additional aid in addressing the issues when designing strategy. Simplified steps to a value network analysis would involve:

1. defining the network;
2. identifying and defining network entities;
3. defining the value each entity perceives from being a network member;
4. identifying and mapping network influences;
5. analysing and shaping the network.

Source: Peppard, J. and Rylander, A. (2006) 'From value chain to value network: insights for mobile operators', *European Management Journal*, 24(2–3): 137; Normann, R. and Ramirez, R. (2006) 'From value chain to value network: designing interactive strategy', *Harvard Business Review*, 71(4): 65–77; Chesbrough, H., Vanhaverbeke, W. and West, J. (2006) *Open Innovation: Researching a New Paradigm*, Oxford University Press.

factor by factor (or capability by capability), thus revealing where it is strongest and weakest, and against whom. Moreover, the overall competitive strength score indicates how all the different factors add up – whether the organization is at a net competitive advantage or disadvantage against each rival. The firm with the largest overall competitive strength rating enjoys the strongest competitive position, with the size of its net competitive advantage reflected by how much its score exceeds the scores of rivals.

In addition, the strength ratings provide guidelines for designing wise offensive and defensive strategies. For example, if ABC Company wants to go on the offensive to win additional sales and market share, such an offensive probably needs to be aimed directly at winning customers away from Rival 2 (which has a lower overall strength score) rather than Rival 1 (which has a higher overall strength score). Moreover, while ABC has high ratings for technological skills (a 10 rating), dealer network/distribution capability (a 9 rating), new product innovation capability (a 9 rating), quality/product performance (an 8 rating) and reputation/image (an 8 rating), these strength measures have low importance weights – meaning that ABC has strengths in areas that do not translate into much competitive strength in the marketplace. Even so, it outclasses Rival 2 in all five areas, plus it enjoys substantially lower costs than Rival 2 (ABC has a 5 rating on relative cost position versus a 1 rating for Rival 2) – and relative cost position carries the highest importance weight of all the strength measures. ABC also has greater competitive strength than Rival 3 as concerns customer service capabilities (which carries the second highest importance weight). Hence, because ABC's strengths are in the very areas where Rival 2 is weak, ABC is in a good position to attack Rival 2; it may well be able to persuade a number of Rival 2's customers to switch their purchases over to ABC's product.

> An organization's competitive strength scores pinpoint its strengths and weaknesses against rivals and point directly to the kinds of offensive/defensive actions it can use to exploit its competitive strengths and reduce its competitive vulnerabilities.

But ABC should be cautious about cutting price aggressively to win customers away from Rival 2, because Rival 1 could interpret that as an attack by ABC to win away Rival 1's customers as well. And Rival 1 is in by far the best position to compete on the basis of low price, given its high rating on relative cost in an industry where low costs are competitively important (relative cost carries an importance weight of 0.30). Rival 1's very strong relative cost position *vis-à-vis* both ABC and Rival 2 arms it with the ability to use its lower-cost advantage to thwart any price cutting on ABC's part; clearly ABC is vulnerable to any retaliatory price cuts by Rival 1 – Rival 1 can easily defeat both ABC and Rival 2 in a price-based battle for sales and market share. If ABC wants to defend against its vulnerability to potential price-cutting by Rival 1, then it needs to aim a portion of its strategy at lowering its costs.

The point here is that a competitively astute organization should utilize the strength scores in deciding what strategic moves to make – what strengths to exploit in winning business away from rivals, which rivals to attack and which competitive weaknesses to try to correct. When an organization has important competitive strengths in areas where one or more rivals are weak, it makes sense to consider offensive moves to exploit rivals' competitive weaknesses. When an organization has important competitive weaknesses in areas where one or more rivals are strong, it makes sense to consider defensive moves to curtail its vulnerability.

Question 6: What Strategic Issues and Problems Merit Priority Managerial Attention?

The final and most important analytical step is to focus in on exactly what strategic issues organization managers need to address – and resolve – for the organization to be more financially and competitively successful in the years ahead. This step involves drawing on the results of both industry analysis and the evaluations of the organization's own competitiveness. The task here is to get a clear understanding on exactly what strategic and competitive challenges confront the organization, which of the organization's competitive shortcomings need fixing, what obstacles stand in the way of improving the organization's competitive position in the marketplace and what specific problems merit priority attention by managers.

The 'worry list' of issues and problems that have to be wrestled with can include such things as:

- *How* to stave off market challenges from new foreign competitors.
- *How* to combat the price discounting of rivals.
- *How* to reduce the organization's high costs and pave the way for price reductions.
- *How* to sustain the organization's present rate of growth in light of slowing buyer demand.
- *Whether* to expand the organization's product line.
- *Whether* to correct the organization's competitive deficiencies by acquiring a rival organization with the missing strengths.
- *Whether* to expand into foreign markets rapidly or cautiously.
- *Whether* to reposition the organization and move to a different strategic group.
- *What to do* about growing buyer interest in substitute products.
- *What to do* to combat the ageing demographics of the organization's customer base.

The worry list thus always centres on such concerns as 'how to . . .', 'what to do about . . .', and 'whether to. . .'. The purpose of the worry list is to identify the specific issues/problems that management needs to address, not to figure out what specific actions to take. Deciding what to do – which strategic actions to take and which strategic moves to take – comes later (when it is time to craft the strategy and choose among the various strategic alternatives).

If the items on the worry list are relatively minor, which suggests that the organization's strategy is mostly on track and reasonably well matched to the organization's overall situation, managers seldom need to go much beyond fine-tuning the present strategy. If, however, the issues and problems confronting the organization are serious and indicate the present strategy is not well suited for the road ahead, the task of crafting a better strategy has got to go to the top of management's action agenda.

Focusing in on the strategic issues an organization faces and compiling a 'worry list' of problems and obstructions creates a strategic agenda of problems that merit prompt managerial attention.

Actually deciding on a strategy and what specific action to take is what comes *after* developing the list of strategic issues and problems that merit prioritized management attention.

A good strategy must contain ways to deal with all the strategic issues and obstacles that stand in the way of the organization's financial and competitive success in the years ahead.

KEY POINTS

There are six key questions to consider in evaluating an organization's ability to compete successfully against market rivals:

1. *How well is the present strategy working?* This involves evaluating the strategy from a qualitative standpoint (completeness, internal consistency, rationale and suitability to the situation) and also from a quantitative standpoint (the strategic and financial results the strategy is producing). The stronger an organization's current overall performance, the less likely the need for radical strategy changes. The weaker an organization's performance and/or the faster the changes in its external situation (which can be gleaned from industry and competitive forces analysis), the more its current strategy must be questioned.

2. *Do the organization's resources and capabilities have sufficient competitive power to give it a sustainable advantage over competitors?* The answer to this question comes from conducting the four tests of a resource's competitive power. If an organization has resources and capabilities that are competitively valuable and rare, the firm will have a competitive advantage over market rivals. If its resources and capabilities are also hard to copy, with no good substitutes, then the firm may be able to sustain this advantage even in the face of active efforts by rivals to overcome it.

3. *Is the organization able to seize market opportunities and overcome external threats to its future well-being?* The answer to this question comes from performing a SWOT analysis. The two most important parts of SWOT analysis are (1) drawing conclusions about what story the compilation of strengths, weaknesses, opportunities and threats tells about the organization's overall situation and (2) acting on the conclusions to better match the organization's strategy to its internal strengths and market opportunities, to correct the important internal weaknesses, and to defend against external threats. An organization's strengths and competitive assets are strategically relevant because they are the most logical and appealing building blocks for strategy; internal weaknesses are important because they may represent vulnerabilities that need correction. External opportunities and threats come into play because a good strategy necessarily aims at capturing an organization's most attractive opportunities and at defending against threats to its well-being.

4. *Are the organization's prices, costs and value proposition competitive?* One telling sign of whether an organization's situation is strong or precarious is whether its prices and costs are competitive with those of industry rivals. Another sign is how it compares with rivals in terms of differentiation – how effectively it delivers on its customer value proposition. Value chain analysis and benchmarking are essential tools in determining whether the organization is performing particular functions and activities efficiently and effectively, learning whether its costs are in line with competitors, whether it is differentiating in ways that really enhance customer value, and deciding which internal activities and business processes need to be scrutinized for improvement. They complement resource and capability analysis by providing data at the level of individual activities that provides more objective evidence of whether individual resources and capabilities, or bundles of resources and linked activity sets, are competitively superior.

5. *On an overall basis, is the organization competitively stronger or weaker than key rivals?* The key appraisals here involve how the organization matches up against key rivals on industry key success factors and other chief determinants of competitive success and whether and why the organization has a *net* competitive advantage or disadvantage. Quantitative competitive strength assessments, using the method presented in Table 4.4, indicate where an organization is competitively strong and weak and provide insight into the organization's ability to defend or enhance its market position. As a rule, an organization's competitive strategy should be built around its competitive strengths and should aim at improving areas where it is competitively vulnerable. When an organization has important competitive strengths in areas where one or more rivals are weak, it makes sense to consider offensive moves to exploit rivals' competitive weaknesses. When an organization has important competitive weaknesses in areas where one or more rivals are strong, it makes sense to consider defensive moves to reduce its vulnerability.

6. *What strategic issues and problems merit front-burner managerial attention?* This analytical step zeros in on the strategic issues and problems that stand in the way of the organization's success. It involves using the results of industry analysis as well as resource and value chain analysis of the organization's

competitive situation to identify a 'worry list' of issues to be resolved for the organization to be financially and competitively successful in the years ahead. The worry list always centres on such concerns as 'how to …', 'what to do about …' and 'whether to … ' – the purpose of the worry list is to identify the specific issues/problems that management needs to address. Actually deciding on a strategy and what specific actions to take is what comes after the list of strategic issues and problems that merit front-burner management attention is developed.

Solid analysis of the organization's competitive situation vis-à-vis *its key rivals, like good industry analysis, is a valuable precondition for good strategy-making.* A competently done evaluation of an organization's resources, capabilities and competitive strengths exposes strong and weak points in the present strategy and how attractive or unattractive the organization's competitive position is and why. Managers need such understanding to craft a strategy that is well suited to the organization's competitive circumstances.

HARIBO

Risk is actually reduced if you focus on what you really master

Hans Riegal

With only a few simple tools, Hans Riegal senior began producing jelly 'dancing bears' in 1922. Growing to become a leading brand in the European sugar confectionery sector, HARIBO now produces 200 different kinds of candy. In addition to its gummies and licorice treats, the company's brands include Maoam (fruit candies) and Dulcia (marshmallow confections). Acquisitions of smaller confectioners have spread the company's manufacturing base across Europe and it exports to more than 100 countries around the globe. The business maintains a strong media presence with ongoing TV commercials, although it has been mindful of local regulations on food advertising to children, and the commercials and slogans are carefully aimed at adults. A strong presence on the web has also been established.

From the post-war period, Brothers Hans and Paul Riegel ran the family company together until Paul's death in 2009. Hans was the innovative businessman, while Paul had an ingrained talent for the technology of candy-making. The third generation of the Riegal family continued the tradition of working in the company, in diverse roles in production management, country management and law.

Haribo invests heavily into R&D and frequently introduces new products, reacting quickly to current trends and bringing 10–15 product innovations onto the market every year. Its 'Gold Bears', however, enjoy a stable popularity, considered by some to have reached cult status. While the bear's recipe and design has not changed much over the years, some of the ingredients have been changed. When European consumers became aware of the potential dangers of some food colours HARIBO started using natural food colourings. When European consumers became concerned about the possible effects of BSE on their health, HARIBO stopped using cattle by-products and switched to gelatin produced from raw material derived from pigs for their fruit gum products. In 2007 one of the new innovations was a HARIBO lite range of fruit-flavoured and fruit-shaped gums with no artificial colours, 30 per cent fewer calories, 40 per cent sugar reduction and a 0.1 per cent fat content per 100 g. Made with a mix of fruit and plant concentrates, HARIBO suggested its low fat and sugar range brought 'something totally new to the category'. The business

believed these products would initially be targeted at young women and teenagers, but it was intended they would find a wider audience of confectionery purchasers. Another release, in 2009, was Funny Mix, a product without gelatin. Marketed clearly as 'suitable for vegetarians', it was developed to meet the growing demand for a larger variety of vegetarian treats.

With presence in over 100 countries, special development of a variety of confectionery is tailored in taste to suit the preferences of each country. The French prefer marshmallow products like 'Tagada' or 'Chamallows' and sugar-coated sweets like 'Dragibus' while in England 'Starmix' is No. 1. In Scandinavia 'Matador Mix' is the top-selling item.

With Hans Riegel heading up new product development, his management style remained consistent through the years. He was criticized by some management consultants and journalists as being patriarchal and old-fashioned, notoriously known for opening every letter addressed to his company to stay on top of things, meeting one-on-one with each of his directors every day to discuss the issues and tasks of each department based on his findings and displaying little belief in the need of modern business management methods. Hans Riegel's management style was also very stable, mainly applied to brand development and finances. While there was a constant stream of new products developed, the advertising and design and slogan for the HARIBO brand remained relatively constant and HARIBO financed its acquisitions with the company's own funds rather than borrowing from banks.

THE CONFECTIONERY INDUSTRY

The confectionery sector is a highly competitive industry in which producers must demonstrate both creativity and innovative abilities to differentiate from competitors. Although the sector has been experiencing a sharp increase, in recent times, the consumption is stagnating. The European confectionery market generated total revenues of €52 billion in 2010, representing a compound annual growth rate (CAGR) of 2.9 per cent for the period spanning 2006–10. Chocolate sales proved the most lucrative for the European confectionery market in 2010, generating total revenues equivalent to 54.2 per cent of the market's overall value. The performance of the market is forecast to decelerate, with an anticipated CAGR of 2.7 per cent for the five-year period 2010–15, which is expected to lead the market to a value of €58 billion by the end of 2015.

Although certain sectors of the confectionery industry have reached maturity in many parts of the

▶

Rank	Company name	HQ	No. of plants	No. of employees	Chocolate	Hard candies	Range Gummies, liquorice, jellies, chews and fruit snacks	Other candy (including jelly beans, marshmallow)	Gum	Reduced-sugar	Energy bars
1	Kraft Foods	USA	223	127,000	X	X	X	X	X	X	X
2	Mars	USA	51	29,000	X	X	X	X	X	X	X
3	Nestlé	Switzerland	443	281,000	X	X	X	X	X	X	X
4	Ferrero	Italy	18	21,736	X	X	–	X	–	–	–
5	Hershey	USA	11	11,300	X	X	X (2)	X	X	X	X
6	Perfetti Van Melle	Italy & The Netherlands	31	18,000	–	X	X	X	X	X	–
7	Haribo	Germany	15	6,000	–	X	X	X	X	(1)	–

¹Haribo does sell bulk packages of 'no-sugar' bears
²Haribo's limited 'Lite' range is included as fruit snacks
Source: Global top 100. www.candyindustry.com (January 2012).

world, the global market continues to grow. Much of this recent growth has come from developing regions and countries, aided by the spread of multinational suppliers and their brands, as well as a growing base of increasingly affluent consumers in places such as Russia, China and India. In the developed markets, one of the biggest trends in the food sector is the health market, which in the confectionery industry translates to 'healthier'. In the developed world, much of the market's recent growth can be attributed to niche sectors, such as low-fat, low-sugar, organic and fair-trade products. New product innovation remains critical to future success within the industry, with many of the world's leading suppliers investing heavily in this area.

QUESTIONS

1. What are the sources of success for HARIBO?

2. Considering current trends, how well positioned is HARIBO to meet the increasingly competitive situation in the confectionery industry?

Sources: Simon, H. (1996) *Hidden Champions: Lessons from 500 of the World's Best* Unknown Companies, Boston MA, Harvard Business School Press; Schons, P. (2003) *The Millionaire and his Candy*, Kultureke, Germanic-American Institute; 'Talking retail', 22 February 2010 Funny Mix – Haribo's latest vegetarian sweet, www.talkingretail.com (accessed 19 March 2012); www.haribo.com (accessed 19 March 2012); *The History of the Cult Mark HARIBO and Its Founder Family*, Bastei Lübbe, Bergisch Gladbach, 2006. Available online at www.live-pr.com/en/confectionery-in-europe-market-research (accessed 19 March 2012).

ASSURANCE OF LEARNING EXERCISES

LO 4.2, LO 4.3, LO 4.4

1. Review the information in Illustration Capsule 4.1 concerning the average costs of producing and selling fair-trade coffee. Then answer the following questions:

   a. Organizations that do not sell fair-trade coffee can buy coffee direct from small farmers for as little as $0.75 per pound. By paying substandard wages, they can also reduce their labour costs of roasting and bagging coffee to $0.70 per pound and reduce their overhead by 20 per cent. If they sell their coffee at the same average price as Just Coffee, what would their profit margin be and how would this compare to Just Coffee's?

   b. How can Just Coffee respond to this type of competitive threat? Does it have any valuable competitive assets that can help it respond, or will it need to acquire new ones? Would your answer change the organization's value chain in any way?

LO 4.1

2. Using the information in Table 4.1 and the financial statement information for Avon Products below, calculate the following ratios for Avon for both 2008 and 2009:

   a. Gross profit margin

   b. Operating profit margin

   c. Net profit margin

   d. Times interest earned coverage

   e. Return on shareholders' equity

   f. Return on assets

   g. Debt-to-equity ratio

   h. Days of inventory

   i. Inventory turnover ratio

   j. Average collection period

3. Based on these ratios, did Avon's financial performance improve, weaken or remain about the same from 2008 to 2009?

Consolidated Statements of Income for Avon Products, Inc., 2008–2009 (in millions, except per-share data)

	Years ended December 31	
	2009	**2008**
Net sales	$10 284.7	$10 588.9
Other revenue	98.1	101.2
Total revenue	10 382.8	10 690.1
Costs, expenses, and other:		
Cost of sales	3888.3	3949.1
Selling, general and administrative expenses	5476.3	5401.7
Operating profit	1018.2	1339.3
Interest expense	104.8	100.4
Interest income	(20.2)	(37.1)
Other expense, net	7.1	37.7
Total other expenses	91.7	101.0
Income before taxes	926.5	1238.3
Income taxes	298.3	362.7
Net income	628.2	875.6

▶

	Years ended December 31	
	2009	2008
Net income attributable to non-controlling interests	(2.4)	(.3)
Net income attributable to Avon	$625.8	$875.3
Earnings per share:		
Basic	$1.45	$2.04
Diluted	$1.45	$2.03

Consolidated Balance Sheets for Avon Products, Inc., 2008–2009 (in millions, except per-share data)

	As of 31 Dec. 2009	As of 31 Dec. 2008
Assets		
Cash and cash equivalents	$1311.6	$1104.7
Accounts receivable (less allowances of $165.5 and $127.9)	779.7	687.8
Inventories	1067.5	1007.9
Prepaid expenses and other	1030.5	756.5
Total current assets	4189.3	3556.9
Property, plant and equipment, at cost Land	144.3	85.3
Buildings and improvements	1048.1	1008.1
Equipment	1506.9	1346.5
Total property, plant and equipment, at cost	2699.3	2439.9
Less accumulated depreciation	(1169.7)	(1096.0)
Net property, plant and equipment	1529.6	1343.9
Other assets	1113.8	1173.2
Total assets	$ 6832.7	$ 6074.0
Liabilities and shareholders' equity		
Debt maturing within 1 year	$138.1	$1,031.4
Accounts payable	754.7	724.3
Accrued compensation	291.0	234.4
Other accrued liabilities	697.1	581.9
Sales and taxes other than income	259.2	212.2
Income taxes	134.7	128.0
Total current liabilities	2274.8	2912.2
Long-term debt	2307.8	1456.2
Employee benefit plans	588.9	665.4
Long-term income taxes	173.8	168.9
Other liabilities	174.8	159.0
Total liabilities	$5520.1	$5361.7
Commitments and contingencies		
Shareholders' equity		
Common stock, par value $.25 – authorized		
1,500 shares; issued 740.9 and 739.4 shares	$186.1	$185.6
Additional paid-in capital	1941.0	1874.1
Retained earnings	4383.9	4118.9
Accumulated other comprehensive loss	(692.6)	(965.9)
Treasury stock, at cost (313.4 and 313.1 shares)	(4545.8)	(4537.8)
Total Avon shareholders' equity	1272.6	674.9
Non-controlling interest	40.0	37.4
Total shareholders' equity	$1312.6	$712.3
Total liabilities and shareholders' equity	$6832.7	$6074.0

Source: Avon Products, Inc., 2009 10-K.

EXERCISES FOR SIMULATION PARTICIPANTS

LO 4.1

1. Using the formulas in Table 4.1 and the data in your organization's latest financial statements, calculate the following measures of financial performance for your organization:

   a. Operating profit margin

   b. Return on total assets

   c. Current ratio

   d. Working capital

   e. Long-term debt-to-capital ratio

   f. Price-earnings ratio

LO 4.1

2. On the basis of your company's latest financial statements and all the other available data regarding your company's performance that appear in the Industry Report, list the three measures of financial performance on which your company did 'best' and the three measures on which your company's financial performance was 'worst'.

LO 4.1, LO 4.2, LO 4.3, LO 4.4, LO 4.5

3. What hard evidence can you cite that indicates your company's strategy is working fairly well (or perhaps not working so well, if your company's performance is lagging that of rival companies)?

LO 4.3

4. What internal strengths and weaknesses does your company have? What external market opportunities for growth and increased profitability exist for your company? What external threats to your company's future well-being and profitability do you and your co-managers see? What does the preceding SWOT analysis indicate about your company's present situation and future prospects – where on the scale from 'exceptionally strong' to 'alarmingly weak' does the attractiveness of your company's situation rank?

LO 4.2, LO 4.3

5. Does your company have any core competences? If so, what are they?

LO 4.4

6. What are the key elements of your company's value chain? Refer to Figure 4.3 in developing your answer.

LO 4.5

7. Using the methodology presented in Table 4.4, do a weighted competitive strength assessment for your company and two other companies that you and your co-managers consider to be very close competitors.

ENDNOTES

1. In recent years, considerable research has been devoted to the role an organization's resources' and competitive capabilities' play in determining its competitiveness, shaping its strategy and impacting its profitability. Following the trailblazing article by Wernerfelt, Birger (1984) 'A resource-based view of the firm', *Strategic Management Journal*, 5(5): 171–80, the findings and conclusions have merged into what is now referred to as the resource-based view of the firm. Other very important contributions include Barney, Jay (1991) 'Firm resources and sustained competitive advantage', *Journal of Management*, 17(1): 99–120; Peteraf, Margaret A. (1993) 'The cornerstones of competitive advantage: a resource-based view', *Strategic Management Journal*, 14(3): 179–91; Wernerfelt, Birger (1995) 'The resource-based view of the firm: ten years after', *Strategic Management Journal*, 16(3): 171–4. A full-blown overview of the resource-based view of the firm, in its most current form, is presented in Barney, Jay B. and Clark, Delwyn N. (2007) *Resource-based Theory: Creating and Sustaining Competitive Advantage*, New York, Oxford University Press.

2. A more detailed explanation of the relationship between resources and capabilities can be found in Amit, R. and Schoemaker, P. (1993) 'Strategic assets and organizational rent', *Strategic Management Journal*, 14: 33–46.

3. See, for example, Barney, Jay B. (1995) 'Looking inside for competitive advantage', *Academy of Management Executive*, 9(4): 49–61; Bartlett, Christopher A. and Ghoshal, Sumantra (2002) 'Building: competitive advantage through people', *MIT Sloan Management Review*, 43(2): 34–41; Miller, Danny, Eisenstat, Russell and Foote, Nathaniel (2002) 'Strategy from the inside out: building capability-creating organizations', *California Management Review*, 44(3): 37–54.

4. See Barney, (2011) 'Firm resources and sustained competitive advantage', pp. 105–9; Peteraf, M. and Barney, J. (2003) 'Unraveling the resource-based tangle', *Managerial and Decision Economics*, 24(4): 309–23.

5. Los Angeles Times (2011) 'Apple's worldwide share of PC market reaches 15-year high', 18 November. Available online at www.latimesblogs.latimes.com/technology/2011/11/apples-worldwide-share-of-pc-market-reaches-15-year-high.html (accessed 18 January 2012).

6. See Amit and Schoemaker, 'Strategic assets and organizational rent', for more on the power of strategic assets to improve an organization's profitability.

7. For a discussion of how to recognize powerful substitute resources, see Peteraf, Margaret A. and Bergen, Mark E. (2003) 'Scanning dynamic competitive landscapes: a market-based and resource-based framework', *Strategic Management Journal*, 24: 1027–42.

8. See Montgomery, C. (1995) 'Of diamonds and rust: a new look at resources', in Montgomery, C. (ed.) *Resource-based and Evolutionary Theories of the Firm*, Boston, Kluwer Academic, pp. 251–68.

9. For a good discussion of what happens when an organization's capabilities grow stale and obsolete, see Leonard-Barton, D. (1992) 'Core capabilities and core rigidities: a paradox in managing new product development', *Strategic Management Journal*, 13: 111–25; Montgomery, 'Of diamonds and rust'.

10. The concept of dynamic capabilities was introduced by Teece, D., Pisano, G. and Shuen, A. (1997) 'Dynamic capabilities and strategic management', *Strategic Management Journal*, 18(7): 509–33. Other important contributors to the concept include Eisenhardt, K. and Martin, J. (2000) 'Dynamic capabilities: what are they?' *Strategic Management Journal*, 21(10–11): 1105–21; Zollo, M. and Winter, S. (2002) 'Deliberate learning and the evolution of dynamic capabilities', *Organization Science*, 13: 339–51; Helfat, C. et al. (2007), *Dynamic Capabilities: Understanding Strategic Change in Organizations*, Malden, MA, Blackwell.

11. For a more extensive discussion of how to identify and evaluate the competitive power of an organization's capabilities, see Birchall, David W. and Tovstiga, George (1999) 'The strategic potential of a firm's knowledge portfolio', *Journal of General Management*, 25(1): 1–16; Bontis, Nick, Dragonetti, Nicola C., Jacobsen, Kristine and Roos, Goran (1999) 'The knowledge toolbox: a review of the tools available to measure and manage intangible resources', *European Management Journal*, 17(4): 391–401. Also see Teece, David (1998) 'Capturing value from knowledge assets: the new economy, markets for know-how, and intangible assets', *California Management Review*, 40(3): 55–79.

12. Leonard-Barton, D. (1992) 'Core capabilities and core rigidities: a paradox in managing new product development', *Strategic Management Journal*, 13: 111–25.

13. Sull, Donald (2005) 'Strategy as active waiting', *Harvard Business Review*, 83(9): 121–2.

14. Ibid., pp. 124–6.

15. See Peteraf, M. (1993) 'The cornerstones of competitive advantage: a resource-based view', *Strategic Management Journal*, March, 179–91.

16. The value chain concept was developed and articulated by Michael Porter in his 1985 best-seller, *Competitive Advantage*, New York, Free Press.

17. For discussions of the accounting challenges in calculating the costs of value chain activities, see Shank, John K. and Govindarajan, Vijay (1993) *Strategic Cost Management*, New York, Free Press, especially chs 2–6, 10 and 11; Cooper, Robin and Kaplan, Robert S. (1988) 'Measure costs right: make the right decisions', *Harvard Business Review*, 66(5): 96–103; Ness, Joseph A. and Cucuzza, Thomas G. (1995) 'Tapping the full potential of ABC', *Harvard Business Review*, 73(4): 130–8.

18. Porter, *Competitive Advantage*, p. 34.

19. The strategic importance of effective supply chain management is discussed in Lee, Hau L. (2004) 'The triple-a supply chain', *Harvard Business Review*, 82(10): 102–12.

20. For more details, see Watson, Gregory H. (1993) *Strategic Benchmarking: How to Rate Your Company's Performance Against the World's Best,* New York, Wiley; Camp, Robert C. (1989) *Benchmarking: The Search for Industry Best Practices that Lead to Superior Performance*, Milwaukee, ASQC Quality Press; Iacobucci, Dawn and Nordhielm, Christie (2000) 'Creative benchmarking', *Harvard Business Review*, 78(6): 24–5.

21. Main, Jeremy (1992) 'How to steal the best ideas around', *Fortune*, 19 October, pp. 102–3.

22. Some of these options are discussed in more detail in Porter, *Competitive Advantage*, ch. 3.

23. Porter discusses options such as these in *Competitive Advantage*, ch. 4.

24. An example of how Whirlpool Corporation transformed its supply chain from a competitive liability to a competitive asset is discussed in Stone, Reuben E. (2004) 'Leading a supply chain turnaround', *Harvard Business Review*, 82(10): 114–21.

Chapter Five

Strategies for competitive advantage: generic strategies and beyond

Competitive strategy is about being different. It means deliberately choosing to perform activities differently or to perform different activities than rivals to deliver a unique mix of value.

Michael E. Porter
Harvard Business School professor and Co-founder of Monitor Consulting

The essence of strategy lies in creating tomorrow's competitive advantages faster than competitors mimic the ones you possess today.

Gary Hamel and C.K. Prahalad
Professors, authors and consultants

Major sustainable competitive advantages are almost non-existent in the field of financial services.

Warren Buffett
CEO Berkshire Hathaway

Learning Objectives

When you have read this chapter you should be able to:

LO 5.1   Explain what distinguishes each of the five most common generic strategies and why some of these strategies work better in certain kinds of industry and competitive conditions than in others.

LO 5.2   Identify the major avenues for achieving a competitive advantage based on lower costs.

LO 5.3   Discuss some of the alternative generic strategy frameworks, including those that argue for competitive advantage based on price.

LO 5.4   Describe the major avenues to a competitive advantage based on differentiating an organization's product or service offering from the offerings of rivals.

LO 5.5   Recognize the attributes of a best-cost provider strategy and the way in which some organizations use a hybrid strategy to go about building a competitive advantage and delivering superior value to customers.

THE END OF HIGHER EDUCATION AS WE KNOW IT?

In July 2010, when Universities Minister, David Willets, announced that he would allow the first new university college in the UK for 30 years, it signalled a major change in the higher education sector. BPP had been delivering a variety of professional qualifications since it was founded in 1976. In 2009 the organization was acquired by the Apollo Group, a for-profit organization based in the USA and the power behind one of the fastest growing private higher education institutions, the University of Phoenix.

BPP Chief Executive Officer (CEO), Carl Lygo, promised to shake up UK higher education and 'challenge the status quo'. The UK's coalition government had already made changes to the way higher education was funded by allowing universities to charge up to £9000 p.a. for tuition in an attempt to create more of a market. BPP chose to charge between £4000–5000 for their degrees, one of the lowest prices in the market. Lygo claimed that BPP were able to do this because they cut back on costs in areas that did not directly affect students. Other universities, such as Coventry, also decided to try this 'no frills' approach.

BPP's approach to higher education was very different from the traditional campus-based, three- and four-year undergraduate degree model. For some programmes they offered an intensive model of delivery without the usual breaks between terms that students could complete in two years. These were offered at £12 000 for the whole degree, compared with £27 000 at a traditional university. Lygo considered that this type of accelerated degree programme would appeal to students wanting work-related qualifications who would live at home while studying.

The organization focused on a relatively small number of degrees and qualifications in professional fields such as law, accountancy, finance and business, although they also had plans to move into health-related degrees. BPP had always recruited professionals from industry to deliver their courses. Its full-time faculty were practitioners who had turned to teaching rather than the traditional university model that focused on research. BPP's learning centres were located in city centre office blocks in 14 locations in the UK. Carl Lygo was confident that his organization's target market was not the sort of student that valued wider campus services such as coffee-bars and swimming pools. BPP's operations also made better utilization of their teaching space than many other higher education providers, with fewer lecture theatres and classrooms standing empty during weekends and outside the traditional university terms.

BPP's focus on teaching rather than research was intended to match their customers' needs more closely despite plans to operate a student/staff ratio of 30:1 against a sector average of 17:1. Carl Lygo's assessment of the typical BPP student's needs was, 'they want more contact time, more feedback, smaller groups, a tutor who knows their name and the chance of a job at the end'. Many of the organization's law students were in full-time employment and its model of delivery had been built on an understanding of their needs.

However, BPP's model had not yet proved itself in the changing UK market. Although the organization had some 6500 students in its business and law schools in 2011 and had trained 30 000 accountants, their profits were yet to fulfil the potential of their $600 million price tag. Many traditional universities would be watching their progress with interest in future.

QUESTIONS

1. What are the main differences between BPP's approach to delivering higher education and those of a more traditional university?

2. Which of the differences you have highlighted are likely to increase BPP's operating costs and which will reduce them in comparison with its competitors?

Sources: Baker, S. (2010) 'Huge BPP write-off announced as Apollo prophesies bleak short-term future for private demand', *Times Higher Education Supplement*, 18 November, No. 1974, News, p. 6; Baker, S. (2011) 'Market failure? BPP write-down raises penetrative questions', *Times Higher Education Supplement*, 6 June, No. 2001, News, p. 6; Coughlan, S. (2010) 'First private university in decades to be created', BBC News, 26 July. Available online at: www.bbc.co.uk/news/uk-10756830 (accessed 19 November 2011); Coughlan, S. (2011) 'Private university's £5,000 tuition fees', BBC News, 6 September. Available online at: www.bbc,co.uk/news/education-14806047 (accessed 19 November 2011); Lygo, C. (2011) 'Universities could cut their fees if they learned to be more business-like', *The Guardian*, 24 October 2011. Available online at: www.guardian.co.uk/education/2011/oct/24/competition-private-universities-reduce-fees (accessed 19 November 2011); Matthews, D. (2011) 'More places, along with more students per lecturer, figure in BPP's plans', *Times Higher Education Supplement*, 28 July, No. 2009, News, p. 6; Murray, J. (2011) 'Education: interview Carl Lygo: Living the American dream in Britain: From free school meals to leader of a university: the head of BPP is setting an example', *The Guardian (London)* 10 May, Education Section, p. 7.

There are several basic approaches to competing successfully and gaining a competitive advantage over rivals, but they all involve the capacity to deliver more customer value than rivals can. Superior value can mean a good product at a lower price, a superior product that is worth paying more for, or a best-value offering that represents an attractive combination of price, features, quality, service and other appealing attributes. But whatever form delivering superior value takes, it nearly always requires performing value chain activities differently than rivals and building competitively valuable resources and capabilities that rivals cannot readily match or beat.

This chapter describes the five best-known *generic competitive strategy options* and considers which environments they are most suitable for. Which of the five to employ is often an organization's or business unit's first and foremost choice in crafting an overall strategy and beginning its quest for competitive advantage. Although we cover these five options in detail, there are other ways of viewing generic strategy options and we will also consider how this element of business-level strategy has developed from a theoretical and a practical standpoint through the Key Debate, Different View, Emerging Theme and Current Practice features.

Generic strategies are frequently used to create and then defend a strong market position in an oligopolistic situation. However, as we saw in Chapter 1, there is a strong body of evidence that suggests sustainable competitive advantage is not possible in environments where disruption is frequent and there is intense competition. The opening case in this chapter can be read in several ways. On the one hand this is a new entrant to the higher education market trying to create a sustainable long-term position by focusing on reducing costs and targeting a particular segment of the market. On the other hand BPP could be seen as a disruptive outsider that is not willing to play the game in the same way as its rivals and is about to push the higher education sector into a period of hypercompetitive activity. If you reread the case in this light, what would your advice be to the senior managers at a traditional university?

The Five Generic Competitive Strategies

An organization's competitive strategy *deals with the specifics of management's approach for competing successfully* – its specific efforts to please customers, its offensive and defensive moves to counter the manoeuvres of rivals, its responses to shifting market conditions, its initiatives to strengthen its market position and the specific kind of competitive advantage it is trying to achieve. As we saw in Chapter 2, these generic strategies are used in individual businesses or business units in a multibusiness organization. Even so, the chances are remote that any two organizations – even organizations in the same industry – will employ competitive strategies that are exactly alike in every detail. Why? Because managers at different organizations always have a slightly different spin on how best to deal with competitive pressures and industry driving forces, what future market conditions will be like and what strategy specifics make the most sense for their particular organization in light of the organization's strengths and weaknesses, its most promising market opportunities and the external threats to its future well-being.

LO
5.1 Explain what distinguishes each of the five most common generic strategies and why some of these strategies work better in certain kinds of industry and competitive conditions than in others.

However, when one strips away the details to get at the real substance, the two factors that tend to distinguish one competitive strategy from another boil down to (1) whether an organization's market target is broad or narrow and (2) whether the organization is pursuing a competitive advantage linked to low costs or product/service differentiation. As shown in Figure 5.1, these two factors give rise to five competitive strategy options for staking out a market position, operating the business and delivering value to customers:[1]

1. *A low-cost provider strategy:* striving to achieve lower overall costs than rivals on products that attract a broad spectrum of buyers.

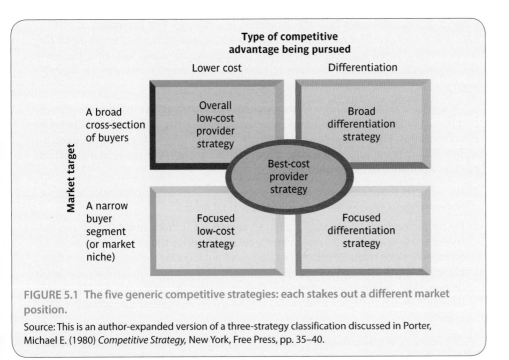

FIGURE 5.1 The five generic competitive strategies: each stakes out a different market position.

Source: This is an author-expanded version of a three-strategy classification discussed in Porter, Michael E. (1980) *Competitive Strategy,* New York, Free Press, pp. 35–40.

2. *A broad differentiation strategy:* seeking to differentiate the organization's product offering from rivals' with attributes that will appeal to a broad spectrum of buyers.

3. *A focused (or market niche) low-cost strategy:* concentrating on a narrow buyer segment and outcompeting rivals on costs, thus being in position to win buyer favour by means of a lower-priced product offering.

4. *A focused (or market niche) differentiation strategy:* concentrating on a narrow buyer segment and outcompeting rivals with a product offering that meets the specific tastes and requirements of niche members better than the product offerings of rivals.

5. *A best-cost provider strategy:* giving customers *more value for the money* by offering upscale product attributes at a lower cost than rivals. Being the 'best-cost' producer of an upscale product allows an organization to underprice rivals whose products have similar upscale attributes. This option is a *hybrid* strategy that *blends elements of differentiation and low-cost strategies* in a unique way.

Low-cost Provider Strategies

Striving to be the industry's overall low-cost provider is a powerful competitive approach in markets with many price-sensitive buyers. An organization achieves **low-cost leadership** when it becomes the industry's lowest-cost provider rather than just being one of perhaps several competitors with comparatively low costs. A low-cost provider's strategic target is to have lower costs than rivals on products of comparable quality. In striving for a cost advantage over rivals, managers must take care to incorporate features and services that buyers consider essential – *a product offering that is too frills-free sabotages the attractiveness of the organization's product and can turn buyers off even if it is cheaper than competing products.* However, context can be very important in this regard. No-frills products and services have made significant gains in developed nations since the financial crisis of 2007/8 and attracted a wide range of customers who would not traditionally have considered trading down (Illustration

Core Concept

A **low-cost leader**'s basis for competitive advantage is lower overall costs than its competitors. Successful low-cost leaders are exceptionally good at finding ways to drive costs out of their businesses and still provide a product or service that buyers find acceptable.

Capsule 5.1 demonstrates how this happened in retailing). For maximum effectiveness, a low-cost provider needs to pursue cost-saving approaches that are difficult for rivals to copy. When it is relatively easy or inexpensive for rivals to imitate the low-cost organization's methods, then any resulting cost advantage evaporates too quickly to gain a very valuable edge in the marketplace.

LO

5.2 Identify the major avenues for achieving a competitive advantage based on lower costs.

A low-cost advantage over rivals has enormous competitive power, sometimes enabling an organization to achieve faster rates of growth (by using price cuts to draw customers away from rivals) and frequently helping to boost an organization's profitability. An organization can translate a low-cost advantage over rivals into attractive profit performance in either of two ways:

1. By using its lower-cost edge to underprice competitors and attract price-sensitive buyers in great enough numbers to increase total profits.

2. By refraining from using price cuts to steal sales away from rivals (which run the risk of starting a price war) and, instead, charging a price roughly equal to those of other low-priced rivals. While this strategy will not increase the organization's market share, it will enable the organization to earn a bigger profit margin per unit sold (because the organization's costs per unit are below the unit costs of rivals) and thereby propel it to higher total profits and return on investment than rivals are able to earn.

A low-cost advantage over rivals can translate into better profitability than rivals attain.

While many organizations are inclined to exploit a low-cost advantage by attacking rivals with lower prices (in hopes that the expected gains in sales and market share will lead to higher total profits), this strategy can backfire if rivals respond with retaliatory price cuts of their own (in order to protect their customer base) and the aggressor's price cuts fail to produce sales gains that are big enough to offset the profit erosion associated with charging a lower price. The bigger the risk that rivals will respond with matching price cuts, the more appealing it becomes to employ the second option for using a low-cost advantage to achieve higher profitability.

The Two Major Avenues for Achieving a Cost Advantage

To achieve a low-cost edge over rivals, an organization's cumulative costs across its overall value chain must be lower than competitors' cumulative costs. There are two ways to accomplish this:[2]

1. Do a better job than rivals of performing value chain activities more cost-effectively.

2. Revamp the organization's overall value chain to eliminate or bypass some cost-producing activities.

Let us look at each of the two approaches to securing a cost advantage.

Cost-efficient Management of Value Chain Activities

For an organization to do a more cost-efficient job of managing its value chain than rivals, managers must launch a concerted, ongoing effort to ferret out cost-saving opportunities in every part of the value chain. To achieve this, managers will often need to put all activities under the same cost-saving scrutiny, and encourage all of an organization's personnel to use their talents and ingenuity to come up with innovative and effective ways to keep costs down. We return to some of these issues again in Chapter 11, where we cover some of the process management tools that help managers and their teams to execute this. All avenues for performing value chain activities at a lower cost than rivals have to be explored. Particular attention, however, needs to be paid to a set of factors known as **cost drivers,** which have an especially strong effect on an organization's costs and which managers can use as levers to push costs down

Core Concept

A **cost driver** is a factor that has a strong influence on an organization's costs.

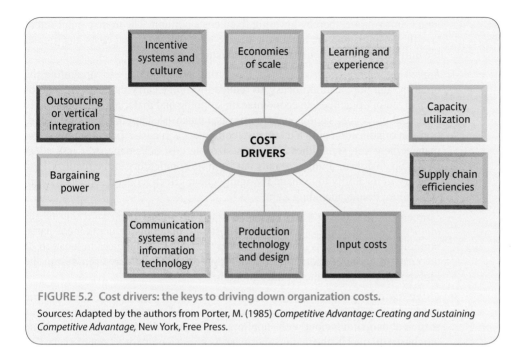

FIGURE 5.2 Cost drivers: the keys to driving down organization costs.

Sources: Adapted by the authors from Porter, M. (1985) *Competitive Advantage: Creating and Sustaining Competitive Advantage*, New York, Free Press.

(Figure 5.2 provides a list of important cost drivers). Cost-cutting methods that demonstrate an effective use of the cost drivers include:

1. *Striving to capture all available economies of scale.* Economies of scale stem from an ability to lower unit costs by increasing the scale of operation, and they can affect the unit costs of many activities along the value chain, including manufacturing, R&D, advertising, distribution and general administration. For example, British Airways, Adidas, BP and EDF have the ability to afford the £40 million for Tier One sponsorship of the 2012 Olympics in London because the cost of such sponsorship can be spread out over the hundreds of millions of units they sell. In contrast, a small organization with a sales volume of only 1 million units would find the £40 million cost of Tier One sponsorship prohibitive – the sponsorship would raise costs over £30 per unit even if it was unusually effective and caused sales volume to jump 25 per cent, to 1.25 million units. Similarly, a large manufacturing plant can be more economical to operate than a smaller one. In global industries, making separate products for each country market instead of selling a mostly standard product world-wide tends to boost unit costs because of lost time in model change-over, shorter production runs and inability to reach the most economic scale of production for each country model.

2. *Taking full advantage of experience and learning-curve effects.* The cost of performing an activity can decline over time as the learning and experience of personnel in the organization builds. Learning/experience economies can stem from debugging and mastering newly introduced technologies, using the experiences and suggestions of workers to install more efficient plant layouts and assembly procedures and the added speed and effectiveness that accrue from repeatedly picking sites for and building new plants, retail outlets or distribution centres. Aggressively managed low-cost providers pay diligent attention to capturing the benefits of learning and experience and to keeping these benefits proprietary to whatever extent possible.

3. *Trying to operate facilities at full capacity.* Whether an organization is able to operate at or near full capacity has a big impact on units costs when its value chain contains activities associated with substantial fixed costs. Higher rates of capacity utilization allow depreciation and other fixed costs to be spread over a

larger unit volume, thereby lowering fixed costs per unit. The more capital-intensive the business and the higher the fixed costs relative to total costs, the greater the unit-cost penalty for underutilizing existing capacity.

4. *Improving supply chain efficiency.* Partnering with suppliers to streamline the ordering and purchasing process, to reduce inventory carrying costs via just-in-time inventory practices, to economize on shipping and materials handling and to ferret out other cost-saving opportunities is a much-used approach to cost reduction. An organization with a distinctive competence in cost-efficient supply chain management can sometimes achieve a sizeable cost advantage over less adept rivals. Spanish firm, Inditex, stands out from its competitors in the retail fashion industry in its ability to manage its supply chain effectively and support its high street retail brands including Zara.

5. *Using lower cost inputs wherever doing so will not entail too great a sacrifice in quality.* Some examples include lower-cost raw materials or component parts, non-union labour 'inputs', and lower rental fees due to differences in location. If the costs of certain factors are 'too high', an organization may even design the high-cost inputs out of the product altogether.

6. *Using the organization's bargaining power* vis-à-vis *suppliers or others in the value chain system to gain concessions.* Tesco and Carrefour, for example, have sufficient bargaining clout with suppliers to win price discounts on large-volume purchases. In the UK the major supermarkets now account for £7 out of every £10 spent on the high street.[3]

7. *Using communication systems and information technology (IT) to achieve operating efficiencies.* For example, data sharing, starting with customer orders and going all the way back to components production, coupled with the use of enterprise resource planning (ERP) and manufacturing execution system (MES) software, can greatly reduce production times and labour costs. Numerous organizations now have online systems and software that turn formerly time-consuming and labour-intensive tasks like purchasing, inventory management, invoicing and bill payment into speedily performed mouse clicks.

8. *Employing advanced production technology and process design to improve overall efficiency.* Examples range from highly automated robotic production technology to computer-assisted design (CAD) techniques to design for manufacture (DFM) procedures that enable more integrated and efficient production. ThyssenKrupp's investment in advanced production facilities at their Duisburg site has made it one of the most efficient steel production mills in the world. They have achieved this through a combination of a shortened production chain and recycling that helps to minimize the use of water and energy at the plant. Other manufacturers have pioneered the use of production or processing technology that eliminates the need for costly investments in facilities or equipment and that requires fewer employees. Organizations can also achieve substantial efficiency gains through process innovation or through approaches such as business process management, business process reengineering and total quality management (TQM) that aim to co-ordinate production activities and drive continuous improvement in productivity and quality.[4] Procter & Gamble is an example of an organization known for its successful application of business process reengineering techniques.

9. *Being alert to the cost advantages of outsourcing or vertical integration.* Outsourcing the performance of certain value chain activities can be more economical than performing them in-house if outside specialists, by virtue of their expertise and volume, can perform the activities at lower cost. Indeed, outsourcing has, in recent years, become a widely used cost reduction approach. On the other hand, there can be times when integrating into the activities of either suppliers or distribution channel allies can lower costs through greater production efficiencies, reduced transaction costs or a better bargaining position. Direct Line

Insurance was one of the pioneers in selling policies directly to customers rather than relying on a network of brokers. They have maintained this strategy despite the rise of online price comparison sites in the UK. We return to this topic in more detail in Chapter 6.

10. *Motivating employees through incentives and organizational culture.* An organization's incentive system can encourage not only greater worker productivity but also cost-saving innovations that come from worker suggestions. The culture of an organization can also spur worker pride in productivity and continuous improvement. (Chapters 11 and 12 provide further coverage of how these factors impact on the execution of an organization's strategy.)

In addition to the above means of performing value chain activities more efficiently than rivals, managers can also achieve important cost savings by deliberately opting for an inherently economic strategy. For instance, an organization can often open up a significant cost advantage over rivals by:

- Having lower specifications for purchased materials, parts and components than do rivals. Thus, a maker of personal computers can use the cheapest hard drives, microprocessors, monitors and other components so as to end up with lower production costs than rival PC makers.

- Stripping frills and features from its product offering that are not highly valued by price-sensitive or bargain-hunting buyers. Deliberately restricting the organization's product offering to 'the essentials' can help an organization cut costs associated with snazzy attributes and a full line-up of options and extras. Activities and costs can also be eliminated by offering buyers fewer services. The opening case on BPP illustrates this sort of approach in the higher education sector by focusing on a core offering, without the additional services associated with a traditional campus experience.

- Offering a limited product line as opposed to a full product line. Pruning slow-selling items from the product line-up and being content to meet the needs of most buyers rather than all buyers can eliminate activities and costs associated with numerous product versions and wide selection.

- Distributing the organization's product only through low-cost distribution channels and avoiding high-cost distribution channels.

- Choosing to use the most economical method for delivering customer orders (even if it results in longer delivery times).

The point here is that a low-cost provider strategy entails not only performing value chain activities cost-effectively but also judiciously choosing cost-saving strategic approaches.

Revamping the Value Chain System to Lower Costs

Dramatic cost advantages can often emerge from redesigning the organization's value chain system in ways that eliminate costly work steps and entirely bypass certain cost-producing value chain activities. While using communication technologies and information systems or business process reengineering (covered in depth in Chapter 11) to drive down costs often involves activities that span the value chain system, other approaches to revamping the value chain system can include:

- *Selling direct to consumers and bypassing the activities and costs of distributors and dealers.* To circumvent the need for distributors-dealers, an organization can (1) create its own direct salesforce (which adds the costs of maintaining and supporting a salesforce but which may well be cheaper than utilizing independent distributors and dealers to access buyers) and/or (2) conduct sales operations at the organization's website (incurring costs for website operations and shipping may be a substantially cheaper way to make sales to customers than going through distributor-dealer channels). Costs in the wholesale/retail portions of the value chain frequently represent 35–50 per cent of the price final consumers pay, so establishing a direct salesforce or selling online may offer big cost savings. The closing case study in Chapter 3 demonstrated how the Internet had enabled some record labels and artists, such as the Arctic Monkeys and Groove Armada, to go directly to their customers without the need to make use of retailers and distributors. However, none of these individuals and organizations had been able to match Apple's iTunes service in terms of reach and convenience. The main losers were the bricks and mortar retailers who have been bypassed or replaced.

- *Co-ordinating with suppliers to bypass the need to perform certain value chain activities, speed up their performance or otherwise increase overall efficiency.* Examples include having suppliers combine particular parts and components into preassembled modules, thus permitting a manufacturer to assemble its own product in fewer work steps and with a smaller workforce, and sharing real-time sales information to lower costs through improved inventory management.

- *Reducing materials handling and shipping costs by having suppliers locate their plants or warehouses close to the organization's own facilities.* Having suppliers locate their plants or warehouses very close to an organization's own plant facilitates just-in-time deliveries of parts and components to the exact workstation where they will be utilized in assembling the organization's product. This not only lowers incoming shipping costs but also curbs or eliminates the need for an organization to build and operate storerooms for incoming parts and components and have plant personnel move the inventories to the workstations as needed for assembly.

Illustration Capsule 5.1 describes how German discount supermarket chains, Aldi and Lidl, have managed to dominate their home market and make gains even against entrenched opposition in a range of new ventures throughout Europe by adopting a low-cost strategy.

Illustration Capsule 5.1

HOW ALDI AND LIDL DEVELOPED LOW-COST STRATEGIES THAT EVEN WAL-MART COULD NOT MATCH

When Wal-Mart, the world's leading supermarket, decided to exit the German market in 2006, Lidl (who are part of the Schwarz group) and, Aldi were cited as the main reason. So how did two hard discount chains that stock mainly own label products, rarely advertise and only carry about 1000 lines (compared with the 40 000 in most supermarkets) beat the competition? The two organizations' cost advantage stems from a series of initiatives and practices:

- By focusing on only a small number of lines both Aldi and Lidl have been able to sell sufficient volumes to increase their bargaining power with their suppliers. The limited range of products and volume of sales has also given them economies of scale and simplifies handling and shipping. They have both expanded their operations into neighbouring countries, such as Poland, the Czech Republic, Hungary, Romania and also further afield into the UK – which has increased the economies of scale they can leverage from headquarters functions and distribution.
- Despite selling mainly own-brand products neither retailer has lost sight of the need to maintain quality despite charging low prices (the stores operate on a gross margin of about 15 per cent – half that of a regular supermarket). Many leading brands have agreed to manufacture for the chains because of their high volume of sales. Nestlé, Unilever and even Kellogg have all manufactured for Aldi's own brand goods.
- Both chains do not accept credit cards or where they do, pass on the full processing fee charged by the provider. By taking only debit cards and cash the firms can save between 1–2 per cent on each transaction.
- The no-frills approach extends to virtually all areas of operation. The discounters operate from smaller stores that require fewer staff. They also spend far less on advertising than rival supermarkets. Operations

▶

◄ are stripped to the bare minimum with goods often displayed in the boxes they arrive in and coin-operated trolleys used at each store to avoid employing staff to collect them after customers have finished with them.

● One other example of low-cost inputs to the businesses is Lidl and Aldi's largely organic growth. Both organizations are privately owned and do not incur some of the expenses associated with public status. The fact that they have been able to fund most of their expansion themselves rather than through taking on debt also reduces the costs they incur.

The firms' entry into the UK market also illustrates that timing can be a key factor in the success of a strategy. Both organizations were able to expand significantly in 2007/8 because the recession had made supermarket customers much more price-sensitive than previously. This allowed Aldi and Lidl to appeal to a broader market in the UK (nearly 90 per cent of German consumers regularly shop at their stores) and record growth of 21 per cent and 13 per cent, respectively. The phenomenon, dubbed the 'Aldi affect', was short-lived, as economic conditions improved and the incumbents in the UK fought back, the discount chains' growth stalled and Aldi's UK operations made a loss in 2010. However, both organizations have learned from the experience and changed their approach in the UK to include more advertising and a higher quality store experience. In the meantime, their rivals have responded with a range of moves, including widening own brand offerings, Tesco even experimented with their own version of a discount store.

Sources: Landler, M. and Barbaro, M. (2006) 'Wal-Mart finds that its formula doesn't fit every culture', *New York Times*, 2 August. Available online at www.nytimes.com/2006/08/02/business/worldbusiness/02walmart.html?pagewanted=all (accessed 28 November 2011); Moreau, R. (2008) 'Aldi and Lidl's global expansion strategies', *The Retail Digest*; Bloomberg (2004) 'The next Wal-Mart', *Business Week*, 26 April. Available online at www.businessweek.com/magazine/content/04_17/b3880010.htm (accessed 28 November 2011); Thompson, J. (2008) 'Lidl and Aldi see sales soar amid economic downturn', *The Independent*, 25 June. Available online at www.independent.co.uk/news/business/news/lidl-and-aldi-see-sales-soar-amid-economic-downturn-853614.html (accessed 28 November 2011).

The Keys to Being a Successful Low-cost Provider

To succeed with a low-cost provider strategy, managers have to scrutinize each cost-creating activity and determine what factors cause costs to be high or low. Then they have to use this knowledge to streamline or reengineer how activities are performed, exhaustively pursuing cost efficiencies throughout the value chain. Normally, low-cost producers try to engage all personnel in continuous cost improvement efforts, and they strive to operate with exceptionally small corporate staffs to keep administrative costs to a minimum. Many successful low-cost leaders also use benchmarking to keep close tabs on how their costs compare with those of rivals and organizations performing comparable activities in other industries.

But while low-cost providers are champions of frugality, they seldom hesitate to spend aggressively on resources and capabilities *that promise to drive costs out of the business*. Indeed, having resources or capabilities of this type and ensuring that they remain competitively superior is essential for achieving competitive advantage as a low-cost provider.

> Success in achieving a low-cost edge over rivals comes from outmanaging rivals in finding ways to perform value chain activities faster, more accurately and more cost-effectively.

Other organizations noted for their successful use of low-cost provider strategies include Hyundai in cars, Briggs & Stratton in small gasoline engines, Bic in ballpoint pens, Ryanair in air travel and Haier in major home appliances.

When a Low-cost Provider Strategy Works Best

A low-cost provider strategy becomes increasingly appealing and competitively powerful when:

1. *Price competition among rival sellers is vigorous.* Low-cost providers are in the best position to compete offensively on the basis of price, to use the appeal of lower

price to take sales (and market share) from rivals, to win the business of price-sensitive buyers, to remain profitable despite strong price competition and to survive price wars.

2. *The products of rival sellers are essentially identical and readily available from many eager sellers.* Look-alike products and/or overabundant product supply set the stage for lively price competition; in such markets, it is the less efficient, higher-cost organizations whose profits get squeezed the most.

3. *There are few ways to achieve product differentiation that have value to buyers.* When the differences between product attributes or brands do not matter much to buyers, buyers are nearly always very sensitive to price differences and market share winners will tend to be those with the lowest-priced products or services.

4. *Most buyers use the product in the same ways.* With common user requirements, a standardized product can satisfy the needs of buyers, in which case low selling price, not features or quality, becomes the dominant factor in causing buyers to choose one seller's product over another's.

5. *Buyers incur low costs in switching their purchases from one seller to another.* Low switching costs give buyers the flexibility to shift purchases to lower-priced sellers having equally good products or to attractively priced substitute products. A low-cost leader is well positioned to use low price to induce its customers not to switch to rival brands or substitutes.

6. *Buyers are large and have significant power to bargain down prices.* Low-cost providers have partial profit-margin protection in bargaining with high-volume buyers, since powerful buyers are rarely able to bargain price down past the survival level of the next most cost-efficient seller.

7. *Industry newcomers use introductory low prices to attract buyers and build a customer base.* A low-cost provider can use price cuts of its own to make it harder for a new rival to win customers. Moreover, the pricing power of a low-cost provider acts as a barrier for new entrants.

As a rule, the more price-sensitive buyers are, the more appealing a low-cost strategy becomes. A low-cost organization's ability to set the industry's price floor and still earn a profit erects protective barriers around its market position.

> A low-cost provider is in the best position to win the business of price-sensitive buyers, set the floor on market price and still earn a profit.

Pitfalls to Avoid in Pursuing a Low-cost Provider Strategy

Perhaps the biggest mistake a low-cost provider can make to spoil the profitability of its low-cost advantage is getting carried away with overly aggressive price-cutting to win sales and market share away from rivals. *Higher unit sales and market shares do not automatically translate into higher total profits.* A low-cost/low-price advantage results in superior profitability only if (1) prices are cut by less than the size of the unit cost advantage or (2) the added gains in unit sales are large enough to bring in a bigger total profit despite lower margins per unit sold. An organization with a 5 per cent per-unit cost advantage cannot cut prices 20 per cent, end up with a volume gain of only 10 per cent, and still expect to earn higher profits.

> Reducing price does not lead to higher total profits unless the incremental gain in total revenues exceeds the incremental increase in total costs.

A lower price improves total profitability only if the price cuts lead to total revenues that are big enough to *more than cover* all the added costs associated with selling more units. When the incremental gains in total revenues flowing from a lower price exceed the incremental increases in total costs associated with a higher sales volume, then cutting price is a profitable move. But if a lower selling price results in revenue gains that are smaller than the increases in total costs, profits end up lower than before and the price cut ends up reducing profits rather than raising them.

> A low-cost provider's product offering must always contain enough attributes to be attractive to prospective buyers – low price, by itself, is not always appealing to buyers.

A second pitfall of a low-cost provider strategy is failing to emphasize avenues of cost advantage that can be kept proprietary or that relegate rivals to playing catch-up. The real value of a cost advantage depends on its sustainability. Sustainability, in turn, hinges on whether the organization achieves its cost advantage in ways difficult for rivals to copy or otherwise overcome.

A third pitfall is becoming too fixated on cost reduction. Low cost cannot be pursued so zealously that an organization's offering ends up being too features-poor to generate buyer appeal. Furthermore, an organization driving hard to push its costs down has to guard against misreading or ignoring increased buyer interest in added features or service, declining buyer sensitivity to price, or new developments that start to alter how buyers use the product. Otherwise, it risks losing market ground if buyers start opting for more upscale or feature-rich products. Illustration Capsule 5.1 about Lidl and Aldi demonstrated that these firms had to adapt their offering in the UK market as consumer's changed their buying habits.

Even if these mistakes are avoided, a low-cost provider strategy still entails risk. An innovative rival may discover an even lower-cost value chain approach. Important cost-saving technological breakthroughs may suddenly emerge. And if a low-cost provider has heavy investments in its present means of operating, then it can prove very costly to quickly shift to the new value chain approach or a new technology.

LO 5.3
Discuss some of the alternative generic strategy frameworks, including those that argue for competitive advantage based on price.

Key Debate 5.1

IS COST LEADERSHIP A DISCRETE POSITION OR JUST ANOTHER TYPE OF DIFFERENTIATION?

In the current global economic climate many organizations are striving to lower their costs, but as Porter (1985) stresses there can only be one cost leader in any industry or serving any particular niche. This suggests that cost leadership is a form of unique position. However, unlike a differentiated position, it may be hard for a consumer to recognize a cost leader in an industry unless they have opted to use their position to offer prices lower than their rivals while maintaining the quality of its product or service. If we assume that some consumers buy on the basis of this lowest price then it could be argued that this is just another form of differentiation (Mintzberg, 1998) because the lowest priced product is clearly in a unique position where its perceived value to the consumer is greater than those of its rivals. Porter's model was also developed before the advent of the Internet, which for many industries has given buyers substantially more knowledge of and access to price information.

Mintzberg's generic strategies are based on six differentiated positions (Table 5.1) and also break down scope into four rather than two categories – unsegmented, segmented, niche and customized. These distinctions help to remove the vagueness around the definition of focus and broad in Porter's framework. Bowman (1988) is another commentator that argues for using price rather than cost to formulate a set of generic strategies. The strategic clock (Figure 5.3.) sets relative price against perceived use value to generate eight distinct positions. Hendry (1990) also provides some interesting cases to argue that in some industries there are only differentiated positions because cost is less relevant. His examples focus on professional services such as architecture and management consultancy where competition is driven by differentiation.

However, none of the generic strategy models covered above can match Porter's concept in terms of simplicity and many of the assumptions about price and cost leadership seem to be an attempt to create limits to the choices available to managers. This can be seen as a strength in a prescriptive model. Getting managers to focus on costs rather than price alone is also another advantage with Porter's model, because without an understanding of the organization's cost base and that of its competitors (see Current Practice 5.1) it is very difficult to make the right moves against low-cost competitors. The more complex models put forward by Mintzberg and Bowman go some way to countering Hendry's criticisms of Porter's approach and appear to reflect economic reality more effectively, making them better as descriptive models for looking at the pattern of strategy in an organization and its immediate competitors.

In Bowman's framework (which is also referred to as the customer matrix in later works – Bowman and Faulkner 1997) the two base generic strategies for success are to reduce price relative to other products with ▶

the same perceived use value (which would move a firm to the left of Figure 5.3 to position **2. Low price**) or to increase the perceived use value of the product or service, while maintaining price parity (which would move the firm to the top of the diagram, to position **4. Differentiation**). However, there are other possible options within the framework. Position **1. No frills**, means the organization has cut its prices but also reduced the perceived value in the eyes of the customer, in some instances this may move the product into a different segment of the market with a different set of competitors. The same is also true of position **5. Focused differentiation**, which increases the perceived use value but also includes a price premium and so would tend to be limited to less price-sensitive segments of the market. According to Bowman and Faulkner (1997) position **3. Hybrid** is the only position that guarantees an increase in market share and it is the hardest to maintain as the firm must be the lowest cost and the most agile (we cover this further in the section on Best Cost). The remaining positions (**6**, **7** and **8**) will only work in certain circumstances such as a monopoly or if all competitors follow suit in increasing prices. The key to applying the framework successfully is to understand how the customer views the product. This may lead to a very different view of the industry than that held by managers in the firm and is an important difference between Bowman and Porter's concepts. Both Bowman and Mintzberg's versions of generic strategy positions suggest that while cost is an important factor, it is not a position on its own and that for generic strategies to be successful they have to be based on something buyers can perceive, as well as an organization's capabilities.

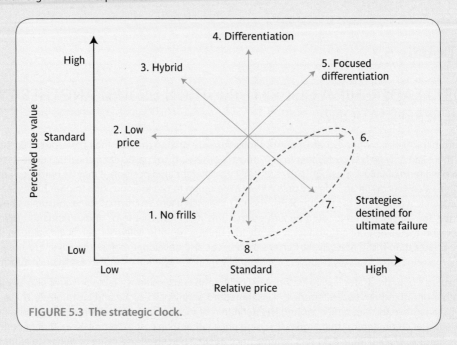

FIGURE 5.3 The strategic clock.

TABLE 5.1 Mintzberg's strategies of differentiation

Strategy	Description
Price differentiation	The product or service is differentiated by charging a lower price relative to competitors. This might be used for commodity products or services with a standard design or by creating a product or service that is intrinsically cheaper
Image differentiation	Advantage based on marketing that creates an image for a product or service so that it appears differentiated but is actually intrinsically the same as the standard industry offering barring cosmetic differences such as packaging
Support differentiation	Again the product itself may be the same as the standard industry offering, but is differentiated on additional support for the product such as extended warranty or credit offers or special after sales service
Quality differentiation	Differentiation based on product features which combine to make a better product than the standard industry offering. This might take the form of enhanced reliability, durability or performance

| Design differentiation | This form of advantage is likely to produce the most differences between the product and service created and the standard industry offering. Features will be unique and the product may not even be similar to the 'dominant design' in the industry |
| Undifferentiation | Where there is sufficient space in a market or industry or managers in an organization do not or will not make a choice on differentiating, the product or service can end up as an undifferentiated offering. This is a common position for copy-cat organizations to occupy |

QUESTION

1. Should managers focus more on price or cost when deciding on competitive strategy?

Sources: Bowman, C. (1988) *Strategy in Practice*, Harlow, Prentice-Hall; Bowman, C. and Faulkner, D. (1997) *Competitive and Corporate Strategy*, London, Irwin; Hendry (1990) 'The problem with Porter's generic strategies', *European Management Journal*, 8(4): 443–50; Mintzberg, H. (1998) 'Generic strategies: toward a comprehensive framework', in Lamb, R. and Shivastava, P. (eds) *Advances in Strategic Management*, JAI Press; Porter, M. (1985) *Competitive Advantage*, New York, Free Press.

Broad Differentiation Strategies

Differentiation strategies are attractive whenever buyers' needs and preferences are too diverse to be fully satisfied by a standardized product offering. Successful product differentiation requires careful study of buyers' needs and behaviours to learn what buyers consider important, what they think has value and what they are willing to pay for.[5] Then the trick is for an organization to incorporate certain buyer-desired attributes into its product offering such that its offering will not only appeal to a broad range of buyers but also be different enough to stand apart from the product offerings of rivals; in regard to the latter, a strongly differentiated product offering is always preferable to a weakly differentiated one. A differentiation strategy calls for a customer value proposition that is *unique*. The strategy achieves its aim when an attractively large number of buyers find the customer value proposition appealing and become strongly attached to an organization's differentiated attributes.

> **Core Concept**
>
> The essence of a broad differentiation strategy is to offer unique product attributes that a wide range of buyers find appealing and worth paying for.

Successful differentiation allows an organization to do one or more of the following:

- Command a premium price for its product/service.
- Increase unit sales (because additional buyers are won over by the differentiating features).
- Gain buyer loyalty to its brand (because some buyers are strongly bonded to the differentiating features of the organization's product/service offering).

> **LO 5.4**
> Describe the major avenues to a competitive advantage based on differentiating an organization's product or service offering from the offerings of rivals.

Differentiation enhances profitability whenever an organization's product can command a sufficiently higher price or produce sufficiently bigger unit sales *to more than cover the added costs of achieving the differentiation*. Organizational differentiation strategies fail when buyers do not value the brand's uniqueness and/or when an organization's approach to differentiation is easily copied or matched by its rivals.

Organizations can pursue differentiation from many angles including: a unique taste (Guinness, Listerine); multiple features (Microsoft Office, the iPhone); wide selection and one-stop shopping (Amazon.com); superior service (FedEx); engineering design and performance (Mercedes, BMW); prestige and distinctiveness (Rolex); design and style (Bang and Olufsen); quality manufacture (Michelin in tyres, Honda in cars); technological leadership (3M Corporation in bonding and coating products); a full range of services (Charles Schwab in stock brokerage); wide product selection (Knorr); and high fashion design (Gucci and Chanel).

Managing the Value Chain to Create the Differentiating Attributes

Although Mintzberg's framework (Table 5.1) lists image, quality and support as three significant ways to differentiate a product or service, differentiation is not something hatched solely in marketing and advertising departments, nor is it limited to the catch-alls of quality and service. Differentiation opportunities can exist in activities all along an industry's value chain (which highlights one of the weaknesses of Mintzberg's generic strategy framework – by being too specific the choices might limit managers and prevent them adopting a more creative and wide-ranging approach). The most systematic approach that managers can take, however, involves focusing on the uniqueness drivers, a set of factors – analogous to cost drivers – that are particularly effective in creating differentiation. Figure 5.4 contains a list of important uniqueness drivers. Ways that managers can enhance differentiation based on these drivers include the following:

> **Core Concept**
>
> A **uniqueness driver** is a factor that can have a strong differentiating effect.

1. *Striving to create superior product features, design and performance.* This applies to the physical as well as functional attributes of a product, including features such as expanded end uses and applications, added user safety, greater recycling capability or enhanced environmental protection. Design features can be important in enhancing the aesthetic appeal of a product. Ducati's motorcycles, for example, are prized for their designs and have been exhibited in the Guggenheim art museum in New York City.[6]

2. *Improving customer service or adding additional services.* Better customer services, in areas such as delivery, returns and repair, can be as important in creating differentiation as superior product features. Examples include superior technical assistance to buyers, higher-quality maintenance services, more and better product information provided to customers, more and better training materials for end-users, better credit terms, quicker order processing or greater customer convenience.

3. *Pursuing production R&D activities.* Engaging in production R&D may permit custom-order manufacture at an efficient cost, provide wider product variety and selection through product 'versioning', improve product quality or make production methods safer for the environment. Many manufacturers have developed flexible manufacturing systems that allow different models and product versions to be made on the same assembly line. Being able to provide buyers with made-to-order products can be a potent differentiating capability.

4. *Striving for innovation and technological advances.* Successful innovation is the route to more frequent first-on-the-market advantage and can be a powerful differentiator. If the innovation proves hard to replicate, through patent protection or other means, it can provide an organization with a first-mover advantage that is sustainable. Chapter 6 covers the advantages and disadvantages of being a first-mover in more depth.

5. *Pursuing continuous quality improvement.* Perceived quality differences can be an important differentiator in the eyes of customers. Quality control processes can be applied throughout the value chain, including after sale customer service activities. They can reduce product defects, prevent premature product failure, extend product life, make it economical to offer longer warranty coverage, improve economy of use, result in more end-user convenience or enhance product appearance. Organizations whose quality management systems meet certification standards,

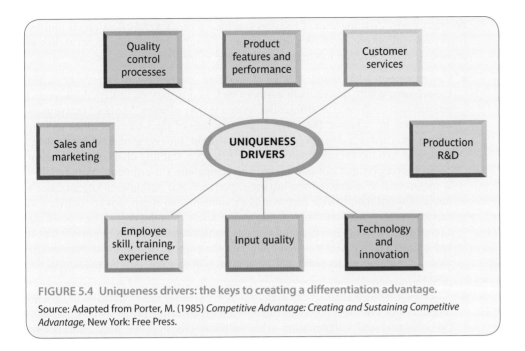

FIGURE 5.4 Uniqueness drivers: the keys to creating a differentiation advantage.

Source: Adapted from Porter, M. (1985) *Competitive Advantage: Creating and Sustaining Competitive Advantage,* New York: Free Press.

such as the ISO 9001 standards, can enhance their reputation for quality with customers. We look at how quality systems play a key role in executing strategy in Chapter 11.

6. *Increasing the intensity of marketing and sales activities.* Marketing and advertising can have a tremendous effect on the value perceived by buyers and therefore their willingness to pay more for the organization's offerings. They can create differentiation even when little tangible differentiation exists otherwise. For example, blind taste tests show that even the most loyal Pepsi or Coke drinkers have trouble telling one cola drink from another.[7] Brands create customer loyalty, which increases the perceived 'cost' of switching to another product. Brand management activities are therefore also important in supporting differentiation.

7. *Seeking out high-quality inputs.* Input quality can ultimately spill over to affect the performance or quality of the organization's end product. Starbucks, for example, gets high ratings on its coffees partly because it has very strict specifications on the coffee beans purchased from suppliers.

8. *Improving employee skill, knowledge and experience through human resource (HR) management activities.* Hiring, training and retaining highly skilled and experienced employees is important since such employees are often the source of creative, innovative ideas that are behind new product development. Moreover, they are essential to performing differentiating activities such as design, engineering, marketing and R&D. Organizational culture and reward systems can help unleash the potential contribution of high-value employees to a differentiation strategy (again, we cover these in more depth in Chapters 11 and 12).

Managers need a keen understanding of the sources of differentiation and the activities that drive uniqueness to evaluate various differentiation approaches and design durable ways to set their product offering apart from rival brands.

Revamping the Value Chain System to Increase Differentiation

Just as pursuing a cost advantage can involve the entire value chain system, the same is true for a differentiation advantage. Activities performed upstream by suppliers or downstream by distributors and retailers can have a meaningful effect on customers' perceptions of an organization's offerings and its value proposition. Approaches to enhancing differentiation through changes in the value chain system include:[8]

- *Co-ordinating with channel allies to enhance customer perceptions of value.* Co-ordinating with downstream partners such as distributors, dealers, brokers and retailers can contribute to differentiation in a variety of ways. Methods that organizations use to influence the value chain activities of their channel allies include setting standards for downstream partners to follow, providing them with templates to standardize the selling environment or practices, training channel personnel or co-sponsoring promotions and advertising campaigns. Co-ordinating with retailers is important for enhancing the buying experience and building an organization's image. Co-ordinating with distributors or shippers can mean quicker delivery to customers, more accurate order filling and/or lower shipping costs. The Coca-Cola Company considers co-ordination with its bottler/distributors so important that it has at times taken over a troubled bottler for the purpose of improving its management and upgrading its plant and equipment before releasing the product to the market.[9]

- *Co-ordinating with suppliers to better address customer needs.* Collaborating with suppliers can also be a powerful route to a more effective differentiation strategy. Co-ordinating and collaborating with suppliers can improve many dimensions affecting product features and quality. This is particularly true for organizations that only engage in assembly operations, such as Dell in PCs and Ducati in motorcycles. Close co-ordination with suppliers can also enhance differentiation by speeding up new product development cycles or speeding delivery to end-customers. Strong relationships with suppliers can also mean that the organization's supply requirements are prioritized when industry supply is insufficient to meet overall demand.

Delivering Superior Value via a Broad Differentiation Strategy

Differentiation strategies depend on meeting customer needs in unique ways or creating new needs, through activities such as innovation or persuasive advertising. The objective is to offer customers something that rivals cannot – at least in terms of the level of satisfaction. There are four basic routes to achieving this aim.

The first route is to incorporate product attributes and user features that *lower the buyer's overall costs* of using the organization's product. This is not obvious and is often an overlooked route to a differentiation advantage. It is a differentiating factor since it can help business buyers be more competitive in their markets and more profitable. Producers of materials and components often win orders for their products by reducing a buyer's raw-material waste (providing cut-to-size components or even reusing and recycling waste materials), reducing a buyer's inventory requirements (providing just-in-time deliveries), using online systems to reduce a buyer's procurement and order processing costs and providing free technical support. This route to differentiation can also appeal to individual consumers who are looking to economize on their overall costs of consumption. Making an organization's product more economical for a buyer to use can be done by incorporating energy-efficient features (energy-saving appliances and light bulbs help cut buyers' utility bills; fuel-efficient vehicles cut buyer costs for gasoline) and/or by increasing maintenance intervals and product reliability so as to lower buyer costs for maintenance and repairs. In Chapter 9, we see that these sorts of differentiating factors are becoming more important because they not only reduce costs, but they also help firms to meet their sustainability targets.

A second route is to incorporate *tangible* features that increase customer satisfaction with the product, such as product specifications, functions and styling. This can be accomplished by including attributes that add functionality, enhance the design, expand the range of uses, save time for the user, are more reliable, or make the product cleaner, safer, quieter, simpler to use, portable, more convenient or longer-lasting than rival brands. Cell phone manufacturers are in a race to introduce next-generation devices capable of being used for more purposes and having simpler menu functionality.

A third route to a differentiation-based competitive advantage is to incorporate *intangible* features that enhance buyer satisfaction in non-economic ways. Toyota's Prius appeals to environmentally conscious motorists not only because these drivers want to help reduce global carbon dioxide emissions but also because they identify with the image conveyed. Rolls-Royce, Ralph Lauren, Tiffany, Rolex and Prada have differentiation-based competitive advantages linked to buyer desires for status, image, prestige, upscale fashion, superior craftsmanship and the finer things in life. Intangibles that contribute to differentiation can extend beyond product attributes to the reputation of the organization and to customer relations or trust.

> Differentiation can be based on *tangible* or *intangible* attributes.

The fourth route is to *signal the value* of the organization's product offering to buyers. Typical signals of value include a high price (in instances where high price implies high quality and performance), more appealing or fancier packaging than competing products, advertising content that emphasizes a product's unique attributes, the quality of brochures and sales presentations, the luxuriousness and ambience of a seller's facilities (important for high-end retailers and for offices or other facilities frequented by customers). They make potential buyers aware of the professionalism, appearance and personalities of the seller's employees and/or make potential buyers realize that an organization has prestigious customers. Signalling value is particularly important (1) when the nature of differentiation is based on intangible features and is therefore subjective or hard to quantify, (2) when buyers are making a first-time purchase and are unsure what their experience with the product will be, and (3) when repurchase is infrequent and buyers need to be reminded of a product's value.

Regardless of the approach taken, achieving a successful differentiation strategy requires, first, that the organization has strengths in capabilities, such as customer service, marketing, brand management and technology that can create and support differentiation. That is, the resources, competences and value chain activities of the organization must be well matched to the requirements of the strategy. For the strategy to result in competitive advantage, the organization's competences must also be sufficiently unique in delivering value to buyers that they help set its product offering apart from those of rivals. They must be competitively superior. There are numerous examples of organizations that have differentiated themselves on the basis of distinctive competences and capabilities. LVMH, the French luxury goods group, has built up a high level of competence in designing and managing retail outlets. The organization's experts will often build scale models to work out customer flows and where the best positions are in department stores. In this they are considered to be the best in the industry. Drinks firm Diageo have superior brand management capabilities and have identified 14 strategic brands that they use to drive growth through investment in consistent marketing programmes on a global basis.

The most successful approaches to differentiation are those that are hard or expensive for rivals to duplicate. Indeed, this is the route to a sustainable differentiation advantage. While resourceful competitors can, in time, clone almost any tangible product attribute, socially complex intangible attributes, such as organizational reputation, long-standing relationships with buyers and image are much harder to imitate. Differentiation that creates switching costs that lock in buyers also provides a route to sustainable advantage. For example, if a buyer makes a substantial investment in learning to use one type of system, that buyer is less likely to switch to a competitor's system (This has kept many users from switching away from Microsoft Office products, despite

> Easy-to-copy differentiating features cannot produce sustainable competitive advantage.

the fact that there are other applications with superior features). As a rule, differentiation yields a longer-lasting and more profitable competitive edge when it is based on a well-established brand image, patent-protected product innovation, complex technical superiority, a reputation for superior product quality and reliability, relationship-based customer service and unique competitive capabilities. Such differentiating attributes are generally tougher and take longer for rivals to match, and buyers widely perceive them as offering superior value.

When a Differentiation Strategy Works Best

Differentiation strategies tend to work best in market circumstances where:

- *Buyer needs and uses of the product are diverse.* Diverse buyer preferences present competitors with a bigger window of opportunity to do things differently and set themselves apart with product attributes that appeal to particular buyers. For instance, the diversity of consumer preferences for menu selection, ambience, pricing and customer service gives restaurants exceptionally wide latitude in creating a differentiated product offering. Similar opportunities exist for the publishers of magazines, the makers of motor vehicles and the manufacturers of cabinetry and countertops.

- *There are many ways to differentiate the product or service that have value to buyers.* There is plenty of room for retail apparel competitors to stock different styles and quality of apparel merchandise but very little room for the makers of paper clips or copier paper or sugar to set their products apart. Likewise, the sellers of different brands of gasoline or orange juice have little differentiation opportunity compared to the sellers of high-definition TVs or patio furniture or breakfast cereal. Basic commodities, such as chemicals, mineral deposits and agricultural products, provide few opportunities for differentiation.

- *Few rival organizations are following a similar differentiation approach.* The best differentiation approaches involve trying to appeal to buyers on the basis of attributes that rivals are not emphasizing. A differentiator encounters less head-to-head rivalry when it goes its own separate way in creating uniqueness and does not try to outdifferentiate rivals on the very same attributes. When many rivals are all claiming 'ours tastes better than theirs' or 'ours gets your clothes cleaner than theirs', the most likely result is weak brand differentiation and 'strategy overcrowding' – competitors end up chasing much the same buyers with much the same product offerings.

- *Technological change is fast-paced and competition revolves around rapidly evolving product features.* Rapid product innovation and frequent introductions of next-version products not only provide space for organizations to pursue separate differentiating paths but also heighten buyer interest. In video game hardware and video games, golf equipment, PCs, cell phones and MP3 players, competitors are locked into an ongoing battle to set themselves apart by introducing the best next-generation products; organizations that fail to come up with new and improved products and distinctive performance features quickly lose out in the marketplace. In mobile telecommunications, handset manufacturers, such as Nokia and Motorola, that were slow to develop smartphones in response to Apple's iPhone, lost ground to nimbler competitors such as HTC and Samsung.

Pitfalls to Avoid in Pursuing a Differentiation Strategy

> Any differentiating feature that works well is a magnet for imitators, although imitation attempts are not always successful.

Differentiation strategies can fail for any of several reasons. *A differentiation strategy is always doomed when competitors are able to quickly copy most or all of the appealing product attributes an organization comes up with.* Rapid imitation means that no rival achieves differentiation, since whenever one organization introduces some aspect of uniqueness that strikes the fancy of buyers, fast-following copycats quickly re-establish similarity. This is why an organization must seek out sources of uniqueness that are time-consuming or burdensome for rivals to match if it hopes to use differentiation to win a lasting competitive edge over rivals.

A second pitfall is that *the organization's attempt at differentiation produces an unenthusiastic response on the part of buyers*. Thus, even if an organization succeeds in setting its product apart from those of rivals, its strategy can result in disappointing sales and profits if buyers find other brands more appealing. If many potential buyers look at an organization's differentiated product offering and conclude 'so what', the organization's differentiation strategy is unlikely to be successful.

The third big pitfall of a differentiation strategy is *overspending on efforts to differentiate the organization's product offering, thus eroding profitability*. Organizational efforts to achieve differentiation nearly always raise costs, often substantially, since marketing and R&D are expensive undertakings. Managers wishing to achieve profitable differentiation have to keep the unit cost of achieving differentiation below the price premium that the differentiating attributes can command in the marketplace (thus increasing the profit margin per unit sold) or to offset thinner profit margins per unit by selling enough additional units to increase total profits. If an organization goes overboard in pursuing costly differentiation efforts and then unexpectedly discovers that buyers are unwilling to pay a sufficient price premium to cover the added costs of differentiation, it ends up saddled with unacceptably thin profit margins or even losses. The need to contain differentiation costs is why many organizations add little touches of differentiation that increase buyer satisfaction but are inexpensive to institute. Upscale restaurants often provide valet parking. Laundry detergent and soap manufacturers add pleasing scents to their products. Ski resorts provide skiers with complimentary coffee or hot apple cider at the base of the lifts in the morning and late afternoon.

Other common mistakes in crafting a differentiation strategy include:[10]

> Over-differentiating and overcharging can be fatal strategy mistakes.

- *Failing to open up meaningful gaps in quality, service or performance features* vis-à-vis *the products of rivals*. Tiny differences between rivals' product offerings may not be visible or important to buyers. If an organization wants to generate the fiercely loyal customer following needed to earn superior profits and open up a differentiation-based competitive advantage over rivals, then its strategy must result in *strong rather than weak product differentiation*. In markets where differentiators do no better than achieve weak product differentiation (because the attributes of rival brands are fairly similar in the minds of many buyers), customer loyalty to any one brand is weak, the costs of brand switching are fairly low and no one organization has enough of a market edge that it can get by with charging a price premium over rival brands.

- *Adding so many frills and extra features that the product exceeds the needs and use patterns of most buyers*. A dazzling array of features and options not only drives up costs (and therefore product price) but also runs the risk that many buyers will conclude that a less deluxe and lower-priced brand is better value since they have little occasion or reason to use some of the deluxe attributes.

- *Charging too high a price premium*. While buyers may be intrigued by a product's deluxe features, they may nonetheless see it as being overpriced relative to the value delivered by the differentiating attributes. Managers need to be aware that certain actions can turn off would-be buyers with what is perceived as 'price gouging'. Normally, the bigger the price premium for the differentiating extras, the harder it is to keep buyers from switching to the lower-priced offerings of competitors.

A low-cost provider strategy can defeat a differentiation strategy when buyers are satisfied with a basic product and do not think 'extra' attributes are worth a higher price.

CURRENT PRACTICE 5.1

COMPETING SUCCESSFULLY WITH LOW-COST RIVALS

As we have seen in the first part of this chapter, low-cost advantage is often leveraged through aligning the whole of an organization's value chain. Improvements to an organization's operations, such as aggressive sourcing of raw materials, reduces costs, while measures like investing in rapid new product development can increase revenue. Both of these feed through into better margins for the organization. Consultants at A.T. Kearney also link cash management and asset utilization to this equation. Actions such as maintaining low stock levels and securing access to low-cost capital can work in combination with effective matching of supply and demand to deliver further advantage through asset effectiveness. Many incumbents in a range of industries have seen their position threatened by low-cost entrants using these techniques in recent years. A.T. Kearney's consultants recommend four preparatory steps and a range of strategic responses to compete against low-cost rivals.

First, organizations need to identify potential low-cost rivals – getting caught off-guard and failing to realize likely competitors are classic errors that incumbents made when organizations like Wal-Mart and Ryanair entered their markets. Organizations that assemble products in low-cost countries or have strong customer bases in emerging economies are some of the key players to watch according to Jim Morehouse and his colleagues. Second, the organization needs to carry out a total cost analysis – this involves making assumptions about how much the competitors' operations cost in a detailed analysis of each stage of the value/supply chain. Looking at operational best practice in every part of the process can help to underpin these assumptions. Next the organization needs to develop a series of scenarios – as we saw in Chapter 3, these can be developed by combining a range of trend information with expert opinion and can then be used to test the organization's strategy and feed into the final step of choosing the best strategic moves.

The consultants recommend both short- and long-term responses to low-cost rivals. Despite the dangers of starting a price war, lowering product/service prices is cited as one of the short-term responses that can buy incumbent firms time and also ascertain how robust the low-cost rival's advantage is. Reinforcing existing sources of differentiation is another approach that can be achieved through promotional and salesforce activity and is a tactic Shell and Apple have used to good effect. Finally, organizations also have the option to walk away from some segments of the market and leave them to the low-cost competitor, especially if those customers are unprofitable. However, to sustain their advantage, incumbent firms must use the time these measures buy them to develop effective long-term responses. Diversifying into related products and markets is a strategy that Cisco has used effectively to compete with Chinese firm Haier. Other organizations have developed their own low-cost operation either as an offshoot or by remodelling their entire organization. For example, IBM chose to bundle products and services in order to create an offer that low-cost rivals would find much harder to imitate.

Source: Morehouse, J., O'Meara, B., Hagen, C. and Huseby, T. (2008) 'Hitting back: strategic responses to low cost rivals', *Strategy and Leadership*, 36(1): 4–13.

Focused (or Market Niche) Strategies

What sets focused strategies apart from low-cost provider and broad differentiation strategies is concentrated attention on a narrow piece of the total market. The target segment, or niche, can be defined by geographic uniqueness, by specialized requirements in using the product, or by special product attributes that appeal only to niche members. Nomad Travel and Outdoor, a UK-based travel equipment retailer, specializes in kit for people going on adventure holidays. The firm has links with a range of travel companies offering everything from activity breaks to safaris. Examples of other organizations that concentrate on a well-defined market niche keyed to a particular product or buyer segment include Helly Hansen (in specialist clothing for sailing, skiing and other outdoor pursuits); Lapierre (in top-of-the-line mountain bikes); Triodos bank (a specialist in providing ethical and sustainable financial services); Ovo (new entrant to the UK energy market specializing in supplying renewable energy); and Match.com (the world's largest online dating service). Microbreweries, bed-and-breakfast providers and local owner-managed retail boutiques have also scaled their operations to serve narrow or local customer segments.

A Focused Low-cost Strategy

A focused strategy based on low cost aims at securing a competitive advantage by serving buyers in the target market niche at a lower cost and lower price than those of rival competitors. This strategy has considerable attraction when an organization can lower costs significantly by limiting its customer base to a well-defined buyer segment. The avenues to achieving a cost advantage over rivals also serving the target market niche are the same as those for low-cost leadership: outmanage rivals in keeping the costs of value chain activities contained to a bare minimum and search for innovative ways to bypass certain value chain activities. The only real difference between a low-cost provider strategy and a focused low-cost strategy is the size of the buyer group that an organization is trying to appeal to – the former involves a product offering that appeals broadly to almost all buyer groups and market segments, whereas the latter aims at just meeting the needs of buyers in a narrow market segment.

Focused low-cost strategies are fairly common. Producers of private-label goods are able to achieve low costs in product development, marketing, distribution and advertising by concentrating on making generic items imitative of name-brand merchandise and selling directly to retail chains wanting a low-priced store brand. McBride is Europe's leading private label company producing a range of household, personal care and health products. In 2011 they achieved sales of more than £812 million, by focusing on producing private-label brands for retailers such as Tesco, Carrefour, Waitrose and Biedronka. Budget hotel chains, like Premier Inn and Travelodge, cater to price-conscious travellers who just want to pay for a clean, no-frills place to spend the night. The opening case to the chapter is another example of an organization taking a focused low-cost position. BPP targets mainly professional and part-time students with a limited range of higher education programmes, while aiming to offer the lowest fees for their degrees by keeping delivery costs low.

A Focused Differentiation Strategy

A focused strategy keyed to differentiation aims at securing a competitive advantage with a product offering carefully designed to appeal to the unique preferences and needs of a narrow, well-defined group of buyers (as opposed to a broad differentiation strategy aimed at many buyer groups and market segments). Successful use of a focused differentiation strategy depends on the existence of a buyer segment that is looking for special product attributes or seller capabilities and on an organization's ability to stand apart from rivals competing in the same target market niche.

Organizations like Gucci, Rolls-Royce, Haägen-Dazs and W.L. Gore (the maker of Gore-Tex) employ successful differentiation-based focused strategies targeted at upscale buyers wanting products and services with world-class attributes. Indeed, most markets contain a buyer segment willing to pay a big price premium for the very finest items available, thus opening the strategic window for some competitors to pursue differentiation-based focused strategies aimed at the very top of the market pyramid. Morgan Cars only produces about 600 cars a year, although prices are not as high as the likes of Ferrari and Maserati, (entry-level models are just over £30 000), each car is hand-built in the firm's factory in Worcestershire and there is normally a one-to two-year waiting list for new models.

Another successful focused differentiator is the Ecology Building Society. Based in Keighley, West Yorkshire, the Ecology specializes in properties that provide an ecological benefit, whether that is through their construction (sustainable use of materials, energy efficiency etc.), use of land or lifestyle. The Ecology Building Society is currently one of the fastest growing financial institutions in the UK and has over 10 000 accounts and assets of over £100 million. The Ecology was started in 1980 with just £5000. It appeals not just to savers looking for a green investment but more specifically to those with a passion for sustainable building and innovative approaches to constructing green buildings.

When a Focused Low-cost or Focused Differentiation Strategy is Attractive

A focused strategy aimed at securing a competitive edge based either on low cost or differentiation becomes increasingly attractive as more of the following conditions are met:

- The target market niche is big enough to be profitable and offers good growth potential.
- Industry leaders do not see that having a presence in the niche is crucial to their own success – in which case focusers can often escape battling head to head against some of the industry's biggest and strongest competitors.
- It is costly or difficult for multi-segment competitors to put capabilities in place to meet the specialized needs of buyers constituting the target market niche and at the same time satisfy the expectations of their mainstream customers.
- The industry has many different niches and segments, thereby allowing a focuser to pick a competitively attractive niche suited to its most valuable resources and capabilities. Also, with more niches there is more room for focusers to avoid each other in competing for the same customers.
- Few, if any, other rivals are attempting to specialize in the same target segment – a condition that reduces the risk of segment overcrowding.
- The focuser has a reservoir of customer goodwill and loyalty (accumulated from having catered to the specialized needs and preferences of niche members over many years) that it can draw on to help stave off ambitious challengers looking to home in on its business.

The advantages of focusing an organization's entire competitive effort on a single market niche are considerable, especially for smaller and medium-size organizations that may lack the breadth and depth of resources to tackle going after a broad customer base with a 'something for everyone' line-up of models, styles and product selection. YouTube has become a household name by concentrating on short video clips posted online. Papa John's and Domino's Pizza have created impressive businesses by focusing on the home delivery segment. Porsche and Ferrari have done well catering to wealthy sports car enthusiasts.

Emerging Theme 5.1

TECHNOLOGY: IS FOCUS THE STRATEGY OF THE FUTURE?

As Chris Anderson pointed out in his 2009 book, *The Longer Long Tail*, the Internet has given e-tailers unlimited shelving and allowed them to stock a far wider choice of products than their bricks and mortar equivalents. What this has uncovered is the latent demand for products that only appeal to niche audiences, with low sales and so are not economic for high street stores to stock. In some cases, like Rhapsody, an online music retailer, those products made up over 45 per cent of their annual sales. While the top selling 100 products in a category such as CDs or books might account for 80 per cent of sales in a traditional retail outlet, with sales falling to an uneconomic level after the 3000th or 4000th best-selling product, online is different. The lack of overheads means that e-tailers can stock the 90 000th or 100 000th best-selling products – even if they only sell a few copies a year. While the hits still make up a substantial percentage of sales, the misses in aggregate also add up to a significant level of income – in what is known as the Long Tail effect. So, many firms such as Amazon, eBay and Netflix are happy to serve niches and provide a platform for producers of niche products. The phenomenon is also moving beyond media products such as film, books and music, with the recent growth in microbreweries and even mainstream firms, such as Anheuser-Busch, launching subsidiaries to deal with niche products (Long

▶

◄

Tail Libations Inc.). 3D printing technology is allowing more and more customization of products and has the potential to allow individuals to become their own producers of goods from coat-hangers to engine components. The changes that technology could bring to a wide range of markets might mean that the current distinction between broad and narrow target markets becomes less relevant as the majority of products can be produced for small groups of customers or even customized for individuals. When a market segment of one can be profitable will most organizations adopt a focus strategy?

Source: Anderson, C. (2009) *The Longer Long Tail*, London, Random House.

The Risks of a Focused Low-cost or Focused Differentiation Strategy

Focusing carries several risks. One is the chance that competitors will find effective ways to match the focused organization's capabilities in serving the target niche – perhaps by coming up with products or brands specifically designed to appeal to buyers in the target niche or by developing expertise and capabilities that offset the focuser's strengths. In the hotel business, large chains like Marriott have launched multibrand strategies that allow them to compete effectively in several segments simultaneously. Marriott has flagship J.W. Marriot and Ritz-Carlton hotels with deluxe accommodation for business travellers and holidaymakers; its Courtyard by Marriott and SpringHill Suites brands cater to business travellers looking for moderately priced lodging; and the Marriott Residence Inns and TownePlace Suites are designed as a 'home away from home' for travellers staying five or more nights. Multi-brand strategies are attractive to large companies like Marriott precisely because they enable an organization to enter a market niche and siphon business away from organizations that employ a focused strategy.

A second risk of employing a focused strategy is the potential for the preferences and needs of niche members to shift over time towards the product attributes desired by the majority of buyers. An erosion of the differences across buyer segments lowers entry barriers into a focuser's market niche and provides an open invitation for rivals in adjacent segments to begin competing for the focuser's customers. A third risk is that the segment may become so attractive that it is soon inundated with competitors, intensifying rivalry and splintering segment profits.

Illustration Capsule 5.2 shows how Danish consumer electronics company Bang & Olufsen has come under increasing pressure from imitators and innovators in its sector.

Illustration Capsule 5.2

BANG & OLUFSEN – CAN FOCUSED DIFFERENTIATION SURVIVE DISRUPTIVE INNOVATION?

Danish firm, Bang & Olufsen (B&O), have turned consumer electronics design into a very profitable cult. Since the company's launch in the 1920s it has always done things differently to its competitors. Its original art deco design for radios used high-quality walnut and maple and was more like high-end furniture, compared with the functional sets other organizations in the industry produced. By the late 1970s B&O's position as designers of the coolest TVs and sound systems was confirmed by an exclusive exhibition held at the Museum of Modern Art in New York in 1978.

▶

◀   B&O's strategy was to differentiate their products by creating the most elegant and deluxe offering in each category. But all this came at a price, so they had a limited pool of customers willing and able to afford the ultra-expensive products. Their latest 3D 85-inch Beovision4 TV has an asking price of £63 200 and even an iPod speaker dock costs £895. However, their greatest threat has come, not from a low-cost rival based in one of the emerging BRIC economies (although Asian manufacturers of high-quality, low-cost TVs have undoubtedly taken some of their market), but another designer of cool products, Apple. The launch of the iPod and iTunes service and more recently the iPhone have undermined one of the key reasons customers were prepared to pay so much for B&O's. The products the organization produced not only looked good, they also lasted for a long time, which meant customers considered them an investment and were prepared to pay a premium price. The rapid changes and almost continuous innovation in consumer electronics have created entirely new platforms – such as Apple's devices and services, and made products seem more disposable than in the past. Investing several thousand pounds in an elegant sound system that may be obsolete in five years does not look like such a good investment and such conspicuous consumption is not seen as desirable in a climate of austerity and economic crisis. The risk for B&O is that they might lose their niche altogether.

A sharp fall in profits and share price in 2008/9 prompted the firm to appoint a new chief executive officer (CEO), Tue Mantoni, who had overseen the revival of British motorcycle manufacturer, Triumph. His answer to the organization's problems is to get closer to its customers and understand what will make the company's products more relevant to their lives, while retaining its distinctive designs.

Sources: Walker, R. (2011) 'Can the cult of Bang & Olufsen last?' *Wired*, October, Bang & Olufsen company website – www.bang-olufsen.com/.

Core Concept

Best-cost provider strategies are a *hybrid* of low-cost provider and differentiation strategies that aim at providing desired quality/features/performance/service attributes while beating rivals on price.

LO 5.5
Recognize the attributes of a best-cost provider strategy and the way in which some organizations use a hybrid strategy to go about building a competitive advantage and delivering superior value to customers.

Best-cost Provider Strategies

Best-cost provider strategies stake out a middle ground between pursuing a low-cost advantage and a differentiation advantage and between appealing to the broad market as a whole and a narrow market niche (see Figure 5.1). Such a middle ground allows an organization to aim squarely at the sometimes great mass of value-conscious buyers looking for a good to very good product or service at an economical price. Value-conscious buyers frequently shy away from both cheap low-end products and expensive high-end products, but they are quite willing to pay a 'fair' price for extra features and functionality they find appealing and useful. The essence of a best-cost provider strategy is giving customers more *value for the money* by satisfying buyer desires for appealing features/performance/quality/service and charging a lower price for these attributes compared to rivals with similar calibre product offerings.[11] From a competitive-positioning standpoint, best-cost strategies are thus a *hybrid,* balancing a strategic emphasis on low cost against a strategic emphasis on differentiation (desirable features delivered at a relatively low price).

To profitably employ a best-cost provider strategy, an organization *must have the resources and capabilities to incorporate attractive or upscale attributes into its product offering at a lower cost than rivals.* When an organization can incorporate appealing features, good to excellent product performance or quality, or more satisfying customer service into its product offering *at a lower cost than rivals,* then it enjoys 'best-cost' status – it is the low-cost provider of a product or service with *desirable attributes*. A best-cost provider can use its low-cost advantage to underprice rivals whose products or services have similarly desirable attributes and still earn attractive profits. It is usually not difficult to entice buyers away from rivals with an equally good product at a more economical price.

Being a best-cost provider is different from being a low-cost provider because the additional attractive attributes entail additional costs (which a low-cost provider can avoid by offering buyers a basic product with few frills). Moreover, the two strategies aim at a distinguishably different market target. *The target market for a best-cost provider is value-conscious buyers* – buyers who are looking for appealing extras and functionality at an appealingly low price. Value-hunting buyers (as distinct from *price-conscious buyers* looking for a basic product at a bargain-basement price) often constitute a very sizeable part of the overall market. Normally, value-conscious buyers are willing to pay a 'fair' price for extra features, but they shy away from paying the top price for items having all the bells and whistles. It is the desire to cater to *value-conscious buyers* as opposed to *budget-conscious buyers* that sets a best-cost provider apart from a low-cost provider – the two strategies aim at distinguishably different market targets.

When a Best-cost Provider Strategy Works Best

A best-cost provider strategy works best in markets where product differentiation is the norm and there is an attractively large number of value-conscious buyers who prefer mid-range products to cheap, basic products or expensive top-of-the-line products. A best-cost provider needs to position itself near the middle of the market with either a medium-quality product at a below-average price or a high-quality product at an average or slightly higher price. The objective is to provide the *best value* for better-quality, differentiated products. Best-cost provider strategies also work well in recessionary times when great masses of buyers become value-conscious and are attracted to economically priced products and services with appealing attributes. *But unless an organization has the resources, know-how and capabilities to incorporate upscale product or service attributes at a lower cost than rivals, adopting a best-cost strategy is ill-advised* – a winning strategy must always be matched to an organization's most valuable resources and capabilities.

Illustration Capsule 5.3 describes how Toyota has applied the principles of the best-cost provider strategy in producing and marketing its Lexus brand.

Illustration Capsule 5.3

TOYOTA'S BEST-COST PROVIDER STRATEGY FOR ITS LEXUS LINE

Toyota Motor Company is widely regarded as a low-cost producer among the world's motor vehicle manufacturers. Despite its emphasis on product quality, Toyota has achieved low-cost leadership because it has developed considerable skills in efficient supply chain management and low-cost assembly capabilities and because its models are positioned in the low-to-medium end of the price spectrum, where high-production volumes are conducive to low-unit costs. But when Toyota decided to introduce its new Lexus models to compete in the luxury-car market segment, it employed a classic best-cost provider strategy. Toyota took the following four steps in crafting and implementing its Lexus strategy:

- Designing an array of high-performance characteristics and upscale features into the Lexus models to make them comparable in performance and luxury to other high-end models and attractive to Mercedes, BMW, Audi and Jaguar buyers.
- Transferring its capabilities in making high-quality Toyota models at low cost to making premium-quality Lexus models at costs below other luxury-car-makers. Toyota's supply chain capabilities and low-cost assembly know-how allowed it to incorporate high-tech performance features and upscale quality into Lexus models at substantially less cost than Mercedes, BMW and other luxury vehicle-makers have been able to achieve in producing their models.
- Using its relatively lower manufacturing costs to underprice comparable Mercedes, BMW, Audi and Jaguar models. Toyota believed that with its cost advantage it could price attractively equipped Lexus cars low enough to draw price-conscious buyers away from comparable high-end brands. Toyota's pricing policy

▶

also allowed it to induce Toyota, Honda, Ford or GM owners desiring more luxury to switch to a Lexus. Lexus's pricing advantage has typically been quite significant. For example, in 2011 prices for the Lexus RX 350, a mid-size SUV, started from £32 000 whereas comparable Mercedes M-class SUVs had price tags in the £42 000–£59 000 range and a comparable BMW X5 SUV could range anywhere from £45 000–£80 000.

● Establishing a new network of Lexus dealers, separate from Toyota dealers, dedicated to providing a level of personalized, attentive customer service unmatched in the industry.

Toyota's best-cost strategy has resulted in growing sales of Lexus models (now over 400 000 vehicles annually). Lexus has consistently ranked first in the widely watched J. D. Power & Associates quality survey, and Lexus owners enjoy both top-notch dealer service and product quality.

Best-cost Provider Strategy – Big Risk or the Only Option in Future?

An organization's biggest vulnerability in employing a best-cost provider strategy is getting squeezed between the strategies of organizations using low-cost and high-end differentiation strategies. Low-cost providers may be able to siphon customers away with the appeal of a lower price (despite less appealing product attributes). High-end differentiators may be able to steal customers away with the appeal of better product attributes (even though their products carry a higher price tag). Thus, to be successful, a best-cost provider must offer buyers *significantly* better product attributes in order to justify a price above what low-cost leaders are charging. Likewise, it has to achieve significantly lower costs in providing upscale features so that it can outcompete high-end differentiators on the basis of a *significantly* lower price.

However, recent developments have shown that emerging market organizations are going beyond the basics of a best-cost approach and changing some of the assumptions that underpin both differentiation and focus strategies. Peter Williamson has termed these moves cost innovation.[12] Emerging multinationals from countries such as China, India and Brazil already benefit from operating at low cost. However, they are also challenging some of the established norms for dealing with low-cost competitors. For example, in high-tech markets, cost innovators are offering high-end products at low cost. Dawning, a Chinese computer manufacturer, is incorporating technology normally found in supercomputers into low-cost servers. Other challengers are providing variety and customization, normally associated with differentiation strategies, at low cost; or successfully moving niche products into the mass market, such as Haier's strategy to open up the wine-storage refrigerator segment via its deal with Wal-Mart subsidiary Sam's Club. Other examples cited by Williamson include Brazilian jet manufacturer, Embraer, Indian firms, Suzlon (wind power generation), Tata (cars etc.), Infosys and Wipro (IT Services). These organizations have the potential to render differentiation and focus advantages redundant, which leaves cost leadership and best cost/cost innovation as the only option open to incumbents. If the strength of cost innovation challengers is as high as being predicted then combining cost and differentiation may become the norm in future rather than a difficult combination achieved by relatively few smart organizations.

The Contrasting Features of the Five Generic Competitive Strategies: a Summary

Deciding which generic competitive strategy should serve as the framework on which to hang the rest of the organization's strategy is not a trivial matter. Each of the five generic competitive strategies *positions* the organization differently in its market and competitive environment. Each establishes a central theme for how the organization will endeavour to outcompete rivals. Each creates some boundaries or guidelines for manoeuvring as market circumstances unfold and as ideas for improving the strategy are debated. Each points to different ways of experimenting and tinkering with the basic strategy – for example, employing a low-cost leadership strategy means experimenting with ways that costs can be cut and value chain activities can be streamlined, whereas a broad differentiation strategy means exploring ways to add new differentiating features or to perform value chain activities differently if the result is to add value for customers in ways they are willing to pay for. Each entails differences in terms of product line, production emphasis, marketing emphasis and means of maintaining the strategy, as shown in Table 5.2.

Thus, a choice of which generic strategy to employ spills over to affect many aspects of how the business will be operated and the manner in which value chain activities need to be managed. Deciding which generic strategy to employ is perhaps the most important strategic commitment an organization makes – it tends to drive the rest of the strategic actions an organization decides to undertake.

Successful Competitive Strategies are Resource-based

For an organization's competitive strategy to succeed in delivering good performance and the intended competitive edge over rivals, it has to be underpinned by an appropriate set of resources, know-how and competitive capabilities. To succeed in employing a low-cost provider strategy, an organization has to have the resources and capabilities needed to keep its costs below those of its competitors; this means having the expertise to cost-effectively manage value chain activities better than rivals and/or having the innovative capability to bypass certain value chain activities being performed by rivals. Successful focused strategies require the capability to do an outstanding job of satisfying the needs and expectations of niche buyers. Success in employing a best-cost strategy requires the resources and capabilities to simultaneously incorporate desirable product or service attributes and deliver them at a lower cost than rivals. To succeed in strongly differentiating its product in ways that are appealing to buyers, an organization must have the resources and capabilities to incorporate unique attributes into its product offering that a broad range of buyers will find appealing and worth paying for. This is easier said than done because, given sufficient time, competitors can clone almost any product feature buyers find quite appealing. Hence, long-term differentiation success is usually dependent on having a hard-to-imitate portfolio of resource capabilities (like patented technology; strong, socially complex skills in product innovation; expertise in relationship-based customer service) that allow an organization to sustain its differentiation-based competitive advantage. Likewise, sustaining the competitive edge inherent in any generic strategy depends on resources, capabilities and competences that rivals have a hard time duplicating and for which there are no good substitutes.

> An organization's competitive strategy is unlikely to succeed unless it is predicated on leveraging a competitively valuable collection of resources and capabilities that match the strategy.

TABLE 5.2 Distinguishing features of the five most common generic competitive strategies

	Low-cost provider	Broad differentiation	Focused low-cost provider	Focused differentiation	Best-cost provider
Strategic target	• A broad cross-section of the market	• A broad cross-section of the market	• A narrow market niche where buyer needs and preferences are distinctively different	• A narrow market niche where buyer needs and preferences are distinctively different	• Value-conscious buyers • A middle market range
Basis of competitive strategy	• Lower overall costs than competitors	• Ability to offer buyers something attractively different from competitors' offerings	• Lower overall cost than rivals in serving niche members	• Attributes that appeal specifically to niche members	• Ability to offer better goods at attractive prices
Product line	• A good basic product with few frills (acceptable quality and limited selection)	• Many product variations, wide selection; emphasis on differentiating features	• Features and attributes tailored to the tastes and requirements of niche members	• Features and attributes tailored to the tastes and requirements of niche members	• Items with appealing attributes; assorted features; better quality, not best
Production emphasis	• A continuous search for cost reduction without sacrificing acceptable quality and essential features	• Build in whatever differentiating features buyers are willing to pay for; strive for product superiority	• A continuous search for cost reduction for products that meet basic needs of niche members	• Small-scale production or custom-made products that match the tastes and requirements of niche members	• Build in appealing features and better quality at lower cost than rivals
Marketing emphasis	• Low prices, good value • Try to make a virtue out of product features that lead to low cost	• Tout differentiating features • Charge a premium price to cover the extra costs of differentiating features	• Communicate attractive features of a budget-priced product offering that fits niche buyers' expectations	• Communicate how product offering does the best job of meeting niche buyers' expectations	• Tout delivery of best value. • Either deliver comparable features at a lower price than rivals or else match rivals on prices and provide better features
Keys to maintaining the strategy	• Economical prices, good value • Strive to manage costs down, year after year, in every area of the business	• Stress constant innovation to stay ahead of imitative competitors • Concentrate on a few key differentiating features	• Stay committed to serving the niche at the lowest overall cost; do not blur the organization's image by entering other market segments or adding other products to widen market appeal	• Stay committed to serving the niche better than rivals; do not blur the organization's image by entering other market segments or adding other products to widen market appeal	• Unique expertise in simultaneously managing costs down while incorporating upscale features and attributes
Resources and capabilities required	• Capabilities for driving costs out of the value chain system • *Examples*: large-scale automated plants, an efficiency-oriented culture, bargaining power	• Capabilities concerning quality, design, intangibles, and innovation • *Examples*: marketing capabilities, R&D teams, technology	• Capabilities to lower costs on niche goods • *Examples*: lower input costs for the specific product desired by the niche, batch production capabilities	• Capabilities to meet the highly specific needs of niche members • *Examples*: custom production, close customer relations	• Capabilities to simultaneously deliver lower cost and higher-quality/ differentiated features • *Examples*: TQM practices, mass customization

A Different View

COMBINING GENERIC STRATEGIES WITH THE RESOURCE-BASED VIEW: THE MARKET-CONTROL/VALUE MATRIX

One of the criticisms of Porter's generic strategy approach is that it is overly focused on the external environment – especially competitors and industry and does not give sufficient weight to resources and capabilities. The debate between followers of the market-based and resource-based views of strategy tends to produce polarized positions and there has been little attempt at integrating the two approaches. Both schools of thought have been criticized for producing static models for what has become a very dynamic business environment. The Internet, globalization and deregulation have all combined to open up markets and make speed of response a critical factor in many industries. As we saw in Chapter 3, industry boundaries in some sectors have become increasingly hard to define. Focusing on the resources and competences that can give organizations a competitive advantage in such environments is something managers need to think about when deciding what strategy to choose.

One alternative put forward by Professor John Parnell is the market-control/value matrix (see Figure 5.5). According to Parnell, his framework gives generic strategies a modern twist by incorporating the resource-based view and also acknowledging some of the work carried out by other academics into generic strategy options since Porter (see Key Debate 5.1). Following on from the work of Bowman and Faulkner, the new matrix has value as one of the dimensions, which allows managers to bring low cost and differentiation concepts into the equation, but without treating them as polar opposites as in Porter's matrix. Parnell treats the two extremes of value – focused differentiation – or a product with high perceived worth to a limited group of customers sold with a price premium – and no frills – or a product that is perceived as of lower worth, but is sold at a more attractive price for a certain group of customers – as extremes on a continuum. Managers can choose any point on the continuum as their position if they believe this gives their firm a competitive advantage by leveraging their key resources and competences. By concentrating on the value proposition rather than focus, low cost or differentiation, hybrid positions, as mentioned above in the best-cost section, are possible.

The second dimension links back to another element we touched on in Chapter 3, market control. Organizations can attempt to control the markets in which they operate through a variety of techniques – including barriers to entry, but also control over suppliers and over customers' switching costs. Including the resource-based view for this dimension is necessary because there are examples of firms that manipulate these control mechanisms (e.g. the large supermarket chains' power over their suppliers or banks making it complex for customers to move their accounts to a competitor) and there are differences in the extent to which individual organizations can achieve market control. Again, Parnell sees this as a continuum with extremes, but also viable positions in between. To illustrate some of the possible positions we can use Figure 5.5.

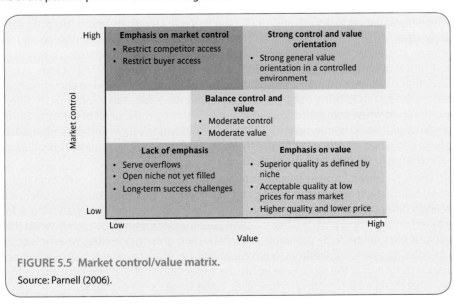

FIGURE 5.5 Market control/value matrix.

Source: Parnell (2006).

▶

◀   Each position is relative to the competitors in the organization's market. Organizations whose main emphasis is on value are usually in a sector where market control is difficult to achieve, so firms here focus on a value proposition that it is difficult for their competitors to imitate. In contrast an organization emphasizing market control will not have a stronger value proposition than its competitors, but will have superior capabilities that enable it to stop customers switching or prevent new entrants to the market.

Organizations that lack emphasis will usually perform poorly in the long term. Those with a strong value proposition and the ability to control their market are able to become dominant in their market space – Microsoft or Wal-Mart might exemplify this position – but they are still vulnerable to bad press and antitrust and other lawsuits. There are positions in between the four already covered – one example would be the central position that strikes a balance between value and market control. Parnell considers this an attractive option for new organizations and also those in stable situations.

Source: Parnell, J. (2006) 'Generic strategies after two decades: a reconceptualization of competitive strategy', *Management Decision*, 44(6): 1139–54.

KEY POINTS

The key points to take away from this chapter include the following:

1. Deciding which of the five generic competitive strategies to employ – overall low cost, broad differentiation, focused low cost, focused differentiation or best cost – is perhaps the most important strategic commitment an organization makes. It tends to drive the remaining strategic actions an organization undertakes and sets the whole tone for pursuing a competitive advantage over rivals.

2. In employing a low-cost provider strategy and trying to achieve a low-cost advantage over rivals, an organization must do a better job than rivals of cost-effectively managing value chain activities and/or it must find innovative ways to eliminate cost-producing activities. Low-cost provider strategies work particularly well when the products of rival sellers are virtually identical or very weakly differentiated and supplies are readily available from eager sellers, when there are not many ways to differentiate that have value to buyers, when many buyers are price-sensitive and shop the market for the lowest price and when buyer switching costs are low.

3. Broad differentiation strategies seek to produce a competitive edge by incorporating tangible and intangible attributes that set an organization's product/service offering apart from rivals in ways that buyers consider valuable and worth paying for. Successful differentiation allows an organization to (1) command a premium price for its product, (2) increase unit sales (because additional buyers are won over by the differentiating features), and/or (3) gain buyer loyalty to its brand (because some buyers are strongly attracted to the differentiating features and bond with the organization and its products). Differentiation strategies work best when diverse buyer preferences open up windows of opportunity to strongly differentiate an organization's product offering from those of rival brands, in situations where few other rivals are pursuing a similar differentiation approach, and in circumstances where organizations are racing to bring out the most appealing next-generation product. A differentiation strategy is doomed when competitors are able to quickly copy most or all of the appealing product attributes an organization comes up with, when an organization's differentiation efforts fail to interest many buyers and when an organization overspends on efforts to differentiate its product offering or tries to overcharge for its differentiating extras.

4. A focused strategy delivers competitive advantage either by achieving lower costs than rivals in serving buyers constituting the target market niche or by developing a specialized ability to offer niche buyers an appealingly differentiated offering that meets their needs better than rival brands do. A focused strategy based on either low cost or differentiation becomes increasingly attractive when the target market niche is big enough to be profitable and offers good growth potential, when it is costly or difficult for multi-segment competitors to put capabilities in place to meet the specialized needs of the target market niche and at the same time satisfy the expectations of their mainstream customers and when few other rivals are attempting to specialize in the same target segment.

5. Best-cost provider strategies combine a strategic emphasis on low cost with a strategic emphasis on more than minimal quality, service, features or performance. The aim is to create competitive advantage by giving buyers *more value for the money for mid-range products* – an approach that entails (1) matching close rivals on key quality/service/features/performance attributes, (2) beating them on the costs of incorporating such attributes into the product or service, and (3) charging a more economical price. A best-cost provider strategy works best in markets with large numbers of value-conscious buyers desirous of purchasing appealingly good products and services for less money.

6. In all cases, competitive advantage depends on having competitively superior resources and capabilities that are a good match for the chosen generic strategy. A sustainable advantage depends on maintaining that competitive superiority with resources, capabilities and value chain activities that rivals have trouble matching and for which there are no good substitutes.

CLOSING CASE

LA FITNESS – MUSCLING UP OR SLIMMING DOWN?

At the end of 2011, Martin Long, CEO of LA Fitness, was in the middle of a three-year overhaul of the UK health club chain. The mid-market firm had made a loss in 2010 (see Exhibit 5.1) and was facing a new threat from low-cost rivals entering the sector.

EXHIBIT 5.1: Selected figures from LA fitness accounts relating to financial years 2008–10 (all figures in £000s)

Item/ Year	2010	2009	2008
Turnover	71 938	76 788	80 542
PBIT	987	2490	5974
NOPAT	(3590)	3509[*]	5457
Fixed assets	70 822	71 991	74 390
Current assets	36 773[†]	31 621	27 894[†]
Current liabilities	(35 954)	(27 631)	(28 936)
Long-term debt/ provisions	(60 248)	(60 997)	(61 873)
Total equity	11 393	14 984	11 475

Notes: Loss from the profit and loss account and liabilities from the balance sheet shown in ()

[*] includes profit from sale of fixed assets amounting to £4 350 704

[†] Cash in hand and at bank £0 on balance sheet for each year at 31 July.

BACKGROUND

LA Fitness was launched in 1996, by gym owners Fred Turok, Jeremy Taylor and David Turner, as a brand for their jointly managed network of clubs. The three founders had originally linked up in 1990 when each owned a single gym. All had a desire to build a chain of health and fitness clubs with first-class facilities. By 1997, LA Fitness was one of the top 10 health club operators in the UK and two years later the firm floated on the London Stock Exchange. However, by 2005, the firm was facing more competition and was finding trading difficult due to a decline in consumer confidence. Share prices, which had remained buoyant on the back of the sector's growth in the 1990s, had collapsed. The fitness sector was undergoing a period of consolidation as the market had become saturated and the owners of LA Fitness knew that they needed to improve their financial position to take advantage of this.

In May 2005 LA Fitness agreed a £140 million take-over by US-based private equity firm, MidOcean Partners. The deal valued the company at £90.3 million and also took on £48 million of debt. LA Fitness then took over Dragon Gyms in 2006 adding further locations to their growing portfolio of clubs. However, the continuing deterioration of the economy was having an impact on the growth rates in the sector and LA Fitness was struggling to recapture its earlier success. Although the new owners retained Fred Turok as chairman, they decided that a new senior management team was needed to take the brand forward. In 2008 they head-hunted Martin Long, CEO at computer retail group, Game, and he began an intensive review of the business covering everything from facilities and branding to customer experience and the financial performance of each club.

MidOcean Partners had challenges of their own and their UK investments had been impacted by the economic downturn in 2008. The buyout group had taken the decision to concentrate its activity in the USA and leave a token presence of three partners in London. The partners retained ownership of LA Fitness and a manufacturer of plastic bags, the Europackaging Group but, apart from this, they had no other interests in the UK.

THE UK HEALTH AND FITNESS INDUSTRY

The UK's fitness sector experienced substantial growth in the 1990s fuelled by changes in social habits around exercise and healthy living. Fitness clubs were able to make rapid profits on the back of this growth and many of the leading players were listed on the London Stock Exchange by the end of the decade. In the early 2000s the trend reversed and most of the big chains became private companies again, often with support from private equity firms. The industry also showed signs of maturity with some consolidation and growth rates reducing to about 2–3 per cent per annum.

By the end of 2011 the health and fitness industry in the UK was valued at anywhere between £2.66 billion and £3.81 billion. There had been limited growth in the sector despite the recession, with reports of a 17 per cent increase in the market for the period 2006–11. The total industry membership base was estimated at approximately 7.3 million or about 12 per cent of the UK population. The majority of the membership base was in the private sector, which accounted for 5.33 million members in 2011. Although it appeared the industry as a whole had not been adversely affected by the economic downturn

▶

EXHIBIT 5.2: Top UK fitness clubs 2011

Brand	Members	Clubs	Members per club
David Lloyd/Next Gen./Harbour Club	450 000	79	5696
Virgin Active/Esporta	419 000	122	3434
Fitness First	400 000	160	2500
DW Sports Fitness	250 000	60	4167
LA Fitness	215 000	80	2688
Bannatyne's Health Club	180 000	59	3051
Nuffield Health, Fitness & Wellbeing	150 000	51	2941

in 2007/8, by 2011 most operators were reporting a downturn in business. Membership numbers had fallen slightly from 2010 to 2011 (by 0.3 per cent) and there had been a net reduction in the number of fitness facilities during the same period (5885 to 5852).

All of the major players in the industry (see Exhibit 5.2) had survived the recession so far. However, the industry was still fragmented with these top seven firms accounting for 39 per cent of membership and 23 per cent of clubs in the private element of the market. Despite continued consolidation in the sector, such as Virgin's acquisition of Esporta in April 2011, many firms were based on single site clubs.

The traditional business model for fitness clubs relied on membership and joining fees, which typically provided 80 per cent of the income for the organization. Companies usually spent 10–15 per cent of their revenue on marketing and sales activity, which was designed to encourage prospects to sign up for a minimum of 12 months and take advantage of the additional services on offer at clubs. However, the economic downturn had put significant pressure on revenue from catering, beauty treatments and other services, leaving most gyms more reliant on their core membership income.

THE CHANGING COMPETITION

LA Fitness was one of several mid-market players in the industry and as such it was potentially vulnerable to a range of rivals. Virgin Active's takeover of premium chain Esporta had allowed it to leapfrog into second place in the market behind David Lloyd, increasing its number of gyms from 71 to 126. Virgin Active was reportedly in talks with a private equity firm CVC to fund further expansion. David Lloyd clubs had fewer sites than many of its rivals but saw itself as a specialist attracting an ABC1 demographic with extensive facilities, including courts for racquet-based sports, and a high level of health and fitness expertise within the staff cohort at each club.

Fitness First was one of the only international players in the UK market. Described as the world's biggest health and fitness chain, the firm had about 435 clubs in 2011, with 150 of these located in the UK. Like LA Fitness, it was listed on the stock exchange in the 1990s and was later bought by private equity firm, BC Partners. At the end of 2011, CEO, Colin Waggett, was planning to float the company again to raise up to £1 billion for further investment, but on the Singapore stock exchange, reflecting Fitness First's increasing interest in expanding into Asia's big cities. The firm had been actively managing its portfolio of clubs in Europe, selling about 100 of its gyms in the Benelux countries, Italy, France and Spain, in order to expand into Asia and focus on the sites in big cities in Europe. Fitness First had also sold some of its clubs in the UK to FitSpace, the first low-cost gym, which entered the UK market in 2006. The company had also closed 10 of its unprofitable clubs in the north of England and the Midlands in July 2011. These clubs were being converted to low-cost gyms at a cost of £600–700 000 each for the launch of a new brand, Klick Fitness. Although Fitness First would still own the clubs they would be marketed as a totally separate brand. The clubs would only employ four staff instead of the usual fifteen and would have less room allocated to features such as locker rooms, saunas and lounges. Membership fees would be between £10–15 per month compared with the £40–50 charged by full-service fitness clubs.

Fitness First's decision to launch the Klick brand highlighted one of the major changes to the industry in recent years, the entry of low-cost operators. Although there were only 70 budget gyms operating in the UK by August 2011, many of the industry incumbents saw the likes of Fitness4less and easyGym as a credible threat. The new breed of fitness clubs aimed to reduce the costs of membership to about a third of that of a traditional gym by cutting all the extras, such as steam rooms, swimming pools and even personal contact with staff, and focusing only on a core offer of classes and basic equipment. Many of the budget gyms were more flexible than their traditional rivals about membership and joining fees. Fitness4less, for example, only required members to sign up for one month at a time. The budget offering appeared to chime with a wide range of consumers looking for value-for-money products and services following the economic downturn.

Since 2007 there had also been growth in other alternatives to gym membership. People had always had access to public sector facilities or outdoor exercise activities such as running and cycling, but other options now included outdoor boot camp operators such as British Military Fitness and indoor exercising using games systems such as Wii Fit.

LONG'S STRATEGY

LA Fitness's CEO realized that the chain needed to develop a consistent strategy to survive in the current environment. Investment in the estate was one strand of the new strategy Long and his senior team now pursued. During 2009 the organization hired 350 more staff and invested £20 million in its 24 clubs in London. Long wanted to make it clear to customers that LA Fitness was not 'a cheap or discounted chain'. In an interview with the *Evening Standard* (London) in October 2009, he stated: 'We're aiming to offer good value, not competing on the basis of bargain'. The review also highlighted six loss-making clubs that Long offloaded to an unnamed buyer at a cost of £1.1 million due to unexpired leases on the properties. Refurbishment of the remaining clubs began in 2010 with a further planned spend of £10 million. Long hoped this would give the firm the scope to challenge the top players in the industry such as Virgin Active and Fitness First.

Long's strategy also placed significant emphasis on ensuring that marketing activity provided a consistent message about the brand and set it apart from its competitors. The marketing strategy was designed to increase retention of the firm's existing members through a mix of social media and digital campaigns. To ensure the new approach was managed effectively, LA Fitness outsourced its entire marketing function to marketing services provider, Bezier. Part of the rebrand also included signing a four-year profit sharing deal with former member of girl band Mis-Teeq, Alesha Dixon. The singer and 'Strictly Come Dancing' star became the face of the company, but also worked with the board as an adviser and developed new products and services for the firm. Dixon would be paid on the basis of improvements in the chain's financial position over the period of her contract.

Despite all the changes Long had made since 2008, the chain's financial performance did not appear to be improving. According to its most recent accounts it made a loss in 2010 after making profits in the previous two years (see Exhibit 5.1). Membership figures were continuing to fall and more competitors were entering the market. Setting the company apart from its competitors was a costly exercise. The firm had taken on additional debt to finance the refurbishment of the clubs in the chain and continued marketing and brand-building would also require further expenditure. This would be critical if LA Fitness was to challenge the top firms in the industry. The organization had also built up expectations of a certain level of service among its core customers. Any change to this might lead to a further decline in the existing membership base. However, there were also the new entrants to the market with their value-for-money offering to consider. Although they were only a small part of the industry now, they could cause the same problems for firms like LA Fitness that the budget airlines had caused the full service providers.

QUESTIONS

1. Which of the five generic strategies is LA Fitness's business following?

2. Evaluate the strategy or strategies you have identified by briefly considering the organization's external environment and its resources and capabilities.

3. What strategies are LA Fitness's competitors following? Should the organization consider rethinking their own strategy in the light of what their competitors are doing?

4. Is LA Fitness's approach a suitable response to low-cost competitors? What should they do differently according to the consultants A.T. Kearney?

5. What potential is there for a best-cost approach in the UK fitness market?

Sources: LA Fitness (2011) 'About us: history'. Available online at www.lafitness.co.uk/about-us/history/ (accessed 24 November 2011); Muspratt, C. (2005) 'LA Fitness snapped up in £140m private equity deal', *The Telegraph* (London), 7 May; Tobin, L. (2009) 'LA Fitness hires 350 in £20m revamp of London's gyms', *London Evening Standard*, Business, 23 October; Barnett, M. (2011) 'Gyms tone up to take on their new low-cost rivals', *Marketing Week*, 23 June; Armitstead, L. and Power, H. (2008) 'LA Fitness owner runs down London operation', *The Telegraph* (London), 13 April; Teather, D. (2010) 'Fred Turok, chairman of LA Fitness', *The Guardian* (London), 20 August; Marketing (2011) 'Health clubs beat the drop', *Marketing*, 3 August, p. 30; FIA (2011) *UK state of the Fitness Industry Report*, FIA; Johnston, C. (2011) 'It's not stretch for budget gyms to flex their muscles', *The Times* (London), Business, 22 August, pp. 32–3; Walsh, D. (2011) 'Flotation means new approach to fitness', *The Times* (London), 2 July, Leisure section; Ho, Geoff (2011) 'LA Fitness struggles to get its figures into shape', *Sunday Express*, 24 April, City & Business; Farey-Jones, D. (2009) 'Alesha Dixon joins LA Fitness in results based deal', *Brand Republic*, 10 December, News Releases, p. 1; LA Fitness (2009) *Annual Accounts for LA Leisure Limited*, Doncaster, LA Fitness Limited; LA Fitness (2010) *Annual Accounts for LA Leisure Limited*, Doncaster, LA Fitness Limited; Mintel (2011) *Health and Fitness Clubs – UK – June 2011*, London, Mintel.

ASSURANCE OF LEARNING EXERCISES

LO 5.1, LO 5.2, LO 5.3, LO 5.4

1. Media Markt/Saturn is the largest consumer electronics retailer in Europe, with 2010 sales of over €20 billion. The organization competes aggressively on price with such rivals as DSG (whose retail brands include Currys and Elkjop), Best Buy Europe and Kesa Electricals (whose retail brands include Darty, BCC and Vanden Borre) but it is also known by consumers for its wide range of brands and eye-catching advertising based on the 'Hey, I'm no fool' slogan (Ich bin doch nicht blöd). The retailer also offers a wide range of after-sales services, including installation and fault diagnosis. How would you characterize Media Markt/Saturn's competitive strategy? Should it be classified as a low-cost provider strategy? A differentiation strategy? A best-cost strategy? Explain your answer.

LO 5.3

2. Stihl is the world's leading manufacturer and marketer of chainsaws, with annual sales exceeding €2 billion. With innovations dating to its 1929 invention of the gasoline-powered chainsaw, the organization holds over 1000 patents related to chainsaws and outdoor power tools. The organization's chainsaws, leaf blowers and hedge trimmers sell at price points well above competing brands and are sold only by its network of over 8000 independent dealers. The organization boasts in its advertisements that its products are rated number one by consumer magazines and are *not* sold at OBI or B&Q. How does Stihl's choice of distribution channels and advertisements contribute to its differentiation strategy?

LO 5.3

3. Explore BMW's website (www.bmw.com), and then click on the link for www.bmwgroup.com. The site you find provides an overview of the organization's key functional areas, including research and development (R&D) and production activities (see the page headings). Under Research and Development, click on Innovation & Technology and explore the links at the sidebar to better understand the types of resources and capabilities that underlie BMW's approach to innovation. Also review the statements under Production focusing on car production world-wide and sustainable production. How do the resources, capabilities and activities of BMW contribute to its differentiation strategy and the unique position in the industry that it has achieved?

LO 5.5

4. Using one of the case studies or illustration capsules from the chapter, apply either Mintzberg's or Bowman's generic strategy model to the organization or organization's described. Comment on how effective the model was in analysing the organization in comparison with Porter's framework.

EXERCISES FOR SIMULATION PARTICIPANTS

LO 5.1, LO 5.2, LO 5.3, LO 5.4

1. Which one of the five generic competitive strategies best characterizes your organization's strategic approach to competing successfully?
2. Which rival organizations appear to be employing a low-cost provider strategy?
3. Which rival organizations appear to be employing a broad differentiation strategy?
4. Which rival organizations appear to be employing some type of focused strategy?

▶

5. Which rival organizations appear to be employing a best-cost provider strategy?

6. What is your organization's action plan to achieve a sustainable competitive advantage over rival organizations? List at least three (preferably more) specific kinds of decision entries on specific decision screens that your organization has made or intends to make to win this kind of competitive edge over rivals.

ENDNOTES

1. This classification scheme is an adaptation of a narrower three-strategy classification presented in Porter, Michael E. (1980) *Competitive Strategy: Techniques for Analyzing Industries and Competitors*, New York, Free Press. For a discussion of the different ways that organizations can position themselves in the marketplace, see Porter, Michael E. (1996) 'What is strategy?' *Harvard Business Review*, 74(6): 65–7.

2. Porter, M. (1985) *Competitive Advantage: Creating and Sustaining Superior Performance*, New York, Free Press, p. 97.

3. Savage, M. (2007) 'The big question: have supermarkets become just too powerful in Britain?', *The Independent*, 21 September. Available online at www.independent.co.uk/news/business/analysis-and-features/the-big-question-have-supermarkets-become-just-too-powerful-in-britain-403010.html (accessed 29 May 2012).

4. Hammer, Michael and Champy, James were the main proponents of business process reengineering. See Hammer, M. and Champy, J. (2008) *Reengineering the Corporation: A Manifesto for Business Revolution,* rev. and updated, New York, HarperBusiness.

5. For a discussion of how unique industry positioning and resource combinations are linked to consumers' perspectives of value and their willingness to pay more for differentiated products or services, see Priem, Richard L. (2007) 'A consumer perspective on value creation', *Academy of Management Review*, 32(1): 219–35.

6. Gavetti, G. (2002) 'Ducati', Harvard Business School case 9-701-132, rev. 8 March.

7. www.jrscience.wcp.muohio.edu/nsfall01/FinalArticles/Final-IsitWorthitBrandsan.html.

8. This section expands on the section on value chain linkages found in Porter, *Competitive Advantage,* p. 125.

9. Yoffie, D. 'Cola Wars continue: Coke and Pepsi in 2006', Harvard Business School case 9-706-447.

10. Porter, *Competitive Advantage,* pp. 160–2.

11. For an excellent discussion of best-cost provider strategies, see Williamson, Peter J. and Zeng, Ming (2009) 'Value-for-money strategies for recessionary times', *Harvard Business Review*, 87(3): 66–74.

12. This work on best-cost or cost innovation strategies is revisited in Williamson, Peter, J. (2010) 'Cost innovation: preparing for a 'value-for-money' revolution', *Long Range Planning*, 43: 343–53.

Chapter Six

Strategies for changing the game

New ways of operating and altering the scope of operations

It was our duty to expand.

Ingvar Kamprad
Founder of IKEA

In the virtual economy, collaboration is a new competitive imperative.

Michael Dell
CEO of Dell Inc.

Our preoccupation in the century to come will be with creating and sustaining a mass innovation economy.

Charles Leadbeater
Author, journalist and consultant

Learning Objectives

When you have read this chapter you should be able to:

LO 6.1 Decide whether and when to pursue offensive or defensive strategic moves to improve a company's market position.

LO 6.2 Recognize when being a first mover or a fast follower or a late mover is most advantageous.

LO 6.3 Explain the strategic benefits and risks of expanding a company's horizontal scope through mergers and acquisitions.

LO 6.4 Discuss the advantages and disadvantages of extending the company's scope of operations via vertical integration.

LO 6.5 Describe the conditions that favour farming out certain value chain activities to outside parties.

LO 6.6 Explain when and how strategic alliances can substitute for horizontal mergers and acquisitions or vertical integration and how they can facilitate outsourcing.

CAN NINTENDO KEEP WINNING IN THE VIDEO GAMES' WAR?

For much of its history, the video game industry has focused on hard-core gamers and ways to improve the speed and realism of their gaming experience. As a business model it had proved highly successful for the three main players in the field, Sony, Microsoft and Nintendo. In recent years, Sony's expertise in engineering and technical capabilities and Microsoft's financial resources had given them a significant advantage over their smaller rival Nintendo. However, in 2006 as a new round of competitive moves began with Microsoft's launch of the Xbox 360, it was Nintendo that came up with the game-winning strategy by creating a new marketplace for its innovative products. In 2005/6 it looked like Microsoft would sweep the board as it had got to market first in November 2005 with its new generation console. Sony's Playstation3 had been dogged with technical problems and was not launched until nearly 12 months after the Xbox 360. Nintendo was also not ready to launch its new offering, the Wii (pronounced 'we') until late 2006.

The Wii console proved to be a winner virtually from the start and beat both the Xbox 360 and Playstation3 during 2007, selling over 16 million units world-wide to Microsoft's 7.85 million and Sony's 7.7 million. The Wii outsold the other consoles and by the end of 2011 had turned over 89 million units world-wide compared with 56 million for the PS3 and 58 million for the Xbox 360. Nintendo's success came from a variety of sources. First, the Wii was a genuinely innovative product. Players used a wand-like controller that was able to detect their hand movements and this translated into much more life-like gaming, especially for sports such as tennis, golf, boxing and bowling. However, the Wii was part of a much broader strategy developed by Nintendo President, Saturo Iwata, to target non-gamers and expand the market for video games as a whole. Nintendo's DS, a hand-held gaming device, was the first element of this strategy. The DS was launched in 2004 and was designed to appeal to occasional gamers with simple controls (touchscreen and stylus) and short, simple games. The Wii continued this approach with its simplicity, but was also promoted as family entertainment. In future gamers would play on their feet and in groups rather than alone and on the couch. The DS also allowed multi-player games through its Wi-Fi connection. In 2008 Nintendo was named as one of the world's 10 most innovative companies by *Business Week* and was the second most valuable listed company in Japan.

However, Nintendo's success was to be relatively short-lived. Despite record sales of its consoles in 2008 and 2009, elements of its strategy were already being imitated by its direct competitors, with Sony and Microsoft both launching competitor products to the Wii, in the form of the Move for the PS3 and Kinect for the Xbox 360. But also the popularity of hand-held consoles and targeting new segments of occasional gamers had been picked up by smartphone manufacturers and their allied software/apps producer networks. 'Angry Birds', a game developed for the smartphone market by Finnish firm, Rovio Mobile, is thought to have sold over 500 million copies in 2011. Having taken gaming to a new market it now seemed that another group of organizations was intent on taking a share of Nintendo's profits using their own integrated platforms. The disruptive possibilities did not stop there either. Brands such as 'World of Warcraft' (a multi-player online fantasy game from Blizzard Entertainment) were benefiting from an increase in group gaming via the Internet thanks to faster broadband. There were also developers, such as Zynga, designing games such as Farmville and Cityville to link with social media sites such as Facebook. In September 2011 Nintendo announced half-year losses of 70.3 billion Yen (€702 million) and saw its share price fall by over 13 per cent following disappointing sales of its latest 3DS hand-held game player. To survive and prosper in the new complex and fragmented world of video games, which it can take much of the credit for creating, Nintendo now needs another game changing strategy.

QUESTIONS

1. Which of the five generic strategies covered in Chapter 5 best describes Nintendo's strategy?

2. Does the generic strategy you have identified cover all the aspects of Nintendo's strategy as described in the case study?

Sources: BBC News (2011) 'Nintendo's net loss widens because of stronger Yen', BBC News, 27 October. Available online at www.bbc. co.uk/news/business-15473961 (accessed 28 December 2011); *The Economist* (2011) 'The business of gaming: thinking out of the box', *The Economist*, Special Report Video Games, 10–16 December, pp. 5–7; McGregor, J. (2008) 'The world's most innovative companies', *Business Week*, 17 April. Available online at www.businessweek.com/magazine/content/08 (accessed 28 December 2011); Nintendo (2011) various annual reports and consolidated financial statements 2007–2010. Available online at www.nintendo.com; VGChartz (2011) 'Hardware annual summary'. Available online at www.vgchartz.com/hw_annual_summary.php (accessed 28 December 2011).

In previous chapters we have looked at how organizations gain competitive advantage through the resources and competences they develop and how these can underpin a particular position in an industry. In the past, aligning a firm's resources and competences to one of the five most common generic strategies may have been sufficient not only to gain, but also to sustain competitive advantage over a period of time. In some industries, especially those with more stable characteristics and more oligopolistic structures, this may still be the case. However, as we have seen in Chapters 1 and 3, there is a body of evidence which suggests that factors such as globalization and technological change can limit the length of time competitive advantage can be sustained. Sometimes generic approaches are not sufficient on their own for incumbent firms to defend their industry position or for challenger companies to break into established marketplaces.[1] The opening case illustrates how Nintendo was able to challenge the market leaders through innovation and by creating a new market for their games, but also how the boundaries of the video games industry have shifted dramatically as a result of the technological developments in mobile telecoms such as smartphones and the growth of the Internet. The case shows the risks that incumbents face from new firms using disruptive innovation to enter a market and some of the approaches they can take to combat this.

This chapter looks at a range of strategic approaches that can help to strengthen an incumbent's position but also provide challengers with a way into an existing industry or a method to create a new market altogether. The chapter considers the choices managers make:

- To proactively exploit opportunities in their industry through offensive moves against their rivals or by attempting to change the boundaries of the industry.
- To leverage their organization's existing assets into new industries and sectors and when to develop new products, processes and knowledge in response to changes in the environment.
- Regarding decisions to change the boundaries of the firm itself, through merging or acquiring other organizations in the same industry, or by integrating backward, or forwards into more stages along the industry's overall value chain, or outsourcing and covering less of the value chain within the firm.
- Around co-operation and strategies that cover groups of connected organizations involved in partnerships, networks and strategic alliances.

This chapter presents the pros and cons of each of these strategy-enhancing measures.

Going on the Offensive – Strategic Options to Improve a Company's Market Position

LO 6.1
Decide whether and when to pursue offensive or defensive strategic moves to improve a company's market position.

As we saw in Chapter 1 (Key Debate 1.1) not all strategy experts agree that it is possible to develop and defend a sustainable competitive advantage in the long term. In high-velocity and hypercompetitive markets,[2] constructing a generic position may actually be damaging for an organizationas; it could prevent it from adapting or maintaining the flexibility needed to survive in a fast-moving environment. In some cases organizations might find an aggressive or disruptive approach is actually more successful than defending a specific position. Firms can prosper by creating a series of temporary advantages over competitors in a series of manoeuvres designed to play to their strengths and their rivals' weaknesses.

Strategic offensives are called for when an organization spots opportunities to gain profitable market share at the expense of rivals or when a company has no choice but to try to whittle away at a strong rival's competitive advantage. The actions of Wal-Mart, Apple and Google are all examples of companies aggressively pursuing competitive advantage and trying to reap the benefits of a leading market share, superior profit margins and more rapid growth, as well as the reputational rewards of being known as a winning company on the move.[3] The best offensives tend to incorporate several principles: (1) focusing relentlessly on building competitive advantage and then striving to convert it into sustainable advantage (as described in Chapter 4); (2) creating and deploying company resources in ways that cause rivals to struggle to defend themselves; (3) employing the element of surprise as opposed to doing what rivals expect and are prepared for; and (4) displaying a strong bias for swift, decisive and overwhelming actions to overpower rivals.[4]

If this sounds rather militaristic in tone, then it is well to remember that some schools of strategic thought believe that their origins are in military strategy and that the teachings of Sun Tzu, Von Clauswitz and other famous soldiers have much to recommend them. Companies from emerging economies can also bring a high level of aggression to their strategic approaches. In China, for example, there is a saying that 'the marketplace is a battlefield'. However, such approaches are not without their risks, as we will see in Chapter 9, used without restraint, aggressive business practices can lead to poor performance and other reputational problems.

Choosing the Basis for Competitive Attack

As a rule, challenging rivals on competitive grounds where they are strong is an uphill struggle.[5] Offensive initiatives that exploit competitor weaknesses stand a far better chance of succeeding than do those that challenge competitor strengths, especially if the weaknesses represent important vulnerabilities and if weak rivals can be caught by surprise with no ready defence.[6]

> The best offensives use a company's most competitively potent resources to attack rivals in the areas where they are weakest.

Strategic offensives should, as a general rule, be based on exploiting a company's strongest strategic assets – its most valuable resources and capabilities, such as a better-known brand name, a more efficient production or distribution system, greater technological capability or a superior reputation for quality. But a consideration of the company's strengths should not be made without also considering the rival's strengths and weaknesses. A strategic offensive should be based on those areas of strength where the company has its greatest competitive advantage over the targeted rivals. If a company has especially good customer service capabilities, it can make special sales pitches to the customers of those rivals that provide sub-par customer service. Aggressors with a recognized brand name and strong marketing skills can launch efforts to win customers away from rivals with weak brand recognition. There is considerable appeal in emphasizing sales to buyers in geographic regions where a rival has a weak market share or is exerting less competitive effort. Likewise, it may be attractive to pay special attention to buyer segments that a rival is neglecting or is weakly equipped to serve.

Ignoring the need to tie a strategic offensive to a company's resources where they are competitively stronger than rivals' can leave an organization in a vulnerable position. For instance, it is foolish for a company with relatively high costs to employ a price-cutting offensive – price-cutting offensives are best left to financially strong companies whose costs are relatively low in comparison to those of the companies being attacked. Likewise, it is ill-advised to pursue a product innovation offensive without having competitively superior expertise in research and development (R&D), new product development and speeding new products to market.

> Sometimes a company's best strategic option is to seize the initiative, go on the attack and launch a strategic offensive to improve its market position.

The principal offensive strategy options include the following:

1. *Using a cost-based advantage to attack competitors on the basis of price or value.* A price-cutting offensive can involve offering customers an equally good or better product at a lower price or offering a low-priced, lower-quality product that gives customers more value for the money. This is the classic offensive for improving a

company's market position *vis-à-vis* rivals, but it works well only under certain circumstances. Lower prices can produce market share gains if competitors do not respond with price cuts of their own and if the challenger convinces buyers that its product offers them a better value proposition. However, such a strategy increases total profits only if the gains in additional unit sales are enough to offset the impact of lower prices and thinner margins per unit sold. Price-cutting offensives are generally successful only when a company *first achieves a cost advantage and then hits competitors with a lower price.*[7] Wal-Mart's rise to dominance in discount retailing and supermarkets was based on just this type of strategic offensive. Ryanair also used this strategy successfully against rivals such as British Airways and Aer Lingus, by first cutting costs to the bone and then targeting leisure passengers who care more about low price than in-flight amenities and service.[8] While some companies have used price-cutting offensives as a means of obtaining the cost advantages associated with greater market share (economies of scale or experience), this has proved to be a highly risky strategy. More often than not, such price-cutting offensives are met with retaliatory attacks that can mire the entire industry in a costly price war.

2. *Leap-frogging competitors by being the first adopter of next-generation technologies or being first to market with next-generation products.* In technology-based industries, the opportune time to overtake an entrenched competitor is when there is a shift to the next generation of the technology. As we saw in the opening case Microsoft got its next-generation Xbox 360 to market a full 12 months ahead of Sony's PlayStation 3 and Nintendo's Wii. In theory this should have helped it to outperform the other firms with their later launches. However, this type of offensive strategy is high-risk since it requires costly investment at a time when consumer reactions to the new technology are yet unknown. In Microsoft's case, the Wii proved to be the product that consumers valued more and both it and Sony were left to play catch-up with features such as the Wii's motion controller.

3. *Pursuing continuous product innovation to draw sales and market share away from less innovative rivals.* Ongoing introductions of new and improved products can put rivals under tremendous competitive pressure, especially when rivals' new product development capabilities are weak. But such offensives can be sustained only if a company has sufficient product innovation skills to keep its pipeline full and maintain buyer enthusiasm for its new and better product offerings.

4. *Adopting and improving on the good ideas of other companies (rivals or otherwise).*[9] Apple's iPod was not the first portable MP3 player; that credit must go to Diamond Multi-media who launched the Rio PMP300 in 1998. However, Apple's product was designed, in part, by learning from the mistakes made by other manufacturers over issues such as size of memory and design. Luxury goods company LVMH has adopted a number of techniques from the car industry to ensure that costs are kept to a minimum in their manufacturing processes without affecting quality. The firm has also employed key quality managers from car parts manufacturers, such as Valeo, to ensure that it is able to access the latest thinking from other sectors.[10] Offensive-minded companies are often quick to take any good idea (not nailed down by a patent or other legal protection), make it their own and then aggressively apply it to create competitive advantage for themselves.

5. *Using hit-and-run or guerrilla warfare tactics to grab sales and market share from complacent or distracted rivals.* Options for 'guerrilla offensives' include occasionally offering substantially lower prices (to win a big order or steal a key account from a rival), surprising key rivals with sporadic but intense bursts of promotional activity (offering a special trial offer for new customers to draw them away from rival brands), or undertaking special campaigns to attract buyers away from rivals plagued with a strike or problems in meeting buyer demand.[11] Guerrilla offensives are particularly well suited to small challengers that have neither the resources nor the market visibility to mount a full-fledged attack on industry leaders and that may not merit a full retaliatory response from larger rivals.[12] Again,

the parallels with military strategy can be seen with both the nature of the techniques used (surprise) and the terminology.

6. *Launching a pre-emptive strike to secure an advantageous position that rivals are prevented or discouraged from duplicating.*[13] What makes a move pre-emptive is its one-of-a-kind nature – whoever strikes first stands to acquire competitive assets that rivals cannot readily match. Examples of pre-emptive moves include: (1) securing the best distributors in a particular geographic region or country; (2) obtaining the most favourable sites in terms of customer demographics, cost characteristics, or access to transportation, raw-material supplies, or low-cost inputs; (3) tying up the most reliable, high-quality suppliers via exclusive partnerships, long-term contracts or acquisition; and (4) moving swiftly to acquire the assets of distressed rivals at bargain prices. To be successful, a pre-emptive move does not have to totally block rivals from following; it merely needs to give a firm a prime position that is not easily replicated or circumvented.

How long it takes for an offensive to yield good results varies with the competitive circumstances.[14] It can be short if buyers respond immediately (as can occur with a dramatic cost-based price cut, an imaginative ad campaign or an especially appealing new product). Securing a competitive edge can take much longer if winning consumer acceptance of an innovative product will take some time or if the firm may need several years to debug a new technology, put new production capacity in place, or develop and perfect new competitive capabilities. But how long it takes for an offensive move to improve a company's market standing (and whether it can do so) also depends on whether market rivals recognize the threat and begin a counter-response. And whether rivals will respond depends on whether they are capable of making an effective response and if they believe that a counter-attack is worth the expense and the distraction.[15]

Choosing Which Rivals to Attack

Offensive-minded firms need to analyse which of their rivals to challenge as well as how to mount the challenge. The following are often considered the best targets for offensive attacks:[16]

- *Market leaders that are vulnerable.* Offensive attacks make good sense when a company that leads in terms of size and market share is not a true leader in terms of serving the market well. Signs of leader vulnerability include unhappy buyers, an inferior product line, a weak competitive strategy with regard to low-cost leadership or differentiation, strong emotional commitment to an ageing technology the leader has pioneered, outdated plants and equipment, a preoccupation with diversification into other industries and mediocre or declining profitability. Toyota's massive product recalls in 2009 and 2010 due to safety concerns presented other car companies with a prime opportunity to attack a vulnerable and distracted market leader. GM and Ford used incentives and low-financing offers aimed at winning over Toyota buyers to increase their market share during this period. Offensives to erode the positions of vulnerable market leaders have real promise when the challenger is also able to revamp its value chain or innovate to gain a fresh cost-based or differentiation-based competitive advantage.[17] To be judged successful, attacks on leaders do not have to result in making the aggressor the new leader; a challenger may 'win' by simply becoming a stronger runner-up. Caution is well advised in challenging strong market leaders – there is a significant risk of squandering valuable resources in a futile effort or precipitating a fierce and profitless industry-wide battle for market share. Managers also need to keep in mind that the market leader may well respond to an attack by putting their own house in order and making good the deficiencies that led to their vulnerability.
- *Runner-up firms with weaknesses in areas where the challenger is strong.* Runner-up firms are an especially attractive target when a challenger's resources and capabilities are well suited to exploiting their weaknesses.

- *Struggling enterprises that are on the verge of going under.* Challenging a hard-pressed rival in ways that further sap its financial strength and competitive position can weaken its resolve and hasten its exit from the market. In this type of situation, it makes sense to attack the rival in the market segments where it makes the most profits, since this will threaten its survival the most.

- *Small local and regional firms with limited capabilities.* Because small firms typically have limited expertise and resources, a challenger with broader and/or deeper capabilities is well positioned to raid their biggest and best customers – particularly those that are growing rapidly, have increasingly sophisticated requirements and may already be thinking about switching to a supplier with more full-service capability. However, managers contemplating this type of approach still need to research such firms, especially if they are unfamiliar with the region or locality. Sometimes there may be reasons other than obvious capabilities for a small firm's success or the loyalty of its customers. For example, links within communities and between families in some parts of the world can have a powerful influence on how business is conducted. This can be particularly important in international markets, which is covered more fully in the next chapter. But managers should keep in mind that giants such as eBay and Google were unable to compete successfully with incumbent Chinese Internet companies, despite having scale advantages and excellent capabilities, and firms such as Mercedes, Kellogg's and Domino's Pizza had to learn painful lessons before they succeeded in entering the Indian market successfully.[18]

Blue Ocean Strategy – a Special Kind of Offensive

> **Core Concept**
>
> A **blue ocean strategy** is based on discovering or inventing new industry segments that create altogether new demand, thereby positioning the firm in uncontested market space offering superior opportunities for profitability and growth.

In Chapter 3 (A Different View) we looked at how an organization using a **blue ocean strategy** seeks to gain a dramatic and durable competitive advantage by abandoning efforts to beat competitors in existing markets and, instead, inventing a new industry or distinctive market segment that renders existing competitors largely irrelevant and allows a company to create and capture altogether new demand.[19] This strategy views the business universe as consisting of two distinct types of market space. One is where industry boundaries are defined and accepted, the competitive rules of the game are well understood by all industry members and companies try to outperform rivals by capturing a bigger share of existing demand; in such markets, lively competition constrains a company's prospects for rapid growth and superior profitability since rivals move quickly to either imitate or counter the successes of competitors. The second type of market space is a 'blue ocean' where the industry does not really exist yet, is untainted by competition and offers wide-open opportunity for profitable and rapid growth if a company can come up with a product offering and strategy that allows it to create new demand.

One example of such wide-open or blue ocean market space is the online auction industry that eBay created and now dominates. Other examples of companies that have achieved competitive advantages by creating blue ocean market spaces include Starbucks in the coffee shop industry, FedEx in overnight package delivery, Swatch in wristwatches and, as we saw earlier, Cirque du Soleil in live entertainment. Companies that create blue ocean market spaces can usually sustain their initial competitive advantage without encountering a major competitive challenge for 10–15 years because of high barriers to imitation and the strong brand-name awareness that a blue ocean strategy can produce.

Zipcar Inc. is presently using a blue ocean strategy to compete against entrenched rivals in the rental-car industry. It rents cars by the hour or day (rather than by the week) to members who pay a yearly fee for access to cars parked in designated spaces located conveniently throughout large cities in the USA, Canada and the UK. By allowing drivers under 25 years of age to rent cars and by targeting city dwellers who need to supplement their use of public transportation with short-term car rentals,

Zipcar entered uncharted waters in the rental-car industry, growing rapidly in the process. Founded in 2000, Zipcar floated on the NASDAQ with a first share issue in December 2010 and a further sale of equity in March 2011. The firm's revenue is increasing but its shares were some way below their peak of $31 by December 2011 ($13) – so only time will tell if a blue ocean approach is going to work in this instance.

Nintendo executives considered their strategy, outlined in the opening case, as blue ocean.[20] When interviewed by *Forbes* magazine in July 2006, their US VP for Marketing, Perrin Kaplan, stated that Nintendo was 'creating a market where there initially was none'. However, Nintendo's strategy was more than this. One of the key tools that Kim and Mauborgne (2005) recommend for both diagnosing the key issues and generating actions is the 'strategy canvas'. The canvas for the video games industry is illustrated in Figure 6.1.[21] The horizontal axis shows the factors that players in the industry compete on, while the vertical axis shows the level of offer buyers receive from each company in the industry in relation to each factor. The top of the axis shows a high score and means that buyers are offered more whereas the bottom indicates a low score. In Figure 6.1 Nintendo's offer does not include DVD/HD integration like its competitors and the Wii offers less impressive graphics and processor. However, the motion sense controller is something that its rivals did not offer until later and the focus on sports/fitness and social gaming was much greater than that of the Xbox and PS3. The strategy canvas for the two other firms is more closely aligned and the figure clearly illustrates Nintendo's break with video game industry norms. To create a blue ocean strategy organizations need to plot the typical industry curve on the strategy canvas and then decide which factors they will eliminate, which they will reduce, which factors need to be created and will be new to the industry and which will be raised above current industry standards.

Although Nintendo's strategy appears to meet the criteria laid down by Kim and Mauborgne in creating a blue ocean, it is still not clear if they will gain a 10–15-year

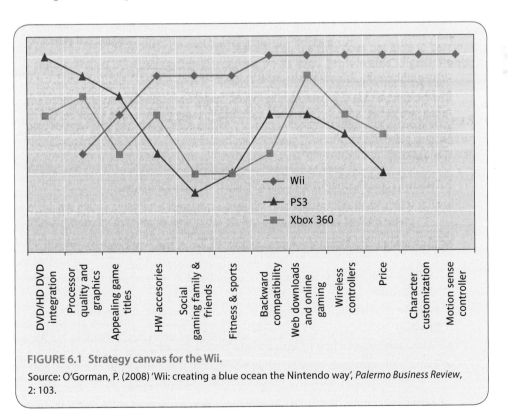

FIGURE 6.1 **Strategy canvas for the Wii.**

Source: O'Gorman, P. (2008) 'Wii: creating a blue ocean the Nintendo way', *Palermo Business Review*, 2: 103.

advantage from this. As we have seen in the opening case, the space they created has attracted many other organizations and their close competitors have been quick to develop their own versions of motion sensing games consoles.

Defensive Strategies – Protecting Market Position and Competitive Advantage

> Good defensive strategies can help protect a competitive advantage but rarely are the basis for creating one.

In a competitive market, firms are subject to offensive challenges from rivals. The main purposes of defensive strategies are to (1) lower the risk of being attacked, (2) weaken the impact of any attack that occurs, and (3) influence challengers to aim their efforts at other rivals. While defensive strategies usually do not enhance a firm's competitive advantage, they can definitely help fortify the firm's competitive position, protect its most valuable resources and capabilities from imitation and defend whatever competitive advantage it might have. Defensive strategies can take either of two forms: actions to block challengers and actions to signal the likelihood of strong retaliation.

Blocking the Avenues Open to Challengers

> There are many ways to throw obstacles in the path of would-be challengers.

The most frequently employed approach to defending a company's present position involves actions that restrict a challenger's options for initiating a competitive attack. There are any number of obstacles that can be put in the path of would-be challengers.[22] A defender can participate in alternative technologies as a hedge against rivals attacking with a new or better technology. A defender can introduce new features, add new models or broaden its product line to close off gaps and vacant niches to opportunity-seeking challengers. It can thwart the efforts of rivals to attack with a lower price by maintaining economy-priced options of its own. It can try to discourage buyers from trying competitors' brands by lengthening warranties, offering free training and support services, developing the capability to deliver spare parts to users faster than rivals can, providing coupons and sample giveaways to buyers most prone to experiment and making early announcements about impending new products or price changes to induce potential buyers to postpone switching. It can challenge the quality or safety of rivals' products. Finally, a defender can grant volume discounts or better financing terms to dealers and distributors to discourage them from experimenting with other suppliers, or it can convince them to handle its product line *exclusively* and force competitors to use other distribution outlets.

Signalling Challengers that Retaliation is Likely

The goal of signalling challengers that strong retaliation is likely in the event of an attack is either to dissuade challengers from attacking at all or to divert them to less threatening options. Either goal can be achieved by letting challengers know the battle will cost more than it is worth. Signals to would-be challengers can be given by:[23]

- Publicly announcing management's commitment to maintaining the firm's present market share.
- Publicly committing the company to a policy of matching competitors' terms or prices.
- Maintaining a war chest of cash and marketable securities.
- Making an occasional strong counter-response to the moves of weak competitors to enhance the firm's image as a tough defender.

Signalling is most likely to be an effective defensive strategy if the signal is accompanied by a credible commitment to follow through.

Timing a Company's Offensive and Defensive Strategic Moves

When to make a strategic move is often as crucial as *what* move to make. Timing is especially important when **first-mover advantages** or **disadvantages** exist.[24] Under certain conditions, being first to initiate a strategic move can have a high payoff in the form of a competitive advantage that later movers can not dislodge. Moving first is no guarantee of success, however, since first movers also face some significant disadvantages. Indeed, there are circumstances in which it is more advantageous to be a fast follower or even a late mover. Because the timing of strategic moves can be consequential, it is important for company strategists to be aware of the nature of first-mover advantages and disadvantages and the conditions favouring each type.[25]

The Potential for First-Mover Advantages

Market pioneers and other types of first movers typically bear greater risks and greater development costs than firms that move later. If the market responds well to its initial move, the pioneer will benefit from a monopoly position (by virtue of being first to market) that enables it to recover its investment costs and make an attractive profit. If the firm's pioneering move gives it a competitive advantage that can be sustained even after other firms enter the market space, its first-mover advantage will be greater still. The extent of this type of advantage, however, will depend on whether and how fast follower firms can piggyback on the pioneer's success and either imitate or improve on its move.

The conditions that favour first-mover advantages, then, are those that slow the moves of follower firms or prevent them from imitating the success of the first mover. There are five such conditions in which first-mover advantages are most likely to arise:

1. *When pioneering helps build a firm's reputation with buyers and creates brand loyalty.* A firm's reputation can insulate it from competition when buyer uncertainty about product quality keeps the firm's customers from trying competitors' offerings and when new buyers minimize their risk by choosing on the basis of reputation. Similarly, customer loyalty to an early-mover's brand can create a tie that binds, limiting the success of later entrants' attempts to poach from the early mover's customer base and steal market share.

2. *When a first-mover's customers will thereafter face significant switching costs.* Switching costs limit the ability of late movers to lure away the customers of early movers by making it expensive for a customer to switch to another company's product or service. Switching costs can arise for a number of reasons. They may be due to the time a consumer invests in learning how to use a specific company's product. They may arise from an investment in complementary products that are also brand-specific. They can also arise from certain types of loyalty programme or long-term contracts that give customers greater incentives to remain with an initial provider.

3. *When property rights protections thwart rapid imitation of the initial move.* In certain types of industries, property rights protections in the form of patents, copyrights and trademarks prevent the ready imitation of an early-mover's initial moves. First-mover advantages in pharmaceuticals, for example, are heavily dependent on patent protections, and patent races in this industry are common. In other industries, however, patents provide limited protection and can frequently be circumvented. Property rights protections also vary among nations, since they are dependent on a country's legal institutions and enforcement mechanisms.

4. *When an early lead enables the first mover to move down the learning curve ahead of rivals.* When there is a steep learning curve and when learning can be kept proprietary, a first mover can benefit from volume-based cost advantages that grow

Core Concept

Because of **first-mover advantages** and **disadvantages**, competitive advantage can spring from *when* a move is made as well as from *what* move is made.

LO 6.2

Recognize when being a first mover or a fast follower or a late mover is most advantageous.

ever larger as its experience accumulates and its scale of operations increases. This type of first-mover advantage is self-reinforcing and, as such, can preserve a first-mover's competitive advantage over long periods of time. Honda's advantage in small multi-use motorcycles has been attributed to such an effect.

5. *When a first mover can set the technical standard for the industry.* In many technology-based industries, the market will converge around a single technical standard. By establishing the industry standard, a first mover can gain a powerful advantage that, like experienced-based advantages, builds over time. The greater the importance of technical standards in an industry, the greater the advantage of being the one to set the standard and the more firmly the first mover will be entrenched. The lure of such an advantage, however, can result in standard wars among early movers, as each strives to set the industry standard. The key to winning such wars is to enter early on the basis of strong fast-cycle product development capabilities, gain the support of key customers and suppliers, employ penetration pricing and make allies of the producers of complementary products or licence the product widely as Pilkington did with its float glass technology.

To sustain any advantage that may initially accrue to a pioneer, a first mover needs to be a fast learner and continue to move aggressively to capitalize on any initial pioneering advantage. It helps immensely if the first mover has deep financial pockets, important competitive capabilities and astute managers. What makes being a first mover strategically important is not being the first company to do something but, rather, being the first competitor to put together the precise combination of features, customer value and sound revenue/cost/profit economics that gives it an edge over rivals in the battle for market leadership.[26] If the marketplace quickly takes to a first mover's innovative product offering, the first mover must have large-scale production, marketing and distribution capabilities if it is to take full advantage of its market lead. If technology is advancing at a torrid pace, a first mover cannot hope to sustain its lead without having strong capabilities in R&D, design and new product development, along with the financial strength to fund these activities.

Illustration Capsule 6.1 describes how Amazon.com achieved a first-mover advantage in online retailing.

The Potential for First-Mover Disadvantages or Late-Mover Advantages

There are circumstances when first movers face significant disadvantages and when it is actually better to be an adept follower than a first mover. First-mover disadvantages *(or late-mover advantages)* arise in the following four instances:

1. *When pioneering is more costly than imitating, and only negligible experience or learning-curve benefits accrue to the leader.* Such conditions allow a follower to end up with lower costs than the first mover and either win customers away with lower prices or benefit from more profitable production.

2. *When the products of an innovator are somewhat primitive and do not live up to buyer expectations.* In this situation, a clever follower can study customers' reactions to the pioneer's products and win disenchanted buyers away from the leader with better-performing products. Moreover, the first mover may find itself saddled with a negative reputation that retards its ability to recover from its early mis-steps.

3. *When rapid market evolution gives fast followers the opening to leap-frog a first-mover's products with more attractive next-version products.* Industries characterized by fast-paced changes in either technology or buyer needs and expectations may present opportunities for second movers to improve on the pioneer's products and offer customers a more attractive value proposition as a result.

4. *When market uncertainties make it difficult to ascertain what will eventually succeed.* Under these conditions, first movers are likely to make numerous mistakes that later movers can avoid and learn from. Even if the pioneer manages to please early adopters, it may turn out that the needs of early adopters are very different from the mass-market needs. Late movers may find it far more advantageous to wait until these needs are clarified and then focus on satisfying the mass-market's demand.

Illustration Capsule 6.1

AMAZON.COM'S FIRST-MOVER ADVANTAGE IN ONLINE RETAILING

Amazon.com's path to becoming the world's largest online retailer began in 1994 when Jeff Bezos, a Manhattan hedge fund analyst at the time, noticed that the number of Internet users was increasing by 2300 per cent annually. Bezos saw the tremendous growth as an opportunity to sell products online that would be demanded by a large number of Internet users and could be easily shipped. Bezos launched the online bookseller Amazon.com in 1995. The start-up's revenues soared to $148 million in 1997, $610 million in 1998 and $1.6 billion in 1999. Bezos' business plan – hatched while on a cross-country trip with his wife in 1994 – made him *Time* magazine's Person of the Year in 1999.

The volume-based and reputational benefits of Amazon.com's early entry into online retailing had delivered a first-mover advantage, but between 2000–2009 Bezos undertook a series of additional strategic initiatives to solidify the company's number one ranking in the industry. Bezos undertook a massive building programme in the late-1990s that added five new warehouses and fulfilment centres totalling $300 million. The additional warehouse capacity was added years before it was needed, but Bezos wanted to move pre-emptively against potential rivals and ensure that, as demand continued to grow, the company could continue to offer its

customers the best selection, the lowest prices and the cheapest and most convenient delivery. The company also expanded its product line to include sporting goods, tools, toys, grocery items, electronics and digital music downloads, giving it another means of maintaining its experience and scale-based advantages. Amazon.com's 2011 revenues of $48 billion (up from $34.2 billion in 2010) made it the world's largest Internet retailer; Jeff Bezos' shares in Amazon.com made him the twenty-sixth wealthiest person in the world in 2012, with an estimated net worth of $18.4 billion.

Moving down the learning curve in Internet retailing was not an entirely straightforward process for Amazon.com. Bezos commented in a *Fortune* article profiling the company, 'We were investors in every bankrupt, 1999-vintage e-commerce start-up. Pets.com, living.com, kozmo.com. We invested in a lot of high-profile flameouts'. He went on to specify that although the ventures were a 'waste of money', they 'didn't take us off our own mission'. Bezos also suggested that gaining advantage as a first mover is 'taking a million tiny steps – and learning quickly from your missteps'.

Sources: Brohan, Mark (2009) 'The Top 500 Guide', *Internet Retailer*, June. Available online at www.internetretailer.com on 17 June 2009; Quittner, Josh (2008) 'How Jeff Bezos rules the retail space', *Fortune*, 5 May, pp. 126–34; Bloomberg (2012) 'Amazon,com inc financials'. Available online at: www.investing.businessweek.com/research/stocks/financials/financials.asp?ticker=AMZN:US (accessed 30 May 2012); Forbes.com (2012) 'The world's billionaires'. Available online at: www.forbes.com/wealth/billionaires/list (accessed 30 May 2012).

To Be a First Mover or Not

In weighing the pros and cons of being a first mover versus a fast follower versus a late mover, it matters whether the race to market leadership in a particular industry is a marathon or a sprint. In marathons, a slow mover is not unduly penalized – first-mover advantages can be fleeting, and there is ample time for fast followers and sometimes even late movers to play catch-up.[27] Thus, the speed at which the pioneering innovation is likely to catch on matters considerably as companies struggle with whether to pursue a particular emerging market opportunity aggressively (as a first mover or fast follower) or cautiously (as a late mover). For instance, it took 18 months for 10 million users to sign up for Hotmail, 5.5 years for world-wide mobile phone use to grow from 10 million to 100 million, and close to 10 years for the number of at-home broadband subscribers to reach 100 million world-wide. The lesson here is that there is a market penetration curve for every emerging opportunity; typically, the curve has an inflection point at which all the pieces of the business model fall into place, buyer demand explodes and the market takes off. The inflection point can come early on a fast-rising curve (as with use of email) or farther on up a slow-rising curve (as with the use of broadband). Any company that seeks competitive advantage by being a first mover thus needs to ask some hard questions:

- Does market take-off depend on the development of complementary products or services that currently are not available?
- Is new infrastructure required before buyer demand can surge?
- Will buyers need to learn new skills or adopt new behaviours? Will buyers encounter high switching costs in moving to the newly introduced product or service?
- Are there influential competitors in a position to delay or derail the efforts of a first mover?

When the answers to any of these questions are yes, then a company must be careful not to pour too many resources into getting ahead of the market opportunity – the race is likely going to be more of a 10-year marathon than a 2-year sprint.[28] On the other hand, if the market is a winner-take-all type of market, where powerful first-mover advantages insulate early entrants from competition and prevent later movers from making any headway, then it may be best to move quickly despite the risks.

CURRENT PRACTICE 6.1

NEW BASES FOR COMPETITIVE ADVANTAGE

In 2009 Michael Deimler and Martin Reeves, two senior partners at BCG argued that the changes many firms are seeing in their environment are placing increasing pressure on traditional approaches to competitive advantage – position and capabilities. In a series of perspectives papers they outlined six new bases for competitive advantage; adaptive, signal, systems, social, simulation and people advantages. These new bases of advantage could be seen as a set of 'generic' capabilities that firms can use to supplement a specific position in the industry or markets they serve. In the same way as other strategies covered in this chapter must be underpinned by relevant resources and competences, these new approaches to competitive advantage will build on an organization's existing capabilities rather than replacing them.

What Deimler and Reeves term 'adaptive advantage' underpins their whole framework. The other five sources of advantage support the adaptive approach (as illustrated in Figure 6.2). Firms with an adaptive advantage are those that are able to marry analytical, deductive and deliberate with emergent and experimental approaches to strategy. These firms recognize the turbulence and unpredictability in markets and are flexible enough to adapt to and benefit from these changes. As we noted in Chapter 1 successful strategy is a blend of proactive initiative and reactive adjustments. Firms that are good at balancing these two elements could be described as possessing an adaptive advantage using the BCG definition. A typical example of this sort of organization is Richard Branson's Virgin Group, through their management of a diverse business portfolio.

A good example of a company with signal advantage is Google. It has been able to optimize its income from its main source of revenue, advertising, by being able to focus on the most relevant information and signals in the environment, process it rapidly and use it effectively to adapt. Firms with signal advantage are able to use the mass of data now available to organizations more effectively than their rivals.

Systems advantage is attained by firms that are able to manage beyond their own value chain and exploit the value system within their extended network of suppliers, complementers, distributors and other partners. In cases like Amazon and Apple it is the ability of the firm to exploit a technology platform such as the Kindle or iPhone through an entire business ecosystem. Advantage comes from the speed at which the members of the network can adapt to changes in the environment, such as exploiting new technologies, and also their ability to access a far greater range of resources and capabilities than a single firm.

Organizations can achieve social advantage by aligning their business with the prevailing social and ecological context. In the past, firms such as the Body Shop and the Co-operative Bank have been able to appeal to sizeable niches through stressing their ethical approaches. However, following the financial crisis, this is an issue that many more main-stream organizations are embracing. To gain advantage organizations have to do more than take a risk management approach to corporate social responsibility. Firms have to understand their customers' ethical and environmental stance and adapt their business model and create value through aligning to this.

Simulation advantage relates to learning curve advantages but is specifically focused on making best use of experi-mentation. As we have seen in this chapter there are many risks involved in being a first mover or pioneer. It is now possible for firms to test their products using virtual or simulated environments, but as more and more real-time data is becoming available it is also feasible to test entire business models and strategies in simulated environments. Procter & Gamble is one of the best-known companies for using virtual environments to test product prototypes.

Finally, firms can gain advantage by harnessing the individuals and groups in their workforce and making use of their creativity and insights by developing a more open and adaptable culture. In organizations with people advantage, there is often greater autonomy and flexibility for the workforce and strategy is as much a bottom-up as a top-down process. As we saw in Chapter 1, Mozilla uses people advantage for its Firefox web browser by leveraging its community of volunteer programmers through a common set of values.

Sources: Reeves, M. and Deimler, M.S. (2009) 'New bases of competitive advantage', *BCG Perspectives*, Boston Consulting Group; Reeves, M., Morieux, Y. and Deimler, M.S. (2010) 'People advantage', *BCG Perspectives*, Boston Consulting Group; Reeves, M. and Deimler, M. (2011) 'Adaptability: the new competitive advantage', *Harvard Business Review*, July–August, pp.134–41; Reeves, M., Heuskel, D. and Lewis, T. (2010) 'Social advantage', *BCG Perspectives*, Boston Consulting Group.

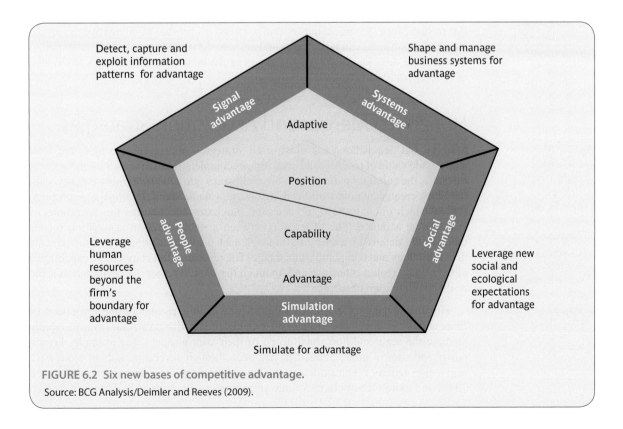

FIGURE 6.2 **Six new bases of competitive advantage.**

Source: BCG Analysis/Deimler and Reeves (2009).

Core Concept

The **scope of the firm** refers to the range of activities that the firm performs internally, the breadth of its product and service offerings, the extent of its geographic market presence and its mix of businesses.

Core Concept

Horizontal scope is the range of product and service segments that a firm serves within its focal market.

Core Concept

Vertical scope is the extent to which a firm's internal activities encompass one, some, many or all of the activities that make up an industry's entire value chain system, ranging from raw-material production to final sales and service activities.

LO 6.3

Explain the strategic benefits and risks of expanding a company's horizontal scope through mergers and acquisitions.

Strengthening an Organization Market Position via its Scope of Operations

Apart from considerations of competitive moves and their timing, there is another set of managerial decisions that can affect the strength of a company's market position. These decisions concern the scope of a company's operations – the breadth of its activities and the extent of its market reach. Decisions regarding the **scope of the firm** focus on which activities a firm will perform internally and which it will not.

Decisions such as these, in essence, determine where the boundaries of a firm lie and the degree to which the operations within those boundaries cohere. They also have much to do with the direction and extent of a business's growth. In this chapter, we introduce the topic of company scope and discuss different types of scope decisions in relation to a company's business-level strategy. In the next two chapters, we develop two additional dimensions of a firm's scope. Chapter 7 focuses on international expansion – a matter of extending the company's geographic scope into foreign markets. Chapter 8 takes up the topic of corporate strategy, which concerns diversifying into a mix of different businesses. Scope issues are at the very heart of corporate-level strategy.

Several dimensions of firm scope have relevance for business-level strategy in terms of their capacity to strengthen a company's position in a given market. These include the firm's **horizontal scope**, which is the range of product and service segments that the firm serves within its market. Mergers and acquisitions involving other market participants provide a means for a company to expand its horizontal scope. Expanding the firm's vertical scope by means of vertical integration can also affect the success of its market strategy. **Vertical scope** is the extent to which the firm engages in the various activities that make up the industry's entire value chain system, from initial activities such as raw-material production all the way to retailing and after-sales service activities. Outsourcing decisions concern another dimension of scope since they involve narrowing the firm's boundaries with respect to its participation in value chain activities. We discuss the pros and cons of each of these options in the sections that follow. Since strategic alliances and partnerships provide an alternative to vertical integration and acquisition strategies and are sometimes used to facilitate outsourcing, we conclude this chapter with a discussion of the benefits and challenges associated with co-operative arrangements of this sort.

Horizontal Merger and Acquisition Strategies

Mergers and acquisitions are much-used strategic options; for example, the total world-wide value of mergers and acquisitions completed in 2010 was $2.4 trillion.[29] A *merger* is the combining of two or more companies into a single corporate entity, with the newly created company often taking on a new name. An *acquisition* is a combination in which one company, the acquirer, purchases and absorbs the operations of another, the acquired. The difference between a merger and an acquisition relates more to the details of ownership, management control and financial arrangements than to strategy and competitive advantage. The resources and competitive capabilities of the newly created enterprise end up much the same whether the combination is the result of acquisition or merger.

Horizontal mergers and acquisitions, which involve combining the operations of firms within the same general industry, provide an effective means for firms to rapidly increase the scale and horizontal scope of their core business. For example, French power and control giant, Schneider, has been through several periods of aggressive acquisition activity to consolidate its position in the electrical industry in the 1980s and 1990s and more recently to move into related industries such as building automation and security. Mergers between airlines, such as the 2010 British Airways/Iberia merger, have increased their scale of operations and extended their reach geographically. The new company created by the merger, International Airlines Group, was the second largest carrier in Europe behind Air France/KLM (the result of an earlier merger) with a market value of €5.3 billion. Companies from developing economies are increasingly expanding their businesses through cross-border acquisitions, as we discuss in the following chapter on international strategy.

Combining the operations of two companies, via merger or acquisition, is an attractive strategic option for strengthening the resulting company's competitiveness and opening up avenues of new market opportunity. Increasing a company's horizontal scope can strengthen its business and increase its profitability in five ways: (1) by improving the efficiency of its operations; (2) by heightening its product differentiation; (3) by reducing market rivalry; (4) by increasing the company's bargaining power over suppliers and buyers; and (5) by enhancing its flexibility and dynamic capabilities (discussed in Chapter 4).

To achieve these benefits, horizontal merger and acquisition strategies typically are generally aimed at any of five outcomes:[30]

1. *Increasing the company's scale of operations and market share.* Many mergers and acquisitions are undertaken with the objective of transforming two or more high-cost companies into one lean competitor with significantly lower costs. When a company acquires another company in the same industry, there is usually enough overlap in operations that less efficient plants can be closed or distribution and sales activities can be partly combined and downsized. Likewise, it is usually feasible to squeeze out cost savings in administrative activities, again by combining and downsizing such activities as finance and accounting, information technology (IT), human resources (HR), and so on. The combined companies may also be able to reduce supply chain costs because of greater bargaining power over common suppliers and closer collaboration with supply chain partners. By helping to consolidate the industry and remove excess capacity, such combinations can also reduce industry rivalry and improve industry profitability.

2. *Expanding a company's geographic coverage.* One of the best and quickest ways to expand a company's geographic coverage is to acquire rivals with operations in the desired locations. If there is some geographic overlap, then one benefit is being able to reduce costs by eliminating duplicate facilities in those geographic areas where undesirable overlap exists. Since a company's size increases with its geographic scope, another benefit is increased bargaining power with the company's suppliers or buyers. For companies whose business customers require national or international coverage, a broader geographic scope can provide differentiation benefits while also enhancing the company's bargaining power. Food products companies like Nestlé, Kraft, Unilever and Procter & Gamble have made acquisitions an integral part of their strategies to expand internationally in order to serve key customers such as Carrefour and Wal-Mart on a global basis. Greater geographic coverage can also contribute to product differentiation by enhancing a company's name recognition and brand awareness. Mexican cement producer, Cemex, has expanded its operations from Central to North and South America, Europe and Asia through a series of acquisitions over the last 25 years.

3. *Extending the company's business into new product categories.* Many times a company has gaps in its product line that need to be filled in order to offer customers a more effective product bundle or the benefits of one-stop shopping.[31] For example, customers might prefer to acquire a suite of software applications from a single vendor that can offer more integrated solutions to the company's problems. Acquisition can be a quicker and more potent way to broaden a company's product line than going through the exercise of introducing a company's own new product to fill the gap. Expanding into additional market segments or product categories

can offer companies benefits similar to those gained by expanding geographically: greater product differentiation, bargaining power and efficiencies. It can also reduce rivalry by helping to consolidate an industry.

4. *Gaining quick access to new technologies or complementary resources and capabilities.* By making acquisitions to bolster a company's technological know-how or to expand its skills and capabilities, a company can bypass a time-consuming and expensive internal effort to build desirable new resources and organizational capabilities. Between 2000–2009, Cisco Systems purchased 85 companies to give it more technological reach and product breadth, thereby enhancing its standing as the world's biggest provider of hardware, software and services for building and operating Internet networks. By acquiring technologies and other resources and capabilities that complement its own set, a company can gain many of the types of benefits available from extending its horizontal scope. Among them is the greater flexibility and dynamic capabilities that spring from greater innovativeness and the ability to compete on the basis of a more effective bundle of resources.

5. *Leading the convergence of industries whose boundaries are being blurred by changing technologies and new market opportunities.* In fast-cycle industries or industries whose boundaries are changing, companies can use acquisition strategies to hedge their bets about the direction that an industry will take, increase their capacity to meet changing demands and respond flexibly to changing buyer needs and technological demands. Such acquisitions add to a company's dynamic capabilities by bringing together the resources and products of several different companies and enabling the company to establish a strong position in the consolidating markets. Microsoft has made a series of acquisitions that have enabled it to launch Microsoft TV Internet Protocol Television (IPTV). Microsoft TV allows broadband users to use their home computers or Xbox game consoles to watch live programming, see video on demand, view pictures and listen to music. News Corporation has also prepared for the convergence of media services with the purchase of satellite TV companies to complement its media holdings in TV broadcasting (the Fox network and TV stations in various countries), cable TV (Fox News, Fox Sports and FX), filmed entertainment (Twentieth Century Fox and Fox studios), newspapers, magazines and book publishing.

Why Mergers and Acquisitions Sometimes Fail to Produce Anticipated Results

All too frequently, mergers and acquisitions do not produce the hoped-for outcomes.[32] Cost savings may prove smaller than expected. Gains in competitive capabilities may take substantially longer to realize or, worse, may never materialize at all. Efforts to mesh the corporate cultures can stall due to formidable resistance from organization members. Managers and employees at the acquired company may argue forcefully for continuing to do things the way they were done before the acquisition. Key employees at the acquired company can quickly become disenchanted and leave; the morale of company personnel who remain can drop to disturbingly low levels because they disagree with newly instituted changes. Differences in management styles and operating procedures can prove hard to resolve. The managers appointed to oversee the integration of a newly acquired company can make mistakes in deciding which activities to leave alone and which activities to meld into their own operations and systems.

A number of mergers/acquisitions have been notably unsuccessful. Ford's $2.5 billion acquisition of Jaguar was a failure, as was its $2.5 billion acquisition of Land Rover (both were sold to India's Tata Motors in 2008 for $2.3 billion). Daimler AG, the maker of Mercedes-Benz and Smart cars, entered into a high-profile merger with Chrysler only to dissolve it in 2007, taking a loss of $30 billion. A number of recent mergers and acquisitions have yet to live up to expectations – prominent examples include Oracle's acquisition of Sun Microsystems, the Fiat-Chrysler deal, Bank of America's acquisition of Merrill Lynch and the merger of Sprint and Nextel in the mobile phone industry. Antitrust concerns on the part of regulatory authorities have prevented the successful conclusion of other mergers and acquisitions. Coca-Cola, for example, failed to win approval in 2009 for its proposed $2.4 billion acquisition of Huiyuan Juice Group under China's new antimonopoly law.

Vertical Integration Strategies

Expanding the firm's vertical scope by means of a vertical integration strategy provides another way to strengthen the company's position in its core market. A **vertically integrated firm** is one that participates in multiple segments or stages of an industry's overall value chain. A good example of a vertically integrated organization is the UK's Co-operative Group. The organization's Co-operative Food supermarkets and local stores are supplied in part from the group's network of farms (The Co-operative Farms is actually Britain's largest farming business). The Farms' business owns its own preparation and packing operation, located in three sites in the UK and washes and packs the farm produce before it is delivered to the stores and sold under the 'Grown by Us' brand. As with many other UK supermarkets, Co-operative Food now also offers home delivery and added value in the form of recipe cards. The only part of the process from field to plate that the group does not perform is the final cooking of the food.[33]

A vertical integration strategy can expand the firm's range of activities *backward* into sources of supply and/or *forward* toward end-users. When Tiffany & Co, a manufacturer and retailer of fine jewellery, began sourcing, cutting and polishing its own diamonds, it integrated backward along the diamond supply chain. Mining giant De Beers Group and Canadian miner Aber Diamond integrated forward when they entered the diamond retailing business.

A firm can pursue vertical integration by starting its own operations in other stages of the vertical activity chain, by acquiring a company already performing the activities it wants to bring in-house, or by entering into a strategic alliance or joint venture. Vertical integration strategies can aim at *full integration* (participating in all stages of the vertical chain) or *partial integration* (building positions in selected stages of the vertical chain). Firms can also engage in *tapered integration* strategies, which involve a mix of in-house and outsourced activity in any given stage of the vertical chain. Oil companies, for instance, supply their refineries with oil from their own wells as well as with oil that they purchase from other producers – they engage in tapered backward integration. Since UK brewing business, Marstons plc., the maker of Pedigree, Hobgoblin and Cumberland ale sells most of its beer through supermarkets, off licences and other pub operators but also operates its own chain of 500 managed pubs and a further 1600 tenanted, licensed and franchised pubs, it practises tapered forward integration.

> **Core Concept**
>
> A **vertically integrated firm** is one that performs value chain activities along several portions or stages of an industry's overall value chain, which begins with the production of raw materials or initial inputs and culminates in final sales and service to the end consumer.

> **LO 6.4**
> Discuss the advantages and disadvantages of extending the company's scope of operations via vertical integration.

The Advantages of a Vertical Integration Strategy

Under the right conditions, a vertical integration strategy can add materially to a company's technological capabilities, strengthen the firm's competitive position and boost its profitability.[34] But it is important to keep in mind that vertical integration has no real payoff strategy-wise or profit-wise unless it produces cost savings and/or differentiation benefits sufficient to justify the extra investment.

Integrating Backward to Achieve Greater Competitiveness

It is harder than one might think to generate cost savings or improve profitability by integrating backward into activities such as parts and components manufacture (which

Core Concept

Backward integration involves performing industry value chain activities previously performed by suppliers or other enterprises engaged in earlier stages of the industry value chain.

could otherwise be purchased from suppliers with specialized expertise in making these parts and components). For backward integration to be a cost-saving and profitable strategy, a company must be able to (1) achieve the same scale economies as outside suppliers and (2) match or beat suppliers' production efficiency with no drop-off in quality. Neither outcome is easy to achieve. To begin with, a company's in-house requirements are often too small to reach the optimum size for low-cost operation – for instance, if it takes a minimum production volume of 1 million units to achieve mass-production economies and a company's in-house requirements are just 250 000 units, then it falls far short of being able to capture the scale economies of outside suppliers (which may readily find buyers for 1 million or more units). Furthermore, matching the production efficiency of suppliers is fraught with problems when suppliers have considerable production experience of their own, when the technology they employ has elements that are hard to master and/or when substantial R&D expertise is required to develop next-version parts and components or keep pace with advancing technology in parts/components production.

But that said, there are still occasions when a company can improve its cost position and competitiveness by performing a broader range of vertical chain activities in-house rather than having certain of these activities performed by outside suppliers. When the item being supplied is a major cost component, when there is a sole supplier, or when suppliers have outsized profit margins, vertical integration can lower costs by limiting supplier power. Vertical integration can also lower costs by facilitating the co-ordination of production flows and avoiding bottleneck problems. Furthermore, when a company has proprietary know-how that it wants to keep from rivals, then in-house performance of value-adding activities related to this know-how is beneficial even if such activities could be performed by outsiders. Apple recently decided to integrate backward into producing its own chips for iPhones, chiefly because chips are a major cost component, they have big profit margins, and in-house production would help co-ordinate design tasks and protect Apple's proprietary iPhone technology. Swiss pharmaceutical giant Roche's takeover of Genentech in 2009 was another example of backward integration. Many of Roche's best-selling cancer drugs are Genentech products, including Avastin and Rituxan. Genentech carried out the fundamental R&D and early clinical trials, while Roche co-ordinated the late-stage trials and sales, marketing and distribution of the medicines. The main purpose for the acquisition was to improve co-ordination between the two organizations on new product development. However, Roche's agreement on marketing rights with the Californian biotech firm was due to expire in 2015, so there were other potential benefits from the purchase.[35]

Backward vertical integration can produce a differentiation-based competitive advantage when performing activities internally contributes to a better-quality product/service offering, improves the calibre of customer service, or in other ways enhances the performance of the final product. On occasion, integrating into more stages along the vertical added-value chain can add to a company's differentiation capabilities by allowing it to build or strengthen its core competencies, better master key skills or strategy-critical technologies, or add features that deliver greater customer value. Spanish clothing maker Inditex has backward integrated into fabric-making, as well as garment design and manufacture, for its successful Zara brand. By tightly controlling the process and postponing dyeing until later stages, Zara can respond quickly to changes in fashion trends and supply its customers with the hottest items. NewsCorp backward integrated into film studios (Twentieth Century Fox) and TV programme production to ensure access to high-quality content for its TV stations (and to limit supplier power).

Core Concept

Forward integration involves performing industry value chain activities closer to the end-user.

Integrating Forward to Enhance Competitiveness

Like backward integration, forward integration can lower costs by increasing efficiency and bargaining power. In addition, it can allow manufacturers to gain better access to end-users, strengthen brand awareness and increase product differentiation. Car-makers, for example, have forward integrated into the lending business in order to exercise more control and make car loans a more attractive part of the car-buying process. Forward integration can also enable companies to make the end-users' purchasing experience a differentiating feature. For example, Ducati and Harley motorcycles both have company-owned retail stores that are essentially little museums, filled with iconography, which provide an environment conducive to selling not only motorcycles and gear but memorabilia, clothing and other items featuring the brand. Insurance companies and brokerages have the ability to make consumers' interactions with local agents and office personnel a differentiating feature by focusing on building relationships.

In many industries, independent sales agents, wholesalers and retailers handle competing brands of the same product; having no allegiance to any one company's brand, they tend to push whatever earns them the biggest profits. Independent mobile telecoms retailers and agents in the UK, such as Carphone Warehouse, often represent a number of different mobile networks and try to find the best match between a customer's requirements and the tariffs and contracts of alternative mobile networks. Under this arrangement, it is possible for an agent or retailer to develop a preference for one company's products and services and neglect other represented mobile networks. A network may conclude, therefore, that it is better off integrating forward and setting up its own retail outlets, as Vodafone did in 1993, or acquiring independent retailers and service providers such as Talkland and People's Phone, which it did in 1996. Likewise, some tyre manufacturers (such as Goodyear) have integrated forward into tyre retailing to exert better control over salesforce/customer interactions. Some producers have opted to integrate forward by selling directly to customers at the company's website. Bypassing regular wholesale/retail channels in favour of direct sales and Internet retailing can have appeal if it reinforces the brand and enhances consumer satisfaction or if it lowers distribution costs, produces a relative cost advantage over certain rivals and results in lower selling prices to end-users. In addition, sellers are compelled to include the Internet as a retail channel when a sufficiently large number of buyers in an industry prefer to make purchases online. However, a company that is vigorously pursuing online sales to consumers at the same time that it is also heavily promoting sales to consumers through its network of wholesalers and retailers is competing directly against its distribution allies. Such actions constitute *channel conflict* and create a tricky route to negotiate. A company that is actively trying to expand online sales to consumers is signalling *a weak strategic commitment to its dealers* and *a willingness to cannibalize dealers' sales and growth potential.* The likely result is angry dealers and loss of dealer goodwill. Quite possibly, a company may stand to lose more sales by offending its dealers than it gains from its own online sales effort. Consequently, in industries where the strong support and goodwill of dealer networks is essential, companies may conclude that it is important to avoid channel conflict and that their websites should be designed to partner with dealers rather than compete against them.

The Disadvantages of a Vertical Integration Strategy

Vertical integration has some substantial drawbacks beyond the potential for channel conflict.[36] The most serious drawbacks to vertical integration include the following concerns:

- Vertical integration raises a firm's capital investment in the industry, *increasing business risk.* What if industry growth and profitability go sour?
- Vertically integrated companies are often *slow to embrace technological advances* or more efficient production methods when they are saddled with older technology or facilities. A company that obtains parts and components from outside suppliers can always shop the market for the latest and best parts and components, whereas a vertically integrated firm that is saddled with older technology or facilities that make items it no longer needs is looking at the high costs of premature abandonment.

- Integrating backward into parts and components manufacture *can impair a company's operating flexibility* when it comes to changing out the use of certain parts and components. It is one thing to design out a component made by a supplier and another to design out a component being made in-house (which can mean laying off employees and writing off the associated investment in equipment and facilities). Most of the world's car-makers, despite their expertise in automotive technology and manufacturing, have concluded that purchasing many of their key parts and components from manufacturing specialists results in higher quality, lower costs and greater design flexibility than does the vertical integration option.

- Vertical integration potentially results in *less flexibility in accommodating shifting buyer preferences* when a new product design does not include parts and components that the company makes in-house. Integrating forward or backward locks a firm into relying on its own in-house activities and sources of supply.

- Vertical integration *may not enable a company to realize economies of scale* if its production levels are below the minimum efficient scale. Small companies in particular are likely to suffer a cost disadvantage by producing in-house when suppliers of many small companies can realize scale economies that a small company cannot attain on its own.

- Vertical integration poses all kinds of *capacity matching problems.* In motor vehicle manufacturing, for example, the most efficient scale of operation for making axles is different from the most economic volume for radiators and different yet again for both engines and transmissions. Building the capacity to produce just the right number of axles, radiators, engines and transmissions in-house – and doing so at the lowest unit costs for each – is much easier said than done. If internal capacity for making transmissions is deficient, the difference has to be bought externally. If internal capacity for radiators proves excessive, customers need to be found for the surplus. And if by-products are generated – as occurs in the processing of many chemical products – they require arrangements for disposal. Consequently, integrating across several production stages in ways that achieve the lowest feasible costs can be a monumental challenge.

- Integration forward or backward often calls for *radical new skills and business capabilities.* Parts and components manufacturing, assembly operations, wholesale distribution and retailing and direct sales via the Internet represent different kinds of businesses, operating in different types of industries, with different key success factors. Managers of a manufacturing company should consider carefully whether it makes good business sense to invest time and money in developing the expertise and merchandising skills to integrate forward into wholesaling or retailing. Many manufacturers learn the hard way that company-owned wholesale/retail networks present many headaches, fit poorly with what they do best and do not always add the kind of value to their core business they thought they would.

In today's world of close working relationships with suppliers and efficient supply chain management systems, *very few businesses can make a case for integrating backward into the business of suppliers* to ensure a reliable supply of materials and components or to reduce production costs. The best materials and components suppliers stay abreast of advancing technology and are adept in improving their efficiency and keeping their costs and prices as low as possible. A company that pursues a vertical integration strategy and tries to produce many parts and components in-house is likely to find itself very hard-pressed to keep up with technological advances and cutting-edge production practices for each part and component used in making its product

Weighing the Pros and Cons of Vertical Integration

All in all, therefore, a strategy of vertical integration can have both important strengths and weaknesses. The tip of the scales depends on (1) whether vertical integration can enhance the performance of strategy-critical activities in ways that lower cost, build expertise, protect proprietary know-how or increase differentiation; (2) the impact of vertical integration on investment costs, flexibility and response times and the administrative costs of co-ordinating operations across more vertical chain activities; and (3) how difficult it will be for the company to acquire the set of skills and capabilities needed to operate in another stage of the vertical chain. *Vertical integration strategies have merit according to which capabilities and value-adding activities truly need to be performed in-house and which can be performed better or cheaper by outsiders.* Without solid benefits, integrating forward or backward is not likely to be an attractive strategy option.

EDF, a large French energy company, has made vertical integration a central part of its strategy but combined this successfully with horizontal integration, as described in Illustration Capsule 6.2.

Illustration Capsule 6.2

EDF'S VERTICAL INTEGRATION STRATEGY

French power firm, EDF (Electricité de France) has had vertical integration at the heart of its strategies since it was founded in 1946 after the nationalization of over 1400 separate gas and electricity generation, transmission and distribution companies. The opening up of European energy markets in the 1990s presented the company with further opportunities to expand beyond their base in France. EDF developed substantial expertise in operating plants to generate electricity, but also in building power stations, one example of backward integration. The firm was at the forefront of France's burgeoning nuclear industry and this enabled them to leverage their capabilities into a range of new markets, including China.

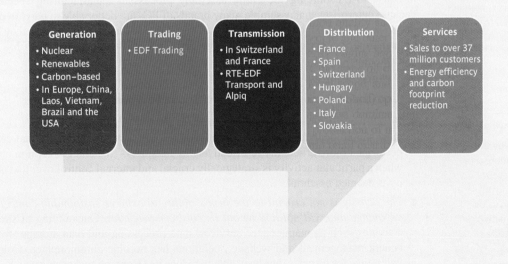

Generation
- Nuclear
- Renewables
- Carbon–based
- In Europe, China, Laos, Vietnam, Brazil and the USA

Trading
- EDF Trading

Transmission
- In Switzerland and France
- RTE-EDF Transport and Alpiq

Distribution
- France
- Spain
- Switzerland
- Hungary
- Poland
- Italy
- Slovakia

Services
- Sales to over 37 million customers
- Energy efficiency and carbon footprint reduction

FIGURE 6.3 The energy value chain for EDF.

From a monopoly position EDF was forced into a competitive environment when the European Union (EU) ordered that 20 per cent of the French electricity market should be opened up to competition in 1999. The French government set up the firm as a limited company that year and in 2004 they were floated on the Paris stock exchange. As European energy markets became more competitive, EDF were able to acquire other generators and distributors extending their operations to the UK, Belgium, Spain and a number of other EU countries. Most recently they acquired Italian energy firm Edison in 2011. Not all the expansion was on the basis of horizontal integration. EDF set up a subsidiary based in London to trade energy on the wholesale markets – linking their generation business to the transmission and distribution elements of the energy value chain (see Figure 6.3 for the value chain and examples of EDF's activity in each element).

At the heart of EDF's current strategy is the desire to reinforce its business model as designer, producer and operator, so the firm has continued to develop its nuclear expertise, but has also invested heavily in generation from renewables. At the other end of the supply chain, they have strengthened their position as a distributor by moving into retail sales in the UK as well as in France and through offering additional services to customers with a focus on energy efficiency – through building design advice and innovative uses of energy in both domestic and commercial environments. EDF employed some 160 000 people world-wide in 2010 and increased its turnover by 4.6 per cent to €65.2 billion. It remains the largest nuclear power firm in the world and the largest hydropower company in Europe.

Sources: Thompson, J. (2011) 'EDF unveils Edison takeover details', *Financial Times*, 27 December. Available online at www.ft.com/cms/s/0/8ed04a18-30a8-11e1-9436-00144feabdc0.html#ixzz1iU8LjhGe (accessed 29 May 2012); Datamonitor (2011) *Company Profile: Electicite de France (EDF)*, Datamonitor, London; EDF company website and documents.

Outsourcing Strategies: Narrowing the Scope of Operations

In contrast to vertical integration strategies, outsourcing strategies narrow the scope of a business's operations (and the firm's boundaries, in terms of what activities are performed internally). Outsourcing involves a conscious decision to forgo attempts to perform certain value chain activities internally and instead to farm them out to outside specialists.[37] Many PC-makers, for example, have shifted from assembling units in-house to outsourcing the entire assembly process to manufacturing specialists because enterprises that assemble many brands of PCs are better able to bargain down the prices of PC components (by buying in very large volumes) and because they have greater expertise in performing assembly tasks more cost-effectively. Nike has outsourced most of its manufacturing-related value chain activities so that it can concentrate on marketing and managing its brand.

Outsourcing certain value chain activities can be advantageous whenever:

● *An activity can be performed better or more cheaply by outside specialists.* A company should generally *not* perform any value chain activity internally that can be performed more efficiently or effectively by outsiders – the chief exception occurs when a particular activity is strategically crucial and internal control over that activity is deemed essential.

● *The activity is not crucial to the firm's ability to achieve sustainable competitive advantage and will not hollow out its core competencies.* Outsourcing of support activities such as maintenance services, data processing and data storage, fringe-benefit management and website operations has become commonplace. Colgate-Palmolive, for instance, has been able to reduce its IT operational costs by more than 10 per cent per year through an outsourcing agreement with IBM. A number of companies have outsourced their call centre operations to foreign-based contractors

Core Concept

Outsourcing involves farming out certain value chain activities to outside vendors.

LO 6.5
Describe the conditions that favour farming out certain value chain activities to outside parties.

that have access to lower-cost labour supplies and can employ lower-paid call centre personnel to respond to customer inquiries or requests for technical support.

● *It streamlines company operations in ways that improve organizational flexibility and speed time to market.* Outsourcing gives a company the flexibility to switch suppliers in the event that its present supplier falls behind competing suppliers. To the extent that its suppliers can speedily get next-generation parts and components into production, then a company can get its own next-generation product offerings into the marketplace quicker. Moreover, seeking out new suppliers with the needed capabilities already in place is frequently quicker, easier, less risky and cheaper than hurriedly retooling internal operations to replace obsolete capabilities or trying to install and master new technologies.

● *It reduces the company's risk exposure to changing technology and/or buyer preferences.* When a company outsources certain parts, components and services, its suppliers must bear the burden of incorporating state-of-the-art technologies and/or undertaking redesigns and upgrades to accommodate a company's plans to introduce next-generation products. If what a supplier provides falls out of favour with buyers, or is designed out of next-generation products, or rendered unnecessary by technological change, it is the supplier's business that suffers rather than a company's own internal operations.

● *It allows a company to assemble diverse kinds of expertise speedily and efficiently.* A company can nearly always gain quicker access to first-rate capabilities and expertise by employing suppliers who already have them in place than it can by trying to build them from scratch with its own company personnel.

● *It allows a company to concentrate on its core business, leverage its key resources and do even better what it already does best.* A company is better able to heighten its own competitively valuable capabilities when it concentrates its full resources and energies on performing those activities internally that it can perform better than outsiders and/or that it needs to have under its direct control. Hewlett-Packard, IBM and others have sold manufacturing plants to suppliers and then contracted to purchase the output.

A Major Risk of Outsourcing Value Chain Activities

Some commentators state that *the biggest danger of outsourcing is that a company will farm out too many or the wrong types of activities and thereby hollow out its own capabilities.*[38] They give examples of companies anxious to reduce operating costs that have opted to outsource such strategically important activities as product development, engineering design and sophisticated manufacturing tasks – the very capabilities that underpin a company's ability to lead sustained product innovation. While these companies may have been able to lower their operating costs by outsourcing these functions to outsiders that can perform them more cheaply, it is argued that *their ability to lead the development of innovative new products has been weakened in the process.*

However, as the Key Debate 6.1 illustrates, some organizations appear to have benefited from adopting a more open approach to core activities such as R&D and innovation. For example, nearly every US brand of laptop and cell phone (with the notable exception of Apple) is not only manufactured but designed in Asia.[39] However, this is not without risk and it can be strategically dangerous for a company to be dependent on outsiders for competitive capabilities that over the long run determine its market success. Companies like IBM and Dell are alert to the danger of farming out the performance of strategy-critical value chain activities and generally only outsource relatively mundane functions: IBM outsources customer support operations, and Dell outsources manufacturing.

Another risk of outsourcing comes from the lack of direct control. It may be difficult to monitor, control and co-ordinate the activities of outside parties by means of contracts and arm's-length transactions alone; unanticipated problems may arise that cause delays or cost overruns and become hard to resolve amicably. Moreover, contract-based outsourcing can be problematic because outside parties lack incentives to make investments specific to the needs of the outsourcing company's value chain.

Key Debate 6.1

IS INNOVATION BETTER SITED WITHIN OR OUTSIDE AN ORGANIZATION?

Ideagoras, open source software, crowdsourcing and a host of other concepts have been put forward as new ways for firms to generate new product ideas, solve technical problems and tap into greater intellectual capacity. It was Henry Chesbrough (2003) that first coined the term 'open innovation' to describe how firms were looking beyond their boundaries for R&D ideas. R&D had been considered a major strategic asset for firms and a significant barrier to entry for new entrants seeking to take on established incumbents in an industry. Chesbrough argued that the closed model of innovation, where firms invested substantial resources in R&D within the company, was not producing the expected competitive advantage. He cited Cisco's successful challenge to Lucent, and Motorola and Siemens' decline in the mobile telecoms sector in the face of new entrant, Nokia.

Other authors have provided further support for the argument that firms should look outside their organization to maximize the competitive advantage they gain from innovation. Tapscott and Williams (2008) give a range of examples involving ideagoras – or online marketplaces for ideas, such as InnoCentive – which involve Fortune 500 companies such as Boeing, Procter & Gamble and Novartis, posting technical problems to the website and offering to pay anyone who can provide a viable solution. Thomke and von Hippel (2002) demonstrated how some firms were turning to their customers and giving them the tools to conduct R&D. As early as the 1970s chip manufacturers such as VLSI provided customers with the tools to design bespoke prototypes that they would manufacture. More recently other firms have seen the advantages and reaped the benefits of this approach in everything from flavours to plastics, T-shirt designs to music and video.

Open innovation's supporters argue that having a good business model and being able to exploit innovations is often more important than getting to market first and in some cases being a fast follower can give firms a stronger position. There are many examples of pioneers failing to capitalize on their inventions, such as Altvista in search engines or Leica in 35 mm cameras (Trott and Hartmann, 2009). But there are also many examples of successful first movers, such as Pilkington and their float glass. Even pioneers that do not succeed with an invention, such as Sony and their Betamax video, can still earn a reputation for technological or scientific innovation by being first movers.

Instances of successful firms who keep their R&D focus largely internal do exist. Ferrero's closed approach to innovation has enabled them to become one of the world's top confectioners. Protecting their secret recipe appears to have been a sound approach. Apple adopted a closed approach to innovation when developing the iPod and similarly Nintendo kept the Wii under wraps (Almirall and Casadesus-Masanell, 2010), yet both products have gone on to revolutionize their respective industries.

Other commentators take a more cautious view of open innovation. Birkinshaw et al. (2011) stated that regarding open innovation as the future was one of the great myths in the field. While their research did show many large companies considered a more open approach to innovation was necessary, there were also many practical issues that had to be addressed. Open innovation carries a high degree of cost because the networks and forums that support the process have to be developed and managed. Firms that have embraced open innovation, such as Lego, Procter & Gamble and Intel have all invested heavily before seeing good returns. Birkinshaw et al. (2011) also point out that open innovation can complicate intellectual property issues and solving this is a further cost to the organization, although firms have been licensing successful technologies for many years. Trott and Hartmann (2009) dispute that closed innovation, as defined by Chesbrough, actually ever existed in commercial organizations. They challenge each of the assumptions put forward as examples of closed attitudes to R&D. For example, in response to the idea that closed firms believe they have to discover and develop ideas to profit from R&D, they cite the development of technology partnerships as early as the 1960s in some industries such as airliner manufacture, typified by the Airbus consortium, which was underpinned by a joint venture between Germany's MBB, France's Aerospatiale, British Aerospace and Spain's CASA.

QUESTIONS

1. What type of approach to innovation should (a) a pharmaceutical and (b) a snack food company follow?

2. What cultural factors might make it difficult for an organization to adopt an open approach to innovation?

Sources: Almirall, E. and Casadesus-Masanell, R. (2010) 'Open versus closed innovation: a model of discovery and divergence', *Academy of Management Review*, 35(1): 27–47; Birkinshaw, J., Bouquet, C. and Barsoux, J-L. (2011) 'The 5 myths of innovation', *MIT Sloan Management Review*, Winter, pp. 43–50; Chesbrough, H. (2003) 'The era of open innovation', *MIT Sloan Management Review*, Spring, pp. 35–41; Tapscott, D. and Williams, A. (2008) *Wikinomics*, Atlantic Books, London; Thomke, S. and von Hippel, E. (2002) 'Customers as innovators: new ways to create value', *Harvard Business Review*, April, pp. 5–11; Trott, P. and Hartmann, D. (2009) 'Why "open innovation" is old wine in new bottles', *International Journal of Innovation Management*, 13(4): 715–36.

Strategic Alliances and Partnerships

Strategic alliances and co-operative partnerships provide one way to gain some of the benefits offered by vertical integration, outsourcing and horizontal mergers and acquisitions while minimizing the associated problems. Companies frequently engage in co-operative strategies as an alternative to vertical integration or horizontal mergers and acquisitions. Increasingly, companies are also employing strategic alliances and partnerships to extend their scope of operations via international expansion and diversification strategies, as we describe in Chapters 7 and 8. Strategic alliances and co-operative arrangements are now a common means of narrowing a company's scope of operations as well, serving as a useful way to manage outsourcing (in lieu of traditional, purely price-oriented contracts).

For example, oil and gas companies engage in considerable vertical integration, but Shell Oil Company and Pemex (Mexico's state-owned petroleum company) have found that joint ownership of their Deer Park Refinery in Texas lowers their investment costs and risks in comparison to going it alone. The colossal failure of the Daimler-Chrysler merger formed an expensive lesson for Daimler AG about what can go wrong with horizontal mergers and acquisitions; its 2010 strategic alliance with Renault-Nissan may allow the two companies to achieve jointly the global scale required for cost competitiveness in cars and trucks while avoiding the type of problems that so plagued Daimler-Chrysler. Many companies employ strategic alliances to manage the problems that might otherwise occur with outsourcing – Cisco's system of alliances guards against loss of control, protects its proprietary manufacturing expertise, and enables the company to monitor closely the assembly operations of its partners while devoting its energy to designing new generations of the switches, routers and other Internet-related equipment for which it is known.

Companies in all types of industries and in all parts of the world have elected to form strategic alliances and partnerships to complement their own strategic initiatives and strengthen their competitiveness in domestic and international markets – the very same goals that motivate vertical integration, horizontal mergers and acquisitions and outsourcing initiatives. This is an about-face from times past, when the vast majority of companies were content to go it alone, confident that they already had or could independently develop whatever resources and know-how were needed to be successful in their markets. But in today's world, large corporations – even those that are successful and financially strong – have concluded that it does not always make good

LO 6.6
Explain when and how strategic alliances can substitute for horizontal mergers and acquisitions or vertical integration and how they can facilitate outsourcing.

strategic and economic sense to be *totally independent* and *self-sufficient* with regard to each and every skill, resource and capability they may need. When a company needs to strengthen its competitive position, whether through greater differentiation, efficiency improvements or a stronger bargaining position, the fastest and most effective route may be to partner with other enterprises having similar goals and complementary capabilities; moreover, partnering offers greater flexibility should a company's resource requirements or goals later change.

A strategic alliance is a formal agreement between two or more separate companies in which there is strategically relevant collaboration of some sort, joint contribution of resources, shared risk, shared control and mutual dependence. Often, alliances involve co-operative marketing, sales or distribution, joint production, design collaboration or projects to jointly develop new technologies or products. They can vary in terms of their duration and the extent of the collaboration; some are intended as long-term arrangements, involving an extensive set of co-operative activities, while others are designed to accomplish more limited, short-term objectives.

Collaborative arrangements may entail a contractual agreement, but they commonly stop short of formal ownership ties between the partners (although sometimes an alliance member will secure minority ownership of another member). A special type of strategic alliance involving ownership ties is the joint venture. A joint venture entails forming a new corporate entity that is jointly owned by two or more companies that agree to share in the revenues, expenses and control of the newly formed entity. Since joint ventures involve setting up a mutually owned business, they tend to be more durable but also riskier than other arrangements. In other types of strategic alliances, the collaboration between the partners involves a much less rigid structure in which the partners retain their independence from one another. If a strategic alliance is not working out, a partner can choose to simply walk away or reduce its commitment to collaborating at any time.

Five factors make an alliance 'strategic', as opposed to just a convenient business arrangement:[40]

1. It helps build, sustain or enhance a core competence or competitive advantage.
2. It helps block a competitive threat.
3. It increases the bargaining power of alliance members over suppliers or buyers.
4. It helps open up important new market opportunities.
5. It mitigates a significant risk to a company's business.

Strategic co-operation is a much-favoured approach in industries where new technological developments are occurring at a furious pace along many different paths and where advances in one technology spill over to affect others (often blurring industry boundaries). Whenever industries are experiencing high-velocity technological advances in many areas simultaneously, firms find it virtually essential to have co-operative relationships with other enterprises to stay on the leading edge of technology and product performance even in their own area of specialization.

The growth in sales of smartphones and tablet computers, coupled with fierce competition from rival firms in Taiwan and South Korea are the main reasons behind the recent joint venture between some of Japan's major display manufacturers. In November 2011, Hitachi, Sony and Toshiba signed a definitive agreement with the government-funded Innovation Network Corporation of Japan (INCJ) to integrate their small- and medium-sized display businesses into a single entity, Japan Display Inc. The new joint venture was launched in April 2012 with an investment of 200 billion yen (about €2 billion).[41]

Since 2003, Samsung Electronics, a global electronics company headquartered in South Korea, has entered into more than 30 major strategic alliances involving such

> **Core Concept**
>
> A **strategic alliance** is a formal agreement between two or more separate companies in which they agree to work co-operatively toward some common objective.

> **Core Concept**
>
> A **joint venture** is a type of strategic alliance in which the partners set up an independent corporate entity that they own and control jointly, sharing in its revenues and expenses.

companies as Sony, Nokia, Intel, Microsoft, Dell, Toshiba, Lowe's, IBM, Hewlett-Packard and Disney Automation; the alliances involved joint investments, technology transfer arrangements, joint R&D projects and agreements to supply parts and components – all of which facilitated Samsung's strategic efforts to globalize its business and secure its position as a leader in the world-wide electronics industry. Microsoft collaborates very closely with independent software developers to ensure that their programs will run on the next-generation versions of Windows. Genentech (now part of Roche), a leader in biotechnology and human genetics, has formed R&D alliances with over 30 companies to boost its prospects for developing new cures for various diseases and ailments. The Star Alliance is a partnership between 28 airlines, including Air Canada, BMI, Lufthansa, Singapore Airlines, Thai and Egyptair. Based in Frankfurt, Germany, the alliance started as a joint marketing vehicle for the airlines, but has extended its scope to include sharing new technologies, co-ordination of schedules between the members and common airport facilities, all aimed at improving customers' travel experience.

Toyota has forged long-term strategic partnerships with many of its suppliers of automotive parts and components, both to achieve lower costs and to improve the quality and reliability of its vehicles. In 2008, when Chrysler found itself unable to build hybrid SUVs and trucks using its two-mode technological innovation (because it lacked the economies of scale necessary to produce proprietary components at a reasonable cost), it entered into a strategic alliance with Nissan whereby Nissan would build Chrysler vehicles with the hybrid technology and Chrysler would take over the production of certain Nissan truck models. Daimler AG has been entering a variety of alliances to lower its risks and improve its prospects in electric cars, where it lacks key capabilities. Its equity-based strategic partnership with Tesla Motors, for example, will allow Daimler to use proven technology to bring its electric vehicles to market quickly, while helping Tesla learn how to mass-produce its electric cars. Daimler's 2010 joint venture with Chinese car maker BYD is intended to help Daimler make and sell electric cars for the Chinese market.

Studies indicate that large corporations are commonly involved in 30–50 alliances and that a number have hundreds of alliances. One study estimated that corporate revenues coming from activities involving strategic alliances have more than doubled since 1995.[42] Another study reported that the typical large corporation relied on alliances for 15–20 per cent of its revenues, assets or income.[43] Companies that have formed a host of alliances have a need to manage their alliances like a portfolio – terminating those that no longer serve a useful purpose or that have produced meagre results, forming promising new alliances and restructuring certain existing alliances to correct performance problems and/or redirect the collaborative effort.[44]

> Company use of alliances is quite widespread.

Why and How Strategic Alliances are Advantageous

The most common reasons companies enter into strategic alliances are to expedite the development of promising new technologies or products, to overcome deficits in their own technical and manufacturing expertise, to bring together the personnel and expertise needed to create desirable new skill sets and capabilities, to improve supply chain efficiency, to share the risks of high-stake, risky ventures, to gain economies of scale in production and/or marketing and to acquire or improve market access through joint marketing agreements.[45] Manufacturers frequently pursue alliances with parts and components suppliers to gain the efficiencies of better supply chain management and to speed new products to market. By joining forces in components production and/or final assembly, companies may be able to realize cost savings not achievable with their own small volumes. Allies can learn much from one another in performing joint research, sharing technological know-how and collaborating on complementary new technologies and products – sometimes enough to enable them to pursue other new opportunities on their own.[46] In industries where

> The best alliances are highly selective, focusing on particular value-creating activities, whether within or across industry boundaries, and on obtaining a specific competitive benefit. They enable a firm to build on its strengths and to learn.

technology is advancing rapidly, alliances are all about fast cycles of learning, staying abreast of the latest developments, gaining quick access to the latest round of technological know-how and developing dynamic capabilities. In bringing together firms with different skills and knowledge bases, alliances open up learning opportunities that help partner firms better leverage their own resources and capabilities.[47]

There are several other instances in which companies find strategic alliances particularly valuable. As we explain in the next chapter, a company that is racing for *global market leadership* needs alliances to:[48]

- *Get into critical country markets quickly* and accelerate the process of building a potent global market presence.
- *Gain inside knowledge about unfamiliar markets and cultures through alliances with local partners.* For example, US, European and Japanese companies wanting to build market footholds in the fast-growing Chinese market have pursued partnership arrangements with Chinese companies to help get products through the customs process, to help guide them through the maze of government regulations, to supply knowledge of local markets, to provide guidance on adapting their products to better match the buying preferences of Chinese consumers, to set up local manufacturing capabilities and to assist in distribution, marketing and promotional activities.
- *Access valuable skills and competencies* that are concentrated in particular geographic locations (such as advertising and marketing expertise in the UK, fashion design skills in Italy and efficient manufacturing skills in Japan and China).

A company that is racing to *stake out a strong position in an industry of the future* needs alliances to:[49]

- *establish a stronger beachhead* for participating in the target industry;
- *master new technologies and build new expertise and competencies* faster than would be possible through internal efforts;
- *open up broader opportunities* in the target industry by melding the firm's own capabilities with the expertise and resources of partners.

Capturing the Benefits of Strategic Alliances

The extent to which companies benefit from entering into alliances and partnerships seems to be a function of six factors:[50]

1. *Picking a good partner.* A good partner must bring complementary strengths to the relationship. To the extent that alliance members have non-overlapping strengths, there is greater potential for synergy and less potential for co-ordination problems and conflict. In addition, a good partner needs to share the company's vision about the overall purpose of the alliance and to have specific goals that either match or complement those of the company. Strong partnerships also depend on good chemistry among key personnel and compatible views about how the alliance should be structured and managed.

2. *Being sensitive to cultural differences.* Cultural differences among companies can make it difficult for their personnel to work together effectively. Cultural differences can be problematic among companies from the same country, but when the partners have different national origins, the problems are often magnified. Unless there is respect among all the parties for company cultural differences, including those stemming from different local cultures and local business practices, productive working relationships are unlikely to emerge.

3. *Recognizing that the alliance must benefit both sides.* Information must be shared as well as gained, and the relationship must remain forthright and trustful. Many

alliances fail because one or both partners grow unhappy with what they are learning. Also, if either partner plays games with information or tries to take advantage of the other, the resulting friction can quickly erode the value of further collaboration. Open, trustworthy behaviour on both sides is essential for fruitful collaboration.

4. *Ensuring that both parties live up to their commitments.* Both parties have to deliver on their commitments for the alliance to produce the intended benefits. The division of work has to be perceived as fairly apportioned, and the calibre of the benefits received on both sides has to be perceived as adequate. Such actions are critical for the establishment of trust between the parties; research has shown that trust is an important factor in fostering effective strategic alliances.[51]

5. *Structuring the decision-making process so that actions can be taken swiftly when needed.* In many instances, the fast pace of technological and competitive changes dictates an equally fast decision-making process. If the parties get bogged down in discussions or in gaining internal approval from higher-ups, the alliance can turn into an anchor of delay and inaction.

6. *Managing the learning process and then adjusting the alliance agreement over time to fit new circumstances.* One of the keys to long-lasting success is adapting the nature and structure of the alliance to be responsive to shifting market conditions, emerging technologies and changing customer requirements. Wise allies are quick to recognize the merit of an evolving collaborative arrangement, where adjustments are made to accommodate changing market conditions and to overcome whatever problems arise in establishing an effective working relationship. Most alliances encounter troubles of some kind within a couple of years – those that are flexible enough to evolve are better able to recover.[52]

Most alliances that aim at sharing technology or providing market access turn out to be temporary, lasting only a few years. This is not necessarily an indicator of failure, however. Strategic alliances can be terminated after a few years simply because they have fulfilled their purpose; indeed, many alliances are intended to be of limited duration, set up to accomplish specific short-term objectives. Longer-lasting collaborative arrangements, however, may provide even greater strategic benefits. Alliances are more likely to be long-lasting when (1) they involve collaboration with partners that do not compete directly, (2) a trusting relationship has been established, and (3) both parties conclude that continued collaboration is in their mutual interest, perhaps because new opportunities for learning are emerging.

The Drawbacks of Strategic Alliances and Partnerships

While strategic alliances provide a way of obtaining the benefits of vertical integration, mergers and acquisitions and outsourcing, they also suffer from some of the same drawbacks. Culture clash and integration problems due to different management styles and business practices can interfere with the success of an alliance, just as they can with vertical integration or horizontal mergers and acquisitions. Anticipated gains may fail to materialize due to an overly optimistic view of the synergies or a poor fit in terms of the combination of resources and capabilities. When outsourcing is conducted via alliances, there is no less risk of becoming dependent on other companies for essential expertise and capabilities; indeed, this may be the Achilles' heel of such alliances.

Moreover, there are additional pitfalls to collaborative arrangements. The greatest danger is that a partner will gain access to a company's proprietary knowledge base, technologies or trade secrets, enabling the partner to match the company's core strengths and costing the company its hard-won competitive advantage. This risk is greatest when the alliance is among industry rivals or when the alliance is for the purpose of collaborative R&D, since this type of partnership requires an extensive exchange of closely held information.

The question for managers is when to engage in a strategic alliance and when to choose an alternative means of meeting their objectives. The answer to this question depends on the relative advantages of each method and the circumstances under which each type of organizational arrangement is favoured.

The principle advantages of strategic alliances over vertical integration or horizontal mergers/acquisitions are threefold:

1. They lower investment costs and risks for each partner by facilitating resource pooling and risk sharing. This can be particularly important when investment needs and uncertainty are high, such as when a dominant technology standard has not yet emerged.

2. They are more flexible organizational forms and allow for a more adaptive response to changing conditions. Flexibility is key when environmental conditions or technologies are changing rapidly. Moreover, strategic alliances under such circumstances may enable the development of each partner's dynamic capabilities.

3. They are more rapidly deployed – a critical factor when speed is of the essence. Speed is of the essence when there is a winner-take-all type of competitive situation, such as the race for a dominant technological design or a race down a steep experience curve, where there is a large first-mover advantage.

The key advantages of using strategic alliances rather than arm's-length transactions to manage outsourcing are (1) the increased ability to exercise control over the partners' activities and (2) a greater willingness for the partners to make relationship-specific investments. Arm's-length transactions discourage such investments since they imply less commitment and do not build trust.

On the other hand, there are circumstances when other organizational mechanisms are preferable to partnering. Mergers and acquisitions are especially suited for situations in which strategic alliances or partnerships do not go far enough in providing a company with access to needed resources and capabilities.[53] Ownership ties are more permanent than partnership ties, allowing the operations of the merger/acquisition participants to be tightly integrated and creating more in-house control and autonomy. Other organizational mechanisms are also preferable to alliances when there is limited property rights protection for valuable know-how and when companies fear being taken advantage of by opportunistic partners.

While it is important for managers to understand when strategic alliances and partnerships are most likely (and least likely) to prove useful, it is also important to know how to manage them.

How to Make Strategic Alliances Work

A surprisingly large number of alliances never live up to expectations. A recent article reported that even though the number of strategic alliances increases by about 25 per cent annually, about 60–70 per cent of alliances continue to fail each year.[54] The success of an alliance depends on how well the partners work together, their capacity to respond and adapt to changing internal and external conditions and their willingness to renegotiate the bargain if circumstances so warrant. A successful alliance requires real in-the-trenches collaboration, not merely an arm's-length exchange of ideas. Unless partners place a high value on the skills, resources and contributions each brings to the alliance and the co-operative arrangement results in valuable win-win outcomes, it is doomed.

While the track record for strategic alliances is poor on average, many companies have learned how to manage strategic alliances successfully and routinely defy these averages. The Samsung Group, which includes Samsung Electronics and had world-wide sales of $117.8 billion in 2009, successfully manages an ecosystem of over 1300 partnerships that enable productive activities from global procurement to local marketing to collaborative R&D. The Samsung Group takes a systematic approach to managing its partnerships and devotes considerable resources to this enterprise. In 2008, for example, it established a Partner Collaboration and Enhancement Office under the direct control of its CEO. The Samsung Group supports its partners with financial help as well as training and development resources to ensure that its alliance partners' technical, manufacturing and management capabilities remain globally competitive. As a result, some of its equipment providers have emerged as the leading firms in their industries while contributing to Samsung's competitive advantage in the global TV market.

Companies that have greater success in managing their strategic alliances and partnerships often credit the following factors:

- *They create a system for managing their alliances.* Companies need to manage their alliances in a systematic fashion, just as they manage other functions. This means setting up a process for managing the different aspects of alliance management from partner selection to alliance termination procedures. To ensure that the system is followed on a routine basis by all company managers, many companies create a set of explicit procedures, process templates, manuals or the like.

- *They build relationships with their partners and establish trust.* Establishing strong interpersonal relationships is a critical factor in making strategic alliances work since they facilitate opening up channels of communication, co-ordinating activity, aligning interests and building trust. Cultural sensitivity is a key part of this, particularly for cross-border alliances. Accordingly, many companies include cultural sensitivity training for their managers as a part of their alliance management programme.

- *They protect themselves from the threat of opportunism by setting up safeguards.* There are a number of means for preventing a company from being taken advantage of by an untrustworthy partner or unwittingly losing control over key assets. Contractual safeguards, including non-competing clauses, can provide some protection. But if the company's core assets are vulnerable to being appropriated by partners, it may be possible to control their use and strictly limit outside access. Cisco Systems, for example, does not divulge the source code for its designs to its alliance partners, thereby controlling the initiation of all improvements and safeguarding its innovations from imitation.

- *They make commitments to their partners and see that their partners do the same.* When partners make credible commitments to a joint enterprise, they have stronger incentives for making it work and are less likely to 'free-ride' on the efforts of other partners. Because of this, equity-based alliances tend to be more successful than non-equity alliances.[55]

- *They make learning a routine part of the management process.* There are always opportunities for learning from a partner, but organizational learning does not take place automatically. Moreover, whatever learning takes place cannot add to a company's knowledge base unless the learning is incorporated into the company's routines and practices. Particularly when the purpose of an alliance is to improve a company's knowledge assets and capabilities, it is important for the company to learn thoroughly and rapidly about its partners' technologies, business practices and organizational capabilities and then transfer valuable ideas and practices into its own operations promptly.

Finally, managers should realize that alliance management is an organizational capability, much like any other. It develops over time, out of effort, experience and learning. For this reason, it is wise to begin slowly, with simple alliances, designed to meet limited, short-term objectives. Short-term partnerships that are successful often become the basis for much more extensive collaborative arrangements. Even when strategic alliances are set up with the hope that they will become long-term engagements, they have a better chance of succeeding if they are phased in so that the partners can learn how they can work together most fruitfully.

KEY POINTS

1. Companies can strengthen their competitive advantage by making further strategic choices regarding (1) competitive actions, (2) timing and (3) scope of operations can complement its competitive approach and maximize the power of its overall strategy.

2. Strategic offensives should, as a general rule, be grounded in a company's strategic assets. The best offensives use a company's resource and capability strengths to attack rivals in the competitive areas where they are comparatively weakest.

3. Companies have a number of offensive strategy options for improving their market positions: using a cost-based advantage to attack competitors on the basis of price or value, leap-frogging competitors with next-generation technologies, pursuing continuous product innovation, adopting and improving the best ideas of others, using hit-and-run tactics to steal sales away from unsuspecting rivals and launching pre-emptive strikes. A blue-ocean type of offensive strategy seeks to gain a dramatic and durable competitive advantage by abandoning efforts to beat out competitors in existing markets and, instead, inventing a new industry or distinctive market segment that renders existing competitors largely irrelevant and allows a company to create and capture altogether new demand.

4. The purposes of defensive strategies are to lower the risk of being attacked, weaken the impact of any attack that occurs and influence challengers to aim their efforts at other rivals. Defensive strategies to protect a company's position usually take one of two forms: (1) actions to block challengers and (2) actions to signal the likelihood of strong retaliation.

5. The timing of strategic moves also has competitive relevance and is especially important when first-mover advantages or disadvantages exist. Company managers are obligated to carefully consider the advantages or disadvantages that attach to being a first mover versus a fast follower versus a wait-and-see late mover.

6. Decisions concerning the scope of a company's operations – which activities a firm will perform internally and which it will not – can also affect the strength of a company's market position. The *scope of the firm* refers to the range of its activities, the breadth of its product and service offerings, the extent of its geographic market presence and its mix of businesses. Companies can expand their scope horizontally (more broadly within their focal market) or vertically (up or down the chain of value-adding activities that start with raw-material production and end with sales and service to the end-consumer). Horizontal mergers and acquisitions (combinations of market rivals) provide a means for a company to expand its horizontal scope. Vertical integration expands a firm's vertical scope.

7. Horizontal mergers and acquisitions can strengthen a firm's competitiveness in five ways: (1) by improving the efficiency of its operations; (2) by heightening its product differentiation; (3) by reducing market rivalry; (4) by increasing the company's bargaining power over suppliers and buyers; and (5) by enhancing its flexibility and dynamic capabilities.

8. Vertical integration, forward or backward, makes strategic sense only if it strengthens a company's position via either cost reduction or the creation of a differentiation-based advantage. Otherwise, the drawbacks of vertical integration (increased investment, greater business risk, increased vulnerability to technological changes, less flexibility in making product changes and the potential for channel conflict) are likely to outweigh any advantages.

9. Outsourcing involves farming out pieces of the value chain formerly performed in-house to outside vendors, thereby narrowing the scope of the firm. Outsourcing can enhance a company's competitiveness whenever: (1) an activity can be performed better or more cheaply by outside specialists; (2) having the activity performed by others will not hollow out the outsourcing company's

core competencies; (3) it streamlines company operations in ways that improve organizational flexibility, speed decision-making and cut cycle time; (4) it reduces the company's risk exposure; (5) it allows a company to access capabilities more quickly and improves its ability to innovate; and (6) it permits a company to concentrate on its core business and focus on what it does best.

10. Strategic alliances and co-operative partnerships provide one way to gain some of the benefits offered by vertical integration, outsourcing and horizontal mergers and acquisitions while minimizing the associated problems. They serve as an alternative to vertical integration and mergers and acquisitions; they serve as a supplement to outsourcing, allowing more control relative to outsourcing via arm's-length transactions.

11. Companies that manage their alliances well, generally, (1) create a system for managing their alliances, (2) build relationships with their partners and establish trust, (3) protect themselves from the threat of opportunism by setting up safeguards, (4) make commitments to their partners and see that their partners do the same, and (5) make learning a routine part of the management process.

CLOSING CASE

SAFARICOM AND M-PESA – INNOVATION THROUGH PARTNERSHIP

Bob Collymore, the CEO of Kenyan mobile telecoms network provider, Safaricom, had plenty to think about at the end of 2011. The firm's key product, M-Pesa, a mobile telecoms-based money transfer system, had exceeded all expectations over the Christmas period, recording 285 transactions per second compared to 154 in the same period the previous year. However, thanks to increasing competition and costs Safaricom had also seen its profits drop by 47 per cent in the first six months of the 2011/12 financial year. Did the firm need a new strategy for the New Year?

BACKGROUND

Safaricom started life as part of the state-owned Kenya Posts and Telecommunications Corporation initially as an analogue mobile network and from 1999 as the main GSM network provider in Kenya. The company was incorporated in 1997 and floated on Kenya's Nairobi Stock Exchange (NSE) as a public company in 2002. The Kenyan Government remained a majority shareholder in the firm via Telkom Kenya until 2008 when it sold just over a third of its shares. The Treasury still retains a 35 per cent holding in the organization.

M-Pesa was first introduced as a pilot at the end of 2005 into the Kenyan financial services market. Aimed at the millions of Kenyans who do not have bank accounts (only 2 million out of 32 million used banks in 2005/6), the service had originally been developed by Susie Lonie and Nick Hughes working for UK mobile telecoms network provider, Vodafone. However, to ensure the launch of the new service was successful Vodafone put together a strategic alliance that included Safaricom, the UK Government's Department for International Development (DFID), Faulu Kenya and Microsave, who provided expertise in microfinance and the Commercial Bank of Africa. Safaricom has had strong links with Vodafone since 2000 when the UK-based telecoms giant bought a substantial shareholding in the business. In 2011, Vodafone owned 40 per cent of Safaricom.

The pilot proved extremely successful and suggested that the take-up of the service would be very rapid and widespread. M-Pesa (the name is a combination of M for mobile and the Swahili word for money, pesa) allowed Safaricom's mobile customers to transfer money electronically to other M-Pesa users and also non-registered users. The company later allowed users to pay bills through the service and purchase mobile airtime. To set up an M-Pesa account, users had to register with one of Safaricom registered retail outlets. This allowed the firm to set up an electronic money account via the users' mobile SIM card and linked to the individual's mobile number. Customers did not pay for registering or depositing money in their M-Pesa account but there was a small fee charged for money transfers, withdrawals and balance inquiries.

M-Pesa could be seen as a data product as the service was delivered by SMS. However, it moved Safaricom into potential competition with financial services firms. Many Kenyans worked in the main cities such as Nairobi, but still had families in rural areas. Money transfer was a service with many potential customers. Before M-Pesa's launch in 2007, Kenyans had limited opportunities to transfer money. The country only had about 800 post offices and a similar number of bank branches. There were only 1500 ATMs and most of these were in urban areas. Transferring money via Posta (the Kenyan Post Office) or Western Union was slow and expensive. There were many small enterprises, often bus and taxi firms, which offered to physically take money along their transport routes, but security and reliability was a major issue with these providers. M-Pesa offered a secure, affordable alternative, which was much faster than the other services as it was SMS-based and was more convenient due to the ability to set up accounts and withdraw cash via Safaricom's network of 19 500 partner M-Pesa stores of which 6000 were registered agents.

PERFORMANCE AND PROBLEMS

The scope of Safaricom's operations and the reach of its network of partners and agents was a key factor in the rapid growth of the M-Pesa service. M-Pesa had 13.8 million users in Kenya by March 2011 that represented 80 per cent of Safaricom's 17.18 million subscribers. This meant that since its full launch in 2007 the service had been adopted by over half of the country's adult population A year earlier, only 60 per cent of subscribers had signed up to the service. Revenue from the new service had grown from 2.93 billion Kenyan Shillings (approximately €27 million) in 2009 to 11.78 billion Kenyan Shillings (approximately €108 million) by 2011, which meant it accounted for 12 per cent of the firm's turnover (see Exhibit 6.1 for selected financial figures).

Safaricom continued to develop the M-Pesa service to strengthen their dominant position. By mid-2011 the company had added Pesapoint, Diamond

EXHIBIT 6.1: Safaricom/M-Pesa key figures

Measure	Financial year			
	2008	2009	2010	2011
Revenue (Kenyan shillings billions)	61.37	70.48	83.96	94.83
Subscribers (millions)	10.23	13.36	15.79	17.18
M-PESA revenue (Kenyan shillings billions)	0.37	2.93	7.56	11.78
M-PESA users (millions)	2.08	6.18	9.48	13.80
Profit (NOPAT) (Kenyan shillings billions)	13.85	10.54	15.15	13.16

Source: Safaricom Annual Reports, 2008–2011.

a further service in partnership with Equity Bank known as M-Kesho, which allowed M-Pesa customers to open a basic bank account and use this to secure micro-loans and to gain interest on positive balances. The M-Kesho product was quickly replicated by other Kenyan banks during the latter half of 2010.

Trust Bank and Equity Bank to their list of partners through an agreement to allow M-Pesa customers to access the three banks' network of ATMs. In March 2011 it concluded an agreement with Western Union to allow Kenyans living and working overseas to transfer money back home. In addition to the PayBill service, Safaricom also developed services to allow customers to use M-Pesa to pay for goods at retail outlets, transfer money onto a prepay Visa card to facilitate shopping and withdrawal of cash on an international basis and to pay for plane, bus and train tickets.

In the initial stages of developing the M-Pesa service the partners had been clear that this was not a bank account. The documents required to open an M-Pesa account were not as extensive as those needed to open a regular bank account. The service was underpinned by partner banks which facilitated the back office processes that underpinned the service. It also meant that Safaricom did not have to meet the many regulatory requirements imposed on banks. However, as the service evolved it was blurring the distinction between mobile data services and financial services. For their many unbanked customers M-Pesa was the closest they had come to having a bank account. There was also a record of their financial transactions that could provide a profile for financial institutions to base lending decisions on. In May 2010 Safaricom launched

The success of the service also started to bring its own problems and the end of 2011 marked a period of technical problems, which started with an upgrade to the service in mid-December, resulting in a failure of various handset transactions including airtime top-ups. The peak money transfer period over Christmas and New Year also saw the firm's capacity unable to cope with the volume of transactions through the M-Pesa service .

A MORE COMPETITIVE INDUSTRY

Up until 2008 Kenya's mobile market had only two players, Safaricom and Zain, who between them had some 15 million subscribers. The entry of the India-based Essar Group under its Yu brand in November 2008 and the extension of Telkom Kenya's services in partnership with France Telecom to include mobile through the Orange brand was to change the industry dynamics. But a more significant event was the purchase of the Zain brand by Indian high-tech giant Airtel in 2010. Airtel acquired Zain's entire portfolio of African mobile businesses and subsequently launched a price war against Safaricom in late 2010. In January 2011 Airtel dropped its tariff to just one Kenyan shilling a minute having previously halved the rate to 3 shillings a minute in late 2010. Safaricom's share price

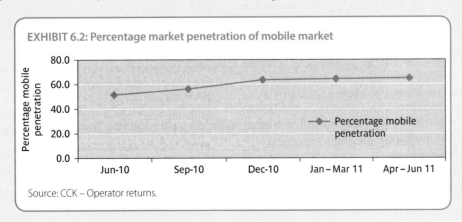

EXHIBIT 6.2: Percentage market penetration of mobile market

Source: CCK – Operator returns.

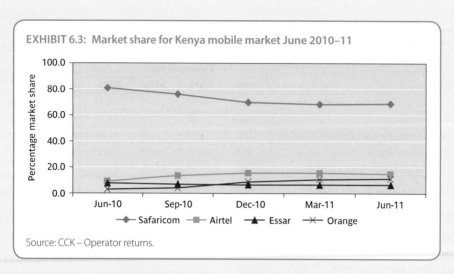

EXHIBIT 6.3: Market share for Kenya mobile market June 2010–11

Source: CCK – Operator returns.

crashed to less than 4.7 Kenyan shillings. This was not the lowest point for the firm's shares. In 2008 they had fallen from a high of just over 7.8 Kenyan shillings to 2.7 Kenyan shillings as the impact of the new entrants to the mobile telecoms market in Kenya become more apparent.

Despite the fact that the total mobile market had been growing rapidly with penetration increasing from 51 per cent to 64 per cent during 2010/11 (see Exhibit 6.2 for further details), the new entrants to the market had also put pressure on Safaricom's market share, which dropped from 80 per cent to 68 per cent in the same period. Both Orange and Airtel increased their share of the market to 10.6 per cent and 14.3 per cent respectively (see Exhibit 6.3 for full details).

M-Pesa had continued to give Safaricom a competitive advantage over its mobile rivals and by 2011 accounted for 70 per cent of financial transactions in Kenya. M-Pesa had also been launched in South Africa and Tanzania. However, the fact that Safaricom had educated customers to use mobile wallet services now meant that their rivals could launch their own versions without the cost of learning from scratch. Airtel launched a mobile money service branded as Zap across its African operations in partnership with Standard Chartered Bank. The service allowed transfers, deposits and withdrawals via Airtel handsets. Then in September 2011, they extended their mobile wallet services, this time in partnership with Mastercard, to allow customers to purchase items from international merchants via their handsets without the need for a credit or debit card. Meanwhile, Orange and Essar had launched rival services to M-Pesa, branded as Iko Pesa and Yu Cash. Orange had also entered into partnership with Equity Bank and Visa in a deal to launch an Iko Pesa debit card. Equity Bank were keen to promote the Iko Pesa mobile banking platform, because, unlike M-Kesho, they had a one-year exclusivity clause and Orange appeared to have ironed out many of the technical problems encountered by their rivals in setting up a mobile banking platform.

THE CEO'S DECISION

Safaricom had taken many steps to strengthen its market leading position since 2007 but by the end of December 2011 its share price had slipped to just 3.1 Kenyan shillings, its market share was heading towards 65 per cent and its profits had slumped. On top of this they had encountered a range of technical problems and some partnership issues that had damaged their reputation. However, they had been the main player in a revolutionary approach to helping their customers gain greater access to a range of financial services and this had produced substantial growth in revenues and subscribers. Bob Collymore had to decide where to take the company next, but this would need a well-crafted approach, one that would help to sustain the firm's competitive advantage, but also keep the investors, partners, agents and customers committed to a future with Safaricom.

QUESTIONS

1. How has Safaricom strengthened its position in the Kenyan mobile market using offensive and defensive strategies?

2. What advantages and disadvantages have resulted from Safaricom's position as first mover in the development of mobile money services?

3. What aspect of managing their strategic alliances and partnerships have Safaricom got right and which could they have improved on?

4. Would a more vertically integrated approach have improved the outcomes for Safaricom?

5. What strategy would you recommend to Bob Collymore for the future?

Sources: Telecompaper (2011) 'Safaricom sets new record with M-pesa transactions', *Telecompaper*, 30 December. Available online at www.telecompaper.com/news/safaricom-sets-new-record-with-m-pesa-transactions (accessed 12 January 2012); Nduati, L. (2011) 'Safaricom now raises the bar for Bonga points reward', *Daily Nation* (Kenya), 17 December. Available online at www.nation.co.ke/business/news/Safaricom+now+raises+the+bar+for+Bonga+points+reward+/-/1006/1291222/-/k4ujl7z/-/ (accessed 12 January 2012); Safaricom (2012) 'Our heritage', Safaricom.co.ke. Available online at www.safaricom.co.ke/index.php?id=331 (accessed 12 January 2012); Safaricom (2011) *Annual Report and Group Accounts 2011*, Safaricom, Nairobi, p 172; Karugu, W. and Mwendwa, T. (2007) *Vodafone and Safaricom Kenya: Extending the Range and Reliability of Financial Services to the Poor in Rural Kenya*, United Nations Development Programme Case Study, New York; Mas, I. and Radcliffe, D. (2010) 'Mobile payments go viral: M-PESA in Kenya', *Yes Africa Can: Success Stories from a Dynamic Continent*, World Bank, August; Hernandez, W. (2011) 'Western union expands M-Pesa funds-transfer service beyond the UK', *CardLine*, 4/1/2011, 11(13); Gordon, J. (2010)

'Tomorrow is here: M-KESHO offers microloans and interest via mobile phone', *MicrofinanceAfrica.net*. Available online at www.microfinanceafrica.net/news/tomorrow-is-here-m-kesho-offers-microloans-and-interest-via-mobile-phone/ (accessed 12 January 2012); Mwaura Kimani and Okuttah Mark (2011) 'Equity's deal with Orange tilts banking landscape', *MicrofinanceAfrica.net*. Available online at www.microfinanceafrica.net/tag/iko-pesa/ (accessed 12 January 2012); Fripp, C. (2011a) 'Safaricom upgrade knocks out M-PESA', IT News Africa. Available online at www.itnewsafrica.com/2011/12/safaricom-upgrade-knocks-out-m-pesa/ (accessed 12 January 2012); Fripp, C. (2011b) 'Kenya's M-Pesa to experience more disruptions', IT News Africa. Available online at www.itnewsafrica.com/2011/12/kenya%E2%80%99s-mpesa-to-experience-more-disruptions/ (accessed 12 January 2012); Adams, J. (2011) 'Mobile goes global in Kenya', *American Banker*, 00027561, 23 Septemper, 176(F337); Githinji, P. (2011) 'Orange Kenya's Iko Pesa raise stakes in mobile money market', *The Standard*, 28 November. Available online at www.standardmedia.co.ke/InsidePage.php?id=2000047465&cid=14&j=&m=&d= (accessed 12 January 2012).

ASSURANCE OF LEARNING EXERCISES

LO 6.1

1. Carry out some research into the European paints and coatings industry. Imagine you are a manager with Akzo Nobel. Analyse their position in the market and decide whether they should follow and offensive or defensive strategy.

LO 6.2

2. Identify the first movers in web browser market in the 1990s? How was Microsoft able to succeed as a later entrant to this market? Who are the key challengers in this sector currently and what strategies could they use to take more of Microsoft's share of the market?

LO 6.3

3. Using your university library's subscription to Lexis-Nexis, EBSCO, or a similar database, perform a search on 'acquisition strategy'. Identify at least two companies in different industries that are using acquisitions to strengthen their market positions. How have these acquisitions enhanced the acquiring companies' competitive capabilities?

LO 6.4

4. Go to www.bridgestone.co.jp/english/ir, and review information about Bridgestone Corporation's tyre and raw-material operations under the About Bridgestone and IR Library links. To what extent is the company vertically integrated? What segments of the vertical chain has the company chosen to enter? What are the benefits and liabilities of Bridgestone's vertical integration strategy?

LO 6.5, L O 6.6

5. Go to www.google.co.uk, and do a search on 'outsourcing'. Identify at least two companies in different industries that have entered into outsourcing agreements with firms with specialized services. In addition, describe what value chain activities the companies have chosen to outsource. Do any of these outsourcing agreements seem likely to threaten any of the companies' competitive capabilities? Are the companies using strategic alliances to manage their outsourcing?

EXERCISES FOR SIMULATION PARTICIPANTS

LO 6.1

1. What offensive strategy options does your company have? Identify at least two offensive moves that your company should seriously consider to improve the company's market standing and financial performance.

LO 6.2

2. What options for being a first mover does your company have? Do any of these first-mover options hold competitive advantage potential?

LO 6.1

3. What defensive strategy moves should your company consider in the upcoming decision round? Identify at least two defensive actions that your company has taken in a past decision round.

LO 6.3

4. Does your company have the option to merge with or acquire other companies? If so, which rival companies would you like to acquire or merge with?

LO 6.4

5. Is your company vertically integrated? Explain.

LO 6.5, L O 6.6

6. Is your company able to engage in outsourcing? If so, what do you see as the pros and cons of outsourcing? Are strategic alliances involved? Explain.

ENDNOTES

1. There is a good discussion on how organizations use a range of strategic approaches to competing in these dynamic environments in Wirtz, B., Mathieu, A. and Schilke, O. (2007) 'Strategy in high-velocity environments', *Long Range Planning*, 40: 295–313.

2. There is a useful summary of the features of hypercompetitive environments and some of the potential strategic approaches open to organizations operating in this type of industry in D'Aveni, R. (1995) 'Coping with hypercomptetition: utilizing the new 7S framework', *Academy of Management Executive*, 9(3): 45–57.

3. An insightful discussion of aggressive offensive strategies is presented in Stalk, George Jr and Lachenauer, Rob (2004) 'Hardball: five killer strategies for trouncing the competition', *Harvard Business Review*, 82(4): 62–71. For a discussion of offensive strategies to enter attractive markets where existing firms are making above-average profits, see Bryce, David J. and Dyer, Jeffrey H. (2007) 'Strategies to crack well-guarded markets', *Harvard Business Review*, 85(5): 84–92. A discussion of offensive strategies particularly suitable for industry leaders is presented in 'Aveni, Richard D. (2002) 'The empire strikes back: counterrevolutionary strategies for industry leaders', *Harvard Business Review*, 8(11): 66–74.

4. Stalk, George (2004) 'Playing hardball: why strategy still matters', *Ivey Business Journal* 69(2): 1–2. See Smith, K.G., Ferrier, W.J. and Grimm, C.M. (2001) 'King of the hill: dethroning the industry leader', *Academy of Management Executive*, 15(2): 59–70; also see Ferrier, W.J., Smith, K.G. and Grimm, C.M. (1999) 'The role of competitive action in market share erosion and industry dethronement: a study of industry leaders and Challengers', *Academy of Management Journal*, 42(4): 372–88.

5. For a discussion of how to wage offensives against strong rivals, see Yoffie, David B. and Kwak, Mary (2002) 'Mastering balance: how to meet and beat a stronger opponent', *California Management Review*, 44(2): 8–24.

6. Stalk, 'Playing hardball', pp. 1–2.

7. MacMillan, Ian C. Alexander, B., van Putten, A.B. and McGrath, Rita Gunther (2003) 'Global Gamesmanship', *Harvard Business Review*, 81(5): 66–67; also see Rao, Ashkay R., Bergen, Mark E. and Davis, Scott (2000) 'How to fight a price war', *Harvard Business Review*, 78(2): 107–16.

8. Yoffie, D.B. and Cusumano, M.A. (1999) 'Judo strategy – the competitive dynamics of Internet time', *Harvard Business* Review, 77(1): 70–81.

9. Stalk and Lachenauer, 'Hardball: five killer strategies', p. 64.

10. *The Economist* (2009) 'LVMH in the recession: the substance of style', *The Economist* 17 September. Available online at www.economist.com/node/14447276 (accessed 30 May 2012).

11. For an interesting study of how small firms can successfully employ guerrilla-style tactics, see Chen, Ming-Jer and Hambrick, Donald C. (1995) 'Speed, stealth, and selective attack: how small firms differ from large firms in competitive behavior', *Academy of Management Journal*, 38(2): 453–82. Other discussions of guerrilla offensives can be found in MacMillan, Ian (1980) 'How business strategists can use guerrilla warfare tactics', *Journal of Business Strategy*, 1(2): 63–5; Rothschild, William E. (1984) 'Surprise and the competitive advantage', *Journal of Business Strategy* 4(3) 10–18; Harrigan, Kathryn R. (1985) *Strategic Flexibility*, (Lexington, MA, Lexington Books, 30–45; Fahey, Liam 'Guerrilla strategy: the hit-and-run attack', in Fahey, Liam (ed.), (1989) *The Strategic Management Planning Reader*, Englewood Cliffs, NJ, Prentice Hall, pp. 194–7.

12. Yoffie and Cusumano, 'Judo strategy'. See also Yoffie, D.B. and Kwak, M. (2002) 'Mastering balance: how to meet and beat a stronger opponent', *California Management Review*, 44(2): 8–24.

13. The use of pre-emptive strike offensives is treated comprehensively in MacMillan, Ian (1983) 'Preemptive strategies', *Journal of Business Strategy*, 14(2): 16–26.

14. MacMillan, Ian C. 'How long can you sustain a competitive advantage?' in Fahey, Liam (ed.) (1989) *The Strategic Planning Management Reader*, Englewood Cliffs, NJ, Prentice Hall, pp. 23–4.

15. For a discussion of competitors' reactions, see Coyne, Kevin P. and Horn, John (2009) 'Predicting your competitor's reactions', *Harvard Business Review*, 87(4): 90–7.

16. Kotler, Philip (1984) *Marketing Management*, 5th edn., Englewood Cliffs, NJ, Prentice Hall, p. 400.

17. Porter, Michael E. (1985) *Competitive Advantage*, New York, Free Press, p. 518.

18. M. Haig (2003) *Brand Failures*, London, Kogan Page, pp. 130-37.

19. Kim, W. Chan and Mauborgne, Renée (2004) 'Blue ocean strategy', *Harvard Business Review* 82(10): 76–84.

20. R. Rosmarin, (2006) 'Nintendo's new look', *Forbes*, 2 February. Available online at www.forbes.com/2006/02/07/xbox-ps3-revolution-cx_rr_0207nintendo.html (accessed 30 May 2012).

21. For a more detailed analysis of Nintendo's blue-ocean strategy, see O'Gorman, P. (2008) 'Wii: creating a blue ocean the Nintendo way', *Palermo Business Review*, 2: 97–108.

22. Porter, *Competitive Advantage,* pp. 489–94.

23. Ibid. pp. 495–7. The list here is selective; Porter offers a greater number of options.

24. Ibid. pp. 232–33.

25. For research evidence on the effects of pioneering versus following, see Covin, Jeffrey G., Slevin, Dennis P. and Heeley, Michael B. (1999) 'Pioneers and followers: competitive tactics, environment, and growth', *Journal of Business Venturing*, 15(2): 175–210; Bartlett, Christopher A. and Ghoshal, Sumantra (2000) 'Going global: lessons from late-movers', *Harvard Business Review*, 78(2): 132–45.

26. Hamel, Gary (2001) 'Smart mover, dumb mover', *Fortune*, 3 September p. 195.

27. Ibid. p. 192; Markides, Costas and Geroski, Paul A. (2004) 'Racing to be 2nd: conquering the industries of the future', *Business Strategy Review*, 15(4): 25–31.

28. For a more extensive discussion, see Suarez, Fernando and Lanzolla, Gianvito (2005) 'The half-truth of first-mover advantage', *Harvard Business Review*, 83(4): 121–27.

29. Gibbon, Henry (2010) 'Worldwide M&A declines 28 per cent to US$2trn', *Acquisitions Monthly*, 303: 4–11.

30. For an excellent review of the strategic objectives of various types of mergers and acquisitions and the managerial challenges that different kinds of mergers and acquisitions present, see Bower, Joseph L. (2001) 'Not all M&As are alike – and that matters', *Harvard Business Review*, 79(3): 93–101.

31. Chatain, O. and Zemsky, P. (2007) 'The horizontal scope of the firm: organizational tradeoffs vs. buyer-supplier relationships', *Management Science*, 53(4): 550–65.

32. For a more expansive discussion, see Dyer, Jeffrey H., Kale, Prashant and Singh, Harbir (2004) 'When to ally and when to acquire', *Harvard Business Review*, 82(4): 109–10.

33. The Co-operative Farms (2012). Available online at www.co-operative.coop/farms/ (accessed 30 May 2012).

34. See Harrigan, Kathryn R. (1986) 'Matching vertical integration strategies to competitive conditions', *Strategic Management Journal*, 7(6): 535–56; for a more extensive discussion of the advantages and disadvantages of vertical integration, see Stuckey, John and White, David (1993) 'When and when not to vertically integrate', *Sloan Management Review*, Spring, pp. 71–83.

35. Pollack, A. (2009) 'Roche agrees to buy Genetech for $46.8 billion', *New York Times,* 12 March. Available online at www.nytimes.com/2009/03/13/business/worldbusiness/13drugs.html (accessed 30 May 2012).

36. The resilience of vertical integration strategies despite the disadvantages is discussed in Osegowitsch, Thomas and Madhok, Anoop (2003) 'Vertical integration is dead, or is it?' *Business Horizons*, 46(2): 25–35.

37. For a good overview of outsourcing strategies, see McIvor, Ronan (2008) 'What is the right outsourcing strategy for your process?' *European Management Journal*, 26(1): 24–34.

38. For a good discussion of the problems that can arise from outsourcing, see Pisano, Gary P. and Shih, Willy C. (2009) 'Restoring American competitiveness', *Harvard Business Review* 87(7–8): 114–25; Barthélemy, Jérôme (2003) 'The seven deadly sins of outsourcing', *Academy of Management Executive*, 17(2): 87–100.

39. Pisano and Shih, 'Restoring american competitivness', pp. 116–17.

40. Wakeam, Jason (2003) 'The five factors of a strategic Alliance', *Ivey Business Journal*, 68(3): 1–4.

41. BBC News (2011) 'Toshiba, Hitacha and Sony to form LCD Display company', BBC News, 31 August. Available online at www.j-display.com/english/news/2012/20120402.html (accessed 30 May 2012).

42. Parise, Salvatore and Sasson, Lisa (2002) 'Leveraging knowledge management across strategic alliances', *Ivey Business Journal,* 66(4): 42.

43. Ernst, David and Bamford, James (2005) 'Your alliances are too stable', *Harvard Business Review*, 83(6): 133.

44. An excellent discussion of the portfolio approach to managing multiple alliances and how to restructure a faltering alliance is presented in Ernst and Bamford, 'Your alliances are too stable', pp. 133–41.

45. Porter, Michael E. *The Competitive Advantage of Nations*, New York: Free Press, 1990, p. 66. For a discussion of how to realize the advantages of strategic partnerships, see Kaplan, Nancy J. and Hurd, Jonathan (2002) 'Realizing the promise of partnerships', *Journal of Business Strategy*, 23(3): 38–42; Parise and Sasson, 'Leveraging knowledge management across strategic alliances', pp. 41–7; Ernst and Bamford, 'Your alliances are too stable', pp. 133–41; and Hughes, Jonathan and Weiss, Jeff (2007) 'Simple rules for making alliances work', *Harvard Business Review*, 85(11): 122–31.

46. For a discussion of how to raise the chances that a strategic alliance will produce strategically important outcomes, see Koza, M. and Lewin, A. (2000) 'Managing partnerships and strategic alliances: raising the odds of success', *European Management Journal,* 18(2): 146–51.

47. Inkpen, A. (1998) 'Learning, knowledge acquisition, and strategic alliances', *European Management Journal*, 16(2): 223–29.

48. Doz, Yves L. and Hamel, Gary (1998) *Alliance Advantage: The Art of Creating Value through Partnering*, Boston, Harvard Business School Press, ch. 1.

49. Ibid.

50. Ibid. chs 4–8; Anslinger, Patricia and Jenk, Justin (2004) 'Creating successful alliances', *Journal of Business Strategy*, 25(2): 18–23; Moss Kanter, Rosabeth (1994) 'Collaborative advantage: the art of the alliance', *Harvard Business Review*, 72(4): 96–108; Bleeke, Joel and Ernst, David (1991) 'The way to win in cross-border alliances', *Harvard Business Review*, 69(6): 127–35; Hamel, Gary Doz, Yves L. and Prahalad, C.K. (1989) 'Collaborate with your competitors – and win', *Harvard Business Review*, 67(1): 133–9; Hughes and Weiss, 'Simple rules for making alliances work'.

51. Cullen, J.B., Johnson, J.L. and Sakano, T. (2000) 'Success through commitment and trust: the soft side of strategic alliance management', *Journal of World Business*, 35(3): 223–40; Das, T.K. and Teng, B.S. (1998) 'Between trust and control: developing confidence in partner cooperation in alliances', *Academy of Management Review*, 23(3): 491–512.

52. Eisenhardt, K.M. and Schoonhoven, C.B. (1996) 'Resource-based view of strategic alliance formation: strategic and social effects in entrepreneurial firms', *Organization Science* 7(2): 136–50; Zollo, M., Reuer, J.J. and Singh, H. (2002) 'Interorganizational routines and performance in strategic alliances', *Organization Science*, 13(6): 701–13.

53. The pros and cons of mergers/acquisitions versus strategic alliances are described in Dyer, Kale and Singh, 'When to ally and when to acquire', pp. 109–15.

54. Hughes and Weiss, 'Simple rules for making alliances work', p. 122.

55. Pan, Y.G. and Tse, D.K. (2000) 'The hierarchical model of market entry modes', *Journal of International Business Studies*, 31(4): 535–54.

Chapter Seven

Strategies for international growth

We're not going global because we want to or because of any megalomania, but because it's really necessary ... The costs are so enormous today that you really need to have world-wide revenues to cover them.

Rupert Murdoch
CEO of the media conglomerate News Corporation

Globalization [provides] a long-lasting competitive advantage. If we build a new gas turbine, in 18 months our competitors also have one. But building a global company is not so easy to copy.

Percy Barnevik
Former CEO of the Swiss-Swedish industrial corporation ABB

Capital, technology, and ideas flow these days like quicksilver across national boundaries.

Robert H. Waterman, Jr
Internationally recognized expert on management practices

Learning Objectives

When you have read this chapter you should be able to:

LO 7.1   Develop an understanding of the primary reasons organizations choose to compete in international markets.

LO 7.2   Learn how and why differing market conditions across countries and industries make crafting international strategy a complex undertaking.

LO 7.3   Learn about the major strategic options for entering and competing in international markets.

LO 7.4   Gain familiarity with the three main strategic approaches for competing internationally.

LO 7.5   Understand how international organizations go about building competitive advantage in foreign markets.

ORIFLAME

Founded in Sweden in 1967 by Jonas and Robert af Jochnick and Bengt Hellsten, and listed on the Nasdaq OMX exchange in 2004, Oriflame is a 'direct sales' multinational beauty company. They are present in more than 60 countries and are the market leader in more than half. The CIS and Baltics, including the former Soviet Republics, is Oriflame's largest region accounting for 57 per cent of total sales. Asia represents 10 per cent of sales, the EMEA region 27 per cent and Latin America 6 per cent. The company has expanded rapidly with more than 40 new market entries undertaken since 1990. Oriflame's regions operate very autonomously, with each country operating as a profit centre and regional directors deciding on supply chain and customer service matters.

With 8000 employees, Oriflame sells a product range of over 1000 products through a salesforce consisting of approximately 3.6 million consultants. The consultants are provided with various incentive schemes to sell as well as bring new consultants into the network.

Oriflame produces around 60 per cent of their products themselves in their five production facilities located in Sweden, Poland, China, Russia and India while the remaining production is outsourced.

Their strategy is 'to build a global brand locally'. Communication can be fine-tuned with a specific target group in mind, emphasizing what is attractive in a specific market, and pricing can differ between markets, but the aim is to keep the perception of Oriflame the same globally to maintain a strong brand identity. Oriflame builds heavily on their Swedish heritage in their branding efforts, promoting values of natural, progressive and ethical.

By 2012, after decades of rapid growth and successful development, particularly in the CIS region, Oriflame was finding it increasingly more difficult to maintain the same pace. They were slower to recover from the financial crisis than they predicted, and other external challenges had arisen. In 2010, for instance, new regulations on product registration in Russia and Indonesia affected sales negatively, and they were shut down in Iran by authorities. They remained positive, however, with plans to work harder with their branding process, and to improve their support services to consultants.

Oriflame positions themselves as a 'cosmetics company selling direct' rather than a direct selling company offering beauty products. Their sales model, adopted from the conception of the organization, eliminates retailers from the distribution chain. The cosmetics industry is recognized as one of the fastest-growing consumer product sectors and is the most important sector for the direct sales industry, representing about one-third of total global direct sales. Direct sales as a channel is estimated to have more than a fifth of the total cosmetics and toiletry market in eastern Europe (global average is 11 per cent). Being a cosmetics company that sells direct means that Oriflame competes with major cosmetics manufacturers as well as other companies selling direct – both for end-consumers and for sales consultants. The industry is highly fragmented and characterized by a high level of rivalry. Oriflame's main identified competitors include L'Oreal, Procter & Gamble and Unilever as well as Avon and Mary Kay.

Products are developed quickly and are regularly discontinued, keeping a constant supply of new products generating sales. The central marketing and sales tool is their product catalogue that is published in 40 languages every three weeks. Each catalogue takes a year of planning prior to publication, and contains a mix of existing products and brands and seasonal and localized offerings for specific markets.

In 2011, two new iPad apps were launched, making the catalogue digital to consultants. The apps, distributed through the iTunes store, were promoted as 'taking direct selling to the next level' and a major step forward in the way Oriflame engages with consultants and consumers world-wide. The apps give access to the latest Oriflame news in 14 languages initially in the EMEA region, with the plan to extend this to 33 languages. The idea was to make the Oriflame catalogue and business opportunity presentation available at any time and in any location. During a business opportunity presentation the prospect can instantly register to become an Oriflame consultant. Michael Cervell, Senior Vice President Global Direct Sales at Oriflame said, 'We have shown once again that we are driving the industry forward by providing world-class service to our consultants and consumers using the latest technologies. This is just the first step in this area, and we expect to extend into other platforms as the technology develops'.

QUESTIONS

1. What are the strengths and weaknesses of Oriflame's strategy and business model when competing internationally?

2. Is the introduction of the Oriflame app, in your view, a major step forward?

Sources: www. Oriflame.com; Oriflame Annual Reports, 2009, 2010, Interim report 2011.

Any organization that aspires to industry leadership in the twenty-first century must think in terms of global, not domestic, market leadership. The world economy is globalizing at an accelerating pace as ambitious growth-minded organizations race to build stronger competitive positions in the markets of more and more countries, as countries previously closed to foreign organizations open up their markets, as organizations in developing countries gain competitive strength, and as advances in information and communication technology (ICT) shrink the importance of geographic distance. The forces of globalization are changing the competitive landscape in many industries, offering organizations attractive new opportunities but at the same time introducing new competitive threats. Organizations in industries where these forces are greatest are therefore under considerable pressure to come up with a strategy for competing successfully in foreign markets.

This chapter focuses on strategy options for expanding beyond domestic boundaries and competing in the markets of either a few or a great many countries. In the process of exploring these issues, we will introduce such concepts as multidomestic, global and transnational strategies; the Porter diamond of national advantage; and cross-country differences in cultural, demographic and market conditions. The chapter also includes sections on strategy options for entering and competing in foreign markets; the importance of locating value chain operations in the most advantageous countries; and the special circumstances of competing in such developing markets as China, India, Brazil, Russia and eastern Europe.

Why Organizations Decide to Enter International Markets

LO 7.1
Develop an understanding of the primary reasons organizations choose to compete in international markets.

An organization may opt to expand outside its domestic market for any of five major reasons:

1. *To gain access to new customers.* Expanding into international markets offers potential for increased revenues, profits and long-term growth and becomes an especially attractive option when an organization's home markets are mature and nearing saturation levels. Organizations often expand internationally to extend the life cycle of their products, as Honda has done with its classic 50 cc motorcycle, the Honda cub (which is still selling well in developing markets, more than 50 years after it was first introduced in Japan). A larger target market also offers organizations the opportunity to earn a return on large investments more rapidly. This can be particularly important in research and development (R&D) intensive industries, where development is fast-paced or competitors imitate innovations rapidly.

2. *To achieve lower costs through economies of scale, experience and increased purchasing power.* Many organizations are driven to sell in more than one country because domestic sales volume alone is not large enough to fully capture economies of scale in product development, manufacturing or marketing. Similarly, firms expand internationally to increase the rate at which they accumulate experience and move down the learning curve. International expansion can also lower an organization's input costs through greater pooled purchasing power. The relatively small size of country markets in Europe and limited domestic volume explains why organizations like Michelin, BMW and Nestlé long ago began selling their products all across Europe and then moved into markets in North America and Latin America.

3. *To further exploit its core competences.* An organization with competitively valuable resources and capabilities can often extend a market-leading position in its home market into a position of regional or global market leadership by leveraging these resources further. Nokia's competences and capabilities in mobile phones have propelled it to global market leadership in the wireless telecommunications business. Walmart is capitalizing on its considerable expertise in discount retailing

to expand into China, Latin America, Japan, South Korea and the UK; Walmart executives believe the organization has tremendous growth opportunities in China. Organizations can often leverage their resources internationally by replicating a successful business model, using it as a basic blueprint for international operations, as Starbucks and McDonald's have done.[1]

4. *To gain access to resources and capabilities located in international markets.* An increasingly important motive for entering international markets is to acquire resources and capabilities that cannot be accessed as readily in an organization's home market. Organizations often enter into cross-border alliances or joint ventures, for example, to gain access to resources and capabilities that complement their own or to learn from their partners.[2] Cross-border acquisitions are commonly made for similar reasons.[3] In other cases, organizations choose to establish operations in other countries to utilize local distribution networks, employ low-cost human resources (HR) or acquire technical knowledge. In a few cases, organizations in industries based on natural resources (e.g. oil and gas, minerals, rubber and lumber) find it necessary to operate in the international arena because attractive raw-material supplies are located in many different parts of the world.

5. *To spread its business risk across a wider market base.* An organization spreads business risk by operating in many different countries rather than depending entirely on operations in a few countries. Thus, when an organization with operations across much of the world encounters economic downturns in certain countries, its performance may be bolstered by buoyant sales elsewhere.

In addition, organizations that are the suppliers of other organizations often expand internationally when their major customers do so to meet their needs abroad and retain their position as a key supply chain partner. Automotive parts suppliers, for example, have followed automobile manufacturers abroad, and retail goods suppliers have followed large retailers into international markets.

Why Competing across National Borders Makes Strategy-making More Complex

Crafting a strategy to compete in one or more countries of the world is inherently more complex because of (1) factors that affect industry competitiveness that vary from country to country, (2) the potential for location-based advantages in certain countries, (3) different government policies and economic conditions that make the business climate more favourable in some countries than in others, (4) the risks of adverse shifts in currency exchange rates, and (5) cross-country differences in cultural, demographic and market conditions.

> **LO 7.2** Learn how and why differing market conditions across countries and industries make crafting international strategy a complex undertaking.

Cross-country Variation in Factors that Affect Industry Competitiveness

Certain countries are known for their strengths in particular industries. For example, Chile has competitive strengths in industries such as copper, fruit, fish products, paper and pulp, chemicals and wine. Japan is known for competitive strength in consumer electronics, cars, semiconductors, steel products and specialty steel. Where industries are more likely to develop competitive strength depends on a set of factors that describe the nature of each country's business environment and vary across countries. Because strong industries are made up of strong firms, the strategies of firms that expand internationally are usually grounded in one or more of these factors. The four[1] major factors are summarized in a framework known as the *Diamond of National Advantage* (see Figure 7.1).[4] While the original Diamond model consists of four main factors, two additional forces are also considered to affect the competitiveness of a

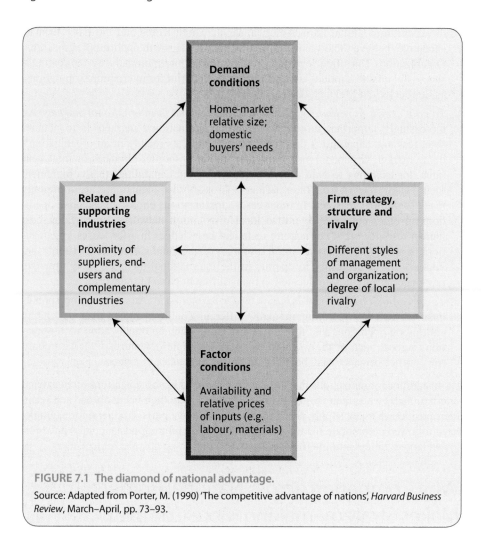

FIGURE 7.1 The diamond of national advantage.

Source: Adapted from Porter, M. (1990) 'The competitive advantage of nations', *Harvard Business Review*, March–April, pp. 73–93.

nation. The role of *chance*; for example, oil shocks and major technological break-throughs, as well as the various roles of *government*, which we deal with separately in this chapter.

Demand Conditions

The demand conditions in an industry's home market include the relative size of the market and the nature of domestic buyers' needs and wants. Industry sectors that are larger and more important in their home market tend to attract more resources and grow faster than others. Demanding domestic buyers for an industry's products spur greater innovativeness and improvements in quality. Such conditions foster the development of stronger industries, with firms that are capable of translating a home-market advantage into a competitive advantage in the international arena.

Factor Conditions

Factor conditions describe the availability, quality and cost of raw materials and other inputs (called *factors)* that firms in an industry require to produce their products and services. The relevant factors vary from industry to industry but can include different types of labour, technical or managerial knowledge, land, financial capital and natural resources. Elements of a country's infrastructure may be included as well, such as its transportation, communication and banking system. For instance, in India there are efficient, well-developed national channels for distributing trucks, scooters, farm equipment, groceries, personal care items and other packaged products to the country's three million retailers, whereas in China distribution is primarily local and there is a limited national network for distributing most products. Competitively strong industries and firms develop where relevant factor conditions are favourable.

Related and Supporting Industries

Robust industries often develop as part of a cluster of related industries, including suppliers of components and capital equipment, end-users and the makers of complementary products, including those that are technologically related. The sports car-makers, Ferrari and Maserati, for example, are located in an area of Italy known as the 'engine technological district' that includes other firms involved in racing, such as Ducati Motorcycles, along with hundreds of small suppliers. The advantage to firms that develop as part of a related-industry cluster comes from the close collaboration with key suppliers and the greater knowledge-sharing throughout the cluster, resulting in greater efficiency and innovativeness.

Firm Strategy, Structure and Rivalry

Different country environments foster the development of different styles of management, organization and strategy. For example, strategic alliances are a more common strategy for firms from Asian or Latin American countries, which emphasize trust and co-operation in their organizations, than for firms from North America, where individualism is more influential. In addition, countries vary in terms of the competitiveness of their industries. Fierce competitive conditions in home markets tend to hone domestic firms' competitive capabilities and ready them for competing internationally.

For an industry in a particular country to become competitively strong, all four factors must be favourable for that industry. When they are, the industry is likely to contain firms that are capable of competing successfully in the international arena. Thus, the diamond framework can be used to reveal the answers to several questions that are important for competing on an international basis. First, it can help predict where foreign entrants into an industry are most likely to come from. This can help managers prepare to cope with new competitors, since the framework also reveals something about the basis of the new rivals' strengths. Second, it can reveal the countries in which international rivals are likely to be weakest and thus help managers decide which international markets to enter first. And third, because it focuses on the attributes of a country's business environment that allow firms to flourish, it reveals something about the advantages of conducting particular business activities in that country. Thus, the diamond framework is an aid to deciding where to locate different value chain activities most beneficially – a topic that we address next.

Locating Value Chain Activities for Competitive Advantage

Increasingly, organizations are locating different value chain activities in different parts of the world to exploit location-based advantages that vary from country to country. This is particularly evident with respect to the location of manufacturing activities. Differences in wage rates, worker productivity, energy costs, environmental regulations, tax rates, inflation rates and the like, create sizeable variations in manufacturing costs from country to country. By locating its plants in certain countries, firms in some industries can reap major manufacturing cost advantages because of lower input costs (especially labour), relaxed government regulations, the proximity of suppliers and technologically related industries, or unique natural resources. In such cases, the low-cost countries become principal production sites, with most of the output being exported to markets in other parts of the world. Organizations that build production facilities in low-cost countries (or that source their products from contract manufacturers in these countries) gain a competitive advantage over rivals with plants in countries where costs are higher. The competitive role of low manufacturing costs is most evident in low-wage countries like China, India, Pakistan, Cambodia, Vietnam, Mexico, Brazil, Guatemala, the Philippines and several countries in Africa and eastern Europe that have become production havens for manufactured goods with high labour content (especially textiles and apparel). Hourly compensation for production workers in 2007 averaged about €0.62 in China versus about €0.83 in the Philippines, €2.21 in Mexico, €4.51 in Brazil, €4.98 in Taiwan, €6.00 in Hungary, €6.26 in Portugal, €14.95 in Japan, €18.62 in the USA, €21.90 in Canada, €28.52 in Germany and €36.78 in Norway.[5] China is fast becoming the manufacturing capital of the world – virtually all of the world's major manufacturing organizations now have facilities in China.

For other types of value chain activities, input quality or availability are more important considerations. Tiffany entered the mining industry in Canada to access diamonds that could be certified as 'conflict free' and not associated with either the funding of African wars or unethical mining conditions. Many US organizations locate call centres in countries such as India and Ireland, where English is spoken and the workforce is well educated. Other organizations locate R&D activities in countries where there are prestigious research institutions and well-trained scientists and engineers. Likewise, concerns about short delivery times and low shipping costs make some countries better locations than others for establishing distribution centres.

The Impact of Government Policies and Economic Conditions in Host Countries

Cross-country variations in government policies and economic conditions affect both the opportunities available to a foreign entrant and the risks of operating within that country. The governments of some countries are anxious to attract foreign investments and go all out to create a business climate outsiders will view as favourable. A good example is Ireland, which has one of the world's most pro-business environments. Ireland offers companies very low corporate tax rates, has a government that is responsive to the needs of industry and aggressively recruits high-tech manufacturing facilities and international organizations. Ireland's policies were a major factor in Intel's decision to locate a €1.9 billion chip manufacturing plant in Ireland that employs over 4000 people. Governments anxious to spur economic growth, create more jobs and raise living standards for their citizens usually enact policies aimed at stimulating business innovation and capital investment. They may provide incentives such as reduced taxes, low-cost loans, site location and site development assistance and government-sponsored training for workers to encourage organizations to construct production and distribution facilities. When new business-related issues or developments arise, pro-business governments make a practice of seeking advice and counsel from business leaders. When tougher business-related regulations are deemed appropriate, they endeavour to make the transition to more costly and stringent regulations somewhat business-friendly rather than adversarial.

On the other hand, governments sometimes enact policies that, from a business perspective, make locating facilities within a country's borders less attractive. For example, the nature of an organization's operations may make it particularly costly to achieve compliance with a country's environmental regulations. Some governments, desirous of discouraging foreign imports, provide subsidies and low-interest loans to domestic organizations (to enable them to better compete against international organizations), enact deliberately burdensome procedures and requirements for imported goods to pass customs inspection (to make it harder for imported goods to compete against the products of local businesses), and impose tariffs or quotas on the imports of certain goods (also to help protect local businesses from foreign competition). They may also specify that a certain percentage of the parts and components used in manufacturing a product be obtained from local suppliers, require prior approval of capital spending projects, limit withdrawal of funds from the country and require minority (sometimes majority) ownership of foreign organization operations by local organizations or investors. Sometimes foreign organizations wanting only to sell their products in a country face a web of regulations regarding technical standards and product certification. Political leaders in some countries may be openly hostile to or suspicious of organizations from certain foreign countries operating within their borders. Moreover, there are times when a government may place restrictions on exports to ensure adequate local supplies and regulate the prices of imported and locally produced goods. Such government actions make a country's business climate less attractive and in some cases may be sufficiently onerous as to discourage an organization from locating production or distribution facilities in that country or maybe even selling its products in that country.

The decision about whether to enter a particular country must take into account the degree of political and economic risk. **Political risks** stem from government hostility to foreign business, weak governments and political instability. In industries that a government deems critical to the national welfare, there is sometimes a risk that the government will nationalize the industry and expropriate the assets of foreign organizations. In 2010, for example, Ecuador threatened to expropriate the holdings of all foreign oil organizations that refused to sign new contracts giving the state control of all production. Other political risks include the loss of investments due to war or political unrest, regulatory changes that create operating uncertainties, security risks due to terrorism and corruption. **Economic risks** are intertwined with political risks but also stem from factors such as inflation rates and the stability of a country's monetary system. The threat of piracy and lack of protection for intellectual property are important sources of economic risk. Another is fluctuation in the value of different currencies – a factor that we discuss in more detail next.

> **Core Concept**
>
> **Political risks** stem from instability or weakness in national governments and hostility to foreign business. **Economic risks** stem from the stability of a country's monetary system, economic and regulatory policies, lack of property rights protections and risks due to exchange rate fluctuation.

The Risks of Adverse Exchange Rate Shifts

When organizations produce and market their products and services in many different countries, they are subject to the impacts of sometimes favourable and sometimes unfavourable changes in currency exchange rates. The rates of exchange between different currencies can vary by as much as 20–40 per cent annually, with the changes occurring sometimes gradually and sometimes swiftly. Sizeable shifts in exchange rates, which tend to be hard to predict because of the variety of factors involved and the uncertainties surrounding when and by how much these factors will change, shuffle the global cards of which countries represent the low-cost manufacturing locations and which rivals have the upper hand in the marketplace.

To understand the economic risks associated with fluctuating exchange rates, consider the case of a Canadian organization that has located manufacturing facilities in Brazil and that exports most of the Brazilian-made goods to markets in the European Union (EU). To keep the numbers simple, assume that the exchange rate is 4 Brazilian reals for 1 euro and that the product being made in Brazil has a manufacturing cost of 4 Brazilian reals (or 1 euro). Now suppose that for some reason the exchange rate shifts from 4 reals per euro to 5 reals per euro (meaning that the real has declined in value and that the euro is stronger). Making the product in Brazil is now more cost-competitive because a Brazilian good costing 4 reals to produce has fallen to only 0.8 euro at the new exchange rate (4 reals divided by 5 reals per euro = 0.8 euro) and this clearly puts the producer of the Brazilian-made good *in a better position to compete* against the European makers of the same good. On the other hand, should the value of the Brazilian real grow stronger in relation to the euro – resulting in an exchange rate of 3 reals to 1 euro – the same Brazilian-made good formerly costing 4 reals (or 1 euro) to produce now has a cost of 1.33 euros (4 reals divided by 3 reals per euro = 1.33 euros) and this puts the producer of the Brazilian-made good in a weaker competitive position *vis-à-vis* European producers of the same good. Clearly, the attraction of manufacturing a good in Brazil and selling it in Europe is far greater when the euro is strong (an exchange rate of 1 euro for 5 Brazilian reals) than when the euro is weak and exchanges for only 3 Brazilian reals.

But there is one more piece to the story. When the exchange rate changes from 4 reals per euro to 5 reals per euro, not only is the cost competitiveness of the Brazilian manufacturer stronger relative to European manufacturers of the same item but the Brazilian-made good that formerly cost 1 euro and now costs only 0.8 euro can also be sold to consumers in the EU for a lower euro price than before. In other words, the combination of a stronger euro and a weaker real acts to *lower the price of Brazilian-made goods* in all the countries that are members of the EU, and this is likely to *spur sales of the Brazilian-made good in Europe and boost Brazilian exports to Europe.* Conversely, should the exchange rate shift from 4 reals per euro to 3 reals per euro – which makes the Brazilian manufacturer less cost competitive with European manufacturers of the same item – the Brazilian-made good that formerly cost 1 euro and now costs 1.33 euros will sell for a higher price in euros than before, thus weakening the demand of European consumers for Brazilian-made goods and acting to reduce Brazilian exports to Europe. Thus *Brazilian exporters are likely to experience (1) rising demand for their goods in Europe whenever the Brazilian real grows weaker relative to the euro and (2) falling demand for their goods in Europe whenever the real grows stronger relative to the euro.*

In so far as US-based manufacturers are concerned, declines in the value of the US dollar against foreign currencies act to reduce or eliminate whatever cost advantage overseas manufacturers might have over US manufacturers and can even prompt overseas organizations to establish production plants in the USA. Likewise, a weak euro versus other currencies enhances the cost competitiveness of manufacturing goods in Europe for export to other markets; a strong euro versus other currencies weakens the cost competitiveness of European plants that manufacture goods for export. The growing strength of the euro relative to the US dollar has encouraged a number of European manufacturers such as Volkswagen, Fiat and Airbus to shift production from European factories to new facilities in the USA. Also, the weakening dollar caused Chrysler to discontinue its contract manufacturing agreement with an Austrian firm for assembly of minivans and Jeeps sold in Europe. Beginning in 2008, Chrysler's vehicles sold in Europe were exported from its factories in Illinois and Missouri. The weak dollar was also a factor in Ford's and GM's recent decisions to begin exporting US-made vehicles to China and Latin America.

It is important to note that *currency exchange rates are rather unpredictable*, swinging first one way and then another way, so the competitiveness of any organization's facilities in any country is partly dependent on whether exchange rate changes over time have a favourable or unfavourable cost impact. Organizations producing goods in one country for export abroad always improve their cost competitiveness when the country's currency grows weaker relative to currencies of the countries where the goods are being exported to, and they find their cost competitiveness eroded when the local currency grows stronger. On the other hand, domestic organizations that are under pressure from lower-cost imported goods become more cost competitive when their currency grows weaker in relation to the currencies of the countries where the imported goods are made; in other words, a manufacturer in England views a weaker pound as a *favourable exchange rate shift* because such shifts help make its costs more competitive than those of international rivals.

> Fluctuating exchange rates pose significant economic risks to an organization's competitiveness in international markets. Exporters are disadvantaged when the currency of the country where goods are being manufactured grows stronger relative to the currency of the importing country.

> Domestic organizations facing competitive pressure from lower-cost imports are benefited when their government's currency grows *weaker* in relation to the currencies of the countries where the lower-cost goods are being made.

Cross-country Differences in Demographic, Cultural and Market Conditions

Differing population sizes, income levels and other demographic factors give rise to considerable differences in market size and growth rates from country to country. Less than 20 per cent of the populations of Brazil, India and China have annual purchasing power equivalent to 19 000 euros. Middle-class consumers represent a much smaller portion of the population in these and other developing countries than in North America, Japan and much of western Europe – China's middle-class numbers about 300 million out of a population of 1.35 billion.[6] At the same time, in developing markets like India, China, Brazil and Malaysia, market growth potential is far higher than it is in the more mature economies of Britain, Denmark, Canada and Japan. The potential for market growth in cars is explosive in China, where 2009 sales of new vehicles amounted to 13.6 million, surpassing US sales of 10 million and making China the world's largest market.[7] Owing to widely differing population demographics and income levels, there is a far bigger market for luxury cars in the USA and Germany than in Argentina, India, Mexico, China and Thailand.

Buyer tastes for a particular product or service sometimes differ substantially from country to country. In France consumers prefer top-loading washing machines, while in most other European countries consumers prefer front-loading machines. Soups that appeal to Swedish consumers are not popular in Malaysia. Italian coffee drinkers prefer espressos, but in North America the preference is for mild-roasted coffees. Sometimes, product designs suitable in one country are inappropriate in another because of differing local standards – for example, in many European countries electrical devices run on 240-volt electric systems, while in the USA the standard is a 110-volt electric system, necessitating the use of different electrical designs and components. Cultural influences can also affect consumer demand for a product. For instance, in South Korea, many parents are reluctant to purchase PCs even when they can afford them because of concerns that their children will be distracted from their schoolwork by surfing the web, playing PC-based video games and becoming Internet 'addicts'.[8]

Consequently, organizations operating in an international marketplace have to wrestle with *whether and how much to customize their offerings in each different country market to match the tastes and preferences of local buyers or whether to pursue a strategy of offering a mostly standardized product world-wide.* While making products that are closely matched to local tastes makes them more appealing to local buyers, customizing an organization's products country by country may have the effect of raising production and distribution costs due to the greater variety of designs and components, shorter production runs and the complications of added inventory handling and distribution logistics. Greater standardization of a multinational organization's product offering, on the other hand, can lead to scale economies and learning curve effects, thus contributing to the achievement of a low-cost advantage. *The tension between the market pressures to localize an organization's product offerings country by country and the competitive pressures to lower costs is one of the big strategic issues that participants in international markets have to resolve.*

CURRENT PRACTICE 7.1

DIAMOND MODEL REVISITED

In Porter's single home-based diamond approach, a firm's capabilities to tap into the location advantages of other nations are viewed as very limited.[9] It has been suggested that a more relevant concept for small, open, trading economies would be a 'double diamond' model.[10] For example, in the case of Canada, an integrated North American diamond (including both Canada and the USA), not just a Canadian one, is more relevant. The double diamond model suggests that managers build upon both domestic and foreign diamonds to become globally competitive.

Further, global instability from 2009 has seen a slowing down of western companies expanding into new markets while some developing economies have grown solidly. This has changed the international competitive landscape as companies in these developing economies have grown to gain strong market positions. It is generally considered that 'rapidly expanding economies', such as China and India, are the most attractive opportunities for western organizations looking to grow, and in assessing the requirements for competing globally under these new conditions the 'Global Advantage Diamond' has been developed by Boston Consulting Group (BCG).[11]

With the assumption that replicating home-country business models is no longer the winning strategy, it is proposed that organizations must adapt and localize their business models to target new groups of customers in developing economies, while also finding ways to integrate these different business models to share best practices and achieve synergies. It is desirable that organizations develop integrated strategies that combine:

- *Market access*. Driving sales growth by targeting new markets and new market segments.
- *Resource access*. Leveraging resources in developing economies.
- *Local adaptations*. Adapting their business to the full range of needs of the new customers, or 'manyness'.
- *Network co-ordination*. Integrating operations to capitalize on the benefits of the organizations' global reach.

The Global Advantage Diamond can be used by established businesses from developed countries and by challengers from the developing economies, although their positioning and actions will typically reflect their different starting points.

The Concepts of Multidomestic Competition and Global Competition

Core Concept

Multidomestic competition exists when the competition among rivals in each country market is localized and not closely connected to the competition in other country markets – there is no world market, just a collection of self-contained local markets.

In crafting a strategy to compete on an international basis, it is essential for managers to recognize that the pattern of international competition varies in important ways from industry to industry.[12] At one extreme is multidomestic competition, in which there is so much cross-country variation in market conditions and in the organizations contending for leadership that the market contest among organizations in one country is localized and not closely connected to the market contests in other countries. The stand-out features of multidomestic competition are that (1) buyers in different countries are attracted to different product attributes, (2) sellers vary from country to country, and (3) industry conditions and competitive forces in each national market differ in important respects. Take the banking industry in Poland, Mexico and Australia as an example – the requirements and expectations of banking customers vary among the three countries, the lead banking competitors in Poland differ from those in Mexico or Australia and the competitive situation among the leading banks in Poland is unrelated to that taking place in Mexico or Australia. Thus, with multidomestic competition, rival firms vie for national championships and success in one country does not necessarily signal the ability to fare well in other countries. In multidomestic competition, the power of an organization's strategy and capabilities in one country has little impact on its competitiveness in other countries where it operates. Moreover, any competitive advantage an organization secures in one country is largely confined to that country; the spillover effects to other countries are minimal to non-existent. Industries characterized by multidomestic competition include radio and TV broadcasting, consumer banking, life insurance, apparel, metals fabrication, many types of food products (coffee, cereals, breads, canned goods, frozen foods) and retailing.

Core Concept

Global competition exists when competitive conditions across national markets are linked strongly enough to form a true world market and when leading competitors compete head to head in many different countries.

At the other extreme is global competition, in which prices and competitive conditions across country markets are strongly linked and the term *global* has true meaning. In a globally competitive industry, much the same group of organizations competes in many different countries but especially in countries where sales volumes are large and where having a competitive presence is strategically important to building a strong global position in the industry. Thus, an organization's competitive position in one country both affects and is affected by its position in other countries. In global competition, a firm's overall competitive advantage grows out of its entire world-wide operations; the competitive advantage it creates at its home base is supplemented by advantages growing out of its operations in other countries (having plants in low-wage countries, being able to transfer expertise from country to country, having

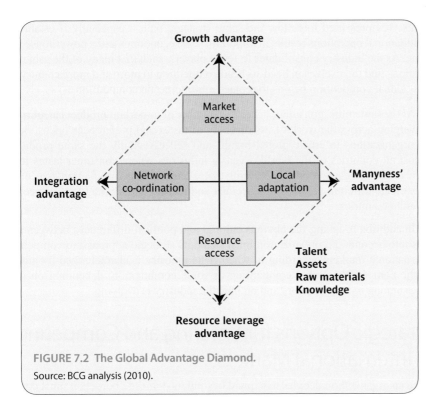

FIGURE 7.2 The Global Advantage Diamond.

Source: BCG analysis (2010).

the capability to serve customers that also have multinational operations and having brand-name recognition in many parts of the world). Firms in globally competitive industries vie for world-wide leadership. Global competition exists in motor vehicles, TVs, tyres, mobile phones, PCs, copiers, watches, digital cameras, bicycles and commercial aircraft.

An industry can have segments that are globally competitive and segments in which competition is country by country.[13] In the hotel/motel industry, for example, the low- and medium-priced segments are characterized by multidomestic competition – competitors mainly serve travellers within the same country. In the business and luxury segments, however, competition is more globalized. Organizations like Nikki (owned by Japan Airlines), Marriott, Sheraton and Hilton have hotels at many international locations, use world-wide reservation systems and establish common quality and service standards to gain marketing advantages in serving businesspeople and other travellers who make frequent international trips. In lubricants, the marine engine segment is globally competitive – ships move from port to port and require the same oil everywhere they stop. Brand reputations in marine lubricants have a global scope, and successful marine engine lubricant producers (ExxonMobil, BP Amoco and Shell) operate globally. In automotive motor oil, however, multidomestic competition dominates – countries have different weather conditions and driving patterns, production of motor oil is subject to limited scale economies, shipping costs are high and retail distribution channels differ markedly from country to country. Thus, domestic firms – like Quaker State and Pennzoil in the USA and Castrol in Great Britain – can be leaders in their home markets without competing globally.

It is also important to recognize that an industry can be in transition from multidomestic competition to global competition. In a number of today's industries – beer and major home appliances are prime examples – leading domestic competitors have begun expanding into more and more overseas markets, often acquiring local organizations or brands and integrating them into their operations. As some industry members start to build global brands and a global presence, other industry members find themselves pressured to follow the same strategic path – especially if establishing multinational operations results in important scale economies and a powerhouse brand name. As the industry consolidates to fewer players, such that many of the same organizations find themselves in head-to-head competition in more and more country markets, global competition begins to replace multidomestic competition.

At the same time, consumer tastes in a number of important product categories are converging across the world. Less diversity of tastes and preferences opens the way for organizations to create global brands and sell essentially the same products in almost all countries of the world. Even in industries where consumer tastes remain fairly diverse, organizations are learning to use 'custom mass production' to economically create different versions of a product and thereby satisfy the tastes of people in different countries.

In addition to taking the obvious cultural and political differences between countries into account, an organization must shape its strategic approach to competing in international markets according to whether its industry is characterized by multidomestic competition global competition or some combination, depending on differences among industry sectors and on how the industry is evolving.

Strategic Options for Entering and Competing in International Markets

LO 7.3 Learn about the major strategic options for entering and competing in international markets.

Once an organization decides to expand beyond its domestic borders it must consider the question of how to enter international markets. There are six primary strategic options for doing so:

1. Maintain a national (one-country) production base and export goods to other markets.
2. License overseas firms to produce and distribute the organization's products abroad.
3. Employ a franchising strategy.
4. Establish a wholly owned subsidiary in the overseas market by acquiring a foreign organization.
5. Create a wholly owned overseas subsidiary from the ground up via a 'greenfield' venture.
6. Rely on strategic alliances or joint ventures to partner with organizations abroad.

Which option to employ depends on a variety of factors, including the nature of the firm's strategic objectives, whether the firm has the full range of resources and capabilities needed to operate abroad, country-specific factors such as trade barriers and the transaction costs involved (the costs of contracting with a partner and monitoring its compliance with the terms of the contract, for example). The options vary considerably regarding the level of investment required and the associated risks, but higher levels of investment and risk generally provide the firm with the benefits of greater ownership and control.

Export Strategies

Using domestic plants as a production base for exporting goods to foreign markets is an excellent initial strategy for pursuing international sales. It is a conservative way to test the international waters. The amount of capital needed to begin exporting is often quite minimal; existing production capacity may well be sufficient to make goods for export. With an export strategy, a manufacturer can limit its involvement in international markets by contracting with foreign wholesalers experienced in importing to handle the entire distribution and marketing function in their countries or regions of the world. If it is more advantageous to maintain control over these functions, however, a manufacturer can establish its own distribution and sales organizations in some or all of the target markets. Either way, a home-based production and export strategy helps the firm minimize its direct investments in foreign countries. Such strategies have been favoured traditionally by Chinese, Korean and Italian organizations – products are designed and manufactured at home and then distributed through local channels in the importing countries; the primary functions performed abroad relate chiefly to establishing a network of distributors and perhaps conducting sales promotion and brand awareness activities.

Whether an export strategy can be pursued successfully over the long run hinges on whether its advantages for the organization continue to outweigh its disadvantages. This depends in part on the relative cost competitiveness of the home-country production base. In some industries, firms gain additional scale economies and learning curve benefits from centralizing production in one or several giant plants whose output capability exceeds demand in any one country market; exporting is one obvious way to capture such economies. However, an export strategy is vulnerable when (1) manufacturing costs in the home country are substantially higher than in foreign countries where rivals have plants, (2) the costs of shipping the product to distant overseas markets are relatively high, or (3) adverse shifts occur in currency exchange rates. The disadvantages of export strategies can also inflate due to high tariffs and other trade barriers, inadequate control over marketing or distribution and an inability to tap into location advantages available elsewhere, such as skilled low-cost labour.

Licensing Strategies

Licensing makes sense when a firm with valuable technical know-how, an appealing brand or a unique patented product has neither the internal organizational capability nor the resources to enter foreign markets. Licensing also has the advantage of avoiding the risks of committing resources to country markets that are unfamiliar, politically volatile, economically unstable or otherwise risky. By licensing the technology, trademark or production rights to foreign-based firms, the firm does not have to bear the costs and risks of entering foreign markets on its own, yet it is able to generate income from royalties. The big disadvantage of licensing is the risk of providing valuable technological know-how to foreign organizations and thereby losing some degree of control over its use; monitoring licensees and safeguarding the organization's proprietary know-how can prove quite difficult in some circumstances. But if the royalty potential is considerable and the organizations to whom the licences are being granted are trustworthy and reputable, then licensing can be a very attractive option. Many software and pharmaceutical organizations use licensing strategies.

Franchising Strategies

While licensing works well for manufacturers and owners of proprietary technology, franchising is often better suited to the international expansion efforts of service and retailing enterprises. McDonald's, Yum! Brands (the parent of Pizza Hut, KFC and Taco Bell), the UPS Store, Jani-King International (the world's largest commercial cleaning franchisor), 7-Eleven and Curves have all used franchising to build a presence in foreign markets. Franchising has much the same advantages as licensing. The franchisee bears most of the costs and risks of establishing overseas locations; a franchisor has to expend only the resources to recruit, train, support and monitor franchisees. The big problem a franchisor faces is maintaining quality control; foreign franchisees do not always exhibit strong commitment to consistency and standardization, especially when the local culture does not stress the same kinds of quality concerns. Another problem that can arise is whether to allow franchisees to make modifications in the franchisor's product offering so as to better satisfy the tastes and expectations of local buyers. Should McDonald's allow its franchised units in Japan to modify Big Macs slightly to suit Japanese tastes? Should the franchised Pizza Hut units in China be permitted to substitute spices that appeal to Chinese consumers? Or should the same menu offerings be rigorously and unvaryingly required of all franchisees world-wide?

Acquisition Strategies

Acquisition strategies have the advantages of a high level of control as well as speed, which can be a significant factor when a firm wants to enter an overseas market on a relatively large scale. When a strong presence in the market or local economies of scale are a significant competitive factor in the market, these advantages may make acquiring a large local firm preferable to most other entry modes. Similarly, when entry barriers are high – whether in the form of trade barriers, access to a local distribution network or building key relationships with local constituents and officials – an acquisition may be the only route to overcoming such hurdles. Acquisition may also be the preferred entry strategy if the strategic objective is to gain access to the core capabilities or well-guarded technologies of a foreign firm.

At the same time, acquisition strategies have their downside as a foreign entry strategy. Acquisition strategies are always costly, since it is necessary to pay a premium over the share-price value of an organization in order to acquire control. This can leave the acquiring organization with a good deal of debt, increasing its risk of bankruptcy and limiting its other investment options. Acquiring a foreign firm can be particularly tricky due to the challenge of international negotiations, the burden of foreign legal and regulatory requirements and the added complexity of post-acquisition integration efforts when organizations are separated by distance, culture and language.[14] While the potential benefits of a cross-border acquisition can be high, the risk of failure is high as well.

Greenfield Venture Strategies

> **Core Concept**
>
> A **greenfield venture** is a subsidiary business that is established by setting up the entire operation from the ground up.

A **Greenfield venture** strategy is one in which the organization creates a subsidiary business in the foreign market by setting up the entire operation (plants, distribution system etc.) from the ground up. Like acquisition strategies, greenfield ventures have the advantage of high control, but to an even greater degree since starting from scratch allows the organization to set up every aspect of the operation to its specifications. Since organizational change is notoriously difficult and hampered by a variety of inertial factors, it is much harder to fine-tune the operations of an acquired firm to this degree – particularly a foreign firm. Entering a foreign market from the ground up provides a firm with another potential advantage: It enables the organization to *learn by doing* how to operate in the foreign market and how to best serve local needs, navigate the local politics and compete most effectively against local rivals. This is not to say, however, that the organization needs to acquire all the knowledge and experience needed from the ground up; in building its operation, the organization can avail itself of local managerial talent and know-how by simply hiring experienced local managers who understand the local market conditions, local buying habits, local competitors and local ways of doing business. By assembling a management team that also includes senior managers from the parent organization (preferably with considerable international experience), the parent organization can transfer technology, business practices and the organizational culture into the new subsidiary and ensure that there is a conduit for the flow of information between the corporate office and local operations.

Greenfield ventures in overseas markets also pose a number of problems, just as other entry strategies do. They represent a costly capital investment, subject to a high level of risk. They require numerous other organization resources as well, diverting them from other uses. They do not work well in countries without strong, well-functioning markets and institutions that protect the rights of foreign investors and provide other legal protection.[15] Moreover, an important disadvantage of greenfield ventures relative to other means of international expansion is that they are the slowest entry route – particularly if the objective is to achieve a sizeable market share. On the other hand, successful greenfield ventures may offer higher returns to compensate for their high risk and slower path.

Alliance and Joint Venture Strategies

Collaborative agreements with organizations abroad in the form of strategic alliances or joint ventures are widely used as a means of entering foreign markets.[16] Often they are used in conjunction with another entry strategy, such as exporting, franchising or establishing a greenfield venture. Historically, firms in industrialized nations that wanted to export their products and market them in less-developed countries sought alliances with local organizations in order to do so – such arrangements were often necessary to win approval for entry from the host country's government. Organizations wanting to set up a manufacturing operation abroad often had to do so via a joint venture with a foreign firm. Over the last 20 years, those types of restrictions have been lifted in countries such as India and China, and organizations have been able to enter these markets via more direct means.[17]

> Collaborative strategies involving alliances or joint ventures with foreign partners are a popular way for organizations to edge their way into the markets of foreign countries.

Today, a more important reason for using strategic alliances and joint ventures as a vehicle for international expansion is that they facilitate resource- and risk-sharing. When firms need access to complementary resources to succeed abroad, when the venture requires substantial investment and when the risks are high, the attraction of such strategies grows. An organization can benefit immensely from a foreign partner's familiarity with local government regulations, its knowledge of the buying habits and product preferences of consumers, its distribution channel relationships and so on. Both Japanese and US organizations are actively forming alliances with European organizations to better compete in the 27-nation EU and to capitalize on emerging but risky opportunities in the countries of eastern Europe. Similarly, many US and European organizations are allying with Asian organizations in their efforts to enter markets in China, India, Thailand, Indonesia and other Asian countries where they lack local knowledge and uncertainties abound. Many organizations are particularly interested in strategic partnerships that will strengthen their ability to gain a foothold in the sizeable US market.

Another potential benefit of a collaborative strategy is the learning and added expertise that come from performing joint research, sharing technological know-how, studying one another's manufacturing methods and understanding how to tailor sales and marketing approaches to fit local cultures and traditions. Indeed, by learning from the skills, technological know-how and capabilities of alliance partners and implanting the knowledge and know-how of these partners in its own employees and organization, an organization can upgrade its capabilities and become a stronger competitor in its home market. DaimlerChrysler's strategic alliance with Mitsubishi, for example, was motivated by a desire to learn from Mitsubishi's technological strengths in small-size vehicles in order to improve the performance of its loss-making 'smart car' division.[18]

> Cross-border alliances enable a growth-minded organization to widen its geographic coverage and strengthen its competitiveness in foreign markets; at the same time, they offer flexibility and allow an organization to retain some degree of autonomy and operating control.

Many organizations believe that cross-border alliances and partnerships are a better strategic means of gaining the above benefits (as compared to acquiring or merging with overseas-based organizations to gain much the same benefits) because they allow an organization to preserve its independence (which is not the case with a merger), retain veto power over how the alliance operates and avoid using scarce financial resources to fund acquisitions. Furthermore, an alliance offers the flexibility to readily disengage once its purpose has been served or if the benefits prove elusive, whereas an acquisition is a more permanent sort of arrangement (although the acquired organization can, of course, be divested).[19]

Illustration Capsule 7.1 provides four examples of cross-border strategic alliances.

Illustration Capsule 7.1

FOUR EXAMPLES OF CROSS-BORDER STRATEGIC ALLIANCES

1. The engine of General Motors' growth strategy in Asia is its three-way joint venture with Wulung, a Chinese producer of mini-commercial vehicles, and SAIC (Shanghai Automotive Industrial Corporation), China's largest automaker. The success of the SAIC-GM-Wulung Automotive Organization is also GM's best hope for financial recovery since it emerged from bankruptcy on 10 July 2009. While GM lost €3.8 billion overall before interest and taxes during the last six months of 2009, its international operations (everything except North America and Europe) earned €1 billion. Its Chinese joint ventures accounted for approximately one-third of that profit, due in part to the success of the no-frills Wulung Sunshine, a lightweight minivan that has become China's best-selling vehicle. In 2010, GM's sales in China topped its US sales – the first time that sales in an overseas market have done so in the 102-year history of the organization. GM is now positioning its Chinese joint venture to serve as a springboard for the organization's expansion in India, with the possibility of launching a product to rival the Tata Nano there. When GM's president of international operations, Timothy E. Lee, was asked about GM's ability to compete in India, he replied, 'When you harvest from your partnerships the collective wisdom of other cultures, it's incredible what you can do'.

2. The European Aeronautic Defence and Space Organization (EADS) was formed by an alliance of aerospace organizations from Britain, Spain, Germany and France that included British Aerospace, Daimler-Benz Aerospace and Aerospatiale. The objective of the alliance was to create a European aircraft organization capable of competing with US-based Boeing Corp. The alliance has proved highly successful, infusing its commercial airline division, Airbus, with the know-how and resources needed to compete head to head with Boeing for world leadership in large commercial aircraft (those designed for over 100 passengers). The organization also established an alliance with US military aircraft manufacturer, Northrop Grumman, to develop a highly sophisticated refuelling tanker based on the A330 airliner for the US Air Force.

3. Cisco, the world-wide leader in networking components, entered into a strategic alliance with Nokia Siemens Networks to develop communications networks capable of transmitting data either across the Internet or by mobile technologies. Nokia Siemens Networks itself was created through a 2006 international joint venture between Siemens AG and Nokia. The Cisco–Nokia Siemens alliance was created to better position both organizations for convergence among Internet technologies and wireless communication devices that was expected to dramatically change how both computer networks and wireless telephones would be used.

4. Verio, a subsidiary of Japan-based NTT Communications and one of the leading global providers of web hosting services and IP data transport, operates with the philosophy that in today's highly competitive and challenging technology market, organizations must gain and share skills, information and technology with technology leaders across the world. Believing that no organization can be all things to all customers in the web hosting industry, Verio executives have developed an alliance-oriented business model that combines the organization's core competences with the skills and products of best-of-breed technology partners. Verio's strategic partners include Accenture, Cisco Systems, Microsoft, Sun Microsystems, Oracle, Arsenal Digital Solutions (a provider of worry-free tape backup, data restore and data storage services), Internet Security Systems (a provider of firewall and intrusion detection systems) and Mercantec (which develops storefront and shopping cart software). Verio's management believes that its portfolio of strategic alliances allows it to use innovative, best-of-class technologies in providing its customers with fast, efficient, accurate data transport and a complete set of web hosting services. An independent panel of 12 judges recently selected Verio as the winner of the Best Technology Foresight Award for its efforts in pioneering new technologies.

Note: Developed with Mukund Kulashekaran.

▶

Sources: Organization websites and press releases; Doz, Yves L. and Hamel, Gary (1998) *Alliance Advantage: The Art of Creating Value through Partnering*, Boston, MA, Harvard Business School Press; Muller, Joanne (2010) 'Can China save GM?' *Forbes.com*, 10 May. Available online at www.forbes.com/forbes/2010/0510/global-2000-10-automobiles-china-detroit-whitacre-save-gm.html; 'GM's first-half china sales surge past the U.S', *Bloomberg Businessweek*, 2 July 2010. Available online at www.businessweek.com/news/2010-07-02/gm-s-first-halfchina-sales-surge-past-the-u-s-.html; Gupta, Nandini Sen (2010) 'General Motors may drive in Nano rival with Chinese help', *Economic Times*, 31 May. Available online at www.economictimes.indiatimes.com/articleshow/5992589.cms.

The Risks of Strategic Alliances with Foreign Partners

Alliances and joint ventures with international partners have their pitfalls, however. Cross-border allies typically have to overcome language and cultural barriers and figure out how to deal with diverse operating practices. The transaction costs of working out a mutually agreeable arrangement and monitoring partner compliance with the terms of the arrangement can be high. The communication, trust-building and co-ordination costs are not trivial in terms of management time.[20] Often, partners soon discover they have conflicting objectives and strategies, deep differences of opinion about how to proceed and/or important differences in corporate values and ethical standards. Tensions build-up, working relationships cool and the hoped-for benefits never materialize.[21] It is not unusual for there to be little personal chemistry among some of the key people on whom success or failure of the alliance depends – the rapport such personnel need to work well together may never emerge. And even if allies are able to develop productive personal relationships, they can still have trouble reaching mutually agreeable ways to deal with key issues or resolve differences. Occasionally, the egos of corporate executives can clash. An alliance between Northwest Airlines and KLM Royal Dutch Airlines resulted in a bitter feud among both organizations' top officials (who, according to some reports, refused to speak to each other).[22] Plus there is the problem of getting alliance partners to sort through issues and reach decisions fast enough to stay abreast of rapid advances in technology or fast-changing market conditions.

One worrisome problem with alliances or joint ventures is that a firm may risk losing some of its competitive advantage if an alliance partner is given full access to its proprietary technological expertise or other unique and competitively valuable capabilities. There is a natural tendency for allies to struggle to collaborate effectively in competitively sensitive areas, thus spawning suspicions on both sides about forthright exchanges of information and expertise. It requires many meetings of many people working in good faith over a period of time to decide what is to be shared, what is to remain proprietary and how the co-operative arrangements will work.

Even if a collaborative arrangement proves to be a win-win proposition for both parties, an organization has to guard against becoming overly dependent on overseas partners for essential expertise and competitive capabilities. If an organization is aiming for global market leadership and needs to develop capabilities of its own, then at some juncture a cross-border merger or acquisition may have to be substituted for cross-border alliances and joint ventures. One of the lessons about cross-border alliances is that they are more effective in helping an organization establish a foothold of new opportunity in world markets than they are in enabling an organization to achieve and sustain global market leadership.

When a Cross-border Alliance May Be Unnecessary

Experienced multinational organizations that market in 50–100 or more countries across the world find less need for entering into cross-border alliances than do organizations in the early stages of globalizing their operations.[23] Multinational organizations make it a point to develop senior managers who understand how 'the system' works in different countries, plus they can avail themselves of local managerial talent and know-how by simply hiring experienced local managers and thereby avoid the problems of collaborative alliances with local organizations. If a multinational enterprise with considerable experience in entering the markets of different countries wants to avoid the hazards of allying with local businesses, it can simply assemble a capable management team consisting of both senior managers with considerable international experience and local managers. The role of its own in-house managers with international business savvy is to transfer technology, business practices and the organizational culture into the organization's operations in the new country market and to serve as conduits for the flow of information between the headquarters and local operations. The role of local managers is to contribute needed understanding of the local market conditions, local buying habits and local ways of doing business and, often, to head up local operations.

Hence, one cannot automatically presume that an organization needs the wisdom and resources of a local partner to guide it through the process of successfully entering new markets. Indeed, experienced multinationals often discover that local partners do not always have adequate local market knowledge – much of the so-called experience of local partners can predate the emergence of current market trends and conditions and sometimes their operating practices can be archaic.[24]

Competing Internationally: the Three Main Strategic Approaches

> **Core Concept**
>
> An **international strategy** is a strategy for competing in two or more countries simultaneously.

Broadly speaking, a firm's **international strategy** is simply its strategy for competing in two or more countries simultaneously. Typically, an organization will start to compete internationally by entering just one or perhaps a select few markets abroad, selling its products or services in countries where there is a ready market for them. But as it expands further internationally, it will have to confront head-on the conflicting pressures of local responsiveness versus efficiency gains from standardizing and integrating operations globally. Moreover, it will have to consider whether the markets abroad are characterized by multidomestic competition, global competition or some mix. The issue of whether and how to vary the organization's competitive approach to fit specific market conditions and buyer preferences in each host country or whether to employ essentially the same strategy in all countries is perhaps the foremost strategic issue that organizations must address when they operate in two or more foreign markets.[25] Figure 7.3 shows an organization's three options for resolving this issue: a *multidomestic, global* or *transnational* strategy.

Multidomestic Strategy – Think Local, Act Local

> **LO 7.4** Gain familiarity with the three main strategic approaches for competing internationally.

A **multidomestic strategy** is one based on differentiating products and services on a country-by-country or regional basis to meet differing buyer needs and to address divergent local market conditions. It is a good choice for organizations that compete primarily in industries characterized by multidomestic competition. This type of strategy involves having plants produce different product versions for different local markets and adapting marketing and distribution to fit local customs, cultures, regulations and market requirements. Castrol, a specialist in oil lubricants, produces over 3000 different formulas of lubricants to meet the requirements of different climates, vehicle types and uses and equipment applications that characterize different country markets. In the food products industry, it is common for organizations to vary the ingredients in their products and sell the localized versions under local brand names to cater to country-specific tastes and eating preferences.

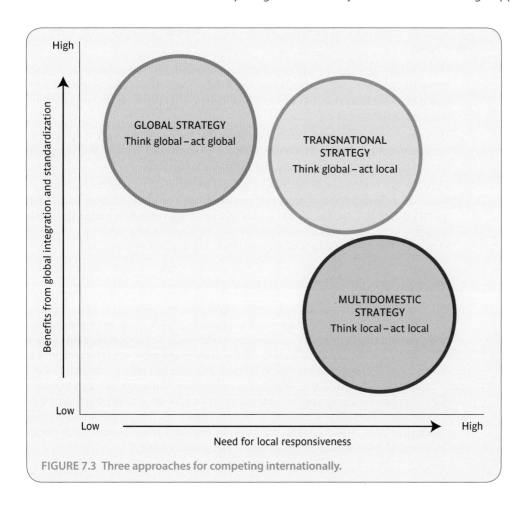

FIGURE 7.3 **Three approaches for competing internationally.**

In essence, a multidomestic strategy represents a **think-local, act-local** approach to international strategy. A think-local, act-local approach is possible only when decision-making is decentralized, giving local managers considerable latitude for crafting and executing strategies for the country markets they are responsible for. Giving local managers decision-making authority allows them to address specific market needs and respond swiftly to local changes in demand. It also enables them to focus their competitive efforts, stake out attractive market positions *vis-à-vis* local competitors, react to rivals' moves in a timely fashion and target new opportunities as they emerge.

A think-local, act-local approach to strategy-making is most appropriate when the need for local responsiveness is high due to significant cross-country differences in demographic, cultural and market conditions and when the potential for efficiency gains from standardization is limited, as depicted in Figure 7.3. Consider, for example, the wide variation in refrigerator usage and preference around the world. Northern Europeans want large refrigerators because they tend to shop once a week in supermarkets; southern Europeans prefer small refrigerators because they shop daily. In parts of Asia refrigerators are a status symbol and may be placed in the living room, leading to preferences for stylish designs and colours – in India bright blue and red are popular colours. In other Asian countries household space is constrained, and many refrigerators are only 4 feet high so that the top can be used for storage. If the minimum efficient scale for producing refrigerators is relatively low, there would be little reason to forgo the benefits of meeting these varying needs precisely in favour of a standardized, one-size-fits-all approach to production.

Core Concept

A **multidomestic strategy** is one in which an organization varies its product offering and competitive approach from country to country in an effort to be responsive to differing buyer preferences and market conditions. It is a **think-local, act-local** type of international strategy, facilitated by decision-making decentralized to the local level.

Despite their obvious benefits, think-local, act-local strategies have three big drawbacks:

1. They hinder transfer of an organization's capabilities, knowledge and other resources across country boundaries, since the organization's efforts are not integrated or co-ordinated across country boundaries. This can make the organization less innovative overall.

2. They raise production and distribution costs due to the greater variety of designs and components, shorter production runs for each product version and complications of added inventory handling and distribution logistics.

3. They are not conducive to building a single, world-wide competitive advantage. When an organization's competitive approach and product offering vary from country to country, the nature and size of any resulting competitive edge also tends to vary. At the most, multidomestic strategies are capable of producing a group of local competitive advantages of varying types and degrees of strength.

Global Strategy – Think Global, Act Global

Core Concept

A **global strategy** is one in which an organization employs the same basic competitive approach in all countries where it operates, sells much the same products everywhere, strives to build global brands and co-ordinates its actions world-wide with strong headquarters control. It represents a **think-global, act-global** approach.

A **global strategy** contrasts sharply with a multidomestic strategy in that it takes a standardized, globally integrated approach to producing, packaging, selling and delivering the organization's products and services world-wide. Organizations employing a global strategy sell the same products under the same brand names everywhere, utilize much the same distribution channels in all countries and compete on the basis of the same capabilities and marketing approaches world-wide. Although the organization's strategy or product offering may be adapted in very minor ways to accommodate specific situations in a few host countries, the organization's fundamental competitive approach (low cost, differentiation, best cost or focused) remains very much intact world-wide and local managers stick close to the global strategy.

A **think-global, act-global** strategic theme prompts organization managers to integrate and co-ordinate the organization's strategic moves world-wide and to expand into most, if not all, nations where there is significant buyer demand. It puts considerable strategic emphasis on building a *global* brand name and aggressively pursuing opportunities to transfer ideas, new products and capabilities from one country to another.[26] Global strategies are characterized by relatively centralized value chain activities, such as production and distribution. While there may be more than one manufacturing plant and distribution centre to minimize transportation costs, for example, they tend to be few in number. Achieving the efficiency potential of a global strategy requires that resources and best practices be shared, value chain activities be integrated and capabilities be transferred from one location to another as they are developed. These objectives are best facilitated through centralized decision-making and strong headquarters control.

Because a global strategy cannot accommodate varying local needs, it is an appropriate strategic choice when there are pronounced efficiency benefits from standardization and when buyer needs are relatively homogeneous across countries and regions. A globally standardized and integrated approach is especially beneficial when high volumes significantly lower costs due to economies of scale or added experience (moving the organization further down a learning curve). It can also be advantageous if it allows the firm to replicate a successful business model on a global basis efficiently or engage in higher levels of R&D by spreading the fixed costs and risks over a higher-volume output. It is a fitting response to industry conditions marked by global competition.

The drawbacks of global strategies are several: (1) They do not enable firms to address local needs as precisely as locally based rivals can; (2) they are less responsive to changes in local market conditions, either in the form of new opportunities or competitive threats; (3) they raise transportation costs and may involve higher tariffs; and (4) they involve higher co-ordination costs due to the more complex task of managing a globally integrated enterprise.

Transnational Strategy – Think Global, Act Local

A **transnational strategy** (sometimes called *glocalization*) incorporates elements of both a globalized and a localized approach to strategy-making. This type of middle-ground strategy is called for when there are relatively high needs for local responsiveness as well as appreciable benefits to be realized from standardization, as Figure 7.3 suggests. A transnational strategy encourages an organization to **think global, act local** to balance these competing objectives.

Often, organizations implement a transnational strategy with mass-customization techniques that enable them to address local preferences in an efficient, semi-standardized manner. Both McDonald's and KFC have discovered ways to customize their menu offerings in various countries without compromising costs, product quality and operating effectiveness. When it first opened Disneyland Paris, Disney learned the hard way that a global approach to its international theme parks would not work; it has since adapted elements of its strategy to accommodate local preferences even though much of its strategy still derives from a globally applied formula. Otis Elevator found that a transnational strategy delivers better results than a global strategy when competing in countries like China where local needs are highly differentiated. In 2000, it switched from its customary single-brand approach to a multibrand strategy aimed at serving different segments of the market. By 2009, it had doubled its market share in China and increased its revenues sixfold.[27]

A transnational strategy is far more conducive than other strategies to transferring and leveraging subsidiary skills and capabilities. But, like other approaches to competing internationally, transnational strategies also have significant drawbacks:

1. They are the most difficult of all international strategies to implement due to the added complexity of varying the elements of the strategy to situational conditions.

2. They place large demands on the organization due to the need to pursue conflicting objectives simultaneously.

3. Implementing the strategy is likely to be a costly and time-consuming enterprise, with an uncertain outcome.

Table 7.1 provides a summary of the pluses and minuses of the three approaches to competing internationally.

> **Core Concept**
>
> A **transnational strategy** is a think-global, act-local approach that incorporates elements of both multidomestic and global strategies.

The Quest for Competitive Advantage in the International Arena

There are three important ways in which a firm can gain competitive advantage (or offset domestic disadvantages) by expanding outside its domestic market.[28] First, it can use location to lower costs or achieve greater product differentiation. Second, it can transfer competitively valuable resources, competences and capabilities from one country to another or share them across international borders to extend and deepen its competitive advantages. And third, it can benefit from cross-border co-ordination in ways that a domestic-only competitor cannot.

> **LO 7.5**
> Understand how international organizations go about building competitive advantage in foreign markets.

Using Location to Build Competitive Advantage

To use location to build competitive advantage, an organization must consider two issues: (1) whether to concentrate each activity it performs in a few select countries or

TABLE 7.1 Advantages and disadvantages of multidomestic, global and transnational approaches

	Advantages	Disadvantages
Multidomestic (think local, act local)	• Can meet the specific needs of each market more precisely	• Hinders resource and capability sharing or cross-market transfers
	• Can respond more swiftly to localized changes in demand	• Higher production and distribution costs
	• Can target reactions to the moves of local rivals	• Not conducive to a world-wide competitive advantage
	• Can respond more quickly to local opportunities and threats	
Transnational (think global, act local)	• Offers the benefits of both local responsiveness and global integration	• More complex and harder to implement
	• Enables the transfer and sharing of resources and capabilities across borders	• Conflicting goals may be difficult to reconcile and require trade-offs
	• Provides the benefits of flexible co-ordination	• Implementation more costly and time-consuming
Global (think global, act global)	• Lower costs due to scale and scope economies	• Unable to address local needs precisely
	• Greater efficiencies due to the ability to transfer best practices across markets	• Less responsive to changes in local market conditions
	• More innovation from knowledge-sharing and capability transfer	• Higher transportation costs and tariffs
	• The benefit of a global brand and reputation	• Higher co-ordination and integration costs

to disperse performance of the activity to many nations; and (2) in which countries to locate particular activities.[29]

When to Concentrate Activities in a Few Locations

It is advantageous for an organization to concentrate its activities in a limited number of locations when:

● *The costs of manufacturing or other activities are significantly lower in some geographic locations than in others.* For example, much of the world's athletic footwear is manufactured in Asia (China and Korea) because of low labour costs; much of the production of circuit boards for PCs is located in Taiwan because of both low costs and the high-calibre technical skills of the Taiwanese labourforce.

● *There are significant scale economies in production or distribution.* The presence of significant economies of scale in components production or final assembly means that an organization can gain major cost savings from operating a few ultra-efficient plants as opposed to a host of small plants scattered across the world. Achieving low-cost provider status often requires an organization to have the largest world-wide manufacturing share (as distinct from brand share or market share), with production centralized in one or a few world-scale plants. Some organizations even use such plants to manufacture units sold under the brand names of rivals to further boost production-related scale economies. Makers of digital cameras and LCD TVs located in Japan, South Korea and Taiwan have used their scale economies to establish a low-cost advantage. Likewise, an organization may be able to reduce its distribution costs by capturing scale economies associated with establishing large-scale distribution centres to serve major geographic regions of the

> Organizations that compete internationally can pursue competitive advantage in world markets by locating their value chain activities in whatever nations prove most advantageous.

world market (e.g. North America, Latin America, Europe–Middle East and Asia-Pacific).

- *There are sizeable learning and experience benefits associated with performing an activity in a single location.* In some industries, a manufacturer can lower unit costs, boost quality or master a new technology more quickly by concentrating production in a few locations. The greater the cumulative volume of production at a plant, the faster the build-up of learning and experience of the plant's workforce, thereby enabling quicker capture of the learning/experience benefits.

- *Certain locations have superior resources, allow better co-ordination of related activities or offer other valuable advantages.* A research unit or a sophisticated production facility may be situated in a particular nation because of its pool of technically trained personnel. Samsung became a leader in memory chip technology by establishing a major R&D facility in Silicon Valley and transferring the know-how it gained back to its operations in South Korea. Organizations also locate activities to benefit from proximity to a cluster of related and supporting industries, as discussed earlier. Cisco Systems, an international firm that sells networking and communications technology, such as routers, restricts its acquisitions to organizations located in one of three well-known clusters of high-tech activity.[30] Where just-in-time inventory practices yield big cost savings and/or where an assembly firm has long-term partnering arrangements with its key suppliers, parts manufacturing plants may be located close to final assembly plants. A customer service centre or sales office may be opened in a particular country to help cultivate strong relationships with pivotal customers located nearby.

When to Disperse Activities across Many Locations

There are several instances when dispersing activities is more advantageous than concentrating them. Buyer-related activities – such as distribution to dealers, sales and advertising and after-sale service – usually must take place close to buyers. This means physically locating the capability to perform such activities in every country market where a firm has major customers (unless buyers in several adjoining countries can be served quickly from a nearby central location). For example, firms that make mining and oil-drilling equipment maintain operations in many locations around the world to support customers' needs for speedy equipment repair and technical assistance. The four biggest public accounting firms have offices in numerous countries to serve the overseas operations of their international corporate clients. Dispersing activities to many locations is also competitively advantageous when high transportation costs, diseconomies of large size and trade barriers make it too expensive to operate from a central location. Many organizations distribute their products from multiple locations to shorten delivery times to customers. In addition, it is strategically advantageous to disperse activities to hedge against the risks of fluctuating exchange rates, supply interruptions (due to strikes, mechanical failures and transportation delays) and adverse political developments. Such risks are usually greater when activities are concentrated in a single location.

As discussed earlier, there are a variety of reasons for locating different value chain activities in different countries – all having to do with location-based advantages that vary from country to country. While the classic reason for locating an activity in a particular country is low cost, input quality and availability are also important considerations.[31] Such activities as materials procurement, parts manufacture, finished-goods assembly, technology research and new product development can frequently be decoupled from buyer locations and performed wherever advantage lies. Components can be made in Mexico; technology research done in Frankfurt; new products developed and tested in Phoenix; and assembly plants located in Spain, Brazil, Taiwan or South Carolina. Capital can be raised in whatever country it is available on the best terms.

Sharing and Transferring Resources and Capabilities across Borders to Build Competitive Advantage

When an organization has competitively valuable resources and capabilities, it may be able to mount a resource-based strategic move to enter additional country markets. If an organization's resources retain their value in international contexts, then entering new markets can extend the organization's resource-based competitive advantage over a broader domain. For example, organizations have used powerful brand names such as Rolex, Chanel and Tiffany to extend their differentiation-based competitive advantages into markets far beyond their home-country origins. In each of these cases, the luxury brand name represents a valuable resource that is *shared among all of the organization's international operations* and allows the organization to command a higher willingness to pay from its customers in each country.

Transferring resources and capabilities across borders provides another means to extend an organization's competitive advantage internationally. For example, if a firm learns how to assemble its product more efficiently at its Brazilian plant, the accumulated expertise can be quickly communicated to assembly plants in other world locations. Whirlpool, the leading global manufacturer of home appliances, with 69 manufacturing and technology research centres around the world and sales in nearly every country, uses an online global information technology (IT) platform to quickly and effectively transfer key product innovations and improved production techniques both across national borders and across its various appliance brands.

Sharing or transferring resources and capabilities across borders provides a way for an organization to leverage its core competences more fully and extend its competitive advantages into a wider array of geographic markets. Thus a technology-based competitive advantage in one country market may provide a similar basis for advantage in other country markets (depending on local market conditions). But since sharing or transferring valuable resources across borders is a very cost-effective means of extending an organization's competitive advantage, these activities can also contribute to an organization's competitive advantage on the costs side, giving multinational organizations a powerful edge over domestic-only rivals. Since valuable resources and capabilities (such as brands, technologies and production capabilities) are often developed at a very high cost, deploying them abroad spreads the fixed development cost over greater output, thus lowering the organization's unit costs. The cost of transferring already developed resources and capabilities is low by comparison. And even if the resources and capabilities need to be fully replicated in the overseas market or adapted to local conditions, this can usually be done at low additional cost relative to the initial investment in capability-building.

Consider the case of Walt Disney's theme parks as an example. The success of the theme parks in the USA derives in part from core resources such as the Disney brand name and characters like Mickey Mouse that have universal appeal and world-wide recognition. These resources can be freely shared with new theme parks as Disney expands internationally. Disney can replicate its theme parks in new countries cost-effectively since it has already borne the costs of developing its core resources, park attractions, basic park design and operating capabilities. The cost of replicating its theme parks abroad should be relatively low, even if they need to be adapted to a variety of local country conditions. By expanding internationally, Disney is able to enhance its competitive advantage over local theme park rivals. It does so by leveraging the differentiation advantage conferred by resources such as the Disney name and the park attractions. And by moving into new overseas markets, it augments its competitive advantage world-wide through the efficiency gains that come from cross-border resource-sharing and low-cost capability transfer and business model replication.

Sharing and transferring resources and capabilities across country borders may also contribute to the development of broader or deeper competences and capabilities – ideally helping an organization achieve *dominating depth* in some competitively valuable area. For example, an international organization that consistently incorporates the same differentiating attributes in its products world-wide has enhanced potential to build a global brand name with significant power in the marketplace. The reputation for quality that Honda established world-wide began in motorcycles but enabled the organization to command a position in both cars and outdoor power equipment in multiple-country markets. A one-country customer base is often too small to support the resource build-up needed to achieve such depth; this is particularly true when the market is developing or protected and sophisticated resources have not been required. By deploying capabilities across a larger international domain, an organization can gain the experience needed to upgrade them to a higher performance standard. And by facing a more challenging set of international competitors, an organization may be spurred to develop a stronger set of competitive capabilities. Moreover, by entering international markets, firms may be able to augment their capability set by learning from international rivals, co-operative partners or acquisition targets.

However, sharing and transferring resources and capabilities across borders cannot provide a guaranteed recipe for competitive success. Because lifestyles and buying habits differ internationally, resources that are valuable in one country may not have value in another. For example, brands that are popular in one country may not transfer well or may lack recognition in the new context and thus offer no advantage against an established local brand. In addition, whether a resource or capability can confer a competitive advantage abroad depends on the conditions of rivalry in each particular market. If the rivals in a foreign country market have superior resources and capabilities, then an entering firm may find itself at a competitive disadvantage even if it has a resource-based advantage domestically and can transfer the resources at low cost.

Using Cross-border Co-ordination for Competitive Advantage

Organizations that compete on an international basis have another source of competitive advantage relative to their purely domestic rivals: They are able to benefit from co-ordinating activities across different countries' domains.[32] For example, an international manufacturer can shift production from a plant in one country to a plant in another to take advantage of exchange rate fluctuations, to cope with components shortages, or to profit from changing wage rates or energy costs. Production schedules can be co-ordinated world-wide; shipments can be diverted from one distribution centre to another if sales rise unexpectedly in one place and fall in another. By co-ordinating their activities, multinational organizations may also be able to enhance their leverage with host-country governments or respond adaptively to changes in tariffs and quotas.

Efficiencies can also be achieved by shifting workloads from where they are unusually heavy to locations where personnel are underutilized. Whirlpool's efforts to link its product R&D and manufacturing operations in North America, Latin America, Europe and Asia allowed it to accelerate the discovery of innovative appliance features, co-ordinate the introduction of these features in the appliance products marketed in different countries and create a cost-efficient world-wide supply chain. Whirlpool's conscious efforts to integrate and co-ordinate its various operations around the world have helped it become a low-cost producer and also speed product innovations to market, thereby giving Whirlpool an edge over rivals world-wide.

Profit Sanctuaries and Cross-Border Strategic Moves

Profit sanctuaries are country markets (or geographic regions) in which an organization derives substantial profits because of its protected market position or unassailable

> **Core Concept**
>
> **Profit sanctuaries** are country markets that provide an organization with substantial profits because of a protected market position or sustainable competitive advantage.

competitive advantage. Japan, for example, is the chief profit sanctuary for most Japanese organizations because trade barriers erected by the Japanese government effectively block foreign organizations from competing for a large share of Japanese sales. Protected from the threat of foreign competition in their home market, Japanese organizations can safely charge somewhat higher prices to their Japanese customers and thus earn attractively large profits on sales made in Japan. Other profit sanctuaries may be protected because an organization has an unassailable market position due to unrivalled and inimitable capabilities. In most cases, an organization's biggest and most strategically crucial profit sanctuary is its home market, but multinational organizations may also enjoy profit sanctuary status in other nations where they have a strong position based on some type of competitive advantage. Organizations that compete world-wide are likely to have more profit sanctuaries than organizations that compete in just a few country markets; a domestic-only competitor, of course, can have only one profit sanctuary at most (see Figure 7.4).

Using Cross-market Subsidization to Make a Strategic Move

Profit sanctuaries are valuable competitive assets, providing the financial strength to support strategic moves in selected country markets. The added financial capability afforded by multiple profit sanctuaries gives an international competitor the financial strength to move proactively against a domestic competitor whose only profit sanctuary is its home market. The international organization has the flexibility of setting

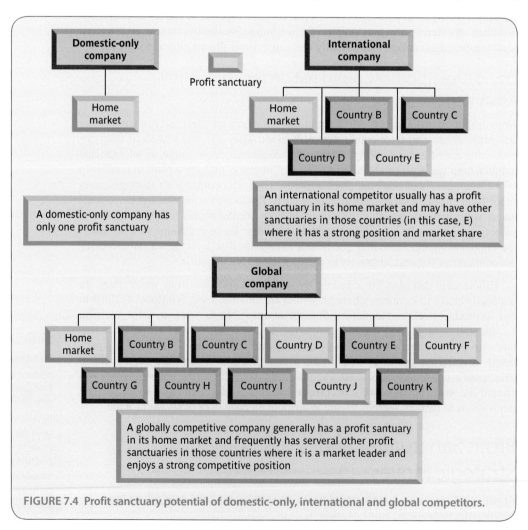

FIGURE 7.4 **Profit sanctuary potential of domestic-only, international and global competitors.**

prices below local competitors or launching high-cost marketing campaigns in the domestic organization's home market and gaining market share at the domestic organization's expense. Low margins or even losses in these markets can be subsidized with the healthy profits earned in its profit sanctuaries – a practice called **cross-market subsidization**. The international organization can adjust the depth of its price-cutting to move in and capture market share quickly, or it can shave prices slightly to make gradual market inroads (perhaps over a decade or more) so as not to threaten domestic firms precipitously and trigger protectionist government actions. If the domestic organization retaliates with matching price cuts or increased marketing expenses, it exposes its entire revenue stream and profit base to erosion; its profits can be squeezed substantially and its competitive strength sapped, even if it is the domestic market leader.

> **Core Concept**
>
> **Cross-market subsidization** – supporting competitive moves in one market with resources and profits diverted from operations in another market – can be competitively powerful.

When taken to the extreme, cut-rate pricing attacks by international competitors may draw charges of unfair dumping. An organization is said to be dumping when it sells its goods in foreign markets at prices that are (1) well below the prices at which it normally sells in its home market or (2) well below its full costs per unit. Organizations that engage in dumping usually keep their selling prices high enough to cover variable costs per unit, thereby limiting their losses on each unit to some percentage of fixed costs per unit.

Dumping can be a tempting strategy in either of two instances: (1) when selling goods abroad at below-market prices can allow a firm to avoid the high costs of idling plants, and (2) when temporary below-cost pricing can allow an organization to make lasting market share gains by driving weak firms from the market. The first may be justified as a legitimate competitive practice, while the latter is usually viewed to be predatory in nature. A charge of unfair dumping is more easily defended when an organization with unused production capacity discovers that it is cheaper to keep producing (as long as the selling prices cover average variable costs per unit) than it is to incur the costs associated with idle plant capacity. By keeping its plants operating at or near capacity, not only may an organization be able to cover variable costs and earn a contribution to fixed costs, but it also may be able to use its below-market prices to draw price-sensitive customers away from foreign rivals. It is wise for organizations pursuing such an approach to court these new customers and retain their business when prices later begin a gradual rise back to normal market levels.

Alternatively, an organization may use below-market pricing to drive down the price so far in the targeted country that domestic firms are quickly put in dire financial straits or in danger of being driven out of business. However, using below-market pricing in this way *runs a high risk of host-government retaliation on behalf of the adversely affected domestic organizations*. Almost all governments can be expected to retaliate against perceived dumping practices by imposing special tariffs on goods being imported from the countries of the guilty organizations. Indeed, as the trade among nations has mushroomed over the past 10 years, most governments have joined the World Trade Organization (WTO), which promotes fair-trade practices among nations and actively polices dumping. Organizations based in France and China were recently found guilty of dumping laminate flooring at unreasonably low prices in Canada to the detriment of Canadian producers.[33] Organizations deemed guilty of dumping frequently come under pressure from their government to cease and desist, especially if the tariffs adversely affect innocent organizations based in the same country or if the advent of special tariffs raises the spectre of an international trade war.

Using Cross-border Tactics to Defend against International Rivals

Cross-border tactics can also be used as a means of defending against the strategic moves of strong international rivals with multiple profit sanctuaries of their own. If an organization finds itself under competitive attack by an international rival in one country market, one way to respond is with a counter-attack against one of the rival's key markets in a different country – preferably where the rival is least protected and has the most to lose. This is a possible option when rivals compete against one another in much the same markets around the world.

For organizations with at least one profit sanctuary, having a presence in a rival's key markets can be enough to deter the rival from making aggressive attacks. The reason for this is that the combination of some market presence (even at small scale) and a profit sanctuary elsewhere can send a signal to the rival that the organization could quickly ramp up production (funded by the profit sanctuary) to mount a competitive attack in that market if the rival attacks one of the organization's key markets in another country.

When international rivals compete against one another in multiple-country markets, this type of deterrence effect can restrain them from taking aggressive action against one another due to the fear of a retaliatory response that might escalate the battle into a cross-border competitive war. Mutual restraint of this sort tends to stabilize the competitive position of multimarket rivals against one another. And while it may prevent each firm from making any major market share gains at the expense of its rival, it also prevents costly competitive battles that would be likely to erode the profitability of both organizations without any compensating gain.

> **Core Concept**
>
> When the same organizations compete against one another in multiple geographic markets, the threat of cross-border counter-attacks may be enough to deter aggressive competitive moves and encourage mutual restraint among international rivals.

Strategies for Competing in the Markets of Developing Countries

Organizations racing for global leadership have to consider competing in developing economy markets like China, India, Brazil, Indonesia, Thailand, Poland, Russia and Mexico – countries where the business risks are considerable but where the opportunities for growth are huge, especially as their economies develop and living standards climb toward levels in the industrialized world.[34] With the world now comprising nearly seven billion people – 40 per cent of whom live in India and China, and hundreds of millions more live in other, less-developed countries in Asia and Latin America – an organization that aspires to world market leadership (or to sustained rapid growth) cannot ignore the market opportunities or the base of technical and managerial talent such countries offer. For example, in 2010, China was the world's second-largest economy (behind the USA), as measured by purchasing power. Its population of 1.4 billion people now consumes a quarter of the world's luxury products, due to the rapid growth of a wealthy class.[35] China is also the world's largest consumer of many commodities. China's growth in demand for consumer goods had made it the world's largest market for vehicles by 2009 and put it on track to become the world's largest market for luxury goods by 2014.[36] Thus, no organization that aspires to global market leadership can afford to ignore the strategic importance of establishing competitive market positions in China, India, other parts of the Asia-Pacific region, Latin America and eastern Europe. Illustration Capsule 7.2 describes Yum! Brands' strategy to increase its sales and market share in China.

Tailoring products to fit market conditions in a developing country like China, however, often involves more than making minor product changes and becoming more familiar with local cultures.[37] Ford's attempt to sell a Ford Escort in India at a price of €16 500 – a luxury-car price, given that India's best-selling Maruti-Suzuki model sold at the time for €8000 or less and that fewer than 10 per cent of Indian households had an annual purchasing power greater than €16 000 – met with a less-than-enthusiastic market response. McDonald's has had to offer vegetable burgers in parts of Asia and to rethink its prices, which are often high by local standards and affordable only by the well-to-do. Kellogg has struggled to introduce its cereals successfully because

Illustration Capsule 7.2

YUM! BRANDS' STRATEGY FOR BECOMING THE LEADING FOOD SERVICE BRAND IN CHINA

In 2010, Yum! Brands operated more than 37 000 restaurants in more than 110 countries. Its best-known brands were KFC, Taco Bell, Pizza Hut, A&W and Long John Silver's. In 2009, its fastest growth in revenues came from its 3369 restaurants in China, which recorded operating profits of $602 million during the year. KFC was the largest

quick-service chain in China, with 2870 units in 2009, while Pizza Hut was the largest casual-dining chain, with 450 units. Yum! Brands planned to open at least 500 new restaurant locations annually in China, including new Pizza Hut Home delivery units and East Dawning units, which had a menu offering traditional Chinese food. All of Yum! Brands' menu items for China were developed in its R&D facility in Shanghai.

In addition to adapting its menu to local tastes and adding new units at a rapid pace, Yum! Brands also adapted the restaurant ambience and decor to appeal to local consumer preferences and behaviour. The organization changed its KFC store formats to provide educational displays that supported parents' priorities for their children and to make KFC a fun place for children to visit. The typical KFC outlet in China averaged two birthday parties per day.

In 2009, Yum! Brands operated 60 KFC, Taco Bell, Pizza Hut, A&W and Long John Silver's restaurants for every 1 million Americans. The organization's more than 3300 units in China represented only two restaurants per 1 million Chinese. Yum! Brands management believed that its strategy keyed to continued expansion in the number of units in China and additional menu refinements would allow its operating profits from restaurants located in China to account for 40 per cent of system-wide operating profits by 2017.

Sources: Yum! Brands 2009 10-K and other information posted at www.yum.com.

consumers in many less-developed countries do not eat cereal for breakfast and changing habits is difficult and expensive. Single-serving packages of detergents, shampoos, pickles, cough syrup and cooking oils are very popular in India because they allow buyers to conserve cash by purchasing only what they need immediately. Thus, many organizations find that trying to employ a strategy akin to that used in the markets of developed countries is hazardous.[38] Experimenting with some, perhaps many, local twists is usually necessary to find a strategy combination that works.

Strategy Options for Competing in Developing Country Markets

There are several options for tailoring an organization's strategy to fit the sometimes unusual or challenging circumstances presented in developing country markets:

● *Prepare to compete on the basis of low price.* Consumers in developing markets are often highly focused on price, which can give low-cost local competitors the edge unless an organization can find ways to attract buyers with bargain prices as well as better products.[39] For example, when Unilever entered the market for laundry detergents in India, it realized that 80 per cent of the population could not afford the brands it was selling to affluent consumers there. To compete against a very low-priced detergent made by a local organization, Unilever developed a low-cost detergent (named Wheel), constructed new low-cost production facilities, packaged the detergent in single-use amounts so that it could be sold at a very low unit price, distributed the product to local merchants by handcarts and crafted an economical marketing campaign that included painted signs on buildings and demonstrations near stores. The new brand quickly captured €80 million in sales and was the number-one detergent brand in India in 2008 based on sales revenue. Unilever later replicated the strategy in India with low-priced packets of shampoos and deodorants and in South America with a detergent brand named Ala.

- *Be prepared to modify aspects of the organization's business model or strategy to accommodate local circumstances (but not to such an extent that the organization loses the advantage of global scale and branding).*[40] For instance, when Dell entered China, it discovered that individuals and businesses were not accustomed to placing orders through the Internet (whereas over 50 per cent of Dell's sales in North America were online). To adapt, Dell modified its direct sales model to rely more heavily on phone and fax orders and decided to be patient in getting Chinese customers to place Internet orders. Further, because numerous Chinese government departments and state-owned enterprises insisted that hardware vendors make their bids through distributors and systems integrators (as opposed to dealing directly with Dell salespeople, as did large enterprises in other countries), Dell opted to use third parties in marketing its products to this buyer segment (although it did sell through its own salesforce where it could). But Dell was careful not to abandon the parts of its business model that gave it a competitive edge over rivals. Similarly, when McDonald's moved into Russia in the 1990s, it was forced to alter its practice of obtaining needed supplies from outside vendors because capable local suppliers were not available; to supply its Russian outlets and stay true to its core principle of serving consistent, quality fast food, McDonald's set up its own vertically integrated supply chain – cattle were imported from Holland and russet potatoes were imported from the USA. McDonald's management also worked with a select number of Russian bakers for its bread, brought in agricultural specialists from Canada and Europe to improve the management practices of Russian farmers, built its own 30 000-square-metre McComplex to produce hamburgers, French fries, ketchup, mustard and Big Mac sauce and set up a trucking fleet to move supplies to restaurants.

- *Try to change the local market to better match the way the organization does business elsewhere.*[41] An international organization often has enough market clout to drive major changes in the way a local country market operates. When Hong Kong-based STAR launched its first satellite TV channel in 1991, it generated profound impacts on the TV marketplace in India. The Indian government lost its monopoly on TV broadcasts, several other satellite TV channels aimed at Indian audiences quickly emerged and the excitement of additional TV channels in India triggered a boom in TV manufacturing in India. When Japan's Suzuki entered India, it triggered a quality revolution among Indian auto parts manufacturers. Local component suppliers teamed up with Suzuki's vendors in Japan and worked with Japanese experts to produce higher-quality products. Over the next two decades, Indian organizations became proficient in making top-notch components for vehicles, won more prizes for quality than organizations in any country other than Japan and broke into the global market as suppliers to many auto-makers in Asia and other parts of the world. Mahindra and Mahindra, one of India's premier manufacturers, has been recognized by a number of organizations for its product quality. Among its most noteworthy awards was its number-one ranking by J.D. Power Asia Pacific in 2007 for new vehicle overall quality.

- *Stay away from developing markets where it is impractical or uneconomic to modify the organization's business model to accommodate local circumstances.*[42] Home Depot expanded into Mexico in 2001 and China in 2006, but it has avoided entry into other developing countries because its value proposition of good quality, low prices and attentive customer service relies on (1) good highways and logistical systems to minimize store inventory costs, (2) employee stock ownership to help motivate store personnel to provide good customer service, and (3) high labour costs for housing construction and home repairs that encourage homeowners to engage in do-it-yourself projects. Relying on these factors in the USA and Canadian markets has worked spectacularly for Home Depot, but the organization has found that it cannot count on these factors in nearby Latin America.

Organizational experiences in entering developing markets like China, India, Russia and Brazil indicate that profitability seldom comes quickly or easily. Building a market for the organization's products can often turn into a long-term process that involves re-education of consumers, sizeable investments in advertising and promotion to alter tastes and buying habits and upgrades of the local infrastructure (transportation systems, distribution channels etc.). In such cases, an organization must be patient, work within the system to improve the infrastructure and lay the foundation for generating sizeable revenues and profits once conditions are ready for market expansion.

> Profitability in developing markets rarely comes quickly or easily – new entrants have to adapt their business models and strategies to local conditions and be patient in earning a profit.

Defending against Global Giants: Strategies for Local Organizations in Developing Countries

If opportunity-seeking, resource-rich multinational organizations are looking to enter developing country markets, what strategy options can local organizations use to survive? As it turns out, the prospects for local organizations facing global giants are by no means grim. Studies of local organizations in developing markets have disclosed five strategies that have proved themselves in defending against globally competitive organizations.[43] Illustration Capsule 7.3 discusses how a travel agency in China used a combination of these strategies to become that country's largest travel consolidator and online travel agent.

1. *Develop business models that exploit shortcomings in local distribution networks or infrastructure.* In many instances, the extensive collection of resources possessed by the global giants is of little help in building a presence in developing markets. The lack of well-established wholesaler and distributor networks, telecommunication systems, consumer banking or media necessary for advertising makes it difficult for large internationals to migrate business models proved in developed markets to developing countries. Such markets sometimes favour local organizations whose managers are familiar with the local language and culture and are skilled in selecting large numbers of conscientious employees to carry out labour-intensive tasks. Shanda, a Chinese producer of massively multiplayer online role-playing games (MMORPG), has overcome China's lack of an established credit card network by selling prepaid access cards through local merchants. The organization's focus on online games also addresses shortcomings in China's software piracy laws. Emerge Logistics has used its understanding of China's extensive government bureaucracy and fragmented network of delivery services to deliver goods for international organizations doing business in China. Many foreign firms have found it difficult to get their goods to market since the average Chinese trucking organization owns only one or two trucks. An India-based electronics organization has been able to carve out a market niche for itself by developing an all-in-one business machine designed especially for India's 1.2 million small shopkeepers that tolerates the frequent power outages in that country.[44]

2. *Utilize keen understanding of local customer needs and preferences to create customized products or services.* When developing country markets are largely made up of customers with strong local needs, a good strategy option is to concentrate on customers who prefer a local touch and to accept the loss of the customers attracted to global brands.[45] A local organization may be able to astutely use its local orientation – its familiarity with local preferences, its expertise in traditional products and its long-standing customer relationships. A small Middle Eastern mobile phone manufacturer competes successfully against industry giants Nokia, Samsung and Motorola by selling a model designed especially for Muslims – it is loaded with the Koran, alerts people at prayer times and is equipped with a compass that points them toward Mecca. Shenzhen-based Tencent has become the leader in instant messaging in China through its unique understanding of Chinese behaviour and culture.

3. *Take advantage of aspects of the local workforce with which large multinational organizations may be unfamiliar.* Local organizations that lack the technological capabilities of foreign entrants may be able to rely on their better understanding of the local labourforce to offset any disadvantage. Focus Media is China's largest outdoor advertising firm and has relied on low-cost labour to update its 130 000 LCD displays and billboards in 90 cities in a low-tech manner, while multinational organizations operating in China use electronically networked screens that allow messages to be changed remotely. Focus uses an army of employees who ride to each display by bicycle to change advertisements with programming contained on a USB flash drive or DVD. Indian IT firms such as Infosys Technologies and Satyam Computer Services have been able to keep their personnel costs lower than those of international competitors EDS and Accenture because of their familiarity with local labour markets. While the large internationals have focused recruiting efforts in urban centres like Bangalore and Delhi, driving up engineering and computer science salaries in such cities, local organizations have shifted recruiting efforts to second-tier cities that are unfamiliar to foreign firms.

4. *Use acquisition and rapid growth strategies to better defend against expansion-minded internationals.* With the growth potential of developing markets such as China, Indonesia and Brazil obvious to the world, local organizations must attempt to develop scale and upgrade their competitive capabilities as quickly as possible to defend against the stronger international's pool of resources. Most successful organizations in developing markets have pursued mergers and acquisitions at a fast pace to build first a nationwide and then an international presence. Hindalco, India's largest aluminium producer, has followed just such a path to achieve its ambitions for global dominance. By acquiring organizations in India first, it gained enough experience and confidence to eventually acquire much larger foreign organizations with world-class capabilities.[46] When China began to liberalize its foreign trade policies, Lenovo (the Chinese PC-maker) realized that its long-held position of market dominance in China could not withstand the onslaught of new international entrants such as Dell and HP. Its acquisition of IBM's PC business allowed Lenovo to gain rapid access to IBM's globally recognized PC brand, its R&D capability and its existing distribution in developed countries. This has allowed Lenovo not only to hold its own against the incursion of global giants into its home market but to expand into new markets around the world.[47]

5. *Transfer organization expertise to cross-border markets and initiate actions to contend on an international level.* When an organization from a developing country has resources and capabilities suitable for competing in other country markets, launching initiatives to transfer its expertise to new markets becomes a viable strategic option.[48] Televisa, Mexico's largest media organization, used its expertise in Spanish culture and linguistics to become the world's most prolific producer of Spanish-language soap operas. Jollibee Foods, a family-owned organization with 56 per cent of the fast-food business in the Philippines, combated McDonald's

entry first by upgrading service and delivery standards and then by using its expertise in seasoning hamburgers with garlic and soy sauce and making noodle and rice meals with fish to open outlets catering to Asian residents in Hong Kong, the Middle East and California. By continuing to upgrade its capabilities and learn from its experience in international markets, an organization can sometimes transform itself into one capable of competing on a world-wide basis, as an emerging global giant.[49] Sundaram Fasteners of India began its foray into new markets as a supplier of radiator caps to GM – an opportunity it pursued when GM first decided to outsource the production of this part. As a participant in GM's supplier network, the organization learned about emerging technical standards, built its capabilities and became one of the first Indian organizations to achieve QS 9000 quality certification. With the expertise it gained and its recognition for meeting quality standards, Sundaram was then able to pursue opportunities to supply automotive parts in Japan and Europe.

Illustration Capsule 7.3

HOW CTRIP SUCCESSFULLY DEFENDED AGAINST INTERNATIONAL RIVALS TO BECOME CHINA'S LARGEST ONLINE TRAVEL AGENCY

Ctrip has utilized a business model tailored to the Chinese travel market, its access to low-cost labour and its unique understanding of customer preferences and buying habits to build scale rapidly and defeat international rivals such as Expedia and Travelocity in becoming the largest travel agency in China. The organization was founded in 1999 with a focus on business travellers, since corporate travel accounts for the majority of China's travel bookings. The organization also placed little emphasis on online transactions, since at the time there was no national ticketing system in China, most hotels did not belong to a national or international chain and most consumers preferred paper tickets to electronic tickets. To overcome this infrastructure shortcoming, the organization established its own central database of 5600 hotels located throughout China and flight information for all major airlines operating in China. Ctrip set up a call centre of 3000 representatives that could use its proprietary database to provide travel information for up to 100 000 customers per day. Because most of its transactions were not done over the Internet, the organization hired couriers in all major cities in China to ride by bicycle or scooter to collect payments and deliver tickets to Ctrip's corporate customers. Ctrip also initiated

a loyalty programme that provided gifts and incentives to the administrative personnel who arranged travel for business executives. By 2009, Ctrip.com held 60 per cent of China's online travel market and planned to enter the Taiwanese tourism market, having just acquired EzTravel, Taiwan's largest online travel site.* By April 2010, its market cap reached €4.24 billion and was creeping up rapidly on Expedia's market cap of €5.75 billion.**

Notes: * 'Ctrip.com Acquires ezTravel', *China Hospitality News*, 11 August 2009. Available online at www.chinahospitalitynews.com/en/2009/08/11/12859-ctrip-com-acquires-eztravel/. ** Schaal, Dennis (2010) 'Online travel powerhouses – Priceline, Expedia . . . and Ctrip?' *Tnooz.co: Talking Travel Tech*, 1 April. Available online at www.tnooz.com/2010/04/01/news/online-travel-powerhouses-priceline-expedia-and-ctrip/.

Source: Based on information in Bhattacharya, Arindam K. and Michael, David C. (2008) 'How local organizations keep multinationals at bay', *Harvard Business Review*, 86(3): 85–95.

Key Debate 7.1

GLOBALIZATION

Globalization refers to the growing economic interdependence among countries, including increasing cross-border flows of goods and services, capital and know-how. While much of the growth in global activity has been spurred by government, multinational organizations are a central driver through cross-border alliances, joint ventures, international mergers and acquisitions, as well as offshoring activities and exporting products world-wide.

Globalization is seen by many organizations as a source of opportunity; however, it is not without opposition. Some elements of globalization are questioned and opposed by different groups. These include developing countries that have seen destabilizing effects, as well as western economies that have had significant job losses as a result of offshoring to low-wage countries. There are also other issues that are debated in both academic circles and among practitioners of international business. Some of the key questions[50] are briefly presented here for you to consider.

1. *Is it really happening?* While it is usually assumed that the world is becoming more global there are some sceptics. The argument is not that there are more interrelations, but that these are not unprecedented in world history, and that these interrelations are heavily concentrated to certain regions – principally western Europe, North America, Japan and more recently the BRIC countries. This means that the world is becoming more international, but not more global.[51] At an individual level, only a minor percentage of the world's population are active participants and considered globalized.

2. *Does it produce convergence?* If the world is becoming more global, some predict that the consequence will be a convergence of societies toward a uniform pattern of economic, political and even cultural organization. The argument is based in the idea that conformity will come from a world culture of rationalized modernity and a consensus on matters of citizen and human rights, the natural world, socio-economic development and education.[52] Alternatively, it has been argued that there will be enduring cross-national differences; for instance, that firms will continue to pursue different modes of economic action and adopt different organizational forms depending on the home countries even as globalization increases.[53]

3. *Does it undermine the authority of nation states?* The spread of multinational organizations has been accused of creating destructive political tensions, reducing government regulatory power and threatening the independent decision-making of states.[54] Others argue that globalization induces a transformation of the role of the state, but does not diminish its role.[55]

4. *Is globality different from modernity?* Globalization is often posited as something new, and the beginning of a new era. However, it can also be seen as just a continuation of the trend toward modernity. Modernity would be considered an outgrowth from the western worldview, whereas globality would denote processes, qualities and conditions that are not dominated by any one model or worldview, and includes a multiplicity of conceptions.[56]

5. *Is a global culture in the making?* With similar products increasingly becoming available in many markets, some argue that mass consumerism is creating a global consumer culture driven by symbols, images and self-image, with a standardization of tastes and desires.[57] Alternatively, it is believed that globalization creates an affirmation of cultural identity and that national cultures, while changing, do so in a path-dependent rather than a convergent manner.[58]

QUESTIONS

1. Which of the globalization debates are most relevant for organizations that conduct operations internationally?

2. Do MNEs have a responsibility to address criticisms of globalization?

KEY POINTS

1. Competing in international markets allows organizations to (1) gain access to new customers; (2) achieve lower costs through greater scale economies, learning curve effects or purchasing power; (3) leverage core competences developed domestically in additional country markets; (4) gain access to resources and capabilities located outside an organization's domestic market; and (5) spread business risk across a wider market base.

2. Organizations electing to expand into international markets must consider five factors when evaluating strategy options: (1) cross-country variation in factors that affect industry competitiveness; (2) location-based drivers regarding where to conduct different value chain activities; (3) varying political and economic risks; (4) potential shifts in exchange rates; and (5) differences in cultural, demographic and market conditions.

3. The strategies of firms that expand internationally are usually grounded in home-country advantages concerning demand conditions, factor conditions, related and supporting industries, and firm strategy, structure and rivalry, as described by the Diamond of National Advantage framework.

4. The pattern of international competition varies in important ways from industry to industry. At one extreme is *multidomestic competition*, in which the market contest among rivals in one country is not closely connected to the market contests in other countries – there is no world market, just a collection of self-contained country (or maybe regional) markets. At the other extreme is *global competition*, in which competitive conditions across national markets are linked strongly enough to form a true world market, wherein leading competitors compete head-to-head in many different countries.

5. There are six strategic options for entering foreign markets. These include: (1) maintaining a national (one-country) production base and exporting goods to foreign markets; (2) licensing foreign firms to produce and distribute the organization's products abroad; (3) employing a franchising strategy; (4) establishing a wholly owned subsidiary by acquiring a foreign organization; (5) creating a wholly owned foreign subsidiary from the ground up via a greenfield venture; and (6) using strategic alliances or other collaborative partnerships to enter a foreign market.

6. An organization must choose among three alternative approaches for competing internationally: (1) a *multidomestic strategy*, which is a *think-local, act-local* approach to crafting international strategy; (2) a *global strategy* – a *think-global, act-global* approach; and (3) a combination *think-global, act-local* approach, known as a *transnational strategy*. A think-local, act-local or multidomestic strategy is appropriate for industries or organizations that must vary their product offerings and competitive approaches from country to country in order to accommodate different buyer preferences and market conditions. The think-global, act-global approach that characterizes a global strategy works best when there are substantial cost benefits to be gained from taking a standardized and globally integrated approach and little need for local responsiveness. A transnational approach (think global, act local) is called for when there is a high need for local responsiveness as well as substantial benefits from taking a globally integrated approach. While this is the most challenging international strategy to implement, it can be used when it is feasible for an organization to employ essentially the same basic competitive strategy in all markets but still customize its product offering and some aspect of its operations to fit local market circumstances.

7. There are three general ways in which a firm can gain competitive advantage (or offset domestic disadvantages) in international markets. One way involves locating various value chain activities among nations in a manner that lowers costs or achieves greater product differentiation. A second way draws on an international competitor's ability to extend or deepen its competitive advantage by cost-effectively sharing, replicating or transferring its most valuable resources and capabilities across borders. A third concerns benefiting from cross-border co-ordination in ways that are unavailable to domestic-only competitors.

8. Profit sanctuaries are country markets in which an organization derives substantial profits because of its protected market position. They are valuable competitive assets, providing organizations with the financial strength to mount strategic moves in selected country markets or to support defensive moves that can ward off mutually destructive competitive battles. They may be used to facilitate

strategic moves in international markets through *cross-subsidization* – a practice of supporting competitive moves in one market with resources and profits diverted from operations in another market. They may be used defensively to encourage *mutual restraint* among competitors when there is international *multimarket competition* by signalling that each organization has the financial capability for mounting a strong counter-attack if threatened. For organizations with at least one profit sanctuary, having a presence in a rival's key markets can be enough to deter the rival from making aggressive attacks.

9. Organizations aiming for global leadership have to consider competing in developing markets like China, India, Brazil, Indonesia and Mexico – countries where the business risks are considerable but the opportunities for growth are huge. To succeed in these markets, organizations often have to (1) compete on the basis of low price, (2) be prepared to modify aspects of the organization's business model or strategy to accommodate local circumstances (but not so much that the organization loses the advantage of global scale and global branding) and/or (3) try to change the local market to better match the way the organization does business elsewhere. Profitability is unlikely to come quickly or easily in developing markets, typically because of the investments needed to alter buying habits and tastes, the increased political and economic risk and/or the need for infrastructure upgrades. And there may be times when an organization should simply stay away from certain developing markets until conditions for entry are better suited to its business model and strategy.

10. Local organizations in developing country markets can seek to compete against large multinational organizations by (1) developing business models that exploit shortcomings in local distribution networks or infrastructure, (2) utilizing superior understanding of local customer needs and preferences or local relationships, (3) taking advantage of competitively important qualities of the local workforce with which large multinational organizations may be unfamiliar, (4) using acquisition strategies and rapid-growth strategies to better defend against expansion-minded multinational organizations, or (5) transferring organization expertise to cross-border markets and initiating actions to compete on a global level.

MANGANESE BRONZE AND GEELY – A CASE OF 'CARRY ON CABBIE'?

When John Russell joined the board of Manganese Bronze in 2007, he became CEO of an increasingly rare type of organization, a UK-owned automobile manufacturer. The firm was the producer of the distinctive black London taxis. Russell was an industry insider having worked at Peugeot, Rover and Harley Davidson, but he also had a long experience of international business and it was this that senior managers at Manganese Bronze hoped would help them to grow the business.

BACKGROUND

The London taxicab has a long history, with claims that the first cab rank in London was set up in 1634 on the Strand. The term 'taxicab' first appeared in 1907 when cabs had to be fitted with taximeters. It was in this period that the demanding 'conditions of fitness' were introduced which meant that, among other things, taxis had to have a 25 foot turning circle (just under 8 metres). This meant that many potential manufacturers abandoned the market and others were put off entering due to the exacting specifications. For the latter half of the twentieth century the market was dominated by Austin/Carbodies of Coventry and dealers Mann and Overton. The FX4 model that they developed in 1958 is the classic London taxi familiar to most people. Manganese Bronze Holdings plc took over Carbodies in 1973, then, in the 1980s Carbodies bought the rights to the FX4 from Austin and acquired the Mann and Overton dealership to form London Taxi International (LTI).

The FX4 proved to be a very durable product and LTI occupied a dominant position in the UK market, with 85 per cent of the market for much of the twentieth century. However, the lack of a new product did bring in competitors, such as Metro-Cammell-Weymann, whose Metrocab launched in 1987 provided an alternative. However, LTI finally launched a new line of TX models starting with the TX1 in 1997. The new models continued to have the spacious interior and high ceiling (a throwback to when taxi passengers still wore top hats) but was wheelchair accessible with wider opening doors, had better visibility and exceeded safety specifications. In response to the competition, but also their demanding and vocal customers, the London cabbies, LTI continued to develop their product until the launch of the TX4 in 2006. The taxi's engine, made by VM Mototi in Italy, met new European emissions standards and the cabs also had ABS brakes and optional air-conditioning. The same year Metrocab's owners ceased production.

As well as manufacturing the taxis, Manganese Bronze also ran some dealerships and provided finance for customers to help with purchasing their new taxis. While some firms ran fleets of taxis there were many independent cabbies and with the cost of a new taxi often exceeding £35 000, the offer of finance often sealed the deal for sales in the UK.

INTERNATIONAL EXPANSION

By the early years of the twenty-first century, the domestic market for taxis in the UK was fairly static. Manganese Bronze rarely sold more than 2400 vehicles in any given year through LTI. Export sales were even smaller with the typical figure around 100 (see Exhibit 7.1 for full details). However, if the firm was going to expand and survive in an increasingly global market, it needed to sell more taxis to the rest of the world. In 2005 the firm was working to expand into Mexico and China, both emerging markets where it considered demand for the product would be high but with lower production costs. In these markets, the cost of UK-produced taxis was too high for local buyers. The company was looking for partners who they would license to produce the taxis locally and sell internationally, although not in the UK, which would continue to be supplied from the Coventry factory.

The company had also tried to penetrate the North American market through a distributor, London Taxis North America (LTNA). In 2003, the owner Larry Smith had estimated that sales of London Taxis could be around 3000 over the four years to 2007. However, despite the fact that Manganese Bronze's taxis met the exacting UK/EU standards, they still required further changes to conform to local US standards, including being painted yellow if they were used in New York. Despite the initial confidence shown in the product and an early jump in sales in 2004, the venture did not produce the anticipated returns. Manganese Bronze initially took a stake in the distributor in 2004 to provide them with finance and by 2005 had acquired the firm outright along with their advertising sales operation in the USA. Sales fell further partly as a result of the downturn in 2007/8. Manganese Bronze managers hoped that lower cost operations in Mexico or China might export a lower priced vehicle to help them open up the US market, but by August 2009, with average annual losses running at over £1 million, they had closed LTNA.

▶

Although they had been negotiating with a Chinese commercial partner (China National Bluestar Corporation) and the local government in the city of Lanzhou since 2003/4, problems with gaining the required permissions from the Chinese Government had delayed setting up a joint venture. Similarly, in Mexico, although they had signed an agreement in 2004 with a local firm to produce the taxis under licence and distribute them throughout South America, there were delays. The firm wanted to carry out tests to ensure that the taxis could operate effectively in the high-altitude environment of Mexico City and finding a suitable manufacturing site was also proving difficult.

THE NEW PARTNERSHIP

Events took a dramatic turn in 2006 with the signing of an agreement with China's Geely Automotive. The company had only started producing cars in 1997, but had grown to be one of the country's largest automotive manufacturers. Geely floated on the Hong Kong stock exchange in 2005. The agreement led to the setting-up of a joint venture in China during 2007, Shanghai London Taxi International (SLTI), of which Manganese Bronze owned 48 per cent with the rest of the new company's shares in the hands of Geely and its subsidiaries. Initial objectives were to produce 20 000 taxis for sale in China and international markets outside the UK. The two companies had put a project team in place by mid-2007, the factory set-up was completed on time and prototypes of the TX4 modified for the Chinese market were ready by mid-2008.

However, other elements of Manganese Bronze's business were not going so well. 2008 was a difficult year for the company; not only were their sales hit by the economic downturn, but also their new model, the TX4, seemed to be prone to under-bonnet fires that resulted in a general product recall being issued in September 2008. Then there was the competition. Modified Mercedes Vito vans satisfied the conditions of fitness for operation in London and provided the first real competitor to the black cabs since the demise of Metrocab. Apart from the small profit generated by the joint venture in China, the only other ray of sunshine for that year was that the company's parts business did well as a result of many cabbies not replacing their existing vehicles with newer models.

By the middle of 2009 the target for the joint venture had been reduced to sales of 8000 vehicles for China and other overseas markets. Production in Shanghai had started in January 2009 and the new vehicles had generated a lot of interest but relatively few sales. The partners expected to sell 1000 vehicles to international markets in 2010, but problems with arranging finance for international customers reduced this to 226. A breakthrough occurred in March 2011, when SLTI finally secured a large order from Azerbaijan of 1000 taxis. The Baku Taxi company was a state-backed operator in the country's capital and insisted the taxis were supplied, not in their traditional black livery but in a distinctive violet hue. The price per vehicle from SLTI was substantially lower, at £18 000 a-piece, than the Coventry-made taxis. The joint venture also reported firm orders for a further 1250 taxis were placed in 2010/11.

EXHIBIT 7.1 Manganese bronze – sales of taxis 2003–2011

	2003	2004	2005	2006	2007*	2008	2009	2010	2011
UK	2253	2271	2412	2388	4147	1951	1724	1653	1502
International	67	223	109	92	52	173	209	226	705
Total	2320	2494	2521	2480	4199	2124	1933	1879	2207

Note: * 2007 was a 17-month period to bring the firm's accounting dates in line with their new partner's.

EXHIBIT 7.2 Manganese bronze – selected financial figures 2003–2011

£ 000	2003	2004	2005	2006	2007*	2008	2009	2010	2011
Turnover	113 259	86 712	87 598	83 824	144 494	77 242	73 100	69 600	75 000
Operating profit/loss	(3974)	(5025)	2532	3236	5575	(5364)	(7000)	(1900)	(1300)
Net assets	22 558	22 818	19 677	21 477	37 530	26 799	27 600	20 200	16 000

Note: * 2007 was a 17 month period to bring the firm's accounting dates in line with their new partner's.

◀

The partnership with Geely also had a profound effect on Manganese Bronze's UK operations. The firm had made losses for six of the last nine years and as the number of taxis sold in the UK reduced, this put increasing pressure on the viability of the firms UK manufacturing operations. In 2007 the firm employed about 500 people in its various operations. By 2011 this had reduced to 288 as the manufacturing operations at Coventry were scaled back and some work was outsourced to the joint-venture company in China. Some of this activity was to reduce costs, but also because the UK no longer had a wealth of automotive suppliers. In 2010, for example, when the company that painted the primer onto the taxi's body panels ceased production, Manganese Bronze managers decided that there were no viable alternatives and relocated the work to SLTI. This resulted in a further 60 job losses at the Coventry plant

CAR DEALERSHIPS

Geely also faced similar issues to Manganese Bronze, in that most of their sales were domestic and they wanted to expand overseas. In 2009 Geely reported sales of 300 000 vehicles in China, mostly through the 500 car dealerships they owned. The Chinese firm initially planned to focus on Russia and the Ukraine. However, once they acquired Volvo from Ford in 2010

their focus moved more to Europe and as a sign of their deepening relationship with Manganese Bronze they also agreed an exclusive deal for the British company to distribute their Geely-branded cars in the UK from the end of 2012. The firm had substantial experience in this area through their dealership, Mann and Overton, which had taken over all sales activity in the UK after the firms that made up the franchise network for taxi sales were given notice in 2009.

QUESTIONS

1. Why did Manganese Bronze and Geely decide to expand internationally?

2. How well does the BCG Diamond model explain the development of the relationship between Manganese Bronze and Geely?

3. What methods have Manganese Bronze used to enter international markets? Why have some approaches been more successful than others?

4. Apply Porter's Diamond model to the case – what advantages does Manganese Bronze have as a result of being based in the UK?

Sources: BBC News items, *Business Week*; London Vintage Taxi Association website; Company annual reports for 2003–2011; Geely automotive website; Manganese Bronze website.

ASSURANCE OF LEARNING EXERCISES

LO 7.2, LO 7.3, LO 7.4

1. Harley-Davidson has chosen to compete in various country markets in Europe and Asia using an export strategy. Go to the Investor Relations section at www.harley-davidson.com and read the sections of its latest annual report related to its international operations. Why does it seem that the organization has avoided developing production facilities outside the USA?

LO 7.3, LO 7.5

2. The Hero Group is among the 10 largest corporations in India, with 20 business segments and annual revenues of €2.6 billion in fiscal 2006. Many of the corporation's business units have utilized strategic alliances with foreign partners to compete in new product and geographic markets. Review the organization's statements concerning its alliances and international business operations at www.herogroup.com/alliance.htm, and prepare a two-page report that outlines the group's successful use of international strategic alliances.

LO 7.2, LO 7.4, LO 7.5

3. Assume you are in charge of developing the strategy for an international organization selling products in 50 different countries around the world. One of the issues you face is whether to employ a multidomestic strategy, a global strategy or a transnational strategy.

▶

◄

a. If your organization's product is mobile phones, do you think it would make better strategic sense to employ a multidomestic strategy, a global strategy or a transnational strategy? Why?

b. If your organization's product is dry soup mixes and canned soups, would a multidomestic strategy seem to be more advisable than a global strategy? Why?

c. If your organization's product is large home appliances such as washing machines, ranges, ovens and refrigerators, would it seem to make more sense to pursue a multidomestic strategy, a global strategy or a transnational strategy? Why?

d. If your organization's product is apparel and footwear, would a multidomestic strategy, a global strategy or a transnational strategy seem to have more appeal? Why?

EXERCISES FOR SIMULATION PARTICIPANTS

The questions below are for simulation participants whose organizations operate in an international market arena. If your organization competes only in a single country, then skip the questions in this section.

LO 7.2

1. Does your organization compete in a world-market arena characterized by multidomestic competition or global competition? Explain why.

LO 7.3, LO 7.4, LO 7.5

2. Which one of the following best describes the strategic approach your organization is taking in trying to compete successfully on an international basis?

- Think local, act local
- Think global, act local
- Think global, act global

Explain your answer, and indicate two or three main elements of your organization's strategic approach to competing in two or more different geographic regions.

LO 7.2

3. To what extent, if any, have you and your co-managers adapted your organization's strategy to take shifting exchange rates into account? In other words, have you undertaken any actions to try to minimize the impact of adverse shifts in exchange rates?

LO 7.2

4. To what extent, if any, have you and your co-managers adapted your organization's strategy to take geographic differences in import tariffs or import duties into account?

ENDNOTES

1. Winter, Sidney G. and Szulanski, Gabriel (2001), 'Replication as strategy', *Organization Science*, 12(6): 730–43; Winter, Sidney G. and Szulanski, Gabriel (2002) 'Getting it right the second time', *Harvard Business Review*, 80(1): 62–9.

2. Inkpen, A.C. and Dinur, A. (1998) 'Knowledge management processes and international joint ventures', *Organization Science*, 9(4): 454–68; Dussauge, P., Garrette, B. and Mitchell, W. (2000) 'Learning from

competing partners: outcomes and durations of scale and link alliances in Europe, North America and Asia', *Strategic Management Journal*, 21(2): 99–126; Dhanaraj, C., Lyles, M.A., Steensma, H.K. et al., (2004) 'Managing tacit and explicit knowledge transfer in IJVs: the role of relational embeddedness and the impact on performance', *Journal of International Business Studies*, 35(5): 428–42; Glaister, K.W. and Buckley, P.J. (1996) 'Strategic motives for international alliance formation', *Journal of Management Studies*, 33(3): 301–32.

3. Anand, J. and Kogut, B. (1997) 'Technological capabilities of countries, firm rivalry and foreign direct investment', *Journal of International Business Studies*, 28(3): 445–65; Anand, J. and Delios, A. (2002) 'Absolute and relative resources as determinants of international acquisitions', *Strategic Management Journal*, 23(2): 119–35; Seth, A., Song, K. and Pettit, A. (2002) 'Value creation and destruction in cross-border acquisitions: an empirical analysis of foreign acquisitions of U.S. firms', *Strategic Management Journal*, 23(10): 921–40; Anand, J., Capron, L. and Mitchell, W. (2005) 'Using acquisitions to access multinational diversity: thinking beyond the domestic versus cross-border M&A comparison', *Industrial & Corporate Change*, 14(2): 191–224.

4. Porter, M. (1990) 'The competitive advantage of nations', *Harvard Business Review*, March–April, pp. 73–93.

5. U.S. Department of Labor (2009) 'International comparisons of hourly compensation costs in manufacturing in 2007', *Bureau of Labor Statistics Newsletter*, 26 March, p. 8.

6. 'China's middle class found wanting for happiness', *The Independent*, 19 March 2010. Available online at www.independent.co.uk/life-style/house-and-home/chinas-middle-class-foundwanting-for-happiness-1924180.html.

7. 'China Car Sales "Overtook the US" in 2009', BBC News, 11 January 2010, www.news. bbc.co.uk/2/hi/8451887.stm.

8. Yoon, Sangwon (2010) 'South Korea targets Internet addicts; 2 million hooked', *Valley News*, 25 April, p. C2.

9. R.M. Grant, (1991) 'Porter's "competitive advantage of nations": an assessment strategic', *Management Journal*, 12: 535–48.

10. Rugman, A.M. and D'Cruz, J.R. (1993) 'The "Double Diamond" model of international competition: the Canadian experience', *Management International Review*, Vol. 33, Extensions of the Porter Porter Diamond Framework, pp. 17–39.

11. 'Competing for advantage: how to succeed in the new global reality', The Boston Consulting Group, January 2010.

12. Michael E. Porter, (1990) *The Competitive Advantage of Nations*, New York, Free Press, pp. 53–4.

13. Ibid., p. 61.

14. Meyer, K.E., Wright, M. and Pruthi, S. (2009) 'Institutions, resources, and entry strategies in emerging economies', *Strategic Management Journal*, 30(5): 61–80; Pablo, E. (2009) 'Determinants of cross-border M&As in Latin America', *Journal of Business Research*, 62(9): 861–7; Olie, R. (1994) 'Shades of culture and institutions in international mergers', *Organization Studies*, 15(3): 381–406.

15. Meyer et al., 'Institutions, resources, and entry strategies in emerging economies'.

16. See Doz, Yves L. and Hamel, Gary (1998) *Alliance Advantage*, Boston, MA, Harvard Business School Press, especially chs 2–4; Bleeke, Joel and Ernst, David (1991) 'The way to win in cross-border alliances', *Harvard Business Review*, 69(6): 127–33; Hamel, Gary, Doz, Yves L. and Prahalad, C.K. (1999) 'Collaborate with your competitors – and win', *Harvard Business Review*, 67(1): 134–35; Porter, *The Competitive Advantage of Nations*, p. 66.

17. Kumar, N. and Chadha, A. (2009) 'India's outward foreign direct investments in steel industry in a chinese comparative perspective', *Industrial and Corporate Change*, 18(2): 249–67; Chittoor, R., Ray, S., Aulakh, P. and Sarkar, M.B. (2008) 'Strategic responses to institutional changes: "indigenous growth" model of the Indian pharmaceutical industry', *Journal of International Management*, 14: 252–69.

18. Froese, F. and Goeritz, L. (2007) 'Integration management of western acquisitions in Japan', *Asian Business and Management*, 6: 95–114.

19. For a discussion of the pros and cons of alliances versus acquisitions, see Dyer, Jeffrey H., Kale, Prashant and Singh, Harbir (2004) 'When to ally and when to acquire', *Harvard Business Review*, 82(7–8): 109–15.

20. For additional discussion of organization experiences with alliances and partnerships, see Doz and Hamel, *Alliance Advantage*, chs 2–7; and Moss Kanter, Rosabeth (1994) 'Collaborative advantage: the art of the alliance', *Harvard Business Review*, 72(4): 96–108.

21. Main, Jeremy (1990) 'Making global alliances work', *Fortune*, 19 December, p. 125.

22. Details are reported in Tully, Shawn (1996) 'The alliance from hell', *Fortune*, 24 June, pp. 64–72.

23. Prahalad, C.K. and Lieberthal, K. (2003) 'The end of corporate imperialism', *Harvard Business Review*, 81(8): 109–17.

24. Ibid.

25. For an in-depth discussion of the challenges of crafting strategies suitable for a world in which both production and markets are globalizing, see Ghemawat, Pankaj (2007) 'Managing differences: the central challenge of global strategy', *Harvard Business Review*, 85(3): 59–68.

26. For more details on the merits of and opportunities for cross-border transfer of successful strategy experiments, see Bartlett, C.A. and Ghoshal, S. (1998) *Managing Across Borders: The Transnational Solution*, 2nd edn. Boston, MA, Harvard Business School Press, pp. 79–80 and ch. 9. Also see Ghemawat, Pankaj (2007) 'Managing differences: the central challenge of global strategy', *Harvard Business Review*, 85(3): 58–68.

27. Paine, Lynn S. (2010) 'The China rules', *Harvard Business Review*, 88(6): 103–8.

28. Porter, *The Competitive Advantage of Nations*, pp. 53–5.

29. Ibid., pp. 55–8.

30. Inkpen, A., Sundaram, A. and Rockwood, K. (2000) 'Cross-border acquisitions of U.S. technology assets', *California Management Review*, 42(3): 50–71.

31. Porter, *The Competitive Advantage of Nations*, p. 57.

32. Prahalad, C.K. and Doz, Yves L. (1987) *The Multinational Mission*, New York, Free Press, pp. 58–60; Ghemawat, 'Managing differences', pp. 58–68.

33. Canadian International Trade Tribunal, findings issued 16 June 2005, and posted at www.citt-tcce.gc.ca (accessed 28 September 2005).

34. This point is discussed at greater length in Prahalad and Lieberthal, 'The end of corporate imperialism', pp. 68–79; also see Arnold, David J. and Quelch, John A. (1998) 'New strategies in emerging markets', *Sloan Management Review*, 40(1): 7–20. For a more extensive discussion of strategy in emerging markets, see Prahalad, C.K. (2005) *The Fortune at the Bottom of the Pyramid: Eradicating Poverty through Profits*, Upper Saddle River, NJ, Wharton, especially chs 1–3.

35. 'Is a luxury good consumption tax useful?' 18 June 2010. Available online at www.bjreview.com.cn/print/txt/2010-06/18/content_280191.htm; 'GM's first-half China sales surge past the U.S.', *Bloomberg Businessweek*, 2 July 2010. Available online at www.businessweek. com/news/2010-07-02/gm-s-first-half-chinasales-surge-past-the-u-s-.html.

36. Muller, Joanne (2010) 'Can China save GM?' 10 May. Available online at www.forbes.com/forbes/2010/0510/global-2000-10-automobileschina-detroit-whitacre-save-gm.html; 'Is a luxury good consumption Tax Useful?'

37. Prahalad and Lieberthal, 'The end of corporate imperialism', pp. 72–73.

38. Khanna, Tarun, Palepu, Krishna G. and Sinha, Jayant (2005) 'Strategies that fit emerging markets', *Harvard Business Review*, 83(6): 63; Bhattacharya, Arindam K. and Michael, David C. (2008) 'How local organizations keep multinationals at bay', *Harvard Business Review*, 86(3): 94–5.

39. Prahalad and Lieberthal, 'The end of corporate imperialism', p. 72.

40. Khanna, Palepu and Sinha, 'Strategies that fit emerging markets', pp. 73–4.

41. Ibid., p. 74.

42. Ibid., p. 76.

43. The results and conclusions from a study of 134 local organizations in 10 emerging markets are presented in Khanna, Tarun and Palepu, Krishna G. (2006) 'Emerging giants: building world-class organizations in developing countries', *Harvard Business Review*, 84(10): 60–9; also, an examination of strategies used by 50 local organizations in emerging markets is discussed in Bhattacharya, Arindam K. and Michael, David C. 'How local organizations keep multinationals at bay', pp. 85–95.

44. Hamm, Steve (2004) 'Tech's future', *Business-Week*, 27 September, p. 88.

45. Dawar, Niroj and Frost, Tony (1999) 'Competing with giants: survival strategies for local organizations in emerging markets', *Harvard Business Review*, 77(1): 122; see also Guitz Ger, (1999) 'Localizing in the global village: local firms competing in global markets', *California Management Review*, 41(4): 64–84; Khanna and Palepu, 'Emerging giants', pp. 63–6.

46. Kumar, N. (2009) 'How emerging giants are rewriting the rules of M&A', *Harvard Business Review*, May, pp. 115–21.

47. Rui, H. and Yip, G. (2008) 'Foreign acquisitions by Chinese firms: a strategic intent perspective', *Journal of World Business*, 43: 213–26.

48. Dawar and Frost, 'Competing with giants', p. 124.

49. Ibid., p. 126; Khanna and Palepu, 'Emerging giants', pp. 60–9.

50. As outlined by Guillen, M. (2001) 'Is Globalization civilizing, destructive or feeble? A critique of five debates in the social science literature', *Annual Review of Sociology*, 27: 235–60.

51. Hirst, P. and Thompson, G. (1996) *Globalization in Question*, London, Polity.

52. Meyer, J., Boli, J., Thomas, G. and Ramirez, F. (1997) 'World society and the nation state', *American Journal of Sociology*, 103(1): 144–81.

53. Orru, M., Biggart, N. and Hamilton, G. (1997) *The Economic Organization of East Asian Capitalism*, Thousand Oaks, CA, Sage.

54. Strange, S. (1996) *The Retreat of the State: The Diffusion of Power in the World Economy*, New York, Cambridge University Press.

55. Cox, R. (1987) *Production, Power and World Order: Social Forces in the Making of History*, New York, Columbia University Press.

56. Guillen, M. (2001) *The Limits of Convergence: Globalization and Organizational Change in Argentina, South Korea, and Spain*, Princeton, NJ, Princeton University Press.

57. Sklair, L. (1991) *Sociology of the Global System*, New York, Harvester Wheatsheaf.

58. Ingelhart, R. and Baker, W. (2000) Modernization, culture change, and the persistence of traditional values, *American Sociology Review*, 65: 19–51.

Chapter Eight

Corporate strategy

Diversification and the multibusiness organization

Fit between a parent and its businesses is a two-edged sword: A good fit can create value; a bad one can destroy it.

Andrew Campbell
Michael Gould and Marcus Alexander

We are quite pragmatic. If a business does not contribute to our overall vision, it has to go.

Richard Wambold
CEO, Pactiv

Make winners out of every business in your company. Don't carry losers.

Jack Welch
Former CEO, General Electric

I think our biggest achievement to date has been bringing back to life an inherent Disney synergy that enables each part of our business to draw from, build upon, and bolster the others.

Michael Eisner
Former CEO, Walt Disney Organization

Learning Objectives

When you have read this chapter you should be able to:

LO 8.1   Understand when and how business diversification can enhance shareholder value.

LO 8.2   Understand how related diversification strategies can produce cross-business strategic fit capable of delivering competitive advantage.

LO 8.3   Become aware of the merits and risks of corporate strategies based on unrelated diversification.

LO 8.4   Gain command of the analytical tools for evaluating an organization's diversification strategy.

LO 8.5   Understand a diversified organization's four main corporate strategy options for solidifying its diversification strategy and improving performance.

SANOFI

Sanofi SA, formerly Sanofi-Aventis, is a global and diversified healthcare company. The organization discovers, develops and distributes therapeutic solutions focusing on the field of healthcare with six growth platforms: diabetes solutions, human vaccines, innovative drugs, consumer healthcare, emerging markets and animal health. Sanofi has a portfolio of prescription drugs, vaccines, generics and consumer healthcare products. The organization is active in over 100 countries, with 110 000 employees.

As of 31 January 2012, the organization's major shareholder was L'Oreal with a stake of 8.82 per cent.

Formed in 2004 when French pharmaceutical major Sanofi-Synthélabo acquired the Franco-German pharmaceutical group Aventis, as of 2012, it was the world's fourth largest pharmaceutical company going by prescription drugs sales. On 6 May 2011, Sanofi-Aventis simplified its name to **Sanofi**.

In 2008, the pharmaceutical industry in general was in the midst of an unprecedented strategic crisis as innovation (accounting for around 20% of drug companies' annual sales) was no longer creating the expected market impact due to a lack of results. Christopher Viehbacher (Viehbacher), from GlaxoSmithKline, took over as CEO of Sanofi-Aventis when the company was going through this difficult phase. At the same time, a growing number of patents were due to expire, reinforcing competition from generic drugs. At Sanofi-Aventis, key drugs like Plavix were due to go into the public domain by 2013, threatening more than one-third of its revenues. Despite having a costly R&D operation, its new drug pipeline was lacking, with little hope of compensating for the loss of sales. In addition, experts felt that Sanofi-Aventis was being run like France's national treasure, making it incapable of keeping up with the rapid changes in the pharmaceutical industry.

After taking charge, Viehbacher restructured top management and the R&D function to transform Sanofi-Aventis from a Europe/US-centric research-based pharmaceutical company into a global diversified healthcare leader. The new strategy focused on a total restructure of the R&D function and enhanced emphasis on emerging markets and diversification into other healthcare segments (non-prescription drugs segments). While the reorganization involved job losses and a reduction in the number of subsidiaries in Europe, Sanofi-Aventis was still acquiring – focusing on bolt-on acquisitions that created value. In contrast, others in the industry were undertaking mega-mergers, being multi-billion dollar deals between two major pharmaceutical companies aimed at creating a company with more drugs and opportunities to cut costs. Analysts appreciated Viehbacher's strategy and leadership but some felt that he faced some serious challenges going forward. The biggest challenge, according to Viehbacher himself, was how to adapt the Sanofi-Aventis model to suit the rapidly changing pharmaceutical environment and create more sustainable growth.

Sanofi believed that as a result of the changing face of the industry, healthcare needs and scientific discovery they needed to diversify and look outside at partnerships and acquisitions to grow the business. The company strategy was based on the idea that the successful companies of tomorrow would be those that went beyond delivering products to delivering real solutions and services. Sanofi identified growth platforms that they believed would drive the business – emerging markets, diabetes, vaccines, consumer healthcare, innovation products and animal health. As such, they underwent a deep transformation including a complete restructure of R&D, expansion of their footprint in biotechnology through the acquisition of Genzyme and a refocusing of their regional operations.

In the industry in general, analysts see further diversification as promising. Recent trends such as the takeovers of Alcon (ophthalmology) and Ebewe Pharma (generics) by Novartis or Oenobiol in France and Chattem in the USA (nutritional supplements) by Sanofi are seen as reflecting the search for new growth areas in human and animal health, ranging from generics to self-medication products. Several drug companies have started to reduce their investment or workforces in R&D: Pfizer, GlaxoSmithKline, AstraZeneca and Roche announced restructuring plans involving up to several thousand researchers in each case.

Several diversification options exist in the pharmaceutical industry. One is risk management: developing areas of activity that are less subject to regulatory constraints or dependent on R&D productivity, for instance, generics and nutritional supplements/health food. Another focus could be segments related to the pharmaceutical companies' core markets, such as diagnostic products or medical equipment, in the search for a therapeutic solution rather than a single molecule. Or, alternatively, horizontal integration, moving the value chain toward sales or care provision.

With the notable exception of Johnson & Johnson, most pharmaceutical players earn less than one-fifth of their sales from their traditional market of prescription medicines. Roche is the most proactive, with 20% of business in new sectors (mainly diagnostics and personalised medicine), while AstraZeneca is the most reluctant, with just 3%. Between these two extremes, companies such as Sanofi are exploring other paths: vaccines, animal health, self-medication and nutrition. Some major players are continuing to place their bets on concentration as the key to success. Thus, in contrast to Johnson & Johnson that is going for diversification, Merck, Novartis and GlaxoSmithKline seem to want to focus on their core business.

Supporters of diversification argue that it is essential to adapt the pharmaceutical industry's offerings in order to offer health solutions rather than just medicines. Medicines will become commodities, particularly in emerging countries where patients pay for their own treatment. Pharmaceutical companies now have to determine whether diversification really is a suitable long-term path, beyond simply making up for revenue erosion in patent-expired medicines, and if so, what the best diversification path might be.

QUESTIONS

1. Based on the current diversification strategy of Sanofi, what risks can you anticipate for the organization?

2. What might be the reasons for the divergent diversification strategies being pursued in the pharmaceutical industry?

Sources: Sanofi Company available online at www.en.sanofi.com/ (accessed 29 March 2012); Fierce Pharma Newsletter 3 August 2011, 'Sanofis European revamp may kill 700 jobs'. Available online at www.fiercepharma.com (accessed 28 March 2012); InPharm, 25 October 2010, www.inpharm.com (accessed 27 March 2012); FierceBiotech, 'The 25 most influential people in biopharma today'. Available online at www.fiercebiotech.com (accessed 27 March 2012).

In this chapter, we move up one level in the strategy-making hierarchy, from strategy making in a single business enterprise to strategy-making in a diversified enterprise. Because a diversified organization is a collection of individual businesses, the strategy-making task is more complicated. In a one-business organization, managers have to come up with a plan for competing successfully in only a single industry environment – the result is what we labelled in Chapter 2 as *business strategy* (or *business-level strategy*). But in a diversified organization, the strategy-making challenge involves assessing multiple industry environments and developing a *set* of business strategies, one for each industry arena in which the diversified organization operates. And top executives at a diversified organization must still go one step further and devise an organization-wide or *corporate strategy* for improving the attractiveness and performance of the organization's overall business line-up and for making a rational whole out of its diversified collection of individual businesses.

In most diversified companies, corporate-level executives delegate considerable strategy-making authority to the heads of each business, usually giving them the latitude to craft a business strategy suited to their particular industry and competitive circumstances and holding them accountable for producing good results. But the task of crafting a diversified organization's overall or corporate strategy falls squarely in the lap of top-level executives and involves four distinct facets:

1. *Picking new industries to enter and deciding on the mode of entry.* The first concerns in diversifying are what new industries to get into and whether to enter by starting a new business from the ground up, acquiring an organization already in the target industry or forming a joint venture or strategic alliance with another organization.

2. *Pursuing opportunities to leverage cross-business value chain relationships and strategic fit into competitive advantage.* An organization that diversifies into businesses with competitively important value chain match-ups (pertaining to common technology, supply chain logistics, production, distribution channels and/or customers) gains competitive advantage potential not open to an organization that diversifies into businesses whose value chains are totally unrelated and that require totally different resources and capabilities. Capturing this competitive advantage potential requires capitalizing on such cross-business opportunities as transferring skills or technology from one business to another, reducing costs via sharing common facilities and resources, utilizing the organization's well-known brand names and distribution muscle to increase the sales of newly acquired products and encouraging knowledge-sharing and collaborative activity among the businesses.

3. *Establishing investment priorities and steering corporate resources into the most attractive business units.* A diversified organization's different businesses are usually not equally attractive from the standpoint of investing additional funds. It is incumbent on corporate management to (a) decide on the priorities for investing capital in the organization's different businesses, (b) channel resources into areas where earnings potentials are higher and away from areas where they are lower, and (c) divest business units that are chronically poor performers or are in an increasingly unattractive industry. Divesting poor performers and businesses in unattractive industries frees up unproductive investments either for redeployment to promising business units or for financing attractive new acquisitions.

4. *Initiating actions to boost the combined performance of the corporation's collection of businesses.* Corporate strategists must craft moves to improve the overall performance of the corporation's business line-up and sustain increases in shareholder value. Strategic options for diversified corporations include (a) sticking closely with

the existing business line-up and pursuing opportunities presented by these businesses, (b) broadening the scope of diversification by entering additional industries, (c) divesting some businesses and retrenching to a narrower collection of diversified businesses with better overall performance prospects, and (d) restructuring the entire organization by divesting some businesses and acquiring others so as to put a whole new face on the organization's business line-up.

The demanding and time-consuming nature of these four tasks explains why corporate executives generally refrain from becoming immersed in the details of crafting and executing business-level strategies, preferring instead to delegate lead responsibility for business strategy and business-level operations to the heads of each business unit.

In the first part of this chapter we describe the various means an organization can use to become diversified, and we explore the pros and cons of related versus unrelated diversification strategies. The second part of the chapter looks at how to evaluate the attractiveness of a diversified organization's business line-up, decide whether the organization has a good diversification strategy and identify ways to improve its future performance. In the chapter's concluding section, we survey the strategic options open to already diversified companies.

When to Diversify

As long as an organization has its hands full trying to capitalize on profitable growth opportunities in its present industry, there is no urgency to pursue diversification. But the opportunities for profitable growth are often limited in mature industries and declining markets. An organization may also encounter diminishing market opportunities and stagnating sales if its industry becomes competitively unattractive and unprofitable. An organization's growth prospects may reduce quickly if demand for the industry's product is eroded by the appearance of alternative technologies, substitute products or fast-shifting buyer preferences. Consider, for example, how digital cameras have virtually destroyed the business of companies dependent on making camera film and doing film processing, how iPods and other brands of digital music players (as well as online music stores) have affected the revenues of retailers of music CDs and how the mushrooming use of mobile phones and Internet-based voice communication have diminished demand for landline-based telecommunication services and eroded the revenues of such once-dominant long-distance providers as AT&T, British Telecommunications and NTT in Japan. Under conditions such as these, diversification into new industries always merits strong consideration, particularly if the resources and capabilities of an organization can be employed more fruitfully in other industries.[1]

An organization becomes a prime candidate for diversifying under the following four circumstances:[2]

1. When it spots opportunities for expanding into industries whose technologies and products complement its present business.
2. When it can leverage its collection of resources and capabilities by expanding into businesses where these resources and capabilities are valuable competitive assets.
3. When diversifying into additional businesses opens new avenues for reducing costs via cross-business-sharing or transfer of competitively valuable resources and capabilities.
4. When it has a powerful and well-known brand name that can be transferred to the products of other businesses and thereby used as a lever for driving up the sales and profits of such businesses.

CURRENT PRACTICE 8.1

While stemming from the 1950s, the Ansoff Matrix still frames management thinking and helps practitioners when determining corporate growth strategies. By considering ways to grow via existing products and new products, and in existing markets and new markets there are four possible combinations, of which diversification is just one.

	Existing products	**New products**
Existing markets	Market penetration	Product development
New markets	Market development	Diversification

Known as *growth vector analysis* the generic strategic options are:

- *Market penetration.* Growth through increasing market share in current market segments
- *Market development.* Targeting existing products and offerings to new market segments, either a new geography or a different customer set.
- *Product development.* Developing and providing new products or services to the existing market segment. These can be additional to the current range, or replacement products and service to replenish outdated offerings
- *Diversification.* Growth through developing new businesses for new markets. Within the diversification category we can classify the options as simply 'related' or 'unrelated' diversification; alternatively, we can talk about Horizontal, Vertical or Conglomerate diversification. Horizontal diversification is the development of activities that are complementary to the firm's current activities; Vertical integration is the development of activities that involve the preceding or succeeding stages in the organization's value chain; Conglomerate diversification is another name for unrelated diversification.

Source: Ansoff, I. (1957) 'Strategies for diversification', *Harvard Business Review*, 35(5): 113–24.

Building Shareholder Value: a Primary Justification for Diversifying

Generally, diversification must do more for an organization than simply spread its business risk across various industries. In principle, diversification cannot be considered a success unless it results in *added long-term economic value for shareholders* – value that shareholders cannot capture on their own by purchasing shares in companies in different industries or investing in mutual funds so as to spread their investments across several industries.

For there to be reasonable expectations of producing added long-term shareholder value, a move to diversify into a new business must pass three tests:[3]

1. *The industry attractiveness test.* The industry to be entered must be attractive enough to yield consistently good returns on investment. Whether an industry is attractive depends mainly on the presence of industry and competitive conditions that are conducive to earning as good or better profits and return on investment than the organization is earning in its present business(es). It is hard to justify diversifying into an industry where profit expectations are *lower* than those in the organization's present businesses.

2. *The cost-of-entry test.* The cost of entering the target industry must not be so high as to erode the potential for good profitability. Industry attractiveness is not a sufficient reason for a firm to diversify into an industry. In fact, the more attractive an industry's prospects are for growth and long-term profitability, the more expensive the industry can be to get into. Entry barriers for start-up companies are likely to be high in attractive industries; were barriers low, a rush of new entrants would soon erode the potential for high profitability. And buying a well-positioned organization in an appealing industry often entails a high acquisition cost that makes passing the cost-of-entry test less likely. Since the owners of a successful and growing organization

LO 8.1
Understand when and how business diversification can enhance shareholder value.

usually demand a price that reflects their business's profit prospects, it is easy for such an acquisition to fail the cost-of-entry test.

3. *The better-off test.* Diversifying into a new business must offer potential for the organization's existing businesses and the new business to perform better together under a single corporate umbrella than they would perform operating as independent, stand-alone businesses – an effect known as synergy. For example, let us say that organization A diversifies by purchasing organization B in another industry. If A and B's consolidated profits in the years to come prove no greater than what each could have earned on its own, then A's diversification will not provide its shareholders with added value. Organization A's shareholders could have achieved the same 1 + 1 = 2 result by merely purchasing shares in organization B. Diversification does not result in added long-term value for shareholders unless it produces a 1 + 1 = 3 effect where the businesses *perform better together* as part of the same firm than they could have performed as independent organizations.

> **Core Concept**
>
> Creating added value for shareholders via diversification requires building a multibusiness organization where the whole is greater than the sum of its parts – an outcome known as synergy.

Diversification moves should generally satisfy all three tests to grow shareholder value over the long term. Diversification moves that can pass only one or two tests would need to be justified on other grounds.

Strategies for Entering New Businesses

The means of entering new businesses can take any of three forms: acquisition, internal start-up or joint ventures with other companies.

Acquisition of an Existing Business

Acquisition is a popular means of diversifying into another industry. Not only is it quicker than trying to launch a brand new operation, but it also offers an effective way to hurdle such entry barriers as acquiring technological know-how, establishing supplier relationships, becoming big enough to match rivals' unit costs, having to spend large sums on introductory advertising and promotions and securing adequate distribution. Acquisitions are also commonly employed to access resources and capabilities that are complementary to those of the acquiring firm and that cannot be developed readily internally. Buying an ongoing operation allows the acquirer to move directly to the task of building a strong market position in the target industry, rather than getting slowed down in trying to develop the knowledge, experience, scale of operation and market reputation necessary for a start-up entrant to become an effective competitor.

> **Core Concept**
>
> An acquisition premium is the amount by which the price offered exceeds the pre-acquisition market value of the target organization.

However, acquiring an existing business can prove quite expensive. The costs of acquiring another business include not only the acquisition price but also the costs of negotiating and completing the purchase transaction and the costs of integrating the business into the diversified organization's portfolio. If the organization to be acquired is a successful organization, the acquisition price will include a substantial *premium* over the pre-acquisition value of the organization. For example, the €4.4 billion that Xerox paid to acquire Affiliated Computer Services in 2010 included a 38 per cent premium over the service organization's market value.[4] Premiums are paid in order to convince the shareholders and managers of the target organization that it is in their financial interests to approve the deal. The average premium in deals between US companies rose to 56 per cent in 2009, but it is more often in the 30–40 per cent range.[5]

The big dilemma an acquisition-minded firm faces is whether to pay a premium price for a successful organization or to buy a struggling organization at a bargain price.[6] If the buying firm has little knowledge of the industry but ample capital, it is often better off purchasing a capable, strongly positioned firm – even if its current owners demand a premium price. However, when the acquirer sees promising ways to transform a weak firm into a strong one and has the resources, the know-how and the patience to do it, a struggling organization can be the better long-term investment.

While acquisitions offer an enticing means for entering a new business, many fail to deliver on their promise.[7] Realizing the potential gains from an acquisition requires a successful integration of the acquired organization into the culture, systems and structure of the acquiring firm. This can be a costly and time-consuming operation. Acquisitions can also fail to deliver long-term shareholder value if the acquirer overestimates the potential gains and pays a premium in excess of the realized gains. High integration costs and excessive price premiums are two reasons that an acquisition might fail the cost-of-entry test. Firms with significant experience in making acquisitions are better able to avoid these types of problems.[8]

Internal Development

Internal development of new businesses has become an increasingly important means for companies to diversify and is often referred to as **corporate venturing** or *new venture development*. It involves building a new business from scratch. Although building a new business from the ground up is generally a time-consuming and uncertain process, it avoids the pitfalls associated with entry via acquisition and may allow the firm to realize greater profits in the end. It may offer a viable means of entering a new or emerging industry where there are no good acquisition candidates.

Entering a new business via internal development also poses some significant hurdles. An internal new venture not only has to overcome industry entry barriers but also has to invest in new production capacity, develop sources of supply, hire and train employees, build channels of distribution, grow a customer base and so on. The risks associated with internal start-ups are substantial, and the likelihood of failure is high. Moreover, the culture, structures and organizational systems of some companies may impede innovation and make it difficult for corporate entrepreneurship to flourish.

Generally, internal development of a new business has appeal only when: (1) the parent organization already has in-house most or all of the skills and resources it needs to piece together a new business and compete effectively; (2) there is ample time to launch the business; (3) the internal cost of entry is lower than the cost of entry via acquisition; (4) the targeted industry is populated with many relatively small firms such that the new start-up does not have to compete head to head against larger, more powerful rivals; (5) adding new production capacity will not adversely impact the supply-demand balance in the industry; and (6) incumbent firms are likely to be slow or ineffective in responding to a new entrant's efforts to compete in the market.[9]

Joint Ventures

Joint ventures entail forming a new business that is owned jointly by two or more organizations. Entering a new business via joint venture can be useful in at least three types of situations.[10] First, a joint venture is a good vehicle for pursuing an opportunity that is too complex, uneconomical or risky for one organization to pursue alone. Second, joint ventures make sense when the opportunities in a new industry require a broader range of competences and know-how than an organization can assemble. Many of the opportunities in satellite-based telecommunications, biotechnology and network-based systems that blend hardware, software and services call for the co-ordinated development of complementary innovations and the tackling of an intricate web of financial, technical, political and regulatory factors simultaneously. In such cases, pooling the resources and competences of two or more organizations is a wiser and less risky way to proceed. Third, organizations sometimes use joint ventures to diversify into a new industry when the diversification move entails having operations in a foreign country – several governments require foreign companies operating

> **Core Concept**
>
> **Corporate venturing** (or *new venture development*) is the process of developing new businesses as an outgrowth of an organization's established business operations. It is also referred to as *corporate entrepreneurship* or *intrapreneurship* since it requires entrepreneurial-like qualities within a larger enterprise.

within their borders to have a local partner that has minority, if not majority, ownership in the local operations. Aside from fulfilling host-government ownership requirements, companies usually seek out a local partner with expertise and other resources that will aid the success of the newly established local operation.

However, as discussed in Chapters 6 and 7, partnering with another organization – in the form of either a joint venture or a collaborative alliance – has significant drawbacks due to the potential for conflicting objectives, disagreements over how to best operate the venture, culture clashes and so on. Joint ventures are generally the least durable of the entry options, usually lasting only until the partners decide to go their own ways.

Choosing a Mode of Entry

The choice of how best to enter a new business – whether through internal development, acquisition or joint venture – depends on the answers to four important questions:

1. Does the organization have all of the resources and capabilities it requires to enter the business through internal development or is it lacking some critical resources?
2. Are there entry barriers to overcome?
3. Is speed an important factor in the firm's chances for successful entry?
4. Which is the least costly mode of entry, given the organization's objectives?

The Question of Critical Resources and Capabilities

If a firm has all the resources it needs to start up a new business or will be able to easily purchase or lease any missing resources, it may choose to enter the business via internal development. However, if missing critical resources cannot be easily purchased or leased, a firm wishing to enter a new business must obtain these missing resources through either acquisition or joint venture. Royal Ahold N.V. a Dutch grocery chain conglomerate purchased Bol.com, another Dutch online mass merchant in 2012, to obtain critical resources in online retailing. The acquisition of these additional capabilities complemented Royal Ahold's existing strengths and enabled them to not only reach a diverse new set of European web shoppers but also to expand to non-food categories. Firms often acquire other companies as a way to enter foreign markets where they lack local marketing knowledge, distribution capabilities and relationships with local suppliers or customers. McDonald's acquisition of Burghy, Italy's only national hamburger chain, offers an example.[11] If there are no good acquisition opportunities or if the firm wants to avoid the high cost of acquiring and integrating another firm, it may choose to enter via joint venture. This type of entry mode has the added advantage of spreading the risk of entering a new business, which is particularly attractive when uncertainty is high. DeBeers's joint venture with the luxury goods organization LVMH provided DeBeers with the complementary marketing capabilities it needed to enter the diamond retailing business, as well as partner to share the risk.

The Question of Entry Barriers

The second question to ask is whether entry barriers would prevent a new entrant from gaining a foothold and succeeding in the industry. If entry barriers are low and the industry is populated with small firms, internal development may be the preferred mode of entry. If entry barriers are high, the organization may still be able to enter with ease if it has the requisite resources and capabilities for overcoming high barriers. For example, entry barriers due to reputational advantages may be surmounted by a diversified organization with a widely known and trusted corporate name. But if the entry barriers cannot be overcome readily, then the only feasible entry route may be through acquisition of a well-established organization. While entry barriers may also be overcome with a strong complementary joint venture, this mode is the more uncertain choice due to the lack of industry experience.

The Question of Speed

Speed is another determining factor in deciding how to go about entering a new business. Acquisition is a favoured mode of entry when speed is of the essence, as is the case in rapidly changing industries where fast movers can secure long-term positioning advantages. Speed is important in industries where early movers gain experience-based advantages that grow ever larger over time as they move down the learning curve and in technology-based industries where there is a race to establish an industry standard or leading technological platform. But in other cases it can be better to enter a market after the uncertainties about technology or consumer preferences have been resolved and learn from the mis-steps of early entrants. In these cases, joint venture or internal development may be preferred.

The Question of Comparative Cost

The question of which mode of entry is most cost-effective is a critical one, given the need for a diversification strategy to pass the cost-of-entry test. Acquisition can be a high-cost mode of entry due to the need to pay a premium over the share price of the target organization. When the premium is high, the price of the deal will exceed the worth of the acquired organization as a stand-alone business by a substantial amount. Moreover, the true cost of an acquisition must include the transaction costs of identifying and evaluating potential targets, negotiating a price and completing other aspects of deal-making. In addition, the true cost must take into account the costs of integrating the acquired organization into the parent organization's portfolio of businesses.

Strategic alliances and other types of partnerships may provide a way to conserve on such entry costs. But even here, there are organizational co-ordination costs and transaction costs that must be considered, including settling on the terms of the arrangement. If the partnership does not proceed smoothly and is not founded on trust, these costs may be significant. In making the choice about how to proceed, the firm should also consider the possibility of even simpler arrangements. If the objective is simply to leverage a brand name and organization logo, for example, a strategic alliance centred on licensing may be the lowest-cost alternative. Licensing is particularly attractive if the organization lacks other resources and capabilities that are needed for an entry move. Harley-Davidson, for example, has chosen to license its brand name to makers of apparel as an alternative to entering the apparel industry, for which it is not well suited.

Choosing the Diversification Path: Related Versus Unrelated Businesses

Once an organization decides to diversify, it faces the choice of whether to diversify into related businesses, unrelated businesses or some mix of both. Businesses are said to be *related* when their value chains exhibit competitively important cross-business relationships. By this, we mean that there is a close correspondence between the businesses in terms of how they perform *key* value chain activities and the resources and capabilities each needs to perform those activities. The big appeal of related diversification is to build shareholder value by leveraging these cross-business relationships into competitive advantages, thus allowing the organization as a whole to perform better than just the sum of its individual businesses. Businesses are said to be *unrelated* when the resource requirements and key value chain activities are so dissimilar that no competitively important cross-business relationships exist.

The next two sections explore the ins and outs of related and unrelated diversification.

> **Core Concept**
>
> **Transaction costs** are the costs of completing a business agreement or deal of some sort, over and above the price of the deal. They can include the costs of searching for an attractive target, the costs of evaluating its worth, bargaining costs and the costs of completing the transaction.

> **Core Concepts**
>
> **Related businesses** possess competitively valuable cross-business value chain and resource match-ups; **unrelated businesses** have dissimilar value chains and resource requirements, with no competitively important cross-business relationships at the value chain level.

> **LO 8.2**
> Understand of how related diversification strategies can produce cross-business strategic fit capable of delivering competitive advantage.

Strategic Fit and Diversification into Related Businesses

Core Concept

Strategic fit exists when the value chains of different businesses present opportunities for cross-business resource transfer, lower costs through combining the performance of related value chain activities or resource-sharing, cross-business use of a potent brand name and cross-business collaboration to build stronger competitive capabilities.

A related diversification strategy involves building the organization around businesses where there is *strategic fit with respect to key value chain activities and competitive assets*. **Strategic fit** exists whenever one or more activities constituting the value chains of different businesses are sufficiently similar as to present opportunities for cross-business-sharing or transferring of the resources and capabilities that enable these activities.[12] Prime examples of such opportunities include:

- *Transferring specialized expertise, technological know-how or other competitively valuable capabilities from one business's value chain to another's.*

- *Combining the related value chain activities of separate businesses into a single operation to achieve lower costs.* For instance, it is often feasible to manufacture the products of different businesses in a single plant, use the same warehouses for shipping and distribution or have a single salesforce for the products of different businesses (because they are marketed to the same types of customers).

- *Exploiting common use of a well-known brand name that connotes excellence in a certain type of product range.* For example, Yamaha's name in motorcycles gave the organization instant credibility and recognition in entering the personal-water-craft business, allowing it to achieve a significant market share without spending large sums on advertising to establish a brand identity for the WaveRunner. Sony's name in consumer electronics made it easier for Sony to enter the market for video games with its PlayStation console and line-up of PlayStation video games. Apple's well-known and highly popular iPods gave the firm instant credibility and name recognition in launching its iPhones and iPads.

- *Sharing other resources that support corresponding value chain activities of the businesses, such as relationships with suppliers or a dealer network.* After acquiring Marvel Comics in 2009, the Walt Disney Company saw to it that Marvel's iconic characters, such as Spiderman, Iron Man and the Black Widow, were shared with many of the other Disney businesses, including its theme parks, retail stores and video game business. (Disney's characters, starting with Mickey Mouse, have always been among the most valuable of its resources.)

- *Engaging in cross-business collaboration and knowledge-sharing to create new competitively valuable resources and capabilities.*

Core Concepts

Related diversification involves sharing or transferring *specialized* resources and capabilities.

Specialized resources and capabilities have very specific applications and their use is limited to a restricted range of industry and business types, in contrast to **generalized resources and capabilities** that can be widely applied and can be deployed across a broad range of industry and business types.

Related diversification is based on value chain match-ups with respect to *key* value chain activities – those that play a central role in each business's strategy and that link to its industry's key success factors. Such match-ups facilitate the sharing or transfer of the competitively important resources and capabilities that enable the performance of these activities and underlie each business's quest for competitive advantage. By facilitating the sharing or transferring of such important competitive assets, related diversification can boost each business's prospects for competitive success.

The resources and capabilities that are leveraged in related diversification are **specialized resources and capabilities**. By this, we mean that they have very *specific* applications; their use is restricted to a limited range of business contexts in which these applications are competitively relevant. Because they are adapted for particular applications, specialized resources and capabilities must be utilized by certain kinds of businesses operating in specific types of industries to have value; they have limited utility outside this specific range of industry and business applications. This is in contrast to **generalized resources and capabilities** (such as general management capabilities, human resource management capabilities and general accounting services), which can be applied usefully across a wide range of industry and business types.

L'Oréal is the world's largest beauty products' organization, with more than €20 billion in revenues and a successful strategy of related diversification built upon leveraging a highly specialized set of resources and capabilities. These include 18 dermatologic and cosmetic research centres, R&D capabilities and scientific knowledge concerning skin and hair care, patents and secret formulas for hair and skin care products and robotic applications developed specifically for testing the safety of hair and skin care products. These resources and capabilities are highly valuable for businesses focused on products for human skin and hair – they are *specialized* to such applications and, in consequence, they are of little or no value beyond this restricted range of applications. To leverage these resources in a way that maximizes their potential value, L'Oréal has diversified into cosmetics, hair care products, skin care products and fragrances (but not food, transportation, industrial services or any application area far from the narrow domain in which its specialized resources are competitively relevant). L'Oréal's businesses are related to one another on the basis of its value-generating specialized resources and capabilities and the cross-business linkages among the value chain activities that they enable.

Corning's most competitively valuable resources and capabilities are specialized to applications concerning fibre optics and specialty glass and ceramics. Over the course of its 150-year history, it has developed an unmatched understanding of fundamental glass science and related technologies in the field of optics. Its capabilities now span a variety of sophisticated technologies and include expertise in domains such as custom glass composition, specialty glass melting and forming, precision optics, high-end transmissive coatings and opto-mechanical materials. Corning has leveraged these specialized capabilities into a position of global leadership in five related market segments: display technologies based on glass substrates, environmental technologies using ceramic substrates and filters, optical fibres and cables for telecommunications, optical biosensors for drug discovery and specialty materials employing advanced optics and specialty glass solutions. The market segments into which Corning has diversified are all related by their reliance on Corning's specialized capability set and by the many value chain activities that they have in common as a result.

US-based General Mills has diversified into a closely related set of food businesses on the basis of its capabilities in the realm of 'kitchen chemistry' and food production technologies. Its businesses include General Mills cereals, Pillsbury and Betty Crocker baking products, yoghurts, organic foods, dinner mixes, canned goods and snacks. Earlier it had diversified into restaurant businesses on the mistaken notion that all food businesses were related. As a result of exiting these businesses in the mid-1990s, the organization was able to improve its overall profitability and strengthen its position in its remaining businesses. The lesson from its experience – and a takeaway for the managers of any diversified organization – is that it is not product relatedness that defines a well-crafted related diversification strategy. Rather, the businesses must be related in terms of their key value chain activities and the specialized resources and capabilities that enable these activities.[13] An example is Citizen Holdings Company, whose products appear to be different (watches, miniature card calculators, hand-held televisions) but are related in terms of their common reliance on miniaturization know-how and advanced precision technologies.[14]

While organizations pursuing related diversification strategies may also have opportunities to share or transfer their *generalized* resources and capabilities (e.g. information systems; human resource management practices; accounting and tax services; budgeting, planning and financial reporting systems; expertise in legal and regulatory affairs; and fringe-benefit management systems), the most competitively valuable opportunities for resource-sharing or transfer always come from leveraging their specialized resources and capabilities. The reason for this is that specialized resources and capabilities drive the key value-creating activities that both connect the businesses (at points where there is strategic fit) and link to the key success factors in the markets

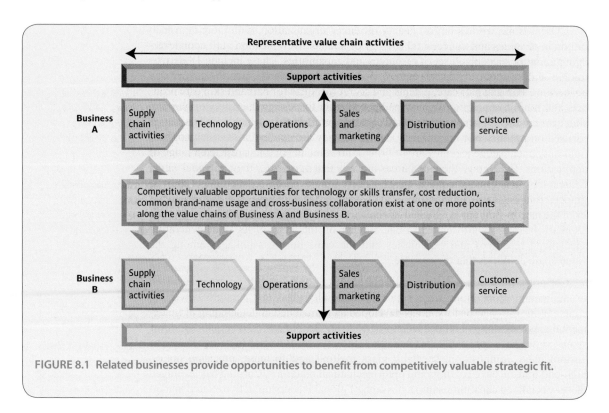

FIGURE 8.1 Related businesses provide opportunities to benefit from competitively valuable strategic fit.

where they are competitively relevant. Figure 8.1 illustrates the range of opportunities to share and/or transfer specialized resources and capabilities among the value chain activities of related businesses. It is important to recognize that even though generalized resources and capabilities may be shared by multiple business units, such resource-sharing alone cannot form the backbone of a strategy based in related diversification.

Identifying Cross-business Strategic Fit along the Value Chain

Cross-business strategic fit can exist anywhere along the value chain – in R&D and technology activities, in supply chain activities and relationships with suppliers, in manufacturing, in sales and marketing, in distribution activities or in customer service activities.[15]

Strategic Fit in Supply Chain Activities

Businesses that have strategic fit with respect to supply chain activities can perform better together because of the potential for skills transfer in procuring materials, the sharing of capabilities in logistics, the benefits of added collaboration with common supply chain partners and/or added leverage with shippers in securing volume discounts on incoming parts and components. Dell Computer's strategic partnerships with leading suppliers of microprocessors, circuit boards, disk drives, memory chips, flat-panel displays, wireless capabilities, long-life batteries and other PC-related components have been an important element of the organization's strategy to diversify into servers, data storage devices, networking components and LCD TVs – products that include many components common to PCs and that can be sourced from the same strategic partners that provide Dell with PC components.

A DIFFERENT VIEW

RELATED DIVERSIFICATION AS A PURSUIT OF MARKET ADJACENCIES

Research at Bain & Company on incidences of sustained, profitable growth found that most growth strategies fail to deliver value, or even destroy it, primarily because they wrongly diversify from the core business. The findings from following over 2000 companies that were focusing on organizational strengths, or in other words the core business, yields higher long-term growth and profit returns. The foundation of profitable growth is therefore proposed as having a clear definition of the organization's core business, being the set of products, capabilities, customers, channels and geographies that defines the essence of what the organization is or aspires to be. With a clear core business, growth opportunities stem from knowledge and understanding of market adjacencies.

Adjacency expansion is an organization's continual moves into logically related segments or businesses that utilize and usually reinforce the strength of the profitable core. It is argued that over time, these sequenced moves can fundamentally redefine the core business by adding new capabilities as well as provide growth in themselves. This view proposes that it is through adjacency expansion that an organization in a stable industry repositions itself to pursue the most attractive opportunities or responds to a changed business environment. Market adjacencies allow an organization to extend the boundaries of its core business. What distinguishes an adjacency from other growth opportunities is the extent to which it draws on customer relationships, technologies or skills in the core business to build competitive advantage in a new, adjacent competitive arena.

The most common identified adjacencies in a core business are:

1. *Interlocking customer and product adjacencies*: Expanding into new customer and product segments
2. *Share-of-wallet adjacencies*: Capturing most of the purchases core customers make can increase loyalty and establish deeper customer relationships.
3. *Capability adjacencies*: Based on deep organizational know-how these can take three forms: technological, business and management processes and knowledge on how to store, manage and obtain value from information.
4. *Network adjacencies*: Adding network connections in a network-dependent business can increase the value of the network to all other users, generating increasing returns to scale.
5. *New-to-the-world adjacencies*: As industry structures become less stable, adjacency expansions into the new uninhabited space can be necessary for future market positions.

Sources: Zook, C. and Allen, J. (2010) *Profit from the Core: a Return to Growth in Turbulent Times*, Cambridge, MA, Harvard Business Press; Zook, C. (2007) 'Finding your next CORE business', *Harvard Business Review*, 85(4).

Strategic Fit in R&D and Technology Activities

Businesses with technology-sharing benefits can perform better together than apart because of potential cost savings in R&D, potentially shorter times in getting new products to market and more innovative products or processes. Moreover, technological advances in one business can lead to increased sales for both. Technological innovations have been the driver behind the efforts of cable TV companies to diversify into high-speed Internet access (via the use of cable modems) and, further, to explore providing local and long-distance telephone service to residential and commercial customers either through a single wire or by means of VoIP (voice over Internet protocol) technology.

Manufacturing-related Strategic Fit

Cross-business strategic fit in manufacturing-related activities can represent an important source of competitive advantage in situations where a diversifier's expertise in quality manufacture and cost-efficient production methods can be transferred to another business. When Emerson Electric diversified into the chain-saw business, it transferred its expertise in low-cost manufacture to its newly acquired Beaird-Poulan business division; the transfer drove Beaird-Poulan's new strategy – to be the low-cost provider of chainsaw products – and fundamentally changed the way Beaird-Poulan chain saws were designed and manufactured. Another benefit of production-related value chain match-ups is the ability to consolidate production into a smaller number of plants and significantly reduce overall production costs. When snowmobile maker Bombardier diversified into motorcycles, it was able to set up motorcycle assembly lines in the same manufacturing facility where it was assembling snowmobiles.

Strategic Fit in Sales and Marketing Activities

Various cost-saving opportunities spring from diversifying into businesses with closely related sales and marketing activities. When the products are sold directly to the same customers, sales costs can often be reduced by using a single salesforce and avoiding having two different salespeople call on the same customer. The products of related businesses can be promoted at the same website and included in the same media ads and sales brochures. After-sale service and repair organizations for the products of closely related businesses can often be consolidated into a single operation. There may be opportunities to reduce costs by consolidating order processing and invoicing and using common promotions. When global power-tool maker Black & Decker acquired Vector Products, it was able to use its own global sales force and distribution facilities to sell and distribute the newly acquired Vector power inverters, vehicle battery chargers and rechargeable spotlights because the types of customers that carried its power tools (discounters, home centres and hardware stores) also stocked the types of products produced by Vector.

A second category of benefits arises when different businesses use similar sales and marketing approaches; in such cases, there may be competitively valuable opportunities to transfer selling, merchandising, advertising and product differentiation skills from one business to another. Procter & Gamble's product line-up includes Folgers coffee, Tide laundry detergent, Crest toothpaste, Ivory soap, Charmin toilet tissue, Gillette razors and blades, Duracell batteries, Oral-B toothbrushes and Head & Shoulders shampoo. All of these have different competitors and different supply chain and production requirements, but they all move through the same wholesale distribution systems, are sold in common retail settings to the same shoppers, are advertised and promoted in much the same ways and require the same marketing and merchandising skills.

Distribution-related Strategic Fit

Businesses with closely related distribution activities can perform better together than apart because of potential cost savings in sharing the same distribution facilities or using many of the same wholesale distributors and retail dealers to access customers. When Conair Corporation acquired Allegro Manufacturing's travel bag and travel accessory business in 2007, it was able to consolidate its own distribution centres for hair dryers and curling irons with those of Allegro, thereby generating cost savings for both businesses. Likewise, since Conair products and Allegro's neck rests, ear plugs, luggage tags and toiletry kits were sold by the same types of retailers (discount stores, supermarket chains and pharmacies) Conair was able to convince many of the retailers not carrying Allegro products to take on the line.

Strategic Fit in Customer Service Activities

Opportunities for cost savings from sharing resources or for greater differentiation through skills transfer can come from strategic fit with respect to customer service activities, just as they do along other points of the value chain. For example, cost savings may come from consolidating after-sales service and repair organizations for the products of closely related businesses into a single operation. Likewise, different businesses can often use the same customer service infrastructure. For instance, an electric utility that diversifies into natural gas, water, appliance sales and repair services and home security services can use the same customer data network, the same customer call centres and local offices, the same invoicing and customer accounting systems and the same customer service infrastructure to support all of its products and services. Through the transfer of best practices in customer service across a set of related businesses or through sharing resources such as proprietary information about customer preferences, a multibusiness organization can create a differentiation advantage through higher-quality customer service.

Strategic Fit, Economies of Scope and Competitive Advantage

What makes related diversification an attractive strategy is the opportunity to convert cross-business strategic fit into a competitive advantage over business rivals whose operations do not offer comparable strategic-fit benefits. The greater the relatedness among a diversified organization's businesses, the bigger an organization's window for converting strategic fit into competitive advantage via (1) transferring skills or knowledge, (2) combining related value chain activities to achieve lower costs, (3) leveraging the use of a well-respected brand name or other differentiation-enhancing resources, and (4) using cross-business collaboration and knowledge sharing to create new resources and capabilities and drive innovation.

The Path to Competitive Advantage and Economies of Scope

Sharing or transferring valuable specialized assets among the organization's businesses can help each business perform its value chain activities more proficiently. This translates into competitive advantage for the businesses in one or two basic ways: (1) the businesses can contribute to greater efficiency and lower costs relative to their competitors; and/or (2) they can provide a basis for differentiation so that customers are willing to pay relatively more for the businesses' goods and services. In either or both of these ways, a firm with a well-executed related diversification strategy can improve the chances of its businesses attaining a competitive advantage.

Related businesses often present opportunities to eliminate or reduce the costs of performing certain value chain activities; such cost savings are termed **economies of scope** – a concept distinct from *economies of scale*. Economies of *scale* are cost savings that accrue directly from a larger-size operation; for example, unit costs may be lower in a large plant than in a small plant, lower in a large distribution centre than in a small one and lower for large-volume purchases of network advertising than for small-volume purchases. Economies of *scope,* however, stem directly from resource-sharing, facilitated by strategic fit along the value chains of related businesses. Such economies are open only to a multibusiness enterprise that enables its businesses to share technology, perform R&D together, use common manufacturing or distribution facilities, share a common salesforce or distributor-dealer network, use the same established brand name and/or share other commonly employed resources and capabilities. *The greater the cross-business economies associated with resource-sharing and strategic fit, the greater the potential for a related diversification strategy to yield a competitive advantage based on lower costs than those of rivals.*

> **Core Concept**
>
> **Economies of scope** are cost reductions that flow from operating in multiple businesses (a *larger scope* of operation), whereas *economies of scale* accrue from a *larger-size* operation.

From Competitive Advantage to Added Profitability and Gains in Shareholder Value

The competitive advantage potential that flows from economies of scope and the capture of other strategic-fit benefits is what enables an organization pursuing related

Diversifying into related businesses where competitively valuable strategic-fit benefits can be captured puts an organization's businesses in the position to perform better financially as part of the organization than they could have performed as independent enterprises, thus providing a clear avenue for improving shareholder value.

diversification to achieve $1 + 1 = 3$ financial performance and the hoped-for gains in shareholder value. The strategic and business logic is compelling: capturing the benefits of strategic fit along the value chains of its related businesses gives a diversified organization a clear path to achieve competitive advantage over undiversified competitors and competitors whose own diversification efforts do not offer equivalent strategic-fit benefits.[16] Such competitive advantage potential provides an organization with a dependable basis for earning profits and a return on investment that exceeds what the organization's businesses could earn as stand-alone enterprises. Converting the competitive advantage potential into greater profitability is what fuels $1 + 1 = 3$ gains in shareholder value – the necessary outcome for satisfying the better-off test and proving the business merit of an organization's diversification effort.

There are four things to bear in mind here:

1. Capturing cross-business strategic-fit benefits via a strategy of related diversification builds shareholder value in ways that shareholders cannot undertake by simply owning a portfolio of shares in companies in different industries.
2. The capture of cross-business strategic-fit benefits is possible only via a strategy of related diversification.
3. The benefits of cross-business strategic fit come from the transferring or sharing of competitively valuable resources and capabilities among the businesses – resources and capabilities that are *specialized* to certain applications and have value only in specific types of industries and businesses.
4. The benefits of cross-business strategic fit are not automatically realized when an organization diversifies into related businesses; *the benefits materialize only after management has successfully pursued internal actions to capture them.*

Diversification into Unrelated Businesses

LO 8.3
Become aware of the merits and risks of corporate strategies based on unrelated diversification.

An unrelated diversification strategy discounts the merits of pursuing cross-business strategic fit and, instead, focuses squarely on entering and operating businesses in industries that allow the organization as a whole to increase its earnings. Companies that pursue a strategy of unrelated diversification generally exhibit a willingness to diversify into *any industry* where senior managers see an opportunity to realize consistently good financial results. Such companies are frequently labelled *conglomerates* because their business interests range broadly across diverse industries. Companies that pursue unrelated diversification nearly always enter new businesses by acquiring an established organization rather than by forming a start-up subsidiary within their own corporate structures or participating in joint ventures.

With a strategy of unrelated diversification, the emphasis is on satisfying the attractiveness and cost-of-entry tests and each business's prospects for good financial performance. Thus, with an unrelated diversification strategy, organization managers spend much time and effort screening acquisition candidates and evaluating the pros and cons of keeping or divesting existing businesses, using such criteria as:

- whether the business can meet corporate targets for profitability and return on investment;
- whether the business is in an industry with attractive growth potential;
- whether the business is big enough to contribute *significantly* to the parent firm's bottom line.

But the key to successful unrelated diversification is to go beyond these considerations and ensure that the strategy passes the better-off test as well. This test requires more than just growth in revenues; it requires *growth in profits* – beyond what could be achieved by a mutual fund or a holding organization that owns the businesses without adding any value. Unless the different businesses are more profitable together under the corporate umbrella than they are apart as independent businesses, *the strategy cannot create economic value for shareholders.* And unless it does so, there is *no primary justification for unrelated diversification.*

Building Shareholder Value via Unrelated Diversification

Given the absence of cross-business strategic fit with which to create competitive advantages, building economic shareholder value via unrelated diversification ultimately hinges on the ability of the parent organization to improve its businesses via other means. Critical to this endeavour is the role that the parent organization plays *as a corporate parent.* To the extent that an organization has strong *parenting capabilities* – capabilities that involve nurturing, guiding, grooming and governing constituent businesses – a corporate parent can propel its businesses forward and help them gain ground over their market rivals. Corporate parents also contribute to the competitiveness of their unrelated businesses by sharing or transferring *generalized resources and capabilities* across the businesses – competitive assets that have utility in any type of industry and that can be leveraged across a wide range of business types as a result. Examples of the kinds of generalized resources that a corporate parent leverages in unrelated diversification include the corporation's reputation, credit rating and access to financial markets; governance mechanisms; an ethics programme; a central data and communications centre; shared administrative resources such as public relations and legal services; and common systems for functions such as budgeting, financial reporting and quality control.

The three principal ways in which a parent organization can further the prospects of its unrelated businesses and increase long-term economic shareholder value are discussed below.

Astute Corporate Parenting

An effective way for a diversified organization to improve the performance of its otherwise unrelated businesses is through astute corporate parenting. *Corporate parenting* refers to the role that a diversified corporation plays in nurturing its component businesses through the provision of top management expertise, disciplined control, financial resources and other types of generalized resources and capabilities such as long-term planning systems, business development skills, management development processes and incentive systems.[17]

One of the most important ways that corporate parents contribute to the success of their businesses is by offering high-level oversight and guidance.[18] The top executives of a large diversified corporation have among them many years of accumulated experience in a variety of business settings and can often contribute expert problem-solving skills, creative strategy suggestions and first-rate advice and guidance on how to improve competitiveness and financial performance to the heads of the organization's various business subsidiaries; this is especially true in the case of newly acquired businesses. Particularly astute high-level guidance from corporate executives can help the subsidiaries perform better than they would otherwise be able to do through the efforts of the business-unit heads alone.[19] The outstanding leadership of Royal Little, the founder of Textron, was a major reason that the organization became an exemplar of the unrelated diversification strategy while he was CEO. Little's bold moves transformed the organization from its origins as a small textile manufacturer into a global powerhouse known for its Bell helicopters, Cessna aircraft and a host of other strong brands in a wide array of industries.

Norm Wesley, CEO of the conglomerate Fortune Brands from 1999 to 2007, is similarly credited with driving the sharp rise in the company's stock price while he was at the helm. Fortune Brands is now the €5.5 billion maker of products ranging from spirits (e.g. Jim Beam bourbon and rye, Gilbey's gin and vodka, Courvoisier cognac) to golf products (e.g. Titleist golf balls and clubs, FootJoy golf shoes and apparel, Scotty Cameron putters) to hardware (e.g. Moen faucets, American Lock security devices, Therma-Tru doors).

Corporate parents can also create added value for their businesses by providing them with other types of generalized or parenting resources that lower the operating costs of the individual businesses or that enhance their operating effectiveness. The administrative resources located at an organization's corporate headquarters are a prime example. They typically include legal services, accounting expertise and tax services and other elements of the administrative infrastructure, such as risk management capabilities, information technology resources and resources concerning public relations and corporate communications. Providing individual business with such types of generalized and support resources and capabilities creates value by lowering organization-wide overhead costs, since each business would otherwise have to duplicate the centralized activities.

Corporate brands that do not connote any specific type of product are another type of generalized corporate resource that can be shared among unrelated businesses. GE's brand is an example, having been applied to businesses as diverse as financial services (GE Capital), medical imaging (GE medical diagnostics) and lighting (GE light bulbs). Corporate brands that are applied in this fashion are sometimes called *umbrella brands*. Utilizing a well-known corporate name (GE) in a diversified organization's individual businesses has the potential not only to lower costs (by spreading the fixed cost of developing and maintaining the brand over many businesses) but also to enhance each business's customer value proposition by linking its products to a name that consumers trust. In similar fashion, a corporation's reputation for well-crafted products, for product reliability or for trustworthiness can lead to greater customer willingness to purchase the products of a wider range of a diversified organization's businesses. Incentive systems, financial control systems and an organization's culture are other types of generalised corporate resources that may prove useful in enhancing the daily operations of a diverse set of businesses.

Judicious Cross-business Allocation of Financial Resources

Widely diversified firms may also be able to create added value by serving as an internal capital market and allocating surplus cash flows from some businesses to fund the capital requirements of other businesses. This can be particularly important when interest rates are high or credit is unusually tight (such as in the wake of the worldwide banking crisis that began in 2008) or in economies with less well-developed capital markets. Under these conditions, an unrelated diversifier with strong financial resources can add value by shifting funds from business units generating excess cash (more than they need to fund their own operating requirements and new capital investment opportunities) to other, cash-short businesses with appealing growth prospects. A parent organization's ability to function as its own internal capital market enhances overall corporate performance and boosts shareholder value to the extent that its top managers have better access to information about investment opportunities internal to the firm than do external financiers and can avoid the costs of external borrowing.

Acquiring and Restructuring Undervalued Companies

One way for parent companies to add value to unrelated businesses is by acquiring weakly performing companies at a bargain price and then *restructuring* their operations (and perhaps their strategies) in ways that produce sometimes dramatic increases in profitability. **Restructuring** refers to overhauling and streamlining the operations of a business – combining plants with excess capacity, selling off redundant or underutilized assets, reducing unnecessary expenses, revamping its product offerings,

Core Concept

Restructuring refers to overhauling and streamlining the activities of a business – combining plants with excess capacity, selling off underutilized assets, reducing unnecessary expenses and otherwise improving the productivity and profitability of an organization.

instituting new sales and marketing approaches, consolidating administrative functions to reduce overhead costs, instituting new financial controls and accounting systems and otherwise improving the operating efficiency and profitability of an organization. Restructuring sometimes involves transferring experienced managers to the newly acquired business, either to replace the top layers of management or to step in temporarily until the business is returned to profitability or is well on its way to becoming a major market contender.

Restructuring is often undertaken when a diversified organization acquires a new business that is performing well below levels that the corporate parent believes are achievable. Diversified companies that have capabilities in restructuring (sometimes called *turnaround capabilities*) are often able to significantly boost the performance of weak businesses in a relatively wide range of industries. Successful unrelated diversification strategies based on restructuring require the parent organization to have considerable expertise in identifying underperforming target companies and in negotiating attractive acquisition prices so that each acquisition passes the cost-of-entry test. The capabilities in this regard of Lords James Hanson and Gordon White, who headed up the storied British conglomerate Hanson Trust, played a large part in Hanson's impressive record of profitability through the early 1990s.

The Path to Greater Shareholder Value through Unrelated Diversification

For a strategy of unrelated diversification to produce organization-wide financial results above and beyond what the businesses could generate operating as stand-alone entities, corporate executives must:

- Do a superior job of diversifying into new businesses that can produce consistently good earnings and returns on investment (to satisfy the attractiveness test).
- Do an excellent job of negotiating favourable acquisition prices (to satisfy the cost-of-entry test).
- Do a superior job of corporate parenting via high-level managerial oversight and resource-sharing, financial resource allocation and portfolio management or restructuring underperforming businesses (to satisfy the better-off test).

> **Core Concept**
>
> A diversified organization has a **parenting advantage** when it is better able than other companies to boost the combined performance of its individual businesses through high-level guidance, general oversight and other corporate-level contributions.

The best corporate parents understand the nature and value of the kinds of resources at their command and know how to leverage them effectively across their businesses. Those that are able to create more value in their businesses than other diversified companies have what is called a **parenting advantage**.[20] When a corporation has a parenting advantage, its top executives have the best chance of being able to craft and execute an unrelated diversification strategy that can satisfy all three tests and truly enhance long-term economic shareholder value.

The Drawbacks of Unrelated Diversification

Unrelated diversification strategies have two important negatives that undercut the pluses: very demanding managerial requirements and limited competitive advantage potential.

Demanding Managerial Requirements

Successfully managing a set of fundamentally different businesses operating in fundamentally different industry and competitive environments is a very challenging and exceptionally difficult proposition.[21] Consider, for example, that organizations like Electrolux and the Virgin Group have dozens of business subsidiaries making hundreds and sometimes thousands of products. While headquarters executives can glean information about the industry from third-party sources, ask lots of questions when making occasional visits to the operations of the different businesses and do their best to learn about the organization's different businesses, they still remain heavily dependent on briefings from business-unit heads and on 'managing by the numbers'; that is, keeping a close track on the financial and operating results of each subsidiary. Managing by the numbers works well enough when business conditions are normal and the heads of the various business units are capable of consistently meeting their numbers. But the problem comes when things start to go awry in a business due to exceptional circumstances and corporate management has to get deeply involved in the problems of a business it does not know all that much about. Because every business tends to encounter difficulties at some juncture, unrelated diversification is thus a somewhat risky strategy from a managerial perspective.[22] Just one or two unforeseen problems or big strategic mistakes (like misjudging the importance of certain competitive forces, not recognizing that a newly acquired business has some serious resource deficiencies and/or competitive shortcomings or being too optimistic about turning around a struggling subsidiary) can cause a precipitous drop in corporate earnings and impact the parent organization's market value.

Hence, competently overseeing a set of widely diverse businesses can turn out to be much harder than it sounds. In practice, comparatively few companies have proved that they have top management capabilities that are up to the task. There are far more companies whose corporate executives have failed at delivering consistently good financial results with an unrelated diversification strategy than there are companies with corporate executives who have been successful.[23] Unless an organization truly has a parenting advantage, the odds are that the result of unrelated diversification will be $1 + 1 = 2$ or less.

Limited Competitive Advantage Potential

Relying solely on the expertise of corporate executives to wisely manage a set of unrelated businesses is *a much weaker foundation for enhancing shareholder value* than is a strategy of related diversification.

The second big negative is that *unrelated diversification offers a limited potential for competitive advantage beyond what each individual business can generate on its own.* Unlike a related diversification strategy, unrelated diversification provides no cross-business strategic-fit benefits that allow each business to perform its key value chain activities in a more efficient and effective manner. A cash-rich corporate parent pursuing unrelated diversification can provide its subsidiaries with much-needed capital, may achieve economies of scope in activities relying on generalized corporate resources and may even offer some managerial know-how to help resolve problems in particular business units, but otherwise it has little to offer in the way of enhancing the competitive strength of its individual business units. In comparison to the highly specialized resources that facilitate related diversification, the generalized resources that support unrelated diversification tend to be relatively low value, for the simple reason that they are more common. Unless they are of exceptionally high quality (such as GE's world-renowned general management capabilities), resources and capabilities that are generalized in nature are less likely to provide a source of competitive advantage for diversified companies. *Without the competitive advantage potential of strategic fit in strategically important value chain activities, consolidated performance of an unrelated group of businesses stands to be little more than the sum of what the individual business units could achieve if they were independent, in most circumstances.*

Inadequate Reasons for Pursuing Unrelated Diversification

When firms pursue an unrelated diversification strategy for the wrong reasons, the odds are that the result will be $1 + 1 = 2$ or less. Rationales for unrelated diversification that are not likely to increase shareholder value include the following:

- *Risk reduction.* Managers sometimes pursue unrelated diversification in order to reduce risk by spreading the organization's investments over a set of truly diverse industries whose technologies and markets are largely disconnected. But this cannot create long-term shareholder value since the organization's shareholders can more flexibly (and more efficiently) reduce their exposure to risk by investing in a diversified portfolio of shares and securities.

- *Growth*. While unrelated diversification may enable an organization to achieve rapid or continuous growth, firms that pursue growth for growth's sake are unlikely to maximize shareholder value. While growth can bring more attention and prestige to a firm from greater visibility and higher industry rankings, only profitable growth – the kind that comes from creating added value for shareholders – can justify a strategy of unrelated diversification.

- *Stabilization*. In a broadly diversified organization, there is a chance that market down trends in some of the organization's businesses will be partially offset by cyclical upswings in its other businesses, thus producing somewhat less earnings volatility. In actual practice, however, there is no convincing evidence that the consolidated profits of firms with unrelated diversification strategies are more stable or less subject to reversal in periods of recession and economic stress than the profits of firms with related diversification strategies.

- *Managerial motives*. Unrelated diversification can provide benefits to managers such as higher compensation (which tends to increase with firm size and degree of diversification) and reduced employment risk. Diversification for these reasons is far more likely to reduce shareholder value than to increase it.

Because unrelated diversification strategies *at their best* have only a limited potential for creating long-term economic value for shareholders, it is essential that managers do not compound this problem by taking a misguided approach toward unrelated diversification, in pursuit of objectives that are more likely to destroy shareholder value than create it.

Key Debate 8.1

THEORY ON DETERMINANTS OF THE BOUNDARIES OF THE FIRM

To what extent firms grow, through related or unrelated diversification, is a question that has generated significant debate in industrial economics, strategy, corporate finance and organization theory. Stemming from Coase's (1937) article 'The nature of the firm' discussion continues on the optimal boundary of the firm across industries.

TRANSACTION COST THEORY

One of the central theories is transaction-cost economics (TCE). TCE is essentially a theory about the costs of contracting, and focuses on the firm's choice to diversify into a new industry rather than contract out any assets that are valuable in that industry.

The transaction-cost rationale for related diversification is that multibusiness firms holding portfolios of similar businesses can obtain transaction efficiency advantages unavailable to non-diversified firms. The view holds that firms diversify when they have valuable and difficult to imitate resources that are valuable across related industries or are complementary to resources in other industries, and when gains related to these resources cannot be realized by contracting among independent firms.

RESOURCE-BASED VIEW

Another theory stream that has created a vast literature on corporate diversification is the resource-based view of the firm. This literature has emphasized the benefits of related diversification. The pure contractual argument of TCE is rejected, and the firm is seen as a repository of distinct productive (technological and organizational) knowledge, and as an entity that can learn, and grow, on the basis of this knowledge. Firms are perceived as

▶

◄

bundles of resources where underutilized resources can be profitably applied elsewhere, hence leading to related diversification. The firm is seen as superior to the market at supplying higher-order organizational principles, including values, a shared language and mechanisms by which to codify technologies, and this explains the efficiency benefits of diversification expansion.

A central argument of both theoretical streams is in principal that related diversification outperforms unrelated, or conglomerate diversification. Unrelated or conglomerate diversification is typically viewed as an anomaly, either a mistake (as in the conglomerate merger wave of the 1960s) or pure luck.

Still, over two-thirds of fortune 500 companies continue to be active in at least five distinct lines of business, and in the developing world conglomerates are even more important, accounting for a large share of economic activity in countries like India and Korea.

The two theory streams have addressed the existence of conglomerate activity with differing explanations. The transaction-cost argument suggests that the benefit of unrelated diversification could come from intra-firm capital allocation. While capital markets act to allocate resources between single-product firms, in the diversified, multidivisional firm, by contrast, resources are allocated through an internal capital market, being the headquarters or corporate parent. The efficiencies of this capital distribution are believed to arise from the increased access to information by the parent through internal reporting procedures and a greater willingness to share information internally by the business divisions, as well as the ability to use directed control rights and selectively intervene.

The resource-based view, in contrast, suggests that firm capabilities are unknown *ex ante*, but must be discovered over time through experimenting with different combinations of business units. Unrelated diversification is therefore thought to be a necessary step toward the discovery of future capabilities, and is thus value creating.

ADDITIONAL READING

Matsusaka, J. (2001) 'Corporate diversification, profit maximisation and organizational capabilities', *Journal of Business*, 74(3): 409–31.
Rumelt, R.P (1974) *Strategy, Structure, and Economic Performance*, Cambridge, Harvard University Press.

Sources: Williamson, O.E. (1985) *The Economic Institutions of Capitalism*, New York, Free Press; Penrose, E.T. (1959) *The Theory of the Growth of the firm*, Oxford, Oxford University Press; Kogut, B. and Zander, U. (1992) 'Knowledge of the firm, combinative capabilities, and the replication of technology', *Organization Science*, 3: 383–97.

Combination Related–Unrelated Diversification Strategies

There is nothing to preclude an organization from diversifying into both related and unrelated businesses. Indeed, in actual practice the business make-up of diversified companies varies considerably. Some diversified companies are really *dominant-business enterprises* – one major 'core' business accounts for 50–80 per cent of total revenues and a collection of small related or unrelated businesses accounts for the remainder. Some diversified companies are *narrowly diversified* around a few (two to five) related or unrelated businesses. Others are *broadly diversified* around a wide-ranging collection of related businesses, unrelated businesses or a mixture of both. And a number of multibusiness enterprises have diversified into unrelated areas but have a collection of related businesses within each area, thus giving them a business portfolio consisting of *several unrelated groups of related businesses*. There is ample room for companies to customize their diversification strategies to incorporate elements of both related and unrelated diversification, as may suit their own competitive asset profile and strategic vision. *Combination related-unrelated diversification strategies have particular appeal for organizations with a mix of valuable competitive assets, covering the spectrum from generalized to specialized resources and capabilities.*

Figure 8.2 shows the range of alternatives for companies pursuing diversification.

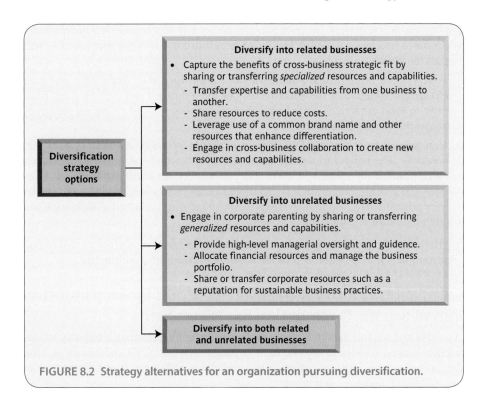

FIGURE 8.2 Strategy alternatives for an organization pursuing diversification.

Evaluating the Strategy of a Diversified Organization

Strategic analysis of diversified companies builds on the concepts and methods used for single business companies. But there are some additional aspects to consider and a couple of new analytical tools to master. The procedure for evaluating the pluses and minuses of a diversified organization's strategy and deciding what actions to take to improve the organization's performance involves six steps:

1. Assessing the attractiveness of the industries the organization has diversified into, both individually and as a group.

2. Assessing the competitive strength of the organization's business units and determining which are strong contenders in their respective industries.

3. Checking the competitive advantage potential of cross-business strategic fit among the organization's various business units.

4. Checking whether the firm's resources fit the requirements of its present business line-up.

5. Ranking the performance prospects of the businesses from best to worst and determining what the corporate parent's priority should be in allocating resources to its various businesses.

6. Crafting new strategic moves to improve overall corporate performance.

The core concepts and analytical techniques underlying each of these steps merit further discussion.

LO 8.4 Gain command of the analytical tools for evaluating an organization's diversification strategy.

Step 1: Evaluating Industry Attractiveness

A principal consideration in evaluating a diversified organization's business make-up and the calibre of its strategy is the attractiveness of the industries in which it has business operations. Answers to several questions are required:

1. *Does each industry the organization has diversified into represent a good market for the organization to be in?* Ideally, each industry in which the firm operates will pass the attractiveness test.

2. *Which of the organization's industries are most attractive, and which are least attractive?* Comparing the attractiveness of the industries and ranking them from most to least attractive is a prerequisite to wise allocation of corporate resources across the various businesses.

3. *How appealing is the whole group of industries in which the organization has invested?* The answer to this question points to whether the group of industries holds promise for attractive growth and profitability. An organization whose revenues and profits come primarily from businesses in relatively unattractive industries probably needs to look at divesting businesses in unattractive industries and entering industries that qualify as highly attractive.

The more attractive the industries (both individually and as a group) a diversified organization is in, the better its prospects for good long-term performance.

Calculating Industry Attractiveness Scores for Each Industry into Which the Organization has Diversified

A simple and reliable analytical tool involves calculating quantitative industry attractiveness scores, which can then be used to gauge each industry's attractiveness, rank the industries from most to least attractive and make judgements about the attractiveness of all the industries as a group.

Assessing industry attractiveness involves a consideration of the conditions of each business's macro-environment as well as its competitive environment – the very same factors that are used to evaluate the strategy of a single business organization, as discussed in Chapter 3. Key indicators of industry attractiveness thus include:

- social, political, regulatory and environmental factors;
- seasonal and cyclical factors;
- industry uncertainty and business risk;
- market size and projected growth rate;
- industry profitability;
- the intensity of competition (five forces);
- emerging opportunities and threats

In addition, it is critically important to consider those aspects of industry attractiveness that pertain *specifically* to an organization's diversification strategy. This involves looking at all the industries in which the organization has invested to assess their resource requirements and to consider whether there is good cross-industry strategic fit. The following measures are typically used to gauge industry attractiveness from this multibusiness perspective:

- *The presence of cross-industry strategic fit.* The more an industry's value chain and resource requirements match up well with the value chain activities of other industries in which the organization has operations, the more attractive the industry is to a firm pursuing related diversification.

- *Resource requirements.* Industries having resource requirements that match those of the parent organization or are otherwise within the organization's reach are more attractive than industries in which capital and other resource requirements could strain corporate financial resources and organizational capabilities.

After a set of attractiveness measures that suit a diversified organization's circumstances has been identified, each attractiveness measure is assigned a weight reflecting its relative importance in determining an industry's attractiveness – it is weak methodology to assume that the various attractiveness measures are equally important. The intensity of competition in an industry should nearly always carry a high weight (say, 0.20–0.30). Strategic-fit considerations should be assigned a high weight in the case of companies with related diversification strategies; but for companies with an unrelated diversification strategy, strategic fit with other industries may be dropped from the list of attractiveness measures altogether. The importance weights must add up to 1.

Next, each industry is rated on each of the chosen industry attractiveness measures, using a rating scale of 1–10 (where a *high* rating signifies *high* attractiveness and a *low* rating signifies *low* attractiveness). *Keep in mind here that the more intensely competitive an industry is, the lower the attractiveness rating for that industry.* Likewise, the more the resource requirements associated with being in a particular industry are beyond the parent organization's reach, the lower the attractiveness rating. On the other hand, the presence of good cross-industry strategic fit should be given a very high attractiveness rating, since there is good potential for competitive advantage and added shareholder value. Weighted attractiveness scores are then calculated by multiplying the industry's rating on each measure by the corresponding weight. For example, a rating of 8 times a weight of 0.25 gives a weighted attractiveness score of 2.00. The sum of the weighted scores for all the attractiveness measures provides an overall industry attractiveness score. This procedure is illustrated in Table 8.1.

Interpreting the Industry Attractiveness Scores

Industries with a score much below 5 probably do not pass the attractiveness test. If an organization's industry attractiveness scores are all above 5, it is probably fair to conclude that the group of industries the organization operates in is attractive as a whole. But the group of industries takes on a decidedly lower degree of attractiveness as the number of industries with scores below 5 increases, especially if industries with low scores account for a sizeable fraction of the organization's revenues.

For a diversified organization to be a strong performer, a substantial portion of its revenues and profits must come from business units with relatively high attractiveness

TABLE 8.1 Calculating weighted industry attractiveness scores*

Industry attractiveness measure	Importance weight	Industry A rating/score	Industry B rating/score	Industry C rating/score	Industry D rating/score
Market size and projected growth rate	0.10	8/0.80	5/0.50	7/0.70	3/0.30
Intensity of competition	0.25	8/2.00	7/1.75	3/0.75	2/0.50
Emerging opportunities and threats	0.10	2/0.20	9/0.90	4/0.40	5/0.50
Cross-industry strategic fit	0.20	8/1.60	4/0.80	8/1.60	2/0.40
Resource requirements	0.10	9/0.90	7/0.70	10/1.00	5/0.50
Seasonal and cyclical influences	0.05	9/0.45	8/0.40	10/0.50	5/0.25
Societal, political, regulatory and environmental factors	0.05	10/0.50	7/0.35	7/0.35	3/0.15
Industry profitability	0.10	5/0.50	10/1.00	3/0.30	3/0.30
Industry uncertainty and business risk	0.05	5/0.25	7/0.35	10/0.50	1/0.05
Sum of the assigned weights	1.00				
Overall weighted industry attractiveness scores		**7.20**	**6.75**	**5.10**	**2.95**

Note: * Rating scale: 1 = very unattractive to organization; 10 = very attractive to organization.

scores. It is particularly important that a diversified organization's principal businesses be in industries with a good outlook for growth and above-average profitability. Having a big fraction of the organization's revenues and profits come from industries with slow growth, low profitability or intense competition tends to drag overall organization performance down. Business units in the least attractive industries are potential candidates for divestiture, unless they are positioned strongly enough to overcome the unattractive aspects of their industry environments or they are a strategically important component of the organization's business make-up.

The Difficulties of Calculating Industry Attractiveness Scores

There are two hurdles to using this method of evaluating industry attractiveness. One is deciding on appropriate weights for the industry attractiveness measures, since they have a subjective component; different analysts may have different views about which weights are appropriate for the different attractiveness measures. The second hurdle is gaining sufficient command of the industry to assign more accurate and objective ratings. Generally, an organization can come up with the statistical data needed to compare its industries on such factors as market size, growth rate, seasonal and cyclical influences and industry profitability. Cross-industry fit and resource requirements are also fairly easy to judge. But the attractiveness measure on which judgement weighs most heavily is intensity of competition. It is not always easy to conclude whether competition in one industry is stronger or weaker than in another industry because of the different types of competitive influences that prevail and the differences in their relative importance. In the event that the available information is too limited to confidently assign a rating value to an industry on a particular attractiveness measure, then it is usually best to use a score of 5, which avoids biasing the overall attractiveness score either up or down.

But despite the hurdles, calculating industry attractiveness scores is a systematic and reasonably reliable method for ranking a diversified organization's industries from most to least attractive – numbers like those shown for the four industries in Table 8.1 help identify the basis for judging which industries are more attractive and to what degree.

Step 2: Evaluating Business-unit Competitive Strength

The second step in evaluating a diversified organization is to appraise how strongly positioned each of its business units is in its respective industry. Doing an appraisal of each business unit's strength and competitive position in its industry not only reveals its chances for industry success but also provides a basis for ranking the units from competitively strongest to competitively weakest and sizing up the competitive strength of all the business units as a group.

Calculating Competitive Strength Scores for Each Business Unit

Quantitative measures of each business unit's competitive strength can be calculated using a procedure similar to that for measuring industry attractiveness. The following factors are used in quantifying the competitive strengths of a diversified organization's business subsidiaries:

> Using relative market share to measure competitive strength is analytically superior to using straight-percentage market share.

● Relative market share. A business unit's *relative market share* is defined as the ratio of its market share to the market share held by the largest rival firm in the industry, with market share measured in unit volume, not a monetary value. A 10 per cent market share, for example, does not signal much competitive strength if the leader's share is 50 per cent (a 0.20 relative market share), but a 10 per cent share is actually quite strong if the leader's share is only 12 per cent (a 0.83 relative market share) – this is why an organization's relative market share is a better measure of competitive strength than an organization's market share based on either monetary value or unit volume.

- Costs relative to competitors' costs.
- Ability to match or beat rivals on key product attributes.
- Brand image and reputation.
- Other competitively valuable resources and capabilities.
- Ability to benefit from strategic fit with the organization's other businesses.
- Ability to exercise bargaining leverage with key suppliers or customers.
- Calibre of alliances and collaborative partnerships with suppliers and/or buyers.
- Profitability relative to competitors. Above-average profitability is a signal of competitive advantage, while below-average profitability usually denotes competitive disadvantage.

After settling on a set of competitive strength measures that are well matched to the circumstances of the various business units, weights indicating each measure's importance need to be assigned. A *case can be made for using different weights* for different business units whenever the importance of the strength measures differs significantly from business to business, but otherwise it is simpler just to go with a single set of weights and avoid the added complication of multiple weights. As before, the importance weights must add up to 1. Each business unit is then rated on each of the chosen strength measures, using a rating scale of 1–10 (where a *high* rating signifies competitive *strength* and a *low* rating signifies competitive *weakness*). In the event that the available information is too skimpy to confidently assign a rating value to a business unit on a particular strength measure, then it is usually best to use a score of 5, which avoids biasing the overall score either up or down. Weighted strength ratings are calculated by multiplying the business unit's rating on each strength measure by the assigned weight. For example, a strength score of 6 times a weight of 0.15 gives a weighted strength rating of 0.90. The sum of the weighted ratings across all the strength measures provides a quantitative measure of a business unit's overall market strength and competitive standing. Table 8.2 provides sample calculations of competitive strength ratings for four businesses.

Interpreting the Competitive Strength Scores

Business units with competitive strength ratings above 6.7 (on a scale of 1–10) are strong market contenders in their industries. Businesses with ratings in the 3.3–6.7 range have moderate competitive strength *vis-à-vis* rivals. Businesses with ratings below 3.3 are in competitively weak market positions. If a diversified organization's business units all have competitive strength scores above 5, it is fair to conclude that its business units are all fairly strong market contenders in their respective industries. But as the number of business units with scores below 5 increases, there is reason to question whether the organization can perform well with so many businesses in relatively weak competitive positions. This concern takes on even more importance when business units with low scores account for a sizeable fraction of the organization's revenues.

Using a Nine-cell Matrix to Simultaneously Portray Industry Attractiveness and Competitive Strength

The industry attractiveness and business strength scores can be used to portray the strategic positions of each business in a diversified organization. Industry attractiveness is plotted on the vertical axis and competitive strength on the horizontal axis. A nine-cell grid emerges from dividing the vertical axis into three regions (high, medium and low attractiveness) and the horizontal axis into three regions (strong, average and weak competitive strength). As shown in Figure 8.3, high attractiveness is associated with scores of 6.7 or greater on a rating scale of 1–10, medium attractiveness to scores of 3.3–6.7 and low attractiveness to scores below 3.3. Likewise, high competitive strength is defined as scores greater than 6.7, average strength as scores of 3.3–6.7 and low strength as scores below 3.3. *Each business unit is plotted on the nine-cell matrix according to its overall attractiveness score and strength score, and then it is shown as a 'bubble'.* The size of each bubble is scaled to the percentage of revenues the business generates relative to total corporate revenues. The bubbles in Figure 8.3 were located on the grid using the four industry attractiveness scores from Table 8.1 and the strength scores for the four business units in Table 8.2.

The locations of the business units on the attractiveness–strength matrix provide valuable guidance in deploying corporate resources to the various business units. In general, *a diversified organization's prospects for good overall performance are enhanced by concentrating corporate resources and strategic attention on those business units having the greatest competitive strength and positioned in highly attractive industries* – specifically, businesses in the three cells in the upper left portion of the attractiveness-strength matrix, where industry attractiveness and competitive strength/ market position are both favourable. The general strategic prescription for businesses falling in these three cells (e.g. business A in Figure 8.3) is 'grow and build', with businesses in the high-strong cell standing first in line for resource allocations by the corporate parent.

Next in priority come businesses positioned in the three diagonal cells stretching from the lower left to the upper right (businesses B and C in Figure 8.3). Such businesses usually merit medium or intermediate priority in the parent's resource allocation ranking. However, some businesses in the medium-priority diagonal cells may

TABLE 8.2 Calculating weighted competitive strength scores for a diversified organization's business units*

Competitive strength measure	Importance weight	Business A in industry A rating/score	Business B in industry B rating/score	Business C in industry C rating/score	Business D in industry D rating/score
Relative market share	0.15	10/1.50	1/0.15	6/0.90	2/0.30
Costs relative to competitors' costs	0.20	7/1.40	2/0.40	5/1.00	3/0.60
Ability to match or beat rivals on key product attributes	0.05	9/0.45	4/0.20	8/0.40	4/0.20
Ability to benefit from strategic fit with organization's other businesses	0.20	8/1.60	4/0.80	8/0.80	2/0.60
Bargaining leverage with suppliers/ buyers; calibre of alliances	0.05	9/0.45	3/0.15	6/0.30	2/0.10
Brand image and reputation	0.10	9/0.90	2/0.20	7/0.70	5/0.50
Competitively valuable capabilities	0.15	7/1.05	2/0.30	5/0.75	3/0.45
Profitability relative to competitors	0.10	5/0.50	1/0.10	4/0.40	4/0.40
Sum of the assigned weights	1.00				
Overall weighted competitive strength scores		**7.85**	**2.30**	**5.25**	**3.15**

Note: * Rating scale: 1 = very weak; 10 = very strong.

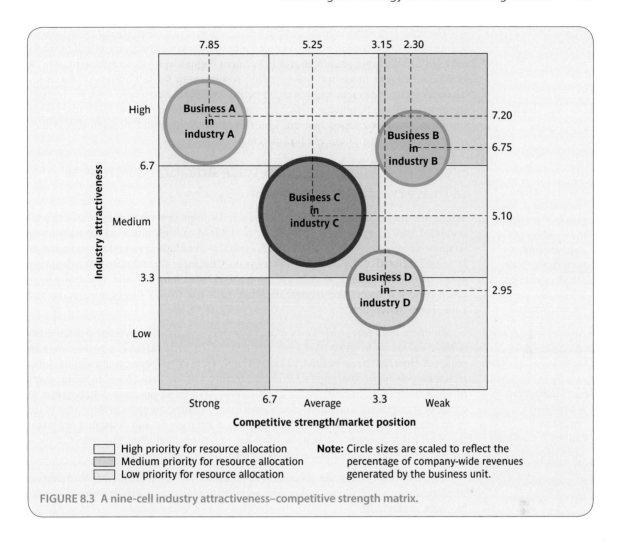

FIGURE 8.3 A nine-cell industry attractiveness–competitive strength matrix.

have brighter or dimmer prospects than others. For example, a small business in the upper right cell of the matrix (like business B), despite being in a highly attractive industry, may occupy too weak a competitive position in its industry to justify the investment and resources needed to turn it into a strong market contender and shift its position leftward in the matrix over time. If, however, a business in the upper right cell has attractive opportunities for rapid growth and a good potential for winning a much stronger market position over time, it may merit a high claim on the corporate parent's resource allocation ranking and be given the capital it needs to pursue a grow-and-build strategy – the strategic objective here would be to move the business leftward in the attractiveness-strength matrix over time.

Businesses in the three cells in the lower right corner of the matrix (like business D in Figure 8.3) typically are weak performers and have the lowest claim on corporate resources. Most such businesses are good candidates for being divested (sold to other companies) or else managed in a manner calculated to wring out the maximum cash flows from operations – the cash flows from low-performing/low-potential businesses can then be diverted to financing expansion of business units with greater market opportunities. In exceptional cases where a business located in the three lower right cells is nonetheless fairly profitable (which it might be if it is in the low-average cell) or has the potential for good earnings and return on investment, the business merits retention and the allocation of sufficient resources to achieve better performance.

The nine-cell attractiveness–strength matrix provides a clear, strong logic for why a diversified organization needs to consider both industry attractiveness and business strength in allocating resources and investment capital to its different businesses. A good case can be made for concentrating resources in those businesses that enjoy higher degrees of attractiveness and competitive strength, being very selective in making investments in businesses with intermediate positions on the grid and withdrawing resources from businesses that are lower in attractiveness and strength unless they offer exceptional profit or cash flow potential.

Step 3: Checking the Competitive Advantage Potential of Cross-business Strategic Fit

While this step can be bypassed for diversified companies whose businesses are all unrelated (since, by design, strategic fit is lacking), a high potential for converting strategic fit into competitive advantage is central to concluding just how good an organization's related diversification strategy is. Checking the competitive advantage potential of cross-business strategic fit involves searching for and evaluating how much benefit a diversified organization can gain from cross-business resource and value chain match-ups.

But more *than just strategic-fit identification is needed. The real test is what competitive value can be generated from strategic fit.* To what extent can cost savings be realized? How much competitive value will come from cross-business transfer of skills, technology or intellectual capital? Will transferring a potent brand name to the products of other businesses increase sales significantly? Will cross-business collaboration to create or strengthen competitive capabilities lead to significant gains in the marketplace or in financial performance? Without significant strategic fit and dedicated organizational efforts to capture the benefits, one has to be sceptical about the potential for a diversified organization's businesses to perform better together than apart.

Figure 8.4 illustrates the process of comparing the value chains of an organization's businesses and identifying opportunities to exploit competitively valuable cross-business strategic fit.

Step 4: Checking for Resource Fit

The businesses in a diversified organization's line-up need to exhibit good **resource fit**. In firms with a related diversification strategy, resource fit exists when the firm's businesses strengthen its overall mix of resources and capabilities and when the businesses have matching resource requirements at points along their value chains that are critical for the businesses' market success. In companies pursuing unrelated diversification, resource fit exists when the parent organization has capabilities *as a corporate parent* of unrelated businesses, resources of a general nature that it can share or transfer to its component businesses and corporate resources sufficient to support its entire group of businesses without being spread too thin. Resource fit in terms of a sufficiency of corporate resources to manage and support the entire enterprise is also relevant for related diversifiers and companies pursuing a mixed diversification strategy; firms pursuing related diversification can also benefit from leveraging the resources of the corporate parent.

Financial Resource Fit

One dimension of resource fit concerns whether a diversified organization can generate the internal cash flows sufficient to fund the capital requirements of its businesses, pay its dividends, meet its debt obligations and otherwise remain financially healthy. While additional capital can usually be raised in financial markets, it is important for a diversified firm to have a healthy **internal capital market** that can support the financial

---

The greater the value of cross-business strategic fit in enhancing an organization's performance in the marketplace or on the bottom line, the more competitively powerful is its strategy of related diversification.

Core Concept

A diversified organization exhibits **resource fit** when its businesses add to an organization's overall resource strengths and have matching resource requirements and/or when the parent organization has adequate corporate resources to support its businesses' needs and add value.

Core Concept

A strong **internal capital market** allows a diversified organization to add value by shifting capital from business units generating *free cash flow* to those needing additional capital to expand and realize their growth potential.

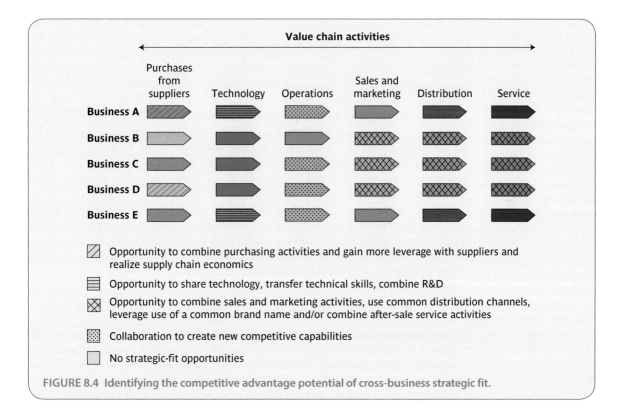

Value chain activities

FIGURE 8.4 **Identifying the competitive advantage potential of cross-business strategic fit.**

requirements of its business line-up. The greater the extent to which a diversified organization is able to fund investment in its businesses through internally generated cash flows rather than from equity issues or borrowing, the more powerful its financial resource fit and the less dependent the firm is on external financial resources. This can provide an important competitive advantage over single business rivals when credit market conditions are tight, as they have been in many countries in recent years.

A *portfolio approach* to ensuring financial fit among a firm's businesses is based on the fact that different businesses have different cash flow and investment characteristics. For example, business units in rapidly growing industries are often **cash hogs** – so labelled because the cash flows they are able to generate from internal operations are not big enough to fund their expansion. To keep pace with rising buyer demand, rapid-growth businesses frequently need sizeable annual capital investments – for new facilities and equipment, for new product development or technology improvements and for additional working capital to support inventory expansion and a larger base of operations. A business in a fast-growing industry becomes an even bigger cash hog when it has a relatively low market share and is pursuing a strategy to become an industry leader.

In contrast, business units with leading market positions in mature industries may be **cash cows** – businesses that generate substantial cash surpluses over what is needed to adequately fund their operations. Market leaders in slow-growth industries often generate sizeable positive cash flows *over and above what is needed for growth and reinvestment* because their industry-leading positions tend to enable them to earn attractive profits and because the slow-growth nature of their industry often entails relatively modest annual investment requirements. Cash cows, although not always attractive from a growth standpoint, are valuable businesses from a financial resource perspective. The surplus cash flows they generate can be used to pay corporate dividends, finance acquisitions and provide funds for investing in the organization's promising cash hogs.

Core Concept

A **cash hog** business generates cash flows that are too small to fully fund its operations and growth and requires cash infusions to provide additional working capital and finance new capital investment.

Core Concept

A **cash cow** business generates cash flows over and above its internal requirements, thus providing a corporate parent with funds for investing in cash hog businesses, financing new acquisitions or paying dividends.

Viewing a diversified group of businesses as a collection of cash flows and cash requirements (present and future) is a major step forward in understanding what the financial ramifications of diversification are and why having businesses with a good financial resource fit can be important. For instance, *a diversified organization's businesses exhibit a good financial resource fit when the excess cash generated by its cash cow businesses is sufficient to fund the investment requirements of promising cash hog businesses.* Ideally, investing in promising cash hog businesses over time results in growing the hogs into self-supporting *star businesses* that have strong or market-leading competitive positions in attractive, high-growth markets and high levels of profitability. Star businesses are often the cash cows of the future – when the markets of star businesses begin to mature and their growth slows, their competitive strength should produce self-generated cash flows more than sufficient to cover their investment needs. The 'success sequence' is thus cash hog to young star (but perhaps still a cash hog) to self-supporting star to cash cow. While the practice of viewing a diversified organization in terms of cash cows and cash hogs has declined in popularity, it illustrates one approach to analysing financial resource fit and allocating financial resources across a portfolio of different businesses.

Aside from cash flow considerations, there are two other factors to consider in assessing whether a diversified organization's businesses exhibit good financial fit:

1. *Does the organization have adequate financial strength to fund its different businesses and maintain a healthy credit rating?* A diversified organization's strategy fails the resource-fit test when the organization's financial resources are stretched across so many businesses that its credit rating is impaired. Severe financial strain sometimes occurs when an organization borrows so heavily to finance new acquisitions that it has to trim way back on capital expenditures for existing businesses and use the big majority of its financial resources to meet interest obligations and to pay down debt. Many of the world's largest banks (e.g. Royal Bank of Scotland, Citigroup, HSBC) recently found themselves so undercapitalized and financially overextended that they were forced to sell off some of their business assets to meet regulatory requirements and restore public confidence in their solvency.

2. *Do any of the organization's individual businesses not contribute adequately to achieving organization-wide performance targets?* A business exhibits a poor financial fit with the organization if it soaks up a disproportionate share of the organization's financial resources, makes subpar bottom-line contributions, is too small to make a material earnings contribution or is unduly risky (such that the financial well-being of the whole organization could be jeopardized in the event it falls on hard times).

Non-financial Resource Fit

Just as a diversified organization must have adequate financial resources to support its various individual businesses, it must also have a big enough and deep enough pool of managerial, administrative, and competitive capabilities to support all of its different businesses. The following two questions help reveal whether a diversified organization has sufficient non-financial resources:

1. *Does the organization have (or can it develop) the specific resources and capabilities needed to be successful in each of its businesses?*[24] Sometimes a diversified organization's resources and capabilities are poorly matched to the resource requirements of one or more businesses it has diversified into. For instance, BTR, a multibusiness organization in Great Britain, discovered that the organization's resources and managerial skills were quite well suited for parenting its industrial manufacturing businesses but not for parenting its distribution businesses (National Tyre Services and Texas-based Summers Group). As a result, BTR

decided to divest its distribution businesses and focus exclusively on diversifying around small industrial manufacturing.[25] For companies pursuing related diversification strategies, a mismatch between the organization's competitive assets and the key success factors of an industry can be serious enough to warrant divesting businesses in that industry or not acquiring a new business. In contrast, when an organization's resources and capabilities are a good match with the key success factors of industries it is not presently in, it makes sense to take a hard look at acquiring companies in these industries and expanding the organization's business line-up.

2. *Are the organization's resources being stretched too thinly by the resource requirements of one or more of its businesses?* A diversified organization must guard against overtaxing its resources and capabilities, a condition that can arise when (1) it goes on an acquisition spree and management is called on to assimilate and oversee many new businesses very quickly or (2) it lacks sufficient resource depth to do a creditable job of transferring skills and competences from one of its businesses to another. The broader the diversification, the greater the concern about whether the organization has sufficient managerial depth to cope with the diverse range of operating problems its wide business line-up presents. Plus, the more an organization's diversification strategy is tied to transferring its existing know-how or technologies to new businesses, the more it has to develop a big enough and deep enough resource pool to supply these businesses with sufficient capability to create competitive advantage.[26] Otherwise, its competitive assets end up being thinly spread across many businesses, and the opportunity for competitive advantage slips through the cracks.

Step 5: Ranking the Performance Prospects of Business Units and Assigning a Priority for Resource Allocation

Once a diversified organization's strategy has been evaluated from the perspective of industry attractiveness, competitive strength, strategic fit and resource fit, the next step is to rank the performance prospects of the businesses from best to worst and determine which businesses merit top priority for resource support and new capital investments by the corporate parent.

The most important considerations in judging business-unit performance are sales growth, profit growth, contribution to earnings and return on capital invested in the business. Sometimes, cash flow is a big consideration. As a rule, the prior analyses, taken together, signal which business units are likely to be strong performers on the road ahead and which are likely to be laggards. And it is a short step from ranking the prospects of business units to drawing conclusions about whether the organization as a whole is capable of strong, mediocre or weak performance in upcoming years.

The rankings of future performance generally determine what priority the corporate parent should give to each business in terms of resource allocation. *Business subsidiaries with the brightest profit and growth prospects and solid strategic and resource fit generally should head the list for corporate resource support.* More specifically, corporate executives must be diligent in steering resources out of low-opportunity areas into high-opportunity areas. Divesting marginal businesses is one of the best ways of freeing unproductive assets for redeployment. Surplus funds from cash cows also can be used to finance the range of chief strategic and financial options shown in Figure 8.5. Ideally, an organization will have enough funds to do what is needed, both strategically and financially. If not, strategic uses of corporate resources should usually take precedence unless there is a compelling reason to strengthen the firm's balance sheet or divert financial resources to pacify shareholders.

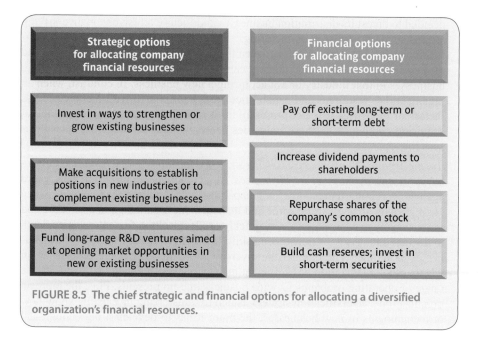

FIGURE 8.5 The chief strategic and financial options for allocating a diversified organization's financial resources.

Step 6: Crafting New Strategic Moves to Improve Overall Corporate Performance

LO 8.5
Understand a diversified organization's four main corporate strategy options for solidifying its diversification strategy and improving organizational performance.

The diagnosis and conclusions flowing from the five preceding analytical steps set the agenda for crafting strategic moves to improve a diversified organization's overall performance. Corporate strategy options once an organization has diversified boil down to four broad categories of actions (see Figure 8.6):

1. Sticking closely with the existing business line-up and pursuing the opportunities these businesses present.

2. Broadening the organization's business scope by making new acquisitions in new industries.

3. Divesting some businesses and retrenching to a narrower base of business operations.

4. Restructuring the organization's business line-up with a combination of divestitures and new acquisitions to put a whole new face on the organization's business make-up.

Sticking Closely with the Existing Business Line-up

The option of sticking with the current business line-up makes sense when the organization's present businesses offer attractive growth opportunities and can be counted on to create economic value for shareholders. As long as the organization's set of existing businesses puts it in a good position for the future and these businesses have a good strategic and resource fit, then major changes in the organization's business mix is unnecessary. Corporate executives can concentrate their attention on getting the best performance from each of the businesses, steering corporate resources into areas of greatest potential and profitability. The specifics of 'what to do' to wring better performance from the present business line-up have to be dictated by each business's circumstances and the preceding analysis of the corporate parent's diversification strategy.

However, in the event that corporate executives are not entirely satisfied with the opportunities they see in the organization's present set of businesses and conclude that changes in the organization's direction and business make-up are in order, they can opt for any of the three other strategic alternatives that follow.

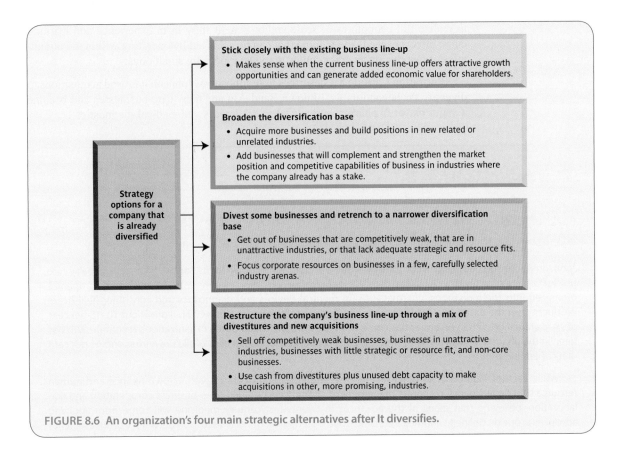

Stick closely with the existing business line-up
- Makes sense when the current business line-up offers attractive growth opportunities and can generate added economic value for shareholders.

Broaden the diversification base
- Acquire more businesses and build positions in new related or unrelated industries.
- Add businesses that will complement and strengthen the market position and competitive capabilities of business in industries where the company already has a stake.

Divest some businesses and retrench to a narrower diversification base
- Get out of businesses that are competitively weak, that are in unattractive industries, or that lack adequate strategic and resource fits.
- Focus corporate resources on businesses in a few, carefully selected industry arenas.

Restructure the company's business line-up through a mix of divestitures and new acquisitions
- Sell off competitively weak businesses, businesses in unattractive industries, businesses with little strategic or resource fit, and non-core businesses.
- Use cash from divestitures plus unused debt capacity to make acquisitions in other, more promising, industries.

Strategy options for a company that is already diversified

FIGURE 8.6 An organization's four main strategic alternatives after It diversifies.

Broadening a Diversified Organization's Business Base

Diversified companies sometimes find it desirable to build positions in new industries, whether related or unrelated. There are several motivating factors. One is the potential for transferring resources and capabilities to other related or complementary businesses. A second is rapidly changing conditions in one or more of an organization's core businesses brought on by technological, legislative or new product innovations that alter buyer preferences and resource requirements. For instance, the passage of legislation in the USA allowing banks, insurance companies and stock brokerages to enter each other's businesses spurred a raft of acquisitions and mergers to create full-service financial enterprises capable of meeting the multiple financial needs of customers.

A third, and often very important, motivating factor for adding new businesses is to complement and strengthen the market position and competitive capabilities of one or more of the organization's present businesses. Procter & Gamble's acquisition of Gillette strengthened and extended P&G's reach into personal care and household products – Gillette's businesses included Oral-B toothbrushes, Gillette razors and razor blades, Duracell batteries and Braun shavers and small appliances. Cisco Systems built itself into a world-wide leader in networking systems for the Internet by making 130 technology-based acquisitions between 1993–2008 to extend its market reach from routing and switching into IP telephony, home networking, wireless LAN, storage networking, network security, broadband and optical and broadband systems.

Another important avenue for expanding the scope of a diversified organization is to grow by extending the operations of existing businesses into additional country markets. Expanding an organization's geographic scope may offer an exceptional competitive advantage potential by facilitating the full capture of economies of scale and learning/experience curve effects. In some businesses, the volume of sales needed to realize full economies of scale and/or benefit fully from experience and learning curve effects exceeds the volume that can be achieved by operating within the boundaries of just one or several country markets, especially small ones.

Illustration Capsule 8.1 describes how Johnson & Johnson has used acquisitions to diversify far beyond its well-known Band-Aid and baby care businesses and become a major player in pharmaceuticals, medical devices and medical diagnostics.

Illustration Capsule 8.1

MANAGING DIVERSIFICATION AT JOHNSON & JOHNSON: THE BENEFITS OF CROSS-BUSINESS STRATEGIC FIT

Johnson & Johnson (J&J), once a consumer products organization known for its Band-Aid line and its baby care products, has evolved into a €47 billion diversified enterprise consisting of some 250-plus operating companies organized into three divisions: pharmaceuticals, medical devices and diagnostics and consumer healthcare products. Over the past decade J&J has made acquisitions totalling more than €39 billion; about 10–15 per cent of J&J's annual growth in revenues has come from acquisitions. Much of the organization's recent growth has been in the pharmaceutical division, which in 2009 accounted for 36 per cent of J&J's revenues and 41 per cent of its operating profits.

While each of J&J's business units sets its own strategies and operates with its own finance and human resource (HR) departments, corporate management strongly encourages cross-business co-operation and collaboration, believing that many of the advances in twenty-first-century medicine will come from applying advances in one discipline to another. J&J's drug-coated stent grew out of a discussion between a drug researcher

and a researcher in the organization's stent business. The innovative product helps prevent infection after cardiac procedures. (When stents are inserted to prop open arteries following angioplasty, the drug coating helps prevent infection.) A gene technology database compiled by the organization's gene research lab was shared with personnel from the diagnostics division, who developed a test that the drug researchers used to predict which patients would most benefit from an experimental cancer therapy. J&J's liquid Band-Aid product (a liquid coating applied to hard-to-cover places like fingers and knuckles) is based on a material used in a wound-closing product sold by the organization's hospital products company. Scientists from three separate business units worked collaboratively toward the development of an absorbable patch that would stop bleeding on contact. The development of the instant clotting patch was expected to save the lives of thousands of accident victims since uncontrolled bleeding was the number one cause of death due to injury.

J&J's corporate management maintains that close collaboration among people in its diagnostics, medical devices and pharmaceutical businesses – where numerous examples of cross-business strategic fit exist – gives J&J an edge on competitors, most of whom cannot match the organization's breadth and depth of expertise.

Sources: Barrett Amy, (2003) 'Staying on top', *Businessweek*, 5 May, pp. 60–8; Johnson & Johnson 2007 Annual Report; www.jnj.com (accessed 29 July 2010).

Divesting Some Businesses and Retrenching to a Narrower Diversification Base

Retrenching to a narrower diversification base is usually undertaken when top management concludes that its diversification strategy has ranged too far afield and that the organization can improve long-term performance by concentrating on building stronger positions in a smaller number of core businesses and industries. Hewlett-Packard spun off its testing and measurement businesses into a stand-alone organization called Agilent Technologies so that it could better concentrate on its PC, workstation, server, printer and peripherals and electronics businesses.

But there are other important reasons for divesting one or more of an organization's present businesses. Sometimes divesting a business has to be considered because market conditions in a once attractive industry have badly deteriorated. A business can become a prime candidate for divestiture because it lacks an adequate strategic or resource fit, because it is a cash hog with questionable long-term potential, or because it is weakly positioned in its industry with little prospect, the corporate parent can realize a decent return on its investment in the business. Sometimes an organization acquires businesses that, down the road, just do not work out as expected even though management has tried all it can think of to make them profitable. Sub-par performance by some business units is bound to occur, thereby raising questions of whether to divest them or keep them and attempt a turnaround. Other business units, despite adequate financial performance, may not combine as well with the rest of the firm as was originally thought. For instance, PepsiCo divested its group of fast-food restaurant businesses to focus its resources on its core soft-drink and snack-food businesses, where their resources and capabilities could add more value.

On occasion, a diversification move that seems sensible from a strategic-fit standpoint turns out to be a poor *cultural fit*.[27] Several pharmaceutical companies had just this experience. When they diversified into cosmetics and perfume, they discovered their personnel had little respect for the 'frivolous' nature of such products compared to the far nobler task of developing miracle drugs to cure the ill. The absence of shared values and cultural compatibility between the medical research and chemical-compounding expertise of the pharmaceutical companies and the fashion/marketing orientation of the cosmetics business was the undoing of what otherwise was diversification into businesses with technology-sharing potential, product-development fit and some overlap in distribution channels.

> Diversified companies need to divest low-performing businesses or businesses that do not fit in order to concentrate on expanding existing businesses and entering new ones where opportunities are more promising.

There is evidence indicating that pruning businesses and narrowing a firm's diversification base improves corporate performance.[28] A useful guide to determine whether or when to divest a business subsidiary is to ask, 'If we were not in this business today, would we want to get into it now?'[29] When the answer is no or probably not, divestiture should be considered. Another signal that a business should become a divestiture candidate is whether it is worth more to another organization than to the present parent; in such cases, shareholders would be well served if the organization sells the business and collects a premium price from the buyer for whom the business is a valuable fit.[30]

Selling a business outright to another organization is by far the most frequently used option for divesting a business. But sometimes a business selected for divestiture has ample resources and capabilities to compete successfully on its own. In such cases, a corporate parent may elect to spin the unwanted business off as a financially and managerially independent organization, either by selling shares to the investing public via an initial public offering or by distributing shares in the new organization to existing shareholders of the corporate parent.

Restructuring a Diversified Organization's Business Line-up through a Mix of Divestitures and New Acquisitions

Core Concept

Organization-wide restructuring (*corporate restructuring*) involves divesting some businesses and acquiring others so as to put a whole new face on the organization's business line-up.

If there is a serious mismatch between the organization's resources and the type of diversification it has pursued, then an **organization-wide restructuring** effort may be called for. Restructuring a diversified organization on an organization-wide basis (*corporate restructuring*) involves divesting some businesses and acquiring others so as to put a whole new face on the organization's business line-up.[31] Performing radical surgery on an organization's group of businesses may also be an appealing strategy alternative when its financial performance is limited or eroded by:

- Too many businesses in slow-growth, declining, low-margin or otherwise unattractive industries (a condition indicated by the number and size of businesses with industry attractiveness ratings below 5 and located on the bottom half of the attractiveness-strength matrix – see Figure 8.3).
- Too many competitively weak businesses (a condition indicated by the number and size of businesses with competitive strength ratings below 5 and located on the right half of the attractiveness-strength matrix).
- Ongoing decline in the market shares of one or more major business units due to strongly increasing competition.
- An excessive debt burden with interest costs that eat deeply into profitability.
- Ill-chosen acquisitions that have not lived up to expectations.

Organization-wide restructuring can also be mandated by the emergence of new technologies that threaten the survival of one or more of a diversified organization's important businesses. On occasion, corporate restructuring can be prompted by special circumstances – such as when a firm has a unique opportunity to make an acquisition so big and important that it has to sell several existing business units to finance the new acquisition or when an organization needs to sell off some businesses in order to raise the cash for entering a potentially big industry with wave-of-the-future technologies or products.

Candidates for divestiture in a corporate restructuring effort typically include not only weak performers or those in unattractive industries but also business units that lack a strategic fit with the businesses to be retained, businesses that are cash hogs or that lack other types of resource fit, and businesses incompatible with the organization's revised diversification strategy (even though they may be profitable or in an attractive industry). As businesses are divested, corporate restructuring generally involves aligning the remaining business units into groups with the best strategic fit and then redeploying the cash flows from the divested business to either pay down debt or make new acquisitions to strengthen the parent organization's business position in the industries it has chosen to emphasise.[32]

Over the past decade, corporate restructuring has become a popular strategy at many diversified companies, especially those that had diversified broadly into many different industries and lines of business. In 2008, GE's CEO Jeffrey Immelt announced that GE would spin off its industrial division, which included GE appliances, lighting and various industrial businesses. Earlier, he had led GE's withdrawal from the insurance business by divesting several companies and spinning off others. He further restructured GE's business line-up with two other major initiatives: (1) spending €7.5 billion to acquire British-based Amersham and extend GE's Medical Systems business into diagnostic pharmaceuticals and biosciences, thereby creating a €11 billion business designated as GE Healthcare, and (2) acquiring the entertainment assets of debt-ridden French media conglomerate Vivendi Universal Entertainment and integrating its operations into GE's NBC division, thereby creating a broad-based €10 billion media business positioned to compete against Walt Disney, Time Warner, Fox and Viacom. Illustration Capsule 8.2 discusses how VF Corporation shareholders have benefited through the organization's large-scale restructuring program.

Illustration Capsule 8.2

VF'S CORPORATE RESTRUCTURING STRATEGY THAT MADE IT THE STAR OF THE APPAREL INDUSTRY

VF Corporation's corporate restructuring, which includes a mix of divestitures and acquisitions, has provided its shareholders with returns that are more than five times greater than shareholder returns provided by competing apparel manufacturers. Its total return to investors in 2009 (a year in which the economy was down and many manufacturers were struggling) was 38.7 per cent. VF's growth in revenue and earnings made it number 310 on *Fortune*'s list of the 500 largest US companies in 2009. In 2010, it earned a spot on *Fortune*'s 'World's Most Admired Companies' list.

The organization's corporate restructuring began in 2000 when it divested its slow-growing businesses, including its namesake Vanity Fair brand of lingerie and sleepwear. The organization's €103 million acquisition of North Face in 2000 was the first in the series of many acquisitions of 'lifestyle brands' that connected with the way people lived, worked and played. Since the acquisition and turnaround of North Face, VF has spent €2.1 billion to acquire 18 additional businesses. New apparel and lifestyle brands acquired by VF Corporation include Vans skateboard shoes, Nautica, Eagle Creek, John Varvatos, 7 For All Mankind sportswear, Reef surf wear and Lucy athletic wear. The organization also acquired a variety of apparel companies specializing in apparel segments such as uniforms for professional baseball and football teams and law enforcement personnel.

VF Corporation's acquisitions came after years of researching each organization and developing a relationship with an acquisition candidate's chief managers before closing the deal. The organization made a practice of leaving management of acquired companies in place, while bringing in new managers only when necessary talent and skills were lacking. In addition, companies acquired by VF were allowed to keep long-standing traditions that shaped culture and spurred creativity. For example, the Vans headquarters in Cypress, California, retained its half-pipe and concrete floor so that its employees could skateboard to and from meetings.

In 2009, VF Corporation was among the most profitable apparel firms in the industry, with net earnings of €348 million. The organization expected new acquisitions that would push VF's revenues to €8 billion by 2012.

Sources: Kapner Suzanne, (2008) 'How a 100-year old apparel firm changed course', *Fortune,* 9 April. Available online at www. vfc.com (accessed 29 July 2010).

KEY POINTS

1. The purpose of diversification is to build shareholder value. Diversification builds shareholder value when a diversified group of businesses can perform better under the auspices of a single corporate parent than they would as independent, stand-alone businesses – the goal is to achieve not just a 1 + 1 = 2 result but, rather, to realize important 1 + 1 = 3 performance benefits. Whether getting into a new business has potential to enhance shareholder value hinges on whether an organization's entry into that business can pass the attractiveness test, the cost-of-entry test and the better-off test.

2. Entry into new businesses can take any of three forms: acquisition, internal start-up or joint venture/ strategic partnership. The choice of which is best depends on the firm's resources and capabilities, the industry's entry barriers, the importance of speed and the relative costs.

3. There are two fundamental approaches to diversification – into related businesses and into unrelated businesses. The rationale for *related* diversification is to benefit from *strategic fit:* diversify into businesses with match-ups along their respective value chains and then capitalize on the strategic fit by sharing or transferring the resources and capabilities that enable the matching value chain activities in order to gain competitive advantage.

4. *Unrelated* diversification strategies surrender the competitive advantage potential of strategic fit at the value chain level in return for the potential that can be realized from superior corporate parenting. An outstanding corporate parent can benefit its businesses through (1) providing high-

level oversight and making available other corporate resources, (2) allocating financial resources across the business portfolio, and (3) restructuring underperforming acquisitions.

5. Related diversification provides a stronger foundation for creating shareholder value than unrelated diversification, since the *specialized resources and capabilities* that are leveraged in related diversification tend to be more valuable competitive assets than the *generalized resources and capabilities* underlying unrelated diversification, which in most cases are relatively common and easier to imitate.

6. Analysing how good an organization's diversification strategy is consists of a six-step process:

   Step 1: *Evaluate the long-term attractiveness of the industries into which the firm has diversified.* Industry attractiveness needs to be evaluated from three angles: the attractiveness of each industry on its own, the attractiveness of each industry relative to the others and the attractiveness of all the industries as a group.

   Step 2: *Evaluate the relative competitive strength of each of the organization's business units.* The purpose of rating the competitive strength of each business is to gain a clear understanding of which businesses are strong contenders in their industries, which are weak contenders and the underlying reasons for their strength or weakness. The conclusions about industry attractiveness can be joined with the conclusions about competitive strength by drawing an industry attractiveness–competitive strength matrix that helps identify the prospects of each business and what priority each business should be given in allocating corporate resources and investment capital.

   Step 3: *Check for cross-business strategic fit.* A business is more attractive strategically when it has value chain relationships with the organization's other business units that offer potential to (1) realize economies of scope or cost-saving efficiencies, (2) transfer technology, skills, know-how or other resource capabilities from one business to another, (3) leverage use of a trusted brand name or other resources that enhance differentiation, and (4) build new resources and competitive capabilities via cross-business collaboration. Cross-business strategic fit represents a significant avenue for producing competitive advantage beyond what any one business can achieve on its own.

   Step 4: *Check whether the firm's resource mix fits the resource requirements of its present business line-up.* In firms with a related diversification strategy, a resource fit exists when the organization's businesses add to its overall resource position and when they have matching resource requirements at the value chain level. In companies pursuing unrelated diversification, a resource fit exists when the parent organization has generalized resources that can add value to its component businesses and when it has corporate resources sufficient to support its entire group of businesses without spreading itself too thin. When there is a financial resource fit among the businesses of any type of diversified organization, the organization can generate internal cash flows sufficient to fund the capital requirements of its businesses, meet its debt obligations and otherwise remain financially healthy.

   Step 5: *Rank the performance prospects of the businesses from best to worst, and determine what the corporate parent's priority should be in allocating resources to its various businesses.* The most important considerations in judging business-unit performance are sales growth, profit growth, contribution to earnings and the return on capital invested in the business. Normally, strong business units in attractive industries have significantly better performance prospects than weak businesses or businesses in unattractive industries. Business subsidiaries with the brightest profit and growth prospects and solid strategic and resource fit generally should head the list for corporate resource support.

   Step 6: *Crafting new strategic moves to improve overall corporate performance.* This step entails using the results of the preceding analysis as the basis for devising actions to strengthen existing businesses, make new acquisitions, divest weak-performing and unattractive businesses, restructure the organization's business line-up, expand the scope of the organization's geographic reach into new markets around the world and otherwise steer corporate resources into the areas of greatest opportunity.

7. Once an organization has diversified, corporate management's task is to manage the collection of businesses for maximum long-term performance. There are four different strategic paths for improving a diversified organization's performance: (1) sticking with the existing business line-up, (2) broadening the firm's business base by diversifying into additional businesses or geographic markets, (3) retrenching to a narrower diversification base by divesting some of its present businesses, and (4) restructuring the organization's business line-up with a combination of divestitures and new acquisitions to put a whole new face on the organization's business make-up.

CLOSING CASE

PHILIPS EXITS TV

The TV market has deteriorated, and the sooner we complete the sale the better

Frans Van Houten, CEO, Philips

Royal Philips Electronics of the Netherlands, known as Philips, is a global leader in healthcare, lighting and consumer lifestyle products, focused on improving people's lives through innovation. Philips' core products have traditionally been consumer electronics and electrical products (including audio equipment, blu-ray players, computer accessories, TVs, small domestic appliances and shavers); healthcare products (including CT scanners, ECG equipment, mammography equipment, monitoring equipment, MRI scanners, radiography equipment, resuscitation equipment, ultrasound equipment and X-ray equipment); and lighting products (including indoor luminaires, outdoor luminaires, lamps, lighting controls and lighting electronics).

Once dominant in consumer electronics, the Dutch firm has developed into a diverse group after strong competition by rivals such as Sony, Samsung and JG Electronics forced them to become a niche player in previously significant product areas such as TVs, appliances, DVDs and audio players. From operating in the first tier of the TV set industry, Philips announced in April 2011 that it was divesting its TV business into a joint venture with China's TVP Technology Ltd. The deal was signed in February 2012 marking the end of an era for Philips. TVP owns 70 per cent of the joint venture, with Philips retaining 30 per cent, with the option to sell this final stake to TVP after six years.

TV MANUFACTURING

Over most of the last decade, TV sets were a strong growth business. Newly affluent Chinese, Indians, Indonesians and Brazilians were buying their first TVs. Then, there was a move from analogue to digital TVs in North American and Europe, so people replaced old sets with new ones. There was also the transition to larger flat-screen TVs. Rather quickly, however, the TV market changed. In early 2008, analysts were forecasting 5 per cent to 6 per cent growth in the global TV business for the coming two years. By 2009, those forecasts were predicting a contraction in global demand of up to 7.5 per cent, more so in Europe. Americans and Europeans were increasingly watching on-demand streaming videos, including TV programmes and movies, on their computers and tablets.

Suddenly, TV manufacturing was not a growth industry anymore. Just about every major TV manufacturer was losing money making TVs. Samsung, Sony, LG and Philips all lost money on TVs in 2009 and 2010. Indeed, Sony and Philips had been making losses on the TV business for over six years. In 2010 Philips had a 3.8 per cent share of the global LCD TV market and in the four years from 2007, Philips' TV unit recorded a loss of almost €1 billion. Every new, sleek, large flat-screen high-definition TV sold actually added to the losses. Many new players entered the market only to fold. Some years ago, Taiwanese player BenQ took the industry by a storm. It rather quickly exited the business and focused on projectors, digital camcorders and computer monitors. Other players such as Apple have been looking at the TV business, but with so much blood-letting in the industry, they need to completely rethink the TV set to make any profit out of it.

TVP

TVP started in the early 1980s as a colour TV maker in Taiwan, doing contract manufacturing for lesser-known brands. In the late 1980s, it switched to designing and manufacturing computer monitors. By 2005, it had become the world's largest computer monitor maker and a key supplier to PC giants such as Hewlett-Packard and Dell. Yet, as personal computing switched from mainly desktops to a combination of desktops and laptops and tablets, TVP diversified its business, returning to its TV manufacturing roots by becoming a contract manufacturer for LCD TVs. TVP is a clear leader in LCD TV OEM manufacturing, serving more than 25 different TV brands globally. The company produced more than 18 million LCD TVs in 2011.

TVP has partnered with Philips for more than a decade. Forming the joint venture to take over the global R&D, manufacturing and sales and marketing of Philips TV is a good way for TVP to diversify away from low-margin computer monitors and merely doing low-end contract manufacturing of TVs.

Having control over the Philips brand brings a lot more name recognition than its own brand, AOC, which is marketed in the USA but is not exactly popular. At the time of the shareholders[7] meeting to approve the new joint venture, the CFO of TVP, Shane Tyau, said:

> *In the TV sector, obviously our brand is not a consumer electronics name. We need a brand name like Philips, in particular. It already has an established market, and that can allow us to promptly reach out to the market in Europe as well as other of Philip's existing markets. The TV business is a fast-changing business with new models and technologies coming up any time. TVP's strength is its speed of innovation.*

▶

◄

Sources: Reuters, www.reuters.com/article/2012/02/22/us-tvp-philips (accessed 18 March 2012); www.//bizmology.hoovers.com/2012/02/24/philips-electronics-sells-tv-division-to-china/ (accessed 17 March 2012); The Final Act: Philips Exits TV FPD Industry News, TVs on April 19, 2011, www.displaysearchblog.com (accessed 18 March 2012); BBC News 18 April 2011, Philips moves to end losses at ailing television arm www.bbc.co.uk (accessed 18 March 2012); The Edge: Singapore. Will TVP walk away from Philips TV deal? www.the edgesingapore.com (accessed 17 March 2012); www.philips.com (accessed 17 March 2012).

QUESTIONS

1. With margins being squeezed in its traditional computer monitor business, which is seen as inextricably linked to desktops, TVP wants to diversify its business. But is buying another low-margin, low-growth business the right solution?

2. Who benefits most from the joint venture, Philips or TVP? What factors would determine if TVP should pay a premium or receive a discount on the business?

ASSURANCE OF LEARNING EXERCISES

LO 8.1, LO 8.2

1. See if you can identify the value chain relationships that make the businesses of the following companies related in competitively relevant ways. In particular, you should consider whether there are cross-business opportunities for (1) transferring skills/technology, (2) combining related value chain activities to achieve economies of scope, and/or (3) leveraging the use of a well-respected brand name or other resources that enhance differentiation.

OSI Restaurant Partners
- Outback Steakhouse
- Carrabba's Italian Grill
- Roy's Restaurant (Hawaiian fusion cuisine)
- Bonefish Grill (market-fresh fine seafood)
- Fleming's Prime Steakhouse & Wine Bar

L'Oréal
- Maybelline, Lancôme, Helena Rubinstein, Kiehl's, Garner and Shu Uemura cosmetics
- L'Oréal and Soft Sheen/Carson hair care products
- Redken, Matrix, L'Oréal Professional and Kerastase Paris professional hair care and skin care products
- Ralph Lauren and Giorgio Armani fragrances
- Biotherm skincare products
- La Roche–Posay and Vichy Laboratories dermocosmetics

Johnson & Johnson
- Baby products (powder, shampoo, oil, lotion)
- Band-Aids and other first-aid products
- Women's health and personal care products (Stayfree, Carefree, Sure & Natural)
- Neutrogena and Aveeno skin care products
- Non-prescription drugs (Tylenol, Motrin, Pepcid AC, Mylanta, Monistat)
- Prescription drugs
- Prosthetic and other medical devices
- Surgical and hospital products
- Acuvue contact lenses

▶

◀

LO 8.1, LO 8.3

2. A defining characteristic of unrelated diversification is few cross-business commonalities in terms of key value chain activities. Peruse the business group listings for Lancaster Colony shown below, and see if you can confirm that it has diversified into unrelated business groups.

Lancaster Colony's business line-up

- Specialty food products: Cardini, Marzetti, Girard's and Pheiffer salad dressings; T. Marzetti and Chatham Village croutons; Jack Daniels mustards; Inn Maid noodles; New York and Mamma Bella garlic breads; Reames egg noodles; Sister Schubert's rolls; and Romanoff caviar
- Candlelite brand candles marketed to retailers and private-label customers chains
- Glassware, plastic ware, coffee urns and matting products marketed to the food service and lodging industry

If need be, visit the organization's website (www.lancastercolony.com) to obtain additional information about its business line-up and strategy.

LO 8.1, L O 8.2, L O 8.3

3. The Walt Disney Organization is in the following businesses:
   - Theme parks
   - Disney Cruise Line
   - Resort properties
   - Movie, video and theatrical productions (for both children and adults)
   - Television broadcasting (ABC, Disney Channel, Toon Disney, Classic Sports Network, ESPN and ESPN2, E!, Lifetime and A&E networks)
   - Radio broadcasting (Disney Radio)
   - Musical recordings and sales of animation art
   - Anaheim Mighty Ducks NHL franchise
   - Anaheim Angels major-league baseball franchise (25 per cent ownership)
   - Books and magazine publishing
   - Interactive software and Internet sites
   - The Disney Store retail shops

   Based on the above listing, would you say that Walt Disney's business line-up reflects a strategy of related diversification, unrelated diversification or a combination of related and unrelated diversification? Be prepared to justify and explain your answer in terms of the nature of Disney's shared or transferred resources and capabilities and the extent to which the value chains of Disney's different businesses seem to have competitively valuable cross-business relationships.

   If need be, visit the organization's website at www.corporate.disney.go.com/index.html?ppLink=pp_wdig to obtain additional information about its business line-up and strategy.

EXERCISES FOR SIMULATION PARTICIPANTS

LO 8.1, LO 8.2, LO 8.3

1. In the event that your organization had the opportunity to diversify into other products or businesses of your choosing, would you opt to pursue related diversification, unrelated diversification or a combination of both? Explain why.

▶

LO 8.1, LO 8.2

2. What specific resources and capabilities does your organization possess that would make diversifying into related businesses attractive? Indicate what kinds of strategic-fit benefits could be captured by transferring these resources and competitive capabilities to newly acquired related businesses.

LO 8.1, LO 8.2

3. If your organization opted to pursue a strategy of related diversification, what industries or product categories could it diversify into that would allow it to achieve economies of scope? Name at least two or three such industries or product categories, and indicate the specific kinds of cost savings that might accrue from entry into each.

LO 8.1, LO 8.2

4. If your organization opted to pursue a strategy of related diversification, what industries or product categories could it diversify into that would allow it to capitalize on using its present brand name and corporate image to good advantage in the newly entered businesses or product categories? Name at least two or three such industries or product categories, and indicate *the specific benefits* that might be captured by transferring your organization's brand name to each.

ENDNOTES

1. For a more detailed discussion of when diversification makes good strategic sense, see Markides, Constantinos C. (1997) 'To diversify or not to diversify', *Harvard Business Review,* 75(6): 93–9.

2. For a discussion of how hidden opportunities within a corporation's existing asset base may offer growth to corporations with declining core businesses, see Zook Chris, (2007) 'Finding your next core business', *Harvard Business Review*, 85(4): 66–75.

3. Porter, Michael E. (1997) 'From competitive advantage to corporate strategy', *Harvard Business Review,* 45(3): 46–9.

4. Nazareth, Rita (2009) 'CEOs Paying 56% M&A premium shows stocks may be cheap (Update 3)'. Available online at www.bloomberg.com/apps/news?pid=20603037&sid=ahPoIYY.zgQ.

5. Ibid.

6. Porter, Michael E. (1980) *Competitive Strategy: Techniques for Analyzing Industries and Competitors*, New York, Free Press, pp. 354–5.

7. Shleifer, A. and Vishny, R. (1991) 'Takeovers in the 60s and the 80s – evidence and implications', *Strategic Management Journal*, 12: 51–9; Brush, T. (1996) 'Predicted change in operational synergy and post-acquisition performance of acquired businesses', *Strategic Management Journal*, 17(1): 1–24; Walsh, J.P. (1988) 'Top management turnover following mergers and acquisitions', *Strategic Management Journal*, 9(2): 173–83; Cannella, A. and Hambrick, D. (1993) 'Effects of executive departures on the performance of acquired firms', *Strategic Management Journal*, 14: 137–52; Roll, R. (1986) 'The hubris hypothesis of corporate takeovers', *Journal of Business*, 59(2): 197–216; Haspeslagh, P. and Jemison, D. (1991) *Managing Acquisitions*, New York, Free Press.

8. Hayward, M.L.A. (2002) 'When do firms learn from their acquisition experience? Evidence from 1990–1995', *Strategic Management Journal*, 23(1): 21–9; Ahuja, G. and Katila, R. (2001) 'Technological acquisitions and the innovation performance of acquiring firms: a longitudinal study', *Strategic Management Journal*, 22(3): 197–220; Barkema, H. and Vermeulen, F. (1998) 'International expansion through start-up or acquisition: a learning perspective', *Academy of Management Journal*, 41(1): 7–26.

9. Haspeslagh and Jemison, *Managing Acquisitions,* pp. 344–5.

10. Doz, Yves L. and Hamel, Gary (1998) *Alliance Advantage: The Art of Creating Value through Partnering*, Boston, MA, Harvard Business School Press, chs 1 and 2.

11. Glover, J. (1996) 'The Guardian', 23 March. Available online at www.mcspotlight.org/media/press/guardpizza_23mar96.html.

12. Porter, Michael E. (1985) *Competitive Advantage*, New York, Free Press, pp. 318–19 and pp. 337–53; Porter, 'From competitive advantage to corporate strategy', pp. 53–7. For an empirical study supporting the notion that strategic fit enhances performance (provided the resulting combination is competitively valuable and difficult to duplicate by rivals), see Markides, Constantinos C. and Williamson, Peter J. (1996) 'Corporate diversification and organization structure: a resource-based view', *Academy of Management Journal*, 39(2): 340–67.

13. Collis, David J. and Montgomery, Cynthia A. (1998) 'Creating corporate advantage', *Harvard Business Review*, 76(3): 72–80; Markides and Williamson, 'Corporate diversification and organization structure'.

14. Markides and Williamson, 'Corporate diversification and organization structure'.

15. For a discussion of the strategic significance of cross-business co-ordination of value chain activities and insight into how the process works, see Liedtka, Jeanne M. (1996) 'Collaboration across lines of business for competitive advantage', *Academy of Management Executive*, 10(2): 20–34.

16. For a discussion of what is involved in actually capturing strategic-fit benefits, see Eisenhardt, Kathleen M. and Galunic, D. Charles (2000) 'Coevolving: at last, a way to make synergies work', *Harvard Business Review*, 78(1): 91–101; Markides, Constantinos C. and Williamson, Peter J. (1994) 'Related diversification, core competences and corporate performance', *Strategic Management Journal*, 15: 149–65.

17. Campbell, A., Goold, M. and Alexander, M. (1995) 'Corporate strategy: the quest for parenting advantage', *Harvard Business Review*, 73(2): 120–32.

18. Montgomery, C. and Wernerfelt, B. (1988) 'Diversification, Ricardian rents, and Tobin-Q', *RAND Journal of Economics*, 19(4): 623–32.

19. Ibid.

20. Ibid.

21. For a review of the experiences of companies that have pursued unrelated diversification successfully, see Anslinger, Patricia L. and Copeland, Thomas E. (1996) 'Growth through acquisitions: a fresh look', *Harvard Business Review*, 74(1): 126–35.

22. Of course, management may be willing to assume the risk that trouble will not strike before it has had time to learn the business well enough to bail it out of almost any difficulty. But there is research that shows this is very risky from a financial perspective; see, for example, Lubatkin, M. and Chatterjee, S. (1994) 'Extending modern portfolio theory', *Academy of Management Journal*, 37(1): 109–36.

23. For research evidence of the failure of broad diversification and trend of companies to focus their diversification efforts more narrowly, see Franko, Lawrence G. (2004) 'The death of diversification? The focusing of the world's industrial firms, 1980–2000', *Business Horizons*, 47(4): 41–50.

24. For an excellent discussion of what to look for in assessing this type of strategic fit, see Campbell, Goold and Alexander, 'Corporate strategy: the quest for parenting advantage'.

25. Ibid. p. 128.

26. A good discussion of the importance of having adequate resources, as well as upgrading corporate resources and capabilities, can be found in Collis, David J. and Montgomery, Cynthia A. (1995) 'Competing on resources: strategy in the 90s', *Harvard Business Review*, 73(4): 118–28.

27. Drucker, Peter F. (1974) *Management: Tasks, Responsibilities, Practices*, New York, Harper & Row, p. 709.

28. See, for, example, Markides, Constantinos C. (1995) 'Diversification, restructuring, and economic performance', *Strategic Management Journal*, 16: 101–18.

29. Drucker, *Management: Tasks, Responsibilities, Practices*, p. 94.

30. Collis and Montgomery, 'Creating corporate advantage'.

31. For a discussion of why divestiture needs to be a standard part of any organization's diversification strategy, see Dranikoff, Lee, Koller, Tim and Schneiders Anton, (2002) 'Divestiture: strategy's missing link', *Harvard Business Review*, 80(5): 74–83.

32. Evidence that restructuring strategies tend to result in higher levels of performance is contained in Markides, 'Diversification, restructuring, and economic performance'.

Chapter Nine

Ethics, corporate social responsibility, environmental sustainability and strategy

Corporate social responsibility is a hard-edged business decision. Not because it is a nice thing to do or because people are forcing us to do it ... because it is good for our business.

Niall Fitzgerald KBE
Deputy Chairman of Thomson Reuters and former CEO of Unilever

It takes many good deeds to build a good reputation and only one bad one to lose it.

Benjamin Franklin
American Statesman, Inventor and Philosopher

Corporations are economic entities, to be sure, but they are also social institutions that must justify their existence by their overall contribution to society.

Henry Mintzberg, Robert Simons and Kunal Basu
Professors

Companies have to be socially responsible or shareholders pay eventually.

Warren Shaw
Former CEO of LG T Asset Management

Learning Objectives

When you have read this chapter you should be able to:

LO 9.1   Explain how the standards of ethical behaviour in business relate to the ethical standards and norms of the larger society and culture in which an organization operates.

LO 9.2   Identify conditions that can give rise to unethical business strategies and behaviour.

LO 9.3   Give examples of the costs of business ethics failures.

LO 9.4   Explain the concepts of corporate social responsibility and environmental sustainability and of how organizations balance these duties with economic responsibilities to shareholders.

BP AND THE GULF OF MEXICO DISASTER

On 20 April 2010 an explosion on the Deepwater Horizon drilling rig in the Gulf of Mexico killed 11 workers and led to the worst oil spillage in US history. Although the rig was operated by Transocean, they were subcontractors of British oil firm BP. Within 10 days of the explosion the rig had sunk and oil had begun to reach the Louisiana shoreline threatening wildlife and the livelihoods of local people who relied on tourism, fishing and a variety of other industries reliant on the fragile ecosystem. By the time the leak was finally capped and secured on 19 September 2010, the equivalent of 4.5 million barrels of oil had spilled in the Gulf of Mexico.

Oil exploration and processing is a risky business and organizations involved in the industry are well aware of the potential harm to the environment that their activities and end product cause. Many oil companies also make substantial profits as their product is seen a strategic resource by other organizations and governments throughout the globe. Prior to the Gulf of Mexico disaster BP's income was in excess of $230 billion and the firm's profit was over $14 billion.

However, BP's record on corporate social responsibility is a mixed one. Despite being one of the first oil companies to recognize their impact and admit the existence of global warming and climate change in 2002 the firm had a poor record on health and safety and oil leaks even prior to 2010. In 2005 BP's Texas City refinery exploded leaving 15 workers dead and 180 injured. In 2006 the firm had to close its pipeline in Prudhoe Bay, Alaska after a leak was discovered that had discharged over a million litres of oil. BP were also accused of acting in an unethical and unfair manner. The corporation was fined for manipulating propane prices in the USA in 2007 and oil prices in Russia in 2008. In Columbia the firm is alleged to have benefited from a paramilitary reign of terror that protected their Ocensa pipeline in the country. BP had been one of the most active oil companies in exploring alternative sources of energy spending about 4 per cent of their exploratory budget on this activity. Marketing campaigns and a forward-looking strategy were underpinned with the slogan 'Beyond Petroleum'.

The positive and negative results of their past strategies have been dwarfed by the events in the Gulf of Mexico. The initial investigation into the disaster blamed systemic management failings for the explosion. By April 2011 BP had set aside $41 billion to cover the costs of the disaster. These will include the work done to cap the leak and clean up the Louisiana coastline, compensation for those that lost livelihoods as a result of the spill, as well as legal fees, and fines levied by the US Environmental Protection Agency. The figure represents over two and a half times BP's annual profit. The disaster also cost BP's then Chief Executive, Tony Hayward, his job. Hayward announced his resignation in July 2010 and left the firm in October.

There is also the issue of reputation to be considered. The events were broadcast globally for weeks with every move the organization made scrutinized by news organizations, not to mention bloggers and citizen journalists. By the end of the disaster BP was possibly the most hated company in the US despite its efforts to clean up the spill and compensate those affected by it. Congress passed legislation restricting its activities in the US and there was even talk of the government nationalising BP's operations in the country. Despite all this BP remains in the Gulf and committed to deep water exploration and drilling. The operations in this part of the world are some of its most lucrative and BP still has to satisfy its many shareholders.

QUESTIONS

1. What were the direct and indirect costs of the Gulf of Mexico disaster for BP?

2. Are these costs just a fact of life for an oil organization like BP and a necessary evil in order to produce the substantial profits required by their shareholders?

Sources: Allen, K. (2010) 'BP profits fall by 45%', *The Guardian*, 2 February. Available online at www.guardian.co.uk/business/2010/feb/02/bp-profits-fall-2009 (accessed 6 August 2011); Mardell, M. (2011) 'The failure of an industry', BBC News, 6 January. Available at www.bbc.co.uk/blogs/thereporters/markmardell/2011/01/the_failure_of_an_industry.html (accessed 6 August 2011); Mervin, J. (2011) 'Counting the cost of the BP disaster one year on', BBC News. Available online at www.bbc.co.uk/news/business-13120605 (accessed 6 August 2011).

Most commercial organizations have a responsibility to make a profit and grow the business – in capitalist or market economies; management's fiduciary duty to create value for shareholders is not a matter for serious debate. Just as clearly, an organization and its personnel also have a duty to obey the law and play by the rules of fair competition. But does an organization have a duty to go beyond legal requirements and operate according to the ethical norms of the societies in which it operates – should all organizational personnel be held to some standard of ethical conduct? And does an organization have a duty or obligation to contribute to the betterment of society independent of the needs and preferences of the customers it serves? Should an organization display a social conscience and devote a portion of its resources to bettering society? How far should an organization go in protecting the environment, conserving natural resources for use by future generations and ensuring that its operations do not ultimately endanger the planet? The opening case on BP provides some stark evidence of what can happen when things go wrong.

The focus of this chapter is to examine what link, if any, there should be between an organization's efforts to craft and execute a good strategy and its duties to (1) conduct its activities in an ethical manner, (2) demonstrate socially responsible behaviour by being a committed corporate citizen and directing corporate resources to the betterment of employees, the communities in which it operates and society as a whole, and (3) adopt business practices that conserve natural resources, protect the interests of future generations, and preserve the well-being of the planet.

What do We Mean by *Business Ethics*?

> **Core Concept**
>
> **Business ethics** is the application of general ethical principles to the actions and decisions of businesses and the conduct of their personnel.

Ethics concerns principles of right or wrong conduct, it is usually thought of as a set of moral standards that governs or influences the way people behave. **Business ethics** is the application of ethical principles and standards to the actions and decisions of business organizations and the conduct of their personnel.[1] Ethical principles in business are not materially different from ethical principles in general because business actions have to be judged in the context of society's standards of right and wrong. There is not a special set of ethical standards applicable only to business situations. If dishonesty is considered unethical and immoral, then dishonest behaviour in business – whether it relates to customers, suppliers, employees, shareholders, competitors, government or society – qualifies as equally unethical and immoral. If being ethical entails not deliberately harming others, then recalling a defective or unsafe product is ethically necessary. If society deems bribery unethical, then it is unethical for organization personnel to make payoffs to government officials or bestow gifts and other favours on prospective customers to win or retain business. In short, ethical behaviour in business situations requires adhering to generally accepted norms about right or wrong conduct. As a consequence, organization managers have an obligation – indeed, a duty – to observe ethical norms when crafting and executing strategy.

Where do Ethical Standards Come From – are They Universal or Dependent on Local Norms?

> **LO 9.1**
> Explain how the standards of ethical behaviour in business relate to the ethical standards and norms of the larger society and culture in which an organization operates.

Notions of right and wrong, fair and unfair, ethical and unethical are present in all societies and cultures. But there are three distinct schools of thought about the extent to which ethical standards travel across cultures and whether multinational organizations can apply the same set of ethical standards in any and all locations where they operate. Illustration Capsule 9.1 describes the difficulties Apple has faced in trying to enforce a common set of ethical standards across its vast global supplier network.

Illustration Capsule 9.1

MANY OF APPLE'S SUPPLIERS FLUNK THE ETHICS TEST

Apple requires its suppliers to comply with the company's Supplier Code of Conduct as a condition of being awarded contracts. To ensure compliance, Apple has a supplier monitoring programme that includes audits of supplier factories, corrective action plans and verification measures. In the company's 25-page 2011 Progress Report on Supplier Responsibility, Apple reported that in 2010 it conducted 127 audits of supplier facilities in such countries as China, the Czech Republic, Malaysia, the Philippines, Singapore, South Korea, Taiwan, Thailand and the USA; 97 of these audits were first-time audits and 30 were repeat audits.

Apple distinguishes among the seriousness of infractions, designating 'core violations' as those that go directly against the core principles of its Supplier Code of Conduct and must be remedied immediately. During the 2010 audits, 36 such violations were discovered, including 10 cases of underage labour, 18 cases involving excessive recruitment fees, 2 cases of improper hazardous waste disposal and 4 cases of deliberately falsified audit records. Apple responded by ensuring that immediate corrective actions were taken, placing violators on probation and planning to audit them again in a year's time. The organization was especially concerned about the growing number of workers aged under 16 it found in suppliers' factories in China; this rose from 11 in 2009 to 91 in 2010.

At 76 of the audited facilities, workers were required to work more than 60 hours per week more than 50 per cent of the time – Apple sets a maximum of 60 hours per week (except in unusual or emergency circumstances). In 74 of the audited facilities, workers were found to have been required to work more than six consecutive days a week at least once per month – Apple requires at least one day of rest per seven days of work (except in unusual or emergency circumstances).

Following the suicides at Foxconn's Shenzhen facility, a team of independent experts led by Apple's COO, Tim Cook, had carried out a detailed investigation with local managers at their suppliers to understand the situation better. The team presented their findings in August 2010 and although it was clear Foxconn had put in  place many effective measures to improve welfare there were still improvements to be made around training care centre counsellors and hotline staff.

Apple also requires suppliers to provide a safe working environment and to eliminate physical hazards to employees where possible. But the 2010 audits revealed that workers were not wearing appropriate protective personal equipment at 54 facilities. The audit also revealed that 137 workers had been poisoned with hydrocarbon n-hexane at one of their factories in China. Violations were found at 95 facilities where workers were improperly trained, where unlicensed workers were operating equipment and where required inspections of equipment were not being conducted. Apple auditors found that 63 facilities had failed to conduct environmental impact assessments, 37 facilities did not have permits for air emissions and 4 facilities did not meet the conditions specified in their emission permits. Moreover, the audits revealed that 53 supplier facilities did not have any personnel assigned to ensuring compliance with Apple's Supplier Code of Conduct. The explosion at the iPad factory at Chengdu in May 2011 that killed two workers illustrates how critical this area is and how far Apple still has to go in ensuring its suppliers are operating to the highest standards.

For Apple, the audits represent a starting point for bringing its suppliers into compliance, through greater scrutiny, education and training of suppliers' personnel, and incentives. Apple collects quarterly data to hold its suppliers accountable for their actions and makes procurement decisions based, in part, on these numbers. Suppliers that are unable to meet Apple's high standards of conduct ultimately end up losing Apple's business.

▶

Sources: Apple's 2011 Progress Report on Supplier Responsibility; Chartier, David (2011) 'Apple Releases 2011 Supplier Responsibility report', 14 February 14. Available online at www.macworld.com/article/157914/2011/02/apple_supplier_responsibility_report.html (accessed 4 August 2010); Andrews, Amanda (2011) 'Apple investigates explosion at iPad factory in China', *The Telegraph*, 21 May. Available online at www.telegraph.co.uk/technology/apple/8527700/Apple-investigates-explosion-at-iPad-factory-in-China.html (accessed 4 August, 2011); Moore, Malcolm (2011) 'Apple's child labour issues worsen', *The Telegraph*, 15 February. Available online at www.telegraph.co.uk/technology/apple/8324867/Apples-child-labour-issues-worsen.html (accessed 4 August 2011); Branigan, Tania (2011) 'Apple report reveals child labour increase', *The Guardian*, 15 February. Available online at www.guardian.co.uk/technology/2011/feb/15/apple-report-reveals-child-labour?INTCMP=SRCH (accessed 4 August 2011).

The School of Ethical Universalism

> **Core Concept**
>
> The school of **ethical universalism** holds that common understandings across multiple cultures and countries about what constitutes right and wrong give rise to universal ethical standards that apply to members of all societies, all organizations and all businesspeople.

According to the school of **ethical universalism**, the most important concepts of what is right and what is wrong are *universal* and transcend culture, society, and religion.[2] For instance, being truthful (or not being deliberately deceitful) strikes a chord of what is right in the peoples of all nations. Likewise, demonstrating integrity of character, not cheating and treating people with courtesy and respect are concepts that resonate with people of virtually all cultures and religions. In most societies, people would concur that it is unethical for organizations to knowingly expose workers to toxic chemicals and hazardous materials or to sell products known to be unsafe or harmful to the users.

Common moral agreement about right and wrong actions and behaviours across multiple cultures and countries gives rise to universal ethical standards that apply to members of all societies, all organizations and all businesspeople. These universal ethical principles set out the traits and behaviours that are considered virtuous and that a good person is supposed to believe in and to display. Thus, adherents of the school of ethical universalism maintain it is entirely appropriate to expect all businesspeople to conform to these universal ethical standards.[3]

The strength of ethical universalism is that it draws on the collective views of multiple societies and cultures to put some clear boundaries on what constitutes ethical business behaviour and what constitutes unethical business behaviour regardless of the country or culture in which an organization's personnel are conducting activities. This means that in those instances where basic moral standards really do not vary significantly according to local cultural beliefs, traditions or religious convictions, a multinational company can develop a code of ethics that it applies more or less evenly across its worldwide operations.[4] It can avoid the slippery slope that comes from having different ethical standards for different company personnel depending on where in the world they are working.

The School of Ethical Relativism

> **Core Concept**
>
> The school of **ethical relativism** holds that differing religious beliefs, customs and behavioural norms across countries and cultures give rise to *multiple sets of standards concerning what is ethically right or wrong*. These differing standards mean that whether business-related actions are right or wrong depends on the prevailing local ethical standards.

Apart from a select set of universal moral prescriptions – like being truthful and trustworthy – that apply in every society and business circumstance, there are meaningful variations in the ethical standards by which different societies judge the conduct of business activities. Indeed, differing religious beliefs, social customs, traditions and behavioural norms frequently give rise to different standards about what is fair or unfair, moral or immoral and ethically right or wrong. The school of **ethical relativism** holds that when there are cross-country or cross-cultural differences in what is deemed ethical or unethical in business situations, it is appropriate for local moral standards to take precedence over what the ethical standards may be in an organization's home market. The thesis is that what constitutes ethical or unethical behaviour on the part of local businesspeople is properly governed by local ethical standards rather than the standards that prevail in other locations.[5] Consider the following examples.

The Use of Under age Labour

In industrialized nations, the use of under-age workers is considered taboo. Social activists are adamant that child labour is unethical and that organizations should neither employ children under the age of 18 as full-time employees nor source any products from foreign suppliers that employ under age workers. Many countries have passed legislation forbidding the use of under-age labour or, at a minimum, regulating the employment of people under the age of 18. However, in India, Bangladesh, Botswana, Sri Lanka, Ghana, Somalia and more than 100 other countries, it is customary to view children as potential, even necessary, workers.[6] Many poverty-stricken families cannot subsist without the income earned by young family members; sending their children to school instead of having them work is not a realistic option. In 2008, the International Labour Organization estimated that 176 million children ages 5–14 were working around the world.[7] If such children are not permitted to work – due to pressures imposed by activist groups in industrialized nations – they may be forced to go out on the streets begging or to seek work in parts of the 'underground' economy such as drug trafficking and prostitution.[8] So if all businesses in countries where employing under-age workers is common succumb to the pressures of activist groups and government organizations to stop employing under-age labour, then have they served the best interests of the under-age workers, their families and society in general?

The Payment of Bribes and Kickbacks

A particularly thorny area facing multinational organizations is the degree of cross-country variability in paying bribes.[9] In many countries in eastern Europe, Africa, Latin America and Asia, it is customary to pay bribes to government officials in order to win a government contract, obtain a licence or permit or facilitate an administrative ruling.[10] Likewise, in many countries it is normal to make payments to prospective customers in order to win or retain their business. In some developing nations, it is difficult for any organization, foreign or domestic, to move goods through customs without paying off low-level officials.[11] A *Wall Street Journal* article reported that 30–60 per cent of all business transactions in eastern Europe involved paying bribes and the costs of bribe payments averaged 2–8 per cent of revenues.[12] Some people stretch to justify the payment of bribes and kickbacks on grounds that bribing government officials to get goods through customs or giving kickbacks to customers to retain their business or win new orders is simply a payment for services rendered, in the same way that people tip for service at restaurants.[13] But while this is a clever rationalization, it rests on moral quicksand.

Organizations that forbid the payment of bribes and kickbacks in their codes of ethical conduct and that are serious about enforcing this prohibition face a particularly vexing problem in countries where bribery and kickback payments are an entrenched local custom.[14] Refusing to pay bribes or kickbacks in these countries (so as to comply with the organization's code of ethical conduct) is very often tantamount to losing business to competitors willing to make such payments – an outcome that penalizes ethical organizations and ethical personnel (who may suffer lost sales commissions or bonuses). On the other hand, the payment of bribes or kickbacks not only undercuts the organization's code of ethics but also risks breaking the law. Many countries have legislation outlawing such practices. In the UK the law was updated in July 2011 when the new Bribery Act came into force. The Act makes bribery illegal and creates offences that carry up to 10 years in prison and unlimited fines. Organizations have to ensure that they have adequate procedures in place to prevent bribery, including training staff, carry out risk assessments for the markets they operate in and due diligence on the organizations they deal with[15]. Germany enacted similar laws in 1997 and it was under this legislation that Siemens was prosecuted. Penalties also include up to a 10-year imprisonment and fines of up to €1 million plus any profit derived from the corrupt practices.[16] The Organization for Economic Co-operation and Development

(OECD) has anti-bribery standards that criminalize the bribery of foreign public officials in international business transactions – as of 2009, the 30 OECD members and 8 non-member countries had adopted these standards.[17] In 2008, Siemens, one of the world's largest corporations and headquartered in Munich, Germany, was fined $1.6 billion (€2 billion) by the US and German governments for bribing foreign officials to help it secure huge public works contracts around the world.[18] Investigations revealed that Siemens created secret offshore bank accounts and used middlemen posing as consultants to deliver suitcases filled with cash, paying an estimated $1.4 billion to over 4000 well-placed government officials in Asia, Africa, Europe, the Middle East and Latin America between 2001–2007. An estimated 300 Siemens sales employees, executives and board members were being investigated in 2009 for their roles in the scheme. The evidence gathered indicated that such bribes were a core element of Siemens' strategy and business model. Illustration Capsule 9.3 shows how Siemens new CEO, Peter Löscher, tackled these issues.

Penalizing organizations for overseas bribes is becoming more widespread internationally. The Serious Fraud Office (SFO) in London held a landmark investigation in December 2009 of DePuy International, a subsidiary of Johnson & Johnson, for bribing Greek officials to purchase products. This comes after DePuy was fined over $311 million by the US government for kickbacks to US surgeons in 2007.[19]

Ethical Relativism Equates to Multiple Sets of Ethical Standards

The existence of varying ethical norms such as those cited above explains why the adherents of ethical relativism maintain that there are few absolutes when it comes to business ethics and thus few ethical absolutes for consistently judging an organization's conduct in various countries and markets. Indeed, ethical relativists argue that while there are some general moral prescriptions that apply regardless of the business circumstance, there are plenty of situations where ethical norms must be contoured to fit the local customs, traditions and notions of fairness shared by the parties involved. They argue that a 'one-size-fits-all' template for judging the ethical appropriateness of business actions and the behaviours of company personnel simply does not exist – in other words, ethical problems in business cannot be fully resolved without appealing to the shared convictions of the parties in question.[20]

> Under ethical relativism, there can be no one-size-fits-all set of authentic ethical norms against which to gauge the conduct of company personnel.

While European and US managers may want to impose standards of business conduct that give heavy weight to such core human rights as personal freedom, individual security, political participation and the ownership of property, managers in China may have a much weaker commitment to these kinds of human rights. Japanese managers may prefer ethical standards that show respect for the collective good of society. Muslim managers may wish to apply ethical standards compatible with the teachings of Mohammed. Clearly, there is some merit in the school of ethical relativism's view that what is deemed right or wrong, fair or unfair, moral or immoral, ethical or unethical in business situations depends partly on the context of each country's local customs, religious traditions and societal norms. Hence, there is a kernel of truth in the argument that businesses need some room to tailor their ethical standards to fit local situations. An organization has to be very cautious about exporting its home-country values and ethics to foreign countries where it operates – 'photocopying' ethics is disrespectful of other cultures and neglects the important role of moral free space (in which there is room to accommodate local ethical standards).

Pushed to the Extreme, Ethical Relativism Breaks Down

While the ethical relativism rule of 'When in Rome, do as the Romans do' appears reasonable, it nonetheless presents a big problem – when the envelope starts to be pushed, as will inevitably be the case, *it is tantamount to rudderless ethical standards*.

Consider, for instance, the following example: in 1992, the owners of the *SS United States*, an ageing luxury ocean liner constructed with asbestos in the 1940s, had the liner towed to Turkey, where a contractor had agreed to remove the asbestos for $2 million (versus a far higher cost in the USA, where asbestos removal safety standards were much more stringent).[21] When Turkish officials blocked the asbestos removal because of the dangers to workers of contracting cancer, the owners had the liner towed to the Black Sea port of Sevastopol, in the Crimean Republic, where the asbestos removal standards were quite lax and where a contractor had agreed to remove more than 500 000 square feet of carcinogenic asbestos for less than $2 million. There are no moral grounds for arguing that exposing workers to carcinogenic asbestos is ethically correct, regardless of what a country's law allows or the value the country places on worker safety.

An organization that adopts the principle of ethical relativism and holds organization personnel to local ethical standards necessarily assumes that what prevails as local morality is an adequate guide to ethical behaviour. This can be ethically dangerous – it leads to the conclusion that if a country's culture is accepting of bribery or environmental degradation or exposing workers to dangerous conditions (toxic chemicals or bodily harm), then so much the worse for honest people and environmental protection and safe working conditions. Such a position is morally unacceptable. Bribery is a common occurrence in Russia, which ranks 154 out of 178 on Transparency International's corruption perception index. When German car-maker, Daimler, admitted that bribery had been carried out by managers in its Russian operations, following a US Justice Department Investigation, it fired all 45 employees implicated in the corruption.[22]

> Codes of conduct based on ethical relativism can be *ethically dangerous* for multinational organizations by creating a maze of conflicting ethical standards.

Moreover, from a global markets perspective, ethical relativism results in a maze of conflicting ethical standards for multinational organizations wanting to address the very real issue of which ethical standards to enforce company-wide. It is a slippery slope indeed to resolve such ethical diversity without any kind of higher-order moral compass. Imagine, for example, that a multinational organization (in the name of ethical relativism) permits personnel to pay bribes and kickbacks in countries where such payments are customary but forbids them to make such payments in countries where bribes and kickbacks are considered unethical or illegal. Or that the organization says it is appropriate to use child labour in its plants in countries where under-age labour is acceptable but inappropriate to employ child labour at the remainder of its plants. Having thus adopted conflicting ethical standards for operating in different countries, managers have little moral basis for enforcing any ethical standards companywide, rather, the clear message to employees would be that the organization has no ethical standards or principles of its own. This is scarcely strong moral ground to stand on.

Ethics and Integrative Social Contracts Theory

Social contracts theory provides a middle position between the opposing views of universalism (that the same set of ethical standards should apply everywhere) and relativism (that ethical standards vary according to local custom).[23] According to **integrated social contracts theory**, universal ethical principles or norms based on the collective views of multiple cultures and societies combine to form a 'social contract' that all individuals, groups, organizations and businesses in all situations have a duty to observe. *Within the boundaries of this social contract*, local cultures or groups can specify what other actions may or may not be ethically permissible. While this system leaves some 'moral free space' for the people in a particular country (or local culture or even a organization) to make specific interpretations of what other actions may or may not be permissible, universal ethical norms always take precedence. Thus, local ethical standards can be *more* stringent than the universal ethical standards, but never less so.

> **Core Concept**
>
> According to **integrated social contracts theory**, universal ethical principles based on the collective views of multiple societies form a 'social contract' that all individuals and organizations have a duty to observe in all situations. *Within the boundaries of this social contract*, local cultures or groups can specify what additional actions may or may not be ethically permissible.

Hence, while organizations, industries, professional associations and other business-relevant groups are 'contractually obligated' to society to observe universal ethical norms, they have the discretion to go beyond these universal norms and specify other behaviours that are out of bounds and place further limitations on what is considered ethical. For example, both the legal and medical professions have standards regarding what kinds of advertising are ethically permissible that extend beyond the universal norm that advertising should not be false or misleading. Similarly, food products companies are beginning to establish ethical guidelines for judging what is and is not appropriate advertising for food products that are inherently unhealthy and may cause dietary or obesity problems for people who eat them regularly or consume them in large quantities.

The strength of integrated social contracts theory is that it accommodates the best parts of ethical universalism and ethical relativism. It is indisputable that cultural differences have an impact on how business is conducted in various parts of the world and that these cultural differences sometimes give rise to different ethical norms. But it is just as indisputable that some ethical norms are more authentic or universally applicable than others, meaning that in many instances of cross-country differences one side may be more 'ethically correct' than another. In such instances, resolving cross-cultural differences over what is ethically permissible entails applying the rule that *universal or 'first-order' ethical norms override the local or 'second-order' ethical norms*. A good example is the payment of bribes and kickbacks. Yes, bribes and kickbacks seem to be common in some countries, but does this justify paying them? Just because bribery flourishes in a country does not mean it is an authentic or legitimate ethical norm. Virtually all of the world's major religions (e.g. Buddhism, Christianity, Confucianism, Hinduism, Islam, Judaism, Sikhism and Taoism) and all moral schools of thought condemn bribery and corruption.[24] Therefore, a multinational organization might reasonably conclude that the right ethical standard is one of refusing to condone bribery and kickbacks on the part of organization personnel no matter what the local custom is and no matter what the sales consequences are.

> According to integrated social contracts theory, adherence to universal or 'first-order' ethical norms should always take precedence over local or 'second-order' norms.

Granting an automatic preference to local-country ethical norms presents vexing problems to multinational company managers when the ethical standards followed in a foreign country are lower than those in its home country or are in conflict with the organization's code of ethics. Sometimes – as with bribery and kickbacks – there can be no compromise on what is ethically permissible and what is not. *This is precisely what integrated social contracts theory maintains – adherence to universal or 'first-order' ethical norms should always take precedence over local or 'second-order' norms.* Consequently, integrated social contracts theory offers managers in multinational organizations clear guidance in resolving cross-country ethical differences: those parts of the organization's code of ethics that involve universal ethical norms must be enforced world-wide, but *within* these boundaries there is room for ethical diversity and opportunity for host-country cultures to exert *some* influence in setting their own moral and ethical standards. Such an approach avoids the discomforting case of a self-righteous multinational organization trying to operate as the standard bearer of moral truth and imposing its interpretation of its code of ethics world-wide no matter what. And it avoids the equally disturbing case for an organization's ethical conduct to be no higher than local ethical norms in situations where local ethical norms permit practices that are generally considered immoral or when local norms clearly conflict with an organization's code of ethical conduct.

How and Why Ethical Standards Impact on the Tasks of Crafting and Executing Strategy

Many organizations have acknowledged their ethical obligations in official codes of ethical conduct and statements of organizational values. In the USA, for example, the

Sarbanes–Oxley Act, passed in 2002, requires that organizations whose shares are publicly traded have a code of ethics or else explain in writing to the Securities and Exchange Commission (SEC) why they do not. The closest equivalent piece of legislation in the UK is the Companies Act 2004. But there is a big difference between having a code of ethics that serves merely as public window dressing and having ethical standards that truly paint the white lines for an organization's actual strategy and business conduct.[25] *The litmus test of whether an organization's code of ethics is cosmetic is the extent to which it is embraced in crafting strategy and in operating the business day to day.*

It is up to senior executives to walk the talk and make a point of considering three sets of questions whenever a new strategic initiative is under review:

1. Is what we are proposing to do fully compliant with our code of ethical conduct? Are there any areas of ambiguity that may be of concern?
2. Is it apparent that this proposed action is in harmony with our core values? Are any conflicts or potential problems evident?
3. Is there anything in the proposed action that could be considered ethically objectionable? Would our stakeholders, our competitors, the SEC, or the media view this action as ethically objectionable?

Unless questions of this nature are posed – either in open discussion or by force of habit in the minds of strategy-makers – there is room for strategic initiatives to become disconnected from the organization's code of ethics and stated core values. If an organization's executives believe strongly in living up to the organization's ethical standards, they will unhesitatingly reject strategic initiatives and operating approaches that do not measure up. However, in organizations with a cosmetic approach to ethics, any strategy-ethics-values linkage stems mainly from a desire to avoid the risk of embarrassment and possible disciplinary action should strategy-makers be held accountable for approving a strategic initiative that is deemed by society to be unethical and perhaps illegal.

While most managers are careful to ensure that an organization's strategy is within the bounds of what is legal, evidence indicates they are not always so careful to ensure that all elements of their strategies and operating activities are within the bounds of what is considered ethical. In recent years, there have been revelations of ethical misconduct on the part of managers at such organizations as Enron, Tyco International, HealthSouth, Adelphia, Royal Dutch/Shell, Parmalat (an Italy-based food products organization), Rite Aid, Mexican oil giant Pemex, AIG, Citigroup, several leading brokerage houses, mutual fund organizations, investment banking firms and a host of mortgage lenders. Much of the crisis in residential real estate that emerged in the USA in 2007/8 stemmed from consciously unethical strategies at certain banks and mortgage companies to boost the fees they earned on processing home mortgage applications by deliberately lowering lending standards and finding ways to secure mortgage approvals for home buyers who lacked sufficient income to make their monthly mortgage payments. Once these lenders earned their fees on the so-called sub-prime loans (a term used for high-risk mortgage loans to home buyers with dubious qualifications to repay the loans), they secured the assistance of investment banking firms to bundle those and other mortgages into collateralized debt obligations (CDOs), found means of having the CDOs assigned triple-A bond ratings and auctioned them to unsuspecting investors, who later suffered huge losses when the high-risk borrowers began to default on their loan payments (government authorities later forced some of the organizations that auctioned off these CDOs to repurchase them at the auction price and bear the losses themselves).

The consequences of crafting strategies that cannot pass the test of moral scrutiny are manifested in sizeable fines, devastating public relations hits, sharp drops in share prices (that cost shareholders billions of euros) and criminal indictments and convictions of company executives. The fall-out from all these scandals has resulted in heightened management attention to legal and ethical considerations in crafting strategy.

What are the Drivers of Unethical Strategies and Business Behaviour?

LO 9.2
Identify conditions that can give rise to unethical business strategies and behaviour.

Confusion over conflicting ethical standards may suggest one reason for the lack of an effective moral compass in business dealings and why certain elements of an organization's strategy may be unethical. But apart from this, three main drivers of unethical business behaviour stand out:[26]

1. Faulty oversight that implicitly allows the overzealous pursuit of personal gain, wealth and self-interest.
2. Heavy pressures on managers to meet or beat short-term performance targets.
3. An organizational culture that puts profitability and business performance ahead of ethical behaviour.

Faulty Oversight and the Overzealous Pursuit of Personal Gain, Wealth and Self-interest

People who are obsessed with wealth accumulation, greed, power, status and their own self-interest often push ethical principles aside in their quest for personal gain. Driven by their ambitions, they exhibit few qualms in skirting the rules or doing whatever is necessary to achieve their goals. A general disregard for business ethics can prompt all kinds of unethical strategic manoeuvres and behaviours at organizations. In December 2010, Calisto Tanzi, the founder and former CEO of Parmalat, an Italian food company, was jailed for 18 years for his part in Europe's biggest corporate fraud. The Italian conglomerate collapsed in 2003 with debts of €14 billion. Tanzi founded the organization in 1961 and by 2003 it had employed 36 000 staff in 30 countries. Much of this growth had been financed with debt. However, Calisto Tanzi with some of his senior managers had included a fictitious bank account in the Cayman Islands containing €4 billion on the organization's balance sheet. This led investors to believe that Parmalat's financial situation was much better than the reality. As well as receiving substantial prison sentences, Tanzi and his fellow executives were also ordered to pay Parmalat €2 billion and reimburse the investors.[27]

Core Concept

Self-dealing occurs when managers take advantage of their position to further their own private interests rather than those of the organization.

Responsible corporate governance and oversight by the organization's corporate board is necessary to guard against self-dealing and the manipulation of information to disguise such actions by an organization's managers. **Self-dealing** occurs when managers take advantage of their position to further their own private interests rather than those of the organization. As discussed in Chapter 2, the duty of the corporate board (and its compensation and audit committees in particular) is to guard against such actions. A strong, independent board is necessary to have proper oversight of the organization's financial practices and to hold top managers accountable for their actions.

A particularly egregious example of the lack of proper oversight is the case of Enron Corporation, a former diversified energy company that has become a symbol of corporate corruption and fraud. Andrew Fastow, Enron's chief financial officer (CFO), set himself up as the manager of one of Enron's off-the-books partnerships and as the part owner of another, allegedly earning extra compensation of $30 million for his owner-manager roles in the two partnerships; Enron's board of directors agreed to suspend the organization's conflict-of-interest rules designed to protect the company from this very kind of executive self-dealing. Although *Fortune* magazine had named Enron 'America's most innovative company' for six years running, in the end it turned out that Enron's real creativity was in its accounting practices. Enron's eventual downfall resulted not only in the organization's bankruptcy in 2001 but also in the dissolution of its auditor, Arthur Andersen, which was one of the top five accounting organizations at the time.[28]

Illustration Capsule 9.2 discusses the more recent multibillion-dollar Ponzi schemes perpetrated at Bernard L. Madoff Investment Securities and alleged at Stanford Financial Group.

Illustration Capsule 9.2

INVESTMENT FRAUD AT BERNARD L. MADOFF INVESTMENT SECURITIES AND STANFORD FINANCIAL GROUP

Bernard Madoff engineered the largest investment scam in history to accumulate a net worth of more than $800 million and build a reputation as one of Wall Street's most savvy investors – he was appointed to various Securities and Exchange Commission panels, invited to testify before Congress on investment matters, made chairman of Nasdaq and befriended by some of the world's most influential people. Madoff deceived Wall Street and investors with a simple Ponzi scheme that promised investors returns that would beat the market by 400–500 per cent. The hedge funds, banks and wealthy individuals that sent Bernard L. Madoff Investment Securities billions to invest on their behalf were quite pleased when their statements arrived showing annual returns as high as 45 per cent. But, in fact, the portfolio gains shown on these statements were fictitious. Funds placed with Bernard Madoff were seldom, if ever, actually invested in any type of security – the money went to cover losses in his legitimate share-trading business, fund periodic withdrawals of investors' funds and support Madoff's lifestyle (including three vacation homes, a $7 million Manhattan condominium, yachts and luxury cars).

For decades, the Ponzi scheme was never in danger of collapse because most Madoff investors were so impressed with the reported returns that they seldom made withdrawals from their accounts, and when they did withdraw funds Madoff used the monies being deposited by new investors to cover the payments. Madoff's deception came to an end in late 2008 when the dramatic drop in world share prices caused so many of Madoff's investors to request withdrawals of their balances that there was not nearly enough new money coming in to cover the amounts being withdrawn. As with any Ponzi scheme, the first investors to ask Madoff for their funds were paid, but those asking later were left empty-handed. All told, more than 1300 account holders lost about $65 billion when Bernard Madoff admitted to the scam in December 2008. As of late July 2011, investigators had located assets of only about $8.6 billion to return to Madoff account holders. Madoff was sentenced to 150 years in prison for his crimes.

Increased oversight at the Securities and Exchange Commission after the December 2008 Madoff confession led to the June 2009 indictment of R. Allen Stanford and five others who were accused of running an investment scheme similar to that perpetrated by Bernard Madoff. Stanford was alleged to have defrauded more than 30 000 Stanford Financial Group account holders out of $7 billion through the sale of spurious certificates of deposit (CDs). The CDs marketed by Stanford Financial Group were issued by the

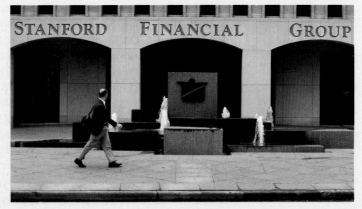

organization's Antiguan subsidiary, Stanford International Bank, and carried rates that were as much as three to four times greater than the CD rates offered by other financial institutions. Stanford claimed that the Stanford

▶

International Bank was able to provide such exceptional yields because of its investment in a globally diversified portfolio of stocks, bonds, commodities and alternative investments and because of the tax advantages provided by the bank's location in Antigua. All the investments made by Stanford International Bank were said to be safe and liquid financial instruments monitored by more than 20 analysts and audited by Antiguan regulators. In fact, the deposits were invested in much riskier private equity placements and real estate investments and were subject to severe fluctuations in value. The statements provided to CD holders were alleged by prosecutors to be based on fabricated performance and phoney financial statements.

Federal prosecutors also alleged that deposits of at least $1.6 billion were diverted into undisclosed personal loans to Allen Stanford. At the time of Stanford's indictment, he ranked 605th on *Forbes* magazine's list of the world's wealthiest persons, with an estimated net worth of $2.2 billion. Stanford was a notable sports enthusiast and philanthropist – he supported a cricket league in Antigua and professional golf tournaments in the USA and contributed millions to the St. Jude Children's Research Hospital and museums in Houston and Miami. Stanford also pledged $100 million to support programmes aimed at slowing global warming. In May 2009, Stanford Investment Bank disclosed that it owed $7.2 billion to about 28 000 account holders. Its total assets at the time stood at $1 billion, including $46 million in cash. Stanford was found guilty of running a Ponzi scheme valued at $7 billion in March 2012 by a court in Houston, Texas.

Note: Developed with C. David Morgan in 2009; updated in 2012.

Sources: Bandler, James, Varchaver, Nicholas and Burke, Doris (2009) 'How Bernie did it', *Fortune Online*, 30 April (accessed 7 July 2009); Greenberg, Duncan (2009) 'Billionaire responds to SEC probe', *Forbes Online*, 13 February (accessed 9 July 2009); Benner, Katie (2009) 'Stanford scandal sets Antigua on edge', *Fortune Online*, 25 February (accessed 9 July 2009); Abkowitz, Alyssa (2009) 'The investment scam-artist's playbook', *Fortune Online*, 25 February (accessed 9 July 2009); Glass, Kathryn (2009) 'Stanford Bank assets insufficient to repay depositors', *Fox Business.com*, 15 May (accessed 9 July 2009); McQuillen, Bill, Blum, Justin and Brubaker Calkins, Laurel (2009) 'Allen Stanford indicted by U.S. in $7 billion scam', *Bloomberg.com*, 19 June (accessed 9 July 2009); Kim, Jane J. (2009) 'The Madoff fraud: SIPC sets payouts in Madoff scandal', *Wall Street Journal* (Eastern Edition), 29 October, p. C4.; BBC News (2011) 'Seven charges against Allen Stanford are dropped', *BBC News*, 5 May. Available online at www.bbc.co.uk/news/world-us-canada-13302864 (accessed 5 August 2011); BBC News (2011) 'Bernard Madoff victims get another $1bn', *BBC News*, 28 July. Available online at: www.bbc.co.uk/news/business-14336043 (accessed 5 August 2011); BBC News (2012) 'Allen Stanford found guilty in $7bn Ponzi Scheme', BBC News, 7 March. Available online at www.bbc.co.uk/news/world-us-canada-17274724 (accessed 27 May 2012).

Heavy Pressures on Managers to Meet or Beat Short-term Earnings Targets

Performance expectations of stock exchange analysts and investors create enormous pressure on management to do whatever it takes to deliver good financial results each and every quarter. Executives at high-performing organizations know that investors will see the slightest sign of a slowdown in earnings growth as a red flag and drive down the organization's stock price. In addition, slowing growth or declining profits could lead to a downgrade of the organization's credit rating if it has used lots of debt to finance its growth. The pressure to 'never miss a quarter' – so as not to upset the expectations of analysts, investors and creditors – prompts near-sighted managers to engage in short-term manoeuvres to make the numbers, regardless of whether these moves are really in the best long-term interests of the organization. Sometimes the pressure induces personnel to continue to stretch the rules until the limits of ethical conduct are overlooked. Once ethical boundaries are crossed in efforts to 'meet or beat their numbers', the threshold for making more extreme ethical compromises becomes lower.

Several top executives at the former telecommunications organization WorldCom were convicted of concocting a fraudulent $11 billion accounting scheme to hide costs and inflate revenues and profit over several years; the scheme was said to have helped the organization keep its stock price propped up high enough to make additional acquisitions, support its nearly $30 billion debt load, and allow executives to cash in on their lucrative stock options. Vivendi ex-CEO Jean-Marie Messier was found guilty by a Paris court in January 2011 of misleading shareholders following a $77 billion spending spree between 1994–2002, during which time the French organization acquired 23 organizations. A 2007 internal investigation at Dell Computer found that executives had engaged in a scheme to manipulate the organization's accounting data to meet investors' quarterly earnings expectations. The fraudulent accounting practices inflated the organization's earnings by $150 million between 2002–2006. The executives were terminated by Dell Computer in 2007.

Organization executives often feel pressured to hit financial performance targets because their compensation depends heavily on the organization's performance. During the late 1990s, it became fashionable for boards of directors to grant lavish bonuses, stock option awards and other compensation benefits to executives for meeting specified performance targets. So outlandishly large were these rewards that executives had strong personal incentives to bend the rules and engage in behaviours that allowed the targets to be met. Much of the accounting manipulation at the root of recent corporate scandals has entailed situations in which executives benefited enormously from misleading accounting or other shady activities that allowed them to hit the numbers and receive incentive awards ranging from €10 million to €100 million.

The fundamental problem with short-termism – the tendency for managers to focus excessive attention on short-term performance objectives – is that it does not create value for customers or improve the organization's competitiveness in the marketplace; that is, it sacrifices the activities that are the most reliable drivers of higher profits and added shareholder value in the long run. Cutting ethical corners in the name of profits carries exceptionally high risk for shareholders – the steep stock price decline and tarnished brand image that accompany the discovery of scurrilous behaviour leave shareholders with an organization worth much less than before – and the rebuilding task can be arduous, taking both considerable time and resources.

> **Core Concept**
>
> **Short-termism** is the tendency for managers to focus excessively on short-term performance objectives at the expense of longer-term strategic objectives. It has negative implications for the likelihood of ethical lapses as well as organizational performance in the longer run.

An Organizational Culture That Puts Profitability and Business Performance Ahead of Ethical Behaviour

When an organization's culture spawns an ethically corrupt or amoral work climate, people have an organization-approved licence to ignore 'what is right' and engage in any behaviour or employ any strategy they think they can get away with.[29] At such organizations, unethical people are given a free reign, and otherwise honourable people may succumb to the many opportunities around them to engage in unethical practices. A perfect example of an organizational culture gone awry on ethics is Enron.[30]

Enron's leaders encouraged company personnel to focus on the current bottom line and to be innovative and aggressive in figuring out how to grow current earnings – regardless of the methods. Enron's annual 'rank and yank' performance evaluation process, in which the lowest-ranking 15–20 per cent of employees were let go, made it abundantly clear that bottom-line results were what mattered most. The name of the game at Enron became devising clever ways to boost revenues and earnings, even if this sometimes meant operating outside established policies. In fact, outside-the-lines behaviour was celebrated if it generated profitable new business.

A high-performance/high-rewards climate came to pervade the Enron culture, as the best workers (determined by who produced the best bottom-line results) received impressively large incentives and bonuses (amounting to as much as $1 million for traders and even more for senior executives). On Car Day at Enron, an array of luxury sports cars arrived for presentation to the most successful employees. Understandably, employees wanted to be seen as part of Enron's star team and partake in the benefits granted to Enron's best and brightest employees. The high monetary rewards, the ambitious and hard-driving people whom the organization hired and promoted and the competitive, results-oriented culture combined to give Enron a reputation not only for trampling competitors at every opportunity but also for internal ruthlessness. The organization's super-aggressiveness and win-at-all-costs mind-set nurtured a culture that gradually and then more rapidly fostered the erosion of ethical standards, eventually making a mockery of the organization's stated values of integrity and respect. When it became evident in autumn 2001 that Enron was a house of cards propped up by deceitful accounting and a myriad of unsavoury practices, the organization imploded in a matter of weeks – one of the biggest bankruptcies of all time, costing investors $64 billion in losses.

More recently, a team investigating an ethical scandal at oil giant Royal Dutch/ Shell Group that resulted in the payment of $150 million in fines found that an ethically flawed culture was a major contributor to why managers made rosy forecasts that they could not meet and why top executives engaged in manoeuvres to mislead investors by overstating Shell's oil and gas reserves by 25 per cent (equal to 4.5 billion barrels of oil). The investigation revealed that top Shell executives knew that a variety of internal practices, together with unrealistic and unsupportable estimates submitted by overzealous, bonus-conscious managers in Shell's exploration and production group, were being used to overstate reserves. An email written by Shell's top executive for exploration and production (who was caught up in the ethical misdeeds and later forced to resign) said, 'I am becoming sick and tired of lying about the extent of our reserves issues and the downward revisions that need to be done because of our far too aggressive/optimistic bookings'.[31]

In contrast, when high ethical principles are deeply ingrained in the corporate culture of an organization, culture can function as a powerful mechanism for communicating ethical behavioural norms and gaining employee buy-in to the organization's moral standards, business principles and corporate values. In such cases, the ethical principles embraced in the organization's code of ethics and/or in its statement of corporate values are seen as integral to the organization's identity, self-image and ways of operating. Stories of former and current moral heroes are kept in circulation, and the deeds of company personnel who display ethical values and are dedicated to walking the talk are celebrated at internal company events. The message that ethics matters – and matters a lot – resounds loudly and clearly throughout the organization and in its strategy and decisions. Illustration Capsule 9.3 discusses Siemens' approach to building a culture that repairs the damage of past scandals and reinforces an ethical approach to business.

Illustration Capsule 9.3

REBUILDING SIEMENS' REPUTATION

When Peter Löscher took over as CEO of engineering giant Siemens in July 2007 he knew that one of his key tasks would be to rebuild the company's tarnished reputation. The German industrial firm had been mired by allegations of bribery and corruption arising from the previous management's conduct in securing contracts in a number of countries. This resulted in the departure of several senior managers and cost Siemens €2 billion in fines and associated fees to settle with the authorities in Germany and the USA during 2008. The firm also lost business; with the Nigerian government just one customer that cancelled contracts after the bribery allegations came to light.

  Peter Löscher made a number of far-reaching changes to the organization's compliance systems. This started with the installation of a much larger compliance unit comprising 600 experts in the field and creating a management board position with responsibility for legal and compliance matters. Siemens had compliance

▶

◀

systems prior to the scandal, but according to Andreas Pohlmann, their chief compliance officer, the values had not been effectively embedded into the culture of the company or communicated effectively.

The development of a clear set of principles was an early step in the process of communicating the new approach Siemens had to compliance. The new mantras were 'only clean business is Siemens business' and that breaches of the laws and regulations covering compliance would not be tolerated. To underline the new approach Löscher signed the letter from the United Nations Global Compact that supports the UN's convention against corruption. However, the firm also realized that compliance had to be more than just a set of principles. Clear responsibilities were embedded throughout the chain of command across the firm's operations in 190 countries. Compliance measures also became part of the company's compensation system and targets set for all senior managers in the organization.

THE THREE PILLARS

Siemens's new compliance system had three key elements; prevent, detect and respond. At the first level the aim was to prevent laws and regulations being broken by staff. Compliance policies and procedures were updated and communicated to staff world-wide through a variety of media and underpinned with extensive training. By 2010 over 228 000 employees had been through the training schemes set up by the organization.

The detection element of the system required the creation of reliable reporting channels. Siemens set up a compliance Ombudsman, Accounting Complaints channel and a Compliance Help Desk 'Tell Us', which crucially was open to suppliers, customers and other stakeholders to report any suspicious activity. The channels also ensured that anyone reporting compliance violations were protected from sanctions provided their reports were made in good faith. In 2010 there were 582 incidents reported via these confidential channels of which 502 merited further investigation. The clearest evidence that the system was working came in June 2011 when evidence of bribery by managers in Kuwait came to light via a report made to the compliance team. The fact that the issue was handled internally showed that the multinational firm had learned from the previous instances of corruption. The case also illustrated the final pillar of the compliance system, response. Siemens made the case public, brought in the relevant public authorities at an early stage and disciplined the staff involved. It is possible that the former managers in the case may have a claim for damages brought against them by the organization.

Sources: Schäfer, D. (2011) 'Siemens uncovers bribery case at Kuwait unit', *The Financial Times*, 10 June. Available online at www.ft.com/cms/s/0/c0c7177e-9380-11e0-922e-00144feab49a.html#ixzz1UBlVNJM2 (accessed 4 August 2011); BBC News (2007) 'Nigeria suspends Siemens dealing', *BBC News*, 6 December. Available online at www.news.bbc.co.uk/1/hi/business/7130315.stm (accessed 4 August 2011); Pohlmann, A. (2008) 'A new direction for Siemens', *Compliance Quarterly*, 2008 (2). Available online at www.enewsbuilder.net/globalcompact/e_article001149152.cfm?x=bd2Hd2m (accessed 4 August 2011); Siemens (2010) *Siemens Sustainability Report 2010*. Available online at http://www.siemens.com/sustainability/en/sustainability/reporting/current_reporting.htm (accessed 4 August 2011).

Why Should an Organization's Strategies be Ethical?

There are two reasons why an organization's strategy should be ethical: (1) because a strategy that is unethical is morally wrong and reflects badly on the character of the company personnel; and (2) because an ethical strategy can be good business and serve the self-interest of shareholders.

The Moral Case for an Ethical Strategy

Managers do not dispassionately assess what strategic course to steer. Ethical strategy-making generally begins with managers who themselves have strong moral character (i.e. who are trustworthy, have integrity and truly care about conducting the organization's business in an honourable manner). Managers with high ethical principles are usually advocates of a corporate code of ethics and strong ethics compliance, and they are genuinely committed to upholding corporate values and ethical business principles. They demonstrate their commitment by displaying the organization's stated values and living up to its business principles and ethical standards. They understand there is a big difference between adopting value statements and codes of ethics and ensuring that they are followed strictly in an organization's actual strategy and business conduct. As a consequence, ethically strong managers consciously opt for strategic actions that can pass the strictest moral scrutiny – they display no tolerance for strategies with ethically controversial components.

Emerging Theme 9.1

TECHNOLOGY AND SOCIO-CULTURAL CHANGE

CAN ORGANIZATIONS HIDE UNETHICAL BEHAVIOUR AND DAMAGE TO THE ENVIRONMENT IN THE INTERNET AGE?

Marketers and customer services professionals have known for years that customers tell far more people about bad experiences than they do about good. One of the heuristics used in the 1990s stated that on average a customer would tell three of their acquaintances about a good experience but fourteen about a bad product or service. Then came Jeff Jarvis and the My Dell hell saga in 2005. Jarvis bought a Dell laptop computer that did not live up to his expectations. As he became more and more frustrated with how the company handled his complaint, he posted each episode to his blog www.buzzmachine.com. What might have reached a few acquaintances before the Internet now had tens of thousands of followers. Dell learned their lesson and is much more focused on creating a dialogue with its customers these days.

Blogging is just one way that angry consumers, employees and other stakeholders can affect an organization's reputation. There are now a whole host of anti-corporate websites following commenting on every move certain organizations make. One of the best known is the anti-supermarket site, www.tescopoly.com, which is dedicated to exposing how Tesco and other major supermarkets behave in their dealings with suppliers, customers and local communities. Other pressure groups register web domain names that disparage the organization or its senior staff. In December 2010 the Bank of America registered over 300 of these sites to prevent activists using them (most were variations on the theme of adding sucks or blows to the name of a senior manager at the bank).

Then there are the whistle-blowing sites, perhaps the most infamous of which is WikiLeaks (www.wikileaks.org). The site publishes everything from diplomatic and government papers to internal company reports and memos as well as press reports removed as a result of legal action. For example, WikiLeaks published a range of articles about Trafigura's activities in the Ivory Coast that conventional media outlets such as the BBC and The Times newspaper had withdrawn.

With the rise of the citizen journalist and the global reach of the Internet, it may be that there really is nowhere to hide.

Sources: Jarvis, J. (2005) 'My Dell hell', The Guardian, 29 August. Available online at www.guardian.co.uk/technology/2005/aug/29/mondaymediasection.blogging (accessed 15 August 2011); Kapner, S. (2010) 'Hundreds of anti BofA websites registered', The Financial Times, 23 December. Available online at www.ft.com/cms/s/0/3993f69e-0e2b-11e0-86e9-00144feabdc0.html#axzz1V2qJn9Aj (accessed 15 August 2011).

LO 9.3 Give examples of the costs of business ethics failures.

The Business Case for Ethical Strategies

In addition to the moral reasons for adopting ethical strategies, there may be solid business reasons. Pursuing unethical strategies and tolerating unethical conduct not only damages an organization's reputation but also may result in a wide-ranging set of other costly consequences. Figure 9.1 shows the types of costs an organization can incur when unethical behaviour on its part is discovered, the wrongdoings of organizational personnel are headlined in the media and it is forced to make amends for its

Visible costs	Internal administrative costs	Intangible or less visible costs
• Government fines and penalities • Civil penalties arising from class-action lawsuits and other litigation aimed at punishing the company for its offence and the harm done to others • The costs to share-holders in the form of a lower stock price (and possibly lower dividends)	• Legal and investigative costs incurred by the company • The costs of providing remedial education and ethics training to company personnel • Costs of taking corrective actions • Administrative costs associated with ensuring future compliance	• Customer defections • Loss of reputation • Lost employee morale and higher degrees of employee cynicism • Higher employee turnover • Higher recruiting costs and difficulty in attracting talented employees • Adverse effects on employee productivity • The costs of complying with often harsher government regulations

FIGURE 9.1 The costs organizations incur when ethical wrongdoing is found out.

Source: Adapted from Thomas, Terry, Schermerhorn, John R. and Dienhart, John W. (2004) 'Strategic leadership of ethical behaviour', *Academy of Management Executive*, 18(2): 58.

behaviour. The more egregious are an organization's ethical violations, the higher the costs and the bigger the damage to its reputation (and to the reputations of the organizational personnel involved). In high-profile instances, the costs of ethical misconduct can easily run into the hundreds of millions and even billions of Euros, especially if they provoke widespread public outrage and many people were harmed. The penalties levied on executives caught in wrongdoing can skyrocket as well, as the 150-year prison term sentence of financier Bernie Madoff illustrates.

The fall-out of ethical misconduct on the part of an organization goes well beyond the costs of making amends for the misdeeds. Rehabilitating an organization's shattered reputation is time-consuming and costly. Many customers shun organizations known for their shady behaviour. Organizations known to have engaged in unethical conduct have difficulty in recruiting and retaining talented employees; indeed, many people take an organization's ethical reputation into account when deciding whether to accept a job offer.[32] Most ethically upstanding people are repulsed by a work environment where unethical behaviour is condoned; they do not want to get entrapped in a compromising situation, nor do they want their personal reputations tarnished by the actions of an unsavoury employer. Creditors are usually unnerved by the unethical actions of a borrower because of the potential business fall-out and subsequent risk of default on loans.

All told, an organization's unethical behaviour risks doing considerable damage to shareholders in the form of lost revenues, higher costs, lower profits, lower stock prices and a diminished business reputation. To a significant degree, therefore, ethical strategies and ethical conduct are *good business*. Most organizations understand the value of operating in a manner that wins the approval of suppliers, employees, investors and society at large. Most businesspeople recognize the risks and adverse fall-out attached to the discovery of unethical behaviour. Hence, organizations have an incentive to employ strategies that can pass the test of being ethical. Even if an organization's managers are not of a strong moral character and personally committed to high ethical standards, they have good reason to operate within ethical bounds, if only to

Conducting business in an ethical fashion is not only morally right – it is in an organization's enlightened self-interest.

Shareholders can suffer major damage when an organization's unethical behaviour is discovered. Making amends for unethical business conduct is costly, and it takes years to rehabilitate a tarnished organizational reputation.

TABLE 9.1 Key drivers towards more ethical business practices

Most important driver, by country

Cost management	Public attitudes/building brand	Recruitment/ retention of staff	Tax relief
Canada*	Argentina	Australia	Germany
China	Armenia	Belgium	Italy
France	Botswana	Canada*	
Georgia	Brazil	Denmark	
Greece	Chile	Japan*	
Hong Kong	Finland	New Zealand	
India	Mexico	Russia	
Ireland	Spain	Switzerland	
Japan*	Sweden	Taiwan	
Malaysia	United States of America	Turkey	
Netherlands	Vietnam		
Philippines			
Poland			
Singapore			
South Africa			
Thailand			
United Arab Emirates			
United Kingdom			

Note: *denotes drivers level

Source: Grant Thornton (2011) *Corporate Social Responsibility: The Power of Perception, Grant Thornton International Business Report*, Grant Thornton International Ltd, London.

(1) avoid the risk of embarrassment, scandal and possible disciplinary action for unethical conduct on their part and (2) escape being held accountable for unethical behaviour by personnel under their supervision and their own lax enforcement of ethical standards.

There are, therefore, significant driving forces in for adopting more ethical business practices. However, not all organizations are driven by the same motives. As part of their annual International Business Report, accountancy organization, Grant Thornton, survey over 7000 businesses globally. The survey records what organizations in different countries regard as their most important reason is for moving towards a more ethical approach. Table 9.1 supports many of the points made in Figure 9.1.

LO 9.4
Explain the concepts of CSR and environmental sustainability and how organizations balance these duties with economic responsibilities to shareholders.

Strategy, Corporate Social Responsibility and Environmental Sustainability

The idea that businesses have an obligation to foster social betterment, a much-debated topic in the past 50 years, took root in the nineteenth century when progressive organizations in the aftermath of the industrial revolution began to provide workers with housing and other amenities. The notion that corporate executives should balance the interests of all stakeholders – shareholders, employees, customers, suppliers, the communities in which they operated and society at large – began to blossom in the 1960s. The first evidence of corporate social responsibility (CSR) style reporting appeared in some annual reports in the 1970s and 1980s. Organizations such as Abt and Associates were pioneers in this style of reporting adding an environmental section to their annual report in 1972. A wider group of organizations began to produce stakeholder reports in the wake of Ben & Jerry's innovative approach in 1988. Shell Canada and the Body Shop were other organizations that reported on the social and environmental impact of their activities at this time. The late 1990s marked the start of more structured CSR reporting based on external standards and capable of certification.[33]

Today, CSR is a concept that resonates in western Europe, the USA, Canada and such developing nations as Brazil and India.

What Do We Mean by *CSR*?

The essence of socially responsible business behaviour is that an organization should balance strategic actions to benefit shareholders against the *duty* to be a good corporate citizen. The underlying thesis is that company managers should display a *social conscience* in operating the business and specifically take into account how management decisions and organizational actions affect the well-being of employees, local communities, the environment and society at large.[34] Acting in a socially responsible manner thus encompasses more than just participating in community service projects and donating monies to charities and other worthy social causes. Demonstrating social responsibility also entails undertaking actions that earn trust and respect from all stakeholders – operating in an honourable and ethical manner, striving to make the organization a great place to work, demonstrating genuine respect for the environment and trying to make a difference in bettering society. As depicted in Figure 9.2, corporate responsibility programmes commonly include the following elements:

> **Core Concept**
>
> **Corporate social responsibility (CSR)** refers to an organization's *duty* to operate in an honourable manner, provide good working conditions for employees, encourage workforce diversity, be a good steward of the environment and actively work to better the quality of life in the local communities where it operates and in society at large.

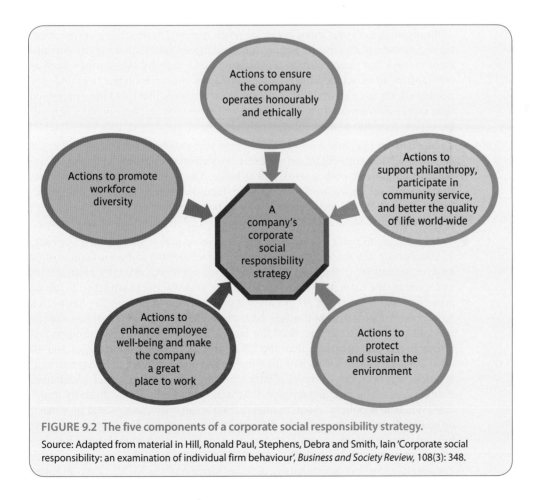

FIGURE 9.2 The five components of a corporate social responsibility strategy.

Source: Adapted from material in Hill, Ronald Paul, Stephens, Debra and Smith, Iain 'Corporate social responsibility: an examination of individual firm behaviour', *Business and Society Review,* 108(3): 348.

- *Making efforts to employ an ethical strategy and observe ethical principles in operating the business.* A sincere commitment to observing ethical principles is a necessary component of a CSR strategy simply because unethical conduct is incompatible with the concept of good corporate citizenship and socially responsible business behaviour.

- *Making charitable contributions, supporting community service endeavours, engaging in broader philanthropic initiatives and reaching out to make a difference in the lives of the disadvantaged.* Some organizations fulfil their philanthropic obligations by spreading their efforts over a multitude of charitable and community activities – for instance, Bayer AG, a German chemical organization, supports around 300 projects around the world ranging from culture and sports to environmental protection and health. Others prefer to focus their energies more narrowly. Schlumberger, an oilfield services provider, supports education-focused community initiatives in 30 countries. Their programmes include science education initiatives and teacher training to improve high school students' access to technical education. Leading prescription drug maker GlaxoSmithKline and other pharmaceutical organizations either donate or heavily discount medicines for distribution in the least developed nations. Organizations frequently reinforce their philanthropic efforts by encouraging employees to support charitable causes and participate in community affairs, often through programmes that match employee contributions.

- *Taking actions to protect the environment and, in particular, to minimize or eliminate any adverse impact on the environment stemming from the organization's own business activities.* Social responsibility as it applies to environmental protection entails actively striving to be a good steward of the environment. This means using the best available science and technology to reduce environmentally harmful aspects of the organization's operations *below the levels required by prevailing environmental regulations.* It also means putting time and money into improving the environment in ways that extend past an organization's own industry boundaries – such as participating in recycling projects, adopting energy conservation practices and supporting efforts to clean up local water supplies. Retailers like B&Q have pressured their suppliers to adopt stronger environmental protection practices in order to lower the carbon footprint of their entire supply chains.

- *Taking actions to create a work environment that enhances the quality of life for employees.* Numerous organizations exert extra effort to enhance the quality of life for their employees, both at work and at home. This can include on-site day care, flexible work schedules, workplace exercise facilities, special leaves for employees to care for sick family members, work-at-home opportunities, career development programmes and education opportunities, special safety programmes and the like.

- *Taking actions to build a workforce that is diverse with respect to gender, race, national origin and other aspects that different people bring to the workplace.* Most large organizations in the USA have established workforce diversity programmes and some go the extra mile to ensure that their workplaces are attractive to ethnic minorities and inclusive of all groups and perspectives. In Europe this has been a more recent process as organizations have responded to their US partners, competitors and head offices. Europe does not have a history of civil rights struggle and also is much less integrated than the USA with 21 recognized languages and 40 other languages spoken. Much of the equality and diversity work in European organizations has been driven by legislation covering age, gender, sexual orientation, disability, ethnicity/race and religion.[35] At some organizations, the diversity initiative extends to suppliers – sourcing items from small businesses owned by women or ethnic minorities, for example. The pursuit of workforce diversity can be good business. At Carrefour, strategic success depends on serving all their retail customers wherever they are located. The organization is present in 14 European countries but also has stores in South America, Asia, Africa and the Middle East. In many cases the stores serve diverse communities and ensuring that their workforce reflects this is a key success factor in engaging with local communities. In Carrefour's French hypermarkets there are over 100 nationalities represented on their staff.[36]

The particular combination of socially responsible endeavours an organization elects to pursue defines its **CSR strategy**. The specific components emphasized in a CSR strategy vary from organization to organization and are typically linked to an organization's core values. Nestlé, for example, talk about creating shared value and relate this approach to their 10 principles of business operation, which include, Nutrition, Health and Wellness and Environmental Sustainability. Marks & Spencer's strategy is referred to as Plan A and focuses on five key elements or pillars; climate change, waste, sustainable raw materials, fair partner and health. Some organizations use other terms, such as *corporate citizenship*, *corporate responsibility* or *sustainable responsible business (SRB)* to characterize their CSR initiatives.

Although there is wide variation in how organizations devise and implement a CSR strategy, communities of organizations concerned with corporate social responsibility (such as CSR Europe) have emerged to help organizations share best CSR practices. Moreover, a number of reporting standards have been developed, including ISO 26000 – a new internationally recognized standard for social responsibility produced by the International Standards Organization (ISO).[37] Organizations that exhibit a strong commitment to corporate social responsibility are often recognized by being included on lists such as *Corporate Responsibility* magazine's '100 Best Corporate Citizens' or *Corporate Knights* magazine's 'Global 100 Most Sustainable Corporations'.

> **Core Concept**
>
> An organization's **CSR strategy** is defined by the specific combination of socially beneficial activities the organization opts to support with its contributions of time, money and other resources.

Key Debate 9.1

WHO IS RESPONSIBLE FOR CSR?

In a recent article in the *Wall Street Journal*, Professor Aneel Karnani, of the University of Michigan, argued that for organizations the idea of CSR was either irrelevant or ineffective. His argument is underpinned by a long line of economists (including Milton Friedman and David Henderson) who have argued that the only purpose of a corporation should be profit maximization for its shareholders. According to Karnani, organizations that address market demands that align to social goals such as healthy foods or cleaner vehicles are making profits and improving social welfare. This makes the concept of CSR irrelevant because each organization's actions to maximize profits are also benefiting society. Where organizations' profits would diminish if they acted in the interests of society, such as an organization using low wage labour or an industry that creates pollution that is expensive to deal with, CSR is ineffective. Karnani views the attempts of such businesses to implement CSR programmes as leading to 'green-washing' or lower profits, which means that the executives are not acting in the best interests of their shareholders. So if organizations are not responsible for CSR, then it falls to governments to regulate and force corporations to act in the interests of society by putting in place punitive fines for behaviour deemed unacceptable.

Some of the assumptions commentators such as Friedman and Karnani make are open to question. Mallen Baker points out that the profit maximization is not a given even for publicly quoted organizations. When shareholders challenged Henry Ford's decision to pay his workers more, because it diminished profits and potential dividends to shareholders, the US courts found in Ford's favour (*Dodge v. Ford*, [1919]). Acting in shareholders' interests involves taking a long-term view according to Rosabeth Moss Kanter, and for most corporations a mission that supports society and strong values has benefits that underpin good performance. These include being able to recruit the most talented employees, the creation of a strong culture and the ability to enter emerging markets. Organizations such as drinks-maker, Innocent, have seen the benefits of this sort of approach in the UK. Both Baker and Kanter talk about CSR being a choice that organizations need to consider, in other words, organizations do not 'accidentally' find themselves in a position where their strategy for making profits is

▶

◄

aligned with social goals. In making that choice they need to understand the needs and aspirations of their existing and potential employees and customers, suppliers and complementors. For companies like Toyota this has led them to build more effective supply chain relationships than their competitors and also to develop products such as the Prius which anticipated society's need for more fuel efficient vehicles. This backs up Kanter's view that thinking about societal problems can drive innovation in organizations. So a stakeholder rather than a shareholder focus is better for the long-term performance of the organization since, as we saw in Chapter 6 (Current Practice 6.1), it can be a source of competitive advantage. Organizations cannot be divorced from the societies and communities they serve and if these are healthy and thriving, then business organizations will prosper.

QUESTION

1. What views would the following groups have in this debate?
   a. Shareholders
   b. Company directors
   c. Customers

Sources: Karnani, A. (2010) 'The case against corporate social responsibility', *Wall Street Journal*, 23 August; Baker, M. (2010) 'Reply to the case against CSR – the latest version', *Business Respect*, 169, 26 August; Moss Kanter, R. (2010) 'How to do well and do good', *MIT Sloan Management Review*, 52(1): 12–15.

Corporate Social Responsibility and the Triple Bottom Line

CSR initiatives undertaken by organizations are frequently directed at improving the organization's 'triple bottom line' – a reference to three types of performance metrics: *economic*, *social* and *environmental*. The goal is for an organization to succeed simultaneously in all three dimensions, as illustrated in Figure 9.3.[38] The three dimensions of performance are often referred to in terms of the 'three pillars' of 'people, planet and profit'. The term *people* refers to the various social initiatives that make up CSR strategies, such as corporate giving, community involvement and organization efforts to improve the lives of its internal and external stakeholders. *Planet* refers to an organization's ecological impact and environmental practices. The term *profit* has a broader meaning with respect to the triple bottom line than it does otherwise. It encompasses not only the profit an organization earns for its shareholders but also the economic impact that the organization has on society more generally, in terms of the overall value that it creates and the overall costs that it imposes on society. For example, The Co-operative Group, a member-owned organization with retail and financial operations in the UK, invests 4 per cent of its profit in local communities and encourages employees to carry out voluntary work. They reduced their carbon footprint by 15 per cent and the amount of packaging used in their stores by 9 per cent in 2010. The Co-operative is also a leading supporter of the fair-trade movement. These and many other initiatives have led to the organization being named as Europe's most sustainable bank by the *Financial Times*, winning the *Grocer* magazine's Green Retailer of the Year Award as well as increasing profits by 14 per cent.[39]

Many organizations now make a point of citing the beneficial outcomes of their CSR strategies in press releases and issue special reports for consumers and investors to review. Staples, the world's largest office products organization, makes reporting an important part of its commitment to corporate responsibility; the organization posts a 'Staples Soul Report' on its website that describes its initiatives and accomplishments in the areas of diversity, environment, community and ethics. Triple bottom line (TBL) reporting is emerging as an increasingly important way for organizations to make the

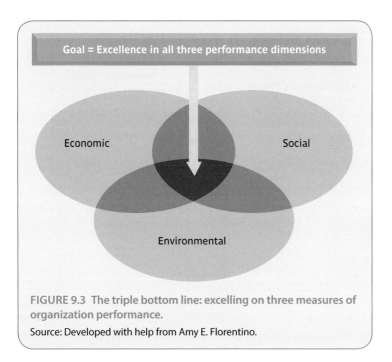

FIGURE 9.3 The triple bottom line: excelling on three measures of organization performance.

Source: Developed with help from Amy E. Florentino.

results of their CSR strategies apparent to stakeholders and for stakeholders to hold organizations accountable for their impact on society. The use of standard reporting frameworks and metrics, such as those developed by the Global Reporting Initiative, promotes greater transparency and facilitates benchmarking CSR efforts across organizations and industries.

CURRENT PRACTICE 9.1

NOVO NORDISK'S TRIPLE BOTTOM LINE

Novo Nordisk, a leading manufacturer of insulin based in Denmark, manages its business using the TBL business principle to ensure that their decisions are long term in scope and balance shareholder value with societal values. The organization's strategy is underpinned by The Novo Nordisk Way – 10 statements that encapsulate its principles:

1. We create value by having a patient centred business approach.
2. We set ambitious goals and strive for excellence.
3. We are accountable for our financial, environmental and social performance.
4. We provide innovation to the benefit of our stakeholders.
5. We build and maintain good relations with our key stakeholders.
6. We treat everyone with respect.
7. We focus on personal performance and development.
8. We have a healthy and engaging working environment.
9. We optimize the way we work and strive for simplicity.
10. We never compromise on quality and business ethics.

In terms of measurable outcomes, these are divided into the three types of TBL metrics detailed below in Figure 9.4

Sources: Novo Nordisk (2011) *Novo Nordisk Annual Report 2010*: 'Financial, social and environmental performance', Novo Nordisk, Bagsvaerd; Novo Nordisk (2011) Company website available at www.novonordisk.com (accessed 18 November 2011).

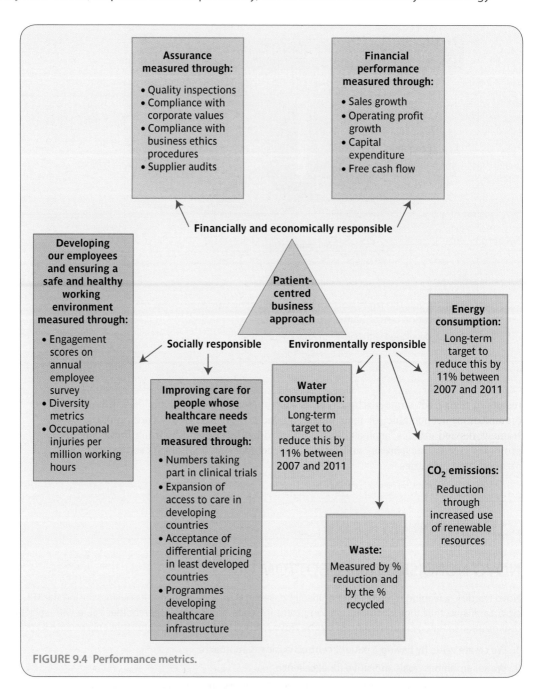

FIGURE 9.4 Performance metrics.

Investment organizations have created mutual funds comprising organizations that are excelling on the basis of the triple bottom line in order to attract funds from environmentally and socially aware investors. In the UK FTSE has produced the FTSE4GOOD index series since 2001. This consists of five indices covering Europe, the USA, Japan, the UK and a global version. To be included in the indices, which are aimed at responsible investors, organizations have to demonstrate they are working toward environmental management, countering bribery, upholding human and labour rights, climate change mitigation and adaption and supply chain labour standards. Organizations dealing with tobacco, nuclear weapons systems and complete arms system manufacturers are excluded.[40]

What Do We Mean by *Sustainability* and *Sustainable Business Practices*?

The term *sustainability* is used in a variety of ways. In many organizations, it is synonymous with CSR; it is seen by some as a term that is gradually replacing CSR in the business lexicon. Indeed, sustainability reporting and TBL reporting are often one and the same, as illustrated by the Dow Jones Sustainability Index, which tracks the same three types of performance measures that constitute the TBL.

More often, however, the term takes on a more focused meaning, concerned with the relationship of an organization to its *environment* and its use of *natural resources*, including land, water, air, plants, animals, minerals, fossil fuels and biodiversity. It is widely recognized that the world's natural resources are finite and are being consumed and degraded at rates that threaten their capacity for renewal. Since corporations are the biggest users of natural resources, managing and maintaining these resources is critical for the long-term economic interests of corporations.

For some organizations, this issue has direct and obvious implications for the continued viability of their business model and strategy. DHL Express UK has been working to reduce its carbon footprint by 10 per cent, the courier organization sees this as vital to cutting costs in a competitive market with well-informed customers.[41] Beverage organizations such as Red Bull and Danone are having to rethink their business models because of the prospect of future world-wide water shortages. For other organizations, the connection is less direct, but all organizations are part of a business ecosystem whose economic health depends on the availability of natural resources. In response, most major organizations have begun to change *how* they do business, emphasizing the use of sustainable business practices, defined as those capable of meeting the needs of the present without compromising the ability to meet the needs of the future.[42] Many have also begun to incorporate a consideration of environmental sustainability into their strategy-making activities.

Environmental sustainability strategies entail deliberate and concerted actions to operate businesses in a manner that protects natural resources and ecological support systems, guards against outcomes that will ultimately endanger the planet and is therefore sustainable for centuries.[43] One aspect of environmental sustainability is keeping use of the Earth's natural resources within levels that can be replenished via the use of sustainable business practices. In the case of some resources (like crude oil, fresh water and the harvesting of edible fish from the oceans), scientists say that use levels either are already unsustainable or will be soon, given the world's growing population and propensity to consume additional resources as incomes and living standards rise. Another aspect of sustainability concerns containing the adverse effects of greenhouse gases and other forms of air pollution so as to reduce global warming and other undesirable climate and atmospheric changes. Other aspects of sustainability include greater reliance on sustainable energy sources, greater use of recyclable materials, the use of sustainable methods of growing foods (so as to reduce topsoil depletion and the use of pesticides, herbicides, fertilizers and other chemicals that may be harmful to human health or ecological systems), habitat protection, environmentally sound waste management practices and increased attempts to decouple environmental degradation and economic growth (according to many scientists, economic growth has historically been accompanied by declines in the well-being of the environment).

Unilever, a diversified producer of processed foods, personal care and home cleaning products, is among the many committed corporations pursuing sustainable business practices. The organization tracks 11 sustainable agricultural indicators in its processed foods business and has launched a variety of programmes to improve the environmental performance of its suppliers. Examples of such programmes include

Core Concept

Sustainable business practices are those that meet the needs of the present without compromising the ability to meet the needs of the future.

Core Concept

An organization's environmental sustainability strategy consists of its deliberate actions to protect the environment, provide for the longevity of natural resources, maintain ecological support systems for future generations and guard against ultimate endangerment of the planet.

special low-rate financing for tomato suppliers choosing to switch to water-conserving irrigation systems and training programmes in India that have allowed contract cucumber growers to reduce pesticide use by 90 per cent while improving yields by 78 per cent. Unilever has also reengineered many internal processes to improve the organization's overall performance on sustainability measures. For example, the organization's factories have reduced water usage by 63 per cent and total waste by 67 per cent since 1995 through the implementation of sustainability initiatives. Unilever has also redesigned packaging for many of its products to conserve natural resources and reduce the volume of consumer waste. For example, the organization's Dove and Sure deodorants were reshaped to use 18 per cent less plastic per pack. As the producer of Lipton Tea, Unilever is the world's largest purchaser of tea leaves; the organization has committed to sourcing all of its tea from Rainforest Alliance Certified farms by 2015, due to their comprehensive triple bottom line approach toward sustainable farm management.

Crafting CSR and Sustainability Strategies

> CSR strategies and environmental sustainability strategies that both provide valuable social benefits *and* fulfil customer needs in a superior fashion can lead to competitive advantage. Corporate social agendas that address only social issues may help boost an organization's reputation for corporate citizenship but are unlikely to improve its competitive strength in the marketplace.[46]

While CSR and environmental sustainability strategies take many forms, those that both provide valuable social benefits *and* fulfil customer needs in a superior fashion may also contribute to an organization's competitive advantage.[44] For example, while carbon emissions may be of some concern for financial institutions such as HSBC, Toyota's sustainability strategy for reducing carbon emissions has produced both competitive advantage and environmental benefits. Its Prius hybrid electric- and gasoline-powered automobile is not only among the least polluting automobiles but is also the best-selling hybrid vehicle in the USA; it has earned the organization the loyalty of fuel-conscious buyers and given Toyota a green image. The welfare of cocoa bean growers and their families is at the heart of Divine Chocolate's strategy. Not only does the £10 million confectionery organization pay fair-trade prices for the beans it buys, it is also part-owned by the farmers. The Kuapa Kokoo is a co-operative in Ghana with 45 000 members and owns 45 per cent of Divine Chocolate and has two seats on the organization's board of directors. Divine was originally a project to help farmers operate further up the value chain and was supported by the Body Shop, Twin Trading and a number of charities including Comic Relief and Christian Aid. Divine pays the farmers a guaranteed minimum of $1600 per tonne and this protects them from the volatility in the market to some degree. They also pay a further premium of $150 per tonne to the Kuapa Kokoo, which the co-operative invests in its own projects, ranging from productivity improvements to education and health schemes. Consumers have embraced the brand that has seen spectacular growth during 2010 in new markets such as Norway (270 per cent) and Denmark (70 per cent).[45]

CSR strategies and environmental sustainability strategies are more likely to contribute to an organization's competitive advantage if they are linked to an organization's competitively important resources and capabilities or value chain activities. Thus, it is common for organizations engaged in natural resource extraction, electric power production, forestry and paper products, motor vehicles and chemical production to place more emphasis on addressing environmental concerns than, say, software and electronics firms or apparel manufacturers. Organizations whose business success is heavily dependent on high employee morale or attracting and retaining the best and brightest employees are somewhat more prone to stress the well-being of their employees and foster a positive, high-energy workplace environment that elicits the dedication and enthusiastic commitment of employees, thus putting real meaning behind the claim 'Our people are our greatest asset'. Ernst & Young, one of the four largest global accounting firms, stresses its 'people first' workforce diversity strategy that is all about respecting differences, fostering individuality and promoting inclusiveness so that its more than 144 000 employees in 140 countries can feel valued, engaged and empowered in developing creative ways to serve the organization's clients. As a service business, Marriot's most competitively important resource is also people. Thus, its social agenda includes providing 180 hours of paid classroom and on-the-job training to the chronically unemployed. Ninety per cent of the graduates from the job training programme take jobs with Marriott, and about two-thirds of those remain with Marriott for more than a year. At Traidcraft plc, a £14 million trading organization specializing in fair-trade products, its strategy to fight world poverty through trade is evident in almost every segment of its organization value chain and is a big part of its differentiation strategy. The organization's procurement policies ensure that suppliers are paid sufficiently to cover the cost of producing the goods and to make a fair profit. They look to build long-term relationships and also to ensure that workers in their suppliers are fairly treated and work in good conditions. The organization is also linked to a charity, Traidcraft Exchange, which supports poor people in Asia and Africa to engage in trading activities, find markets and grow their businesses as a way to escape poverty.[47]

Not all organizations choose to link their corporate environmental or social agendas to their value chain, their business model or their industry. For example, LVMH, a luxury goods organization, which is active in several sectors including wines and spirits, fashion and leather goods, watches, jewellery and perfume, has a foundation that invests in the restoration of historic monuments. However, unless an organization's social responsibility initiatives become part of the way it operates its business every day, the initiatives are unlikely to catch fire and be fully effective. As an executive at Royal Dutch/Shell put it, corporate social responsibility 'is not a cosmetic; it must be rooted in our values. It must make a difference to the way we do business'.[48] The same is true for environmental sustainability initiatives.

The Moral Case for CSR and Environmentally Sustainable Business Practices

The moral case for why businesses should act in a manner that benefits all of the organization's stakeholders – not just shareholders – boils down to 'It's the right thing to do'. Ordinary decency, civic-mindedness and contributions to the well-being of society should be expected of any business.[49] In today's social and political climate, most business leaders can be expected to acknowledge that socially responsible actions are important and that businesses have a duty to be good corporate citizens. But there is a complementary school of thought that business operates on the basis of an implied social contract with the members of society. According to this contract, society grants a business the right to conduct its business affairs and agrees not to unreasonably restrain its pursuit of a fair profit for the goods or services it sells. In return for this 'licence to operate', a business is obligated to act as a responsible citizen, do its fair share to promote the general welfare and avoid doing any harm. Such a view clearly puts a moral burden on an organization to take corporate citizenship into consideration and do what is best for shareholders within the confines of discharging its duties to operate honourably, provide good working conditions to employees, be a good environmental steward and display good corporate citizenship.

> Every action an organization takes can be interpreted as a statement of what it stands for.

The Business Case for CSR and Environmentally Sustainable Business Practices

Whatever the moral arguments for socially responsible business behaviour and environmentally sustainable business practices, it has long been recognized that it is in the enlightened self-interest of organizations to be good citizens and devote some of their energies and resources to the betterment of employees, the communities in which they operate and society in general. In short, there are reasons why the exercise of social and environmental responsibility may be good business:

- *Such actions can lead to increased buyer patronage.* A strong visible social responsibility or environmental sustainability strategy may give an organization an edge in differentiating itself from rivals and in appealing to consumers who prefer to do business with organizations that are good corporate citizens. Ben & Jerry's, Innocent Drinks, Divine Chocolate and the Body Shop have definitely expanded their customer bases because of their visible and well-publicized activities as socially conscious organizations. More and more organizations are also recognizing the cash register payoff of social responsibility strategies that reach out to people of all cultures and demographics (women, retirees and ethnic groups).

- *A strong commitment to socially responsible behaviour reduces the risk of reputation-damaging incidents.* Organizations that place little importance on operating in a socially responsible manner are more prone to scandal and embarrassment. Consumer, environmental and human rights activist groups are quick to criticize businesses whose behaviour they consider to be out of line, and they are adept at getting their message into the media and onto the Internet. Pressure groups can generate widespread adverse publicity, promote boycotts and influence like-minded or sympathetic buyers to avoid an offender's products. Research has shown that product boycott announcements are associated with a decline in an organization's share price.[50] When a major oil organization suffered damage to its reputation on environmental and social grounds, the CEO repeatedly said that the most negative impact the organization suffered – and the one that made him fear for the future of the organization – was that bright young graduates were no longer attracted to working for the organization.[51] For many years, Nike received stinging criticism for not policing sweatshop conditions in the Asian factories that produced Nike footwear, causing Nike cofounder and former CEO Phil Knight to observe that 'Nike has become synonymous with slave wages, forced overtime, and arbitrary abuse'.[52] In 1997, Nike began an extensive effort to monitor conditions in the 800 factories of the contract manufacturers that produced Nike shoes. As Knight said, 'Good shoes come from good factories and good factories have good labour relations'. Nonetheless, Nike has continually been plagued by complaints from human rights activists that its monitoring procedures are flawed and that it is not doing enough to correct the plight of factory workers. As this suggests, a damaged reputation is not easily repaired.

  The higher the public profile of an organization or its brand, the greater the scrutiny of its activities and the higher the potential for it to become a target for pressure group action.

- *Socially responsible actions and sustainable business practices can lower costs and enhance employee recruiting and workforce retention.* Organizations with deservedly good reputations for social responsibility and sustainable business practices are better able to attract and retain employees, compared to organizations with tarnished reputations. Some employees just feel better about working for an organization committed to improving society.[53] This can contribute to lower turnover, better worker productivity and lower costs for staff recruitment and training. For example, smoothie and juice manufacturer, Innocent, is said to enjoy much lower rates of employee turnover because of the organization's socially responsible practices as well as superior employee benefits and management efforts to make Innocent a great place to work. Making an organization a great place to work pays dividends in recruitment of talented workers, more creativity and energy on the part of workers, higher worker productivity and greater employee commitment to the organization's business mission/vision and success in the marketplace (we cover this aspect of strategy execution in more depth in Chapter 11 when we look at motivation). Sustainable business practices are often concomitant with greater operational efficiencies. For example, Dutch flooring manufacturer, Desso, has instituted a closed loop supply chain approach across a range of its products referred to as Cradle to

Cradle™. Their products are designed to be easily disassembled and reused in producing more flooring or composted. The organization also offers to collect used carpets that they have not manufactured and along with recycling their own products this reduces their cost of raw materials.[54]

- *Opportunities for revenue enhancement may also come from CSR and environmental sustainability strategies.* The drive for sustainability and social responsibility can spur innovative efforts that, in turn, lead to new products and opportunities for revenue enhancement. Electric cars such as the Peugeot iOn and the Nissan Leaf are one example. In many cases, the revenue opportunities are tied to an organization's core products. PepsiCo and Coca-Cola, for example, have expanded into the juice business to offer a healthier alternative to their carbonated beverages. General Electric (GE) has created a profitable new business in wind turbines. In other cases, revenue enhancement opportunities come from innovative ways to reduce waste and use the by-products of an organization's production. Tyre company, Michelin, now uses recycled truck tyres to provide the surfaces for children's playgrounds. British Gypsum and Taylor Woodrow plc, two firms in the construction sector, have become partners in a novel scheme to recycle plasterboard. Seventy-two per cent of the components of the board were recycled with the paper element being used by British Gypsum to make fertilizer.[55]

- *Well-conceived CSR strategies and sustainable business practices are in the best long-term interest of shareholders.* Social responsibility strategies and strategies to promote environmental sustainability can work to the advantage of shareholders in several ways. They help avoid or pre-empt legal and regulatory actions that could prove costly and otherwise burdensome. In addition, when CSR and sustainability strategies increase buyer patronage, offer revenue-enhancing opportunities, lower costs, increase productivity and reduce the risk of reputation-damaging incidents, they contribute to the total value created by an organization and improve its profitability. In this manner, well-conceived socially and environmentally responsible strategies can enhance shareholder value even as they address the needs of other organization stakeholders. While some question whether addressing social needs is truly in the interest of an organization's shareholders, the answer depends on how well such strategies are crafted and whether they contribute to the success of the organization's business model. A review of 135 studies indicated there is a positive, but small, correlation between good corporate behaviour and good financial performance; only 2 per cent of the studies showed that dedicating corporate resources to social responsibility harmed the interests of shareholders.[56] Another indicator is the performance of mutual funds dedicated to socially responsible investments (SRIs) relative to other types of funds. The longest-running SRI index, the Domini 400, has continued to perform competitively, slightly outperforming the S&P 500 (the top-500 organizations in the Standard & Poor's Index).[57] Similarly, the Dow Jones Sustainability Index has performed comparably to the Dow Jones Large Cap and Total Market Indexes.[58]

> Socially responsible strategies that create value for customers and lower costs can improve organization profits and shareholder value at the same time that they address other stakeholder interests.

In sum, organizations that take social responsibility and environmental sustainability seriously can improve their business reputations and operational efficiency while also reducing their risk exposure and encouraging loyalty and innovation. Overall, organizations that take special pains to protect the environment (beyond what is required by law), are active in community affairs and are generous supporters of charitable causes and projects that benefit society are more likely to be seen as good investments and as good organizations to work for or do business with. Shareholders are likely to view the business case for social responsibility as a strong one, particularly when it results in the creation of more customer value, greater productivity, lower operating costs and lower business risk – all of which should increase organization profitability and enhance shareholder value even as the organization's actions address broader stakeholder interests.

> There is little hard evidence indicating shareholders are disadvantaged in any meaningful way by an organization's actions to be socially responsible.

Organizations are, of course, sometimes rewarded for bad behaviour – an organization that is able to shift environmental and other social costs associated with its activities onto society as a whole can reap large short-term profits. The major cigarette producers for many years were able to earn greatly inflated profits by shifting the health-related costs of smoking onto others and escaping any responsibility for the harm their products caused to consumers and the general public. Only recently have they been facing the prospect of having to pay high punitive damages for their actions. Unfortunately, the cigarette-makers are not alone in trying to evade paying for the social harms of their operations for as long as they can. Calling a halt to such actions usually hinges on (1) the effectiveness of activist social groups in publicizing the adverse consequences of an organization's social irresponsibility and marshalling public opinion for something to be done, (2) the enactment of legislation or regulations to correct the inequity, and (3) widespread actions on the part of socially conscious buyers to take their business elsewhere.

KEY POINTS

1. Ethics concerns standards of right and wrong. Business ethics concerns the application of ethical principles and standards to the actions and decisions of business organizations and the conduct of their personnel. Ethical principles in business are not materially different from ethical principles in general.

2. There are three schools of thought about ethical standards for organizations with international operations:
   - According to the *school of ethical universalism,* common understandings across multiple cultures and countries about what constitutes right and wrong behaviours give rise to universal ethical standards that apply to members of all societies, all organizations and all businesspeople.
   - According to the *school of ethical relativism,* different societal cultures and customs have divergent values and standards of right and wrong. Thus, what is ethical or unethical must be judged in the light of local customs and social mores and can vary from one culture or nation to another.
   - According to the *integrated social contracts theory,* universal ethical principles or norms based on the collective views of multiple cultures and societies combine to form a 'social contract' that all individuals in all situations have a duty to observe. Within the boundaries of this social contract, local cultures or groups can specify what additional actions are not ethically permissible. However, when local ethical norms are more permissive than the universal norms, universal norms always take precedence.

3. Confusion over conflicting ethical standards may provide one reason why some organization personnel engage in unethical strategic behaviour. But three other factors prompt unethical business behaviour: (1) faulty oversight that implicitly sanctions the overzealous pursuit of wealth and personal gain; (2) heavy pressures on organization managers to meet or beat short-term earnings targets; and (3) an organization culture that puts profitability and good business performance ahead of ethical behaviour. In contrast, culture can function as a powerful mechanism for promoting ethical business conduct when high ethical principles are deeply ingrained in the culture of an organization.

4. Business ethics failures can result in three types of costs: (1) visible costs, such as fines, penalties and lower stock prices; (2) internal administrative costs, such as legal costs and costs of taking corrective action; and (3) intangible costs, such as customer defections and damage to the organization's reputation.

5. The term *corporate social responsibility* concerns an organization's *duty* to operate in an honourable manner, provide good working conditions for employees, encourage workforce diversity, be a good steward of the environment and support philanthropic endeavours in local communities where it operates and in society at large. The particular combination of socially responsible endeavours an organization elects to pursue defines its CSR strategy.

6. The triple bottom line refers to organization performance in three realms: economic, social and environmental. Increasingly, organizations are reporting their performance with respect to all three performance dimensions.

7. *Sustainability* is a term that is used in various ways, but most often it concerns an organization's relationship to the environment and its use of natural resources. Sustainable business practices are those capable of meeting the needs of the present without compromising the world's ability to meet future needs. An organization's environmental sustainability strategy consists of its deliberate actions to protect the environment, provide for the longevity of natural resources, maintain ecological support systems for future generations and guard against ultimate endangerment of the planet.

8. CSR strategies and environmental sustainability strategies that both provide valuable social benefits *and* fulfil customer needs in a superior fashion can lead to competitive advantage.

9. The moral case for social responsibility boils down to a simple concept: it is the right thing to do. There are also solid reasons why CSR and environmental sustainability strategies may be good business – they can be conducive to greater buyer patronage, reduce the risk of reputation-damaging incidents, provide opportunities for revenue enhancement and lower costs. Well-crafted CSR and environmental sustainability strategies are in the best long-term interest of shareholders for the reasons above and because they can avoid or pre-empt costly legal or regulatory actions.

Closing Case

NEWS CORPORATION AT BAY

The events of July 2011 provided a dramatic example of the impact of allegations of unethical and illegal activity anywhere in an organization on its ability to execute strategy. By the end of that month News Corporation's senior managers had been quizzed by members of the UK Parliament, lost the chief executives of two of its business subsidiaries, discontinued a 168-year-old brand and withdrawn from the major acquisition of a satellite TV broadcaster.

BACKGROUND

The scandal first broke back in 2005 when Clive Goodman, the royal editor on the *News of the World* (a British Sunday newspaper and part of News Corporation's News International subsidiary – see Exhibit 9.1 for an overview of the organization's structure), wrote a story about Prince William, a member of the British Royal Family. Some of the information in the piece appeared to have come from the Prince's voicemail and the police were called in to investigate illegal phone hacking. This led to the arrest and later conviction of Goodman and a private investigator, Glenn Mulcaire, for illegally accessing the messages. These events were dismissed as the actions of a rogue reporter after investigations by News International senior managers. However, new evidence began to

come to light after *The Guardian*, a rival British newspaper, reported that it had evidence of up to 3000 people having their voicemails hacked by *News of the World* journalists and alleged that three leading figures from the world of football had been paid £1million to settle out of court. The *News of the World* vehemently denied these claims. However, in September 2010 an ex-*News of the World* journalist, Sean Hoare, turned whistle-blower and made further allegations of widespread phone hacking at the newspaper. This and other evidence of an out of court settlement with public relations (PR) guru, Max Clifford, prompted the Metropolitan Police to reopen their investigation in January 2011.

In February 2011, the High Court demanded that Glenn Mulcaire surrender documents relating to the case and this was swiftly followed by the arrest of three *News of the World* journalists. Despite this News International senior managers continued to deny knowledge of the alleged activities of their staff but did offer apologies to several public figures. While the focus of the investigation was on celebrities the fall-out from the scandal appeared to be manageable. However, at the beginning of July events to a dramatic turn as *The Guardian* reported allegations that the *News of the World* had hacked into the phone of Milly Dowler, a schoolgirl murdered in 2002. At this point the newspaper's reputation went into free-fall and on 7 July, three

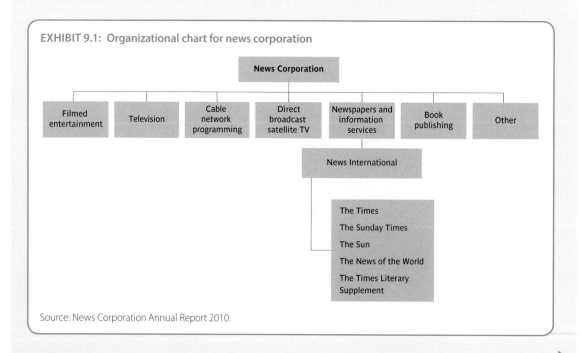

EXHIBIT 9.1: Organizational chart for news corporation

Source: News Corporation Annual Report 2010.

▶

days after the allegations were reported, James Murdoch, News International's chairman, announced that the *News of the World* would close with the final issue appearing on Sunday 10 July 2011 (a full timeline of events is provided in Exhibit 9.2).

THE CULTURE AT NEWS CORPORATION

News Corporation had a reputation for an aggressive, even brutal approach to business. The organization had been happy to upset governments, regulators and competitors. In the short term this had proved successful and the organization has steadily expanded on the back of significant profits from the various elements of its media empire. However, this approach had made News Corporation a string of enemies and it is likely that *The Guardian* and the *New York Times* had competitive as well as journalistic motives for pushing their investigations into the *News of the World's* activities.

As the phone hacking scandal gathered pace during July a number of ex-employees of the *News of the World* and News International made further allegations

---

EXHIBIT 9.2: Timeline for the scandal

Date	Event
May 2000	Rebekah Brooks (nee Wade) became editor of the *News of the World*
January 2003	Andy Coulson becomes editor of the *News of the World* as Rebekah Brooks moves to take editorship of *The Sun* newspaper
November 2005–August 2006	Following the publication of an article on Prince William, the *News of the World* royal editor, Clive Goodman, is arrested along with Glenn Mulcaire, a private investigator for hacking phones
January 2007	Mulcaire and Goodman are found guilty and jailed. Andy Coulson resigns as editor of the *News of the World*
May 2007	David Cameron, then leader of the opposition, hires Coulson as his media adviser
July 2009	*The Guardian* newspaper alleges that phone hacking was far more widespread than News International have admitted
September 2009	Rebekah Brooks is appointed as chief executive of News International
June 2010	News Corporation launches its takeover bid for BSkyB
September 2010	Further allegations of widespread phone hacking by the *News of the World* appears in *The Guardian* and *New York Times*
January 2011	Scotland Yard opens up a new investigation into phone hacking allegations
February 2011	The High Court orders Glenn Mulcaire to reveal who told him to hack phones
April 2011	Police arrest three former *News of the World* journalists
4 July 2011	The Dowler family's lawyer alleges that their daughter's phone was hacked by the *News of the World* after her murder in 2002
7 July 2011	James Murdoch announces the closure of the *News of the World*
8 July 2011	Andy Coulson is arrested. David Cameron, the British Prime Minister, announced there will be two inquiries into the scandal. One will be led by a judge
10 July 2011	Final edition of the *News of the World* comes out
11 July 2011	Further claims of phone hacking surface from other political figures. News Corporation's bid for BSkyB is referred to the Competition Commission
13 July 2011	News Corporation withdraws its planned bid for BSkyB
14 July 2011	The scandal spreads to the USA after allegations that 9/11 victims phones were hacked
15 July 2011	Rebekah Brooks resigns as CEO of News International
17 July 2011	Brooks is arrested by Police
19 July 2011	Rupert Murdoch, his some James and Rebekah Brooks, are summoned to appear before members of the UK Parliament to answer questions about the scandal

Sources: *The Economist* (2011) 'How to lose friends and alienate people', 16 July; BBC News 'Phone-hacking scandal timeline'. Available online at www.bbc.co.uk/news/uk-14124020 (accessed 8 August 2011); *The Economist* (2011) 'Wider still and wider', 23 July.

about the way the organization was managed. Charles Begley, a former reporter on the paper, and Matt Driscoll, a sports reporter, were both victims of the culture of bullying at the paper between 2000–7. Driscoll reportedly received a pay-out of £800 000 for unfair dismissal at an Employment Tribunal. Other former reporters on the paper alleged that there was a 'macho' culture centred on taking risks and eschewing respectable journalistic methods.

BRIBERY ALLEGATIONS

There is some debate as to whether News Corporation has also breached anti-corruption laws in the USA and the UK. Allegations that police officers were paid for information into crimes and contact details have surfaced as well as reports that *News of the World* staff attempted to purchase personal details of 9/11 victims from a New York police officer. The scale of alleged bribery was exposed by *The Guardian* on 7 July when it reported that the Metropolitan Police were investigating claims that £100 000 had been paid to five officers. The case was seen as so serious that the Independent Police Complaints Commission was brought in to oversee the investigation. Such activity had been in sharp focus in the UK after a new Bribery Act came into force on 1 July 2011. It was not clear whether this would cover the bribing of police officers for information. However, just being connected to News International appeared to be sufficient to damage senior police officers. By the end of July Britain's senior policeman, the Metropolitan Police Commissioner, Sir Paul Stephenson and one of his deputies, Assistant Commissioner John Yates, had resigned. Both had been involved in employing the former *News of the World* journalist, Neil Wallis, who was arrested as part of the new enquiry on 14 July 2011.

CONSEQUENCES

If Rupert Murdoch, News Corporation's boss, thought that his organization could weather the storm at the beginning of July, he had a much clearer idea of the true consequences of the scandal by the end of the month. The UK government's Culture Secretary, Jeremy Hunt, partly in response to hostile public opinion, referred the News Corporation's takeover bid for British satellite broadcaster BSkyB to the Competition Commission on 11 July. Two days later the firm withdrew its bid and accepted that, at least in the short term, its strategy for moving the emphasis of the media empire from newspapers to TV and consolidating its various European businesses could not now be implemented.

The scandal has also damaged News Corporation's finances directly. After the scandal broke at the beginning of July 2011, the firm's shares fell by 14 per cent wiping $5 billion off its value. At the beginning of August 2011 the News Corporation shares were trading at $14.01 on the NASDAQ, compared to a high of $19.08 in March 2011 (details of the changes in share price in 2010/11 are in Exhibit 9.3). News International lost substantial revenue prior to the closure of the *News of the World* as a result of a string of major customers pulling their advertising from the paper. The loss of revenue from closing the paper is not significant in the context of the group's overall income but it is still a loss.

The organization also lost some of its key members of staff during July. Rebekah Brooks, who was the editor of the *News of the World* when some of the alleged phone hacking occurred in 2002, had risen to chief executive of News International. Brooks resigned on 15 July 2011 and was arrested and questioned by police two days later. Les Hinton, the former head of the News International from 1996–2007, also resigned from his post at News Corporation's financial news service Dow Jones.

When the various investigations complete their work, News Corporation may also have to face significant fines from authorities on both sides of the Atlantic. If any of the *News of the World's* activities contravened the US's Foreign and Corrupt Practices Act, the fines could be substantial. Siemens had to pay $800 million in 2008. The scandal could also damage the News Corporation's ability to bid for broadcast TV licences. The US Federal Communications Commission could remove existing licences and prevent the organization from bidding in future. This could be particularly damaging as the TV elements of the News Corporation are its best performing business units. Their film-making and newspaper operations are far less successful partly due to the impact of the Internet on their business models. News Corporation's foray into new media has been even less successful. It lost money on the acquisition and then disposal of MySpace, a social networking site that was purchased for $580 million in 2005 and sold in June 2011 for $35 million.

Finally, the scandal was a humiliation for the organization and its boss, Rupert Murdoch. Whether all the allegations proved to be true or not, Murdoch and News Corporation had been forced to apologise to a wide range of institutions, individuals and other organizations. Their reputation, which had been under fire after a series of poorly performing acquisitions, had suffered further. Putting a true cost on that could prove impossible.

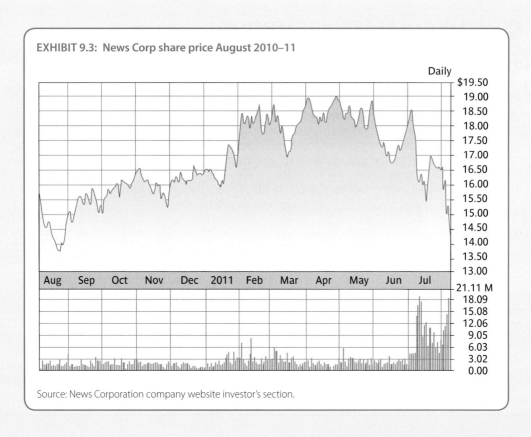

EXHIBIT 9.3: News Corp share price August 2010–11

Source: News Corporation company website investor's section.

QUESTIONS

1. What were the main drivers of the unethical behaviour of staff at the *News of the World* newspaper?

2. What costs did News Corporation incur when the wrongdoing at their subsidiary was found out?

3. What steps would you advise the organization to take in order to improve its reputation and put its strategy back on track?

Sources: BBC News (2007) 'Pair jailed over royal phone taps', BBC News, 26 January. Available online at www.news.bbc. co.uk/1/hi/uk/6301243.stm (accessed 8 August 2011); Robinson, J. and Davies, C. (2009) 'News of the World phone hacking: Guardian shows MPs new evidence', *The Guardian*, 14 July. Available online at www.guardian.co.uk/media/2009/ jul/14/news-world-new-evidence?INTCMP=SRCH (accessed 8 August 2011); Van Natta, D., Becker, J. and Bowley, G. (2010) 'Tabloid hack attack on the Royals and beyond', *The New York Times Magazine*, 1 September. Available online at www. nytimes.com/2010/09/05/magazine/05hacking-t.html (accessed 8 August 2011); Davies, N. and Evans, R. (2010) 'Max Clifford drops News of the World phone hacking action in £1m deal', *The Guardian*, 9 March. Available online at www. guardian.co.uk/media/2010/mar/09/clifford-news-of-the-world-phone-hacking?INTCMP=SRCH (accessed 8 August 2011); BBC News (2011) 'Phone-hacking scandal timeline', BBC News. Available online at www.bbc.co.uk/news/ uk-14124020 (accessed 8 August 2011); *The Economist* (2011) 'How to lose friends and alienate people', *The Economist,* 16 July, pp. 25–7; Prodhan, G. and Holton, K. (2011) 'Special report: inside Rebekah Brooks', *News of the World*', Reuters, 16 July. Available online at www.reuters.com/article/2011/ 07/16/us-newscorp-notw-brooks-idUSTRE76F0O420110716 (accessed 8 August 2011); Porter, H. (2011) 'Phone-hacking scandal has exposed a culture of bullying and intimidation at News International', *The Observer*, 24 July. Available online at www.guardian.co.uk/media/2011/jul/24/phone-hacking-scandal-bullying-intimidation (accessed 8 August 2011); *The Economist* (2011) 'Officers down', *The Economist,* 23 July, pp. 23–4; *The Economist* (2011) 'Wider still and wider', *The Economist,* 23 July, pp. 20–2; BBC News (2011) 'News Corp profits fall on sale of MySpace website', BBC News, 11 August. Available online at www.bbc.co.uk/news/business-14483682 (accessed 11 August 2011).

ASSURANCE OF LEARNING EXERCISES

LO 9.1, LO 9.2, LO 9.3, LO 9.4

1. Assume that you are the sales manager at a European organization that makes sleepwear products for children. Organization personnel discover that the chemicals used to flameproof the organization's line of children's pyjamas might cause cancer if absorbed through the skin. After this discovery, the pyjamas are banned from sale in the European Union (EU) and the USA, but senior executives of your organization learn that the children's pyjamas in inventory and the remaining flameproof material can be sold to sleepwear distributors in certain east European countries where there are no restrictions against the material's use. Your superiors instruct you to make the necessary arrangements to sell the inventories of banned pyjamas and flameproof materials to east European distributors. How would you handle this situation?

LO 9.4

2. Review Marks and Spencer's commitments in Plan A at www.plana.marksandspencer.com/. How does the organization's commitment to the five pillars provide positive benefits for its stakeholders? How does Marks and Spencer plan to improve the livelihoods of their suppliers and their communities through its fair partner initiative? Why is this important to Marks and Spencer shareholders?

LO 9.4

3. Go to www.nestle.com, and read the organization's latest sustainability report. What are Nestlé's key sustainable environmental policies? How is the organization addressing social needs? How do these initiatives relate to the organization's principles, values and culture and its approach to competing in the food industry?

EXERCISES FOR SIMULATION PARTICIPANTS

LO 9.1

1. Is your organization's strategy ethical? Why or why not? Is there anything that your organization has done or is now doing that could legitimately be considered 'shady' by your competitors?

LO 9.4

2. In what ways, if any, is your organization exercising corporate social responsibility (CSR) and good corporate citizenship? What are the elements of your organization's CSR strategy? Are there any changes to this strategy that you would suggest?

LO 9.3, LO 9.4

3. If some shareholders complained that you and your co-managers have been spending too little or too much on corporate social responsibility, what would you tell them?

LO 9.4

4. Is your organization striving to conduct its business in an environmentally sustainable manner? What specific *additional* actions could your organization take that would make an even greater contribution to environmental sustainability?

LO 9.4

5. In what ways is your organization's environmental sustainability strategy in the best long-term interest of shareholders? Does it contribute to your organization's competitive advantage or profitability?

ENDNOTES

1. Post, James E., Lawrence, Anne T. and Weber, James (2002) *Business and Society: Corporate Strategy, Public Policy, Ethics*, 10th edn. Burr Ridge, IL, McGraw-Hill Irwin, p. 103.

2. For research on what are the universal moral values (six are identified – trustworthiness, respect, responsibility, fairness, caring and citizenship), see Schwartz, Mark S. (2005) 'Universal moral values for corporate codes of ethics', *Journal of Business Ethics*, 59(1): 27–44.

3. See Schwartz, Mark. S. (2002) 'A code of ethics for corporate codes of ethics', *Journal of Business Ethics*, 41(1–2): 27–43.

4. Ibid: pp. 29–30.

5. Beauchamp, T.L. and Bowie, N.E. (2001) *Ethical Theory and Business*, Upper Saddle River, NJ, Prentice-Hall, p. 8.

6. Based on information in US Department of Labor, (2003) 'The Department of Labor's 2002 findings on the worst forms of child labour.' Available online at www.dol.gov/ILAB/media/reports.

7. Diallo, Yacouba, Hagemann, Frank, Etienne, Alex, Gurbuzer, Yonca and Mehran, Farhad (2010) *Global Child Labour Developments: Measuring Trends from 2004 to 2008*, ILO, Geneva. Available online at www.ilo.org/ipecinfo/product/viewProduct.do?productId=13313.

8. Greenfield, W.M. (2004) 'In the name of corporate social responsibility', *Business Horizons*, 47(1): 22.

9. For a study of why such factors as low per-capita income, lower disparities in income distribution and various cultural factors are often associated with a higher incidence of bribery, see Sanyal, Rajib (2005) 'Determinants of bribery in international business: the cultural and economic factors', *Journal of Business Ethics*, 59(1): 139–45.

10. For data relating to bribe-paying frequency in 30 countries, see Transparency International, *2007 Global Corruption Report*, p. 332, and *2008 Global Corruption Report*, p. 306. Available online at www.globalcorruptionreport.org.

11. Donaldson, Thomas and Dunfee, Thomas W. (1999) 'When ethics travel: the promise and peril of global business ethics', *California Management Review*, 41(4): 53.

12. Reed, John and Portanger, Erik (1999) 'Bribery, corruption are rampant in eastern Europe, survey finds', *Wall Street Journal*, 9 November, p A21.

13. For a study of 'facilitating' payments to obtain a favour (such as expediting an administrative process, obtaining a permit or licence or avoiding an abuse of authority), which are sometimes condoned as unavoidable or are excused on grounds of low wages and lack of professionalism among public officials, see Argandoña, Antonio (2005) 'Corruption and companies: the use of facilitating payments', *Journal of Business Ethics*, 60(3): 251–64.

14. Donaldson and Dundee, 'When Ethics Travel', p. 59.

15. BBC News (2011) 'Bribery act targets corrupt firms', BBC News, 1 July. Available online at: www.bbc.co.uk/news/uk-13983256 (accessed 27 May 2012).

16. Dogra, S. and Chatzinerantzis, A. (2010) *Foreign Corrupt Practices 2010 – Your Guide*, Linklaters LLP, London.

17. See 'OECD (2009) Convention on combating bribery of foreign public officials in international business transactions'. Available online at www.oecd.org/document/21/0,3343, en_2649_34859_2017813_1_1_1_1,00.html (accessed 22 May 2009).

18. BBC News (2008) 'Siemens in corruption settlement', *BBC News*, 15, December. Available online at: www.news.bbc.co.uk/1/hi/business/7784512.stm (accessed 27 May 2012).

19. Peel, Michael (2009) 'Landmark bribery case goes to trial', *Financial Times*, 2 December, p. 4 (accessed 27 December 2009 from ABI/INFORM Global, document ID: 1913325051).

20. Donaldson, Thomas and Dunfee, Thomas W. (1999) *Ties That Bind: A Social Contracts Approach to Business Ethics*, Boston, MA, Harvard Business School Press, pp. 35 and 83.

21. Based on a report in Satchell, M.J. (1994) 'Deadly trade in toxics', *U.S. News & World Report, 7* March p. 64, and cited in Donaldson and Dunfee, 'When ethics travel', p. 46.

22. BBC News (2010) 'US charges car firm Daimler with violating bribery laws', *BBC News;* 23 March. Available online at www.news.bbc.co.uk/1/hi/business/8584158.stm (accessed 27 May 2012).

23. Two of the definitive treatments of integrated social contracts theory as applied to ethics are Donaldson, Thomas and Dunfee, Thomas W. (1994) 'Towards a unified conception of business ethics: integrative social contracts theory', *Academy of Management Review*, 19(2): 252–84, and Donaldson and Dunfee, *Ties That Bind*, especially chs 3, 4 and 6. See also Spicer, Andrew, Dunfee, Thomas W. and Bailey, Wendy J. (2004) 'Does national context matter in ethical decision making? An empirical test of integrative social contracts theory', *Academy of Management Journal*, 47(4): 610.

24. Nichols, P.M. (1997) 'Outlawing transnational bribery through the World Trade Organization', *Law and Policy in International Business*, 28(2): 321–2.

25. For an overview of widely endorsed guidelines for creating codes of conduct, see Paine Lynn, Deshpandé Rohit, Margolis Joshua D. and Bettcher Kim Eric (2005) 'Up to code: does your company's conduct meet world-class standards?' *Harvard Business Review*, 83(12): 122–33.

26. For survey data on what managers say about why they sometimes behave unethically, see Veiga, John F. Golden, Timothy D. and Dechant, Kathleen (2004) 'Why managers bend company rules', *Academy of Management Executive*, 18(2): 84–9.

27. BBC News (2010) 'Parmalat founder given 18-year jail term over fraud', *BBC News*, 9 December. Available online at www.bbc.co.uk/news/business-11958133 (accessed 27 May 2012).

28. For more details, see Sims, Ronald R. and Brinkmann, Johannes (2003) 'Enron ethics (or: culture matters more than codes)', *Journal of Business Ethics*, 45(3): 244–6.

29. Veiga, Golden and Dechant, 'Why managers bend company rules', p. 36.

30. The following account is based largely on the discussion and analysis in Sims and Brinkmann, 'Enron ethics', pp. 245–52. Perhaps the definitive book-length account of the corrupt Enron culture is Eichenwald, Kurt (2005) *Conspiracy of Fools: A True Story*, New York, Broadway Books.

31. Cummins, Chip and Latour, Almar (2004) 'How Shell's move to revamp culture ended in scandal', *Wall Street Journal*, 2 November p. A14.

32. Carroll, Archie B. 'The four faces of corporate citizenship', *Business and Society Review* 100/101, September, p. 6.

33. Tepper Marlin, A. and Tepper Marlin, J. (2003) 'A brief history of social reporting'. Available online at www.mallenbaker.net/csr/page.php?Story_ID=857 (accessed 27 May 2012).

34. For an argument that the concept of corporate social responsibility is not viable because of the inherently conflicted nature of a corporation, see Devinney, Timothy M. (2009) 'Is the socially responsible corporation a myth? The good, the bad, and the ugly of corporate social responsibility', *Academy of Management Perspectives*, 23(2): 44–56.

35. Stuber, M. (2007) 'Rethinking diversity for a global scope: A European/EMEA perspective', *The Changing Currency of Diversity*, 15(1).

36. EMCC (2007) 'Case example of carrefour SA', European Monitoring Centre on Change. Available online at www.eurofund.europa.eu (accessed 18 November 2011).

37. Henriques, Adrian (2010) 'ISO 26000: a new standard for human rights?' Institute for Human Rights and Business, 23 March. Available online at www.institutehrb.org/blogs/guest/iso_26000_a_new_standard_for_human_rights.html?gclid5CJih7NjN2aICFVs65QodrVOdyQ (accessed 7 July 2010).

38. Zetsloot, Gerald I.J.M. and van Marrewijk Marcel N.A. (2004) 'From quality to sustainability', *Journal of Business Ethics* 55(2): 79–82.

39. Co-operative Group (2012) *Our Plan*. Available online at www.co-operative.coop/join-the-revolution/our-plan/ (accessed 29 May 2012).

40. FTSE (2012) FTSE4Good index series: Inclusion Criteria. Available online at www.ftse.com/Indices/FTSE4Good_Index_Series/Downloads/F4G_Criteria.pdf (accessed 29 May 2012).

41. Article 13 (2010) 'DHL Express UK revisited case study'. Available online at www.article13.com/A13_ContentList.asp?strAction=GetPublication&PNID=1444 (accessed 18 November 2011).

42. This definition is based on the Brundtland Commission's report, which described sustainable development in a like manner: United Nations General Assembly, (1987) 'Report of the World Commission on Environment and Development: Our Common Future'. Available online at www.un-documents.net/wced-ocf.htm, transmitted to the General Assembly as an annex to document A/42/427 – 'Development and International Co-operation: Environment' (accessed 15 February 2009).

43. See, for example, Goodland, Robert (1995) 'The concept of environmental sustainability', *Annual Review of Ecology and Systematics*, 26: 1–25; Speth, J.G. (2008) *The Bridge at the End of the World: Capitalism, the Environment, and Crossing from Crisis to Sustainability*, New Haven, CT, Yale University Press.

44. For an excellent discussion of crafting corporate social responsibility strategies capable of contributing to an organization's competitive advantage, see Porter, Michael E. and Kramer, Mark R. (2006) 'Strategy & society: the link between competitive advantage and corporate social responsibility', *Harvard Business Review*, 84(12): 78–92.

45. Further information about Divine Chocolate can be found on the organization's website, which contains a wide range of resources for academics, teachers and students. Available online at: www.divinechocolate.com/about/resources.aspx (accessed 29 May 2012).

46. For a discussion of how organizations are connecting social initiatives to their core values, see Hess, David, Rogovsky, Nikolai and Dunfee, Thomas W. (2002) 'The next wave of corporate community involvement: corporate social initiatives', *California Management Review*, 44(2): 110–25. See also Aaronson, Susan Ariel (2003) 'Corporate responsibility in the global village: the british role model and the American laggard', *Business and Society Review*, 108(3): 323.

47. Tradicraft's website contains a range of resources explaining the organization's business model and its recently published strategy for 2011–14. Available online at www.traidcraft.co.uk/about_traidcraft (accessed 29 May 2012).

48. Smith, N. Craig (2003) 'Corporate responsibility: whether and how', *California Management Review*, 45(4): 63.

49. For an excellent discussion of the social responsibilities that corporations have in emerging countries where many people live in poverty, see Brugmann, Jeb and Pralahad, C.K. (2007) 'Cocreating business's new social compact', *Harvard Business Review*, 85(2): 80–90.

50. Davidson, Wallace N., El-Jelly, Abuzar and Worrell, Dan L. (1995) 'Influencing managers to change unpopular corporate behaviour through boycotts and divestitures: a stock market test', *Business and Society*, 34(2): 171–96.

51. Ibid., p. 3.

52. McCawley, Tom (2000) 'Racing to improve its reputation: nike has fought to shed its image as an exploiter of third-world labour yet it is still a target of activists', *Financial Times*, December, p. 14; Smith, 'Corporate responsibility', p. 61.

53. Smith, 'Corporate responsibility', p 63; see also World Economic Forum, 'Findings of a survey on global corporate leadership'. Available online at www.weforum.org/corporatecitizenship (accessed 11 October 2003).

54. Desso's website clearly explains the closed loop supply chain principles. Available online at www.desso.com/Desso/EN/EN-Cradle_to_Cradle/EN-Cradle_to_Cradle-Cradle_to_Cradleampltsupampgtampltsupampgt.html (accessed 29 May 2012).

55. Article 13 (2005) Taylor Woodrow plc case study available online at www.article13.com/A13_ContentList.asp?strAction=GetPublication&PNID=1358 (accessed 29 May 2012).

56. Margolis, Joshua D. and Elfenbein, Hillary A. (2008) 'Doing well by doing good: don't count on it', *Harvard Business Review*, 86(1): 19–20. Of some 80 studies that examined whether an organization's social performance is a good predictor of its financial performance, 42 concluded yes, 4 concluded no and the remainder reported mixed or inconclusive findings. See Smith, 'Corporate responsibility', p. 65; Preston, Lee E. and O'Bannon, Douglas P. (1997) 'The corporate social-financial performance relationship', *Business and Society*, 36(4): 419–29; Roman, Ronald M., Hayibor, Sefa and Agle, Bradley R. (1999) 'The relationship between social and financial performance: repainting a portrait', *Business and Society*, 38(1): 109–25; Margolis, Joshua D. and Walsh, James P. (2001) *People and Profits*, Mahwah, NJ, Lawrence Erlbaum.

57. 'Performance and Socially Responsible Investments', *The Social Investment Forum*, 2009. Available online at www.socialinvest.org/resources/performance. cfm (accessed 15 November 2009).

58. Cheney, Glenn 'Sustainability looms as a bigger issue', *Accounting Today*, 18 May. Available online at www.accessmylibrary.com/article-1G1-199972817/sustainability-looms-biggerissue. html (accessed 15 November 2009).

Chapter Ten

Building an organization capable of good strategy execution

People, capabilities and structure

Strategies most often fail because they aren't executed well.

Larry Bossidy and Ram Charan
CEO Honeywell International; author and consultant

People are not your most important asset. The right people are.

Jim Collins
Professor and author

The companies that look after their people are the companies that do really well.

Sir Richard Branson
Entrepreneur, founder and chairman of the Virgin Group

Learning Objectives

When you have read this chapter you should be able to:

LO 10.1   Describe the actions managers can take to execute strategy successfully.

LO 10.2   Explain why hiring, training and retaining the right people constitute key components of the strategy execution process.

LO 10.3   Recognize how continuously building and upgrading the organization's resources and capabilities contributes to good strategy execution.

LO 10.4   Identify what issues to consider in establishing a strategy-supportive organizational structure and organizing the work effort.

LO 10.5   Discuss the pros and cons of centralized and decentralized decision-making in implementing the chosen strategy.

THE NATIONAL TRUST – GOING LOCAL

Founded in 1895, the National Trust is a very unique social enterprise, combining a philanthropic mission to save Britain's heritage and open spaces for the nation with the corporate infrastructure required to run a large-scale tourism and property business. The Trust was started by a group of radical Christian Socialists, led by Octavia Hill, and funded by several paternalistic aristocrats. In its 116 years of operation the organization has come to own most of the land and houses of that founding group and many more besides. It derives much of its income from membership, generated by fees from its 3.8 million members and in 2010/11 had a turnover in excess of £400 million.

The Trust had a rather elitist and aloof reputation despite its founding principles and had developed into a bureaucratic and very hierarchical organization. By 2001, despite becoming one of the biggest landowners in the UK, the Trust was facing an uncertain future after a series of events in its external environment that had substantially reduced its revenue. Falling stocks affected income from its investments and donations, terrorist attacks had put off many wealthy US tourists from travelling and visitor numbers at many of its historic houses and properties had fallen, and income from its land had been affected by foot and mouth disease. Fiona Reynolds, a former senior civil servant, was appointed Director General in 2001 to turn the charity's fortunes around. Reynolds' initial strategy focused on changing the culture of the organization and bringing its management and operations into the twentyfirst century. There was a damaging tension between two camps in the organization: on the one hand, those engaged with attracting visitors to the properties and enhancing their experience; on the other, those who felt the preservation of the properties was the most important goal for the organization and this should not be compromised by the need to raise funds from visitors. Many staff in the organization did not feel that either their members or visitors were customers.

Many of the changes proposed in the new Director General's strategy proved controversial for the organization and it was soon clear that the main strategy-making part of the organization, a 52-member council, part-elected by members and part-nominees from stakeholder organizations, was not fit for purpose. However, such was the position the Trust held in managing the UK's heritage and landscape that changing this was no easy matter. Finally, in 2005 an Act of Parliament was passed to change the management from the unwieldy council to a tighter board of trustees. A new Chairman, appointed in 2008, journalist and writer, Simon Jenkins, also helped to push Reynolds' agenda to modernize, reduce the bureaucracy and increase responsiveness. By the late 2000s, the National Trust's finances and performance had improved substantially and there was a general feeling that the needs of the access-oriented and conservation-minded factions within the organization were both being met as Reynolds' first 10-year strategy came to its end. Her next vision for the organization was to prove just as controversial. Launched in 2009/10, the 'Going Local' strategy would have a root and branch impact on the organization.

As a charity the Trust relied on 61 000 volunteers in addition to around 5 000 members of staff. The new strategy planned a decrease in the number of regional staff by 20 per cent and central staff by 10 per cent, balanced by an increase in those working at the local properties. But, perhaps more importantly, the strategy was aimed at delegating more power to local groups and encouraging a more bottom-up approach to managing the organization and generating ideas and policy. Although the Trust is only two years into the new strategy, the effects are already showing in a variety of ways. The nine regional offices have been slimmed down to six and many of their functions delegated to local property-based teams. In a radical break with tradition, one of the Trust's newest acquisitions, Seaton Delaval House in Northumberland, was acquired through the fundraising efforts of 11 000 local people and was then opened to the public, on the basis of local views, after less than five months and before most of the major restoration projects had been completed. In the past, the Trust had closed new properties for 18 months while professional teams overhauled them and prepared them for visitors.

The Trust has also invested in a different calibre of senior manager, in 2011 the number of staff earning over £100 000 went from 11 to 18. The Trust has continued to invest in marketing expertise with Claire Mullin, ex-Dyson marketing chief, recruited as its first brand and marketing director for the Trust in 2011, to lead a restructured marketing function focused on member and customer acquisition.

Most importantly the new strategy is also improving the Trust's performance in a wide range of areas. Visitor satisfaction rose from 59 per cent in 2008 to 71 per cent in 2011. Staff satisfaction remains stable despite the structural changes that have included redundancies and redeployments. Significantly, middle managers and staff in the properties have recorded a substantial increase in satisfaction. The Trust has also continued to grow its revenues from £406 million in 2009/10 to £412 million in 2010/11 despite the recession.

QUESTIONS

1. What were the major changes in terms of people, capabilities and structure resulting from the National Trust's two 10-year strategies?

2. Could the Going Local strategy have been envisaged or implemented without the changes made to the organization prior to 2009?

Sources: Henley, J. (2010) 'How the National Trust is finding its mojo', *The Guardian*, 10 February. Available on-line at www.guardian.co.uk/culture/2010/feb/10/national-trust-opens-its-doors (accessed 29 May 2012); Marketing Week (2011) 'National Trust picks ex-Dyson marketer to boost brand', *Marketing Week*, 3 February, p. 4; National Trust (2011) *Going Local: Annual Report 2010/11*, National Trust, London; National Trust (2010) *Going Local: Fresh Tracks Down Old road, Our Strategy for the Next Decade*, National Trust, Swindon; Nordberg, D. (2005) 'National Trust out of the woods', *Market Leader*, Spring, pp. 56–8; Sidders, J. (2010) 'National Trust staff to enter consultation over job cuts', *Horticulture Week*, 13 August, p. 6.

As we have seen from the opening case, once managers have decided on a strategy, the emphasis turns to converting it into actions and good results. Putting the strategy into place and getting the organization to execute it well call for different sets of managerial skills. Whereas crafting strategy is largely a market-driven and resource-driven activity, executing strategy is an operations-driven activity revolving around the management of people and business processes. Whereas successful strategy-making depends on strategic vision, solid industry and competitive analysis and shrewd market positioning, successful strategy execution depends on doing a good job of working with and through others; allocating resources; building and strengthening competitive capabilities; creating an appropriate organizational structure; instituting strategy-supportive policies, processes and systems; motivating and rewarding people; and instilling a discipline of getting things done. Executing strategy is an action-oriented, make-things-happen task that tests a manager's ability to direct organizational change, achieve continuous improvement in operations and business processes, create and nurture a strategy-supportive culture and consistently meet or beat performance targets.

Most experienced managers are clear that it is much easier to develop a sound strategic plan than it is to execute the plan and achieve the desired outcomes. According to one executive, 'It's been rather easy for us to decide where we wanted to go. The hard part is to get the organization to act on the new priorities'.[1] In a recent study of 1000 companies, government agencies and not-for-profit organizations in over 50 countries, 60 per cent of employees rated their organizations poor in terms of strategy implementation.[2] *Just because senior managers announce a new strategy does not mean that organization members will embrace it and move forward enthusiastically to implement it.* Senior executives cannot simply direct immediate subordinates to abandon old ways and take up new ways, and they certainly cannot expect the needed actions and changes to occur in rapid-fire fashion and still lead to the desired outcomes. Some managers and employees may be sceptical about the merits of the strategy, seeing it as contrary to the organization's best interests, unlikely to succeed or threatening to their departments or careers. Moreover, employees may have misconceptions about the new strategy or have different ideas about what internal changes are needed to execute it. Long-standing attitudes, vested interests, inertia and ingrained organizational practices do not melt away when managers decide on a new strategy and begin efforts to implement it, especially if only a few people have been involved in crafting the strategy or if the rationale for strategic change requires quite a bit of salesmanship. It takes adept managerial leadership to convincingly communicate a new strategy and the reasons for it, overcome pockets of doubt and disagreement, secure the commitment and enthusiasm of key personnel, gain agreement on how to implement the strategy and move forward to get all the pieces into place. Company personnel must understand – in their heads and hearts – why a new strategic direction is necessary and where the new strategy is taking them.[3] Instituting change is, of course, easier when the problems with the old strategy have become obvious and/or the company has spiralled into a financial crisis. It is likely that the initial strategy developed by the National Trust in 2001 was easier to implement due to the charity's poor financial performance and threat-filled environment.

But the challenge of successfully implementing new strategic initiatives goes well beyond managerial adeptness in overcoming resistance to change. What really makes strategy execution a tougher, more time-consuming management challenge than crafting strategy are the wide array of managerial activities that need to be addressed and the number of complex issues that must be worked out. Managers need to have a clear idea of what has to be done to put new strategic initiatives in place and, further, how best to get these things done in a timely manner that yields good results. Demanding people-management skills and perseverance are required to get a variety of initiatives launched and moving and to integrate the efforts of many different work groups into a smoothly functioning whole. Depending on how much consensus-building and organizational change is involved, the process of implementing strategy

> **Core Concept**
>
> Good strategy execution requires a *team effort*. All managers have strategy-executing responsibility in their areas of authority, and all employees are active participants in the strategy execution process.

changes can take several months to several years. To achieve *real proficiency* in executing the strategy can take even longer.

Even traditional firms with pyramidal hierarchies find that like crafting strategy, *executing strategy is a job for the whole organisation, not just a few senior managers.* In such firms, while the chief executive officer and the heads of major units (business divisions, functional departments and key operating units) are ultimately responsible for seeing that strategy is executed successfully, the process typically affects every part of the firm – all value chain activities and all workgroups. Top-level managers must rely on the active support and co-operation of middle- and lower managers to institute whatever new operating practices are needed in the various functional areas and operating units to achieve proficient strategy execution. It is middle-and lower-level managers who ultimately must ensure that workgroups and front-line employees do a good job of performing strategy-critical value chain activities and produce operating results that allow company-wide performance targets to be met. In consequence, strategy execution requires every manager to think through the answer to the question: *'What does my area have to do to implement its part of the strategic plan, and what should I do to get these things accomplished efficiently and effectively?'* In organizations with flatter structures or with more emergent strategy processes, managers tend to have more of a co-ordinating role and have to strike a balance between empowering staff to unleash their creativity and ensuring consistency with the overall goals and vision of the organization's top-level strategy.

A Framework for Executing Strategy

LO 10.1
Describe the actions managers can take to execute strategy successfully.

Executing strategy entails figuring out the specific techniques, actions and behaviours that are needed for a smooth strategy-supportive operation, and then following through to get things done and deliver results. With new strategic direction often the first step in implementing strategic change is for management to communicate the case for organizational change clearly and persuasively to internal stakeholders such as employees so that they find ways to put the strategy into place, make it work and meet performance targets. Management's handling of the strategy implementation process can be considered successful if and when the company achieves the targeted strategic and financial performance and shows good progress in making its strategic vision a reality.

The specifics of how to execute a strategy – the exact items that need to be placed on management's action agenda – always need to be customized to fit the particulars of a company's situation. The challenges for successfully executing a low-cost provider strategy are different from those for executing a high-end differentiation strategy. Implementing a new strategy for a struggling company in the midst of a financial crisis is a different job from that of making minor improvements to strategy execution in a company that is doing relatively well. Moreover, some managers are more adept than others at using particular approaches to achieve the desired kinds of organizational changes. Hence, there is no definitive managerial recipe for successful strategy execution that cuts across all company situations and all types of strategies or that works for all types of managers. Rather, the specific actions required to implement a strategy – the 'to do list' that constitutes management's action agenda – always represents management's judgement about how best to proceed in light of prevailing circumstances.

The Principal Components of the Strategy Execution Process

Despite the need to tailor a company's strategy-executing approaches to the particulars of its situation, there are key elements of the organization's architecture or its configuration[4] which managers need to attend to in designing a firm that is fit for executing their chosen strategy. Structure, systems and culture are inextricably linked in any change at a strategic level and this gives rise to three distinct but interconnected areas of activity encompassing 10 basic managerial tasks that crop up repeatedly in company efforts to execute strategy (see Figure 10.1):

1. Staff the organization with managers and employees capable of executing the strategy well.

2. Build the organizational capabilities required for successful strategy execution.

3. Create a strategy-supportive organizational structure.

4. Allocate sufficient budgetary (and other) resources to the strategy execution effort.

5. Institute policies and procedures that facilitate strategy execution.

6. Adopt best practices and business processes that drive continuous improvement in strategy execution activities.

7. Install information and operating systems that enable company personnel to carry out their strategic roles proficiently.

8. Tie rewards and incentives directly to the achievement of strategic and financial targets.

9. Instil a corporate culture that promotes good strategy execution.

10. Exercise the internal leadership needed to propel strategy implementation forward.

In devising an action agenda for executing strategy, managers often start with *an assessment of what the organization must do differently to carry out the strategy successfully*. They then consider *how to make the necessary internal changes* as rapidly as possible. Successful strategy implementers have a knack for diagnosing what their organizations need to do to execute the chosen strategy well and figuring out how to

> When strategies fail, it is often because of poor execution. Strategy execution is therefore a critical managerial endeavour.

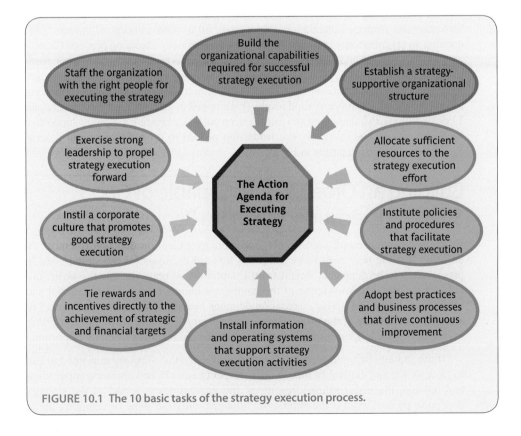

FIGURE 10.1 The 10 basic tasks of the strategy execution process.

get things done cost-efficiently and with all deliberate speed. They are skilled at promoting results-oriented behaviours on the part of company personnel and following through on making the right things happen in a timely fashion.[5]

In big organizations with geographically scattered operating units, the action agenda of senior executives mostly involves communicating the case for change, building consensus for how to proceed, installing strong managers to move the process forward in key organizational units, directing resources to the right places, establishing deadlines and measures of progress, rewarding those who achieve implementation milestones and personally leading the strategic change process. Thus, the bigger the organization, the more that successful strategy execution depends on the co-operation and implementing skills of operating managers who can promote needed changes at the lowest organizational levels and deliver results. In small organizations, top managers can deal directly with front-line managers and employees, personally orchestrating the action steps and implementation sequence, observing firsthand how implementation is progressing and deciding how hard and how fast to push the process along. Regardless of the organization's size and whether implementation involves sweeping or minor changes, the most important leadership trait is a strong, confident sense of what to do and how to do it. Having a strong grip on these two things comes from understanding the circumstances of the organization and the requirements for effective strategy execution. Then it remains for company personnel in strategy-critical areas to step up to the plate and produce the desired results.

> The two best signs of good strategy execution are whether a company is meeting or beating its performance targets and performing value chain activities in a manner that is conducive to company-wide operating excellence.

What's Covered in Chapters 10, 11 and 12

In the remainder of this chapter and the next two chapters, we discuss what is involved in performing the 10 key managerial tasks that shape the process of executing strategy. This chapter explores the first three of these tasks (highlighted in blue in Figure 10.1). We start with the most concrete and action-based elements of organised change – *people* and *facilities/competences*[6] – which correspond to (1) staffing the organization with people capable of executing the strategy well, (2) building the organizational capabilities needed for successful strategy execution and then move on to more conceptual matters – (3) creating an organizational *structure* supportive of the strategy execution process. Chapter 11 concerns *systems* and *programmes*, including the tasks of allocating resources, instituting strategy-facilitating policies and procedures, employing business process management tools and best practices, installing operating and information systems and tying rewards to the achievement of good results (highlighted in green in Figure 10.1). Chapter 12 deals with the two remaining and most conceptual tasks: creating a strategy-supportive corporate *culture* and exercising the leadership needed to drive the execution process forward (highlighted in purple in Figure 10.1).

Building an Organization Capable of Good Strategy Execution: Where to Begin

Building an organization capable of good strategy execution depends foremost on ensuring that the resources and capabilities that are the basis for the strategy are in place, ready to be deployed. Recall from Chapter 4 that these include the skills, talents, experience and knowledge of the company's human resources (managerial and otherwise). Proficient strategy execution depends heavily on competent personnel of all types, but because of the many managerial tasks involved and the role of leadership in strategy execution, assembling a strong management team is especially important.

If the strategy being implemented is a new strategy, the company may need to add to its resource and capability mix in other respects as well. But renewing, upgrading and revising the organization's resources and capabilities is a part of the strategy execution process even if the strategy is fundamentally the same or changing on an

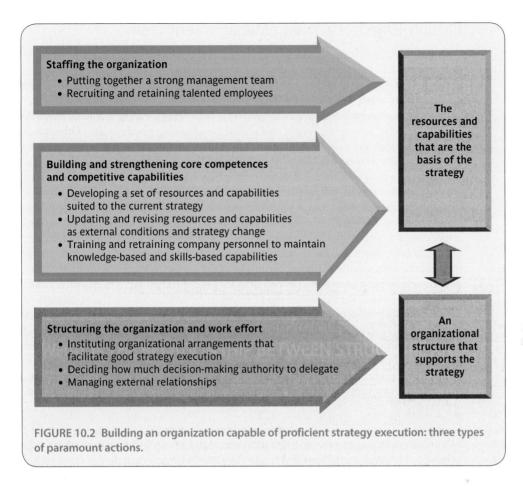

FIGURE 10.2 Building an organization capable of proficient strategy execution: three types of paramount actions.

incremental basis over time, since resources depreciate and conditions are always changing. Thus, augmenting and strengthening the firm's core competences and seeing that they are suited to the current strategy are also top priorities.

Structuring the organization and work effort is another critical aspect of building an organization capable of good strategy execution. An organization structure that is well matched to the strategy can help facilitate its implementation; one that is not well suited can lead to higher bureaucratic costs and communication or co-ordination breakdowns. As shown in Figure 10.2, three types of organization-building actions are paramount:

1. *Staffing the organization*: putting together a strong management team, and recruiting and retaining employees with the needed experience, technical skills and intellectual capital.

2. *Building and strengthening core competences and competitive capabilities:* developing proficiencies in performing strategy-critical value chain activities and updating them to match changing market conditions and customer expectations.

3. *Structuring the organization and work effort:* organizing value chain activities and business processes, establishing lines of authority and reporting relationships, deciding how much decision-making authority to delegate to lower-level managers and front-line employees and managing external relationships.

Staffing the Organization

Organizations will find it hard to perform the activities required for successful strategy execution without attracting and retaining talented managers and employees with suitable skills and intellectual capital.

LO 10.2
Explain why hiring, training and retaining the right people constitute key components of the strategy execution process.

Putting Together a Strong Management Team

> Putting together a talented management team with the right mix of experiences, skills and abilities to get things done is one of the first strategy-implementing steps.

Assembling a capable management team is a cornerstone of the organization-building task.[7] While different strategies and company circumstances sometimes call for different mixes of backgrounds, experiences, management styles and know-how, some commentators state that *the most important consideration is to fill key managerial slots with smart people who are clear thinkers, capable of figuring out what needs to be done, good at managing people and skilled in delivering good results.*[8] Other studies are clear that the task of implementing challenging strategic initiatives must be assigned to executives who have the skills and talents to turn their decisions into results that meet or beat the established performance targets. They state that without a smart, capable, results-oriented management team, the implementation process is likely to be hampered by missed deadlines, misdirected or wasteful efforts and managerial ineptness.[9] By the same token, there is a view that weak executives are serious impediments to getting optimal results because they are unable to differentiate between ideas that have merit and those that are misguided – the calibre of work done under their supervision usually suffers accordingly.[10] In contrast, managers with strong strategy-implementing capabilities have a talent for asking tough, incisive questions; they know enough about the details of the business to be able to ensure the soundness of the decisions of the people around them, and they can discern whether the resources people are asking for to put the strategy in place make sense. They are good at getting things done through others, partly by making sure they have the right people under them and that these people are put in the right jobs.[11] They consistently follow through on issues, monitor progress carefully, make adjustments when needed and keep important details from slipping through the cracks. In short, they understand how to drive organizational change, and they have the managerial skills and discipline requisite for first-rate strategy execution.

Sometimes a company's existing management team is up to the task; at other times it may need to be strengthened or expanded by promoting qualified people from within or by bringing in outsiders whose experiences, talents and leadership styles better suit the situation. In turnaround and rapid-growth situations, and in instances when a company does not have insiders with the requisite know-how, filling key management slots from the outside is a fairly standard organization-building approach. In addition, it is important to ferret out and replace managers who, for whatever reasons, either do not buy into the case for making organizational changes or do not see ways to make things better.[12] Industry experts state that for a management team to be truly effective at strategy execution, it must be composed of managers who recognize that organizational changes are needed and who are ready to get on with the process. Weak executives and die-hard resisters have to be replaced or side-lined, perhaps by shifting them to areas where they cannot hamper new strategy execution initiatives.

The overriding aim in building a management team should be to assemble a *critical mass* of talented managers who can function as agents of change and further the cause of first-rate strategy execution. Every manager's success is enhanced (or limited) by the quality of his or her managerial colleagues and the degree to which they freely exchange ideas, debate ways to make operating improvements and join forces to tackle issues and solve problems.[13] When a first-rate manager enjoys the help and support of other first-rate managers, it is possible to create a managerial whole that is greater than the sum of individual efforts – talented managers who work well together as a team can produce organizational results that are dramatically better than what one or two star managers acting individually can achieve.[14]

Illustration Capsule 10.1 describes General Electric's (GE's) widely acclaimed approach to developing a top-calibre management team.

Illustration Capsule 10.1

HOW GE DEVELOPS A TALENTED AND DEEP MANAGEMENT TEAM

GE is widely considered to be one of the best-managed companies in the world, partly because of its concerted effort to develop outstanding managers. It ranked number one among the best companies for leadership in the most recent global survey conducted by the Hay Group. For starters, GE strives to hire talented people with a high potential for executive leadership; it then goes to great lengths to expand the leadership, business and decision-making capabilities of all its managers. The company spends about $1 billion annually on training and education programmes. In 2009, all of its 191 most senior executives had spent at least 12 months in training and professional development during their first 15 years at GE.

Four key elements undergird GE's efforts to build a talent-rich stable of managers:

1. GE makes a practice of transferring managers across divisional, business or functional lines for sustained periods of time. Such transfers allow managers to develop relationships with colleagues in other parts of the company, help break down insular thinking in business 'silos', promote the sharing of cross-business ideas and best practices and build a mind-set open and adaptive to international markets. There is an enormous emphasis at GE on transferring ideas and best practices from business to business and making GE a 'boundaryless' company.

2. In selecting executives for key positions, GE is strongly disposed to candidates who exhibit what are called the four E's – enormous personal *energy*, the ability to *energize* others, *edge* (a GE code word for instinctive competitiveness and the ability to make tough decisions in a timely fashion – saying yes or no, and not maybe) and *execution* (the ability to carry things through to fruition). Considerable attention is also paid to problem-solving ability, experience in multiple functions or businesses and experience in driving business growth (as indicated by good market instincts, in-depth knowledge of particular markets, customer touch and technical understanding).

3. All managers are expected to be proficient at what GE calls *workout* – a process in which managers and employees come together to confront issues as soon as they come up, pinpoint the root cause of the issues and bring about quick resolutions so that the business can move forward. Workout is GE's way of training its managers to diagnose what to do and how to do it.

4. Each year GE sends about 10 000 newly hired and long-time managers to its John F. Welch Leadership Development Centre (generally regarded as one of the best corporate training centres in the world) for a three-week course on the company's Six Sigma quality initiative. GE's Leadership Development Centre also offers advanced courses for senior managers that may focus on a single management topic for a month. All classes involve managers from different GE businesses and different parts of the world. Some of the most valuable learning comes between formal class sessions when GE managers from different businesses trade ideas about how to improve processes and better serve the customer. This knowledge-sharing not only spreads best practices throughout the organization but also improves each GE manager's knowledge.

◄

One of the keys to the success of the management development process at GE is its ability to be adapted to a changing environment: 'It's a constant evolution', according to chief learning officer Susan Peters.* Under the leadership of Jack Welch, GE's CEO from 1980 to 2001, training activities were focused around cost-cutting, efficiency and deal-making. His successor, Jeffrey Immelt, adapted the focus of development programmes to drive toward new goals of risk-taking, innovation and customer focus. Recently, GE has tackled the ascendancy of emerging markets by an increased focus on global capability development, including the development of the China Learning Centre in Shanghai. This has had a visible impact on the organization: in the last seven years the proportion of non-US executives has doubled, from 15 per cent to more than 30 per cent.

As a key part of talent development, talent assessment and feedback are approached with characteristic GE energy. Each of GE's 85 000 managers and professionals is graded in an annual process that divides them into five tiers: the top 10 per cent, the next 15 per cent the middle 50 per cent, the next 15 per cent and the bottom 10 per cent. Everyone in the top tier gets stock awards, nobody in the fourth tier gets shares of stock and most of those in the fifth tier become candidates for being weeded out. Business heads are pressured to wean out 'C' players. The CEO Jeffrey Immelt personally reviews the performance reviews of the top 600 employees each year, as part of GE's intensive, months-long performance review process.

* Brady, D. (2010) 'Can GE still manage?' *Bloomberg Businessweek*, 25, April pp. 26–32.

Note: Developed with Jeffrey L. Boyink.

Sources: GE website (accessed 2010 June); Hewitt Associates, 'Managing leadership in turbulent times – why and how the global top companies for leaders optimize leadership talent in emerging markets' (White Paper). Available online at www. hewittassociates.com/_MetaBasicCMAssetCache_/Assets/Articles/2009/Managing_Leadership_Turbulent_Times_033009. pdf; Brady, D. (2010) 'Can GE still manage?' *Bloomberg Businessweek*, 25 April 2010, pp. 26–32; 'Hay group study identifies best companies for leadership,' *Bloomberg Businessweek.com*, 18 February 2010. Available online at www.greatleadershipbydan. com/2010/02/bloomberg-businessweek comhay-group.html.

Recruiting, Training and Retaining Capable Employees

> In many industries, adding to a company's talent base and building intellectual capital are more important to good strategy execution than additional investments in capital projects.

Assembling a capable management team is not enough. Staffing the organization with the right kinds of people must go much deeper than managerial jobs in order for strategy-critical value chain activities to be performed competently. *The quality of an organization's people is always an essential ingredient of successful strategy execution – knowledgeable, engaged employees are a company's best source of creative ideas for the nuts-and-bolts operating improvements that lead to operating excellence.* Companies like Google, Microsoft, McKinsey & Company, KPMG, Cisco Systems, Amazon.com, Unilever, Britvic, Adidas, SAP, Goldman Sachs and Intel make a concerted effort to recruit the best and brightest people they can find and then retain them with excellent compensation packages, opportunities for rapid advancement and professional growth and interesting assignments. Even though many employers have scaled down their talent management programmes during the recession, those that have learned the lessons of previous downturns keep investing in their workforce and seek to retain their best people.

> The best companies make a point of recruiting and retaining talented employees – the objective is to make the company's entire workforce (managers and rank-and-file employees) a genuine competitive asset.

The NHS operates a scheme called Gateway that seeks outsiders with the skills and experience to undertake director-level roles. It also provides support and development to help them find suitable roles in the organization.[15] McKinsey & Company, one of the world's premier management consulting firms, recruits only cream-of-the-crop MBAs from Europe's top business schools; such talent is essential to McKinsey's strategy of performing high-level consulting for the world's top corporations. The leading global accounting firms screen candidates not only on the basis of their accounting expertise but also on whether they possess the people skills needed to relate well with clients and colleagues. In high-tech companies, the challenge is to staff workgroups with gifted, imaginative and energetic people who can bring life to new ideas quickly and inject into the organization what one Dell executive calls 'hum'.[16] The saying 'People are our most important asset' may seem trite, but it fits high-tech companies precisely. Besides checking closely for functional and technical skills, Dell tests applicants for their tolerance of ambiguity and change, their capacity to work in teams and their ability to learn on the fly. Companies like Amazon.com, Google and Cisco Systems have broken new ground in recruiting, hiring, cultivating, developing and retaining talented employees – almost all of whom are in their 20s and 30s. Cisco goes after the top 10 per cent, raiding other companies and endeavouring to retain key people at the companies it acquires. Cisco executives believe that a cadre of star engineers, programmers, managers, salespeople and support personnel is the backbone of the company's efforts to execute its strategy and remain the world's leading provider of Internet infrastructure products and technology.

The practices listed below are common among companies dedicated to recruiting, training and retaining the most capable people they can find:

1. Spending considerable effort on screening and evaluating job applicants — selecting only those with suitable skill sets, energy, initiative, judgement, aptitude for learning and personality traits that mesh well with the company's work environment and culture.

2. Putting employees through training programmes that continue throughout their careers.

3. Providing promising employees with challenging, interesting and skill-stretching assignments.

4. Rotating people through jobs that span functional and geographic boundaries. Providing people with opportunities to gain experience in a variety of international settings is increasingly considered an essential part of career development in multinational or global companies.

5. Making the work environment stimulating and engaging so that employees will consider the company a great place to work. Progressive companies work hard at creating an environment in which employees are made to feel that their views and suggestions count.

6. Striving to retain talented, high-performing employees via promotions, salary increases, performance bonuses, stock options and equity ownership, fringe-benefit packages and other perks.

7. Coaching average performers to improve their skills and capabilities, while weeding out underperformers and benchwarmers.

Building and Strengthening Core Competences and Competitive Capabilities

High among the organization-building priorities in the strategy execution process is the need to build and strengthen competitively valuable core competences and capabilities. As explained in Chapter 4, a company's ability to perform the value-creating activities that express its strategy derives from its resources and capabilities. In the course of crafting strategy, managers identify the resources and capabilities that will enable the firm's strategy. In executing the strategy, managers deploy those resources and capabilities in the form of value-creating activities. But the first step is to ensure that the necessary resources and capabilities are in place and that they are renewed, upgraded or augmented, as needed.

If the strategy being implemented is new, company managers may have to acquire new resources, significantly broaden or deepen certain capabilities or even add entirely new competences in order to put the strategic initiatives in place and execute them proficiently. But even if the strategy has not changed materially, good strategy execution

> **LO 10.3**
> Recognize how continuously building and upgrading the organization's resources and capabilities contributes to good strategy execution.

involves refreshing and strengthening the firm's resources and capabilities to keep them in top form. Moreover, it involves augmenting and modifying them to keep pace with evolving market needs and competitive conditions.

Three Approaches to Building and Strengthening Capabilities

> Building new competences and capabilities is a multi-stage process that occurs over a period of months and years. It is not something that is accomplished overnight.

Building core competences and competitive capabilities is a time-consuming, managerially challenging exercise. While some assistance can be got from discovering how best-in-industry or best-in-world companies perform a particular activity, trying to replicate and then improve on the competences and capabilities of others is, however, much easier said than done.

With deliberate effort, well-orchestrated organizational actions and continued practice, however, it is possible for a firm to become proficient at capability-building despite the difficulty. Indeed, by making capability-building activities a routine part of their strategy execution endeavours, some firms are able to develop *dynamic capabilities* that assist them in managing resource and capability change, as discussed in Chapter 4. The most common approaches to capability-building include (1) internal development, (2) acquiring capabilities through mergers and acquisitions, and (3) accessing capabilities via collaborative partnerships.[17]

Developing Capabilities Internally

Capabilities develop incrementally along an evolutionary development path as organizations search for solutions to their problems. The process is a complex one, since capabilities are the product of bundles of skills and know-how that are integrated into organizational routines and deployed within activity systems through the combined efforts of teams and workgroups that are often cross-functional in nature, spanning a variety of departments and locations. For instance, the capability of speeding new products to market involves the collaborative efforts of personnel in R&D, engineering and design, purchasing, production, marketing and distribution. Similarly, the capability to provide superior customer service is a team effort among people in customer call centres (where orders are taken and inquiries are answered), shipping and delivery, billing and accounts receivable and after-sales support. The process of building a capability begins when managers set an objective of developing a particular capability and organize activity around that objective.[18] Managers can ignite the process by having high aspirations and setting 'stretch goals' for the organization.[19]

Because the process is incremental, the first step is to develop the *ability* to do something, however imperfectly or inefficiently. This entails selecting people with the requisite skills and experience, upgrading or expanding individual abilities as needed, and then moulding the efforts of individuals into a collaborative effort to create an organizational ability. At this stage, progress can be fitful since it depends on experimentation, active search for alternative solutions and learning through trial and error.[20]

> A company's capabilities must be continually refreshed and renewed to remain aligned with changing customer expectations, altered competitive conditions and new strategic initiatives.

As experience grows and company personnel learn how to perform the activities consistently well and at an acceptable cost, the ability evolves into a tried-and-true competence or capability. Getting to this point requires a continual investment of resources and systematic efforts to improve processes and solve problems creatively as they arise. Improvements in the functioning of a capability come from task repetition and the resulting learning by doing of individuals and teams.[21] But the process can be accelerated by making learning a more deliberate endeavour and providing the incentives that will motivate company personnel to achieve the desired ends.[22] This can be critical to successful strategy execution when market conditions are changing rapidly. Here the dynamic capabilities can be classed as *incremental* or *renewing*, but also *regenerative*.[23] This last type of capability is one that changes the nature of other dynamic capabilities in the organization and can be particularly important in the types of hyper-competitive environments discussed in Chapters 1 and 3. By helping an organization to refresh its resources and competences, regenerative dynamic capabilities are able to help break away from a strategic path that is no longer helping them to perform well in a changed environment. For example, if an organization has developed strong capabilities in R&D, with substantial investments in facilities, scientists and engineers, these may aid the creation of new products and also other useful resources and competences. The experimentation and creative skills might also be leveraged into other parts of the business and help to renew the resource base. However, in a changing environment, where customers want an increased role in product creation, there might be a significant advantage for this organization to develop dynamic capabilities in managing open innovation (see Key Debate 6.1 in Chapter 6 for more on this topic). This would change the resource base of the organization, but also the nature of the dynamic capabilities, because incorporating customers into the new product development process would fundamentally change the way the organization operated. Instead of just being good at leveraging ideas between Strategic Business Units (SBUs), the organization would need to excel at co-ordinating external relationships.

It is generally much easier and less time-consuming to update and remodel a company's existing capabilities as external conditions and company strategy change than it is to create them from scratch. Maintaining capabilities in top form may simply require exercising them continually and fine-tuning them as necessary. Refreshing and updating capabilities require only a limited set of modifications to a set of routines that is otherwise in place. Phasing out an existing capability takes significantly less effort than adding a brand-new one. Replicating a company capability, while not an easy process, still begins with an established template.[24] Even the process of augmenting a capability may require less effort if it involves the recombination of well-established company capabilities and draws on existing company resources.[25] Companies like Cray in large computers and Honda in gasoline engines, for example, have leveraged the expertise of their talent pool by frequently re-forming high-intensity teams and reusing key people on special projects designed to augment their capabilities. Canon combined miniaturization capabilities that it developed in producing calculators with its existing capabilities in precision optics to revolutionize the 35-mm camera market.[26] Toyota, en route to overtaking General Motors as the global leader in motor vehicles, has aggressively upgraded its capabilities in fuel-efficient hybrid engine technology and constantly fine-tuned its famed Toyota Production System to enhance its already proficient capabilities in manufacturing top-quality vehicles at relatively low costs – see Illustration Capsule 10.2.

Illustration Capsule 10.2

TOYOTA'S LEGENDARY PRODUCTION SYSTEM: A CAPABILITY THAT TRANSLATES INTO COMPETITIVE ADVANTAGE

The heart of Toyota's strategy in motor vehicles is to outcompete rivals by manufacturing world-class, quality vehicles at lower costs and selling them at competitive price levels. Executing this strategy requires top-notch manufacturing capability and super-efficient management of people, equipment, and materials. Toyota began conscious efforts to improve its manufacturing competence over 50 years ago. Through tireless trial and error, the company gradually took what started as a loose collection of techniques and practices and integrated them into a full-fledged process that has come to be known as the Toyota Production System (TPS). The TPS drives all

▶

plant operations and the company's supply chain management practices. TPS is grounded in the following principles, practices, and techniques:

- *Use just-in-time delivery of parts and components to the point of vehicle assembly.* The idea here is to cut out all the bits and pieces of transferring materials from place to place and to discontinue all activities on the part of workers that don't add value (particularly activities where nothing ends up being made or assembled).

- *Develop people who can come up with unique ideas for production improvements.* Toyota encourages employees at all levels to question existing ways of doing things — even if this means challenging a boss on the soundness of a directive. Former Toyota president Katsuaki Watanabe encouraged the company's employees to 'pick a friendly fight.' Also, Toyota doesn't fire its employees who, at first, have little judgement for improving work flows; instead, the company gives them extensive training to become better problem solvers.
- *Emphasize continuous improvement.* Workers are expected to use their heads and develop better ways of doing things, rather than mechanically follow instructions. Toyota managers tout messages such as 'Never be satisfied' and 'There's got to be a better way.' Another mantra at Toyota is that the *T* in TPS also stands for 'Thinking.' The thesis is that a work environment where people have to think generates the wisdom to spot opportunities for making tasks simpler and easier to perform, increasing the speed and efficiency with which activities are performed, and constantly improving product quality.
- *Empower workers to stop the assembly line when there's a problem or a defect is spotted.* Toyota views worker efforts to purge defects and sort out the problem immediately as critical to the whole concept of building quality into the production process. According to TPS, 'If the line doesn't stop, useless defective items will move on to the next stage. If you don't know where the problem occurred, you can't do anything to fix it.'
- *Deal with defects only when they occur.* TPS philosophy holds that when things are running smoothly, they should not be subject to control; if attention is directed to fixing problems that are found, quality control along the assembly line can be handled with fewer personnel.
- *Ask yourself 'Why?' five times.* While errors need to be fixed whenever they occur, the value of asking 'Why?' five times enables identifying the root cause of the error and correcting it so that the error won't recur.
- *Organize all jobs around human motion to create a production/assembly system with no wasted effort.* Work organized in this fashion is called 'standardized work' and people are trained to observe standardized work procedures (which include supplying parts to each process on the assembly line at the proper time, sequencing the work in an optimal manner, and allowing workers to do their jobs continuously in a set sequence of sub processes).
- *Find where a part is made cheaply, and use that price as a benchmark.*

The TPS utilizes a unique vocabulary of terms (such as *kanban, takt-time, jikoda, kaizen, heijunka, monozukuri, poka yoke,* and *muda*) that facilitates precise discussion of specific TPS elements. In 2003, Toyota established its Global Production Centre to efficiently train large numbers of shop-floor experts in the latest TPS methods and better operate an increasing number of production sites worldwide. Since then, additional upgrades and refinements have been introduced, some in response to the large number of defects in Toyota vehicles that surfaced in 2009–2010.

There is widespread agreement that Toyota's ongoing effort to refine and improve on its renowned TPS gives it important manufacturing capabilities that are the envy of other motor vehicle manufacturers. Not only

▶

◀

have such auto manufacturers as Ford, Daimler, Volkswagen and General Motors attempted to emulate key elements of TPS, but elements of Toyota's production philosophy have been adopted by hospitals and postal services.

However, Toyota's systems are not without their critics and one former employee, Darius Mehri, has claimed that many of the productivity improvements have been made at the expense of health and safety of employees and are actually underpinned by social control and a bullying culture.

Sources: Information posted at www.toyotageorgetown.com; Hirotaka, Takeuchi, Osono, Emi and Shimizu, Norihiko (2008) 'The contradictions that drive Toyota's success,' *Harvard Business Review*, 86(6): 96–104; Ohno, Taiichi (1988) *Toyota Production System: Beyond Large-Scale Production,* New York, Sheridan; Mehri, D. (2006) 'The darker side of lean: an insider's perspective on the realities of the Toyota Production System', *Academy of Management Perspective*, May, pp. 21-42.

Managerial actions to develop core competences and competitive capabilities generally take one of two forms: either strengthening the company's base of skills, knowledge, and intellect or co-ordinating and integrating the efforts of the various work groups and departments. Actions of the first sort can be undertaken at all managerial levels, but actions of the second sort are best orchestrated by senior managers who not only appreciate the strategy-executing significance of strong capabilities but also have the clout to enforce the necessary co-operation and co-ordination among individuals, groups, departments and external allies.[27]

Acquiring Capabilities through Mergers and Acquisitions

Sometimes a company can refresh and strengthen its competences by acquiring another company with attractive resources and capabilities.[28] An acquisition aimed at building a stronger portfolio of competences and capabilities can be every bit as valuable as an acquisition aimed at adding new products or services to the company's line-up of offerings. The advantage of this mode of acquiring new capabilities is primarily one of speed, since developing new capabilities internally can take many years of effort. Capabilities-motivated acquisitions are essential (1) when a market opportunity can slip by faster than a needed capability can be created internally and (2) when industry conditions, technology or competitors are moving at such a rapid speed that time is of the essence.

At the same time, acquiring capabilities in this way is not without difficulty. Capabilities involve tacit knowledge and complex routines that cannot be transferred readily from one organizational unit to another. This may limit the extent to which the new capability can be utilized. French advertising firm, the Publicis Groupe, have had to become highly skilled in ensuring that their horizontal acquisitions bring their full value to the parent organization. Talent in global advertising is highly mobile and account directors and creatives can often take major clients with them if they decide to leave post-merger. Publicis CEO, Maurice Lévy went to great lengths in 2000 to ensure the group's acquisition of Saatchi & Saatchi[29] kept the talent and knowledge the British firm had built up over many years. The Publicis Groupe was restructured to give the UK firm equal billing with Publicis Worldwide, the French firm's original advertising agency arm and Saatchi executives were invited to lead post-acquisition integration talks. Integrating the capabilities of two firms involved in a merger or acquisition may pose an additional challenge, particularly if there are underlying incompatibilities in their supporting systems or processes. Moreover, since internal fit is important, there is always the risk that under new management the acquired capabilities may not be as productive as they had been. In a worst case scenario, the acquisition process may end up damaging or destroying the very capabilities that were the object of the acquisition in the first place.

Accessing Capabilities through Collaborative Partnerships

Another method of acquiring capabilities from an external source is to access them via collaborative partnerships with suppliers, competitors or other companies having the cutting-edge expertise. There are three basic ways to pursue this course of action:

1. *Outsource the function requiring the capabilities to a key supplier or another provider.* Whether this is a wise move depends on what can be safely delegated to outside suppliers or allies versus what internal capabilities are key to the company's long-term success. As discussed in Chapter 6, outsourcing has the advantage of conserving resources so that the firm can focus its energies on those activities most central to its strategy. It may be a good choice for firms that are too small and resource-constrained to execute all the parts of their strategy internally.

2. *Collaborate with a firm that has complementary resources and capabilities in a joint venture, strategic alliance or other type of partnership established for the purpose of achieving a shared strategic objective.* This requires launching initiatives to identify the most attractive potential partners and to establish collaborative working relationships. Since the success of the venture will depend on how well the partners work together, potential partners should be selected as much for their management style, culture and goals as for their resources and capabilities. As we saw in the closing case of Chapter 6, UK telecoms company, Vodafone, collaborated with Kenyan mobile network, Safaricom, to pilot their mobile money service M-Pesa. Vodafone had the technological expertise, but Safaricom had the network of agents and the knowledge of the local Kenyan market.

3. *Engage in a collaborative partnership for the purpose of learning how the partner does things, internalizing its methods and thereby acquiring its capabilities.* Since this method involves an abuse of trust, it not only puts the co-operative venture at risk but also encourages the firm's partner to treat the firm similarly or refuse further dealings with the firm.

Upgrading Employee Skills and Knowledge Resources

Good strategy execution also requires that employees have the skills and knowledge resources they will need to perform their tasks well. Employee training thus plays an important role in the strategy execution process. Training and retraining are important when a company shifts to a strategy requiring different skills, competitive capabilities and operating methods. Training is also strategically important in organizational efforts to build skills-based competences. And it is a key activity in businesses where technical know-how is changing so rapidly that a company loses its ability to compete unless its employees have cutting-edge knowledge and expertise. Successful strategy implementers see to it that the training function is both adequately funded and effective. If the chosen strategy calls for new skills, deeper technological capability or the building and using of new capabilities, training should be placed near the top of the action agenda.

The strategic importance of training has not gone unnoticed. Over 600 companies have established internal 'universities' to lead the training effort, facilitate continuous organizational learning and help upgrade company capabilities. One of the world's leading hotel companies, Paris-based Accor, has had a corporate 'university' since 1985, the Academie Accor. This underpins much of the firm's career development for its employees and the Academie now has 17 locations world-wide to underpin Accor's diverse global workforce. Many companies conduct orientation sessions for new employees, fund an assortment of competence-building training programmes, and reimburse employees for tuition and other expenses associated with obtaining additional college education, attending professional development courses and earning professional certification of one kind or another. A number of companies offer online, just-in-time training courses to employees around the clock. Increasingly, employees at all levels are expected to take an active role in their own professional development and assume responsibility for keeping their skills up to date and in line with the company's needs.

Strategy Execution Capabilities and Competitive Advantage

As firms get better at executing their strategies, they develop capabilities in the domain of strategy execution much as they build other organizational capabilities. Superior strategy execution capabilities allow companies to get the most from their organizational resources and competitive capabilities. In this way they contribute to the success of a firm's business model. But excellence in strategy execution can also be a more direct source of competitive advantage, since more efficient and effective strategy execution can lower costs and permit firms to deliver more value to customers. Superior strategy execution capabilities may also enable a company to react more quickly to market changes and beat other firms to the market with new products and services. This can allow a company to profit from a period of uncontested market dominance.

> Superior strategy execution capabilities are the only source of sustainable competitive advantage when strategies are easy for rivals to copy.

Because strategy execution capabilities are socially complex capabilities that develop with experience over long periods of time, they are hard to imitate. And there is no substitute for good strategy execution. (Recall the tests of resource advantage from Chapter 4.) As such, they may be as important a source of sustained competitive advantage as the capabilities that drive a firm's strategies. Indeed, they may be a far more important avenue for securing a competitive edge over rivals in situations where it is relatively easy for rivals to copy promising strategies. In such cases, the only way for firms to achieve lasting competitive advantage is to out-execute their competitors.

Organizing the Work Effort with a Supportive Organizational Structure

> **LO**
> **10.4** Identify what issues to consider in establishing a strategy-supportive organizational structure and organizing the work effort.

There are few hard-and-fast rules for organizing the work effort to support good strategy execution. Every firm's organization chart is partly a product of its particular situation, reflecting prior organizational patterns, varying internal circumstances, executive judgements about reporting relationships and the politics of who gets which assignments. Moreover, every strategy is grounded in its own set of organizational capabilities and value chain activities. But some considerations in organizing the work effort are common to all companies. These are summarized in Figure 10.3 and discussed in the following sections.

Deciding Which Value Chain Activities to Perform Internally and Which to Outsource

The advantages of a companys having an outsourcing component in its strategy were discussed in Chapter 6, but there is also a need to consider the role of outsourcing in executing the strategy. Aside from the fact that another company (because of its experience, scale of operations and specialized know-how) may be able to perform certain value chain activities better or cheaper than a company can perform them internally, outsourcing can also sometimes make a positive contribution to better strategy execution. Managers too often spend inordinate amounts of time, mental energy and resources haggling with functional support groups or other internal bureaucracies over needed services, leaving less time for them to devote to performing strategy-critical activities in the most proficient manner.

> Wisely choosing which activities to perform internally and which to outsource can lead to several strategy-executing advantages – lower costs, heightened strategic focus, less internal bureaucracy, speedier decision-making and a better arsenal of organizational capabilities.

One way to reduce such distractions is to outsource the performance of assorted administrative support functions and perhaps even selected primary value chain activities to outside vendors, thereby enabling the company to concentrate its full

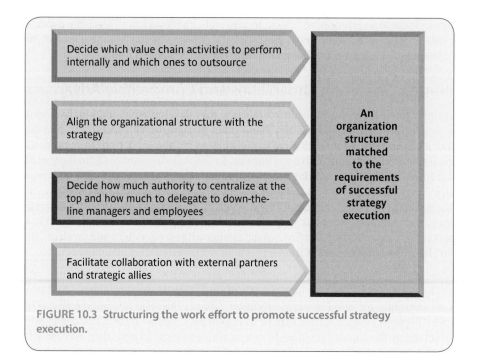

FIGURE 10.3 Structuring the work effort to promote successful strategy execution.

energies on performing the value chain activities that are at the core of its strategy, where it can create unique value. For example, E&J Gallo Winery outsources 95 per cent of its grape production, letting farmers take on weather-related and other grape-growing risks while it concentrates its efforts on wine production and sales.[30] Broadcom, a global leader in chips for broadband communication systems, outsources the manufacture of its chips to Taiwan Semiconductor, thus freeing company personnel to focus their full energies on R&D, new chip design and marketing. Nike concentrates on design, marketing and distribution while outsourcing virtually all production of its shoes and sporting apparel.

Such heightened focus on performing strategy-critical activities can yield three important execution-related benefits:

1. *The company improves its chances for outclassing rivals in the performance of strategy-critical activities and turning a core competence into a distinctive competence.* At the very least, the heightened focus on performing a select few value chain activities should promote more effective performance of those activities. This could materially enhance competitive capabilities by either lowering costs or improving quality. ING Insurance, Hugo Boss, Japan Airlines and Chevron have outsourced their data-processing activities to computer service firms, believing that outside specialists can perform the needed services at lower costs and equal or better quality. A relatively large number of companies outsource the operation of their websites to web design and hosting enterprises. Many business that get a lot of inquiries from customers or that have to provide 24/7 technical support to users of their products across the world have found that it is considerably less expensive to outsource these functions to specialists (often located in foreign countries where skilled personnel are readily available and worker compensation costs are much lower) than to operate their own call centres.

2. *The streamlining of internal operations that flows from outsourcing often serves to decrease internal bureaucracies, flatten the organizational structure, speed internal decision-making and shorten the time it takes to respond to changing market conditions.*[31] In consumer electronics, where advancing technology drives new product innovation, organizing the work effort in a manner that expedites getting

next-generation products to market ahead of rivals is a critical competitive capability. The world's motor vehicle manufacturers have found that they can shorten the cycle time for new models by outsourcing the large majority of their parts and components from independent suppliers and then working closely with their vendors to swiftly incorporate new technology and better integrate individual parts and components to form engine cooling systems, transmission systems and electrical systems.

3. *Partnerships can add to a company's arsenal of capabilities and contribute to better strategy execution.* By building, continually improving and then leveraging partnerships, a company enhances its overall organizational capabilities and strengthens its competitive assets – assets that deliver more value to customers and consequently pave the way for competitive success. Soft-drink and beer manufacturers cultivate their relationships with their bottlers and distributors to strengthen access to local markets and build loyalty, support and commitment for corporate marketing programmes, without which their own sales and growth are weakened. In the global hotel industry, many of the major players such as Accor and Intercontinental Hotel Group (IHG) have moved to a more 'asset-light' business model, so instead of owning hotel properties, they either manage them on behalf of real-estate partners or they provide support to franchisees, which benefit from their global brands and successful formula. Taking this approach has proved beneficial as it has released large amounts of capital previously tied up in physical assets and allowed the firms to use the cash to invest in emerging markets such as China and India. Companies like Boeing, Aerospatiale, Verizon Communications and Dell have learned that their central R&D groups cannot begin to match the innovative capabilities of a well-managed network of supply chain partners.[32]

However, as was emphasized in Chapter 6, a company must guard against going overboard on outsourcing and becoming overly dependent on outside suppliers. A company cannot be the master of its own destiny unless it maintains expertise and resource depth in performing those value chain activities that underpin its long-term competitive success.[33] As a general rule, therefore, it is the strategically less important activities – like handling customer enquiries and providing technical support, doing the payroll, administering employee benefit programmes, providing corporate security, managing stockholder relations, maintaining fleet vehicles, operating the company's website, conducting employee training and managing an assortment of information and data-processing functions – for which outsourcing makes the most strategic sense.

Aligning the Firm's Organizational Structure with Its Strategy

The design of the firm's **organizational structure** is a critical aspect of the strategy execution process. The organizational structure comprises the formal and informal arrangement of tasks, responsibilities and lines of authority and communication by which the firm is administered.[34] It specifies the linkages among parts of the organization, the reporting relationships, the direction of information flows and the decision-making processes. It is a key factor in strategy implementation since it exerts a strong influence on how well managers can co-ordinate and control the complex set of activities involved.[35]

A well-designed organizational structure is one in which the various parts (e.g. decision-making rights, communication patterns) are aligned with one another and also matched to the requirements of the strategy. With the right structure in place, managers can orchestrate the various aspects of the implementation process with an even hand and a light touch. Without a supportive structure, strategy execution is more likely to become bogged down by administrative confusion, political manoeuvring and bureaucratic waste.

> **Core Concept**
>
> A firm's **organizational structure** comprises the formal and informal arrangement of tasks, responsibilities, lines of authority and reporting relationships by which the firm is administered.

Good organizational design may even contribute to the firm's ability to create value for customers and realize a profit. By enabling lower bureaucratic costs and facilitating operational efficiency, it can lower a firm's operating costs. By facilitating the co-ordination of activities within the firm, it can improve the capability-building process, leading to greater differentiation and/or lower costs. Moreover, by improving the speed with which information is communicated and activities are co-ordinated, it can enable the firm to beat rivals to the market and profit from a period of unrivalled advantage.

Making Strategy-Critical Activities the Main Building Blocks of the Organizational Structure

In any business, some activities in the value chain are always more critical to successful strategy execution than others. For instance, a ski apparel manufacturer must be good at styling and design, low-cost manufacturing, distribution (convincing an attractively large number of retailers to stock and promote the company's brand) and marketing and advertising (building a brand image that generates buzz and appeal among ski enthusiasts). In discount stock brokerage, the strategy-critical activities are fast access to information, accurate order execution, efficient record-keeping and transactions processing and good customer service. In specialty chemicals, the critical activities are R&D, product innovation, getting new products onto the market quickly, effective marketing and expertise in assisting customers. Where such is the case, it is important for management to build its organizational structure around proficient performance of these activities, making them the centre-pieces or main building blocks in the enterprise's organizational structure.

The rationale for making strategy-critical activities the main building blocks in structuring a business is compelling: if activities crucial to strategic success are to have the resources, decision-making influence and organizational impact they need, they have to be centre-pieces in the organizational scheme. Making them the focus of structuring efforts will also facilitate their co-ordination and promote good internal fit — an essential attribute of a winning strategy, as summarized in Chapter 1. To the extent that implementing a new strategy entails new or altered key activities or capabilities, different organizational arrangements may be required.[36]

Matching Type of Organizational Structure to Strategy Execution Requirements

Organizational structures can be classified into a limited number of standard types. The type that is most suitable for a given firm will depend on the firm's size and complexity as well as its strategy. As firms grow and their needs for structure evolve, their structural form is likely to evolve from one type to another. The four basic types are the *simple structure*, the *functional structure*, the *multidivisional structure* and the *matrix structure*, as described below.

1. **Simple structure** — A **simple structure** is one in which a central executive (often the owner-manager) handles all major decisions and oversees the operations of the organization with the help of a small staff.[37] Simple structures are also known as *line-and-staff structures*, since a central administrative staff supervises line employees who conduct the operations of the firm, or *flat structures*, since there are few levels of hierarchy.[38] It is characterized by limited task specialization; few rules; informal relationships; minimal use of training, planning and liaison devices; and a lack of sophisticated support systems. It has all the advantages of simplicity, including low administrative costs, ease of co-ordination, flexibility, quick decision-making, adaptability and responsiveness to change.[39] Its informality and lack of rules may foster creativity and heightened individual responsibility.

Simple organizational structures are typically employed by small firms and entrepreneurial start-ups. The simple structure is the most common type of organizational

Core Concept

A **simple structure** consists of a central executive who handles all major decisions and oversees all operations with the help of a small staff.

Simple structures are also called *line-and-staff* structures or *flat* structures.

structure since small firms are the most prevalent type of business. As an organization grows, however, this structural form becomes inadequate to the demands that come with size and complexity. In response, growing firms tend to alter their organizational structure from a simple structure to a functional structure.

2. **Functional structure** — A functional structure is one that is organized along functional lines, where a function represents a major step in the firm's value chain, such as R&D, engineering and design, manufacturing, sales and marketing, logistics and customer service. Each functional unit is supervised by functional line managers who report to the CEO and a corporate staff. This arrangement allows functional managers to focus on their area of responsibility, leaving it to the CEO and headquarters to provide direction and ensure that their activities are co-ordinated and integrated. Functional structures are also known as *departmental structures,* since the functional units are commonly called departments, and *unitary structures* or *U-forms*, since a single unit is responsible for each function.

In large organizations, functional structures lighten the load on top management, relative to simple structures, and make for a more efficient use of managerial resources. Their primary advantage, however, is due to greater task specialization, which promotes learning, enables the realization of scale economies and offers productivity advantages not otherwise available. Their disadvantage is that the departmental boundaries can inhibit the flow of information and limit the opportunities for cross-functional co-operation and co-ordination.

It is generally agreed that some type of functional structure is the best organizational arrangement when a company is in just one particular business (regardless of which of the five generic competitive strategies it opts to pursue). For instance, a technical instruments manufacturer may be organized around R&D, engineering, supply chain management, assembly, quality control, marketing and technical services. A discount retailer, such as Lidl or Aldi, may organize around such functional units as purchasing, warehousing and distribution, store operations, advertising and sales, merchandising and customer service. Functional structures can also be appropriate for firms with high-volume production, products that are closely related and a limited degree of vertical integration.

As firms continue to grow, they often become more diversified and complex, placing a greater burden on top management. At some point, the centralized control that characterizes the functional structure becomes a liability, and the advantages of functional specialization begin to break down. To resolve these problems and address a growing need for co-ordination across functions, firms generally turn to the multidivisional structure.

3. **Multidivisional structure** — A multidivisional structure is a decentralized structure consisting of a set of operating divisions organized along market, customer, product or geographic lines, and a central corporate headquarters, which monitors divisional activities, allocates resources, performs assorted support functions and exercises overall control. Since each division is essentially a business, the divisions typically operate as independent profit centres (i.e. with profit/loss responsibility) and are organized internally along functional lines.[40] Division managers oversee day-to-day operations and the development of business-level strategy, while corporate executives attend to overall performance and corporate strategy, the elements of which were described in Chapter 8. Multidivisional structures are also called *divisional structures* or *M-forms*, in contrast to the U-form (functional) structure.

Multidivisional structures are common among companies pursuing some form of diversification strategy or global strategy, with operations in a number of businesses or countries. When the strategy is one of unrelated diversification, as in a conglomerate or holding company, the divisions generally represent separate industries. When the strategy is based on related diversification, the divisions may be organized according to

Core Concept

A **functional structure** is organized into functional departments, with departmental managers who report to the CEO and small corporate staff.

Functional structures are also called *departmental* structures, *unitary* structures or *U-forms*.

Core Concept

A **multidivisional structure** is a decentralized structure consisting of a set of operating divisions organized along business, product, customer group or geographic lines, and a central corporate headquarters that allocates resources, provides support functions and monitors divisional activities.

Multidivisional structures are also called *divisional* structures or *M-forms*.

markets, customer groups, product lines, geographic regions or technologies. In this arrangement, the decision about where to draw the divisional lines depends foremost on the nature of the relatedness and the strategy-critical building blocks, in terms of which businesses have key value chain activities in common. For example, a company selling closely related products to business customers as well as two types of end-consumers – online buyers and in-store buyers – may organize its divisions according to customer groups since the value chains involved in serving the three groups differ. Another company may organize by product line due to commonalities in product development and production within each product line. Multidivisional structures are also common among vertically integrated firms. There the major building blocks are often divisional units performing one or more of the major processing steps along the value chain (e.g. raw-material production, components manufacture, assembly, wholesale distribution, retail store operations).

Multidivisional structures offer significant advantages over functional structures in terms of facilitating the management of a complex and diverse set of operations.[41] Putting business-level strategy in the hands of division managers while leaving corporate strategy to top executives reduces the potential for information overload and improves the quality of decision-making in each domain. This also minimizes the costs of co-ordinating division-wide activities while enhancing top management's ability to control a diverse and complex operation. Moreover, multidivisional structures can help align individual incentives with the goals of the corporation and spur productivity by encouraging competition for resources among the different divisions.

But a divisional business-unit structure can also present some problems to a company pursuing related diversification, because having independent business units – each running its own business in its own way – inhibits cross-business collaboration and the capture of cross-business synergies. To solve this type of problem, firms turn to more complex structures, such as the matrix structure.

4. **Matrix structure** — A matrix structure is a combination structure in which the organization is organized along two or more dimensions at once (e.g. business, geographic area, value chain function) for the purpose of enhancing cross-unit communication, collaboration and co-ordination. In essence, it overlays one type of structure onto another type. Matrix structures are managed through multiple reporting relationships, so a middle manager may report to several bosses. For instance, in a matrix structure based on product line, region and function, sales managers for plastic containers in Dubai and Frankfurt might report to the manager of the plastics division, the head of the EMEA sales region and the head of marketing.

Matrix organizational structures have evolved from the complex, over-formalized structures that were popular in the 1960s, 1970s and 1980s but often produced inefficient, unwieldy bureaucracies. The modern incarnation of the matrix structure is generally a more flexible arrangement, with a single primary reporting relationship that can be overlaid with a temporary secondary reporting relationship as need arises. For example, a software company that is organized into functional departments (software design, quality control, customer relations) may assign employees from those departments to different projects on a temporary basis, so an employee reports to a project manager as well as to his or her primary boss (the functional department head) for the duration of a project.

Matrix structures are also called *composite structures* or *combination structures*. They are often used for project-based, process-based or team-based management. Such approaches are common in businesses involving projects of limited duration, such as consulting, architecture and engineering services. The type of close cross-unit collaboration that a flexible matrix structure supports is also needed to build competitive capabilities in strategically important activities, such as speeding new products to

Core Concept

A matrix structure is a structure that combines two or more organizational forms, with multiple reporting relationships. It is used to foster cross-unit collaboration.

Matrix structures are also called *composite* structures or *combination* structures.

market, which involve employees scattered across several organizational units.[42] Capabilities-based matrix structures that combine process departments (like new product development) with more traditional functional departments provide a solution.

An advantage of matrix structures is that they facilitate the sharing of plant and equipment, specialized knowledge and other key resources – they lower costs by enabling the realization of economies of scope. They also have the advantage of flexibility in form and may allow for better oversight since supervision is provided from more than one perspective. A disadvantage is that they add an additional layer of management, thereby increasing bureaucratic costs and decreasing response time to new situations.[43] In addition, there is a potential for confusion among employees due to dual reporting relationships and divided loyalties. While there is some controversy over the utility of matrix structures, the modern approach to matrix structures does much to minimize their disadvantages.[44]

Key Debate 10.1

WHAT IS THE RELATIONSHIP BETWEEN STRUCTURE AND STRATEGY?

In his seminal work of 1962, Alfred D. Chandler, put forward the view that structure followed strategy based on his research of the growth of multidivisional organizations in the USA. He observed that firms, who adopted a strategy of diversification, subsequently developed a divisional structure or M-Form structure, with each division possessing its own operational functions and a degree of autonomy. This structure enabled the expansion into new product and geographic areas, because it allowed the firm to maintain its administrative performance. This strategy leads to structure hypothesis has been supported by other authors looking at different contexts including Channon, Rumelt and later Pavan – most recently a study of firms in Spain by Galan and Sanchez-Bueno (published in 2009) came to similar conclusions. The opening case in this chapter could also be seen as providing a good example of the structure of an organization being changed following a new strategy being crafted. The National Trust's reduction of the number of regional offices and moving functions and power to the managers in its properties was a clear result of their 'Going Local' strategy.

However, Chandler's work is not without its critics. His study was based on historical data relating to US corporations in the first half of the twentieth century. Some commentators have argued that this was a time of relative stability in the external environment and that more recently the growth in hyper-competitive or high-velocity environments mean that organizations improvise rather than restructure. New structures such as matrix and network forms are better at adapting to new strategies without the need for major restructuring programmes. Galan and Sanchez-Beuno's work suggest that many of these criticisms may have been overstated as their study of 100 Spanish firms between 1993 and 2003 confirmed that companies following a strategy of diversification had a high probability of adopting a divisionalized structure.

One further argument put forward by Robert Burgelman against structure following strategy is that it was based on a top-down conception of strategy. In the 1970s, Bower found that more decentralized organizations could result in entrepreneurial behaviour among middle managers or unit heads which could then produce diversified strategy, which senior managers may subsequently need to respond to. Even Chandler's study suggested that the change of structure documented at firms such as DuPont and General Motors led to a greater role for top management in controlling corporate strategy. So to some extent it is arguable that strategy follows structure. In the opening case there is some evidence that the structure the National Trust had prior to 2005 limited its ability to follow particular strategic directions. The changes to the charity's governance, with the council playing an advisory role, meant that some stakeholders had less influence on strategy-making and was a prerequisite to delegating power to the local staff at properties. Galan and Sanchez-Beuno's paper acknowledges that changes to structure can lead to changes in strategy, as firms with a divisionalized form were more likely to subsequently pursue a diversified strategy.

▶

◄

QUESTION

1. To what extent does an organization's context determine the relationship between strategy and structure?

Sources: Bower, J.L. (1974) 'Planning and control: bottom up or top down?' *Journal of General Management*, 1: 20–31; Burgelman, R. (1983) 'A model of the interaction of strategic behaviour, corporate context and the concept of strategy', *Academy of Management Review*, 8(1): 61–70; Chandler, A. (1962) *Strategy and Structure*, Cambridge, MA, MIT Press; Channon, D.F. (1973) *The Strategy and Structure of British Entreprise*, London, Macmillan Press; Eisenhardt, K.M. and Brown, S.L. (1999) 'Patching, restitching business portfolios in dynamic markets', *Harvard Business Review*, 77: 72–82, Galan, J. and Sanchez-Bueno, M. (2009) 'The continuing validity of the strategy-structure nexus, new findings, 1993–2003', *Strategic Management Journal*, 30: 1234–43; Pavan, R.J. (1976) 'Strategy and structure: the italian experience', *Journal of Economics and Business*, 28(3): 254–60; Rumelt, R. (1974) *Strategy, Structure and Economic performance*, Boston, MA, Harvard Business School Press.

Determining How Much Authority to Delegate

LO 10.5

Discuss the pros and cons of centralized and decentralized decision-making in implementing the chosen strategy.

On average, larger companies with more complex organizational structures are more decentralized in their decision making than smaller firms with simple structures – by necessity and by design. Under any organizational structure, however, there is still room for considerable variation in how much authority top managers retain and how much is delegated to down-the-line managers and employees. In executing strategy, then, companies must decide how much authority to delegate to the managers of each organizational unit – especially the heads of divisions, functional departments and other operating units – and how much decision-making latitude to give individual employees in performing their jobs. The two extremes are to centralize decision-making at the top (the CEO and a few close lieutenants) or to decentralize decision-making by giving managers and employees considerable decision-making latitude in their areas of responsibility. As shown in Table 10.1, the two approaches are based on sharply different underlying principles and beliefs, with each having its pros and cons.

Centralized Decision-making: Pros and Cons

In a highly centralized organizational structure, top executives retain authority for most strategic and operating decisions and keep a tight rein on business-unit heads, department heads and the managers of key operating units; comparatively little discretionary authority is granted to front-line supervisors and rank-and-file employees. The command-and-control paradigm of centralized structures is based on the underlying assumptions that front-line personnel have neither the time nor the inclination to direct and properly control the work they are performing and that they lack the knowledge and judgement to make wise decisions about how best to do it – hence the need for managerially prescribed policies and procedures, close supervision and tight control. The thesis underlying authoritarian structures is that strict enforcement of detailed procedures backed by rigorous managerial oversight is the most reliable way to keep the daily execution of strategy on track.

One advantage of an authoritarian structure is tight control by the manager in charge – it is easy to know who is accountable when things do not go well. This structure can also reduce goal conflict among managers from different parts of the organization who may have different perspectives, incentives and objectives. For example, a manager in charge of an engineering department may be more interested in pursuing a new technology than is a marketing manager who doubts that customers will value the technology as highly. Another advantage of a command-and-control structure is that it can enable a more uniform and swift response to a crisis situation that affects the organization as a whole.

TABLE 10.1 **Advantages and disadvantages of centralized versus decentralized decision-making**

Centralized organizational structures	Decentralized organizational structures
Basic tenets	**Basic tenets**
• Decisions on most matters of importance should be in the hands of top-level managers who have the experience, expertise, and judgement to decide what is the best course of action. • Lower-level personnel have neither the knowledge, the time, nor the inclination to properly manage the tasks they are performing. • Strong control from the top is a more effective means for co-ordinating company actions.	• Decision-making authority should be put in the hands of the people closest to, and most familiar with, the situation. • Those with decision-making authority should be trained to exercise good judgement. • A company that draws on the combined intellectual capital of all its employees can outperform a command-and-control company.
Chief advantages	**Chief advantages**
• Fixes accountability through tight control from the top. • Eliminates goal conflict among those with differing perspectives or interests. • Allows for quick decision-making and strong leadership under crisis situations.	• Encourages company employees to exercise initiative and act responsibly. • Promotes greater motivation and involvement in the business on the part of more company personnel. • Spurs new ideas and creative thinking. • Allows fast response to market change. • May entail fewer layers of management.
Primary disadvantages	**Primary disadvantages**
• Lengthens response times by those closest to the market conditions because they must seek approval for their actions. • Does not encourage responsibility among lower-level managers and rank-and-file employees. • Discourages lower-level managers and rank-and-file employees from exercising any initiative.	• Top management lacks 'full control' – higher-level managers may be unaware of actions taken by empowered personnel under their supervision. • Puts the organization at risk if empowered employees happen to make 'bad' decisions. • Can impair cross-unit collaboration.

But there are some serious disadvantages as well. Hierarchical command-and-control structures make a large organization with a complex structure sluggish in responding to changing market conditions because of the time it takes for the review/approval process to run up all the layers of the management bureaucracy. Furthermore, to work well, centralized decision-making requires top-level managers to gather and process whatever information is relevant to the decision. When the relevant knowledge resides at lower organizational levels (or is technical, detailed or hard to express in words), it is difficult and time-consuming to get all the facts and nuances in front of a high-level executive located far from the scene of the action – full understanding of the situation cannot be readily copied from one mind to another. Hence, centralized decision-making is often impractical – the larger the company and the more scattered its operations, the more that decision-making authority must be delegated to managers closer to the scene of the action.

Decentralized Decision-making: Pros and Cons

In a highly decentralized organization, decision-making authority is pushed down to the lowest organizational level capable of making timely, informed, competent decisions. The objective is to put adequate decision-making authority in the hands of the people closest to and most familiar with the situation and train them to weigh all the factors and exercise good judgement. Decentralized decision-making means, for example, that employees with customer contact are empowered to do what it takes to please customers. At Starbucks, for example, employees are encouraged to exercise initiative in promoting customer satisfaction – there is the oft-repeated story of a store employee

> The ultimate goal of decentralized decision-making is to put authority in the hands of those persons or teams closest to and most knowledgeable about the situation.

who, when the computerized cash register system went offline, enthusiastically offered free coffee to waiting customers.[45]

The case for empowering front-line managers and employees to make decisions regarding daily operations and strategy execution is based on the belief that a company that draws on the combined intellectual capital of all its employees can outperform a command-and-control company.[46] The challenge in a decentralized system is in maintaining adequate control. With decentralized decision-making, top management maintains control by determining the limits to authority for each type of position, installing company-wide strategic control systems, holding people accountable for their decisions, instituting compensation incentives that reward people for doing their jobs in a manner that contributes to good company performance and creating a corporate culture where there is strong peer pressure on individuals to act responsibly.[47]

Decentralized organization structures have much to recommend them. Pushing decision-making authority down to subordinate managers, workteams and individual employees shortens organizational response times and spurs new ideas, creative thinking, innovation and greater involvement on the part of all company personnel. Moreover, in worker-empowered structures, jobs can be defined more broadly, several tasks can be integrated into a single job and people can direct their own work. Fewer layers of managers are needed because deciding how to do things becomes part of each person's or team's job. Today's online communication systems and smartphones make it easy and relatively inexpensive for people at all organizational levels to have direct access to data, other employees, managers, suppliers and customers. They can access information quickly (via the Internet or company network), readily check with superiors or whoever else as needed, and take responsible action. Typically, there are genuine gains in morale and productivity when people are provided with the tools and information they need to operate in a self-directed way.

But decentralization also has some disadvantages. Top managers lose an element of control over what goes on (since empowered subordinates have authority to act on their own) and may thus be unaware of actions being taken by personnel under their supervision. Such a lack of control can put a company at risk in the event that empowered employees make unwise decisions. Moreover, because decentralization gives organizational units the authority to act independently, there is a risk of too little collaboration and co-ordination between different organizational units.

Many companies have concluded that the advantages of decentralization outweigh the disadvantages. Over the past 15–20 years, there has been a decided shift from authoritarian multilayered hierarchical structures to flatter, more decentralized structures that stress employee empowerment. This shift reflects a strong and growing consensus that authoritarian, hierarchical organizational structures are not well suited to implementing and executing strategies in an era when extensive information and instant communication are the norm and when a big fraction of the organization's most valuable assets consists of intellectual capital and resides in the knowledge and capabilities of its employees.

Capturing Cross-business Strategic Fit in a Decentralized Structure

> Efforts to decentralize decision-making and give company personnel some leeway in conducting operations must be tempered with the need to maintain adequate control and cross-unit co-ordination.

Diversified companies striving to capture the benefits of synergy between separate businesses have to beware of giving business-unit heads full rein to operate independently. Cross-business strategic fit typically has to be captured either by enforcing close cross-business collaboration or by centralizing performance of functions requiring close co-ordination at the corporate level.[48] For example, if businesses with overlapping process and product technologies have their own independent R&D departments – each pursuing its own priorities, projects and strategic agendas – it is hard for the corporate parent to prevent duplication of effort, capture either economies of scale or economies of scope or encourage more collaborative R&D efforts. Where the potential for cross-business R&D synergies exist, the best solution is usually to centralize the R&D function and have a co-ordinated corporate R&D effort that serves the interests of both the individual businesses and the company as a whole. Likewise, centralizing the related activities of separate businesses makes sense when there are opportunities to share a common salesforce, use common distribution channels, rely on a common field service organization, use common e-commerce systems and so on.

A Different View

THE EMPTY BIRD'S NEST

Some of the most commonly found organizational structures stem from the early part of the twentieth century, when entrepreneurs, such as Henry Ford, found that to manufacture complex products on an economic scale, hierarchies and planners were needed to control the work done. More diversified organizations adapted divisional structures to cope with the complexities of broad portfolios of increasingly unrelated products and services with control sitting with a corporate centre and based on performance measures. Organizations with these structures will have top-down processes but while what Mintzberg (1989) referred to as the machine organization is generally centralized, the diversified organization will often be looser with each division having a certain amount of latitude in how it meets its performance targets. Neither would be classed as extreme examples of decentralization.

According to leading management thinker Charles Leadbeater, author of *We-think* (2009), the Internet has given rise to organizations that are changing a lot of the assumptions managers make about what structures and control systems are needed to implement strategy successfully. Some of these organizations, such as Wikipedia, are described as anarchic or as Leadbeater states (2009, p. 19) are 'like a vast bird's nest of knowledge, each piece of information carefully resting on another. Yet this is a bird's nest with no bird in charge of where to put each piece. It has almost constructed itself'. In the same way that the early pioneers of mass production and multinational corporations experimented with organizational structures to develop a suitable model, Leadbeater contends that Internet-based innovators, such as Jimmy Wales, the founder of Wikipedia, are exploring new forms of organization based around self-organizing networks.

Although there can be no doubt that Wikipedia has achieved much in the few years since its inception in 1999, it is not without its critics. The site has not produced a substantial economic return for its founder and some commentators claim that it has far more errors than a print encyclopaedia produced through more traditional means such as Britannica. However, Wikipedia can correct mistakes within minutes of their discovery and in a study carried out by *Nature* magazine in 2005 the researchers found an average of 2.92 errors per article in Britannica compared to 3.86 for Wikipedia. In January 2011, the online encyclopaedia also had over 17 million entries in 250 languages compared to Britannica's 120 000 in English (Bennett, 2011). Wikipedia is also not the only organization to have used self-organizing networks to disrupt (intentionally or unintentionally) the status quo in an industry. The Mozilla and Linux networks have successfully competed with IT giants such as Microsoft and firms such as Trip Advisor and Yelp have created distinctive websites based on user-generated content that a regular review publication relying on paid journalists would find it impossible to imitate (Bennett, 2011).

So, can managers learn anything from entities that are organized without formal organizational features such as job titles, hierarchies and functional departments? Leadbeater argues that the success of such enterprises is the result of three key elements 'participation, recognition and collaboration' (2009, p. 21). Therefore organizations that make it easy for people with the right skills to participate in crafting and executing strategy, find ways to recognize their contribution to the process in ways they will value, and put in place mechanisms that allow effective collaboration where the ideas generated collectively can be screened and evaluated have the potential to maximize the potential of their people.

Sources: Bennett, D. (2011) 'Assessing Wikipedia, Wiki-style, on its 10th anniversary', *Business Week*, 6 January. Available online at www.businessweek.com/magazine/content/11_03/b4211057979684.htm (accessed 25 March 2012); Leadbeater, C. (2009) *We-think*, Profile Books, London; Mintzberg, H. (1989) *Mintzberg on Management: Inside our Strange World of Organisations*, Free Press, New York.

Facilitating Collaboration with External Partners and Strategic Allies

Organizational mechanisms – whether formal or informal – are also required to ensure effective working relationships with each major outside constituency involved in strategy execution. Strategic alliances, outsourcing arrangements, joint ventures and co-operative partnerships present immediate opportunities and open the door to future possibilities, but little of value can be realized without active management of the relationship. Unless top management sees that constructive organizational bridge-building with strategic partners occurs and that productive working relationships emerge, the value of co-operative relationships is lost and the company's power to execute its strategy is weakened. If close working relationships with suppliers are crucial, then supply chain management must enter into considerations regarding how to create an effective organizational structure. If distributor/dealer/franchisee relationships are important, someone must be assigned the task of nurturing the relationships with forward channel allies. If working in parallel with providers of complementary products and services contributes to enhanced organizational capability, then co-operative organizational arrangements have to be put in place and managed to good effect.

Building organizational bridges with external allies can be accomplished by appointing 'relationship managers' with responsibility for making particular strategic partnerships or alliances generate the intended benefits. Relationship managers have many roles and functions: getting the right people together, promoting good rapport, seeing that plans for specific activities are developed and carried out, helping adjust internal organizational procedures and communication systems, ironing out operating dissimilarities and nurturing interpersonal co-operation. Multiple cross-organization ties have to be established and kept open to ensure proper communication and co-ordination.[49] There has to be enough information-sharing to make the relationship work and periodic frank discussions of conflicts, trouble spots and changing situations.

> **Core Concept**
>
> A **network structure** is the arrangement linking a number of independent organizations involved in some common undertaking.

Organizing and managing a network structure provides another mechanism for encouraging more effective collaboration and co-operation among external partners. A network structure is the arrangement linking a number of independent organizations involved in some common undertaking. A well-managed network structure typically includes one firm in a more central role, with the responsibility of ensuring that the right partners are included and the activities across the network are co-ordinated. The high-end Italian motorcycle company Ducati operates in this manner, assembling its motorcycles from parts obtained from a hand-picked integrated network of parts suppliers.

Further Perspectives on Structuring the Work Effort

All organization designs have their strategy-related strengths and weaknesses. To do a good job of matching structure to strategy, strategy implementers first have to pick a basic design and modify it as needed to fit the company's particular business line-up. They must then (1) supplement the design with appropriate co-ordinating mechanisms (cross-functional task forces, special project teams self-contained workteams, and so on) and (2) institute whatever networking and communications arrangements it takes to support effective execution of the firm's strategy. Some companies may avoid setting up 'ideal' organizational arrangements because they do not want to disturb existing reporting relationships or because they need to accommodate other situational idiosyncrasies, yet they must still work toward the goal of building a competitively capable organization.

The ways and means of developing stronger core competences and organizational capabilities (or creating altogether new ones) have to fit a company's own circumstances. Not only do different companies and executives tackle the capabilities-building challenge in different ways, but the task of building different capabilities requires different organizing techniques. Thus, generalizing about how to build capabilities has to be done cautiously. What can be said unequivocally is that building a capable organization entails a process of consciously knitting together the efforts of individuals and groups. Organizational capabilities emerge from establishing and nurturing co-operative working relationships among people and groups to perform activities in a more efficient, value-creating fashion. While an appropriate organizational structure can facilitate this, organization-building is a task in which senior management must be deeply involved. Indeed, effectively managing both internal organization processes and external collaboration to create and develop competitively valuable organizational capabilities remains a top challenge for senior executives in today's companies.

KEY POINTS

1. Executing strategy is an action-oriented, operations-driven activity revolving around the management of people and business processes. The way for managers to start in implementing a new strategy is with *a probing assessment of what the organization must do differently to carry out the strategy successfully*. They should then consider *precisely how to make the necessary internal changes* as rapidly as possible.

2. Good strategy execution requires a *team effort*. All managers have strategy-executing responsibility in their areas of authority, and all employees are active participants in the strategy execution process.

3. Ten managerial tasks crop up repeatedly in company efforts to execute strategy: (1) staffing the organization well; (2) building the necessary organizational capabilities; (3) creating a supportive organizational structure; (4) allocating sufficient resources; (5) instituting supportive policies and procedures; (6) adopting processes for continuous improvement; (7) installing systems that enable proficient company operations; (8) tying incentives to the achievement of desired targets; (9) instilling the right corporate culture; and (10) exercising internal leadership.

4. The two best signs of good strategy execution are whether a company is meeting or beating its performance targets and performing value chain activities in a manner that is conducive to company-wide operating excellence. *Shortfalls in performance signal weak strategy, weak execution or both.*

5. Building an organization capable of good strategy execution entails three types of organization-building actions: (1) *staffing the organization* – assembling a talented management team, and recruiting and retaining employees with the needed experience, technical skills and intellectual capital; (2) *building and strengthening core competences and competitive capabilities* – developing proficiencies in performing strategy-critical value chain activities and updating them to match changing market conditions and customer expectations; and (3) *structuring the organization and work effort* – instituting organizational arrangements that facilitate good strategy execution, deciding how much decision-making authority to delegate and managing external relationships.

6. Building core competences and competitive capabilities is a time-consuming, managerially challenging exercise that can be approached in three ways: (1) developing capabilities internally; (2) acquiring capabilities through mergers and acquisitions; and (3) accessing capabilities via collaborative partnerships.

7. In building capabilities internally, the first step is to develop the *ability* to do something, through experimentation, active search for alternative solutions and learning by trial and error. As experience grows and company personnel learn how to perform the activities consistently well and at an acceptable cost, the ability evolves into a tried-and-true capability. The process can be accelerated by making learning a more deliberate endeavour and providing the incentives that will motivate company personnel to achieve the desired ends.

8. As firms get better at executing their strategies, they develop capabilities in the domain of strategy execution. Superior strategy execution capabilities allow companies to get the most from their organizational resources and competitive capabilities. But excellence in strategy execution can also be a more direct source of competitive advantage, since more efficient and effective strategy execution can lower costs and permit firms to deliver more value to customers. Superior strategy

execution capabilities are hard to imitate and have no good substitutes. As such, they can be an important source of *sustainable* competitive advantage. Any time rivals can readily duplicate successful strategies, making it impossible to *out-strategize* rivals, the chief way to achieve lasting competitive advantage is to *out-execute* them.

9. Structuring the organization and organizing the work effort in a strategy-supportive fashion has four aspects: (1) deciding which value chain activities to perform internally and which ones to outsource; (2) aligning the firm's organizational structure with its strategy; (3) deciding how much authority to centralize at the top and how much to delegate to down-the-line managers and employees; and (4) facilitating the necessary collaboration and co-ordination with external partners and strategic allies.

10. To align the firm's organizational structure with its strategy, it is important to make strategy-critical activities the main building blocks. There are four basic types of organizational structures: the simple structure, the functional structure, the multidivisional structure and the matrix structure. Which is most appropriate depends on the firm's size, complexity and strategy.

CLOSING CASE

LEGO – THE COMEBACK KIDS

A COMPANY IN CRISIS

When Jørgen Vig Knudstrop became LEGO's CEO in 2004 (see Exhibit 10.1 for a brief biography), the Danish toy company was in deep trouble. Despite having secured an exclusive licensing deal with Lucasfilm to develop *Star Wars*-themed toys in the late 1990s, the firm had also made a series of ill-fated strategic moves which had seen sales plummet by up to 30 per cent in a single year. The company had diversified into theme parks back in 1968, when they launched the first LEGOLAND in their home town of Billund. However, new parks launched in 1996 near Windsor in Britain and in 1999 in California, USA had both been unprofitable. A range of new products, such as an action figure called Galidor, and Clikits, a building system aimed at girls,

Exhibit 10.2 for selected figures), up 17 per cent on the previous year and an increase in operating profits of over 13 per cent. LEGO's share of the traditional toys and games sector had risen to over 5 per cent of the market world-wide and construction toys were being hailed as the most dynamic part of a buoyant global market. In contrast the video game element of the industry saw a decline for the second consecutive year. Some of this resurgence in the traditional element of the industry had been attributed to LEGO's amazing turnaround.

MANAGING CREATIVITY

Innovation had always played a large role in the toys and games industry. LEGO was typical in having superior capabilities in developing new products. In the 1980s, a partnership with MIT researching links between learning and technology had enabled the company to create toys like LEGO Technic and LEGO Mindstorms, a robotic construction toolset. The firm had also branched out into toys for younger children with Duplo and, in 2004, LEGO Quatro. The turnaround in the firm's fortunes came from more than just good new product development pro-

---

EXHIBIT 10.1: Jørgen Vig Knudstrop: brief biography

1968	Born Fredericia, Denmark
1988–97	BA, Master's degree and PhD in Economics, Aarhus University
1998	Joined McKinsey & Co. as a consultant and later became head of recruitment for their European operations
2001	Joined LEGO
2002	Appointed Head of LEGO's Strategy Department
2003	Acting Chief Financial Officer for LEGO, then Chief Vice-President for Corporate Affairs
2004	Appointed CEO of LEGO

---

had failed and, by 2004, the firm was near bankruptcy. Its own estimates were that it was losing close to €750 000 a day.

LEGO was famous as the producer of the LEGO brick, the main component of its interlocking building system. The firm was founded in 1932 in Denmark by carpenter Ole Kirk Christiansen and the name is a contraction of the Danish words for 'play good'. The toy became very popular because it could be used to build a huge range of models from houses to cars, boats, aeroplanes and trains. However, in the early 2000s it began to look as if such a traditional toy would inevitably lose ground to the Internet and technology-based products.

By 2011 the story was very different, LEGO had posted one of their best years with revenues rising to €2.5 billion for the year ended December 2011 (see

cesses. LEGO created a new structure (see Exhibit 10.3) to ensure that its innovation activities were co-ordinated at a strategic level by an Executive Innovation Governance Group. This body made sure developments were mutually reinforcing and consistent with the organization's overall strategy. The Group also acted as investor by allocating resources to specific projects. Rather than focusing on a single type of innovation, LEGO's strategy aimed to embrace eight key areas at three different levels from incremental changes to fundamentally new products. Alongside new product development, a team was charged with innovating core and enabling processes. Other areas of the firm worked on innovating business models and platforms as well as making effective use of LEGO's many fans through seeking user generated ideas.

One of the major issues that Knudstrop and his senior team identified was the mismatch between

▶

EXHIBIT 10.2 LEGO selected financial data 2002–2011

mDKK	2011	2010	2009	2008	2007	2006	2005	2004	2003	2002
Income Statement:										
Revenue	18731	16014	11661	9526	8027	7823	7050	6315	6792	9601
Expenses	(13 065)	(10 899)	(8659)	(7522)	(6556)	(6475)	(6582)	(6252)	(7902)	(8795)
Operating profit	5666	4973	2902	2100	1449	1528	459	(1162)	(1565)	806
Financial income and expenses	(124)	(84)	(15)	(248)	(35)	34	(3)	(75)	67	(189)
Profit/(loss) before tax	5542	4889	2887	1852	1414	1562	456	(1237)	(1498)	617
Net profit/ (loss) for the year	4160	3718	2204	1352	1028	1430	505	(1931)	(935)	326
Balance Sheet:										
Total assets	12904	10972	7788	6496	6009	9022	7689	8089	10 049	12 560
Equity	6975	5473	3291	2066	1679	4727	3589	2948	4892	6478
Liabilities	5929	5499	4497	4430	4330	4295	4100	4731	5157	6082

what LEGO's designers were producing and what their customers' valued. In the year's prior to 2004, the firm's designers had been given a free rein as a way of fostering their creativity. Design was seen as one of LEGO's core competences and a major source of competitive advantage over some the lower-priced, low-cost competitors, such as Mega Brands and Tyco Toys. However, by delegating many of the design and product decisions to the designers, LEGO ended up producing toys that no longer appealed to their customers and increasing costs as the number of components required for LEGO kits rose from 7000 to 12 400. The restructuring of innovation was one way that Knudstrop planned to change this situation. By getting the designers to work more closely with other teams, such as marketing, supply chain and manufacturing, rather than as an isolated and untouchable group, the CEO hoped to create a more commercial focus. In a counter-intuitive move, the designers were given less flexibility and control over design decisions. New components were only manufactured if they

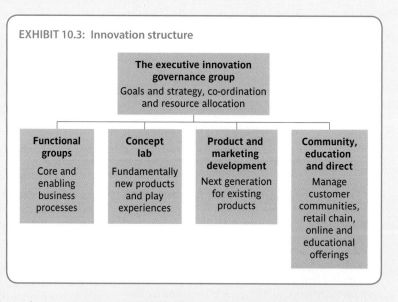

EXHIBIT 10.3: Innovation structure

The executive innovation governance group
Goals and strategy, co-ordination and resource allocation

Functional groups
Core and enabling business processes

Concept lab
Fundamentally new products and play experiences

Product and marketing development
Next generation for existing products

Community, education and direct
Manage customer communities, retail chain, online and educational offerings

won a vote from a majority of designers. Working with manufacturing teams also helped to keep the costs under control and within a couple of years the number of components being manufactured had fallen to its 1997 level of 7000. Opening the innovation process to many of LEGO's user communities also had an impact on the process of design. The design teams had more customer feedback and the links to observational market research data gave them much more insight about how children played with the toys they created. The firm had always struggled to connect with girls and had seen a number of failed product lines aimed at this market segment. The knowledge generated by the anthropologists employed by the firm led to the launch of the LEGO Friends line in 2011.

LEGO also developed partnerships with a wide range of other organizations. Some of their most successful collaborations now came from working with firms in the film industry. Building on their experience of the *Star Wars* franchise, LEGO also formed alliances with Disney and Warner Bros to create toys based on other popular films such as *Indiana Jones*, *Harry Potter* and *Pirates of the Caribbean*. This led to cross-over products such as websites and video games allowing LEGO to extend their brand from the traditional part of the market into the electronic world, which had appeared to be such a threat in the past. But as well as benefiting from the strength of other brands, LEGO's own reputation proved a source of significant advantage. Named the toy of the century in 2000 by *Fortune* magazine, LEGO licensed its brand to other firms manufacturing everything from clothing and watches to bags and sunglasses. This enabled the company to benefit from its brand reputation without having to build capabilities in manufacturing a wide range of products.

Despite its unique heritage and strong brand, LEGO's turnaround was also underpinned with an aggressive cost-reduction programme. Knudstrop's first priority on becoming CEO in 2004 was to reduce production costs by 20 per cent. This was followed by a series of plant closures as manufacturing capacity was concentrated in Kladno in the Czech Republic. Between 2004–6 restructuring had cost the firm €96 million in additional expenses. By 2008 only premium brands were still being manufactured in the Billund factory in Denmark. The new CEO also had to make some tough decisions about what the firm did and what it should outsource. LEGO's theme parks, developed with Blackstone, a key partner, had been flagships for the company since 1968, but were a drain on resources and did not fit with the organization's core capabilities. In 2005, all the LEGOLAND parks were sold to Merlin Entertainments for $800 million.

Knudstrop's assessment of the firm in 2004 was that 'LEGO had lost its identity. The company strayed too far from having the building system at its core'. Eight years on LEGO had become a major player in video games, developed online communities to support innovation and tied itself to film companies, and brick by brick it had come back from the brink.

QUESTIONS/ACTIVITIES

1. How did the execution of LEGO's strategy strengthen its core competences and competitive capabilities?

2. Explain the structural changes that resulted from the new strategy.

3. Comment on the part staffing decisions played in LEGO's turnaround.

Sources: License Europe (2006) 'Rebuilding LEGO', *License Europe*, November–December, pp. 24–9; Datamonitor (2011) *The LEGO Group: Company Profile*, Datamonitor.com, London; License Europe (2006) op. cit.; Robertson, D. and Hjuler, P. (2009) 'Innovating a turnaround at LEGO', *Harvard Business Review*, September, pp. 20–1; Weiners, B. (2011) 'Lego is for girls', *Bloomberg Businessweek*, 14, December. Available online at www.businessweek.com/magazine/lego-is-for-girls-12142011.html (accessed 15 March 2012); Wallop, H. (2012) 'LEGO sees its profits continue to stack up', *Daily Telegraph*, Business, 2 March, p. 3; Passport (2012) *Toys and Games: Trends, Developments and Prospects*, Euromonitor, February. *Marketing* (2011) 'Lego', *Marketing*, July 13, p.16; Greene, J. (2010) 'How LEGO revived its brand', *Bloomberg Businessweek*, 23 July. Available online at www.businessweek.com/innovate/content/jul2010/id20100722_781838.htm; Euromonitor (2010) *LEGO Group – Toys and Games – World*, Euromonitor International April; Lego (2006–2011) Various Annual Reports.

ASSURANCE OF LEARNING EXERCISES

LO 10.2, LO 10.3

1. Review the Careers link on L'Oréal's world-wide corporate website (go to www.loreal.com and click on the company's world-wide corporate website option). The section provides extensive information about personal development, international learning opportunities, integration of new hires into existing teams and other areas of management development. How do the programmes discussed help L'Oréal to hire good people and build core competences and competitive capabilities? Please use the chapter's discussions of recruiting, training and retaining capable

▶

employees and building core competences and competitive capabilities as a guide for preparing your answer.

LO 10.4

2. Examine the overall corporate organizational structure chart for Exelon Corporation. The chart can be found by going to www.exeloncorp.com and using the website search feature to locate 'organizational charts'. Does it appear that strategy-critical activities are the building blocks of Exelon's organizational arrangement? Is its organizational structure best characterized as a departmental structure tied to functional, process, or geographic departments? Is the company's organizational structure better categorized as a divisional structure? Would you categorize Exelon's organizational structure as a matrix arrangement? Explain your answer.

LO 10.5

3. Using Google Scholar or your university library's access to EBSCO, InfoTrac or other online databases, do a search for recent writings on decentralized decision-making and employee empowerment. According to the articles you find in the various management journals, what are the conditions under which decision-making should be pushed down to lower levels of management?

EXERCISES FOR SIMULATION PARTICIPANTS

LO 10.5

1. How would you describe the organization of your company's top management team? Is some decision-making decentralized and delegated to individual managers? If so, explain how the decentralization works. Or are decisions made more by consensus, with all co-managers having input? What do you see as the advantages and disadvantages of the decision-making approach your company is employing?

LO 10.3

2. What specific actions have you and your co-managers taken to develop core competences or competitive capabilities that can contribute to good strategy execution and potential competitive advantage? If no actions have been taken, explain your rationale for doing nothing.

LO 10.1, LO 10.4

3. What value chain activities are most crucial to good execution of your company's strategy? Does your company have the ability to outsource any value chain activities? If so, have you and your co-managers opted to engage in outsourcing? Why or why not?

ENDNOTES

1. As quoted in Floyd, Steven W. and Wooldridge, Bill (1992) 'Managing strategic consensus: the foundation of effective implementation', *Academy of Management Executive*, 6(4): 27.
2. As cited in Neilson, Gary L., Martin, Karla L. and Powers, Elizabeth (2008) 'The secrets of successful strategy execution', *Harvard Business Review*, 86(6): 61–2 .
3. Welch, Jack with Welch, Suzy (2005) *Winning*, New York, HarperBusiness, p. 135.

 4. Mintzberg, H. (1979) *The Structuring of Organizations*, Englewood Cliffs, NJ, Prentice Hall.

 5. For an excellent and very pragmatic discussion of this point, see Bossidy, Larry and Charan, Ram (2002) *Execution: The Discipline of Getting Things Done*, New York, Crown Business), ch. 1.

 6. A good discussion of managed change and a classification of the different organisational changes, their links to changes in different elements of a firms strategy and their relative position on a concrete – conceptual continuum, can be found in Mintzberg, H. and Westley, F. (1992) 'Cycles of organizational change', *Strategic Management Journal*, 13: 39–59.

 7. For an insightful discussion of how important staffing an organization with the right people is, see Bartlett, Christopher A. and Ghoshal, Sumantra (2002) 'Building competitive advantage through people', *MIT Sloan Management Review*, 43(2): 34–41.

 8. The importance of assembling an executive team that has an exceptional ability to gauge what needs to be done and an instinctive talent for figuring out how to get it done is discussed in Menkes, Justin (2005) 'Hiring for smarts', *Harvard Business Review*, 83(11): 100–9, and Menkes, Justin (2005) *Executive Intelligence*, New York, HarperCollins, especially chs 1–4.

 9. See Bossidy and Charan, *Execution: The Discipline of Getting Things Done,* ch. 1.

10. Menkes, *Executive Intelligence*, pp. 68 and 76.

11. Bossidy and Charan, *Execution: The Discipline of Getting Things Done*, ch. 5.

12. Welch with Welch, *Winning*, pp. 141–42.

13. Menkes, *Executive Intelligence*, pp. 65–71.

14. Collins, Jim (2001) *Good to Great*, New York, HarperBusiness, p. 44.

15. Cook, S. and Macaulay, S. (2009) 'Talent management: key questions for learning and development', *Training*, July, pp. 37–41.

16. Byrne, John (1999) 'The search for the young and gifted', *Businessweek*, 4, October p. 108.

17. See chs 5 and 6 in Helfat et al. (2007) *Dynamic Capabilities: Understanding Strategic Change in Organizations*, Malden, MA, Blackwell; Grant, R. (2008) *Contemporary Strategy Analysis*, 6th edn, Malden, MA, Blackwell.

18. Helfat, C. and Peteraf, M. (2003) 'The dynamic resource-based view: capability lifecycles', *Strategic Management Journal,* 24(10): 997–1010.

19. Hamel, G. and Prahalad, C.K. (1993) 'Strategy as stretch and leverage', *Harvard Business Review*, 71(2): 75–84.

20. Dosi, G., Nelson, R. and Winter, S. (eds) (2001) *The Nature and Dynamics of Organizational Capabilities*, Oxford, Oxford University Press).

21. Helfat, C. and Peteraf, M. 'The dynamic resource-based view: capability lifecycles'.

22. Winter, S. (2000) 'The satisficing principle in capability learning', *Strategic Management Journal*, 21(10/11): 981–6; Zollo, M. and Winter, S. (2002) 'Deliberate learning and the evolution of dynamic capabilities', *Organization Science*, 13(3): 339–51.

23. The idea of regenerative dynamic capabilities is discussed at length in Ambrosini, V. C. Bowman, and Collier, N. (2009) 'Dynamic capabilities: an exploration of how firms renew their resource base', *British Journal of Management* 20: S9–S24.

24. Szulanski, G. and Winter, S. (2002) 'Getting it right the second time', *Harvard Business Review*, 80: 62–9; Winter, S. and Szulanski, G. (2001) 'Replication as strategy', *Organization Science*, 12(6): 730–43.

25. Kogut, B. and Zander, U. (1972) 'Knowledge of the firm, combinative capabilities, and the replication of technology', *Organization Science*, 3(3) 383–97.

26. Helfat, C. and Raubitschek, R. (2000) 'Product sequencing: co-evolution of knowledge, capabilities and products', *Strategic Management Journal*, 21(10/11) 961–80.

27. Hayes, Robert H., Pisano, Gary P. and Upton, David M. (1996) *Strategic Operations: Competing through Capabilities*, New York, Free Press, pp. 503–7. Also see Ridderstråle, Jonas (2003) 'Cashing in on corporate competences', *Business Strategy Review*, 14(1): 27–38; Miller, Danny, Eisenstat, Russell and Foote, Nathaniel (2002) 'Strategy from the inside out: building capability-creating organizations', *California Management Review*, 44(3): 37–55.

28. Karim, S. and Mitchell, W. (2000) 'Path-dependent and path-breaking change: reconfiguring business resources following business', *Strategic Management Journal*, 21(10/11): 1061–2; Capron, L., Dussague, P. and Mitchell, W. (1998) 'Resource redeployment following horizontal acquisitions in Europe and North America, 1988–1992', *Strategic Management Journal*, 19(7): 631–62.

29. R.M. Kanter, (2009) 'Mergers that stick', *Harvard Business Review*, October, pp. 121–26.

30. Quinn, J.B. (1992) *Intelligent Enterprise*, New York, Free Press, p. 43.

31. Ibid., pp. 33 and 89; Quinn, J.B. and Hilmer, F. (1995) 'Strategic outsourcing', *McKinsey Quarterly*, 1: 48–70; Heikkilä, Jussi and Cordon, Carlos (2002) 'Outsourcing: a core or non-core strategic management decision', *Strategic Change*, 11(3): 183–93; and Quinn, J.B. (1999) 'Strategic outsourcing: leveraging knowledge capabilities', *Sloan Management Review*, 40(4): 9–21. A strong case for outsourcing is presented in Pralahad, C.K. (2005) 'The art of outsourcing', *Wall Street Journal*, 8 June, p. A13. For a discussion of why outsourcing initiatives fall short of expectations, see Barthélemy, Jérôme (2003) 'The seven deadly sins of outsourcing', *Academy of Management Executive*, 17(2): 87–98.

32. Quinn, 'Strategic outsourcing: leveraging knowledge capabilities', p. 17.

33. Quinn, *Intelligent Enterprise*, pp. 39–40; also see Pisano, Gary P. and Shih, Willy C. (2009) 'Restoring American competitiveness', *Harvard Business Review*, 87(7–8): 114–25; Barthélemy, 'The seven deadly sins of outsourcing'.

34. Chandler, A. (1962) *Strategy and Structure*, Cambridge, MA, MIT Press.

35. Olsen, E., Slater, S. and Hult, G. (2005) 'The importance of structure and process to strategy implementation', *Business Horizons*, 48(1): 47–54; Barkema, H., Baum, J. and Mannix, E. (2002) 'Management challenges in a new time', *Academy of Management Journal*, 45(5): 916–30.

36. The importance of matching organization design and structure to the particular requirements for good strategy execution was first brought to the forefront in a landmark study of 70 large corporations conducted by Professor Alfred Chandler of Harvard University. Chandler's research revealed that changes in an organization's strategy bring about new administrative problems that, in turn, require a new or refashioned structure for the new strategy to be successfully implemented and executed. He found that structure tends to follow the growth strategy of the firm, but often not until inefficiency and internal operating problems provoke a structural adjustment. The experiences of these firms followed a consistent sequential pattern: new strategy creation, emergence of new administrative problems, a decline in profitability and performance, a shift to a more appropriate organizational structure and then recovery to more profitable levels and improved strategy execution. See Chandler, *Strategy and Structure*.

37. Mintzberg, H. (1979) *The Structuring of Organizations*, Englewood Cliffs, NJ, Prentice Hall; Levicki, C. (1999) *The Interactive Strategy Workout*, 2nd edn, London, Prentice Hall.

38. Chandler, *Strategy and Structure*.

39. Mintzberg, *The Structuring of Organizations*.

40. Chandler, *Strategy and Structure*.

41. Williamson, O. (1975) *Market and Hierarchies*, New York, Free Press; Burton, R.M. and Obel, B. (1980) 'A computer simulation test of the M-form hypothesis', *Administrative Science Quarterly*, 25: 457–76.

42. Baum, J. and Wally, S. (2003) 'Strategic decision speed and firm performance', *Strategic Management Journal*, 24: 1107–29.

43. Bartlett, C. and Ghoshal, S. (1990) 'Matrix management: not a structure, a frame of mind', *Harvard Business Review*, July–August, pp. 138–45.

44. Goold, M. and Campbell, A. (2003) 'Structured networks: towards the well designed matrix', *Long Range Planning*, 36(5): 427–39.

45. Somerville, Iain and Mroz, John Edward (1997) 'New competences for a new world', in Hesselbein, Frances, Goldsmith, Marshall and Beckard, Richard (eds), *The Organization of the Future*, San Francisco, CA, Jossey-Bass, p. 70.

46. The importance of empowering workers in executing strategy and the value of creating a great working environment are discussed in Fawcett, Stanley E., Rhoads, Gary K. and Burnah, Phillip (2004)

'People as the bridge to competitiveness: benchmarking the "ABCs" of an empowered workforce', *Benchmarking: An International Journal*, 11(4): 346–60.

47. A discussion of the problems of maintaining adequate control over empowered employees and possible solutions is presented in Simons, Robert (1995) 'Control in an age of empowerment', *Harvard Business Review*, 73: 80–8.

48. For a discussion of the importance of cross-business co-ordination, see Liedtka, Jeanne M. (1996) 'Collaboration across lines of business for competitive advantage', *Academy of Management Executive*, 10(2): 20–34.

49. Kanter, Rosabeth Moss (1994) 'Collaborative advantage: the art of the alliance', *Harvard Business Review*, 72(4): pp. 105–6.

Chapter Eleven

Managing internal operations

Actions that promote good strategy execution

True motivation comes from achievement, personal development, job satisfaction, and recognition.

Frederick Herzberg
Expert on motivation

Note to salary setters: Pay your people the least possible and you'll get the same from them.

Malcolm Forbes
Late publisher of Forbes magazine

We are what we repeatedly do. Excellence, then, is not an act but a habit.

Aristotle
Greek Philosopher

Learning Objectives

When you have read this chapter you should be able to:

LO 11.1   Explain why resource allocation should be based on strategic priorities.

LO 11.2   Describe how well-designed policies and procedures can facilitate good strategy execution.

LO 11.3   Explain how process management tools that drive continuous improvement in the performance of value chain activities can help an organization achieve superior strategy execution.

LO 11.4   Recognize the role information and operating systems play in enabling organization personnel to carry out their strategic roles proficiently.

LO 11.5   Discuss how and why well-designed incentives and rewards can be used to promote adept strategy execution and operating excellence.

ROGUE TRADERS OR SYSTEMS FAILURE – A PROBLEM FOR BANKING

Since Nick Leeson brought down Barings Bank in 1995, racking up $1.4 billion of losses in unauthorized trades, the world has become more aware of the risks and rewards banks manage in their investment arms. However, it is not clear if the financial services industry has improved its execution of strategy through incentives and monitoring employee performance in what is one of their highest risk areas of operation. The Rusnak affair at the Allied Irish Bank US subsidiary Allfirst in 2002 had many similarities to the Barings case. More recently two rogue traders, Jerome Kerviel, who lost French bank Société Générale nearly €5 billion in 2008, and then in 2011, Kweku Adoboli, whose trading losses amounted to $2.3 billion while working for Swiss bank UBS, have shown that the problem is far from solved.

In each case, part of the blame for the failure has been tied to a lack of adequate controls in the banks' operating systems. Traders are set limits they must trade within and are subject to disciplinary action if they persistently operate outside these boundaries. The traders form part of what is known as the 'front office' and are the people who make the deals by effectively placing bets on the way the market will move in particular areas, such as commodities futures, stocks and shares, interest rates or currency exchange rates. Before the deals are signed off, the traders send the details through to the bank's 'back office' functions that confirm the deals and focus on risk control. One thing most of the rogue traders mentioned above were supposed to have had in common was a good knowledge of both front and back office functions. According to the banks, this enabled them to circumvent the monitoring and quality control systems the banks have put in place to prevent rogue trading. However, in the Rusnak case, the investigation that followed the losses at Allfirst pointed out that the managers at the organization simply failed to supervise Rusnak adequately and that procedures and systems were fundamentally flawed or not followed. Jerome Kerviel alleged that his bosses at Société Générale turned a blind eye to his increasingly risky trades because he had made the bank substantial profits in the past.

The second element of the equation that led to the rogue behaviour has been cited as the incentive schemes the banks used to motivate traders. By linking the trader's bonus to the organization's profit at the end of the year, banks have been accused of encouraging reckless attitudes to risk. Some commentators have suggested that smaller bonuses and a greater threat of punishment might deter future rogue traders, but many of the top investment banks dispute this argument. Whatever the solution to the banks' problem, the outcome of failing to address the issue is not in dispute. For Barings Bank, the Leeson affair led to bankruptcy. At UBS the losses have dented the bank's profits and led to the resignation of CEO, Oswald Gruebel. More importantly the failings, real or perceived, in the organizations' systems have damaged their reputations, which ultimately can be just as damaging to their ability to execute strategy.

QUESTION

1. Has the problem of rogue traders been the result of individuals manipulating the system or a failure of management to manage strategy execution effectively through internal operations?

Sources: Knight, L. (2011) 'Q&A: "rogue trader" allegations', BBC News, 18 September. Available online at www.bbc.co.uk/news/business-14929257 (accessed 1 June 2012); BBC News (2011) 'UBS "rogue trader": loss estimate raised to $2.3bn,' BBC News, 18 September. Available online at www.bbc.co.uk/news/business-14965438 (accessed 1 June 2012); Schofield, H. (2010) 'Jerome Kerviel: rogue trader or folk hero?', BBC News, 5 October. Available online at www.bbc.co.uk/news/world-europe-11478129 (accessed 1 June 2012).

In Chapter 10, we emphasized the importance of building organization capabilities and structuring the work effort so as to perform execution-critical value chain activities in a co-ordinated and competent manner. This covered changes to an organization's *people* and *structure*. In this chapter, we discuss five additional managerial actions that promote good strategy execution and are focused on changes to an organization's *systems*:

- Allocating resources to the drive for good strategy execution.
- Instituting policies and procedures that facilitate strategy execution.
- Using process management tools to drive continuous improvement in how value chain activities are performed.
- Installing information and operating systems that enable organization personnel to carry out their strategic roles proficiently.
- Using rewards and incentives to promote better strategy execution and the achievement of strategic and financial targets.

As we can see from the opening case, getting the systems element of implementation wrong can have a devastating effect on the execution of strategy and the reputation/performance of the organization. Systems help managers to measure and monitor the effectiveness of strategy execution, so as much care needs to be taken with designing these as with crafting the original strategy in the first place.

Allocating Resources to the Strategy Execution Effort

Early in the process of implementing a new strategy, managers need to determine what resources (in terms of funding, people etc.) will be required for good strategy execution and how they should be distributed across the various organizational units involved. An organization's ability to marshal the resources needed to support new strategic initiatives has a major impact on the strategy execution process. Too little funding slows progress and impedes the efforts of organizational units to execute their pieces of the strategic plan proficiently. Too much funding wastes organizational resources and reduces financial performance. Both outcomes argue for managers to be deeply involved in reviewing budget proposals and directing the proper amounts of resources to strategy-critical organizational units. This includes carefully screening requests for more people and new facilities and equipment, approving those that hold promise for making a contribution to strategy execution and turning down those that do not. Should internal cash flows prove insufficient to fund the planned strategic initiatives, then management must raise additional funds through borrowing or selling additional shares of stock to willing investors.

LO 11.1
Explain why resource allocation should be based on strategic priorities.

A change in strategy nearly always calls for budget reallocations and resource shifting. Previously important units having a lesser role in the new strategy may need downsizing. Units that now have a bigger strategic role may need more people, new equipment, additional facilities and above-average increases in their operating budgets. Implementing a new strategy requires managers to take an active and sometimes forceful role in shifting resources, downsizing some functions and upsizing others, not only to amply fund activities with a critical role in the new strategy but also to avoid inefficiency and achieve profit projections. The National Trust case in the last chapter illustrated this, with regional and central services being cut in order to shift emphasis and resources to the local groups and managers. Implementing a new strategy also requires putting enough resources behind new strategic initiatives to fuel their success and making the tough decisions to kill projects and activities that are no longer justified. Honda's strong support of research and development (R&D) activities allowed it to develop the first motorcycle airbag, the first low-polluting four-stroke outboard marine engine, a wide range of ultra-low-emission cars, the first hybrid car (Honda

Insight) in the US market and the first hydrogen fuel cell car (Honda Clarity). However, Honda managers had no trouble stopping production of the Honda Insight in 2006 when its sales failed to take off and then shifting resources to the development and manufacture of other promising hybrid models, including a totally redesigned Insight that was launched in Europe in 2009.

Visible actions to reallocate operating funds and move people into new organizational units signal a determined commitment to strategic change and frequently are needed to catalyse the implementation process and give it credibility. Microsoft has made a practice of regularly shifting hundreds of programmers to new high-priority programming initiatives within a matter of weeks or even days. Fast-moving developments in many markets are prompting organizations to abandon traditional annual or semi-annual budgeting and resource allocation cycles in favour of resource allocation processes supportive of more rapid adjustments in strategy.

> The funding requirements of good strategy execution must drive how capital allocations are made and the size of each unit's operating budget. Underfunding organizational units and activities pivotal to the strategy impedes successful strategy implementation.

The bigger the change in strategy (or the more obstacles that lie in the path of good strategy execution), the bigger the resource shifts that will likely be required. Merely fine-tuning the execution of an organization's existing strategy seldom requires big movements of people and money from one area to another. The desired improvements can usually be accomplished through above-average budget increases to organizational units launching new initiatives and below-average increases (or even small budget cuts) for the remaining organizational units. However, there are times when strategy changes or new execution initiatives need to be made without adding to total organization expenses. In such circumstances, managers have to work their way through the existing budget line by line and activity by activity, looking for ways to trim costs and shift resources to higher-priority activities where new execution initiatives are needed. In the event that an organization needs to make significant cost cuts during the course of launching new strategic initiatives, then managers have to be especially creative in finding ways to do more with less and execute the strategy more efficiently. Indeed, it is not unusual for strategy changes and the drive for good strategy execution to be conducted in a manner that entails achieving considerably higher levels of operating efficiency and, at the same time, making sure key activities are performed as effectively as possible.

> An organization's operating budget should be both *strategy-driven* (in order to amply fund the performance of key value chain activities) and *lean* (in order to operate as cost-efficiently as possible).

Instituting Policies and Procedures that Facilitate Strategy Execution

An organization's policies and procedures can either support or obstruct good strategy execution. Any time an organization moves to put new strategy elements in place or improve its strategy execution capabilities, some changes in work practices and the behaviour of organization personnel are usually required. Managers are thus well advised to examine whether existing policies and procedures support such changes and to proactively revise or discard those that are out of line.

As shown in Figure 11.1, well-conceived policies and operating procedures facilitate strategy execution in three ways:

> **LO 11.2**
> Describe how well-designed policies and procedures can facilitate good strategy execution.

● *They provide top-down guidance regarding how things need to be done.* Policies and procedures provide organization personnel with a set of guidelines for how to perform organizational activities, conduct various aspects of operations, solve problems as they arise and accomplish particular tasks. In essence, they represent a store of organizational or managerial knowledge about efficient and effective ways of doing things. They clarify uncertainty about how to proceed in executing strategy and align the actions and behaviour of organization personnel with the requirements for good strategy execution. Moreover, they place limits on ineffective independent action. When they are well matched with the requirements of the strategy implementation plan, they channel the efforts of individuals along a path that supports the plan and facilitates good strategy execution. When existing ways

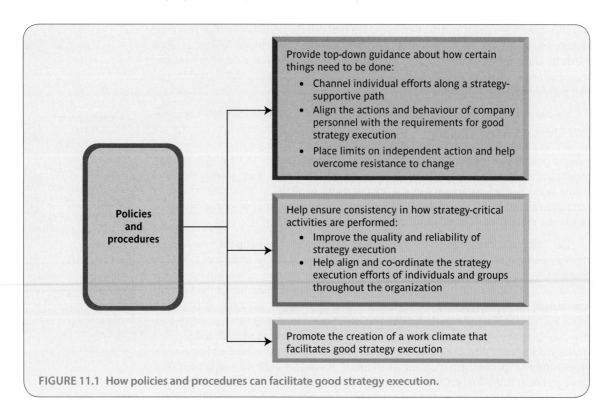

FIGURE 11.1 How policies and procedures can facilitate good strategy execution.

of doing things are misaligned with strategy execution initiatives, actions and behaviours have to be changed. Under these conditions, the managerial role is to establish and enforce new policies and operating practices that are more conducive to executing the strategy appropriately. Policies are a particularly useful way to counteract tendencies for some people to resist change. People generally refrain from violating organization policy or going against recommended practices and procedures without gaining clearance and having strong justification. As we saw in the Siemens illustration in Chapter 9, changing and enforcing the organization's ethical policies was a vital step in Peter Löscher's strategy to turn the German engineering giant around.

● *They help ensure consistency in how execution-critical activities are performed.* For some organizations, policies and procedures serve to standardize the way that activities are performed and encourage strict conformity to the standardized approach. This is important for ensuring the quality and reliability of the strategy execution process. It helps align and co-ordinate the strategy execution efforts of individuals and groups throughout the organization – a feature that is particularly beneficial when there are geographically scattered operating units. For example, eliminating significant differences in the operating practices of different plants, sales regions, customer service centres or the individual outlets in a chain operation helps an organization deliver consistent product quality and service to customers. Good strategy execution often entails an ability to replicate product quality and the calibre of customer service at every location where the organization does business.

● *They promote the creation of a work climate that facilitates good strategy execution.* An organization's policies and procedures help to set the tone of an organization's work climate and contribute to a common understanding of 'how we do things around here'. Because discarding old policies and procedures in favour of new ones invariably alters the internal work climate, managers can use the policy-changing process as a powerful lever for changing the corporate culture in ways that produce a stronger fit with the new strategy.

To ensure consistency in product quality and service behaviour patterns, McDonald's policy manual spells out detailed procedures that personnel in each McDonald's unit are expected to observe. For example, 'Cooks must turn, never flip, hamburgers. If they haven't been purchased, Big Macs must be discarded in 10 minutes after being cooked and French fries in 7 minutes. Cashiers must make eye contact with and smile at every customer'. To ensure that its R&D activities are responsive to customer needs and expectations, Hewlett-Packard requires its R&D people to make regular visits to customers to learn about their problems and learn their reactions to HP's latest new products.

One of the big policy-making issues concerns what activities need to be rigidly prescribed and what activities ought to allow room for independent action on the part of empowered personnel. Few organizations need thick policy manuals to direct the strategy execution process or prescribe exactly how daily operations are to be conducted. Too much policy can be as much of a hindrance as wrong policy and as confusing as no policy. There is wisdom in a middle approach: *prescribe enough policies to give organization members a clear direction and to place reasonable boundaries on their actions; then empower them to act within these boundaries in whatever way they think makes sense.* Allowing organization personnel to act with some degree of freedom is especially appropriate when individual creativity and initiative are more essential to good strategy execution than standardization and strict conformity. Instituting policies that facilitate strategy execution can therefore mean more policies, fewer policies or different policies. It can mean policies that require things be done according to a strictly defined standard or policies that give employees substantial leeway to do activities the way they think best.

Using Process Management Tools to Strive for Continuous Improvement

Organization managers can significantly advance the cause of superior strategy execution by using various process management tools to drive continuous improvement in how internal operations are conducted. One of the most widely used and effective tools for gauging how well an organization is executing pieces of its strategy entails benchmarking the organization's performance of particular activities and business processes against 'best-in-industry' and 'best-in-world' performers.[1] It can also be useful to look at 'best-in-organization' performers of an activity if an organization has a number of different organizational units performing much the same function at different locations. Identifying, analysing and understanding how top-performing organizations or organizational units conduct particular value chain activities and business processes provides useful yardsticks for judging the effectiveness and efficiency of internal operations and setting performance standards for organizational units to meet or beat.

How the Process of Identifying and Incorporating Best Practices Works

A **best practice** is a technique for performing an activity or business process that has been shown to consistently deliver superior results compared to other methods.[2] To qualify as a legitimate best practice, the technique must have a proven record in significantly lowering costs, improving quality or performance, shortening time requirements, enhancing safety or delivering some other highly positive operating outcome. Best practices thus identify a path to operating excellence. For a best practice to be valuable and transferable, it must demonstrate success over time, deliver quantifiable and highly positive results and be repeatable.

As discussed in Chapter 4, *benchmarking* is the backbone of the process of identifying, studying and implementing best practices. An organization's benchmarking

> **LO 11.3**
> Explain how process management tools that drive continuous improvement in the performance of value chain activities can help an organization achieve superior strategy execution.

> **Core Concept**
> A **best practice** is a method of performing an activity that has been shown to consistently deliver superior results compared to other methods.

effort looks outward to find best practices and then proceeds to develop the data for measuring how well an organization's own performance of an activity stacks up against the best-practice standard. For individual managers, benchmarking involves being humble enough to admit that others have come up with world-class ways to perform particular activities yet wise enough to try to learn how to match, and even surpass them. But, as shown in Figure 11.2, the payoff of benchmarking comes from adapting the topnotch approaches pioneered by other organizations to the organization's own operation and thereby boosting, perhaps dramatically, the proficiency with which strategy-critical value chain tasks are performed.

However, benchmarking is more complicated than simply identifying which organizations are the best performers of an activity and then trying to imitate their approaches, especially if these organizations are in other industries. Normally, the outstanding practices of other organizations have to be *adapted* to fit the specific circumstances of an organization's own business, strategy and operating requirements. Since each organization is unique, the telling part of any best-practice initiative is how well the organization puts its own version of the best practice into place and makes it work.

> The more that organizational units use best practices in performing their work, the closer an organization comes to achieving effective and efficient strategy execution.

Indeed, a best practice remains little more than another organization's interesting success story unless the organization personnel buy into the task of translating what can be learned from other organizations into real action and results. The agents of change must be front-line employees who are convinced of the need to abandon the old ways of doing things and switch to a best-practice mind-set. *The more that organizational units use best practices in performing their work, the closer an organization moves toward performing its value chain activities as effectively and efficiently as possible.* As we saw in Chapter 5, performing value chain activities at lower costs than rivals is key to underpinning a cost leadership position in an industry.

Many organizations across the world now engage in benchmarking to improve their strategy execution efforts. Scores of trade associations and special-interest organizations have undertaken efforts to collect best-practice data relevant to a particular industry or business function and make their databases available online to members. Benchmarking and best-practice implementation have clearly emerged as legitimate and valuable managerial tools for promoting operational excellence and enhancing strategy execution.

Business Process Reengineering, Total Quality Management (TQM) and Six Sigma Quality Programmes: Tools for Promoting Operating Excellence

In striving for operating excellence, many organizations have also come to rely on three other potent process management tools: business process reengineering, total

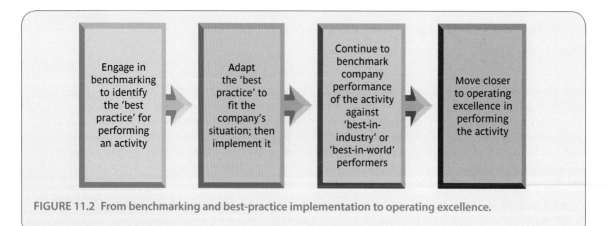

FIGURE 11.2 From benchmarking and best-practice implementation to operating excellence.

quality management (TQM), and Six Sigma quality control techniques. Indeed, these three tools have become globally pervasive techniques for implementing strategies keyed to cost reduction, defect-free manufacture, superior product quality, superior customer service and total customer satisfaction. Again, these techniques can underpin the generic strategies in Chapter 5. The following sections describe how business process reengineering, TQM and Six Sigma programmes can contribute to good strategy execution and operating excellence.

Business Process Reengineering

Organizations scouring for ways to improve their operations have sometimes discovered that the execution of strategy-critical activities is hindered by an organizational arrangement where pieces of the activity are performed in several different functional departments, with no one manager or group being accountable for optimal performance of the entire activity. This can easily occur in such inherently cross-functional activities as customer service (which can involve personnel in order-filling, warehousing and shipping, invoicing, accounts receivable, after-sale repair and technical support), new product development (which typically involves personnel in R&D, design and engineering, purchasing, manufacturing and sales and marketing) and supply chain management (which cuts across such areas as purchasing, inventory management, manufacturing and assembly, warehousing and shipping).

To address the suboptimal performance problems that can arise from this type of situation, many organizations have opted to *reengineer the work effort,* pulling the pieces of strategy-critical activities out of different departments and creating a single department or workgroup to take charge of the whole process and perform it in a better, cheaper and more strategy-supportive fashion. The use of cross-functional teams has been popularized by the practice of business process reengineering, which involves radically redesigning and streamlining the workflow (often enabled by cutting-edge use of online technology and information systems), with the goal of achieving quantum gains in performance of the activity.[3]

When done properly, business process reengineering can produce dramatic operating benefits. Hallmark reengineered its process for developing new greeting cards, creating teams of mixed-occupation personnel (artists, writers, lithographers, merchandisers and administrators) to work on a single holiday or greeting card theme; the reengineered process speeded development times for new lines of greeting cards by up to 24 months, was more cost-efficient and increased customer satisfaction.[4] Northwest Water, a British utility, used process reengineering to eliminate 45 work depots that served as home bases to crews who installed and repaired water and sewage lines and equipment. Under the reengineered arrangement, crews worked directly from their vehicles, receiving assignments and reporting work completion from computer terminals in their trucks. Crew members became contractors to Northwest Water rather than employees, a move that not only eliminated the need for the work depots but also allowed Northwest Water to eliminate a big percentage of the bureaucratic personnel and supervisory organization that managed the crews.[5]

Reengineering of value chain activities has been undertaken at many organizations in many industries all over the world, with excellent results at some organizations.[6] At organizations where it has produced only modest results, this is usually because of ineptness and/or lack of wholehearted commitment from the top. While business process reengineering has been criticized for its use by some organizations as an excuse for downsizing, it has nonetheless proved itself as a useful tool for streamlining an organization's work effort and moving closer to operational excellence. It has also inspired more technologically based approaches to integrating and streamlining business processes, such as *enterprise resource planning,* a software-based system implemented with the help of consulting organizations such as SAP (the leading provider of business software).

> **Core Concept**
>
> **Business process reengineering** involves radically redesigning and streamlining how an activity is performed, with the intent of achieving dramatic improvements in performance.

Business process reengineering is not without its critics. Originally developed by academic Professor Michael Hammer and management consultant James Champy in the early 1990s, it was readily adopted by organizations seeking to reduce costs in a time of economic decline. The idea has been seen as a return to some of the mechanistic management techniques of the early twentieth century – a modern-day version of Taylorism or as an excuse for corporations to make swingeing cuts to their operations.[7] There is no doubt that the technique has been used in a political manner in some organizations and even Champy later (1994) wrote about some of the abuses he saw in its use in reality.

TQM Programs

Total quality management (TQM) is a philosophy of managing a set of business practices that emphasizes continuous improvement in all phases of operations, 100 per cent accuracy in performing tasks, involvement and empowerment of employees at all levels, team-based work design, benchmarking and total customer satisfaction.[8] While TQM concentrates on producing quality goods and fully satisfying customer expectations, it achieves its biggest successes when it is extended to employee efforts in *all departments* – for example, human resources (HR), billing, accounting and information systems – that may lack pressing, customer-driven incentives to improve. It involves reforming the corporate culture and shifting to a total quality/continuous improvement business philosophy that permeates every facet of the organization.[9] TQM aims at instilling enthusiasm and commitment to doing things right from the top to the bottom of the organization. Management's job is to kindle an organization-wide search for ways to improve, a search that involves all organization personnel exercising initiative and using their ingenuity. TQM doctrine preaches that there is no such thing as 'good enough' and that everyone has a responsibility to participate in continuous improvement. TQM is thus a race without a finish. Success comes from making little steps forward each day, a process that the Japanese call *kaizen*.

TQM takes a fairly long time to show significant results – very little benefit emerges within the first six months. The long-term payoff of TQM, if it comes, depends heavily on management's success in implanting a culture within which the TQM philosophy and practices can thrive. TQM is a managerial tool that has attracted numerous users and advocates over several decades, and it can deliver good results when used properly.

Six Sigma Quality Programmes

Six Sigma programmes offer another way to drive continuous improvement in quality and strategy execution. This approach entails the use of advanced statistical methods to identify and remove the causes of defects (errors) and variability in performing an activity or business process. When performance of an activity or process reaches 'Six Sigma quality', there are *no more than 3.4 defects per million iterations* (equal to 99.9997 per cent accuracy).[10]

There are two important types of Six Sigma programmes. DMAIC (define, measure, analyse, improve and control) is an improvement system for existing processes falling below specification and needing incremental improvement. The DMADV process of define, measure, analyse, design and verify is used to develop *new* processes or products at Six Sigma quality levels. DMADV is sometimes referred to as a Design for Six Sigma, or DFSS. Both Six Sigma programmes are overseen by personnel who have completed Six Sigma 'master black belt' training and are executed by personnel who have earned Six Sigma 'green belts' and Six Sigma 'black belts'. According to the Six Sigma Academy, personnel with black belts can save organizations approximately $230 000 per project and can complete four to six projects a year.[11]

The statistical thinking underlying Six Sigma is based on the following three principles: all work is a process, all processes have variability and all processes create data that explain variability.[12]

Core Concept

Total quality management (TQM) entails creating a total quality culture bent on continuously improving the performance of every task and value chain activity.

Core Concept

Six Sigma programmes utilize advanced statistical methods to improve quality by reducing defects and variability in the performance of business processes.

CURRENT PRACTICE 11.1

SIX SIGMA AT A DISPLAY MANUFACTURER

Three researchers from I-Shou University in Kaohsiung, Taiwan, Hsiang-chin Hung, Tai-chi Wu and Ming-hsien Sung recently documented how these three principles drove the metrics of DMAIC, at a TFT-LCD manufacturer based in Taiwan. The organization had four factories producing display components for use in laptop and desktop computer monitors. The organization wanted to reduce the number of defective products they produced because this would reduce losses but also, because of the chemicals and components used, it would reduce their negative impact on the environment. The organization's Six Sigma team pursued quality enhancement and continuous improvement via the DMAIC process as follows:

- *Define.* Because Six Sigma is aimed at reducing defects, the first step is to define what constitutes a defect. The Six Sigma team members decided to focus on the bonding process where adhesive sealant stuck the TFT (thin film transistor), colour filter and LCD layers of the display unit together. If this did not work effectively, the unit would not be sealed properly and this might lead to bubbles between the layers (in which case the display was useless) or the leakage of the liquid crystal (in which case there was a risk of polluting the environment).

- *Measure.* The next step was to collect data to find out why, how and how often this defect occurred. The team started by creating a process flow diagram to map all the different cells in the manufacturing process. They then produced a cause and effect diagram to factor in the impact of staff, machines, materials and methods. The team then combined these two to create a cause and effect matrix.

- *Analyse.* After the data were gathered and the statistics analysed, the organization's Six Sigma team discovered that there was a significant relationship between three of the factors measured and the seal faults. The gap between the machine that dispensed the sealant and the layers, the speed at which the sealant was dispensed and the pressure under which it was then put were shown to be the most critical elements.

- *Improve.* The Six Sigma team then designed a modified process for sealing the displays, but only ran this on two production lines as an initial pilot. The defect rates on the pilot lines were reduced significantly and the new settings for the sealant process were then rolled out to all the production lines.

- *Control.* The organization updated its documentation including the standard operation procedure manual, associated diagrams, training materials for staff and the process check list, so that the improvements were embedded into the production process.

Source: Hung, H., Wu, T. and Sung, M. (2011) 'Application of Six Sigma in the TFT-LCD industry: a case study', *International Journal of Organizational Innovation*, 4(1): 74–93.

Six Sigma's DMAIC process is a particularly good vehicle for improving performance when there are *wide variations* in how well an activity is performed.[13] For instance, airlines striving to improve the on-time performance of their flights have more to gain from actions to curtail the number of flights that are late by more than 30 minutes than from actions to reduce the number of flights that are late by less than 5 minutes. Likewise, FedEx might have a 16-hour average delivery time for its overnight package service operation, but if the actual delivery time varies around the 16-hour average from a low of 12 hours to a high of 26 hours, such that 10 per cent of its packages are delivered over 6 hours late, then it has a huge reliability problem of the sort that Six Sigma programmes are well suited to address.

Since the mid-1990s, thousands of organizations and non-profit organizations around the world have used Six Sigma programmes to promote operating excellence. Such manufacturers as Motorola, Caterpillar, DuPont, Xerox, Alcan Aluminium, BMW, Volkswagen, Nokia, Owens Corning, Boeing and Emerson Electric have employed Six Sigma techniques to improve their strategy execution and increase production quality. French glass producer, Saint-Gobain, used Six Sigma and Lean techniques to streamline operations at its Pisa factory. The organization had unacceptably high inventory levels, which they diagnosed were the result of mismatches between sales forecasting and production planning, problems with product flows and inefficient warehouse operations. Changes to the practices in all these areas over a nine-month period reduced the working capital and cost of inventory and led to tangible savings of €600 000 at this single site.[14] Illustration Capsule 11.1 describes Kuehne + Nagel's use of Six Sigma in its global logistics business.

Illustration Capsule 11.1

KUEHNE + NAGEL'S USE OF SIX SIGMA TO DRIVE CONTINUOUS IMPROVEMENT

One of the largest logistics organizations in the world, Swiss/German organization, Kuehne + Nagel (K + N), had over 1000 offices around the world in 2012. Its sales from operations in 100 countries totalled CHF19.5 billion in 2011. At the heart of the organization's mission is providing 'integrated logistics solutions of outstanding quality and operational excellence'.

One of management's chief objectives in pursuing this vision is to optimize costs at the same time as increasing share. The organization has ambitious growth plans aimed at doubling their operations by 2014 and developing its core competences around detailed knowledge of its customers and the sectors in which they operate. Executing this strategy through K + N's business units covering sea freight (where it is the global market leader), airfreight (where it is one of the top three players), contract logistics (where it also ranks in the top three) and road and rail logistics (where it is one of the top six providers in Europe) has involved a strong focus on continuous improvement, lean capabilities and a drive for operating excellence. To marshal the efforts of its 63 000 employees in executing the strategy successfully, management developed a comprehensive programme based on Lean and Six Sigma principles, known as the Kuehne + Nagel Production System (KNPS).

The KNPS initiative, which began in 2008, has helped K + N deliver a 15 per cent improvement in productivity in its first three years. The project has been driven by a network of regional managers in nine locations worldwide. In common with Six Sigma principles the project started with data-gathering so that each site could have access to its own performance information and begin to look for areas to improve. The roll-out of the system has also involved training staff throughout the organization in Lean and Six Sigma techniques. By February 2012 the organization had trained 136 green belts and 21 black belts. Many other staff, including most senior managers attended one-day awareness courses. The organization's continuous improvement manager, Dean Harrison, consider the involvement of employees as a vital element in the success of the scheme, 'Most of our projects involve the workforce both in concept and delivery, and that has really helped to engage people in what we are trying to achieve'.

K + N's management believe that the organization's KNPS will be a major contributor in sustaining its position as a leading global logistics organization and in delivering its ambitious growth targets over the next few years.

Sources: www.kn-portal.com (accessed 2 April 2012); Organization Annual Report 2010; Sinclair, N. (2012), 'People power,' *UK Excellence*, February, pp. 10–13.

Six Sigma is, however, not just a quality-enhancing tool for manufacturers. At one organization, product sales personnel typically wined and dined customers to close their deals, but the costs of such entertaining were viewed as excessively high.[15] A Six Sigma project that examined sales data found that although face time with customers was important, wining, dining and other types of entertainment were not. The data showed that regular face time helped close sales, but that time could be spent over a cup of coffee instead of golfing at a resort or taking clients to expensive restaurants. In addition, analysis showed that too much face time with customers was counterproductive. A regularly scheduled customer picnic was found to be detrimental to closing sales because it was held at a busy time of year, when customers preferred not to be away from their offices. Changing the manner in which prospective customers were wooed resulted in a 10 per cent increase in sales. Six Sigma has also been used to improve processes in air travel. Heathrow Airport operator, BAA, used Six Sigma to improve the customer experience and improve customer satisfaction. At the start of the project in 2007 Heathrow was ranked 13th out of 13 major European airports for customer satisfaction. Analysis focused on those customers who had to make transfers within the airport to continue their journeys. In 2006, 70 per cent had to change terminals because most transfers were to airlines within a particular alliance and Heathrow's terminals were not configured to take account of this. The project made use of the opening of Terminal 5 to relocate airlines closer to their alliance partners. The result was a reduction in transfer passengers changing terminals (30 per cent) and a dramatic improvement in customer satisfaction (Heathrow was 7th out of 13 in 2009).[16] The Bank of America, Starwood Hotels, SAP AG, Scottish Widows, Alstom Power, Amazon.com, Philips, Vodafone and BP also have reportedly used Six Sigma techniques successfully in their operations.

While many enterprises have used Six Sigma methods to improve the quality with which activities are performed, there is evidence that Six Sigma techniques can stifle innovation and creativity.[17] The essence of Six Sigma is to reduce variability in processes, but creative processes, by nature, include quite a bit of variability. In many instances, breakthrough innovations occur only after thousands of ideas have been abandoned and promising ideas have gone through multiple iterations and extensive prototyping. Google CEO Eric Schmidt has commented that the innovation process is 'anti-Six Sigma' and that applying Six Sigma principles to those performing creative work at Google would choke off innovation at the organization.[18]

James McNerney, a General Electric (GE) executive schooled in the constructive use of Six Sigma, became CEO at 3M Corporation and proceeded to institute a series of Six Sigma –based principles. McNerney's dedication to Six Sigma and his elimination of 8 per cent of the organization's workforce did cause 3M's profits to jump shortly after his arrival, but the application of Six Sigma in 3M's R&D and new product development activities soon proved to stifle innovation and new product introductions, undermining the organization's long-standing reputation for innovation. 3M's researchers complained that the innovation process did not lend itself well to the extensive data collection and analysis required under Six Sigma and that too much time was spent completing reports that outlined the market potential and possible manufacturing concerns for projects in all stages of the R&D pipeline. Six Sigma rigidity and a freeze on 3M's R&D budget from McNerney's first year as CEO through 2005 was blamed for the organization's drop from 1st to 7th place on the Boston Consulting Group's Most Innovative Organizations list.[19]

A blended approach to Six Sigma implementation that is gaining in popularity pursues incremental improvements in operating efficiency, while R&D and other processes that allow the organization to develop new ways of offering value to customers are given a freer rein. Managers of these *ambidextrous organizations* are adept at employing continuous improvement in operating processes but allowing R&D to operate under a set of rules that allows for the development of breakthrough innovations. However, the two distinctly different approaches to managing employees must be carried out by tightly integrated senior managers to ensure that the separate and diversely oriented units operate with a common purpose. Ciba Vision, a global leader in contact lenses, has dramatically reduced operating expenses through the use of continuous improvement programmes, while simultaneously and harmoniously developing a new series of contact lens products that have allowed its revenues to increase by 300 per cent over a 10-year period.[20] An enterprise that systematically and wisely applies Six Sigma methods to its value chain, activity by activity, can make major strides in improving the proficiency with which its strategy is executed without sacrificing innovation. As is the case with TQM, obtaining managerial commitment, establishing a quality culture and fully involving employees are all of critical importance to the successful implementation of Six Sigma quality programmes.[21]

The Difference between Business Process Reengineering and Continuous Improvement Programmes like Six Sigma and TQM

Business process reengineering and continuous improvement efforts like TQM and Six Sigma both aim at improved productivity and reduced costs, better product quality and greater customer satisfaction. The essential difference between business process reengineering and continuous improvement programmes is that reengineering aims at *quantum gains* on the order of 30–50 per cent or more, whereas programmes like TQM and Six Sigma stress *incremental progress,* striving for inch-by-inch gains again and again in a never-ending stream. The two approaches to improved performance of value chain activities and operating excellence are not mutually exclusive; it makes sense to use them in tandem. Reengineering can be used first to produce a good basic design that yields quick, dramatic improvements in performing a business process. Total quality programmes can then be used as a follow-on to reengineering and/or best-practice implementation, delivering gradual improvements over a longer period of time. Such a two-pronged approach to implementing operational excellence is like a marathon race in which you run the first four miles as fast as you can and then gradually pick up speed the remainder of the way.

> Business process reengineering aims at one-time quantum improvement, while continuous improvement programmes like TQM and Six Sigma aim at ongoing incremental improvements.

Capturing the Benefits of Initiatives to Improve Operations

The biggest beneficiaries of benchmarking and best-practice initiatives, reengineering, TQM, and Six Sigma are organizations that view such programmes not as ends in themselves but as tools for implementing organization strategy more effectively. The skimpiest payoffs occur when organization managers seize on them as something worth trying – novel ideas that could improve things. In most such instances, they result in strategy-blind efforts to simply manage better.

There is an important lesson here. Business process management tools all need to be linked to an organization's strategic priorities to contribute effectively to improving the strategy's execution. Only strategy can point to which value chain activities matter and what performance targets make the most sense. Without a strategic framework, managers lack the context in which to fix things that really matter to business-unit performance and competitive success.

To get the most from initiatives to execute strategy more proficiently, managers must have a clear idea of what specific outcomes really matter. Is it high on-time delivery, lower overall costs, fewer customer complaints, shorter cycle times, a higher percentage of revenues coming from recently introduced products or what? Benchmarking best-in-industry and best-in-world performance of most or all value chain activities provides a realistic basis for setting internal performance milestones and longer-range targets.

Once initiatives to improve operations are linked to the organization's strategic priorities, then comes the managerial task of building a total quality culture that is genuinely committed to achieving the performance outcomes that strategic success requires.[22] Managers can take the following action steps to realize full value from TQM or Six Sigma initiatives and promote a culture of operating excellence:[23]

1. Visible, unequivocal and unyielding commitment to total quality and continuous improvement, including a vision concerned with quality and specific, measurable objectives for increasing quality and making continuous improvement.

2. Nudging people toward quality-supportive behaviours by:
   a. Screening job applicants rigorously and hiring only those with attitudes and aptitudes right for quality-based performance.
   b. Providing quality training for most employees.

c. Using teams and team-building exercises to reinforce and nurture individual effort (the creation of a quality culture is facilitated when teams become more cross-functional, multitask-oriented and increasingly self-managed).

d. Recognizing and rewarding individual and team efforts to improve quality regularly and systematically.

e. Stressing prevention (doing it right the first time), not inspection (instituting ways to correct mistakes).

3. Empowering employees so that authority for delivering great service or improving products is in the hands of the doers rather than the overseers – *improving quality has to be seen as part of everyone's job.*

4. Using online systems to provide all relevant parties with the latest best practices, thereby speeding the diffusion and adoption of best practices throughout the organization. Online systems can also allow organization personnel to exchange data and opinions about how to upgrade the prevailing best practices.

5. Emphasizing that performance can, and must, be improved because competitors are not resting on their laurels and customers are always looking for something better.

If the quality initiatives are linked to the strategic objectives and if all organization members buy into a supporting culture of operating excellence, then an organization's continuous improvement practices become decidedly more conducive to proficient strategy execution.

> The purpose of using benchmarking, best practices, business process reengineering, TQM and Six Sigma programmes is to improve the performance of strategy-critical activities and thereby enhance strategy execution.

In summary, benchmarking, the adoption of best practices, business process reengineering, TQM and Six Sigma techniques all need to be seen and used as part of a bigger-picture effort to execute strategy proficiently. Used properly, all of these tools are capable of improving the proficiency with which an organization performs its value chain activities. Not only do improvements from such initiatives add up over time and strengthen organizational capabilities, but they also help build a culture of operating excellence. All this lays the groundwork for gaining a competitive advantage.[24] While it is relatively easy for rivals to also implement process management tools, it is much more difficult and time-consuming for them to instil a deeply ingrained culture of operating excellence (as occurs when such techniques are enthusiastically employed and top management exhibits lasting commitment to operational excellence throughout the organization).

Installing Information and Operating Systems

Organization strategies cannot be executed well without a number of internal systems for business operations. Southwest Airlines, Singapore Airlines, Lufthansa, British Airways and other successful airlines cannot hope to provide a passenger-pleasing service without a user-friendly online reservation system, an accurate and speedy baggage handling system and a strict aircraft maintenance programme that minimizes problems requiring at-the-gate service that delay departures. FedEx has internal communication systems that allow it to co-ordinate its over 80 000 vehicles in handling an average of 8 million packages a day. Its leading-edge flight operations systems allow a single controller to direct as many as 200 of FedEx's 664 aircraft simultaneously, overriding their flight plans should weather problems or other special circumstances arise. In addition, FedEx has created a series of e-business tools for customers that allow them to ship and track packages online, create address books, review shipping history, generate custom reports, simplify customer billing, reduce internal warehousing and inventory management costs, purchase goods and services from suppliers and respond to quickly changing customer demands. All of FedEx's systems support the organization's strategy of providing businesses and individuals with a broad array of package delivery services (from premium next-day to economical five-day deliveries) and enhancing its competitiveness against United Parcel Service and DHL.

> **LO 11.4**
> Recognize the role information and operating systems play in enabling organization personnel to carry out their strategic roles proficiently.

In mining and quarrying one of the most important pieces of equipment is the fleet of vehicles that transport materials, such as ore or coal around the site. These large trucks rely on specialist off-road tyres that have to withstand an often hostile environment. Tyre organizations such as OTR and Michelin have developed tyre monitoring systems that detect pressure, temperature and depth of tread without the need to stop the trucks from working. Michelin's system is within the tyre itself and transmits data to the control centre at the mine or quarry via a tyre management system. Hand-held units are used to monitor tread depth and external condition of the tyres. Using these sorts of systems has allowed mining organizations, such as Norwegian iron ore producer Sydvaranger, to increase productivity by reducing the amount of downtime required for inspecting their vehicles.[25]

Amazon.com ships customer orders of books, CDs, toys and a myriad other items from fully computerized warehouses with a capacity of over 17.5 million square feet in 2010. The warehouses are so technologically sophisticated that they require about as many lines of code to run as Amazon's website does. Using complex picking algorithms, computers initiate the order-picking process by sending signals to workers' wireless receivers, telling them which items to pick off the shelves in which order. Computers also generate data on misboxed items, chute backup times, line speed, worker productivity and shipping weights on orders. Systems are upgraded regularly, and productivity improvements are aggressively pursued. In 2003 Amazon turned their inventory over 20 times annually in an industry whose average was 15 turns; by 2009 its industry turnover had decreased to an unprecedented 12. Amazon's warehouse efficiency and cost per order filled was so low that one of the fastest-growing and most profitable parts of Amazon's business was using its warehouses to run the e-commerce operations of other large retail chains.

Most telephone organizations, electric utilities and TV broadcasting systems have online monitoring systems to spot transmission problems within seconds and increase the reliability of their services. At eBay, there are systems for real-time monitoring of new listings, bidding activity, website traffic and page views. Chelsea and Westminster Healthcare Trust, which operates hospital sites in West London, installed an e-pharmacy system with a robotic dispenser and linked e-procurement system in 2004. The system improved the accuracy of the operations by reducing prescribing errors as well as reducing waiting times for patients and overtime for staff.[26] IBM makes extensive use of social software applications such as Lotus Connections to support its 1796 online communities, having discovered that many of its employees depend on these tools to do their work.[27] In businesses such as public accounting and management consulting, where large numbers of professional staff need cutting-edge technical know-how, organizations have developed systems that identify when it is time for certain employees to attend training programmes to update their skills and know-how. Many organizations have catalogued best-practice information on their intranets to promote faster transfer and implementation organization-wide.[28]

Well-conceived state-of-the-art operating systems not only enable better strategy execution but also strengthen organizational capabilities – sometimes enough to provide a competitive edge over rivals. For example, an organization with a differentiation strategy based on superior quality (covered in Chapter 5) has added capability if it has systems for training personnel in quality techniques, tracking product quality at each production step and ensuring that all goods shipped meet quality standards. If the systems it employs are advanced systems that have not yet been adopted by rivals, the systems may provide the organization with a competitive advantage as long as the costs of deploying the systems do not outweigh their benefits. Luxury chocolate maker, Godiva, makes use of an Electronic Resource Planning system (ERP) and a tailored Customer Relationship Management system (CRM) to manage operations in its diverse markets (North America, Europe, Hong Kong and Japan). The various systems have been integrated with an e-commerce platform.[29] Similarly, an organization striving to be a low-cost provider is competitively stronger if it has an unrivalled benchmarking system that identifies opportunities to implement best practices and drive costs out of the business. Fast-growing organizations get an important lift from having capabilities in place to recruit and train new employees in large numbers and from investing in infrastructure that gives them the capability to handle rapid growth as it occurs. It is nearly always better to put infrastructure and support systems in place before they are actually needed than to have to scramble to catch up to customer demand.

Instituting Adequate Information Systems, Performance Tracking and Controls

Accurate and timely information about daily operations is essential if managers are to gauge how well the strategy execution process is proceeding. Information systems need to cover five broad areas: (1) customer data; (2) operations data; (3) employee data; (4) supplier/partner/collaborative ally data; and (5) financial performance data. All key strategic performance indicators must be tracked and reported in real time where possible. Long the norm, monthly profit-and-loss statements and monthly statistical summaries are fast being replaced with daily statistical updates and even up-to-the-minute performance monitoring, made possible by online technology. Most retail organizations have automated online systems that generate daily sales reports for each store and maintain up-to-the-minute inventory and sales records on each item. Manufacturing plants typically generate daily production reports and track labour productivity on every shift. Many retailers and manufacturers have online data systems connecting them with their suppliers that monitor the status of inventories, track shipments and deliveries and measure defect rates.

Real-time information systems permit organization managers to stay on top of implementation initiatives and daily operations and to intervene if things seem to be drifting off course. Tracking key performance indicators, gathering information from operating personnel, quickly identifying and diagnosing problems, and taking corrective actions are all integral pieces of the process of managing strategy implementation and exercising adequate control over operations. A number of organizations have recently begun creating 'electronic scorecards' for senior managers that gather daily or weekly statistics from different databases about inventory, sales, costs and sales trends; such information enables these managers to easily stay abreast of what is happening and make better on-the-spot decisions.[30] Telephone organizations have elaborate information systems to measure signal quality, connection times, interrupts, wrong connections, billing errors and other measures of reliability that affect customer service and satisfaction. British Petroleum (BP) has fitted out rail wagons carrying hazardous materials with sensors and global-positioning systems (GPS) so that it can track the status, location and other information about these shipments via satellite and relay the data to its corporate intranet. Organizations that rely on empowered customer-contact personnel to act promptly and creatively in pleasing customers have installed online information systems that make essential customer data accessible to such personnel through a few keystrokes; this enables them to respond more effectively to customer inquiries and deliver personalized customer service.

> Having state-of-the-art operating systems, information systems and real-time data is another way organizations can facilitate superior strategy execution and operating excellence.

Statistical information gives managers a feel for the numbers; briefings and meetings provide a feel for the latest developments and emerging issues; and personal contacts add a feel for the people dimension. All are good barometers. Managers must identify problem areas and deviations from plans before they can take action to get the organization back on course, by either improving the approaches to strategy execution or fine-tuning the strategy. Jeff Bezos, Amazon's CEO, is an ardent proponent of managing by the numbers. As he puts it, 'Math based decisions always trump opinion and judgment. The trouble with most corporations is that they make judgment-based decisions when data-based decisions could be made'.[31]

Monitoring Employee Performance

Information systems also provide managers with a means for monitoring the performance of empowered workers to see that they are acting within the specified limits.[32] Leaving empowered employees to their own devices in meeting performance standards without appropriate checks and balances can expose an organization to excessive risk.[33] As we saw in the opening case study, instances abound of employees' decisions or behaviour having gone awry, sometimes costing an organization huge sums or producing lawsuits aside from just generating embarrassing publicity.

Scrutinizing daily and weekly operating statistics is one of the important ways in which managers can monitor the results that flow from the actions of empowered subordinates without resorting to constant over-the-shoulder supervision; if the operating results flowing from the actions of empowered employees look good, then it is reasonable to assume that empowerment is working. But close monitoring of operating performance is only one of the control tools at management's disposal. Another valuable lever of control in organizations that rely on empowered employees, especially in those that use self-managed workgroups or other such teams, is peer-based control. Because peer evaluation is such a powerful control device, organizations organized into teams can remove some layers of the management hierarchy and rely on strong peer pressure to keep team members operating between the white lines. This is especially true when an organization has the information systems capability to monitor team performance daily or in real time.

A DIFFERENT VIEW

DYNAMIC CONTROL SYSTEMS

Harvard Professor, Robert Simons (1995), identified four types of control system he described as 'levers' (see Figure 11.3). Use of these four levers in combination, he argued, help to retain flexibility as well as giving managers control, especially in organizations operating in dynamic or high-velocity environments. The levers are all linked to the organization's business strategy and cover the following:

1. *Diagnostic control systems*: these are the systems that measure key outputs and allow managers to track progress against strategically significant goals. The systems allow managers to make adjustments based on periodic feedback and realign processes and inputs to ensure that future outputs meet the desired goals.

2. *Belief systems*: these are the business's core values. They need to be broad enough to appeal to the different groups in the organization, from sales and marketing to production and clerical personnel. Senior managers use belief systems to orient

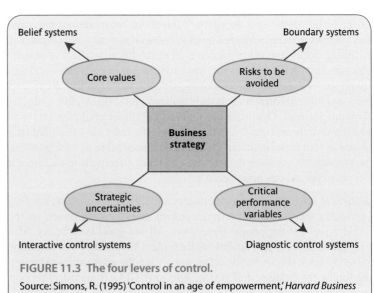

FIGURE 11.3 The four levers of control.

Source: Simons, R. (1995) 'Control in an age of empowerment,' *Harvard Business Review*, 73(2): 80–8.

▶

◄ employees and promote commitment to the organization's vision. They can encapsulate the ways of working employees are expected to embrace – 'respect for the individual', 'pursuit of excellence', and so on.

3. *Boundary systems*: these show employees what the limits of acceptable activity are. Using standard operating procedures and rules to state what staff are allowed to do can stifle creativity, defining what employees should not do promotes innovation, although there are still limits managers set by stating the acceptable scope of activities. Boundary systems are often stated as minimum standards or in codes of ethical conduct. They act as the 'organization's brakes'.

4. *Interactive control systems*: these are important to help organizations deal with strategic uncertainties. In large organizations these are often formal systems that help managers to pick up on emerging information. They support the development of new strategies by allowing managers to sense and respond to threats and opportunities in the organization's environment. These systems are distinct from diagnostic control in that they relate to changing factors such as trends in consumer behaviour, changes to government regulation, new technologies and the moves of existing and potential competitors.

Using all the levers in combination allows managers to unleash the creative talents of their workforce without losing ultimate control of the operational activities that are critical to the execution of the organization's strategy.

Activity

Reread the opening case in this chapter and apply Simon's framework to the various examples. Which of the control levers did management fail to use effectively in each case?

Tying Rewards and Incentives to Strategy Execution

In order to focus staff on performance targets that are critical to the successful execution of a strategy, organization managers typically use an assortment of motivational techniques and rewards to enlist organization-wide commitment to the strategic plan. A properly designed reward structure can be a powerful tool for mobilizing organizational commitment to successful strategy execution. But incentives and rewards do more than just strengthen the resolve of organization personnel to succeed – they also focus their attention on the accomplishment of specific strategy execution objectives. Not only do they spur the efforts of individuals to achieve those aims, but they can also help to co-ordinate the activities of individuals throughout the organization by aligning their personal motives with the goals of the organization. In this manner, reward systems serve as an indirect type of control mechanism that conserves on the more costly control mechanism of supervisory oversight.

> **LO 11.5**
> Discuss how and why well-designed incentives and rewards can be used to promote adept strategy execution and operating excellence.

To win employees' sustained, energetic commitment to the strategy execution process, management must be resourceful in designing and using motivational incentives – both monetary and non-monetary. The more a manager understands what motivates his or her team and the more he or she relies on motivational incentives as a tool for achieving the targeted strategic and financial results, the greater will be employees' commitment to good day-in, day-out strategy execution and achievement of performance targets.[34]

> A properly designed reward structure is a powerful tool for mobilizing organizational commitment to successful strategy execution and aligning efforts throughout the organization with strategic priorities.

Incentives and Motivational Practices that Facilitate Good Strategy Execution

Financial incentives are still an important motivating tool for gaining employee commitment to good strategy execution and focusing attention on strategic priorities. They

Core Concept

Financial rewards can provide high-powered incentives when rewards are tied to specific outcome objectives.

can provide high-powered incentives for some individuals to increase their efforts when rewards are tied to specific outcome objectives. An organization's package of monetary rewards typically includes some combination of base-pay increases, performance bonuses, profit-sharing plans, stock awards, organization contributions to employee pensions and piecework incentives (in the case of production workers). But most successful organizations and managers also make extensive use of non-monetary incentives. Some of the most important non-monetary approaches organizations can use to enhance motivation are listed below:[35]

- *Provide attractive perks and fringe benefits.* The various options include full coverage of health insurance premiums, college tuition reimbursement, generous paid leave allowances, on-site child care, on-site fitness centres, holiday opportunities at organization-owned recreational facilities, personal concierge services, subsidized cafeterias and free lunches, casual dress every day, personal travel services, paid sabbaticals, maternity and paternity leaves, paid leaves to care for ill family members, telecommuting, compressed work weeks (four 10-hour days instead of five 8-hour days), flexitime (variable work schedules that accommodate individual needs), college scholarships for children and relocation services.

- *Give awards and other forms of public recognition to high performers, and celebrate the achievement of organizational goals.* Many organizations hold award ceremonies to honour top-performing individuals, teams and organizational units and to showcase organization successes. This can help create healthy competition among units and teams within the organization, but it can also create a positive *esprit de corps* among the organizations as a whole. Other examples include special recognition at informal organization gatherings or in the organization newsletter, tangible tokens of appreciation for jobs well done and frequent words of praise.

- *Rely on promotion from within whenever possible.* The practice of promoting from within helps bind workers to their employer, and employers to their workers, providing strong incentives for good performance. Moreover, promoting from within helps ensure that people in positions of responsibility have knowledge specific to the business, technology and operations they are managing.

- *Invite and act on ideas and suggestions from employees.* Many organizations find that their best ideas for nuts-and-bolts operating improvements come from the suggestions of employees. Moreover, research indicates that the moves of many organizations to push decision-making down the line and empower employees increases employees' motivation and satisfaction as well as their productivity. The use of self-managed teams has much the same effect.

- *Create a work atmosphere in which there is genuine caring and mutual respect among workers and between management and employees.* A 'family' work environment where people are on a first-name basis and there is strong camaraderie promotes teamwork and cross-unit collaboration.

- *State the strategic vision in inspirational terms so that employees feel they are a part of something very worth while in a larger social sense.* There is a strong motivating power associated with giving people a chance to be part of something exciting and personally satisfying. Jobs with noble purpose tend to inspire employees to give their all. As described in Chapter 9, this not only increases productivity but reduces turnover and lowers costs for staff recruitment and training as well.

- *Share information with employees about financial performance, strategy, operational measures, market conditions and competitors' actions.* Broad disclosure and prompt communication send the message that managers trust their workers and regard them as valued partners in the enterprise. Keeping employees in the dark denies them information useful to performing their jobs, prevents them from being intellectually engaged, saps their motivation and detracts from performance.

- *Maintain attractive office space and facilities.* A workplace environment that is attractive and comfortable usually has decidedly positive effects on employee morale and productivity. An appealing work environment is particularly important when workers are expected to spend long hours at work.

For specific examples of the motivational tactics employed by several prominent organizations (many of which appear on the list of the 100 best organizations to work for in Europe), see Illustration Capsule 11.2.

Illustration Capsule 11.2

WHAT ORGANIZATIONS DO TO MOTIVATE AND REWARD EMPLOYEES

Organizations have come up with an impressive variety of motivational and reward practices to help create a work environment that energizes employees and promotes better strategy execution. Here is a sample of what organizations are doing:

- London and Quadrant Housing Trust is one of the largest providers of social housing in London. The housing association employs 1100 people and manages over 67 000 homes. In 2008 the organization developed a Leadership Academy for its managers, which runs a three-day residential programme to develop their leadership skills to foster collaborative working. All staff participate in a bonus scheme that is linked to resident satisfaction and can be up to 5 per cent of salary.

- Baringa Partners, a management consultancy specializing in energy and utilities markets, start their motivational tactics while they are still recruiting staff. New members of staff are sent a bottle of champagne and at their first organization meeting presented with a branded T-shirt as a sign they have joined the team. New members of staff are assigned a 'buddy' who acts as a mentor. The organization has a quarterly award of £500 for exceptional contributions by any individual employee as well as Star Player and Team of the Year, Cheerleader and One to Watch awards. Other rewards include dinners and weekend breaks for teams that hit significant milestones.

- Centor Insurance is a financial services organization, based in London, which employs just 38 people but has an employee retention rate of 94 per cent and several staff in line for their 20-year-long service award, which is remarkable in an industry where staff tend to change jobs every three or four years. The organization operates a 'War Stories' scheme so that staff who have performed well or overcome particular problems are encouraged to pass on their learning and gain the respect of their colleagues. The organization also has very flexible working practices and is committed to helping its staff achieve a good work–life balance. Jobs have been redesigned to suit part-time hours and home working is facilitated through dedicated technical support.

- At W.L. Gore (the maker of GORE-TEX), which employs over 1000 people in its European operations, employees get to choose what project/team they work on, and each team member's compensation is based on other team members' rankings of his or her contribution to the enterprise.

- Jewellery retailer Beaverbrook's motivates its employees by building a high level of trust through listening and acting on their suggestions. Although the organization runs 66 retail outlets in the UK, the managing director and other senior managers try to do most of their communication with staff face to face by visiting the stores and holding focus groups. This access to the top team extends to Beaverbrook's suggestion scheme. A member of the executive team responds personally to every request made.

- Lansons Communications is one of the top independent PR agencies in the UK. The organization offers a mix of hard and soft benefits to its employees including a share ownership scheme, pensions, a savings scheme and a bonus scheme that is funded with a third share of the annual profits. Lansons also provides subsidized massages, manicures and pedicures as well as buying gifts for children's birthdays and giving staff time off for school plays.

Sources: www.greatplacetowork.co.uk and organization websites (accessed March 2012).

Striking the Right Balance between Rewards and Punishment

Decisions on salary increases, incentive compensation, promotions, key assignments and the ways and means of awarding praise and recognition are potent attention-getting, commitment-generating devices. Such decisions seldom escape the closest employee scrutiny, thus saying more about what is expected and who is considered to be doing a good job than virtually any other factor. While most approaches to motivation, compensation and people management accentuate the positive, organizations also combine positive rewards with the risk of punishment. A number of organizations deliberately give employees heavy workloads and tight deadlines – personnel are pushed hard to achieve 'stretch' objectives and are expected to put in long hours (nights and weekends if need be). At most organizations, senior executives and key personnel in underperforming units are pressured to raise performance to acceptable levels and keep it there or risk being replaced.

Some organizations feel it is unwise to take off the pressure for good individual and group performance or play down the adverse consequences of shortfalls in performance. High-performing organizations often have a cadre of ambitious people who relish the opportunity to climb the ladder of success, love a challenge, thrive in a performance-oriented environment and find some competition and pressure useful to satisfy their own drives for personal recognition, accomplishment and self-satisfaction. However, there is also research which shows that other employees may be more motivated by intrinsic factors (see Key Debate 11.1 for a fuller discussion).

However, if an organization's motivational approaches and reward structure induce too much stress, internal competitiveness, job insecurity and fear of unpleasant consequences, the impact on workforce morale and strategy execution can be counterproductive. Evidence shows that managerial initiatives to improve strategy execution should incorporate more positive than negative motivational elements because when co-operation is positively enlisted and rewarded, rather than coerced by orders and threats (implicit or explicit), people tend to respond with more enthusiasm, dedication, creativity and initiative.[36]

Linking Rewards to Strategically Relevant Performance Outcomes

To create a strategy-supportive system of rewards and incentives, organizations usually reward people for accomplishing results, not for just dutifully performing assigned tasks. To make the work environment results-oriented, managers will focus jobholders' attention and energy on what to *achieve* as opposed to what to *do*. It is flawed management to tie incentives and rewards to satisfactory performance of duties and activities instead of desired business outcomes and organization achievements.[37] In any job, performing assigned tasks is not equivalent to achieving intended outcomes. Diligently showing up for work and attending to one's job assignment does not, by itself, guarantee results.

> The key to creating a reward system that promotes good strategy execution is to make measures of good business performance and good strategy execution the *dominating basis* for designing incentives, evaluating individual and group efforts and handing out rewards.

Ideally, performance targets should be set for every organizational unit, every manager, every team or workgroup and perhaps every employee – targets that measure whether strategy execution is progressing satisfactorily. If the organization's strategy is to be a low-cost provider, the incentive system must reward actions and achievements that result in lower costs. If the organization has a differentiation strategy based on superior quality and service, the incentive system must reward such outcomes as Six Sigma defect rates, infrequent need for product repair, low numbers of customer complaints, speedy order processing and delivery and high levels of customer satisfaction. If an organization's growth is predicated on a strategy of new product innovation, incentives should be tied to factors such as the percentages of revenues and profits coming from newly introduced products.

Incentive compensation for top executives is typically tied to such financial measures as revenue and earnings growth, stock price performance, return on investment and creditworthiness or to strategic measures such as market share growth. However, incentives for department heads, teams and individual workers may be tied to performance outcomes more closely related to their strategic area of responsibility. In manufacturing, incentive compensation may be tied to unit manufacturing costs, on-time production and shipping, defect rates, the number and extent of work stoppages due to equipment breakdowns and so on. In sales and marketing, there may be incentives for achieving sales or unit volume targets, market share, sales penetration of each target customer group, the fate of newly introduced products, the frequency of customer complaints, the number of new accounts acquired and customer satisfaction. Which performance measures to base incentive compensation on depends on the situation – the priority placed on various financial and strategic objectives, the requirements for strategic and competitive success and what specific results are needed in different facets of the business to keep strategy execution on track.

Once an organization's incentive plan is designed, it is then communicated and explained. Everybody needs to understand how his or her incentive compensation is calculated and how individual/group performance targets contribute to organizational performance targets. The pressure to continuously improve strategy execution and achieve performance objectives should be unrelenting, with no loopholes for rewarding shortfalls in performance. Organizations relying on this approach need to ensure that people at all levels are held accountable for carrying out their assigned parts of the strategic plan, and they must understand that their rewards are based on the calibre of results achieved. But with the pressure to perform should come meaningful rewards that will effectively motivate the workforce.

Key Debate 11.1

WHAT REALLY MOTIVATES EMPLOYEES?

Many of the examples in this chapter appear to reinforce the view that extrinsic rewards (those external to the job or task being performed), such as piece rates, performance related pay and significant bonuses, are an important way to align employees' activity with strategy execution. In economic theory these performance contingent rewards are one of the main ways to overcome some of the problems associated with the principal–agent relationship. However, the opening case shows that this concept is less than perfect in helping managers to understand the complexities of motivation in the workforce.

Many professionals are now turning to psychology and education for a deeper analysis of what really motivates employees. Performance contingent rewards used in experiments in these fields have shown that they can actually damage performance and employees find them dehumanizing and alienating. Extrinsic rewards have been found to increase compliance and performance, but usually only in the short term, and over a longer period they have been shown to be damaging, with the performance of groups who received no rewards outpacing the groups being rewarded. This experimental data is also being backed up with practical examples. Daniel Pink's (2009) book, *Drive*, cites a number of examples where the removal of extrinsic rewards actually improved performance. Red Gate, a specialist software organization based in Cambridge, scrapped commission payments for their sales teams after the organization's boss found that his managers were spending most of their time monitoring the system to ensure that the sales force were not gaming it to maximize their income. Removing commissions from the equation not only simplified the pay system but also led to an increase in sales and better employee retention. So, if extrinsic rewards are not the best way to motivate the workforce, what is? According to Pink, reward and punishment are still useful motivators, but intrinsic rewards, those inherent to the job itself, prove far more powerful in aligning people to long-terms goals.

The global downturn has brought the differences between intrinsic and extrinsic rewards into sharp relief. With less financial resources many organizations are finding it hard to invest in traditional rewards. The near

▶

collapse of the banking system in 2007/8 has also caused organizations to question the wisdom of short-term performance-based rewards. According to Kenneth Thomas, extrinsic rewards were necessary in the past when work was more bureaucratic and routine, but in many workplaces employees are coping with rapidly changing environments and are expected to act with less supervision. Thomas identifies four intrinsic rewards that are commonly found in high-performing organizations. First, employees need to feel that their work is worth while and that there is a clear sense of direction or purpose to their activities. They also value the right to choose how they carry out their work, to make sense of what they are being asked to accomplish. Ensuring that employees feel competent in their work is a further intrinsic reward, which allows them to feel a sense of pride in what they achieve. Finally, an open approach to performance measurement is seen as a strong motivator, with employees given the chance to monitor their own performance and also group and individual celebration of milestones achieved. Intrinsic motivation can be much harder to measure and the rewards tend to be much more personal, so moving to this sort of reward system can be tough for organizations who are still wedded to command and control.

FIGURE 11.4 Relationship between reward and culture and its impact on strategy implementation.

Source: Bushardt, S., Glascoff, D. and Doty, D. (2011) 'Organizational culture, formal reward structure, and effective strategy implementation: a conceptual model', *Journal of Organizational Culture, Communications and Conflict*, 15(2): 57–70.

Motivating employees to execute strategy effectively requires more than traditional rewards, organizations also need to give their workforce a sense of purpose and take steps to give them more control over the work they do. However, recent research suggests that aligning rewards with the organizations' culture is a way to maximize the effectiveness of more formal systems (see Figure 11.4). The University of Texas study argued that this was especially important in organizations with strong cultures. If the rewards system did not match the culture of the organization then implementation of strategy had limited effectiveness.

Where the reward system was not configured with the strategy, employees would be confused or cynical about the organization. In a situation with a strong culture, they would follow the group norms rather than behave in a manner dictated by the reward system. Where the reward system and culture reinforced each other the organization would enjoy high levels of effectiveness in executing its strategy.

ACTIVITY

1. Reread the short examples in illustration Capsule 11.2 and the opening case. How do the concepts covered in this debate help to explain the outcomes reported in each situation?

Sources: Benabou, R. and Tirole, J. (2003) 'Intrinsic and extrinsic motivation', *Review of Economic Studies*, 70: 489–520; Deci, E. and Ryan, R. (1985) *Intrinsic Motivation and Self-determination in Human Behavior*, New York, Plenum Press; Bushardt, S., Glascoff, D. and Doty, D. (2011) 'Organizational culture, formal reward structure, and effective strategy implementation: a conceptual model', *Journal of Organizational Culture, Communications and Conflict*, 15(2): 57–70; Gibbons, R. (1997), 'Incentives and careers in organizations', in Kreps, D. and Wallis, K. (eds) *Advances in Economic Theory and Econometrics*, Vol. II, Cambridge, Cambridge University Press; Lazear, E. (2000) 'Performance, pay and productivity', *American Economic Review*, 90(5): 1346–61; Fehr, E. and Schimdt, K. (2000), 'Fairness, incentives, and contractual choices', *European Economic Review*, 44(4): 1057–68; Kohn, A. (1993) *Punished by Rewards*, New York, Plenum Press; Pink, D. (2009) *Drive: The Surprising Truth About What Motivates Us*, London, Canongate Books; Oloffson, K. (2010) 'Business guru Daniel Pink on what fuels good work', *Time,* 12 January. Available online at www.time.com/time/business/article/0,8599,1952993,00.html#ixzz1r13WMIQD (accessed 3 June 2012); Thomas, K. (2009) 'The four intrinsic rewards that drive employee engagement', *Ivey Business Journal*, November/December. Available online at www. iveybusinessjournal.com/topics/the-workplace/the-four-intrinsic-rewards-that-drive-employee-engagement (accessed 3 June 2012).

KEY POINTS

1. Implementing and executing a new or different strategy calls for managers to identify the resource requirements of each new strategic initiative and then consider whether the current pattern of resource allocation and the budgets of the various subunits are suitable.

2. Organization policies and procedures facilitate strategy execution when they are designed to fit the strategy and its objectives. When an organization alters its strategy, managers should review existing policies and operating procedures and replace those that are out of line with the new direction of the organization. Well-conceived policies and procedures aid the task of strategy execution by (1) providing top-down guidance to organization personnel regarding how certain things need to be done and what the boundaries are on independent actions and decisions, (2) enforcing consistency in the performance of strategy-critical activities, thereby improving the quality of the strategy execution effort and aligning the actions of organization personnel, however widely dispersed, and (3) promoting the creation of a work climate conducive to good strategy execution.

3. Competent strategy execution can be effectively supported by visible, strong managerial commitment to best practices and continuous improvement. Benchmarking, best-practice adoption, business process reengineering, TQM and Six Sigma programmes are important process management tools for promoting better strategy execution.

4. Organization strategies can not be implemented or executed well without a number of support systems to carry on business operations. Real-time information systems and control systems further aid the cause of good strategy execution.

5. Strategy-supportive motivational practices and reward systems are powerful management tools for gaining employee commitment and focusing their attention on the strategy execution goals.

CLOSING CASE

DEVON COUNTY COUNCIL – LEAN TIMES

John Hart, the Leader of Devon County Council and Phil Norrey, his chief executive, had an unenviable task at the end of 2010. They had to reduce the organization's budget substantially while still delivering a wide range of public services to their local community. Local government in England was facing its toughest challenge in living memory, with government funding set to fall to its lowest level for a generation and a host of new policies coming through from the UK's recently elected Coalition Government.

BACKGROUND

Devon County Council was one of 33 top-tier councils in England, which along with unitary authorities and district councils made up the system of local government (see Exhibit 11.1 for Devon's key statistics). In many places like Devon there were two layers of local government, a county council covering a large area and responsible for the delivery of public services such as schools, libraries, public transport and social services, and several district councils that covered a smaller area and provided local services, including rubbish collection, recycling, planning and environmental health. Some services, such as police and fire and rescue, were run jointly by more than one county council. Services provided by local authorities were classed as mandatory (those the council must provide) and discretionary (those the council could choose to provide). Local authorities received their funding from the UK government in the form of grants and also from local taxes, the council tax and business rates.

Devon County Council was responsible for one of the largest (by area) rural counties in England. The county, located in the South West, had a population of just under 750 000 in 2008 and this was expected to grow by about 20 per cent by 2033. However, Devon was considered an attractive part of the UK and many people wanted to retire there. Coupled with an ageing population, this presented long-term challenges for the Council's social services function as it was estimated that over 25 per cent of the county's population would be over 65 by 2031. Devon's rural nature also meant that the cost of infrastructure and services could be much higher. Although there were many positive economic factors, such as high employment rates in the county, most of the businesses (96 per cent) in Devon were small enterprises employing less than 20 people. The county relied heavily on public sector employers in providing jobs. In some areas, such as Exeter, nearly 40 per cent of the working population were employed by the public sector.

POLICY IMPERATIVES

Within a month of forming a government in May 2010, the Conservative/Liberal Democrat coalition announced £1.1 billion of cuts to central funding for local authorities. At the same time, Communities Secretary, Eric Pickles, the minister responsible for local government, pledged to cut the amount of top-down monitoring of councils by Whitehall. The Audit Commission, which had been one of the key agencies that inspected and

---

EXHIBIT 11.1: Devon County Council key statistics

Gross budget £1.385 billion
- Key investments include:
  - Schools £374 million
  - Adult and Community Services £217 million
  - Environment, Economy and Culture £106 million
  - Children and Young People £115 million

Political make-up
- County Council seats: 62
  - 41 Conservative
  - 13 Liberal Democrat
  - 5 Labour
  - 2 Independent
  - 1 Green Party

Key statistics
- Population: 750 100
- Schools maintained by DCC: 319
- Academies (previously maintained by DCC): 44
- Pupils: 96 200
- Children looked after: 700
- Adults helped to live at home: 18 956
- Residential and nursing care: 3564 adults
- Libraries and Mobile Libraries: 58
- Roads: 12 850 km (7985 miles)
- Bridges: 3500
- Public Rights of Way: 4940 km or 3070 miles
- Streetlights: 71 000
- Illuminated road signs: 10 917
- Recycling Centres: 19
- Recycling rate: 55 per cent

▶

monitored local councils, was scrapped. The coalition's new policies on local government marked a fundamental change for the sector. The local electorate were to be given a much greater say in how services were funded and delivered, including the right to veto local tax rates if they were above a certain level and the ability to bid to run services through community groups and social enterprises.

The government set out its vision for the sector in a White Paper in July 2011 called 'Open Public Services'. The changes envisaged in this document would fundamentally alter the role of local government. They would involve devolving power and decisions on local services to a micro-level wherever possible, giving local citizens choices over which organizations would provide services, which meant that local authorities would have to open up public services to external providers. Councils would cease to be monopoly providers of many public services and instead they would commission other organizations to deliver on their behalf.

PUBLIC SECTOR PEOPLE

In the UK, in 2012, the public sector accounted for over 20 per cent of jobs. Public sector workers were much more likely to be in a union than their private sector colleagues. However, there was a significant debate around how their pay and conditions differed from the average private sector employee's. Some commentators stated that figures from the Office of National Statistics showed that public sector workers were paid more than £4000 per annum, on average than their private sector equivalents, as well as receiving much more generous pensions on retirement.

Despite the apparent benefits of being a public sector worker, in 2011 a survey found that only 31 per cent of UK public servants were happy in their jobs. Morale was seen a major issue in many councils with similar issues to Devon as staff were being asked to make changes in their working practices and to deliver the same or enhanced services with less resource. The same survey showed that only about 14 per cent were motivated to stay in their current jobs by the benefits and rewards on offer. Two in five respondents stated that 'making a difference' was the most important reason for staying in their current role. Public sector staff also valued the work–life balance the sector offered as an important factor in their choice of role.

The Coalition Government's cuts to public sector budgets as part of their austerity package were predicted to result in the loss of up to 725 000 jobs in the sector by 2015. However, there was little prospect for those whose posts were made redundant finding work in the private sector. A survey by Chartered Institute of Management Accountants (CIMA) in 2011 found that private sector employers were unlikely to

---

EXHIBIT 11.2: Strategic Plan 2011–15 – vision, values and priorities

Vision for 2020
- A flourishing and balanced economy, with strong economic growth and high-quality employment.
- Influencing people and communities for better health and well-being.
- A safe place to live where those at risk of harm are well protected.
- Conservation and enhancement of Devon's environment.
- Greater influence, choice and control over decisions that affect communities and services that they use.

Priorities 2011–13
- Remove barriers to growth.
- Protect and support the most vulnerable.
- Promote early action and provide greater choice and control.
- Help communities help themselves.
- Make the most of Devon's natural assets.

Values
- Enterprise: To promote enterprise and help develop a competitive economy as the key to a better quality of life for all.
- Care: To promote high-quality services that care for, support and protect the people of Devon.
- Community: To work with local people to help build strong and prosperous communities and ensure a sustainable future for all.
- Value: To be a business-like Council that is lean and focused, providing good value for money.

◄

hire former public servants as they felt that they lacked the necessary skills and attitude required to succeed in a more commercial environment.

Performance-related pay (PRP) and bonuses had been a contentious issue in the public sector for some time leading up to the General Election in 2010. Some senior managers' bonuses and reward packages had been heavily criticized by politicians, especially when the packages for some local council chief executives were higher than the Prime Minister's pay. However, according to the Chartered Institute of Personnel and Development (CIPD), in 2010 only 44 per cent of public sector organizations used bonuses and incentive payments, compared to nearly double that percentage in the private sector. The CIPD advocated the introduction of PRP in the sector to help retain and recruit talent while the government cuts were resulting in overall pay restraint and less attractive pension packages. PRP would also help staff to focus on the critical activities needed to deliver effective public services with fewer resources. However, not all senior managers in the sector agreed with this approach. Although some county councils, such as Cambridgeshire, supported the idea of PRP, other human resource (HR) directors at Somerset and Westminster felt that the introduction of these systems would increase the pay bill without necessarily producing tangible results. The complex nature of public sector services meant that collaboration was often a key success factor and incentives aimed at individuals might produce unintended consequences.

STRATEGY, STRUCTURE AND SYSTEMS

At the end of 2011, the Council's chief executive and his team developed a new strategic plan for 2011–15, *Backing Devon*. The plan was intended to address the changes that the Council would need to make in the light of the new policy direction being set by central government and the reduced funding available to the council (for the vision, values and priorities from the plan see Exhibit 11.2).

Devon had already embarked on a cost-cutting exercise in 2009 as the effects of the downturn in the global economy were becoming apparent

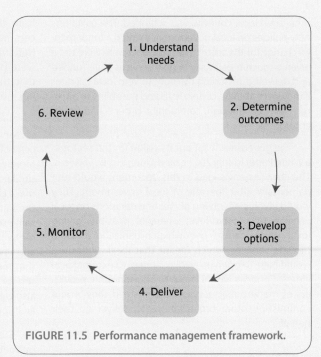

FIGURE 11.5 Performance management framework.

in the UK. The Council had frozen recruitment, which had saved it from 800 redundancies through not replacing staff who had left between December 2009 and the end of 2010. However, the cuts proposed between 2011–2013 would amount to £55 million and the council estimated that this would result in a further 900 job losses over that period out of a total workforce of just over 15 000. According to Unison (a public sector work-

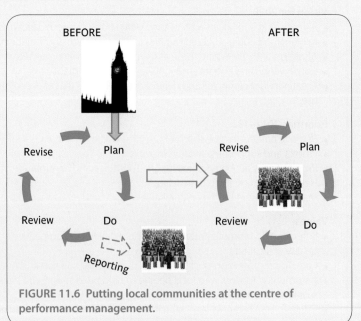

FIGURE 11.6 Putting local communities at the centre of performance management.

▶

ers union) representative, Karen Williams, the reduction in staffing was having a 'devastating' effect on staff.

The streamlining of the council was not just confined to those lower in the hierarchy. During 2011 the Council restructured, reducing its number of senior managers from 29 to 18, the four directors were reduced to two with the new divisions covering 'Place'-based services such as highways, economy and enterprise and 'people'-based services, including social care and education. A corporate services function, with legal, financial, HR and strategic sections supported the two other directorates, with managers reporting directly to the chief executive.

The new strategic plan also pledged to involve the local population much more in decisions over and implementation of the Council's strategy. Backing Devon stated that the role of the Council in delivering services would reduce but that its influencing, leading and, perhaps most importantly, its commissioning roles would increase. To support this change of emphasis the Council planned to invest in leadership and management skills in its remaining workforce as well as developing enhanced capabilities in commissioning, which would be required because it would be working through a wide range of delivery organizations from multinational private sector contractors to local social enterprises and co-operatives.

The way the Council managed its performance would also need to change. In the past performance management had tended to be reactive and was often driven by the needs of central government organizations, such as the National Audit Office. Now the system needed to be more proactive and take account of the views of local people. Performance information would need to be used to drive improvement in services. The leadership also needed to change how the organization and managers viewed performance management from something routine and necessary to a more dynamic perspective. Devon's new performance management framework comprised six stages. Each would require the use of new information systems in order to put the local community at the heart of the process. Managers would need to start by working with a range of data, policy documents and local communities to understand the needs for each of the services the Council delivered or commissioned, after which they would determine the outcomes in terms of objectives and priorities. Again this would be carried out in consultation with local communities. The third stage required managers to develop different options and other ways of delivering the services. This would be particularly important in overcoming the reduced budgets.

The delivery stage would involve allocating resources to the chosen options, which would increasingly be through partners in the community and voluntary sector. The services would be monitored against the milestones and targets linked to the objectives set in stage two. Systems would need to be modified to include an increased level of monitoring by citizens. Finally, there was a review stage that would tackle poor performance and ensure this was corrected as well as communicating where improvements had taken place (see Figure 11.3 for coverage of the framework).

The leader of the Council, John Hart, had set out a clear mission to create a more business-like organization that was more responsive to local needs but which was also more effective and efficient in delivering services. Now it was the task of the Council's managers and officers to execute that strategy though the new structure, systems and relationships that were being developed.

QUESTIONS

1. What changes has Devon County Council's leadership made to the way it allocates resources to support the new strategic plan?

2. How does the Council's new strategic plan embed continuous improvement systems?

3. What factors are most likely to motivate staff at Devon County Council to work on executing the new strategy?

Sources: Devon County Council (2011) 'Backing Devon – Strategic Plan 2011–2015'; Devon County Council (2011) 'Performance Strategy 2011–2015'; Devon County council website; BBC News (2010) 'Details of English councils' £1.1bn budget cut revealed; BBC News 10 June. Available online at www.bbc.co.uk/news/10285951 (accessed 4 June 2012); BBC News (2010) 'Council "league tables" to be scrapped to save money', BBC News, 25 June. Available online at www.bbc.co.uk/news/10406010 (accessed 4 June); Devon County Council (2011) 'Cabinet Committee minutes'. Available online at www.devon.gov.uk/index/councildemocracy/decision_making/cma/cma_document.htm?cmadoc=minutes_exc_20111109.html (accessed 4 June); Directgov.co.uk (2012) 'Local government powers and finance'. Available online at: www.direct.gov.uk/en/Governmentcitizensandrights/UKgovernment/Localgovernment/DG_073311 (accessed 4 June 2012); Directgov.co.uk (2012) 'Local government structure'. Available online at www.direct.gov.uk/en/Governmentcitizensandrights/UKgovernment/Localgovernment/DG_073310 (accessed 4 June); Stevens, M. (2012) 'Two in five public-sector workers still want to strike', People Management. Available online at: www.peoplemanagement.co.uk/pm/articles/2012/03/two-in-five-public-sector-workers-still-want-to-strike.htm (accessed 4 June); Public Serivce.co.uk (2011) 'Public sector employees want to stay', Public service.co.uk, 16 August. Available online at www.publicservice.co.uk/news_story.asp?id=17180 (accessed 4 June); Huber, N. (2010) 'Analysis: calls for more performance-related pay in the public sector splits HR and employment experts', *Personnel Today*, 17 June. Available online at www.personneltoday.com/articles/2010/06/17/ 55989/analysis-calls-for-more-performance-related-pay-in-the-public-sector-splits-hr-and-employment.html (accessed 4 June 2012); Barrow, B. (2011) 'Public sector workers earn £4000 a year premium compared to private staff', *Mail*, 24 November. Available online at

www.dailymail.co.uk/news/article-2065479/Public-sector-workers-earn-4-000-year-pay-premium-compared-private-staff. html (accessed 4 June); Baker, K. (2010) 'Performance-related pay for the public sector rejected by Personnel Today's austerity panel', *Personnel Today*, 17 June. Available online at www. personneltoday.com/Articles/17/06/2010/55987/Performance-related-pay-for-the-public-sector-rejected-by-Personnel-To-day39s. Austerity.htm (accessed 4 June 2012).

ASSURANCE OF LEARNING EXERCISES

LO 11.3

1. Using your favourite search engine, do a search on the term *best practices*. Browse through the search results to identify at least five organizations that have gathered a set of best practices and are making the best-practice library they have assembled available to members.

LO 11.3

2. Read some of the recent Six Sigma articles posted at www.sixsigma.com. Prepare a one-page report for your tutor detailing how Six Sigma is being used in various organizations and what benefits these organizations are reaping from Six Sigma implementation.

LO 11.5

3. Using Google Scholar or your university library's access to online business periodicals, search for the term *performance-related pay* (PRP) and prepare a 1–2-page report for your tutor discussing the successful (or unsuccessful) use of PLP plans by various organizations. Based on the research you found, what factors seem to determine whether PRP plans succeed or fail?

EXERCISES FOR SIMULATION PARTICIPANTS

LO 11.1

1. Have you and your co-managers allocated ample resources to strategy-critical areas? If so, explain how these investments have contributed to good strategy execution and improved organization performance.

LO 11.3

2. Is benchmarking data available in the simulation exercise in which you are participating? If so, do you and your co-managers regularly study the benchmarking data to see how well your organization is doing? Do you consider the benchmarking information provided to be valuable? Why or why not? Cite three recent instances in which your examination of the benchmarking statistics has caused you and your co-managers to take corrective actions to boost organization performance.

▶

◀

LO 11.2, LO 11.3, LO 11.4

3. What actions, if any, is your organization taking to pursue continuous improvement in how it performs certain value chain activities?

LO 11.5

4. Does your organization have opportunities to use incentive compensation techniques? If so, explain your organization's approach to incentive compensation. Is there any hard evidence you can cite that indicates your organization's use of incentive compensation techniques has worked? For example, have your organization's compensation incentives actually increased productivity? Can you cite evidence indicating that the productivity gains have resulted in lower labour costs? If the productivity gains have *not* translated into lower labour costs, is it fair to say that your organization's use of incentive compensation is a failure?

LO 11.2, LO 11.3, LO 11.4

5. Are you and your co-managers consciously trying to achieve 'operating excellence'? What are the indicators of operating excellence at your organization? Based on these indicators, how well does your organization measure up?

LO 11.3

6. What hard evidence can you cite that indicates your organization's management team is doing a *better* or *worse* job of achieving operating excellence and executing your strategy than are the management teams at rival organizations?

ENDNOTES

1. For a discussion of the value of benchmarking in implementing and executing strategy, see Bogan, Christopher, E. and English, Michael, J. (1994) *Benchmarking for Best Practices: Winning through Innovative Adaptation*, New York, McGraw-Hill chs 2 and 6; Ungan, Mustafa (2004) 'Factors affecting the adoption of manufacturing best practices,' *Benchmarking: An International Journal*, 11(5): 504–20; Hyland, Paul and Beckett, Ron (2002) 'Learning to compete: the value of internal benchmarking', *Benchmarking: An International Journal*, 9(3): 293–304; Ohinata, Yoshinobu, (1994) 'Benchmarking: the Japanese experience', *Long-range Planning*, 27(4): 48–53.

2. www.businessdictionary.com/definition/best-practice.html (accessed 2 December, 2009).

3. Hammer, M. and Champy, J. (1993) *Reengineering the Corporation: A Manifesto for Business Revolution*, New York, Harper Collins Publishers, pp. 26–7.

4. Information on the greeting card industry is posted at www.answers.com (accessed 8 July 2009); 'Reengineering: beyond the buzzword', *Business Week*, 24 May 1993. Available online at www. businessweek.com (accessed 8 July 2009).

5. Hall, Gene, Rosenthal, Jim and Wade, Judy (1993) 'How to make reengineering really work', *Harvard Business Review*, 71(6): 119–31.

6. For more information on business process reengineering and how well it has worked in various organizations, see Quinn, James Brian (1992) *Intelligent Enterprise*, New York, Free Press, p. 162; Majchrzak, Ann and Wang, Qianwei (1996) 'Breaking the functional mind-set in process organizations', *Harvard Business Review*, 74(5): 93–9; Walston, Stephen L., Burns, Lawton R. and Kimberly, John R. (2000) 'Does reengineering really work? An examination of the context and outcomes of hospital reengineering initiatives', *Health Services Research*, 34(6): 1363–88; Ascari, Allessio, Rock, Melinda and Dutta, Soumitra (1990) 'Reengineering and organizational change: lessons from a comparative analysis of organization experiences', *European Management Journal*, 13(1): 1–13. For a review of why some organization personnel embrace process reengineering and some do not, see Burke, Ronald J. (2004) 'Process reengineering: who embraces it and why?' *TQM Magazine,* 16(2): 114–19.

7. The Economist (2009) 'Ideas: total quality management', *The Economist,* 16 November. Available online at: www.economist.com/node/14301657 (accessed 5 June 2012).

8. For some of the seminal discussions of what TQM is and how it works, written by ardent enthusiasts of the technique, see Walton, M. (1986) *The Deming Management Method,* New York, Pedigree; Juran, J. (1992) *Juran on Quality by Design,* New York, Free Press; Crosby, Philip (1979) *Quality Is Free: The Act of Making Quality Certain,* New York, McGraw-Hill; George, S. (1992) *The Baldrige Quality System,* New York, Wiley. For a critique of TQM, see Zbaracki, Mark J. (1998) 'The rhetoric and reality of total quality management', *Administrative Science Quarterly,* 43(3): 602–36.

9. For a discussion of the shift in work environment and culture that TQM entails, see Amsden, Robert T., Ferratt, Thomas W. and Amsden, Davida M. (1996) 'TQM: core paradigm changes', *Business Horizons,* 39(6): 6–14.

10. For easy-to-understand overviews of what Six Sigma is all about, see Pande, Peter S. and Holpp, Larry (2002) *What Is Six Sigma?,* New York, McGraw-Hill; Antony, Jiju (2004) 'Some pros and cons of Six Sigma: an academic perspective', *TQM Magazine,* 16(4): 303–6; Pande, Peter S., Neuman, Robert P. and Cavanagh, Roland R. (2000) *The Six Sigma Way: How GE, Motorola and Other Top Organizations Are Honing Their Performance,* New York, McGraw-Hill; Gordon, Joseph, and Gordon, M. Joseph Jr (2002) *Six Sigma Quality for Business and Manufacture,* New York, Elsevier. For how Six Sigma can be used in smaller organizations, see Wessel, Godecke and Burcher, Peter (2004) 'Six Sigma for small and medium-sized enterprises', *TQM,* 16(4): 264–72.

11. Based on information posted at www. isixsigma.com (accessed 4 November 2002).

12. Smith, Kennedy (2003) 'Six Sigma for the service sector', *Quality Digest,* May. Available online at www. qualitydigest.com (accessed 28 September 2003).

13. Jones, Del (2002) 'Taking the Six Sigma approach', *USA Today,* 31 October, p. 5B.

14. Bargionio, L. (2010) 'A transparent success', *UK Excellence,* July, pp. 13–15.

15. Smith, 'Six Sigma for the service sector'.

16. Brown, P. and Gilbert, A. (2011) 'High flyers', *UK Excellence,* April, pp. 16–18.

17. See, for example, 'A dark art no more', (2007) *Economist,* 385(8550): 10; Hindo, Brian (2007) 'At 3M, a struggle between efficiency and creativity', *Business Week,* 11 June, pp. 8–16.

18. As quoted in 'A dark art no more'.

19. Hindo, 'At 3M, a struggle between efficiency and creativity'.

20. For a discussion of approaches to pursuing radical or disruptive innovations while also seeking incremental gains in efficiency, see O'Reilly, Charles A. and Tushman, Michael L. (2004) 'The ambidextrous organization', *Harvard Business Review,* 82(4): 74–81.

21. Lee, Terry Nels, Fawcett, Stanley E. and Briscoe, Jason (2002) 'Benchmarking the challenge to quality program implementation', *Benchmarking: An International Journal,* 9(4): 374–87.

22. For a recent study documenting the imperatives of establishing a supportive culture, see Ambrož, Milan (2004) 'Total quality system as a product of the empowered corporate culture', *TQM Magazine,* 16(2): 93–104. Research confirming the factors that are important in making TQM programs successful in both Europe and the USA is presented in Dayton, Nick A. (2003) 'The demise of total quality management', *TQM Magazine,* 15(6): 391–96.

23. Olian, Judy D. and Rynes, Sara L. (1991) 'Making total quality work: aligning organizational processes, performance measures, and stakeholders', *Human Resource Management,* 30(3): 310–11; Goodman, Paul S. and Darr, Eric D. (1996) 'Exchanging best practices information through computer-aided systems', *Academy of Management Executive,* 10(2): 7.

24. Powell, Thomas C. (1995) 'Total quality management as competitive advantage', *Strategic Management Journal,* 16: 15–37. See also Hodgetts, Richard M., (1994) 'Quality lessons from America's Baldrige winners', *Business Horizons,* 37(4): 74–9; Reed, Richard, Lemak, David J. and Montgomery, Joseph C. (1996) 'Beyond process: TQM content, and organization performance', *Academy of Management Review,* 21(1): 173–202.

25. Mining and Quarrying World (2009) '"Pneu" data capture system for OTR', *Mining and Quarrying World*, 6(1): 41.

26. e-business W@tch (2006) 'Case study: e-pharmacy at Chelsea and Westminster Hospital UK'. Available online at www.ehealth-impact.org (accessed 30 May 2012).

27. Mustapha, Aishah (2009) 'Net value: social software a new way to work', *The Edge Malaysia (Weekly)*, 16 February.

28. Such systems speed organizational learning by providing fast, efficient communication, creating an organizational memory for collecting and retaining best-practice information, and permitting people all across the organization to exchange information and updated solutions. See Goodman and Darr, 'Exchanging best practices information through computer-aided systems', pp. 7–17.

29. e-business W@tch (2008) 'Case study: ICT in support of CRM at Godiva Chocolatier Europe'. Available online at www.ebusiness-watch.org (accessed 31 May 2012).

30. 'The Web Smart 50', pp. 85–90.

31. Vogelstein, Fred (2003) 'Winning the Amazon way', *Fortune*, 147(10): 60–9.

32. For a discussion of the need for putting appropriate boundaries on the actions of empowered employees and possible control and monitoring systems that can be used, see Simons, Robert (1995) 'Control in an age of empowerment', *Harvard Business Review*, 73: 80–8.

33. Ibid. Also see Band, David C. and Scanlan, Gerald (1995) 'Strategic control through core competences', *Long Range Planning*, 28(2): 102–14.

34. The importance of motivating and empowering workers so as to create a working environment that is highly conducive to good strategy execution is discussed in Fawcett, Stanley E., Rhoads, Gary K. and Burnah, Phillip (2004) 'People as the bridge to competitiveness: benchmarking the 'ABCs' of an empowered workforce', *Benchmarking: An International Journal*, 11(4): 346–60.

35. Pfeffer, Jeffrey and Veiga, John F. (1999) 'Putting people first for organizational success', *Academy of Management Executive*, 13(2): 37–45; Stroh, Linda K. and Caliguiri, Paula M. (1998) 'Increasing global competitiveness through effective people management', *Journal of World Business*, 33(1): 1–16; articles in *Fortune* on the 100 best organizations to work for (various issues).

36. Christensen, Clayton M., Marx, Matt and Stevenson, Howard (2006) 'The tools of cooperation and change', *Harvard Business Review*, 84(10): 73–80.

37. See Kerr, Steven (1995) 'On the folly of rewarding a while hoping for B', *Academy of Management Executive*, 9(1): 7–14; Kerr, S. and Davies, E. (1996) 'Risky business: the new pay game', *Fortune*, 134(2): 94–6; and Twer, Doran (1994) 'Linking pay to business objectives', *Journal of Business Strategy*, 15(4): 15–18.

Chapter Twelve

Organizational culture and leadership

Keys to good strategy execution

The biggest levers you've got to change a company are strategy, structure, and culture. If I could pick two, I'd pick strategy and culture.

Wayne Leonard
Chairman and CEO, Entergy Corporation

The soft stuff is always harder than the hard stuff.

Roger Enrico
Former CEO of PepsiCo

Success goes to those with a corporate culture that assures the ability to anticipate and meet customer demand.

Tadashi Okamura
Former Chairman and CEO of Toshiba Corporation

Learning Objectives

When you have read this chapter you should be able to:

LO 12.1 Identify the key features of an organization's culture and appreciate the role of an organization's core values and ethical standards in building culture.

LO 12.2 Understand how and why an organization's culture can support proficient strategy execution and operating excellence.

LO 12.3 Identify the kinds of actions management can take to change a problem organizational culture.

LO 12.4 Understand what constitutes effective managerial leadership in achieving superior strategy execution.

EXPRESSING SMALL TOWN VALUES IN A GLOBAL ORGANIZATION: IKEA

Maintaining a strong IKEA culture is one of the most crucial factors behind the continued success of the IKEA concept

Ingvar Kamprad

The well-renowned organizational culture of IKEA has been strongly influenced by the founder, Ingvar Kamprad who, in turn, attributes much of his own philosophy to the small town of Småland where he spent his formative years.

Anders Dahlvig, CEO of IKEA between 1999–2009, described the IKEA culture as follows:

It is a very informal type of culture. It's based on a few values that have their roots in Smålandish or Swedish Culture. Things like informality, cost consciousness, and a very humble 'down to earth' approach. Also letting people have responsibilities. So there are a number of core values and intentions that we always describe in communication and training. For IKEA it has always been one very important part of our culture. We think that the organizational culture is important for the business and in some ways for industrial investors. We do give it a lot of attention in terms of marketing and sales as well as development, training and recruitment. The culture is a very important part of a company in the sense that the values of the culture really influence the business itself. I think it is pretty logical and transparent in our company, like cost consciousness for example. It is an important value that I think we have. It has a bearing on the company since it is our strategy to be a low-price company.

A critical method of ensuring continuity and consistency in the IKEA organizational culture is a strong focus is recruiting individuals with values that are aligned with those that the company wishes to embody. Additional insight into the IKEA organizational culture can be gleamed from the recruitment site of the IKEA website. Here, IKEA states what they look for in a job candidate:

An ability to get the job done is obviously the starting point. But beyond that we look for many other personal qualities such as the strong desire to learn, the motivation to continually do things better, simplicity and common sense, the ability to lead by example, efficiency and cost-consciousness. These values are important to us because our way of working is less structured than that of other organizations.

A Corporate Culture Based on shared Values

At IKEA, we do not just want to fill jobs; we want to partner with people. We want to recruit unique individuals who share our values. Co-workers are not restricted at IKEA; we listen and support each individual to identify his or her needs, ambitions and capabilities.

Here are a few of our shared values:

Togetherness, Cost-consciousness, Respect, Simplicity

Småland, where the company's founder was born and raised can be easily identified as the source of our shared values. Simplicity, humility, thrift and responsibility are all eveident in the lifestyle, attitude and customs of the place where IKEA began.

IKEA

When IKEA began as a mail order company in 1943, Ingvar Kamprad was only 17 years old. The IKEA concept as we know it today began in the 1950s, with catalogue marketing along with a showroom to allow customers to see and touch the products. The three distinct features were function, quality and low price. In the 1960s, the warehouse concept was introduced – customers could take the products from the shelves themselves. Internationalization began in 1963, with the first store opening in Norway. In 2012, IKEA is a market leader in home furnishing, with success on a global scale, operating with over 330 stores in 38 countries.

QUESTIONS

1. Why would it be important for an organization's long-term success to be truthful in their external statements about their organizational culture? Under what circumstances would you expect an organization to describe their organizational culture in a way that differs from reality?

2. What organizational culture challenges might IKEA face when operating globally?

Sources: www.IKEA.com (accessed 8 April 2012); Dahlvig, A., Kling, K. and Goteman, I. (2003) 'IKEA CEO Anders Dahlvig on international growth and IKEA's unique corporate culture and brand identity', *The Academy of Management Executive*, 17(1): 31–7.

In the previous two chapters, we examined six of the managerial tasks that drive good strategy execution: building a capable organization, bringing together the needed resources and steering them to strategy-critical operating units, establishing appropriate policies and procedures, driving continuous improvement in value chain activities, creating the necessary operating systems and providing the incentives needed to ensure employee commitment to the strategy execution process. In this chapter, we explore the two remaining managerial tasks that contribute to good strategy execution: creating a strategy-supportive organizational culture and providing the internal leadership needed to drive the implementation of strategic initiatives forward and achieve higher plateaus of operating excellence.

Instilling an Organizational Culture that Promotes Good Strategy Execution

Every organization has its own unique culture. The character of an organization's culture or work climate is a product of the core values and business principles that executives espouse, the standards of what is ethically acceptable and what is not, the work practices and norms of behaviour that define 'how we do things around here', the approach to people management and style of operating, the 'chemistry' and the 'personality' that permeates the work environment and the stories that get told over and over to illustrate and reinforce the organization's values, business practices, and traditions. The meshing together of shared values, beliefs, business principles and traditions into a style of operating, behavioural norms, ingrained attitudes and work atmosphere defines an organization's culture.[1] An organization's culture is important because it influences the organization's actions and approaches to conducting business – in a very real sense, the culture is the organization's automatic, self-replicating 'operating system' – it can be thought of as the organizational DNA.[2] As we learned in Chapter 4, a superior organizational culture can also be a source of sustainable competitive advantage under some circumstances.

> **Core Concept**
>
> **Organizational culture** refers to the character of an organization's internal work climate – as shaped by a system of *shared* values, beliefs, ethical standards and traditions that define behavioural norms, ingrained attitudes, accepted work practices and styles of operating.

Organizational cultures vary widely. For instance, the bedrock of Walmart's culture is dedication to the pursuit of low costs and frugal operating practices, a strong work ethic, ritualistic headquarters meetings to exchange ideas and review problems, and organization executives' commitment to visiting stores, listening to customers and soliciting suggestions from employees. General Electric's (GE's) culture is founded on a hard-driving, results-oriented atmosphere; extensive cross-business sharing of ideas, best practices and learning; reliance on 'workout sessions' to identify, debate and resolve burning issues; a commitment to Six Sigma quality; and a globalized approach to operations. At Nordstrom, the organizational culture is centred on delivering exceptional service to customers – the organization's motto is 'Respond to unreasonable customer requests', and each out-of-the-ordinary request is seen as an opportunity for a 'heroic' act by an employee that can further the organization's reputation for unparalleled customer service. Nordstrom makes a point of promoting employees noted for their heroic acts and dedication to outstanding service; the organization motivates its salespeople with a commission-based compensation system that enables Nordstrom's best salespeople to earn more than double what other department stores pay. Illustration Capsule 12.1 relates how Google and Alberto-Culver describe their organizational cultures.

Identifying the Key Features of an Organization's Culture

An organizational culture is mirrored in the character or 'personality' of its work environment – the factors that underlie how the organization tries to conduct its business and

Illustration Capsule 12.1

THE ORGANIZATIONAL CULTURES AT GOOGLE AND ALBERTO-CULVER

Founded in 1998 by Larry Page and Sergey Brin, two Ph.D. students in computer science at Stanford University, Google has become world-renowned for its search engine technology. Google.com was the most frequently visited Internet site in 2009, attracting over 844 million unique visitors monthly from around the world. Google has some unique ways of operating, and its culture is also rather quirky. The organization describes its culture as follows:

Though growing rapidly, Google still maintains a small organization feel. At lunchtime, almost everyone eats in the office café, sitting at whatever table has an opening and enjoying conversations with Googlers from different teams. Our commitment to innovation depends on everyone being comfortable sharing ideas and opinions. Every employee is a hands-on contributor, and everyone wears several hats. Because we believe that each Googler is an equally important part of our success, no one hesitates to pose questions directly to Larry or Sergey in our weekly all-hands ('TGIF') meetings – or spike a volleyball across the net at an organizational officer.

We are aggressively inclusive in our hiring, and we favour ability over experience. We have offices around the world and dozens of languages are spoken by Google staffers, from Turkish to Telugu. The result is a team that reflects the global audience Google serves. When not at work, Googlers pursue interests from cross-country cycling to wine tasting, from flying to frisbee.

As we continue to grow, we are always looking for those who share a commitment to creating search perfection and having a great time doing it.

Our organizational headquarters, fondly nicknamed the Googleplex, is located in Mountain View, California. Today it's one of our many offices around the globe. While our offices are not identical, they tend to share some essential elements. Here are a few things you might see in a Google workspace:

- *Local expressions of each location, from a mural in Buenos Aires to ski gondolas in Zurich, showcasing each office's region and personality.*
- *Bicycles or scooters for efficient travel between meetings; dogs; lava lamps; massage chairs; large inflatable balls.*
- *Googlers sharing cubes, yurts and huddle rooms – and very few solo offices.*
- *Laptops everywhere – standard issue for mobile coding, email on the go and note-taking.*
- *Foosball, pool tables, volleyball courts, assorted video games, pianos, ping pong tables, and gyms that offer yoga and dance classes.*
- *Grassroots employee groups for all interests, like meditation, film, wine tasting and salsa dancing.*
- *Healthy lunches and dinners for all staff at a variety of cafés.*
- *Break rooms packed with a variety of snacks and drinks to keep Googlers going.*

The Alberto-Culver Company, with fiscal 2009 revenues of more than €1.1 billion, is the producer and marketer of Alberto VO5, TRESemmé, Motions, Soft & Beautiful, Just for Me and Nexxus hair care products; St. Ives skin care products; and such brands as Molly McButter, Mrs. Dash, Sugar Twin and Static Guard. Alberto-Culver brands are sold in more than 120 countries.

At the careers section of its website, the organization described its culture in the following words:

Building careers is as important to us as building brands. We believe that passionate people create powerful growth. We believe in a workplace built on values and believe our best people display those same values in their families and their communities. We believe in recognizing and rewarding accomplishment and celebrating our victories.

We believe the best ideas work their way– quickly – up an organization, not down. We believe that we should take advantage of every ounce of your talent on teams and cross-functional activities, not just assign you to a box.

▶

We believe in open communication. We believe that you can improve what you measure, so we survey and spot check all the time. For that same reason, everyone has specific goals so that their expectations are in line with their managers' and the organization's.

We believe that victory is a team accomplishment. We believe in personal development. We believe if you talk with us you will catch our enthusiasm and want to be a part of the Alberto-Culver team.

Sources: Information posted at www.google.com and www.alberto.com (accessed 30 June 2010); McClellan, S. (2010) 'Alberto Culver launches global search: the client's annual U.S. ad spending alone touches $100 Mil', *Adweek*, 29 January. Available online at www. adweek.com/aw/content_display/news/account-activity/e3i68e64a3cf2727350dd0013083626e8ae.

the behaviours that are held in high esteem. Some of these factors are readily apparent, and others operate quite subtly. The main things to look for include the following:

LO 12.1
Identify the key features of an organization's culture and appreciate the role of an organization's core values and ethical standards in building organizational culture.

- The values, business principles and ethical standards that management preaches and *practices* – these are the key to an organization's culture, but actions speak much louder than words here.

- The organization's approach to people management and the official policies, procedures and operating practices that provide guidelines for the behaviour of employees.

- The atmosphere and spirit that pervades the work climate. Is the workplace vibrant and fun? Methodical and all business? Tense and harried? Highly competitive and politicized? Are people excited about their work and emotionally connected to the organization's business, or are they just there to get a salary? Is there an emphasis on empowered worker creativity, or do people have little discretion in how jobs are done?

- The way managers and employees interact and relate to one another – the reliance on teamwork and open communication, the extent to which there is good camaraderie, whether people are called by their first names, whether co-workers spend little or lots of time together outside the workplace and what the dress codes are (the accepted styles of attire).

- The strength of peer pressure to do things in particular ways and conform to expected norms – what actions and behaviours are encouraged on a peer-to-peer basis?

- The actions and behaviours that are explicitly encouraged and rewarded by management in the form of compensation and promotion.

- The organization's revered traditions and oft-repeated stories about 'heroic acts' and 'how we do things around here'.

- The manner in which the organization deals with external stakeholders (particularly vendors and local communities where it has operations) – whether it treats suppliers as business partners or prefers arm's-length business arrangements, and the strength and genuineness of the commitment to organizational citizenship and environmental sustainability.

The values, beliefs and practices that undergird an organization's culture can come from anywhere in the organizational hierarchy, most often representing the business philosophy and managerial style of influential executives but also resulting from exemplary actions on the part of organization personnel and consensus agreement about appropriate norms of behaviour.[3] Typically, key elements of the culture originate with a founder or certain strong leaders who articulated them as a set of business principles, organizational policies, operating approaches and ways of dealing with employees, customers, vendors, shareholders and local communities where the organization has operations. Over time, these cultural underpinnings take root, become embedded in how the organization conducts its business, come to be accepted by managers and employees alike, and then persist as new employees are encouraged to embrace the organization's values and adopt the implied attitudes, behaviours and work practices.

The Role of Core Values and Ethics

The foundation of an organizational culture nearly always resides in its dedication to certain core values and the bar it sets for ethical behaviour. The culture-shaping significance of core values and ethical behaviours accounts for one reason why so many companies have developed a formal values statement and a code of ethics. Many executives want the work climate at their organizations to mirror certain values and ethical standards, partly because they are personally committed to these values and ethical standards but also because they are convinced that adherence to such values and ethical principles will promote better strategy execution, make the organization a better performer and improve its image.[4] And, not incidentally, strongly ingrained values and ethical standards reduce the likelihood of lapses in ethical and socially approved behaviour that damage an organization's reputation and put its financial performance and market standing at risk, as discussed in Chapter 9.

As depicted in Figure 12.1, an organization's stated core values and ethical principles have two roles in the culture-building process. First, an organization that works hard at putting its stated core values and ethical principles into practice fosters a work climate in which organization personnel share strongly held convictions about how the organization's business is to be conducted. Second, the stated values and ethical principles provide employees with guidance about the manner in which they are to do their jobs — which behaviours and ways of doing things are approved (and expected) and which are out of bounds. These values-based and ethics-based cultural norms serve as measures for gauging the appropriateness of particular actions, decisions and behaviours, thus helping steer employees toward both doing things right and doing the right thing.

> An organization's culture is grounded in and shaped by its core values and ethical standards.

Transforming Core Values and Ethical Standards into Cultural Norms

Once values and ethical standards have been formally adopted, they must be institutionalized in the organization's policies and practices and embedded in the conduct of

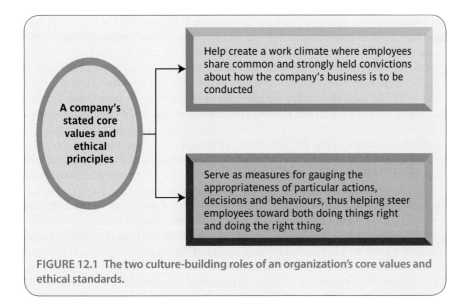

FIGURE 12.1 The two culture-building roles of an organization's core values and ethical standards.

> An organization's values statement and code of ethics communicate expectations of how employees should conduct themselves in the workplace.

employees. This can be done in a number of different ways.[5] Tradition-steeped companies with a rich folklore rely heavily on word-of-mouth indoctrination and the power of tradition to instil values and enforce ethical conduct. But most companies employ a variety of techniques, drawing on some or all of the following:

1. Giving explicit attention to values and ethics in recruiting and hiring to screen out applicants who do not exhibit compatible character traits.

2. Incorporating the statement of values and the code of ethics into orientation programmes for new employees and training courses for managers and employees.

3. Having senior executives frequently reiterate the importance and role of organizational values and ethical principles at events and in internal communications to employees.

4. Using values statements and codes of ethical conduct as benchmarks for judging the appropriateness of organizational policies and operating practices.

5. Making the display of core values and ethical principles a big factor in evaluating each person's job performance – there is no better way to gain attention and commitment of employees than by using the degree to which individuals observe core values and ethical standards as a basis for compensation increases and promotion.

6. Making sure managers, from the CEO down to front-line supervisors, are diligent in stressing the importance of ethical conduct and observance of core values. Line managers at all levels must give serious and continuous attention to the task of explaining how the values and ethical code apply in their areas.

7. Encouraging everyone to use his or her influence in helping enforce observance of core values and ethical standards – strong peer pressure to exhibit core values and ethical standards is a deterrent to wayward behaviour.

8. Periodically having ceremonial occasions to recognize individuals and groups who display the organizational values and ethical principles.

9. Instituting ethics enforcement procedures.

To deeply ingrain the stated core values and high ethical standards, companies must turn them into *strictly enforced cultural norms*. They must make it unequivocally clear that living up to the organization's values and ethical standards has to be 'a way of life' at the organization and that there will be little toleration of errant behaviour.

The Role of Stories

Frequently, a significant part of an organization's culture is captured in the stories that get told over and over again to illustrate to newcomers the importance of certain values and the depth of commitment that various employees have displayed. One of the stories at FedEx, world renowned for the reliability of its next-day package delivery guarantee, is about a deliveryman who had been given the wrong key to a FedEx drop box. Rather than leave the packages in the drop box until the next day when the right key was available, the deliveryman unbolted the drop box from its base, loaded it into the truck and took it back to the station. There, the box was pried open and the contents removed and sped on their way to their destination the next day. Nordstrom keeps a scrapbook commemorating the heroic acts of its employees and uses it as a regular reminder of the above-and-beyond-the-call-of-duty behaviours that employees are encouraged to display. When a customer was unable to find a shoe she was looking for at Nordstrom, a salesman found the shoe at a competing store and had it shipped to her at Nordstrom's expense.[6] At Frito-Lay, there are dozens of stories about truck drivers who went to extraordinary lengths in overcoming adverse weather conditions in order to make scheduled deliveries to retail customers and keep store shelves stocked with Frito-Lay products. At Microsoft, there are stories of the long hours programmers put in, the emotional peaks and valleys in encountering and overcoming coding problems, the exhilaration of completing a complex programme on schedule, the satisfaction of working on cutting-edge projects, the rewards of being part of a team responsible for a popular new software program and the tradition of competing aggressively. Such stories serve the valuable purpose of illustrating the kinds of behaviour the organization reveres and inspiring organization personnel to perform similarly. Moreover, each retelling of a legendary story puts a bit more peer pressure on organization personnel to display core values and do their part in keeping the organization's traditions alive.

Perpetuating the Culture

Once established, organizational cultures are perpetuated in six important ways: (1) by screening and selecting new employees that will fit in well with the culture; (2) by systematic coaching of new members in the culture's fundamentals; (3) by the efforts of senior managers to reiterate core values in daily conversations and pronouncements; (4) by the telling and retelling of organizational legends; (5) by regular ceremonies honouring employees who display desired cultural behaviours; and (6) by visibly rewarding those who display cultural norms and penalizing those who do not.[7] *The more new employees an organization employ's, the more important it becomes to screen job applicants every bit as much for how well their values, beliefs and personalities match up with the culture as for their technical skills and experience.* For example, an organization that stresses operating with integrity and fairness has to employ people who themselves have integrity and place a high value on fair play. An organization whose culture revolves around creativity, product innovation and leading change has to screen new employees for their ability to think outside the box, generate new ideas and thrive in a climate of rapid change and ambiguity. Qatar Airlines, one of the only airlines in the world with a five-star rating ensure that this level is maintained by going to considerable lengths to employ the right cabin crew. Qatar Air explicitly recruit individuals with resilience and who are committed to a high degree of personal fitness and well-being, while exuding warmth, charisma and professionalism. Fast-growing companies risk creating a culture by chance rather than by design if they rush to employ people mainly for their talents and credentials and neglect to screen candidates whose values, philosophies and personalities are not a good fit with the organizational character, vision and strategy being articulated by senior executives.

As a rule, organizations are careful to employ people who they believe will fit in and embrace the prevailing culture. And, usually, job-seekers lean toward accepting jobs at organizations where they feel comfortable with the atmosphere and the people they will be working with. Employees who do not fit in well at an organization tend to leave quickly, while employees who thrive and are pleased with the work environment stay on, eventually moving up the ranks to positions of greater responsibility. The longer people stay at an organization, the more they come to embrace and mirror the organizational culture – their values and beliefs tend to be moulded by mentors, co-workers, organizational training programmes and the reward structure. Normally, employees who have worked at an organization for a long time play a major role in coaching new employees into the culture.

Forces that Cause an Organization's Culture to Evolve

However, cultures are not static – just like strategy and organization structure they evolve. New challenges in the marketplace, revolutionary technologies and shifting internal conditions – especially eroding business prospects, an internal crisis or top executive turnover – tend to breed new ways of doing things and, in turn, drive cultural evolution. An incoming CEO who decides to shake up the existing business and take it in new directions often triggers a cultural shift, perhaps one of major proportions. Likewise, diversification into new businesses, expansion into foreign countries, rapid growth that brings an influx of new employees and merger with or acquisition of another organization can all precipitate significant cultural change.

A Different View

SCHEIN'S LEVELS OF CULTURE

Edgar Schein identifies three distinct levels in organizational cultures:

1. artefacts and behaviours;
2. espoused values;
3. assumptions.

The three levels refer to the degree to which the different cultural phenomena are visible to the observer, and can be used as a basis to 'map', interpret and understand the culture of an organization (see Figure 12.2).

Artefacts are the most visible level and include any tangible, overt or verbally identifiable elements in an organization. The way people dress, the office architecture, furniture layout and office jokes all exemplify organizational artefacts. Artefacts are the visible elements in a culture and they can be observed by people not part of the culture, but can be difficult for outsiders to decipher.

Espoused values are the organization's stated values and rules of behaviour. It is how the members represent the organization both to themselves and to others. This is often expressed in official philosophies and public statements of identity. It can sometimes be a projection for the future, of what the members hope to become. Examples of this would be employee professionalism, or a 'family first' mantra.

Shared basic assumptions are deeply embedded, taken-for-granted beliefs and facts. They are usually unconscious, but constitute the essence of culture. These assumptions are typically so well integrated in the office dynamic that they are hard to recognize from within. To really understand culture, we have to get to this deepest level, the level of **assumptions** and **beliefs**. Schein contends that underlying assumptions grow out of values, until they become taken for granted and drop out of awareness.

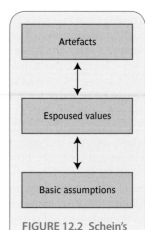

FIGURE 12.2 Schein's three levels of organizational culture.

Source: Schein, E. (2010) *Organizational Culture and Leadership*, San Francisco, CA, Jossey-Bass.

Organizational Cultures can be Strongly or Weakly Embedded

Organizational cultures vary widely in strength and influence. Some are strongly embedded and have a big influence on an organization's operating practices and the behaviour of employees. Others are weakly ingrained and have little effect on behaviours and how activities are conducted.

Strong-culture Companies

Core Concept

In a **strong-culture company**, deeply rooted values and norms of behaviour are widely shared and regulate the conduct of the organization's business.

The main feature of a **strong-culture company** is the dominating presence of certain deeply rooted values, behavioural norms and operating approaches that are widely shared and 'regulate' the conduct of an organization's business and the climate of its workplace.[8] Strong cultures emerge over a period of years (sometimes decades) and are never an overnight phenomenon. In strong-culture companies, senior managers make a point of reiterating the organization's principles and values to organization members and explaining how they relate to its business environment. But, more importantly, the managers make a conscious effort to display these principles in their own actions and behaviour – they walk the talk and *insist* that *organizational values* *and business principles be reflected in the decisions and actions taken by all employees.* An unequivocal expectation that employees will act and behave in accordance with the adopted values and ways of doing business leads to two important outcomes: (1) over time, the values come to be widely shared by employees – people who dislike the culture tend to leave – and (2) individuals encounter strong peer pressure from co-workers to observe the culturally approved norms and behaviours. Hence, a strongly implanted organizational culture ends up having a powerful influence on behaviour because so many employees are accepting of cultural traditions and because this acceptance is reinforced by both management expectations and co-worker peer pressure to conform to cultural norms.

Two factors contribute to the development of strong cultures: (1) a founder or strong leader who established core values, principles and practices that are viewed as having contributed to the success of the organization; and (2) a sincere, long-standing organizational commitment to operating the business according to these established traditions and values, thereby creating an internal environment that supports decision-making based on cultural norms. Continuity of leadership, low workforce turnover, geographic concentration and considerable organizational success all contribute to the emergence and sustainability of a strong culture.[9]

In strong-culture companies, values and behavioural norms are so ingrained that they can endure leadership changes at the top – although their strength can erode over time if new CEOs cease to nurture them or move aggressively to institute cultural adjustments. The cultural norms in a strong-culture organization typically do not change much as strategy evolves, either because the culture constrains the choice of new strategies or because the dominant traits of the culture are somewhat strategy-neutral and compatible with evolving versions of the organization's strategy.

Weak-culture Companies

In direct contrast to strong-culture companies, weak-culture companies lack values and principles that are consistently preached or widely shared (sometimes because the organization has had a series of CEOs with differing values and differing views about how the organization's business ought to be conducted). As a consequence, few widely revered traditions and few culture-induced norms are evident in employee behaviour or operating practices. Because top executives at a weak-culture organization do not repeatedly espouse any particular business philosophy or exhibit long-standing commitment to particular values or behavioural norms, individuals encounter little pressure to do things in particular ways. A weak organizational culture breeds no strong employee allegiance to what the organization stands for or to operating the business in well-defined ways. While individual employees may well have some bonds of identification with and loyalty toward their department, their colleagues, their union or their immediate boss, there is neither passion about the organization nor emotional commitment to what it is trying to accomplish – a condition that often results in many employees viewing their organization as just a place to work and their job as just a way to make a living.

As a consequence, *weak cultures provide little or no assistance in executing strategy* because there are no traditions, beliefs, values, common bonds or behavioural norms that management can use as levers to mobilize commitment to executing the chosen strategy. The only plus of a weak culture is that it does not usually pose a strong barrier to strategy execution, but the negative of not providing any support means that culture-building has to be high on management's action agenda. Without a work climate that channels organizational energy in the direction of good strategy execution, managers are left with the options of either using compensation incentives and other motivational devices to mobilize employee commitment, supervising and monitoring employee actions more closely, or trying to establish cultural roots that will in time start to nurture the strategy execution process.

Cultural Web

While organizational culture can be elusive, approaches have been developed to help us look at it in a systematic way. Such approaches can play a key role in formulating strategy or planning change.

The cultural web provides one such approach for examining and changing an organization's culture. Using it, cultural assumptions and practices can be exposed and the organizational elements can be aligned with one another, and with the strategy.

The cultural web identifies six interrelated elements that help to make up the paradigm of the organizations internal environment. By analysing the factors in each, the bigger picture of the culture emerges: what is working, what is not working and what needs to be changed. The six elements are:

1. **Stories** – the past events and people talked about inside and outside the company. Who and what the company chooses to immortalize says a great deal about what it values, and perceives as the right behaviour.

2. **Rituals and routines** – the daily behaviour and actions of people that signal acceptable behaviour. This determines what is expected to happen in given situations, and what management values.

3. **Symbols** – the visual representations of the company including, for example, logos, the offices and the dress codes.

4. **Organizational structure** – this includes both the structure defined by the organization chart, and the unwritten lines of power and influence that indicate whose contributions are most valued.

5. **Control systems** – the ways that the organization is controlled. These include financial systems, quality systems and rewards (including the way they are measured and distributed within the organization.)

6. **Power structures** – The pockets of real power in the company. This may involve one or two key senior executives, a whole group of executives or even a department. The key is that these people have the greatest amount of influence on decisions, operations and strategic direction.

These elements combine to influence the cultural paradigm (see Figure 12.3).

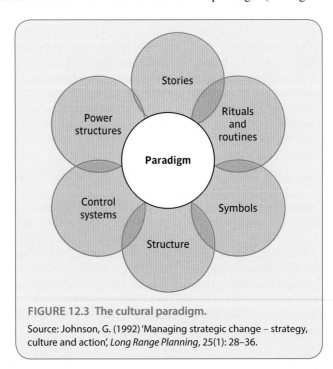

FIGURE 12.3 The cultural paradigm.

Source: Johnson, G. (1992) 'Managing strategic change – strategy, culture and action', *Long Range Planning*, 25(1): 28–36.

Why Organizational Cultures Matter to the Strategy Execution Process

Unlike weak cultures, strong cultures can have a powerful effect on the strategy execution process. This effect may be *positive or negative* since an organization's present culture and work climate may or may not be compatible with what is needed for effective implementation and execution of the chosen strategy. When an organization's present culture promotes attitudes, behaviours and ways of doing things that are conducive to first-rate strategy execution, the culture functions as a valuable support in the strategy execution process.

For example, an organizational culture characterized by frugality and thrift, such as that found at IKEA, nurtures employee actions to identify cost-saving opportunities – the very behaviour needed for successful execution of a low-cost leadership strategy. A culture built around such business principles as outstanding customer satisfaction, operating excellence and employee empowerment promotes employee behaviours and an *esprit de corps* that facilitate execution of strategies linked to high-product quality and superior customer service. A culture in which taking initiative, exhibiting creativity, taking risks and embracing change are the behavioural norms is conducive to successful execution of product innovation and technological leadership strategies.[10]

A culture that is grounded in actions, behaviours and work practices that are conducive to good strategy implementation assists the strategy execution effort in three ways:[11]

1. *A culture that is well matched to the requirements of the strategy execution effort focuses the attention of employees on what is most important to this effort.* Moreover, it directs their behaviour and serves as a guide to their decision-making. In this manner, it can align the efforts and decisions of employees throughout the firm and minimize the need for direct supervision.

2. *Culture-induced peer pressure further induces employees to do things in a manner that aids the cause of good strategy execution.* The stronger the culture (the more widely shared and deeply held the values), the more effective peer pressure is in shaping and supporting the strategy execution effort. Research has shown that strong group norms can shape employee behaviour even more powerfully than can financial incentives.[12]

3. *An organizational culture that is consistent with the requirements for good strategy execution can energize employees, deepen their commitment to execute the strategy flawlessly and enhance worker productivity in the process.* When an organization's culture is grounded in many of the needed strategy-executing behaviours, employees feel genuinely better about their jobs, the organization they work for and the merits of what the organization is trying to accomplish. As a consequence, greater numbers of employees exhibit passion in their work and exert their best efforts to execute the strategy and achieve performance targets.

In contrast, when a culture is in conflict with what is required to execute the organization's strategy well, a strong culture becomes a hindrance to the success of the implementation effort.[13] Some of the very behaviours needed to execute the strategy successfully run contrary to the attitudes, behaviours and operating practices embedded in the prevailing culture. Such a clash poses a real dilemma for employees. Should they be loyal to the culture and organizational traditions (to which they are likely to be emotionally attached) and thus resist or be indifferent to actions that will promote better strategy execution – a choice that will certainly weaken the drive for good strategy execution? Alternatively, should they go along with the strategy execution effort and engage in actions that run counter to the culture – a choice that will likely impair morale and lead to a less-than-wholehearted commitment to management's strategy execution efforts? Neither choice leads to desirable outcomes. Culture-bred resistance to the actions and behaviours needed for good strategy execution, particularly if strong

LO 12.2
Understand how and why an organization's culture can support proficient strategy execution and operating excellence.

A strong culture that encourages actions, behaviours and work practices conducive to good strategy execution adds significantly to the power and effectiveness of an organization's strategy execution effort.

and widespread, poses a formidable hurdle that must be cleared for a strategy's execution to get very far.

This says something important about the task of managing the strategy execution process: *Closely aligning organizational culture with the requirements for proficient strategy execution merits the full attention of senior executives.* The culture-building objective is to create a work climate and style of operating that mobilize the energy and behaviour of employees squarely behind efforts to execute strategy competently. The more deeply that management can embed execution-supportive ways of doing things, the more that management can rely on the culture to automatically steer employees toward behaviours and work practices that aid good strategy execution and veer from doing things that impede it. Moreover, culturally astute managers understand that nourishing the right cultural environment not only adds power to their push for proficient strategy execution but also promotes strong employee identification with and commitment to the organization's vision, performance targets and strategy.

> It is in management's best interest to dedicate considerable effort in establishing an organizational culture that encourages behaviours and work practices conducive to good strategy execution.

Healthy Cultures that Aid Good Strategy Execution

A strong culture, provided it embraces execution-supportive attitudes, behaviours and work practices, is definitely a healthy culture. Two other types of cultures exist that tend to be healthy and largely supportive of good strategy execution: high-performance cultures and adaptive cultures.

High-performance Cultures

Some companies have so-called high-performance cultures where the stand-out traits are a 'can-do' spirit, pride in doing things right, no-excuses accountability and a pervasive results-oriented work climate in which people go all out to meet or beat stretch objectives.[14] In high-performance cultures, there is a strong sense of involvement on the part of employees and emphasis on individual initiative and effort. Performance expectations are clearly delineated for the organization as a whole, for each organizational unit and for each individual. Issues and problems are promptly addressed; there is a focus on what needs to be done. The clear and unyielding expectation is that all employees, from senior executives to front-line employees, will display high-performance behaviours and a passion for making the organization successful. Such a culture – supported by constructive pressure to achieve good results – is a valuable contributor to good strategy execution and operating excellence. Results-oriented cultures are permeated with a spirit of achievement and have a good track record in meeting or beating performance targets.[15]

The challenge in creating a high-performance culture is to inspire high loyalty and dedication on the part of employees, such that they are energized to put forward their very best efforts to do things right and be unusually productive. Managers have to reinforce constructive behaviour, reward top performers and get rid of habits and behaviours that stand in the way of high productivity and good results. They must work at knowing the strengths and weaknesses of their subordinates, so as to better match talent with task and enable people to make meaningful contributions by doing what they do best.[16] They have to stress learning from mistakes and building on strengths and must put an emphasis on moving forward and making good progress; in effect, there has to be a disciplined, performance-focused approach to managing the organization.

Adaptive Cultures

The hallmark of adaptive organizational cultures is willingness on the part of organization members to accept change and take on the challenge of introducing and executing new strategies.[17] Employees share a feeling of confidence that the organization can deal with whatever threats and opportunities arise; they are receptive to risk-taking, experimentation, innovation and changing strategies and practices. The work climate is supportive of managers and employees at all ranks who propose or initiate useful change. Internal entrepreneurship on the part of individuals and groups is encouraged and rewarded. Senior executives seek out, support and promote individuals who exercise initiative, spot opportunities for improvement and display the skills to implement them. Managers openly evaluate ideas and suggestions, fund initiatives to develop new or better products and take prudent risks to pursue emerging market opportunities. As in high-performance cultures, the organization exhibits a proactive approach to identifying issues, evaluating the implications and options and moving ahead quickly with workable solutions. Strategies and traditional operating practices are modified as needed to adjust to or take advantage of changes in the business environment.

But why is change so willingly embraced in an adaptive culture? Why are organization members not fearful of how change will affect them? Why does an adaptive culture not break down from the force of ongoing changes in strategy, operating practices and approaches to strategy execution? The answers lie in two distinctive and dominant traits of an adaptive culture: (1) any changes in operating practices and behaviours must *not* compromise core values and long-standing business principles (since they are at the root of the culture); and (2) the changes that are instituted must satisfy the legitimate interests of stakeholders – customers, employees, shareowners, suppliers and the communities where the organization operates.[18] In other words, what sustains an adaptive culture is that organization members perceive the changes that management is trying to institute as *legitimate* and in keeping with the core values and business principles that form the heart and soul of the culture.[19] Not surprisingly, employees are usually more receptive to change when their employment security is not threatened and when they view new duties or job assignments as part of the process of adapting to new conditions. Should workforce downsizing be necessary, it is important that job losses be handled humanely and employee departures be made as painless as possible.

> As an organization's strategy evolves, an adaptive culture is a definite support in the strategy-implementing, strategy-executing process as compared to cultures that are resistant to change.

Technology companies, software companies and Internet-based companies are good illustrations of organizations with adaptive cultures. Such companies thrive on change – driving it, leading it and capitalizing on it. Companies like Google, Intel, Cisco Systems, eBay, Amazon.com and Apple cultivate the capability to act and react rapidly. They are avid practitioners of entrepreneurship and innovation, with a demonstrated willingness to take bold risks to create altogether new products, new businesses and new industries. To create and nurture a culture that can adapt rapidly to shifting business conditions, they make a point of staffing their organizations with people who are flexible, who rise to the challenge of change, and who have an aptitude for adapting well to new circumstances.

In fast-changing business environments, an organizational culture that is receptive to altering organizational practices and behaviours is a virtual necessity. However, adaptive cultures work to the advantage of all companies, not just those in rapid-change environments. Every organization operates in a market and business climate that is changing to one degree or another and that, in turn, requires internal operating responses and new behaviours on the part of organization members.

Unhealthy Cultures that Impede Good Strategy Execution

The distinctive characteristic of an unhealthy organizational culture is the presence of counter-productive cultural traits that adversely impact the work climate and organizational performance.[20] Five particularly unhealthy cultural traits are hostility to change, heavily politicized decision-making, insular thinking, behaviours that are driven by greed and a disregard for ethical standards and the presence of incompatible, clashing subcultures.

Change-resistant Cultures

In contrast to adaptive cultures, change-resistant cultures – where scepticism about the importance of new developments and a fear of change are the norm – place a premium on not making mistakes, prompting managers to lean toward safe, conservative options intended to maintain the status quo, protect their power base and guard the interests of their immediate workgroups. When such organizations encounter business environments with accelerating change, going slow on altering traditional ways of doing things can be a serious liability. Under these conditions, change-resistant cultures encourage a number of undesirable or unhealthy behaviours – viewing circumstances myopically, avoiding risks, not capitalizing on emerging opportunities, taking a lax approach to both product innovation and continuous improvement in performing value chain activities and responding more slowly than is warranted to market change. In change-resistant cultures, word quickly gets around that proposals to do things differently face an uphill battle and that people who champion them may be seen as something of a nuisance. Executives who do not value managers or employees with initiative and new ideas put a damper on product innovation, experimentation and efforts to improve. At the same time, change-resistant organizations have little appetite for being first movers or fast followers, believing that being in the forefront of change is too risky and that acting too quickly increases vulnerability to costly mistakes. Hostility to change is most often found in companies with multi-layered management bureaucracies that have enjoyed considerable market success in years past and that are wedded to the 'We have done it this way for years' syndrome. Before filing bankruptcy in 2009, General Motors was a classic example of an organization whose change-resistant bureaucracy was slow to adapt to fundamental changes in its markets, preferring to cling to the traditions, operating practices and business approaches that had at one time made it the global industry leader.

Politicized Cultures

What makes a politicized internal environment so unhealthy is that political infighting consumes a great deal of organizational energy, often with the result that what is best for the organization takes a backseat to political manoeuvring. In organizations where internal politics pervades the work climate, empire-building managers jealously guard their decision-making prerogatives. They have their own agendas and operate the work units under their supervision as autonomous 'fiefdoms'; the positions they take on issues are usually aimed at protecting or expanding their own turf. Collaboration with other organizational units is viewed with suspicion, and cross-unit co-operation occurs grudgingly. The support or opposition of politically influential executives and/or coalitions among departments with vested interests in a particular outcome tends to shape what actions the organization takes. All this political manoeuvring takes away energy from efforts to execute strategy with real proficiency and frustrates employees who are less political and more inclined to do what is in the organization's best interests.

Insular, Inwardly Focused Cultures

Sometimes an organization reigns as an industry leader or enjoys great market success for so long that its employees start to believe they have all the answers or can develop them on their own. There is a strong tendency to neglect what customers are saying and how their needs and expectations are changing. Such confidence in the correctness of its approach to business and an unflinching belief in the organization's competitive superiority breeds arrogance, prompting employees to discount the merits of what outsiders are doing and the payoff from studying best-in-class performers. Insular thinking, internally driven solutions and a must-be-invented-here mind-set come to permeate the organizational culture. An inwardly focused organizational culture gives rise to managerial inbreeding and a failure to recruit people who can offer fresh thinking and outside perspectives. The big risk of insular cultural thinking is that the organization can underestimate the capabilities and accomplishments of rival companies and overestimate its own progress – until its loss of market position makes the realities obvious.

Unethical and Greed-driven Cultures

Organizations that have little regard for ethical standards or that are run by executives driven by greed and ego gratification are scandals waiting to happen, as discussed in Chapter 9. Executives exude the negatives of arrogance, ego, greed and an 'ends-justify-the-means' mentality in pursuing stretch revenue and profitability targets.[21] Senior managers wink at unethical behaviour and may cross over the line to unethical (and sometimes criminal) behaviour themselves. They are prone to adopt accounting principles that make financial performance look better than it really is. Legions of companies have fallen prey to unethical behaviour and greed, most notably WorldCom, Enron, Quest, HealthSouth, Adelphia, Tyco, Parmalat, Rite Aid, Hollinger International, Refco, Marsh & McLennan, Siemens, Countrywide Financial and Stanford Financial Group, with executives being indicted and/or convicted of criminal behaviour.

Incompatible Subcultures

Although it is common to speak about organizational culture in the singular, it is not unusual for organizations to have multiple cultures (or subcultures).[22] Values, beliefs and practices within an organization sometimes vary significantly by department, geographic location, division or business unit. As long as the subcultures are compatible with the overarching organizational culture and are supportive of the strategy execution efforts, this is not problematic. Multiple cultures pose an unhealthy situation when they are composed of incompatible subcultures that embrace conflicting business philosophies, support inconsistent approaches to strategy execution and encourage incompatible methods of people management. Clashing subcultures can prevent an organization from co-ordinating its efforts to craft and execute strategy and can distract employees from the business of business. When incompatible subcultures encourage the emergence of warring factions within the organization, they are not just unhealthy – they are downright poisonous.

Incompatible subcultures arise most commonly because of important cultural differences between an organization's culture and that of a recently acquired organization or because of a merger between companies with cultural differences. Organizations with M&A experience are quite alert to the importance of cultural compatibility in making acquisitions and the need to integrate the cultures of newly acquired companies – cultural due diligence is often as important as financial due diligence in deciding whether to go forward on an acquisition or merger. On a number of occasions, organizations decided to pass on acquiring particular companies because of culture conflicts they believed would be hard to resolve.

A Different View

A TAXONOMY OF ORGANIZATIONAL CULTURE

Charles Handy (1996)[23] suggests that we can classify organizations into a broad range of four cultures. The formation of culture will depend on many factors including organizational history, ownership, organizational structure, technology, critical business incidents and environment and so on.

The purpose of the analysis is to assess the degree to which the predominant culture reflects the real needs and constraints of the organization. The four cultures identified are 'power', 'role', 'task' and 'people'.

▶

◀

THE POWER CULTURE

The power culture is described as a 'web'. This reflects the concentration of power of a family-owned business, which can either be extremely large or small. The family operation with strict responsibilities going to family members and responsibility given to personalities rather than expertise creates the power structure of the 'web'.

Power is concentrated in a small area, the centre of which is the wheel or the centre of the web. Power radiates out from the centre, usually a key personality, to others in the family who send information down to departments, functions or units.

The important point to note is that because power and decision-making is concentrated in just a few hands, the strategists and key family members create situations that others have to implement. It is difficult for others outside the 'family network' to influence events.

The ability of the power culture to adapt to changes in the environment is very much determined by the perception and ability of those who occupy the positions of power within it. The power culture has more faith in individuals than committees and can either change very rapidly and adapt or 'fail to see the need for change' and die.

THE ROLE CULTURE

This is typified as a Greek temple and is stereotyped as portraying bureaucracy in its purest form. The apex of the temple is where the decision-making takes place, the pillars of the temple reflect the functional units of the organization that have to implement the decisions from the apex. The strength of the culture lies in specialization within its pillars. Interaction takes place between the functional specialism by job descriptions, procedures, rules and systems. Authority is not based on personal initiative but is dictated by job descriptions.

Co-ordination is by a narrow band of senior staff. This is the only co-ordination required as the system provides the necessary integration. In this culture, the job description is more important than the skills and abilities of the people. Performance beyond the role prescription is not required or encouraged.

The authority of position power is legitimate. Personal power is not. System effectiveness depends on adherence to principles rather than personalities.

This culture is appropriate in organizations that are not subject to constant change. The culture functions well in a stable environment, but is insecure in times of change. The role culture is typified in government departments, local authorities, public utilities and the public sector in general. This sort of culture finds it extremely difficult to change rapidly. The role culture is typified by rationality and size.

THE TASK CULTURE

This is characteristic of organizations that are involved in extensive research and development (R&D) activities and they are much more dynamic. They are constantly subject to change and have to create temporary task teams to meet their future needs. Information and expertise are the skills that are of value here. The culture is represented best by a net. There is a close liaison between departments, functions and specialities. Liaison, communication and integration are the means whereby the organization can anticipate and adapt to change quickly.

Influence in this team culture is based upon expertise and up-to-date information. The dangers for this culture exist when there is a restriction in resources causing it to become more 'power'- or 'role'-oriented.

THE PERSON CULTURE

This is characteristic of the consensus model of management, where the individuals within the structure determine collectively the path that the organization pursues. If there is a formalized structure, it tends to service the needs of the individuals within the structure. Organizations that portray this culture reject formal hierarchies for 'getting things done' and exist solely to meet the needs of their members. Formal 'management control' and 'reporting relationships' are mainly rejected within this culture, and it is therefore not ideally suited for organizations focused on profit maximization.

▶

◀

THE RIGHT CULTURE

Handy's typologies of organization structures suggest that the culture should be matched with the external demands and constraints on the organization.

One factor that must be kept in mind is that different operating units within the organization require different structures. Some units or functions will be operating in a steady-state environment, where there are very few changes and the future is reasonably predictable, whereas others are subject to a great deal of change not just in what they do but also in how they do it. Consequently, it is desirable to have different approaches to managing and different 'cultures' in different units.

Source: Handy, C. (1996) *Gods of Management: The Changing Work of Organizations*, Oxford, Oxford University Press.

Changing a Problem Culture: The Role of Leadership

When a strong culture is unhealthy or otherwise out of sync with the actions and behaviours needed to execute the strategy successfully, the culture must be changed as rapidly as can be managed. While correcting a strategy-culture conflict can occasionally mean revamping an organization's approach to strategy execution to better fit the organization's culture, more usually it means altering aspects of the mismatched culture to better enable first-rate strategy execution. The more entrenched the mismatched or unhealthy aspects of an organization culture, the more likely the culture will impede strategy execution and the greater the need for change.

Changing a problem culture is among the toughest management tasks because of the heavy anchor of ingrained behaviours and attitudes. It is natural for employees to cling to familiar practices and to be wary, if not hostile, to new approaches of how things are to be done. Consequently, it takes concerted management action over a period of time to root out unconstructive behaviours and replace them with new ways of doing things deemed more conducive to executing the strategy.

The single most visible factor that distinguishes successful culture-change efforts from failed attempts is competent leadership at the top. Great power is needed to force major cultural change and overcome the resistance of entrenched cultures – and great power is possessed only by the most senior executives, especially the CEO. However, while top management must be out front leading the effort, marshalling support for a new culture and instilling the desired cultural behaviours is a job for the whole management team. Middle managers and front-line supervisors play a key role in implementing the new work practices and operating approaches, helping gain acceptance of and support for the desired behavioural norms.

As shown in Figure 12.4, the first step in fixing a problem culture is for top management to identify those facets of the present culture that are dysfunctional and pose obstacles to executing new strategic initiatives and meeting organizational performance targets. Second, managers must clearly define the desired new behaviours and features of the culture they want to create. Third, managers have to convince employees of why the present culture poses problems and why and how new behaviours and operating approaches will improve organizational performance – the case for cultural reform has to be persuasive. Fourth, and most important, all the talk about remodelling the present culture has to be followed swiftly by visible, forceful actions to promote the desired new behaviours and work practices – actions that employees will interpret as a determined top management commitment to bring about a different work climate and new ways of operating.

Making a Compelling Case for Culture Change

The way for management to begin a major remodelling of the organizational culture is by convincing employees of the need for new-style behaviours and work practices.

LO 12.3
Identify the kinds of actions management can take to change a problematic organizational culture.

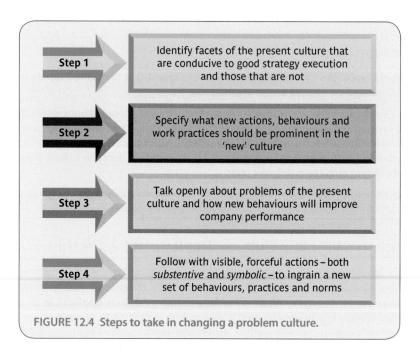

Step 1 Identify facets of the present culture that are conducive to good strategy execution and those that are not

Step 2 Specify what new actions, behaviours and work practices should be prominent in the 'new' culture

Step 3 Talk openly about problems of the present culture and how new behaviours will improve company performance

Step 4 Follow with visible, forceful actions – both *substentive* and *symbolic* – to ingrain a new set of behaviours, practices and norms

FIGURE 12.4 Steps to take in changing a problem culture.

This means making a compelling case for why the culture-remodelling efforts are in the organization's best interests and why employees should support the effort to doing things somewhat differently. Sceptics and opinion leaders have to be convinced that all is not well with the current situation. This can be done by:

- explaining why and how certain behavioural norms and work practices in the current culture pose obstacles to good execution of strategic initiatives;
- explaining how new behaviours and work practices will be more advantageous and produce better results. Effective culture-change leaders are good at telling stories to describe the new values and desired behaviours and connect them to everyday practices;
- citing reasons why the current strategy has to be modified, if the need for cultural change is due to a change in strategy. This includes explaining why the new strategic initiatives will improve the organizations' competitiveness and performance and how a change in culture can help in executing the new strategy.

It is essential for the CEO and other top executives to talk personally to employees all across the organization about the reasons for modifying work practices and culture-related behaviours. Senior officers and department heads have to play a lead role in explaining the need for a change in behavioural norms to those they manage – and the explanations will likely have to be repeated many times. For the culture-change effort to be successful, front-line supervisors and employee opinion leaders must be convinced of the merits of *practising* and *enforcing* cultural norms at every level of the organization, from the highest to the lowest. Arguments for new ways of doing things and new work practices tend to be embraced more readily if employees understand how they will benefit stakeholders (particularly customers, employees and shareholders). Until a large majority of employees accept the need for a new culture and agree that different work practices and behaviours are called for, there is more work to be done in convincing on the whys and wherefores of culture change. Building widespread organizational support requires taking every opportunity to repeat the message of why the new work practices, operating approaches, and behaviours are good for stakeholders.

Management's efforts to make a persuasive case for changing what is deemed to be a problem culture must be *followed quickly* by forceful, high-profile actions across several fronts. The actions to implant the new culture must be both substantive and symbolic.

Substantive Culture-changing Actions

No culture change effort can get very far with just talk about the need for different actions, behaviours and work practices. Executives must give the culture-change effort some credibility by initiating *a series of actions* that employees will see as unmistakably indicative of the seriousness of management's commitment to cultural change. The strongest signs that management is truly committed to instilling a new culture include:

- replacing key executives who are stonewalling needed organizational and cultural changes;
- promoting individuals who have stepped forward to advocate the shift to a different culture and who can serve as role models for the desired cultural behaviour;
- appointing outsiders with the desired cultural attributes to high-profile positions – bringing in new-breed managers sends an unmistakable message that a new era is dawning;
- screening all candidates for new positions carefully, hiring only those who appear to fit in with the new culture;
- mandating that all employees attend culture-training programmes to learn more about the new work practices and to better understand the culture-related actions and behaviours that are expected;
- designing compensation incentives that boost the pay of teams and individuals who display the desired cultural behaviours. Employees are more inclined to exhibit the desired kinds of actions and behaviours when it is in their financial best interest to do so;
- revising policies and procedures in ways that will help drive cultural change.

Executives must take care to launch enough organization-wide culture-change actions at the outset so as to leave no room for doubt that management is serious about changing the present culture and that a cultural transformation is inevitable. The series of actions initiated by top management must create lots of corridor talk across the whole organization, get the change process off to a fast start and be followed by unrelenting efforts to firmly establish the new work practices, desired behaviours and style of operating as 'standard'.

Symbolic Culture-changing Actions

There is also an important place for symbolic managerial actions to alter a problematic culture and tighten the strategy-culture fit. The most important symbolic actions are those that top executives take to *lead by example*. For instance, if the organization's strategy involves a drive to become the industry's low-cost producer, senior managers must display frugality in their own actions and decisions: inexpensive decorations in the executive suite, conservative expense accounts and entertainment allowances, a lean staff in the office, scrutiny of budget requests, few executive perks and so on. At Walmart, all the executive offices are simply decorated; executives are habitually frugal in their own actions, and they are zealous in their efforts to control costs and promote greater efficiency. At Nucor, one of the world's low-cost producers of steel products, executives fly economy class and use taxis at airports rather than limousines. If the culture-change imperative is to be more responsive to customers' needs and to pleasing customers, the CEO can instil greater customer awareness by requiring all officers and executives to spend a significant portion of each week talking with customers about their needs. Top executives must be alert to the fact that other employees will be watching their actions and decisions to see if their actions match their rhetoric. Hence, they need to make sure their current decisions and behaviours will be construed as consistent with the new-culture values and norms.[23]

Another category of symbolic actions includes holding ceremonial events to single out and honour people whose actions and performance exemplify what is called for in the new culture. A point is made of holding events to celebrate each culture-change success (and any other outcome that management would like to see happen again). Executives sensitive to their role in promoting strategy-culture fit make a habit of appearing at ceremonial functions to praise individuals and groups that exemplify the desired behaviours. They show up at employee training programmes to stress strategic priorities, values, ethical principles and cultural norms. Every group gathering is seen as an opportunity to repeat and ingrain values, praise good deeds, expound on the merits of the new culture and cite instances of how the new work practices and operating approaches have worked to good advantage.

The use of symbols in culture-building is widespread. Many universities give outstanding teacher awards each year to symbolize their commitment to good teaching and their esteem for instructors who display exceptional classroom talents. Numerous businesses have employee-of-the-month awards. The military has a long-standing custom of awarding ribbons and medals for exemplary actions. Oriflame awards an array of prizes ceremoniously to its beauty consultants for reaching various sales levels.

How Long Does It Take to Change a Problem Culture?

Planting and growing the seeds of a new culture require a determined effort by the chief executive and other senior managers. A sustained and persistent effort to reinforce the culture at every opportunity through both word and deed is required. Changing a problem culture is never a short-term exercise. It takes time for a new culture to emerge and prevail; overnight transformations simply do not occur. And it takes even longer for a new culture to become deeply embedded. The bigger the organization and the greater the cultural shift needed to produce an execution-supportive fit, the longer it takes. In large companies, fixing a problem culture and instilling a new set of attitudes and behaviours can take 2–5 years. In fact, it is usually tougher to reform an entrenched problematic culture than it is to instil a strategy-supportive culture from scratch in a brand new organization.

Illustration Capsule 12.2 discusses the approaches used at Chrysler in 2009/10 to change a culture that was grounded in a 1970s' view of the automobile industry.

Illustration Capsule 12.2

CHANGING THE 'OLD DETROIT' CULTURE AT CHRYSLER

When Chrysler Group LLC emerged from bankruptcy in June 2009, its road to recovery was far from certain. 'It was questionable whether they'd survive 2010', said Michelle Krebs, an analyst with auto information provider Edmunds.com. One thing that was holding Chrysler back was its culture – a legacy of 'the Old Detroit', that was characterized by finger-pointing and blame-shifting whenever problems arose.[a]

Chrysler's management had long been aware of its culture problem. In 2008, Robert Nardelli, Chrysler's autocratic new CEO, placed himself in charge of a wide-ranging culture-change programme designed to break the ingrained behaviours that had damaged the organization's reputation for quality. Chrysler's slide into bankruptcy was hardly the comeback that the controversial Nardelli envisioned when he was hired for the job by private-equity firm Cerberus Capital Management (which controlled Chrysler from 2007 until 2009).

A strategic partnership ceding management control to Italian automaker Fiat SpA was part of the deal for Chrysler's bankruptcy reorganization, with Fiat's CEO, Sergio Marchionne, becoming Chrysler's CEO as well.

▶

In discussing his five-year plan for Chrysler, Marchionne remarked, 'What I've learned as a CEO is that culture is not part of the game – it is the game!'[b]

Marchionne put Doug Betts, a veteran of Toyota Motor Corp. and Nissan Motor Co., in charge of a systematic overhaul of Chrysler quality, with cultural change as the fundamental driver. Betts began by creating new cross-functional teams designed to break down Chrysler's silos of manufacturing and engineering. Whereas problems were formerly handed off from one department to another, delaying action for an average of 71 days, quality teams are now encouraged to take ownership of solutions.[c] Betts has also taken aim at the climate of fear, replacing concerns over recrimination and retribution with a positive focus on team empowerment and problem-solving. By the end of 2009, Betts was saying, 'It's different now. People are talking openly about problems now and how to fix [them].'[d] By May 2010, confidence in Chrysler was increasing and sales were up by 33 per cent over the same period in the previous year. Analysts were hopeful that Chrysler had finally begun to get it right.

Notes:

[a]Hirsch, Jerry (2010) 'Chrysler performance exceeds expectations: the Fiat-managed company cut its losses to $197 million and recorded a $143-million operating profit in the first quarter of the year', *Los Angeles Times*, 22 April. Available online at www.articles.latimes.com/2010/apr/22/business/la-fi-chrysler-20100422 .

[b]Howes, Daniel 'Chrysler's last chance to get it right', *Detroit News*, Business section, 1-dot edition, p. 4B.

[c]Ibid.

[d]Priddle, Alisa '"Different" Chrysler zeroes in on quality', *Detroit News*, Business section, 2-dot edition, p. 1A.

Note: Developed with Amy Florentino.

Sources: Snell, Robert (2010) 'Chrysler sales up 33% for May; Ford, GM rise 23%, 16.6%', *Detroit News*, last updated 2 June. Available online at www.detnews.com/article/20100602/AUTO01/6020390/Chrysler-sales-up-33—for-May—Ford—GM-rise-23—16.6-#ixzz0sNQX7iWR; www.topics.nytimes.com/top/reference/timestopics/people/n/robert_l_nardelli/index.html, updated 1 May 2009; Boudette, Neal E. (2008) 'Nardelli tries to shift Chrysler's culture', *Wall Street Journal*, 18 June, p. B1.

Leading the Strategy Execution Process

LO 12.4
Understand what constitutes effective managerial leadership in achieving superior strategy execution.

For an enterprise to execute its strategy in a truly proficient fashion and approach operating excellence, top executives have to take the lead in the implementation/execution process and personally drive the pace of progress. They have to be out in the field, seeing for themselves how well operations are going, gathering information firsthand and gauging the progress being made. Proficient strategy execution requires managers to be diligent and adept in spotting problems, learning what obstacles lie in the path of good execution and then clearing the way for progress – the goal must be to produce better results speedily and productively. There has to be constructive, but unrelenting, pressure on organizational units to (1) demonstrate excellence in all dimensions of strategy execution; and (2) do so on a consistent basis – ultimately, that is what will enable a well-crafted strategy to achieve the desired performance results.

The strategy execution process must be driven by mandates to get things on the right track and show good results. The specifics of how to implement a strategy and deliver the intended results must start with understanding the requirements for good strategy execution. Afterwards comes a diagnosis of the organization's preparedness to execute the strategic initiatives and decisions as to which of several ways to proceed to move forward and achieve the targeted results.[24] In general, leading the drive for good strategy execution and operating excellence calls for three actions on the part of the manager in charge:

- Staying on top of what is happening and closely monitoring progress.
- Putting constructive pressure on the organization to execute the strategy well and achieve operating excellence.
- Initiating corrective actions to improve strategy execution and achieve the targeted performance results.

Staying on Top of How Well Things are Going

To stay on top of how well the strategy execution process is going, senior executives have to tap into information from a wide range of sources. In addition to talking with key subordinates and reviewing the latest operating results, watching the competitive reactions of rival firms and visiting with key customers and suppliers to get their perspectives, they usually make regular visits to various company facilities and talk with many different employees at many different organization levels – a technique often labelled **managing by walking around (MBWA)**. Most managers attach great importance to spending time with people at company facilities, asking questions, listening to their opinions and concerns and gathering firsthand information about how well aspects of the strategy execution process are going. Facilities tours and face-to-face contacts with operating-level employees give executives a good grasp of what progress is being made, what problems are being encountered and whether additional resources or different approaches may be needed. Just as important, MBWA provides opportunities to give encouragement, lift spirits, shift attention from the old to the new priorities and create some excitement – all of which can boost strategy execution efforts.

> **Core Concept**
>
> **Management by walking around (MBWA)** is one of the techniques that effective leaders use to stay informed about how well the strategy execution process is progressing.

Jeff Bezos, Amazon.com's CEO, is noted for his practice of MBWA, firing off a battery of questions when he tours facilities and insisting that Amazon managers spend time with their employees to prevent getting disconnected from the reality of what is happening.[25] Walmart executives have had a long-standing practice of spending 2–3 days every week visiting Walmart's stores and talking with store managers and employees. Sam Walton, Walmart's founder, insisted, 'The key is to get out into the store and listen to what the associates have to say'. Jack Welch, the highly effective CEO of GE from 1980 to 2001, not only spent several days each month personally visiting GE operations and talking with major customers but also arranged his schedule so that he could spend time exchanging information and ideas with managers from all over the world who were attending classes at the organization's leadership development centre near their headquarters.

Many manufacturing executives make a point of strolling the factory floor to talk with workers and meeting regularly with union officials. Some managers operate out of open cubicles in big spaces populated with open cubicles for other personnel so that they can interact easily and frequently with co-workers. Managers at some companies host weekly get-togethers (often on Friday afternoons) to create a regular opportunity for information to flow freely between down-the-line employees and executives.

Putting Constructive Pressure on Organizational Units to Execute the Strategy Well and Achieve Operating Excellence

Managers have to be out front in mobilizing organizational energy behind the drive for good strategy execution and operating excellence. Part of the leadership task entails

Key Debate 12.1

WHAT IS ORGANIZATIONAL CULTURE?

The concept of organizational culture is by far not a simple one and there are multiple alternative views on the phenomena. Two of the most prominent views are to see culture as something that an organization 'has', versus viewing it as something that an organization 'is'. These different views give rise to different beliefs as to how malleable an organizational culture can be, and what would need to be done to create a culture change.

If culture is something that an organization 'has' then it is a variable that organizations produce. This variable is accompanied by more or less distinct cultural traits, such as values, norms, rituals, ceremonies and verbal expressions that affect the behaviour of managers and employees. In this view we find the strongest arguments that organizational culture contributes to the effectiveness of an organization, and that strong cultures are to be preferred over weak cultures. We also find the belief that we can somehow 'measure' culture. The improvement of organizational culture is often viewed as a matter of achieving planned cultural change. Getting the right culture in place is expected to have recognizable effects on important outputs like loyalty and productivity.

The alternative view of culture as something that an organization 'is' stresses that the organization is a culture, or can be seen as if it is a culture. According to this perspective organizational culture is not just another subsystem of the organization, it 'is' the organization. When culture is seen as a variable, we can talk about outcomes such as 'a misfit between strategy and culture', but when culture is seen as permeating the entire organization then it is believed that the culture is expressed and reproduced in all aspects of the organization – like the structure and strategy. Rather than consider cultures as strong or weak, the consistency and degree of uniformity of behaviour and beliefs in the organization is just another reflection of the culture.

The subjectivist perspective of culture as constructed by people also means that the pragmatic results of using culture to improve effectiveness are downplayed. When culture is seen as a variable, then the focus is on cultural engineering by leaders. When culture is seen as permeating all aspects of the organization then it follows that organizational culture is relatively resistant to control and change and only occasionally manageable. Therefore, the general understanding and reflection on what 'is' becomes the focus. The awareness of the culture becomes the management tool in that management needs to be aware of what is possible or impossible within a given culture, and how to go about anchoring action within the prevailing culture. Leaders in this view are formed by culture, rather than being the 'captains of culture', except in very special circumstances such as during a fundamental crisis in the organization.

Sources: Alvesson, M. (2002) *Understanding Organizational Culture*, London, Sage Publications; L. Smircich (1983) 'Concepts of culture and organizational analysis', *Administrative Science Quarterly*, 28(3): 339–58.

nurturing a results-oriented work climate, where performance standards are high and a spirit of achievement is pervasive. Successfully leading the effort to foster a results-oriented, high-performance culture generally entails such leadership actions and managerial practices as:

● *Treating employees as valued partners in the drive for operating excellence and good business performance.* Some companies symbolize the value of individual employees and the importance of their contributions by referring to them as cast members (Disney), crew members (McDonald's), job owners (Graniterock), partners (Starbucks) or associates (Walmart and Marriott International). Very often, there is a strong organizational commitment to provide thorough training, offering attractive compensation and career opportunities, emphasizing promotion from within, providing a high degree of job security and otherwise making employees feel well treated and valued.

● *Fostering an* esprit de corps *that energizes organization members.* The task here is to skilfully use people-management practices calculated to build morale, foster pride in doing things right, promote teamwork, create a strong sense of involvement on the part of employees, win their emotional commitment and inspire them to do their best.[26]

- *Using empowerment to help create a fully engaged workforce.* Top executives must seek to engage the full organization in the strategy execution effort. A fully engaged workforce, one where individuals bring their best to work every day, is necessary to produce great results.[27] So is having a group of dedicated managers committed to making a difference in their organization. The two best things top-level executives can do to create a fully engaged organization are: (1) delegate authority to middle- and lower-level managers to get the implementation/execution process moving; and (2) empower employees to act on their own initiative. Operating excellence requires that everybody contribute ideas, exercise initiative and creativity in performing his or her work and have a desire to do things in the best possible manner.

- *Making champions out of the people who head up new ideas and/or perform exceptionally.* The best champions and change agents are persistent, competitive, tenacious, committed and fanatical about seeing their ideas through to success. It is particularly important that people who champion an unsuccessful idea are not punished or sidelined but, rather, be encouraged to try again. Encouraging lots of 'tries' is important, since many ideas will not pan out.

- *Setting stretch objectives and clearly communicating an expectation that employees are to give their best in achieving performance targets.* Stretch objectives – those beyond an organization's current capacities – can sometimes spur organizational members to increase their resolve and redouble their efforts to execute the strategy flawlessly and ultimately reach the stretch objectives. When stretch objectives are met, the satisfaction of achievement and boost to employee morale can result in an even higher level of organizational drive.

- *Using the tools of benchmarking best practices, business process reengineering, total quality management (TQM) and Six Sigma to focus attention on continuous improvement.* These are proven approaches to getting better operating results and facilitating better strategy execution.

- *Using the full range of motivational techniques and compensation incentives to inspire employees, nurture a results-oriented work climate and enforce high-performance standards.* Managers cannot mandate innovative improvements by simply exhorting people to 'be creative', nor can they make continuous progress toward operating excellence with directives to 'try harder'. Rather, they must foster a culture where innovative ideas and experimentation with new ways of doing things can blossom and thrive. Individuals and groups should be strongly encouraged to brainstorm, let their imaginations fly in all directions and come up with proposals for improving how things are done. This means giving employees enough autonomy to stand out, excel and contribute. And it means that the rewards for successful champions of new ideas and operating improvements should be large and visible.

- *Celebrating individual, group and organizational successes.* Top management should miss no opportunity to express respect for individual employees and appreciation of extraordinary individual and group effort.[28] Companies like Mary Kay Cosmetics, Tupperware and McDonald's actively seek out reasons and opportunities to give pins, ribbons, buttons, badges and medals for good showings by average performers – the idea being to express appreciation and give a motivational boost to people who stand out in doing ordinary jobs. GE and 3M Corporation make a point of ceremoniously honouring individuals who believe so strongly in their ideas that they take it on themselves to hurdle the bureaucracy, manoeuvre their projects through the system, and turn them into improved services, new products or even new businesses.

While leadership efforts to instil a results-oriented, high-performance culture usually accentuate the positive, negative reinforcers abound too. Managers whose units consistently perform poorly must be replaced. Low-performing workers and people who reject the results-oriented cultural emphasis must be weeded out or at least employed differently. Average performers should be candidly counselled that they have limited career potential unless they show more progress in the form of additional effort, better skills and improved ability to execute the strategy well and deliver good results.

Leading the Process of Making Corrective Adjustments

Since strategy execution takes place amid changing environmental and organizational circumstances, there is often a need for corrective adjustments. The process of making corrective adjustments in strategy execution varies according to the situation. In a crisis, taking remedial action fairly quickly is of the essence. But it still takes time to review the situation, examine the available data, identify and evaluate options (crunching whatever numbers may be appropriate to determine which options are likely to generate the best outcomes) and decide what to do. When the situation allows managers to proceed more deliberately in deciding when to make changes and what changes to make, most managers seem to prefer a process of incrementally solidifying commitment to a particular course of action.[29] The process that managers go through in deciding on corrective adjustments is essentially the same for both proactive and reactive changes: they sense needs, gather information, broaden and deepen their understanding of the situation, develop options and explore their pros and cons, put forward action proposals, strive for a consensus and finally formally adopt an agreed-on course of action.[30] The time frame for deciding what corrective changes to initiate can be a few hours, a few days, a few weeks or even a few months if the situation is particularly complicated.

Success in making corrective actions hinges on (1) a thorough analysis of the situation, (2) the exercise of good business judgement in deciding what actions to take, and (3) good implementation of the corrective actions that are initiated. Successful managers are skilled in getting an organization back on track rather quickly. They (and their staff) are good at discerning what actions to take and in bringing them to a successful conclusion. Managers who struggle to show measurable progress in implementing corrective actions in a timely fashion are often candidates for being replaced.

The challenges of making the right corrective adjustments and leading a successful strategy execution effort are, without question, substantial.[31] Because each instance of executing strategy occurs under different organizational circumstances, the managerial agenda for executing strategy always needs to be situation-specific – there is no generic procedure to follow. But the job is definitely doable. Although there is no prescriptive answer to the question of exactly what to do, any of several courses of action may produce good results. And, as we said at the beginning of Chapter 10, executing strategy is an action-oriented, make-the-right-things-happen task that challenges a manager's ability to lead and direct organizational change, create or reinvent business processes, manage and motivate people and achieve performance targets.

A Final Word on Leading the Process of Crafting and Executing Strategy

In practice, it is hard to separate leading the process of executing strategy from leading the other pieces of the strategy process. As we emphasized in Chapter 2, the job of crafting, implementing and executing strategy consists of five interrelated and linked stages, with much looping and recycling to fine-tune and adjust the strategic vision, objectives, strategy and implementation/execution approaches to fit one another and to fit changing circumstances. The process is continuous, and the conceptually separate acts of crafting and executing strategy blur together in real-world situations. The best tests of good strategic leadership are whether the organization has a good strategy and business model, whether the strategy is being competently executed and whether the enterprise is meeting or beating its performance targets. If these three conditions exist, then there is every reason to conclude that the organization has good strategic leadership and is a well-managed enterprise.

KEY POINTS

1. Organizational culture is the character of an organization's internal work climate – as shaped by a system of *shared* values, beliefs, ethical standards and traditions that, in turn, define behavioural norms, ingrained attitudes, accepted work practices and styles of operating. An organization's culture is important because it influences the organization's actions and approaches to conducting business. In a very real sense, the culture is the organization's DNA.

2. The key features of an organization's culture include the organization's values and ethical standards, its approach to people management, its work atmosphere and organization spirit, how its personnel interact, the behaviours awarded through incentives (both financial and symbolic), the traditions and oft-repeated 'myths', and its manner of dealing with stakeholders.

3. An organization's culture is grounded in and shaped by its core values and ethical standards. Core values and ethical principles serve two roles in the culture-building process: (1) they foster a work climate in which employees share common and strongly held convictions about how organization business is to be conducted, and (2) they serve as measures for gauging the appropriateness of particular actions, decisions and behaviours, thus helping steer organization personnel toward both doing things right and doing the right thing.

4. Organizational cultures vary widely in strength and influence. Some are strongly embedded and have a big impact on an organization's practices and behavioural norms. Others are weak and have comparatively little influence on operations.

5. Strong organizational cultures can have either positive or negative effects on strategy execution. When they are well matched to the behavioural requirements of the organization's strategy implementation plan, they can be a powerful aid to strategy execution. A culture that is grounded in the types of actions and behaviours that are conducive to good strategy execution assists the effort in three ways:
   - By focusing employee attention on the actions that are most important in the strategy execution effort.
   - Through culture-induced peer pressure for employees to contribute to the success of the strategy execution effort.
   - By energizing employees, deepening their commitment to the strategy execution effort and increasing the productivity of their efforts

6. It is thus in management's best interest to dedicate considerable effort to establishing a strongly implanted organizational culture that encourages behaviours and work practices conducive to good strategy execution.

7. Strong organizational cultures that are conducive to good strategy execution are healthy cultures. So are high-performance cultures and adaptive cultures. The latter are particularly important in dynamic environments. Strong cultures can also be unhealthy. The five types of unhealthy cultures are: (1) those that are change-resistant, (2) those that are characterized by heavily politicized decision-making; (3) those that are insular and inwardly focused; (4) those that are ethically unprincipled and infused with greed; and (5) those that are composed of incompatible subcultures. All five impede good strategy execution.

8. Changing an organization's culture, especially a strong one with traits that do not fit a new strategy's requirements, is a tough and often time-consuming challenge. Changing a culture requires competent leadership at the top. It requires making a compelling case for cultural change and

employing both symbolic actions and substantive actions that unmistakably indicate serious commitment on the part of top management. The more that culture-driven actions and behaviours fit what is needed for good strategy execution, the less managers must depend on policies, rules, procedures and supervision to enforce what people should and should not do.

9. Leading the drive for good strategy execution and operating excellence calls for three actions on the part of the manager in charge:

   * Staying on top of what is happening and closely monitoring progress. This is often accomplished through MBWA.

   * Putting constructive pressure on the organization to execute the strategy well and achieve operating excellence.

   * Initiating corrective actions to improve strategy execution and achieve the targeted performance results.

TELIA – SUBCULTURES AT A TIME OF CHANGE

The introduction of new technologies can fundamentally alter the way an organization works, and can in some cases be a strong driver of organizational culture change. One such major technology-based change driver of the last few decades is the Internet, which is still revolutionizing industries and organizations from within, including those in music, publishing and retail.

Telia, now TeliaSonera, is Europe's fifth largest telecom operator in 2012. In 1999, Telia InfoMedia was one of Telia's eight business areas. They worked with the gathering, packaging and distribution of information. The company operated in the 'infocom' market, characterized by rapid changes. Telia Infomedia Reklam, one of the companies in the catalogue branch of Telia InfoMedia, had a long history and had been a part of a number of reorganizations. Telia InfoMedia Reklam was very decentralized, and in many ways the business lines operated as separate companies. InfoMedia Reklam consisted internationally of 3000 employees, 900 of whom were in Sweden.

Two of the business lines in Sweden were Gula Sidorna Internet (GSI) and Gula Sidorna Directories (GSD). GSD was responsible for sale and distribution of catalogue information in the traditional paper format, while GSI had the task of creating a functional business model of the same fundamental task using the Internet as a new distribution channel.

The two groups were located in the same building, although on different floors, and the core teams were approximately the same size of 10–15 people. The teams consisted of a business manager, business controllers and assistant controllers and those responsible for business development, marketing, technical competence (in GSI) and a webmaster (GSI). In both teams more than half of the employees came to their current division directly after having worked elsewhere within Telia. The GSI team on average had been in their current line of business for considerably less time than those in the GSD team. The majority of the GSD team had been with their present division for more than three years, while the majority of the GSI team had been employed for less than three years. The average age of the two groups also differed – the GSD team averaged 43 years while the Internet team has an average age of approximately 32 years.

GULA SIDORNA DIRECTORIES

The 'Gula Sidorna' or 'Yellow Pages' concept originated in 1978. Over the years there were many company name changes and reorganizations. Gula Sidorna Directories did not form part of the core business of Telia, but was very important as a strong source of revenue, and had enjoyed a successful history. It has been a facet of their business that for much of their history they could work with a certain degree of mistakes and inefficiencies and still remain a successful group.

The GSD team were located in the same building as GSI, although on another floor. The desks were placed quite close together and desk dividers were used. The actual floor plan was open, although this was a recent change. Previously the Telia InfoMedia Reklam sales management and business area employees had their own rooms. The seating arrangements were based on convenience. Those who needed to converse more often were seated in closer proximity. Everyone had their own desks and there were no plans to change the seating arrangements. The team believed that there was some level of status inherent in their floor allocation – being on level 8 mean that they sat closest to the top management of Telia InfoMedia and that this was not coincidental.

New ideas within this group come from above – mainly the president and the top-level management team. The manager listened to ideas from the rest of the team but made the final decisions. In doing so, he wanted the expression of full support from the others involved in the discussion. Goals and responsibilities were decided by the top level. The business manager aimed to *'get the responsibility out'*. The process involves defining and drawing very clear boundaries regarding the areas in which an employee was empowered to make a decision. Team members should have very defined areas, and within this area they should make the decisions where necessary, but they also needed to understand that if a decision was to be made outside this area they needed to go to their superior. Competence evaluations and clear feedback, what could be done better, was considered important to the optimal functioning of both the sales and management groups.

The ideal GSD employee was someone who others could believe in; they needed very good people skills first and foremost, high integrity while being very focused on the goals and loyal to the management and the company.

▶

The manager described his role as *'if I am away for a week then there should be no consequences, they should not feel it'*. He wanted people to know what they could do, making their own decisions within their frame, the goals should be very clear and they should have such confidence in their abilities that they could drive themselves.

The manager believed that he needed to make a platform for the people, build on the people, talk with and interact with them so that they would feel human. *'Things which in a normal life are so clear, in some companies here it isn't. Sit down, have a coffee, be a part of it'*. But he wanted people to understand that when it was work it was work, and when it was social time it was social time.

Consensus was worked at, he liked to be able to say, *'these are the reasons we can't go this way – are you in agreement?'*, instead of *'this is the way we are going – don't argue'*.

GULA SIDORNA INTERNET

The product Gula Sidorna Internet was launched in 1996. The GSI team office was open plan, a demand made by the management when planning the layout. The GSI sales and business managers were very involved in the layout details. The belief was that effort and money should be invested in the work environment as it was not an issue when the employees were worth a *'couple of million'* each and there was so much to do.

The first entrance area was an open modern kitchen with coffee and soft drinks available. The bar height tables and stools provide an informal area where discussions could be carried out. The adjacent area to the kitchen was a smaller coffee/break room, the only area where smoking was permitted, and this room was often full. This room was frequented by the business manager and was an important strategic meeting ground. It was common for employees to join in on the unplanned breaks as not to do so might leave them out of important communication opportunities. The main working area was divided down the middle by an open area – sales on one side and product development and marketing on the other. The business group was seated in clusters of three or four, and it was planned to change the groupings every few months to enhance creativity. No status or prestige, or lack thereof, was thought to be inherent in the building or floor location.

It was thought within GSI that good ideas could come from anywhere, and that there would be a positive response from bringing up a subject that you actually had thought a bit about. All ideas were considered good until proven otherwise, so nobody was afraid of bringing up something that sounded a little 'crazy'. The response to new ideas was for others to listen, think and challenge. New ideas were generally brought up in the bi-monthly meetings, or in the small coffee room. It was expected that the group members would contribute in this way. The employees were extremely engaged in their work, and the manager believed that *'here you must work with your heart and your brain'*. Decisions were made by the group, although some decisions were made exclusively by the manager. Decisions made by the manager rarely resulted in opposition because they generally followed the strategy of the group that was well accepted and integrated. The managers' focus on revenue was very clear and the group appreciated his ability to make tough decisions to keep the strategy on track.

Definitions of the work roles were purposely left unclear, as they wanted to put effort into different areas at different times. Employees were assigned basic responsibilities and then worked on projects that were rapidly changing. It was believed that prioritizing along the projects was one of the key issues to success. The main work was performed in groups and not separately.

The emphasis at GSI was on having strong, independent people working very much on their own, but willing to help each other. The business manager only looked at the goals on a higher level, did not want the role of 'coach' and did not want to see everything that the employees did. He believed that time spent on strategy built some control, but how and when the work was actually done – *'I don't mind, I don't care, as long as they are doing the right thing according to our strategy'*.

The atmosphere was described as 'informal', and the business manager tried to talk to everyone in an informal way every day. Mistakes were tolerated well and as expressed by the employees it was well understood that *'everything is a trial'*.

The employees described themselves as *'strong individuals'* and said they were not afraid of conflict within the group, or outside with the other companies they dealt with. *'It's OK to have conflict about work because you have to – if you always avoid conflict then you shouldn't work here, you need to be able to deal with the conflict if you are right'*. Personal conflict was considered differently, but there had been no problems in the group in this respect.

QUESTIONS

1. Identify the dominant artefacts, norms and beliefs of the two workgroups, GSI and GSD. Would you assess these to be significantly different from each other, or relatively compatible?

◀

2. These two workgroups were merged together as part of a spin-off, creating Eniro AB in 2000. As a senior executive, how would you have managed this integration? Can the ways of working be merged together, or should one be dominant?

Source: Sutton, C. (2000) *Gula Sidorna Internet, an Internet Subculture?* Stockholm, Stockholm School of Economics.

ASSURANCE OF LEARNING EXERCISES

LO 12.1, LO 12.2

1. Go to www.google.com. Click on the About Google link and then on the Organizational Info link. Under the Culture link, read what Google has to say about its culture. Also, in the 'Our Philosophy' section, read 'Ten things Google has found to be true'. How do the 'ten things' and Google's culture aid in management's attempts to execute the organization's strategy?

LO 12.1, LO 12.2

2. Go to the career section at www.carrefour.com, and see what Carrefour has to say about its culture. Does what is on this website appear to be just recruiting propaganda, or does it convey the type of work climate that management is actually trying to create? Explain your answer.

LO 12.3

3. Using Google Scholar or your university library's access to EBSCO, Lexis-Nexis or other databases, search for recent articles in business publications on 'culture change'. Give examples of three companies that have recently undergone culture-change initiatives. What are the key features of each organization's culture-change programme? What results did management achieve at each organization?

LO 12.1, LO 12.2

4. Go to www.jnj.com, the website of Johnson & Johnson, and read the J&J Credo, which sets out the organization's responsibilities to customers, employees, the community and shareholders. Then read the 'Our Company' section. Why do you think the credo has resulted in numerous awards and accolades that recognize the organization as a good corporate citizen?

LO 12.4

5. In the last couple of years, Liz Claiborne, Inc., has been engaged in efforts to turn around its faltering Mexx chain. Search for information on the turnaround plan at Mexx, and read at least two articles or reports on this subject. Describe in 1–2 pages the approach being taken to turn around the Mexx chain. In your opinion, have the managers involved been demonstrating the kind of internal leadership needed for superior strategy execution at Mexx? Explain your answer.

EXERCISES FOR SIMULATION PARTICIPANTS

LO 12.1, LO 12.2

1. If you were making a speech to employees, what would you tell them about the kind of organizational culture you would like to have at your organization? What specific cultural traits would you like your organization to exhibit? Explain.

▶

◄

LO 12.1

2. What core values would you want to ingrain in your organization's culture? Why?

LO 12.3, LO 12.4

3. Following each decision round, do you and your co-managers make corrective adjustments in either your organization's strategy or how well the strategy is being executed? List at least three such adjustments you made in the most recent decision round. What hard evidence (in the form of results relating to your organization's performance in the most recent year) can you cite that indicates the various corrective adjustments you made that either succeeded or failed to improve your organization's performance?

LO 12.4

4. What would happen to your organization's performance if you and your co-managers stick with the status quo and fail to make any corrective adjustments after each decision round?

ENDNOTES

1. Chatham, Jennifer A. and Cha, Sandra E. (2003) 'Leading by leveraging culture', *California Management Review*, 45(4): 20–34.

2. Reid, Joanne and Hubbell, Victoria (2005) 'Creating a performance culture', *Ivey Business Journal*, 69(4): 1.

3. Kotter, John P. and Heskett, James L. (1992) *Organizational Culture and Performance*, New York, Free Press, p. 7. See also Goffee, Robert and Jones, Gareth (1998) *The Character of a Corporation*, New York, HarperCollins.

4. For several perspectives on the role and importance of core values and ethical behaviour, see Badaracco, Joseph L. (1997) *Defining Moments: When Managers Must Choose Between Right and Wrong*, Boston, MA, Harvard Business School Press; Badaracco, Joe and Webb, Allen P. (1995) 'Business ethics: a view from the trenches', *California Management Review*, 37(2): 8–28; Murphy, Patrick E. (1995) 'Organizational ethics statements: current status and future prospects', *Journal of Business Ethics*, 14: 727–40; and Sharp Paine, Lynn (1994) 'Managing for organizational integrity', *Harvard Business Review*, 72(2): 106–17.

5. For a study of the status of formal codes of ethics in large corporations, see Carasco, Emily F. and Singh, Jang B. (2003) 'The content and focus of the codes of ethics of the world's largest transnational corporations', *Business and Society Review*, 108(1): 71–94, and Murphy, Patrick E. (1995) 'Organizational ethics statements: current status and future prospects', *Journal of Business Ethics*, 14: 727–40. For a discussion of the strategic benefits of formal statements of organizational values, see Humble, John, Jackson, David and Thomson, Alan (1994) 'The strategic power of organizational values', *Long Range Planning*, 27(6): 28–42. An excellent discussion of whether one should assume that organization codes of ethics are always ethical is presented in Schwartz, Mark S. (2002) 'A code of ethics for organizational codes of ethics', *Journal of Business Ethics*, 41(1–2): 27–43.

6. Chatham and Cha, 'Leading by leveraging culture'.

7. Kotter and Heskett, *Organizational Culture and Performance*, pp. 7–8.

8. Deal, Terrence E. and Kennedy, Allen A. (1982) *Organizational Cultures*, Reading, MA, Addison-Wesley, p. 22. See also Deal, Terrence E. and Kennedy, Allen A. (1999) *The New Organizational Cultures: Revitalizing the Workplace after Downsizing, Mergers, and Reengineering*, Cambridge, MA, Perseus Publishing; Chatham and Cha, 'Leading by leveraging culture'.

9. Sathe, Vijay (1985) *Culture and Related Organizational Realities*, Homewood, IL, Irwin.

10. Jassawalla, Avan R. and Sashittal, Hemant C. (2002) 'Cultures that support product-innovation processes', *Academy of Management Executive*, 16(3): 42–54.

11. Kotter and Heskett, *Organizational Culture and Performance*, pp. 15–16. Also see Chatham and Cha, 'Leading by leveraging culture'.

12. Chatham and Cha, 'Leading by leveraging culture'.

13. Kotter and Heskett, *Organizational Culture and Performance*, p. 5.

14. For a discussion of how to build a high-performance culture, see Reid and Hubbell, 'Creating a performance culture', pp. 1–5.

15. A strategy-supportive, high-performance culture can contribute to competitive advantage; see Barney, Jay B. and Clark, Delwyn N. (2007) *Resource-based Theory: Creating and Sustaining Competitive Advantage*, New York, Oxford University Press, ch. 4.

16. Reid and Hubbell, 'Creating a performance culture', pp. 2 and 5.

17. This section draws heavily on the discussion of Kotter and Heskett, *Organizational Culture and Performance*, ch. 4.

18. There is no inherent reason why new strategic initiatives should conflict with core values and business principles. While conflict is always possible, most strategy-makers lean toward choosing strategic initiatives that are compatible with the organization's character and culture and that do not go against ingrained values and beliefs. After all, the organization's culture is usually something that strategy-makers have had a hand in building and perpetuating, so they are not often anxious to undermine core values and business principles without serious soul-searching and compelling business reasons.

19. For a more in-depth discussion of using values as legitimate boundaries, see Moss Kanter, Rosabeth (2008) 'Transforming giants', *Harvard Business Review*, 86(1): 43–52.

20. Ibid., ch. 6.

21. See Eichenwald, Kurt (2005) *Conspiracy of Fools: A True Story*, New York, Broadway Books.

22. Ibid., p. 5.

23. Olian, Judy D. and Rynes, Sara L. (1991) 'Making total quality work: aligning organizational processes, performance measures, and stakeholders', *Human Resource Management*, 30(3): 324.

24. For excellent discussions of the problems and pitfalls in leading the transition to a new strategy and to fundamentally new ways of doing business, see Bossidy, Larry and Charan, Ram (2004) *Confronting Reality: Doing What Matters to Get Things Right*, New York, Crown Business; Bossidy, Larry and Charan, Ram (2002) *Execution: The Discipline of Getting Things Done*, New York, Crown Business, especially chs 3 and 5; Kotter, John P. (1995) 'Leading change: why transformation efforts fail', *Harvard Business Review*, 73(2): 59–67; Hout, Thomas M. and Carter, John C. (1995) 'Getting it done: new roles for senior executives', *Harvard Business Review*, 73(6): 133–45; Ghoshal, Sumantra and Bartlett, Christopher A. (1995) 'Changing the role of top management: beyond structure to processes', *Harvard Business Review*, 73(1): 86–96.

25. Fred Vogelstein, (2003) 'Winning the amazon way', *Fortune*, 26 May, p. 64.

26. For a more in-depth discussion of the leader's role in creating a results-oriented culture that nurtures success, see Schneider, Benjamin, Gunnarson, Sarah K. and Niles-Jolly, Kathryn (1994) 'Creating the climate and culture of success', *Organizational Dynamics*, Summer, pp. 17–29.

27. Kanazawa, Michael T. and Miles, Robert H. (2008) *Big Ideas to Big Results*, Upper Saddle River, NJ, FT Press, p. 96.

28. Pfeffer, Jeffrey (1995) 'Producing sustainable competitive advantage through the effective management of people', *Academy of Management Executive*, 9(1): 55–69.

29. Quinn, James Brian (1980) *Strategies for Change: Logical Incrementalism*, Homewood, IL, Richard D. Irwin, pp. 20–2.

30. Ibid., p. 146.

31. For a good discussion of the challenges, see Goleman, Daniel (1998) 'What makes a leader', *Harvard Business Review*, 76(6): 92–102; Heifetz, Ronald A. and Laurie, Donald L. (1997) 'The work of leadership', *Harvard Business Review*, 75(1): 124–34; Farkas, Charles M. and Wetlaufer, Suzy (1996) 'The ways chief executive officers lead', *Harvard Business Review*, 74(3): 110–22. See also Porter, Michael E., Lorsch, Jay W. and Nohria, Nitin (2004) 'Seven surprises for new CEOs', *Harvard Business Review*, 82(10): 62–72.

Part Two   Cases in crafting and executing strategy

Section A

1	Reinventing Accor	456
2	Apple and the retail industry for specialist consumer electronics in the United Kingdom	466
3	Netflix: can it recover from its strategy mistakes?	474
4	The O-Fold innovation for preventing wrinkles: a good business opportunity?	499
5	Studio 100: a showcase in show business	512
6	Ferretti Group: navigating through stormy seas	527
7	Starbucks: evolving into a dynamic global organization	538
8	Rhino capture in Kruger National Park	570
9	Robin Hood	585
10	NIS: geopolitical breakthrough or strategic failure?	587
11	Kyaia	595
12	Microsoft's strategic alliance with Nokia	607

Case 1

Reinventing Accor

Alex Janes
University of Exeter

Denis Hennequin became chief executive officer (CEO) of the Accor Group in December 2010 with the vision to make the firm one of the world's top three leading hotel groups by 2015. The group had decided to focus on its hotel brands in 2009, but it had taken over a year to demerge this part of the business from its prepaid business services division, Accor Services (re-named Edenred in 2010). The stage was now set for a new strategy to take the hotel group to 2015. An initial announcement had been promised for September 2011 with further details to follow as Hennequin's vision was fleshed out by the other senior executives in the firm.[1]

The Accor Group had a 2.9 per cent share of the global hotel market in 2010[2] with revenues of $7.9 billion (€5.9 billion)[3] (see Exhibit 1 for selected financial data on Accor), but this put the firm some way behind the top three in the industry, US based groups Marriot International and Hilton Worldwide, and InterContinental Hotels whose headquarters were in London. There were also other challengers in the industry vying to break into the top group. Starwood Hotels & Resorts and Wyndham Worldwide had both achieved significant growth between 2005 and 2010 (see Exhibit 2 for Global Hotel figures).

Accor were well positioned to achieve a leading position in the industry. They were the leading hotel group in Western Europe, the Middle East and Africa and had a strong position in Eastern Europe and in many emerging markets in Asia-Pacific and South America. The group had 145 000 employees and over 4200 hotels in 90 countries in August 2010.[4] Accor's portfolio of hotels offered substantial breadth as well as depth, from luxury brands, such as Sofitel, through mid-market chains such as Novotel and Mercure, to economy and no-frills offerings such as Ibis and Motel6 (see Exhibit 3 for details of Accor's portfolio of brands).

History of Accor

The Accor Group was created in 1983 and brought together the various hotel brands that Paul Dubrule and Gerard Pelisson had developed or acquired since starting the Novotel hotel chain in the 1960s. The two entrepreneurs, neither of whom had a background in hospitality, opened their first Novotel in 1967 adjacent to Lille airport. Their formula for success was very different from the established strategies followed by hotels in the 1960s and 1970s. Novotel took the idea of the standardised hotel concept, popular in the USA and transported it to Europe. They introduced a range of innovations for the 3 star hotels, such as a bathroom for every guest room, telex facilities, direct dial telephones in guest bedrooms and outdoor amenities such as swimming pools, children's play areas and free car parking, all of which quickly became standard

EXHIBIT 1: Selected financial data on Accor SA

In € millions	2009	2010	2011
Revenue	5490	5948	6100
Operating expense	(3972)	(4134)	(4177)
EBITDAR	1518	1814	1923
Rental expense	(854)	(934)	(995)
EBITDA	664	880	928
Operating profit before tax	(263)	(12)	326
Profits after taxes	(295)	(404)	52
Assets			
Assets held for sale	144	813	386
Non-current assets	7290	5555	5038
Current assets	4312	2310	2576
Total assets	11 746	8678	8000
Equity/Liabilities			
Equity	3254	3949	3768
Long-term liabilities	2818	2015	1850
Current liabilities	5670	2336	2293
Liability on assets held for sale	4	378	89
Total liabilities and equity	11 746	8678	8000

Sources: Accor (2012) *New Frontiers in Hospitality: 2011 Annual Report*, Paris, Accor; Accor (2012) *New Frontiers in Hospitality: 2011 Registration Document and Annual Financial Report*, Paris, Accor.

EXHIBIT 2: Global hotel industry key figures

Company	2005 % value share	2010 % value share	2010 value sales, US$ mn	% growth 2005/2010	% CAGR 2005-2010
Marriott International Inc	4.6	4.8	19 812.5	24.4	4.5
Hilton Worldwide	–	4.1	17 029.8	–	–
InterContinental Hotels Group Plc	3.4	3.7	15 130.1	27.7	5.0
Accor Group	2.6	2.9	11 740.5	31.2	5.6
Starwood Hotels & Resorts Worldwide	2.2	2.5	10 103.6	31.9	5.7
Wyndham Worldwide Corp	–	1.9	7620.0	–	–
Choice Hotels International Inc	1.6	1.5	6262.0	9.5	1.8
Best Western International Inc	1.7	1.5	6030.4	0.5	0.1
Hyatt Hotels Corp	–	0.9	3764.7	–	–
Carlson Cos Inc	0.8	0.7	2998.9	12.0	2.3

Source: Euromonitor International (2011) *Passport – Global Hotels: Reshaping Hotel Experiences*, London, Euromonitor International, p.16.

in the new breed of out of town hotels. The hotel chain also treated its staff very differently with much less hierarchy and job specialisation, employees were encouraged to move location and learn a range of functions to maximise flexibility. The group created its own corporate university in 1985, the Academie Accor.

EXHIBIT 3: Accor's brands in 2011/12

Adagio – was a European brand offering apartments, but with some hotel-type features. The apartments ranged from economy to upscale and the services on offer could be tailored to the needs of individual guests – but each apartment was fully equipped. There were 99 Adagio 'Aparthotels' in nine countries at the end of 2011.
All Seasons – was one of the economy products offered by Accor. All Seasons hotels were located in business areas of towns and cities and were non-standardized, despite being all-inclusive. The hotels were rebranded as Ibis Styles during 2011 and consisted of 149 hotels in 14 countries.
Etap – was another of the firm's economy brands. The no-frills brand was renamed as Ibis Budget (which also replaced Hotel Formule 1 outside Europe) in 2011 and had 522 hotels in 18 countries. The brand mainly appealed to business travellers.
Grand Mercure (or Mei Jue) – was launched in 2011/12 and aimed specifically at the upscale market in China. By the end of 2011 there were nine hotels.
HotelF1- was a no-frills brand with 243 hotels in France
Ibis – as noted above, Ibis was revamped to become the umbrella brand for most of Accor's economy brands in 2011. However, the Ibis hotels continued to operate alongside Ibis Styles and Ibis Budget. Ibis Hotels was the largest element of the Ibis brand in 2011 with 933 hotels in 53 countries. The hotels offered as standardized product appealing to both business and leisure travellers.
Mercure – offered a boutique hotel-style experience to mid-scale travellers and was aimed at both leisure and business travellers. Locations were city and rurally based. There were 716 hotels in 49 countries at the end of 2011.
MGallery – had grown rapidly since its launch in 2009 with 49 hotels in 19 countries by the end of 2011. These hotels were upscale and intended to appeal to both business and leisure travellers. The brand's appeal was similar to that of many boutique hotels with distinctive identities in each location and less of a chain hotel feel.
Motel 6 – was another one of Accor's regional hotel chains, operating only in the USA and Canada. In 2011 the 1028 economy motels attracted mainly leisure travellers, although it was rumoured that Accor had plans to sell off the brand.
Novotel – probably the best known of Accor's brands, there were 394 hotels in 56 countries at the end of 2011. The mid-scale chain was intended to appeal to both leisure and business travellers, with dual purpose rooms and meeting spaces, restaurants and so on. The hotels were located in major city centres throughout the globe. The Suite Novotel was a separate product offering long-stay, flexible room spaces for business and leisure guests.
Pullman – was an upscale brand, mainly aimed at business travellers. These hotels were mainly located in regional/international hub cities. There were 20 Pullman hotels in 20 countries in 2011.
Sofitel – was Accor's luxury hotel brand, consisting of non-standardized accommodation, which were generally sited in prestigious city centre locations and were reflective of the local culture as well as the group's French roots. There were 112 Sofitels in 39 countries in 2011.
Studio6 – was a North American brand of extended-stay budget accommodation, with hotel facilities. This could be seen as an economy version of Adagio. Accor had 66 of these hotels in 2011, but as with Motel6, appeared to be looking for a buyer for the brand.

Sources: Accor (2012) *New Frontiers in Hospitality: 2011 Annual Report*, Paris, Accor; Accor (2012) *New Frontiers in Hospitality: 2011 Registration Document and Annual Financial Report*, Paris, Accor.

Note: Accor announced the sale of the Motel6 and Studio6 brands to Blackstone Real Estate for $1.9 billion in May 2012.

Pelisson and Dubrule expanded their business by building new hotels and then acquiring other chains. During the 1970s Novotel was growing by an average of one hotel per month. The company began its international growth in 1973 with its first hotel outside France in Warsaw, Poland. In 1974 the firm launched a new 2 star hotel brand with the first Ibis hotel, which opened in Bordeaux. This was followed in 1975 by the acquisition of rival 3 star operator, Mercure. 1980 saw the firm make its most dramatic acquisition yet, with the purchase of 4 star deluxe hotel chain, Sofitel.[5] They now had nearly 200 hotels in 22 countries.[6]

The group then expanded into related businesses. In 1982, the acquisition of Jacques Borel International took them into the catering and food services sector with the Ticket Restaurant concept. By the time the Accor group was formally created in 1983, they had 440 hotels, 1500 restaurants and 35 000 employees in 45 countries. The group's growth continued throughout the rest of the 1980s and 1990s. Accor entered the budget end of the market in 1985 with the creation of Formule 1, a one star motel brand and in 1990 it acquired the Motel6 chain which gave it a larger presence in the USA. The firm also expanded in Asia with developments in China and Thailand. The early 1990s were a tough time for the group in the aftermath of the First Gulf War with the subsequent reduction in travel. However, Accor proved it was capable of reinventing itself and in 1993 completed a comprehensive overhaul of the Novotel brand and its business model, which had become rather tired and much imitated. They also launched a new economy brand of hotel, Etap, in 1991 in response to the tough economic conditions.

In 2001, Accor started to move into a wider range of businesses with the acquisition of Employee Advisory Resource Ltd in the UK, which specialized in employee assistance programmes. The following year it acquired Davidson Trahaire, Australia's leading human resources (HR) consulting firm. The services business had grown from the pre-paid ticket restaurants part of the business and in 2005 it launched services in Mexico and later India. This part of Accor's business continued to expand with the acquisition of a controlling stake in Motivano in 2008, an employee benefits firm in the UK and Quasar which offered similar programmes in Germany. In 2009 Accor further consolidated their position as a provider of pre-pay services through a joint venture with MasterCard to offer service throughout Europe.

Meanwhile the firm's hotel and leisure business was also showing significant growth. Accor created a long stay hotel brand aimed at executive customers, Suite Novotel in 1999. This provided 30 sq.m. suites in city centre location for more flexible accommodation with lounge and catering facilities as well as meeting spaces. Accor continued to refresh and expand their existing brands, installing WiFi into both their economy and luxury ranges from 2003 and renaming their Formule 1 brand hotelF1 in 2008. They opened their first Ibis hotel in China in 2003 and continued to expand rapidly in Asia. The group also opened a series of Ibis and Formule 1 hotels in Brazil from 2008 onwards. Accor also launched a new business hotel brand, Pullman, and a new chain of individual economy hotels, All Seasons in 2007. Their non-standardized offering was also extended to the upscale sector of the industry with the launch of MGallery hotels in 2008. Accor had even made a move into casinos and gambling with the creation of Groupe Lucien Barrière as a joint venture with Colony Capital in 2004.

The group divested hotels that were not performing and also sold them to property firms and investment companies to release the capital in the asset. Some of the hotels sold were leased back. Accor released €518 million in 2007 with the sale of 57 hotels in France and Switzerland to a consortium of real estate investment companies. This release of capital could support the two brands launched that year.[7] In 2009 Accor sold 158 of its hotelF1 properties in France for €272 million. The capital generated by sales of real estate and divestment of underperforming hotels also supported the firm's expansion in new faster growing markets such as China, India and Brazil. In 2009 the group opened more luxury hotels under its Sofitel brand in China.

Demerger

The rapid growth of the services and hotel businesses coupled with a poor performance in 2009 which saw the hospitality operations record a net loss of €262 million prompted Gilles Pelisson, the group Chairman and CEO, to start the process of demerging the two elements of the business. The board of directors and other stakeholders finally agreed the separation of the services and hotel businesses in February 2010 with the actual demerger taking place in June. The firm's rationale for the split centred on the view that the businesses now operated in very different business environments and needed very different resources and skills to excel in their contrasting environments.[8] Each business was also very capital intensive and as separate entities they would be better placed to attract a larger number of investors. The demerger left the majority of the group's €1.6 billion consolidated debt with the new hotel company, Accor SA, with Edenred, the renamed services company taking on €0.4 billion and Accor €1.2 billion. The hotel business had a substantially larger tangible asset base against which to offset debt. Both firms would be able to increase their level of equity funds by appealing to investors with different goals. There would be no capital ties between the firms. The demerger was also sold to stakeholders on the basis of its impact on partnerships and strategic alliances. Each of the new firms would be free to pursue different partners without the baggage of the other's business model or capital structure limitations.

The Global Hotel Industry

History

Offering hospitality and accommodation to travellers for payment dates back to antiquity and there are many examples of spas, inns and taverns in the Greek and Roman worlds as well as outside Europe. In fact, the oldest hotel in the world is the Hoshi ryokan in Komatsu, Japan, which has been run by the same family for 46 generations and dates back to 717.[9] However, the growth of the global industry is a much more recent phenomenon. Most hotels were and still are individual enterprises or family run businesses centring on a single location. It was in the nineteenth century that large scale hotels were constructed in Europe as railways replaced the stagecoach as the dominant form of transport. A further boom in hotel construction occurred in the 1920s, particularly in North America, but the real genesis of the global industry began in the 1950s and 1960s when franchising and branded chain hotels allowed rapid expansion and the development of operationally effective, standardised offerings at a national and international level.[10, 11]

The 1970s marked the start of another key phase in the global industry, driven by middle-eastern states and their oil revenues, the growth of mass tourism and the opening up of China and other Asian countries. This led to a 1980s' boom as hotels were built in increasing numbers next to airports, and in a wide range of new resort destinations, catering for both tourists on vacation and commercial audiences as the conference trade grew and business became more globalized.[12] The 1980s also marked the start of the consolidation of the industry through a series of high profile mergers and acquisitions.[13] If the 1980s were the boom, then the 1990s were the bust. The First Gulf War in 1991 created uncertainly in world travel markets and led to a decline in revenues for many hotel based businesses. The decade also saw the beginning of a greater emphasis on environmental issues for the industry as well as a range of new strategies and business models. Some hotel operators ceased to own their hotels and moved to a management company role, leasing or renting their premises, others invested heavily in customer loyalty schemes and brand extensions to cater for a wider range of tastes and wallets. Technology also had a profound effect through the introduction of the Internet, electronic reservation systems and a range of computerized systems, from stock ordering to point of sales facilities in restaurants and bars.

In the last 10 years, many of these trends have accelerated as the industry becomes more competitive and technology more pervasive. The advent of web 2.0 has meant that consumers have far more access to information about hotels, from prices to reviews, and a stronger voice in the marketplace. Guests expected to be able to use their laptops in their rooms, have access to a range of satellite channels on the TV, access a wide choice of dining styles from fast food to á la carte, keep fit in the in-house gym or indulge in a range of beauty and wellness therapies. Like other travel sector companies, hotel firms have also found that there are many advantages in partnerships both within the industry and with a wide range of other organizations.

Current Trends

Globally, the hotel sector was valued at between $415 billion and $544 billion in 2010.[14, 15] There is agreement that the sector has bounced back from the recession after it contracted by some 2.8 per cent worldwide in 2009. Growth of between 4 and 7.8 per cent CAGR (Compound Annual Growth Rate) was being forecast for the period 2010–15. Commentators were predicting that most of this growth would come from the Asia Pacific market which had been increasing at more than 7 per cent as opposed to Europe, where growth was less than 1 per cent in 2010. The leisure part of the hotel industry was still dominant in 2010, accounting for over three-quarters of the market value, with business making up the remainder. Europe and the Americas were the most valuable element of the global market, making up 39 per cent and 31 per cent of the total value of the industry in 2010.[16] Asia Pacific accounted for just over a quarter of the global industry's value with the remainder of the market (4.2 per cent) in the Middle East and Africa.

Brands continued to be an important element in the global hotel industry and after the 2009 dip many of the biggest chains began upgrading and refreshing their different lines. The US market was particularly sensitive to this sort of activity due to the fact that 70 per cent of hotels are branded chain outlets. Re-branding in the hotel sector is far more than just a new advertising campaign. Refreshing a hotel brand often involves new interior design schemes for lobbies, communal and dining areas as well as guest rooms. New furniture is often part of the package and new amenities in the hotel itself, from gym and fitness facilities to spa and health and beauty treatments. The staffing profile in hotels may also be altered as a result. In some cases it will result in the disposal of hotel properties that no longer fit the new brand and development of new properties in new locations that do. This makes this element of strategy implementation one of the most expensive for firms in the industry. In 2010/1 most of the key players were moving away from a traditional look and feel – even in their no-frills offerings – to a minimalist, contemporary atmosphere.

Despite the investment in brands and the growth of loyalty schemes, such as Hilton's HHonours and IHG's Priority Club Rewards,[17] it cost consumers very little to switch providers and this led to an increasingly competitive marketplace. Few of the major players competed on price alone, despite the fact that many consumers were price sensitive in the light of the global downturn. As part of their branding, hotel chains also adopted a highly segmented approach to marketing their ranges of hotels. Innovation also played a key role in attracting and retaining customers and many of the hotel firms were focused on extending their offer and reducing costs in all but the premium sector of the market.

In terms of geographic expansion, most of the main hotel chains were focusing on Asia Pacific as their main growth market. North America and Europe were considered mature markets where growth was difficult to achieve without potential retaliation from other incumbents, although there was some scope for consolidation in Europe are most hotels remained independently owned. The top players in the global industry all had plans to significantly increase their penetration of the Indian and Chinese markets. Starwood announced plans to double their number of hotels in China from 150 to 300 by 2012 and Marriott were planning to develop a further 100 hotels in India and China between 2010 and 2015 to add to their existing stock of 131. However, most hotel firms have focused on the larger cities in each country and this has meant that real estate prices and local taxes have risen in response to demand/opportunity in cities such as Mumbai and Shanghai. Second and third tier destinations, such as Huangshan and Wuzhen are becoming increasingly popular because demand is still outstripping supply and there is significant potential for growth.[18]

Spas have long provided destinations for travellers interested in improving their health and social changes to people's attitudes towards health and fitness are providing a new lease of life for this style of hotel and destination.[19] Investment in facilities to cater for the growing interest in wellness has taken place in a wide range of hotels. This can include indoor and outdoor exercise facilities, and spaces for a range of therapies, from use of special muds and minerals to traditional geo-thermal and sea water based cures. Hilton launched the first of 80 planned in-house spas in October 2010. Globally, the largest growth in this sector is predicted for India, Vietnam and the Philippines.[20] Hotels are also increasingly developing holistic packages to include food, room features, and wellness classes. As consumers become more interested in how and where their food is produced and demand more healthy options, such as anti-energy or relaxation drinks, hotels have had to respond. Westin Hotels announced a $30 million investment in promoting and delivering well-being throughout their chain of hotels in 2011–2.[21]

Consumers' environmental concerns were also driving change in the hotel industry, with a number of the main players using ISO14001 or LEED (Leadership in Energy and Environmental Design) certification as the basis for improving their sustainability. Hotel firms had then found that the changes they made improved operational effectiveness, InterContinental Hotel Group (IHG) found that their Green Engage programme not only gained them LEED certification in January 2011, but it also produced 20 per cent savings due to reduced energy use in their premises. Hilton's LightStay system, launched in 2010, produced similar savings in energy and water use, which helped to reduce operating costs. Extensive re-branding activities have enabled firms such as Marriott and Starwood to change menus and make use of low energy lighting, green bedding and beauty/personal care products.[22]

The Internet and a range of other technologies have had a profound effect on the global hotel industry. The rise of online booking websites such as Lastminute.com, Expedia.com and TripAdvisor.co.uk which also carry reviews meant customers had access to much more information about hotels and the deals they could offer. However, this also made social media an increasingly important tool for marketing. The major chains now had access to much more information about their customers and could make use of advocates with large followings on Facebook or Twitter to help spread positive messages about their hotels and resorts. Marriott ran this sort of campaign for its SpringHill Suites chain by offering a variety of incentives to guests willing to enthuse their friends about the hotel.[23]

The hotel industry had always been a capital intensive industry, because of the amount of equipment and furniture needed to run a full-service establishment and the cost of the real estate in the first place. Increasing reliance on and need for technology had increased this in the last few years. Hotels now had a whole range of procurement and reservation systems, databases and associated networks, plus a whole host of expert suppliers that provided these products and services.[24] In 2011 several hotel chains were experimenting with digital concierges – especially in mid-market and economy hotels. Further changes were being seen from the growth in the use of mobile technology for everything from booking and checking in to providing special maps and even, like IHG, allowing guests to use their smartphones in place of room keys.[25]

Accor's Strategy

Since its separation from the services business, Accor SA had followed an ambitious expansions strategy, mainly focusing on emerging markets in the Asia Pacific region. In October 2011, the firm announced[26] plans to add more than 200 hotels to its existing portfolio of 450 by 2014. The expansion would mainly focus on China, India and Indonesia, with some more limited growth in Australia and Vietnam. Accor's strategy was to seek to increase its level of activity in fast-growing emerging country economies outside Europe. Within Europe, where the company remained the largest player in the market, expansion would be in the economy segment of the industry.[27] Europe still accounted for over 70 per cent of the group's revenue in 2010.

Like most of its competitors, Accor needed to find funds to pay for their expansion into faster growth segments and regions. The decision to focus on hotels following the demerger, led to the sale of some of the group's related businesses, such as casinos and catering.[28] Accor sold its rail catering business Compagnie des Wagon-lit in 2010 and its 49 per cent stake in casino group Lucien Barriere in March 2011. Its gourmet dining brand, Lenôtre, was sold for €75 million the same year. However, most of the capital for expansion was raised by the sale and leaseback of the group's owned hotel properties in Europe and North America. One of the key aims of Accor's strategy under Denis Hennequin was to reduce their proportion of owned hotels and those on fixed leases from 60 per cent to between 20 and 30 per cent of the total.[29] Again, this was becoming a common trend in the industry as firm's sought to avoid taking on a high burden of debt, through what was becoming known as an 'asset light' approach. Rather than owning hotels, firms would use franchise contracts or manage the hotel under contract to the owners or rent the property through a variable lease. Accor felt that this approach to managing its existing portfolio and developing new hotels through franchise agreements and management contracts would allow it to grow rapidly and take advantage of the new markets in emerging economies. Accor's expansion in Australia and New Zealand in 2011 was mainly facilitated through the purchase of hotel management firm, Mirvac, rather than the acquisition or development of hotel real estate.[30]

Hennequin also recognized that the effective management of Accor's portfolio of brands would be critical to the firm's success. The group covered a wide range of segments with their 14 hotel brands. Much of their strength lay in their economy and no-frills brands such as Ibis, hotelF1 and Motel 6. The firm's roots were in the mid-market brands, such as Novotel and Mercure, but they also had the capabilities to manage and create upscale brands such as Pullman and MGallery and succeed with luxury establishments such as their Sofitel chain. Accor's brands combined regional offerings (Motel 6 was specific to the USA) with global hotels such as Ibis. The firm also covered the extended stay segment with an economy brand in the USA, Studio 6, and Suite Novotel, internationally.

However, it was the economy brands that were the best performers in the firm's portfolio showing year on year growth of +6.3 per cent at the end of 2011 compared with +5.0 per cent growth in the upscale and midscale hotels.[31] Accor's strategy was to focus on the Ibis mega-brand and align the other international no-frills brands, Etap and Hotel Formula 1 under the Ibis Budget brand and its other economy brand, All Seasons, under the Ibis Style brand. The positioning for the Ibis umbrella brand would be captured by the concepts of 'modernity, simplicity and well-being'.[32]

Another aspect of Accor's strategy was its focus on sustainable initiatives. The group's Earth Guest programme covers a range of activities from encouraging the procurement of fair trade goods for use in hotels, to recycling glass, cardboard and paper. By 2011, 495 of Accor's hotels had achieved ISO14001 and over 90 per cent subscribed to the Hotel Operator's Environmental Charter. Accor was listed on the four main international indexes: Ethibel, FTSE4Good, Dow Jones Sustainability and ASPI Eurozone.[33]

Key Players in the Global Hotel Industry

Marriott Corporation entered the hotel business a decade before Accor and by 2011 was the leading global hotel company. They had flagship J.W. Marriott and Ritz-Carlton hotels with deluxe accommodation for business travellers and holidaymakers; its Courtyard by Marriott and SpringHill Suites brands catered to business travellers looking for moderately priced lodging; and the Marriott Residence Inns and TownePlace Suites were designed as a 'home away from home' for travellers staying five or more nights. The company operated in 70 countries and had over 3500 hotels in 2011, using both an owned and a franchised business model. Marriott also operated over 2000 rental houses and condominiums for corporates. The corporation recorded revenues of $11.7 billion for the financial year ending December 2010 and employed 129 000 staff.[34]

Hilton Worldwide was also headquartered in the USA and employed a similar number of staff to Marriott (130 000 in 2011). Hilton operated 3750 hotels in 84 countries world-wide. The firm was originally known as the Hilton Hotel Corporation until it was acquired by Blackstone and taken private in 2007. Founded by Conrad Hilton in 1919, the firm owns, manages and franchises a wide range of hotels. Its portfolio of brands ranged from luxury hotels such as the Waldorf Astoria and the Conrad, through mid-priced accommodation such as Hilton and Doubletree, to value brands such as Hampton. Hilton also catered for the extended stay, executive sector through its Homewood and Home2 Suites.[35]

InterContinental Hotel Group (IHG) had adopted a different approach to most of its rivals and although its company revenues were substantially lower than the other players at the top of the market, it had more hotels than Hilton, Marriott or Accor. However, most of the hotels were operated under franchise agreements. InterContinental had 4520 hotels globally in 2011 operating in 100 countries under the Intercontinental, Crowne Plaza, Hotel Indigo, Holiday Inn, Staybridge and Candlewood brands. Their portfolio covered both business and leisure sectors and offered everything from economy brands, such as Holdiay Inn Express to the medium stay suite products such as Candlewood. Based in the UK, the group directly employed just over 7000 staff and generated revenues of $1.6 billion in 2010 and an operating profit of $459 million. The vast majority of their hotels were operated under franchise agreements (over 3700 properties fell into this category), so the group had strong skills in working with hotel owners. About 15 per cent of their hotels were operated on a managed basis and the group only owned 15 hotels itself in 2010.[36]

Starwood was one of the fastest growing hotel and leisure groups in the world in 2010/11. The firm's headquarters were on the US East coast in New York. Starwood employed 145 000 staff in 2010 and had revenues in excess of $5 billion. The company's main focus was in the luxury end of the market and they operated hotels and resorts. Brands included, Sheraton, Le Meridien, Westin, St Regis, Element and Aloft. About half of the firm's hotels are franchised and the rest managed on behalf of property owners or owned outright by Starwood. The company has been a relatively late entrant to a number of emerging markets, such as India and China. It opened its first hotel in Russia in 2011. Starwood was founded in 1969 and incorporated in 1980. The company has plans for significant expansion in the Middle East, South America and India over the next few years.[37]

Becoming one of the top 3

It was clear from their end of year figures for December 2011 that Accor was back on track after their demerger and the losses of 2009. However, with other strong competitors in its market and new trends in the industry there were no guarantees that its strategy would be capable of providing a sustainable competitive advantage. Accor's greatest successes had often been achieved by adopting a different approach to the rest of the hotel trade. Was Accor's current strategy distinctive enough to take it the next step and join the best in the world?

ENDNOTES

1. Accor (2011a) 'Accor's strategic vision'. Available online at www.accor.com/en/group/accor-strategic-vision.html (accessed 1 February 2012).

2. Euromonitor (2011) *Global Hotels: Shaping Hotel Experiences*, August, Euromonitor.com, London.

3. Datamonitor (2011a) *Global Hotels and Motels*, October 2011, Datamonitor.com, London.

4. Accor (2011b) 'Accor in brief'. Available online at www.accor.com/fileadmin/user_upload/Contenus_ Accor/Franchise_Management/Documents_utiles/General_information/accor_in_brief__uk_ dec_2011.pdf (accessed 1 February 2012).

5. Accor (2011c) 'Chronology'. Available online at www.accor.com/en/group/history/chronology.html (accessed 1 February 2012).

6. Datamonitor (2011b) *Accor SA Company Profile*, June, Datamonitor.com, London.

7. Ibid.

8. Accor (2010) 'Demerging the two businesses and details of the demerger process', 24 February, press release. Available online at www.accor.com/fileadmin/user_upload/Contenus_Accor/Finance/ Pressreleases/2010/EN/20100224_CPScission_EN.pdf (accessed 1 February 2012).

9. The most famous hotels in the world (2010) 'Hoshi Ryokan: the world's oldest guest house', 17 April 2010. Available online at www.famoushotels.org/article/1013 (accessed 1 February 2012).

10. IRS (2007) 'Hotel industry overview', August. Available online at www.irs.gov/businesses/ article/0,,id=174494,00.html (accessed 1 February 2012).

11. Levy-Bonvin, J. (2003) 'Hotels: a brief history'. Available online at www.hospitalitynet.org/ news/4017990.search (accessed 1 February 2012).

12. Ibid.

13. IRS (2007) op. cit.

14. Euromonitor (2011) op. cit.

15. Datamonitor (2011a) op. cit.

16. Ibid.

17. Euromonitor (2011) op. cit.

18. Ibid.

19. Crook, Y. and Stevens, T. (2009) 'Wellness tourism: back to basics', *Health Tourism Magazine*. Available online at www.healthtourismmagazine.com/article/Back-Basics.html (available 1 February 2012).

20. Euromonitor (2011) op. cit.

21. Ibid.

22. Ibid.

23. Ibid.

24. Datamonitor (2011a) op. cit.

25. Euromonitor (2011) op. cit.

26. Saminather, N. (2011) 'Accor plans Asia-Pacific expansion with 200 hotels in pipeline', *Bloomberg Business Week*, 14 October.

27. Accor (2012) 'Sustained revenue growth in 2011', press release, 17 January. Available online at www. accor.com/fileadmin/user_upload/Contenus_Accor/Finance/Pressreleases/2012/EN/20120117_pr_ ca_t4_2011.pdf (accessed 1 February 2012).

28. Kenna, A. (2011) 'Accor buys Mirvac Hotels for $254 million to grow in Australia' *Bloomberg Business Week*, 16 December.

29. Saminather, N. (2011) op. cit.

30. Kenna, A. (2011) op. cit.

31. Accor (2012) op. cit.

32. Ibid.

33. Accor (2011b) op. cit.

34. Datamonitor (2011c) *Marriott International, Inc. company profile*, July, datamonitor.com, London.

35. Datamonitor (2011d) *Hilton Worldwide company profile*, October, datamonitor.com, London.

36. Datamonitor (2011e) *InterContinetal Hotel Group plc. company profile*, October, datamonitor.com, London.

37. Datamonitor (2011f) *Starwood Hotels and Resorts Worldwide, Inc. company profile*, August, datamonitor.com, London.

Case 2

Apple and the retail industry for specialist consumer electronics in the United Kingdom

Dr John Sanders

Heriot-Watt University

Background

In general the retail industry for consumer electronics (brown goods) sells personal computers, telephones, MP3 players, audio equipment, televisions, digital cameras, camcorders and DVD players. In 2011 UK consumers spent £21.5 billion on consumer electronics in general, which was a fall of 4 per cent from the previous year (source: Mintel). This decline in consumer spending arose from the global credit crisis and subsequent recession in 2008.

Prior to the recession the retail sales of brown goods had been relatively static for many years. Static sales meant the rivalry between UK retailers was intense as they jostled to maintain or grow profitability. Falling sales due to the recession heightened the already intense rivalry among UK retailers.

Apart from the recession there are two other elements that shape the retail industry for brown goods. First, the leading UK retailers find it difficult to differentiate themselves from each other. The lack of differentiation arises because leading UK retailers of brown goods generally sell products from the same manufacturers. As a consequence, UK customers in general base their purchase choices on price alone. The major winners from price competition have been UK supermarkets and online retailers like Amazon, because they are perceived as being cheaper. For example, Amazon has been gradually increasing its share of industry sales at the expense of leading retailers. Leading brown good retailers have also been guilty of neglecting their customer service activities.

Second, technological convergence is affecting the ability of many specialist retail chains or independent stores to maintain or continue to emphasize differences in their services and activities compared to mainstream stores. For example, specialist camera stores are struggling, because the benefits of purchasing a standalone camera from them are being eroded by the widespread inclusion of digital cameras within other products like mobile phones, tablets, personal computers, laptop computers and other devices at increasingly low prices.

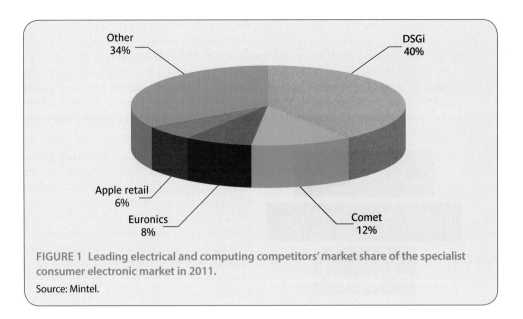

FIGURE 1 Leading electrical and computing competitors' market share of the specialist consumer electronic market in 2011.

Source: Mintel.

The major electrical and computing competitors and their share of the specialist brown goods market in 2011 are shown in Figure 1. In the main industry competitors try to serve the mass market for consumer electronics.

Major Industry Participants

DSGi

DSGi (Dixons Store Group International) operates three retail chains in the UK known as Currys, Currys.digital and PC World. The company has extensive overseas interests in electrical retailing, and therefore has strong buying power due to its  broad geographical coverage. In the UK the company operates a total of 519 Currys and Currys.digital stores, while it has 161 PC World stores. Its broad range of good quality international branded products attracts a wide cross-section of consumers from different ages and economic backgrounds. The company also sells some superior quality and value brands at premium and low budget prices respectively. However, the vast majority of the branded products are sold at prices around the industry average. The Group also run e-commerce operations to support the Currys and PC World brands. Currys and Currys.digital stores differ in regard to size and location. Currys. digital stores are smaller outlets located in high street locations and offer a small selection of popular consumer electronics, telephones and photographic equipment. On the contrary, Currys stores are larger, positioned in retail parks and offer a large selection of consumer electronics, telephones, photographic equipment and household appliances (white goods). PC World stores concentrate on selling computing and photographic equipment although large screen televisions, home cinema systems and DVD players are increasingly prominent in these stores. The company also operates two online retail web sites under the Dixons and Pixmania brand names. Dixons focuses on selling consumer electronics and white goods, while Pixmania retails consumer electronics as well as a wide range of other products such as home and garden products, jewellery, watches, toys, and health and beauty products. Both of these operations focus on low price to compete with online retailers.

For many years across all three store formats (PC World, Currys and Currys.digital) poor-quality customer service has been a major problem for DSGi. Certainly, annual customer satisfaction surveys conducted by 'Which? Magazine'[1] have demonstrated that UK customers find the service at all these stores to be below standard on an annual basis. These stores achieve scores in the forties and fifties out of a total possible score of 100 per cent. In contrast, superior UK retail stores in the same annual surveys score in the seventies and eighties like Apple Retail, John Lewis Partnership and IKEA.

To better survive lower consumer spending and rectify its poor customer service record, DSGi implemented three major changes across its retail stores and web sites. First, across all of its branded web sites major improvements were made to the product information provided and services offered such as instant or three hour delivery and installation. Second, the level of customer support was increased to aid customer installation issues, improved in-store, home and telephone technical advice, reduced repair times and the introduction of a loyalty club. Third, the appearance and layout of its retail branded stores (Currys, Currys.digital and PC World) were renewed and larger store formats introduced. The layout and design of Currys and PC World stores were made visually more appealing and easier to navigate for customers to find products. As far as larger store formats, Currys' branded stores began a gradual movement into larger-sized outlets called megastores, so a much deeper assortment of branded products can be displayed. The company has also launched a small number of 'Currys/PC World' retail stores. These stores combine the range of products usually sold separately by Currys and PC World stores into one convenient location. The Megastores and combined stores are part of DSGi's long-term strategy to have fewer, but larger outlets in cheaper out-of-town retail parks. Underperforming stores have also been closed. These changes attempt to enhance the customer experience by offering improved stores, better online selling processes and support activities.

Vitally DSGi has built strong relationships with suppliers of branded products so it is able to rapidly and efficiently replenish stock. It has managed to gain growing support from a number of premium brand suppliers as well.

Comet

After spending several months in administration, it was announced November 2012 that Comet would be closing the doors to its 250 stores in the UK. Until November 2011, Comet had been owned by Kesa Electricals who decided to sell it after suffering losses of £9 million in 2010/11. The new owners were a London-based private investment firm called OpCapita, who ultimately failed to halt its decline.

Due to the company's large network of stores it always had some power over the manufacturers of consumer electronics, and continually liaised with them to maintain good working relationships. Comet targeted a wide array of customers with a broad choice of good quality products from mainstream international brands. Like DSGi, Comet sold some superior quality and value brands at premium and budget prices respectively, but in the main it sold branded products priced around the industry average.

Comet stores were regularly criticised for poor customer service issues and inadequately trained sales staff in a similar vein to DSGi. Indeed, under Kesa Electricals,

Comet did try to remedy its customer service issues by enhancing the customer experience. The company's efforts to enhance the customer experience had included improvements in their home delivery service, more installation options, customer credit, a 24 hour helpline, and a free 30-day telephone helpline on TVs and home cinema systems. Comet had also improved its web site for customers by revamping its appearance, improving navigation, including product videos, providing customer reviews and offering online delivery tracking. Interestingly a survey commissioned by Mintel Group, a market research company, found that UK consumers perceived Currys and Comet as being impossible to tell apart. Retail experts state that Comet outlets looked dull and drab compared to refurbished Currys and Currys.digital stores (source: Mintel).

Independents

Besides these large retail chains there are over 5000 small independent consumer electronics retailers in the UK. These independent retailers are often family-run with less than 10 employees. Independent retailers have been having a tough time competing with the large retail chains on price and product range. The disadvantages of less space, narrow ranges and above industry prices are eroding their market position over time. Internet use is generally unsophisticated as most independents do not employ a transactional web site. In its place, independent web sites tend to be for informational purposes only.

Euronics

Some small UK independents have attempted to bolster their position by joining together with other European independents to form a cooperative buying group called EURONICS. EURONICS is the largest electrical buying group in Europe with nearly 9000 members across 25
European countries. Over 600 small UK independent stores have joined the buying group, but membership numbers are volatile. Joining the EURONICS buying group enables independent stores to obtain industry competitive prices from international suppliers. EURONICS source a narrower assortment of good quality brands from far fewer suppliers than the industry leaders, but this increases its buying power. EURONICS has also undertaken advertising on behalf of its members, in order to boost public awareness of the brand. The group operates on behalf of its members an e-commerce web site as well. Independents belonging to the EURONICS group charge prices around the industry average.

Apart from the above independents, a small number of them charge premium prices and focus on a few unique or specialize products and services to survive like high-end audio and/or visual products (i.e. home cinema systems). These specialized independent retailers argue that they can offer better service through in-depth personal knowledge of their products, understanding their local customer base more thoroughly, exclusive availability of certain upmarket or superior quality brands and retaining staff for longer to provide product familiarity.

Apple Retail

While most of the previous companies have struggled in the downturn of consumer spending, one company has thrived and achieved impressive sales growth. This company is Apple Incorporated via its UK retail operations. Since November 2004, Apple Incorporated, the iconic US multinational company that designs and markets consumer electronics (e.g. iPhones, iPods, iPod accessories, iPads and Apple TV), computer software and personal computers, has rapidly strengthened its retail presence in the UK. Particularly between 2007 and 2009, the company's retail outlet numbers doubled, while its revenues tripled. At present Apple have 28 stores in the UK. It operates a mixture of flagship stores (stand-alone stores located in high profile locations such as London's Covent Garden) and small retail outlets, which are inside shopping malls. In spite of this increase in retail outlets, it is worth mentioning that Apple generates a large proportion of its turnover from online sales in the UK as well.

Despite selling just its own narrow product range, Apple's turnover has proven to be exceptionally resilient during the downturn. This resilience is due to the strong loyalty of its customers. The company is well known for its passionate and dedicated customer base. Apple's foray into the UK retail sector has not disrupted its activities as a supplier of its products to other third party retailers like DSGi, Comet, Tesco, Asda and Amazon. The company stores sell the entire Apple product range, while its retail customers usually stock a much narrower selection. Apple's products are perceived as being of superior quality than other brands. This perception of superiority enables Apple to charge premium prices. Apple's retail stores also provide product presentations, repairs, expert advice and support. Without doubt Apple stores are perceived by loyalty customers as a haven for sharing their passion with other users, they also give them a sense of belonging to an exclusive, technological astute community that appreciates innovative design, style and quality. The stores reflect the aforementioned attributes as they are modern and spacious. In particular, the flagship stores have gained design awards for their stunning interiors and exteriors. Regardless of Apple products being available from other retailers discussed, Apple customers are known to travel long distances to visit Apple retail stores to make their purchases. No matter the retail location, Apple's range of products attracts a premium price.

Many industry analysts were sceptical of Apple's move into retailing. Certainly, when the first Apple store opened in the USA in 2001 it was viewed as a strategic mistake, because Dell's avoidance of retail stores and its online selling of computers had been extremely successful at that time.[2] Moreover, Gateway, the US-based computer designer, manufacturer and marketer was closing stores at that time as well. However, by the late 2000s, Apple stores had become an iconic presence in stylish high street locations and represented a key element of Apple's marketing strategy.

When Apple was developing its retail strategy, the company wanted to offer their customers an experience unlike those of other companies within the computer industry. Certainly, the customer shopping experience at an Apple retail store contrasts sharply with those previously described at DSGi and Comet Group stores. Visitors to an Apple store are greeted by numerous well-trained and enthusiastic employees wearing colourful Apple T-shirts.[3] The recruitment of Apple store personnel is undertaken very carefully by the company. Getting a job in an Apple retail store requires six to eight interviews.[4] Ron Johnson, who created and developed the Apple store format, states that the intensive staff selection process means people who are hired feel honoured to be part of the team.[5] This is a very different philosophy than trying to recruit somebody at the lowest possible cost.

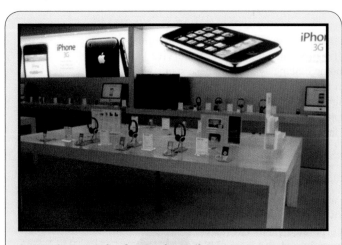

An Interior example of an Apple retail store.

An important ingredient of the Apple store experience is the Genius Bar. Genius Bars attempt to replicate a five star hotel's concierge desk where face-to-face support, information and advice can be readily obtained.[6] The employees or 'Geniuses' staffing the bar will look at any Apple product for free, regardless of whether it was bought at one of its stores.[7] They even offer advice about non-technical support issues like how to use Apple software or attempt to fix non-Apple software issues. The Genius Bars are now so popular that Apple uses a reservation system to manage the demand. No charges are made for this support, customers just pay for repairs for out-of-warranty goods.[8] 'Geniuses' also have latitude to waiver these fees. Genius Bars are a loss leader for the company as it believes customers will probably invest in other Apple products before they leave the store.[9] The company believes customers prefer face-to-face contact offered by Genius Bars rather than telephone and web support, which are often frustrating and ineffective. Apple's retail strategy is also about restoring and enhancing customer relationships that may have been damaged by product problems. The essence of Apple retail stores is to really build a face-to-face relationship that deepens a connection and trust with its customers.[10]

Apple's retail stores provide it with invaluable product information as well. The sales data obtained from its physical and online stores enable Apple to track demand and adjust production accordingly. Certainly if component shortages become apparent the company can rapidly deploy resources to get around any bottlenecks.

Apple Suppliers

Most Apple components are manufactured in Korea, Japan and Taiwan.[11] Generally, Apple wields immense power and influence over its key suppliers. This influence results from Apple's ability to prepay its key suppliers. Prepayment ensures availability and low prices for Apple – and sometimes limits the component options for its competitors. For instance, before the release of the iPhone 4 in June 2010, rivals such as HTC couldn't buy screens they needed because contract manufacturers were using available stock to fill Apple orders.[12]

Due to high volumes, suppliers have done very well from their relationship with Apple, but it is a demanding purchaser. The company requires very detailed breakdowns of its suppliers' material and labour costs, and projected profit levels.[13] Apple's bargaining tactics tend to exert downward pressure on prices, leading to lower profits and margins. In addition, Apple requires many key suppliers to keep two weeks of inventory within a mile of Apple's assembly plants in Asia.[14]

Nevertheless, Apple is not always in a powerful position versus its suppliers. Some key components are obtained from single or limited sources, which subject it to significant supply and pricing risks.

Apple's control over suppliers reaches its pinnacle in the lead-up to product launches. For weeks in advance of a product launch, factories work overtime to build hundreds of thousands of devices. Apple engineers closely monitor suppliers and manufacturers, helping refine processes that transform prototypes into mass-produced devices. For new designs such as the MacBook's unibody shell, cut from a single piece of aluminium, Apple's designers worked with suppliers to create new tooling equipment.[15]

Apple's effort to tightly control its suppliers payoffs as its gross margins are estimated to be around 40 per cent per product, compared with 10 to 20 per cent for most other hardware companies. Those margins increase markedly when Apple sells the products via its website or stores.[16]

Others

Competition from non-specialists such as supermarkets and Internet-based only companies has put pressure on prices

particularly as the current economic outlook encourages consumers to focus on low prices. Without doubt an increasing number of consumers are using the Internet to research products and use price comparison services. Greater use of the Internet is inevitably leading consumers to the price-led online companies, which makes it very difficult for Currys and PC World to show the added value they can offer via customer service. The largest online retailer of consumer electronics in the UK is Amazon. The company sells some superior quality and value brands at premium and low budget prices, respectively, but in the main it sells a broad range of good quality consumer electronics at prices below or around the industry average. Retail experts estimate its sales of consumer electronics was around £400 million in 2009 (source: Mintel). Amazon has considerable purchasing power due to the scale of its global operation.

Taking advantage of their customer loyalty, supermarkets have aggressively moved into the retailing of consumer electronics both in their stores and online. Prices are generally low or below the industry average with a moderate range of consumer electronics compared to the industry leaders. Tesco is without doubt the most important supermarket to enter the industry. The company is the UK's biggest supermarket chain and Europe's second largest retailer. The company has the largest customer base in the UK, strong brand loyalty and recognition, and high purchasing power due to its size. It has recently set a target of becoming the second largest retailer of consumer electronics in the UK. Tesco operates 2306 stores in the UK. Asda, the UK's second largest supermarket, is also strong in consumer electronics. The company has 340 supermarkets of various sizes and layouts. US retailer Wal-Mart, the largest retailer in the world, owns Asda. As a subsidiary of Wal-Mart, Asda has higher purchasing power than most of the other incumbents in the industry. Other notable participants in the industry are John Lewis Department store and Argos Catalogue Company. US multinational retailer, Best Buy, opened its first store in the UK in April 2010 and by November 2011 had established 11 stores. However, due to substantial losses during that period decided to close these stores. Best Buy's business strategy for consumer electronics was very similar to DGSi and Comet.

In summary, the leading industry participants' look and behave the same, with the notable exception of Apple. The inability of rivals to differentiate themselves has left customers with nothing but price as a basis for their choice. In consequence, the retail industry for brown goods is dominated by price competition. UK supermarkets and online retailers have benefited from this price competition as they are perceived as being cheaper.

Apple's modest share places it in fourth place. However, Apple store sales are expected to grow due to the anticipated release of more innovative, must-have gadgets. Apple unlike the other leading retailers has created superior value for its customers by performing activities in a different way and also by offering activities that competitors don't

Apple retail store in London's Regent Street.

perform. For example, its products are stylish and innovative. While a visit to any Apple store demonstrates a very different customer service experience compared to other retailers. The physical appearance and layout of Apple retail stores is inspired. The customer service experience also allows customers to interact with the products and ask questions of enthusiastic and knowledgeable staff. The Genius Bars located in every Apple store provides customers with free assistance as well. What happens within the Apple stores demonstrates that it is possible to counter the trend towards price competition within the retail industry of brown goods.

ENDNOTES

1. *Which*? magazine is a well-known consumer watchdog organization in the UK.
2. Helft, M. (2011) 'Steve Jobs' real legacy: Apple Inc', *Fortune* (cited 4 April 2012). Available online at www.tech.fortune.cnn.com/2011/09/08/steve-jobs-real-legacy-apple-inc/.
3. Ibid.
4. Morse, G. (2011) 'Retail isn't broken, stores are', Interview with Ron Johnson, *Harvard Business Review*, 79: 78–82.
5. Ibid.
6. Manjoo, F. (2010) 'Apple nation', *Fast Company*, Issue 147, July/August (cited 9 April 2012). Available online at www.fastcompany.com/magazine/147/apple-nation.html.
7. Ibid.
8. Ibid.
9. Ibid.
10. Morse, op, cit.
11. Wright, A. (2012) 'Analyzing apple products', *Communications of the ACM*, January, 55(1).
12. Satariano, A. and Burrows, P. (November 7–November 13, 2011) 'Apple's supply-chain secret? Hoard lasers', *Bloomberg Business Week: Technology* (cited 9 April 2012). Available online at www.businessweek.com/magazine/apples-supplychain-secret-hoard-lasers-11032011.html.
13. Ibid.
14. Ibid.
15. Ibid.
16. Ibid.

Case 3

Netflix: can it recover from its strategy mistakes?

Arthur A. Thompson

University of Alabama

Throughout 2010 and the first 6 months of 2011, Netflix was on a roll. Film enthusiasts were flocking to become Netflix subscribers in unprecedented numbers, and shareholders were exceptionally pleased with Netflix's skyrocketing stock price. During those 18 months from January 1, 2010 through June 30, 2011, the number of Netflix subscribers in the US alone doubled from 12.3 million to 24.6 million, quarterly revenues climbed from $445 million to $770 million, and quarterly operating income climbed from $53 million to $125 million. Netflix's swift growth in the U.S. and its promising potential for expanding internationally pushed the company's stock price to an all-time high of $304.79 on July 13, 2011, up from a close of $55.19 on December 31, 2009. Already solidly entrenched as the biggest and best-known Internet subscription service for watching TV shows and movies, the only question in mid-2011 seemed to be how big and pervasive might Netflix's service one day become in the larger world market for renting movies and TV episodes.

Then, over the next 4 months, Netflix announced a series of strategy changes and new initiatives that tarnished the company's reputation and sent the company's stock price into a tailspin:

- In mid-July 2011, Netflix announced a new pricing plan that effectively raised the monthly subscription price by 60 percent for customers who were paying $9.99 per month for the ability to (1) receive an unlimited number of DVDs each month (delivered and returned by mail 1 title out-at-a-time) and (2) watch an unlimited number of movies and TV episodes streamed over the Internet. The new arrangement called for total separation of unlimited DVDs and unlimited streaming to better reflect the different costs associated with the two delivery methods and to give members a choice: a DVD-only plan, a streaming-only plan, or the option to subscribe to both. The monthly subscription price for the unlimited streaming plan was set at $7.99 a month. The monthly subscription price for DVDs-only, one-out-at-a-time, was also set at $7.99 a month. If customers wanted both unlimited streaming and unlimited DVDs, they had to sign up for both plans and pay a total of $15.98 a month ($7.99 + $7.99) – Netflix said it was discontinuing all plans that included both streaming and DVDs by mail. For new Netflix members, the changes were effective immediately. For existing members, the new pricing started for charges on or after September 1, 2011.

- Customer reaction was decidedly negative. Unhappy subscribers posted thousands of comments on Netflix's site and Facebook page. Over the next 8 weeks, Netflix's stock price dropped steadily to around $210–$220 per share, partly because of rumors that perhaps as many as 600 000 Netflix customers had cancelled their subscriptions.

- The stock price slide was exacerbated by media reports that Starz, a premium movie channel offered by many multi-channel TV providers, had broken off talks with Netflix regarding renewal of the contract whereby Starz supplied Netflix with certain Starz-controlled movies and TV shows that Netflix could then provide either on DVDs or via streaming to its subscribers. The substance of the breakdown in negotiations centered on the much higher price that Starz was asking Netflix to pay to renew its rights to distribute Starz content to Netflix subscribers – Starz was rumored to have demanded as much as $300 million annually to renew its license with Netflix, versus the $30 million annually that Netflix had been paying.[1] (Netflix's licensing agreement with Starz later expired in March 2012, and the content was removed from its library of offerings to subscribers.)

- On September 18, 2011, in an attempt at damage control, Netflix chief executive officer (CEO) Reed Hastings in a post on the Netflix blog at http://blog.netflix.com/ apologetically said that the basis for the new pricing had been poorly communicated and personally took the blame for the miscue. He elaborated on the rationale behind the new pricing plans and then, in something of a bombshell, went on to reveal that Netflix was separating its DVD-by-mail subscription service and its unlimited streaming subscription service into two business operating at different websites. Hastings said the DVD-by-mail service would be renamed Qwikster, with its own website (www.qwikster.com) and its own billing. Current Netflix subscribers who wanted DVDs-by-mail would have to go to www.qwikster.com and sign up for the plan. He indicated that the Qwikster website would be operational in a matter of weeks – see Exhibit 1 for the full text of Hastings' post.

EXHIBIT 1: Reed hasting's blog posting, September 18, 2011

An explanation and some reflections

Reed Hastings

I messed up. I owe everyone an explanation.

It is clear from the feedback over the past two months that many members felt we lacked respect and humility in the way we announced the separation of DVD and streaming, and the price changes. That was certainly not our intent, and I offer my sincere apology. I'll try to explain how this happened.

For the past five years, my greatest fear at Netflix has been that we wouldn't make the leap from success in DVDs to success in streaming. Most companies that are great at something – like AOL dialup or Borders bookstores – do not become great at new things people want (streaming for us) because they are afraid to hurt their initial business. Eventually these companies realize their error of not focusing enough on the new thing, and then the company fights desperately and hopelessly to recover. Companies rarely die from moving too fast, and they frequently die from moving too slowly.

When Netflix is evolving rapidly, however, I need to be extra-communicative. This is the key thing I got wrong.

In hindsight, I slid into arrogance based upon past success. We have done very well for a long time by steadily improving our service, without doing much CEO communication. Inside Netflix I say, 'Actions speak louder than words,' and we should just keep improving our service.

But now I see that given the huge changes we have been recently making, I should have personally given a full justification to our members of why we are separating DVD and streaming, and charging for both. It wouldn't have changed the price increase, but it would have been the right thing to do.

So here is what we are doing and why:

Many members love our DVD service, as I do, because nearly every movie ever made is published on DVD, plus lots of TV series. We want to advertise the breadth of our incredible DVD offering so that as many people as possible know it still exists, and it is a great option for those who want the huge and comprehensive selection on DVD. DVD by mail may not last forever, but we want it to last as long as possible.

(Continued)

EXHIBIT 1: (Continued)

I also love our streaming service because it is integrated into my TV, and I can watch anytime I want. The benefits of our streaming service are really quite different from the benefits of DVD by mail. We feel we need to focus on rapid improvement as streaming technology and the market evolve, without having to maintain compatibility with our DVD by mail service.

So we realized that streaming and DVD by mail are becoming two quite different businesses, with very different cost structures, different benefits that need to be marketed differently, and we need to let each grow and operate independently. It's hard for me to write this after over 10 years of mailing DVDs with pride, but we think it is necessary and best: In a few weeks, we will rename our DVD by mail service to 'Qwikster'.

We chose the name Qwikster because it refers to quick delivery. We will keep the name 'Netflix' for streaming.

Qwikster will be the same website and DVD service that everyone is used to. It is just a new name, and DVD members will go to qwikster.com to access their DVD queues and choose movies. One improvement we will make at launch is to add a video games upgrade option, similar to our upgrade option for Blu-ray, for those who want to rent Wii, PS3 and Xbox 360 games. Members have been asking for video games for many years, and now that DVD by mail has its own team, we are finally getting it done. Other improvements will follow. Another advantage of separate websites is simplicity for our members. Each website will be focused on just one thing (DVDs or streaming) and will be even easier to use. A negative of the renaming and separation is that the Qwikster.com and Netflix.com websites will not be integrated. So if you subscribe to both services, and if you need to change your credit card or email address, you would need to do it in two places. Similarly, if you rate or review a movie on Qwikster, it doesn't show up on Netflix, and vice-versa.

There are no pricing changes (we're done with that!). Members who subscribe to both services will have two entries on their credit card statements, one for Qwikster and one for Netflix. The total will be the same as the current charges.

Andy Rendich, who has been working on our DVD service for 12 years, and leading it for the last 4 years, will be the CEO of Qwikster. Andy and I made a short welcome video. (You'll probably say we should avoid going into movie making after watching it.) We will let you know in a few weeks when the Qwikster.com website is up and ready. It is merely a renamed version of the Netflix DVD website, but with the addition of video games. You won't have to do anything special if you subscribe to our DVD by mail service.

For me the Netflix red envelope has always been a source of joy. The new envelope is still that distinctive red, but now it will have a Qwikster logo. I know that logo will grow on me over time, but still, it is hard. I imagine it will be the same for many of you. We'll also return to marketing our DVD by mail service, with its amazing selection, now with the Qwikster brand.

Some members will likely feel that we shouldn't split the businesses, and that we shouldn't rename our DVD by mail service. Our view is with this split of the businesses, we will be better at streaming, and we will be better at DVD by mail. It is possible we are moving too fast – it is hard to say. But going forward, Qwikster will continue to run the best DVD by mail service ever, throughout the U. S. Netflix will offer the best streaming service for TV shows and movies, hopefully on a global basis. The additional streaming content we have coming in the next few months is substantial, and we are always working to improve our service further.

I want to acknowledge and thank our many members that stuck with us, and to apologize again to those members, both current and former, who felt we treated them thoughtlessly.

Both the Qwikster and Netflix teams will work hard to regain your trust. We know it will not be overnight. Actions speak louder than words. But words help people to understand actions.

Respectfully yours,
Reed Hastings, Co-Founder and CEO, Netflix
Source: Posting at Netflix Blog, http://blog.netflix.com/, September 18, 2011 (accessed 6 March 2012).

- Hastings' announcement of Netflix's strategy to split the DVDs-by-mail business from the Internet streaming business and to create Qwikster sparked a second furor from already disgruntled subscribers and further adverse investor reaction (the stock price plunged from around $208 per share to about $115 per share over the next three weeks). Netflix's strategy to split the DVDs-by-mail business from the Internet streaming business drew harsh criticism from Wall Street analysts and business commentators; virtually all knowledgeable industry observers expressed amazement that Netflix executives would even contemplate such a move.

- On October 10, 2011, three weeks after Hastings disclosed the plan to divide Netflix into two standalone businesses, Netflix sent personal e-mails to all U.S. subscribers stating that it was scrapping its Qwikster proposal and that U.S. members would continue to use one website, one account, and one password for their movie and TV watching enjoyment under the Netflix brand. Simultaneously, Netflix issued a press release and posted statements on the Netflix blog at http://blog.netflix.com/ saying that it was abandoning the Qwikster strategy. In the blog, Reed Hastings said, 'It is clear that for many of our members two websites would make things more difficult. So we are going to keep Netflix as one place to go for streaming and DVDs.'

- On October 24, 2011, Netflix announced that in early 2012 it would begin offering unlimited TV shows and movies instantly streamed over the Internet to some 26 million households in the UK and Ireland – 20 million of these households had high-speed broadband Internet service and thus could stream movies to their TVs, computers, or other devices. This move represented the third strategic initiative to expand Netflix's international reach. Netflix began streaming to members in Canada in 2010 and, in September 2011, initiated streaming services to 43 countries in Latin America and the Caribbean; there were 4 times as many households with high-speed broadband service in these 43 countries as there were in Canada. In all three cases, Netflix estimated that it would take about two years after initial launch to attract sufficient subscribers to generate a positive 'contribution profit' –Netflix defined 'contribution profit (loss)' as revenues less cost of revenues and marketing expenses; cost of revenues included subscription costs and order fulfillment costs.

- In announcing the company's entry into Latin America and the Caribbean, Netflix said it was establishing a single low monthly price of 99 pesos for subscribers in Mexico and a price of US$7.99 for customers in the 42 countries in Central America, South America, and the Caribbean. In Brazil, Netflix content was available in Portuguese; in 8 other South American countries and all of the Central America countries, Netflix content was made available in Spanish; in the Caribbean, Netflix was available in English and Spanish. As part of its September entry into Latin America and the Caribbean, Netflix had entered into regional license agreements to obtain movies and TV shows in Spanish and Portuguese from a big variety of major motion picture and television studios, including Walt Disney Studios, Paramount Studios, Sony Pictures Television, NBCUniversal International Television, CBS Television, MGM, Lionsgate, Summit, Relativity, BBC Worldwide, TV Bandeirantes, Televisa, Telemundo, TV Azteca, TV Globo, Caracol, Telefe, and RCTV.

- Also, on October 24, Netflix announced that the number of domestic subscribers dropped by a net of 810 000 during the third quarter of 2011, thus resulting in operating profits, net income and earnings per share that were below Wall Street estimates and investor expectations. Internationally, the company said it had reached 1 million subscribers in Canada and that member counts in Latin America and the Caribbean should exceed 500 000 by year-end 2011. However, Netflix's contribution losses from international operations jumped from ($9.3 million) in the second quarter of 2011 to ($23.3 million) in the third quarter of 2011, owing to increased expenses associated with the startup of operations in Latin America and the Caribbean.

- On the day following the release of Netflix's third quarter financial results, the company's stock price dropped from $118.84 to close at $77.37.

- On November 21, 2011, Netflix announced that it had raised $400 million in new capital by (1) selling 2.86 million shares of common stock to certain mutual funds and accounts managed by T. Rowe Price Associates for $70 per share (which generated proceeds of $200 million) and (2) selling $200 million aggregate principal amount of Zero Coupon Convertible Senior Notes due December 1, 2018 to a private party. Any time after 6 months, Netflix had the option of converting the Zero Coupon Notes into shares of Netflix common stock at an initial conversion rate of 11.6533 shares of common stock per $1000 principal amount, subject to the satisfaction of certain conditions. Netflix executives said that the company did not intend to spend any of the newly-raised capital. Rather, the company intended to use the capital as a safety-net, since the company's cash on hand and future cash flows from operations would likely be squeezed in upcoming quarters by the ongoing need to:

- Make cash payments for additions to its library of titles available for streaming.

- Absorb the expected contribution losses from international operations over the next 5 to 7 quarters.

In the weeks following the announcement of the $400 million in new financing, Netflix's stock price dropped to as low as $62.37 and traded in the range of $65 to $71 for most all of December 2011.

Financial statement data for Netflix for 2000–2011 are shown in Exhibits 2 and 3.

Industry Environment

Since 2000, the introduction of new technologies and electronics products had rapidly multiplied consumer opportunities to view movies. It was commonplace in 2012 for movies to be viewed at theaters, on airline flights, in hotels, from the rear seats of motor vehicles equipped with video consoles, in homes, or most anywhere on a laptop PC or handheld device like an Apple iPhone, iPad, or iPod Touch. Home viewing was

EXHIBIT 2: Netflix's consolidated statements of operations, 2000–2011 (in millions, except per share data)

	2000	2005	2007	2009	2010	2011
Revenues	$35.9	$682.2	$1205.3	$1670.3	$2162.6	$3205.6
Cost of Revenues:						
Subscription costs	24.9	393.8	664.4	909.5	1,154.1	1789.6
Fulfillment expenses	10.2	72.0	121.3	169.8	203.2	250.3
Total cost of revenues	35.1	465.8	786.2	1079.3	1357.4	2039.9
Gross profit	0.8	216.4	419.2	591.0	805.3	1164.7
Operating expenses						
Technology and development	16.8	35.4	71.0	114.5	163.3	259.0
Marketing	25.7	144.6	218.2	237.7	293.8	402.6
General and administrative	7.0	35.5	52.4	51.3	64.5	117.9
Other	9.7	(2.0)	(14.2)	(4.6)	–	9.0
Total operating expenses	59.2	213.4	327.4	399.1	521.6	788.8
Operating income	(58.4)	3.0	91.8	191.9	283.6	376.1
Interest and other income (expense)	(0.2)	5.3	20.1	0.3	(15.9)	(16.5)
Income before income taxes	–	8.3	110.9	192.2	267.7	359.5
Provision for (benefit from) income taxes	–	(33.7)	44.3	76.3	106.8	133.4
Net income	$(58.5)	$42.0	$66.7	$115.9	$160.8	$226.1
Net income per share:						
Basic	$(20.61)	$0.79	$0.99	$2.05	$3.06	$4.28
Diluted	(20.61)	0.64	0.97	1.98	2.96	4.16
Weighted average common shares outstanding:						
Basic	2.8	53.5	67.1	56.6	52.5	52.8
Diluted	2.8	65.5	68.9	58.4	54.3	54.4

Note: Totals may not add due to rounding.
Source: Company 10-K reports for 2003, 2006, and 2009.

EXHIBIT 3: Selected balance sheet and cash flow data for Netflix, 2000–2011 (in millions of $)

	2000	2005	2007	2009	2010	2011
Selected balance sheet data						
Cash and cash equivalents	$14.9	$212.3	$177.4	$134.2	$194.5	$508.1
Short-term investments	–	–	207.7	186.0	155.9	290.0
Current assets	n.a.	243.7	432.4	416.5	637.2	1830.9
Net investment in content library	n.a.	57.0	128.4	146.1	362.0	1966.6
Total assets	52.5	364.7	679.0	679.7	982.1	3069.2
Current liabilities	n.a.	137.6	208.9	226.4	388.6	1225.1
Working capital*	(1.7)	106.1	223.5	190.1	248.6	605.8
Stockholders' equity	(73.3)	226.3	429.8	199.1	290.2	642.8
Cash flow data						
Net cash provided by operating activities	$(22.7)	$157.5	$277.4	$325.1	$276.4	$317.7
Net cash used in investing activities	(25.0)	(133.2)	(436.0)	(246.1)	(116.1)	(265.8)
Net cash provided by (used in) financing activities	48.4	13.3	(64.4)	(84.6)	(100.0)	261.6

* Note: Defined as current assets minus current liabilities.

Sources: Company 10-K Reports for 2003, 2005, 2007, 2008, 2009, and 2011.

possible on PCs, TVs connected to a digital video disc (DVD) player, and video game consoles. As of 2012, more than 90 percent of U.S. households had DVD players connected to their TVs, enabling them to play movie DVDs. Households with big-screen high-definition TVs and a Blu-ray player could rent a Blu-ray DVD and enjoy a significantly higher picture quality. In recent years, millions of households had upgraded to high-speed or broadband Internet service and purchased Blu-ray DVD devices, video game consoles, and/or TVs with built-in connectivity to the Internet, enabling them to view content streamed over the Internet. However, heading into 2012, it was clear that the 134 million U.S. households with high speed Internet service and Internet-connected Blu-ray players, video game consoles, TVs, computers, tablets, and/or smartphones were rapidly shifting from renting physical DVDs to watching movies and TV episodes streamed over the Internet.

Increasing numbers of devices had recently appeared in electronics stores (or become available from cable, satellite, and fiber-optic TV providers) that enabled TVs to be connected to the Internet and receive streamed content from online providers with no hassle. These devices made it simple for households to order streamed movies with just a few clicks instead of traveling to a video rental store or waiting for a disk to be delivered through the mail. In 2012, more than 700 different devices were capable of streaming content from Netflix.

Consumers could obtain or view movie DVDs and TV episodes through a wide variety of distribution channels and providers. The options included:

- Watching movies on assorted cable channels included in the TV and entertainment packages provided by traditional cable providers (such as Time Warner, Comcast, Cox, and Charter), direct broadcast satellite providers (such as DirecTV and DISH Network), or fiber-optics providers (like AT&T and Verizon that had installed thousands of miles of fiber-optic cable that enabled them to simultaneously provide TV packages, telephone, and Internet services to customers).

- Subscribing to any of several movie-only channels (such as HBO, Showtime, and Starz) through a cable, satellite, or fiber-optics provider.

- Using a TV remote to order movies instantly streamed directly to a TV on a pay-per-view basis (generally referred to as 'video-on-demand' or VOD). Cable, satellite, and fiber-optic providers of multi-channel TV packages were promoting their VOD services and making more movie titles available to their customers. In 2011, about 40 million U.S. households (15 percent) spent about $1.3 billion on VOD movie rentals.[2]

- Purchasing DVDs from such retailers as WalMart, Target, Best Buy, Toy-R-Us, and Amazon.com. DVD sales, however, had declined for the past three years, partially a reflection of growing consumer preferences to rent rather than purchase DVDs of movies and TV episodes.

- Renting DVDs from Blockbuster and other local retail stores or from standalone rental kiosks like Redbox and Blockbuster Express. Physical-disc rentals at traditional brick-and-mortar locations had been trending downward for 5–8 years, but the downward spiral accelerated in 2010–2011. Blockbuster's share of physical disc rentals dropped from 23 per cent in 2010 to 17 percent in 2011.[3] The chief beneficiary of declining rentals at brick-and-mortar movie rental locations was Redbox. Since 2007, when Redbox first began deploying its distinctive red vending machine kiosks, Redbox's share of physical-disc DVD and Blu-ray movie rentals in the U.S. had mushroomed to 37 percent as of 2011 (up from 25 percent in 2010).

- Renting DVDs online from Netflix, Blockbuster, and several other subscription services that either mailed DVDs directly to subscribers' homes or streamed the content to subscribers via broadband Internet connections. In 2011, Netflix had about a 30 percent share of the physical DVD rental market and about a 56 percent share of streaming rentals.[4]

- Utilizing the rental or download services of such providers as Apple's iTunes store, Amazon Instant Video, Hulu.com, Vudu.com, Best Buy CinemaNow, Sony PlayStation Network, and Google's YouTube.

- Most recently, a new class of user interface apps had become available that enabled subscribers to the services of multi-channel TV providers (like cable or satellite operators) to watch certain TV shows, movies, and other programs at their convenience rather than at scheduled broadcast times. This service – called TV Everywhere – gave subscribers to watch programs on Internet connected TVs and computers, iPads, iPhones, Android phones, and other devices. HBO's TV Everywhere application – called HBO GO – enabled HBO subscribers to have anytime, anywhere access to all HBO shows, hit movies, and other programs through participating multi-channel TV providers. In 2012, most multi-channel TV providers and the owners of most channels carried on cable and satellite networks were exploring TV Everywhere options and packages for interested viewers.

- Pirating files of movies and other content from Internet sources via the use of illegal file-sharing software. Piracy was widely thought to be a contributing factor to declining sales of movie DVDs. In 2011–2012, movie studios were becoming increasingly concerned that digital piracy could become a tidal wave.[5] Much of Netflix's streaming library was rumored to be available through online piracy.

In recent years, movie studios had released filmed entertainment content for distribution to movie DVD retailers and to companies renting movie DVDs about 17 weeks after a film first began showing in theaters. After about 3 months in theaters, movie studios usually released first-run films to pay-per-view and video-on-demand (VOD) providers (prior to the last several years, the release window had been about 6 months). In 2011, a few studios experimented with charging up to $30 for films released to pay-per-view and VOD providers for showing after 8 weeks in theaters, but quickly ceased because of disappointingly small purchase volumes.[6] However, in October 2011, a Kevin Spacey film was released in theaters and through both Netflix and Time Warner Cable on the same day; the movie grossed $3.5 million at theaters and the studio realized more than $5 million each from Netflix and Time Warner Cable.[7] Premium TV channels like HBO, Starz, Cinemax, and Showtime were next in the distribution window, typically getting access to premium films one year after initial theater showings. Movie studios released films for viewing to basic cable and network TV some 2 to 3 years after theatrical release. TV episodes were often made available for Internet viewing shortly after the original airing date.

Recently, however, some movie studios had experimented with shortened release periods, including making new release titles available to video-on-demand providers or for online purchase on the same date DVDs could be sold by retailers. Other movie studios had implemented or announced their intention to implement policies preventing movie rental providers from renting movie DVDs until 30 to 60 days following the date DVD titles could be sold by retailers. For example, in January 2012, Warner Home Entertainment increased the availability date for rental DVDs top kiosks and subscription-by-mail services to 58 days. Movie studios and TV networks were expected to continue to experiment with the timing of the releases to various distribution channels and providers, in an ongoing effort to discover how best to maximize revenues.

Market Trends in Home Viewing of Movies

The wave of the future in the market for renting movies and TV content was unquestionably in streaming movies and TV shows to Internet-connected TVs, computers, and mobile devices. Streaming had the advantage of allowing household members to order and instantly watch the movies and TV programs they wanted to see. Renting a streamed movie could be done either by utilizing the services of Netflix, Blockbuster Online, Amazon Instant Video, Apple's iTunes, and other streaming video providers or by using a TV remote to place orders with a cable, satellite, or fiber-optics provider to instantly watch a movie from a list of several hundred selections that changed periodically. With a few exceptions, rental prices for pay-per-view and VOD movies ranged from $1 to $6, but the rental price for popular recently-released movies was usually $3.99 to $5.99. During 2011, several movie studios had experimented with charging up to $30 for films released to pay-per-view and VOD providers for showing after 8 weeks in theaters, but disappointingly small viewer response to such high-priced rentals quickly put an end to this strategy.[8] However, in October 2011, a Kevin Spacey film was released in theaters and through both Netflix and Time Warner Cable on the same day; the movie grossed $3.5 million at theaters and the studio realized more than $5 million each from Netflix and Time Warner Cable.[9] In 2012, many in-home movie viewers saw unlimited Internet streaming from subscription services as a better value than pay-per-view – the rental costs for 2 pay-per-view movies usually exceeded the $7.99 monthly price for unlimited streaming currently being charged by Netflix.

Several strategic initiatives to promote increased use of streaming video were underway in 2012.

● The owners of Hulu – Providence Equity Partners, The Walt Disney Company (owner of the ABC network), News Corp. (the parent of Fox Broadcasting and Fox Entertainment) and Comcast (the owner of NBCUniversal) – had for several years offered a free online video service at (www.hulu.com) where viewers could watch a selection of hit TV shows and movies from the libraries of ABC, NBC, Fox Broadcasting, Walt Disney Studios, Universal Studios, Fox Entertainment, and a few others; the revenues to support the free Hulu site came from advertisers whose commercials were inserted into all of the free programs. But in mid-2011, three years after creating the Hulu site, the owners became reluctant to continue giving their content away for free and began an effort to sell the venture. In October 2011, the sales process was abandoned; Google, the Dish Network, Amazon, and Yahoo were rumored to have contemplated or made offers to acquire Hulu. Shortly thereafter, Hulu began actively promoting an advertising-supported unlimited streaming service called Hulu Plus where, for $7.99 per month, subscribers could watch a much larger selection of premium movies and primetime TV shows interspersed with commercials.

- Time Warner Cable, Comcast, Charter, Dish Network, DirecTV, HBO, Showtime, and others were in the early stages of promoting their TV Everywhere concept and program offerings that enabled customers to watch certain TV shows free at any time on any Internet-connected device (including computers and such mobile devices as iPads and smart phones) so long as they were paying subscribers. For example, DirecTV had created a device called Nomad to help subscribers watch their recorded programs anywhere; Nomad allowed subscribers to synchronize their smartphone, laptop, or tablet with recorded content on their DVRs and watch the recorded programs anywhere, anytime. Dish Network had introduced a 'Sling Adapter' that – in conjunction with an Internet-connected DVR and a free Dish remote access app downloaded onto a mobile device –enabled customers to watch TV programs at their convenience on any Internet-connected device. However, for TV everywhere to reach its full potential, each cable, satellite, and fiber-optic multi-channel TV provider had to negotiate agreements for online rights to each channel's programming. As of early 2012, just a few multi-channel TV providers had secured online rights to as many as 15 channels, but this was expected to be temporary.

- Google and Apple were rolling out new versions of their Google TV and Apple TV products to try to win traction with consumers. Google had partnered with LG, Vizio, and Samsung to introduce TVs equipped with Google TV and was rapidly expanding its library of apps optimized for Google TV, all in an attempt to facilitate easy consumer discovery of content that was available for streaming to TVs and/or Android devices. In addition, Google had invested in a new subsidiary called Google Fiber that was actively exploring plans to enter the Internet service and/or TV provider marketplaces by offering a one-gigabit-per-second Internet service coupled with an on-demand TV service that enabled customers to watch what they wanted when they wanted without ever having to record anything. In March 2012, Google filed applications with the Missouri Public Service Commission and the Kansas Corporation Commission for approval to offer a video service to subscribers in the Kansas City area – the proposal called for Google to use national and regional programming collection points to send IPTV (a television-over-Internet technology) across its private fiber-optic network (Google Fiber) to subscribers in Kansas City. It remained to be seen whether Google could secure broadcast rights from the owners of various TV channels and Hollywood movie studios to lure customers; however, Google's YouTube was spending hundreds of millions of dollars funding new TV channels that were scheduled to be available online and could be a part of Google's TV package. Time Warner Cable was the dominant TV provider in Kansas City, while Direct TV, Dish Network, and AT&T's Uverse had smaller customer bases.

Apple TV was a tiny box that enabled users to play high-definition content from iTunes, Netflix, YouTube, and live sports events (professional baseball, hockey, and basketball) on TVs, or to stream content to TVs from an iPad, iPhone or iPod touch, or to stream music and photos from computers to TVs. In March 2012, Netflix and Apple implemented an agreement whereby Apple TV users could sign up for Netflix services directly through their Apple TV device, using their iTunes account.

IHS Screen Digest Research had forecast that streaming content would exceed 3.4 billion views in 2012.[10] It also expected that movie viewing online in 2012 would exceed combined viewing on DVDs and Blu-ray devices for the first time.[11]

Competitive Intensity

The movie rental business was intensely competitive in 2012. Local brick-and-mortar stores that rented DVD discs were in the throes of a death spiral, as a growing number of their customers switched either to obtaining their DVDs at Redbox vending kiosks or utilizing Internet streaming services of one kind or another. Blockbuster, once a movie rental powerhouse with over $4.5 billion in annual rental revenues and more than 9000 company-owned and franchised stores in a host of countries, was a shadow of its former self in 2012. After losing over $4 billion during the 2002–2010 period, closing thousands of store locations, and launching several unsuccessful strategic attempts to rejuvenate revenues and return to profitability, Blockbuster filed for Chapter 11 bankruptcy protection in September 2010. Following a bankruptcy court auction, Dish Network emerged in April 2011 as the owner of Blockbuster's operations in the U.S. and certain foreign countries for a winning bid valued at $321 million. From the acquisition date of April 26, 2011 through December 31, 2011, Blockbuster operations contributed $975 million in revenue and $4 million in net income to Dish Network's consolidated results of operations. Going into 2012, Blockbuster was operating some 1500 retail stores in the U.S., but Dish Network management had announced that it expected to close over 500 domestic Blockbuster stores during the first half of 2012 as a result of weak store-level financial performance and that additional stores might also need to be closed. For the time being, Blockbuster was offering movies and video games for sale and rental through its retail stores, the blockbuster.com website (via a DVDs-by-mail subscription service), and pay-per-view VOD service. In addition, Dish Network subscribers could access Blockbuster@ Home to obtain movies, video games, and TV shows through Internet streaming, mail and in-store exchanges, and online downloads.

Movie Gallery, once the second largest movie rental chain, filed for Chapter 11 bankruptcy protection in February 2010 and, shortly thereafter, opted to liquidate its entire movie rental business and close 1871 Movie Gallery, 545 Hollywood Video, and 250 Game Crazy store locations. Within months, Movie Gallery ceased to exist.

The big winner in renting DVD discs was Redbox. Redbox had entered the movie rental business in 2007 with a vending machine-based strategy whereby Redbox self-service DVD kiosks were placed in leading supermarkets, drug stores, mass merchants like Walmart, convenience stores, and fast-food restaurants (McDonald's). Customers could rent new release movie DVDs for $1 per day (the price was raised to $1.20 per day in Fall 2011). Retailers with Redbox kiosks were paid a percentage of the rental revenues. Going into 2012, Redbox had deployed 35 400 of its vending machine kiosks in 29 300 locations in every state of the U.S. and in Puerto Rico. In February 2012, Redbox agreed to acquire about 9000 Blockbuster-branded DVD kiosks operated by NCR Corp. Redbox and Netflix (with its DVDs-by-mail subscription option) were positioned to dominate the physical DVD rental segment for the foreseeable future.

The main battle in the movie rental marketplace was in the VOD and Internet streaming segments where several classes of competitors employing a variety of strategies were maneuvering to win the viewing time of consumers, capture enough revenue to be profitable, and become one of the market leaders. Competitors offering pay-per-view and VOD rentals were popular options for households and individuals that rented movies occasionally (once or at most twice per month), since the rental costs tended to be less than either the monthly subscription prices for unlimited streaming or the monthly fees to access premium movie channels like HBO, Starz, Cinemax, and Showtime. However, competitors offering unlimited Internet streaming plans tended to be the most economical and convenient choice for individuals and households that watched an average of three or more titles per month and for individuals that wanted to be able to watch movies or TV shows on mobile devices.

Netflix was the clear leader in Internet streaming in 2012, with over 23 million streaming subscribers that watched an average of 30 hours of video monthly and some 60 000 titles that could viewed on an Internet-connected device.[12] But Netflix had numerous ambitious rivals that saw huge revenue and profit opportunities in using online technology to provide movies, TV programming, and other entertainment content to all types of Internet-connected devices on an anywhere, anytime basis.

Netflix's two most important subscription-based instant streaming rivals included:

- Hulu Plus – The subscription fee for Hulu Plus was $7.99 per month for unlimited streaming, and new subscribers got a 1-week free trial. All Hulu Plus content included advertisements as a means of helping keep the monthly subscription price low. The Hulu Plus library of offerings included all current season episodes of popular TV shows, over 15 000 back season episodes of 380+ TV shows, and over 425 movies, many in high-definition.

- Amazon Prime Instant Video – This service entailed becoming an Amazon Prime member for a fee of $79 per year (after a 1-month free trial). All Amazon Prime members were entitled to free 2-day shipping on *all Amazon orders*, unlimited commercial-free streaming of 17 000 movies and TV programs, one free Kindle book rental each month, and assorted other perks. In March 2012, there were an estimated 3.5 to 5 million Amazon Prime members. New Amazon Prime members were entitled to a 1-month free trial. While Amazon had originally created its Amazon Prime membership program as a means of providing unlimited 2-day shipping to customers that frequently ordered merchandise from Amazon and liked to receive their orders quickly, in 2012 it was clear that Amazon was also endeavoring to brand Amazon Prime as a standalone streaming service at a subscription price below that of Netflix. In addition, Amazon competed with Netflix's DVDs-by-mail subscription service and with VOD and pay-per-view providers via its Amazon Instant Video offering, which enabled any visitor to the Amazon website to place an online order to instantly watch on a pay-per-view basis any of the 42 000 movies or TV shows in Amazon's rental library.

In February 2010, Wal-Mart Stores announced its intention to distribute movies over the Internet and had acquired Vudu, a leading provider of digital technologies that enabled online delivery of entertainment content. In 2012, Vudu was the largest home entertainment retailer in the U.S. with the capability to stream about 20 000 movie titles (including some 4000 HD titles with Dolby Surround Sound) to Internet-connected TVs, Blu-ray players, computers, iPads and other tablets, and video game consoles (XBox 360 and PlayStation 3). Movies were available the same day they were released on DVD or Blu-ray discs and could be purchased or rented without a subscription; the rental fee was $2 per night for 2 nights. First-time users were eligible for free Vudu movie credits that could be used for a 1-month trial period. In April 2012, Wal-mart initiated an exclusive in-store disc-to-digital service powered by Vudu technology which enabled people to bring their DVD and Blu-ray collections from partnering movie studios (Paramount, Sony, Fox, Universal, and Warner Bros.) to a Wal-mart Photo Center and have digital copies of the DVDs placed in a personal Vudu account. Then Vudu account holders could log on to Vudu.com and view their movies any time, any place on more than 300 different Internet-connected devices.

The growing rush among multi-channel TV providers to offer subscribers attractive TV Everywhere packages signaled a widespread belief that using Internet streaming to enable subscribers to watch certain TV shows or movies free at any time on any Internet-connected device was the best long-term solution for competing effectively with Netflix's Internet streaming service. In 2012, most every major network broadcaster, multi-channel TV provider, and premium movie channel was investing in Internet apps for all types of Internet-connected TVs, laptops, video game consoles, tablets and smart phones and otherwise positioning themselves to offer attractive TV Everywhere packages. HBO with its HBO GO offering (www.hbogo.com) and Showtime with its Showtime Anytime offering (www.showtimeanytime.com) were both trying to gain more viewing hours with their subscribers. Pricing for TV Everywhere offerings was simple – users just entered an authentication code verifying their subscription status at the appropriate website. Subscribers then clicked on whichever offering interested them to initiate instant streaming to their device.

According to market research done by The NPD Group, 15 percent of U.S. consumers ages 13 and older used pay-TV VOD services from their multi-channel cable, satellite, and fiber-optic providers in the 12 months ending August 2011; this translated into 40 million users and rental revenues of $1.1 billion.[13] However, there were 4 million fewer VOD users who paid additional fees to watch movies from these same providers in August 2011 compared to August 2010. This was attributed to the growing number of attractive VOD offerings from rival online VOD providers such as iTunes, Amazon Instant Video, Vudu, and others that instantly streamed rentals over the Internet. The NPD Group estimated that Internet streaming accounted for 1 out of every 6 VOD rentals in 2011 and that the share of Internet-streamed VOD rentals was likely to continue to grow, chiefly because many consumers saw the prices of Internet-streamed rentals as a better value and believed such providers had more movie-title selections.[14]

Netflix's Business Model and Strategy

Since launching the company's online movie rental service in 1999, Reed Hastings, founder and CEO of Netflix, had been the chief architect of Netflix's subscription-based business model and strategy that had transformed Netflix into the world's largest online entertainment subscription service and revolutionized the way that many people rented movies and previously broadcast TV shows. Hastings' goals for Netflix were simple: Build the world's best Internet movie service, keep improving Netflix's offerings and services faster than rivals, attract growing numbers of subscribers every year, and grow long-term earnings per share. Hastings was a strong believer in moving early and fast to initiate strategic changes that would help Netflix outcompete rivals, strengthen its brand image and reputation, and fortify its position as industry leader.

Netflix's Subscription-based Business Model

Netflix employed a subscription-based business model. Members could choose from a variety of subscription plans whose prices and terms had varied over the years. Originally, all of the subscription plans were based on obtaining and returning DVDs by mail, with monthly prices dependent on the number of titles out at a time. But as more and more households began to have high-speed Internet connections, Netflix began bundling unlimited streaming with each of its DVD-by-mail subscription options, with the long-term intent of encouraging subscribers to switch to watching instantly-streamed movies rather than using DVD discs delivered and returned by mail. The DVDs-by-mail part of the business had order fulfillment costs and postage costs that were bypassed when members opted for instant streaming.

The DVD-by-vMail Option

Subscribers who opted to receive movie and TV episode DVDs by mail went to Netflix's website, selected one or more movies from its DVD library of over 120 000 titles, and received the movie DVDs by first-class mail generally within 1 business day – more than 97 percent of Netflix's subscribers lived within 1-day delivery of the company 50 distribution centers (plus 50 other shipping points) located throughout the U.S. During the 2004–2010 period, Netflix had aggressively added more distribution centers and shipping points in order to provide members with 1-business-day delivery on DVD orders. Subscribers could keep a DVD for as long as they wished, with no due dates, no late fees, no shipping fees, and no pay-per-view fees. Subscribers returned DVDs via the U.S. Postal Service in a prepaid return envelope that came with each movie order. The address on the return envelope was always the closest distribution center/shipping point so that returned DVDs could quickly be returned to inventory and used to fill incoming orders from subscribers.

Exhibit 4 shows Netflix's various subscription plan options during 2010-2012. The most popular DVD-by-mail plans were those with one, two, or three titles out-at-a-time.

The Streaming Option

Netflix launched its Internet streaming service in January 2007, with instant-watching capability for 2000 titles on personal computers. Very quickly, Netflix invested aggressively to enable its software to instantly stream content to a growing number of 'Netflix-ready' devices, including Sony's PlayStation 3 consoles, Microsoft's Xbox 360, Nintendo's Wii, Internet-connected Blu-ray players and TVs, TiVo DVRs, and special Netflix players made by Roku and several other electronics manufacturers. At the same time, it began licensing increasing amounts of digital content that could be instantly streamed to subscribers. Initially, Netflix took a 'metered' approach to streaming, offering, in essence, an hour per month of instant watching on a PC for every dollar of a subscriber's monthly subscription plan. For example, subscribers on the $16.99 per month plan, which provides unlimited DVD rentals with three discs out at a time, received 17 hours a month of movies and TV episodes watched instantly on their PCs while those on the $4.99 limited plan were entitled to 5 hours of instant

EXHIBIT 4: Netflix's subscription plans, 2010–2012

Subscription plan choices	Monthly subscription price		
	June 2010	November 22, 2010 through June 2011	September 2011 through 2012
Unlimited DVD plans:			
1 title out at a time	$8.99 plus unlimited streaming	$9.99 plus unlimited streaming	$7.99
2 titles out at a time	$13.99 plus unlimited streaming	$14.99 plus unlimited streaming	$11.99
3 titles out at a time	$16.99 plus unlimited streaming	$19.99 plus unlimited streaming	$15.99
4 titles out at a time	$23.99 plus unlimited streaming	$27.99 plus unlimited streaming	$21.99
5 to 8 titles out at a time	$29.99–$47.99 plus unlimited streaming	$34.99–$53.99 plus unlimited streaming	$27.99–$43.99
Unlimited streaming (no DVDs)	Not available	$7.99	$7.99
Unlimited streaming plus DVDs			
Unlimited streaming plus 1 DVD title out at a time	–	–	$15.98
Unlimited streaming plus 2 DVD titles out at a time	–	–	$19.98
Unlimited streaming with 3–8 DVDs			$23.98–$51.98
Limited plan:			
• 1 DVD title out a time	$4.99	$4.99	$4.99
• A maximum of 2 DVD rentals per month			
• 2 hours of video streaming to a PC or Apple Mac per month (this plan did not allow members to stream movies to TVs via a Netflix-ready device)			
• Limited streaming selection			

Source: Company records and postings at www.netflix.com.

streaming. In January 2009, Netflix switched to an unlimited streaming option on all of its monthly subscription plans for unlimited DVD rentals; the limited plan continued to have a monthly streaming limit. Netflix had about 6000 movie titles available for streaming as of January 2009 and about 20 000 titles in mid-2010.

Then in July 2011, Netflix announced that effective September 1, 2011 it would no longer offer a single subscription plan including both DVD-by-mail and streaming in the U.S. Domestic subscribers who wished to receive DVDs-by-mail and also watch streamed content had to elect both a DVD-by-mail subscription plan and a streaming subscription plan. At December 31, 2011, Netflix had a total of 21.7 million domestic streaming subscribers (including 1.52 million who were in their free-trial period) and 11.2 million domestic DVD-by-mail subscribers (including 210 000 who were in their free-trial period); almost 6.6 million Netflix members had both a streaming subscription and a DVD-by mail subscription.

All new Netflix subscribers received a free 1-month trial. At the end of the free trial period, members automatically began paying the monthly fee, unless they canceled their subscription. All paying subscribers were billed monthly in advance. Payments were made by credit card or debit card. Subscribers could cancel at any time.

Exhibit 5 shows trends in Netflix's subscriber growth in the U.S. Exhibit 6 shows quarterly trends in Netflix subscriptions and profitability by market segment.

New subscribers were drawn to try Netflix's online movie rental service because of (1) the wide selection, (2) the extensive information Netflix provided about each movie in its rental library (including critic reviews, member reviews, online trailers, and subscriber ratings), (3) the ease with which they could find and order movies, (4) Netflix's policies of no late fees and no due dates on DVD rentals (which eliminated the hassle of getting DVDs back to local rental stores by the designated due date), (5) the convenience of being provided a postage-paid return envelope for mailing DVDs back to Netflix, and (6) the convenience of ordering and instantly watching movies streamed to their TVs or computers with no additional pay-per-view charge.

Management believed that Netflix's subscriber base consisted of three types of customers: those who liked the convenience of home delivery and/or instant streaming, bargain-hunters who were enthused about being able to watch many movies for an economical monthly price, and movie buffs who wanted the ability to choose from a very wide selection of films and TV shows.

Netflix's Strategy

Netflix had a multi-pronged strategy to build an ever-growing subscriber base that included:

- Providing subscribers with a comprehensive selection of DVD titles.
- Acquiring new content by building and maintaining mutually beneficial relationships with entertainment video providers.
- Making it easy for subscribers to identify movies and TV shows they were likely to enjoy and to put them in a queue for either instant streaming or delivery by mail.
- Giving subscribers a choice of watching streaming content or receiving quickly delivered DVDs by mail.
- Spending aggressively on marketing to attract subscribers and build widespread awareness of the Netflix brand and service.
- Promoting rapid transition of U.S. subscribers to streaming delivery rather than mail delivery.
- Expanding internationally.

EXHIBIT 5: Domestic subscriber data for Netflix, 2000–2011

	2000	2005	2007	2009	2010	January 1–June 30, 2011	July 1–December 31, 2011
Total subscribers at beginning of period	107 000	2 610 000	6 316 000	9 390 000	12 268 000	19 501 000	24 594 000
Gross subscriber additions during period	515 000	3 729 000	5 340 000	9 322 000	15 648 000	11 614 000	9 930 000
Subscriber cancellations during the period	330 000	2 160 000	4 177 000	6 444 000	8 415 000	6 521 000	10 129 000
Total subscribers at end of period	292 000	4 179 000	7 479 000	12 268 000	19 501 000	24 594 000	24 395 000
Net subscriber additions during the period	185 000	1 569 000	1 163 000	2 878 000	7 233 000	5 093 000	(199 000)
Free trial subscribers at end of period	n.a.	153 000	153 000	376 000	1 566 000	1 331 000	1 537 000
Subscriber acquisition cost	$49.96	$38.78	$40.86	$25.48	$18.21	$14.70	$15.41
Average monthly revenue per paying subscriber	n.a.	$17.94	$14.95	$13.30	$12.20	$11.49	$12.35

Note: n.a. = not available.

Sources: Netflix's 10-K Reports, 2010, 2009, 2005, and 2003 and Netflix Quarterly Report for the period ending June 30, 2011, posted in the investors relations section at www.netflix.com (accessed March 16, 2012).

A Comprehensive Library of Movies and TV Episodes

Since its early days, Netflix's strategy had been to offer subscribers a large and diverse selection of DVD titles. It was aggressive in seeking out attractive new titles to add to its offerings. Its library of offerings had grown from some 55 000 titles in 2005 to about 120 000 titles in 2012, although the number of titles available for streaming was only about 30 000 as mid-2012 approached. The lineup included everything from the latest available Hollywood releases to releases several decades old to movie classics to independent films to hard-to-locate documentaries to TV shows and how-to videos, as well as a growing collection of cartoons and movies for children 12 and under. Netflix's DVD library far outdistanced the selection available in local brick-and-mortar movie rental stores and the 200 to 400 titles available in Redbox vending machines, but it was on a par with the number of titles available at Amazon. In mid-2012, Netflix's streaming library contained more titles than any other streaming service.

EXHIBIT 6: Quarterly trends in Netflix subscriptions and profitability, by market segment, quarter 3, 2011 through quarter 1, 2012 (in 000s)

	Three months ended		
	September 30, 2011	December 31, 2011	March 31, 2012
Domestic streaming			
Free subscriptions at end of period	937	1518	
Paid subscriptions at end of period	20 511	20 153	
Total subscriptions at end of period	21 448	21 671	
Revenue	n.a.	$476 334	
Cost of revenues and marketing expenses	n.a.	424 224	
Contribution profit		52 110	
International streaming			
Free subscriptions at end of period	491	411	
Paid subscriptions at end of period	989	1447	
Total subscriptions at end of period	1480	1858	
Revenue	$22 687	$28 988	
Cost of revenues and marketing expenses	46 005	88 731	
Contribution profit	$(23 318)	$(59 743)	
Domestic DVDs-by-mail			
Free subscriptions at end of period	115	126	
Paid subscriptions at end of period	13 813	11 039	
Total subscriptions at end of period	13 928	11 039	
Revenue		$370 253	
Cost of revenues and marketing expenses		176 488	
Contribution profit		$193 765	
Consolidated operations			
Free unique subscribers at end of period*	1437	1948	
Paid unique subscribers at end of period*	23 832	24 305	
Total unique subscribers at end of period*	25 269	26 253	
Revenue	$821 839	$875 575	
Cost of revenues and marketing expenses	625 725	689 443	
Contribution profit	196 114	186132	
Other operating expenses	99 272	124 260	
Operating income	96 842	61872	
Other income (expense)	(3219)	(5037)	
Provision for income taxes	31 163	21 616	
Net income	$62 460	$35 219	

Note: Netflix defined 'contribution profit (loss)' as revenues less cost of revenues and marketing expenses. Cost of revenue includes expenses related to the acquisition and licensing of content (streaming content license agreements, DVD direct purchases and DVD revenue sharing agreements with studios, distributors and other content suppliers), as well as content delivery costs related to providing streaming content and shipping DVDs to subscribers (which includes the postage costs to mail DVDs to and from our paying subscribers, the packaging and label costs for the mailers, all costs associated with streaming content over the Internet, the costs of operating and staffing shipping centers and customer service centers, DVD inventory management expenses, and credit card fees).

*Since some Netflix members in the U.S. subscribed to both streaming and DVD-by-mail plans, they were counted as a single unique subscriber to avoid double counting the same subscriber.

n.a. = not applicable. During July and August of the third quarter of 2011, Netflix's domestic streaming content and DVD-by-mail operations were combined. Subscribers in the U.S. were able to receive both streaming content and DVDs under a single hybrid plan. Accordingly, revenues were generated and marketing expenses were incurred in connection with the subscription offerings as a whole. Therefore, the company did not allocate revenues or marketing expenses for the domestic streaming and domestic DVD segments prior to the fourth quarter of 2011.

Source: Netflix records posted in the Financial Statements portion of the investor relations section at www.newtflix.com (accessed 19 March 2012).

New Content Acquisition

Over the years, Netflix had spent considerable time and energy establishing strong ties with various entertainment video providers and leveraging these ties to both expand its content library and gain access to new releases as early as possible – the time frame that Netflix gained access to films after their theatrical release was an important item of negotiation for Netflix (in 2011 Netflix was able to negotiate access to certain films produced by Lionsgate within one year of their initial theatrical release for showing to members in the UK and Ireland). Also, in 2011, Netflix had successfully negotiated *exclusive* rights to show a number of titles produced by several studios.

In August 2011, Netflix introduced a new 'Just for Kids' section on its website that contained a large selection of kid-friendly movies and TV shows. In March 2012, all of the Just for Kids selections became available for streaming on PlayStation 3 game consoles. As of early March 2012, over 1 billion hours of Just for Kids programming had been streamed to Netflix members.

New content was acquired from movie studios and distributors through direct purchases, revenue-sharing agreements, and licensing agreements to stream content. Netflix acquired many of its new release movie DVDs from studios for a low upfront fee in exchange for a commitment for a defined period of time either to share a percentage of subscription revenues or to pay a fee based on content utilization. After the revenue-sharing period expired for a title, Netflix generally had the option of returning the title to the studio, purchasing the title, or destroying its copies of the title. On occasion, Netflix also purchased DVDs for a fixed fee per disc from various studios, distributors and other suppliers. Netflix had about 140 000 titles in its DVD library as of April 2012.

In the case of movie titles and TV episodes that were delivered to subscribers via the Internet for instant viewing, Netflix generally paid a fee to license the content for a defined period of time, with the total fees spread out over the term of the license agreement (so as to match up content payments with the stream of subscription revenues coming in for that content). Following expiration of the license term, Netflix either removed the content from its library of streamed offerings or negotiated extension or renewal of the license agreement. Netflix greatly accelerated its acquisition of new streaming content in 2010 and 2011, growing its streaming library to around 60 000 titles, up from about 17 000 titles in 2009. Netflix's payments to movie studios for streaming rights in 2010–2011 exceeded its payments for DVD distribution rights – see Exhibit 7. In 2010–2011, Netflix's rapidly growing subscriber base gave movie studios and the network broadcasters of popular TV shows considerably more bargaining power to negotiate higher prices for the new content that Netflix sought to acquire for its content library. Netflix management was fully aware of its weakening bargaining position in new content acquisition, and the higher prices it was having to pay to secure streaming rights largely accounted for why the company's contribution profits from streaming were lower than from DVD rentals – see Exhibit 6. However, Netflix executives expected that long-term growth in the number of streaming subscribers would enable the company to earn attractive profits on its streaming business, despite the increased costs of acquiring attractive new content.

Netflix had incurred obligations to pay $3.91 billion for streaming content as of December 31, 2011, up from $1.12 billion as of December 31, 2010. Some of these obligations did not appear on the company's year-end 2011 balance sheet because they did not meet content library asset recognition criteria (either the fee was not known or reasonably determinable for a specific title or the fee was known but the title was not yet available for streaming to subscribers). Certain of Netflix's new licensing agreements also had variable terms and included renewal provisions that were solely at the option of the content provider. The expected timing of the Netflix's streaming content payments was as follows:[15]

EXHIBIT 7: Netflix's quarterly expenditures for additions to content library, 2009–2011

	Expenditures for additions to DVD library (in 000s)	Expenditures for additions to streaming content library (in 000s)	Total expenditures for new content (in 000s)
2009			
Quarter 1	$46 499	$22 091	$68 590
Quarter 2	43 224	9343	52 567
Quarter 3	46 273	9998	56 271
Quarter 4	57 048	22 785	79 833
Annual Total	$193 044	$64 217	$257 261
2010			
Quarter 1	$36 902	$50 475	$87 377
Quarter 2	24 191	66 157	90 348
Quarter 3	29 900	115 149	145 049
Quarter 4	32 908	174 429	207 337
Annual Total	$123 901	$406 210	$530 111
2011			
Quarter 1	$22 119	$192 307	$214 426
Quarter 2	19 065	612 595	631 660
Quarter 3	20 826	539 285	560 111
Quarter 4	23 144	976 545	999 689
Annual Total	$85 154	$2 320 732	$2 405 886

Source: Company cash flow data, posted in the investor relations section at www.netflix.com (accessed 16 March 2012).

Less than one year	$797.6 million
Due after one year and through 3 years	2384.4
Due after 3 years and through 5 years	650.5
Due after 5 years	74.7
Total streaming obligations	$3907.2 million

Netflix's Convenient and Easy-to-Use Movie Selection Software

Netflix had developed proprietary software technology that allowed members to easily scan a movie's length, appropriateness for various types of audiences (G, PG, or R), primary cast members, genre, and an average of the ratings submitted by other subscribers (based on 1 to 5 stars). With one click, members could watch a short preview if they wished. Most important, perhaps, was a personalized 1- to 5-star recommendation for each title that was based on a subscribers' own ratings of movies previously viewed, movies that the member had placed on a list for future streamed viewing and/or mail delivery), and the overall or average rating of all subscribers.

Subscribers often began their search for movie titles by viewing a list of several hundred personalized movie title 'recommendations' that Netflix's software automatically generated for each member. Each member's list of recommended movies was the product of Netflix-created algorithms that organized the company's entire library of titles into clusters of similar movies and then sorted the movies in each cluster from most liked to least liked based on over 3 billion ratings provided by subscribers. In 2010–2011, Netflix added new movie ratings from subscribers to its database at a rate of about 20 million per week. Those subscribers who rated similar movies in similar clusters were categorized as like-minded viewers. When a subscriber was online and browsing through the movie selections, the software was programmed to check the clusters the subscriber had rented/viewed in the past, determine which movies the customer had yet to rent/view in that cluster, and recommended only those movies in the cluster that had been highly rated by viewers. Viewer ratings determined which available titles were displayed to a subscriber and in what order. When streaming members came upon a title they wanted to view, that title could with a single click be put on their 'instant queue' – a list for future viewing. A member's instant queue was immediately viewable with one click whenever the member went to Netflix's website; with one additional click, any title on a member's instant queue could be activated for immediate viewing. In Spring 2011, a number of the world's leading consumer electronics companies began placing a Netflix button on their remotes for operating newly-purchased TVs, Blu-ray disc players, and other devices that had built-in Internet connections – the button provided Netflix subscribers with a one-click connection to their instant queue. Clicking on a remote with a Netflix button resulted in all of the titles in a subscriber's instant queue appearing on the TV screen within a few seconds; streaming was instantly initiated by clicking on whichever title the subscriber wished to watch. In the case of members with DVD-by-mail subscriptions, members browsing the title library on Netflix's website could with one click place a title on their list (or queue) to receive by mail. DVD subscribers specified the order in which titles in their personal queue were to be mailed out and could alter the lists or the mailing order at any time. It was also possible to reserve a copy of upcoming releases. Netflix management saw the movie recommendation tool as a quick and personalized means of helping subscribers identify titles they were likely to enjoy.

Netflix management believed that over 50 percent of the titles selected by subscribers came from the recommendations generated by its proprietary software. The software algorithms were thought to be particularly effective in promoting selections of smaller, high-quality films to subscribers who otherwise might not have discovered them in the company's massive and ever-changing collection. On average, about 85 percent of the titles in Netflix's content library were rented each quarter, an indication of the effectiveness of the company's recommendation software in steering subscribers to movies of interest and achieving broader utilization of the company's entire library of titles.

A Choice of Mail Delivery Versus Streaming

Until 2007-2008 when streaming technology had advanced to the point that made providing video-on-demand a viable option, Netflix concentrated its efforts on speeding the time it took to deliver subscriber orders via mail delivery. The strategy was to establish a nationwide network of distribution centers and shipping points with the capability to deliver DVDs ordered by subscribers within 1 business day. To achieve quick delivery and return capability, Netflix created sophisticated software to track the location of each DVD title in inventory and determine the fastest way of getting the DVD orders to subscribers. When a subscriber placed an order for a specific DVD, the system first looked for that DVD at the shipping center closest to the customer. If that center didn't have the DVD in stock, the system then checked for availability at the next closest center The search continued until the DVD was found, at which point the regional distribution center with the ordered DVD in inventory was provided with the information needed to initiate the order fulfillment and shipping process. If the DVD was unavailable anywhere in the system, it was wait-listed. The software system then moved to the customer's next choice and the process started all over. And no matter where the DVD was sent from, the system knew to print the return label on the pre-paid envelope to send the DVDs to the shipping center closest to the customer to reduce return mail times and permit more efficient use of Netflix's DVD inventory. No subscriber orders were shipped on holidays or weekends.

By early 2007, Netflix had 50 regional distribution centers and another 50 shipping points scattered across the U.S., giving it 1 business-day delivery capability for 95 percent of its subscribers and, in most cases, also enabling 1-day return times. As of 2010, additional improvements in Netflix's distribution and shipping network had resulted in 1 business-day delivery capability for 98 percent of Netflix's subscribers.

In 2007, when entertainment studios became more willing to allow Internet delivery of their content (since recent technological advances prevented streamed movies from being pirated), Netflix moved quickly to better compete with the growing numbers of video-on-demand providers by adding the feature of unlimited streaming to its regular monthly subscription plans. The market for Internet delivery of media content consisted of three segments: the rental of Internet delivered content, the download-to-own segment, and the advertising-supported online delivery segment (mainly, YouTube, and Hulu). Netflix's objective was to be the clear leader in the rental segment via its instant watching feature.

Giving subscribers the option of watching DVDs delivered by mail or instantly watching movies streamed to subscribers' computers or TVs had considerable strategic appeal to Netflix in two respects. One, giving subscribers the option to order and instantly watch streamed content put Netflix in position to compete head-to-head with the growing numbers of video-on-demand providers. Second, providing streamed content to subscribers had the attraction of being cheaper than (1) incurring the postage expenses on DVD orders and returns, (2) having to obtain and manage an ever-larger inventory of DVDs, and (3) covering the labor costs of additional distribution center personnel to fill a growing volume of DVD orders and handle increased numbers of returned DVDs. But streaming content to subscribers was not cost-free; it required server capacity, software to authenticate orders from subscribers, and a system of computers containing copies of the content files placed at various points in a network so as to maximize bandwidth and allow subscribers to access a copy of the file on a server near the subscriber. Having subscribers accessing a central server ran the risk of an Internet transmission bottleneck. Netflix also utilized third party content delivery networks to help it efficiently stream movies and TV episodes in high volume to Netflix subscribers over the Internet. According to one report, Netflix incurred a cost of about 5 cents to stream a movie to a subscriber compared to costs of about $1 in roundtrip mailing and labor fees for a DVD.[16]

Netflix executives believed that the strategy of combining streaming and DVDs-by-mail into a single monthly subscription price between 2007–September 2011 period enabled Netflix not only to offer members an attractively large selection of movies for one low monthly price but also to enjoy a competitive advantage vis-à-vis rivals as compared to providing a postal-delivery-only or Internet-delivery-only subscription service. Furthermore, Netflix management believed the company's combination postal-delivery/streaming service delivered compelling customer value and customer satisfaction by eliminating the hassle involved in making trips to local movie rental stores to choose and return rented DVDs.

In March 2012, 6 months after instituting separate plans for streaming and DVDs-by-mail, Netflix instituted as yet unannounced and somewhat subtle changes at its website. A support page appeared at www.netflix.com that sent people registering for a free trial subscription to 'dvd.netflix.com' if they wanted to sign up for a DVD-by-mail-only account.[17] In addition, Netflix began redirecting DVD-by-mail customers to a separate web page when they tried to rate movies on Netflix's main site, and DVD-by-mail-only subscribers that searched for movie titles were only shown titles that were also available for streaming rather than the heretofore full library of DVD titles.[18] Furthermore, ratings and recommendations by DVD and streaming customers were separated.

Marketing and Advertising

Netflix used multiple marketing channels to attract subscribers, including online advertising (paid search listings, banner ads, text on popular sites such as AOL and Yahoo, and permission-based e-mails), radio stations, regional and national TV, direct mail, and print ads. The costs of free monthly trials were treated as a marketing expense. It also participated in a variety of cooperative advertising programs with studios through which Netflix received cash consideration in return for featuring a studio's movies in its advertising. In recent years, Netflix had worked closely with the makers of Netflix-ready electronics devices to expand the number of devices on which subscribers could view Netflix-streamed content; these expenses were all considered as marketing expenses and sometimes took the form of payments to various consumer electronics partners for their efforts to produce and distribute these devices.

Management had boosted marketing expenditures of all kinds (including paid advertising) from $25.7 million in 2000 (16.8 percent of revenues) to $142.0 million in 2005 (20.8 percent of revenues) to $218.2 million in 2007 (18.1 percent of revenues). When the recession hit in late 2007 and 2008, management trimmed 2008 marketing expenditures to $199.7 million (14.6 percent of revenues) as a cost containment measure but in 2009 marketing expenditures resumed their upward trend, climbing to $237.7 million (14.2 percent of revenues). Marketing expenses rose to even more dramatically to $298.8 million in 2010 and to $402.6 million in 2011 owing to:

- Increased adverting efforts, particularly in the newly-entered countries of Canada, Latin America, the UK, and Ireland.
- Increased costs of free trial subscriptions.
- Increased payments to the company's consumer electronics partners.

Advertising campaigns of one type or another were underway more or less continuously, with the lure of 1-month free trials usually being the prominent ad feature. Advertising expenses totaled approximately $205.9 million in 2009, $181.4 million in 2008 and $207.9 million in 2007 – ad expenses for 2011 and 2010 were not publicly reported.

Transitioning to Internet Delivery of Content

Netflix's core strategy in 2012 was to grow its streaming subscription business domestically and globally. Since launching streaming to Internet-connected devices in 2007, the company had continuously improved the streaming experience of subscribers in three major ways:

- Expanding the size of its streaming content library, currently about 60 000 titles.
- Working with consumer electronics partners to increase the number of Internet-connected devices that could be used to view Netflix-streamed content.
- Improving the ease with which subscribers could navigate Netflix's website to locate and select content they wanted to watch.

The result had been rapidly growing consumer acceptance of and interest in the delivery of TV shows and movies directly over the Internet. Netflix subscribers watched over 2 billion hours of streaming video in the fourth quarter of 2011, an average of approximately 30 hours per member per month (which equated to a cost of $0.27 per hour of viewing, given the current $7.99 subscription price).[19] During this same period, the company realized a contribution profit of $52.1 million on its domestic streaming business segment (see Exhibit 6).

Going forward, Netflix executives expected that the number of members with DVD-by-mail subscriptions would decline, as subscribers migrated from DVD-by-mail plans to Internet streaming plans and as subscribers with both DVD-by-mail and streaming subscriptions opted for streaming-only subscriptions. An ever-smaller fraction of new subscribers was expected to opt for the DVD-by-mail plan. Management saw no need to proactively encourage or try to accelerate the decline in domestic DVD-by-mail subscriptions beyond the actions already taken – rather the strategy was to simply let subscribers choose whichever plan or plans they wished, since the company had ample ability to provide a satisfying experience to both DVD and streaming subscribers. Netflix management projected that the number of domestic DVD subscribers would decline from just over 11.0 million at the end of 2011 to about 9.5 million at the end of March 2012, with smaller sequential declines in future quarters. Early indications were that the number of Netflix streaming subscribers in the U.S.would rise by about 1.7 million in the first quarter of 2012.

In the near term, the falloff in revenues from declining domestic DVD subscriptions was projected to be offset by revenue gains from ongoing growth in the numbers of domestic streaming subscribers. Domestic DVD contribution margins were expected to remain healthy despite shrinking volume, due to the lower postage costs and order fulfillment costs associated with declines in the number of DVD discs being ordered by DVD-by-mail subscribers.

In March 2012, there were reports that Netflix was in exploratory discussions with multi-channel TV providers about offering its streaming content as an add-on option alongside such pvremium movie channels as HBO, Showtime, and Starz.[20] One benefit from such a strategic approach was said to be the likelihood that customers who purchased Netflix through a multi-channel TV provider would be more likely to remain a subscriber. Anywhere from 30 percent to 70 percent of Netflix's subscribers canceled their subscriptions each year (see Exhibit 3) – the percentage of existing subscribers that canceled their subscriptions was referred to as the 'churn rate.' For Netflix to grow its subscriber base in upcoming years, it had to overcome its churn rate by attracting enough new subscribers to more than offset subscriber cancellations. The appeal of offering Netflix through multi-channel TV providers was that pay-television channels had a customer churn rate of only 20 to 25 percent. At an investor event in San Francisco in late February 2012, Reed Hastings said partnering with cable companies to offer Netflix streaming as an add-on option was a natural progression for the company.[21]

International Expansion Strategy

Making Netflix's streaming service available to growing numbers of households and individuals outside the U.S. was a central element of Netflix's long-term strategy to grow revenues and profits. Netflix executives were fully aware that international expansion would temporarily depress overall company profitability since it took roughly 2 years to build a sufficiently large subscriber base in newly-entered country markets to have sufficient revenues to cover all the associated costs. The biggest cost to enter new countries was the expense of obtaining licenses from movie studios and the owners of TV shows to stream their content to subscribers in these countries. The second biggest cost related to the incremental advertising and marketing expenses needed to attract new subscribers and grow subscription revenues fast enough to achieve profitability within the targeted 2-year time frame.

In 2011, Netflix's international streaming segment (Canada and Latin America) reported a contribution loss of $103.1 million. Top management had projected that the added international expenses of expanding service to the UK and Ireland in January 2012 would result in total international contribution losses for Canada, Latin America, UK, and Ireland of between $108 million and $118 million in Quarter 1 of 2012.

Netflix planned to continue to invest in expanding its streaming content libraries in Latin America, the UK, and Ireland throughout 2012 and beyond, just as it had done since launching its service in Canada. According to CEO Reed Hastings and chief financial officer (CFO) David Wells, a bigger content library:[22]

> *improves the consumer experience, builds strong word of mouth and positive brand awareness, and drives additional acquisition [of new subscribers], all elements of a strong foundation for long-term success.*

Nonetheless, Netflix's entry into Latin America presented unique challenges not encountered in the other international markets. The concept of on-demand streaming video (outside of piracy and YouTube) was not something most Latin American households were familiar with, which required Netflix to do more work in driving consumer understanding and acceptance of the company's streaming service. Moreover, in Latin America, a smaller fraction of households had fewer internet-connected TVs, Blu-ray players, and other devices that readily connected to Netflix's service, plus in many locations there was an under-developed Internet infrastructure, relatively low credit card usage among households and individual, and consumer payment challenges for ecommerce. Many Latin American banks turned down all ecommerce debit card transactions due to fraud risk.

Netflix's Performance Prospects in 2012

At the time of printing, management's latest forecast for 2012 called for modest quarterly losses throughout 2012 and a loss for the whole year, due entirely to the sizable contribution losses in the international segment. However, continued growth in the number of domestic streaming subscribers was expected to produce contribution margins of 10–12 percent during 2012, comfortably above the company's long-term domestic streaming target of 8 percent and in line with the 10.9 percent domestic streaming contribution margin in the fourth quarter of 2011. Netflix management said that until the company returned to global profitability, it did not intend to launch additional international expansion.

Highlights of Netflix's Performance in the First Quarter of 2012

For the first three months of 2012, Netflix reported revenues of $869.8 million (21.0 percent higher than the revenues of $718.6 million in the first quarter of 2011) and a net loss of $4.6 million (versus net income of $60.2 million in the first quarter of 2011). The net loss for the quarter stemmed from contribution losses of $102.7 million in the international streaming segment; however, Netflix added 1 million more paying international subscribers during the first Quarter and had another 600 000 international subscribers enrolled in free trials. International streaming revenues were $43.4 million in the first quarter, versus revenues of $29.0 million for the fourth quarter of 2011 and $12.3 million for the first quarter of 2011.

In the U.S. the total number of streaming subscribers (including free trial subscribers) rose from 21.7 million at the end of the fourth quarter of 2011 to 23.4 million at the end the first quarter of 2012. Total paying subscribers jumped by 1.85 million during the quarter (from 20.15 million as of December 31, 2011 to 22.0 million as of March 31, 2012). Not surprisingly, the number of domestic DVD subscribers dropped by almost 1.1 million during the quarter to a total of 10.1 million as of March 31; nonetheless, the customer count exceeded management's expectations and contribution profits from this segment were $146.1 million – 7 million of the DVD subscribers were also streaming subscribers. Viewing per member was at a record high level during the quarter.

Reed Hastings indicated that Netflix would likely add a net of 7 million domestic streaming subscribers during 2012 (about the same number added in 2010) and end the year with approximately 27.2 million domestic streaming customers. He also said that:

- It would take longer than 8 quarters after initial entry for the company's operations in Latin America, the UK, and Ireland to reach sustained profitability, owing to ongoing investments in content improvements and somewhat slower-than-expected growth in membership.

- The company expected to return to global profitability in the second quarter of 2012 because of increasing contribution profits in domestic streaming, slow erosion of contribution profits in the domestic DVD segment, and narrowing contribution losses in the international streaming segment. Netflix had positive free cash flow of $2 million during the first three months of 2012.

- Given the strong response to the launch of the company's service in the UK, the company planned to enter another European market in the fourth quarter of 2012. Quickly investing the growing profits from the company's domestic business in additional global expansion had two key advantages, One, entering foreign markets ahead of other streaming rivals made it easier for Netflix to build a profitable subscriber base. Two, having growing numbers of subscribers in a growing number of countries enabled Netflix to more quickly reach the global scale needed to license global content rights economically.

Initial investor reaction to all this was decidedly negative. In the week following the April announcement of Netflix's first quarter results, full-year expectations, and future plans, Netflix's stock price – which had climbed to $129 per share in mid-February before falling back to the $105–$110 range in mid-April – dropped about $25 per share and then over the next 10 days slid further, trading as low as $72.49.

ENDNOTES

1. Michael Liedtke, 'Netflix's Online Gaps Likely to Continue,' Associated Press, April 9, 2012, accessed April 16, 2012 at www.sltrib.com/sltrib/money/538815.

2. NPD Group press release, February 16, 2012, accessed March 13, 2012 at www.npd.com.

3. NPD Group press release, January 19, 2012, accessed March 13, 2012 at www.npd.com.

4. Ibid.

5. See Daniel Frankel, 'Analyst to Studios: It's Time to Force Early VOD on Theater Chains,' posted at www.paidcontent.org, accessed March 12, 2012.

6. See, for example, Bret Lang, 'Lionsgate Tests Early VOD Waters with Taylor Lautner's "Abduction," The Wrap, posted at www.thewrap.com, August 10, 2011, accessed March 12, 2012 and also Frankel, 'Analyst to Studios: It's Time to Force Early VOD on Theater Chains.'

7. Frankel, 'Analyst to Studios: It's Time to Force Early VOD on Theater Chains.'

8. See, for example, Bret Lang, 'Lionsgate Tests Early VOD Waters with Taylor Lautner's "Abduction," *The Wrap*, posted at www.thewrap.com, August 10, 2011, accessed March 12, 2012 and also Frankel, 'Analyst to Studios: It's Time to Force Early VOD on Theater Chains.'

9. Frankel, 'Analyst to Studios: It's Time to Force Early VOD on Theater Chains.'

10. According to information in Amanda Alix, 'Is Netflix Trying to Pull Another Quikster?' The Motley Fool, posted March 29, 2012 at www.fool.com and accessed on March 30, 2012.

11. William Launder, 'Online Movie Viewing to Outpace DVD, Blu-ray Views This Year,' *The Wall Street Journal*, posted at http://online.wsj.com on March 23, 2012, accessed March 30, 2012.

12. Michael Liedtke, 'Netflix's Online Gaps Likely to Continue,' Associated Press, April 9, 2012, accessed April 16, 2012 at www.sltrib.com/sltrib/money/538815.

13. NPD Group press release, February 16, 2012, accessed March 13, 2012 at www.npd.com.

14. Ibid.

15. Netflix's 2011 10-K Report, p. 62.

16. Michael V. Copeland, 'Reed Hastings: Leader of the Pack,' *Fortune*, December 6, 2010, p. 128.

17. Amanda Alix, 'Is Netflix Trying to Pull Another Quikster?' *The Motley Fool*, posted March 29, 2012 at www.fool.com and accessed on March 30, 2012.

18. Ibid.

19. Letter to Shareholders, January 25, 2012, p. 1; posted in the investor relations section at www.netflix.com, accessed March 28, 2012.

20. Angela Moscaritolo, 'Report: Netflix Looking to Partner with Cable Companies,' *PC Magazine*, posted at www.PCMag.com on March 7, 2012, accessed March 7, 2012 and John Jannarone, 'Netflix Risks Tangle with Cable,' *The Wall Street Journal*, March 29, 2012, p. C12.

21. Moscaritolo, 'Report: Netflix Looking to Partner with Cable Companies.'

22. Letter to Shareholders, January 25, 2012, p. 6; posted in the investor relations section at www.netflix.com, accessed March 28, 2012.

Case 4

The O-Fold innovation for preventing wrinkles: a good business opportunity?

A. J. Strickland

University of Alabama

Jimmy Marquis

University of Alabama, Faculty Scholar

Alex Richards, a junior at a well-respected university, was double-majoring in finance and accounting. He took his schoolwork very seriously and had maintained a 4.0 grade point average. Richards had always dreamed of becoming a corporate executive and assisting in the strategic direction of an established company. He had been told by friends and professors that starting in public accounting and getting a Certified Public Accountant (CPA) was a traditional stepping-stone to a corporate executive position. What attracted Richards to his dream job was not just the compensation package but also the fact that he could set the direction of a company and see his strategy unfold before his eyes. Richards's father was a controller at a medium-size private company, and his mother was a homemaker. While Richards grew up in comfort, he by no means could have been considered from 'old money.'

During the summer between his sophomore and junior years, Richards flew out to Colorado to propose to his fiancée. Now engaged, Richards planned to get married right after graduation but also to hold off on having children for at least seven years. His fiancée had decided to become a physician's assistant, which would require three years of additional school right after her undergraduate degree (she was also a junior).

Before his trip to Colorado, Richards was debating whether to bring a suit to wear. He didn't want to wear it on the airplane or pay to check a suitcase, so he thought about packing the suit in his carry-on bag. In imagining how wrinkled his suit would end up after being stuffed into his carry-on, Richards realized that clothing wrinkled when it came in contact with an edge. That was when he came up with the idea behind O-Fold and created a rough model (see the following Figure).

Suits could be wrapped around the cylindrical O-Fold, secured with straps, packed into tight spaces, and arrive at the destination wrinkle-free. The traveler could store items within the O-Fold's hollow interior and thus would not lose any valuable space. With no edges on the O-Fold, the traveler could pack delicate clothing without the fear of wrinkles.

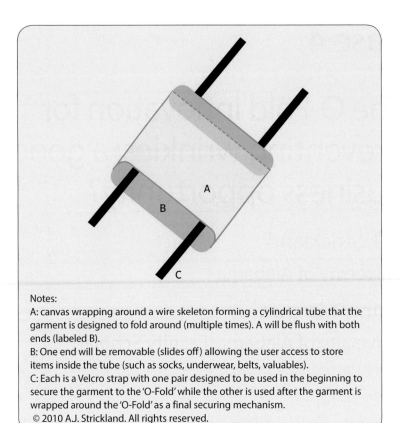

Notes:
A: canvas wrapping around a wire skeleton forming a cylindrical tube that the garment is designed to fold around (multiple times). A will be flush with both ends (labeled B).
B: One end will be removable (slides off) allowing the user access to store items inside the tube (such as socks, underwear, belts, valuables).
C: Each is a Velcro strap with one pair designed to be used in the beginning to secure the garment to the 'O-Fold' while the other is used after the garment is wrapped around the 'O-Fold' as a final securing mechanism.
© 2010 A.J. Strickland. All rights reserved.

A couple of days later, Richards got on the computer to perform a preliminary patent search online to see if anyone had already patented such an idea. Not finding anything to discourage him, Richards decided that he might want to consider doing something with his idea. He realized that he might be able to patent the O-Fold and sell the rights to it, or he could start a company with the O-Fold as the flagship product. Richards was aware that creating a company required a tremendous commitment in both time and money; however, he still enjoyed dreaming about raking in the millions.

With a great Grade Point Average (GPA) and a competitive résumé, Richards knew he should be able to get a good job after graduation if he desired it. With the plan of getting married, Richards was unsure whether starting a company right away would be wise. The opportunity cost of starting a company – giving up a likely good job – was steep in both a financial sense and a security sense. While considering his options, Richards decided to do some preliminary research about the luggage industry.

The Luggage Industry

The luggage industry evolved over time to answer the needs that different modes of travel presented. With more than $5 billion in sales, the industry expected strong growth as the baby boomer generation reached the peak travel years. Average household luggage spending was highest in households with adults ages 35 to 64. And with the peak age group of 45–54, the baby boomer generation was expected to boost demand as they increased their travel time. The luggage industry took a major hit from the September 11, 2001, terrorist attacks. As might be expected, people who feared traveling were reluctant to replace their existing luggage with new pieces. The industry rebounded nicely within two years as Americans once again began to view traveling as a right.

Prior to 9/11, profit margins in the industry were very healthy and had been improving: Average gross plant profit margins were 28.9 per cent in 1990, 41 per cent in 1995, and 45.9 per cent in 2000. Part of the growth in profits could be attributed to overseas manufacturing. Beginning in the late 1980s, there was a push for American-made products. Yet the luggage industry began importing close to 75 per cent of the merchandise while manufacturing 25 per cent (often solid-surface suitcases, which are expensive to import) in the United States. As one industry insider put it, 'Almost all nylon goods, whether it's Samsonite, American Tourister, Verdi, it's all imported. It has the good old American name, but basically it's an import.'

The global recession starting in 2007/8 produced a downward trend in sales, with many categories of travel goods seeing volumes dropping below 2004 levels in the USD market by 2009 (see Exhibit 1) although there were predictions that the global market would bounce back after 2011 (see Exhibit 2).

Another important trend in the luggage industry was the emergence of the businesswoman. Back in 1977, only 3 per cent of business travelers were women; now that number was 45 per cent. With women also making 80 per cent of the household purchases, luggage manufacturers had to begin catering their products to a female taste. Luggage colors moved from the traditional blacks to basic colors to hot pink with polka dots as travelers began to use their luggage to make a fashion statement. Luggage began to come in different shapes with different fabrics and new compartments.

Another trend was a premium put on lightweight luggage. With fuel costs rising, airlines began lowering the maximum weight of checked bags while enforcing a financial penalty on those who checked overweight bags. Travelers also needed their luggage to be smaller as well as more easily manageable. With more security checks after 9/11, travelers began to seek ways to save time; many decided to forgo checking bags in favor of using carry-ons. Allison Polish, senior marketing manager for Victorinox (which popularized the Swiss Army brand), noted, 'We've seen a reduction of the sales of 30-inch uprights; the move to lightweight luggage has meant a boom. The premium on these has soared.'

Travel goods sales for 2004–2009 could be broken down into the following categories: luggage, brief/computer cases, travel/sports bags, handbags, flat goods, and backpacks. Exhibit 1 shows sales of travel goods in the US by sector.

Exhibits 2 and 3 show the global market potential for luggage in 2011, with projections of growth up to 2016. Worldwide demand for luggage was dominated by three areas: Asia-Pacific, The Americas and Europe. Latent demand signified the potential demand if market variables turned out to favor the luggage industry. It was also used to signify market potential.

After researching the luggage industry, Richards went to talk to one of his professors about his idea. His professor recommended looking into early-stage investing

---

EXHIBIT 1: Dollar volume of travel goods by sector, 2004–09 ($ millions)

Category	2004	2005	2006	2007	2008	2009
Luggage	2014.4	2217.1	2100.9	2282.6	1802.3	1521.1
Brief/computer cases	833.2	829.2	1021.1	977.2	885.3	679.0
Travel/sports bags	4931.0	5495.7	6147.3	7387.6	6036.7	5095.0
Handbags	6701.8	7680.7	7971.1	9040.8	7901.2	6431.6
Flat goods	2120.2	2204.8	2105.1	2282.7	1929.0	1610.7
Backpacks	1155.2	1169.2	1357.2	1365.0	1313.1	1335.4
Total	17 755.8	19 596.8	20 702.8	23 335.8	19 867.6	16 672.8

Source: Euromonitor International, from trade sources. Euromonitor (2010) *Travel Goods US*, London, Euromonitor International.

EXHIBIT 2: Estimated worldwide market potential for luggage and leather goods, 2011–16 ($ billions/€ billion)

Year	$ billion	€ billion	% growth
2011	69.7	52.5	6.5%
2012	73.3	55.2	5.1%
2013	76.7	57.8	4.7%
2014	80.6	60.7	5.0%
2015	85.4	64.3	6.0%
2016	90.7	68.3	6.2%
CAGR: 2011–16			5.4%

Source: MarketLine (2012) *Marketline Industry Profile: Global Luggage and Leather Goods*, February, London, Marketline, p. 7.

EXHIBIT 3: Global luggage and leather goods market geography segmentation: $ billion, by value, 2011(e)

Geography	2011	%
Americas	26.9	38.6
Asia-Pacific	23.6	33.8
Europe	15.7	22.5
Middle East & Africa	3.6	5.1
Total	69.7	100%

Source: MarketLine (2012) *Marketline Industry Profile: Global Luggage and Leather Goods*, February, London, MarketLine, p. 9.

and examining what it was like trying to raise money for a new business. Richards's professor mentioned that he might want to specifically look into angel investing due to the infancy of Richards's idea. However, having had experience with angel investors before, his professor quickly warned against making any assumption relating an angel investor to some kind of generous benefactor.

Angel Investing

Angel investors, in contrast with venture capital firms, typically made investments in the range of $25 000–$50 000. In contrast, venture capital (VC) firms regularly made investments in the range of $5–$10 million. In 2008, angel investors invested 16 per cent of their funds in health care, 13 per cent in software, 12 per cent in retail, 11 per cent in biotech, 8 per cent in industrial/energy, and 7 per cent in media. Mergers and acquisitions (M&As) made up 70 per cent of angel exits in 2008, while 26 per cent of exits were bankruptcies and 4 per cent were initial public offerings (IPOs). Average annual returns, while quite variable, were 22 per cent for M&A and IPO exits. The number of companies that received funding from angel investors had declined steadily from 23 per cent in 2005 to 10 per cent in 2008.

The angel investing community was made up largely of wealthy individuals who invested in start-up and early-stage companies. The two main criteria in judging a potential investment – the business and the entrepreneur – were weighted according to what stage in the investing process they were in. In the beginning, a group of angel investors looked over the business plan with the goal of determining whether there would be enough demand for the company to survive and eventually thrive. Once a start-up passed this first test, quality of management typically became a very important factor because angel investing was indeed a partnership. Angel investors would be willing to use, and often required, a hands-on approach with the companies in which they invested; they filled an important gap in the funding process for start-up companies where the risk was too high for VC firms and the amount of money needed was too large for many entrepreneurs to raise on their own or from family and friends. Exhibit 4 shows the change in a company's capital needs over time.

The landscape of angel investing had changed along with many other facets of the economy during the 2008–2009 economic downturn. Through the second quarter of 2008, angel investments totaled $12.4 billion, up 4.2 per cent from the preceding year. However, only 23 000 ventures received those funds, signifying a 3.8 per cent drop. Angel investors were still investing in a shaky economy, but they were not investing in as many ventures as before. Marianne Hudson, executive director of the Angel Capital Association, said, 'There's safety in numbers. Angels see syndication not only as a way of reducing risk, but also as a means of ensuring that good companies are properly funded.' In the recessionary climate, it was not impossible to receive angel investing; however, entrepreneurs had to be extremely prepared when pitching an idea to angel investors. The rules for pitching to angel investors (be succinct, avoid jargon, have an exit strategy) were even more important in the recession because a misstep could result in losing a potential investor.

Angel investing in the economic downturn was very much a buyer's market. During a recession, as unemployment went up, the number of would-be start-ups also typically increased as people who had lost their job looked for other ways to make money. Also, investors began to worry about how the recession would endanger their prior investments and prepared to circle the wagons around the companies in which they already had an interest. The increased demand for funds with a decreased supply of funds for new ventures created a shortage of funds for the would-be start-ups. It was not impossible to get funding, but entrepreneurs had to be prepared to give up more control while also accepting a lower valuation. John May, managing partner of New Vantage Group in Vienna, Virginia, stated, 'I'm not saying we are going to be angels from hell, but we are not going to be stupid about how to price.'

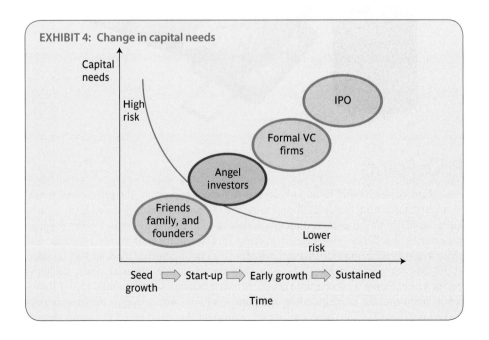

EXHIBIT 4: Change in capital needs

Substitutes

Fighting wrinkles on the road was not a new problem for business travelers. In the past, airlines had allowed garment bags as a carry-on item. Given new size restrictions on carry-on items, travelers moved to more creative solutions to fight the wrinkling of their business clothes.

Plastic was a unique material in that it combated friction, which could cause wrinkles. With this knowledge, some travelers creatively used dry-cleaning bags when they were traveling. They could minimize wrinkles by placing one article of clothing in a dry-cleaning bag and then rolling it up and placing it in a carry-on. This was obviously an inexpensive solution that many business travelers currently were using.

Samsonite had also responded to the wrinkle problem by offering carry-on luggage with a garment bag built in. This allowed the convenience of traveling with just a carry-on without having to forgo a garment bag. The Samsonite Silhouette 11, a 22-inch upright garment bag (shown in the photo), retailed at $440.

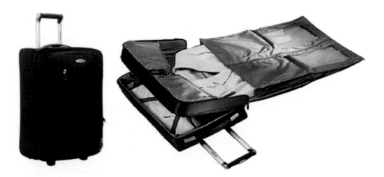

Price Points

Alex Richards knew that if the O-Fold was to have any success, the price point would be a key determining factor. Before pricing the O-Fold, Richards decided he needed to know more about the cost of direct materials as well as the pricing of other luggage accessories. Richards remembered hearing in class that retail stores typically had close to a 100 per cent price markup, whereas the manufacturing markup was broader, at 50–200 per cent. Unsure of how to estimate wholesale material costs, Richards decided to examine a comparable product from a materials and manufacturing standpoint, price out the corresponding markups, and end with a rough direct materials budget per unit. The key here was to pick a product that used about the same amount of material and was similar in manufacturing complexity, so Richards picked a log carrier that retailed at $10.25, measured 36½ inches wide and 17½ inches long, and was made of a heavy-duty canvas similar to the type of material the O-Fold would be made of. Because the log carrier retailed at $10.25, Richards reasoned, the wholesale price to the retailer was probably around $5.25.

All that was left to price out was the manufacturer markup, but Richards was unsure of which percentage to use. Richards took this problem to one of his finance professors to see what she thought. Richards's finance professor asked him, 'If you were to begin producing O-Folds tomorrow, do you think you would pay more or less for your materials than an established company?' Richards responded with 'More' because he would have to develop supplier relationships as well as eventually achieve some economies of scale from a production standpoint. The professor agreed with him and then suggested using the 50 per cent manufacturing markup so that Richards could initially factor in the markup start-up companies have to fight against when competing with other companies that have achieved greater economies of scale and can buy materials at a deeper discount. Pricing out the manufacturer's 50 per cent markup, Richards arrived at a raw material price per unit of around $3.50.

When looking for a retail price comparable, Richards decided to focus on products similar in function and utility to the O-Fold. He began looking at luggage accessories and came across Eagle Creek Pack-It Folders (shown in photo). Eagle Creek Pack-It Folders were designed to fit in a suitcase or briefcase as a supplemental travel accessory. A traveler could place shirts inside the folder for protection while traveling. Although the Pack-It Folder did not offer the wrinkle protection of the O-Fold, it did offer similar utility. Also, the Pack-It Folder came in three widths: 15, 18, and 20 inches. This was important to Richards because it did not limit the potential market by clothing size. The price points for the Pack-It-Folder were $24.00, $27.50, and $30.00 for the 15-, 18-, and 20-inch models, respectively. The price increments were obviously due to the increase in materials required by the larger pieces, a problem that Richards was likely to run into with the O-Fold.

To simplify his business model, Richards decided that he would price all O-Fold sizes the same, at $25.00 retail per unit. Richards knew that $25.00 was just what the ultimate consumer would likely pay for an O-Fold, while he would be able to sell the items wholesale at around $12.50 a unit (given the already-mentioned 100 per cent retail markup). At a wholesale price of $12.50 per unit, with materials costing $3.50 per unit, Richards now had to estimate his manufacturing costs.

Before estimating the costs, Richards purchased materials to make an O-Fold so that he could see how long it would take someone to complete the assembly process. The first step in making an O-Fold was creating the casing for the canvas to be wrapped around; this was achieved by putting together a wire skeleton. Richards spent 10 minutes creating the skeleton, 6 minutes sewing the canvas (with a sewing machine), 3 minutes sewing on the straps (also with a sewing machine), and estimated an additional 5 minutes for packaging. In sum, Richards found that he could produce one O-Fold every 24 minutes, or 2.5 O-Folds per hour. Exhibit 5 shows the O-Fold manufacturing time estimate.

EXHIBIT 5: O-Fold manufacturing time,
Alex Richards alone (minutes)

Manufacturing activity	Time (minutes)
Casing assembly	10
Canvas sewing	6
Strap sewing	3
Packaging	5
Total	24

Richards then recruited his brother to work the sewing machine and set up a two-person assembly line. As a team, Richards and his brother were able to complete seven O-Folds per hour. The assembly-line approach increased the per-person output per hour from 2.5 O-Folds to 3.5 O-Folds while still only requiring the use of a single sewing machine. Richards realized that his brother was using the sewing machine almost the entire time; he was therefore unsure whether adding more people per machine would greatly improve the per-person hourly output. For the sake of the business model, Richards decided to set the standard at 3.5 O-Folds per hour per person per machine.

Wanting to keep his options open, Richards figured he should look into what it would cost him to hire some people to produce the O-Folds for him. One of his professors suggested that Richards look at possibly hiring some people from the more rural part of the state to help produce the O-Folds. Richards called the Terry County Career Center and spoke with the director, Francine Bassett. Bassett explained to Richards that Terry County was known economically for its quilt barns. A quilt barn was a place – literally a barn – in which some of the older women from around the community produced handmade quilts for sale. Quilters recruited some younger women as well. The quilts could fetch a pretty good price, with some of the nicer ones retailing at more than $2000. With little education, a lot of the quilters had begun producing quilts at a young age, and they continued quilting professionally well into their 60s and 70s. Bassett offered to take Richards to see one of the quilting barns in action, and Richards happily agreed.

Mama Gee's Quilting has been around for more than 100 years and was one of the original quilt barns in Terry County. Richards met with the current owner, Gladys Smith, the granddaughter of the founder. Smith informed Richards that quilting allowed women of all ages to help make a living and provide for their families. A lot of young girls in the community would come to her and ask to work free so that they could learn the quilt-making trade. Mama Gee's Quilting employed around 30 women and had more than $400 000 in revenue last year, all without owning a single computer. Smith did not pay by the hour; rather, she sold the quilts on consignment, with a worker making money only if her quilt sold. Bassett informed Richards that minimum wage would be very desirable and that Terry County certainly had a sewing background. At a minimum wage of $7.25 per hour, and a production rate of 3.5 O-Folds per hour, each O-Fold will cost $2.10 in labor to make.

The $2.10 per unit in manufacturing cost plus the $3.50 in material cost placed the finished O-Fold in Richards's possession with a per-unit cost of $5.60. Richards could then sell finished O-Folds wholesale at $12.50 per unit, representing a 123 per cent markup and a contribution margin of $6.90. Richards was young and new at business, so he reasoned there would be more variable costs that he was not yet aware of, such as shipping and returns. Richards rationalized an additional 'cookie-jar' (i.e., contingency) cost estimated at $2.25 per unit for budgeting reasons. This cookie-jar cost would, he hoped, alleviate some of the turmoil caused by unforeseen costs and still leave a healthy per-unit contribution margin of $4.65.

Patent

While Richards was unsure of the structure of the start-up, he was fairly certain that he would need at least to secure a patent in order to protect the idea behind the O-Fold. After doing some research, Richards budgeted $10 000 for obtaining a patent and related fees. Assuming the $4.65 contribution margin, Richards calculated that he would have to sell 2000 units to cover the cost of the patent. While a patent was certainly not cheap, Richards believed it to be necessary if the O-Fold was going to have a chance at being successful. Richards didn't have $10 000 sitting in his back pocket, so the need for outside investors began to become more and more unavoidable. While researching patents, Richards came up with an interesting strategy regarding the timeline for obtaining a patent. The U.S. government provided a one-year patent grace period for inventors by allowing the inventors one year to patent their invention. The grace period began when one of four conditions was met:

1. The invention was placed on sale to the public.
2. A description of the invention was published.
3. A detailed description of the product was presented at a public meeting.
4. The invention was placed into the hands of the public.

Richards believed the grace period provided an opportunity for the product to be market-tested before a patent became necessary. Richards assumed that if he could meet one of the four grace-period conditions, he could begin production and see if the market provided signs that the O-Fold was a viable product. Also, making use of the patent grace period would put Richards in a better position with potential investors because he would then have some real market data to provide credibility to his business model and lower the risk for potential investors.

Business Models

Richards now faced the difficult decision of determining how to design a business model that would give the O-Fold the best chance of being profitable. Each business model would be evaluated on its leverage, risk, probability of success, potential profits, and exit strategy. Richards came up with four potential basic business models for the O-Fold: sell the idea, license the idea, outsource production, and use a crawl-walk-run strategy.

Sell the Idea

Richards's first potential business model – sell the idea – provided a clear exit strategy. Theoretically, the only thing needed for this business model was a patent; however, without market data, it was unlikely that anyone would be willing to pay a large premium for the patent. Although this option would get him out of the game quickly with a little money in his pocket, Richards was unsure whether anyone would be willing to pay what he believed the O-Fold idea to be worth. It could be challenging to convince someone to buy something that hadn't been tested or proved in the marketplace. However, although Richards was by no means rich, he believed he would have enough money to go this route on his own without any outside investors. Exhibit 6 shows Richards's costs, and Exhibit 7 includes the break-even quantity.

License the Idea

Richards's second potential business model was to license the idea. While the perceived cost of licensing a product might seem low, Richards believed it would be wise to bring in an angel investor not just for the money but for the business connections as well. The ideal licensing agreement, in Richards's opinion, would be one in which he received

EXHIBIT 6: Fixed costs for O-Fold production

Patent	$10 000.00
Prototype	500.00
Professional fees	1000.00
Total	$11 500.00

EXHIBIT 7: Fixed costs plus break-even amount for O-Fold production

Patent	$10 000.00
Prototype	500.00
Professional fees	1000.00
Total	$11 500.00
Break-even quantity ($4.65 profit per quantity sold)	2473

some money up front and then a royalty on the back end for each unit sold. Not only did Richards lack the business connections, but he also knew close to nothing about licensing contracts. The knowhow and expertise of an angel investor might be worth even more than the loan itself in terms of total value added by the partnership.

Another positive for licensing the idea was that it would take a lot of the operational elements out of Richards's hands, thus freeing him to pursue other opportunities. This would also put the O-Fold into the hands of a more experienced person who would know how to bring a product such as the O-Fold to the marketplace. The feasibility of this strategy relied heavily on Richard's ability to get his foot in the door at a company that would be interested in licensing the O-Fold. Richards, not the best networker by any means, knew that he could not go this path alone and would need outside help to make it work.

A potential negative was that if the O-Fold proved to be a great idea, Richards would likely be leaving some money on the table when compared to producing and selling the product himself. As with just selling the idea, it would certainly be better if Richards had some type of market data to back up his business model. Being an inexperienced entrepreneur, Richard would find that a lot of people would question the legitimacy of his estimates. While Richards could not fix his inexperience in the short term, he could seek out proven comparables to back up his numbers in order to somewhat increase their reliability.

Outsource Production

The third potential business model took a giant leap in terms of Richards's involvement. Richards could outsource the manufacturing of the O-Fold and sell the finished items himself. This would allow Richards to keep a larger portion of the profits while also allowing him to maintain some control over the strategic direction of the O-Fold. Using Terry County as a potential outsourcing location, Richards would be able to produce an O-Fold with direct materials and direct labor totaling $5.60 per unit and overhead totaling $2.25 per unit. Richards believed that this option would almost certainly require the money and expertise of an angel investor. While the risks were greater with the outsourcing option, the idea of running his own company was very appealing to Richards. He likely would have to put some of his own money at stake; he would also probably have to make this his job. Forgoing the more traditional accounting route, Richards would have to factor in the opportunity cost of giving up a steady salary as well as factoring in the uncertainty of future cash flows associated with the O-Fold. If Richards decided to go this route, he would also have to provide more information about what he believed the strategic direction of the O-Fold should be. Exhibit 8 presents an outsource production strategy break-even analysis for the O-Fold.

Distribution

If he chose the outsourcing business model, Richards would have to answer the question of distribution. There were many options here for Richards to consider. First, he

EXHIBIT 8: Outsource production strategy break-even analysis

	Start-up	Year 1	Year 2	Year 3
Fixed costs				
Patent	$10000			
Prototype	500			
Professional fees	1000			
Website	1000			
Computer and software	$1500	$500	$500	$500
Telephone	600	600	600	600
Office supplies	500	500	500	500
Website management	100	100	100	100
Total:	$15200	$1700	$1700	$1700
Variable costs				
Direct materials	$3.50	$3.50	$3.50	$3.50
Direct labor	2.10	2.10	2.10	2.10
Unexpected costs	2.25	2.25	2.25	2.25
Break-even quantity	3269	366	366	366

could go the traditional retail route by selling in bulk to retailers at the wholesale price. Selling to retail stores was one option where it could be tough to get a foot in the door. Second, he could sell the O-Fold through a website; this represented a cheaper option than the retail route. Richards could post videos about the O-Fold, provide packing tutorials, and take orders all from one website. He would have to work hard at marketing with the online route in order to generate some online traffic. Third, he could advertise the O-Fold in travel magazines and/or airline catalogs. This option would help isolate the target market in terms of marketing effectiveness. Delta's *SkyMall* magazine was placed on all Delta flights, featured merchandise that travelers might be interested in, and provided a way for the customer to place an order. What better way to focus on your market than to advertise a way to pack clothes without wrinkles to people who had just packed clothes themselves? The distribution question was an important one that would have to be answered for the angel investors.

Marketing

Another important question was how to get the word out about the O-Fold. Richards could simply rely on store shelf advertising if he went the retail route, or he could consider online, print, or many other forms of advertising. Working under the assumption that there was a need for the O-Fold out there, Richards would have to find a way to identify, locate, and sell to the customers who would fall in his target market.

Exit Strategy

Angel investors would be very interested to know what Richards envisioned the end game to be for the O-Fold. They would also be interested, even more so, in when they would exit the venture. Companies like this could sometimes have a 'market cap' in terms of limiting how much of the market they could control. If an entrepreneur made too much noise, one of the bigger fish in the market would find a way to attack his or her market share, thus limiting how much the new company could grow. One strategy was to grow while staying unnoticed by the major players in the market. There were several options to pursue for the exit strategy all the way from an IPO to selling the company to a competitor. The angel investors would want to know when they would get their money back, how much certainty there was of getting their money back, and what return they could expect on their investment.

Use a Crawl-Walk-Run Strategy

The crawl-walk-run strategy was a three-step process of growing a company.

1. **Crawl** In the crawl stage, Richards would likely recruit his brother and start making some O-Folds. He then would find a way to sell the finished products either online, door to door, or by some other fairly simple means of distribution. While the profits were certainly limited, this part of the strategy would provide Richards with a type of low-risk market research. At the crawl stage, Richards possibly would not need angel investors; beginning on his own could be of benefit to him later by showing that he bore all the initial risk and garnered some market data to back up the legitimacy of his idea. He could almost certainly get a better valuation with a company that had actually sold something than he could with a company that existed only on paper. Richards would also be able to get a feel for what the day-to-day process of running a business looks like, only on a much smaller scale. This could prove to be beneficial later on when he moved up to the walk stage.

2. **Walk** At this point Richards would likely want to bring in some angel investors to help finance the expansion. As stated above, he could expect a higher valuation once he had some market data to back up his claims. At this stage he would need to move from actually making the O-Folds to outsourcing their production. He would also need to have a patent, a developed distribution channel, and a marketing strategy. These factors would provide a potential early exit strategy for some of the investors if revenues and profits grew accordingly and some other company offered to buy O-Fold.

3. **Run** The run stage was achieved when the company was producing large quantities and enjoying economies of scale. It would be difficult for the start-up to go unnoticed at this stage – new entrants into the market would be attracted – and the entrepreneur would certainly have to have an exit strategy in mind. If Richards could make it to this stage and sold his interest in the company, he could stand to make a fairly large sum of money. Typically, risk followed reward, and failing at this level would result in some people losing a substantial amount of money. Exhibit 9 shows the volume necessary to reach breakeven.

EXHIBIT 9: Crawl-walk-run strategy break-even analysis

	Start-up	Year 1	Year 2	Year 3
Fixed costs				
Website	$1000	$100	$100	$100
Patent	10 000			
Professional fees	2000			
Sewing machine	100			
Computer and software	1500			
Telephone	600	600	600	600
Office supplies	500	500	500	500
Administrative salary	35 000	40 000	40 000	45 000
Building lease	12 000	12 000	12 000	12 000
Equipment lease	24 000	24 000	24 000	24 000
Total	$86 700	$77 200	$77 200	$82 200
Variable costs				
Direct materials	$3.50	$3.50	$3.50	$3.50
Direct labor	2.10	2.10	2.10	2.10
Unexpected costs	2.25	2.25	2.25	2.25
Break-even quantity	18 645	16 602	16 602	17 677

Decision

Richards met with one of his professors to go over some of the different business models and decide which, if any, he should pursue. The professor told Richards that he could line up a meeting with some angel investors if that was what Richards desired. While Richards had enjoyed researching some ideas about starting a company, now a decision was required of him. Should he meet with the angel investors and, if so, what should his pitch be?

Case 5

Studio 100: a showcase in show business[*]

Kurt Verweire

Vlerick Business School

Studio 100 is an international family entertainment group founded in 1996 in Belgium. Some years earlier, Hans Bourlon, Gert Verhulst, and Danny Verbiest had made a production called *'Samson & Gert'* for the national Belgian television station (BRT), which was very successful in Flanders, the northern part of Belgium. Samson's success led to TV and theatre shows. The three programme makers decided to leave the BRT to create their own production house so that they could build a business around the characters they had created. They started the company without any help from investors and bought an office in Schelle, a town close to Antwerp (Belgium) where they created new characters, recorded television shows and rehearsed for the theatre shows. The company started with five people in an office building that was much too large.

Fifteen years later, Studio 100 has more than 1000 employees and dozens of popular characters, it is the owner of one of the largest independent catalogues of children's TV series in the world, and distributes TV series in more than 120 countries.[1] The company's revenues have increased from 5.6 million euro in 1996 to 170.2 million euro in 2011 (see Exhibit 1 for an overview of key financial figures). How has the company been able to achieve this phenomenal growth?

Studio 100's Early Years

New Characters

Soon after the company was founded, Studio 100 created a new format called *'Plop the Gnome'*. This format was broadcast on the Flemish commercial television station and was a big success too. In the years that followed, Studio 100 created other formats, such as *'Pirate Pete'*, *'Bumba'*, and *'Big & Betsy'* (see Exhibit 2) which were broadcast in Flanders and the Netherlands on the most important TV channels.[2] Studio 100 also created stage shows and movies. Studio 100 became the market leader in theatre shows for children and families in Belgium and the Netherlands. These shows are based on the Studio 100 characters or on a classic fairy tale such as

---

* This case study is based on a Vlerick publication 'Studio 100: a showcase in show business', written by Kurt Verweire and MBA students Kristoff Lievens, Nicolas Van Boven, and Pascal Vercruysse in 2009, and a report written by MBA students Annick Bolland, Leonardo Fininzola e Silva, Stefan Keereman, Jef Laurijssen, Werner Roelandt, and Alex Waterinkx (2009) 'Studio 100 – growth strategy' for the Vlerick strategy course.

EXHIBIT 1:   (A) Studio 100's revenue evolution (million euro).

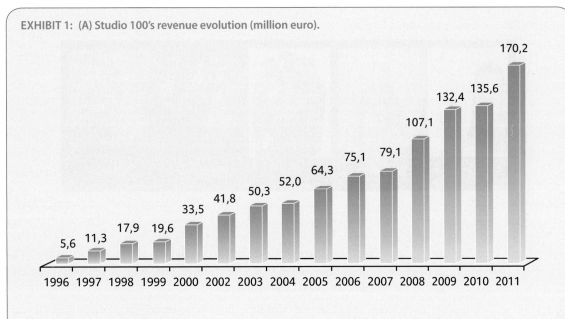

(B) 2007 sales per activity.

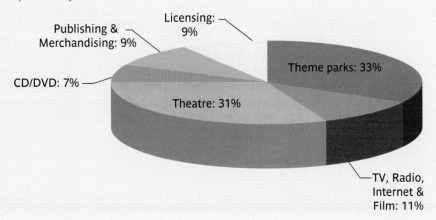

(C) 2011 sales per activity.

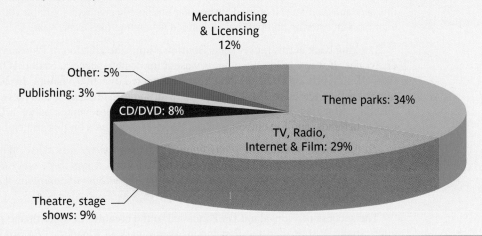

EXHIBIT 2: Some early Studio 100 formats

Samson & Gert   Big & Betsy   Plop   Pirate Pete   Bumba

'Pinocchio', 'Robin Hood', or *'Snow White'.* In addition, Studio 100 has released on average two or three movies per year. Every movie is an original adventure related to one of the well-known Studio 100 characters.

Even today, the characters that were introduced on television more than 10 years ago are still on prime time in Belgium and the Netherlands. The success of Studio 100's characters can be attributed to the fact that the characters are timeless: it is the good versus the bad and there is always the happy end. Another reason for the success is the omnipresence of the Studio 100 characters. They record songs, they appear in books, newspapers and magazines, and they go live on stage in theatres, concerts, or musicals. This means that the characters of Studio 100 are part of the daily life of the Belgian and Dutch children and their (grand)parents. A final element is that Studio 100's characters are very Flemish and Dutch. This provides the company with a significant advantage over many international production companies, since many audiences prefer local TV programming.[3]

Theme Parks

The end of the previous decade saw some new initiatives from Studio 100. One of those new initiatives was the opening of a theme park, called *'Plopsaland'* (see Exhibit 3). Studio 100 bought the old 'Meli-Park', a theme park near the town of De Panne on the Belgian coast. The Meli-Park was originally created by a honey company and based on a bee theme. However, during the 1990s the theme park lost much of its appeal and the number of visitors dropped drastically. Hans Bourlon and Gert Verhulst decided to buy this park and thematize it around the popular Studio 100 characters. Studio 100 invested a lot in extra catering and parking and added new attractions every year.

Looking back at this move, Hans Bourlon admits the creation of Plopsaland was a crazy idea. It was a risky move but it was an immediate success. Studio 100 opened the park in April 2000. In the first year, it attracted 575 000 visitors. In 2004, that number had increased to 781 000. In 2010, with some 35 attractions and more than 1,1 million visitors per year, Plopsaland is one of the most frequented parks in Belgium, the Netherlands, and Luxembourg. Hans Bourlon comments on this strategic move:

> *To be honest, none of the plans about Plopsaland made any sense. We had never imagined that we would have so many visitors ... and three other theme parks some 8 years later ... But that is how it goes within our company. We are always open to new things.*

The success of Plopsaland De Panne led to the creation of other theme parks. In 2005 Studio 100 opened the first indoor theme park in Flanders: *'Plopsa Indoor'.* This park is open 300 days per year and offers some 20 attractions. A third park has

EXHIBIT: 3 Plopsaland De Panne

been added to the list: *'Plopsa Coo'*, located at the Coo waterfalls, a popular tourist attraction in the southern part of Belgium. Besides the spectacular falls, Plopsa Coo also offers 15 attractions and a wildlife park. In April 2010, Studio 100 opened its first theme park in the Netherlands in Coevoorden. And in that same year, the company bought Holiday Park in Germany as well.

A Girl's Band

In 2002, Studio 100 acquired '*K3*', a Flemish girl's band. K3 was founded in 1999 but when they became fully part of Studio 100 in 2002, K3 exploded. The three girls of K3 are solely responsible for creating a new phenomenon in the Belgian and Dutch market: toddler pop. The girls released 35 singles and with the constant rotation of their music videos, six successful feature films and many sold out concerts, the girls are unstoppable. '*The world of K3*', a weekly magazine show, has towering ratings and the girls are superstars, adored by the public and feted by the media. What is more, K3 have their own line of clothing and accessories. There are comic books, magazines, posters, and daily newspaper adventures. MP3 players come pre-loaded with K3 songs. There are K3 cookies for the peckish K3 mega fan, K3 lunchboxes to put the cookies in, and K3 backpacks to put the lunchboxes in.

Merchandising and Licensing

Merchandising and licensing is extremely important for Studio 100. In 2010, 15 per cent of the 135,6 million euro turnover came from these activities. The company has developed a multi-track merchandising strategy aimed at maximizing revenue streams while keeping a tight control on image and brand. A significant part of the revenues comes from merchandising. Merchandising lines are developed and designed in-house and sold to wholesalers and retailers. Depending on the character, one or two merchandising lines are developed each year.[4] Local teams of in total about 20 people manage the contracts with the licence holders in Belgium, the Netherlands, France, and Germany. Every activity that connects Studio 100 with the outside world and that could affect the company's image is formalized and controlled. The company receives many requests to licence their characters. The reputation of the characters results in significant extra sales for the licence holders. But obviously, Studio 100 wins too. Tom Grymonprez, commercial director, explains:

> We ask ourselves a series of questions. Is there a fit with our company? What about the quality of the product? Where is the product sold? And last but not least: does the product fit in the world of our target audience? You won't see Bumba toy guns in the product assortment.[5]

More Formats

Studio 100 has continuously added new formats to its product portfolio. In 2002, the company introduced *'Spring'* targeting the 'older tweens'. In the years that followed, Studio 100 further expanded and created *'TopStars'*, *'Mega Mindy'*, *'Anubis House'*, *'Amika'*, *'Galaxy Park'*, *'Rox'*, *'Dobus'*, *'Bobo'*, and *'Hotel 13'* (see Exhibit 4 for some examples). And after the TV series came the CDs, games, merchandizing, movies, and musicals. In this way, Studio 100 has become the largest provider of family and children entertainment in the Benelux. Common features to all of these programmes have been the high production quality, the clear focus on the target audience of children – segmented by age and gender (see Exhibit 5) – and the family-friendly entertaining value.[6]

Studio 100 is not afraid to apply some radical changes to existing formats. This has helped to create a boost in the formats that had reached the saturation phase. A great example is how the musical 'The Three Piglets' gave a new boost to K3's career. Hans Bourlon reflects:

> One day, we were searching for a way to boost the career of K3, our girl band. One of our employees, who was sitting at the conference table, said: 'Turn them into piglets and make them the main characters in a new musical called 'The 3 Piglets'. We couldn't stop laughing. But one year later, the musical 'The 3 Piglets' was completely sold out. It was a major success. You don't get such

EXHIBIT 4: Some later Studio 100 formats

Spring   TopStars   Mega Mindy   Amika   Anubis House

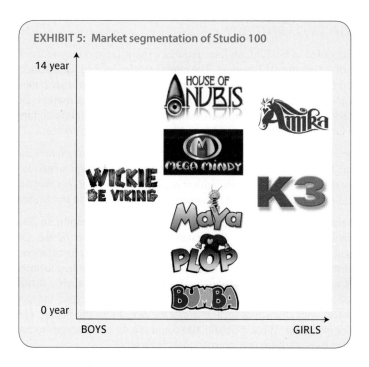

EXHIBIT 5: Market segmentation of Studio 100

ideas out of a market study. If we had asked the public via market research to say what they expected the next K3 show to be like, we would simply have ended up with a 'greatest hits' extravaganza.

Some Challenges

Despite the many successes of the firm, Studio 100 has faced significant challenges over the years. New initiatives have not always been successful. '*Radio Bembem*', the radio station project for children, was stopped. And sometimes key people leave. In December 2004, Danny Verbiest, the founder who had lent his voice to Samson for 15 years, decided to retire and sell his shares of Studio 100. In 2009, Belgium was shocked when Kathleen – the 'blonde' singer of K3 – decided to quit the band. The company turned a problem into an opportunity and set up a reality show '*K2 searching for K3*', where they found a new, Dutch K3 member.

International Exploration and Exploitation

Expansion to French-speaking Belgium

In 2005, Studio 100 set another milestone. For the first time TV content was made in a different language than Dutch, namely French, for the market of southern Belgium (Wallonia). In that year, the company did remakes of the Plop shows which were aired on the Wallonian TV. The shows were now called 'Le Lutin Plop' and featured characters such as 'Lutin Dordebou' ('Lazy'), 'Lutin Pipolette' ('Chatter'), and 'Lutin Bric' ('Chore'). Studio 100 also did remakes of every Samson & Gert show, which in French were translated as *'Fred & Samson'*. The main driver for offering TV shows in French was to convince the Belgian national retail chains to distribute the merchandized material. But since Wallonia is rather small, the revenues and profits of this expansion were rather limited. Would they be able to expand internationally? Studio 100 has always been successful because its characters were Dutch and Flemish. Could they just export these characters to different markets?

Expansion into Germany

Studio 100 decided to bet high on international expansion and they recruited Jo Daris as Director of International Business. The company also looked for additional funding and founded Studio 100 Media in Munich in 2007. This unit distributes TV series worldwide and was the first entry of Studio 100 in the German market. But Jo Daris discovered soon that the international TV stations were hardly interested in the stories of Plop the Gnome, Pirate Pete, and Mega Mindy. Jo Daris comments:

> *The people at Studio 100 are used to having everything they touch turn into gold. This time, however, many eggs were touched, but none of them turned to gold. It was very difficult to convince the buyers at the television stations that our characters could be successful in other countries than Belgium and the Netherlands.*[7]

Nevertheless, the company continued with the internationalization. In 2008 the international expansion process was accelerated by the acquisition of the German EM Entertainment Group. Studio 100 paid 41 million euro for EM Entertainment and got an enormous distribution network; EM delivered children programmes to more than 120 countries. It would have taken decades for Studio 100 to build such a distribution network. But what was more: EM Entertainment also has an impressive independent catalogue of content with characters such as *Maya the Bee*, *Vicky the Viking*, *Heidi*, *Lassie*, and *Pippi Longstocking*. What if Studio 100 could use its competences to revitalize and commercialize these well-known international characters?

Studio 100 Animation

With the acquisition of EM Entertainment Studio 100 also became the owner of Flying Bark, an Australian animation studio. In that same year, Studio 100 opened an animation studio in Paris. Studio 100 Animation develops, finances, and produces series and feature films in 2D or 3D. The Paris studio produces mainly TV series while feature films are the mainstay of production in Sydney.[8] Studio 100 is working on remakes of classics such as Maya the Bee and Heidi.

Germany is now the spearhead for Studio 100's international expansion as the company purchased in November 2010 the German leisure park *Holiday Park*. Studio 100 transformed this park into a theme park where German children can meet their favorite characters such as Tabaluga, Maya the Bee, and Vicky the Viking, much like what happened in Belgium with Plopsaland.

Further Internationalization

Studio 100 internationalized in other markets as well. It started a coproduction, called '*Big & Small*' with Kindle Entertainment, 3J's Productions, the BBC and Treehouse TV. The show is a live action comedy filmed in the UK with British actors. Because of the high quality of the show, Studio 100 has managed to get a foot in the door with the BBC, a distribution channel that is envied by many competitors. In the meantime, Studio 100 has set up another coproduction with the BBC, called '*Kerwhizz*'.

Studio 100 also has expanded in the US. The company remade '*The House of Anubis*', originally a teen drama mystery TV series for the Belgian and Dutch market. The company sold the series to Nickelodeon, a US children's channel, which made a very successful German remake of the series, and later a US remake. Again, the series was a success both in Germany and in the UK and US and this helped to boost merchandizing and publishing revenues in those countries significantly.

Studio 100's Special DNA

The success rate of many of Studio 100's initiatives is high. This is because the two managing directors (and founders), Gert Verhulst and Hans Bourlon, have not only focused on creating new characters and exploiting that content in many different ways, but also because the two managers have been able to build a very specific organizational culture. The two managers have been awarded 'Managers of the Year' in 2008 and the company was named 'Company of the Year' in 2009 in Belgium. But Hans Bourlon hates the word 'management':

> *A company starts to get in trouble when it only organizes, plans and structures what is already there – which is what I call 'management'. That is why I am more afraid that we will lose that creative drive. If we start to do 'more of the same' and exploit rather than explore, then that is the end of Studio 100.*

Creativity, Entrepreneurship, and Innovation

The DNA of Studio 100 can be described as 'boundless creativity and innovation'. The essence of Studio 100 is about discovery: creating new ideas, every day, over and over again, starting from a white piece of paper. What makes Studio 100 unique is the fact that the shareholders and founders of the company are still involved in the conceptual and creative side of the business. This does not often happen in media companies: the creative minds usually stay as far away as possible from the business brains. But in Studio 100, doing business and being creative are inextricably linked, and therein lies the company's success. But there is a clear understanding that creativity comes first, because it is these creative impulses which keep pushing the company forward.[9]

Creativity helps the company to cope with difficult times. Expanding a business is full of unexpected changes and indefinite opportunities. When the company was founded, the CD sale was its biggest success. Ten years later, the audio market had collapsed. But by then, the shows in the theme parks and in theatres have become the money makers.

Gert Verhulst and Hans Bourlon see it as their major task to push creativity down in the organization. Although both managers are still heavily involved with the new projects they 'manage' new ideas rather than 'developing and creating' the ideas themselves. This means challenging the people, providing feedback, giving advice, and coaching. Leading a creative environment means detecting and recognizing strong ideas and promoting them within the company.

> *It goes without saying that we are always open to new ideas, although it is obvious that in first instance people are expected to do what we pay them for.[10] But overall I think that people with great ideas have the opportunity to develop them. For example, our cost controller has developed a new quiz program. And the guy who develops our websites has produced a board game.*

From Ideas to Business

Generating ideas however is only a first step. Equally important is to make everyone in the organization believe in a great idea and go for it. This implies for many people forgetting about their own ideas. In a creative media company this is often a challenging task. And it requires that the company looks for a special type of person. The company prefers a thirty-year-old, who has already had a few other jobs. Someone who understands that drawing is a craft and who is happy to do his best to draw Plop in exactly the same way as the other cartoonists. Someone who is not necessarily interested in 'standing out' but wants to deliver quality, time after time.

Gert Verhulst and Hans Bourlon stimulate people to generate and work out ideas in team. The power of Studio 100 is its integrated business model. TV and music are the primary platforms for launching new characters. Then the company further builds the content and characters in multimedia such as theme parks, theatre shows, movies, CDs, books, merchandising, and licensing. All elements are crucial in Studio 100's business model. And this requires that teams from different departments work together seamlessly. The marketing department of Studio 100 plays a very important role in this process. In many media companies, the marketing department is a separate entity, cut off from the creative process. At Studio 100, the two sides have to work together. Creative ideas are only supported when they can be commercialized. Studio 100 is business-driven and no-nonsense. The company has clear goals. That makes it different from many other creative companies, who do not make plans and just carry on, relying on a hazy form of artistry...

Managing People through an Appropriate Organizational Climate

Stimulating creativity is above all providing the people with a warm nest, an environment that gives them the possibility to slowly rise and shine. The management team of Studio 100 sees this as one of their major tasks: 'We, as an employer, have to create that environment and above all, need to mingle with them.' There's a lot of energy going round at Studio 100. Very often, you can hear music in the corridors: an orchestra is rehearsing, there are ballet lessons or some of the characters are learning new songs.

According to Jo Daris, 'most synergy is created when employees – whatever is their function or their department – meet each other continuously. An open workspace promotes all that'. Indeed, there are some offices in the Studio 100 building, but most of the space goes to studios, rehearsal rooms, ballet rooms, and the clothing department where the costumes are made. That is where the employees write songs, create new shows, invent new attractions for the theme parks and make sceneries. On the tables, you will find models of the theme park attractions or sceneries. And rhyming dictionaries are more commonly used than calculators. At noon, the restaurant looks like carnival: pirates, gnomes, piglets, and mermaids are all sitting at one table. And while they are having lunch, new ideas bubble up. The food is provided for free.

Studio 100 pays a lot of attention to attracting the right people. In a fast-growing company, the question whether you have the right people is a vivid one. The company looks for energized and engaged people. There is a deliberate choice not to attract famous actors for a particular character. The total picture should be right. You just can't play Pirate Pete for one year, earn a lot of money, and then leave the company.

Everybody in Studio 100 gets a fixed pay, even the sales people. This is a quite conservative rewarding system, yet it focuses on the equal importance of all factors in the creation and sale of qualitative products. When somebody, e.g. an actor, asks for more than a fair pay, this might be a reason to change the format and exclude the actor. These discussions occur from time to time. In order to counter these problems, Studio 100 tries to create a group feeling, where everybody feels at home and earns well. The company offers people a long-term perspective, although some people feel they should receive part of the income of their successful project. But Studio 100 is very strict here. Employees might get an extra fee only if they perform *more*; you do not get a bonus for contributing to a successful project. Motivated, creative, and committed employees obviously get more promotion opportunities. In 2009 Studio 100 introduced an option plan for all employees, but Hans Bourlon doubts whether this was really necessary. He wonders whether money really drives commitment.

The company has no trade unions because there have never been candidates. Studio 100 has flexible working hours and does whatever possible to create an energizing and positive environment. The company organizes power yoga sessions, there are quiz teams, and so on. The real writing often takes place late in the evening, in groups and certainly not in suits. In short, the classic 9 to 5 clerk is not around at Studio 100.[11]

Control

In Studio 100, the command-and-control style has given way to a 'softer control' with more emphasis on output control. Although the firm uses clear performance measures to track the progress of specific projects, most attention is paid to a more personal form of control and coaching. Some projects are monitored extensively by the top managers, for others there is the confidence that the organization will bring the projects to a good end. One could say that control is primarily done through creating an appropriate culture in the organization, a culture built around creativity, entrepreneurship, and informality.[12]

A Structured Approach

Creativity and entrepreneurship are core in Studio 100. That does not mean that the company thrives on chaos. In the earlier years, the two managers were entrepreneurial and made decisions without business plans. But today, the company underpins its new strategic ideas with business plans that are used flexibly.

The creative process has become more structured as well and tends to follow a certain process. For example, the creation of a new character takes three phases. The first phase is the development of the baseline for the character. Gert Verhulst and Hans Bourlon are involved frequently in this phase. In a second phase, the characters are further fed into small creative cells to be elaborated upon. Here, the deepening of the characters takes place. The small cells are also responsible for the creation of the derivatives that are based on the core character like games, publishing, shows, movies, etc. The last phase is the development of the character. In this phase the characters are stable, have proven themselves and are simply further developed through, for instance, licensing and merchandising. At this point in time, every employee can contribute ideas or concepts. Though in phase 1 and 2 this is also welcomed it is noticed that in the early phases creativity experts are in place. (Exhibit 6 provides an overview of these phases for 'Plop the Gnome'.)

Portfolio Management

Over the years, Studio 100 has developed strong competences in portfolio management. The different characters have their own strategy and life cycle. Formats targeted to older children, such as *The House of Anubis* or *Mega Mindy* are more prone to hypes and have the potential to generate substantial cash flows in short time frames. Formats direct towards younger children, such as Bumba or Plop have longer life cycles and the potential to generate steady cash flows over longer periods (see Exhibit 7). The goal of portfolio management is to create the right mix of formats and characters that generate shorter-term, potentially more volatile cash flows, counterbalanced with concepts generating longer-term steady cash flows.[13]

Communication

In a fast-growing company, it is important to keep employees informed about the strategic projects and key challenges of the organization. Studio 100 organizes 'strategy meetings' every 2 to 3 months. These meetings can take an entire afternoon. The management presents what and how well the company is doing. It also formulates questions, and presents where it has doubts. Furthermore, people are asked to present in about 15 minutes what they are doing. And of course, this is also the forum where new commercial projects are presented. If an employee at home sees a commercial on TV for a new show of Studio 100, then it is important that (s)he can explain to his/her family what it is about.

> *We are very open in this company. There is no hidden agenda. Some people are sceptical about all that. But I feel this leads to involvement and motivation. A good idea can come from anyone and anywhere.*

EXHIBIT 6: The 'product development process' in Studio 100 – example: Plop the Gnome

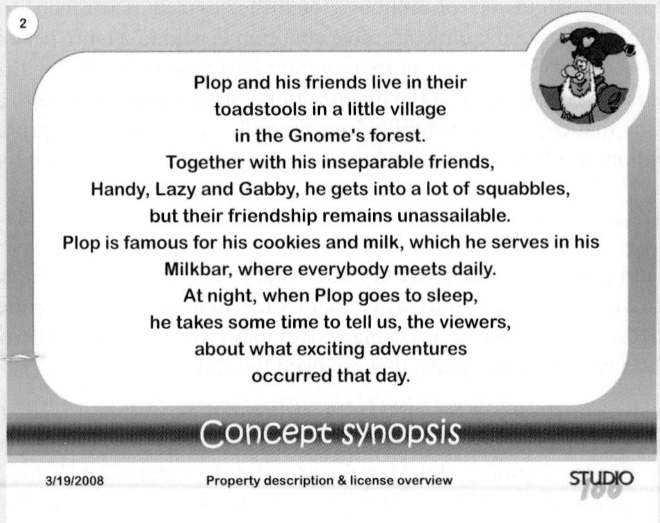

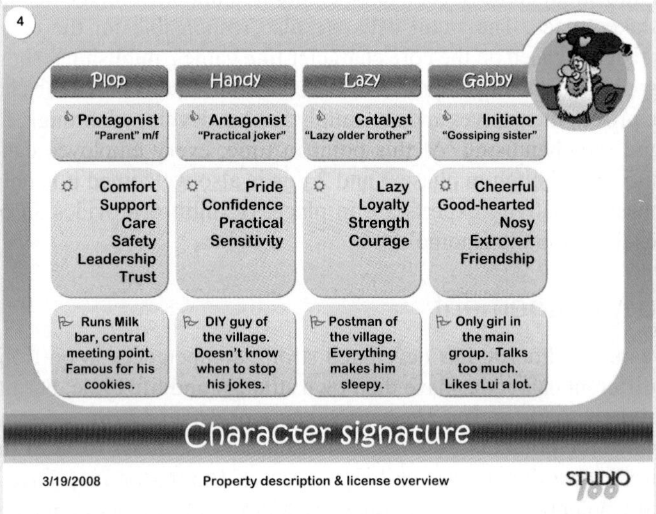

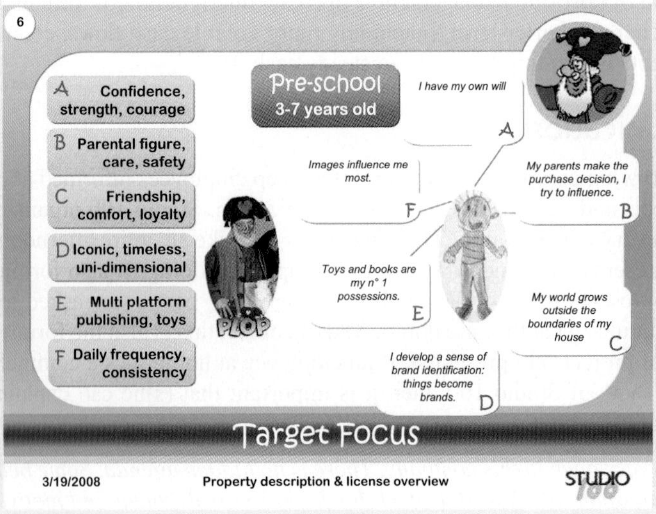

2

Plop and his friends live in their
toadstools in a little village
in the Gnome's forest.
Together with his inseparable friends,
Handy, Lazy and Gabby, he gets into a lot of squabbles,
but their friendship remains unassailable.
Plop is famous for his cookies and milk, which he serves in his
Milkbar, where everybody meets daily.
At night, when Plop goes to sleep,
he takes some time to tell us, the viewers,
about what exciting adventures
occurred that day.

Concept synopsis

3/19/2008   Property description & license overview   STUDIO 100

4

Plop	Handy	Lazy	Gabby
Protagonist "Parent" m/f	Antagonist "Practical joker"	Catalyst "Lazy older brother"	Initiator "Gossiping sister"
Comfort Support Care Safety Leadership Trust	Pride Confidence Practical Sensitivity	Lazy Loyalty Strength Courage	Cheerful Good-hearted Nosy Extrovert Friendship
Runs Milk bar, central meeting point. Famous for his cookies.	DIY guy of the village. Doesn't know when to stop his jokes.	Postman of the village. Everything makes him sleepy.	Only girl in the main group. Talks too much. Likes Lui a lot.

Character signature

3/19/2008   Property description & license overview   STUDIO 100

6

A   Confidence, strength, courage

B   Parental figure, care, safety

C   Friendship, comfort, loyalty

D   Iconic, timeless, uni-dimensional

E   Multi platform publishing, toys

F   Daily frequency, consistency

Pre-school
3-7 years old

I have my own will   A

Images influence me most.   F

My parents make the purchase decision, I try to influence.   B

Toys and books are my n° 1 possessions.   E

My world grows outside the boundaries of my house   C

I develop a sense of brand identification: things become brands.   D

Target Focus

3/19/2008   Property description & license overview   STUDIO 100

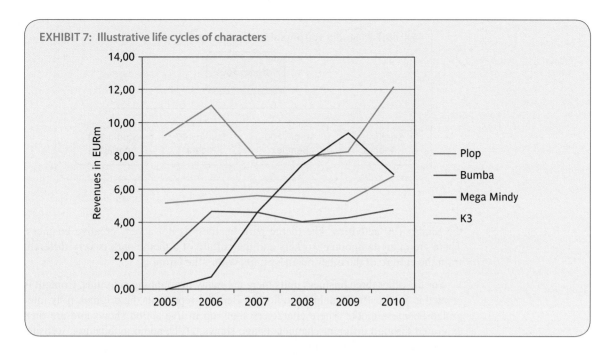

EXHIBIT 7: Illustrative life cycles of characters

Apart from these formal meetings, both Gert Verhulst and Hans Bourlon provide employees with a lot of input and market information. Says Hans Bourlon:

Every morning, I search on the websites of a few newspapers for articles that are related to Studio 100 in one way or another. And I forward these articles to employees that can use them. Everything you see in the world can be a source of inspiration for a story, a new concept or project. Our employees need to know what is on television these days, what are big hits and what interests' people have at this moment. Information should be available to the people who need it.

Creativity Embedded in the Organization Structure

Creative companies stimulate imagination and out-of the box thinking, which implies a certain chaos in the organization. Studio 100 is no exception. It has quite a flexible and fluid organization. The company has set up creative cells that create new characters and monitor the correct interpretation of and alignment with the character over all different departments, such as the TV department, the merchandising department, the theatre department, and the marketing department.

Both the creative cells and the departments have a direct link to the executive management team. This makes decision lines very short. And it results in a balanced organization. This structure also offers the best guarantees that the main ideas and philosophies of the top are transferred to every part of the organization.

Expanding the DNA Abroad

The internationalization of Studio 100 from 2007 onwards necessitated a change in the company's organization structure. The company has created a new organization structure since December 2010 with four main business units: Studio 100 Benelux, Studio 100 Plopsa (theme parks), Studio 100 Media, and Studio 100 Animation (see Exhibit 8). All these units have their own executive teams.

The theme park business was always considered a separate activity. The activities and the risks associated with running this business are very different from the rest of

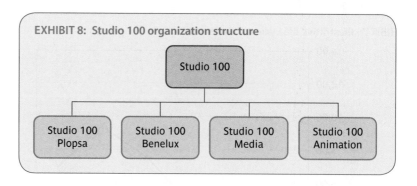

EXHIBIT 8: Studio 100 organization structure

the Studio 100 activities. The theme park business is not a very creative business. There are many temporary workers and the culture of a theme park is very different from the culture of the other business units within the Group.

For the other three business units there are many overlapping activities. Content is created in Studio 100 Benelux. Studio 100 Benelux represents the original, fully integrated business model where characters show up in live action shows and are then exploited through different channels (stage shows, DVD, audio, publishing, website, merchandising, and licensing).

Studio 100 Media focuses on selling and distributing Studio 100 programmes to TV broadcasters. No content is created in this unit. The managers of Studio 100 tried to export the organizational climate of the Belgian unit to the German unit but that did not work well. In 2012, about 40 people work on the sales and marketing of the international portfolio and is responsible for 15 per cent of the company's revenues.

Studio 100 Animation is a rather new activity in the group's portfolio as it develops, finances, and produces animated series and feature films. This unit operates from Paris and Sydney (because of more favourable financing conditions in those countries). The development of new series and concepts is undertaken in close collaboration with Studio 100 Benelux. But the business model of Animation is different than the traditional Studio 100 business model. The business model of Animation is more complex, more global, and the process to bring a character to TV takes much longer. On average, it takes one year to get the financing for a movie and making the movie adds another two years. This means that it takes a few years before the first productions go to market. An important advantage of animations is that these can be truly international products that need little tailoring for local markets. They allow for proper exploitation of economies of scale and can be sold in very large volumes once successful.[14]

Studio 100 realized that its traditional model with live action shows is rather unique in the world. And Jo Daris, the International Business Director (now Director Business Development), could convince the management team of Studio 100 to enter the market of animations. Jo Daris and Koen Peeters, the Chief Financial Officers (CFOs) of the company, believe that this animation silo offers great potential and might very well become the biggest driver of profits in the long run. As Exhibit 9 indicates, this is not yet the case.

Over the years, Studio 100 has developed a clear and winning business model in Belgium and the Netherlands, built around 'boundless creativity and innovation'. The company has been able to leverage its competences in an international context, but Jo Daris and Koen Peeters agree that the international expansion is a challenging task. You cannot just copy a successful business model from one country to another.

EXHIBIT 9: Financial figures of different business units

	2006	2007	2008	2009	2010	2011
Revenues (k EUR)	**75.125**	**79.128**	**107.099**	**132.419**	**135.572**	**170.205**
Benelux				71.091	67.548	83.500
Plopsa				38.749	43.681	58.300
Media				14.965	19.484	22.700
Animation				7.609	4.859	5.500
Business development and corporate				5	0	
Recurring EBITDA (k EUR)	**13.995**	**14.846**	**17.842**	**28.199**	**30.090**	**38.085**
Benelux	6.914	4.750	7.420	10.645	7.177	6.150
Plopsa	8.081	10.276	11.488	15.889	17.168	24.571
Media			3.474	4.652	5.820	6.493
Animation			−1.973	−226	2.659	4.350
Business development and corporate	−1.000	−422	−2.567	−2.761	−2.735	−3.478
EBITDA in % of sales	18,6%	18,8%	16,7%	31,1%	29,9%	22,4%
Net result (k EUR)	**6.159**	**2.036**	**55**	**7.316**	**4.611**	**329**
Profit margin	8,2%	2,6%	0,1%	5,5%	3,4%	0,0%

Source: Company information.

Nevertheless, Studio 100 is determined to further enlarge the international business in its corporate portfolio.

ENDNOTES

1. Corporate Overview Studio 100. Available online at www.studio100.tv/sites/default/files/pdf/corporate_overview.pdf, accessed 25 May 2012.

2. People in Flanders and the Netherlands speak Dutch. That is why Studio 100 has quickly reached out to the Dutch market. In the southern part of Belgian, the main language is French.

3. Ghemawat, P. (2001) 'Distance still matters: the hard reality of global expansion', *Harvard Business Review*, September, pp. 137–147.

4. Studio 100 (2011) *Preliminary Offering Memorandum*, Studio 100, p. 60.

5. Petitjean, F. (2009) 'De nv Kristel, Karen en Kathleen', *De Standaard*, 28 March.

6. Bolland, A., Fininzola e Silva, L., Keereman, S., Laurijssen, J., Roelandt, W. and Waterinckx, A. (2009) 'Studio 100 – growth strategy', *Assignment Strategic Management Part-Time MBA Vlerick Leuven Gent Management School*, Gent/Leuven.

7. Ibid., p. 9.

8. Studio 100 (2011) *Preliminary Offering Memorandum*, Studio 100, p. 68.

9. Schelfout, S. And Spyns, P. (2009) 'Combining business and creativity, therein lies the success of Studio 100: an interview with Hans Bourlon', Manager of the Year and co-founder of Studio 100', *EWI Review (Periodical of the Department of Economy, Science, and Innovation)*, September, p. 41.

10. Ibid., p. 43.

11. Bourlon, H. (2009), Speech for the International Full-time MBA students of Vlerick Leuven Gent Management School, 12 March.

12. Bontinck, W., Conings, L., Devisch, S., Leirman, L., Loeckx, D., Pelemans, E. and Vandecruys, A. (2008) 'Studio 100 case', *Assignment Strategic Management Part-Time MBA Vlerick Leuven Gent Management School*, Gent/Leuven.

13. Studio 100 (2011) *Preliminary Offering Memorandum*, Studio 100, pp. 55–6.

14. Bolland, A., Fininzola e Silva, L., Keereman, S., Laurijssen, J., Roelandt, W. and Waterinckx, A. (2009) 'Studio 100 – growth strategy', *Assignment Strategic Management Part-Time MBA Vlerick Leuven Gent Management School*, Gent/Leuven.

Case 6

Ferretti Group: navigating through stormy seas

Roger Dence*

Introduction

At the time of its 40th anniversary in mid-2008, Ferretti Group, the Italian luxury yacht builder, appeared to be 'riding on the crest of a wave'. However, as for many other organizations, the onset of the global financial crisis in 2007 heralded a period of uncertainty.

The decade from the mid/late-1990s onwards had been a good time for luxury yacht builders. Growth in many parts of the world economy had led to continued demand from already rich and newly wealthy populations in the wider luxury goods market. In this period, Ferretti had become one of the leading yacht building companies in the world. It positioned itself as a global player with a presence in all significant segments, with the medium-term objective of becoming the world's Number 1 manufacturer of luxury motor yachts.

By the end of 2008 though, the effects of the world-wide financial crisis and economic downturn were clearly in evidence. Early in 2009, Ferretti defaulted on its debt repayments forcing a financial restructuring that avoided the immediate risk of going into administration or foundering altogether. While it appeared to have bought itself time to ride out the storm, many strategic issues needed to be addressed as the Ferretti board and senior management plotted a new course towards a less certain future in the decade ahead.

The Luxury Yacht Market and Industry

Prices for new boats are anywhere between €1 million and €150 million plus and with significant annual operating costs to take into account in aspiring to a luxury lifestyle afloat. Annual growth in industry orders for large luxury yachts had risen steadily since the early years of the decade (Table 1) and the industry's order book for the very largest yachts had risen considerably (Table 2).

On the supply side of the industry, the market leader in terms of numbers of players and boats produced in the superyacht category (over 24m/80ft in length) was Italy, followed by the USA, the Netherlands, Germany and the UK. In the 2000s,

---

* Roger Dence is an Associate Tutor at the University of Leicester School of Management. This case study has been produced primarily from published sources. It is intended as a basis for class discussion rather than to illustrate either effective or ineffective handling of a management or administrative situation.

© Roger Dence.

TABLE 1 Industry yacht orders, 1999–2012*

1998	1999	2000	2001	2002	2003	2004	2005	2006	2007	2008	2009	2010	2011	2012
279	283	327	428	507	482	507	651	688	777	916	1016	763	749	728

Sources: ShowBoats International *Global Order Books* for 2009 to 2012 inclusive, published annually in December of each preceding year.

Note* These figures show the state of the industry order book at 1 September of each preceding year (i.e. 2012 = 1 September 2011).

TABLE 2 Yacht orders by length, 2003–12*

Length (ft)	2003	2004	2005	2006	2007	2008	2009	2010	2011	2012
80–89	132	140	207	216	207	253	286	187	158	178
90–99	54	67	71	86	109	114	117	89	78	70
100–119	114	112	145	146	155	179	190	144	151	151
120–149	84	83	115	110	152	175	193	150	155	150
150–199	72	68	84	90	108	125	145	112	132	109
200–249	16	22	21	28	28	47	40	41	45	43
250 +	10	15	9	12	18	23	21	30	30	27
Total projects	482	507	652	688	777	916	992 ^	753+	749	728

Sources: ShowBoats International *Global Order Books* for 2009 to 2012 inclusive, published annually in December of each preceding year.

Notes* These figures show the state of the industry order book at 1 September of each preceding year (i.e. 2012 = 1 September 2011).

^The 2009 figures do not include 16 projects from Lürssen and Amels not identified by length.

+ The 2010 figures do not include 10 projects from Amels not identified by length.

competition had intensified as new shipyards entered the market from countries such as Australia, Brazil, China, France, New Zealand, Russia, Taiwan and Turkey.

While new competitors enjoyed a lower cost base than European yards and competed effectively on price alone in certain market sectors, some lacked the design flair and technical skills of more established rivals. However, with well-regarded design bureaux, brokers and project management teams operating in the USA and Europe, such skills could be bought in as part of the business model or while their own capabilities were developed. These factors promised more direct competition in the future.

At the end of 2008, many European yacht builders had healthy order books, particularly at the higher end of the market where deliveries of new yachts ordered took several years to complete. In steady or growing market conditions, managing the 'pipeline' from marketing to order, through design and production, to commissioning and delivery was an easier, if still challenging, task.

However, the sector-wide situation now was marked by slackening customer demand and downward pressures on pricing and with limited financing available for working capital and investment. Several well-established European boatyards went out of business, fuelling consolidation of the industry. As traditional markets suffered in the economic downturn, market focus became more important, with the potential of emerging markets receiving greater attention.

While the ability of the industry to remain aligned with the needs of the market was not in doubt, the reality of retrenchment was evident. The general sense was that times were going to get tougher and that the achievements of the previous decade would be difficult to replicate. Hard decisions would have to be made and there would be further casualties in the luxury yacht building industry.

Ferretti Group Profile

Organization

Founded in 1968 as a family-owned builder of small boats, in the 1980s Ferretti began to focus on the design and production of luxury motor yachts. Through organic growth and acquisition, the company grew to become one of the leading yacht builders in the world. By 2010, it comprised a portfolio of nine separate brands each covering different segments of the market.[1]

The group also included several wholly or majority owned subsidiaries engaged in related activities that provided an integrated approach to yacht design, manufacture, service and support. These companies were involved in the production of components for yacht interiors, moulds and fibreglass products, wooden fixtures and furnishings, and the painting and refitting of yachts.

The ethos of the group was founded on attributes such as imaginative design (covering both exterior and interior aspects), technological innovation and engineering excellence in meeting customers' tastes and aspirations. These qualities can be seen in the statements of mission and values adopted by the group and some of its companies. For example, the group logo carried the slogan 'Luxury Innovation Excellence'. Ferretti Yachts, the founding company of the group, proclaimed its vision to be: 'We make our customers dreams come true' and its mission as: 'We will achieve excellence before, during and after the purchase of the world's best flybridge motor yachts'.

Marketing, Sales and Distribution

The marketing activities for Ferretti are conducted through a network of dealerships and distributors in primary markets, supporting local and regional customers and monitoring market trends from both customer and competitor viewpoints. Its Service University for training sales dealers and service agents is seen by the group as an important differentiator within the sector.

Given the nature of the customer base, emphasis is placed on corporate and marketing communications to build the profile of individual brands and their reputation for quality, design and performance. Brand/product advertising in yachting and high-end lifestyle media is a key part of the approach. A number of brand affiliations also have been created with international businesses in complementary luxury goods and lifestyle product segments.

Regular attendance at international boat shows serving regional markets is another aspect of the marketing strategy. The schedule of shows is seasonal in nature, the larger established events taking place in Europe and the USA in the Autumn and the New Year with newer regional events in the Middle and Far East in the first five months of the year. Such events provide an opportunity for distributors to present the products and to meet with existing and potential customers, as well as for yacht brokers dealing with new build, sales and charter enquiries and for other intermediaries.

Engineering and Manufacturing

A key element in Ferretti's reputation has been its focus on innovation in developing new solutions to the challenges of designing, building and operating modern luxury yachts. Its early involvement in offshore powerboat competitions required research that could be applied to yachts in volume production, as well as providing a high public profile.

A separate Engineering Division was formed in 1989 for all matters connected with research and design in the naval/marine sector. In 2006, this division was renamed

Advanced Yacht Technology (AYT) as a centre of excellence for the whole group. Among the technological innovations introduced were the Ferretti Wave Efficient Yacht hull concept and an anti-rolling gyro stabilization system.

A new hybrid propulsion system allowing yachts over 20m in length to cruise in a 'zero emission mode' to meet fuel economy and environmental pollution concerns was developed in collaboration with Diesel Center, an affiliate with expertise in propulsion system design and integration. An integrated data system for monitoring a yacht's performance was developed in partnership with the University of Pisa. Tested initially on Pershing boats, the system now provides standardised measurement procedures for comparison with a vessel's reference specifications.

The group's manufacturing capabilities combine an artisanal, craft-based approach, with a focus on the use of traditional materials and fine workmanship, with the needs of a capital-intensive industrial complex employing modern production techniques. By 2010, nine main sites were engaged in the production and assembly of yachts for specific Ferretti brands. The main strategic locations at Torre Annunziata, La Spezia and Ancona also provided regional service centres for Ferretti's important Italian home market, covering the Tyrrhenian, Ligurian and Adriatic Seas respectively.

Strategic Development

Early Growth

Ferretti was established when brothers Alessandro and Norberto Ferretti founded a nautical division of the family-owned car dealership in Bologna. The first agency agreement was to represent Chris Craft, a US-based motorboat producer. In 1971, a 10m wooden motor sailing yacht was produced as its first boat. After a successful few years, the brothers decided to devote themselves exclusively to the boating industry, with Alessandro Ferretti taking charge of commercial matters while Norberto Ferretti dealt with design and production.

In 1982, the company introduced its first motor-only yacht, and began to build sportsfishing, open and flybridge craft under the Ferretti name. Gradually the production of motorsailers was reduced and the company invested more in motor vessel design and production. This set the scene for the company's future development and its reputation for innovative design and an international presence. In 1987, Ferretti inaugurated a new shipyard in Forlì, which is still the headquarters of the group.

By the early 1990s, Ferretti had established itself as one of the leading companies in the production of flybridge yachts of up to 25m in length. In 1993, Ferretti of America Inc was founded to market yachts in The Americas, thus extending the existing sales network, and a year later the company began building a network of dealers outside of Europe and The Americas.

In 1995, Alessandro Ferretti died suddenly, and his brother Norberto Ferretti took over responsibility for running the company. However, reaching agreement with other family shareholders over the company's future direction was to prove difficult.

A Period of Expansion

The year 1998 saw institutional investors acquire a majority share in the company and a strategy set in place to expand through the acquisition of other yacht-building companies.

This initiative started with the purchase of the Cantieri Navali dell'Adriatico shipyard, which built open motorboats under the Pershing name. The same year, the US company Bertram Yacht of Miami was acquired, strengthening Ferretti's international presence. Then, in 1999, Ferretti purchased CRN, a producer of large yachts over 30m in length.

TABLE 3 Ferretti Group revenue, 1997–2011 (€ million) *

1997	1998	1999	2000	2001	2002	2003	2004	2005	2006	2007	2008	2009	2010	2011
47	57	121	188	262	337	390	557	653	770	933	900	800	500	521

Sources: Permira case study presentation from meeting on 'Impact investing: looking at things differently' held 15 November 2005, plus subsequent annual news releases and public statements.

Note: *Figures are preliminary for the year ending 31 August annually; that for 2010 reflects the 2009/10 disposals; some figures are cited as 'value of production' rather than revenue or turnover; the basis and characterisation of some inter-year comparisons differs.

The period 2000 to 2002 saw more acquisitions that extended the group's portfolio of products and brands and furthered its ambition to become the world's leading builder of luxury yachts. In 2000, Ferretti purchased Riva, an old-established shipyard famous for its iconic open boats. Then in 2001, shipyard assets in La Spezia were acquired, allowing the Riva company to produce larger luxury fibreglass craft. The same year, the Apreamare and the Mochi Craft shipyards, both producing working boat designs, were purchased.

In 2002, the group moved into related activities with the acquisition of a company in the nautical furnishings sector. A further shipyard in Ancona was also acquired, enabling CRN to extend its operations through an Italian subsidiary producing wooden manufactures and furnishings and a Spanish affiliate Pinmar, a yacht painting and refitting company.

The following year, in 2003, the Ferretti Group signed a sales agreement with MarineMax, a leading US distributor of pleasure crafts, covering the Ferretti European brands in the USA, Bahamas and Caribbean. After a pause in the pace of acquisitions, Itama, specializing in open motor yachts, was acquired in 2004 through the Pershing operation.

The Private Equity Role

Between 1997 and 2000, Ferretti's sales increased almost four-fold to €188 million on the back of the acquisitions (Table 3). These deals had been made possible by the injection of capital from the private equity fund Schroder Ventures (later to become Permira) in February 1998. This resulted in private equity interests owning almost 55 per cent of the company, with Norberto Ferretti holding almost 30 per cent and other management and private investors the balance.

The rationale for this external financial involvement had been based on a two-fold strategic assessment. First, that the luxury yacht building in Italy was a fragmented and inefficient manufacturing industry ripe for consolidation. And second, that Ferretti's expansion had been constrained by family tensions following Alessandro Ferretti's death in 1995.

From 1998 onwards, the private equity partners led the acquisitions programme. In parallel, these produced synergies in purchasing, product development, manufacture and distribution. Such internal developments benefited the whole group, together with Ferretti's growing capabilities and profile as a leading and successful player in an expanding international industry.

A Period of Public Ownership ... and then Private Again

In 2000, it was decided to seek a listing on the Official Italian Stock Exchange, with the aim of consolidating growth and facilitating further expansion. At the public flotation in June 2000, the company was capitalised at €382 million. As a result, the private equity interest realized 65 per cent of its initial investment in Ferretti at a UK£15.2 million premium to the June 1999 valuation, while its shareholding fell to just over 23 per cent. The public then held 35 per cent of the shares, with Norberto Ferretti 28 per cent and management and private investors retaining 13 per cent.

Following the 11th September 2001 ('9/11') attack on New York's World Trade Centre, and the ensuing uncertainty in financial and other markets, it was decided in 2002 to take the company private again. This move was motivated also by continuing increases in sales and gross profits, with sales up from €188 million in 2000 to €337 million in 2002 (Table 3) and associated profits rising from €31 million to €69 million in the same period. The move was aimed at 'consolidating the leadership of the company in [the] world market ... in a 5 to 7 years period' and undertaking further expansion, with an eventual return to a stock market listing again planned at the end of that period.

A public purchase offer backed by Permira valued the company at €674 million in July 2002 as a prelude to delisting. This offer was accepted by 93.7 per cent of shareholders, the balance being subject to a residual takeover completed in January 2003. Subsequently, in the three years from 2003, the quoted annual revenues almost doubled with annual profits growth of 24 per cent being claimed, the growth being both organic and derived from acquisitions.

A New Investor Appears

After the period of profitable growth, the scene was set for the planned return to a stock market listing. Then, in late 2006, an approach was made by Candover, a UK-based private equity house, that resulted in the sale of a majority stake in Ferretti. The secondary buy-out was completed in January 2007 valuing the company at €1685 million. The shareholdings comprised Candover at 50.2 per cent, with Permira retaining 10.7 per cent and the balance of 39.1 per cent being held between Norberto Ferretti and the group management team.

For Permira, the transaction realised €833 million from its 2002 investment of €277 million, while retaining a minority stake in the company. In this five-year period, the company's management had been consolidated and internal processes enhanced. A push had been made into new markets, especially in Asia and the USA, and the international distribution network strengthened. Production capacity had been enhanced with the number of sites doubling and many new products introduced.

Subsequent progress provided a sense of continued optimism. Figures for the year ending 31st August 2007 included an increase of 21 per cent in the value of production to €933 million (Table 3), and a 34 per cent increase in EBITDA of €158 million. The reported order book exceeded €1000 million, giving order cover of some 70 per cent of annual production, with export sales accounting for 70 per cent of the output of the Italian brands.

For Candover too, its investment as majority shareholder seemed to be fulfilling its early promise. Figures for its own direct portfolio investment of UK£32.3 million in Ferretti – as opposed to the larger institutional investment of UK£195.5 million made through its 2005 Fund – showed an increase of 9.8 per cent in 2007 and a further 5.9 per cent in the first half of 2008.

The Situation in 2008/9

As 2008 began, seemingly it was a case of 'business as usual'. Plans for the further expansion of Ferretti's facilities and product range were being implemented. The schedule of marketing events at international boat shows was in place. And thoughts were turning again towards an eventual public flotation through a relisting on the stock exchange.

Business Development Activities

In the first quarter of 2008, Ferretti's boat show programme included events in Mumbai, Dubai and Shanghai covering the Indian, Middle Eastern and Far Eastern markets that were of increasing importance.

In August 2008, a new US strategy was put in place with the acquisition of the Allied Richard Bertram Marine Group. Renamed as the Allied Marine Group, this US$50 million acquisition was positioned as enabling Ferretti to address higher added-value sectors of the US yachting market, including distribution and after-sales assistance services. Allied Marine's facility in Fort Lauderdale became the main US office for Ferretti in the USA and the sole distributor for all of the Ferretti European brands in the USA.

Management and Financial Developments

In December 2008, the Ferretti chief executive officer (CEO), Vincenzo Cannatelli, resigned with immediate effect, in order to pursue 'other entrepreneurial activities'. The company announcement highlighted the need to 'extend the timetable' for the potential flotation in the light of the financial market crisis, together with the need for an organizational structure 'more consistent' with prevailing market conditions.

The company had been expected to announce operating profits of some €150 million for the year ending 30th August 2008, against sales revenues of some €900 million. However, demand for all classes of yachts, and particularly the smaller boats, fell dramatically as the year progressed. In uncertain conditions, orders and down payments anticipated from boat shows in Europe and the USA had not materialized.

Then, early in 2009, the company defaulted on its debt repayments, forcing a financial restructuring. A programme was put in place reducing long-term debt and strengthening short-term banking facilities and medium-term credit. In addition, the group's capital was increased by €85 million in new funds, €70 million being under-written by Norberto Ferretti and members of the group management and the remaining €15 million by Mediobanca, the company's Italian banking partner.

On the terms proposed, the two private equity investors, Permira and Candover, together owning almost 60 per cent of Ferretti's shares, decided not to participate in the restructuring or in the future shareholding structure. Their investments made two years previously were written off. As a result, 53 per cent of the equity in the newly recapitalised company was owned by the senior loan and mezzanine finance lenders led by Royal Bank of Scotland (RBS), the balance being held by Norberto Ferretti and the group's management (38.5 per cent) and Mediobanca (8.5 per cent). Under the new arrangements, 100 per cent of the voting rights were retained by Norberto Ferretti, senior management and Mediobanca.

The View from the Bridge

Amid the turmoil of the restructuring from January to April 2009, the company still needed to run its business while addressing longer-term strategic issues. On the basis of the changes, Ferretti believed it would have the capital strength and financial flexibility to face future market challenges in the short to medium term and to continue to maintain and develop its position as a leader in the industry.

With the restructuring, the company had avoided going into administration or liquidation. However, it had a debt burden to service, it was majority owned by the banks, and its business prospects were uncertain. A key concern was where and how future profitable growth was to be found, given ongoing turbulence in financial and customer markets.

The consolidation of the industry meant that a smaller number of European and US yards producing luxury yachts were chasing a smaller pool of potential new orders, inducing more price competition, including from recent market entrants from low production cost countries. Yards that had taken yachts in part-exchange for new vessels now had inventories of pre- owned yachts for which there were fewer customers, creating further pressure on pricing in that segment of the market.

Getting and Staying Shipshape

While the external environment posed particular challenges for Ferretti, the internal aspects of the company's operations also demanded attention. Costs would need to be looked at closely and some slimming down and scaling back of operations was inevitable.

However, the investments made in marketing, design, technology, manufacturing and support during the Permira years, and the modern facilities now in place, should stand the company in good stead. Most of the senior management had worked together during the growth years, had considerable commercial experience inside and outside of the luxury yacht industry, and arguably were well placed to direct the company's efforts during the difficult period ahead.

At the top level of management, Norberto Ferretti had co-founded the company in 1968 when he was only 20 years old. He was now in his early 60s, holding the combined roles of Chairman and CEO at a difficult time for the company. To a large extent he was 'the company' with a major financial stake in the business, but the issue of mid-term management succession needed to be considered.

The decade from 1998 onwards had perhaps been the most exciting period in Ferretti's 40-year history. What challenges would the next 10 years hold? How could Ferretti position itself to take advantage of the opportunities presented to it, while managing to deal successfully with difficulties that might threaten its longer-term future and survival? These were questions that would exercise the management team beyond 2009.

Setting and Steering a New Course

Planning for Recovery

In the aftermath of the turbulent business environment in the late 2000s, there were strategic imperatives for the company to address in terms of its recovery. The debt restructuring process was completed in late July 2009 with the purchase of the former Ferretti SpA group by a new entity, Ferretti Holdings SpA. A new board of directors was appointed for the period 2009 to 2011, suggesting an initial two-year recovery period was foreseen.

Norberto Ferretti reassumed the role of Chairman and a new CEO, Salvatore Basile, with international and turnaround/recovery experience in engineering industries was appointed. In addition, two new executive directors with prior company experience were appointed, namely Giancarlo Galeone, a former Ferretti CEO, and Lamberto Tacoli, a former general manager of CRN/Custom Yacht. Two new independent directors were also appointed, one being the former administrator of the bankrupt Italian state airline, Alitalia.

An Industrial Plan was formulated to '... allow the group to consolidate its leadership in the boating sector and to continue the process of growth'. In a *Financial Times* interview on the 29th July 2009, the new CEO, Salvatore Basile, noted that the '... debt restructuring agreement ... was an essential step on the road to recovery, not the end of the journey'.

He observed: 'In the short term, it has solved our problems and given us breathing space, but it cannot solve our longer-term problems [on its own]'. And added that: '...

My feeling is that Ferretti lost its direction in the past five years, and shifted its focus from its customers and its products to its financial performance … We need to go back to fundamentals'.

Also highlighted was the need for Ferretti to adjust its business to a shrinking market. In 2007, Ferretti had produced some 500 vessels, but in 2009 expected to make only about 200 concentrating on larger vessels. Other measures were implemented, aimed at strengthening group synergies, to improve flexibility and decision making, and to better understand and anticipate clients' demands. The internal organizational structure was changed, with new central staff functions covering industrial and commercial, organization and human resources, finance and strategic planning affairs, while retaining the distinctiveness of each brand.

Continued Business Development Efforts

At the Cannes Boat Show in September 2009, preliminary revenues for the year ending 31 August 2009 were reported at around €800 million (Table 3), less than 12 per cent down compared with €900 million the previous year, a result seen as better than the market average given trading conditions.

The group's commercial focus on Europe and the Mediterranean continued, together with the emerging markets of Eastern Europe and the Far and Middle East, while the US market remained as a strategic area following the 2008 acquisition of Allied Marine. The company also established a permanent 'private boat show' facility at its Cattolica marina to enhance customer services for wealthy clients with onboard visits and sea trials and providing a showcase for interior designers and yacht-fitting suppliers.

At the October 2009 Genoa Boat Show, a common design project was unveiled for a new line of CRN and Riva yachts measuring 50m to 80m to provide 'a fleet of the future'. And in 2010, the company announced two Riva design partnerships to produce limited edition Aquariva yachts in collaboration with international designer Marc Newson and with Gucci.

Structural Developments

Key steps in helping Ferretti to refocus onto its core business and raise cash were two disposals. Its 60 per cent interest in the Spanish company Pinmar was sold to the company's management in November 2009. And the sale of Ferretti's 70 per cent interest in Apreamare to its former owners was announced in March 2010 together with the Torre Annunziata, Naples shipyard with its 100-berth private wet dock.

A management buy-out offer for Pershing was not accepted after considering '… the brand's strategic importance, the significance of the Mondolfo production facility and the technical and human value of the people working there …'. The offer, although valuable in cash terms, was rejected on account of the brand's popularity in the US market and the fact that its two most direct European competitors, Mangusta and Leopard, were in financial trouble.

In a move focusing on an emerging market, Ferretti signed an agreement in April 2010 with Spirit, a Brazilian company based in Sao Paolo engaged in the production and sale of new and pre-owned yachts. This agreement provided for the sale and after sales support of all Ferretti Group brand yachts under the name of Ferrettigroup Brasil.

Improving Prospects … and a Setback

At in-house event in May 2010, tentative signs of a market recovery were reported despite the macro-economic situation remaining uncertain. The first seven months of the 2009/10 financial year had seen a doubling of orders compared to the previous year.

Commentators noted that the large yacht business was the most buoyant new-build market sector and that the Ferretti large yacht company CRN was seen as 'keeping the rest of the group afloat'. Much of the action in early/mid-2010 remained in the pre-owned yacht sector, rather than in new construction, but competition to secure new-build orders was fierce and many shipyards reported increasing levels of new enquiries and orders.

At the Cannes Show in September 2010, Ferretti reported turnover of over €500 million (Table 3). Cost reductions of some €50 million had been made over the previous year, with disposals helping to reduce the net debt to some €590 million. An improved order position was reported, with a portfolio of €270 million and new orders of €460 million.

The 2010 year end also brought good news for Ferretti in gaining the Number 1 position in the annual league table of yacht builders published by *ShowBoats International* in its *2011 Global Order Book*, with 76 large yacht projects under construction or on order with an average length of 104ft.

Then, in April 2011, a setback occurred with the death of the CEO, Salvatore Basile, who had been in the post for less than two years and was the main architect of the recovery plan. Continuity in the plan's implementation was ensured by Giancarlo Galeone being named as successor, a main board member and shareholder and formerly CEO and then Vice Chairman from 1995 to 2006 during the company's earlier growth period.

At the next Cannes Show in September 2011, Ferretti reported further improvements in its financial position, the 2010/11 value of production increasing 12 per cent over the previous year to reach some €520 million (Table 3). Compared with the 2009/10 figures, the order portfolio had increased by some 55 per cent to reach €401 million with the volume of new orders up by 27 per cent to €552 million.

A New Strategic Development

In the meantime, in July 2011, Ferretti had announced a non-binding memorandum of understanding (MoU) with a Chinese company, Shandong Heavy Industry Group (SHIG), for a joint venture for the design, production and sale of new brands and models of yachts in the Greater China market and other emerging markets. This agreement included the possibility of SHIG, a company with interests in engines, generators and propulsion systems, taking a minority shareholding in Ferretti.

Come October 2011, Ferretti announced that it was in discussions with lenders about a further restructuring of its capital base through a debt reduction and by raising new money.

Then in January 2012, SHIG announced that it had reached agreement to acquire a controlling interest in Ferretti through an equity investment of €178 million and providing debt financing of €196 million. This gave SHIG a controlling 75 per cent interest in the group, with existing creditors acquiring the remaining 25 per cent through a €25 million equity injection and debt-to-equity swap. These moves increased Ferretti's equity capital by €100 million and reduced its debt to around €120 million.

These developments would pose many questions for the company and for its management, employees, suppliers, distributors and customers. What challenges and opportunities might the future hold? With continuing turbulence in international financial markets and economic uncertainty, would the new corporate situation and financial base enable Ferretti to maintain its position and reputation as leading designers and producers of luxury yachts?

Would its new relationship give it competitive advantages in penetrating the Greater China market, seen as one of the main potential growth areas for luxury yachts? What role would its new owners play in developing Ferretti's capabilities? What potential synergies might become available to Ferretti as a member of a larger, diversified technology-based group of companies?

These and many other questions of a strategic nature would have to wait for answers.

Postscript

Following the completion of the takeover of Ferrettti Group by SHIG in January 2012, a new top-level management structure was announced in August 2012. The company's co-founder and former chairman, Norberto Ferretti, became honorary chairman and an ambassador for the group, with Tan Xuguang, the chairman of Weichai Group Holdings and its subsidiary SHIG, becoming the new Ferretti Group chairman. At the same time, Giancarlo Galeone, named CEO on the death of Salvatore Basile in April 2011, stepped down to be succeeded by Ferruccio Rossi, the managing director of Riva and country manager of Ferretti Group America.

At the September 2012 Cannes Boat Show, the relationship with Weichai-SHIG was highlighted in terms of a strategic partnership facilitating the sharing of resources, reducing costs, and strengthening marketing and after-sales services. A focus on expanding in emerging markets in the Asia Pacific and Latin American regions was emphasised, together with reinforcing the group's presence and facilities in North America based on the Allied Marine and Bertram brands. A month later, an agreement with the Industrial and Commercial Bank of China was signed, by which an initial 200 million credit was made available to support future expansion.

Later in October 2012, an operational restructuring of the company took place, aimed at further strengthening its presence in key markets. A more globalised approach to marketing, sales and service was introduced based on a regional structure covering Europe, Middle East and Africa, the Americas and the Asia Pacific, with local distribution and service operations within each region, with manufacturing continuing in Italy and in the USA. Several senior management appointments were made to support the new approach, including the chief technical officer also assuming responsibility for the Asia Pacific region and a chief marketing officer being appointed.

ENDNOTE

1. Ferretti's portfolio of yacht brands in 2010 comprised: Ferretti Yachts, Riva and Custom Line (flybridge yachts; open yachts; tri-deck GRP hulled yachts); Pershing and Itama (open yachts); Apreamare and Mochi Craft (classical working boat-based designs); Bertram (sportsfishing yachts); and CRN (large yachts over 50m in length). A flybridge yacht has a steering position at the highest point of a vessel's superstructure, most often open to the elements, as opposed to an enclosed bridge situated at a lower level; most vessels have both.

Case 7

Starbucks: evolving into a dynamic global organization

Arthur A. Thompson

University of Alabama

Since its founding in 1987 as a modest nine-store operation in Seattle, USA, Starbucks had become the premier roaster and retailer of specialty coffees in the world, with over 17 400 store locations in more than 55 countries as of April 2012 and annual sales that were expected to exceed $13 billion in fiscal 2012. The sudden and sharp economic downturn that plagued much of the world's economy in late 2008 and all of 2009 hit Starbucks hard. Declining sales at Starbucks' stores prompted management to close 800 underperforming stores in the US and an additional 100 stores in other countries, reduce the number of planned new store openings, trim its workforce by about 6700 employees, and institute a rigorous cost containment program. On the heels of these retrenchment moves, the company's founder and chief executive officer (CEO), Howard Schultz, launched a series of wide-sweeping transformation initiatives to elevate the customer experience at Starbucks' stores, including:

- Conducting a special retraining program for all store employees aimed at reigniting their emotional attachment to customers (a longstanding tradition at Starbucks stores), and refocusing their attention on the details of delivering superior customer service and pleasing customers. Starbucks' stores were closed worldwide for three hours to allow all employees to go through the hands-on training exercise.
- Sharing of best practices across all stores worldwide.
- Refreshing the menu offerings at Starbucks' stores.
- Introducing improved and more environmental-friendly designs for future Starbucks' stores'.
- Providing additional resources and tools for store employees, including laptops, an Internet-based software for scheduling work hours for store employees, and a new point-of-sale system for all stores in the US, Canada, and the United Kingdom.
- Insisting that the entire Starbucks' organization put renewed emphasis on product innovation and differentiation.
- Reinstituting efforts to add more retail stores and expand Starbucks' global footprint.

Starbucks' robust recovery and performance in fiscal years 2010–2011 suggested that Schultz's efforts were successful and that Starbucks was once again poised to deliver sustained growth in revenues and profits. In describing Starbucks' performance for the second quarter of fiscal 2012, Howard Schultz said:[1]

Starbucks record Q2 performance demonstrates the strength of our business, the increasing power and global relevance of our brand, and the success of our unique Blueprint for Profitable Growth business strategy. In Q2 we expanded our retail presence, recorded our seventh consecutive quarter of over 20 per cent sales growth in China, introduced new products into multiple channels, and more than offset high legacy commodity costs through increased efficiencies. I could not be more excited or more optimistic about the future of our company as we pursue disciplined, profitable growth all around the world.

On the strength of Starbucks recent performance, executives announced that the company was accelerating new store growth in fiscal 2012 to approximately 1000 net new stores globally. Exhibit 1 provides an overview of Starbucks performance during fiscal years 2007–2011.

Company Background

Starbucks' Coffee, Tea, and Spice

Starbucks got its start in 1971 when three academics, English teacher Jerry Baldwin, history teacher Zev Siegel, and writer Gordon Bowker – all coffee aficionados – opened Starbucks' Coffee, Tea, and Spice in touristy Pikes Place Market in Seattle. The three partners shared a love for fine coffees and exotic teas and believed they could build a clientele in Seattle that would appreciate the best coffees and teas. They each invested $1350 and borrowed another $5000 from a bank to open the Pikes Place store. Customers were encouraged to learn how to grind the beans and make their own freshly brewed coffee at home. The store did not offer fresh-brewed coffee sold by the cup, but tasting samples were sometimes available. Initially, Zev was the only paid employee. He wore a grocer's apron, scooped out beans for customers, extolled the virtues of fine, dark-roasted coffees, and functioned as the partnership's retail expert. The other two partners kept their day jobs, but came by at lunch or after work to help out. During the start-up period, Jerry kept the books and developed a growing knowledge of coffee; Gordon served as the 'magic, mystery, and romance man.'[2] The store was an immediate success, with sales exceeding expectations, partly because of interest stirred by a favorable article in the *Seattle Times*. Initially, Starbucks ordered its coffee bean supplies from a specialty coffee retailer in Berkeley, California, but toward the end of the first year, the partners purchased a used roaster from Holland, set up roasting operations in a nearby ramshackled building, and came up with their own blends and flavors.

By the early 1980s, the company had four Starbucks' stores in the Seattle area and had been profitable every year since opening its doors. But then Zev Siegel experienced burnout and left the company to pursue other interests. Jerry Baldwin took over day-to-day management of the company and functioned as CEO; Gordon remained involved as an owner, but devoted most of his time to his advertising and design firm, a weekly newspaper he had founded, and a microbrewery that he was launching known as the Redhook Ale Brewery.

Howard Schultz Enters the Picture

In 1981, Howard Schultz, vice president and general manager of US operations for a Swedish maker of stylish kitchen equipment and coffeemakers, decided to pay Starbucks a visit – he was curious why Starbucks was selling so many of his company's products. When he arrived at the Pikes Place store, a solo violinist was playing Mozart at the door (his violin case open for donations). Schultz was immediately taken by the powerful and pleasing aroma of the coffees, the wall displaying coffee beans, and the rows of coffeemakers on the shelves. As he talked with the clerk behind the counter, the clerk scooped out some Sumatran coffee beans, ground them, put the

EXHIBIT 1: Financial and operating summary for Starbucks Corporation, fiscal years 2007–11
($ in millions, except for per share amounts)

	October 2, 2011	October 3, 2010	September 27, 2009	September 28, 2008	September 30, 2007
Income statement data					
Net revenues:					
Company-operated stores	$9632.4	$8963.5	$8180.1	$8771.9	$7998.3
Licensed stores	1007.5	875.2	795.0	779.0	660.0
Consumer products, foodservice and other	1060.5	868.7	799.5	832.1	753.2
Total net revenues	$11700.4	$10707.4	$9774.6	$10383.0	$9411.5
Cost of sales, including occupancy costs	$4949.3	$4458.6	$4324.9	$4645.3	$3999.1
Store operating expenses	3665.1	3551.4	3425.1	3745.3	3215.9
Other operating expenses	402.0	293.2	264.4	330.1	294.2
Depreciation and amortization expenses	523.3	510.4	534.7	549.3	467.2
General and administrative expenses	636.1	569.5	453.0	456.0	489.2
Restructuring charges	0.0	53.0	332.4	266.9	–
Total operating expenses	10175.8	9436.1	9334.5	9992.7	8465.6
Income from equity investees and other	203.9	148.1	121.9	113.6	108.0
Operating income	1728.5	1419.4	562.0	503.9	1053.9
Net earnings attributable to Starbucks	$1245.7	$945.6	$390.8	$315.5	$672.6
Net earnings per common share – diluted	$1.62	$1.24	$0.52	$0.43	$0.87
Balance sheet data					
Current assets	$3794.9	$2756.5	$2035.8	$1748.0	$1696.5
Current liabilities	2973.1	2703.6	1581.0	2189.7	2155.6
Total assets	7360.4	6385.9	5576.8	5672.6	5343.9
Short-term borrowings	–	–	–	713	710.3
Long-term debt (including current portion)	549.5	549.4	549.5	550.3	550.9
Shareholders' equity	$4384.9	$3674.7	$3045.7	$2490.9	$2284.1
Other financial data					
Net cash provided by operating activities	$1612.4	$1704.9	$1389.0	$1258.7	$1331.2
Capital expenditures (additions to property, plant and equipment)	$531.9	$440.7	$445.6	$984.5	$1080.3
Store information					
Stores open at year-end					
United States					
Company-operated stores	6705	6707	6764	7238	6793
Licensed stores	4082	4424	4364	4329	3891
International					
Company-operated stores	2326	2182	2198	2093	1831
Licensed stores	3890	3545	3309	3020	2496
Percentage change in sales at company-operated stores open 13 months or longer					
United States	8%	7%	(6)%	(5)%	4%
International	5%	6%	(2)%	2%	7%
Worldwide average	7%	7%	(5)%	(3)%	5%

Source: 2011, 2009, and 2007 10-K Reports.

grounds in a cone filter, poured hot water over the cone, and shortly handed Schultz a porcelain mug filled with freshly brewed coffee. After only taking three sips of the brew, Schultz was hooked. He began asking questions about the company, the coffees from different parts of the world, and the different ways of roasting coffee.

Later, when he met with Jerry Baldwin and Gordon Bowker, Schultz was struck by their knowledge about coffee, their commitment to providing customers with quality coffees, and their passion for educating customers about the merits of dark-roasted coffees. Baldwin told Schultz, 'We don't manage the business to maximize anything other than the quality of the coffee.'[3] The company purchased only the finest Arabica coffees and put them through a meticulous dark-roasting process to bring out their full flavors. Jerry explained that the cheap robusta coffees used in supermarket blends burned when subjected to dark roasting. He also noted that the makers of supermarket blends preferred lighter roasts because it allowed higher yields (the longer a coffee was roasted, the more weight it lost).

Schultz was also struck by the business philosophy of the two partners. It was clear that Starbucks stood not just for good coffee, but also for the dark-roasted flavor profiles that the founders were passionate about. Top quality, fresh-roasted, whole-bean coffee was the company's differentiating feature and a bedrock value. It was also clear to Schultz that Starbucks was strongly committed to educating its customers to appreciate the qualities of fine coffees. The company depended mainly on word-of-mouth to get more people into its stores, then built customer loyalty cup-by-cup as buyers gained a sense of discovery and excitement about the taste of fine coffee.

On his return trip to New York, Howard Schultz could not stop thinking about Starbucks and what it would be like to be a part of the enterprise. Schultz recalled, 'There was something magic about it, a passion and authenticity I had never experienced in business.'[4] By the time he landed at Kennedy Airport, he knew in his heart he wanted to go to work for Starbucks. Shortly thereafter, Schultz asked Baldwin whether there was any way he could fit into Starbucks. But it took a year, numerous meetings at which Schultz presented his ideas about the tremendous potential of expanding the Starbucks' enterprise outside Seattle and exposing people all over America to Starbucks coffee, and a lot of convincing to get Baldwin, Bowker, and their silent partner from San Francisco to agree to hire him, chiefly because they were nervous about bringing in an outsider, especially a high-powered New Yorker, who had not grown up with the values of the company. Then, in Spring 1982, following another round of meetings and discussions with the three owners, Schultz was offered the job of heading marketing and overseeing Starbucks' retail stores. In September 1982, Howard Schultz took over his new responsibilities at Starbucks.

Starbucks and Howard Schultz: The 1982–85 Period

In his first few months at Starbucks, Schultz spent most of time in the four Seattle stores – working behind the counters, tasting different kinds of coffee, talking with customers, getting to know store personnel, and learning the retail aspects of the coffee business. By December, Jerry Baldwin concluded Schultz was ready for the final part of his training, that of actually roasting the coffee. Schultz spent a week getting an education about the colors of different coffee beans, listening for the telltale second pop of the beans during the roasting process, learning to taste the subtle differences among the various roasts, and familiarizing himself with the roasting techniques for different beans.

Schultz overflowed with ideas for the company. However, his biggest inspiration and vision for Starbucks' future came during the spring of 1983 when the company sent him to Milan, Italy, to attend an international housewares show. While walking from his hotel to the convention center, he spotted an espresso bar and went inside to look around. The cashier beside the door nodded and smiled. The 'barista' behind the counter greeted Schultz cheerfully and began pulling a shot of espresso for one customer and handcrafting a foamy cappuccino for another, all the while conversing merrily with patrons standing at the counter. Schultz thought the barista's performance was 'great theater.' Just down the way on a side street, he went in an even more crowded espresso bar where the barista, which he surmised to be the owner, was greeting customers by name; people were laughing and talking in an atmosphere that plainly was comfortable and familiar. In the next few blocks, he saw two more espresso bars. That afternoon, Schultz walked the streets of Milan to explore more espresso bars. Some were stylish and upscale; others attracted a blue-collar clientele. Most had few chairs and it was common for Italian opera to be playing in the background. What struck Schultz was how popular and vibrant the Italian coffee bars were. Energy levels were typically high and they seemed to function as an integral community gathering place. Each one had its own unique character, but they all had a barista that performed with flair and there was camaraderie between the barista and the customers.

Schultz remained in Milan for a week, exploring coffee bars and learning as much as he could about the Italian passion for coffee drinks. Schultz was particularly struck by the fact that there were 1500 coffee bars in Milan, a city about the size of Philadelphia, and a total of 200 000 in all of Italy. In one bar, he heard a customer order a 'caffe latte' and decided to try one himself – the barista made a shot of espresso, steamed a frothy pitcher of milk, poured the two together in a cup, and put a dollop of foam on the top. Schultz liked it immediately, concluding that lattes should be a feature item on any coffee bar menu even though none of the coffee experts he had talked to had ever mentioned coffee lattes.

Schultz's 1983 trip to Milan produced a revelation: the Starbucks stores in Seattle completely missed the point. There was much more to the coffee business than just selling beans and getting people to appreciate grinding their own beans and brewing fine coffee in their homes. What Starbucks needed to do was serve fresh brewed coffee, espressos, and cappuccinos in its stores (in addition to beans and coffee equipment) and try to create a US version of the Italian coffee bar culture. Going to Starbucks should be an experience, a special treat, a place to meet friends and visit. Re-creating the authentic Italian coffee bar culture in the US could be Starbucks' differentiating factor.

Schultz Becomes Frustrated

On Schultz's return from Italy, he shared his revelation and ideas for modifying the format of Starbucks' stores with Baldwin and Bowker, but they strongly resisted, contending that Starbucks was a retailer, not a restaurant or coffee bar. They feared serving drinks would put them in the beverage business and diminish the integrity of Starbucks' mission as a purveyor of fine coffees. They pointed out that Starbucks had been profitable every year and there was no reason to rock the boat in a small, private company like Starbucks. It took Howard Schultz nearly a year to convince Jerry Baldwin to let him test an espresso bar. Jerry relented when Starbucks opened its sixth store in April 1984. It was the first store designed to sell beverages and it was the first store located in downtown Seattle. Schultz asked for a 1500 square foot space to set up a full-scale Italian-style espresso bar, but Jerry agreed to allocating only 300 square feet in a corner of the new store. The store opened with no fanfare as a deliberate experiment to see what happened. By closing time on the first day, some 400 customers had been served, well above the 250-customer average of Starbucks' best performing stores. Within two months the store was serving 800 customers per day. The two baristas could not keep up with orders during the early morning hours, resulting in lines outside the door onto the sidewalk. Most of the business was at the espresso counter; while sales at the regular retail counter were only adequate.

Schultz was elated at the test results, expecting that Baldwin's doubts about entering the beverage side of the business would be dispelled and that he would gain approval to pursue the opportunity to take Starbucks to a new level. Every day he went into Baldwin's office to show him the sales figures and customer counts at the new downtown store. But Baldwin was not comfortable with the success of the new store, believing that it felt wrong and that espresso drinks were a distraction from the core business of marketing fine arabica coffees at retail.[5] While he didn't deny that the experiment was succeeding, Baldwin didn't want to go forward with introducing beverages in other Starbucks' stores, although to avoid a total impasse Baldwin finally did agree to let Schultz put espresso machines in the back of one or two other Starbucks stores.

Over the next several months, Schultz made up his mind to leave Starbucks and start his own company. His plan was to open espresso bars in high-traffic downtown locations, serve espresso drinks and coffee by the cup, and try to emulate the friendly, energetic atmosphere he had encountered in Italian espresso bars. Baldwin and Bowker, knowing how frustrated Schultz had become, supported his efforts to go out on his own and agreed to let him stay in his current job and office until definitive plans were in place. Schultz left Starbucks in late 1985.

Schultz's Il Giornale Venture

With the aid of a lawyer friend who helped companies raise venture capital and go public, Schultz began seeking out investors for the kind of company he had in mind. Ironically, Jerry Baldwin committed to investing $150 000 of Starbucks' money in Schultz's coffee bar enterprise, thus becoming Schultz's first investor. Baldwin accepted Schultz's invitation to be a director of the new company and Gordon Bowker agreed to be a part-time consultant for six months. Bowker proposed that the new company be named Il Giornale Coffee Company (pronounced il jor nahl' ee), a suggestion that Howard accepted. In December 1985, Bowker and Schultz made a trip to Italy where they visited some 500 espresso bars in Milan and Verona, observing local habits, taking notes about décor and menus, snapping photographs, and videotaping baristas in action.

By the end of January 1986, Schultz had raised about $400,000 in seed capital, enough to rent an office, hire a couple of key employees, develop a store design, and open the first store. But it took until the end of 1986 to raise the remaining $1.25 million needed to launch at least eight espresso bars and prove that Schultz's strategy and business model were viable. Schultz made presentations to 242 potential investors, 217 of which said 'no.' Many who heard Schultz's hour-long presentation saw coffee as a commodity business and thought that Schultz's espresso bar concept lacked any basis for sustainable competitive advantage (no patent on dark roast, no advantage in purchasing coffee beans, no ways to bar the entry of imitative competitors). Some noted that coffee couldn't be turned into a growth business –consumption of coffee had been declining since the mid-1960s. Others were skeptical that people would pay $1.50 or more for a cup of coffee, and the company's unpronounceable name turned some off. Nonetheless, Schultz maintained an upbeat attitude and displayed passion and enthusiasm in making his pitch. He ended up raising $1.65 million from about 30 investors; most of the money came from nine people, five of whom became directors.

The first Il Giornale store opened in April 1986. It had 700 square feet and was located near the entrance of Seattle's tallest building. The décor was Italian and there were Italian words on the menu. Italian opera music played in the background. The baristas wore white shirts and bow ties. All service was stand up – there were no chairs. National and international papers were hung on rods on the wall. By closing time on the first day, 300 customers had been served – mostly in the morning hours. But while the core idea worked well, it soon became apparent that several aspects of the format were not appropriate for Seattle. Some customers objected to the incessant opera music, others wanted a place to sit down; many people did not understand the Italian words on the menu. These 'mistakes' were quickly fixed, but an effort was made not to compromise the style and elegance of the store. Within six months, the store was serving more than 1000 customers a day. Regular customers had learned how to pronounce the company's name. Because most customers were in a hurry, it became apparent that speedy service was essential.

Six months after opening the first store, a second store was opened in another downtown building. In April 1987, a third store was opened in Vancouver, British Columbia, to test the transferability of the company's business concept outside Seattle. Schultz's goal was to open 50 stores in five years and he needed to dispel his investors' doubts about geographic expansion early on to achieve his growth objective. By mid-1987 sales at each of the three stores were running at a rate equal to $1.5 million annually.

Il Giornale Acquires Starbucks

In March 1987 Jerry Baldwin and Gordon Bowker decided to sell the whole Starbucks' operation in Seattle – the stores, the roasting plant, and the Starbucks' name. Schultz knew immediately that he had to buy Starbucks; his board of directors agreed. Schultz and his newly-hired finance and accounting manager drew up a set of financial projections for the combined operations and a financing package that included a stock offering to Il Giornale's original investors and a line of credit with local banks. Within weeks Schultz had raised the $3.8 million needed to buy Starbucks. The acquisition was completed in August 1987. The new name of the combined companies was Starbucks Corporation. Howard Schultz, at the age of 34, became Starbucks' president and CEO.

Starbucks as a Private Company: 1987–92

The following Monday morning, Howard returned to the Starbucks' offices at the roasting plant, greeted all the familiar faces, and accepted their congratulations. Then, he called the staff together for a meeting on the roasting plant floor:[6]

> *All my life I have wanted to be part of a company and a group of people who share a common vision ... I'm here today because I love this company. I love what it represents ... I know you're concerned ... I promise you I will not let you down. I promise you I will not leave anyone behind ... In five years, I want you to look back at this day and say 'I was there when it started. I helped build this company into something great.'*

Schultz told the group that his vision was for Starbucks to become a national company with values and guiding principles that employees could be proud of. He aspired for Starbucks to become the most respected brand name in coffee and for the company to be admired for its corporate responsibility. He indicated that he wanted to include people in the decision-making process and that he would be open and honest with them. For Schultz, building a company that valued and respected its people, that inspired them, and that shared the fruits of success with those who contributed to the company's long-term value was essential, not just an intriguing option. He made the establishment of mutual respect between employees and management a priority.

The business plan Schultz had presented investors called for the new nine-store company to open 125 stores in the next five years – 15 the first year, 20 the second, 25 the third, 30 the fourth, and 35 the fifth. Revenues were projected to reach $60 million in 1992. But the company lacked experienced management. Schultz had never led a growth effort of such magnitude and was just learning what the job of CEO was all about, having been the president of a small company for barely two years. Dave Olsen, a Seattle coffee bar owner who Schultz had recruited to direct store operations at Il

Giornale, was still learning the ropes in managing a multi-store operation. Ron Lawrence, the company's controller, had worked as a controller for several organizations. Other Starbucks' employees had only the experience of managing or being a part of a six-store organization.

Schultz instituted a number of changes in the first several months. To symbolize the merging of the two companies and the two cultures, a new logo was created that melded the designs of the Starbucks' logo and the Il Giornale logo. The Starbucks' stores were equipped with espresso machines and remodeled to look more Italian than Old World nautical. Il Giornale green replaced the traditional Starbucks brown. The result was a new type of store – a cross between a retail coffee bean store and an espresso bar/café – that is now Starbucks' signature.

By December 1987, the mood at Starbucks was distinctly upbeat, with most all employees buying into the changes that Schultz was making and trust beginning to build between management and employees. New stores were on the verge of opening in Vancouver and Chicago. One Starbucks' store employee, Daryl Moore, who had started working at Starbucks in 1981 and who had voted against unionization in 1985, began to question the need for a union with his fellow employees. Over the next few weeks, Moore began a move to decertify the union. He carried a decertification letter around to Starbucks' stores securing the signatures of employees who no longer wished to be represented by the union. He got a majority of store employees to sign the letter and presented it to the National Labor Relations Board. The union representing store employees was decertified. Later, in 1992, the union representing Starbucks' roasting plant and warehouse employees was also decertified.

Market Expansion Outside the Pacific Northwest

Starbucks' entry into Chicago proved far more troublesome than management anticipated. The first Chicago store opened in October 1987 and three more stores were opened over the next six months. Customer counts at the stores were substantially below expectations. Chicagoans did not take to dark-roasted coffee as fast as Schultz had anticipated. It was more expensive to supply fresh coffee to the Chicago stores out of the Seattle warehouse (the company solved the problem of freshness and quality assurance by putting freshly-roasted beans in special FlavorLock bags that utilized vacuum packaging techniques with a one-way valve to allow carbon dioxide to escape without allowing air and moisture in). Rents were higher in Chicago and so were wage rates. The result was a squeeze on store profit margins. Gradually, customer counts improved, but Starbucks lost money on its Chicago stores until, in 1990, prices were raised to reflect higher rents and labor costs, more experienced store managers were hired, and a critical mass of customers caught on to the taste of Starbucks' products.

Portland, Oregon was the next market entered, and Portland coffee drinkers took to Starbucks' products quickly. Store openings in Los Angeles and San Francisco soon followed. LA consumers embraced Starbucks quickly and the *Los Angeles Times* named Starbucks as the best coffee in the US before the first store opened.

Starbucks' store expansion targets proved easier to meet than Schultz had originally anticipated and he upped the numbers to keep challenging the organization. Starbucks opened 15 new stores in fiscal 1988, 20 in 1989, 30 in 1990, 32 in 1991, and 53 in 1992 – producing a total of 161 stores, significantly above his original 1992 target of 125 stores.

From the outset, the strategy was to open only company-owned stores; franchising was avoided so as to keep the company in full control of the quality of its products and the character and location of its stores. But company ownership of all stores required Starbucks to raise new venture capital to cover the cost of new store expansion. In 1988 the company raised $3.9 million; in 1990, venture capitalists provided an additional $13.5 million; and in 1991 another round of venture capital financing generated $15 million. Starbucks was able to raise the needed funds despite posting losses of $330 000 in 1987, $764 000 in 1988, and $1.2 million in 1989. While the losses were troubling to Starbucks' board of directors and investors, Schultz's business plan had forecast losses during the early years of expansion. At a particularly tense board meeting where directors sharply questioned Schultz about the lack of profitability, Schultz said:[7]

> *Look, we're going to keep losing money until we can do three things. We have to attract a management team well beyond our expansion needs. We have to build a world-class roasting facility. And we need a computer information system sophisticated enough to keep track of sales in hundreds and hundreds of stores.*

Schultz argued for patience as the company invested in the infrastructure to support continued growth well into the 1990s. He contended that hiring experienced executives ahead of the growth curve, building facilities far beyond current needs, and installing support systems laid a strong foundation for rapid, profitable growth on down the road. His arguments carried the day with the board and with investors, especially since revenues were growing approximately 80 per cent annually and customer traffic at the stores was meeting or exceeding expectations.

Starbucks became profitable in 1990. Profits had increased every year since 1990 except for fiscal year 2000 (because of $58.8 million in investment write-offs in 4 dot. com enterprises) and for fiscal year 2008 (when the sharp global economic downturn hit the company's bottom line very hard – see Exhibit 1).

Starbucks' Stores: Design, Ambience, and Expansion of Locations

Store Design

Starting in 1991, Starbucks created its own in-house team of architects and designers to ensure that each store would convey the right image and character. Stores had to be custom-designed because the company didn't buy real estate and build its own freestanding structures; rather each space was leased in an existing structure, making each store differ in size and shape. Most stores ranged in size from 1000 to 1500 square feet and were located in office buildings, downtown and suburban retail centers, airport terminals, university campus areas, and busy neighborhood shopping areas convenient for pedestrian foot traffic and/or drivers. A few were in suburban malls. Four store templates – each with its own color combinations, lighting scheme, and component materials – were introduced in 1996; all four were adaptable to different store sizes and settings (downtown buildings, college campuses, neighborhood shopping areas).

But as the number of stores increased rapidly in the 2000–2003, greater store diversity and layout quickly became necessary. Some stores were equipped with special seating areas to help make Starbucks a desirable gathering place where customers could meet and chat or simply enjoy a peaceful interlude in their day. Flagship stores in high-traffic, high-visibility locations had fireplaces, leather chairs, newspapers, couches, and lots of ambience. Increasingly, the company began installing drive-through windows at locations where speed and convenience were important to customers and utilizing kiosks in supermarkets, building lobbies, and other public places.[8] As of 2012, about 25 per cent of Starbucks' locations in the US were equipped with drive-thru windows.

A new global store design strategy was introduced in 2009. Core design characteristics included: celebration of local materials and craftsmanship, a focus on reused and recycled elements, exposure of structural integrity and authentic roots, the absence of features that distracted from an emphasis on coffee, seating layouts that facilitated customer gatherings, an atmosphere that sought to engage all five customer senses (sight, smell, sound, hearing, and feel), and flexibility to meet the needs of many customer types.[9] Each new store was to be a reflection of the environment in which it operated and be environmentally friendly. In 2010, Starbucks began an effort to achieve LEED (Leadership in Energy and Environmental Design) Certification for all new company-owned stores (a LEED-certified building had to incorporate green building design, construction, operations, and maintenance solutions).[10] Exhibit 2 shows the diverse nature of Starbucks stores.

To better control average store opening costs, the company centralized buying, developed standard contracts and fixed fees for certain items, and consolidated work under those contractors who displayed good cost control practices. The retail operations group outlined exactly the minimum amount of equipment each core store needed, so that standard items could be ordered in volume from vendors at 20 to 30 per cent discounts, then delivered just-in-time to the store site either from company warehouses or the vendor. Modular designs for display cases were developed. The layouts for new and remodeled stores were developed on a computer, with software

EXHIBIT 2: Scenes from Starbucks' stores

that allowed the costs to be estimated as the design evolved. All this cut store opening and remodeling costs significantly and shortened the process to about 18 weeks.

Store Ambience

Starbucks management viewed each store as a billboard for the company and as a contributor to building the company's brand and image. The company went to great lengths to make sure the store fixtures, the merchandise displays, the colors, the artwork, the banners, the music, and the aromas all blended to create a consistent, inviting, stimulating environment that evoked the romance of coffee and signaled the company's passion for coffee. To try to keep the coffee aromas in the stores pure, smoking was banned, and employees were asked to refrain from wearing perfumes or colognes. Prepared foods were kept covered so customers would smell coffee only. Colorful banners and posters were used to keep the look of Starbucks' stores fresh and in keeping with seasons and holidays. The thesis was that every detail mattered in making Starbucks' stores a welcoming and pleasant 'third place' (apart from home and work) where people could meet friends and family, enjoy a quiet moment alone with a newspaper or book, or simply spend quality time relaxing – and, most importantly have a satisfying experience.

Starting in 2002, Starbucks began providing Internet access capability and enhanced digital entertainment to patrons at over 1200 Starbucks' locations. The objective was to heighten the 'third place' Starbucks' experience, entice customers into perhaps buying a second latte or espresso while they caught up on email, listened to digital music, put the finishing touches on a presentation, or surfed the Internet. Since then, wireless Internet service had been added at all company operated store locations in the US and at growing numbers of locations world-wide.

Store Expansion Strategy

In 1992 and 1993 Starbucks began concentrating its store expansion efforts on locations with favorable demographic profiles that also could be serviced and supported by the company's operations infrastructure. For each targeted region, Starbucks selected a large city to serve as a 'hub'; teams of professionals were located in hub cities to support the goal of opening 20 or more stores in the hub within two years. Once a number of stores were opened in a hub, then additional stores were opened in smaller, surrounding 'spoke' areas in the region. To oversee the expansion process, Starbucks had zone vice presidents that oversaw the store expansion process in a geographic region and that were also responsible for instilling the Starbucks culture in the newly opened stores.

More recently, Starbucks' strategy in major metropolitan cities had been to blanket major cities with stores, even if some stores cannibalized a nearby store's business. While a new store might draw 30 per cent of the business of an existing store two or so blocks away, management believed a 'Starbucks everywhere' strategy cut down on delivery and management costs, shortened customer lines at individual stores, and increased foot traffic for all the stores in an area. In 2002, new stores generated an average of $1.2 million in first-year revenues, compared to $700 000 in 1995 and only $427 000 in 1990. The steady increases in new-store revenues were due partly to growing popularity of premium coffee drinks, partly to Starbucks' growing reputation, and partly to expanded product offerings. But the strategy of saturating big metropolitan areas with stores ended up cannibalizing sales of existing stores to such an extent that average sales per store in the US dropped under $1 000 000 annually in 2008–2009 and pushed store operating margins down from 14.3 per cent in fiscal 2007 to 6.0 per cent in fiscal 2008 and 7.5 per cent in fiscal 2009. Because Starbucks' long-term profitability target for its retail stores in the US was an operating profit margin in the high teens, Starbucks management cut the number of metropolitan locations when it closed 900 underperforming Starbucks' locations in 2008–2009 (some 75 per cent of the closed stores were within three miles of another Starbucks' store).

Despite the mistake of over-saturating portions of some large metropolitan areas with stores, Starbucks was regarded as having the best real estate team in the coffee bar industry and a core competence in identifying good retailing sites for its new stores. The company's sophisticated methodology enabled it to identify not only the most attractive individual city blocks but also the exact store location that was best. It also worked hard at building good relationships with local real estate representatives in areas where it was opening multiple store locations.

Licensed Starbucks Stores

In 1995 Starbucks began entering into licensing agreements for store locations in areas where it did not have ability to locate its own outlets. Two early licensing agreements were with Marriott Host International to operate Starbucks retail stores in airport locations and with Aramark Food and Services to put Starbucks stores on university campuses and other locations operated by Aramark. Very quickly, Starbucks began to make increased use of licensing, both domestically and internationally. Starbucks preferred licensing to franchising because it permitted tighter controls over the operations of licensees.

Starbucks received a license fee and a royalty on sales at all licensed locations and supplied the coffee for resale at these locations. All licensed stores had to follow Starbucks' detailed operating procedures and all managers and employees who worked in these stores received the same training given to managers and employees in company-operated Starbucks' stores. As of April 2012, Starbucks had 4161 licensed stores in the US and 4124 licensed stores internationally.

International Expansion

In markets outside the continental US, Starbucks had a two-pronged store expansion: either open company-owned and -operated stores or else license a reputable and capable local company with retailing know-how in the target host country to develop and operate new Starbucks' stores. In most countries, Starbucks utilized a local partner/licensee to help it recruit talented individuals, set up supplier relationships, locate suitable store sites, and cater to local market conditions. Starbucks looked for partners/licensees that had strong retail/restaurant experience, had values and a corporate culture compatible with Starbucks, were committed to good customer service, possessed talented management and strong financial resources, and had demonstrated brand-building skills. In those foreign countries where business risks were deemed relatively high, most if not all Starbucks stores were licensed rather than being company-owned and operated.

Exhibit 3 shows the speed with which Starbucks had expanded its network of company-operated and licensed retail stores during the period from 1987 through April 2012. Starbucks' long-term profitability target for its international operations was an operating profit margin in the mid-to-high teens. But the international store margins in recent years had been below the target: 8.1 per cent in fiscal 2007, 5.2 per cent in fiscal 2008, 4.8 per cent in fiscal 2009, 9.8 per cent in fiscal 2010, and 13.3 per cent in fiscal 2011.

Starbucks' Strategy to Expand Its Product Offerings and Enter New Market Segments

In the mid-1990s, Howard Schultz began a long-term strategic campaign to expand Starbucks' product offerings beyond its retail stores and to pursue sales of Starbucks'

EXHIBIT 3: Company-operated and licensed Starbucks' stores

A. Number of Starbucks' store locations world-wide, fiscal years 1987–2011 and April 1, 2012

End of fiscal year*	Company-operated store locations		Licensed store locations		World-wide total
	United States	International	United States	International	
1987	17	0	0	0	17
1990	84	0	0	0	84
1995	627	0	49	0	676
2000	2446	530	173	352	3501
2005	4918	1263	2435	1625	10 241
2006	5728	1521	3168	2023	12 440
2007	6793	1831	3891	2496	15 011
2008	7238	2093	4329	3020	16 680
2009	6764	2141	4364	3366	16 635
2010	6707	2126	4424	3601	16 858
2011	6705	2326	4082	3890	17 003
April 1, 2012	6714	2421	4161	4124	17 420

B. International Starbucks' store locations, april 1, 2012

International locations of company-operated Starbucks' stores		International locations of licensed Starbucks' stores			
		Americas		**Europe/Africa/Middle East**	
Canada	851	Canada	295	Turkey	162
United Kingdom	603	Mexico	342	United Kingdom	138
China	330	Other	113	United Arab Emirates	98
Germany	153			Spain	75
Thailand	146	Asia-Pacific		Saudi Arabia	63
Other	333	Japan	955	Kuwait	67
		South Korea	415	Russia	56
Total	2416	Taiwan	264	Greece	46
		China	247	Other	194
		Philippines	190		
		Malaysia	125		
		Indonesia	122	Licensed total world-wide	4124
		Other	157		

Note: *Starbucks fiscal year ends on the Sunday closest to September 30.

Source: Company 10-K Reports, various years, and company records posted in the investor relations section at www.starbucks.com, accessed May 4, 2012.

products in a wider variety of distribution channels and market segments. The strategic objectives were to capitalize on Starbucks' growing brand awareness and brand-name strength and create a broader foundation for sustained long-term growth in revenues and profits.

The first initiative involved the establishment of an in-house specialty sales group to begin marketing Starbucks' coffee to restaurants, airlines, hotels, universities, hospitals, business offices, country clubs, and select retailers. Early users of Starbucks' coffee included Horizon Airlines, a regional carrier based in Seattle, and United Airlines. There was much internal debate at Starbucks about whether it made sense for Starbucks' coffee to be served on all United flights (since there was different coffee-making equipment on different planes) and the possible damage to the integrity of the

Starbucks' brand if the quality of the coffee served did not measure up. It took seven months of negotiations for Starbucks and United to arrive at a mutually agreeable way to handle quality control on United's various types of planes. The specialty sales group then soon won accounts at Hyatt, Hilton, Sheraton, Radisson, and Westin hotels, resulting in packets of Starbucks' coffee being in each room with coffee-making equipment. Later, the specialty sales group began working with leading institutional foodservice distributors, including SYSCO Corporation and US Foodservice, to handle the distribution of Starbucks' products to hotels, restaurants, office coffee distributors, educational and healthcare institutions, and other such enterprises. In fiscal 2009, Starbucks' generated revenues of $372.2 million from providing whole bean and ground coffees and assorted other Starbucks products to some 21 000 foodservice accounts.

The second initiative came in 1994 when PepsiCo and Starbucks entered into a joint venture arrangement (now called the North American Coffee Partnership) to create new coffee-related products in bottles or cans for mass distribution through Pepsi channels. Howard Schultz saw the venture with PepsiCo as a major paradigm shift with the potential to cause Starbucks business to evolve in heretofore unimaginable directions. The joint venture's first new product, a lightly flavored carbonated coffee drink, was a failure. Then, at a meeting with Pepsi executives, Schultz suggested developing a bottled version of Frappuccino, a new cold coffee drink Starbucks began serving at its retail stores in the summer of 1995 that quickly became a big hot weather seller. Pepsi executives were enthusiastic. Sales of Frappuccino ready-to-drink beverages reached $125 million in 1997 and achieved national supermarket penetration of 80 per cent. Sales of ready-to-drink Frappuccino products began in 2005 in Japan, Taiwan, and South Korea, chiefly through agreements with leading local distributors; the ready-to-drink beverage market in these countries represented more than $10 billion in annual sales.[11] In 2007, the PepsiCo-Starbucks partnership introduced a line of chilled Starbucks' Doubleshot® espresso drinks in the US. Also in 2007, PepsiCo and Starbucks entered into a second joint venture agreement called the International Coffee Partnership (ICP) for the purpose of introducing Starbucks-related beverages in country markets outside of North America; one of ICP's early moves was to begin marketing Frappuccino in China.[12] In 2010, sales of Frappuccino products worldwide reached $2 billion annually.[13]

In 2008, Starbucks partnered with Suntory to begin selling chilled ready-to-drink Doubleshot® drinks in Japan. In 2010, Starbucks partnered with Arla Foods to begin selling Doubleshot products and Starbucks Discoveries chilled cup coffees in retail stores across the United Kingdom (as well as in Starbucks retail stores in the United Kingdom).

In October 1995 Starbucks partnered with Dreyer's Grand Ice Cream to supply coffee extract for a new line of coffee ice cream made and distributed by Dreyer's under the Starbucks' brand. Starbucks' coffee-flavored ice cream became the number-one-selling super-premium brand in the coffee segment in mid-1996. In 2008, Starbucks discontinued its arrangement with Dreyer's and entered into an exclusive agreement with Unilever to manufacture, market, and distribute Starbucks-branded ice creams in the US and Canada. Unilever was the global leader in ice cream with annual sales of about $6 billion; its ice cream brands included Ben & Jerry's, Breyers, and Good Humor. There were seven flavors of Starbucks ice cream and two flavors of novelty bars being marketed in 2010.

In 1997, a Starbucks' store manager who had worked in the music industry and selected the music Starbucks played as background in its stores suggested that Starbucks begin selling the background music on tapes (and later on CDs as they become the preferred format). The Starbucks tapes/CDs proved a significant seller. Later, Starbucks began offering customers the option of downloading music from the company's 200 000-plus song library and, if they wished, having the downloaded songs burned onto a CD for purchase. In 2008, Starbucks, in partnership with Apple's iTunes, began offering a Pick of the Week music card at its stores in the US that allowed customers to download each week's music selection at iTunes.[14] In 2012, Starbucks was continuing to offer CDs with handpicked music and new CDs featuring particular artists; the CDs were typically priced at $12.95.

In 1998 Starbucks' licensed Kraft Foods to market and distribute Starbucks' whole bean and ground coffees in grocery and mass merchandise channels across the US. Kraft managed all distribution, marketing, advertising, and promotions and paid a royalty to Starbucks based on a per centage of net sales. Product freshness was guaranteed by Starbucks' FlavorLock packaging, and the price per pound paralleled the prices in Starbucks' retail stores. Flavor selections in supermarkets were more limited than the varieties at Starbucks' stores. The licensing relationship with Kraft was later expanded to include the marketing and distribution of Starbucks coffees in Canada, the United Kingdom, and other European countries. Going into 2010, Starbucks' coffees were available in some 33 500 grocery and warehouse clubs in the US and 5500 retail outlets outside the US; Starbucks' revenues from these sales were approximately $370 million in fiscal 2009.[15] During fiscal 2011 Starbucks discontinued its distribution arrangement with Kraft and instituted its own in-house organization to handle direct sales of packaged coffees to supermarkets and to warehouse club stores (chiefly Costco, Sam's Club, and BJ's Warehouse).

In 1999, Starbucks purchased Tazo Tea for $8.1 million. Tazo Tea, a tea manufacturer and distributor based in Portland, Oregon, was founded in 1994 and marketed its teas to restaurants, food stores, and tea houses. Starbucks proceeded to introduce hot and iced Tazo Tea drinks in its retail stores. As part of a long-term campaign to expand the distribution of its lineup of super-premium Tazo teas, Starbucks expanded its agreement with Kraft to market and distribute Tazo teas worldwide. In August 2008, Starbucks entered into a licensing agreement with a partnership formed by PepsiCo and Unilever (Lipton Tea was one of Unilever's leading brands) to manufacture, market, and distribute Starbucks super-premium Tazo Tea ready-to-drink beverages (including iced teas, juiced teas, and herbal-infused teas) in the US and Canada – in 2012, the Pepsi/Lipton Tea partnership was the leading North American distributor of ready-to-drink teas. In fiscal 2011, when Starbucks broke off its arrangement with Kraft and created its own in-house organization to handle direct sales of Starbucks' coffees to supermarkets and warehouse clubs, it also broke off its arrangement with Kraft for distribution of Tazo tea and began selling Tazo teas direct to supermarkets (except for Tazo Tea ready-to-drink beverages).

In 2001, Starbucks introduced the Starbucks Card, a reloadable card that allowed customers to pay for their purchases with a quick swipe of their card at the cash register and also to earn and redeem rewards. Cardholders were entitled to free select syrups, milk options, and refills on tea or brewed coffee during a store visit, and Gold Level members earned a free drink after 15 purchases at participating Starbucks' stores. The company's My Starbucks Rewards™ program had 3.5 million members in late 2011. In addition, in 2011 close to 25 million payments at Starbucks stores were being made on cell phones equipped with the Starbucks Card Apps for iPhones and Android-based smart phones.

In 2003, Starbucks spent $70 million to acquire Seattle's Best Coffee, an operator of 540 Seattle's Best coffee shops, 86 Seattle's Best Coffee Express espresso bars, and marketer of some 30 varieties of Seattle's Best whole bean and ground coffees. The decision was made to operate Seattle's Best as a separate subsidiary. Very quickly, Starbucks expanded its licensing arrangement with Kraft Foods to include marketing, distributing, and promoting the sales of Seattle's Best coffees and by 2009, Seattle's Best coffees were available nationwide in supermarkets and at more than 15 000 food-service locations (college campuses, restaurants, hotels, airlines, and cruise lines). A new Seattle's Best line of ready-to-drink iced lattes was introduced in April 2010 in major grocery and convenience stores in the western US; the manufacture, marketing, and distribution of the new Seattle's Best beverages was managed by PepsiCo as part of the long-standing Starbucks-PepsiCo joint venture for ready-to-drink Frappuccino products. In 2010, Starbucks introduced new distinctive red packaging and a red logo for Seattle's Best Coffee, boosted efforts to open more franchised Seattle's Best cafés, and expanded the availability of Seattle Best coffees to 30 000 distribution points, including 7250 Burger King outlets in the US, 9000 Subway locations, and some 299 AMC movie theaters in five countries. During fiscal 2011, the licensing agreement with Kraft to handle sales and distribution of Seattle's Best coffee products was terminated and responsibility for the sales and distribution of these products was transitioned to the same in-house sales force that handled direct sales and distribution of Starbucks-branded coffees and Tazo tea products to supermarkets and warehouse clubs. The Seattle's Best subsidiary generated revenues of approximately $150 million in fiscal 2010 and $175 million in fiscal 2011.

In 2008, Starbucks introduced a new coffee blend called Pike Place™ Roast that would be brewed everyday, all day in every Starbucks store.[16] Before then, Starbucks rotated coffees through its brewed lineup, sometimes switching them weekly, sometimes daily. While some customers liked the ever-changing variety, the feedback from a majority of customers indicated a preference for a consistent brew that customers could count on when they came into a Starbucks' store. Pike Place Roast™ was brewed in smaller batches in 30 minute intervals to ensure that customers were provided the freshest coffee possible. The new Pike Place™ Roast was created by Starbucks' master roasters and coffee quality team using input from nearly 1000 customers – it was smoother than Starbucks' other signature dark roast coffee varieties. In January 2012, after eight months of testing over 80 different recipe and roast iterations, Starbucks introduced three blends of lighter-bodied and milder-tasting Starbucks® Blonde Roast coffees to better appeal to an estimated 54 million coffee drinkers in the US who said they liked flavorful, lighter coffees with a gentle finish. The Blonde Roast blends were available as a brewed option in Starbucks' stores in the US and in packaged form in Starbucks' stores and supermarkets. Because the majority of coffee sales in supermarkets were in the light and medium roast categories, Starbucks' management saw its new Blonde Roast coffees blends as being a $1 billion market opportunity in the US alone.

In Fall 2009, Starbucks introduced Starbucks VIA® Ready Brew, packets of roasted coffee in an instant form, in an effort to attract a bigger fraction of on-the-go and at-home coffee drinkers. VIA was made with a proprietary, microground technology that Starbucks claimed represented a breakthrough.[17] Simply adding a packet of VIA to a cup of hot or cold water produced an instant coffee with a rich, full-bodied taste that closely replicated the taste, quality, and flavor of traditional freshly-brewed coffee. Starbucks stores held a four-day Starbucks VIA Taste Challenge promotional where customers were invited to compare the difference between Starbucks VIA and fresh-brewed Starbucks' coffee. During the 2009 holiday season, Starbucks VIA Ready Brew was one of the top-selling coffee products at Amazon.com. Encouraged by favorable customer response, Starbucks expanded the distribution of VIA to some 25 000 grocery, mass merchandise, and drugstore accounts, including Kroger, Safeway, Walmart, Target, Costco, and CVS. Instant coffee made up a significant fraction of the coffee purchases in the United Kingdom (80 per cent), Japan (53 per cent), Russia (85 per cent), and other countries where Starbucks' stores were located – in both the United Kingdom and Japan, sales of instant coffee exceeded $4 billion annually. Globally, the instant and single-serve coffee category was a $23 billion market. In early 2010, Starbucks introduced VIA in all of the Starbucks stores in the UK and Japan.[18] By the end of fiscal 2011, VIA products were available at 70 000 locations and generated total sales of $250 million.

In Fall 2011, Starbucks began selling Starbucks-branded coffee K-Cup® Portion Packs for the Keurig® Single-Cup Brewing system its retail stores; the Keurig® Brewer was produced and sold by Green Mountain Coffee Roasters. Starbucks entered into a strategic partnership with Green Mountain to manufacture the Starbucks-branded portion packs and also to be responsible for marketing, distributing, and selling them to major supermarket chains, drugstore chains, mass merchandisers and wholesale clubs, department stores, and specialty retailers throughout the US and Canada. The partnership made good economic sense for both companies. Green Mountain could manufacture the single-cup portion packs in the same plants where it was producing its own brands of single-cup packs and then use its own internal resources and capabilities to market, distribute and sell Starbucks'-branded single-cup packs alongside its own brands of single-cup packs. It was far cheaper for Starbucks to pay Green Mountain to handle these functions than to build its own manufacturing plants and put its own in-house resources in place to market, distribute, and sell Starbucks single-cup coffee packs. Both partners expected their arrangement would help accelerate growth of the single-cup serving segment of the coffee market. Initially, the Starbucks' single-cup packs were available in five blends of coffee and two blends of Tazo tea. Single-cup coffee packs represented a $3 billion market and the premium single-cup segment was the fastest growing part of the coffee market in the US; globally, single-cup coffee constituted 8 per cent of total coffee revenue. Just two months after launch, shipments of Starbucks-branded single-cup portion packs had exceeded 100 million units and the packs were available in about 70 per cent of the targeted retailers; company officials estimated that Starbucks had achieved an 11 per cent dollar share of the market for single-cup coffee packs in the US.[19]

In March 2012, Starbucks announced that it would begin selling its first at-home premium single-cup espresso and brewed coffee machine, the Verismo™ system by Starbucks, at select Starbucks' store locations, online, and upscale specialty stores in late 2012. The Verismo system was a high-pressure system with the capability to brew both coffee and Starbucks-quality espresso beverages, from lattes to americanos, consistently and conveniently one cup at a time; sales of the Verismo single-cup machine put Starbucks into head-to-head competition with Nestlé's Nespresso machine and, to a lesser extent, Green Mountain's popular lineup of low-pressure Keurig brewers. Howard Schultz said that the move to begin sales of its own brewing system and single-serve coffee packs was 'not about any disappointment with Green Mountain; it's about controlling our own destiny.'[20] The global market for premium at-home espresso/coffee machines was estimated $8 billion.[21] The introduction of the Verismo was the last phase of Starbucks' strategic plan to have coffee products covering all aspects of the single-cup coffee segment – instant coffees (with its VIA offerings), single portion coffee packs for single-cup brewers, and single-cup brewing machines.

Also in March 2012, Starbucks and Green Mountain announced expansion of their strategic partnership to include the manufacturing, marketing, distribution and sale of Starbucks-branded Vue™ packs for use in Green Mountain's recently introduced Keurig® Vue™ Brewer that used Keurig Vue™ packs to brew coffee, tea, hot cocoa, and iced beverages. The expanded partnership called for Green Mountain initially to distribute the Starbucks Vue™ coffee packs to specialty retailers, department stores, and mass merchandisers in the US as well as sell them on Green Mountain's consumer direct website.

In response to customer requests for more wholesome food and beverage options and also to bring in business from non-coffee drinkers, Starbucks in 2008 altered its menu offerings in stores to include fruit cups, yogurt parfaits, skinny lattes, banana walnut bread (that was nearly 30 per cent real banana), a 300-calorie farmer's market salad with all-natural dressing, and a line of 250-calorie 'better-for-you' smoothies.[22] In 2009–2011, the company continued to experiment with healthier, lower calorie selections and reformulated its recipes to include whole grains and dried fruits and to cut back on or eliminate the use of artificial flavorings, dyes, high-fructose corn syrup, and artificial preservatives. As of May 2012, retail store menus included an assortment of pastries and bakery selections, prepared breakfast and lunch sandwiches and wraps, a selection of bistro boxes (cheese and fruit, tuna salad, sliced chicken and hummus, chicken lettuce wraps), oatmeal, salads, parfaits, juices, and bottled water – at most stores in North America, food items could be warmed. Most recently, Starbucks had announced that it would soon add beer, wine, and complementary food offerings to its menu to help its stores become an attractive and relaxing after-work destination.

Starbucks overall sales mix in its retail stores in fiscal 2011 was 75 percent beverages, 19 percent food, 2 percent coffee-making equipment and other merchandise, and 3 per cent whole bean, ground, and instant coffees.[23] However, the product mix in each store varied, depending on the size and location of each outlet. Larger stores carried a greater variety of whole coffee beans, gourmet food items, teas, coffee mugs, coffee grinders, coffee-making equipment, filters, storage containers, and other accessories. Smaller stores and kiosks typically sold a full-line of coffee beverages, a limited selection of whole bean and ground coffees and Tazo teas, and a few coffee-drinking accessories. Moreover, menu offerings at Starbucks' stores were typically adapted to local cultures; for instance, the menu offerings at stores in North America included a selection of muffins but stores in France had no muffins and instead featured locally-made French pastries.

Starbucks' Consumer Products Group

In 2010, Starbucks formed a new Consumer Products Group (CPG) to be responsible for sales of Starbucks' products sold in all channels other than Starbucks' company-operated and licensed retail stores and to manage the company's partnerships and joint ventures with PepsiCo, Unilever, Green Mountain Coffee Roasters, and others. Exhibit 4 shows the recent performance of the Consumer Products Group. Starbucks' executives considered that the sales opportunities for Starbucks' products in distribution channels outside Starbucks' retail stores were quite attractive from the standpoint of both long-term growth and profitability.

In the first quarter of fiscal 2012, Starbucks expanded the CPG's portfolio of product offerings by spending $30 million to acquire Evolution Fresh, Inc., a maker of super-premium juices that were sold mostly at Whole Foods Market, the biggest organic and natural foods supermarket chain in North America. The strategic purpose of this acquisition was not only to use Starbucks' sales and marketing resources to grow the sales of Evolution Fresh and capture a bigger share of the $3.4 billion super-premium juice segment but also to begin a long-term campaign to pursue growth opportunities in the $50 billion health and wellness sector of the US economy. Starbucks opened its first Evolution Fresh retail store in Bellevue, Washington, in March 2012; more openings of Evolution Fresh stores were planned for later in 2012 and beyond. Starbucks also began selling Evolution Fresh juices in supermarket channels in March 2012.

EXHIBIT 4: Performance of Starbucks' Consumer Products Group, fiscal years 2009–11 (in millions)

Consumer Product Group Operations	Fiscal year		
	2011	**2010**	**2009**
Total net revenues	$860.5	$707.4	$674.4
Operating income	$273.0	$261.4	$281.8
Operating income as a percentege of total net revenues	31.7%	37.0%	41.8%

Source: 2011 10-K Report, p. 76.

Advertising

Starbucks spent sparingly on advertising, preferring instead to build the brand cup-by-cup with customers and depend on word-of-mouth and the appeal of its storefronts. Advertising expenditures were $141.4 million in fiscal 2011, $176.2 million in fiscal 2010, $126.3 million in fiscal 2009, $129.0 million in fiscal 2008, and $103.5 million in 2007. Starbucks stepped up advertising efforts in 2008 to combat the strategic initiatives of McDonald's and several other fast-food chains to begin offering premium coffees and coffee drinks at prices below those charged by Starbucks. In 2009, McDonald's reportedly spent more than $100 million on television, print, radio, billboard, and online ads promoting its new line of McCafé coffee drinks. Starbucks countered with the biggest advertising campaign the company had ever undertaken.[24]

Vertical Integration

Howard Schultz saw Starbucks as having a unique strategy compared to the strategies pursued by its many coffeehouse competitors. He observed:[25]

> *People sometimes fail to realize that almost unlike any retailer or restaurant, we are completely vertically integrated. We source coffee from 30 countries. We have a proprietary roasting process. We distribute to company owned stores, and finally serve the coffee. Others are resellers of commodity-based coffees.*

Howard Schultz's Efforts to Make Starbucks a Great Place to Work

Howard Schultz deeply believed that Starbucks' success was heavily dependent on customers having a very positive experience in its stores. This meant having store employees who were knowledgeable about the company's products, who paid attention to detail in preparing the company's espresso drinks, who eagerly communicated the company's passion for coffee, and who possessed the skills and personality to deliver consistent, pleasing customer service. Many of the baristas were in their 20s and worked part-time, going to college on the side or pursuing other career activities. The challenge to Starbucks, in Schultz's view, was how to attract, motivate, and reward store employees in a manner that would make Starbucks a company that people would want to work for and that would generate enthusiastic commitment and higher levels of customer service. Moreover, Schultz wanted to send all Starbucks' employees a message that would cement the trust that had been building between management and the company's workforce.

Instituting Health-care Coverage for All Employees

One of the requests that employees had made to the prior owners of Starbucks was to extend health-care benefits to part-time workers. Their request had been turned down, but Schultz believed that expanding health-care coverage to include part-timers was something the company needed to do. His father had recently passed away with cancer and he knew from having grown up in a family that struggled to make ends meet how difficult it was to cope with rising medical costs. In 1988 Schultz went to the board of directors with his plan to expand the company's health-care coverage to include part-timers who worked at least 20 hours per week. He saw the proposal not as a generous gesture but as a core strategy to win employee loyalty and commitment to the company's mission. Board members resisted because the company was unprofitable and the added costs of the extended coverage would only worsen the company's bottom line. But Schultz argued passionately that it was the right thing to do and would not be as expensive as it seemed. He observed that if the new benefit reduced turnover, which he believed was likely, then it would reduce the costs of hiring and training – which equaled about $3000 per new hire; he further pointed out that it cost $1500 a year to provide an employee with full benefits. Part-timers, he argued, were vital to Starbucks, constituting two-thirds of the company's workforce. Many were baristas who knew the favorite drinks of regular customers; if the barista left, that connection with the customer was broken. Moreover, many part-time employees were called upon to open the stores early, sometimes at 5:30 or 6 a.m.; others had to work until closing, usually 9 p.m. or later. Providing these employees with health-care benefits, he argued, would signal that the company honored their value and contribution.

The board approved Schultz's plan and part-timers working 20 or more hours were offered the same health coverage as full-time employees starting in late 1988. Starbucks paid 75 per cent of an employee's health-care premium; the employee paid 25 percent. Over the years, Starbucks extended its health coverage to include preventive care, prescription drugs, dental care, eye care, mental health, and chemical dependency. Coverage was also offered for unmarried partners in a committed relationship. Since most Starbucks' employees were young and comparatively healthy, the company had been able to provide broader coverage while keeping monthly payments relatively low.

A Stock Option Plan for Employees

By 1991 the company's profitability had improved to the point where Schultz could pursue a stock option plan for all employees, a program he believed would have a positive, long-term effect on the success of Starbucks.[26] Schultz wanted to turn every Starbucks' employee into a partner, give them a chance to share in the success of the company, and make clear the connection between their contributions and the company's market value. Even though Starbucks was still a private company, the plan that emerged called for granting stock options to every full-time and part-time employee in proportion to their base pay. In May 1991, the plan, dubbed Bean Stock, was presented to the board. Though board members were concerned that increasing the number of shares might unduly dilute the value of the shares of investors who had put up hard cash, the plan received unanimous approval. The first grant was made in October 1991, just after the end of the company's fiscal year in September; each partner was granted stock options worth 12 per cent of base pay. When the Bean Stock program was initiated, Starbucks dropped the term employee and began referring to all of its people as 'partners' because every member of Starbucks' workforce became eligible for stock option awards after six months of employment and 500 paid work hours.

Starbucks went public in June 1992, selling its initial offering at a price of $17 per share. Starting in October 1992 and continuing through October 2004, Starbucks granted each eligible employee a stock option award with a value equal to 14 percent of base pay. Beginning in 2005, the plan was modified to tie the size of each employee's stock option awards to three factors: (1) Starbucks' success and profitability for the fiscal year, (2) the size of an employee's base wages, and (3) the price at which the stock option could be exercised. Since becoming a public company, Starbucks' stock had split 2-for-1 on five occasions; the stock traded at an all-time high of $62 per share in April 2012. As of October 2, 2011, Starbucks' partners held 45.3 million shares in stock option awards that had a weighted average contractual life of 6.4 years; these shares had a weighted average exercise price of $18.57 and an aggregate value of $848 million.[27]

Starbucks Stock Purchase Plan for Employees

In 1995, Starbucks implemented an employee stock purchase plan that gave partners who had been employed for at least 90 days an opportunity to purchase company stock through regular payroll deductions. Partners who enrolled could devote anywhere from 1 to 10 per cent of their base earnings (up to an annual maximum of

$25 000) to purchasing shares of Starbucks stock. After the end of each calendar quarter, each participant's contributions were used to buy Starbucks' stock at a discount of 5 percent of the closing price on the last business day of the each calendar quarter (the discount was 15 percent until March 2009).

Since inception of the plan, some 24.8 million shares had been purchased by partners; roughly 30 percent of Starbucks' partners participated in the stock purchase plan during the 2000–2011 period.

The Workplace Environment

Starbucks' management believed its competitive pay scales and comprehensive benefits for both full-time and part-time partners allowed it to attract motivated people with above-average skills and good work habits. An employee's base pay was determined by the pay scales prevailing in the geographic region where an employee worked and by the person's job, skills, experience, and job performance. About 90 percent of Starbucks' partners were full-time or part-time baristas, paid on an hourly basis. After six months of employment, baristas could expect to earn $8.50 to $9.50 per hour. In 2009, experienced full-time baristas in the company's US stores earned an average of about $37 800; store managers earned an average of $44 400.[28] Voluntary turnover at Starbucks' was 13 percent in 2009.[29] Starbucks executives believed that efforts to make the company an attractive, caring place to work were responsible for its relatively low turnover rates. Starbucks received 225 000 job applications in 2008 and 150 000 job applications in 2009.

Surveys of Starbucks' partners conducted by *Fortune* magazine in the course of selecting companies for inclusion on its annual list of the '100 Best Companies to Work For' indicated that full-time baristas liked working at Starbucks because of the camaraderie, while part-timers were particularly pleased with the health insurance benefits (those who enrolled in Starbucks' most economical plan for just routine health care paid only $6.25 per week).[30] Starbucks had been named to *Fortune's* list in 1998, 1999, 2000, and every year from 2002 through 2012.

Starbucks' management utilized annual 'Partner View' surveys to solicit feedback from its workforce, learn their concerns, and measure job satisfaction. The 2002 survey revealed that many employees viewed the benefits package as only 'average,' prompting the company to increase its match of 401(k) contributions for those who had been with the company more than three years and to have these contributions vest immediately. In a survey conducted in fiscal 2008, 80 per cent of Starbucks' partners reported being satisfied.[31]

Schultz's approach to offering employees good compensation and a comprehensive benefits package was driven by his belief that sharing the company's success with the people who made it happen helped everyone think and act like an owner, build positive long-term relationships with customers, and do things in an efficient way. Schultz's rationale, based on his father's experience of going from one low-wage, no-benefits job to another, was that if you treat your employees well, that is how they will treat customers.

Exhibit 5 summarizes Starbucks' fringe benefit package.

Employee Training and Recognition

To accommodate its strategy of rapid store expansion, Starbucks put in systems to recruit, hire, and train baristas and store managers. Starbucks' vice president for human resources used some simple guidelines in screening candidates for new positions, 'We want passionate people who love coffee ... We're looking for a diverse workforce, which reflects our community. We want people who enjoy what they're doing and for whom work is an extension of themselves.'[32]

EXHIBIT 5: Starbucks fringe benefit program, 2012

- Medical insurance
- Sick time
- Dental and vision care
- Paid vacations (up to 120 hours annually for hourly workers with 5 or more years of service at retail stores and up to 200 hours annually for salaried and non-retail hourly employees with 10 or more years of service)
- Seven paid holidays
- One paid personal day every six months for salaried and non-retail hourly partners
- A 30 per cent discount on purchases of beverages, food, and merchandise at Starbucks stores
- Mental health and chemical dependency coverage
- 401 (k) retirement savings plan–the company matched 100 per cent on the first 3 per cent of eligible pay that a participant contributed, plus 50 per cent of the next 2 per cent of eligible pay contributed OR 100 per cent on the first 6 per cent of eligible pay a participant contributed. Starbucks matching contributions to the 401(k) plans worldwide totaled $45.5 million in fiscal 2011 and $23.5 million in fiscal 2010.
- Short- and long-term disability
- Stock purchase plan – eligible employees could buy shares at a 5 per cent discount through regular payroll deductions of between 1 and 10 per cent of base pay.
- Life insurance
- Short- and long-term disability insurance
- Accidental death and dismemberment insurance
- Adoption assistance
- Financial assistance program for partners that experience a financial crisis
- Stock option plan (Bean stock); shares were granted to eligible partners based on the company's performance and how many shares the company's board of directors made available.
- Pre-tax payroll deductions for commuter expenses
- Free coffee and tea products each week
- Tuition reimbursement program

Source: Information in the Careers section at www.starbucks.com, accessed May 3, 2012 and Starbucks 2011 10-K Report, p. 69.

Every partner/barista hired for a retail job in a Starbucks' store received at least 24 hours training in their first two to four weeks. The topics included classes on coffee history, drink preparation, coffee knowledge (four hours), customer service (four hours), and retail skills plus a four-hour workshop on 'Brewing the Perfect Cup.' Baristas spent considerable time learning about beverage preparation – grinding the beans, steaming milk, learning to pull perfect (18- to 23-second) shots of espresso, memorizing the recipes of all the different drinks, practicing making the different drinks, and learning how to customize drinks to customer specifications. There were sessions on cash register operations, how to clean the milk wand on the espresso machine, explaining the Italian drink names to unknowing customers, selling home espresso machines, making eye contact with customers and interacting with them, and taking personal responsibility for the cleanliness of the store. And there were rules to be memorized: milk must be steamed to at least 150 degrees Fahrenheit but never more than 170 degrees; every espresso shot not pulled within 23 seconds must be tossed; never let coffee sit in the pot more than 20 minutes; always compensate dissatisfied customers with a Starbucks' coupon that entitles them to a free drink.

Management trainees attended classes for 8 to 12 weeks. Their training went much deeper, covering not only coffee knowledge and information imparted to baristas but also going into the details of store operations, practices and procedures as set forth in the company's operating manual, information systems, and the basics of managing people. Starbucks' trainers were all store managers and district managers with on-site experience. One of their major objectives was to ingrain the company's values, principles, and culture and to pass on their knowledge about coffee and their passion about Starbucks.

When Starbucks opened stores in a new market, it sent a Star team of experienced managers and baristas to the area to lead the store opening effort and to conduct one-on-one training following the company's formal classes and basic orientation sessions at the Starbucks Coffee School in San Francisco. From time to time, Starbucks conducted special training programs, including a coffee masters program for store employees, leadership training for store managers, and career programs for partners in all types of jobs.

To recognize partner contributions, Starbucks had created a partner recognition program consisting of 18 different awards and programs. Examples included Coffee Master awards, Certified Barista awards, Spirit of Starbucks awards for exceptional achievement by a partner, a Manager of the Quarter for store manager leadership, Green Apron Awards for helping create a positive and welcoming store environment, Green Bean Awards for exceptional support for company's environmental mission, and Bravo! awards for exceeding the standards of Starbucks' customer service, significantly increasing sales, or reducing costs.

Starbucks' Values, Business Principles, and Mission

During the early building years, Howard Schultz and other Starbucks' senior executives worked to instill some key values and guiding principles into the Starbucks' culture. The cornerstone value in their effort 'to build a company with soul' was that the company would never stop pursuing the perfect cup of coffee by buying the best beans and roasting them to perfection. Schultz was adamant about controlling the quality of Starbucks' products and building a culture common to all stores. He was rigidly opposed to selling artificially-flavored coffee beans – 'we will not pollute our high-quality beans with chemicals'; if a customer wanted hazelnut-flavored coffee, Starbucks would provide it by adding hazelnut syrup to the drink, rather than by adding hazelnut flavoring to the beans during roasting. Running flavored beans through the grinders left chemical residues behind that altered the flavor of beans ground afterward.

Starbucks' management was also emphatic about the importance of employees paying attention to what pleased customers. Employees were trained to go out of their way, and to take heroic measures if necessary, to make sure customers were fully satisfied. The theme was 'just say yes' to customer requests. Further, employees were encouraged to speak their minds without fear of retribution from upper management – senior executives wanted employees to be vocal about what Starbucks was doing right, what it was doing wrong, and what changes were needed. The intent was for employees to be involved in and contribute to the process of making Starbucks a better company.

Starbucks' Mission Statement

In early 1990, the senior executive team at Starbucks went to an off-site retreat to debate the company's values and beliefs and draft a mission statement. Schultz wanted the mission statement to convey a strong sense of organizational purpose and to articulate the company's fundamental beliefs and guiding principles. The draft was submitted to all employees for review and several changes were made based on employee comments. The resulting mission statement and guiding principles are shown in Exhibit 8. In 2008, Starbucks partners from all across the company met for several months to refresh the mission statement and rephrase the underlying guiding principles; the revised mission statement and guiding principles are also shown in Exhibit 6.

EXHIBIT 6: Starbucks' mission statement, values, and business principles

Mission statement, 1990–October 2008

Establish Starbucks as the premier purveyor of the finest coffee in the world while maintaining our uncompromising principles as we grow.

The following six guiding principles will help us measure the appropriateness of our decisions:

- Provide a great work environment and treat each other with respect and dignity.
- Embrace diversity as an essential component in the way we do business.
- Apply the highest standards of excellence to the purchasing, roasting, and fresh delivery of our coffee.
- Develop enthusiastically satisfied customers all of the time.
- Contribute positively to our communities and our environment.
- Recognize that profitability is essential to our future success.

Mission statement, October 2008–present

Our mission: to inspire and nurture the human spirit – one person, one cup, and one neighborhood at a time.

Here are the principles of how we live that every day:

Our coffee

It has always been, and will always be, about quality. We're passionate about ethically sourcing the finest coffee beans, roasting them with great care, and improving the lives of people who grow them. We care deeply about all of this; our work is never done.

Our partners

We're called partners, because it's not just a job, it's our passion. Together, we embrace diversity to create a place where each of us can be ourselves. We always treat each other with respect and dignity. And we hold each other to that standard.

Our customers

When we are fully engaged, we connect with, laugh with, and uplift the lives of our customers – even if just for a few moments. Sure, it starts with the promise of a perfectly made beverage, but our work goes far beyond that. It's really about human connection.

Our stores

When our customers feel this sense of belonging, our stores become a haven, a break from the worries outside, a place where you can meet with friends. It's about enjoyment at the speed of life – sometimes slow and savored, sometimes faster. Always full of humanity.

Our neighborhood

Every store is part of a community, and we take our responsibility to be good neighbors seriously. We want to be invited in wherever we do business. We can be a force for positive action – bringing together our partners, customers, and the community to contribute every day. Now we see that our responsibility – and our potential for good – is even larger. The world is looking to Starbucks to set the new standard, yet again. We will lead.

Our shareholders

We know that as we deliver in each of these areas, we enjoy the kind of success that rewards our shareholders. We are fully accountable to get each of these elements right so that Starbucks – and everyone it touches – can endure and thrive.

Source: Company documents and postings at www.starbucks.com, accessed May 15, 2012.

Starbucks' Coffee Purchasing Strategy

Coffee beans were grown in 70 tropical countries and were the second most traded commodity in the world after petroleum. Most of the world's coffee was grown by some 25 million small farmers, most of whom lived on the edge of poverty. Starbucks' personnel traveled regularly to coffee-producing countries, building relationships with growers and exporters, checking on agricultural conditions and crop yields, and searching out varieties and sources that would meet Starbucks' exacting standards of quality and flavor. The coffee-purchasing group, working with Starbucks' personnel in roasting operations, tested new varieties and blends of green coffee beans from different sources. Sourcing from multiple geographic areas not only allowed Starbucks to offer a greater range of coffee varieties to customers but also spread its risks regarding weather, price volatility, and changing economic and political conditions in coffee-growing countries.

Starbucks' coffee sourcing strategy had three key elements:

- Make sure that the prices Starbucks' paid for green (unroasted) coffee beans was high enough to ensure that small farmers were able to cover their production costs and provide for their families.

- Utilize purchasing arrangements that limited Starbucks' exposure to sudden price jumps due to weather, economic and political conditions in the growing countries, new agreements establishing export quotas, and periodic efforts to bolster prices by restricting coffee supplies.

- Work directly with small coffee growers, local coffee-growing cooperatives, and other types of coffee suppliers to promote coffee cultivation methods that protected biodiversity and were environmentally sustainable.

Pricing and Purchasing Arrangements

Commodity-grade coffee was traded in a highly competitive market as an undifferentiated product. However, high-altitude Arabica coffees of the quality purchased by Starbucks were bought on a negotiated basis at a substantial premium above commodity coffee. The prices of the top-quality coffees sourced by Starbucks depended on supply and demand conditions at the time of the purchase and were subject to considerable volatility due to weather, economic and political conditions in the growing countries, new agreements establishing export quotas, and periodic efforts to bolster prices by restricting coffee supplies.

Starbucks bought coffee using fixed-price and price-to-be-fixed purchase commitments, depending on market conditions, to secure an adequate supply of quality green coffee. Price-to-be-fixed contracts were purchase commitments whereby the quality, quantity, delivery period, and other negotiated terms were agreed upon, but the date at which the base price component of commodity grade coffee was to be fixed was as yet unspecified. For these types of contracts, either Starbucks or the seller had the option to select a date on which to 'fix' the base price of commodity grade coffee prior to the delivery date. As of October 2, 2011, Starbucks had a total of $1.0 billion in purchase commitments, of which $193 million represented the estimated cost of price-to-be-fixed contracts. All price-to-be-fixed contracts as of October 2, 2011 gave Starbucks the right to fix the base price component of commodity grade coffee. Management believed that its purchase agreements as of October 2, 2011 would provide an adequate supply of green coffee through fiscal 2012.[33]

Starbucks Ethical Sourcing Practices for Coffee Beans

Starbucks was committed to buying green coffee beans that were responsibly grown and came from sources that guaranteed small coffee growers received prices for their green coffee beans sufficiently high to allow them to pay fair wages to their workers and earn enough to reinvest in their farms and communities, develop the business skills needed to compete in the global market for coffee, and afford basic health care, education, and home improvements. The company's supplies of green coffee beans were chiefly grown on tens of thousands of small family farms (less than 30 acres) located in low-income countries in Central America, East Africa, and Asia.

Since 1998, Starbucks had partnered with Conservation International's Center for Environmental Leadership to develop specific guidelines (called Coffee and Farmer Equity, or C.A.F.E., Practices) covering four areas: product quality, the price received by farmers/growers, safe and humane working conditions (including compliance with minimum wage requirements and child labor provisions), and environmentally responsible cultivation practices.[34] Some 100,000 small coffee bean farms employing more than 1 million workers were operating according C.A.F.E. Practices in 2010. Numerous other small coffee growers were members of cooperatives that were associated with one of the 25 members of Fairtrade International that (1) helped small farmers get fair prices for their products and develop market opportunities, (2) set international Fairtrade standards, and (3) oversaw companies that wanted to market their products as Fairtrade certified. Increasingly, many small farmers were growing their coffees 'organically' without the use of pesticides, herbicides, or chemical fertilizers; organic cultivation methods resulted in clean ground water and helped protect against degrading of local ecosystems, many of which were fragile or in areas where biodiversity was under severe threat.

Top management at Starbucks had set a goal that by 2015, all of the green coffee beans purchased from growers would be C.A.F.E. Practice certified, Fair Trade certified, organically-certified, or certified by some other equally acceptable third-party. In 2011, 86 percent of Starbucks' purchases of green coffee beans were C.A.F.E. Practices-verified sources and about 8 percent were from Fairtrade certified sources. Starbucks was among the world's largest purchasers of Fair Trade certified coffee beans, and it marketed Fairtrade-certified coffees at most of its retail stores and through other locations that sold Starbucks coffees.

Starbucks' Tazo tea operation was a member of the Ethical Tea Partnership and worked with other tea buyers to improve conditions for workers on tea estates. Through the CHAI (Community Health and Advancement Initiative) project, a joint partnership with Mercy Corps, Starbucks supported tea-growing communities with health services and economic development.

Small Farmer Support Programs

Because many of the tens of thousands of small family farms with less than 30 acres that grew coffees purchased by Starbucks often lacked the money to make farming improvements and/or cover all expenses until they sold their crops, Starbucks provided funding to organizations that made loans to small coffee growers. In 2010, $14.6 million was loaned to nearly 56 000 farmers who grew green coffee beans for Starbucks in 10 countries; in 2011, $14.7 million was loaned to over 45 000 farmers who grew green coffee beans for Starbucks in seven countries. Starbucks' goal was to increase funding to $20 million by 2015. In addition, the company funded Starbucks Farmer Support Centers in Central America, East Africa, and Asia where Starbucks' agronomists and quality experts helped local coffee farmers implement environmentally responsible growing practices, improve the quality and size of their harvests, and ultimately earn better prices.

Coffee Roasting Operations

Starbucks considered the roasting of its coffee beans to be something of an art form, entailing trial-and-error testing of different combinations of time and temperature to get the most out of each type of bean and blend. Recipes were put together by the coffee department, once all the components had been tested. Computerized roasters guaranteed consistency. Highly trained and experienced roasting personnel monitored the process, using both smell and hearing, to help check when the beans were perfectly done – coffee beans make a popping sound when ready. Starbucks' standards were so exacting that roasters tested the color of the beans in a blood-cell analyzer and discarded the entire batch if the reading wasn't on target. After roasting and cooling, the coffee was immediately vacuum-sealed in bags that preserved freshness for up to 26 weeks. As a matter of policy, however, Starbucks removed coffees on its shelves after three months and, in the case of coffee used to prepare beverages in stores, the shelf life was limited to seven days after the bag was opened.

Starbucks had roasting plants in Kent, Washington; York, Pennsylvania; Minden, Nevada; Charleston, South Carolina; and The Netherlands. In addition to roasting capability, these plants also had additional space for warehousing and shipping coffees. In keeping with Starbucks' corporate commitment to reduce its environmental footprint, the state-of-the-art roasting plant built in South Carolina in 2009 had been awarded LEED Silver Certification for New Construction by the US Green Building Council. Twenty percent of materials used in the construction of the building were from recycled content and over 75 percent of the waste generated during construction was recycled. In addition, the facility utilized state-of-the-art light and water fixtures and was partly powered by wind energy. Some of the green elements in the South Carolina plant were subsequently implemented in the other roasting plants as part of the company's initiative to achieve LEED Certification for all company-operated facilities by the end of 2010.[35]

Starbucks' Corporate Social Responsibility Strategy

Howard Schultz's effort to 'build a company with soul' included a long history of doing business in ways that were socially and environmentally responsible. A commitment to do the right thing had been central to how Starbucks operated since Howard Schultz first became CEO in 1987, and one of the core beliefs at Starbucks was that 'the way to build a great, enduring company is to strike a balance between profitability and a social conscience.' The specific actions comprising Starbucks' social responsibility strategy had varied over the years but the intent of the strategy was consistently one of contributing positively to the communities in which Starbucks had stores, being a good environmental steward, and conducting its business in ways that earned the trust and respect of customers, partners/employees, suppliers, and the general public.

In 2008-2012, Starbucks' corporate social responsibility strategy had four main elements:

1. Ethically sourcing all of its products – This included promoting responsible growing practices for the company's coffees and teas (and the cocoa contained in the beverages it served) and striving to buy the manufactured products and services it needed from suppliers who had a demonstrated commitment to social and environmental responsibility. Company personnel purchased paper products with high levels of recycled content and unbleached fiber. Suppliers were encouraged to provide the most energy-efficient products within their category and eliminate excessive packaging; Starbucks had recently instituted a set of Supplier Social Responsibility Standards covering the suppliers of all the manufactured goods and services used in the company's operations. No genetically modified ingredients were used in any food or beverage products that Starbucks served, with the exception of milk (US labeling requirements did not require milk producers to disclose the use of hormones aimed at increasing the milk production of dairy herds).

In 2011, Starbucks audited 129 supplier factories and found 38 that failed its zero-tolerance standards. Purchases from 26 of these factories were discontinued for standards issues, although purchases from 14 previously-dropped factories were later resumed when they achieved compliance. Since initiating audits of supplier compliance in 2006, Starbucks had conducted more than 500 factory assessments and continued to work with more than 100 of these factories on programs to improve their standards. Also in 2011, Starbucks became a member of the Global Social Compliance Program, a business-driven effort to promote the continuous improvement of environmental and working conditions at supplier factories worldwide.

2. Community involvement and corporate citizenship – Active engagement in community activities and display of good corporate citizenship had always been core elements in the way Starbucks conducted its business. Starbucks' stores and employees regularly volunteered for community improvement projects and initiatives that would have a meaningful impact on the localities in which Starbucks had a presence. The company had a goal of getting Starbucks' partners and customers to contribute more than 1 million hours of community service annually by 2015; service contributions totaled 246 000 hours in 2008, 186 000 hours in 2009, 191 000 hours in 2010, and 442 000 hours in 2011. In addition, Starbucks had a goal of annually engaging 50 000 young people to help meet needs and solve problems they saw in their neighborhoods. Toward this end, Starbucks made a series of Youth Action Grants each year to involve young people in community improvement projects – these Youth Action Grants totaled $2.1 million in fiscal 2009 and $1.6 million in fiscal 2010. To celebrate the 40 anniversary of the opening of the first Starbucks' Coffee store at Pike Place in Seattle, during fiscal 2011 the company sponsored a special global month of service in which more than 60 000 people in 30 countries volunteered for over 150 000 service hours and completed 1400 community-service projects. Starbucks held its second global month of service in April 2012.

3. Environmental stewardship – Initiatives here included a wide variety of actions to increase recycling, reduce waste, be more energy efficient, use renewable energy sources, conserve water resources, make all company facilities as green as possible by using environmentally friendly building materials and energy efficient designs, and engage in more efforts to address climate change. Beginning in January 2011, all new company-owned retail stores globally were built to achieve LEED certification. In 2008 Starbucks set a goal of reducing water consumption by 25 percent in company-owned stores by 2015, and after two years had implemented proactive measures that had decreased water use by almost 22 percent. Also in 2008, Starbucks undertook actions to purchase renewable energy equivalent to 50 percent of the electricity used in its North American company-owned stores; that goal was achieved during 2009, at which point Starbucks set a goal to increase its renewable energy purchases to 100 percent of the energy used in all company-owned stores worldwide. The Environmental Protection Agency named Starbucks as one of the Top Five Green Power Purchasers in the US in 2010 and 2011. Starbucks had a program in place to achieve a 25 percent reduction in energy use by 2015. In 2011, nearly 80 percent of company-owned Starbucks stores in North America were recycling cardboard boxes and other back-of-store items; efforts were underway to have front-of-store recycling bins in place in all company-owned locations in North America by 2015 (however, Starbucks faced significant challenges in implementing recycling at its 17 000-plus stores worldwide because of wide variations in municipal recycling capabilities). Since 1985 Starbucks had given a $0.10 discount to customers who brought reusable cups and tumblers to stores for use in serving the beverages they ordered – in 2011 some 34.1 million beverages were served in customers' containers. The company's goal was to serve 5 percent of the beverages made in its stores in reusable containers by 2015. Stores participated in Earth Day activities each year with in-store promotions and volunteer efforts to educate

employees and customers about the impacts their actions had on the environment. Starbucks was a founding member of the Business for Innovative Climate and Energy Policy coalition, where it worked with other companies to advocate stronger clean energy and climate policies.

4. Charitable contributions – The Starbucks Foundation, set up in 1997, oversaw a major portion of the company's philanthropic activities; it received the majority of its funding from Starbucks Coffee Company and private donations. In 2010, the Starbucks Foundation made more than 100 grants to nonprofit organizations totaling $5.4 million, including $1 million to the American Red Cross efforts for the Haiti earthquake relief effort; the Foundation made 145 grants totaling $13.5 million to various nonprofit organizations in fiscal 2011. The 2011 grants included financial support to the American Red Cross for ongoing relief to US communities experiencing severe tornado damage, floods, and other natural disasters; the Japan Earthquake Relief Fund; communities in the tea-growing regions of Darjeeling, India; and Save the Children for efforts to improve education, health, and nutrition in both Guatemala and Indonesia. In 2010, Starbuck Corporation made charitable contributions totaling $10.3 million in cash and $6.7 million in in-kind contributions toward community-building programs. In 2011, it made cash contributions of $30.5 million and in-kind contributions of $17.3 million. For a number of years, Starbucks had made donations to the Global Fund and Product (RED)™ to provide medicine to people in Africa with AIDS; so far Starbucks had made contributions equaling more than 18 million doses of medicine daily. In years past, Starbucks had made a $5 million, five-year commitment to long-term relief and recovery efforts for victims of hurricanes Rita and Katrina and committed $5 million to support educational programs in China.[36]

Water, sanitation, and hygiene education programs in water-stressed countries were supported through the Starbucks Foundation's Ethos Water Fund. For each bottle of Ethos water purchased at Starbucks stores, Starbucks donated $.05 ($0.10 in Canada) to the Ethos Water Fund. Since 2005, the Fund had made $6 million in grants, benefitting more than 420,000 people around the world. (Starbucks had acquired Ethos Water for $8 million in 2005 and sold Ethos-branded bottled water in its stores. The production, distribution, and marketing of Ethos water products was handled by PepsiCo, as part of its longstanding joint venture with Starbucks.)

In 2012 Starbucks was named to *Corporate Responsibility Magazine's* list of the 100 Best Corporate Citizens for 2010, the 12th time that Starbucks had been named to the magazine's list. The 100 Best Corporate Citizens List was based on more than 360 data points of publicly available information in seven categories: Environment, Climate Change, Human Rights, Philanthropy, Employee Relations, Financial Performance, and Governance. Over the years, Starbucks had received over 25 awards from a diverse group of organizations for its philanthropic, community service, and environmental activities.

Top Management Changes: Changing Roles for Howard Schultz

In 2000, Howard Schultz decided to relinquish his role as CEO, retain his position as chairman of the company's board of directors, and assume the newly-created role chief strategic officer. Orin Smith, a Starbucks' executive who had been with the company since its early days, was named CEO. Smith retired in 2005 and was replaced as CEO by Jim Donald who had been president of Starbucks' North American division. In 2006, Donald proceeded to set a long-term objective of having 40 000 stores worldwide and launched a program of rapid store expansion in an effort to achieve that goal.

But investors and members of Starbucks' board of directors (including Howard Schultz) became uneasy about Donald's leadership of the company when the company's stock price drifted downward through much of 2007, customer traffic in Starbucks' stores in the US began to erode in 2007, new store openings worldwide were continuing at the rate of six per day, and Donald kept pressing for increased efficiency in store operations at the expense of good customer service. Schultz had lamented in an internal company email in 2007 (which was leaked to the public) that the company's aggressive growth had led to 'a watering down of the Starbucks experience.'[37] In January 2008, Starbucks board asked Howard Schultz to return to his role as CEO and lead a major restructuring and revitalization initiative.

Howard Schultz's Campaign to Reinvigorate Starbucks, 2008–11

Immediately upon his return as Starbucks CEO, Schultz revamped the company's executive leadership team and changed the roles and responsibilities of several key executives.[38] Believing that Starbucks in recent years had become less passionate about customer relationships and the coffee experience that had fueled the company's success, Schultz hired a former Starbucks' executive to fill the newly-created position of chief creative officer responsible for elevating the in-store experience of customers and achieving new levels of innovation and differentiation. He then proceeded to launch a series of actions to recast Starbucks into the company he envisioned it ought to be, push the company to new plateaus of differentiation and innovation, and prepare for renewed global expansion of Starbucks' retail store network. This transformation effort, which instantly became the centerpiece of his return as company CEO, had three main themes: strengthen the core, elevate the experience, and invest and grow. Schultz's cost containment and efficiency campaign produced gratifying results – the productivity of Starbucks' employees in US company-operated retail stores increased from an average of 9.8 transactions per labor hour in fiscal 2008 to 11.3 transactions per labor hour in fiscal 2011.[39] In addition, the percentage change in sales at company-operated retail stores open at least 13 months had had risen from −9 percent in Q1 of fiscal 2009 to +4 percent in Q1 of fiscal 2010 to +9 percent in Q3 of fiscal 2010 and then remained in the range of +7 to +9 percent very quarter through Q2 of fiscal 2012.

In 2010, as part of Schultz's 'invest and grow' aspect of transforming Starbucks, the company began formulating plans to open 'thousands of new stores' in China over time.[40] Japan had long been Starbucks' biggest foreign market outside North America, but Howard Schultz said that, 'Asia clearly represents the most significant growth opportunity on a go-forward basis.'[41] Schultz also indicated that Starbucks was anxious to begin opening stores in India and Vietnam, two country markets that Starbucks believed were potentially lucrative. During fiscal 2011, Starbucks opened its 500th store in mainland China but, as of April 2012, no stores had yet opened in either Vietnam or India. Top management expected that China would remain the focal point of the company's global expansion efforts and become its largest market outside of the US, with more than 1500 stores by 2015.

Starbucks' Future Prospects

Starbucks reported strong performance for its first two quarters of fiscal 2012:

- Revenues were $6.6 billion, up 16 percent over the first six months of fiscal 2011.
- Operating income was $986.4 million, up 12 percent compared to the first half of fiscal 2011.
- Earnings per share were $0.90, up 14 percent over the prior year.

- Sales at all company-operated retail stores open 13 months or longer rose 8 percent during the first two quarters of fiscal 2012.
- In the second quarter, sales growth at company-operated stores in China open at least 13 months exceeded 20 percent for the seventh consecutive quarter.

In addition, top management provided the following updated performance targets for full-year 2012:

- Opening a net of 500 new stores in the Americas, with licensed stores comprising approximately one-half of the new additions.
- Opening a net of 400 new stores in the China/Asia Pacific region (including 200 in China), with licensed stores comprising approximately two-thirds of the new additions.
- Maintaining its plan to open a net of 100 new stores in Europe, the Middle East, Russia, and Africa (EMEA), with licensed stores comprising approximately two-thirds of the new stores.
- Achieving revenue growth in the low teens, driven by mid-single-digit comparable store sales growth, 1000 net new store openings, and continued strong growth in the Consumer Products Group segment.
- Achieving earning per share of $1.81 to $1.84, representing a 19 to 21 percent increase over fiscal 2011 EPS of $1.52. EPS growth was expected to be approximately 25 to 29 percent in the second half of fiscal 2012.[42]

Management also indicated that it expected to encounter higher commodity costs of approximately $230 million in fiscal 2012, with the majority of this already reflected in the results for the first half of the year. Capital expenditures for fiscal 2012 were expected to be about $900 million.

In January 2012, Howard Schultz said:[43]

Starbucks future has never been brighter. Our foundation never more solid. We are remarkably well positioned to pursue our diversified, multichannel, multibrand business model.

He believed that Starbucks was firing on all cylinders and ready to take full advantage of the many global opportunities that lay ahead.[44]

ENDNOTES

Copyright © 2012 by Arthur A. Thompson. All rights reserved.

1. Company press release, April 26, 2012.

2. Howard Schultz and Dori Jones Yang, *Pour Your Heart Into It* (New York: Hyperion, 1997), p. 33.

3. Ibid., p. 34.

4. Ibid., p. 36.

5. Schultz and Yang, *Pour Your Heart Into It*, pp. 61–62.

6. Schultz and Yang, *Pour Your Heart Into It*, pp. 101–102.

7. Schultz and Yang, *Pour Your Heart Into It*, pp.142.

8. 2009 Annual Report, pp. 3 and Starbucks webcast, March 8, 2012.

9. 'Starbucks Plans New Global Store Design', *Restaurants and Institutions,* June 25, 2009, accessed at www.rimag.com on December 29, 2009.

10. Starbucks Global Responsibility Report for 2009, p. 13.

11. Company press releases, May 31, 2005 and October 25, 2005.

12. Company press release, November 1, 2007.

13. As stated by Howard Schultz in an interview with *Harvard Business Review* editor-in-chief Adi Ignatius; the interview was published in the July–August 2010 of the *Harvard Business Review*, pp. 108–115.

14. 'Starbucks and iTunes Bring Complimentary Digital Music and Video Offerings with Starbucks Pick of the Week,' *Starbucks.com,* April 15, 2008, http://news.starbucks.com/article_display.cfm?article_id=93, accessed June 8, 2010.

15. 2009 Annual Report, p. 5.

16. Company press release, April 7, 2008.

17. Company press release, February 19, 2009.

18. Company press release, April 13, 2010.

19. Company press release, January 26, 2012.

20. Starbucks webcast, March 8, 2012; also quoted in Christelle Agboka, 'Verisimo to Give Starbucks an Edge in Single-Cup Coffee Market', posted at www.reportlinker.com on March 14, 2012, accessed May 17, 2012.

21. Starbucks management presentation at UBS Global Consumer Conference, March 14, 2012; accessed at www.starbucks.com on May 18, 2012.

22. Company press release, July 14, 2008.

23. 2009 Annual Report, p. 4.

24. Claire Cain Miller, 'New Starbucks Ads Seek to Recruit Online Fans', *The New York Times,* May 18, 2009, accessed at www.nytimes.com on January 3, 2010.

25. Andy Server, 'Schultz' Plan to Fix Starbucks', *Fortune*, January 18, 2008, accessed at www.fortune.com on June 21, 2010.

26. As related in Schultz and Yang, *Pour Your Heart Into It*, pp. 131–36.

27. 2011 10-K Report, p. 67.

28. As cited in Fortune's 2010 list of the '100 Best Companies to Work For'. http://money.cnn.com/magazines/fortune/bestcompanies/2010/snapshots/93.html, accessed June 9, 2010.

29. Ibid.

30. Company news release, May 21, 2009, accessed at www.starbucks.com on June 14, 2010.

31. Starbucks 2008 Global Responsibility Report.

32. Kate Rounds, 'Starbucks Coffee', *Incentive*, 167(7): 22.

33. 2011 10-K Report, p. 6.

34. Information posted in the corporate responsibility section at www.starbucks.com, accessed on June 18, 2010.

35. Company press release, February 19, 2009.

36. Company press release, January 18, 2010.

37. As reported in 'Shakeup at Starbucks,' www.cbsnews.com, January 7, 2008, accessed June 16, 2010.

38. Transcript of Starbucks Earnings Conference Call for Quarters 1 and 3 of fiscal year 2008, posted at http://seekingalpha.com and accessed June 16, 2010.

39. Starbucks management presentation at UBS Global Consumer Conference, March 14, 2012, accessed at www.starbucks.com on May 18, 2012.

40. Mariko Sanchanta, 'Starbucks Plans Major China Expansion', Wall Street Journal, April 13, 2010, accessed at http://online.wsj.com on June 10, 2010.

41. Ibid.

42. Company press release, January 26, 2012.

43. Letter to the shareholders, Starbucks 2011 Annual Report, p. 2.

44. Company press release, January 26, 2012.

Case 8

Rhino capture in Kruger National Park

A. J. Strickland

University of Alabama

William E. Mixon

University of Alabama
MBA Candidate

Dr. Markus Hofmeyr, head of Veterinary Wildlife Services for South African National Parks (SANParks), returned from another rhino capture with his team. They had captured their 252nd rhino for the year before the rainy season set in, with heat and rain making it almost impossible to continue the capture program. As Hofmeyr and his team were winding down another successful year, given that each rhino was worth between $30 000 and $35 000,[1] he began to reflect on next year's game capture. Hofmeyr faced the daunting question of how to continue to supplement the funding for SANParks' Park Development Fund. Over the years, the budget for his unit had been reduced, and pressure for self-funding of SANParks was increasing.

Some of the funding for SANParks' operations had long been provided by the South African national government in the form of an annual grant. That began to change in 2010, however, when a budget shortfall forced the government to initiate the removal of the grant over three years. The South African government shifted its strategy toward building a new South Africa, focused on providing additional funds for education, job creation through infrastructure expansions, better health care for all South Africans, and economic prosperity. Funding cuts outside of these priority areas threatened the ability of SANParks' Veterinary Wildlife Services to continue delivering normal veterinary and operational services – services that were beneficial to all SANParks wildlife and the habitat in which the wildlife had roamed for centuries. SANParks' budget allocation is shown in Exhibit 1.

EXHIBIT 1: SANParks budget allocation (in U.S. Dollars)	
Kruger National Park Budget	$4 951 900
Poaching	$275 100
Infrastructure	$275 100

EXHIBIT 2: Rhino population in South Africa		
	2007	**2010**
White rhinos	15 000	17 500
Black rhinos	1500	4200

Kruger National Park

Kruger National Park was established in South Africa in 1898 to protect the nation's fast-dwindling wildlife areas. By the turn of that century, it was estimated that white rhinos were extinct in Kruger. The first translocation of white rhinos to Kruger National Park occurred in 1961, and a total of 345 white rhinos had been relocated from the parks in Kwa Zulu Natal by the mid-1970s. In 2007, an assessment by the African Rhino Specialist Group estimated that 15 000 white rhinos and 1500 black rhinos existed in South Africa. As of 2009, research indicated that 10 000 white rhinos and 500 black rhinos existed within Kruger National Park, making it home to the largest rhino population in the world. Population estimates for rhinos in South Africa are shown in Exhibit 2.[*]

Kruger National Park covered 7722 square miles (20 000 square kilometers) of conservation area, with eight gates that controlled the flow of unauthorized traffic into the park. Since its establishment, it had become known for its unrivaled wildlife diversity and easy viewing and for its world leadership in advanced environmental management techniques, research, and policies. Many viewed Kruger as the best national park in all of Africa in all aspects – management, infrastructure, and, of course, biodiversity. The flagship of South Africa's 22 national parks, Kruger held a variety of species: 336 trees, 49 fish, 34 amphibians, 114 reptiles, 507 birds, and 147 mammals. Over time, the park had developed into a tourist attraction because of the wildlife and the beautiful scenery, which was representative of South Africa's Lowveld region. (The Lowveld consisted of areas around the eastern part of the country where the altitude was about 1000 feet.)

Tourist operations at Kruger were quite large, with the park offering 21 rest camps, 7 private lodge concessions, and 11 private safari lodges. Lodges that previously had been private were operated in partnership between communities and private companies, which provided concessions for parcels of land. The concessions were placed on tender, and areas were allocated for 25- to 30-year leases, during which operational activities linked with tourism were allowed. At the end of the period, the fixed assets became the property of SANParks, which could decide to extend the lease or retender the concession. An integral part of Kruger National Park's conservation effort was game capture. Traditionally, capturing game allowed Kruger to reintroduce certain species to previously uninhabited areas of the park, as well as to introduce rhino to the other national parks in South Africa and neighboring countries.

Game capture also enabled the park to better manage rare species by placing them in breeding enclosures. In some instances, game capture was used to reduce populations where that goal was impeded by natural regulatory mechanisms. Traditional game capture evolved into an income-generating operation as the demand for rhinos increased.

Income Generation from Game Capture

The sale of wildlife for income generation was accepted and supported by South Africa's National Environmental Management Act (2004). SANParks maximized income from wildlife sales by concentrating on selling high-value species. The two species sold without clearly required ecological reasons for their sale were white rhinos from Kruger National Park and disease-free buffalos from other parks. The only condition required when an animal was sold was that its removal could not negatively impact the populations from which it came. In 2009, 500 rhinos were sold in South Africa. Kruger National Park claimed 252 of these transactions; the others were sold from provincial parks and the private sector. A flow chart of sales transactions is shown in Exhibit 3. The average selling price for a white rhino was $30 300. Many wildlife biologists and other experts feared that these rhinos would eventually fall into the hands of private game hunters. Rhino hunting and rhino breeding for future sales or hunting were driving up the price for a rhino. SANParks accepted hunting as a legal form of wildlife utilization but did not support unethical put-and-take hunting practices because it was very difficult to determine what happened to a rhino after leaving SANParks. SANParks was not responsible for enforcing hunting regulations on wildlife; instead, this responsibility was passed on to each respective South African province. However, many provinces were understaffed, which weakened the regulation of hunting activities.

The most common method for selling rhinos outside Kruger National Park was through provincial and private-sector auctions. In 2009, 45 auctions accounted for most rhino sales outside SANParks. During that year, 252 rhinos on a direct tender were captured in the bush and sold at three auctions held by SANParks. The revenue generated from rhino sales in 2009 totaled $7 033 400. These revenue sales supplemented the conservation budget for SANParks' Park Development Fund. The buyers of the live rhinos were dealers who specialized in wild game or private owners who bought directly from SANParks. Rhinos were typically sold to a private game reserve for either tourist viewing or hunting. Rhinos were also sold or donated by SANParks to neighboring countries. Rhinos purchased in the private sector were sometimes sold internationally to zoos or to buyers who dealt in wild game.

Typically, white rhinos were sold more often than black rhinos, since black rhinos were rarer and much more aggressive. SANParks had sold only two black rhino bulls; the other black rhinos moved from Kruger were donated as part of conservation efforts to reestablish them in countries where they had gone extinct. The private sector bought black rhinos from Kwa Zulu Natal Wildlife, where the remaining black rhinos survived with white rhinos at the turn of the twentieth century. Kwa Zulu Natal moved from completely selling black rhinos to retaining full ownership of the adults and partial ownership of the offspring. Offspring were placed into a custodianship program that split the rights between two or more parties. North West Province

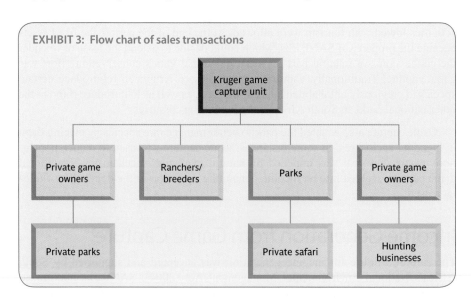

EXHIBIT 3: Flow chart of sales transactions

sold black rhinos, as did the private sector. Compared with white rhinos, black rhinos were more difficult to introduce and had a higher intraspecies mortality rate from fighting. The tendency to fight made black rhinos a riskier investment than white rhinos, which bred and coexisted much better than black rhinos. The majority of white rhinos were purchased in cow/calf combinations, which were not hunted. White rhino bulls were much more likely than white rhino cows to be purchased for hunting. However, most provinces had regulations that limited the number of rhinos eligible to be hunted. Before a rhino was killed, it had to have lived on the current property for more than two years; however, this regulation was very difficult to enforce. Park Services was a critical component of conservation for rhinos and other animals within the park.

Park Services

Veterinary Wildlife Services (VWS) offered a variety of operational and veterinary services for Kruger National Park. Veterinarian operations were critical to the conservation of wildlife within and outside the park. The service's operations included wildlife capture, holding, and translocation; park development; species conservation management; wildlife sales; animal exchanges and contractual commitments; regional cooperation; and research. VWS's aims and objectives and responsibilities are shown in Exhibit 4. Game capture operations began in the 1980s for Kruger National Park; Kruger had also operated game capture in other parks. In the 1990s, a second unit was established for operations outside Kruger. Both units were combined to form VWS in 2002, ensuring that the service was serving SANParks' objectives and not just those of Kruger. Kruger aimed for VWS to 'provide ethical and professional services relating to capture, holding, translocation and research pertaining to wildlife.'[2] Some of the values and functions associated with VWS are shown in Exhibit 5.

SANParks' Game Capture Unit

SANParks' game capture unit had branch offices in three locations in South Africa: Kruger, Kimberley, and Port Elizabeth. The capture, translocation and reestablishment functions of SANParks' Veterinary Wildlife Services are shown in Exhibit 6.

Population growth, sex and age structure, spatial use, natural dispersal, resource distribution, and population dynamics were considered when making the decision to sell an animal to a private buyer. According to SANParks' chief executive officer, Dr. David Mabunda, 'SANParks, by selling or donating rhino, is assisting in the process of recolonization of the range in the country and outside. It should be noted that it would be foolhardy if South Africa were to have its only rhino population residing in the Kruger, because we run the danger of losing them should there be a major outbreak of disease or rampant poaching. We would be sitting ducks.' Bovine tuberculosis and anthrax were two diseases being monitored by VWS in efforts to better understand how to contain them, which in turn would lead to better decisions about disease management where required. Intervention was not always needed in wildlife populations, but an understanding of how a disease influenced population dynamics was. VWS disease management services are shown in Exhibit 7. In addition to these issues, SANParks concerned itself with Kruger National Park's capability to assess and evaluate financial implications and the risks imposed to its white rhino population by intense localized removals and emerging diseases.[3]

Capturing a Rhino

The rhino capture process involved the use of state-of-the-art equipment accompanied by a team of experts. A game capture team included a helicopter pilot, a veterinarian,

EXHIBIT 4: Aims, objectives, and responsibilities of SANParks' Veterinary Wildlife Services

The SANParks Strategic Organizational Objectives Framework

Prioritizational of services according to resources, ethical and legal constraints

Optimal utilization of resources

Development and training of the wildlife profession

Recognition that SANParks concerns itself with populations rather than individuals

The leveraging of information and skills developed in SANParks to the benefit of the SADC region

The recognition of the importance of the wildlife and ecological socio-interfaces

Coordination of research on wildlife diseases and their impact on human livelihoods, wildlife itself, and livestock

Implementation of wildlife capture and translocation programs

Reintroducing populations into national parks

Enhancing the conservation status of rate and threatened species

Controlling over-abundant wildlife populations to avert the threats of habitat degradation and loss of biodiversity

Generating revenue for SNAParks through wildlife sales

Enhancing breeding projects involving valuable and rare species

Building capacity in the veterinary and wildlife capture fields, particularly in persons from historically disadvantaged population groups

an operational coordinator, a veterinary technician, five capture staff personnel, and two drivers for the translocation and crane trucks. Selected operating expenses of a rhino capture are shown in Exhibit 8.

Once a rhino was located, the capture process consisted of darting it with a drug combination from a helicopter. The fast-acting drug combination made the whole capture process less dangerous to the capture unit by rendering the rhino unconscious for evaluation before relocation. Once the rhino was unconscious, a team from the game capture unit moved in to examine it. The game capture unit conducted a medical examination of the rhino by taking blood samples to test for any signs of disease. At this point in the game capture process, three radio-frequency identification (RFID) microchips were tagged on the rhino for identification purposes. Inserting an RFID

EXHIBIT 5: Veterinary Wildlife Services' values and functions

Veterinary Wildlife Values

VWS is a service delivery department for SANParks, providing specialist veterinary and wildlife handling and translocation support

The SANParks strategic organizational objectives framework of biodiversity, balancing, people and enabling systems will guide these services

The resource, ethical, and legal constraints as well as other drivers will make it necessary to prioritize the services that can be delivered. (Guided by the Wildlife Management Commitee recommendations.)

Optimal utilitization of resources

The leveraging of information and skills developed in SANParks to the benefit of the SADEC region, particularly in SANParks TFC involment

Development and training of the wildlife profession

The recognition of the importance of wildlife and ecological and diagnostic test development

Veterinary Wildlife Functions

Service to scientific services and park managment with regard to implementing veterinary aspects of removals and introductions into our parks, collar fitting, sample taking and any other activities that require handling of wildlife

Disease monitoring, management and surveillance (including sample taking, storing and distribution aid research)

Development of current veterinary aspects of capture, translocation and animal husbandry techniques

Veterinary support to special species management related to approved plans (e.g., predator management plans)

Conservation medicine (implementing and integrating disease and ecological principles in our function)

Veterinary research relevant to the service delivery component of VWS

Liaison and education at the appropriate national and international level

microchip involved drilling into the horn, which is made of keratin, a material similar to that which human hair and fingernails are composed of. Photos of the game capture process are shown in Exhibit 9.

Park officials used tagging as a method to better understand the rhinos' movement within their landscape. South African law mandated the tagging of any rhino darted as well. Park services were also looking at ways to place tracking devices on rhinos to increase the capability of understanding rhino movements within their landscape. Prevention was the main emphasis of the rhino poaching counteroffensive in Kruger. It was thought that these potential tracking devices would help deter poaching, but the main deterrent was gaining information from informants on possible plans for rhino poaching.

EXHIBIT 6: The capture, translocation and reestablishment functions of SANParks' Veterinary Wildlife Services

Capture, Translocation and Reestablishment Functions
Operational capture, care and translocation of wildlife species aligned with SANParks requirements
Import species and disease-free breeding projects
Coordination of game sales
Transfrontier development
International translocations
Coordination of capture by external entities

EXHIBIT 7: Veterinary Wildlife Service's disease management services

Disease Management Services
BTB monitoring in Buffalo and Lion within Kruger
Monitoring in all parks when opportunities arise
Sarcoid research in Mountain Zebra in Bontebok NP
Disease prevention principles applied to animal movements and quarantine facilities both in Kruger and Kimberley

EXHIBIT 8: Selected operating expenses of rhino capture

Game capture operating expenses	Cost per rhino	Cost per hour	Cost per day	Cost per year	Unit cost
Helicopter	N/A	$800	N/A	N/A	N/A
Transportation of rhino	$300	N/A	N/A	$11 000	N/A
Truck	N/A	N/A	$300	N/A	N/A
Boom	N/A	N/A	$300	N/A	N/A
Capture team	N/A	$200	$1400	N/A	N/A
RFID microchip	$50	N/A	N/A	N/A	$17

After the evaluation and tagging process, a partial antidote was administered to partially wake up the rhino but keep it in a semi-anesthetized state. Partial antidotes were necessary to protect the game capture team while walking the rhino into the transportation crate. After the rhino was successfully loaded into a transportation crate, a boom truck lifted the crate onto the translocation truck. A boom truck was needed since an average rhino weighed 3300 pounds (1500 kilograms). Typically, the average distance traveled by a rhino captured from Kruger National Park was 50 miles

EXHIBIT 9: The game capture process

The game capture unit follows the helicopter in pursuit of a rhino.

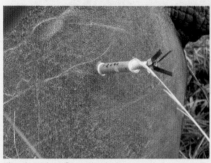

The dart shot from the helicopter is inspected by game capture personnel.

Game capture unit personnel inspect the sedated rhino.

Game capture personnel drill a hole in the rhino's horn to insert the RFID microchip.

Game capture personnel inspect the sedated rhino.

Boom trucks are needed to load the rhino.

After the antidote is given, the staff helps the rhino stand up.

(80 kilometers), at a cost of $300 per rhino per 16 miles. The next translocation process was maintenance in holding facilities (see Exhibit 10). Rhinos were placed in *bomas* (holding pens). *Bomas* allowed a rhino to become accustomed to a new habitat by slowly facilitating a passive release. Once released, the rhino was typically still confined to a larger pen or fenced-in area, depending on the buyer's intentions. It was estimated that 50 percent of the bulls transferred to private hunting companies were killed within two years, at a price of $2800 per inch of rhino horn.

Rhino Hunting

A typical rhino hunt could cost $82 400 per hunter. In 2009, South Africa generated an estimated $6.9 billion in revenues from tourist attractions; of that amount, hunting accounted for about 70 percent, or about $4.8 billion.[4] The cost of booking a rhino hunt varied depending on the safari company, as detailed in Exhibit 11. Most safari companies required a deposit of 50 percent of the basic cost of a safari, which was fully refundable until within three months of the contracted safari date. Accommodations varied according to packages offered by each safari company and were considered

EXHIBIT 10: Dr. Markus Hofmeyr standing above several *Bomas* (holding pens)

EXHIBIT 11: Selected company safari expenses and trip details

Africa Sport Hunting Safaris

Services offered
- First-class rifle and bow hunting
- Ethical, professional hunters
- Personal attention to all our clients
- Family and photographic tours
- Specialized, well-maintained vehicles
- Luxury accommodation
- Excellent cuisine
- Dedicated staff

Firearms and calibers
- Rhino legal minimum .375 caliber and 3–9 × 40 variable-power telescope
- Ammunition recommended minimum of 40 full metal jacket/solids in addition to soft point bullets

Travel information
- Valid passport required

Trophy handling
- All animals will be skinned by our very experienced skinners, as well as marked, salted, and dried prior to being sent to a taxidermist. All documentation will be handled by Africa Sport Hunting Safaris

Clothing and other requirements
- Three sets of hunting clothing: long pants (zip-offs), long-sleeve shirts, socks, and underwear
- Hunting boots/shoes – comfortable
- Casual/running shoes
- Sweater/warm jacket
- Flip flops/sweat suit
- Cap/wide-brimmed hat
- Casual clothes
- Adjust your clothing to the time of year your hunt takes place.
- Winter May–August (35–70°F)
- Summer September–April (50–90°F)

(Continued)

EXHIBIT 11: (Continued)

Personal – Personal medical kit – Sunblock – minimum 30 SPF – Mosquito repellent – Pair of sunglasses – Toiletries	
Additional equipment – Small day pack – Flashlight with spare batteries – Binoculars – Camera with spare film and batteries – Pocket knife	
Accommodation: luxury thatched chalets with a true African ambience – Private rooms with ensuite bathrooms – Running hot and cold water – Electricity with converters – Flush toilets	
Food and beverages – Traditional South African cuisine. For dietary requirements such as diabetes and high cholesterol, please make arrangements on booking of the safari	
Additional services – Facials and full body massages – Manicures and pedicures – Day excursions	
South African hunting areas price list Limpopo Province 2010 – White Rhino – White Rhino (Green-Hunt)	 $45 000 $13 000
Daily rate: South Africa – Dangerous Game – Plains Game – 1 Hunter × 1 Professional Hunter: – 2 Hunters × 1 Professional Hunter: – All non-hunters are welcome at:	 $800 $400 $300 $200
Included in daily rate – Pick up and drop off at Polokwane International Airport – Hunting licenses and fees – Transportation to and from hunting concessions – Field preparation of trophies – Professional hunters, trackers, skinners, and camp staff – Fully equipped hunting vehicles – Luxury accommodation and meals – Drinks and beverages in moderation – Daily laundry services	
Excluded from daily rates – Flights: international and domestic – Charter flights where applicable – All animals shot and wounded will be charged per price list – Dipping, packing, taxidermy cost – Non-hunting, traveling days at $150 per day – Accommodation before and after hunt – Any additional tours or excursions	

(Continued)

EXHIBIT 11: (Continued)

Methods of payment accepted – U.S. currency – Traveler's checks – Wire transfers – Credit cards – Personal checks with prior approval	
Members of: – Professional Hunters Association South Africa – Accredited Tour Guides – Safari Club International – North American Hunters Association – National Rifle Association	
Chattaronga Safaris	
Daily fees hunter 1 2 3 4 Observer	 $400 $350 $300 $300 $200
Included tariffs – Accommodation including full board – Liquor and beverages served in camp – Full-time service of experienced professional hunter. – Trained staff – Trackers – Skinners – Field preparation of trophies – All transportation within hunting areas – All hunting licenses – Pickup and drop-off at international airport: Limpopo-Polokwane, Kwa-Zulu Natal-Johannesburg, Mpumalanga-Johannesburg	
Excluded tariffs – International and domestic flights – Traveling day (non-hunting days) at $180 per day – Trophy fees of animal shot or wounded – Rifle hire (firearms may be rented at $80 per day) – Ammunition is available at cost – Dipping, packing, taxidermy, and shipping – Air charters and accommodation before and after safari – Tips for staff, telephone calls, and curio purchases	
Rhino safari 7 Day 1 × 1 Includes representative 20′ fake horn (because it is not standard practice to cut off the horn of a rhino).	$60 000
Dumukwa	
Daily rates 1 hunter/1 professional hunter 2 hunters/1 professional hunter Non-hunters/observers Rhino dart 5 day 1 × 1 Hunt	 $400 $300 $200 $8500

(Continued)

EXHIBIT 11: (Continued)

Included in daily rates
 – Full accommodation, meals, and use of camp facilities
 – All liquid refreshments including wine, beer, bottled water, and sodas
 – Daily laundry
 – Service of professional hunter with his team of skinners and trackers
 – Field preparation of trophies
 – Transport of raw trophies to local taxidermist for the area you in hunt in
 – All transportation during the safari including from and to the airport
 – 14 percent value added tax (VAT) on all packages

Excluded in daily rates
 – Internet, faxes, and telephone calls
 – Airfare
 – Hotel accommodation before and after the contracted safari
 – Dipping and packing or mounting of trophies
 – Shipping of trophies back to your country
 – Optional hire of firearms

Zingeli Safaris

Included in daily rates
 – Full board and lodging with traditional catering
 – South African wines and beer in moderation, and soft drinks
 – Experienced professional hunter and trained staff
 – Trackers and skinners
 – Field preparation, salting and packing
 – Transportation of trophies to reliable and qualified taxidermist who will follow your instructions and fulfill the necessary requirements
 – Use of hunting vehicle
 – Laundry services
 – Transportation to the ranch and return to Johannesburg International Airport or charter plane

Excluded in daily rates
 – Air travel before, during and after the contracted period of the safari
 – Accommodation and travel charges incurred before and after the contracted period of the safari
 – Trophy fees for animals taken or wounded
 – Value added tax (VAT) 14 percent on daily rates
 – Air charters
 – Gratuities to professional hunters and staff
 – Preparation, packing, documentation, and export of trophies from South Africa

comparable to those of any other tourist attraction in the world. Some safari companies offered photo safaris and wedding packages, in addition to hunting services, to further generate revenue for operations.

Typically, each safari company recommended certain equipment and clothing for hunters to bring along with them. This list varied by season, since temperatures could range between 30°F (low) in the winter and 90°F (high) in the wet summer season. Expenses also varied according to the specific details of a trip such as length of stay, trophy fees, number of hunters and observers, and the daily rate charged per hunter. Airfare to and from South Africa also varied depending on how far in advance travel arrangements were made and whether the flight was direct. Typically, coach seating ranged from $800 to $1100, whereas first-class price ranges easily approached $3000. Rifles, bows, and darting weapons were offered in some packages, but rifles could be imported into South Africa under strict guidelines and regulations. However, hunters were not allowed to import automatic or semiautomatic weapons.

Some companies charged high trophy fees and low daily rates, in contrast to low trophy fees and high daily rates. Trophy fees varied according to the specific animal wounded or killed and were typically not paid until the end of the safari. Daily rates depended on the services offered and could include or exclude a number of amenities necessary to hunt in South Africa. In general, some safari companies offered a lower daily rate as a marketing tool to increase their customer base; a large trophy fee reflected the fact that a safari company's profits depended on a successful hunt by the customer. As Zingeli Safaris stated in its brochure, 'If you don't get your animal we lose; this is your guarantee that we will do our best to find you your dream trophy!' Customers incurred taxidermist fees, in addition to trophy fees, if they desired to have something tangible to take home.

Poaching

Demand for rhino horn in emerging markets such as Asia and India made rhino poaching highly profitable. In 2009, rhino horn was sold on the black market at $3600 per pound, but by 2010 the price was reported to be $7200 per pound. An average rhino horn weighed six to eight pounds. Businesses with ties to political insiders were entering the market to supply and sell rhino horn as wealth creation resulted from the growth of Asia's and India's economies.

The market for raw rhino horn was mainly driven by demand in China and Vietnam. Cultural beliefs, combined with increasing wealth, were creating a strong foundation for the demand of rhino horn. Asians believed that rhino horn was a very beneficial aphrodisiac, and Indians desired rhino horn daggers. These beliefs and desires were strong enough to produce enough capital to entice the illegal killing of rhinos without regard to law enforcers such as the SANParks Environmental Crimes Unit, South African Police Service, and park rangers.

Poachers were well equipped with highly sophisticated transportation such as helicopters and the latest military weaponry available in the region. They were able to strike fast within even the most protected game conservation areas. Poaching was even a problem in Kruger National Park, home to what some considered the best antipoaching unit in South Africa. In 2006, two rhinos were even poached by staff members employed by SANParks. In 2009 alone, there were about 50 rhinos poached in Kruger and 100 poached in South Africa as a whole. As of January 22, 2010, poachers had killed 14 rhinos in Kruger National Park as well.

Poachers were ruthless in the slaughtering of rhinos. They typically cut off the rhino's horns after darting it with a deadly poison (see Exhibit 12). Poachers also darted rhinos with an immobilizing antidote that sometimes left the rhino helpless in the wild to be eaten by other game. SANParks' CEO, Dr. David Mabunda, described poachers as 'dangerous criminals.' Their exploits were not limited to killing rhinos, but also included human trafficking, arms smuggling, prostitution, and drug trafficking.

'Poachers must beware,' Mabunda said in a statement announcing a $250 000 funding boost, in addition to the $5.2 million allocated to train and prepare the SANParks Environmental Crimes Unit and South African Police Service. Fifty-seven rangers equipped with night vision goggles and high-powered motorbikes had been dispatched to guard highly poached areas of the park day and night. Said Mabunda, 'This war we plan on winning.' In addition to the funding boost, plans were considered to guard the porous border near Kruger National Park with military personnel. Elisabeth McLellan, a species expert with the World Wildlife Foundation (WWF), was quoted as saying, 'The situation is bad for rhino worldwide, in terms of poaching.' Conservationists were facing an environment that had evolved into an industry, as world trade had reached a 15-year high for illegal rhino horn trading.

Kenyan authorities at Jomo Kenyatta International Airport had seized a 662-pound load of elephant tusk and rhino horn believed to have come from South Africa. It was

EXHIBIT 12: Rhino left to die after poachers cut off horn

speculated that the load, valued at approximately $1 million, was destined for China. Industry experts suggested that the high value placed on elephant tusk and rhino horn by consumers was driving the demand for both substances.

Animal Supermarket

Kruger National Park was determined to win the war against poaching, but determination alone wasn't enough to protect the rhino. Primary-market transactions involved buyers that protected the rhino – such as other national parks, private game farms, game dealers, and photography safari business owners – but secondary markets from the sale of captured rhinos had also developed. Hunters had become the most numerous buyers in the secondary market, which wasn't aligned with Kruger National Park's mission. Animal rights activists dubbed the sale of animals at Kruger National Park an 'animal supermarket.' Many believed that the commercial trade posed a greater threat than poaching did. Many also felt it was fundamentally wrong to herd animals from a popular wildlife reserve and sell them in efforts at 'conservation.' Wildlife activists accused SANParks of misusing the park by serving as nothing more than a private game breeder, and experts feared that the vast majority of the rhinos sold by SANParks would fall into the hands of private hunters.

SANParks' Justification

SANParks was guided in its decision to sell wildlife by Clause 55(2)(b) of the Protected Areas Act No. 57 of 2003 (as amended), which stated that 'SANParks may, in managing national parks, sell, exchange or donate any animal, plant, or other organism occurring in a park, or purchase, exchange or otherwise acquire any indigenous species which it may consider desirable to reintroduce into a specific park.' SANParks believed that it was critical to its conservation efforts to maintain the sale of animals to private entities. For years, SANParks had sold animals to fund conservation efforts, and in many cases the park had traded animals to obtain other species. Also, SANParks screened animals and buyers to ensure that animals were released not arbitrarily, but to buyers with the proper permits and intentions. Decisions to sell or donate wildlife were scientifically determined according to population dynamics, sex and age structure, spatial use, natural dispersal, and resource distribution.

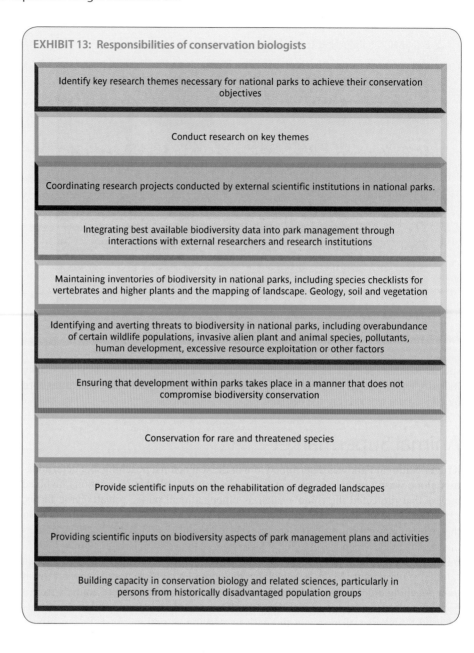

EXHIBIT 13: Responsibilities of conservation biologists

Identify key research themes necessary for national parks to achieve their conservation objectives

Conduct research on key themes

Coordinating research projects conducted by external scientific institutions in national parks.

Integrating best available biodiversity data into park management through interactions with external researchers and research institutions

Maintaining inventories of biodiversity in national parks, including species checklists for vertebrates and higher plants and the mapping of landscape. Geology, soil and vegetation

Identifying and averting threats to biodiversity in national parks, including overabundance of certain wildlife populations, invasive alien plant and animal species, pollutants, human development, excessive resource exploitation or other factors

Ensuring that development within parks takes place in a manner that does not compromise biodiversity conservation

Conservation for rare and threatened species

Provide scientific inputs on the rehabilitation of degraded landscapes

Providing scientific inputs on biodiversity aspects of park management plans and activities

Building capacity in conservation biology and related sciences, particularly in persons from historically disadvantaged population groups

SANParks' strategy was informed by the following objectives: population control, broadening of the range for populations, spreading the risk of managing wildlife, making the populations more resilient and viable, and fund-raising for specific conservation and land-expansion programs. The responsibilities of SANParks' conservation biologists are shown in Exhibit 13. The challenge facing SANParks was how to effectively communicate that selling rhinos was for the greater good.

ENDNOTES

* © 2010 by A.J. Strickland. All rights reserved.
1. All monetary amounts in this case are in U.S. dollars.
2. *Wildlife Research Magazine.*
3. Sam Ferreira & Travis Smith Scientific Services, SANParks, Skukuza, South Africa.
4. *Wildlife Research Magazine.*

Case 9

Robin Hood

Joseph Lampel
New York University

It was in the spring of the second year of his insurrection against the High Sheriff of Nottingham that Robin Hood took a walk in Sherwood Forest. As he walked he pondered the progress of the campaign, the disposition of his forces, the Sheriff's recent moves, and the options that confronted him.

The revolt against the Sheriff had begun as a personal crusade. It erupted out of Robin's conflict with the Sheriff and his administration. However, alone Robin Hood could do little. He therefore sought allies, men with grievances and a deep sense of justice. Later he welcomed all who came, asking few questions and demanding only a willingness to serve. Strength, he believed, lay in numbers.

He spent the first year forging the group into a disciplined band, united in enmity against the Sheriff and willing to live outside the law. The band's organization was simple. Robin ruled supreme, making all important decisions. He delegated specific tasks to his lieutenants. Will Scarlett was in charge of intelligence and scouting. His main job was to shadow the Sheriff and his men, always alert to their next move. He also collected information on the travel plans of rich merchants and tax collectors. Little John kept discipline among the men and saw to it that their archery was at the high peak that their profession demanded. Scarlock took care of the finances, converting loot to cash, paying shares of the take, and finding suitable hiding places for the surplus. Finally, Much the Miller's son had the difficult task of provisioning the ever-increasing band of Merrymen.

The increasing size of the band was a source of satisfaction for Robin, but also a source of concern. The fame of his Merrymen was spreading, and new recruits were pouring in from every corner of England. As the band grew larger, their small bivouac became a major encampment. Between raids the men milled about, talking and playing games. Vigilance was in decline, and discipline was becoming harder to enforce. 'Why,' Robin reflected, 'I don't know half the men I run into these days.'

The growing band was also beginning to exceed the food capacity of the forest. Game was becoming scarce, and supplies had to be obtained from outlying villages. The cost of buying food was beginning to drain the band's financial reserves at the very moment when revenues were in decline. Travelers, especially those with the most to lose, were now giving the forest a wide berth. This was costly and inconvenient to them, but it was preferable to having all their goods confiscated.

Robin believed that the time had come for the Merrymen to change their policy of outright confiscation of goods to one of a fixed transit tax. His lieutenants strongly resisted this idea. They were proud of the Merrymen's famous motto: 'Rob the rich and give to the poor.' 'The farmers and the townspeople,' they argued, 'are our most important allies. How can we tax them, and still hope for their help in our fight against the Sheriff ?'

Robin wondered how long the Merrymen could keep to the ways and methods of their early days. The Sheriff was growing stronger and becoming better organized. He now had the money and the men and was beginning to harass the band, probing for its weaknesses. The tide of events was beginning to turn against the Merrymen. Robin felt that the campaign must be decisively concluded before the Sheriff had a chance to deliver a mortal blow. 'But how,' he wondered, 'could this be done?'

Robin had often entertained the possibility of killing the Sheriff, but the chances for this seemed increasingly remote. Besides, killing the Sheriff might satisfy his personal thirst for revenge, but it would not improve the situation. Robin had hoped that the perpetual state of unrest, and the Sheriff's failure to collect taxes, would lead to his removal from office. Instead, the Sheriff used his political connections to obtain reinforcement. He had powerful friends at court and was well regarded by the regent, Prince John.

Prince John was vicious and volatile. He was consumed by his unpopularity among the people, who wanted the imprisoned King Richard back. He also lived in constant fear of the barons, who had first given him the regency but were now beginning to dispute his claim to the throne. Several of these barons had set out to collect the ransom that would release King Richard the Lionheart from his jail in Austria. Robin was invited to join the conspiracy in return for future amnesty. It was a dangerous proposition. Provincial banditry was one thing, court intrigue another. Prince John had spies everywhere, and he was known for his vindictiveness. If the conspirators' plan failed, the pursuit would be relentless, and retributions swift.

The sound of the supper horn startled Robin from his thoughts. There was the smell of roasting venison in the air. Nothing was resolved or settled. Robin headed for camp promising himself that he would give these problems his utmost attention after tomorrow's raid.

© 1991, by Joseph Lampel.

Case 10

NIS: geopolitical breakthrough or strategic failure?*

On December 24th, 2008, after a meeting at which both Dmitry Medvedev, President of Russia, and Boris Tadic, President of Serbia, were present, JSC Gazprom Neft (GPN) signed an agreement to acquire a 51% stake in Naftna Industrija Srbije (NIS) from the Serbian government. The €400 million deal was concluded in light of an oil and gas treaty between the two countries, which also provided for a branch of the South Stream gas pipeline and Banatsky Dvor, a major gas storage facility, to be constructed on Serbian territory. The contract specified obligations for both parties: for GPN to fund an investment programme of more than €500 million, and for the Serbian government to grant tax concessions to NIS for the first two years. Further, it was agreed that 19.34% of NIS shares owned by the Republic of Serbia would be distributed among the country's citizens.

The project provoked sharp controversy from the outset. Headlines in the Russian and pro-Russian press in Serbia hailed the deal as a 'geopolitical breakthrough in the Balkans', but criticized the 'flagging morale of the company and the consequently disappointing choices that Gazprom has made in Europe', adding that 'Given the current price of oil, the package should have come at half the price.' The Serbian press called for 'an end to the gas mafia' and argued that the government should not 'bargain away the diamond of the Serbian economy'.

Western European and American media focused on the political element of the deal, describing it as the 'the indulgence of Serbia's imperial ambitions in the Balkan region'. An independent international survey carried out in the summer of 2009 showed that the majority of respondents in Russia and Serbia perceived the transaction as politically motivated.

The presidents of the two countries and the Gazprom executives set ambitious goals for the company: to 'win leadership in the Balkan and East European oil markets', to 'lay the foundations for energy security in Europe' and to sustain a permanent 'increase in investments' during its development. They projected these goals in spite of NIS' rocky financial situation, which had been revealed by GPN's due diligence and was echoed in pessimistic forecasts by industry specialists.

Why did the experts and politicians have such conflicting opinions on the success of this venture?

* This case was written by Dr Kirill Kravchenko under the supervision of Stanislav Shekshnia, Affiliate Professor of Entrepreneurship and Family Enterprise at INSEAD. It is intended to be used as a basis for class discussion rather than to illustrate either effective or ineffective handling of an administrative situation.

© 2012 INSEAD

NIS (Naftna Industrija Srbije)

NIS, one of the largest vertically-integrated oil companies in Eastern Europe, and the largest economic entity, employer and taxpayer in Serbia, explores, produces and refines oil and gas. It sells a broad range of refined products. With headquarters and key production facilities in the Republic of Serbia, over 10% of its revenue was generated abroad, from an oil concession in Angola, oil service activities in Africa and Central Asia, and from exporting around 15% of its oil products.

It produces around 1 million tons of oil equivalent a year. The estimated capacity of the company's two refineries is 7.3 million tons. NIS operates a gas-processing plant, an extensive network of oil and gas storage facilities, 500 fuel trucks and rail cars, and over 500 gas stations. It employs nearly 12 000 people, with another 3000 employed in leasing entities, working for NIS. The company owns significant non-core assets, including vacation residences and hotels in a number of countries, a mineral water bottling factory and commercial real estate.

Taxes paid by NIS accounted for more than a quarter of the budget of the Republic of Serbia. The company regularly sponsored the ruling political party and was a source of 'extra income' for different influential political groups, both in Serbia and abroad. Over the last decade the management of NIS had been replaced nearly every year, each time a new government came to power. These changes had resulted in a largely ineffective system of governance, demotivated personnel and a lack of strategic focus.

In light of Serbia's recent history of Serbia – the collapse of Yugoslavia, a series of wars, the longstanding economic blockade imposed by NATO countries, and frequent changes of government – any decision to sell a significant entity of the Serbian economy would inevitably involve a political choice of strategic partner. With the need to focus on the multi-faceted development of Serbia, all the big players in the economy – the country's telecommunications operator, key mass media, entities operating in the oil, metal and chemical sectors – would be instrumental in determining the direction of this development.

Players who had attempted to acquire the Serbian strategic asset in the past included the Austrian company OMV, the British corporation BP, Hungary's MOL and Russia's Lukoil. All attempts had failed, in part due to political instability in the country, in part to misguided negotiation strategies and inadequate valuations of the business. The Serbian government had also made a number of unsuccessful attempts to privatise the company.

The EU, US and Russia were the main contenders vying for influence in Serbia as the trading and geographical centre of the Balkan region. Serbia and Russia had a longstanding friendship based on shared ethnic and linguistic roots as well as cultural affinities. The Orthodox religion, a common socialist past, similar stances on a number of international issues, and mutual support in times of conflict had brought them closer together, fostering goodwill their respective citizens. Many Serbs spoke Russian. After the 1917 Communist revolution, when millions of Russians fled their country, Serbia hosted the second-largest community of Russian émigrés in the world.

Conversely, Serbia's geographical position made it a natural candidate for accession to the EU, while the ever-increasing political and economic activity of the US in the region had encouraged a gradual restoration of cooperation with NATO countries.

Thus, the sale of 51% of NIS' shares as part of the package agreed for the construction of the South Stream pipeline offered an opportunity for Russia to consolidate its influence in Serbia and the Balkans, while for Serbia it was another geopolitical step towards strategic cooperation with Russia.

What was the main motivation behind the decision? Was it the political sympathies and economic benefits in light of the South Stream pipeline construction, or the cultural and historical ties between Russia and Serbia? Mostly likely, it was all of the above. But the deal was not an easy choice for GPN, as a public company. Although the acquisition of vast refining and retail capabilities in Europe fitted neatly with its strategy, economically the project was not the best option among those available to GPN in Europe.

JSC Gazprom Neft

JSC Gazprom Neft was one of the major vertically-integrated oil and gas companies in Russia and the CIS. It had oil reserves in excess of 1.3 billion tons and annual production of around 50 million tons, 60% of which was processed at its own refineries. GPN had full or partial ownership of seven oil refineries in Russia, Belarus and Italy. Its retail network included around 1500 gas stations in Russia, Kazakhstan and Kyrgyzstan.

A public company with JSC Gazprom as its majority shareholder, GPN employed 49 000 people. GPN had extensive experience working within joint-venture frameworks, the largest of which were Slavneft and Tomskneft. Most of its performance indicators put it at the top of the Russian oil industry.

The acquisition of a controlling stake in NIS was GPN's first major project abroad undertaken in alignment with a strategy to achieve a more than two-fold increase in size and to transfer 30% of its business activities abroad by 2020.

Republic of Serbia

Located at the heart of the Balkans, Serbia has a population of 7.5 million people (not including 2 million residing in Kosovo). Despite the absence of sea access, the country is a natural regional transport hub thanks to the River Danube, an extensively developed rail network, and major roads connecting southern and central Europe. Its main sources of revenue include the petrochemical industry, telecommunications and agriculture. Serbia's GDP per capita was $10 800 in 2009. The official rate of unemployment was 27%.

Serbia is a parliamentary republic with two autonomous territories: Kosovo and Vojvodina. The head of state is the president, a position held by the leader of the Democratic Party, Boris Tadic, since 2004. In 2009, Serbia had a coalition government. The political climate in the country was unstable: in the last 8 years, 10 political parties had been in office. During that period, Serbia had been seriously affected by separatism arising after the collapse of Yugoslavia. It had endured bombing by NATO, an economic blockade, the partition of the country, and conflict with Kosovo. In 2008, the Provisional Institutions of Self-Government Assembly in Kosovo unilaterally declared independence; a status subsequently recognised by more than 60 states. These traumatic experiences had left their mark on the national psyche.

Over the last five years, the Serbian economy had grown at more than 5% per year. In 2009, GDP reached $80 billion in terms of purchasing power parity. In late 2008, however, Serbia was hit by the global economic crisis, resulting in the devaluation of the national currency by more than 20%, falling gold and currency reserves, an increase in its external debt to $27.5 billion, a 40% decline in foreign trade, and a budget deficit in excess of 5%. Lacking the internal resources to remain immune to the effects of the global crisis, Serbia became increasingly dependent on attracting external funds in the form of loans and selling off state assets. The most obvious partners for Serbia in such transactions were Russia and the EU.

NIS: Challenges and Solutions

The negotiations between GPN and the Serbian government went on for more than two years. Yet the deal was ultimately closed promptly and the transition to new management had to be completed within a month of the signing. GPN's first move was to appoint a team of 50 managers to fill key positions, thereby taking operational control of the venture. In light of limited international experience and the simultaneous execution of several major projects, Gazprom Neft hired a number of executives from outside to work at NIS: of the nine new members of the management board, only two were former GPN executives. Some new managers such as vice-presidents for Investment, Security and Organizational Development were selected for their international experience and knowledge of foreign languages but had no industry experience. For key positions such as CFO and vice-presidents for Down-stream and Up-stream, a knowledge of the oil industry was considered essential, and the appointees came from large oil companies.

Another delicate task was to maintain a balance between Serbian and foreign executives. Although GPN was the majority shareholder, the Serbian government still had significant influence over the board of directors, since it owned 49% of the company. It had a strong say in the board's decisions such as the appointment of the management board members. Moreover, the lion's share of NIS' business was in Serbia.

Initially the 'hamburger' model was adopted, whereby Serbian executives became the heads of the three main divisions, with Russian managers as their deputies. Expatriates were appointed to run key functions such as Finance, HR and Legal, but it was understood that Serbian successors would be appointed soon afterwards. As a result, expatriates filled most of the senior leadership positions.

The first challenge for the new management of NIS was to take control of the company's catastrophic financial situation. At the time of the acquisition, NIS had made a loss for three years running, its debt had reached $800 million (the debt-to-EBITDA ratio was 2.5 times higher than in similar companies), and cash flow was negative. It had around $500 million in accounts receivable (75% of which were overdue), more than double its level of accounts payable, and around 3800 court cases pending with total potential liabilities of $1.5 billion. Only 2% of its assets were registered and a significant proportion of these were disputed.

After six months, the outlook on most of these counts became more positive. This allowed the company to address long-term strategy, pursuing the ambitious goal that the presidents of the two countries and GPN executives had set: to attain a position of leadership in the oil market of the Balkan region.

NIS executives identified three strategic challenges.

1. The political challenge: How to become a global company in a region plagued with problems between Serbia and its neighbours; how to handle Gazprom's reputation as a Russian 'political weapon,' when its influence was being strenuously resisted not only by other governments in the region, but also by the US and many EU countries?

2. The cultural challenge: Given Serbia's decision to open its markets to foreign players, how to modernise the company to make the transition from 'socialism' to 'capitalism' in the shortest possible time?

3. The economic challenge: How to survive in the oversupplied market of the Baltic region while bearing the burden of social responsibility and outdated technology? Should they aim to be a national leader or a regional player?

Politics

Modern-day Serbia, fragmented by internal political controversy, had to choose which direction to take: whether to cooperate with NATO countries or devise a balancing strategy of cooperation not only with the EU and the US but also with Russia.

The Serbian government was heavily influenced by public opinion, which was largely shaped by the mass media and a number of public organizations. The press in Serbia was almost a political institution in its own right. Taking advantage of this, American and Western European organizations, albeit guided by different interests, systematically pursued a common strategy that yielded positive results. European and American companies financed numerous NGO projects, provided more than 150 advisors to the Serbian government, acquired mass media and lobbied directly to create an atmosphere of goodwill around their business projects in Serbia.

Russia, on the other hand, was only just beginning the task of organizing systemic support for its business interests in the region. Pro-Russian media were still virtually absent or poorly rated. In light of Russia's absence from the informational sphere, Serbia's youth (including the country's future leaders) were heavily influenced by Western culture and less-well informed about Russian activity. For example, following a mass media campaign in favour of the Nabucco pipeline, a significant part of the Serbian public regarded the Russia-sponsored South Stream project as unpromising.

At the same time, internal politics remained tense. With oversight from the EU, the country had been divided into seven main regions: Vojvodina, Belgrade, Western, Eastern, Central, South, Kosovo and Metohija. In order to implement regionalisation, constitutional changes had to be made and significant authority was delegated to the individual regions. NIS' main assets were situated in the most autonomous region, Vojvodina, which carried additional risks for both the business and its shareholders.

Serbia was still in conflict with some of its neighbours. The collapse of Yugoslavia, subsequent wars for independence and religious differences had seriously strained relations between the republics of former Yugoslavia, from battles over cases of expropriation of personal property to the breaking off of diplomatic relations. The legacy of its former struggle for supremacy in the Balkans had prevented Serbia from stabilising relations with Bulgaria, with which it did not even have air communication. Hungary was one of Serbia's more developed partners, but at the same time its most threatening rival. In addition to a history of conflict between the Austro-Hungarian Empire and the Kingdom of Serbia, further points of tension arose from Hungary's influence on the degree of autonomy of the Serbian region of Vojvodina and competition in the energy sector. Serbia's political relations with Romania were relatively peaceful, though in the economic sphere conflicts of interest often arose. Greece was the traditional exception to the rule, sharing close cultural, spiritual and economic ties.

Although Gazprom Neft was generally well perceived in Serbia, its image was less positive in Albania, while attitudes in Hungary and Bulgaria were cautious. This negative image was the result of several factors. Due to the nature of GPN's ties with Russia, the company was perceived as a vehicle for pushing Russia's political agenda. Negative memories of the Communist era, conflicts over gas between Russia and neighbouring countries along the pipeline, as well as the rivalry between the Nabucco and the South Stream projects, also reflected negatively on GPN.

Another politically delicate aspect of the deal was the relationship between the company's shareholders. As in any joint venture, differences of opinion could arise between the two main shareholders, GPN and the Serbian government, and these could be political in nature. For example, if 5 million Serbs were to become NIS minority shareholders, then all Serbian voters would have a direct stake in the company and its business, and serious impact on how the government is represented on the board of directors.

The delicate political situation that underpinned the project of developing NIS into a serious Balkan player in the oil market raised a number of challenges. How to form partnerships and alliances in these uncertain circumstances? How to develop business in neighbouring countries in light of unresolved property disputes? How to surmount mutual distrust and the historic rivalry for leadership in the Balkans on an emotional level? And, finally, under what branding should NIS proceed: the existing Gazprom brand or a new brand?

Culture

When GPN executives were sent to work at NIS, most of them assumed that the main obstacles to their integration would be the language barrier (since the vast majority of their Serbian colleagues spoke neither English nor Russian) or cultural differences. But they soon understood that the real problem was the corporate culture that had developed within NIS. Over the years, the government-run company had turned into a 'safe haven' where everybody was guaranteed a job that provided a modest but stable salary and created opportunities for additional 'informal' income.

To get hired at NIS people had to have either family or friendship ties with existing employees. When the management changed, executives never left the company but were simply demoted. In 2009, average employee seniority was more than 25 years, and average employee age was over 48 years (cf. an average in the worldwide oil sector of 38). The reward system was rigid and took no account of individual or group initiative. Essentially, people were paid simply for showing up at work. Important decisions were taken collectively according to the principle of joint responsibility. Discipline was weak at every level of the business – problems with lateness and cigarette breaks and more serious misdemeanours went unpunished. This way of working was considered normal practice by both managers and employees. Poorly paid and protected by the doctrine of collective responsibility, managers tended to abuse their positions.

The generally lax and unconcerned attitude reminded the Russian newcomers of their socialist past. They soon labelled the corporate culture of NIS 'socialism'. Several of them also saw it as characteristic of southerners, particularly those with Slavic roots, but there were positive traits too: local employees had a detailed knowledge of the company and respect for the brand, as well as being friendly and willing to help.

The new managers recognised the need to change the prevailing culture. In light of the scale of the overhaul and the potential risks, however, they chose to cooperate with the Serbian management to reform the values and priorities of the company rather than mounting a cavalier ambush. The overhaul began with a programme that allowed employees to leave NIS with a settlement of €750 for every year that they had worked in the company. Even here, 'socialist' habits shone through. In the process of forming lists of those who had signed up to the programme, Serbian managers often took decisions that stemmed from family or friendship ties rather than taking into account professional qualities of the employees. The risk was that expertise would be lost in place of employees who were simply 'of their own'. To keep the best employees, management had to find an objective external system. Ultimately, employees were given the choice to either leave the company with compensation, or to accept a different job in NIS such as describing goods for compiling inventories or working in NIS petrol stations. Most preferred to take on these new jobs, even though they were less prestigious and had lower salaries. The 'socialist' legacy would not easily be overcome.

While all parties agreed that NIS could clearly not continue as before, there was no consensus on the alternative business strategy that ought to be adopted.

Economics

NIS extracted two kinds of quality crude oil in Serbia. Its oilfields were in their third or fourth (final) stage of development, which meant they had a high degree of water contamination and declining production levels. Internal production, even at its maximum capacity, was not sufficient to meet more than a quarter of the company's processing needs. The company produced a modest amount of oil from a concession in Angola, which was not currently processed by the company's refineries, hence NIS began examining options to exchange its assets in Angola for other more suitable assets in North Africa or the Balkan region.

Serbia's oil reserves were limited (estimated at 20 million tons). Further development downstream would require entering markets unfamiliar to NIS and significant investments, which currently seemed unrealistic given the company's debt. Although NIS's oil service business was fairly sophisticated, it was underused and incurred high expenses: lifting costs were $23 per barrel, compared to a regional average of $12. This significantly blunted the competitive edge of the company's most lucrative division.

The core of the company was always its oil refining division (downstream). With a maximum refining capacity of 7.3 million tons of crude oil per annum, the company continued to produce out-dated products such as diesel fuel with a high sulphur content and leaded gasoline fuels, which were banned in EU member states. To boost its competitive edge, NIS had made a major investment to modernise its refineries, in a project costing more than €500 million. The project's completion, scheduled for summer 2012, should signal the opportunity for NIS to curtail production of its outdated oil products, but also to make enough Euro 5 diesel fuel to meet demand in the Serbian market, which had better growth prospects. Demand from the local Serbian market in which NIS operated was 4.1 million tons, more than 50% of which was NIS' share (in the retail market its share was just over a third). Accordingly, even if NIS retained or improved its share of the Serbian market, a significant chunk of its output would have to find customers abroad (taking into account existing anti-monopoly restrictions).

The Balkan region had a highly competitive market with excess production capacity. By 2014, its refining facilities were expected to produce a 32% surplus. Moreover, according to Purvin & Gertz, the majority of NIS' competitors had already completed the modernisation of their production facilities or were in the final stages (Romania, Bulgaria, Croatia, and Bosnia and Herzegovina). There were limited options for business cooperation or potential acquisitions. Of the few options available, most were either modestly sized chains of petrol stations which could be consolidated, or larger companies without their own refineries.

In comparison to its competitors in the region NIS had a number of significant weaknesses. First, the company was highly dependent on imported crude oil. Also, transport to NIS' oil processing plants was logistically difficult, since Serbia had no access to the sea nor a major pipeline. Secondly, refining costs were fairly high due to a host of factors: outdated technology, overstaffing due to a heavy burden of social responsibility and restrictions (for example, the fact that employees could only be sacked with their consent and a significant and compulsory pay-out), and the necessity to create extensive reserves to cover overdue debt and legal liabilities. Thirdly, the difficult financial situation of the company meant that it did not have the resources to invest. This created problems for projects such as the modernisation of outdated petrol stations, sustained growth of the company's own production, and even more so for large-scale acquisitions abroad. Further weaknesses were the relaxed work ethic, poorly qualified staff, and low-quality suppliers and contractors.

Nevertheless, NIS' dominant position in the Serbian market, the potential to improve operations with little or no capital investment, and strong support from both shareholders (in the form of investment and high-level political backing) partly compensated for the above shortcomings and formed a base on which to build an effective, Balkan vertically-integrated company.

For the NIS executives it was time to make a decision regarding what kind of strategy to pursue: the simpler option of keeping NIS in the Serbian market as a modestly-sized oil company, or the more complex and risky strategy of developing NIS into a serious Balkan player? They had to find a way to reconcile the expectations of shareholders with their own ambitions and with the realities of the business that had fallen into their hands.

Case 11

Kyaia

Shoes that fly off the shelves*

Introduction

Portugal's shoemaking industry has struggled against the massive clout of China, by far the number one footwear exporter in the world (Exhibit 1). In fact, China's predominance, based on low production costs and favourable exchange rates, has led to the unbeatable average price of three dollars per shoe, compared with 24 dollars for Portuguese shoes.

Despite this, Kyaia's management is confident that the success story of its global-orientated Fly London brand will continue. By improving its distribution networks and implementing a robust brand management policy, Kyaia has gained market share and turned the tables regarding its positioning. As a result, Kyaia keeps on growing at double digit percentage levels, even in times of financial crises and decreasing consumption levels.

Kyaia's inroads into the worldwide markets were the result of a brand strategy that has been, from its outset, directed towards the penetration of international markets. The road to internationalisation has not been an easy one. Kyaia had to overcome a number of obstacles through the development of a strong brand name, the re-configuration of its value chain and the adoption of a strong market orientation.

The Portuguese Footwear Industry

Due to the development of communication and computer technologies, the footwear industry has experienced a process of modernization in the last 40 years, especially in terms of quality and flexibility. Despite this, the industry is considered to be labour-intensive, with labour costs accounting for a large proportion of the total production costs.

The growth of the Portuguese footwear industry between the 1970's and the end of 1980's, was based on Portugal's low labour costs and was reinforced by the favourable exchange rate of the Portuguese currency. During this period, firms imported machinery and equipment specialized in high-volume production of standardized products. The largest share of production was directed to large distribution chains and outsourcing multinational companies, which were located both within

* This case was written by Professors Susana Costa e Silva and Rui Soucasaux Sousa and student Louis Oberdieck, Catolica Porto Business School. It is intended to be used as the basis for class discussion rather than to illustrate either effective or ineffective handling of a management situation. The case was made possible by the co-operation of Fortunato Frederico at Kyaia.

©2011, Catolica Porto Business School.

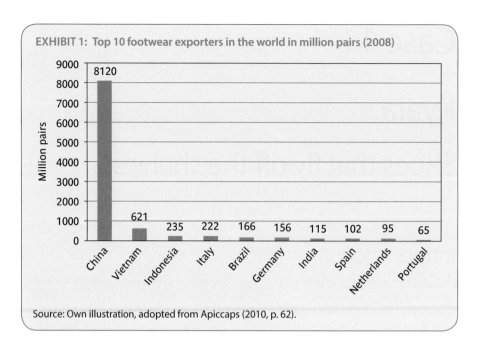

EXHIBIT 1: Top 10 footwear exporters in the world in million pairs (2008)

Source: Own illustration, adopted from Apiccaps (2010, p. 62).

and outside Portugal. This period of accelerated growth came to an end in the nineties, when the impacts of globalisation started to noticeably affect the sector (see Exhibit 2). The immense salary cost differentials between EU countries and developing countries, made it difficult for the former to stay competitive within the same market segments. As a consequence, foreign direct investments left the country and production orders were shifted to Asian countries, like China or Vietnam, with even lower labour costs.

At the same time, changes in consumer behaviour from 'an economy of needs' towards an 'economy of desire and dreams' were reflected in new lifestyles and consumption patterns, giving fashion a crucial role in view of product differentiation. The

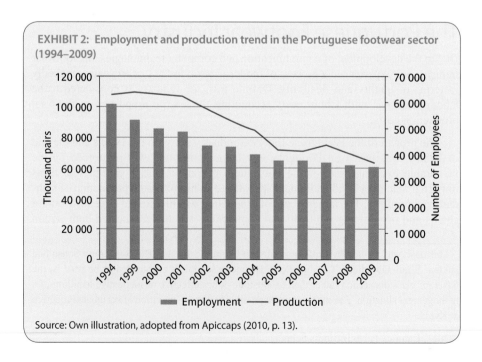

EXHIBIT 2: Employment and production trend in the Portuguese footwear sector (1994–2009)

Source: Own illustration, adopted from Apiccaps (2010, p. 13).

search for new trends and new possibilities for expressing uniqueness and social status leveraged the importance of the creative dimension in the footwear industry. As a consequence, the design component gained an increased role in adding value, at the expense of labour. Moreover, consumers in developed countries became increasingly concerned not only with the aesthetic aspects of their footwear, but also with the utilitarian aspect. Hence, consumers' decision making process includes the assessment of aspects such as comfort, durability and practicability. Technical attributes and processed materials that determine perspiration and the ergonomics characteristics of the footwear are, therefore of crucial importance for certain market segments.

In order to compete in this new context, the Portuguese footwear companies had to change their strategic positioning, targeting specific (lower volume) market niches, demanding high levels of quality, design and branding. But there was a lack of technology for this repositioning, since the formerly imported machines and equipment were not capable of coping with flexible production processes. Moreover, the existing logistic and distribution networks were impeding the efficient and timely distribution of the new kind of demanded footwear. Following this, several companies – including Kyaia – reengineered their manufacturing processes, investing in flexible processes which were able to cope with small production orders. This strategic reorientation enabled companies that used to produce only large-scale orders of thousands of pairs to accept orders of just a few and to respond to these orders in a short period of time. Furthermore, the companies started focusing on market segments with greater added value, establishing the image of fashion creators. Instead of replicating styles from their former subcontracting clients, they concentrated on developing their own brands and started to produce products with greater added value, following a strategy based on differentiation.

History of the Kyaia Group

The Kyaia Group is the work of a lifetime, founded by a self-made man, called Fortunato Frederico who started at the bottom rung of the ladder. At the early age of 14 he got his first job in a footwear factory, named 'Campeão Português', where he cleaned the factory floor and maintained the machines. He learned the handcraft of footwear by working his way up from the bottom and one day he was promoted and put in charge of an assembly line. But his dream was to have his own company and while he had to interrupt his job at the footwear company – due to his military service in Angola – he found the time to elaborate this loose idea.[1]

After his return from Angola, he went back to work for 'Campeão Português'. With the opening of Portugal to the world in 1975, the ensuing growth made business opportunities start to become a reality. It took 9 more years to gather the financial resources necessary for the opening of a private company. Thus, in 1984, Fortunato Frederico finally realized his dream and founded the Kyaia Company, together with two old work-mates – Amflcar Monteiro and José Azevedo. Fortunato Frederico received a 50.1% stake in the company, while the remaining shares were split on an equitable basis between the other two founders. The name Kyaia derives from the place in Angola where Fortunato spent the best time of his military service and which had a significant influence on his future business planning.

In its first year, the company had a production capacity of 500 pairs per day and 50 employees. It made 750 thousand Euros and produced exclusively for export. At that time, Kyaia did not possess its own brand, and thus produced exclusively for other companies, as subcontractor. The decision to locate the company in Guimarães, in the northern part of Portugal, was due to the region's low cost and specialized workforce. But soon Kyaia realized that this decision was problematic, as many multinational companies from the textile, footwear and wiring sectors had also become attracted to the advantages of this region. The effects of such demanding competition for workers threatened Kyaia's growth and put its objective of conquering international markets in question. As a result of this, Kyaia decided to shift part of its production away from the Headquarters in Guimaraes to a less developed city, Paredes de Coura, located 80 Km north of Guimaraes.

Paredes de Coura's economy was at that time heavily concentrated on the agricultural sector, but this was about to change. Farming lost its importance and the workforce released from the primary sector was soon placed at Kyaia's disposal. This additional labour pool and investments in modern production technologies enabled Kyaia to expand its production capacity and the number of its employees. In the beginning of the 90s, Kyaia produced 3000 pairs per day and employed 320 workers. In the following years, Kyaia managed to achieve stability. But it was still producing only for other companies. In addition, Portugal's advantage of low labour costs, which constituted the building block of its footwear industry, was vanishing, putting the future of many Portuguese footwear companies at stake.

It is in this context that Fortunato Frederico realized the need for a new business strategy, based on differentiation, with a focus on the design, functionality and quality aspects of the products, thereby avoiding competition with Asian producers in lower market segments. As a result, Kyaia began focusing on the creation of strong global brands with high added value, aiming towards the more demanding, but also more valuable market segments.

This strategic move started with the introduction of the brand M.C. Power, characterized by a classical design. This brand was not able to achieve a market breakthrough and was therefore replaced by two other brands – Overcube and Fungi – which embodied a more unique and original style. Simultaneously, Kyaia created a mainstream brand with a conventional design, named after the Company itself: Kyaia. These brands achieved only moderate success and did not stay in the market for long. Hence, Kyaia was forced to maintain a strong focus on its role as a subcontractor for other companies.

The branding breakthrough occurred in 1994, when Kyaia bought the brand Fly London which ultimately became its star brand. Despite the fact that at present Kyaia still provides 35% to 40% of its production capacity for subcontracting orders from other brands (e.g., Camel Active and Johnston and Murphy), Fly London effectively made Kyaia independent of subcontracting orders, accounting for 70% of the current overall profit of the Kyaia Group.

In order to promote the internationalization of the Fly London brand, Kyaia invested strongly in the new technologies, the distribution network and marketing. Additionally, the Kyaia Group has extended its brand portfolio by reactivating its Fungi Brand (this time as a brand for children) and introducing a new brand called Softinos. At present, the Kyaia Group comprises 13 companies and employs about 600 employees.

Organizational Structure

The Kyaia Group was built up and consolidated in a time period of 25 years. The Group comprises 13 companies: 9 located in Portugal, 3 in the European Union and 1 in India (see Exhibit 3). The head office of the group is located in Guimarães and is led by the founding father Fortunato Frederico (who holds a 75% stake in the group, after the pull-out of José Azevedo) and his founding partner Amílcar Monteiro (who owns 25%). Thus, Fortunato Frederico possesses a dominant position in the decision making process. The individual companies within the Group operate independently, but do not compete which each other. The industrial area of the group comprises the Kyaia headquarters factory, the Kyaia Fábrica de Gáspeas, the Alfos Fábrica Solas e Accessories Lda, and the Kello Fábrica Calgado Lda. The headquarters

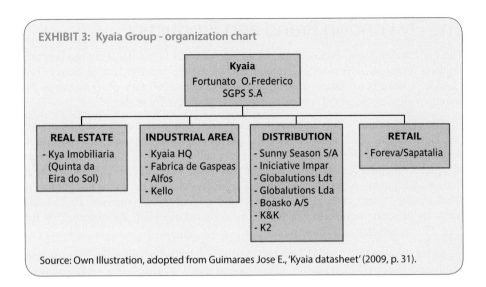

EXHIBIT 3: Kyaia Group - organization chart

Kyaia
Fortunato O.Frederico
SGPS S.A

REAL ESTATE
- Kya Imobiliaria
  (Quinta da
  Eira do Sol)

INDUSTRIAL AREA
- Kyaia HQ
- Fabrica de Gaspeas
- Alfos
- Kello

DISTRIBUTION
- Sunny Season S/A
- Iniciative Impar
- Globalutions Ldt
- Globalutions Lda
- Boasko A/S
- K&K
- K2

RETAIL
- Foreva/Sapatalia

Source: Own Illustration, adopted from Guimaraes Jose E., 'Kyaia datasheet' (2009, p. 31).

factory is located in Guimarães and incorporates a factory outlet store. The other three units are all based in Paredes de Coura. Each factory specializes in one part of the production process. Fábrica de Gáspeas does the stitching, Alfos Fábrica manufactures the soles, and Kello and the headquarters factory assemble the different parts of the footwear.

The Kyaia Group holds stakes in local distributors inside and outside of Portugal (in form of FDI's), as follows:

- Iniciativa Impar: Located in the headquarters in Guimaraes; responsible for the distribution in Portugal.

- Sunny Season S.A.: Located in Luxemburg; responsible for the distribution of the Fly London and Softinos brands in Switzerland, Austria and Germany.

- Globalutions Europa, Lda.: Located in the headquarters in Guimarães; responsible for the distribution of the Softinos products.

- Globalutions Designs PVT, Ldt: FDI in India. This company takes on two key roles for the Kyaia Group: firstly, as a supplier for leather and uppers; secondly, as a distributor for the Indian market.

- Boasko A/S: Located in Denmark; responsible for the distribution in the important Scandinavian markets of Denmark, Finland, Sweden and Norway.

- K&K: Located in Porto; responsible for distribution in Spain and Portugal.

In 2005, the Kyaia Group entered retail by acquiring the Foreva/Sapatalia retail store network. Despite giving the Group an enlarged clout, it also added a significant amount of real estate to its assets.

Located close to the Kyaia Group headquarter, the Quinta da Eira do Sol, a farming estate, plays a special role inside the Group. The estate works as a meeting point for all kinds of stakeholders within the group. Instead of accommodating its stakeholders (including clients) in different hotels, the Group provides them with a pleasant and exclusive place for personal interaction shared between suppliers, customers, employees, designers and technicians. Besides encouraging personal relationships and company loyalty, it also fosters the transfer of information between the different stakeholders. In addition, it creates additional revenues: when the estate is not being used by the Kyaia Group, it can be booked as a hotel by external parties.

The Fly London Brand and Products

The Fly London brand is positioned as an international brand. Its main markets are England, Portugal, Denmark, Germany, Spain, Japan, and the United States. Fly London is worn in all five continents and sold in over 2000 PoS. Its presence in 50 countries all over the world is responsible for 70% of Kyaia's profit.[2]

The main attribute of Fly London shoes is the distinctive style of the outsoles design (see Figure 1), the combination of colours, and the employed materials, geared towards prime quality, durability and comfort. For every collection, Fly London offers a range of about 45 model lines. A model line consists of the same sole and the same shape. Each model line offers two to four different products, which differ in the use of materials, fastening (velcro, lace, zip) etc. This results in an overall average of 120–150 different styles per collection, of which 70% are designed especially for women, 20% for men, 5% for children and 5% unisex.

Kyaia develops two collections per year; one for the spring/summer season and one for the autumn/winter season. Every type of style is available in a great variety of designs, colours and cuts.

Internationalization and Overall Control of the Value Chain

Kyaia was forced to go international since the very beginning in order to overcome the lower quality and high prices of Portuguese leather suppliers. This move began with a visit of Fortunato Frederico to a trade fair in Paris in 1989 to establish business relationships with raw materials suppliers. There, he initiated a partnership with a leather supplier from Pakistan. This company came to supply Kyaia for ten years with the essential raw materials at competitive prices, something almost impossible to achieve with Portuguese suppliers. The success of this partnership motivated Kyaia in 1986 to extend its raw materials supply chain in Pakistan to include uppers, another critical part of the shoe. Recently, the Kyaia Group has secured a high quality and stable supply of leather and uppers, by acquiring an upstream supplier in India. This backward vertical integration enables Kyaia to improve supply chain coordination and to capture upstream profit margins. This backward integration is complemented by forward vertical integration through FDI's in local distributors in nearly all of the main markets in

FIGURE 1 Fly London distinctive style shoes.

Central Europe, in order to be in charge of the distribution channels and to obtain a better access to the end customer.

As illustrated in Figure 2, Kyaia's main aim is the control of all activities in the value chain, with a particular emphasis on production in order to avoid the transfer of value to economic agents outside the firm. Thus, the key challenge for the Group is to link, integrate, coordinate and supervise the value chain including product design, production, distribution and retail. This is accomplished by the vertical integration of production, strategic partnerships and a high level of internationalisation. In particular, the critical stages of the footwear manufacturing process (like assembling and finishing), branding and retailing, are under the control of Kyaia. The strong international Fly London brand protects the company's products from being easily imitated or reproduced, even though there is already a grey market for Fly London. Furthermore, the brand increases the transfer of value deriving from the widespread subcontracted companies that are responsible for the less sophisticated and more labour intensive production stages, and enforces the international nature of the production process. Product design is highly specialized, drawing on a large network of experts, stylists and designers located in the most famous European fashion capitals. A close interaction with shoe component firms ensures the integration of technological knowledge and fashion trends. As a result, the Kyaia Group and its Fly London brand are considered to be trend setters in the industry.[3]

In order to gain control over the retailing activity of the value chain, in 2005 the Kyaia Group bought the domestic shoe retailers Foreva/Sapatalia for 7.5 million Euros. The acquisition integrated in the Kyaia Group 150 employees and a network of 63 PoS under the name Foreva and 17 under the name of Sapatalia. As part of this move, the management of Foreva/Sapatalia was moved from its existing location in

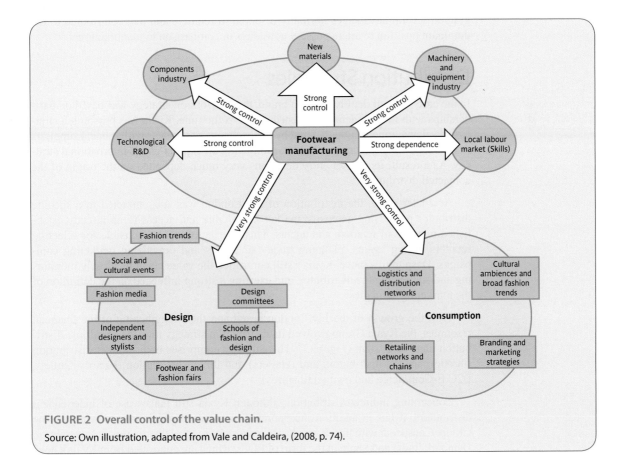

FIGURE 2 Overall control of the value chain.

Source: Own illustration, adapted from Vale and Caldeira, (2008, p. 74).

Alverca, in the Lisbon area, to the headquarters of the Kyaia Group in Guimaraes, close to top management. The Group invested 1.2 million Euros in new facilities for the acquired retailer, including offices, two pilot stores (one for each brand), a permanent show room and a factory outlet. Additionally, the new location was closer to suppliers, since about 70% of them are situated in the northern region of Portugal. Moreover, this move increased the goodwill and reputation of the Group among the local communities in the northern region.

The new facilities in Guimaraes made Foreva/Sapatalia a key player in the commercial and production strategy of the Kyaia Group. Considered by many as a risky investment due to Foreva/Sapatalia's precarious business position before the acquisition, it turned itself into a stable business unit inside the Group. Having accomplished consolidation, Foreva is now investing heavily in its internationalization. The Kyaia Group is not selling its Fly London products in the Foreva/Sapatalia chain stores since their medium-high price level does not fit the medium-low product assortment of the retailer. Moreover, most products in the stores, including the retailer's own brand Foreva, are outsourced and produced by other Portuguese footwear companies. The only products that are manufactured by the Kyaia Group and offered in the stores are Softinos and Fungi shoes.

In summary, the acquisition of the Foreva/Sapatalia network did not simply raise the commercial dimension of the group, but also made it more homogenous, by gaining more influence at the PoS. The underlying strategy was to acquire a position in the retail trade which, combined with production and distribution of footwear, enabled the Group to control a larger portion of the value chain. In addition, the proximity to the consumer at the PoS offers Kyaia new possibilities for developing relationships with end consumers and data collection (e.g., customer loyalty instruments and collection of data regarding buyer's behaviour and product feedback). This acquisition also granted several advantages normally reserved to retailers and that contributed to the dominant position retailers possess nowadays in comparison to manufacturers.[4]

Distribution Strategies

In the early days of the Fly London brand, the distribution strategy was based on partnerships with independent local distributors. At the time, Kyaia was pursuing a strategy of seizing opportunities offered by the exchange of contacts with reliable suppliers in international trade fairs, rather than following an explicit going-international strategy. As a result, its market entry decisions very much depended on the origin of the contacted distributors.

At a later stage, the distribution of Fly London was subcontracted to a specific distributor possessing extensive market knowledge and access to an already established network of retailers and agents. This distributor was responsible for selecting retailers, hiring agents, planning trade fair events and organizing marketing campaigns. Despite this move, Kyaia's still controlled the value chain by closely monitoring and supporting the distributor, and exerting a strong influence on the definition of the marketing strategies.

With the growth of the Fly London brand and the strengthening of the financial resources, the Kyaia Group evolved its distribution strategy towards a multiple distribution channel system (Figure 3). This strategy comprises both indirect distribution (through agents, distributors and retailers) and direct distribution (Factory Outlets, B2C E-Commerce and own retail stores).

Concerning indirect distribution, although Kyaia still makes use of independent distributors, it has in addition incorporated distributors which are co-owned by the Group. Consistent with this, Kyaia has taken a stake in local distributors in Luxemburg, Denmark, India and Spain in the form of FDI's, which are controlled from Kyaia's head

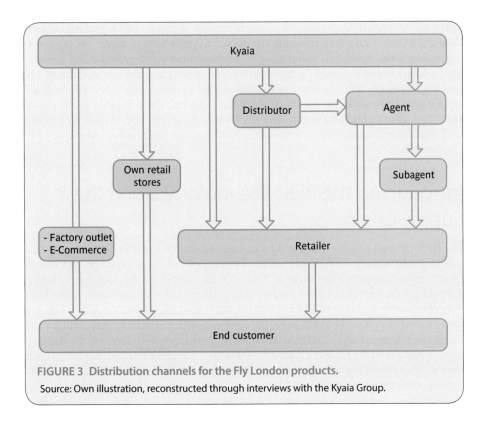

FIGURE 3 Distribution channels for the Fly London products.
Source: Own illustration, reconstructed through interviews with the Kyaia Group.

office in Portugal. The distributors either distribute directly to retailers or engage agents that are responsible for selecting and distributing to the retailers. In some cases, depending on the amount of retailers in the market, these agents in turn have subagents. In any case, the firm does not give up of its control over the distribution channels.

Besides indirect distribution, Kyaia also applies direct distribution channels in forms of Factory Outlets, B2C E-Commerce and own retail stores. Since there are no intermediaries involved, Kyaia sells directly to the end customer and therefore increases its profit margin. Furthermore, the E-Commerce B2C distribution channel provides Kyaia with the possibility to offer Fly London's wide range of products without any shelf space constraints and to receive orders for products which are out of stock at a particular time. Hence, the end customer can take a virtual look at products that may not be available at that time, but which can be ordered and shipped in a period of about three weeks.

Even though Fly London's target consumers are young and very active online, online sales do not replace Fly London's traditional distribution. In particular, shoes are products that many consumers like to touch and feel before making a purchase decision. In summary, Kyaia's B2C E-commerce direct marketing channel is a useful extension of the traditional distribution channels, but the latter still reflects at its best the buying habits of the Fly London end customers.

Beside the online shops, Kyaia sells directly to the end customer through its Factory Outlet, which is located at the production facilities in Guimaraes. The goal of the outlet is to minimize losses from unsold and overstocked products from the different brands, especially Foreva, Sapatalia and Fungi, which are taking up valuable store space. Instead of taking a complete loss on these products, Kyaia sells them off for a discount price.

The Fly London's flagship own retail stores that were recently opened in three major European cities play a special position in Kyaia's distribution strategy. These stores are located in first class locations in Lisbon, London and Copenhagen with Berlin and Barcelona being currently considered as potential candidates for the opening of additional stores. An important goal of these stores is to promote and upgrade Fly London's brand image. As a consequence, the stores carry the whole range of Fly London's products in an exclusive environment with qualified employees, who capture and forward the customers' feedback about the products. Thus, flagship stores play a key role in distributing and positioning Fly London as an upmarket brand. Consistent with this, the mid-range network of Foreva and Sapatalia stores is not used to sell Fly London shoes.

Introducing the RFID Technology along the Supply Chain

The RFID project was led by a Portuguese company called Creative Systems, specialized in implementing RFID applications. The purpose of the Shoe ID project was to explore possible application areas of the RDIF technology in the footwear industry, from the production facilities to the PoS. The pilot project was conducted in the flagship store of Fly London in Lisbon. During the manufacturing process, Fly London shoes intended to be sold at the store, get equipped with a RDIF tag that included the item's stock-keeping unit (SKU), style and size. When the shoes arrive at the flagship store, handheld RFID readers capture the individual tag identification number of each shoe without direct line of sight and without the need to open the shoebox. The information collected by handheld devices is sent via Wi-Fi to the stores software, where the inventory records are continuously updated. Hence, the tag improves supply chain management by providing the store's management with information about the current status of what is in stock, what is in the sales area, and what needs to be reordered.

Kyaia also makes use of the RDIF technology in innovative solutions concerning consumer's interaction with the products in stores. At the flagship store in Lisbon, customers see a projection of themselves on a screen when they try on a pair of shoes. This screen does not simply reproduce the image of the customer wearing the shoes, but also gives the illusion that he/she is in a crowded street in New York, Tokyo or London. Which city is displayed in the background, depends on the style of the shoe the customer is trying on. The technology behind this feature is based on an interactive floor with a built-in RFID reader and antenna. The moment a customer wearing a tagged shoe steps on the floor, the unique identification number of the specific shoe is captured by the antenna via the RFID technology. This number is sent by radio signal to the store's software, which decodes the signal and categorizes the shoe on the basis of its style into the previously mentioned three cities. A signal is then sent back to the video unit that in turn portrays a live image on a flat screen of the customer in the corresponding city.

The aim of this innovation is to add value in-store by augmenting the shopping experience of the customer. This enhanced experience prolongs the stay of the customer in the store and strengthens Fly London's image as a differentiated and innovative footwear brand. As a result of its success, in 2011 the Kyaia's RFID project received the European technology award in the category 'Best Enterprise Solution of the Year'.[5]

The Single-sequence Production Technology

A key part of Kyaia's manufacturing strategic re-orientation towards low volume, customized products was the development of the single-sequence shoe production technology. The objective of the technology is to enable all the tasks associated with the production of a shoe (from cutting to assembly) to occur in a single sequence in the manufacturing line, regardless of shoe type. The system comprises an internal ring, an external ring and crossovers which allow for different routes, customized for each specific type of shoe build. When no tasks are executed on a shoe, the system automatically bypasses the associated work posts. Hence, it is possible to mix different shoe styles and sizes requiring different types of operations in one sequence. The implementation involved a new automated system and software, which in combination with the use of RIDF tags, minimizes hold ups, downtimes and work-in-progress inventory.

Exhibit 4 illustrates the results of the technology after being in use in the Kyaia factory for 9 months. Before the new system was implemented, the Kyaia Group was able to produce only one shoe model at a given time. Thanks to the one step production process, Kyaia is now capable of producing four different shoe models simultaneously. Although the energy costs increased from 2 EUR to 7 EUR per hour the benefits clearly outweighed the costs and the payback period for the initial investment of 100 000 Euro was only 24 months.

Conclusion

This case describes how a firm located in a country that was, for many years, associated with labour cost competitive advantages in the footwear industry, managed to shift from a undifferentiated product, mainly sold through subcontracting, to an internationally competitive firm selling futuristic shoes with a high design content. Much of this shift was accomplished by a strong investment in internationalization and value chain strategies. This move emerged as a response to fierce competition from Asian producers and consisted of strong differentiation through product design, quality and an upmarket positioning of the brands. This was complemented by the hiring of designers of different ages, nationalities and backgrounds, who, based on their own countries and immersed in their own cultural background, conduct research on the new market trends, visit fairs, shops, discos and so on, looking for inspiration. These strategic market moves were matched by consistent investments in suitable manufacturing processes, oriented towards low volume production of a high variety of products. Subsequently, Kyaia emphasized the establishment of strong global brands with high added value targeting the more demanding, but also more valuable market segments. Several attempts were made until the Kyaia Group finally accomplished an international breakthrough with its brand Fly London.

The success of the Fly London brand generated sufficient financial resources that were invested in gaining increased control of the value chain by means of backward and forward vertical integrations at the national and international level. By linking, integrating and coordinating all activities along the chain, the Group was able to

---

EXHIBIT 4: Before and after the implementation of the single-sequence production technology

	Before the implementation	After the implementation
Type of shoe construction produced simultaneously	1	4
Pairs produced per day		+25%
Time in production (making and finishing)		−45%
Stock in production		−90%
Number of operators	26	26
Energy consumption/hour	2€	7€
Machine utilization	70%	95%

Source: Mr. Lufs Gongalves, Public Relations, Kyaia, Guimaraes, e-mail message to author, March 22, 2011.

capture most of the chain's value. Throughout the process, Kyaia understood the crucial importance of international events in the world of fashion products, since fashion trends are defined outside of the local production system in metropolises like Milan and Paris. The Group invested heavily in the presence in international trade fairs, generating brand awareness and creating business connections that proved critical for the development of commercialisation and distribution networks. This combined approach designed to focus on value creation is responsible for a sales turnover of 64 million Euros, with the Kyaia shoes being sold in more than 1500 points of sales all around the world. These are unquestionably 'shoes that fly off the shelves'.

Printed with permission from authors and www.ecch.com.

References

Alfaia, Catarina. 'A mosca do calgado.' *Marketeer,* November 2010: 46–48.

Apiccaps. Footwear, Components and Leather Godds – Statistical Study 2010. Porto: Publicagoes Apiccaps Gabinete do Estudos, 2010.

Guimarães, Jose E. 'Kyaia Datasheet (Paper presented at the 25th anniversary of the Kyaia company).' Guimarães, 2009.

Instalação Profissional. 'Kyaia integra tecnologia RFID premiada na Europa.' 2011: 28.

Vale, Mário, Caldeira, Josué. 'Fashion and the Governance of Knowledge in a traditional Industry: The Case of the Footwear Sectoral Innovation System in the northern Region of Portugal.' *Econ. Innov. New Techn.* 17, Nos. 1&2, 2008: 61–78.

Respondents

Head of the Marketing Department, Kyaia – Fortunato O. Frederico SGPS S.A, Guimarães, personal interview on the 18th of May 2011.

Luis Gonçalves, Public Relations, Kyaia – Fortunato O. Frederico SGPS S.A, Guimarães, personal interview on the 4th of March 2011.

ENDNOTES

1. Guimarães Jose E., 'Kyaia datasheet' (Paper presented at the 25th anniversary of the Kyaia Group, Guimarães, 2009): 55.
2. Catarina Alfaia, 'A mosca do calgado,' *Marketeer,* 72 (2010): 47.
3. Vale, Mario, and Josué Caldeira. 'Fashion and the Governance of Knowledge in a traditional Industry: The Case of the Footwear Sectoral Innovation System in the northern Region of Portugal.' *Econ. Innov. New Techn.* 17, nos. 1&2, 2008: 75–78.
4. Guimaraes Jose E., 'Kyaia datasheet' (Paper presented at the 25th anniversary of the Kyaia Group, Guimaraes, 2009): 21–23.
5. Instalação Profissional 35 (2011): 28.

Case 12

Microsoft's strategic alliance with Nokia[*]

I am excited about this partnership with Nokia. Ecosystems thrive when fueled by speed, innovation, and scale. The partnership announced today provides incredible scale, vast expertise in hardware and software innovation, and a proven ability to execute.[1]

Steven A. Ballmer, Microsoft CEO, on February 11, 2011

I do want a strong third OS out there. It gives the carriers more flexibility and balances the interests of all the parties. But I still have doubts whether Microsoft will get the traction they are hoping for with Windows Phone 7.[2]

Tony Melone, Verizon Communications[3] CTO, on February 17, 2011

Joining Forces in the Smartphone Wars

In September 2011, Microsoft Corp. (Microsoft), the US-based computing industry major, and Nokia Corp. (Nokia),[4] the Finland-based communication company, launched a toolkit that would allow developers to port Symbian operating system (OS)[5] applications to the Windows Phone OS. The package was expected to help Symbian developers learn to develop Windows Phone. 'This helpful package contains the tools and documentation to help you along the path to learning Windows Phone development',[6] said Jean-Christophe Cimetiere, senior technical evangelist, Microsoft.

Earlier in February 2011, Microsoft had entered into a strategic alliance with Nokia. The alliance envisaged combining the traditional strengths of the two companies to create synergies. In the face of stiff competition from Google's Android[7] and Apple's iOS[8], Microsoft' s share in the mobile OS market had been shrinking. And Nokia was struggling to compete with Samsung Electronics (Samsung),[9] Apple,[10] and HTC Corp.[11] in the smartphone market as most buyers perceived its Symbian OS as being outdated and lacking in many of the features that were available in competing operating systems. The strategic alliance was expected to help the two companies build a new mobile eco-system. Nokia was to gradually migrate away from the Symbian OS to Windows Phone. It was hoped that Nokia Windows Phones would offer a compelling alternative to prospective smartphone customers.

With Google, Inc.[12] purchasing Motorola Mobility[13] in August 2011, the smartphone market seemed to be in the middle of a profound change. Barring Microsoft, all major OS vendors now had a presence in the smartphone hardware market. According to some analysts, this could be disadvantageous for Microsoft. As Nokia

* This case was written by **Sachin Govind**, under the direction of **Debapratim Purkayastha**, IBS Hyderabad. It was compiled from published sources, and is intended to be used as a basis for class discussion rather than to illustrate either effective or ineffective handling of a management situation.

© 2012, IBS Center for Management Research.

had a negligible presence in the US, the world's largest smartphone market, industry observers felt that it would be an uphill task for Microsoft and the alliance to make headway there. Also, with Google and Apple succeeding in creating a thriving ecosystem of apps, it was felt that it would be extremely difficult for a third entity to challenge their hegemony.

About Microsoft

Bill Gates (Gates) dropped out of Harvard University to establish Micro-soft in 1975 in a hotel room in Albuquerque, New Mexico. Initially, Gates, together with high school friend Paul Allen (Allen), developed a version of BASIC, a programming language. The duo sold the modified version of the software to other companies.

In 1979, Gates shifted Micro-soft to his hometown Seattle. In 1980, IBM Corp.[14] selected the firm, which by then had been renamed Microsoft, to develop the operating system for its new computing machines. Later, Gates purchased QDOS (Quick & Dirty Operating System) for $50 000 from a programmer. He called it MS-DOS (Microsoft Disk Operating System). In 1983, Allen resigned from Microsoft on health grounds.

In the mid-1980s, Microsoft launched Windows, a graphics-based version of MS-DOS. In 1986, the company went public. Windows NT was launched in 1993; the newer version competed with the UNIX operating system. In the early 1990s, the company was embroiled in legal battles as monopoly charges had been pressed against it. In 1995, the US Department of Justice (DoJ) objected to Microsoft's proposed acquisition of Intuit, a company that developed software for the personal finance industry, on antitrust concerns.

Microsoft was a little late in jumping on to the Internet bandwagon. In 1995, the company launched Microsoft Network (MSN). It also introduced the Internet Explorer, a web browser, in that year. In 1998, the DoJ filed antitrust charges against Microsoft, contending that the Seattle-based company limited consumer choice in the Internet browser market by choking competition. In the same year, Gates appointed Steve Ballmer (Ballmer) as the president.

In 1999, Microsoft announced that it would purchase a minority stake in AT&T[15] for $5 billion. Microsoft also bought Visio, a company that specialized in Windows-based technical drawing software, for $1.3 billion. In the [same] year, it sold [its] stake in Expedia to the public.

In 2000, Ballmer replaced Gates as CEO. Gates continued as chairman; he also gave himself the title of chief software architect. In the same year, Microsoft entered into an agreement with the DoJ. Under this, the company agreed to 'uniformly license' its Windows operating systems, include competing software in its operating system, and stop offering exclusive contracts with manufacturers.

In 2002, Netscape Communications[16] sued Microsoft, seeking damages and injunctions against the company's alleged antitrust actions. In 2003, Microsoft decided to settle the private antitrust suit filed by Netscape; it agreed to pay AOL, Netscape's parent company, $750 million.

In 2003, the company declared dividends for the first time. In 2004, it stated that it would repurchase up to $30 billion of its own stock over the next four years.

In 2005, the company reorganized its divisions in an effort to improve decision-making and execution abilities. After the reorganization, the company's units included Microsoft Business (Information Worker Group, Microsoft Business Solutions), Microsoft Platform Products and Services (Windows Client Group, Server and Tools Group, MSN), and Entertainment and Devices (Home and Entertainment Group, Mobile and Embedded Devices Group).

In 2005, the company made a series of acquisitions. It purchased FolderShare (file synchronization specialist), Groove Networks, a collaboration software developer, Alacris (specializing in identity management software), Sybari Software, a company that developed anti-virus technology, FrontBridge Technologies (specializing in email security), and media-streams.com, a developer of Voice over Internet Protocol technology.

In 2007, Microsoft acquired aQuantive for about $6 billion. This was to strengthen its presence in the online advertising and search market, where Google was making rapid strides. In October 2007, Microsoft entered into a strategic alliance with Facebook, a social networking site. The deal involved expanding the advertising partnership that the companies had entered into. Microsoft was also to purchase a minority equity stake in Facebook for $240 million.

In 2008, Microsoft acquired Fast Search & Transfer ASA (FAST), a technology company that specialized in Internet search and business intelligence applications, for around $1.2 billion. This move was expected to strengthen the company's enterprise search offerings.

In the mid-2000s, Microsoft settled its legal disputes with Sun Microsystems (paid $1.6 billion and agreed to pay royalty on certain technologies), Novell (paid $536 million to settle a suit tied to Novell's NetWare software), Gateway (paid $150 million), IBM (paid $775 million), and RealNetworks ($761 million in cash and promotions).

In 2007–2008, Microsoft joined hands with Hewlett-Packard (HP), a major computer hardware and software company, and Motorola, a US-based mobile devices maker, to develop mobile phones and tablets that used Microsoft Windows Mobile and Windows Media software. In order to strengthen Windows Mobile, the company also acquired Parlano, a chat specialist, Multimap, a company that specialized in online mapping services, and Danger, a mobile software developer, in this period.

In 2008, Microsoft offered to acquire Yahoo![17] repeatedly in an attempt to strengthen its Internet search services so as to compete better with Google. However, Yahoo!'s board of directors rejected the multiple offers.

In 2009, Microsoft revamped its search business; it launched a new search engine called bing.com, which replaced its Live Search product. The same year, Yahoo! and Microsoft signed a 10-year agreement, which involved Microsoft taking charge of the search engine function on Yahoo!. Yahoo! would receive 88% of all search-related advertising revenue for the first five years.

Microsoft and the Mobile OS Space

Microsoft entered the mobile operating software (OS) market on April 19, 2000, with the launch of Pocket PC 2000 (codenamed Rapier). This software, based on Windows CE 3.0,[18] was meant for Pocket PC devices.[19] The OS came with Pocket Office, Pocket Internet Explorer, Microsoft Reader (software that allowed users to read e-books), Windows Media Player, Notes (note-taking application), Microsoft Money (personal finance software), etc.

In October 2001, Microsoft launched Pocket PC 2002, an improved version of Pocket PC 2000. This software was also based on Windows CE 3.0. For the first time, this OS was used on smartphones. The new version had a host of features such as Enhanced UI,[20] VPN[21] support, MSN Messenger, Pocket Outlook, in addition to updated versions of Pocket Office, Microsoft Reader, and Windows Media Player.

In June 2003, Microsoft launched a new OS under the 'Microsoft Windows Mobile' banner. Windows Mobile 2003, as it was called, came in four editions[22] and included features such as Bluetooth headset support, support for add-on keyboards, SMS reply options, etc.

In the first quarter of 2004, Microsoft launched Windows Mobile 2003 Second Edition. This edition came with portrait and landscaping switching, support for higher resolution of up to 640x480, Wi-Fi Protected Access support, etc.

Windows Mobile 5 (codenamed Magneto) was officially launched in May 2005. This edition featured a newer version of Pocket Office called Office Mobile. It also had nifty features such as photo caller ID, default QWERTY keyboard support, picture and video package, etc.

In February 2007, Microsoft launched Windows Mobile 6. This version supported higher screen resolution of up to 800x480 and came with features like VoIP support, improved Internet sharing, etc. Between April 2008 and January 2010, the company introduced WM 6.1, WM 6.5, WM 6.5.1, and WM 6.5.3, with new features and improved functionality.

On October 21, 2010, Microsoft launched Windows Phone 7 in Australia, Singapore, and Europe; and later, on November 08, 2010, it launched the software in the US, and Canada. According to reports, Microsoft had initially planned to launch WM 7, an updated version of WM 6.5.3. However, unexpected delays and rapidly changing competition compelled the company to launch Phone 7, based on a completely new platform.

The Changing Mobile OS Market

In 2003, when Microsoft launched WM 2003, Palm Inc.[23] was the leader in the smartphone market. Palm devices used proprietary software, called Palm OS. However, companies like HP, Hitachi, and Dell incorporated Pocket PC 2002 or Mobile 2003 in their smartphone models. In the first quarter of 2004, Microsoft was able to capture 40 per cent of the smartphone OS market. By the third quarter, sales of Microsoft CE-based phones exceeded that of Palm OS phones.

In the mid-2000s, Nokia's Symbian OS and the Blackberry OS of Research in Motion's (RIM)[24] made rapid strides. Later, the smartphone market saw the entry of new players who would transform the market in a matter of a few years. Starting in 2007, Symbian's market share in the smartphone space began to slide with the entry of Apple and Google in the mobile software space.

In January 2007, Steve Jobs, CEO, Apple, Inc., launched the iPhone. The iPhone operated on Mac OS (iOS), a proprietary technology. Apple made a huge splash in the smartphone market with the iPhone, with hundreds of people crowding stores all over the US to buy these touch-screen devices. The company sold around 6 million units of the original iPhone over five quarters. In July 2008, an updated version of the original iPhone, called iPhone 3G, was launched in 22 countries around the world. Subsequently, the company launched iPhone 3GS in June 2009 and iPhone 4 in June 2010. By early 2012, the company had sold more than 100 million iPhones.

Meanwhile, in November 2007, Google founded the Open Handset Alliance (OHA),[25] a consortium of more than 80 companies in the software, hardware, and telecommunication space. The alliance was meant to develop open standards for mobile devices. Earlier in 2005, Google had acquired Android Inc., the original developer of Android OS. The Android OS was based on the Linux[26] kernel, with middleware[27] and APIs[28] written in C.[29] The Android code was released by Google under the Apache License, a free software license. Although the search engine giant would not be paid for the license, the company expected to earn ad revenues by extending its search application to mobile devices. All Android-based phones would come embedded with Google Search.

EXHIBIT I (a): Worldwide OS market shares based on smartphone sales

OS vendor	2007	2008	2009	2010	Q1 2011	Q2 2011	Q3 2011
Symbian	63.5%	52.4%	46.9%	37.6%	27.4%	22%	16.9%
Android	N/A	0.5%	3.9%	22.7%	36%	43%	52.5%
BBOS	9.6%	16.6%	19.9%	16.0%	12.9%	12%	11%
iOS(Apple)	2.7%	8.2%	14.4%	15.7%	16.8%	18%	15%
Windows Phone	**12%**	**11.8%**	**8.7%**	**4.2%**	**3.6%**	**2%**	**1.5%**
Others	12.1%	10.5%	6.1%	3.8%	3.3%	1%	1.4%

Source: Gartner.

EXHIBIT I (b): Smartphone market shares in the US by OS

OS vendor	Q1 2010	Q3 2010	Q3 2011	Q4 2011
Symbian	10.1%		1.8%	1.4%
Android	19.0%	43.6%	44.8%	47.3%
BBOS	32.5%	24.2%	18.9%	16.0%
iOS	21.1%	26.2%	27.4%	29.6%
Windows Phone	**12.8%**	**3.0%**	**5.6%**	**4.7%**
Others	4.5%		1.4%	1.0%

Source: ComScore, Canalys.

In April 2010, HP announced that it would acquire Palm for $1 billion. Later in July 2010, HP completed the acquisition.

The global smartphone market expanded rapidly in the mid to late 2000s. However, Microsoft was unable to cash in on this growth. The market share of Google's Android, Apple's iOS, and RIM's Blackberry OS in the smartphone market increased at the expense of Microsoft Windows Mobile and Symbian, Nokia's mobile OS **(Refer to Exhibit I (a) for Worldwide OS market shares by smartphone sales between 2007 and 2011 and to I (b) for US smartphone market shares by OS)**.

Apple's iPhone was a game changer. In addition to the sleek design, nifty operating system, and attractive features, customers found the thousands of applications or apps particularly appealing. These apps were developed by third party vendors and were sold by Apple on iTunes, the company's online market place. Google, too, was successful in creating an ecosystem of app developers and an online market place.

According to a report released by Canalys,[30] global smartphone sales in Q3 2010 touched 81 million units, clocking 95 percent growth, compared to the corresponding period in 2009. Sales of Android-based phones reached 20 million units in the quarter, up 1309 percent compared to the same period the previous year. Top smartphone makers such as HTC, Samsung, Sony Ericsson, Motorola, etc., marketed a range of Android-based mobile phones at various price points, which helped the platform grow at the blistering pace that it did. 'Google is being far more aggressive in building its platform than Microsoft ever was',[31] said Bill Gurley, a partner at Benchmark Capital.[32]

With iPhone 4 doing well, Apple was able to garner 17 percent of the worldwide market for smartphones in the period. RIM took 15 percent of the smartphone market. While Nokia's Symbian led the pack with a 33 percent market share, it was rapidly losing ground to Android and iOS. According to the report, sales of Microsoft-based phones accounted for a mere 3 percent of smartphones shipped. Speaking on

Microsoft's problems, David Roberts, chief executive of *PopCap*, a games developer, said, 'Microsoft has a perception problem. Everyone thinks of them as a distant third, but they've got a good product'.[33]

Microsoft and Nokia Forge Strategic Alliance

On February 11, 2011, Nokia and Microsoft announced a roadmap for a broad strategic partnership. The partnership was to exploit the strengths of both companies and 'build a new mobile eco-system'. The proposed partnership included the following:

- Nokia would largely use Windows Phone OS for its smartphone models. The Finnish company would develop enhancements on top of the platform in areas such as imaging, where it was a market leader.
- Nokia would use its hardware design, language support capabilities, and its global reach to develop Windows Phone-based smartphones at various price points, and in diverse market segments and regions.
- Nokia and Microsoft would work together on joint marketing initiatives
- The two companies would share a 'development roadmap'.
- Bing, Microsoft's search engine, would be integrated into Nokia devices and services. Microsoft adCenter would provide search advertising services on Nokia's line of devices and services.
- Nokia Maps would be at the center of Microsoft's mapping services.
- Nokia's extensive operator billing agreements were expected to allow consumers to purchase Nokia Windows Phone services with ease, especially in countries where credit-card use was low.
- Microsoft development tools would be used to create applications to run on Nokia Windows Phones.
- Nokia's content and application store would be assimilated into Microsoft Marketplace.

Although Microsoft did not say if the deal included cash payments, some media reports indicated that the software giant would pay $1 billion to Nokia for R&D, promotion, technology royalties, etc., in the next five years.[34] Nokia would start paying royalty to Microsoft once it started selling phones installed with Windows Phone.

In an open letter, which seemed more like a war cry, Nokia CEO Stephen Elop (Elop) and Microsoft CEO Steve Balmer stated, 'There are other mobile ecosystems. We will disrupt them. There will be challenges. We will overcome them. Success requires speed. We will be swift. Together, we see the opportunity, and we have the will, the resources, and the drive to succeed'.[35]

In the days following the announcement, Elop, who had earlier headed the Business Division at Microsoft, explained how the partnership would be taken forward. Elop stated that he expected to sell about 150 million Symbian-based phones before the OS was abandoned. Nokia would launch the first Windows Phone-based smartphone in the last quarter of 2011. The new phones would have map apps by Navteq,[36] location-based services and advertising, Bing search, Xbox Live, and Zune Music.[37] The changes that Nokia would introduce to WP7 would be available to other handset vendors.

Elop declared that he would cut jobs at Nokia; however, he did not specify how many jobs would be cut. He hinted that Nokia may not make profits while the Symbian-to-Windows Phone transition took place **(Refer to Exhibit II for financial information on Nokia)**. And when Elop was asked if Nokia would enter the tablet market, he was evasive. 'We aren't announcing *today* a specific tablet strategy. We could see the advantages of a family [of devices] that uses the Microsoft ecosystem',[38] he said. He said that Nokia Windows Phone devices would start shipping in volume in 2012. In

EXHIBIT II: Financial information on Nokia

Mn €	2007	2008	2009	2010	Q2 2011
Net sales	51 058	50 710	40 984	42 446	9275
Operating profit	7985	4966	1197	2070	−487
Profit before taxes	8268	4970	962	1786	–

Source: http://investors.nokia.com.

June 2011, he gave a sneak preview of the first Nokia Windows Phone, dubbed 'Sea Ray'.

Microsoft's and Nokia's announcement on forging a special relationship sparked interest and debates in the mobile phone industry. Google's VP, Vic Gundotra, tweeted 'Two turkeys do not make an eagle',[39] hinting that the partnership would not have any impact on the market.

According to some analysts, the partnership between Microsoft and Nokia was a win-win arrangement (Refer to Table 1 for a brief overview on strategic alliances). Nokia was the largest mobile device maker with global reach and proven product development skills, they said. The Finnish company was also expected to contribute software and services to the Windows Phone platform.

In April 2011, in a press release,[40] Gartner, Inc., a leading research firm, forecast market shares of major mobile OS vendors by the year 2015. In what seemed like an endorsement of the Nokia-Microsoft deal, the research firm predicted that the Windows Phone OS would garner close to 20% market share by 2015, from around 4% in 2010. According to the report, the Android OS would have the largest market share, rising from 23% in 2010 to 49% in 2015. In June 2011, IDC, another research firm, predicted that Microsoft might hold a 20.3% market share in 2015.

However, there were others who weren't convinced that the strategic alliance with Nokia would help Microsoft in reviving its fortunes in the mobile OS market. Some industry analysts felt that the two companies did not have any choice but to come together. 'They're like the two people left at the end of the disco who think 'oh, you'll do', said one industry observer.[41]

According to some analysts, the success of an OS depended on the number of applications or apps that it supported. As smartphone users had taken to apps in a big way **(Refer to Exhibit III for a list of popular apps)**, the OS that offered a good choice of apps would win more customers, it was argued. iOS with around 300 000 third-party apps[42] and Android with around 200 000 third-party apps[43] were in a very comfortable position as far as apps were concerned, whereas Windows Phone 7 offered

EXHIBIT III: Popular mobile applications

Mobile app	OS vendor
1. Facebook, Angry Birds Lite, Words with Friends Free, Skype, Doodle Jump, Fruit Ninja, Gamebox 1	Apple iOS
2. Gmail, Google Maps, Flash Player 10.1, Angry Birds, Facebook for Android	Android
3. Mp3 ringtone creator, Relaxing sounds, A+ Picture Effects and Photo Editor, Catapult, Doodles	Blackberry OS
4. Fruit Ninja, Need for Speed Undercover, Crackdown 2, The Oregon Trail HD	Windows Phone 7

Sources: http:appworld.blackberry.com, www.independent.co.uk, and www.techcrunch.com.

EXHIBIT IV: Legal suits among OS vendors

	Complainant	Defendant	Date	Issue
1	Apple	HTC	02.03.2010	Infringement of 20 Apple patents relating to user interface, architecture, and hardware
2	Apple	Nokia	12.12.2009	Infringement of 13 patents relating to touch-screen scroll
3	Nokia	Apple	October 2009	Infringement of 10 patents relating to wireless data, speech coding, security, and encryption
4	Nokia	Samsung	December 2009	Colluding to fix prices of Liquid Crystal Displays
5	Nokia	Qualcomm	2005–2007	Infringement of patents relating to mobile downloading of software apps and mobile TV broadcasts
6	Qualcomm	Nokia	November 2005	Infringement of 12 patents relating to manufacture of equipment that complies with the GPRS, GSM, EDGE standards
7	RIM	Motorola	December 2008	For not allowing former Motorola employees from working for RIM

Sources: www.theregister.co.uk, www.nytimes.com, news.cnet.com, www.businessweek.com, and www.engadget.com.

less than one-tenth of what Apple offered. According to analysts, Microsoft and Nokia were not doing enough to woo third-party developers. And third-party app developers would not want to develop apps for a platform that had no takers.

Nokia's decision to kill the Symbian OS came in for some flak. When Nokia's employees at Tampere, Finland, learnt that the Symbian would be killed off, over a thousand of them staged a walk-out in protest. Analysts were of the view that most Symbian developers would probably now develop apps for iOS or Android rather than for Nokia Windows Phone.

According to industry observers, the two companies would find it hard to increase Windows Phone's market share in the US, where the Nokia's smartphone market share had shrunk to a little more than 1% **(Refer to Exhibit IV for smartphone shipments by OS vendor in the US)**. According to analysts, Nokia brand value in the US, the largest smartphone market in the world, had eroded and it may be next to impossible to recover lost ground.

In July 2011, Microsoft announced the launch of a new version of Windows Phone OS, called Mango. The first Nokia Windows Phone was expected to be based on this latest version of Windows Phone.

Google Buys Motorola Mobility

In August 2011, Google purchased Motorola Mobility for $12.5 billion. According to analysts, the search engine giant took this step in response to the legal threats by

EXHIBIT V: Microsoft's five-year financial highlights

Mn $	2007	2008	2009	2010	2011
Net sales	51 122	60 420	58 437	62 484	69 943
Operating income	18 438	22 271	20 363	24 098	27 161
Net income	14 065	17 681	14 569	18 760	23 150

Source: www.microsoft.com.

Microsoft and Apple. 'Google gets Motorola Mobility's portfolio (17,000 patents) … it may position Google to defend itself against more fundamental IP attacks, and increase counter-threat and leverage in global patent negotiations and litigation',[44] said Mike Abramsky, an analyst at RBC Capital Markets.[45] According to analysts, Google's purchase of Motorola Mobility, a leading manufacturer of cable set-tops and mobile phones, was expected to help it extend its search business to cable TV and mobile devices.

Google's decision to acquire Motorola ruffled more than a few feathers. Some OHA members, such as Samsung Electronics, now started to regard Google as a potential rival. According to Korean media reports,[46] Chairman Lee Kun-hee asked top Samsung executives to take steps to improve the company's software abilities. Lee was also reported to have said that Samsung should pay attention to the fact that IT power was moving away from hardware companies to software companies.[47] Samsung had developed its own OS, christened Bada; however, the Korean giant's Android-based smartphone models made up the lion's share of its global smartphone sales. Samsung also sold phones running Microsoft's Windows Mobile.

Verizon Communications, an important US-based carrier, did not explicitly endorse the deal. However, John Thorne, Verizon's senior vice president and deputy general counsel, hoped that the acquisition would stop the legal wrangles among the OS vendors **(Refer to Exhibit V for legal suits among mobile OS vendors)**. 'We will be looking with interest as further details of the proposed transaction become clear. But, at first glance, to the extent that this deal might bring some stability to the ongoing smartphone patent disputes, that would be a welcome development'.[48]

Following HP's decision to stop selling devices with its WebOS software, it was expected that the number of application developers for Windows Phone would increase. HP was expected to sell off WebOS (formerly Palm OS).

The Road Ahead

In 2010, Microsoft had reported net income of nearly $19 billion, up from around $15 billion in 2009 **(Refer to Exhibit VI for Microsoft's 5-year financials and a comparison of financials of Microsoft, Apple, and Google).** Microsoft was betting big on online services, search, entertainment, mobile computing, cloud computing, etc. However, in the mobile OS market, the company continued to cede market share to Apple and Google in 2010 and in 2011.

In May 2011, Microsoft entered into handset agreements with Acer Inc., Fujitsu Ltd. and ZTE Corp. It also announced that it would add around 500 features in the fall release of Windows Phone 7, christened Mango. The newest version would include functions such as extended voice recognition for writing, face detection in photos, and support for 15 additional European and Asian languages. Mango would also allow users to synchronize Microsoft Office documents with cloud versions in Microsoft's Office 365 and SkyDrive.

EXHIBIT VI: Comparison of financials of Microsoft, Apple and Google for 2010

	Microsoft	Apple	Google
Annual sales (in millions)	$69 943	$65 225	$29 321
Employees	89 000	49 400	24 400
Market cap (in millions)	$199 450.68	$259 906.50	$188 747.03
Profitability			
Gross profit margin	77.73%	39.82%	65.18%
Pre-tax profit margin	40.13%	30.78%	34.01%
Net profit margin	33.10%	23.53%	27.05%
Return on equity	44.84%	41.99%	19.47%
Return on assets	23.77%	27.53%	15.97%
Return on invested cap	38.23%	41.99%	17.85%
Valuation			
Price/sales ratio	3.10	3.48	5.41
Price/earnings ratio	9.36	14.79	20.00
Price/book ratio	3.70	5.00	3.46
Price/cash flow ratio	8.02	10.65	13.42
Operations			
Days of sales o/s	73.06	17.37	42.62
Inventory turnover	14.75	65.94	–
Days cost of goods sold in inventory	24.74	5.53	–
Asset turnover	0.72	1.17	0.59
Net receivables turnover flow	5.00	21.01	8.56
Effective tax rate	17.53%	23.54%	20.47%
Financial			
Current ratio	2.6	2.01	4.16
Quick ratio	2.35	1.72	4.00
Leverage ratio	1.90	1.57	1.25
Total debt/equity	0.21	–	0.07
Interest coverage	96.16	–	–
Per share data			
Revenue per share	$8.14	$107.41	$103.10
Dividend per share	$0.61	$0	–
Cash flow per share	$3.14	$35.10	$40.53
Working capital per share	$5.51	$22.60	$97.76
Growth			
12-month revenue growth	11.94%	52.02%	23.98%
12-month net income growth	23.4%	70.16%	30.44%
12-month EPS growth	28.10%	66.85%	28.91%
12-month dividend growth	17.31%	–	–

Source: www.hoovers.com.

In July 2011, at the Microsoft Windows Partner Conference, Andy Lees, president of the Windows Phone Division, explained the new benefits for Microsoft partners. He said, 'This is a really exciting time for Windows Phone. With Windows Phone 7 and our upcoming 'Mango' release, we bring a familiar platform and tools together with the breadth of Microsoft products to help partners scale and reach new customers. This represents a huge opportunity for partners to thrive and grow their business in the rapidly expanding Windows Phone ecosystem'.[49] Lees said that the number of

Windows Phone applications had increased from 8000 in February 2011 to more than 22 000 in July 2011. He further stated that vigorous efforts would be made to expand the Windows Phone ecosystem further.

In late October, Nokia launched two new Windows Phone 7-based mobile phones in the UK. Christened Lumia 800 (US\$ 584) and Lumia 710 (US\$ 375), the phones sported a fresh look **(Refer to Exhibit VII for images of Lumia phones)** and came with applications such as Nokia Drive, a voice guided navigation application, and Nokia Music, a music service. The phones were initially sold in Europe and later were launched in China, India, and other emerging markets. Meanwhile, Nokia's market share in the smartphone market continued to fall **(Refer to Exhibit VIII for smartphone market shares by manufacturer).** Nokia launched these models in the US in January 2012. Initial reports indicated that the Windows Phone-based phones failed to make an impact in the market. These new devices were based on a

EXHIBIT VII: Photo of Nokia's Lumia series phones

Source: www.online.wsj.com.

EXHIBIT VIII: World-wide smartphone market shares by manufacturer

Manufacturer	Apple	Nokia	Samsung	Others
Market share in Q2 2011	18.5 %	**15.2 %**	17.5 %	48.8 %
Market share in Q4 2011	23.5 %	**12.4 %**	22.8 %	41.3 %

Source: Strategy Analytics, IDC.

EXHIBIT IX: IDC's forecast of worldwide smartphone operating system 2011 and 2015 market share and 2011–2015 CAGR

Operating system	2011 market share	2015 market share	2011–2015 CAGR
Android	39.50%	45.40%	23.80%
BlackBerry	14.90%	13.70%	17.10%
iOS	15.70%	15.30%	18.80%
Symbian	20.90%	0.20%	−65.00%
Windows Phone 7/Windows Mobile	5.50%	20.90%	67.10%
Others	3.50%	4.60%	28.00%
Total	100.00%	100.00%	19.60%

Source: IDC Worldwide Quarterly Mobile Phone Tracker, March 29, 2011.

concept of 'tiles' and infinite scrolling to give users access to the services that they liked to use. According to some observers, smartphones users and software writers had already adopted a new interaction involving a combination of touch, gestures, and apps, and hence Microsoft and Nokia would find it very difficult to gain v with its offering.[50]

Shortly after the announcement of the strategic alliance between Microsoft and Nokia, IDC had predicted that Microsoft which till then had steadily lost market share in the Mobile OS market, would gain in subsequent years and that by 2012, Windows Phone would be the #2 OS worldwide behind Android (**Refer to Exhibit IX for IDC's forecast**).[51] However, there were many sceptics. They said that it would not be easy for Microsoft to topple Apple in the smartphones wars. In the words of one expert: 'In PCs, it was business leading consumers . . . This is a different game: consumers leading business.'[52]

Printed with permission from author and www.ecch.com.

ENDNOTES

1. Marius Oiaga, 'Nokia Plus Windows Phone will Disrupt Android and iPhone Mobile Ecosystems', http://news.softpedia.com, February 11, 2011.
2. Marguerite Reardon, 'Microsoft's Ecosystem is a Tough Sell to Verizon', www.reviews.cnet.com, February 15, 2011.
3. Verizon Communications Inc., incorporated in Delaware in 2000, and based in New York City, is a provider of broadband, video, and other wireless and wireline communication services.
4. Headquartered in Helsinki, Finland, Nokia Corporation is a major manufacturer and marketer of mobile phones and smart devices. The company traces its origins to 1865, when Fredrik Idestam set up a wood pulp mill. The company diversified into rubber, cables, and electronics in the 1960s. However, it was in mobile technology that the company achieved world-wide success. In 2010, Nokia's sales turnover touched €42 446 million (Source: www.nokia.com).
5. Symbian OS was originally developed by Symbian Ltd. Nokia purchased Symbian Ltd. in December 2008.
6. 'Microsoft and Nokia Launch Toolkit for Porting Symbian Apps to Windows Phone', www.computerweekly.com, September 21, 2011.
7. Android, developed by Open Handset Alliance and led by Google, is an operating system for mobile devices.
8. iOS (formerly called iPhone OS) is Apple's operating system for mobile devices.
9. Samsung Electronics is a Korea-based multinational corporation that manufactures and markets consumer electronics and IT products.
10. Apple Inc. is a US-based multinational corporation that develops and markets consumer electronics, software, and computers.
11. HTC Corp. (formerly called High-Tech Computer Corporation) is a Taiwan-based manufacturer and marketer of mobile devices.
12. Headquartered in Mountain View, California, and incorporated in 1998, Google is a major technology company that has a world-wide presence. It is a major player in the online search market. In 2011, the company's sales turnover was US $37.9 billion. (Source: investor.google.com)
13. Motorola Mobility, Inc., based in Illinois, USA, is a major mobile handset and tablet company. In 2010, the company was spun off from Motorola, Inc.
14. Headquartered in New York, International Business Machines Corporation or IBM Corp. is a provider of an array of services such as IT, business consultancy, application, outsourcing, etc. In 2010, the company earned US $99.9 billion in revenues.

15. AT&T Inc. is a major player in the telecommunications arena providing services such as digital TV, high-speed internet, DSL, wireless, etc. The company is headquartered in Dallas, Texas. It earned revenues of US $35 billion (cash from operating activities) in 2010.

16. Netscape Communications Corp. is a computer services company that was a major player in the web browser market in the early 1990s. The company's browser, Netscape Navigator, lost the first browser war to Microsoft's Internet Explorer. In 1998, Netscape was acquired by AOL and became a holding company.

17. Headquartered in Sunnyvale, California, Yahoo! Inc. is a multi-national internet company. It is popular for its web portal, email services, directory, search engine, etc. The company earned revenues of US $6.32 billion in 2010.

18. Windows CE 3.0 is an operating system developed by Microsoft for embedded systems such as hand-held devices and mobile phones, which had slower processors and less memory space than PCs.

19. According to Microsoft, a Pocket PC is 'a hand-held device that enables users to store and retrieve email, contacts, appointments, tasks; play multimedia files and games; exchange text messages with Windows Live Messenger (formerly known as MSN Messenger), browse the Web, and more'.

20. UI or User Interface refers to the space where interaction between humans and machines takes place.

21. VPN or Virtual Private Network is a network that makes use of public telecommunication infrastructure, such as the Internet to provide traveling users or remote offices access to a central organizational network. (Source: www.wikipedia.org)

22. The four editions were Pocket PC Premium Edition, Pocket PC Professional Edition, Smartphone, and Pocket PC Phone Edition.

23. Palm Inc. was a smartphone maker based in Sunnyvale, California. The company launched a slew of smartphones such as Pre, Pixi, Treo, Centro, etc., in the late 1990s and early 2000s.

24. Research in Motion (RIM) is a Waterloo, Canada-based multinational telecommunications company that manufactures and markets wireless handsets.

25. The Open Handset Alliance was a consortium of 84 companies including Broadcom Corporation, Google, HTC, Intel, LG, Marvell Technology Group, Motorola, Nvidia, Qualcomm, Samsung Electronics, Sprint Nextel, T-Mobile, Texas Instruments, etc.

26. Linux is a computer operating system based on free and open source software. The OS kernel was created by Linus Torvalds in 1992.

27. Middleware refers to computer software that connects software components or people and their applications. (Source: www.wikipedia.org)

28. API or Application Programming Interface refers to specifications and codes that programs can follow to communicate with each other.

29. C is a general purpose computer programming language developed by Dennis Ritchie at the Bell Telephone Labs between 1969 and 1973.

30. Canalys, headquartered in Palo Alto, California, is a research, analytics and consultancy firm. The company also has offices in Shanghai, Singapore, and Reading, UK.

31. Peter Burrows, 'Mobile Wars! Apple vs. Google vs. Those Other Guys', www.businessweek.com, February 16, 2011.

32. Benchmark Capital is a venture capital firm based in Menlo Park, California. The firm has invested in companies in the Internet, mobile, cloud, hardware, and software as a service (SaaS) sectors. Some notable companies include ebay, Nordstrom, Yelp, Twitter, etc.

33. Randall Stross, 'Microsoft + Nokia = A Challenge for Apple', *The New York Times,* April 2, 2011.

34. 'Microsoft Paying Nokia $1 Billion for 5 Years Plus Deal', www.mobiletechworld.com, March 7, 2011.

35. 'Open Letter from CEO Stephen Elop, Nokia and CEO Steve Ballmer, Microsoft', http://conversations.nokia.com, February 11, 2011.

36. Navteq, based in Illinois, is a wholly-owned subsidiary of Nokia but operates independently. It is a major player in the electronic navigable maps market.

37. Zune Music is part of the Zune Marketplace, an online store developed and operated by Microsoft. As of mid-2011, there were more than 11 million songs that could be downloaded in mp3 format at up to 320 kbps and are DRM-free.

38. Jonathan Angel, 'Nokia Goes for Windows Phone 7, Will Drop Symbian', www.linuxfordevices.com, February 11, 2011.

39. Charles Arthur, 'Nokia and Microsoft: Turkey or Eagle?' www.guardian.co.uk, February 11, 2011.

40. 'Gartner Says Android to Command Nearly Half of Worldwide Smartphone Operating System Market by Year-end 2012', www.gartner.com, April 7, 2011.

41. Charles Author, 'Nokia tie-up with Microsoft: turkey or eagle', www.guardian.co.uk, February 11, 2011.

42. Brennon Slattery, 'App Overload: Apple Passes 300k Apps', www.pcworld.com, October 18, 2010.

43. Ionut Arghire, 'New Android Market Stats Out, Over 200K Apps Available', http://news.softpedia.com, December 28, 2010.

44. 'Google-Motorola Deal: Implications for Microsoft, RIM and Apple', www.ibtimes.com, August 17, 2011.

45. RBC Capital Markets is a Canada-based investment bank.

46. 'Samsung Chief Stresses Software after Google-Motorola deal', english.yonhapnews.co.kr, August 17, 2011.

47. 'The Google-Motorola deal makes Samsung worried about its software competitiveness', August 17, 2011.

48. Greg Bensinger, 'Verizon Hopes Google Deal Calms Patent Spats', http://online.wsj.com, August 17, 2011.

49. 'Microsoft President Announces New Partner Benefits and Underscores Opportunity with Windows Phone 'Mango', www.microsoft.com, July 12, 2011.

50. Om Malik, 'Nokia & Microsoft's Real Challenge', http://gigaom.com, October 27, 2011.

51. 'IDC Forecasts Worldwide Smartphone Market to Grow by Nearly 50% in 2011', www.idc.com, March 29, 2011.

52. Randall Stross, 'Microsoft + Nokia = A Challenge for Apple', *The New York Times*, April 2, 2011.

Index

3M Corporation 401
Accor: case study 456–65
accounting
    corporate governance 46, 48
    failures in corporate governance at Fannie Mae and
        Freddie Mac 47–8
acquisition premium 272–3
acquisition strategies 194–7
    capabilities-motivated 367
    corporate parent restructuring undervalued
        companies 284–5
    diversification 272–3
    international markets 236
    unsuccessful outcomes 196–7
activity ratios 103
aircraft manufacturing: strategic alliances 238
airlines: strategic alliances 207
Alberto-Culver: organizational culture 425–6
Aldi 150–1
Amazon.com 444
    first-mover advantage 191
    warehouse information and operating systems 404
Ansoff Matrix 271
Apple
    case study 3, 469–71, 472–3
    Supplier Code of Conduct 315–16
AstraZeneca: vision statement 30
Audi: case study of takeover of Lamborghini 25–6
audit committees 48
    corporate governance failures at Fannie Mae and
        Freddie Mac 47–8
automobile industry
    Lamborghini and Audi case study 25–6
    Manganese Bronze and Geely case study 259–61
    strategic alliances 207
    Toyota Production System (TPS) 365–7

balanced scorecard 37
Bang and Olufsen 165–6
banking
    business model of Zopa.com and First Direct
        compared 13–14
    problem of rogue traders 391
barriers to entry see entry barriers
benchmarking 121–2
    ethical conduct 123
    linking an organization's strategic priorities 402–3
    strategy execution enhanced by 395–6
best practice 121–2, 395–6
    linking an organization's strategic priorities 402–3
best-cost provider strategies 166–9, 170

Toyota Lexus cars 167–8
Bezos, Jeff 191, 444
blue-ocean strategy 86–7, 186–8
    Nintendo 187–8
board of directors
    fiduciary duty 48
    independence 48
    role 45–9
bonuses
    corporate governance failures at Fannie Mae and
        Freddie Mac 47–8
    directors 46
    rewards and incentives 408
Boston Consulting Group (BSG)
    Global Advantage Diamond model 231–2
    new approaches to competitive advantage 192–3
BP: case study on the Gulf of Mexico disaster 313
BPP: case study 143
brands 105, 106
    customer loyalty 69
bribery 317–18, 319, 320
    Siemens 318, 326–7
BSG see Boston Consulting Group
business ethics
    Apple's Supplier Code of Conduct 315–16
    BP and the Gulf of Mexico disaster case study 313
    bribery 317–18, 319, 320
    child labour 317
    cultural differences 320
    drivers of unethical business behaviour 322–6, 437
    News Corporation case study 344–7
    relativism 316–18
    Starbucks 562–3
business model of organization
    customer value proposition 12, 13–14
    operating model 12, 14
    relationship with strategy 11–12
    Zopa.com and First Direct compared 13–14
business process reengineering 396–8
    compared to Six Sigma and TQM programmes 402
    linking an organization's strategic priorities 402–3
business strategy 41, 42, 43, 269
    ethical strategies 328–30
buyers
    bargaining power 73–4
    demographics 79, 231

capability
    accessing through partnerships 368
    acquiring through mergers and acquisitions 367
    building and strengthening 363–9

capability *continued*
  definition 105
  dynamic 109–10, 364–5
  identifying 106–7
  internal development 364–7
cars *see* automobile industry
case studies
  Accor 456–65
  Amazon.com 191
  Apple 3, 469–71, 472–3
  BP and the Gulf of Mexico disaster 313
  BPP 143
  consumer electronics retailers 466–73
  Devon County Council 414–18
  EDF (Electricité de France) 201–2
  Ferrero and Nestlé 18–20
  Ferretti Group 527–37
  H&M 99
  Haribo 135–6
  IKEA 423
  innovative travel goods 499–511
  Kruger National Park 570–84
  Kuehne + Nagel 400
  Kyaia 595–606
  LA Fitness 174–6
  Lamborghini and Audi 25
  Lego 383–5
  McDonalds 8
  Manganese Bronze and Geely 259–61
  National Trust 353–4
  Netflix 474–98
  News Corporation 344–7
  NIS (Nafta Industrija Srbije) 587–94
  Oriflame 223
  Philips 307–8
  Robin Hood 585–6
  Safaricom and M-Pesa 214–17
  Sanofi SA 267–8
  Scandic hotels 51–2
  scenario planning at VisitScotland 62, 63
  Six Sigma quality programme 399, 400
  Spotify digital music downloads 91–4
  Starbucks 538–69
  strategic alliance between Microsoft and Nokia 607–20
  Studio 100 entertainment company 512–26
  TeliaSonera 450–2
  'Tesco Law' 57
  video game industry 181
  Yum! Brands in China 251
cash cows 297
cash hogs 297
CEOs
  board of directors to oversee actions of 48
  corporate governance failures at Fannie Mae and Freddie Mac 47–8
  strategy-making role 39–40, 46
change
  adaptive organizational cultures 434–5
  impact on competition 77–83
  organizational culture 439–43
  organizational cultures resistant to 436
  strategy adjustments in preparation for 82–3
  TeliaSonera case study 450–2
  see also drivers of industry change; strategy execution
channel conflict 199
charitable giving: corporate social responsibility 332
chief executive officers *see* CEOs
child labour 317
China
  purchasing power 250, 251
  Yum! Brands 251
Chrysler: culture-change 442–3
Cirque du Soleil 86–7
Cisco: strategic alliances 238
climate change: environmental sustainability strategies 337
Coca-Cola: vision statement 30
coffee shops: Starbucks case study 538–69
Comet: case study 468–9
compensation
  corporate governance failures at Fannie Mae and Freddie Mac 47–8
  executives 46, 411
  rewards and incentives 408, 411
competence
  assessing 110–13
  definition 110
competition
  analysis 64–77
  approaches by industry type 67, 68
  buyer bargaining power 73–4
  new entrants 68–70
  Porter's five-forces model 64, 65, 68, 75–7
  response to change 77–83
  rivalry among competing sellers 64–8, 80
  substitute products 70–1, 80
  supplier bargaining power 71–3
competitive advantage
  adaptive advantage 192–3
  best-cost provider strategies 166–9, 170
  country variations 225–7
  CSR combining sustainability strategies 338–9
  differentiation 126
  differentiation strategies 153–61, 170
  first-mover 69, 157, 184, 189–90, 191
  focused differentiation strategy 163–4, 165–6, 170
  focused low-cost strategy 163–4, 165, 170
  focused strategies 162–6
  international organizations 243–7
  late-mover 190–1
  location-based 227–8, 243–5
  low-cost provider strategies 145–55, 162, 170
  market-control/value matrix strategy 171–2
  meaning of concept 7–10
  new approaches from BSG 192–3
  overall assessment of organization 127–32
  profit sanctuaries 247–9

related business diversification 281–2
  Scandic hotels 51–2
  sustainable 7–10, 107–10
  value chain activities 125–7
competitive assets 104–7
competitive intelligence 85–6
complementors 76–7
confectionery industry
  Ferrero and Nestlé case study 18–20
  Haribo case study 135–6
conglomerates 282, 288
consumer electronics
  Apple case study 3, 469–71, 472–3
  retail case study 466–73
consumers
  cross-country differences 231
  developing countries 250–5
control systems
  employees 406
  information and tracking 405–6
  levers of control 406–7
  organizational culture 432
Co-operative Group 197, 334
core competence
  building and strengthening 363–9
  definition 110–11
core values 34–6
  FedEx 34
  organizational culture 427–8
  Zappos Family of Companies 35–6
Corning 277
corporate culture *see* organizational culture
corporate governance
  failures at Fannie Mae and Freddie Mac 47–8
  role of board of directors 45–9, 322
corporate parenting 283–5
  acquiring and restructuring undervalued
    companies 284–5
  cross-business allocation of finance 284
  provision of generalized resources and capabilities 283–4
corporate social responsibility (CSR) 49
  argument against 333–4
  BP and the Gulf of Mexico disaster case study 313
  charitable giving 332
  cigarette producers 342
  combining environmentally sustainable practices 339–42
  development 330–1
  elements of CSR strategy 331–6
  employees 332–3, 340
  ISO 26000 333
  News Corporation case study 344–7
  Nike 340
  Starbucks 564–6
  strategies combining sustainability 338–9
  triple bottom line 334–6
  see also business ethics; sustainability

corporate strategy 40–2, 43
  Ansoff Matrix 271
  ethical strategies 327–30
  see also diversification
corporate venturing 273
cosmetic industry: Oriflame case study 223
cost advantages 69
  approaches to achieving 146–50
  location-based 227–8, 244
cost drivers 146–7
cost innovation 168
costs: competitiveness 115–27
country business environment
  corporate social responsibility 332–3
  cost advantages of certain locations 227–8, 244
  demographic and cultural differences 230–1
  ethical differences 320
  foreign exchange risk 229–30
  government policies and economic conditions 228–9
  mission statement differences 33–4
  variation in competitiveness 225–7, 231–2
cross-market subsidization 249
CSR *see* corporate social responsibility
Ctrip: case study 255
cultural forces 60
  cross-country differences 231
  ethical differences 320
  strategic alliances 208
  see also organizational culture
currency risk 229–30
Currys: case study 467–8
customer loyalty: brands 69
customer service: strategic fit benefits of
    diversification 280–1
customer value: competitiveness 115–27
customers: bargaining power 73–4

D'Aveni, R. 9–10
decision-making
  centralized 376–7
  decentralized 377–8
Dell computers 252
demographics 60
  buyers 79, 231
  cross-country differences 230–1
developing countries
  Ctrip case study 255
  local organizations defence against global giants 253–5
  strategies for competing 250–5
Devon County Council: case study 414–18
differentiation
  advantage 126
  Bang and Olufsen 165–6
  focused strategies 163–4, 165–6, 170
  overspending 161
  strategies 153–61, 170
digital music industry: Spotify case study 91–4
Direct Line Insurance 148–9

direct sales: Oriflame case study 223
directors: compensation 46, 411
distinctive competence 111
distribution activities: strategic fit benefits of
    diversification 280
diversification 267–305
    acquisition of an existing business 272–3
    adjacency expansion of core business 279
    better-off (synergy) test 272, 282
    checking competitive advantage potential of strategic
        fit 296, 297
    checking for resource fit 296–9
    choice of modes of entry 274–5
    combination related-unrelated strategies 288–9
    competitive advantage through strategic fit 281–2
    Corning 277
    cost-of-entry test 271–2, 275
    entry barriers 271–2, 274–5
    evaluating competitive strength of business units 292–6
    evaluating industry attractiveness 289–92
    evaluating the strategy 289–302
    financial resource fit 296–8
    General Mills 277
    generalized resources and capabilities 276, 277, 278, 283–4
    industry attractiveness test 271
    internal development (corporate venturing) 273
    Johnson & Johnson case study 302
    joint ventures 273–4
    L'Oreal 277
    licensing 275
    partnerships 275
    related businesses 275–82, 289
    restructuring 304–5
    retrenching 303
    Sanofi SA case study 267–8
    shareholder value enhancement 271–2, 281–5
    specialized resources and capabilities 276, 277–8
    speed as factor in mode of entry 275
    strategic alliances 275
    strategic fit benefits 276–82
    tasks for corporate-level executives 269–70
    theories 287–8
    timing 270–1
    transaction costs 275
    unrelated businesses 275, 282–7, 289
Divine Chocolate 338
Dixons: case study 467–8
drivers of industry change
    buyer demographics 79
    globalization 78–9
    identifying factors 78–82
    impact of factors 82
    industry growth rate 78
    Internet 79–80, 81–2
    technology 79
dumping 249

e-business
    information and operating systems 403–7

    Spotify case study 91–4
e-tailing *see* online retailing
ecological forces 60
economic risk 229
    exchange rate fluctuations 229–30
economies of scale 68–9, 147, 281
    international expansion 224, 244–5
economies of scope: related business diversification 281
economy 60
    cross-country variations 228–9
EDF (Electricité de France): vertical and horizontal
        integration strategies 201–2
employees
    communicating strategic vision to 29–31
    corporate social responsibility 332–3, 340
    differentiation strategy 157
    empowerment 395, 403, 406
    incentives 149, 407–12
    monitoring performance 406
    motivation 407–12
    organizational culture 427–8, 429, 433–4, 440
    overcoming resistance to new strategies 355
    peer evaluation 406
    recruiting 362–3
    retaining 363
    Starbucks 556–60
    training 368–9
empowerment 395, 403, 406
Enron 322–3, 325–6
enterprise resource planning 397
entertainment industry: Studio 100 case study 512–26
entry barriers 68–70
    diversification 271–2, 274–5
    restrictive government policies 69, 80
environmental forces 60
environmental responsibility 49, 332
    Scandic hotels 51–2
    sustainability strategies 337–42
    triple bottom line 334–6
ethics
    benchmarking 123
    codes of conduct 320–2
    corporate strategy 327–30
    impact of technology and social media on reporting
        unethical behaviour 328
    integrated social contracts theory 319–20
    organizational culture 427–8
    universal standards 316
    see also business ethics
exports 234–5
external environment *see* macro-environment

Fannie Mae: corporate governance failure 47–8
fashion retail: H&M case study 99
FedEx
    core values 34
    information and operating systems 403
Ferrero: case study 18–19
Ferretti Group: case study 527–37

Traidcraft 339
travel agencies: Ctrip case study 255
triple bottom line (TBL) 334–6
  FTSE4GOOD index 336
  Novo Nordisk 335–6

UBS: vision statement 30
Unilever 252, 337–8
uniqueness drivers 156, 157

value chain 117–27
  benchmarking 121–2, 123
  comparison of rival organizations 117–19
  competitive advantage 125–7
  cost-efficient management of activities 146–9
  differentiation strategies 156–61
  Just Coffee 119
  system for an entire industry 120–1
value innovation 86–7
value network concept 130–1
values *see* core values
Verio: strategic alliances 238
vertical integration strategies 148, 197–202
  advantages 197–9
  backward integration 197–8, 200
  disadvantages 199–200
  EDF combines horizontal strategies 201–2
  forward integration 198–9
  pros and cons 200–1
vertical scope 194
video game industry
  case study 181

Nintendo 181, 187–8
vision 27–31
  communication to employees 29–31
vision statements 28–9
  AstraZeneca 30
  Coca-Cola 30
  country-specific differences 33–4
  functions 31
  Scandic hotels 51–2
  slogans 31
  UBS 30
  wording 29
VisitScotland: scenario planning 62, 63
Vodafone: Safaricom and M-Pesa case study 214–17, 368

Walmart 444
weaknesses 111–13
Welch, Jack 444
World Trade Organization (WTO) 249
WorldCom 324–5

Xerox 121–2

yacht building: Ferretti Group case study 527–37
Yum! Brands 251

Zappos Family of Companies: mission and core
    values 35–6
Zara 99, 148
Zipcar Inc. 186–7
Zopa.com: business model compared with First Direct
    13–14

distribution activities 280
manufacturing-related activities 279–80
related business diversification 276–82
research and development (R&D) 279
sales and marketing activities 280
supply chain 278
technology 279
strategic group mapping 83
analysis 84–5
creation 83–4
strategic intent 43
strategic objectives
company examples 38
compared with financial objectives 36–7
strategic plan: meaning 43–4
strategy
defensive 188
deliberate/proactive 11
emergent/reactive 11
evolving nature 10
meaning of concept 4–11
offensive 182–8
tests for good strategy 12–15
strategy execution 44–5, 353–81
aligning the firm's organizational structure 371–80
allocating resources 392–3
board of directors role 45–9
continuous improvement using process management
tools 395–403
core competence and capability building and
strengthening 363–9
corrective adjustments 45, 447
evaluating performance 45
framework 356–8
impact of organizational culture 433–43
information and operating systems 403–7
internal operations 391–418
joint ventures 368
leadership 443–7
Lego case study 383–5
National Trust case study 353–4
organizing the work effort 369–81
outsourcing 368, 369–71, 380
partnerships 368, 371, 380
policies and procedures 393–5
process 356–8
relationships with partners and strategic alliances 380
rewards and incentives facilitating 407–12
staffing the organization 359–63
strategic alliances 368, 380
team effort 355–6
strategy management 16–17, 27–45
crafting a strategy 39–44
executing the strategy see strategy execution
setting objectives 36–9
shareholder versus stakeholder approaches 49
vision, mission and core values 27–36
strategy simulations

BSG (Business Strategy Game) xxv–xxviii, xxix–xxx
GLO-BUS xxv–xxvii, xxviii–xxx
strategy-making: managerial hierarchy 39–43
strengths 110, 111–13
Studio 100: case study 512–26
substitute products
competitive pressure 70–1, 80
costs of switching 71, 73
price and quality 71, 80
technological advances 79
suppliers
bargaining power 71–3
differentiation strategy 158
dominance of Microsoft and Intel 71–2
supply chain
management 148
strategic fit benefits of diversification 278
sustainability 7–10, 107–10
Divine Chocolate 338
environmental strategies 337–42
Scandic hotels 51–2
strategies combining CSR 338–9
Toyota's strategy 338
Unilever's commitment 337–8
see also corporate social responsibility (CSR)
SWOT analysis 110–15
overall assessment of organization 128–32
shortfalls 116

tangible resources 105–6
technology 60
change 79
impact of social media on reporting unethical
behaviour 328
information and operating systems 403–7
strategic fit benefits of diversification 279
telecommunications: TeliaSonera case study 450–2
TeliaSonera: case study 450–2
Tesco: consumer electronics retailer 472
'Tesco Law': case study 57
threats 112–14
tobacco industry: corporate social responsibility (CSR)
342
total quality management (TQM) 148, 398
compared to business process reengineering 402
linking an organization's strategic priorities 402–3
tourism
Ctrip travel agency 255
Kruger National Park case study 570–84
National Trust case study 353–4
scenario planning at VisitScotland 62, 63
Toyota
Lexus cars 167–8
Prius cars 338
product recall 185
Production System 365–7
toys: Lego case study 383–5
TQM see total quality management

political forces 60
  cross-country variations 228–9
  organizational culture 436
political risk 229
Porter, M. 9–10
  Diamond of National Advantage framework 225–7,
    231–2
  five-forces model of competition 64, 65, 68, 75–7
price
  competitiveness 115–27
  cutting 183–4
price sensitivity 73–4
  low-cost provider strategies 145–55, 162
production: strategic fit benefits of diversification 279–80
profit sanctuaries 247–9
profitability ratios 102
public sector: Devon County Council case study 414–18

quality
  differentiation strategy 157–8
  Six Sigma programmes 398–402
  total quality management (TQM) 148, 398

regulation 60, 76
  impact on competition 80
relationship managers 380
research and development (R&D)
  open versus closed innovation 204–5
  Six Sigma quality programmes claim to stifle
    innovation 401
  strategic fit benefits of diversification 279
resource
  definition 105
  dynamic 109–10
  tangible and intangible 105–6
  types of organizational 105–6
resource and capability analysis 104–10
  competitive value 108, 109, 126–7
  identifying a resource and capability 104–7
  imitation 108, 109
  rarity 108, 109
  starting up a new business 274
  substitutability 108, 109
  sustainability of competitive advantage 107–10
  SWOT analysis 110–15, 116, 128–32
  value network concept 130–1
resource bundles 107
  assessing competitive power 127
restaurants
  McDonalds case study 8
  Yum! Brands in China 251
retailers
  Apple and consumer electronics case study 466–73
  Lidl and Aldi 150–1
rewards *see* incentives

Saint-Gobain 399–400
salaries

directors 46
rewards and incentives 408
sales activities: strategic fit benefits of diversification 280
Samsung Group: strategic alliances 206–7, 210–11
Sanofi SA: case study 267–8
Scandic hotels
  case study 51–2
  vision and mission 32, 51–2
scenario planning 59–62
  VisitScotland 62, 63
Schein, E. 430
scope of the firm 194
self-dealing 322
shareholder value
  business case for CSR and sustainability practices 341
  diversification to achieve gains 271–2, 281–5
  increasing value via unrelated diversification 283–5
  versus stakeholder value 49
Shell 326
shoemaking industry: Kyaia case study 595–606
short-termism 325
Siemens 318, 326–7
Simons, R. 406–7
Six Sigma quality programmes 398–402
  compared to business process reengineering 402
  innovation and R&D issues 401
  Kuehne + Nagel case study 400
  linking an organization's strategic priorities 402–3
slogans 31
socio-cultural forces 60
  cross-country differences 231
  impact of technology and social media on reporting
    unethical behaviour 328
  strategic alliances 208
Sompo Japan Insurance Company of Europe: mission
  statement 32
Spotify: case study 91–4
stakeholder versus shareholder value 49
Stanford, R. Allen 323–4
Starbucks: case study 538–69
strategic alliances 205–12
  advantages 207–9, 210
  airlines 207
  automotive industry 207
  case study of Microsoft and Nokia 607–20
  cultural differences 208
  disadvantages 209–10
  diversification 275
  examples of cross-border alliances 238–9
  international markets 237–40
  requirements for success 208–9, 210–12
  risks of cross-border alliances 239
  Safaricom and M-Pesa case study 214–17, 368
  Samsung Group 206–7, 210–11
  strategy execution 368, 380
strategic fit
  customer service 280–1
  decentralized organization structure 378–9

mission statements 31–4
  country-specific differences 33–4
  Microsoft 32
  Scandic hotels 32, 51–2
  Sompo Japan Insurance Company of Europe 32
  Starbucks 560–1
  Zappos Family of Companies 35–6
mobile telecommunications
  Apple case study 3, 469–71, 472–3
  Safaricom and M-Pesa case study 214–17, 368
  strategic alliance between Microsoft and Nokia case
    study 607–20
motivation
  employees 407–12
  examples of employee rewards used 409
  psychology of 411–12
movie rentals: case study 474–98
Mozilla 6

national parks: Kruger National Park case study 570–84
National Trust: case study 353–4
natural resources: sustainability strategies 337–42
Nestlé: case study 19–20
Netflix: case study 474–98
network structure 380
new entrants: competitive pressure 68–70
new products
  hurdles for new entrants 68–70
  impact on competition 80
News Corporation: case study 344–7
newspaper industry: News Corporation case study 344–7
niche markets
  Bang and Olufsen 165–6
  e-tailers 164–5
  see also focused strategies
Nike 340
Nintendo
  blue-ocean strategy 187–8
  case study 181
NIS (Nafta Industrija Srbije): case study 587–94
no-frills products and services 145, 149
  Lidl and Aldi 150–1
Nokia: strategic alliance with Microsoft case
    study 607–20
Nordstrom: company objectives 38
Novo Nordisk: triple bottom line (TBL) 335–6

objectives
  company examples 38
  extension throughout the organization 39
  financial versus strategic 36–7
  setting 36–9
  short-term and long-term 39
oil and gas industry
  case study on BP and the Gulf of Mexico disaster 313
  NIS (Nafta Industrija Srbije) case study 587–94
online retailing
  Amazon.com first-mover advantage 191

  channel conflict 199
  niche products 164–5
open innovation 204–5
operating strategies 41, 42–3
opportunities 112–13
organizational culture 423–43
  adaptive cultures 434–5
  Alberto-Culver 425–6
  change 439–43
  change-resistant cultures 436
  Chrysler's change of culture 442–3
  classification 437–9
  control systems 432
  core values 427–8
  cultural web 432
  employees 427–8, 429, 433–4, 440
  ethics 427–8
  evolution 429–30
  Google 425
  high-performance cultures 434
  IKEA case study 423
  impact on strategy execution 433–43
  incompatible subcultures 437
  insular/inwardly focused cultures 436–7
  key features 424, 426–9
  levels 430
  meaning of concept 445
  perpetuation 429
  person culture 438
  politicized cultures 436
  power culture 438
  problem culture 439–43
  rituals and routines 432
  role culture 438
  stories 428–9, 432
  strong-culture companies 430–1
  symbols 432
  task culture 438
  TeliaSonera case study 450–2
  unethical/greed-driven cultures 322–6, 437
  weak-culture companies 431
Oriflame: case study 223
outsourcing 148, 202–5
  risks 203–4
  strategy execution 368, 369–71, 380
overseas markets *see* international markets

partnerships 205–12
  disadvantages 209–10
  diversification 275
  strategy execution 368, 371, 380
PC World: case study 467–8
performance measurement
  balanced scorecard 37
  benchmarking 121–2, 123, 395–6
  financial ratios 102–4
performance targets *see* objectives
pharmaceutical industry: Sanofi SA case study 267–8

international markets *continued*
  demographic and cultural differences 230–1
  developing countries 250–5
  Diamond of National Advantage framework 225–7, 231–2
  dumping 249
  ethical differences 320
  exports 234–5
  foreign exchange risk 229–30
  franchising 235–6
  Global Advantage Diamond model 231–2
  government policies and economic conditions 228–9
  greenfield ventures 236–7
  joint ventures 237–40
  licensing 235
  location-based advantages 227–8, 243–5
  Manganese Bronze and Geely case study 259–61
  motives for expansion into 224–5
  multidomestic and/or global competition 232–4
  mutual restraint by competing rivals 250
  Oriflame case study 223
  strategic alliances 237–40
  strategy *see* international strategy
  see also globalization
international strategy
  global (think-global, act-global) strategy 241, 242–3, 244
  multidomestic (think-local, act-local) strategy 240–2, 244
  transnational (think-global, act-local) strategy 241, 243, 244
Internet
  drivers of industry change 79–80, 81–2
  Finnish magazine publishing 81–2
Internet retailing *see* online retailing
Ireland: pro-business government policies 228

Johnson & Johnson: diversification case study 302
joint ventures 206
  diversification 273–4
  international markets 237–40
  Manganese Bronze and Geely case study 259–61
  Philips and TVP 307
  risks of cross-border alliances 239
  strategy execution 368
Just Coffee: value chain 119

kaizen 398
key success factors (KSFs) 87–8
Kruger National Park: case study 570–84
Kuehne + Nagel 400
Kyaia: case study 595–606

L'Oreal 277
LA Fitness: case study 174–6
Lamborghini: case study of takeover by Audi 25–6
late-mover advantage 190–1
  pros and cons 192

lawyers: 'Tesco Law' case study 57
leadership
  managers at General Electric 361–2
  strategy execution 443–7
learning curve effects 68–9, 147
legal factors 60
legal profession: 'Tesco Law' case study 57
Lego: case study 383–5
leverage ratios 103
licensing
  diversification 275
  international markets 235
Lidl 150–1
liquidity ratios 102
local authorities: Devon County Council case study 414–18
logistics industry: Kuehne + Nagel case study 400
low-cost leadership 145–55, 162
  focused strategies 163–4, 165, 170
  Lidl and Aldi 150–1

McDonalds
  case study 8
  company objectives 38
  policy manual 395
macro-environment 58–94
  analysis 62–89
  competitive forces 64–77
  competitive intelligence 85–6
  components 58–9, 60
  drivers of industry change 77–83
  key success factors 87–8
  strategic groups 83–5
Madoff, Bernard 323
managers
  General Electric 361–2
  strategic issues meriting priority attention 132
  strategy implementation process 360–2
  strategy-making role 39–43
managing by walking around (MBWA) 444
Manganese Bronze: case study on joint venture with Geely 259–61
manufacturing: strategic fit benefits of diversification 279–80
marketing activities: strategic fit benefits of diversification 280
Marriott hotels 165, 338–9
media: Internet impact on Finnish magazine publishing 81–2
merger strategies 194–7
  capabilities-motivated 367
  unsuccessful outcomes 196–7
Michelin 404
Microsoft 6
  company objectives 38
  mission statement 32
  strategic alliance with Nokia case study 607–20
  supplier dominance 71–2

film rentals: case study 474–98
financial objectives
    company examples 38
    compared with strategic objectives 36–7
financial ratios 102–4
financial reporting: corporate governance 46, 48
financial resources: diversified firm 296–8
financial services
    business model of Zopa.com and First Direct
        compared 13–14
    problem of rogue traders 391
firm
    centralized decision-making 376–7
    decentralized decision-making 377–8
    functional structure 373
    matrix structure 374–5
    multidivisional structure 373–4
    organizational structure 371–80
    relationship between structure and strategy 375–6
    scope 194
    simple structure 372–3
    without formal organizational structure 379
    see also international firms
First Direct: business model compared with Zopa.
    com 13–14
first-mover advantage 69, 157, 184, 189–90
    Amazon.com 191
    pros and cons 192
first-mover disadvantage 190–1
focused strategies 162–6
    Bang and Olufsen 165–6
    differentiation strategy 163–4, 165–6, 170
    low-cost strategy 163–4, 165, 170
footwear: Kyaia case study 595–606
foreign exchange risk 229–30
foreign markets *see* international markets
franchising 235–6
fraud
    Enron 322–3, 325–6
    Madoff and Stanford Ponzi schemes 323–4
    WorldCom 324–5
Freddie Mac: corporate governance failure 47–8
FTSE4GOOD index 336
functional area strategies 41, 42, 43

Geely: case study on joint venture with Manganese
    Bronze 259–61
General Electric (GE) 444
    management talent 361–2
    strategy-making 40
General Mills 277
General Motors: strategic alliances 238
global forces 60
global warming: environmental sustainability
    strategies 337
globalization 78–9, 223–56
    IKEA case study 423
    Manganese Bronze and Geely case study 259–61

    see also international markets
Google: organizational culture 425
Google Chrome 6
greenfield ventures: international markets 236–7
guerrilla offensives 184–5

H&M: case study 99
Handy, C. 437–9
Haribo: case study 135–6
health and fitness industry: LA Fitness case study 174–6
healthcare industry *see* pharmaceutical industry
Heathrow Airport 401
higher education: BPP case study 143
Honda 392–3
horizontal scope 194
    EDF combines vertical integration strategies 201–2
    mergers and acquisitions 194–7
hotels
    Accor case study 456–65
    Scandic hotels 32, 51–2
hypercompetition 9–10

IKEA: case study 423
image 105, 106
imitation
    differentiation strategy to avoid 160–1
    resource and capability analysis 108, 109
    see also substitute products
incentives
    employees 149, 407–12
    examples of rewards used to motivate employees 409
    intrinsic versus extrinsic rewards 411–12
    linking to performance outcomes 410–11
information: competitive intelligence 85–6
information systems 403–7
    monitoring employee performance 406
    tracking systems 405–6
innovation
    blue-ocean strategy 86–7, 186–8
    case study 499–511
    differentiation strategy 157, 160
    impact on competition 80
    offensive strategy 184
    open versus closed innovation 204–5
    Six Sigma quality programmes claim to stifle R&D 401
intangibles 105–6
    differentiation strategy 159
Intel: supplier dominance 71–2
intellectual capital 105, 106
international firms
    co-ordinating activities 247
    competitive advantage quest 243–7
    profit sanctuaries 247–9
    resources and capabilities sharing 246–7
international markets
    acquisition strategies 236
    corporate social responsibility 332–3
    cross-country variation in competitiveness 225–7, 231–2